W9-DGS-625

THE U.S. GOVERNMENT AND THE VIETNAM WAR

THE U.S. GOVERNMENT AND THE VIETNAM WAR

Executive and Legislative Roles and Relationships

PART IV: JULY 1965–JANUARY 1968

WILLIAM CONRAD GIBBONS

PRINCETON UNIVERSITY PRESS
PRINCETON, NEW JERSEY

Published by Princeton University Press, 41 William Street,
Princeton, New Jersey 08540
In the United Kingdom: Princeton University Press, Chichester, West Sussex

Library of Congress Cataloging-in-Publication Data
(Revised for volume 4)
Gibbons, William Conrad.
The U.S. government and the Vietnam war.
"Prepared for the Committee on Foreign Relations,
United States Senate, by the Congressional Research
Service, Library of Congress."
"Originally published by the U.S. Government
Printing Office in June 1994"—T.p. verso.
Includes bibliographical references and indexes.
Contents: pt. 1. 1945-1960—pt. 2, 1961-1964—
pt. 3. Jan.-Jul. 1963—pt. 4. Jul. 1965-Jan. 1968
1. Vietnamese Conflict, 1961-1975—United States.
2. Indochinese War, 1946-1954—United States. 3. United
States—Politics and government—1945-
I. United States. Congress. Senate. Committee on
Foreign Relations. II. Library of Congress. Congressional
Research Service. III. Title. IV. Title:
US government and the Vietnam War.
DS558.G52 1986 959.704'33'73 86-3270
ISBN 0-691-00636-9 (v. 4.: alk. paper)
ISBN 0-691-00635-0 (pbk.: v. 4)

This book was prepared for the Committee on Foreign Relations of the United States Senate by the Congressional Research Service of the Library of Congress. It was originally published by the U.S. Government Printing Office in June 1994. The "Letter of Submittal" and "Foreword" are deleted and some typographical corrections have been made. Otherwise, contents and pagination are the same.

Princeton University Press books are printed on acid-free paper and meet the guidelines for permanence and durability of the Committee on Production Guidelines for Book Longevity of the Council on Library Resources

Printed in the United States of America by Princeton Academic Press

1 3 5 7 9 8 6 4 2
1 3 5 7 9 8 6 4 2 (Pbk.)

For my grandchildren, Benjamin Gibbons and Alexander and Stephanie Meier-Gibbons, and for my children Ashley and Justin, who joined our family in June 1994, with love.

PREFACE

This, the fourth of a five-part policy history of the U.S. Government and the Vietnam war, covers the critical period of active American involvement from the decision in July 1965 to send large-scale troops, to January 1968, just before the beginning of the Tet offensive and the decision to stop bombing North Vietnam and to seek a negotiated settlement. Parts I, II, and III covered the periods 1945–1960, 1961–1964, and January–July 1965. Part V will cover the period from January 1968 to May 1975.

The goal here, as in previous volumes, is to describe and analyze major developments in U.S. policy—political, military, and diplomatic—and, by drawing on a wide variety of sources including interviews and previously classified documents, to present a comprehensive view of the decisions that were reached and the courses of action that were taken. The perspective is primarily that of the participants, and the judgments expressed and conclusions reached are generally drawn from their experiences.

Following a summary of the evolution of the decision to use U.S. forces in Vietnam, the study traces the efforts to "win" the limited war being waged, while avoiding a larger, more general war or jeopardizing other important U.S. interests. There are detailed discussions of the search for an effective political and military strategy, of differences of opinion within the government (including strong differences within the military), and of the process by which major policy and operational choices were made.

Included in this analysis is the question of maintaining political and legislative support for the war, as well as the problems encountered in fighting the war while expanding domestic programs. Also included are public reactions to the war, the activities of antiwar groups, and the responses of elected officials to pressures from the electorate.

Extensive consideration is given to the responses of the U.S. Congress to the war and the positions taken by various members and committees on funds and policy, as well as to interaction between the President and Congress. Political party activities are also considered, along with the effect of the war on congressional and presidential elections.

Events in South Vietnam are an important aspect of this study, and considerable attention is paid to American efforts to influence the South Vietnamese and to South Vietnamese reactions to their situation and the role of the United States.

There is also major emphasis on efforts to find a political/diplomatic settlement of the war, especially contacts between the U.S. and other major powers, as well as direct and indirect secret negotiations between the U.S. and the North Vietnamese.

Sources for this volume consisted primarily of White House and other records at the Lyndon Baines Johnson Library; State Department files; U.S. Army records, especially the papers of General William C. Westmoreland, and the 135 interviews conducted by the author with the help of Patricia McAdams and, for a portion of the early interviews, Dr. Anna Kasten Nelson. Also consulted were oral histories at the Johnson Library and at the U.S. Army Military History Institute at Carlisle Barracks, Pennsylvania. Materials on Congress were obtained from the papers of the Senate Foreign Relations Committee at the National Archives and from the Committee, White House, and other records at the Johnson Library, and interviews with Members of Congress and their staffs.

A number of persons have contributed to this part of the study. The continued support of the Senate Foreign Relations Committee and of Senator Claiborne Pell and Geryld B. Christianson, who were Chairman and Staff Director of the Committee at the time this volume was completed, is deeply appreciated. The Committee's Editor, Donald McDonald, and Leon Stern, Assistant to the Editor, were very helpful in coding the manuscript and arranging for printing.

Reviewers of earlier parts who also examined all or parts of this volume were William P. Bundy, General Andrew J. Goodpaster, Chester Cooper, and Norvill Jones. (Their credentials were described in earlier volumes.) General Douglas Kinnard, who served in Vietnam in several capacities, and is the author of *The War Managers* (cited below), was also helpful, as were Generals William C. Westmoreland, Bruce Palmer, Jr., and Frederick C. Weyand. General Volney Warner provided useful information on PROVN.

The author owes a special debt to Professor Richard H. Immerman of Temple University, for his excellent critique of the draft manuscript.

Tom Johnson, former Press Secretary to President Lyndon Johnson and now the President of Cable News Network (CNN), kindly allowed the author to use and quote at length from his notes of meetings of the President and his advisers (the Tuesday Lunch).

Professor George Herring of the University of Kentucky generously made available page proofs of his new book, *LBJ and Vietnam* (cited below).

Mary Blake French, editor of *Army* magazine, suggested useful sources and materials.

In the Congressional Research Service, very helpful reviews were provided by Joan M. Davenport, Review Specialist in the Office of the Director, who studied Asian affairs and has lived in the region and who combines knowledge and excellent editorial judgment; Dr. Robert G. Sutter, Project Manager, an Asian specialist who was former Chief and now serves as a Senior Specialist of the Foreign Affairs and National Defense Division; and Robert L. Goldich, a Specialist in National Defense who was the supervisor of this project during several years as a section head in the Foreign Affairs and National Defense Division.

Others in the Congressional Research Service who have provided vital support include the former Director, Joseph E. Ross and his successor, Daniel P. Mulhollan; Charlotte P. Preece, Chief of the Foreign Affairs and National Defense Division; Edgar Glick and Jeanne Hamilton who handled contract arrangements; and Cynthia

A. Wilkins, Personnel Security Officer for the Library of Congress, who arranged for security clearances.

At George Mason University, where the author is a Visiting Professor, important contributions have been made by Dr. Louise White, Chair of the Public and International Affairs Department, and Virginia V. McCaslin, Secretary, as well as the Office of Grants Administration and Mary F. Blackwell, Coordinator of Office Support Services.

At the Department of State, where the author spent many months examining classified materials, Teresa Farrell, Chief of the Research Branch of the Foreign Affairs Information Management Center, and Charles N. Mills, the former chief, were very cooperative in efforts to locate and declassify relevant documents. Others who were helpful included those former Foreign Service Officers who reviewed the material (but who, understandably, prefer anonymity) and others who processed the hundreds of documents that the author had requested.

At the Defense Department, W. M. McDonald, Director, Freedom of Information and Security Review, was again very helpful in processing Freedom of Information Act requests.

At the U.S. Army Center of Military History, Dr. John Carland, Historian, was very cooperative. Hannah Zeidlik, Chief of the Historical Resources Branch, was helpful in arranging for access to classified military records. Ted Ballard, Archivist Historian, assisted with access to the papers of General Westmoreland. The declassification of important Army documents was very competently and skillfully performed by Wanda Radcliffe.

At the U.S. Army Military History Institute, David A. Keough, Assistant Archivist/Historian, and John J. Slonaker, Chief, Historical Reference Branch, were very helpful in making available information from that important archival source.

The most important source of materials used in this volume has been the papers in the Lyndon B. Johnson Library in Austin, Texas, where a small staff handles with skill and tact an enormous and complicated workload of requests. Thanks go to the Director, Harry Middleton; the Supervisory Archivist, Tina Houston; the Senior Archivist, Regina Greenwell, and her illustrious predecessor, Dr. David C. Humphrey (now a historian in the State Department); and Archivist Linda Hansen, for their splendid contribution. Archivist John Wilson, who bore with superb patience and good will the brunt of the author's many requests, deserves special recognition and appreciation for his excellent service.

Also helpful were Betty Austin, Special Collections, University of Arkansas Libraries; Sheryl B. Vogt, Head of the Richard B. Russell Library at the University of Georgia; Jill Christiansen and Peter Drummey at the Massachusetts Historical Society; David S. Sheaves, Applications Analyst/Programmer at the Institute for Research in Social Science, University of North Carolina; and Leah D. W. Stoker, Media Correspondent, the Gallup Organization, Inc.

Above all, the author wishes to thank his assistant at George Mason University, Anne G. Bonanno, whose continued hard work, abundant tact and good will, and awesome pursuit of the smallest error are deeply appreciated. For 14 years she has been solely responsible for the entire support side of this project, and deserves great credit for what has been accomplished.

Note:

After the publication of Part III of this study, the author received a letter from Allan W. Cameron commenting on the discussion on page 266 of the student people-to-people program sponsored by the U.S. Government in the summer of 1965 for a small group of American college students. Contrary to the statement in the text, Cameron says that the program was not coordinated by the American Friends of Vietnam but by the Institute of International Education under a grant from the Agency for International Development. He adds that the program was repeated in the summer of 1966 with 40 students (30 in South Vietnam and 10 in Laos), and that he was employed as the Field Representative and Team Leader for the group.

In reference to the question of the government's exploitation of the students in supporting U.S. policy, Cameron says that "after our return, there was absolutely no effort made to exploit my knowledge or that of another student from the same graduate school. Indeed, we were disappointed by the lack of interest in Washington, which contrasted starkly with the level of interest in Saigon."

CONTENTS

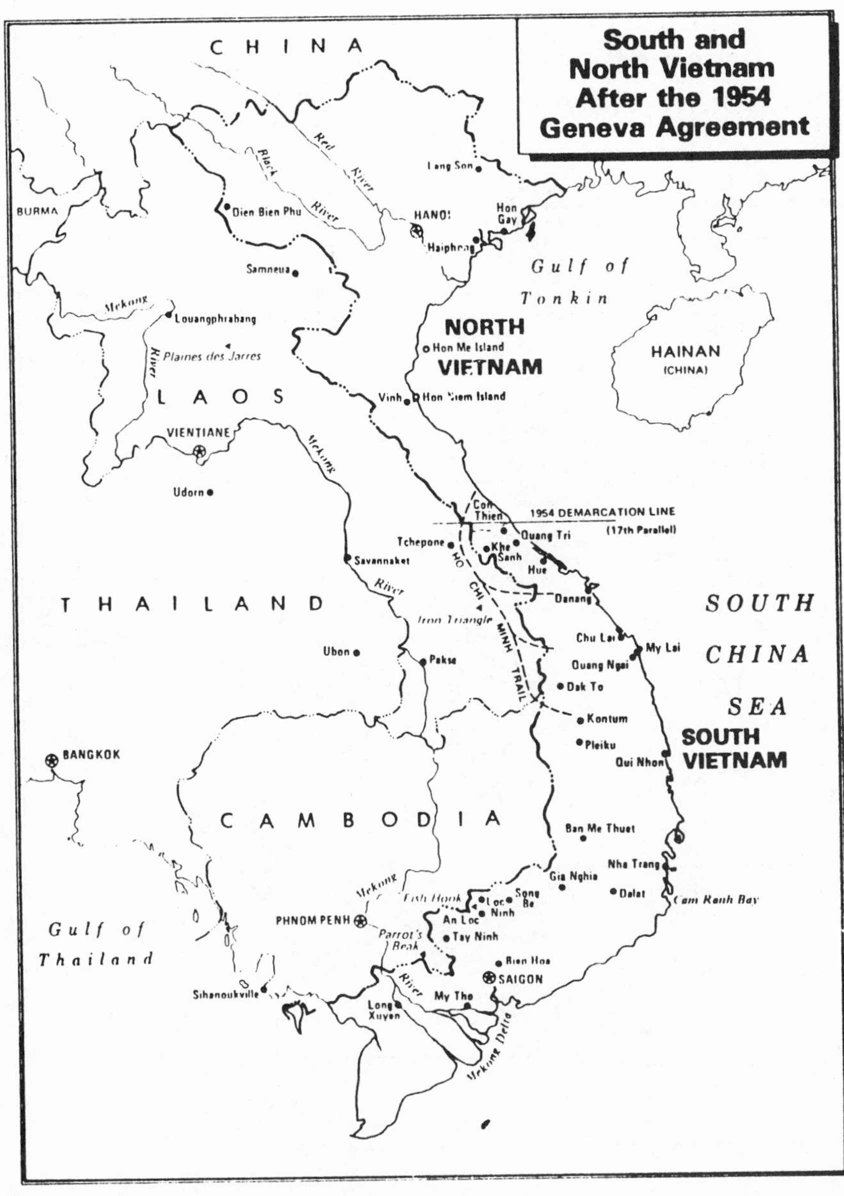
South and
North Vietnam
After the 1954
Geneva Agreement
CHINA
BURMA
Red River
Black River
Lang Son
Dien Bien Phu
HANOI
Hon Gay
Haiphong
Gulf of Tonkin
Samneua
Mekong
Louangphrabang
Plaines des Jarres
River
LAOS
NORTH VIETNAM
Hon Me Island
Vinh
HAINAN (CHINA)
VIENTIANE
Mekong
Udorn
Con Thien
1954 DEMARCATION LINE (17th Parallel)
Quang Tri
Tchepone
Khe Sanh
Hue
Savannaket
River
HO CHI MINH TRAIL
THAILAND
Danang
SOUTH CHINA SEA
Iron Triangle
Chu Lai
My Lai
Ubon
Pakse
Quang Ngai
Dak To
Kontum
Pleiku
SOUTH VIETNAM
BANGKOK
Qui Nhon
CAMBODIA
Ban Me Thuet
Nha Trang
Gia Nghia
Dalat
Cam Ranh Bay
Mekong
Fish Hook
Loc Ninh
Song Be
An Loc
PHNOM PENH
Tay Ninh
Gulf of Thailand
Parrot's Beak
Bien Hoa
SAIGON
Sihanoukville
River
My Tho
Long Xuyen
Mekong Delta

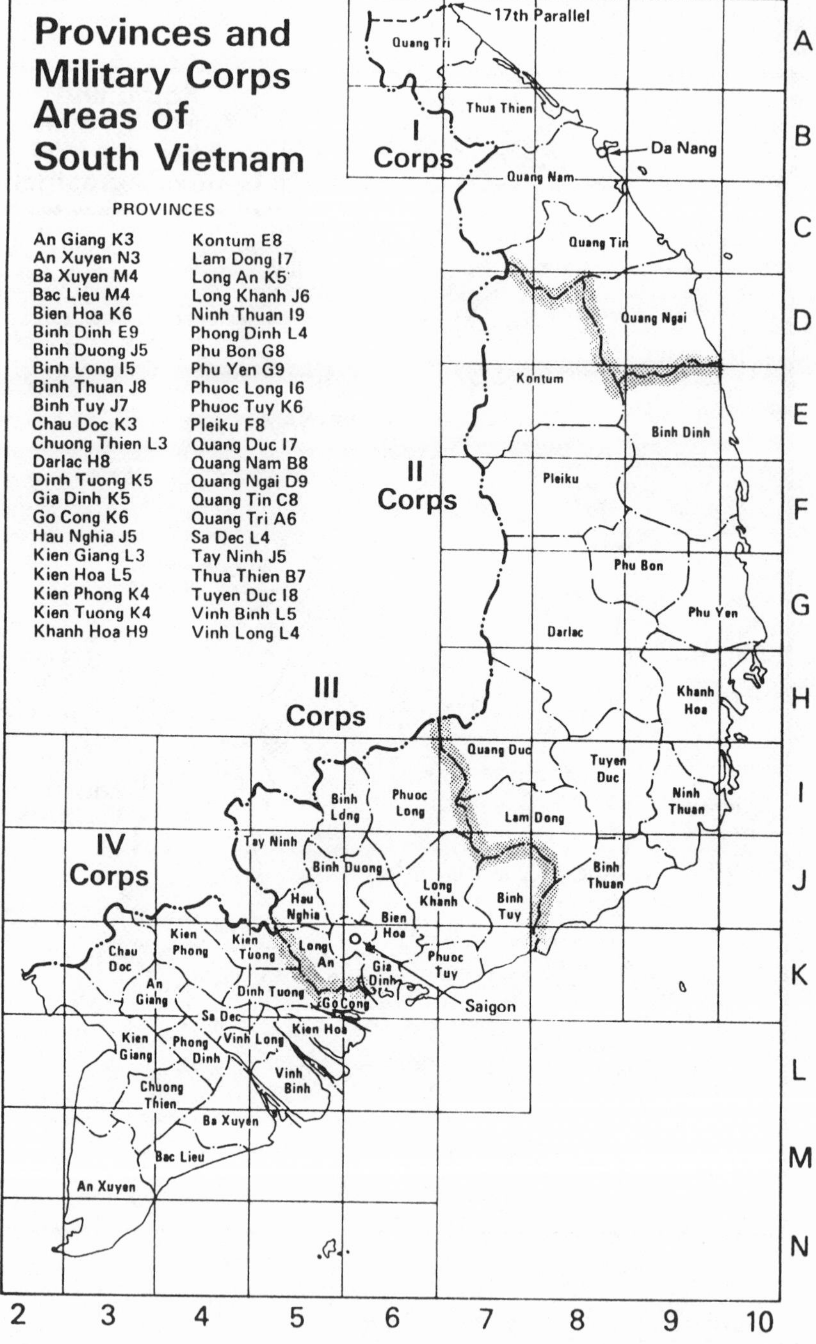

Provinces and Military Corps Areas of South Vietnam
PROVINCES
An Giang K3
An Xuyen N3
Ba Xuyen M4
Bac Lieu M4
Bien Hoa K6
Binh Dinh E9
Binh Duong J5
Binh Long I5
Binh Thuan J8
Binh Tuy J7
Chau Doc K3
Chuong Thien L3
Darlac H8
Dinh Tuong K5
Gia Dinh K5
Go Cong K6
Hau Nghia J5
Kien Giang L3
Kien Hoa L5
Kien Phong K4
Kien Tuong K4
Khanh Hoa H9
Kontum E8
Lam Dong I7
Long An K5
Long Khanh J6
Ninh Thuan I9
Phong Dinh L4
Phu Bon G8
Phu Yen G9
Phuoc Long I6
Phuoc Tuy K6
Pleiku F8
Quang Duc I7
Quang Nam B8
Quang Ngai D9
Quang Tin C8
Quang Tri A6
Sa Dec L4
Tay Ninh J5
Thua Thien B7
Tuyen Duc I8
Vinh Binh L5
Vinh Long L4
17th Parallel
Quang Tri
Thua Thien
I Corps
Da Nang
Quang Nam
Quang Tin
Quang Ngai
Kontum
Binh Dinh
II Corps
Pleiku
Phu Bon
Phu Yen
Darlac
Khanh Hoa
III Corps
Quang Duc
Tuyen Duc
Ninh Thuan
Binh Long
Phuoc Long
Lam Dong
Tay Ninh
IV Corps
Binh Duong
Binh Thuan
Long Khanh
Binh Tuy
Hau Nghia
Bien Hoa
Kien Phong
Kien Tuong
Chau Doc
Long An
Phuoc Tuy
Gia Dinh
An Giang
Dinh Tuong
Go Cong
Saigon
Sa Dec
Kien Hoa
Kien Giang
Phong Dinh
Vinh Long
Vinh Binh
Chuong Thien
Ba Xuyen
Bac Lieu
An Xuyen
A B C D E F G H I J K L M N
2 3 4 5 6 7 8 9 10

CHAPTER 1

THE IDIOM OF POWER

On July 28, 1965, President Lyndon B. Johnson announced that the United States was deploying additional troops to South Vietnam and declared that the U.S. would use its forces to defend South Vietnam from the "growing might and grasping ambition of Asian communism." This action, he said, was necessary in order to maintain the credibility of U.S. power and commitments. "If we are driven from the field in Vietnam," he said, "then no nation can ever again have the same confidence in American promises, or in American protection."[1]

The goal, the President stated, was to convince the Communists that they could not win in Vietnam by force of arms. Once this was accomplished, a peaceful solution to the conflict was "inevitable." He declined to predict how long the war might last, saying that it would take "months or years or decades," but he warned that there was no "quick solution." In response to a question about the economic effects of the decision, he said that the U.S. was in a period of unprecedented prosperity and that there was no need to declare a national emergency (under which the government could have exercised various economic and other controls). Although he did not say so publicly, he had been advised by the Chairman of his Council of Economic Advisers that the additional military expenditures required by the decision to use U.S. forces would have a favorable effect on the economy, at least in the short-run.[2]

The President's decision was based on the recommendations of most of his foreign policy and military advisers and all of his three principal advisers—Secretary of State Dean Rusk, Secretary of Defense Robert S. McNamara, and the Presidential Special Assistant for National Security Affairs, McGeorge Bundy—that the military situation was becoming more critical, and that if the U.S. did not intervene in force, there was an imminent threat that the Communists would take control of South Vietnam. Failure to act would have far-reaching consequences, according to Rusk, not only in Southeast Asia but worldwide: "The integrity of the U.S. commitment is the principal pillar of peace throughout the world. If that commitment becomes unreliable, the communists would draw conclusions that would lead to our ruin and almost certainly to a catastrophic war. So long as the South Vietnamese are prepared to

[1] U.S. President, *Public Papers of the Presidents of the United States*, Lyndon B. Johnson, 1965 (Washington, D.C.: Office of the Federal Register, National Archives and Records Service, 1966), p. 794. For Johnson's explanation of his reasons for this decision, see his memoirs, *The Vantage Point: Perspectives of the Presidency* (New York: Holt, Rinehart & Winston, 1971), pp. 151–152.

[2] For a detailed discussion of these and other aspects of the July 28, 1965 decision, see pt. III of this study, ch. 6.

fight for themselves, we cannot abandon them without disaster to peace and to our interests throughout the world."[3]

Evolution of the Decision to Use U.S. Forces

The decision to use U.S. forces to defend South Vietnam was the culmination of 20 years of political and military actions by which the United States had become progressively involved in preventing Communist domination of Vietnam. In 1945, President Harry S Truman agreed to let the French resume control of Indochina (the three "Associated States" of Vietnam, Laos and Cambodia), and from then until the French withdrew in 1954 the U.S. provided financial and military assistance directly or indirectly to French forces fighting in Vietnam.[4]

In the spring of 1950, after the Communists had taken control of China, the U.S. decided to increase its assistance to the French as well as to begin providing military assistance directly to the Associated States. A small U.S. military mission was established in each of the three countries to aid in these efforts. The position of the U.S., as expressed in the policy decision of President Truman, National Security Council (NSC) Directive 64, April 24, 1950, "The Position of the United States With Respect to Indochina," was that, "It is important to United States security interests that all practicable measures be taken to prevent further Communist expansion in Southeast Asia," and that, "The neighboring countries of Thailand and Burma could be expected to fall under Communist domination if Indochina were controlled by a Communist-dominated government. The balance of Southeast Asia would then be in grave danger."[5]

After the Korean war began in the summer of 1950, the U.S. was concerned about possible Communist designs on Southeast Asia, and some consideration was given to using U.S. forces, including ground forces, in Indochina. Gen. J. Lawton Collins, Chief of Staff of the Army, stated in a memorandum on October 18, 1950, that as a last resort and under certain conditions the U.S. should use its ground forces in Indochina to stop the Communists.[6] In November, however, with U.S. forces tied down in Korea, the Joint Chiefs of Staff (JCS) took the position, based on a study by the JCS's Joint Strategic Survey Committee, that the U.S. should not use its own forces in Indochina but, rather, should seek to get the French to do more to gain support of the people. According to the Survey Committee, "While minor commitments of United States military forces [in addition to French and indigenous forces] might be sufficient to defeat the Viet Minh [the Communists] in Indochina, it is more probable that such commitments would lead to a major involvement of the United States in that area similar to that in Korea or even to global war. Accordingly, there would be great potential danger to the security interests of the United States in the commitment of any 'token' or 'minor' United States forces in Indochina."[7]

---

[3] Johnson Library, NSF NSC History, Deployment of Forces, Rusk Memorandum to the President, July 1, 1965.

[4] For background on U.S. involvement in Vietnam prior to 1965 see pts. I and II of this study.

[5] For NSC 64, see pp. 66–67 of pt. I of this study.

[6] *Ibid.*, p. 81.

[7] *Ibid.*, p. 83.

In 1953–1954, the newly elected President Dwight D. Eisenhower and his associates also debated whether and under what circumstances to use U.S. forces in Indochina. In October 1953, Eisenhower approved a broad National Security Council directive which took an even stronger view of the strategic importance of Indochina than had the Truman administration. Indochina, the directive said, was "of such strategic importance" that an attack on it from outside (i.e., China) "probably would compel the United States to react with military force either locally at the point of attack or generally against the military power of the aggressors."[8]

The Army became concerned, however, about the gap between policy and capability, and in late 1953 a study was conducted by the Army Plans Division of the requirements for U.S. forces if the French withdrew from Indochina. It was estimated that seven U.S. Army divisions and one Marine division, a total of 275,000–300,000 men including support forces (but not including naval and air forces), would be required to replace the French, and that it would take five to eight years to pacify the country using the techniques successfully employed by the British in Malaya.[9] The Plans Division concluded that there were not enough troops to fill such a requirement while still meeting other U.S. commitments. The Joint Strategic Plans Committee of the JCS, however, recommended, and the JCS approved, that if necessary to prevent Communist control the U.S. should use its forces in Indochina.[10]

At a meeting of the National Security Council on January 8, 1954, to consider whether U.S. forces should be used, Eisenhower expressed strong opposition to the use of U.S. ground forces in Vietnam:[11] "For himself, said the President with great force, he simply could not imagine the United States putting ground forces anywhere in Southeast Asia, except possibly in Malaya, which one would have to defend as a bulwark to our off-shore island chain. But to do this anywhere else was simply beyond his contemplation. Indeed, the key to winning this war was to get the Vietnamese to fight. There was just no sense in even talking about United States forces replacing the French in Indochina. If we did so, the Vietnamese could be expected to transfer their hatred of the French to us. I can not tell you, said the President with vehemence, how bitterly opposed I am to such a course of action. This war in Indochina would absorb our troops by divisions!" Eisenhower did not necessarily oppose the use of some U.S. personnel and equipment, especially from the Air Force and the CIA, to assist the French, and he was in favor of having the U.S. take over most of the train-

---

[8] *Ibid.*, p. 146.

[9] *Ibid.*, p. 147.

[10] At least one military official disagreed. In a memorandum in early January 1964, Vice Adm. Arthur C. Davis, Director of the Office of Foreign Military Affairs in the International Security Affairs Division of the Defense Department, made this memorable statement (*ibid.*, p. 150):

"Involvement of U.S. forces in the Indochina war should be avoided at all practical costs. If, then, National Policy determines no other alternative, the U.S. should not be self-duped into believing the possibility of partial involvement—such as 'Naval and Air units only.' One cannot go over Niagara Falls in a barrel only slightly. . . . If it is determined *desirable* to introduce air and naval forces in combat in Indochina it is difficult to understand how involvement of ground forces could be avoided. Air strength sufficient to be of worth in such an effort would require bases in Indochina of considerable magnitude. Protection of those bases and port facilities would certainly require U.S. ground force personnel, and the force once committed would need ground combat units to support any threatened evacuation. It must be understood that there is no cheap way to fight a war, once committed." (emphasis in original)

[11] *Ibid.*, p. 153.

ing of local forces in Indochina. He also agreed with a statement by Secretary of State John Foster Dulles in another NSC meeting on January 14, 1954 that if the French withdrew, the U.S., without intervening directly, could support a guerrilla operation inside Vietnam.[12]

During the battle of Dien Bien Phu in the early months of 1954, Eisenhower agreed to provide France with aircraft and aircraft technicians, as well as the use of the CIA in ferrying troops and supplies into Dien Bien Phu. As the battle worsened, the French asked the U.S. to bomb the attacking forces. This or any other intervention by U.S. forces was considered and rejected, in part because of the opposition of key Members of Congress, but primarily because of the President's opposition to the use of U.S. forces in this manner, which was buttressed by similar opposition from Army Chief of Staff Matthew B. Ridgway. According to Ridgway, "The adverse conditions prevalent in this area [Indochina] combine all those which confronted U.S. forces in previous campaigns in the South and Southwest Pacific and Eastern Asia, with the additional grave complication of a large native population, in thousands of villages, most of them about evenly divided between friendly and hostile." Moreover, he said, "Such use of United States armed forces, apart from any local successes they might achieve, would constitute a dangerous strategic diversion of limited United States military capabilities, and would commit our armed forces in a non-decisive theatre to the attainment of non-decisive local objectives."[13]

Following the partition of Vietnam at the Geneva Conference in the summer of 1954, the French withdrew, and the U.S. assumed responsibility for helping the new South Vietnamese Government. Eisenhower increased the size of the U.S. military mission to about 700 (only 342 were permitted by the Geneva Agreement; the others were considered "temporary"). Although the Communists became more active toward the end of the 1950s and steps were taken to provide for increased U.S. assistance, especially covert action in Laos, the U.S. military role remained limited during Eisenhower's Presidency.

In 1961, the newly elected President, John F. Kennedy, turned first to the problem of Laos, which appeared to be more critical than Vietnam.[14] He considered sending U.S. forces to Laos, either unilaterally or as part of a multilateral force under the Southeast Asia Treaty (SEATO). For a variety of reasons, not the least of which was the strong opposition of key congressional leaders to

---

[12] *Ibid.*, pp. 153–155.

[13] *Ibid.*, pp. 203, 237.

[14] By late 1960, as he was leaving office, Eisenhower was very concerned about the situation in Laos. In a meeting with President-elect John F. Kennedy in January 1961, he was reported by Clark M. Clifford, who was present, to have said, "with considerable emotion," that the U.S. could not afford to let the Communists take Laos, the "key to the whole area." Clifford's notes of the meeting also state that Eisenhower told Kennedy that if all else failed the U.S. would have to intervene, alone if necessary. See pt. II of this study, p. 9. Notes on the meeting by Robert McNamara, which were declassified in 1985 after the publication of pt. II, state, however, that although Eisenhower told Kennedy that if Laos were "lost" all of Southeast Asia would be also, he advised against unilateral action by the U.S. Johnson Library, NSF Memos to the President—McGeorge Bundy, attachment to Memorandum for the President, Aug. 26, 1965.

For a detailed explanation see Fred I. Greenstein and Richard H. Immerman, "What Did Eisenhower Tell Kennedy about Indochina? The Politics of Misperception," *Journal of American History*, 79 (September 1992), pp. 568–587.

U.S. military intervention in Laos, Kennedy decided to negotiate a settlement in Laos but to strengthen the U.S. role in Vietnam.

A few days after taking office, Kennedy approved a new counterinsurgency program for Vietnam which had been developed during 1960 by the Eisenhower administration, under which the U.S. increased its assistance to Vietnam. He also established a high-level interdepartmental Counterinsurgency Group and exhorted his advisers to give priority to the development of counterinsurgency doctrine and capabilities.

On May 11, 1961, Kennedy approved NSC 52, which reaffirmed the U.S. commitment to Vietnam and authorized a sweeping program of action. The objective, it said, was "to prevent Communist domination of South Vietnam; to create in that country a viable and increasingly democratic society, and to initiate, on an accelerated basis, a series of mutually supporting actions of a military, political, economic psychological and covert character designed to achieve this objective."[15]

The JCS took the position that, consistent with NSC 52, the U.S. should deploy its own forces to South Vietnam in order to:[16]

A. Provide a visible deterrent to potential North Vietnam and/or Chinese Communist action.

B. Release Vietnam forces from advanced and static defense positions to permit their fuller commitment to counterinsurgency actions.

C. Assist in training the Vietnamese forces to the maximum extent consistent with their mission.

D. Provide a nucleus for the support of any additional major U.S. or SEATO military operation in Southeast Asia.

E. Indicate the firmness of our interest to all Asian nations.

Kennedy's response to the JCS was to ask for a study of the question of using U.S. forces. He also sounded out South Vietnamese President Ngo Dinh Diem, who said he would welcome more military advisers but that he did not want U.S. forces to become involved in the war.

In June 1961, Kennedy and Russian Premier Nikita Khrushchev met in Vienna, and although Khrushchev appeared to agree to a negotiated settlement for Laos he was very belligerent with respect to making a peace treaty with Germany. Kennedy apparently felt he was being tested, and that steps would have to be taken to prove U.S. resolve. As he was reported to have said, "Now we have a problem in making our power credible, and Vietnam looks like the place."[17]

In the summer of 1961, as Laos negotiations began but tension between the U.S. and the U.S.S.R. increased over the German question, some of Kennedy's advisers recommended that the U.S. should seek to convince the Communists to agree to a reasonable settlement in Laos, as well as to make clear U.S. determination to defend Indochina and other American interests, by establishing a military headquarters in Thailand and by sending some troops to Vietnam and to Thailand. These advisers also suggested that if ne-

---

[15] See pt. II of this study, p. 40.
[16] *Ibid.*, p. 39, from JCS memorandum of May 9, 1961.
[17] *Ibid.*, p. 48.

gotiations were not successful, the U.S., in concert with Thailand and South Vietnam, should take and hold the southern part of Laos, or, with or without SEATO, send combat forces to South Vietnam on the border area adjacent to the southern part of Laos. There was also some discussion of the bombing of North Vietnam and a naval blockade as part of a plan for applying "graduated pressure" on the North Vietnamese. Kennedy voiced considerable skepticism about U.S. military involvement in Laos, however, and said he wanted to pursue negotiations. Secretary of State Dean Rusk and Secretary of Defense McNamara agreed.[18]

By the fall of 1961, the situation in Laos had stabilized and negotiations for a settlement were proceeding satisfactorily. With respect to Vietnam, however, there was widespread concern among U.S. policymakers that the situation was deteriorating, and a feeling that the U.S. would have to play a more active role. On October 10, 1961, a paper, "Concept for Intervention in Vietnam," which combined the ideas of the State and Defense Departments and the JCS, was presented to President Kennedy.[19] It proposed the deployment in the highlands of Vietnam (Pleiku) of a SEATO (primarily U.S.) force of 11,000 ground combat troops supported by 11,800 air, naval and other forces. "To clean up the Viet Cong threat," the paper said, might require 40,000 combat forces (all services) or more, depending on whether the North Vietnamese increased their aid to the South or if the Chinese intervened. Ultimately, there could be a need for as many as four ground combat divisions (160,000–200,000 including support forces).

The paper discussed the pros and cons of sending a SEATO force into South Vietnam. Among the "cons" was: "The plan itself would not itself solve the underlying problem of ridding SVN of communist guerrillas." Also, "It breaks the Geneva Accords and puts responsibility on the U.S. for rationalizing the action before the U.N. and the world." Furthermore, there would be the "risk of being regarded as interlopers á la the French. . . ." In addition, the Communists might react by a "change of tactics back to small-scale operations [which] might leave this force in a stagnant position."

Among the "pros" was that such a move could strengthen the Vietnamese as well as U.S. influence with the Vietnamese and the U.S. bargaining position with the Russians. Moreover, "If we go into South Viet-Nam now with SEATO, the costs would be much less than if we wait and go in later, or lose SVN."

The paper took the position that because the deployment of such combat forces would represent a decision to intervene militarily in the war, it was a step which "cannot be taken without accepting as our real and ultimate objective the defeat of the Viet Cong and making Viet-Nam secure in the hands of an anti-Communist government."

At a meeting with his advisers on October 11, 1961, President Kennedy agreed to send a U.S. Air Force squadron to Vietnam, but decided that before acting on the recommendation for using ground forces he would send Gen. Maxwell D. Taylor, then serving on the

---

[18] See *ibid.*, pp. 58–68.
[19] *Ibid.*, p. 69.

White House staff, and Walt W. Rostow, a deputy to McGeorge Bundy, to Vietnam to examine the situation. Taylor and Rostow, who had been advocating intervention with U.S. forces, reported after their trip that, "vigorous American action is needed to buy time for Vietnam to mobilize and organize its real assets; but the time for such a turn around has nearly run out. And if Vietnam goes, it will be exceedingly difficult if not impossible to hold Southeast Asia. What will be lost is not merely a crucial piece of real estate, but the faith that the U.S. has the will and the capacity to deal with the Communist offensive in that area."[20] They recommended, among other things, that the U.S. should send 6,000–18,000 ground combat and logistical troops to Vietnam to serve as a deterrent as well as a demonstration of U.S. resolve.

In early November 1961 there was considerable discussion of the Taylor-Rostow recommendation for sending U.S. troops. Most of the President's principal advisers, including McNamara, McGeorge Bundy and the JCS, were in favor of the proposal, but only, as the paper on intervention had also advised, if the U.S. made a categorical commitment to defend South Vietnam. McNamara, for himself and for Deputy Secretary of Defense Roswell L. Gilpatric and the JCS, sent a memorandum to the President in which he argued that the fall of South Vietnam would have "extremely serious" strategic implications in Asia as well as worldwide. Moreover, "The chances are against, probably sharply against, preventing that fall by any measures short of the introduction of U.S. forces on a substantial scale." McNamara, Gilpatric and the JCS supported the Taylor-Rostow plan for a limited deployment, but said that the Communists would not be convinced of American resolve unless the U.S. also announced its commitment to defend South Vietnam and sent word to the North Vietnamese that continued support by them of the Communists in the South would lead to punitive retaliation by the U.S. against the North.

If the U.S. took these actions, the memorandum added, the possible extent of the military commitment would have to be faced. "I believe we can assume," McNamara said, "that the maximum U.S. forces required on the ground in Southeast Asia will not exceed 6 divisions, or about 205,000 men. . . ."

Secretary of State Rusk, however, had reservations, and in a cable from Tokyo he questioned whether a small number of U.S. troops could be a decisive factor unless the performance of the South Vietnam improved: "While attaching greatest possible importance to security in Southeast Asia, I would be reluctant to see U.S. make major additional commitment American prestige to a losing horse."

In order to present the President with a unified recommendation, Rusk and McNamara sent him a joint memorandum in mid-November 1961 in which, after restating the importance of defending South Vietnam, they proposed that the U.S. should be prepared to use its own forces "if that should become necessary for success." Moreover, it might also be necessary for the U.S. "to strike at the source of the aggression in North Vietnam." They recommended that plans should be made for using U.S. forces, but pointed out

[20] *Ibid.*, p. 73.

that it would be preferable to postpone a decision to send forces until after the Laotian settlement had been completed.

In meetings with his advisers during November, President Kennedy agreed with the recommendation that combat forces should not be sent at that time, partly because of his concern about having the support of Congress, the public, and other countries before doing so. He approved, however, a major new program of U.S. assistance to South Vietnam, including a greatly increased number of U.S. military advisers, and the assignment of U.S. military units to provide direct support to the South Vietnamese military (airlift, reconnaissance by air and sea, intelligence, communications, etc.).[21]

Although Kennedy agreed with his advisers that U.S. combat forces should not be sent at that time, in a cable to Lodge, the language of which Kennedy personally cleared,[22] the State Department said "We do not propose to introduce into the GVN [Government of Vietnam] U.S. combat troops now, but we do propose a phase of intense public and diplomatic activity designed to focus on the infiltration of men from the North. We shall decide what course of action we shall take later should infiltration not be radically reduced. . . . Very strictly for your own information, you should know that the Department of Defense has been instructed to prepare plans for the use of U.S. combat forces in South Vietnam under the various contingencies that can be foreseen, including stepped-up infiltration from the North as well as organized Communist military intervention into South Vietnam. However, you should be entirely clear that it must be the objective of our policy to do all possible to accomplish our purpose with respect to GVN without the use of U.S. combat forces."

After these decisions were made in November of 1961, the Kennedy administration attempted through this program of increased assistance to provide support to South Vietnam without committing U.S. forces to the war. (Although by the fall of 1963 there were more U.S. military forces in Vietnam than had been recommended in the fall of 1961, and although many of these "advisers" were engaged in combat, there were no U.S. military units engaged in combat, nor had there been any attacks by U.S. forces on North Vietnam.) By the end of 1962, however, there were increasing signs that the situation was continuing to deteriorate, and in November 1963, after months of preliminary activity, the U.S., in hopes of getting stronger indigenous leadership, supported a coup against President Diem. On November 22, Kennedy was assassinated, and Lyndon Johnson became President.

In a meeting with his senior advisers on November 24, 1963, President Johnson said that he "approached the situation [Vietnam] with some misgivings," but added, "we have to see that our objectives are accomplished."[23] A few days later, he reaffirmed the

---

21 For a critique of Kennedy's actions on the Taylor-Rostow recommendations, see Worth H. Bagley, "Kennedy and Taylor: Vietnam, 1961," *Proceedings* of the U.S. Naval Institute (May 1993), pp. 106–115. At the time, then Lt. Commander Bagley was an assistant to Taylor, accompanied him to Vietnam, and was present at the meeting of Taylor with the President after the trip.

22 See the clearances listed at the bottom of the first page of the cable, Washington to Saigon 618, Nov. 15, 1961, in the Kennedy Library, Papers of Theodore Sorenson, Vietnam File. This cable is not included in U.S. Department of State, *Foreign Relations of the United States*, 1961–1963, Vietnam, vol. I (Washington, D.C.: U.S. Govt. Print. Off., 1988).

23 See pt. III of this study, p. 1.

U.S. commitment by approving National Security Action Memorandum (NSAM) 273, based on agreements reached by his military and civilian advisers at a conference in Honolulu on November 20, which stated in part: "It remains the central object of the United States in Vietnam to assist the people and Government of that country to win their contest against the externally directed and supported Communist conspiracy."[24]

On December 21, 1963, McNamara, after a brief trip to Vietnam, reported to the President that "The situation is very disturbing. Current trends, unless reversed in the next 2–3 months, will lead to neutralization at best and most likely to a Communist-controlled state."[25] McNamara took the position that U.S. resources and personnel "cannot usefully be increased substantially," (at the time there were 20,000 U.S. military personnel in South Vietnam) but he recommended several steps, including new covert operations against North Vietnam, the so-called OPLAN (operations plan) 34–A. On January 22, 1964, Gen. Maxwell Taylor, now Chairman of the Joint Chiefs of Staff, sent a JCS memorandum to Secretary of Defense McNamara proposing that to carry out NSAM 273 the U.S. must take steps to "make plain to the enemy our determination to see the Vietnam campaign through to a favorable conclusion."[26] U.S. failure in Vietnam, the memorandum declared, would not only have a direct effect on the neighboring countries of Asia and on the U.S. position in Asia, but because it was "the first real test of our determination to defeat the communist wars of national liberation formula, it is not unreasonable to conclude that there would be a corresponding unfavorable effect upon our image in Africa and in Latin America."

The JCS memorandum argued that "self-imposed restrictions" on the U.S., which included limiting the war geographically to the territory of South Vietnam, avoiding the direct use of U.S. combat forces, and limiting the role of the U.S. to that of giving advice to the South Vietnamese, were forcing the U.S. and South Vietnam to fight on the enemy's terms. "He has determined the locale, the timing, and the tactics of the battle while our actions are essentially reactive." A more aggressive attitude was needed, and a "much higher level of activity . . . to make plain our resolution, both to our friends and to our enemies."

"It is our conviction," the JCS memorandum concluded, "that if support of the insurgency from outside South Vietnam in terms of operational direction, personnel and material were stopped completely, the character of the war in South Vietnam would be substantially and favorably altered."

---

[24] See pt. III of this study, p. 3.

For President Johnson's handling of the war during the 1963–1965 period, see George Herring, *LBJ and Vietnam: A Different Kind of War* (Austin: Univ. of Texas Press, 1994); Larry Berman, *Planning a Tragedy: The Americanization of the War in Vietnam* (New York: W. W. Norton, 1981), and *Lyndon Johnson's War: The Road to Stalemate in Vietnam* (New York: W. W. Norton, 1989); and Brian VanDeMark, *Into the Quagmire: Lyndon Johnson and the Escalation of the Vietnam War* (New York: Oxford Univ. Press, 1981). See also the analysis of Paul Y. Hammond, *LBJ and the Presidential Management of Foreign Relations* (Austin: Univ. of Texas Press, 1992).

[25] See pt. II of this study, pp. 211–212.

[26] For the text, see the *Pentagon Papers*, Gravel ed., vol. III, pp. 496–499 (hereafter cited as *PP*). This edition of the *Pentagon Papers* was published in 1971 in four volumes by the Beacon Press of Boston, based on material made available by Senator Mike Gravel (D/Alaska).

The JCS recommended "bolder actions which may embody greater risks," including making the U.S. military commander [in South Vietnam] responsible for all U.S. programs, civilian as well as military, and persuading the South Vietnamese to let the U.S. military commander assume ("temporarily") tactical direction of the war and full responsibility for all operations against North Vietnam. Operations against the North would be intensified. U.S. planes "under Vietnamese cover" would bomb the North, and the U.S. would equip and advise the South Vietnamese in their own program of bombing and mining harbors, as well as commando raids on the coast. The U.S. would also encourage South Vietnam to conduct ground operations in Laos against the Ho Chi Minh Trail. Finally, the memorandum recommended that additional U.S. forces be committed "as necessary" in South Vietnam, and "as necessary" in attacks on North Vietnam.

In mid-March 1964, President Johnson again sent McNamara to Vietnam (accompanied, among others, by General Taylor), and then approved the report of the trip in its entirety, designating it as NSAM 288.[27] This document reiterated the objective of the U.S.—"an independent, non-Communist South Vietnam"—and the dire consequences which would occur if South Vietnam fell to the Communists. Once again, McNamara took the position that although the situation was worse, substantial increases in U.S. resources and personnel still were not needed. He proposed a number of steps to aid the South Vietnamese, predicting that the situation should improve in four—six months if the new government acted vigorously. (In January 1964, Gen. Nguyen Khanh had taken control of the government, previously headed since the Diem coup by Gen. Duong Van Minh.) He also recommended, however, that the U.S. should prepare for possible "graduated covert military pressure" against North Vietnam. A few weeks later, the JCS submitted a plan to implement NSAM 288, OPLAN 37–64, April 17, 1964, which proposed a three-phase program of graduated military pressure against North Vietnam and infiltration routes in Laos and Cambodia,[28] and on May 28 the JCS, under the acting chairmanship of the Air Force Commander, Gen. Curtis E. LeMay, argued that the only way to prevent the North Vietnamese from supporting the insurgency in the South was to destroy their ability to do so.[29]

Meanwhile, in mid-May 1964 the President directed his advisers to prepare proposals for increased military and non-military actions. On May 25, Rusk, McNamara and McGeorge Bundy sent a memorandum to the President in which they recommended "a Presidential decision that the U.S. will use selected and carefully graduated military force against North Vietnam" unless other efforts were able to produce "a sufficient improvement of non-Communist prospects in South Vietnam and Laos to make military actions

---

[27] See pt. II of this study, p. 238.

[28] Phase I provided for air and ground strikes against targets in South Vietnam and "hot pursuit" into border areas of Laos and Cambodia. Phase II provided for "tit-for-tat" airstrikes and related military operations against North Vietnam. Phase III provided for more severe actions against North Vietnam. As part of its work on OPLAN 37, the JCS developed a list of targets for bombing the North, which became known as the "94 target list."

[29] The memorandum proposed airstrikes against infiltration points at Dien Bien Phu and Vinh. JCS Chairman Taylor told McNamara that he agreed with the proposals to increase military pressure on the North, but preferred less risky targets.

against North Vietnam unnecessary." Force would be used to achieve the politico-military goal of deterring the North Vietnamese and causing them to desist, rather than defeating them militarily: "Our clear purpose in this decision," the memorandum said, "should be to use all our influence to bring about a major reduction or elimination of North Vietnamese influence in Laos and in South Vietnam, and *not* to unroll a scenario aimed at the use of force as an end in itself." (emphasis in original)

The recommendations of Rusk, McNamara and McGeorge Bundy were based on these premises:[30]

(1) that the U.S. cannot tolerate the loss of Southeast Asia to Communism;

(2) that without a decision to resort to military action if necessary, the present prospect is not hopeful, in South Vietnam or in Laos;

(3) that a decision to use force if necessary, backed by resolute and extensive deployment, and conveyed by every possible means to our adversaries, gives the best present chance of avoiding the actual use of such force.

The Bundy memorandum further recommended that deployment of U.S. forces to South Vietnam should be "on a very large scale" to maximize the impact of such a move.

At a meeting in early June 1964 of the President's civilian and military advisers it was agreed, however, that U.S. military action was not necessary at the time and that more preparations were needed to secure public and international support for such a move.[31]

---

[30] Pt. II of this study, p. 257. Notes of the preceding meeting on May 24, 1964, of Rusk, McNamara, McGeorge Bundy and other key officials involved in preparing the plans for increased action were declassified in 1990 and are available at the Johnson Library, NSF NSC History.

[31] At this meeting (June 10, 1964), there was also a discussion, based on a paper prepared by William P. Bundy, of whether or not to seek a congressional resolution. The decision was made to defer action. See pt. II of this study, p. 266. Subsequent to publication of pt. II, a document was declassified in 1990 (Johnson Library, NSF Files of McGeorge Bundy, "Summary Record of the Meeting on Southeast Asia," June 10, 1964) that sheds new light on the factors involved. During the meeting, William Bundy, Assistant Secretary of State for the Far East, said that because of the legislative calendar, the resolution would need to be sent to Congress in ten days or two weeks. McNamara said, without explanation, "we would not be in a position" to send it before July 1, adding that "a congressional resolution before September was unlikely unless the enemy acts suddenly in the area, which is also unlikely. Our actions to date are not such as to require a resolution." Rusk agreed, saying, "We should ask for a resolution only when the circumstances are such as to require action, and, thereby, force Congressional action." There would be "great difficulties in getting congressional approval," he said, prior to "basic decisions by the President on the U.S. course of action in Southeast Asia." Attorney General Nicholas deB. Katzenbach agreed, saying that "It would be much simpler to obtain approval of a resolution if U.S. actions are forcing the pace." "Heavy groundwork with Congressmen will be necessary," he added. McGeorge Bundy said that such groundwork would be difficult if the Executive was not committed to seek a resolution. He also "asked that the group not dismiss the proposal to seek a Congressional resolution without taking into account the great benefit such a resolution would have in conveying our firmness of purpose in Southeast Asia."

Secretary of the Treasury C. Douglas Dillon pointed out that the argument "could be reversed"—that if a resolution were passed and the U.S. did not act promptly, there could be a "crisis of morale."

McGeorge Bundy raised the question of military actions that would be taken "without taking actions which could be initiated only with a Congressional resolution." McNamara replied that all of the actions he had recommended fell in that category, and that they would "go quite far." CIA Director John A. McCone commented that "putting U.S. troops on the ground in Southeast Asia would require a Congressional resolution."

In discussing the question of preparing the public for possible U.S. military action, McNamara suggested that there should be a "press campaign . . . of such a nature as to avoid building up public pressure for drastic action." Rusk responded that the Members of Congress to whom he had talked acted unconcerned, and did not seem to feel that there was a crisis. McNamara

Continued

In early August 1964, after a U.S. destroyer was attacked in the Gulf of Tonkin off the coast of North Vietnam, the President approved the first direct U.S. air attack on North Vietnam. He also used the occasion to get congressional approval of the Gulf of Tonkin Resolution authorizing him to "take all necessary steps" to defend South Vietnam, including the use of U.S. forces.

In the weeks that followed, the President's advisers continued to prepare for the use of U.S. forces in Vietnam and/or increased pressure on North Vietnam. At the time, however, the political situation in South Vietnam was very unstable, and in a meeting with his advisers in early September 1964 the President said that with such a "weak and wobbly situation" the U.S. could not act until there was a "base" on which to build. He said he would be ". . . ready to do more, when we had a base." He "did not wish to enter the patient in a 10-round bout when he was in no shape to hold out for one round." Accordingly, NSAM 314, September 10, 1964, directed that additional steps should be taken to prepare for increased U.S. intervention, but stressed the need to strengthen the South Vietnamese Government in order to create the necessary base.[32]

On November 1, 1964, the Communists attacked an American base and the President was urged by Maxwell Taylor, U.S. Ambassador to South Vietnam, as well as Gen. William C. Westmoreland, Commander of U.S. Forces in South Vietnam (COMUSMACV), and other military advisers, to retaliate by bombing North Vietnam. He declined to do so with the Presidential election campaign in its final days, but immediately after being elected on November 3 he directed his advisers to prepare alternative courses of action for the U.S. In early December, the President, saying that the "day of reckoning" was coming, approved a plan for graduated pressure by the U.S. on North Vietnam. He reiterated, however, the importance of strengthening the South Vietnamese Government before taking such action.[33]

In late December, the Communists bombed a U.S. officers' billet in Saigon, and Taylor and the military again recommended retaliation against North Vietnam. The President, with advice from Rusk and McNamara, declined to do so, citing the political confusion in South Vietnam. He also told Taylor that instead of bombing the North, he favored increasing U.S. combat forces in order to take stronger action against the guerrillas in the South.[34]

> Every time I get a military recommendation it seems to me that it calls for large-scale bombing: I have never felt that this war will be won from the air, and it seems to me that what is much more needed and would be more effective is a larger and stronger use of Rangers and Special Forces and Marines, or other appropriate military strength on the ground and on the scene. I am ready to look with great favor on that kind of

---

replied that there was, however, congressional dissatisfaction with what the U.S. was doing. He suggested that "in the event of a dramatic event in Southeast Asia we would go promptly for a Congressional resolution, but we would not plan on one and that our public information program would not be aimed at getting support for a resolution."

[32] Pt. II of this study, pp. 353–354.

[33] *Ibid.*, p. 376.

[34] Johnson Library, NSF NSC History, Deployment of Forces, CAP 64375 from the President to Taylor, Dec. 30, 1964.

increased American effort, directed at the guerrillas and aimed to stiffen the aggressiveness of Vietnamese military units up and down the line. Any recommendation that you or General Westmoreland make in this sense will have immediate attention from me, although I know that it may involve the acceptance of larger American sacrifices. We have been building our strength to fight this kind of war ever since 1961, and I myself am ready to substantially increase the number of Americans in Vietnam if it is necessary to provide this kind of fighting force against the Viet Cong.

In his reply a few days later, Taylor included an analysis prepared by Westmoreland and his staff. The U.S. advisory effort, MACV said, had "gone about as far . . . as it is practical to go without passing the point of clearly diminishing returns." As for the direct use of U.S. forces in a non-advisory role, MACV examined several alternatives and concluded that the political disadvantages of using U.S. forces outweighed the military advantages:[35]

> The Vietnamese have the manpower and the basic skills to win this war. What they lack is motivation. The entire advisory effort has been devoted to giving them both skill and motivation. If that effort has not succeeded there is less reason to think that U.S. combat forces would have the desired effect. In fact, there is good reason to believe that they would have the opposite effect by causing some Vietnamese to let the U.S. carry the burden while others, probably the majority, would actively turn against us. Thus intervention with ground combat forces would at best buy time and would lead to ever increasing commitments until, like the French, we would be occupying an essentially hostile foreign country.

Moreover, a review of tactical operations during 1963–1964, the MACV analysis said, indicated that the instances where the use of U.S. ground combat forces would have been desirable and feasible were "few and far between," and that "In balance, they do not seem to justify the presence of U.S. units, even disregarding the political problems involved."

MACV recommended, therefore, that the U.S. continue to use the advisory system, providing some additional manpower and operational support as necessary.

At the end of January 1965, after it appeared that the political and military situation in South Vietnam was getting worse, McGeorge Bundy and McNamara urged the President not to wait for a stronger political base, but to "use our military power in the Far East and to force a change of Communist policy." Continued inaction, they said, would lead to "disastrous defeat." Rusk did not agree, feeling that the consequences of escalation (or withdrawal) were so serious that the U.S. had to find a way to make existing programs effective. Except for Rusk, however, William P. Bundy says that McGeorge Bundy and McNamara's memorandum "summed up all of the feelings of all of us at that moment."[36]

After he received the McGeorge Bundy-McNamara recommendation, the President sent McGeorge Bundy to Vietnam for a report.

---

35 Same location, Saigon to Washington 2058, Jan. 6, 1965.
36 Pt. III of this study, p. 47.

During the last day of the visit, when Bundy's report, which recommended that the U.S. begin applying "sustained pressure" on North Vietnam (Phase II of the plan approved in December), was being completed, the Communists attacked the U.S. base at Pleiku, and McGeorge Bundy joined Ambassador Maxwell Taylor and General Westmoreland in recommending that the U.S. bomb North Vietnam. At an NSC meeting that night (February 6, 1965) which the Democratic leaders of Congress, John W. McCormack (D/Mass.), Speaker of the House, and Mike Mansfield (D/Mont.), majority leader of the Senate, attended, it was agreed by all except Mansfield that the U.S. should respond by a retaliatory airstrike on North Vietnam.

After another NSC meeting the next day (February 8), the President sent a cable to Ambassador Taylor in which he said that, despite the weaknesses of the South Vietnamese Government, he had decided to begin sustained reprisal ("continuing action") against North Vietnam (Phase II of the plan approved in December 1964). Shortly thereafter, the U.S. began the air war, codenamed ROLLING THUNDER.[37]

During the spring of 1965, after McNamara, at the direction of the President, had told the military in early March that there would be no limitation on funds, equipment or personnel,[38] increasing numbers of U.S. forces were approved for Vietnam (82,000 by June of 1965). In mid-March, Gen. Harold K. Johnson, Army Chief of Staff, after a trip to Vietnam on which he had been sent by the President to recommend ways to "get things bubbling,"[39] proposed, based on discussions with Westmoreland and Ambassador Taylor, a number of specific steps to provide more support for the South Vietnamese, as well as the deployment of additional U.S. ground combat units.[40] He recommended that an Army combat division be sent either to enclaves on the coastal region or to the highlands (the area of Pleiku). He said he preferred the latter, but recognized that coastal enclaves "may be the maximum action that is politically possible within the U.S. at this time."

General Johnson said it might also be necessary to send additional forces to interdict infiltration from the North, and he suggested, as he had in August 1964 when he became Chief of Staff of the Army, that this be done by invoking the Southeast Asia Treaty (SEATO) and deploying an international force (primarily or entirely Americans) of four divisions along the 17th parallel (the 1954 demarcation line between the North and the South) from the Gulf of Tonkin to Savannakhet on the Mekong River in Laos.

The President approved most of General Johnson's recommendations, but he waited a few weeks before approving the deployment of the U.S. division, and, according to available records, did not indicate whether he would approve the international force.

---

[37] For these developments, as well as the events leading up to the July 28, 1965 decision, see *ibid.*

[38] See *ibid.*, p. 149. This was not the open-ended authorization it may have appeared to be, however, as the military were soon to learn.

[39] *Ibid.*

[40] Taylor wanted to increase bombing of the North and was leery of sending more U.S. ground combat troops to the South. Westmoreland, however, thought U.S. forces would have to play a stronger role, and that more ground combat units would be needed. See *ibid.*, pp. 158–160.

In early June 1965, General Westmoreland, concluding that there was imminent danger of a Communist victory, requested large-scale deployment of U.S. combat forces—the "44 Battalion" request—"to take the war to the enemy."[41] He recommended that U.S. ground combat forces be increased to 175,000 by the end of 1965 and to 275,000 in 1966, and that they be deployed on the coast as well as inland and used both offensively and defensively. Although U.S. forces had not yet become involved in major combat against the Communists, Westmoreland said he was "convinced that U.S. troops with their energy, mobility, and firepower can successfully take the fight to the VC."[42]

In the following weeks, Westmoreland's request was discussed by the President and his advisers. Papers were prepared summarizing major points of view, and a report was filed by McNamara after a trip which he and others made to Vietnam in mid-July. In addition, the JCS prepared a study, at McNamara's request on behalf of the President, on the question, "Can we win if we do everything we can?" (The answer was, yes, but with a number of provisos.)[43]

In connection with McNamara's trip to Vietnam, Westmoreland was asked a series of questions pertaining to the use of large-scale U.S. forces, one of which was: "How long do you think it will take with your recommended forces (a) to seize the initiative, (b) to prove to the Viet Cong that they cannot win, and (c) thereby to force them to a settlement on our terms?" Westmoreland's reply was that U.S. forces would dislodge the Communists from local areas, but that this would not have a "lasting effect" unless the South Vietnamese were able to retain control over such areas. Therefore, he concluded, in a very significant caveat, "The objective of forcing the VC to the conclusion that he cannot win is considered to reside in a campaign of uncertain duration."[44]

Between July 21 and 28, 1965, a number of meetings were held by the President to discuss McNamara's report prior to a decision on Westmoreland's request. These appear to have been conducted primarily for instrumental rather than substantive purposes—how to tailor and present to the public the decision approving troops rather than whether to approve the request to send large-scale U.S. forces. The President apparently had already decided that he was going to approve the request,[45] and although the meetings were proclaimed by the White House to be deliberations on policy, they were, in fact, directed primarily at building and shaping a consensus in the Executive, Congress, and the public as the basis for gaining support for the President's decision.[46]

---

[41] *Ibid.*, p. 277.

[42] *Ibid.*

[43] *Ibid.*, pp. 359 ff.

[44] U.S. Department of State, Lot File 67 D 45. For the list of questions see pt. III of this study, pp. 372–373.

[45] On July 17, Deputy Secretary of Defense Cyrus Vance sent a "literally eyes only" message to McNamara in Vietnam stating that it was the President's "current intention" to approve Westmoreland's request. See *ibid.*, p. 381.

[46] John P. Burke and Fred I. Greenstein, in *How Presidents Test Reality: Decisions on Vietnam* (New York: Russell Sage Foundation, 1989), argue that in making decisions on Vietnam President Johnson did not adequately organize and use his advisory system, and that this, together with his other factors in his handling of the Presidency, adversely affected the quality of those decisions. "The Johnson policy process," they say (p. 259), "had some of the qualities of an unassembled jigsaw puzzle. There was much information and analysis, but nowhere within the na-

Continued

The question of "winning" was one of the issues discussed during these meetings, including whether U.S. forces could fight effectively in the kind of war being waged in South Vietnam. McNamara and JCS Chairman Earle G. Wheeler assured the President that U.S. forces could fight effectively, and that, in the words of McNamara's report, there was "a good chance of achieving an acceptable outcome within a reasonable period of time." When Adm. William F. Raborn, Director of the CIA, reported that in the opinion of the CIA the Communists would avoid major confrontations with U.S. forces, thus frustrating plans by the U.S. to engage and defeat main force units, McNamara replied, "U.S. forces can engage guerrillas as well as main force units." General Wheeler said that because of harassment by U.S. forces, the Communists "will have to 'come out and fight.'"

In a meeting of the President with the members of the Joint Chiefs of Staff other assurances were given by the military. In view of the difficulty of predicting how many U.S. forces might be needed and what the results might be, the President asked whether the U.S. should pause before making a further commitment. The reply from Adm. David L. McDonald, Chief of Naval Operations, was, "Sooner or later we'll force them to the conference table." The President then asked: "If we put in 100,000 would they put in an equal number?" General Wheeler replied that although the North Vietnamese might increase the deployment of their regular forces in the South, "they can't match us on buildup." Moreover, Admiral McDonald said, the threat of more troops from North Vietnam could be countered by increased bombing of the North. And in response to a question by the President as to whether bombing had been as effective as expected, Gen. John P. McConnell, Air Force Chief of Staff, said that it had been in the South but less so in the North because "we are not striking the targets that hurt them," implying that if the President would authorize striking such targets, bombing would be effective.

In a televised news conference on July 28, 1965, President Johnson announced that the U.S. would use its forces to defend South Vietnam. He said he was sending 50,000 more troops, (raising the total to 125,000), and that more would be needed and would be sent "as requested." For domestic and international political reasons, he did not reveal that he had already approved the deployment of another 50,000 (for a total of 175,000), and that another 100,000 (for a total of 275,000) were scheduled to be deployed in 1966.[47]

On August 5, the President met from 6:00 p.m. to 7:10 p.m. with the members of the NSC.[48] General Maxwell Taylor, who had just

---

tional security apparatus were the various pieces assembled, posing the President and his aides with coherent proposals and counterproposals."

[47] See pt. III of this study, for further details.

[48] Johnson Library, NSF NSC Meetings File. Present were the President, Vice President Hubert H. Humphrey, Rusk, McNamara, McGeorge Bundy, Secretary of the Treasury Henry H. Fowler, Ambassador Henry Cabot Lodge, Jr., George W. Ball, Cyrus Vance, William Bundy, David E. Bell (Administrator of the Agency for International Development), John T. McNaughton (Assistant Secretary of Defense) Ambassador at Large W. Averell Harriman, General Wheeler, Raborn, Richard Helms, Taylor, Ambassador Llewellyn Thompson, U.N. Ambassador Arthur Goldberg, Leonard H. Marks (Director of USIA), John Chancellor (director of the Voice of America), and Barry Zorthian, who was in charge of public affairs at the U.S. Mission in Saigon. Also present were Clark Clifford and NSC and White House staff members Bill D. Moyers, Chester L. Cooper, Douglass Cater, Bromley Smith and Joseph A. Califano, Jr.

been replaced as U.S. Ambassador to South Vietnam by Henry Cabot Lodge, Jr., told the group that the decision to increase U.S. forces "gave a lift to the South Vietnamese." "The present military situation is serious but not desperate. No one knows how much Viet Cong resilience is still left. The arrival of additional U.S. forces [the 1st Brigade of the 101st Airborne Division had arrived on July 29] must have convinced Hanoi that their chance of winning the war is lessening." "By the end of 1965," Taylor added, "the North Vietnamese offensive will be bloodied and defeated without having achieved major gains. Hanoi may then decide to change its policy. 1965 could be a decisive year."[49]

1964–1965 Pentagon Games and Intelligence Estimates Predict Problems

Even as the decision to send large-scale forces to Vietnam was being made and Taylor was forecasting decisive U.S. military victories, SIGMA II–65, a "politico-military" game (broader in scope than the usual "war" game), which was conducted at the Pentagon July 26-August 5, 1965, once again raised serious questions about further U.S. military involvement in the war. Four previous games in 1963, 1964 and 1965 had suggested that the bombing of North Vietnam and the use of large-scale U.S. ground forces in the South would not defeat the Communists, who would respond with greater force in an effort to inflict increasing casualties and to compel the U.S. to withdraw.[50]

---

[49] In a long cable to Washington (drafted by the Mission Intelligence Committee) on Aug. 26, 1965 from Lodge, in which Westmoreland concurred, a similar opinion was expressed: "Lack of complete success of their summer campaign has frustrated Viet-Cong aims for 1965. If they have not done so thus far, the Communists must soon acknowledge their inability either to achieve an early victory or to dislodge the growing military strength of the U.S. forces in the South." U.S. Department of State, Central File, Pol 27 Viet S, Saigon to Washington 624, Aug. 26, 1965.

[50] SIGMA I–63 was held in the spring of 1963, SIGMA I–64 in April 1964, SIGMA II–64 in September 1964, SIGMA I–65 in May 1965, and SIGMA II–65 in August 1965. These games were conducted by the Politico-Military Branch, Cold War Division, Joint War Games Agency of the Joint Chiefs of Staff. For SIGMA I–63, see pt. II of this study, p. 354, fn. 27. (There is an error in the footnote. The date was 1963 rather than 1964.) The report on SIGMA I–64 is available at the Johnson Library, NSF Agency File, JCS. For SIGMA II–64, see pt. II of this study, p. 353 and the article by Harold P. Ford cited below. The report on SIGMA II–65, declassified for the author by the JCS, is in the author's files.

The purpose of these games was to help those involved in policymaking in the executive branch, primarily the White House, the State and Defense Departments and the military services, together with the CIA, to gain a better understanding of the outcomes and consequences of U.S. actions in the context of those of other parties or countries involved in the conflict. In the words of the final report on SIGMA II–65, "The purpose of SIGMA II–65 is to explore current problems in Southeast Asia using an interagency United States/Republic of Vietnam team as well as selected teams of area experts representing other nations and influences concerned. It is hoped that examination of familiar problems and constraints from several national viewpoints under conditions of simulated crises will lead to: a. New perspectives on the overall politico-military situation. b. Better insight into potential problems or windfall opportunities. c. Ideas to enhance current plans and programs. d. An array of realistic scenario concepts against which current and future contingency plans can be evaluated." *SIGMA II–65 Final Report*, Aug. 20, 1965, p. H–1.

Each game involved 50 or so participants from the executive branch offices mentioned above. In SIGMA I–63, SIGMA I–64 and SIGMA I–65, played by working-level officials, senior or cabinet-level officials participated as members of policy review teams. In SIGMA II–64, senior officials participated as players. In SIGMA II–65, senior officials met after the game was completed to review and discuss a video-summary. (For the list of those on the SIGMA II–65 teams and in the senior review group see pp. A–4-A–8 of *ibid.)*

In each game, teams were designated by color. For SIGMA II–65, for example, there were the following: Blue—U.S. and South Vietnam, Red—North Vietnam, Black—the "Vietcong" (Communists of South Vietnam), Yellow—China, Green—U.S.S.R. There was also a control team for each of the games which helped to establish the framework for the game by providing the opening scenario as well as subsequent scenarios for the game as it progressed. Control, which was neutral, also handled all communications between national teams, answered substantive and

Continued

In the 1963 game (SIGMA I–63), according to former Ambassador William H. Sullivan, one of the participants, who was very closely associated with Southeast Asian affairs during his career in the State Department, by 1970, when the scenario of the game ended, the U.S. would have 500,000 troops in Vietnam and would be faced with a military stalemate and with draft riots at home.[51]

In the case of the August 1965 game, SIGMA II–65,[52] according to the final report,

> There was a marked asymmetry in the objectives of the opposing teams. The Blue team [U.S.-South Vietnam] assumed a significant commitment by the Viet Cong to major military victories in the short term and attached principal importance to the short term objective of preventing such victories. The Red [North Vietnam] and Black [Vietcong] teams in fact, however, discounted the importance of an early military victory and were unperturbed at the prospect of decreasing military activity in the short-run in the face of the U.S. build-up. Their attention was focused on the longer term results of their efforts to disrupt the economy, terrorize the opposition, and destroy political order and they read the results in these areas as pointing to eventual victory for their side.

The Red and Black teams, the report added, "were thinking in terms of the 1968 U.S. elections, ten and even twenty years beyond, and they did not think they needed early victory."[53]

With respect to the use of large-scale U.S. ground combat forces, "there was considerable feeling among SIGMA II–65 participants that Viet Cong adoption of the strategy of avoiding major engagements with U.S. forces *would* make it extremely difficult to find and fix enemy units. . . . Viet Cong experience in the jungles, guerrilla warfare, intelligence capabilities would pose serious problems, even for well-equipped and highly mobile U.S. regulars." (emphasis in original)[54]

With respect to bombing North Vietnam, "there was considerable feeling among *all* of the Communist teams that punishment being imposed could and would be absorbed by the Hanoi leadership. This thought was based on the fact that the country is basically a subsistence economy centering on the self-sustaining village. Isolation and disruption of the Hanoi-Haiphong-complex transport systems would pose serious urban and military problems but the DRV still had its ports and although electric power and petroleum were becoming critical [according to the scenario there had been U.S. attacks on power plants and petroleum supplies], major industry had not been hit. Industrial activities constitute such a limited portion of the total economy that even this disruption seemed an acceptable price."[55]

---

procedural questions, and attempted to guide the game toward the achievement of game objectives.

[51] William H. Sullivan, *Obbligato, 1939–1979* (New York: W. W. Norton, 1984), pp. 178–181.

[52] *SIGMA II–65 Final Report*, B–4.

[53] *Ibid.*, p. C–2.

[54] *Ibid.*, p. D–4.

[55] *Ibid.*, p. D–5.

In a memorandum to William Bundy on August 5, W. W. Rostow, head of the Department of State's Policy Planning Council, who had participated in SIGMA II–65, commented on the game:[56]

> What I draw from this afternoon's critique of Sigma 2–65 is the following:
>
> 1. An indecisive engagement of large numbers of U.S. troops on the ground, for a protracted period, with rising casualties, could produce political frustration in the U.S. and in South Vietnamese politics.
>
> 2. Air and other direct pressure on the North is a critical variable, notably if the gamesters are correct that Peiping can't think of anything useful to do if we up the ante—and, by and large, I believe they are right.
>
> 3. The development of political unity, momentum, and a sense of direction in South Vietnamese politics is as important as we're all saying it is. We've got to start running right now for that supervised election which, after all, represents for us an optimum outcome of the war; and winning elections takes the political organization we don't now have.

The conclusions of SIGMA II–65 participants closely paralleled intelligence findings. (There were CIA and other intelligence officials participating in the game, of course, and other participants had read the intelligence estimates.) In SNIE (Special National Intelligence Estimate) 10–9–65, July 23, 1965,[57] the U.S. Intelligence Board (composed of representatives from the intelligence offices of relevant agencies and departments) concluded that if the U.S. sent large-scale troop deployments to South Vietnam, as the President was then in the final stages of deciding to do, the Communists would respond by augmenting their own forces, including sending more North Vietnamese troops to the South, and by avoiding direct confrontation with U.S. forces. In response to heavier bombing of the North, the North Vietnamese would ask the Russians for greater air defense assistance, but even with heavier bombing of military and industrial targets their will to persist would not be significantly affected.

The strategy of the Communists, the intelligence estimate concluded, would depend upon the course of the war. If it appeared that they were going to be defeated, they would probably show some interest in negotiating. Otherwise, they would wait, in the belief that the U.S. would not have the will to persist.

Responses to the President's Decision to Send Large-Scale U.S. Forces to Vietnam

The response to the President's decision to send large-scale U.S. forces to Vietnam was generally favorable, both in and out of the government. In the small circle of Presidential advisers, only George Ball, the Under Secretary of State, and Clark Clifford, a

[56] U.S. Department of State, S/P Chron File.

[57] Johnson Library, NSF NSC History, Deployment of Forces. For a summary of twelve intelligence estimates during 1974–1965, see pt. III of this study, pp. 463–467. See also the excellent article by Harold P. Ford, who at the time of the July 1965 decision was a senior CIA officer, "The U.S. Decision to Go Big in Vietnam," *Studies in Intelligence* (Spring 1985), pp. 1–15, which concludes with a very thoughtful analysis of why national intelligence had made "so slight an impact" on the decision. *Studies in Intelligence* is a classified in-house publication of the CIA, but this article, which was kindly provided by Mr. Ford, has been declassified.

Washington lawyer who was very close to the President and was serving at the time as the non-paid chairman of the President's Foreign Intelligence Advisory Board, expressed disagreement, but both men said that they would support the President's decision. In the case of Ball, although the President appeared to respect his views and usually accorded them a full hearing, Ball was performing a role as "devil's advocate"—according to Rusk, Ball had been "named" by the President to play that role[58]—and his viewpoint was judged in that context. In addition, the President gave more weight to Rusk's views, partly because of his greater respect for him, and because Rusk was the Secretary of State and Lyndon Johnson generally tended to respect rank and position.

In the case of Clark Clifford, although the President had great respect for Clifford, and looked to him and to Washington lawyer Abe Fortas for a wide range of personal advice, he did not consider Clifford a foreign policy or military expert, nor did Clifford have the kind of information and current knowledge of the situation that was possessed by the Secretary of State and the Secretary of Defense.

Another dissenter was the Vice President, Hubert H. Humphrey, but the President had limited respect for his knowledge and judgment in foreign policy and military matters. Humphrey's role as Vice President, with no significant operational responsibility or access to information except from his statutory membership on the NSC, also tended to remove him from policymaking and the operations of the White House, and Johnson, like most Presidents, including Kennedy when Johnson was Vice President, treated Humphrey as something of an outsider, especially with respect to the making of foreign policy. Johnson also expected his Vice President to be loyal, and when Humphrey objected to escalating the U.S. role in the war in February 1965 Johnson reacted by excluding him from any involvement in Vietnam policymaking until 1966, when Humphrey became more supportive.[59]

---

[58] Pt. III of this study, p. 90, fn. 121.

[59] See *ibid.*, pp. 95–96. It is not clear how Humphrey felt about the July 28 decision. For whatever reasons, he did not attend the meetings which preceded it except for one meeting on July 26 and a Cabinet meeting on July 27. The notes of those two meetings do not indicate that he made any comments during either meeting.

In "The Mythology Surrounding Lyndon Johnson, His Advisers, and the 1965 Decision to Escalate the Vietnam War," *Political Science Quarterly*, 103, No. 4 (1988), pp. 637–664, and subsequently in *Uncertain Warriors: Lyndon Johnson and His Vietnam Advisers* (Lawrence, Kans.: Univ. Press of Kansas, 1993), David M. Barrett argues that President Johnson "was not a victim of groupthink and that he received and listened to significant advice warning him against sending troops to Vietnam." Although the article and the book provide a useful summary of the views of six men who gave the President such advice—Ball, Clifford, Humphrey, Mansfield, J. William Fulbright (D/Ark.), and Richard B. Russell (D/Ga.), Barrett fails to demonstrate either that the President was not a "victim of groupthink" or that he "listened" to the arguments of the six men.

Barrett seems to conclude that Johnson's "insecurity vis-á-vis the 'intellectuals'" from the Kennedy administration, namely, Rusk, McNamara and McGeorge Bundy, led him to be "unduly influenced" by them. Even accepting Barrett's characterization of these three men as "intellectuals" (would he argue that, by comparison, Ball, Fulbright, Clifford, Mansfield, Russell and Humphrey were not?), it also happens that Rusk, McNamara and McGeorge Bundy were the President's three principal advisers and the members of the small group to which, by virtue of their positions as well as his respect for them, he turned for advice. Was the President "unduly influenced" by them because they were "intellectuals," or was he influenced by them because they were the Secretary of State, the Secretary of Defense and the National Security Adviser? And if the President was "unduly influenced" by them—and Barrett does not attempt to define what he means by that expression—could it be that he was, to use the concept employed by Barrett, a "victim of groupthink" rather than a victim of his own insecurity?

Barrett also describes at length the views of each of the six men who advised against sending troops, but he does not analyze the relationships of the President with the six to ascertain

There were several dissenters among staff-level officials in the White House and the State Department who were involved in Vietnam policymaking,[60] but the President, if, in fact, he knew about it, paid little if any attention to their doubts and criticism.

There was also considerable dissent in the CIA, as might be expected given the agency's estimates about the prospects for U.S. success. One example was the position taken by Harold P. Ford, a very experienced and sagacious CIA officer, who had been the agency's representative on the inter-agency task force that developed the graduated pressure plan in November 1964. On April 8, 1965, Ford, who was Chief of the Estimates Staff of the Office of National Estimates, sent a memorandum, "Into the Valley," to the Director of the CIA that read in part:[61]

> This troubled essay proceeds from a deep concern that we are becoming progressively divorced from reality in Vietnam, that we are proceeding with far more courage than wisdom—towards unknown ends, and that we are perhaps about to compound our already difficult predicament if we indeed commit several divisions of U.S. ground troops to combat in South Vietnam.
>
> We do not have the capability to achieve the goals we have set for ourselves in Vietnam, yet we think and act as if we do.
>
> In view of the enemy's power in the Vietnam countryside and of the narrow and fragile political base we have in the GVN, we are asking a steep price indeed of the enemy in asking him to call off the VC and to cease DRV support and direction of it.
>
> There seems to be a congenital American disposition to underestimate Asian enemies. We are doing so now. We cannot afford so precious a luxury. Earlier, dispassionate estimates, war games, and the like, told us that the DRV/VC would persist in the face of such pressures as we are now exerting on them. Yet we now seem to expect them to come running to the conference table, ready to talk about our high terms.
>
> The chances are considerably better than even that the U.S. will in the end have to disengage in Vietnam, and do so considerably short of our present objectives.

Within the military, there was strong support for the President's action. The decision not to invoke a national emergency and to mobilize and call up the Reserves, however, was bitterly criticized by military leaders, especially in the Army, the service which would be most deeply affected by the decision. It is reported that General Johnson, Chief of Staff of the Army, was so incensed, and so convinced that the Army should not be asked to go to battle under such a handicap, that he considered resigning:[62]

> After the [President's July 27] speech, he [General Johnson] closed the door of his office and put on his best dress uniform. When he emerged he ordered his driver to get his car; he was

whether he was likely, in fact, to "listen" to their advice. Nor does he analyze the President's attitudes toward taking advice from persons who were not members of his official advisory group and who were not, except for Ball, experienced in the conduct of national security policy or privy to information which was available to his advisers.

[60] See pt. III of this study, pp. 96, 449–450.

[61] Harold Ford, "The U.S. Decision to Go Big in Vietnam," cited above, pp. 10–11.

[62] Mark Perry, *Four Stars* (Boston: Houghton Mifflin, 1989), p. 156.

going to talk to the president, he told his staff. On the way into Washington, Johnson reached up and unpinned the stars from his shoulders, holding them lightly in his hands. When the car arrived at the White House gates, he ordered the driver to stop. He stared down at his stars, shook his head, and pinned them back on. Years later he reflected on the incident, regretting his own decision. "I should have gone to see the President," he reportedly told one colleague. "I should have taken off my stars. I should have resigned. It was the worst, the most immoral decision I've ever made."

In Congress, the reaction to the President's July 1965 decision was mixed. Although some Members praised it and only a few Members were publicly critical, many Members appeared to be apprehensive about the situation and were relieved that the President had not called up the Reserves, declared a national emergency, or asked for large new appropriations. At a meeting of 11 congressional leaders with the President the day before the decision was announced, the only dissenter was Senate Majority Leader Mansfield, (although Bourke B. Hickenlooper (R/Iowa), the senior Republican on the Senate Foreign Relations Committee, appeared to be very dubious), but the lack of enthusiasm for using large-scale U.S. forces in the war was also apparent. The mood, as Senator Hickenlooper expressed it, was one of supporting the President rather than approving what he had decided to do.[63]

A few senior Members of the Senate, including three prominent Democrats in key roles—Mansfield, Richard B. Russell (D/Ga.), the powerful chairman of the Armed Services Committee who had been Lyndon Johnson's mentor in the Senate, and J. William Fulbright (D/Ark.), the chairman of the Foreign Relations Committee, who also had been close to the President—had also met on the day before the President's decision was announced, and, according to Mansfield's summary for the President of the group's conclusion, "there was full agreement that insofar as Vietnam is concerned we are deeply enmeshed in a place where we ought not to be; that the situation is rapidly going out of control; and that every effort should be made to extricate ourselves."[64]

A few days later, Russell was interviewed on the CBS television program "Face the Nation." In commenting on the mistakes the U.S. had made he said, "Our greatest mistake there has been in overemphasizing the military and not putting sufficient emphasis on the civilian side." "The people there don't have much sense of nationalism to start with," he said, "and no cause can ever win that hasn't got a champion that the people admire." He thought it would be "highly likely" that in a free election the South Vietnamese would choose Ho Chi Minh in preference to the existing South Vietnamese Government officials. "One of the vital things there," he added "is getting a stable civil government and unless we get that basis the war can run on there interminably."

---

[63] See pt. III of this study, p. 429.

[64] *Ibid.*, p. 435. See also Caroline F. Ziemke, "Senator Richard B. Russell and the 'Lost Cause' in Vietnam, 1954–1968," *Georgia Historical Quarterly*, LXXII (Spring 1988), pp. 30–71.

For a general commentary on Russell and Vietnam, see the chapter on Vietnam in Gilbert C. Fite, *Richard B. Russell, Jr., Senator From Georgia* (Chapel Hill: Univ. of North Carolina Press, 1991).

Russell was also asked whether a defeat in Vietnam would be a "strategic blow" for the U.S. He replied that it "would be a worse blow to our world prestige and to our reputation for keeping our word under all conditions than it would be from either a strategic or a tactical or an economic standpoint. I don't think it has any value strategically. . . . I am fairly familiar with the domino theory that if South Vietnam falls that all the other falls. I don't think that is necessarily true. I don't agree with that completely."[65]

Outside the Government, there was also a mixed reaction to the President's decision. Among prominent leaders with experience in foreign policy and military affairs as represented by the "Wise Men,"[66] as well as among the "defense intellectuals" who served as civilian strategists for the Pentagon, there was widespread support for the decision.[67] (The Wise Men, otherwise known as the President's Consultants on Foreign Affairs, consisted at that time of Dean G. Acheson, Eugene R. Black, Omar N. Bradley, John Cowles, Arthur H. Dean, Allen W. Dulles, Roswell Gilpatric, Paul G. Hoffman, George B. Kistiakowsky, Arthur Larson, Morris I. Leibman, Robert A. Lovett, John J. McCloy, Teodoro Moscoso, James Perkins and James J. Wadsworth.)[68] In private meetings with Rusk and others shortly before the decision was made, the Wise Men concluded that the stakes were so high that the U.S. had to use whatever combat forces were required to prevent the Communists from taking control of South Vietnam.[69]

The "defense intellectuals" from major American universities and research centers such as Harvard University, the Massachusetts Institute of Technology, and the RAND Corporation, also supported the decision. One of the principal strategic theorists of the period, Bernard Brodie, said later that he knew of no one among the civilian strategists (he included himself) "who by the end of 1965 had manifested any misgivings about the course that President Johnson had embarked upon." On the contrary, he said, for some of them

---

[65] Transcript of "Face the Nation," Aug. 1, 1965.

[66] See pt. III of this study, pp. 347–350.

[67] *Ibid.*, pp. 452–453.

[68] All of these distinguished men had been very active in public affairs, and most of them had served in high positions in the Government. Acheson, a Washington lawyer, had been Secretary of State in the Truman administration; Black had been president of the World Bank; Bradley had been an outstanding military leader, serving as Army Chief of Staff and Chairman of the JCS; Cowles was the publisher of the *Minneapolis Star and Tribune* and the *Des Moines Register;* Dean, a partner in the New York law firm of Sullivan and Cromwell, had held a number of Government posts; Dulles was Director of the CIA in the Eisenhower administration; Gilpatric, a member of the New York law firm of Cravath, Swaine and Moore, was Deputy Secretary of Defense in the Kennedy administration; Hoffman, a former automobile company executive and Director of the Marshall Plan, was managing director of the U.N. Special Fund; Kistiakowsky, former science adviser to President Eishenhower, was a professor of chemistry at Harvard University; Larson, Director of the U.S. Information Agency in the Eisenhower administration, was head of the Rule of Law Center at Duke University; Leibman was a prominent Chicago lawyer who had active connections with the White House and the Defense Department; Lovett, who, among other things, had been Secretary of Defense in the last two years of the Truman administration, was a partner in the New York investment firm of Brown Brothers, Harriman; McCloy, who had held a number of government posts, was a partner in the New York law firm of Milbank, Tweed, Hadley and McCloy; Moscoso, a businessman and former government official in Puerto Rico, had been director of the State Department program for Latin America, the Alliance for Progress, in the Kennedy administration; Perkins, a former foundation executive, was president of Cornell University; Wadsworth was a government consultant who had held many posts, especially in the U.S. Mission to the U.N.

[69] See pt. III of this study, pp. 347–350. Larson was not fully convinced, and preferred greater emphasis on diplomacy.

". . . it was precisely the kind of application of their ideas which they could not help but relish."[70]

The President's decision was also generally well-received by the press. "Few Americans," the *New York Times* said in an editorial, "will quarrel with President Johnson's determined conclusion to hold on in Vietnam.[71] The reaction of the public is difficult to gauge. There were no polls on public attitudes toward the President's July 28 decision. The results of a Gallup poll in late August on the question, *"Do you approve or disapprove of the way the Johnson Administration is handling the situation in Vietnam?"* could be interpreted as indicative of stronger public support for the administration's position after the President's decision:[72]

[In percent]

	Late-August 1965	*Mid-July 1965*	*Mid-June 1965*
Approve	57	52	48
Disapprove	25	26	28
No Opinion	18	22	24

A question of this kind tends, however, to evoke a partisan response, thus affecting its reliability as an indicator of general public opinion.[73]

---

[70] Bernard Brodie, "Why Were We So (Strategically) Wrong," *Foreign Policy* 5 (Winter 1971–72), pp. 151–163 at 158.

[71] *New York Times*, July 29, 1965. The *Times* warned, however, that the war could last for years or decades (as the President himself had said in response to a question at the July 28 press conference), and stressed the importance of using the minimum force necessary to prove to the North Vietnamese and Chinese "that military aggression is not worthwhile and never will be."

[72] *Washington Post*, Aug. 27, 1965. For a breakdown of the responses to the Poll in late August by sex, race, education, occupation, age, religion, politics, region, income and community size, see *Vietnam War, A Compilation: 1964–1990*, Public Opinion and the Vietnam War, National and International Opinion, 3 vols. (Princeton, N.J.: Gallup Poll, n.d.), vol. 1, no pagination. This very useful compilation reprints the Gallup press releases on polls, which frequently contained more detailed information than appeared in newspaper accounts, or *The Gallup Poll: Public Opinion, 1935–1971* (New York: Random House, 1972).

[73] See John E. Mueller, *War, Presidents and Public Opinion* (New York: Wiley, 1973), p. 116. The following table *(ibid.*, p. 271, from Gallup Poll data), shows the effect of partisanship on support for the war. For each group, the numbers represent the percentages in support of the war, in opposition and no opinion. (*Note*: These data indicate support for the war, not for the way Johnson was handling the war.)

	Republican			*Democrat*			*Independent*		
May 1965	54	27	19	54	25	21	46	29	25
August 1965	57	28	16	62	22	16	60	26	14
November 1965	61	25	14	65	18	17	67	21	12
March 1966	56	27	17	60	24	16	59	27	14
May 1966	47	42	11	50	32	18	49	37	14
September 1966	43	42	15	49	32	19	51	32	17
November 1966	52	34	14	52	28	20	50	32	18
May 1967	45	43	12	55	31	14	47	41	12
July 1967	41	51	8	55	33	12	43	46	11
October 1967	37	54	9	48	41	11	44	48	8
Early February 1968	39	53	8	45	41	14	40	47	13
March 1968	39	53	8	46	43	11	39	54	7
April 1968	39	52	9	43	43	14	38	52	10
August 1968	31	58	11	37	50	13	37	54	9
Early October 1968	35	57	8	40	52	8	38	53	9
February 1969	36	54	10	44	47	9	35	59	6
September 1969	35	57	8	31	59	10	30	60	10
January 1970	36	53	11	32	56	12	30	64	6
April 1970	38	49	13	33	49	18	33	57	10
March 1970	38	54	8	33	58	9	37	55	8
January 1971	32	61	7	30	59	11	31	60	9
May 1971	31	58	11	27	64	9	29	60	11

Also in August, Gallup asked for the first time a question that was asked 24 additional times between then and 1971—the only question on the war to be asked in the same wording and over an extended period of time—the so-called "mistake" question:[74]

"In view of developments since we entered the fighting in Vietnam, do you think the U.S. made a mistake sending troops to fight in Vietnam?"

[In percent]

	August 1965
Not a mistake	61
Mistake	24
No opinion	15

The percentage in this poll of those who thought it was not a mistake to send troops was the highest of the entire war.[75]

According to a Harris Survey taken in late August and released in mid-September 1965,[76] "the American people are nearly 70–30 behind the proposition that Vietnam should be the ground on which the United States should take its stand against communism in Asia." Moreover, there was apparently general recognition that the war could last for a long time. "Only a relatively small minority any longer expects a quick settlement of the war. More than twice as many, in fact a majority of the public, believe that the Vietnam fighting will go on for several years. . . . There is little doubt now that most Americans appear ready for a long haul in Vietnam, as distasteful as the sacrifice and suffering might be."

[74] *Ibid.*, p. 54.

[75] These are the results from all of the "mistake" questions asked by Gallup during the war (*ibid.*, pp. 54–55):

[In percent]

	Not a mistake	*Mistake*	*No opinion*
August 1965	61	24	15
March 1966	59	25	16
May 1966	49	36	15
September 1966	48	35	17
November 1966	51	31	18
Early February 1967	52	32	16
May 1967	50	37	13
July 1967	48	41	11
October 1967—Bunker, Westmoreland visit to Washington	44	46	10
December 1967	46	45	9
Tet offensive—Early February 1968	42	46	12
March 1968	41	49	10
April 1968	40	48	12
August 1968	35	53	12
Early October 1968—Nixon elected	37	54	9
February 1969	39	52	9
September 1969	32	58	10
January 1970	33	57	10
March 1970	32	58	10
April 1970—Cambodia invaded	34	51	15
May 1970	36	56	8
January 1971	31	59	10
May 1971	28	61	11

It should be noted, however, that data from the "mistake" question, while useful, are not a reliable index of support for and opposition to the war because of the wording of the question and the lack of follow-up questions. For an explanation, see pt. III of this study, p. 142.

[76] *Washington Post*, Sept. 12, 1965.

In this poll, Louis Harris used a question which he had used several times before, beginning in November 1964:[77]

> *"What course do you feel the United States should follow in the Vietnam fighting—carry the ground fighting to North Vietnam, at the risk of bringing Red China into the war, negotiate a settlement, or hold the line to keep the Communists from taking over South Vietnam?"*

[In percent]

	September 1965	*July 1965*	*May 1965*
Hold the line	49	45	42
Negotiate	25	30	36
Carry the war north	26	25	22

Harris gave this explanation of the results of this poll: "The bulk of Americans—the 49 percent who want to hold the line in South Vietnam—feel almost as strongly about that view [as the 26 percent who wanted to carry the war north]. Ninety-five percent of them say they are willing to give up last year's tax cut to maintain that position. Seventy-three percent say they are for holding the line even if it means a land war as in Korea. Sixty-nine percent say they are for holding the line even if it means Russia and China join with North Vietnam. And 58 percent are for staying in South Vietnam even if it means the eventual use of atom bombs against China.

"In sharp contrast, the 25 percent of the public who want to end the fighting in Vietnam with the best settlement we can get is far less solid in its views. Seventy percent of these people say they would change their minds about our course in Vietnam if it means that Communists would use similar tactics on other continents. Almost two-thirds say they would change their minds if negotiating our way out of Vietnam means that the Communists would take over all of southeast Asia or that Americans would be fighting against Communist 'wars of liberation' in other places in the next 15 years."

In the same survey Harris also asked a question on U.S. military tactics, the responses to which also tended to support the Johnson administration (although there was a large percentage of "not sure"):[78]

> *"I want to read off to you a number of positions the Johnson Administration has taken on Vietnam. For each, I wish you would tell me if you think the Administration is more right or more wrong."*

[In percent]

	More Right	*More Wrong*	*Not Sure*
Not using tactical atomic ground weapons	67	14	19
Not bombing the China mainland	65	13	22
Not bombing Hanoi	47	20	33
Not blockading North Vietnam ports	31	38	31

[77] It should be noted that, unlike earlier surveys in which this question was asked, this survey does not provide the percentage of "Not sure" answers. For earlier surveys, see pt. III of this study, pp. 145, 353.

[78] *Washington Post*, Sept. 13, 1965.

The Reaction of Antiwar Groups

Peace and antiwar groups responded to the President's decision by creating the first national end-the-war organization and by increasing the number of teach-ins and demonstrations. On August 6–9, 1965, a demonstration was held in Washington at the instigation of some of the older leaders of traditional peace groups, including the Reverend A. J. Muste, the 81-year old head of the Fellowship of Reconciliation and the Committee for Nonviolent Action, and David Dellinger, editor of *Liberation* magazine, together with younger antiwar leaders such as Professor Staughton Lynd of Yale University.[79] Civil rights leaders were also involved as were students in the antiwar and civil rights movements, but the "new left" Students for a Democratic Society (SDS) did not participate directly. In its national meeting in June, the group had been unable to agree on what it should do about the war, although it did agree that local SDS chapters could give it priority in their own programs.

During the demonstration, the 1,000 protestors who had gathered in Washington, calling themselves the "Assembly of Unrepresented People," discussed the need for developing a broad national program for coordinating antiwar activities, and agreed to establish a National Coordinating Committee to End the War in Vietnam in which 23 organizations, including the SDS, would be represented.[80] Those present at the meeting also agreed to engage in civil disobedience as a way of showing their opposition to the war. Accordingly, on August 9, when they marched toward the Capitol, the demonstrators refused to stop at police lines and 350 were arrested.[81] Clearly, many antiwar activists were becoming impatient with less confrontational methods such as the teach-ins, and, based on experience in the civil rights movement, wanted to take direct action to express their opposition to the war.

On August 12, 1965, Dr. Martin Luther King, Jr., head of the Southern Christian Leadership Conference, who was opposed to the war, called on President Johnson to agree to negotiate with the National Liberation Front, and announced that he was considering making an effort to end the fighting by appealing directly to gov-

---

[79] For general treatments of antiwar organizations and activities see Charles DeBenedetti (with Charles Chatfield, assisting author), *An American Ordeal: The Antiwar Movement of the Vietnam Era* (Syracuse, N.Y.: Syracuse Univ. Press, 1990). Also useful are Nancy Zaroulis and Gerald Sullivan, *Who Spoke Up? American Protest Against the War in Vietnam, 1963–1975* (Garden City, N.Y.: Doubleday, 1984), Thomas Powers, *The War at Home: Vietnam and the American People, 1964–1968* (New York: Grossman, 1973) and Tom Wells, *The War Within: America's Battle Over Vietnam* (Berkeley: Univ. of California Press, 1994). For the August 1965 demonstration and subsequent protests, see, among other personal accounts by antiwar activists, David Dellinger's *From Yale to Jail: The Life Story of a Moral Dissenter* (New York: Pantheon Books, 1993).

[80] By the end of 1966, this was replaced by the Spring Mobilization Committee to End the War in Vietnam, which, in the fall of 1967, became the National Mobilization Committee to End the War in Vietnam, known as the Mobe. In 1969–70, as the SDS became more radical, the name was changed to the New Mobilization Committee to End the War in Vietnam (it was still called the Mobe). By the spring of 1970, it had become defunct.

[81] See Powers, *The War at Home*, pp. 81–82.

On August 6, several representatives from the group met at the White House with Chester Cooper, McGeorge Bundy's deputy for Asian affairs to discuss Vietnam. In an August 9 weekly report on Asia to Bundy (from Cooper, and NSC staffers James C. Thomson, Jr. and Donald Ropa, who was on detail to the NSC from the CIA) Cooper said that he had ". . . spent Friday afternoon coping with the Reverend Muste, Joan Baez and some very limp young men. So far as he [Cooper] knows, no crockery was broken." Johnson Library, NSF Name File, Cooper Memos.

ernments on both sides.[82] He dropped the idea, however, after pressure from other civil rights leaders and his staff not to "confuse" the civil rights issue with the war.[83]

Starting in early August 1965, and continuing periodically into September, antiwar protestors in the San Francisco-Berkeley area, many of whom were students at the University of California (Berkeley), also began to take more direct action by attempting to stop trains carrying U.S. troops to the Oakland Army Terminal for embarkation to Vietnam, as well as demonstrating at ports where ships were being loaded for Vietnam.[84] Several U.S. Senators, led by Senator Frank J. Lausche (D/Ohio), responded by introducing legislation (which was not enacted) to establish criminal penalties for interference with troops or supplies.[85]

Draft card burning as a form of protest, a practice which had begun during the spring of 1965, was also increasing, and Congress, spurred by the march on the Capitol during the August demonstration in Washington and by the incidents in Oakland, vented its feelings by enacting by a vote of 393–1 in the House of Representatives and a voice vote in the Senate a new law imposing a fine of up to $10,000 and imprisonment for up to 5 years for the willful or knowing destruction or mutilation of a draft card.[86]

The bill was passed by the House on August 10, the day after the arrests during the march on the Capitol. Republican William G. Bray of Indiana, the ranking minority member of the House Armed Services Committee, probably expressed the attitude of many Members of Congress when he said:[87]

> The need of this legislation is clear. Beatniks and so-called "campus-cults" have been publicly burning their draft cards to demonstrate their contempt for the United States and our resistance to Communist takeovers. Such actions have been suggested and led by college professors—professors supported by taxpayers' money. . . .
>
> Just yesterday such a mob attacking the United States and praising the Vietcong attempted to march on the Capitol but were prevented by the police from forcibly moving into our Chambers. They were led by a Yale University professor [Staughton Lynd]. They were generally a filthy, sleazy beatnik gang; but the question which they pose to America is quite serious. . . .

---

[82] *New York Times*, Aug. 13 and 14, 1965. The White House replied to King through Robert C. Weaver, an African-American who was Secretary of Labor. Weaver said that criticism of U.S. policy by prominent civil rights leaders might lead to miscalculations by the Communists. *Ibid.*, Aug. 20, 1965.

[83] See Adam Fairclough, *To Redeem the Soul of America: The Southern Christian Leadership Conference and Dr. Martin Luther King, Jr.* (Athens: Univ. of Georgia Press, 1987), pp. 271–274.

[84] *New York Times*, Aug. 7, 8, 24, 1965.

[85] For Lausche's speech, in which he included the text of one of the statements being handed out at the protest, see *Congressional Record*, vol. 111 (Washington, D.C.: U.S. Govt. Print. Off.), pp. 22316–22317 (hereafter referred to as *CR*). A similar bill passed the House of Representatives in 1966, but was not acted on by the Senate.

[86] *Ibid.*, pp. 19871–19872, 20433–20434. The only Member of the House to be recorded against the bill was a Republican from New York, Henry P. Smith. On Oct. 15, 1965, David Miller, a pacifist, after a brief speech at a demonstration against the war, burned his draft card. He was arrested and sentenced to five years in jail (he served two). For his account, see Joan Morrison and Robert K. Morrison, *From Camelot to Kent State: The Sixties Experience in the Words of Those Who Lived It* (New York: Times Books, 1987), pp. 107–111.

[87] *CR*, vol. 111, p. 19871.

> The Communists are planning to use the "Judas goats" to lead those who are free to defect from freedom. So-called "students" and Communist stooges here and abroad, by demonstrations of anti-American feeling, by belittling, and by vilification are to downgrade the United States in the eyes of the world and shake the confidence and faith of our citizens in our democratic way of life. They hope to attain victory over freedom by subversion within the United States and by erosion of our national pride and confidence in the greatness of America and our national heritage. . . .

On September 2, the National Student Association (NSA), an organization of student governments from about 300 colleges and universities, "overwhelmingly" adopted a resolution at its national conference calling on the U.S. Government to stop the bombing of North Vietnam and other offensive actions, and to seek negotiations, in which representatives of the "Vietcong" should be included.[88] Ironically, at the time NSA was actively and secretly cooperating with the CIA in various ways, including receiving CIA funding for U.S. student representatives to international student conferences.[89]

The White House Mounts a Campaign to Support U.S. Policy

Meanwhile, a number of steps were being taken by the Johnson administration to justify the President's decision to the public and to develop public support for U.S. policy in Vietnam.

In a luncheon meeting on August 19 at the State Department with the Secretary and senior department officers, the President talked at length about the state of public opinion. He said that support for the administration's policy in Vietnam was "generally satisfactory at present, but that this would become more doubtful if the conflict were prolonged another year or more." He urged the group to be "as active as possible in getting the Administration point of view fully expressed in public forums, and also in dealing with critical segments of the press such as the *New York Times* and, occasionally, the 'Kennedy Columnists.'"[90] As a part of this

---

[88] *New York Times*, Sept. 3, 1965. Working through the American Friends of Vietnam, an organization of prominent public figures founded in 1955 which advocated an active U.S. role in Vietnam (for background, see pts. I and III of this study), the White House attempted to influence action on the resolution, and a memorandum to McGeorge Bundy on September 7 from Cooper, Thomson, and Ropa (Johnson Library, NSF Country File, Vietnam) reported: "Ropa was on the phone several times during the week to monitor the effort of the American Friends of Vietnam to blunt the strong momentum at the NSA convention for condemning present policies in Vietnam. The resolution that passed was critical and not too helpful; it would have been an even more serious indictment of present policies had the American Friends not proselytized there."

In an earlier memorandum (July 12) to Presidential Assistant Douglass Cater, who was a former president of the NSA, Cooper said that the NSA was preparing to consider and would probably adopt such a resolution, and that such a move could "add appreciably to the momentum building up for a more extensive array of hostile teach-ins next fall." He suggested that Cater, Senator Walter F. Mondale (D/Minn.) and others in the government who had been active in NSA should appear before the convention to explain and justify the Vietnam policy of the Johnson administration. Johnson Library, NSF Country File, Vietnam.

[89] U.S. Congress, Senate, Select Committee to Study Government Operations with Respect to Intelligence Activities, Final Report, *Foreign and Military Intelligence*, Book I, S. Rept. 94–755, April 26, 1976, 94th Cong., 2d sess. (Washington, D.C.: U.S. Govt. Print. Off., 1976), p. 184 (hereafter this will be referred to as Final Report, Book I of the Senate Select Committee to Study Intelligence Activities).

[90] U.S. Department of State, Lot File 85 D 240 (William Bundy Papers), William Bundy notes, Aug. 26, 1965, on points discussed by the President during the meeting.

promotional campaign, the White House issued on August 20, 1965 a compilation of statements on the background and reasons for the role of the United States in Vietnam, beginning with Eisenhower's statements in 1954. (There was no reference to the initial commitment by Truman in 1950.) James C. Thomson, Jr., of the NSC staff, who had become opposed to the war, was assigned the task of preparing the booklet, *Why Vietnam.* "In a gesture toward my conscience," he said later, "I fought—and lost—a battle to have the title followed by a question mark." [91]

On September 9, announcement was made of a new public group, the Committee for an Effective and Durable Peace in Asia, chaired by Arthur Dean, one of the Wise Men, the purpose of which was to help promote the administration's case.[92] In its statement, the committee, which had been organized at the initiative of the White House,[93] declared:

> In order to meet the increased aggression against South Vietnam and to convince the Government of North Vietnam that such aggression cannot be successful, it has become necessary for the President of the United States to increase defense expenditures and to commit large American forces to supplement the forces of the South Vietnamese. At the same time the President has given ample evidence of his willingness to commit the United States to serious negotiations designed to bring about a cessation of bloodshed and Communist aggression.
>
> The Committee believes the President has acted rightly and in the national interest in taking these steps and that he is entitled to the support of the responsible citizens of this country. The Committee intends to do what it can to assist the President to achieve his objectives of peace and the ending of aggression.[94]

The President's assistants, primarily Douglass Cater and Chester L. Cooper, Bundy's deputy for Vietnam on the NSC staff, as well as Press Secretary Bill D. Moyers, and Special Assistant Jack J. Valenti, were also working with the State and Defense Departments to develop ways of promoting public support.

On August 3, 1965, there was a dinner meeting at the White House on the Government's "information problem" organized and chaired by Cater and attended also by McGeorge Bundy, Cooper, Joseph A. Califano, Jr., an assistant to the President who worked

---

[91] James C. Thomson, Jr., "How Could Vietnam Happen?" *Atlantic* (April 1968), p. 50.

[92] Of the 48 members listed in the initial announcement, 6—Dean Acheson, Eugene Black, John Cowles, Arthur Dean, Roswell Gilpatric, and John McCloy—were Wise Men. The others were also prominent persons in American life, both Democrats and Republicans, including James B. Conant, C. Douglas Dillon, Oveta Culp Hobby, James R. Killian, Jr., Benjamin E. Mays, Lewis F. Powell, David Rockefeller.

McCloy at first objected to the establishment of the committee, saying that the President was doing well and did not need that kind of support, and that it might lead to formation of an opposing group. He relented, however, after conferring with McGeorge Bundy and others. See McCloy memoranda and letters of Aug. 2, 10, 11, 20, 1965, in the Johnson Library, NSF Country File, Vietnam.

[93] See pt. III of this study, pp. 397–398 for background on the origins of the committee. For documentation of the role of the White House and the State Department in the organization of the group and the development of its statement of purpose see the folder "Arthur Dean Committee" in the Johnson Library, NSF Country File, Vietnam, Box 195.

[94] *New York Times*, Sept. 9, 1965. In the advertisement in which this statement and the list of members appeared there was also a more detailed statement of principles by the committee.

largely on domestic affairs, Leonard H. Marks, a Washington lawyer and lobbyist and friend of President Johnson, who was Director of the U.S. Information Agency (USIA), John Chancellor, a newsman serving as Deputy Director of USIA, James L. Greenfield, Assistant Secretary of State for Public Affairs, William J. Jorden, a member of Greenfield's staff, Morris Leibman, a Chicago attorney who was one of the "Wise Men," and Gordon Chase, a member of the NSC staff.[95]

In advance of the meeting, Cater sent each participant a list of questions as well as a copy of a memorandum drafted by Leibman on the broad problem of developing and maintaining public support for the conduct of "twilight wars" such as Vietnam. These were Leibman's "assumptions":[96]

1. That we are going to have a 10 to 20 year period of "twilight war."

 a. Caveat: We could have 2 or 3 Vietnams or Dominican Republics at once.

 b. Caveat: Situations like South Korea, South Vietnam or the Dominican Republic will not be "finally resolved."

2. The President of the United States will have to have *great* flexibility and discretion.

3. This will require a basic and sophisticated consensus of the American people.

 a. How do you avoid polarization and extremism?

 b. How do you communicate complexity as against simplicity?

 c. How do you establish "partial mobilization" on the home front over long periods of time?

 d. How do you avoid the syndrome of frustration, hostility, etc. (emphasis in original)

The next day (August 4), there was another meeting that was attended by Cater, Chester Cooper, Greenfield, Jorden, Chase, and Leibman. The group agreed that there were four basic questions with respect to the information problem: "First, how can we get the private sector to take some of the information burden with respect to U.S. policy on Vietnam? Second, how can we do a better job of creating an image of a President who has something besides Vietnam on his mind? Third, how do we convey to the American people the concept of a twilight war and of the U.S. role in it? Fourth, how do we coordinate and manage more effectively our information effort?"[97]

During the meeting, Cooper mentioned the usefulness for public information purposes of the American Friends of Vietnam (AFV), the organization founded in 1955 to support an active U.S. role in Vietnam. "While we have been careful to keep our hand fairly hidden," Cooper said, "we have, in fact, spent a lot of time on it and have been able to find them some money." The group agreed that efforts should be made to raise more money for the AFV. In a

---

[95] Gordon Chase summarized the meeting in a memorandum to the President on Aug. 4, 1965, Johnson Library, NSF Country File, Vietnam.

[96] Leibman's memorandum is attached to the memorandum on July 28, 1965 from Cater to participants in the August 3 meeting.

[97] Johnson Library, NSF Country File, Vietnam, Memorandum for the Record Aug. 4, 1965, "August 4 Luncheon Meeting on the Information Problem."

memorandum to McGeorge Bundy on August 9, Cooper said that he intended "to exploit Leibman for the American Friends of Vietnam," and in a memorandum on August 16 he reported that Leibman had agreed to buy and distribute 5,000 copies of a new journal, *Vietnam Perspectives*, being issued by the AFV, one of the purposes of which was to counteract the *Viet-Report*, an anti-war newsletter.[98]

Following the meeting on August 4, a decision was made to create a Public Affairs Policy Committee for Vietnam, chaired by McGeorge Bundy, with about 10 representatives from the White House (Cater and Cooper) the State and Defense Departments, and the U.S. Information Agency. For at least the next several months the committee met about once a week, primarily to discuss relations with the media, but it did not take on operational responsibilities.[99]

Cooper, particularly, continued to be involved in operations, however, including such activities as arranging for briefings of public officials and groups, assisting various persons seeking to support the President, meeting with teach-in groups and representatives of various groups opposed to the war, and countering anti-war activities.[100]

Congress Supports the President and Approves New Funds

As noted, Congress generally supported the President's decision to send U.S. forces to Vietnam, although several prominent leaders and a few other Members were opposed to further U.S. involvement and a number of Members were apprehensive. Broadly speaking, at the time there were 10–12 Senators and 35–40 Representatives who were actively and openly opposed to the use of large-scale U.S. forces.

Once U.S. forces were committed to battle, and patriotic feelings were aroused, even the strongest critics of U.S. involvement were put in the position of having to approve the necessary funds or suffer the political consequences. This had been demonstrated the pre-

---

[98] Johnson Library, NSF Name File, Cooper Memos, and Cooper memorandum, "Financial Support to the American Friends of Vietnam," Sept. 10, 1965, Johnson Library, NSF Country File, Vietnam. Historian Melvin Small, who has used the AFV archives, concludes that, ". . . the White House apparently did not pull out all of the stops for the AFV. The organization was in constant difficulty trying to make ends meet and almost was unable to raise the rather modest $58,000 it needed to operate in 1965." Small, *Johnson, Nixon, and the Doves* (New Brunswick, N.J.: Rutgers Univ. Press, 1988), p. 47.

Viet-Report, first issued in July 1965, was published for three years. Staughton Lynd was a member of its advisory board. Sponsors included the University Committee to Protest the War in Vietnam (the group which, among other things, was promoting the Vietnam teach-ins), and Benjamin Spock, a nationally known New York pediatrician who was becoming very active in the anti-war movement.

[99] Material pertaining to the committee is located in the Johnson Library, NSF Country File, file folder labeled "Public Affairs Policy Committee." Notes on meetings of the committee cease after December 1965.

In addition to the Public Affairs Policy Committee for Vietnam, the Interdepartmental Vietnam Coordinating Committee, chaired by the State Department, had a Public Affairs Subcommittee that was active in recommending ways of promoting U.S. policy.

[100] There are brief reports of Cooper's public affairs activities, as well as those of Donald Ropa, a member of the NSC staff on detail from the CIA, and Thomson, in weekly reports on "The Asian Week" to McGeorge Bundy from Cooper, Ropa and Thomson which are in the Johnson Library, some in NSF Name File, Cooper Memos, and others in the NSF Country File, Vietnam. One of the projects on which Cooper worked during the fall of 1965 was the unsuccessful effort to establish an American-Southeast Asia Foundation to assist with programs in Vietnam conducted by U.S. voluntary agencies, both to promote such efforts, and, through such programs, to gain greater public support for U.S. policy. At Cooper's urging, Dr. Howard Rusk of New York City agreed to sponsor such a move, but for various reasons the idea was eventually abandoned.

vious May when Congress, after only two days of consideration, had approved the President's request for new funds for the war with only seven dissenting votes in the House and three in the Senate. Likewise, a request from the President in early August 1965 for a supplemental appropriation of $1.7 billion, the "Southeast Asia Emergency Fund," to cover the additional cost of the war until the end of 1965, at which time there would be a request for additional funds, was quickly approved by Congress by an even wider margin than in May. Senator Wayne Morse (D/Ore.), a very vocal critic of U.S. military involvement in the war, who voted for the appropriation, explained why: "As long as they [U.S. forces] are there, they must have every possible bit of protection than can be given to them. . . ."[101]

On August 4, 1965, Secretary McNamara accompanied by General Wheeler, Chairman of the JCS, testified on the $1.7 billion request in an executive (closed) session of the Defense Subcommittee of the Senate Appropriations Committee, chaired by Senator John C. Stennis (D/Miss.), who was also the ranking Democrat on the Armed Services Committee.[102] "What is at stake," McNamara said, "is the ability of the free world to block Communist armed aggression and prevent the loss of all of Southeast Asia, a loss which in its ultimate consequences could drastically alter the strategic situation in Asia and the Pacific to the grave detriment of our own security and that of our allies." North Vietnam and China, he said, had chosen to make South Vietnam the test case for a "war of national liberation." If this were successful, the Chinese not only would be in a better position "to seize control of the world Communist movement," but their prestige and power would be enhanced in other countries, thus increasing the likelihood of other wars of national liberation.

In South Vietnam, McNamara explained, the Communists had decided "to wage an all-out attempt to bring down the Government." Greater U.S. assistance was needed to meet the threat, he said, but U.S. objectives would remain the same:

> We have no desire to widen the war. We have no desire to overthrow the North Vietnamese regime, seize its territory, or achieve the unification of North and South Vietnam by force of arms. We have no need for permanent military bases in South Vietnam or for special privileges of any kind. What we are seeking through the planned military buildup is to block the Vietcong offensive, to give the people of South Vietnam and their Armed Forces some relief from the unrelenting Communist pressures—to give them time to strengthen their Government, to reestablish law and order, and to revive their economic life which has been seriously disrupted by Vietcong harassment and attack in recent months.

---

[101] *CR*, vol. 111, p. 21732.

[102] U.S. Congress, Senate, Committee on Appropriations Defense Subcommittee, *Department of Defense Appropriations for 1966*, Hearings, 89th Cong., 1st sess. (Washington, D.C.: U.S. Govt. Print. Off., 1965), pp. 731 ff. On August 5, McNamara also testified before the House Defense Appropriations Subcommittee, but the testimony, taken in executive session, was not printed or released.

Although the hearing was rather perfunctory, there were some significant questions and answers.[103] In response to one question about the bombing of North Vietnam, McNamara stated that there was only a "very small" difference between what the Joint Chiefs of Staff had recommended and the program that was being carried out. General Wheeler was invited to comment but his response was deleted. Senator Stennis then asked, "Is the Secretary substantially correct?" to which General Wheeler replied: "Yes. Any difference is primarily one of tempo."

At least two Senators on the committee, A. Willis Robertson of Virginia and Allen J. Ellender of Louisiana, both conservative Democrats, expressed their opposition to further U.S. involvement in the war, a position both men had begun to take in preceding months.[104] Senator Stuart Symington (D/Mo.) a member of the Armed Services Committee (as well as the Committee on Foreign Relations), continued to argue that the U.S. should apply greater military pressure in order to "win," or that it should "get out."

In a meeting of the NSC the next day (August 5), McNamara told the President that in the Senate and House Armed Services Committees "there is broad support, but this support is thin. There is a feeling of uneasiness and frustration."[105] "The Republicans," he added, "are making political capital by overstating the effect on the U.S. economy of the cost of the Vietnam war."

Rusk, however, said that in his testimony before the House Foreign Affairs Committee a few days earlier there appeared to be good support for U.S. policy.

In an effort to placate congressional critics and to maintain Congress' support for the war, the President invited all of the Members of the Senate and the House to off-the-record White House briefings on Vietnam in mid-August. At the meetings, attended by 74 Senators and 336 Representatives, the President made brief statements, followed by remarks by Taylor, Rusk, and McNamara. In addition, Ambassador at Large W. Averell Harriman reported on his talks with the Russians and U.N. Ambassador Arthur Goldberg discussed his visit with U.N. Secretary General U Thant. Eugene Black, former head of the World Bank, who had been appointed by the President to develop plans for a large Mekong River aid project, discussed that initiative.[106]

On August 10, the day after he attended one of these briefings, Senator Wayne Morse, who for many years had been the Senate's strongest critic of U.S. military involvement in Vietnam, declared in a Senate speech: "Yesterday the White House sponsored another of its attempts to disguise the war in Vietnam to make it palatable to Members of Congress."[107] "All the same dogmas were repeated," he said, "just as though nothing had changed since Mr. McNamara went over to Vietnam in October of 1963, and told us when he re-

[103] Unfortunately, most of the answers as well as parts of some of the questions were deleted by the Defense Department before the printed hearings were made public by the committee.

[104] For the position taken earlier by Robertson and Ellender see pt. III of this study, pp. 135, 305.

[105] Johnson Library, NSF NSC Meetings File.

[106] This information was taken from notations in the President's Daily Diary. There are partial transcripts of the meetings of August 10 and 11 in the Johnson Library, Transcripts of Vietnam Briefings.

[107] *CR*, vol. 111, p. 19840.

turned that things looked so good the boys would all be home by 1965."

"Thanks to General Taylor and Secretary McNamara," Morse added, "the Communists have proved to the world that the United States cannot cope with insurgency on its own terms, but can only fight it by turning a guerrilla war into a conventional war fought by American forces." He continued:

> The recitation of how things are improving in Vietnam is a depressing thing to hear when a comparison with a year ago, or 2 years ago, or 4 years ago, or 10 years ago, shows only that the American position and the position of the South Vietnam Government have steadily eroded and deteriorated. It is a remarkable thing to be able to go up to the White House periodically and hear how things are improving when each visit is occasioned by a new step the United States has had to take in order to stabilize a deteriorating situation. It is an Alice-in-Wonderland exhibition of how the unpleasant can be evaded and the failures ignored.
>
> In light of this most recent exhibition, I have no hope or confidence whatever that the conventional war we are now undertaking in Vietnam under the same men who failed to win a guerrilla war, will have any more favorable result. For another element in the so-called briefings of the administration is a total vacuity in the political surroundings of the struggle itself.
>
> It has been the ignorance of the politics of war that has brought us into this situation. . . .
>
> To the administration, the war in Vietnam is a matter of military tactics. That is the sad but plain truth. We have based our policy there on nothing more than military tactics and we have been losing. We are continuing to base our policy there on military tactics and we are going to continue to lose.

The President was apparently interested in what Morse had to say—Morse had, after all, raised the subject of impeachment following the President's July 28 announcement—judging by the fact that he received a summary of the speech the next day from McGeorge Bundy and Thomson of the NSC staff.[108]

A comment by former President Eisenhower a few days later caused considerably more consternation in the White House, however. In a news conference on August 17, Eisenhower said that the Communists must be stopped in Vietnam, but, contrary to President Johnson's frequent assertion that U.S. military actions in Vietnam resulted from the commitment made by Eisenhower's October 1955 letter to President Ngo Dinh Diem, Eisenhower said there had been no commitment of a military nature at that time.[109]

---

[108] Johnson Library, Presidential Chron File, 7/65–8/65, James Thomson. For Morse's comments on impeachment, see pt. III of this study, p. 447.

[109] *New York Times*, Aug. 18, 1965.

Eisenhower, who, at President Johnson's direction, was being briefed frequently by Gen. Andrew J. Goodpaster, special assistant to the Chairman of the Joint Chiefs of Staff, took the position that, having decided to go to war, the U.S. should use overwhelming force against the enemy. He was opposed to "dribbling" forces into Vietnam. He was also opposed to detailed control of military operations by Washington, saying that tactical decisions should be made by the field commander. Johnson Library, NSF Name File, President Eisenhower, Goodpaster Memorandum for the Record, "Meeting with General Eisenhower, 3 August 1965."

Continued

Johnson's reaction was conveyed in a 9:50 p.m. memorandum on August 18 from Presidential Assistant Bill Moyers to McGeorge Bundy, the President's National Security Adviser, after Bundy had submitted to the President the staff work he had requested:

> The President asked me to tell you that this is not enough. He wants—"by the time I get up in the morning"—everything "that was pertinent in the SEATO [Southeast Asia Treaty] debates, everything every Republican Senator and Congressman—and Democrats alike—said which indicates that SEATO requires us to give arms to SEATO countries or Protocol states—the whole debate—everything Eisenhower said in office that builds our case—the full text of his letter to Churchill and Diem. I want the kind of brief Abe Fortas would prepare on Gideon [a famous Supreme Court case argued by Fortas]. It's got to be full and convincing.
>
> "Then, I want Mac to get Goodpasture *[sic]* [Gen. Andrew J. Goodpaster, assistant to the Chairman of the Joint Chiefs of Staff] to helicopter up to Gettysburg tomorrow. I want him to go 'to brief the General on the battle we have just had out in Vietnam,' but I want him to take this letter to Ike and I want him to take a copy of all the material that Mac Bundy is going to get overnight.
>
> "Tell Mac to get that fellow Tom [Thomas L.] Hughes [the State Department's Director of Intelligence and Research] out of bed over at State and make him do all this research tonight, and his people."
>
> And that, my unfortunate friend, is almost all verbatim.[110]

Goodpaster, who had served on Eisenhower's White House staff, met with Eisenhower the next morning, and in his report to McGeorge Bundy he said that Eisenhower "stressed strongly that there is no question in any of this about his support for what the President is doing. . . . The real point is that action has now taken a different form from that of ten years ago, while the policy aim of course remains the same." Goodpaster added: "I suggested as a summary that there has been continuity of purpose and policy, together with evolution of means and action. General Eisenhower added that there has also been an evolution in the situation and in what is needed, in view of what the enemy has done."[111]

After meeting with Goodpaster, whose visit to Gettysburg was not publicly announced, Eisenhower told the press that he continued to support the President's position on Vietnam. As he and Goodpaster had agreed, Eisenhower also said that the circumstances had changed. In 1954 it was hoped that the Com-

---

In a conversation with Ambassador Lodge, who was asked by the President to see Eisenhower before leaving for Saigon, Eisenhower also stressed, as Lodge reported to the President, the "overriding importance of Viet Nam wanting to be free. We should do everything to inculcate such a desire. They must have 'heart' or, after we have achieved a successful outcome, they will slump right back. It would be tragic if a successful outcome were followed by an election in which the people voted for the Viet Cong. I told him our plans regarding [Edward G.] Lansdale were aimed precisely at such a contingency." (Same location, Memorandum from Lodge to the President, Aug. 11, 1965.) Lansdale was Lodge's assistant for pacification activities.

[110] Johnson Library, NSF Memos to the President—McGeorge Bundy. The letter attached to this memorandum is not in the file. For the 1955 letter from Eisenhower to Diem, see pt. I of this study, p. 286.

[111] This and a number of other Goodpaster memoranda on his discussions with Eisenhower, as well as a folder containing the material which Goodpaster took to Gettysburg on August 19, are in the Johnson Library, NSF Name File, President Eisenhower.

munists could be defeated without recourse to U.S. arms, but this hope was not realized, and he supported Johnson's decision to send U.S. forces. "When our country is in a position of crisis," he said, "there is only one thing a good American can do, and that is to support the President."[112]

In Congress, however, Republicans in the House continued their efforts to place the onus of the war on the Democrats. On August 24, 1965, the House rejected, 139–263, a Republican move to send a supplemental appropriations bill for domestic programs back to committee.[113] Melvin R. Laird (R/Wisc.), who made the motion, argued that "the large-scale needs of a war situation are now upon us. To attempt to finance them by additional deficit financing without first bending every effort to tighten the Nation's belt in the nondefense spending area is to court an economic situation that will further erode the value of the dollar, more deeply threaten the economic well-being of low and middle-income citizens, and the economic health of the Nation." He added that in order to act responsibly on the budget, and to prevent inflationary spending, Congress should be given estimates of the cost of the war during the fiscal year then underway (FY 1966, ending on June 30, 1966), and, in view of predictions that the administration would be returning to Congress in January 1966 to ask for an additional $10–12 billion for the war, that Congress should not act on separate, smaller requests.

Laird's motion was supported by most of the Republicans and a few Southern Democrats, but was opposed by most Democrats, including all of the liberals.

The next day (August 25), House Republicans issued a "white paper," "Vietnam: Some Neglected Aspects of the Historical Record," which asserted that the crisis in Vietnam had occurred since 1960 under the Democrats. These were its conclusions:[114]

> The policy of the Democratic administration has too often been uncertain, providing a basis for miscalculation by the Communists. Policy has been altered abruptly. Conflicting statements have been issued. Deeds have not matched words. Among the specific features of policy subject to this criticism have been the whole handling of the problem of Laos, the reversal of the position of the United States toward the Diem regime, the cover-up of the gravity of the desperate dangers of the situation in Vietnam, President Johnson's campaign victory of 1964, and the progressive dilution of official statements of the Nation's objectives in Vietnam.

Later that day, McGeorge Bundy told the President that it was the unanimous view of McNamara, Ball, William Bundy, and Presidential Assistant Bill Moyers that the Republican white paper "is a pretty feeble effort and that it does not deserve top level reply." Senator Everett McKinley Dirksen (R/Ill.), Senate Republican leader, he said, had already disavowed it, and Eisenhower had repeated his support for the President. "In sum, this document imports into

---

[112] *New York Times*, Aug. 20, 1965.

[113] *CR*, vol. 111, pp. 21549–21571. The bill provided funds for the Departments of Labor, and Health, Education and Welfare.

[114] *Ibid.*, pp. 21838–21844.

the discussion of foreign affairs the very spirit of narrow partisanship which you have been trying to exclude."[115]

That same day (August 25), the Senate approved the $1.7 billion request for additional funds for the war (as an amendment to the FY 1966 Department of Defense Appropriations bill) by a vote of 89–0.[116] On September 17, the House, which had passed the appropriations bill in June before the supplemental request was made, approved the conference report, which provided for the $1.7 billion, by a vote of 382–0.[117]

Fulbright Despairs of Persuading the President

Meanwhile, Senate Foreign Relations Committee Chairman Fulbright, disillusioned about Vietnam, and disturbed about Johnson's handling of the Dominican Republic situation in May 1965, which had been the subject of Foreign Relations Committee hearings during July, was considering making a public statement on the conduct of the Dominican Republic affair that would also be a touchstone for more general criticism of the handling of major U.S. foreign policy issues, including Vietnam. In a memorandum on August 17, Carl Marcy, chief of staff of the Foreign Relations Committee, proposed to Fulbright that he consider making a speech on the changes in the past two years that had led to a situation in which "the United States is feared today as the nation most likely to precipitate a nuclear war."[118] "What has happened in the past two years to thrust the hopes of the world for peace into the abyss of fear of world war? What has happened to turn the liberal supporters of President Kennedy into opponents of the policies of President Johnson? What has happened to turn the right wing opponents of Eisenhower and Kennedy into avid supporters of the policies of the present Administration?" The principal cause, Marcy said, was that the U.S. had "tried to force upon the rest of the world a righteous American point of view. . . ." Another reason was the American penchant for demanding immediate results.

"Such a speech," Marcy told Fulbright, "would break you with the Administration and make Borah and Hiram Johnson and Cabot Lodge, Sr. [Senators who had challenged the President on foreign policy issues in the early 1900s], look like pikers. But it is a line of action that you should consider." He added, however, "I don't know whether I would do this if I were you!"[119]

---

[115] Johnson Library, NSF Memos to the President—McGeorge Bundy.

[116] Senator Ernest Gruening (D/Alaska), who had voted with Morse against the request in May, but who supported the $1.7 billion request, had, at the President's request, which was "quickly agreed to by the President," talked about Vietnam with Johnson on August 19. *New York Times*, Aug. 20, 1965.

[117] *CR*, vol. 111, p. 24262.

[118] A copy of Marcy's memorandum is in the University of Arkansas Library, Fulbright Papers, series 48, box 16.

[119] Two days earlier (August 15), Fulbright had invited McGeorge Bundy to meet with the Foreign Relations Committee at an informal "coffee." Bundy declined, saying that on the instructions of "higher authority"—the President—he could not meet with the committee. In a memorandum to Fulbright reporting on Bundy's reaction, Marcy said, "The higher authority suggested that he did not want to get into the habit of sending Presidential aides to the Hill." National Archives, Record Group (hereafter referred to as RG) 46, Marcy Chron File. Instead, Bundy said, the President had suggested that the committee meet with Bundy for a drink in his office or at his home. There is no record of what further action, if any, may have been taken on this matter, but the committee did not accept the offer from the President and Bundy. Several years later, as will be seen (pt. V of this study, forthcoming), Henry A. Kissinger, who was then serving as President Richard M. Nixon's National Security Adviser, held a couple of informal meetings with the Foreign Relations Committee at private locations in Washington.

By the end of August, Fulbright after receiving a strong indictment of the administration's role in the Dominican Republic affair from Pat M. Holt, who handled Latin America for the Foreign Relations Committee, and Seth Tillman, another committee staffer who worked closely with Fulbright, debated whether to communicate privately with the President or to make a public statement. Action by the Foreign Relations Committee was almost out of the question. As Tillman said in a later interview, "It seemed certain at the time that the committee itself would not go on record criticizing the administration. This was just not something you did in those days." [120]

Holt and Tillman were in favor of a public statement. Marcy and Lee Williams, Fulbright's administrative assistant and the principal political adviser on his personal staff, were concerned about the effect on Fulbright's relationship with Johnson and on Fulbright's role. As Williams said in a later interview: [121]

> I felt I knew something about the nature of the man, Johnson, and I think I said at the time, "Look, do you understand that if you do this, it's over between you and Johnson. He'll never let you in the door again. I mean that's over. And I think you have to weigh whether if you give this speech at this time the value of it is going to be enough that you're willing to give up the kind of relationship you've enjoyed with Johnson and the opportunity to have the kind of input to him that you've had before." . . . I thought Johnson was getting a lot of poor advice at that time, and I wanted him to have Fulbright available to be a balance wheel . . . to terminate that kind of relationship was bad for the country, in my opinion . . . and by Fulbright, I don't mean Fulbright alone; I mean the voice of Fulbright as he represented the views of a significant segment of this country and of Congress, as a spokesman for that point of view.

Marcy told Fulbright that he, too, thought such a speech would lead to a break with the President. Fulbright replied that he would take care of the politics; he wanted to know if the speech was accurate. Marcy said that it was.

[120] Congressional Research Service (CRS) Interview with Seth Tillman, Feb. 9, 1979.
[121] CRS Interview with Lee Williams, Mar. 13, 1979.

Fulbright decided to make the speech. "In September of '65," he said later, "I gave up hope of persuading him [the President]."[122] This was Tillman's explanation:[123]

> I think it was in large part because of his feeling that he just wasn't getting anywhere with them through private channels of communication; that the personal relationship with Johnson, which had been very serviceable during the Senate years, had ceased to be so; and that he, Fulbright, was not bringing to bear any significant influence on these central issues through the private means of communication.

After the speech, according to one description, there was "No more access. No more phone calls. No more warmth. No more Air Force One."[124] (This situation changed somewhat in June 1966, however, as will be seen.) Marcy was also shunned. In an interview some years later he recalled that he went to a meeting at the White House soon after the speech, "and as I sought to shake hands Lyndon looked at me, right through me, and said: 'What are you doing here?' I was never invited back."[125]

Johnson's aides immediately began supplying him with material critical of Fulbright. On the day after the speech, Presidential Assistant Douglass Cater sent the President, apparently at his request, a sampling of Fulbright's votes since 1961 and a note saying that earlier votes were being compiled. In a separate memorandum, Cater said that Fulbright's speech "contains this inexcusable sneer: 'We are not, as we like to claim in Fourth of July speeches, the most revolutionary nation on earth; we are, on the contrary, much closer to being the most unrevolutionary nation on earth.'" Cater suggested that, in a speech he was drafting for Johnson to give at a celebration at the Smithsonian Institution in which the American Revolution was to be mentioned, these words be added: "a revolution not always supported by some who lament our lack of revolu-

---

[122] CRS Interview with J. William Fulbright, Feb. 18, 1983.

In the speech, which he delivered in the Senate on Sept. 15, 1965, Fulbright said that the U.S. had intervened in the Dominican Republic not to save American lives, as the President had contended, but out of fear that the Communists were behind the revolution and the result would be "another Cuba." (*CR*, vol. 111, pp. 23855–23861.) In its handling of the Dominican crisis, he said, the U.S. had allied itself with a "corrupt and reactionary military oligarchy" rather than seeking to understand and support the non-Communist revolutionaries who, as in other countries in Latin America, could provide the alternative to a Cuban-type Communist revolution. In addition, U.S. armed intervention in the Dominican crisis was illegal, based on treaty provisions that prohibit intervention in the affairs of any country in the Americas, or the use of force by one country against another except, based on agreement of the members of the Organization of American states, for actions to maintain peace and security.

Fulbright was also critical of the "bad advice" which he said U.S. officials had given President Johnson about the degree of Communist influence among the rebels, as well as exaggerated reports of atrocities and the danger to American lives.

On the morning of the day he delivered the speech, Fulbright sent a copy of it to Johnson with an accompanying note which said:

"Public—and I trust, constructively—criticism is one of the services that a senator is uniquely able to perform. There are many things that members of your administration, for quite proper reasons of consistency and organization, cannot say, even though it is in the long term of interests of the administration that they be said. A senator, as you well know, is under no such restrictions. It is in the sincere hope of assisting your administration in this way, and of advancing the objective of your policy in Latin America, that I offer the enclosed remarks." (Haynes Bonner Johnson and Bernard M. Gwertzman, *Fulbright, The Dissenter* [Garden City, N. Y.: Doubleday, 1968], p. 218.

[123] CRS Interview with Seth Tillman, Feb. 9, 1979.

[124] David Halberstam, *The Powers That Be* (New York: Knopf, 1979), p. 502.

[125] U.S. Congress, Senate, Office of the Senate Historian, Oral History Interview with Carl Marcy, Oct. 5, 1983, conducted by Dr. Donald Ritchie.

tionary spirit." "This would be interpreted," Cater said, "as a dig at Fulbright's hypocrisy on racial matters."[126]

When Johnson was hospitalized for an operation a short while later, Fulbright sent a letter expressing his hopes for recovery, and added these words:[127]

> I sense from various sources that you were displeased by my recent speech. I regret this. I sincerely believe that in the long run it will help you in your relations with the countries of Latin America. I admit, of course, that my judgment could be wrong, but there is already a very considerable response from here and abroad which supports my basic premise.
>
> Regardless of the validity of my judgment in this instance, I have done in the past, and shall continue to do in the future, what I can to help you to the best of my ability. I make no secret of the fact that I think you were the best Majority Leader the Senate has ever had, and that I believe you are and will continue to be a great President. It does not seem to me that I can be of any help to you by always agreeing with every decision or every opinion of your Administration. These are necessarily, in many cases, collective opinions, and like all others may sometimes be in error. As I understand the function of a senator, especially one who is deeply interested in the success of his President, it is his duty whenever there is any question about a policy to raise the matter for clarification and for correction if the resulting discussion reveals the need therefor. Subservience cannot, as I see it, help develop new policies or perfect old ones.
>
> As you know, I have been in the Congress a long time. I desire no other office. I only wish to contribute whatever I can in my present position to the success of your Administration and, thereby to the welfare of the people of my State and Country.

Fulbright never received a reply to the letter, and he continued to be criticized for taking issue with the administration. Even though some public figures came to his defense, he said privately that he could not encourage other Senators to speak out: "I can't advise them to speak out, because if you do then everyone jumps down your throat. This country has gotten to where you are not supposed to speak out."[128]

Several weeks later, Fulbright is said to have confided to a colleague, "My God, I feel so alone. No one seems to give a damn. I feel at times that I am walking among the blind and the deaf."[129]

This incident helped to pave the way for the Senate Foreign Relations Committee's hearings on Vietnam early the following year,

---

[126] Cater's memorandum is in the Johnson Library, WHCF, Fulbright.

[127] Johnson and Gwertzman, p. 220.

[128] *Ibid.* In another Senate speech on Oct. 22, 1965 (*CR*, vol. 111, pp. 28372 ff.) Fulbright defended his public criticism of the President, saying, among other things: "A consensus is a fine thing insofar as it represents a genuine reconciliation of differences; it is a miscarriage of democratic procedures insofar as it represents the concealment of differences. I think we Americans tend to put too high a value on unanimity, as if there were something dangerous and illegitimate about honest differences of opinion honestly expressed by honest men. Probably because we have been united about so many things for so long, we tend to be mistrustful of intellectual dissent, confusing it with personal hostility and political disloyalty."

[129] Tristam Coffin, *Senator Fulbright: Portrait of a Public Philosopher* (New York: Dutton, 1966), p. 264.

as well as to create doubts about the President's credibility and his handling of the Vietnam situation. As Pat Holt, later the chief of staff of the committee explained several years later:[130]

> There were doubts in the Senate about the wisdom of U.S. policy in Vietnam even during the Kennedy administration, but before the Dominican intervention there was a predisposition to give the President the benefit of those doubts. Afterward, this predisposition was reversed. . . . An increasingly common view on Capitol Hill was, as one senator expressed in privately at the time, "If we know the President was impetuous in the Dominican Republic and exaggerated the situation there to the point of falsifying it, how can we trust him anywhere else?

[130] *Washington Post*, May 2, 1977, Pat M. Holt, "Residue from the 1965 Dominican Intervention."

CHAPTER 2

FORMULATING U.S. STRATEGY AND PLANS

After the President's decision in July to send large-scale forces, American troops began streaming into South Vietnam during August and September.[1] According to a plan of operations developed by Westmoreland and his staff, U.S. forces, together with other third country forces (largely South Korean and Australian) and South Vietnamese forces (which would be responsible primarily for the area around Saigon and in the delta—IV Corps), were to exert military pressure on the Communists to compel them to accept a settlement—to "grind down the enemy," while at the same time building up the South Vietnamese, militarily and politically.[2]

The newly appointed U.S. Ambassador to South Vietnam, Henry Cabot Lodge, disagreed with Westmoreland's proposed plan of operations. In a memorandum to McGeorge Bundy on July 7, 1965, (as well as in a memorandum to the President on July 20 in connection with McNamara's report of that date),[3] Lodge argued against a large-scale deployment of U.S. forces and against "search-and-destroy" (attrition), and in favor of smaller forces and what he called a "coastal strategy" ("enclaves"). In his unpublished "Vietnam Memoir," he said, summarizing the July 7 memorandum, that there were, "broadly speaking," two possible strategies:[4]

> A. One strategy is that of "seek-out-and-destroy." To this there are very heavy objections
>
> 1. It might not achieve a true victory in a situation which is still essentially a political movement.
>
> 2. It would tie down the U.S. troops which might be needed elsewhere and which could not be quickly extricated.
>
> 3. The climate, terrain, etc., are about the worst in the world for American soldiers.
>
> 4. To put an army of this size into the field might create a violently bad reaction in U.S. public opinion and this in turn might compromise the ability of the U.S. Government to carry out any kind of intelligent or farsighted policy.

---

[1] By the end of October 1965, 35 combat battalions (about 215,000 men, including support forces) had been deployed or approved for deployment—an increase of about 130,000 over the number in Vietnam at the time of the President's decision in July. These included the 1st Cavalry Division (Airmobile) and 1st Brigade of the 101st Airborne Division, which were sent to II Corps in the Central Highlands, the 1st Infantry Division and the 173rd Airborne Brigade, which were sent to III Corps in the area around Saigon, and the 3rd Marine Amphibian Force (which consisted of the 3rd Marine Division and elements of the 1st Marine Division), which was given responsibility for I Corps in the northern part of South Vietnam. In addition, a South Korean division arrived in II Corps in early November.

[2] Center for Military History (CMH), Westmoreland Papers, History File, Presentation by Westmoreland to a group of U.S. Army officers, Nov. 9, 1968.

[3] See pp. 386–387 of pt. III of this study.

[4] Massachusetts Historical Society, Lodge Papers, unpublished "Vietnam Memoir," pt. IV, ch. I, p 7.

Basically, the only purpose of military activity is to provide the opportunity for the Vietnamese to carry out their revolution for a new and better life. The strategy of "seek-out-and-destroy" only reaches that aim indirectly, if at all.

B. Alternative is neither to extend or to withdraw, but to operate differently by what may roughly be called coastal tactics. Under such a scheme, United States troops would do the following:

1. Help the Government of Viet-Nam in pitched battles against large units of the Viet Cong and the PAVN;

2. Guard the perimeters—be they seaports or airfields or both;

3. If necessary, help to hold Saigon;

4. Make occasional forays to attractive targets which can be reached from these places;

5. And thus, free the ARVN for the work for countersubversion-terrorism in the hamlets which it alone can do.

This must be accompanied by a new, lively, professional political campaign so that we can work out from the secure areas. But the accomplishments of this political campaign must be solid and enduring and not series of flashy quickies.

On September 1, 1965, a concept paper, "Concept of Operations in the Republic of Vietnam," was issued by Westmoreland's headquarters.[5] The U.S. objective in Vietnam, it declared, was "To end the war in Vietnam by convincing the Viet Cong and the DRV that military victory is impossible, thereby forcing an agreement favorable to the RVN and the United States." There were three assumptions with respect to U.S. operations:

(1) That the VC will continue to fight and will continue to be supported by the DRV until the conviction that military victory is impossible makes the absorption of further punishment unendurable.

(2) That Communist China will continue military aid and advice but will not actively intervene.

(3) That friendly forces will maintain control of the air and lines of communication in RVN.

In addition, the achievement of the U.S. objective "presupposed the removal of restrictions, delays and planning uncertainties. . . ."[6] The paper did not state what, specifically, should be removed.

---

[5]National Archives, Westmoreland-CBS Papers, "Concept of Operations in the Republic of Vietnam," Sept. 1, 1965, 535 pp. On Sept. 17, 1965, Westmoreland's headquarters issued more detailed guidance for the use of U.S. forces: "Tactics and Techniques for Employment of U.S. Forces in the Republic of Vietnam," MACV Directive 525–4 (a revision and expansion of the July MACV statement), CMH, Westmoreland Papers, History File.

[6]In pointing out the importance of lifting some of these limitations and restrictions, Westmoreland's concept paper was consistent with and followed the line of reasoning of the special study (Goodpaster Report) in July 1965 by the staff of the JCS, at the request of McNamara for the President, of the question, "Can we win if we do everything we can?" (See pt. III of this study, pp. 359 ff.) The JCS study had concluded that the U.S. could win if the following assumptions held true:

"a. China and Russia will not intervene with armed forces, overtly or covertly, so long as there is no US/SVN land invasion of NVN.

"b. Restrictions on US/SVN use of force do not exceed the following:

"(1) No land invasion of NVN by US/SVN forces.

"(2) No use of nuclear weapons or chemical weapons.

According to the MACV paper, there would be two and possibly three phases: first, stopping the Communist offensive; second, resuming the offensive against Communist forces and reinstituting rural reconstruction (pacification) programs in high-visibility areas. If the insurgency continued, there would then be a third phase in which U.S. and other forces would apply greater military pressure on Communist forces "to destroy or render militarily ineffective the remaining organized VC units and their base areas," together with pacification of all of South Vietnam.

The timetable for the three phases was to be:

Phase I—September 1, 1965-December 31, 1965
Phase II—January 1, 1966-June 30, 1966
Phase III—July 1, 1966 to July 1 or December 31, 1967.

After the Communists had been compelled to end the war, U.S. forces could be "gradually removed, consistent with the capability of GVN to maintain internal order and protect its own boundaries."

Although U.S. forces would play the leading role in offensive military operations, "For political and psychological reasons," the concept paper stated, "the conflict must retain primarily a Vietnamese character at all times."

While Westmoreland was issuing the concept paper for operations containing these guidelines for the employment of U.S. forces, the Joint Chiefs of Staff were seeking approval of the Secretary of Defense and, through him, of the President, of an overall "concept" (strategy) for the conduct of the war. In a memorandum for the Secretary of Defense on August 27, 1965, "Concept for Vietnam," the JCS discussed the U.S. objective and the proposed plan for achieving it.[7] The memorandum began with a statement that seemed to suggest the after-the-fact nature of the request for approval of strategic planning: "In the light of the introduction of major U.S. combat units into Southeast Asia, the Joint Chiefs of Staff consider it essential that we further formalize our concept for the future conduct of the war."

The U.S. "objective" in Vietnam, the memorandum said, as stated by NSAM 288 (March 1964), was a "stable and independent noncommunist government."[8] It went on to explain, however, that although this was the stated objective, there was much more at stake:

> The RVN [Republic of Vietnam—South Vietnam] is a politico/military keystone in Southeast Asia and is symbolic of U.S. determination in Asia as Berlin is in Europe—to prevent Communist expansion. The United States is committed to the de-

---

"(3) No mass bombing of population per se.

"c. Once the concept envisaged in this study is approved by higher authority, operations within the scope of the proposed strategy will not be subject to restriction, delay or planning uncertainties. This implies that the GVN will cooperate as necessary to this end.

"d. Operational coordination between US and SVN forces meets minimum acceptable professional standards of effectiveness.

"e. Neither the government nor the population of SVN turns against the US and demands withdrawal."

Another assumption, which was not included in this summary of "major assumptions," but which was stated subsequently and appears to have been one of the most important assumptions of the study, was that while American forces along with some South Vietnamese and third country forces were conducting offensive military operations against main force units, the South Vietnamese would provide local security against Communist guerrillas.

[7] Johnson Library, NSF NSC History, Deployment of Forces, JCSM-652-65, Aug. 27, 1965.

[8] For NSAM 288, see pt. II of this study, p. 238.

> fense of the RVN in order to assist a free people to remain free. In addition to the freedom of the RVN, U.S. national prestige, credibility, and honor with respect to world-wide pledges, and declared national policy are at stake. Further, it is incumbent upon the United States at this stage to invalidate the communist concept of "wars of national liberation."

According to the JCS memorandum, "The war in Vietnam is the single most critical international problem facing the United States today, and it portends the most serious immediate threat to continued U.S. world leadership and national security."

These were the "major problems to be dealt with in the conduct of the war":

> (1) The continued direction and support of Viet Cong operations by the DRV [Democratic Republic of Vietnam—North Vietnam], infiltration from the north, and the apparent attendant Viet Cong capability to provide materiel support and to replace heavy personnel losses.
>
> (2) The continued existence of a major Viet Cong infrastructure, both political and military, in the RVN.
>
> (3) The greater growth rate of Viet Cong strength as compared to that of the South Vietnamese ground forces.
>
> (4) The continued loss of LOCs [lines of communication], food-producing areas, and population to Viet Cong control.
>
> (5) The lack of a viable politico/economic structure in the RVN.
>
> (6) The threat of CHICOM [Chinese Communist] intervention or aggression in Southeast Asia and elsewhere in the Western Pacific.
>
> The basic military tasks, of equal priority, are:
>
> (1) To cause the DRV to cease its direction and support of the Viet Cong insurgency.
>
> (2) To defeat the Viet Cong and to extend GVN control over all of the RVN.
>
> (3) To deter Communist China from direct intervention and to defeat such intervention if it occurs.

The JCS memorandum went on to discuss the strategy the U.S. should employ to deal with these problems:

> The US basic strategy for accomplishing the above tasks should be: to intensify military pressure on the DRV by air and naval power; to destroy significant DRV military targets, including the base of supplies; to interdict supporting LOCs in the DRV [this would include the mining of ports]; to interdict the infiltration and supply routes into the RVN; to improve the combat effectiveness of the RVNAF [Republic of Vietnam Armed Forces]; to build and protect bases; to reduce enemy reinforcements; to defeat the Viet Cong, in concert with RVN and third country forces; and to maintain adequate forces in the Western-Pacific and elsewhere in readiness to deter and to deal with CHICOM aggression. By aggressive and sustained exploitation of superior military force, the United States/Government of Vietnam would seize and hold the initiative in both the DRV and RVN, keeping the DRV, the Viet Cong, and the PL/VM [Pathet Lao/Viet Minh] at a disadvantage, progres-

sively destroying the DRV war-supporting power and defeating the Viet Cong. The physical capability of the DRV to move men and supplies through the Lao Corridor, down the coastline, across the demilitarized zone, and through Cambodia must be reduced to the maximum practical extent by land, naval, and air actions in these areas and against infiltration connected targets. Finally, included within the basic U.S. military strategy must be a buildup in Thailand to ensure attainment of the proper U.S.-Thai posture to deter CHICOM aggression and to facilitate placing U.S. forces in an advantageous logistic position if such aggression occurs.

"Our strategy for Vietnam should not allow the communists to keep pace with or more than match our military efforts," the Chiefs said. Yet, as they also pointed out, "For the most part, the Viet Cong have sought to avoid a large-scale restrained battle with US/GVN forces. Instead their tactics have been to maximize the advantages of initiative and surprise and to strike at weakness with overwhelming strength, 'fading away' when the combat strength ratio is unfavorable to them." For this reason, the Chiefs said, it was essential to have the support of the people and the control of resources in those areas of South Vietnam—the Saigon area, the Mekong delta, the coastal plain, and the central highlands—which were of major military significance.

The JCS memorandum was less explicit, however, with respect to how U.S. forces could be effectively used in South Vietnam in a guerrilla warfare situation in which, as the JCS recognized, the support of the people was required in order to wage a successful counterguerrilla campaign. According to the memorandum, the strategy to be used in the South would be to establish secure areas on the coast and elsewhere, and then to enlarge and expand those areas through "search and destroy operations" conducted by the U.S. and other third country forces, while providing support to South Vietnamese forces responsible for "clearing and securing operations" for "rural reconstruction." There was no explanation in the JCS memorandum as to how U.S. forces could accomplish their assigned tasks. It seemed to be taken for granted that the "Viet Cong" could and would be "defeated."

This JCS strategy paper of August 27, 1965 was never approved by civilian authorities. A copy of the paper was sent to McGeorge Bundy on August 30 by Col. Richard C. Bowman, the NSC liaison officer with the JCS, with a memorandum that said merely "The attached JCSM contains the most recent JCS views on military strategy in Vietnam."[9] There is no record that Bundy sent the report to the President or that any other action with respect to the report was taken at the White House.

After receiving the JCS paper, McNamara asked that it be reviewed by the Office of International Security Affairs of the Department of Defense, headed by Assistant Secretary of Defense John T. McNaughton. In a memorandum to McNamara on September 8, 1965, McNaughton said that the plan proposed by the JCS, while generally acceptable, contained a number of suggestions that were "clearly controversial and raise far-reaching policy issues (e.g.,

[9] Johnson Library, NSF Country File, Vietnam.

blockade and mining of DRV, U.S. buildup in Thailand, intensified RT [ROLLING THUNDER]).” “In my judgment,” McNaughton said, “an over-all approval of the concept proposed by the JCS is not required at this time and would not significantly increase U.S. capabilities and planning in dealing with the situation in SEA [Southeast Asia] in the foreseeable future. Accordingly, I recommend that the concept proposed not be specifically approved at this time. Instead I recommend that you indicate to the Chairman, JCS, that you have studied the referenced JCSM and agree to the use of the proposed concept in the formulation of specific recommendations for future operations in SEA.”[10] Copies of the JCS memorandum, McNaughton said, were being sent to McGeorge Bundy and to William Bundy, Assistant Secretary of State for the Far East.

In a memorandum on September 11 to JCS Chairman Wheeler, McNamara said merely, “I agree that recommendations for future operations in SEA should be formulated. Such recommendations should be submitted for individual consideration as they are developed.”[11] He added that he had sent a copy of the JCS memorandum to the State Department and the White House “for use in future deliberations.”

The lack of approval by civilian authorities of the JCS strategy paper for Vietnam—the most definitive statement of its kind during the entire course of U.S. involvement in the war—“left Westmoreland,” as General Bruce B. Palmer, Jr. (who served as the Army's Deputy Chief of Staff for Operations during the early part of 1965), has suggested, “to invent his own strategic concept . . . a war of attrition.”[12]

In an interview several years later, General Palmer said, “Basically, the strategy of attrition was wrong. . . . And I blame myself as much as anybody. I thought for a while that the attrition strategy ought to make them get awful tired of what was happening and change their strategy, their objectives, but they never did.”[13] Palmer adds that after he became Westmoreland's Deputy Commander of U.S. Army forces in Vietnam, he, Westmoreland and Gen. Creighton Abrams, who, as will be seen, also was critical of attrition, (Abrams became Commander of U.S. forces in Vietnam in the spring of 1967), “had many, many conversations about whether we were doing the right thing. Nobody really knew the answer.”

---

[10] National Archives, RG 330, JS ISA/EAP, Vietnam 381, Memorandum from McNaughton to McNamara, “Concept for Vietnam,” Sept. 8, 1965.

[11] Same location, McNamara Memorandum for the Chairman of the JCS, “Concept for Vietnam,” Sept. 11, 1965.

[12] Commentary by Gen. Bruce B. Palmer, Jr., in *The Second Indochina War*, John Schlight (ed.) (Washington, D.C.: U.S. Army Center for Military History, 1986), p. 155.

According to Herbert Y. Schandler, a retired Army colonel who had served in Vietnam and helped to write the *Pentagon Papers*, “Left with no guidance from their civilian superiors, the Joint Chiefs of Staff continued to formulate recommendations for future operations along the same lines. Throughout the war their recommendations continued to take the form of requests for additional American troops in South Vietnam and for expanded operational authority outside South Vietnam. Since Secretary McNamara, or higher civilian authority, had failed to provide them with any national objectives, missions, or strategic concepts other than the very general ones of ‘resisting’ or ‘insuring a non-Communist South Vietnam,’ the military leaders virtually were forced to adopt their own concept for conducting their war and to continue to press for its approval.” Herbert Y. Schandler, *The Unmaking of a President: Lyndon Johnson and Vietnam* (Princeton, N.J.: Princeton Univ. Press, 1977), p. 35. See also Schandler's paper, “America and Vietnam: The Failure of Strategy, 1964–67,” in *Vietnam as History*, Peter Braestrup (ed.) (Washington, D.C.: Univ. Press of America, 1984), pp. 23–32.

[13] U.S. Army Military History Institute, Carlisle Barracks, Carlisle, Pa., Oral History, Bruce Palmer, Jr., 1975.

For his part, Westmoreland has argued that he had no choice, especially after his civilian superiors declined to act on the JCS strategy paper:[14]

> What alternative was there to a war of attrition? A grand invasion of North Vietnam was out, for the U.S. national policy was not to conquer North Vietnam but to eliminate the insurgency inside South Vietnam, and President Johnson had stated publicly that he would not "broaden" the war. Because the number of American troops at my disposal would for long be limited, attacking the enemy inside Laos and Cambodia would be beyond my means for months, even years; I would grapple with restrictions on those operations when the time came, although I was destined never to overcome the restrictions. Meanwhile I had to get on with meeting the crisis within South Vietnam, and only by seeking, fighting, and destroying the enemy could that be done.

Andrew F. Krepinevich argues, however, that Westmoreland "simply developed a strategy to suit the Army's preferred *modus operandi,* force structure, and doctrine." "The Army," Krepinevich says, "being denied the opportunity to win a decisive battle of annihilation by invading North Vietnam, found the attrition strategy best fit the kind of war it had prepared to fight." "The Army's attrition strategy," he adds, "was nothing more than the natural outgrowth of its organizational recipe for success—playing to America's strong suits, material abundance and technological superiority, and the nation's profound abhorrence of U.S. casualties."[15]

---

[14] William C. Westmoreland, *A Soldier Reports* (New York: Doubleday, 1976), p. 153.

[15] Andrew F. Krepinevich, *The Army and Vietnam* (Baltimore, Md.: Johns Hopkins Univ. Press, 1986), pp. 164, 196. Krepinevich's major point is that the failure of the Army to adapt its doctrine, force structure, and strategy to the circumstances of the Vietnam war caused it to fail in its mission (*ibid.,* p. 259):

"MACV's strategy of attrition represented a comparatively expensive way of buying time for South Vietnam, in human and material resources. The strategy's great reliance on large amounts of firepower did not in the long run serve, as in previous wars, to reduce U.S. casualties and wear down the enemy. . . . The nature of insurgency warfare . . . made such a strategic approach a high-cost, high-risk option for MACV by mandating a quick victory before the American people grew weary of bearing the burden of continuing the war."

He adds: "In developing its Vietnam strategy to use operational methods successful in previous wars, the Army compromised its ability to successfully combat lower-phase insurgency operations at anything approaching an acceptable cost. In focusing on the attrition of enemy forces rather than on defeating the enemy through denial of his access to the population, MACV missed whatever opportunity it had to deal the insurgents a crippling blow at a low enough cost to permit a continued U.S. military pressure in Vietnam in the event of external, overt aggression. Furthermore, in attempting to maximize Communist combat losses, the Army often alienated the most important element in any counterinsurgency strategy—the people."

Eric M. Bergerud argues, however, that the war—to oversimplify his analysis—was probably unwinnable no matter what military strategy or tactics or political or economic programs might have been used by the U.S. "The United States did not fail in Vietnam because of tactical errors that were open to remedy," he says. "The errors made were on a much higher level. The American military seriously underestimated the difficulties involved in dealing with enemy forces. And the civilian leadership, particularly under Johnson, underestimated the strength and tenacity of the enemy and overestimated the willingness of its own people and soldiers to continue the struggle indefinitely. In short, American leaders, both civilian and military, committed a strategic blunder that has brought many a general to grief: They chose the wrong battlefield." *The Dynamics of Defeat: The Vietnam War in Hau Nghia Province* (Boulder, Colo.: Westview Press, 1991), p. 335.

Gen. Phillip B. Davidson, who served as Westmoreland's chief of intelligence, has criticized U.S. strategy in his study, *Vietnam War: The History, 1945–1975* (Novato, Calif.: Presidio Press, 1988). In a chapter on "Why We Lost the War," he says (pp. 796–797) that the primary reason for the Communists' victory was that "they had a superior ground strategy . . . the strategy of revolutionary war." U.S. strategy, "in theory, at least . . . should have been to avoid a protracted war and to strike the Viet Cong and North Vietnam as soon as possible with enough military force to bring the war to a quick and satisfactory solution." Having chosen not to wage

Continued

Gen. William E. DePuy, who was Westmoreland's J–3 (Operations) officer and his principal strategist during 1965, says that the U.S. "eventually learned that we could not bring them [the Communists] to battle frequently enough to win a war of attrition." "We thought probably we could. We were arrogant, because we were Americans and we were soldiers or Marines and we could do it, but it turned out that it was a faulty concept, given the sanctuaries, given the fact that the Ho Chi Minh Trail was never closed, it was a losing concept of operation." [16]

Westmoreland as well as DePuy and other key military leaders argue, however, that the "strategy of attrition" was, as Westmoreland has said, "an interim situation pending a change in policy." Westmoreland says he hoped "that in due time political authority would grant the flexibility required" for a strategy that would allow U.S. forces to conduct operations against the sanctuaries and against the Communists' logistical pipeline—the Ho Chi Minh Trail.[17]

The Joint Chiefs of Staff have been criticized for not taking a stronger stand with civilian authorities on behalf of the military's preferred strategy. General Palmer, among others, argues that the Chiefs failed "to articulate an effective military strategy that they could persuade the commander-in-chief and secretary of defense to adopt." Moreover, Palmer adds, "Not once during the war did the JCS advise the commander-in-chief or the secretary of defense that the strategy being pursued most probably would fail and that the United States would be unable to achieve its objectives." "The only explanation of this failure," he says, "is that the chiefs were imbued with the 'can do' spirit and could not bring themselves to make such a negative statement or to appear to be disloyal." [18]

In a later interview, General Wheeler, the Chairman of the Joint Chiefs, commented that "among the sins of omission he regretted committing during the course of the war, the one he would emphasize was his failure to insist that McNamara take some formal action on that concept of the Joint Chiefs [the strategy paper of August 27, 1965] and forward it to the President." [19]

For his part, President Johnson apparently believed that he would be better able to perform his role and carry out his purposes if strategy and plans were not too specific or explicit, at least with respect to what was Presidentially approved. He tended to prefer not to make advance commitments that might affect his freedom of

---

that kind of warfare, the U.S., Davidson says, was in the position of having to develop a counterstrategy to revolutionary war. But leaders of the U.S. Government did not understand revolutionary war, and even if they had, they could not "for political, psychological, institutional, and bureaucratic reasons," have developed any effective counterstrategy. Thus, he concludes (p. 811), "the United States lost the war in the way all wars are lost—to a superior strategy which availed itself of our political and psychological vulnerabilities while negating our great military strength."

[16] CRS Interview with Gen. William E. DePuy, Aug. 1, 1988. See also his article, "Our Experience in Vietnam: Will We Be Beneficiaries or Victims?" *Army* (June 1987).

[17] CMH, Westmoreland Papers, letter from Westmoreland to Henry Kissinger commenting on a reference in Kissinger's memoirs (*The White House Years,* [New York: Little, Brown, 1979], p. 1004) to Westmoreland's "substitution of logistics for strategy." See also Westmoreland's chapter, "Evolution of Strategy," in his memoir, *A Soldier Reports.*

[18] Gen. Bruce B. Palmer, Jr., *The 25 Year War: America's Military Role in Vietnam* (Lexington: Univ. Press of Kentucky, 1984), pp. 45–46. A similar conclusion about the role of the JCS was reached by two other military analysts, Schandler, *The Unmaking of a President,* pp. 57–59, 336–338, and Harry G. Summers, Jr., *On Strategy* (Carlisle Barracks, Pa: Strategic Studies Institute, U.S. Army War College, 1981 and Novato, Calif.: Presidio Press, 1982).

[19] See Braestrup, *Vietnam as History,* pp. 38–39.

action at a future date, and he usually reacted strongly against any attempts to commit him to a course of action or to divulge what he planned to do.

Faced with the problem of maintaining his political support and gaining approval of his domestic program, the President also seemed to feel the need to minimize or to conceal actions that might have resulted in greater opposition, while keeping a tight rein on decisions that might have an adverse effect on his program and goals, either domestic or foreign.

Although there was no formally approved strategy for fighting the war, there was a prevailing assumption as to how the U.S. could make the most effective use of its power, how it could "win," namely, that through the application of graduated or measured pressure ("calibration" and "fine tuning" were terms used at the time) the U.S. could convince the Communists that they could not win, and they would then relent and fade away or agree to some kind of settlement.[20] As Bill Moyers, one of the President's prin-

---

[20] See pt. II of this study, pp. 211–214, 233–237 and 366 ff. and pt. III, pp. 6, 18–19.

One of the leading proponents of graduated pressure was Walt W. Rostow, who had been a professor and a member of the staff of a research center at MIT, and in 1961 had joined the Kennedy administration as the NSC staff member principally responsible for Vietnam, after which he served as Director of Policy Planning in the State Department and then returned to the White House in 1966 as the President's National Security Adviser. The graduated pressure concept was, in fact, dubbed the "Rostow thesis."

According to Rostow, "By applying limited, graduated military actions reinforced by political and economic pressures on a nation providing external support for insurgency, we should be able to cause that nation to decide to reduce greatly or eliminate altogether support for the insurgency." *PP*, Gravel ed., vol. IV, p. 337. The objective would not be to destroy the ability of that nation to provide support, but to affect its "calculation of interests" with respect to the consequences if it did not reduce or eliminate such support.

For an incisive analysis of the development of the "strategy of calibrated escalation" in relation to the doctrine of "flexible response," see John Lewis Gaddis, *Strategies of Containment: A Critical Appraisal of Postwar American National Security Policy* (New York: Oxford Univ. Press, 1982), especially chs. 7 and 8. Gaddis concludes that "calibration" strategy was a failure. "What strikes one in retrospect about the strategy of calibrated escalation," he says, "is the extent to which, as so often happened in Vietnam, the effects produced were precisely opposite from those intended." (p. 249) He continues (p. 254): "'[The] central object of U.S. military policy is to create an environment of stability in a nuclear age,' Rostow wrote in 1966; 'this requires as never before that military policy be the servant of political purposes and be woven intimately into civil policy.' To be sure, this had been the objective all along of the 'calibration' strategy: it reflected the immense confidence in the ability to 'manage' crises and control bureaucracies that was characteristic of 'flexible response,' the concern to integrate force and rationality, to find some middle ground between the insanity of nuclear war and the humiliation of appeasement. But it was also a curiously self-centered strategy, vague as to the objects to be deterred, heedless of the extent to which adversaries determined its nature and pace, parochial in its assumption that those adversaries shared its own preoccupations and priorities, blind to the extent to which the indiscriminate use of force had come to replace the measured precision of the original concept."

For theoretical treatments as well as critiques of graduated pressure as a function or instrumentality of "coercive diplomacy" see the references cited in pt. II of this study, p. 342, and pt. III, p. 118.

There has been remarkably little reassessment and reconsideration of the application of coercive diplomacy in Vietnam, or the use of graduated pressure, on the part of those who played leading roles in explicating these ideas, or who, like W. W. Rostow, were advocates while serving in the government. The best available critiques besides Gaddis are Alexander L. George, David K. Hall and William E. Simons, *The Limits of Coercive Diplomacy: Laos, Cuba, Vietnam* (Boston: Little, Brown, 1971), and Wallace J. Thies, *When Governments Collide* (Berkeley: Univ. of California Press, 1980).

Even more remarkable is the fact that the U.S. Government itself does not seem to have felt the need for a reappraisal of the use of coercive diplomacy and the use of graduated pressure in Vietnam. A large and expensive research project conducted in 1979–1980 by the BDM Corporation on *The Strategic Lessons Learned in Vietnam* for the Strategic Studies Institute of the U.S. Army War College (McLean, Va.: 1980), for example, scarcely touches the subject. The only relevant studies by persons associated with the government are Krepinevich, *The Army and Vietnam*, and Mark Clodfelter, *The Limits of Air Power: The American Bombing of North Vietnam* (New York: Free Press, 1989), both written by career military officers. (Krepinevich has since retired.) Both are very useful, but Clodfelter's deals more directly with the question of co-

Continued

cipal assistants during 1964–1966, said about the mood of the President and his associates: "There was a belief that if we indicated a willingness to use our power, they would get the message and back away from an all-out confrontation. . . . There was a confidence . . . that when the chips were really down, the other people would fold."[21]

A similar assessment was given by Deputy Secretary of Defense Cyrus Vance:[22]

> I think that a lot of us felt that by the gradual application of force the North Vietnamese and the NLF would be forced to seek a political settlement of the problem. We had seen the gradual application of force applied in the Cuban missile crisis, and had seen a very successful result.[23] We believed that if this same gradual and restrained application of force were applied in South Vietnam, that one could expect the same kind of result; that rational people on the other side would respond to increasing military pressure and would therefore try and seek a political solution.

What was President Johnson's own view of the use of graduated pressure? This is difficult to discern from the available evidence, but his actions in approving plans based on this approach and in rejecting or postponing proposals for a more rapid and larger use of force, as well as the importance he obviously attached to such detailed controls on escalation as the approval of bombing targets, suggest that he was inclined to prefer "progressive squeeze and talk" to "full/fast-squeeze," to use the terminology of Assistant Secretary of Defense McNaughton.[24] This was doubtless due in part to the President's desire to keep the war limited in size, scope, and level of violence, and to keep it from interfering with his other programs and goals, but he also seems to have felt that this was the preferred method for responding to the threat—that it was more likely to produce the desired result with fewer adverse consequences than would a full/fast squeeze.

Graduated pressure was also a method of influencing behavior which was personally congenial to Johnson and compatible with his style of dealing with people and events. As Doris Kearns writes, "Johnson had grounded his actions all his life on the conviction that every man had his price. That must also be true of Ho Chi Minh. . . ."[25] In a meeting with Senator George S. McGovern (D/

---

ercive diplomacy/graduated pressure. See also the critical study by Earl H. Tilford, Jr., a retired Air Force officer who was one of the historians in the Office of Air Force History, *Crosswinds: The Air Force's Setup in Vietnam* (College Station, Tex.: Texas A & M Univ. Press, 1992), and the monograph by Col. Dennis M. Drew, director of the Airpower Research Institute, *ROLLING THUNDER 1965: Anatomy of a Failure,* Airpower Research Institute Report No. AU–ARI–CP–86–3 (Maxwell Air Force Base, Ala.: Air Univ. Press, 1986).

[21] "Bill Moyers Talks About the War and LBJ, An Interview," *Atlantic* (July 1968). Paul Hammond concludes that "the tone and outcome of Johnson's Vietnam deliberations cannot be explained without employing hubris as an explanatory factor. I mean to say that Johnson's advisors, and Johnson himself, in their failure to address from the outset the prospect of failure, particularly in the context of setting severe constraints on the employment of military force, assumed that failure was beyond serious consideration." Hammond, *LBJ and the Management of Foreign Relations,* p. 197.

[22] Johnson Library, Cyrus Vance Oral History, 1970.

[23] According to Gaddis, *Strategies of Containment,* p. 231, the Kennedy administration regarded its handling of the Cuban missile crisis as, "a textbook demonstration of 'flexible response' in action, and, hence, as a model to be followed elsewhere."

[24] See pt. III of this study, p. 18.

[25] Doris Kearns, *Lyndon Johnson and the American Dream* (New York: Harper and Row, 1976), p. 266.

S. Dak.) in early 1965, after the U.S. began bombing the North as part of its graduated pressure plan, the President explained that he was "'going up old Ho Chi Minh's leg an inch at a time.'"[26]

Can the graduated pressure plan that had been developed in November-December 1964 and accepted, in principle at least, by the President (who also approved the beginning of operations carried out according to the plan), be considered to have been a strategy? In one sense, this plan, which comes as close to being a statement of strategy as any plan developed and used during the war, was at least the beginning of a strategy: it was directed to the pursuit of a specific national goal and prescribed the way in which national power could be used for the achievement of that goal. Yet it did not qualify as a strategy in other respects. As approved by the President's principal advisers and subsequently accepted if not explicitly approved by the President, it was not a statement of the problem facing the United States, of U.S. goals, of available and appropriate means, and of whether those means were sufficient to achieve the stipulated ends. Moreover, it failed to address the major question which confronted the U.S. in 1965, namely, whether and how U.S. ground forces should be used.

The plan also did not specifically address some of the major strategic questions with respect to how the war should be fought, especially whether it should be limited to South Vietnam, what restraints should be applied vis-à-vis China and Russia, what limits to place on bombing, whether the U.S. should use nuclear weapons. Other major questions which were not addressed were whether the U.S. should use its ground forces if the political situation in South Vietnam continued to be so unstable, what kind of a role the U.S. should play in the war if it decided to intervene more directly and extensively in the South, how American ground forces should be used if the U.S. decided to expand its role, and how and whether those forces could be used effectively under the conditions and circumstances which prevailed.[27]

Although the graduated pressure plan as approved by the President provided for a possible diplomatic outcome, the questions of how negotiations might be facilitated and what U.S. tactics and goals might be were given even less attention than military aspects of the plan.

Above all, the plan was silent about what the U.S. should do if the North Vietnamese did not respond to pressure as expected and

---

[26] George McGovern, *Grassroots* (New York: Random House, 1977), p. 194.

[27] During the deliberations of the Working Group which developed the plan (see pt. II of this study, p. 375), there were papers on and discussions of a number of aspects, including such questions as whether to use nuclear weapons, whether and when to use U.S. ground forces, what kind of military operations to conduct in Laos, whether to conduct an amphibious landing in North Vietnam. Unfortunately, there apparently are no notes of most of these meetings or other sources from which to discern what was discussed and how and why the content of the final position paper presented to the President on Dec. 1, 1964 was determined.

Nor do the tabbed materials which accompany the position paper shed much light on the subject. Tab D states in very cryptic fashion the actions which would occur during the first 30 days (Phase I), the transition from Phase I to Phase II, and the next 2–6 months (Phase II). In Phase II, in addition to airstrikes, the plan called for deployment of additional U.S. forces "as necessary" as well as aerial mining of North Vietnamese ports coupled with a U.S. naval blockade.

Tab F, which dealt with possible Communist reactions and U.S. countermoves, stated that in the event of a ground attack by the North on the South, the U.S., in addition to using its forces to defend the South, would "consider seizing and occupying all of NVN." In the event of a ground attack by the Chinese, the U.S. would use its forces to attack China, with "nuclear strikes if necessary."

a different approach were required—either some form of settlement or withdrawal or another kind of persuasion/coercion.[28] Little if any consideration seems to have been given to the possibility that, rather than for the U.S. to succeed in coercing the Communists, the Communists, by protracting the war and attriting U.S. forces, could coerce the United States and force it to seek a negotiated withdrawal.

The graduated pressure plan, however, while coming as close as any other statement or plan during the war, was not intended to be a statement of strategy or even a general plan of action. William Bundy, who was in charge of developing the November-December 1964 plan, says that it had only "short-term validity, giving initial guidance for a bombing program. The group certainly did not think of itself as prescribing an overall strategy if the North Vietnamese kept coming, Saigon could not hold them, and large-scale U.S. forces were sent in."[29]

Although the graduated pressure plan did not stipulate any limits on the war, there were limits imposed by the Johnson administration. One very important limit was the *de facto* ceiling on manpower that resulted from the President's rejection in July 1965 of the proposal by McNamara and the military to order national mobilization, which would have allowed the Reserves to be called up as well as invoking various economic controls.[30] There were also limits on the conduct of the war: no land invasion of North Vietnam, no serious encroachment on China, only limited covert operations in Laos and Cambodia, no use of nuclear or chemical weapons, no mass bombing of population centers or civilian targets, no mining of harbors.

The military, McGeorge Bundy said later in an interview, were allowed by civilian authorities to do "whatever they were not forbidden to do." "It may have been quixotic to suppose that you could conduct a military campaign with an essentially political purpose. But, of course, that was what Vietnam was all about all the way."[31]

---

[28] Douglas Pike says that the U.S. effort was afflicted by "strategic ambiguity," which resulted from the fact that "we first committed ourselves to the war and then began to think about it comprehensively. The highest level leadership did not initially sit down and address in detailed and extended fashion its strategic position, did not discuss and analyze enemy strengths, weaknesses, and probable strategies, did not wrangle and argue and finally hammer out a fully articulated strategy.

"There was in this behavior a sense of enormous self-confidence, indeed a kind of unconscious arrogance on the part of the Americans."

Moreover, he notes, "we entered the war without fully appreciating the enemy's strategy. Worse, we never made a serious effort to correct this shortcoming. The highest leadership never devoted itself to systematically learning about Hanoi's strategic thinking and doctrine." Pike, "Conduct of the War: Strategic Factors, 1965–1968," in *The Second Indochina War*, John Schlight (ed.), p. 112.

[29] Communication from William P. Bundy to the author, July 1993.

[30] As Gen. Douglas Kinnard has observed, "This [the 500,000 limitation], rather than any specific strategic or tactical plan, was the basis of the manpower goal which the Military Assistance Command [Westmoreland's headquarters] sought." Kinnard, *The War Managers* (New York: Da Capo Press, 1992, 3d. ed., 1977), p. 36. General Kinnard served in Vietnam in 1966–1967 as Chief of Operations Analysis in Westmoreland's J-3 (Operations), and 1969–1970 as Commanding General of the II Field Force Artillery and then as Chief of Staff of the II Field Force Vietnam.

See also Schandler, *The Unmaking of a President*, p. 56, and Summers, *On Strategy*, p. 74, and John Stuckey and Joseph H. Pistorius, "Mobilization for the Vietnam War: A Political and Military Catastrophe," *Parameters* (Spring 1988).

[31] CRS Interview with McGeorge Bundy, Jan. 8, 1979.

Finally, as suggested by Bundy's comments, there is the relationship of political policy and strategy (national policy) and military strategy and plans—of military means and political ends. Military leaders in the American system of political control operate within an uncertain environment that can—and did in the case of Vietnam—produce confusion and frustration in carrying out politically determined policy. Based on a survey of U.S. generals with command positions in Vietnam during 1965–1972, Douglas Kinnard concluded:[32]

> Apparently, translating the overall United States objectives into something understandable to the general officers of the war was not successfully accomplished by policymakers. It is possible for lower-level soldiers and officials to fight a war without being sure of their objectives, but that almost 70 percent of the Army generals who managed the war were uncertain of its objectives mirrors a deep-seated strategic failure: the inability of policymakers to frame tangible, obtainable goals.

The President and perhaps others responsible for the political direction of the war, however, apparently did not feel the need to frame "tangible, obtainable goals," in the sense of providing written directives that would be considered adequate by the military in translating political policy and strategy into military strategy, plans and operations. In part, as reinforced by the President's own penchant for not becoming committed in advance, this resulted from concern about approving statements of strategy and plans that went beyond what those in political authority were willing to approve, or which could be construed by the military to convey authority or justify actions that might be contrary to politically determined policy. Rather, the President and his associates seem to have believed that the general statements of policy that were approved, together with limitations on operations that were stipulated, were adequate for the understanding on the part of the military as to what was being required of them. Beyond that, because it was being fought as a limited war and in a highly political/military context involving the U.S.S.R. and China, especially the risk of Chinese military intervention, as well as sensitive relations with the South Vietnamese, close control by political policymakers was thought to be essential in order to keep the war limited, and, through graduated pressure, to employ military means effectively in securing political ends. Such controls were also important to avoid domestic consequences if the public became aroused because of the apparent lack of success of U.S. efforts or the cost in men and money, or through an excess of patriotic zeal.[33]

Preparing for the "Other War": Pacification and Development

While the military buildup was taking place in August-October 1965 and plans for the use of U.S. forces were being proposed, new efforts were also underway with respect to the nonmilitary side of the war. Recognizing that the war could not be "won" and U.S. ob-

---

[32] Kinnard, *The War Managers*, p. 25.

[33] For a very cogent analysis of the expectation of U.S. military leaders regarding the availability of resources needed to "win" the war, and the effect of this innovation on military strategy and tactics, see Hammond, *LBJ and the Presidential Management of Foreign Relations*, pp. 186 ff.

jectives achieved unless and until national and local governments became more viable, the U.S. and the South Vietnamese began taking steps to strengthen the institutions of government and to promote the security and well-being of people, especially in the rural areas where the Communists held sway.

In his unpublished memoir, Lodge said that upon arrival in Saigon in early August 1965 he took several steps along these lines. He told the CIA station chief that he was depending on him to have a current list of South Vietnamese commanders "who might be eligible for diplomatic recognition as head of a government in the event that the Communists subverted the then government of Viet-Nam." He told Philip Habib, chief of the Political Section of the U.S. Embassy, to prepare a study on what would constitute a "satisfactory outcome" of the war. And he told his new assistant, Edward G. Lansdale, to advise Nguyen Cao Ky "so that he would become a true political leader," and to use his staff to protect Ky's physical safety and to advise him about possible coup attempts.[34]

State Department policy planners also stressed the need for political development. In "Politics and Victory in South Vietnam," W. W. Rostow, chairman of State's Policy Planning Council (formerly on the NSC staff), argued that unless there could be "some effective political expression of South Vietnamese anti-Communist nationalism," military and diplomatic successes could come to naught.[35] "Thus," the paper said, "we must turn to the problem of the political life of South Vietnam with a seriousness which matches that now accorded to military and diplomatic aspects of the crisis; and with far more creative imagination, because our margin of influence is less and the techniques of operation less familiar." The "greatest single weakness of the U.S. Government in dealing with developing nations is our weakness in doing this kind of job on a systematic high-priority basis."

The "working hypothesis" of the paper, as had been suggested earlier by, among others, George A. Carver, Jr. of the CIA, was that a revolutionary process was occurring in South Vietnam in which, according to the paper, "the trend is toward the emergence of a rather typical proud and assertive young nationalism. . . ." The paper quoted Carver's argument that if this process, which was represented by the rise of the Buddhists and the younger military officers like Ky and Nguyen Van Thieu, could produce a political balance arrived at by the Vietnamese themselves—"a balance embodied in an institutional framework adopted to Vietnamese needs and realities and supported by the rising emotions of Vietnamese nationalists," and if this regenerated government could then enlist the support of people in the provinces, the counterinsurgency program "would be well launched on the road to genuine progress."[36]

---

[34] Massachusetts Historical Society, Lodge Papers, unpublished "Vietnam Memoir," pt. IV, ch. IX, pp. 1–2.

[35] There is a copy of the paper, dated August 1965, with a cover memorandum from W. W. Rostow, Chairman of the Policy Planning Council, dated August 2 and 3 respectively, in the Johnson Library, NSF Name File, Chester Cooper Memos, and in the State Department, Lot File 72 D 139.

[36] Carver's article, "The Real Revolution in South Vietnam," in which he was not identified as working for the CIA, appeared in *Foreign Affairs* (April 1965). Frances FitzGerald, whose father had been a leading CIA official, called the article "a sublime example of American official scholarship," and said that the rise of the young officers was merely "a change of men," and

Rostow's paper suggested a "working agenda" for this new program. First, it was essential for the South Vietnamese military to have a common view of the future of the country, and to play a role in preventing a Communist takeover while helping with the establishment of civilian leadership. But it should not continue to exercise such leadership directly. Second, "It may be time for South Vietnam to develop a modern revolutionary party which would seek to embrace within it all the major groups in the society except the Communists and those irreversibly discredited by their past association with French colonialism, appeasement of Hanoi, etc. . . . a political organization to focus the authentic nationalism which suffuses the country into an instrument capable of coping with Communist organizational techniques. . . ." This would require the development of a political program around which the major groups could rally, which would involve: "a stance of independence towards all foreigners; national unity in the South, with all Vietnamese unity as a long-run objective; an end to corruption; rapid industrial development; land reform and other measures which would ease the burden on the farmer; anti-Communism; etc."

Work should be started, the paper said, on a five-year "reconstruction development program," which would include the strengthening of local institutions to encourage citizen participation in development, specifically community development programs, trade unions, farmers' associations and cooperatives.

In order for this program to succeed, the paper concluded, "the whole of the U.S. Government, from the President down, [must] accept this kind of effort as equivalent in priority to what we do in Vietnam in the military and diplomatic fields," and the U.S. Mission in Saigon would have to be organized for such a campaign and "equipped with men who command the rare skills necessary for this kind of enterprise."

The paper did not question whether such an agenda could be implemented in a country disrupted by war, and whose culture was so very different from that of the United States on which the political concepts and the proposals of the paper were based. Just as the military assumed that U.S. forces could fight effectively in Vietnam, so the Chairman of the State Department Policy Planning Council appeared to have assumed that the U.S. should help to bring about this kind of political change ("development") in South Vietnam and other "developing" nations, and to have assumed implicitly that this could and would be done successfully.

These views about the importance of political development in South Vietnam were widely shared throughout the U.S. Government, both in the Executive and in Congress.[37] President Johnson himself appears to have been very concerned about this aspect of the war. Partly as a result of the Diem coup, which he had opposed, he was determined to secure and maintain a stable and effective government.

---

that, "Probity, a desire for social justice and equal opportunity for all—such virtues might more reasonably be expected in the heads of a Mafia ring than in those generals who had spent their formative years struggling to the top of the corrupt, inefficient, and demoralized army of the Diem regime." *Fire in the Lake* (Boston: Little, Brown, 1972), pp. 251–253.

[37] For some expressions of congressional views, see pt. III of this study, pp. 263–265.

Moreover, the new team in the U.S. Mission in Saigon was committed to political development. Ambassador Lodge viewed the war as a politico-military struggle,[38] as did Lansdale, a CIA officer known for helping to suppress the Communists in the Philippines and for his experience and skill in dealing with the Vietnamese.[39] During his previous term as Ambassador, Lodge, as a way of focusing U.S. and South Vietnamese counterinsurgency programs, and in order to demonstrate how an important area dominated by the Communists could be pacified, proposed that the seven provinces adjacent to Saigon, which had long been a Communist stronghold, be singled out for attention. This program, called Hop Tac (the words mean "cooperation"), began in September 1964, but little progress had been made by the time Lodge was reappointed Ambassador in July 1965.

In a "working paper" on "Solving the 'Politico' Part of the 'Politico-Military' Vietnam Problem," Lodge told Lansdale that he would be responsible for getting the Hop Tac program and those in other areas "moving—always with solid, durable growth; never with bogus statistics."[40] This task, Lodge said, "entails nothing less than starting a true political movement with all the requisite practical and ideological aspects for a new and better life for the Vietnamese people. It means real—and not pretend—social revolution and social justice."[41] "This," he added, "would be the ultimate body blow to the Viet Cong and would guarantee U.S. success."

---

[38] For Lodge's views see pt. III of this study, pp. 153–262, 386–387, and *PP*, Gravel ed., vol. II, pp. 527 ff.

[39] For Lansdale, see the entries under his name in the index of pts. I and II of this study, his memoir, *In the Midst of Wars* (New York: Harper and Row, 1972), and his article "Viet Nam: Do We Understand Revolution?" *Foreign Affairs* (October 1964).

In the summer of 1964, Lansdale, apparently hoping and possibly anticipating that his original team would be reactivated, prepared two long memoranda, one on the development of the South Vietnamese political system, and the other, "Concept for Victory in Vietnam," June 8, 1964. Copies are in the Massachusetts Historical Society, Lodge Papers.

See also the biography by Cecil B. Currey, Edward *Lansdale: The Unquiet American* (Boston: Houghton-Mifflin, 1988), especially pp. 279–282. There are also some valuable insights with respect to Lansdale in Zalin Grant's interesting and provocative book *Facing the Phoenix* (New York: W. W. Norton, 1991).

Early in his first appointment to Vietnam in 1963–1964, Lodge had requested that Lansdale be assigned to be the head of the CIA station in South Vietnam where he could be "a sort of 'Lawrence of Arabia' to take charge under my supervision of all U.S. relationships with the change of government here." This was not approved. (Lodge Papers, "Vietnam Memoir," pt. II, p. 6.) See also U.S. Department of State, *Foreign Relations of the United States*, 1961–1963, vol. IV, Vietnam, August-December 1963 (Washington, D.C.: U.S. Govt. Print. Off., 1991), pp. 205, 240, 753.

[40] Johnson Library, NSF Country File, Vietnam. This paper was originally prepared in May 1965 as instructions for John McNaughton, Lodge's choice for the post of Chief of Staff in the Embassy (according to Lodge, the President also preferred McNaughton). In a discussion with the President on May 27, Lodge said that "this was the one man I was asking for and that it was clear that the job in Vietnam was far more important than the job which McNaughton held in Washington." (Lodge's memorandum on this conversation, as well as the conversation on March 25 in which the President mentioned his preference for McNaughton are in pt. III of Lodge's "Vietnam Memoir.") On June 22, however, Lodge talked to McGeorge Bundy, who said that William Bundy thought McNaughton was "too inflexible," and preferred William Sullivan, who subsequently held the post for a few months prior to taking up his new position as Ambassador to Laos. (The memorandum on this conversation is also in pt. III of Lodge's "Vietnam Memoir.") William Bundy, however, says that while Sullivan was well qualified, that he preferred William Porter (who subsequently was appointed to the post, after Sullivan became Ambassador.) (Communication from William Bundy to the author, July 1993.)

[41] In their practical application, Lodge's lofty ideas tended at times to become quite prosaic and to reflect American concepts of promoting social and political satisfaction—especially when the situation seemed to call for prompt action—through steps to improve the material conditions of life. In a cable to President Johnson Lodge said, for example, that Saigon "contains more examples of grinding and desperate poverty than ever before. This is objectionable on humanitarian grounds. It is also extremely dangerous. The ability to cope basically with the overcrowding, the undernourishment and the filth would take years. But I am studying things which we could do quickly, one of which assuredly is keeping the price of rice under control. Another is

"We have had everything in Vietnam except good practical politics," Lodge said. "Only by working at the grass roots—militarily, politically and socially—is victory in Viet Nam possible. The effort must start in the 12,000 hamlets, among the real hamlet people who owe their position to their fellows and not to government appointment. From them a 'People's Force' must be created."[42]

Such a "competitive political movement," Lodge said, also was needed for success against the Communists worldwide: "There is clearly a limit to our ability to meet force with force. If we send troops to enough places, we—not the Communists—will be con-

---

cloth, another is the feasibility of putting in latrines and electric lights in the many places where both are lacking." U.S., Department of State, Central File, Pol 27 Viet S, Saigon to Washington 621, Aug. 26, 1965.

[42]On September 27, Lodge held a meeting at which he presented a working paper for purposes of illustrating the steps which should be taken, as he reported in a cable to the President on September 30 (U.S. Department of State, Central File, Pol 27 Viet S, Saigon to Washington 1100) "in order to hasten the day when a true precinct organization exists which will destroy the Viet Cong in small groupings." This was the text of the paper:

"In each city precinct and each rural hamlet immediately adjacent to a thoroughly pacified city (i.e. the smallest unit from a public safety standpoint) the following program should be undertaken in the following order:

"A. Saturate the minds of the people with some socially conscious and attractive ideology, which is susceptible of being carried out.

"B. Organize the people politically with a hamlet chief and committee whose actions would be backed by the police or the military using police-type tactics. This committee should have representatives of the political, military, economic and social organizations and should have an executive who directs.

"C. With the help of the police or military, conduct a census.

"D. Issue identification cards.

"E. Issue permits for the movement of goods and people.

"F. When necessary, hold a curfew.

"G. Thanks to all those methods, go through each hamlet with a fine tooth comb to apprehend the terrorists.

"H. At the first quiet moment, bring in agricultural experts, school teachers, etc.

"I. The hamlet should also be organized for its own defense against small Viet Cong external attacks.

"J. When the above has been done, hold local elections."

Progress along military lines, Lodge said, was considerably ahead of progress along civil and political lines. "Yet civil-political progress is utterly indispensable to a successful outcome. For one thing, the majority of Viet Cong are probably still in small groups rather than in main force units and will thus not be reached by the planned military offensives. These small VC groups cannot be overcome without the support of the population, organized on a precinct basis. If these VC are not overcome, the worst of the aggression will still be going on, requiring continuing presence of American ground troops.

"It seems clear that U.S. military can prevent the Viet Cong from taking over the state, can destroy or neutralize main force units, and can destroy hitherto impregnable redoubts. These are very big achievements indeed. But they do not prevent the Viet Cong from continuing to have a disruptive and debilitating effect on the country which would mean that as soon as we left, the Viet Cong would take over again. In other words, a durable result would not have been accomplished."

In another cable to the President Lodge described what he and members of the U.S. Mission Council would consider to be a "satisfactory outcome" of the pacification program (U.S. Department of State, Central File, Pol 27 Viet S, Saigon to Washington 1377, Oct. 21, 1965):

"1. The area around Saigon and south of Saigon (all of the Delta) must be pacified. . . . 'Pacified' is defined as the existence of a state of mind among the people that they have a stake in the government as shown by the holding of local elections. It also means a proper local police force. . . .

"2. The thickly populated northeastern strip along the coast . . . would be completely pacified.

"3. The GVN would retain its present control of all cities and all provincial capitals.

"4. All principal roads would be open to the Vietnamese military day and night.

"5. Those areas not pacified would not be safe havens for the VC but would be contested by energetic offensive forays to prevent consolidation of a communist base.

"6. The VC disarms; and their weapons and explosives are removed from their hands. Their main force units would be broken up.

"7. North Vietnam stops its infiltration.

"8. North Vietnam stops its direction of the war.

"9. Chieu Hoi rehabilitation would be extended to individual Viet Cong who are suitable. . . .

"10. Hardcore VC to go to North Vietnam.

"11. GVN to approve."

tained [a reference to the "containment" of communism]. A competitive political movement is the answer."[43]

Lansdale replied in a memorandum, a portion of which Lodge, who had done so with his own memorandum, sent to the President.[44] This was Lansdale's response to Lodge:

> The military can suppress the Communist forces, even keep them suppressed by continued military action, but cannot defeat them short of genocide unless our side puts the war on a political footing in Viet Nam.
>
> The enemy in Vietnam understands thoroughly the political nature of the war he is waging. The enemy sees his every act as a political act, and uses psychological, military, and socioeconomic weapons to gain his political goals. This is a strict rule the enemy borrowed from Clausewitz. Lenin, Mao, Ho, and Giap have been clear and firm on this basic rule. The Viet Cong have obeyed it amazingly well. Our side has broken this rule over and over again. It is being broken daily right now.
>
> Thus, when you ask my help to get a Counter Subversion/Terrorism program moving, you really are asking me to help you to get our side to start obeying and applying the prime rule of the war in Vietnam. It isn't separate from the other programs. It is the basis upon which the war in Vietnam will be won or lost. The psychological, military, and socio-economic programs are its instruments, not ends in themselves. Political bankruptcy in Vietnam and the direct use of U.S. combat forces complicate your task vastly. (A U.S. commander, tasked to attack a suspected enemy position, is going to clobber it first by bombing or artillery to cut his own U.S. casualties to a minimum when they attack; casualties of Vietnamese noncombatants must be secondary to his responsibility to his own command and mission.) I point this out to underscore the fact that something brand new, perhaps of considerable difference from anything previous, will have to be worked out in Vietnam to put the war on the essential political footing. It might require heroic measures, such as moving noncombatants out of Central Vietnam into the far South, to permit the military threat to be resolved conclusively in Central Vietnam by military means while non-combatant refugees get a real chance at a new life. Again, this could be a wrong move. You are going to need some exceptionally expert help to solve this vital problem; for many reasons, it's your biggest.

When McGeorge Bundy gave this memorandum to the President he said in his cover note: "Lansdale appears quite ready to take

---

[43] In 1984, shortly before he died, Lodge sent a letter to his old friend and former classmate at Harvard University, Corliss Lamont. In a letter in November 1965 which Lodge apparently had never answered, Lamont had urged him to "stop abetting President Johnson's evil actions and design in Vietnam," and to resign as Ambassador and "help transform the Republican Party into the great American Peace Party." In his letter to Lamont in 1984, thanking him for a copy of his autobiography, Lodge said regarding Lamont's 1965 letter: "You were right—we were wrong and we failed—I should have resigned sooner." *Harvard Magazine*, November-December 1985, "The Lamont-Lodge Letters."

[44] Johnson Library, NSF Memos to the President—McGeorge Bundy. Lansdale's memorandum is in the Massachusetts Historical Society, Lodge Papers, memorandum to Lodge from Lansdale, "Your Working Paper on the 'Politico' Part of the Vietnam Problem," July 29, 1965.

over MACV—and yet he's not all wrong. Can we afford some creative tension?"[45]

Lansdale's official position was Senior Liaison Officer, and his team of about ten, primarily members of his earlier teams in the Philippines in the late 1940s-early 1950s and his 1954 Vietnam team, was known as the SLO team. He was given the title of chairman of the U.S. Mission Liaison Group, a position in which, as Lodge said in a cable to the President, Lansdale would be "the spokesman [for pacification] for the whole U.S. Mission" in relations with the Government of South Vietnam.[46] His role was never well defined, partly because neither he nor Lodge saw the need for it, and partly because of the amorphous nature of the task he had been assigned, based on the idea that the U.S. could and should seek to bring about major political change and development in South Vietnam.[47]

Shortly after he arrived in Saigon on August 20, 1965, Lodge was contacted by another advocate of the idea of waging a counter revolution to defeat the Communists, John Paul Vann, a former U.S. Army officer and military adviser in Vietnam, who had returned as a civilian representative for pacification programs in Hau Nghia Province, located between Saigon and the border of Cambodia. During his service as a military adviser, Vann became convinced that the struggle could be won only if there were a government with popular support through which the goals of the "social revolution," which he felt was occurring in South Vietnam, could be realized. This, he argued in a paper which he wrote in the summer of 1965, required U.S. intervention in the affairs of South Vietnam "to insure the emergence of a government responsive to a majority of its

---

[45] Johnson Library, NSF Memos to the President—McGeorge Bundy.

[46] *PP*, Gravel ed., vol. II, pp. 530–531, Lodge to the President, Saigon to Washington 716, Sept. 2, 1965.

[47] For Lodge's memorandum to Lansdale describing Lansdale's role, see the Lodge Papers, Lodge to Lansdale, Aug. 9, 1965. According to the memorandum, Lansdale and his staff would be responsible only to Lodge.

There is very little public information on the activities of Lansdale and his team. He sent copies of many of his reports to William Bundy, beginning with the report on Sept. 17, 1965, Saigon to Washington 333, and there are copies of these in the Department of State, Central File, Pol 27 Viet S.

Frances FitzGerald, (*Fire in the Lake*, p. 269), depicts the problems faced by Lansdale:

"Again at the behest of the CIA, Lansdale returned to Vietnam at the end of 1965 with a team of enthusiastic young men and the general mission of injecting some new ideas into the counterinsurgency program. This vague definition of role did not serve him as it once had. Lansdale's zeal for political conversion and his disapproval of the very scale on which the American operations were now conducted made him an uncomfortable neighbor for the 'regulars' at the mission. In a series of careful jurisdictional maneuvers, the bureaucrats narrowed his 'area of responsibility' to the point where they had effectively cut him off from the mission command and from all work except that of a symbolic nature. For the next few years Lansdale would spend most of his time in talk with Vietnamese intellectuals, a few ex-Viet Minh officers, and his own American devotees. Living in his grand villa, isolated from the press, he would become an American counterpart to the elusive Vietnamese 'Third Force,' a hero to idealistic young American officials who saw the failure of American policy as a failure of tactics. Lansdale's bureaucratic defeat was only an indication of the general shift in emphasis of American policy. With the commitment of American troops Washington began to look upon the war as an American affair. The Vietnamese seemed to recede into the background, and along with them those Americans who had spent years in Vietnam and believed in the regeneration of a non-Communist nationalism. The romantic warriors, such as Frank Scotton and Jean Sauvageot, who, like Lansdale, spoke and thought Vietnamese, who loved the exoticism of the villages and believed with fervor in a non-Communist liberation front—they were to remain merely the 'characters' in a generally faceless enterprise. With all the civilian infighting, the talk of political strategies and 'winning the hearts and minds of the Vietnamese people,' the American war was to be a conventional military operation."

people."[48] The existing government exploited the people. "It is, in fact, a continuation of the French colonial system of government with upper-class Vietnamese replacing the French." Moreover, the system was inefficient and should be simplified and made less cumbersome in order to provide better service to the public.

Vann proposed that there should be a three-year pilot project in three provinces in which authority would be decentralized to the provinces from the central government. Provincial officials would be given control over programs, personnel, and the allocation of resources. All U.S. assistance programs in each province would be unified under a single American adviser. There would be "political indoctrination and motivational training" of all South Vietnamese governmental personnel in the provinces as well as American advisers. South Vietnamese military units in the province would also be trained for civic action and psychological warfare.

In the paper, Vann was critical of the way in which the war was being fought: "Emphasis is placed upon the use of physical obstacles to provide population security rather than the fostering of a spirit of resistance." "Gadgetry, air power, and artillery continue to be substituted for the discriminate ground actions required to prosecute the military side of this war without unduly alienating the civilian population."

Vann said that every effort should be made to "sell" the proposed program to the Government of South Vietnam, but that, "If this cannot be done without compromising the principal provisions of the proposal, then GVN [Government of Vietnam] must be *forced* to accept U.S. judgment and direction." (emphasis in original)

Vann submitted his proposal to a number of U.S. officials, including Ambassador Lodge (with whom he had become acquainted after leaving the Army and before returning to Vietnam when he helped with the Lodge for President campaign in Colorado). In a letter to Lodge in July 1965, Vann proposed that Lodge appoint him as his assistant for pacification to keep himself personally informed about the situation. Lodge saw Vann briefly in September, after Lansdale and some members of his team had visited Vann in Hau Nghia Province, but nothing came of the meeting nor did Vann receive the expected invitation to join Lansdale's team.[49]

One of the members of Lansdale's team was Daniel Ellsberg (later an antiwar activist who achieved notoriety when he made public the Defense Department's internal history of the Vietnam war, the *Pentagon Papers*). Ellsberg, who at the time was a strong supporter of the war, had just come from Washington where he had been special assistant to John McNaughton, Assistant Secretary of

---

[48] John Paul Vann, "Harnessing the Revolution in South Vietnam," Sept. 10, 1965, U.S., Department of State, Central File, Pol 27 Viet S. See also Neil Sheehan, *A Bright Shining Lie: John Paul Vann and America in Vietnam* (New York: Random House, 1988), pp. 535–539, and Bergerud, *The Dynamics of Defeat: The Vietnam War in Hau Nghia Province*, pp. 107–110.

Vann's paper was prepared in collaboration with three of his associates, Douglas Ramsey, (a CIA officer who was then acting under the cover of a Foreign Service officer) who was Vann's Assistant Provincial Representative in Hau Nghia Province and was later captured in 1966 by the Communists and imprisoned until the end of the war, Everet Bumgardner, who had been in Vietnam with the U.S. information program in 1954 and returned in 1965 as head of the program's field operations (propaganda and psychological warfare), and Frank Scotton, Bumgardner's principal field operative. In 1964, Scotton and others had organized 45-man propaganda/paramilitary teams in Quang Ngai Province. For more information on these men and their relationships with Vann, see Sheehan, *A Bright Shining Lie*.

[49] See *ibid.*, pp. 544–548, 552–553.

Defense for International Security Affairs.[50] He had been with Lansdale on his visit to Vann, and returned alone for a three-day visit in October 1965. In a report, "Visit to an Insecure Province," he described the situation in Hau Nghia Province and explained Vann's ideas.[51] Vann, he said, believed that it was necessary to find a way of infusing the South Vietnamese system with greater efficiency, honesty, and sense of purpose, and that to do so "we should be exerting very heavy American influence (not 'heavy-handed,' but 'effective'), by intervening in specific cases where necessary, to change the Vietnamese administrative pattern of ignoring talent, experience and competent performance in handing out jobs and promotions in favor of political and family associations, conservatism and payoff." Initially, the U.S. should intervene in selected provinces in an effort to shift responsibility from the older, ensconced leaders to "*new,* younger, competent leadership with roots in the provinces and with social consciousness and energy." (emphasis in original) This should be done gradually and without publicity. "[M]aximum effort should be taken throughout to preserve 'face' and the facade of Vietnamese authority and control, and to gain the acquiescence of present incumbents. . . ."

Ellsberg said that there were some "obvious objections" to Vann's proposal, especially the charge of "colonialism"—"the closest analogy would be that of a 'good' colonialist power" such as the British in Malaya—but Vann's proposal "has the merit of being relevant to some profoundly serious problems of implementation, and its radical nature is appropriate to the urgency and intractability of these problems."

Ellsberg added:

> The familiar postulate that "The war must be won by the Vietnamese" usually conceals the hidden assumption that the war must be won by "*these*" Vietnamese, the ones who head and run the system right now, in Saigon, Corps and provinces. It is not logically guaranteed that this particular set of Vietnamese—with their constricted backgrounds and orientation (quite apart from their competence or dedication, which may be considerable)—will or can win this war. It may be that new leadership is, very simply, a requirement: as one analyst puts it, "leaders who came from, think like, and are responsive to the majority of the population." If so, is the present leadership class going to allow these new leaders to emerge, in time, without considerable U.S. intervention?
>
> We may believe the present leadership group *can* reform itself, and that our best course is to help it do so. Or, we may pin our hopes on starting an evolutionary process in motion—perhaps by the beginnings of representative government—that will eventually transform the nature of the government, its personnel and its elan. In either case, it is still important to

---

[50] When he went to Vietnam in 1965 Ellsberg volunteered to become a Marine combat infantry officer—a post he had held during three years in the Marines in the 1950s—but he was barred from doing so because his position in the Pentagon had exposed him to highly sensitive information that would be of value to the enemy if he were captured. See the comments in Currey, *Edward Lansdale,* pp. 295–296. McNaughton apparently was not unhappy to see Ellsberg go—see Sheehan, *A Bright Shining Lie,* p. 593.

[51] A copy of Ellsberg's report is in the Kennedy Library, James Thomson Papers. See also Bergerud, *The Dynamics of Defeat,* pp. 79–81.

> see clearly what the natural workings of the present system are, and how they must change. It is no longer sound to hope that all difficulties will dissolve eventually in the friendly atmosphere engendered by Candide-like "optimism" and self-maintained ignorance of realities. . . .

Ellsberg continued:

> To say, as Vann does, that the present leaders, bureaucrats and province and district officials *do not* come from or think like the majority of the population, do not know much at all about rural majority, and for the most part are not very interested in making government responsive to the wishes of the majority, may be unpleasant. But it is to say something that is very important about the nature of the problems here.
>
> To say, as Vann does, that ARVN/RF/PF forces [Army of the Republic of Vietnam, Regional Forces, Popular Forces], with relatively rare exceptions, abandon the countryside to the VC every night; do not use recon patrols to develop or check intelligence; do not seek ground contact with the VC, and do not maintain it or pursue when the VC are encountered; do not control by observers the artillery fire by which (along with air) they produce most casualties (enemy and friendly); do not take steps to maintain the security of their operations; do huddle in static, defensive positions and take nearly all their casualties on the defensive; is to say a lot of nasty things, not only about the ARVN but about the effective influence of U.S. advisors, who have harped on these matters for four years. It is also to say some true and important things about the reasons for VC military growth and success, and to suggest the need for putting teeth in the advisory system or else finding an alternative to it. . . .

Vann played a very important role in the pacification program until his death in 1972 in a helicopter crash, but although his ideas about winning the war were well-received by some, and proposals such as that for unifying U.S. operations in each province may have had some influence,[52] there was less support for his proposal for pressuring the South Vietnamese to accept American direction,[53] and after several months Daniel Ellsberg himself concluded that it was not possible for the U.S. to bring about the development of an American-style representative government in South Vietnam.[54]

By the fall of 1965, the American presence and role in Vietnam were becoming so dominant, and the use of military force so paramount, that "nation building" was becoming an adjunct to military operations and the "Americanization" of the war was, as William Bundy and others had feared, proceeding apace. As James Reston said in a series of articles he wrote for the *New York Times* during a trip to Vietnam in August 1965, "When Uncle Sam moves in, somebody has to move over."[55] According to Bui Diem, then Ky's

---

[52] Sheehan, *A Bright Shining Lie*, p. 552.

[53] *Ibid.*, p. 557.

[54] A copy of Ellsberg's memorandum to Vann, "Some Vietnamese Thoughts on Representative Institutions in Vietnam," July 26, 1966, is in the files of the Senate Committee on Foreign Relations, National Archives, RG 46.

[55] *New York Times*, Aug. 29, 1965.

assistant, "The Americans came in like bulldozers," and the war "was now undisputably an American enterprise."[56]

In Washington, there was some concern that the large increase in nonmilitary personnel and activities projected for the coming months could have an adverse effect on "nation-building."[57] One of the principal Foreign Service Officers dealing with Vietnam was Robert H. Miller, the State Department's desk officer for Vietnam and head of the East Asia Bureau's Vietnam Working Group who was also a State Department representative on the interagency Vietnam Coordinating Committee. On October 20, 1965, the committee met to consider a paper prepared by Miller on the future course of the nonmilitary program. In the paper, during the discussion, and in a subsequent memorandum, Miller questioned whether the nonmilitary program was accomplishing its intended purpose or whether changes should be made.[58] The nonmilitary program consisted, he said, of an accumulation of projects "developed in a crisis atmosphere over the past few years. . . . Each project has been conceived as an urgent requirement demanding priority effort until the point has been reached where all projects are urgent, all are high priority." "This atmosphere," Miller said, "is conducive to the development of massive programs but not to a careful appraisal of programs in Vietnam."

Moreover, Miller said, nonmilitary programs had not had any "measurable success." "The Vietnamese peasant has an infinite capacity to absorb economic and social benefits without returning an ounce of loyalty. This is primarily because, without security, the program impact on the peasant's heart and mind is virtually nil." He concluded that the first priority of nonmilitary programs should be to help provide security, but that this was "a problem that has never been licked, and a problem that in the last analysis must be dealt with by the Vietnamese."

Miller questioned whether the expansion of U.S. nonmilitary programs was hurting rather than helping the South Vietnamese in their efforts to strengthen their institutions and their services to the public:

> I cannot escape the conviction that the general thrust of our present effort in Vietnam is increasingly in the direction of assuming governmental functions for ourselves and pushing the GVN aside because of its general inadequacy and incom-

---

The problem posed for the political program by the increasing role of the military can be seen in the decision in the fall of 1965 to provide for joint civilian-military participation in the administration of the program of rural development, the key to Lodge's concept that the Communists would eventually fade away. Lansdale was responsible for liaison with the new South Vietnamese Ministry of Rural Construction. The U.S. military command, which Lansdale proposed should be an observer in this process, successfully insisted on sharing the role of representation, however, and Lansdale's role was thereby weakened from the outset. This decision, in turn, tended to subordinate the use of political means to the military means then in ascendancy.

See William E. Colby and Peter Forbath, *Honorable Men: My Life in the CIA* (New York: Simon and Schuster, 1978), pp. 230–236, and Douglas S. Blaufarb, *The Counterinsurgency Era* (New York: Free Press, 1977), ch. 7.

[56] Bui Diem with David Chanoff, *In the Jaws of History* (Boston: Houghton Mifflin, 1987), p. 153.

[57] Plans for the next fiscal year (July 1, 1966-June 30, 1967) provided for large increases in projects and in personnel. Total "direct hire" staff—U.S. Government employees—would increase from 1,000 to a proposed 3,000. Personnel employed under contracts with private companies and organizations would also expand.

[58] Miller's paper of Oct. 20, 1965 is located in U.S. Department of State, Lot File 72 D 207. His subsequent notes of the meeting and his memorandum of October 25 are in Lot File 71 D 88.

petence. At the same time, our effort is not attacking what remains the essential Communist challenge—gaining control of the country through erosion and subversion at the village and hamlet level. I fear that our present course could lead increasingly to something resembling a U.S. occupation of South Vietnam without our getting at this real, long-term Communist challenge. Under these conditions, I fear that the U.S. could in fact become an occupation force faced with the need to pacify not just the Viet Cong controlled areas but a growing proportion of the total population.

The proposed program for 1966–1967, Miller said, "raises real questions as to whether U.S. nonmilitary programs are rapidly reaching the point where they are beyond both the economic and administrative capacity of South Vietnam to absorb, and whether, if this apparently spiralling situation continues, it could lead to an upsurge of popular feeling against the American presence to the point of undermining our entire effort."

On the other hand, Miller said that he was encouraged by the efforts of Lansdale and his team to stimulate Vietnamese leaders to develop "*Vietnamese* solutions" (emphasis in original) which could contribute to the "real nation-building process needed to defeat the Viet Cong." [59]

During the discussion by the Vietnam Coordinating Committee of Miller's paper, there was, as Miller reported in his subsequent memorandum, some support for his analysis, but several members, particularly those from AID and the Department of Defense, "stressed that the U.S. had to undertake many tasks because the GVN was incapable of undertaking them effectively, that Mission programs require our full support, and that it would be wrong to think of changing or redirecting our effort when the new U.S. team in Saigon has only begun to take hold."

During the ensuing months, as the U.S. presence in South Vietnam continued to grow and the problems essayed by Miller became more severe, there were, from time to time, recurrent expressions of doubt about the effectiveness of such large-scale intervention, and some efforts were made to limit the U.S. role. More extreme proposals, such as that of John Paul Vann noted earlier, were rejected as unworkable. By and large, however, U.S. nonmilitary programs in South Vietnam continued to expand rapidly in scope and

---

[59] In part, this was a reference to a proposal being developed by Lansdale and his team for creating a "National Revolutionary Movement," based on a "revolutionary village" program, representatives of which would comprise a "National Council" of village elders to advise the government and, as soon as a majority of villages were considered "revolutionary," to elect a group to draft a constitution for the country. In order for a village to be designated as a revolutionary village it would have to inform the government that it was "free of the VC" and ready to receive a government inspection team which could live safely in the village. The inspection team would certify that the report was correct, and would help the village elect its leaders and its delegate to the National Council. (Massachusetts Historical Society, Lodge Papers, Memorandum to Lodge from Lansdale, "A National Council," Oct. 30, 1965, enclosing the draft of the plan, "Proposal: A True Vietnamese Revolution," Oct. 30, 1965, prepared by George Melvin and Daniel Ellsberg.)

Of the 2,685 villages and city villages (districts) officially listed, it was estimated that 765 (which included 129 districts in Saigon and other major cities), most of which were controlled by Catholics or by political sects, were eligible to be designated as revolutionary villages.

As conceived by the Lansdale team, this proposal would provide a mechanism for developing a form of self-government that would give people a voice in determining their own affairs while also enabling the choosing of representatives from rural areas "at a time when a large proportion of the individuals in the countryside are subject to coercion by Communist political agents, backed up by terrorists, guerrillas and regular troops."

size during the U.S. buildup. The results, it could be argued, were similar to those on the military side, as Miller had predicted; that is, that large U.S. programs did not create loyalty among the peasants or help significantly in developing the kind of self-government which the country needed to survive after American withdrawal.

September 1965: Washington Begins to Worry

By early September 1965, only six weeks after the United States had confidently begun to prepare for major military and nonmilitary offensives, key Washington policymakers were expressing concern about the lack of progress and were raising some basic questions about U.S. assumptions, plans and expectations.

On the military side, despite reports of the beneficial effects of the presence of U.S. troops on South Vietnamese forces,[60] there were disturbing signs that Communist forces, despite superior U.S. firepower, could adapt their strategy and tactics to take advantage of U.S. limitations and weaknesses and the constraints that had been placed on U.S. military operations. Rather than yielding, either to ROLLING THUNDER or to the escalation of the ground war, the Communists were increasing their own efforts—recruiting more troops in the South, strengthening their air and other defenses in the North, and increasing the infiltration of men and supplies into the South, including North Vietnamese regulars. They showed no serious interest in negotiations.[61]

On the nonmilitary side, it was estimated that little if any progress was being made toward pacification and reconstruction. Although the Ky-Thieu government was still in power, it seemed to have made little headway, and there was some renewed discontent among the Buddhists and others who were opposed to the continuation of military rule.[62]

Initially, the news from the military front had been encouraging as U.S. forces claimed to have won a significant victory in their first major engagement. The battle occurred on August 18–21, 1965, when the Marines, acting on intelligence from a Communist deserter, made an amphibious/heliborne assault (Operation STARLITE) against a Communist regiment on the Batangan Peninsula in Quang Ngai Province south of the Marine base at Chu Lai. The Marines reportedly killed 623 of the enemy against their own loss

---

[60] According to Ambassador Lodge in a cable to Washington on Sept. 13, 1965, (*PP*, Gravel ed., vol. II, p. 366, Saigon to Washington 888), "All reports indicate that the American troops are having a very beneficial effect on VN troops, giving them greater confidence and courage. I am always mindful of the possibility that the American presence will induce the VN to slump back and 'Let George do it.' But there seems to be no sign of this.

"I wish I could describe the feeling of hope which this great American presence on the ground is bringing. There can no longer be the slightest doubt that persistence will bring success, that the aggression will be warded off and that for the first time since the end of W W II, the cause of free men will be on an upward spiral."

[61] For a highly secret U.S. diplomatic probe beginning in July 1965, which seemed at first to interest the North Vietnamese but which they ultimately rejected, see pt. III of this study, pp. 442–443.

[62] In a cable to President Johnson on September 22, Ambassador Lodge said that the continuing existence of the Ky-Thieu government was due "in large part to the conviction that the U.S. is truly committed to staying as long as is necessary and to doing whatever is necessary to ward off the Viet Cong aggression. . . . In other words, your decision on troops is not only a great thing militarily, but is paying big dividends politically." U.S. Department of State, Central File, Pol 27 Viet S, Saigon to Washington 991, Sept. 22, 1965. "Let us hope that this stability continues," Lodge added," and I try to leave no stone unturned to see that it does. I have made it clear in strategic places that a coup would be most unwelcome. I also am taking steps to make sure we are organized to hear about coup plotting in time to do something about it."

of 51 dead and 203 wounded.[63] In a cable to President Johnson on August 26, Ambassador Lodge said that the attack "could be a milestone which has not only blunted the Viet Cong's pickaxe in this particular place, but appears to show that the U.S. can with relative certainty prevent the Viet Cong from ever becoming a regular army. It is a maxim of guerrilla warfare that, as Che Guevara [a Cuban Communist guerrilla leader] and other authorities have said, 'Triumph will always be the product of a regular army, even though its origins are with a guerrilla army.' If the Viet Cong cannot somewhere, sometime, transform themselves into a regular army, they cannot reasonably hope militarily to conquer the country. The victory at Chu Lai, therefore, may constrain them seriously to call into question the tactics which they have been following."[64]

The Communists, on the other hand, claimed that the battle was proof of their ability to withstand American forces, and at least one American commander on the scene was said to have been surprised by how well they fought.[65]

In Operation STARLITE, as well as in other military actions during these early weeks of fighting by U.S. forces, it was apparent that, besides stirring up U.S. public opinion, the destructive effects of such operations could adversely affect pacification. In Operation STARLITE, according to a history prepared by the Marine Corps, "Civilians in the combat zone presented complications. The first attempts to evacuate them were difficult; the people were frightened and did not trust the Marines. Eventually most of the local populace were placed in local collective points where they were fed and provided with medical attention. Although attempts were made to avoid civilian casualties, some villages were completely destroyed by supporting arms [artillery or aircraft] when it became obvious the enemy occupied fortified positions in them."[66]

In an earlier incident, which received considerable publicity when shown on American television, U.S. Marines had virtually destroyed the hamlet of Cam Ne near the American air base at Danang in an area controlled by the Communists. The scene of a U.S. Marine setting fire to a house in Cam Ne with a Zippo lighter while an old woman pleaded with him not to was filmed by a CBS crew headed by reporter Morley Safer and was telecast in the Unit-

---

[63] Jack Shulimson and Maj. Charles M. Johnson, USMC, *U.S. Marines in Vietnam: The Landing and the Buildup, 1965,* Marine Corps History and Museums Division (Washington, D.C.: U.S. Govt. Print. Off., 1978), pp. 69–83. For a good description of this and other major battles during the war, see Shelby L. Stanton (a retired Army Captain who was a Special Forces adviser and combat infantry platoon leader in Vietnam), *The Rise and Fall of an American Army, U.S. Ground Forces in Vietnam,* 1965–1973 (Novato, Calif.: Presidio Press, 1985).

[64] U.S. Department of State, Central File, Pol 27 Viet S, Saigon to Washington 621, Aug. 26, 1965.

[65] Sheehan, *A Bright Shining Lie,* p. 537; William S. Turley, *The Second Indochina War, A Short Political and Military History, 1954–1975* (Boulder, Colo.: Westview Press, 1986); and *The Anti-U.S. Resistance War for National Salvation, 1954–1975: Military Events,* prepared by the War Experiences Recapitulation Committee of the High Level Military Institute (Hanoi: People's Army Publishing House, 1980), p. 79, translation by the U.S. Government's Foreign Broadcast Information Service, and published by the Joint Publications Research Service.

[66] Schulimson and Johnson, *U.S. Marines in Vietnam: The Landing and the Buildup,* 1965, cited above, p. 82.

ed States on the night of August 5, 1965.[67] In his commentary, Safer said, among other things:[68]

> The day's operation burned down 150 houses, wounded three women, killed one baby, wounded one Marine and netted them four prisoners. Four old men who could not answer questions put to them in English. Four old men who had no idea what an I.D. card was. Today's operation is the frustration of Vietnam in miniature. There is little doubt that American firepower can win a victory here. But to a Vietnamese peasant whose home means a lifetime of backbreaking labor it will take more than presidential promises to convince him that we are on his side.

Safer says that the Marines were very upset about his report and "were quick to retaliate. First with direct threats at the press center. A drunken major stood outside our room a few nights later screaming 'Communists Broadcasting System' as he emptied his pistol in the air. Had the place not been filled with other reporters, I genuinely believe that Ha Thuc Can [Safer's cameraman] and I would have been killed. Then Marine Corps headquarters in Washington claimed that the film of a Marine setting fire to a roof with a Zippo lighter had been faked: that I had given the Marine the lighter and had asked him to burn down the house. This was quickly squelched when the private in question could not be produced to repeat the story."[69] The only time in Vietnam that I carried a weapon," Safer says, "was on my visit back to Danang following the broadcast of the Cam Ne incident. I had been told that there might be 'a little accident.'"[70]

When the film was received in the U.S., CBS network executives, aware of its sensitivity, reviewed and discussed it before broadcasting it. The next day, CBS President Frank Stanton received a harsh telephone call from President Johnson asking "how could CBS employ a Communist like Safer, how could they be so unpatriotic as to put on enemy film like this?"[71] A few days later, according to Safer, the President "summoned" Stanton to the White House, where he and Press Secretary Bill Moyers "continued the harangue." "Johnson," Safer says, "threatened that unless CBS got

---

[67] For a description of the incident and reaction to it, see Morley Safer, *Flashbacks* (New York: Random House, 1990), pp. 88–97, and the *New York Times* for this period. See also William M. Hammond's account of the incident and its aftermath, *Public Affairs: The Military and the Media, 1962–1968,* a volume in the series, *The United States Army in Vietnam* (Washington, D.C.: Center of Military History, U.S. Army, U.S. Govt. Print. Off., 1988), pp. 185–193.

Secretary of the Navy Paul H. Nitze defended the burning of the houses (the Marines were under his jurisdiction) as a necessary component of military action in a guerrilla warfare situation. See the *New York Times,* Aug. 15, 1965.

The Marine Corps' own history says that the Marines were particularly sensitive to the need to win the support of the people, but contends that the hamlet was occupied and fortified by the Communists, and that the Marines had come under fire when they entered it previously. See Shulimson and Johnson, *U.S. Marines in Vietnam: The Landing and the Buildup, 1965,* p. 64.

See also the hearings of the U.S. Congress, Senate, Committee on Foreign Relations, *News Policies in Vietnam,* Hearings, August 17 and 31, 1966, 89th Cong., 2d sess. (Washington, D.C.: U.S. Govt. Print. Off., 1966).

[68] Daniel C. Hallin, *The "Uncensored War": The Media and Vietnam* (New York: Oxford Univ. Press, 1986), p. 132.

[69] Safer, *Flashbacks,* p. 93.

[70] *Ibid.,* p. 88.

[71] See Halberstam, *The Powers That Be,* p. 490.

rid of me and 'cleaned up its act,' the White House would 'go public' with information about Safer's 'Communist ties.'"[72]

Safer, a Canadian, was subjected to a full investigation by the U.S. Government, and the President told the JCS to investigate the officer in charge of the patrol "to make sure that he had not been bribed by a Communist reporter. . . ."[73]

The Cam Ne incident and its impact on the U.S. and international public opinion were discussed at the White House on September 12 at an hour-long meeting, chaired by Moyers, of the group that was considering public affairs aspects of the war and formulating plans for the creation of the Public Affairs Policy Committee for Vietnam.[74] James Greenfield, head of public affairs in the State Department, said that Cam Ne and other such incidents were causing "very serious problems here and abroad. . . . Alleged mistreatment of Vietnamese civilians and civilian facilities is a moral and humanitarian concern for many Americans. We must recognize this as a serious, long-run problem." Arthur Sylvester, the Defense Department's press secretary, replied that the problem was "unfriendly correspondents" in Vietnam who "appear to miss no chance to embarrass us." He said that the Cam Ne incident "was not typical" and that it "conveyed an inaccurate impression." He thought steps should be taken to get better information officers in Vietnam and "to inform our personnel of the press problem stemming from such pictures and stories, so that they don't lend themselves to this kind of coverage. . . ." Greenfield retorted that "we couldn't pull a curtain on the problem. There were too many reporters covering this war. It isn't just a problem of a few bad apples. We have to get used to fighting in the open. This is a new kind of war, a war in which the basic goal is people, not territory. You can't win the people in Vietnam by burning their villages. . . . We have to take steps to prevent these things from happening, not just to make sure reporters don't see them."

Chester Cooper agreed, saying "at issue here is how the war should be fought." "We should examine carefully the usefulness of such actions as bombing raids by the Vietnamese Air Force and our own planes against Vietnamese villages. Our object is not so much to destroy an enemy as to win a people. . . ."

In a memorandum to Moyers the next day (August 13), Greenfield discussed the various public affairs problems of the war, and recommended a "thorough review of military actions and techniques . . . such things as the use of artillery against occupied villages, serial bombing and the use of napalm in populated areas, military attacks on villages, etc. . . . We are not making progress

---

[72] Safer, *Flashbacks,* p. 95.

[73] *Ibid.* James Reston says in his memoirs that when he returned from a trip to Vietnam in early September, during which, as noted, he did a series of reports for the *New York Times,* "The president called me to the White House and gave me 'the works.' He denounced my colleagues in Saigon in terms I could hardly bear after my trip [at the end of the trip, the Navy aircraft carrying Reston crash-landed and he was badly bruised], and he asked me, 'Why don't you get on the team? You have only one president.' I had heard it all before and said I thought he was trying to save face. He stood up and showed me to the door. 'I'm not trying to save my face,' he said, 'I'm trying to save my ass.'" James Reston, *Deadline* (New York: Random House, 1991), p. 321.

[74] Johnson Library, NSF Country File, Vietnam, "Memorandum of Discussion on Meeting in Mr. Moyer's Office, The White House, August 10, 1965—5:30–6:30 p.m."

if we kill 50 Viet Cong but provide them with 150 potential recruits in the process."[75]

In a cable to Westmoreland the next day (August 14), JCS Chairman Wheeler asked about the use of U.S. troops in village-clearing operations, saying, "I recall one of the concepts in your estimate of the situation was that US and GVN forces would be used against VC units, but that GVN forces would have to perform the pacification task." Wheeler also asked about the use of U.S. airpower against villages, and whether a clear distinction was made between villages controlled by the Communists and those which were not.[76] Westmoreland's response was that, to be effective, U.S. forces would have to be used in populated areas.[77] "The final battle," he said, "is for the hamlets themselves and this inevitably draws the action toward the people and the places where they live."[78] With respect to airstrikes, he said that villages in the areas controlled by the Communists were considered to be "fair game," but, at the same time, their future pacification had to be kept in mind. "In short," he concluded, "we have a genuine problem which will be with us as long as we are in Vietnam. Commanders must exercise restraint unnatural to war and judgment not often required of young men."

There were three steps, Westmoreland added, that must be taken to reduce the adverse publicity resulting from media coverage of damage suffered by noncombatants: (1) explanation in U.S. of the nature of the war, (2) "some control over press and photographic coverage so that we do not suffer from self-inflicted wounds," (3) intensification of indoctrination of U.S. commanders and troops on the "great importance" of minimizing non-combatant casualties.

This and other incidents prompted the U.S. Mission to hold a conference in Saigon in early September to discuss the psychological aspects of the war, at which U.S. commanders were told to consider psychological as well as military factors when conducting military operations. Westmoreland issued a new directive on minimizing noncombatant battle casualties and created an inter-service

---

[75] Same location, Memorandum for Moyers from Greenfield, "Public Affairs Problems in the Vietnam Conflict," Aug. 13, 1967.

[76] CMH, Westmoreland Papers, History File, JCS 3041–65, Wheeler to Westmoreland, Aug. 14, 1965.

[77] Same location, Message Files, MAC 4171 and 4382, Aug. 18 and 28, 1965.

[78] John Paul Vann argued that it was a tactic of the Communists to draw American forces into attacking hamlets, and that such attacks were usually a mistake (quoted in Guenter Lewy, *America in Vietnam* (New York: Oxford Univ. Press, 1978), pp. 103–104, from a memorandum by Vann):

"I have witnessed the enemy's employment of this tactic for the past 10 years. His specific objective is to get our friendly forces to engage in suicidal destruction of hard-won pacification gains. Invariably he is successful since in the heat of battle rational thinking and long term effects usually play second fiddle to short term objectives.

"In the last decade I have walked through hundreds of hamlets that have been destroyed in the course of a battle, the majority as the result of the heavier friendly fire. The overwhelming majority of hamlets thus destroyed failed to yield sufficient evidence of damage to the enemy to justify the destruction of the hamlet. Indeed, it has not been unusual to have a hamlet destroyed and find absolutely no evidence of damage to the enemy. I recall in May 1959 the destruction and burning by air strike of 900 houses in Chou Doc Province without evidence of a single enemy being killed. . . ."

Vann added: "The destruction of a hamlet by friendly firepower is an event that will always be remembered and practically never forgiven by those members of the population who lost their homes."

Tactical Air Firepower Board to recommend better ways of handling the problem.[79]

Despite signs that U.S. forces were going to encounter greater difficulties than had been anticipated, and that there might be basic flaws in the U.S. plan of attack, McNamara, in a memorandum to the President on September 1, asked for the deployment of six additional maneuver (combat) battalions. Instead of asking for 50,000 men, as stipulated in July, the request was for 85,000–90,000 men which, if approved, would have brought the total of authorized U.S. forces to 210,000 or more by the end of 1965 rather than the 175,000 approved in July for the entirety of Phase I (1965).[80] On Saturday, September 11, in preparation for a meeting with the President on the following Monday, the three principal Presidential advisers—Rusk, McNamara, McGeorge Bundy—together with George Ball, met to review the situation in Vietnam and the request for deployment of the remainder of the Phase I forces. In a memorandum to the President the next day, McGeorge Bundy reported on the meeting.[81] He said that the group's "most difficult and inconclusive discussions" turned on what the U.S. should do in response to avoidance by the Communists of major combat with U.S. forces. Rusk questioned "whether we really need to move up toward 200,000 men." "McNamara continues to feel that we do," Bundy said, "and I agree." "The problem is to make sure that the role of our troops is so understood that neither the country nor the troops themselves get frustrated if the scene of major action shifts toward smaller terrorist activities in which our troops cannot play the dominant role."

On the question of ROLLING THUNDER, Bundy said that McNamara was having a "running discussion with the Chiefs," and needed guidance from the President.[82] McNamara, he said, felt that there should be a continuation of attacks on clearly defined military targets, while avoiding targets in the Hanoi-Haiphong area that could lead to direct engagements with North Vietnamese

[79] According to the directive, "The use of unnecessary force leading to non-combatant battle casualties in areas temporarily controlled by the VC will embitter the population, drive them into the arms of the VC, and make the long range goal of pacification more difficult and more costly." CMH, Westmoreland Papers, History File, MACV Directive 525–3, Sept. 7, 1965. Guidelines were issued to commanders of all U.S. forces, who were told: "Commanders will consider both the military and psychological objective of each operation. Prestrikes in populated areas [airstrikes before ground attacks], reconnaissance by fire into hamlets [firing before entering to see if there is return fire] and poorly selected harassing and interdiction fire [indiscriminate shelling or bombing of areas controlled by the Communists—"freestrike zones"] are examples of military measures which will be counterproductive in the long run."

For Westmoreland's briefing of the Tactical Air Firepower Board on Sept. 15, 1965, see the Memorandum for the Record, serial no. 00884, Sept. 15, 1965, same location.

[80] McNamara's September 1 memorandum is in the Johnson Library Meetings Notes File.

[81] Johnson Library, NSF Memos to the President—McGeorge Bundy.

[82] As noted above, the JCS had proposed on Aug. 27, 1965 a military "concept" under which, the U.S. air war against North Vietnam would be increased for the purpose of "progressively destroying the DRV war-supporting power." This proposal was not acted upon. On September 2 the JCS recommended a program of increased U.S. airstrikes on North Vietnam on September 17–30 which would include such "lucrative" targets as airfields (including Phuc Yen, the major North Vietnamese air force base), power plants, and rail and highway routes. (JCSM–670–65, Sept. 2, 1965, described in *PP*, Gravel ed., vol. IV, p. 29.) For a summary and discussion of intelligence estimates of probable Communist reactions to such attacks see JCSM–686–65, Sept. 11, 1965, Johnson Library, NSF Country File, Vietnam. For McNamara's response on September 15 to JCSM 670–65, see below.

For the views of McNamara and McNaughton on the air war against North Vietnam see McNaughton's paper of Aug. 5, 1965, "Analysis of the Program of Bombing North Vietnam," (Johnson Library, NSF Country File, Vietnam), a revision of an earlier paper of July 30 (same location).

military aircraft. Rusk, he said, was opposed to extending the existing pattern of bombing into the area northeast of Hanoi (near China), and McNamara "accepted this advice."

The group also discussed the diplomatic situation, and in his memorandum to the President McGeorge Bundy said that the highly secret contact initiated in August by the U.S. with a North Vietnamese diplomat in Paris[83] was not proving fruitful, and the group agreed "that we ought not now to look as if we were very eager for more talks . . . we should adopt a public posture that our position on negotiations is now totally clear and that the next move is up to the Communists." He added: "I take it from our phone conversation yesterday that this is your [the President's] own general view."

The group also agreed on the primary importance of pacification: "We seem to have got past the big monsoon dangers, and we need to be sure that we have an agreed program for the continuing contest of pacification . . . all of us feel that this is the most important area of effort for the coming weeks and months."

On Monday, September 13, the President met from 1:16 p.m. to 2:20 p.m. with the four advisers—Rusk, McNamara, Ball and McGeorge Bundy.[84] CIA Director Raborn also attended, as well as Bill Moyers and Joseph Califano from the President's staff. According to the notes of the meeting, of those subjects included in McGeorge Bundy's memorandum on the September 11 meeting the only one raised in the September 13 meeting was the question of bombing. McNamara told the President that the JCS (JCSM 670–65, September 2) had recommended bombing (during September 17–30) surface-to-air missile (SAMs) sites, airfields where North Vietnamese fighter-bombers were located, and other sites in the Hanoi-Haiphong area as well as others closer to China. McNamara said he was opposed to such a "significant expansion" of the war. Rusk agreed. McNamara said he would have the issue studied by the CIA and would then raise it again with the President. The notes do not indicate that the President replied to McNamara's statement.

On September 15, McNamara responded to the JCS bombing request, saying, "At this date I am not persuaded by the reasoning of JCSM 670–65 that the military advantages the Joint Chiefs of Staff state would flow from the proposed strike efforts outweigh the military and political risks involved in implementing the proposal." Such attacks, he said, might lead to increased efforts by the North to aid forces in the South, and "would not at this time significantly injure the VC ability to persevere in the South or persuade the Hanoi Government that the price of persisting was unacceptably high." "More important," McNamara said, "is the risk of a US-Chinese confrontation . . . there is a substantial risk that a strike program of the weight recommended would induce the Chinese Communists to intervene in the air from Chinese bases." It had therefore been decided, he concluded, that the program proposed for September 17–30 would not be approved at that time, and that a new intelligence estimate would be obtained on the likely reaction of

---

[83] For an explanation of the Paris contact see pt. III of this study, pp. 442–443.

[84] Califano's notes on the meeting are in the Johnson Library, Diary Backup for Sept. 13, 1965.

North Vietnam, the U.S.S.R. and China to such a bombing program.[85]

After the White House meeting on September 13, a cable was sent to Lodge on September 14 asking for his and Westmoreland's assessment of the situation.[86] "Informal high-level review over weekend [the meeting of Rusk, McNamara, McGeorge Bundy and Ball on September 11]," it stated, "leaves us with feeling situation has more major uncertainties, variables and possibly occasions for changes in our actions than for some time past." With respect to military operations, it "Seems likely increasing US ground strength is driving Hanoi/VC to avoid major unit actions and in effect revert to pattern of placing primary emphasis on small scale actions. Quite possibly we may be faced with VC tactics of prolonged small-scale struggle in which they will rely on international pressures and their doubtless exaggerated view of our internal political opposition to bring about eventual reduction in our effort, while they also hope and work for adverse internal political developments in GVN." This tactic raised the question of how best to use U.S. forces, including whether and how to use U.S. forces for pacification. Referring to the request of the military for 85,000 more troops, the cable said, "There is even a residual question whether further increases in strength at presently planned pace are wise, or whether we should in some small degree defer further increases. . . . In short, if we move rapidly up in force strength, question is bound to arise of effective employment [of] these forces and exactly what concept and strategy we should follow against VC lie-low tactics."[87]

On ROLLING THUNDER, there was a need, the cable said, for better evaluation of results. One possibility would be to send to Saigon a survey group comparable to that which produced the bombing survey after World War II.

With respect to pacification/reconstruction, the cable suggested that, with South Vietnamese forces being assisted by U.S. deployments, there could be "far more steam" put into pacifying the area around Saigon (Hop Tac) and other key areas. Another possibility was to consider applying key elements of the "Acheson-Ball plan" to the entire country, or the entire plan in one or two areas (especially IV Corps—the delta).[88]

The cable to Lodge added that "internal political progress" in the Government of South Vietnam "naturally remains basic to any lasting solution whether by negotiation or by course of events without any 'settlement.'" "We have impression," it said, "Ky Government

---

[85] National Archives, RG 330, JS IAA/EAP, Vietnam 381, Memorandum from McNamara to the Chairman, Joint Chiefs of Staff, "Air Strikes Against North Vietnam," Sept. 15, 1965.

[86] U.S. Department of State, Central File, Pol 27 Viet S, Washington to Saigon 753, Sept. 14, 1965.

[87] According to his memoirs, (*A Soldier Reports*, p. 161) Westmoreland was irate: "By nobody's rule were matters such as that valid considerations for the Department of State. Even if they were, what did they think we were doing in Saigon? Did the military do no planning, never look ahead? Would I, a military man, presume to tell a team of surgeons how to operate? What special audacity prompted civilian bureaucrats to deem they knew better how to run a military campaign than did military professionals? Is no special knowledge or experience needed? Had the would-be strategists taken the trouble to examine my cable traffic with the Joint Chiefs or had they consulted General Wheeler, they would have had their answers many times over."

[88] The Acheson-Ball plan provided for social and political reconstruction leading to the establishment of a constitutional government, after which all foreign troops would be withdrawn. For details see pt. III of this study, pp. 260–263.

settling down somewhat and generally acting wisely, with your advice, to deal with possible threats from various quarters," but suggestions would be welcomed, especially with respect to "prospects for generating younger, more energetic, and more cohesive leadership group, and winning more positive popular support."

With respect to negotiations, the cable said, the Washington principals agreed with the feeling in the Saigon Mission that the U.S. should proceed with caution, and that "we do not need to add to the record or to state our position further except in response to clear need." [89]

Lodge responded in a cable on September 18 that was coordinated with Westmoreland.[90] The Mission, Lodge said, agreed with the observations of the Washington principals that the situation "has more imponderables than usual," but took a much more optimistic view. "U.S. military presence," the cable said, "appears to have blunted VC offensive, improved Vietnamese morale and given us great opportunity. . . ."

The fact that the Communists were emphasizing small-scale military actions was considered a "big dividend" by Lodge and Westmoreland, who took the position that the Vietnamese were responsible for dealing with these kinds of guerrilla attacks, but that "the presence of U.S. forces does provide the opportunity for thorough pacification of the areas in which they are stationed and full advantage should be taken of this opportunity." [91] "We are already discussing with the Vietnamese the possibility of singling out areas that look like good prospects . . . and then pacifying them so as to get a little smell of across-the-board success in the air."

With respect to the question of further troop deployment, Lodge's cable said, Westmoreland "feels strongly" about receiving on schedule the full complement of forces approved for Phase I. "We need sufficient strength to insure the success of our strategy and tactics.

---

[89] In a very private letter to the President on Aug. 26, 1965 (Johnson Library, NSF Country File, Vietnam) Lodge said that he was opposed to negotiations. Although he recognized the President's need to stress U.S. willingness to seek peace, he did not believe that the war would be ended by a diplomatic settlement. He thought that the emphasis should be on achieving a satisfactory "outcome," which he defined as either a decision by the Communists to stop fighting, or effective U.S. and South Vietnamese control over the more populous areas of South Vietnam. He told the President, "if you make a 'settlement' and diplomatic 'negotiations' as a symbol of success, you are really reaching for the moon."

[90] U.S. Department of State, Central File, Pol 27 Viet S, Saigon to Washington 953, Sept. 18, 1965. On September 23, McGeorge Bundy sent the President a memorandum summarizing the cables to and from Lodge. Johnson Library, NSF Memos to the President—McGeorge Bundy.

The draft which Lodge sent to Westmoreland for review and comment is in CMH, Westmoreland Papers, History File.

[91] In a cable to General Wheeler on September 22 (CMH, Westmoreland Papers, Message Files, CINCPAC 220725Z) Admiral Ulysses S. Grant Sharp, Jr., Commander in Chief, Pacific (CINCPAC), commented on the dual role of U.S. forces: "If the Viet Cong stay above ground in large formations, this will be to our advantage. With ARVN help we may be able to find, fix and destroy them. If the Viet Cong go underground and revert to small-scale actions, we should employ U.S. forces in coordination with the ARVN and proceed with securing and pacifying areas as fast as we can." "This is a counterinsurgency war . . . the primary object is to restore security to the population. . . . If we are to succeed we must do a number of things at the same time and do them differently than we did in past conflicts. . . . The Viet Cong must be cleared from an area and the area then held and secured. This must be followed by continuing actions to consolidate the gains achieved, develop the area and enlarge it." He added: "The performance and results achieved by U.S. forces in pacification operations came about from advantages we have the ARVN does not. U.S. forces possess an inherent faith and courage in this type of undertaking and understanding of it. They demonstrate their interest in the South Vietnamese people and provide a major incentive for them. Our professionalism in certain fields, technical qualifications and special equipment cannot be duplicated by the ARVN in pacification operations, . . . At the same time, we destroy Viet Cong main force units, kill or capture guerrillas and, alongside our ARVN compatriots, demonstrate how this can be done."

As we succeed it becomes more difficult for the Viet Cong to marshal main-force units and the pressure will be on them to withdraw such units to more remote areas and/or to transform themselves into small units. This is a considerable triumph for us, because it means that the U.S. presence has in effect fragmented the main force, prevented it from coming into being, or at least has forced it to play a lesser role."

With respect to the bombing of North Vietnam, Lodge replied that plans were being made to use air power more effectively and there was no need for a survey group.

On pacification, Lodge said that priority was being given to Hop Tac,[92] and that, with respect to the Acheson plan, the development of the electoral process "from the rice roots up" was being emphasized.

On the political situation, Lodge said that the existing leadership was "sufficiently 'young and energetic,'" and that it was his hope that "with the passage of time and with our advice plus his own natural aptitude, General Ky can become a really effective political leader."

---

[92] A report to Lodge on Sept. 10, 1965 from Richard Holbrooke, a member of his staff, concluded that the original goals of Hop Tac were "completely unrealistic and did not take into account the difficulty of the task." Moreover, "The GVN [Government of Vietnam] has never considered Hop Tac its own plan and it own number one priority. The staff planning for the plan was done almost entirely by the United States, and then translated into Vietnamese. It is, in the eyes of many Vietnamese, 'the plan of the Americans.'" Massachusetts Historical Society, Lodge Papers, Memorandum of Richard Holbrooke, "HOP TAC—Preliminary Thoughts," September 1965, cited also in *PP*, Gravel ed., vol. II, pp. 524–525.

Westmoreland and his associates, however, thought the plan could be revived and successfully implemented. See his Sept. 14, 1965 memorandum to Lodge, "Hop Tac," and the briefing on Hop Tac which MACV gave to the Mission Council on Sept. 21, 1965, both located in CMH, Westmoreland Papers, History File. The briefing, referring to Hop Tac as "a laboratory experiment" in pacification, noted that "If in the shadow of the flagpole [i.e., in Saigon] where we have ready access to top level ministerial talent we cannot successfully achieve pacification, how can we expect rural construction to succeed in the far reaches of the realm?"

CHAPTER 3

TRYING TO FIND A KEY

By the end of September 1965, there was a "twinge of optimism" in Washington as a result of Lodge's reports together with the leveling off since August of Communist military activity.[1] On September 29, 1965, the President met from 12:29 p.m. to 1:20 p.m. with McNamara, Ball, McGeorge Bundy, Raborn and Helms from the CIA, and Califano and Moyers from the White House staff, to consider the request for deployment of the remainder of Phase I forces and for the next phase in the bombing of North Vietnam.[2] McNamara reviewed the request, noting that the estimate of 175,000 troops for Phase I had been increased to 210,000. He said he would like to have authorization for 195,000, and that he would request the remaining 15,000 in November. The President approved the request, saying, according to the notes of the meeting, that "it was a situation in which he had no choice but to approve the increase." The brief notes, taken by Califano, do not contain any other reference to comments by the President that might help to explain this statement, or any comments on the question of troop increases by other participants.

McGeorge Bundy said he was "inclined to the view" that the President should make a public statement about U.S. nonmilitary efforts. The press tended to give substantial coverage to such effects, he said, only when the President drew attention to them, adding that it was important to obtain favorable press coverage "in view of the world opinion and forthcoming student demonstrations."

The group, with the exception of Raborn and Helms, then continued the meeting at a luncheon at 1:40 p.m. to discuss the bombing of North Vietnam. McNamara recommended a bombing program that provided for gradual escalation but excluded sensitive targets. He also discussed the question of the "hardening attitude" of the North Vietnamese. (The notes of the meeting do not explain what was meant by the term but it apparently referred to North Vietnamese resistance to negotiations.) He noted that, in response to the request he had made after the September 13 meeting with the President, the CIA's Board of National Estimates had prepared a Special National Intelligence Estimate (SNIE 10–11–65) on the subject which, he said, concluded that "Hanoi's attitude was hardening largely because we were not rough enough in our bombing."[3]

---

[1] For this and subsequent observations which will be cited as Bundy MS, CRS is indebted to William P. Bundy for permission to quote from his unpublished manuscript, written in 1970–72, dealing with key decisions concerning Southeast Asia in the period from early 1961 to early 1966. The quotation here is from ch. 31, p. 31.

[2] For Califano's notes of the meeting see Johnson Library, NSF Memos to the President—W. W. Rostow.

[3] SNIE 10–11–65, still classified, apparently concluded, among other things, that if targets were bombed in the Hanoi-Haiphong area the North Vietnamese would be more inclined toward a political and diplomatic initiative.

He pointed out, however, that the SNIE had been prepared without the help of key experts in the Government, and he urged the President to direct several of these to conduct a study of the reasons for Hanoi's hardening attitude. The President approved both the recommended bombing program and the proposed study.

Those selected for the study were William Bundy, John McNaughton, General Maxwell Taylor (who, after being replaced by Lodge in July 1965 as U.S. Ambassador to South Vietnam, had become a special consultant to the President), and Llewellyn Thompson, a highly respected Foreign Service Officer who was the Department of State's leading expert on the U.S.S.R. This became known as the Thompson group, and the study, completed on October 11, 1965, was called the Thompson study.[4]

The Thompson study, following its examination of the hardening of Hanoi's attitudes, recommended a course of action for bombing the North as well as touching on general questions of U.S. policy and strategy. The conclusions of the group closely paralleled the views expressed by Rusk, McNamara, Ball and McGeorge Bundy in September. Bombing should be leveled off. Escalation of the air war could produce a strong military reaction by the Russians and Chinese. Mining the harbor at Haiphong was rejected because it could lead to the sinking of Russian ships. It could also lead to increased dependence on overland transport from China, thereby increasing Chinese influence on the North Vietnamese.

As explained later by William Bundy, "the first rule in the [bombing] program was to avoid action that could lead China to conclude that it was the American objective to destroy North Vietnam or undermine its regime." A second point was "to do nothing that could impair Soviet leverage in Hanoi. The quiet hope that at some point this leverage would be exerted to ease the situation prevailed as a central point in American policy."[5]

Escalation of bombing could also adversely affect diplomatic efforts to end the war. There were already signs, the study stated, that bombing had increased the support of the North Vietnamese public for the war effort. Moreover, bombing may have been having the opposite effect from that intended. Rather than making the North Vietnamese more amenable to negotiations, there were signs that they were less willing to negotiate while under attack.[6]

---

[4] A copy of the Thompson study, Oct. 11, 1965, is in the Department of State, Lot File 85 D 240 (William Bundy Papers).

[5] William Bundy MS, ch. 31, p. 33. According to the biography by his associate, Thomas J. Schoenbaum, *Waging Peace and War: Dean Rusk in the Truman, Kennedy, and Johnson Years* (New York: Simon and Schuster, 1988), p. 453, "Rusk believed that the Russians were the key to getting peace talks going. He had long private discussions with both [Andrei A.] Gromyko [Foreign Minister of the U.S.S.R.] and [Anatole] Dobrynin [Ambassador of the U.S.S.R. to the U.S.], and from these talks he became convinced that the Russians were trying to help and had little interest in seeing the United States bogged down in Vietnam."

[6] A similar position was taken by the small group of U.S. intelligence officers who were monitoring events in China from their post at the U.S. Consulate in Hong Kong. In a letter to Washington on Nov. 10, 1965, the Consul General, Edmund E. Rice, a veteran Foreign Service Officer and China specialist, said that he and the members of his China Mainland Section (other members of the Consulate General staff might have different opinions, he said) doubted whether air attacks on targets in the Hanoi-Haiphong area would induce the North to negotiate. (U.S. Department of State, Central File Pol 27 Viet S.) The North Vietnamese, he said, were girding for a protracted conflict in the confidence that eventually world and domestic opinion would force the U.S. to desist.

Moreover, Rice and his colleagues continued to express concern about the possible effects on the Chinese of an action by the U.S. that might be considered serious enough to cause China to intervene more actively in the war. (For earlier views of Rice on this subject, see pt. III of this study.) "Our consensus here," the letter said, "is that if there were a 'provocation' in Viet-

The Thompson group recommended, as a way of testing whether the Communists would negotiate, as well as to establish a basis for U.S. escalation if they refused, that there be a long pause in U.S. bombing of the North. If the response to such a pause were not satisfactory, bombing should be resumed and intensified.

The group also concluded—as had Rusk, McNamara, McGeorge Bundy and Ball—that the Communists appeared to be avoiding combat with American forces. According to the study, they "probably [would] decide in the near future to break up most of their large units and move toward one or the other of two strategies: They may change their tactics in the direction of small acts or sabotage; or less likely, they could adopt an even more passive strategy of apparently 'fading into the woodwork.'" The second and more likely strategy would be "a strategy of guerrilla hit-and-run strikes, terror and sabotage."

With respect to the prospects for negotiations, the group concluded that the Communists "would continue to oppose negotiations except on their own terms until such time as it becomes clear to them that we will stay the course and successfully, if gradually, push them back into the woodwork and begin a discernible trend toward pacification of most of the country."

Thus, the Thompson group disposed of the issue of strategy in the ground war by assuming that if the U.S. were able to "stay the course" successfully, while making progress toward pacification, the Communists would eventually negotiate, capitulate, or fade away.

General Taylor prepared a separate memorandum in which he recommended increased bombing of the North but advised against substantial increases in U.S. forces. If the Communists continued to fight primarily a guerrilla war, he said, the U.S. might have to deploy up to one million men. Instead, he proposed that the U.S. should help the South Vietnamese build their own forces.[7]

The Thompson study, together with the discussions of these issues by Rusk, McNamara and McGeorge Bundy, raised what could have been viewed as disturbing questions about the role of the United States in the war. If the Communists were going to fight primarily a guerrilla war, in which, as McGeorge Bundy said in his September 12 memorandum to the President, U.S. forces "cannot play the dominant role," then the U.S. might not be able to fight

nam which might be considered sufficiently grave the Chinese might decide that the time had finally come to play a more directly active role. A U.S. campaign against the Hanoi-Haiphong complex, particularly if it were a massive one, might be considered as such a 'provocation.'"

Such attacks might also increase the aid being given to North Vietnam by the Russians, Rice said, as well as making it more difficult for the Russians to act as a moderating influence on the North.

[7] A copy of Taylor's memorandum, "Possible Alternatives in Vietnam—The Future of Rolling Thunder," Oct. 11, 1965, is in the Department of State, Lot File 85 D 240 (William Bundy Papers).

In a column in the *Washington Post* on Sept. 30, 1965, Washington journalist Walter Lippmann, who was known for his astute analysis of problems and trends in U.S. foreign policy, said that although U.S. forces had thwarted Communist military progress, the U.S. was not achieving its objectives: "The war in Vietnam is like pushing a tub full of water. While the Americans can seize almost any place they choose to attack, the Vietcong will almost surely come back once the Americans leave. So we shall be forced to face the fact that in order to win the war in South Vietnam we shall have to occupy South Vietnam with American troops. A few months ago Mr. Hanson Baldwin, the military correspondent of the *New York Times*, called for a million men for Vietnam. It sounded fantastic at the time in the light of what President Johnson was saying about not wanting a wider war. But it is beginning to look very much as if Mr. Baldwin had made an informed and realistic estimate of what a military solution would require."

the war for which it was preparing. According to the original plan, as noted earlier, U.S. forces were to be used to destroy Communist main force units. When questioned during the meetings in July on what the U.S. would do if the Communists avoided major confrontations with U.S. forces, McNamara and General Wheeler said that U.S. forces could engage guerrillas as well as main force units, and through harassment could force the Communists to come out and fight.[8] Unless the Communists could be forced to come out and fight, it might be necessary for the U.S. to revise its strategy and to play a supporting role while the South Vietnamese carried on the counterguerrilla war. And if U.S. pressure on the Communists in the North and the South did not succeed in forcing the enemy to negotiate, capitulate or fade away, and the Communists were only gradually pushed back into the woodwork, as the Thompson report stated, the war could last considerably longer than had been predicted.

There was also the question of whether, if the Communists did not come out and fight, interdiction bombing of the North would be effective. McNamara had been told by U.S. officials in Saigon in July that to wage guerrilla warfare at the level being carried out at the time the Communists only needed about 14 tons of supplies per day, an amount so small that it could not be interdicted by bombing.[9] Only if the Communists decided to come out and fight—which, U.S. officials assumed, would thereby substantially increase their need for supplies—could interdiction bombing of North Vietnamese infiltration routes into South Vietnam become effective.

Phase II and the Policy Choices Facing the U.S.

Toward the end of October 1965, Washington officials began to review the projected needs for Phase II of the U.S. plan of military operations. Under the original conception of Phase II in July 1965—the "strategic offense" phase, which would occur during January 1-June 30, 1966—U.S. forces would conduct offensive operations in high priority areas "necessary to destroy enemy forces and reinstitution of rural construction activities." According to this plan, an additional 100,000 U.S. troops (24 combat battalions) would be deployed during Phase II, bringing U.S. forces to 275,000 by July 1966.[10]

In meetings during October 18–22 with the Joint Chiefs as well as with the Secretary of Defense and the Service Secretaries (Army, Navy, Air Force), followed by a meeting with Rusk, McNamara, Ball, William Bundy, McGeorge Bundy, McNaughton, Vance, General Wheeler, Llewellyn Thompson, Maxwell Taylor and McNaughton, Westmoreland's J–3, General DePuy, presented MACV's (Military Assistance Command, Vietnam) proposal for 1966. It was, according to William Bundy, "a sobering picture. . . . Instead of a situation brought back into balance by the end of 1965, with significant gains early in 1966, as Westmoreland had seemed to predict in June and July, DePuy now thought that it would take most of 1966 to get slowly on top of the situation, with gains only

[8] See pt. III of this study, p. 401.
[9] *Ibid.*, p. 376.
[10] *Ibid.*, p. 384.

commencing thereafter."[11] Rather than 100,000 additional troops, DePuy estimated that 115,000 would be needed, which, added to the increases that had already been made in Phase I forces from the original 175,000 to 210,000, would raise the level of U.S. forces to 325,000 in 1966, even before the completion of Phase I, compared to the 275,000 provided for Phase II by the original plan.[12]

On October 23, William Bundy prepared a top secret memorandum, "Policy Choices and Decision-Making Procedures on Vietnam," copies of which were sent only to Rusk, McNamara, Ball, McGeorge Bundy and Thompson, on the policy choices facing the U.S.[13] Based on DePuy's presentation, the proposal of the Thompson Group for a bombing pause,[14] and a message from Ambassador Lodge expressing concern about the adverse effects on South Vietnam of possible negotiations to end the war,[15] the memorandum began with a discussion of the "elements of the problem." The U.S. military command in Vietnam, Bundy said, had made a strong case for the need to increase U.S. forces in Phase II to 325,000 men in order to achieve U.S. objectives, and even then there was no "absolute assurance that we are going to get there." He added that although DePuy predicted little increase in U.S. casualties, "Nonetheless, we are faced with the pressures from various quarters, symbolized by General LeMay and the [Gerald R.] Ford, [Mich.]/[E. Ross] Adair [Ind.] line [Ford and Adair were leading Republican Members of the House of Representatives], to hit the North substantially harder."

---

[11] William Bundy MS, ch. 31, pp. 31–32.

[12] On October 16, Westmoreland met in Saigon with Henry Kissinger, a professor at Harvard University who was in Vietnam at the request of Lodge to analyze and report on various aspects of the situation. According to Westmoreland (CMH, History File, History Notes), Kissinger was "attempting to make some projection as to how long it will take our programmed military efforts to accomplish the objective of pacifying the country." Westmoreland told him that Phase I U.S. forces and South Vietnamese forces could have 60 percent of the population under government control in 18 months, and that in another 18 months Phase II forces could have 80 percent of the population under control."

Westmoreland said he told Kissinger that it was important to continue to deploy U.S. forces in Vietnam "to maintain the initiative and to go for victory, not a stalemate," and that "Kissinger said that he fully agreed with this thesis."

[13] U.S. Department of State, Lot File 85 D 240 (William Bundy Papers).

[14] According to William Bundy (MS, ch. 33, p. 3), Ball and McNamara, "took up the [pause] proposal with zeal." At Ball's direction, William Bundy prepared a memorandum, "Elements of a Second Pause Scenario," Oct. 22, 1965, a copy of which is in the Johnson Library, NSF Country File, Vietnam.

[15] U.S. Department of State, Central File, Pol 27 Viet S, Saigon to Washington 1377, Oct. 21, 1965. Lodge argued that the South Vietnamese Government was not yet strong enough to survive the "political warfare" with the Communists which would result from negotiations. (This point had been emphasized by Ky in a meeting with Lodge and Kissinger the previous day. See in the Johnson Library, NSF Country File, Vietnam, Saigon to Washington 1361, Oct. 20, 1965.)

Lodge also took the position, contrary to the State Department's negotiating position, that not all Communist military activity in South Vietnam would have to cease. He argued that negotiations could be based on pacification of the area around Saigon and on the coast, and on maintaining existing control by the government of cities and province capitals, with major roads open day and night, provided that the North Vietnamese ceased their infiltration and the Communists in the South disbanded their "formal" military units.

On November 10, Rusk personally drafted a reply to Lodge in which he stated that although negotiations did not appear likely, it was important, both from the standpoint of U.S. and world opinion, to demonstrate that the United States would be willing to negotiate. (U.S. Department of State, Lot file 85 D 240 (William Bundy Papers.) "The point which would concern me most," Rusk said, "would be the idea that the war must be continued because the South Vietnamese authorities with whom we are dealing are afraid of peace. . . . I see great difficulty in accepting the internal political difficulties of the South Vietnamese as a war aim of the United States." He added: "Frankly, I do not know whether the negotiations will come about in the near future or at all. I know that it will be contrary to our most fundamental policy to permit negotiations to accomplish what we have resisted by force."

If the American people and "international opinion" were going to be persuaded to accept such an expansion of the U.S. effort, a convincing case would have to be made, Bundy said, that the U.S. had "exhausted all avenues" to negotiation. However, a move toward negotiations, including a bombing pause in the near future, could, as Lodge had warned, produce an adverse reaction in South Vietnam and damage efforts to create a "real political structure" in Saigon.

Another element concerned the role of the U.S.S.R. There had been a report, Bundy noted, that the Russians wanted a pause of at least three weeks in order to generate diplomatic pressures that might nudge the North Vietnamese toward negotiations, and this "vital Soviet factor argues strongly for a pause" as well as against any substantial increase in bombing the North.[16]

There were, said William Bundy, three broad policy choices for the U.S.:

(1) A serious pause for a month, followed—if it fails—by decisions on Phase II deployment and possibly by some step-up in the bombing of the North.

(2) Finish up Phase I deployments and proceed to Phase II decisions and actions without any major action such as a pause, or any appreciable change in the bombing pattern against the DRV.

(3) Complete Phase I deployments and stop at that point for perhaps three months before going further, while continuing present bombing pace against the North.

As will be seen, this memorandum became the basis in early November of a staff paper for the President. Meanwhile, on October 26 McGeorge Bundy circulated the draft of a joint Defense Department-State Department-White House message to Lodge asking for his comments on the situation and the U.S. course of action.[17] Referring to DePuy's presentation of Phase II, and noting that the plan envisioned that U.S. forces would play the dominant combat role, it questioned whether "what began as a Vietnamese war with U.S. assistance may end as a U.S. war with only passive Vietnamese cooperation." It would be useful, the draft said, if Lodge could explain how Vietnamese forces would be strengthened. Also, what should the U.S. do about the air war, and should there be a pause before Phase II deployments?

From available records, it is not clear whether this message was sent, but on November 3 Lodge sent a letter to President Johnson that appears to be an answer to the message, in which he said, "Herewith is my best attempt to peer into the future."[18] McGeorge Bundy gave Lodge's letter to the President with a note saying that he had given copies to Rusk and McNamara, but not to Arthur Goldberg (U.S. Ambassador to the U.N.), "because I am afraid it would only stir him to a very strong reaction." (Goldberg was in favor of trying to find a way to negotiate an end to the war.) "We

[16] For an interesting analysis of possible Russian moves toward becoming more involved in Indochina, and the importance of recognizing that this could benefit the U.S. in its effort to contain the North Vietnamese and the Chinese, see the message from the U.S. Ambassador to Laos, William Sullivan, an experienced and astute diplomat, Vientiane to Washington 437, Nov. 3, 1965, in the Johnson Library, NSF Memos to the President—McGeorge Bundy.

[17] U.S. Department of State, Lot File 85 D 240 (William Bundy Papers).

[18] U.S. Department of State, Central File, Pol 27 Viet S.

are beginning," Lodge said, "to master the technique of thwarting and eventually overcoming the Viet Cong main force units and military redoubts. The process will be long and difficult, but we know what is required to accomplish it. The next step must be to eliminate Viet Cong terrorism and to smash Viet Cong organization in the villages. The GVN, with our help is just beginning this process. If governmental stability is maintained, I believe that the GVN, with our help, can succeed." He added:

> If the pacification program moves forward as we intend, I would expect that, within six months, about 300 additional villages of the 2,685 in the country for a total of about 1,000 will have been pacified in the three different areas which are the initial objective. From then on, it will be straight forward, if slow, ploughing ahead with the light at the end of the tunnel growing brighter all the time.

"The three most embarrassing things which I can think of now," Lodge said, "are: 1. a cease-fire; 2. an end to the bombing of the North; and 3. recognition of the Viet Cong (self-styled National Liberation Front) in some form." It was also his opinion that a cease-fire without supervision and troop withdrawal would demoralize the South Vietnamese Government and military forces, as would an end to bombing without gaining something in return. Moreover, any recognition of the "Viet Cong," except as members of a North Vietnamese negotiating delegation, would lead to the collapse of the South Vietnamese Government.[19]

---

[19] Lodge's views and recommendations were generally supported by Henry Kissinger in a letter to Lodge on November 10: "You are engaged in a noble enterprise on which the future of free peoples everywhere depends." (This and other Kissinger letters referred to here, each of which he marked "For the Ambassador's Eyes Only," are in the Massachusetts Historical Society, Lodge Papers.) On November 23, Kissinger wrote to Lodge that he had been in Washington conferring with most of the principal officials dealing with Vietnam in the White House, State, Defense and the CIA, and that Lodge's position in Washington "seems to me extremely strong. Bill Bundy volunteered the information that the reporting from Saigon is at the highest level ever. McGeorge Bundy said that the President has overcome any lingering suspicion from the time [1964] when you were a Presidential contender and has absolute confidence in you as a man in addition to being very pleased with your performance."

Kissinger said he would suggest "tempering extremely optimistic predictions somewhat. Failure to realize them will undermine your influence when it counts." He also said that "Washington is intellectually unprepared for negotiations but committed to them as soon as the DRV asks for them," and he recommended that the U.S. Mission should develop a "concrete" negotiating position.

Kissinger also told Lodge that Washington was very concerned about pacification, and in a long letter on December 3, in which he reiterated his belief in the importance of the U.S. effort in Vietnam—"I am deeply persuaded that Vietnam is the hinge of our national effort where success and failure will determine our world role for decades to come—he discussed the question of pacification. The Government of South Vietnam, he said, was "in a precarious position. . . . Its authority in the countryside is still weak. It must be nurtured carefully." "In the provinces, the civil war and political turmoil in Saigon have produced a combination of attentisme, demoralization and lethargy." "Overshadowing everything," he added, "is a social or maybe even philosophical problem: The Vietnamese have a strong sense of being a distinct people but little sense of nationhood. Our deepest challenge then is to discover how a nation can be built when the society is torn by internal schisms and in the middle of a civil war."

Kissinger said that the pacification program "needs above all some clear and unambiguous success," which could then have a "multiplier effect." But, given the inadequacy of Vietnamese provincial administration "and the American tendency to do too much too quickly on too vast a scale," pilot projects should be emphasized. (He said he thought well of Lansdale's proposal for "revolutionary villages," but added that the plan should be carefully designed to avoid another failure like the "strategic hamlets" of the early 1960s.)

In the course of his letter, Kissinger commented on the various elements of the U.S. pacification effort. Lansdale's group, he said, "in many respects is the most complex, the most promising and also the most difficult to assess. Lansdale is without doubt a man of extraordinary gifts. He is an artist in dealing with Asians. He is patient, inspirational, imaginative. . . . At the same time, the artistic and highly individualistic temperament of Lansdale and his group have

Continued

McNamara Revises His Position

On November 3, McNaughton's Office of International Security Affairs drafted a memorandum for McNamara to send to the President, "Courses of Action in Vietnam," based on William Bundy's earlier paper of October 23 on policy choices.[20] It began with this statement of "U.S. strategy":

> The February decision to bomb North Vietnam and the July approval of Phase I deployments make sense only if they are in support of a long-run United States policy to contain Communist China. China—like Germany in 1917, like Germany in the West and Japan in the East in the late 30s, and like the U.S.S.R. in 1947—looms as a major power threatening to undercut our importance and effectiveness in the world and, more remotely but more menacingly, to organize all of Asia against us. The long-run U.S. policy is based upon an instinctive understanding in our country that the peoples and resources of Asia could be effectively mobilized against us by China or by a Chinese coalition and that the potential weight of such a coalition could throw us on the defensive and threaten our security. This understanding of a straightforward security threat is interwoven with another perception—namely, that we have our view of the way the U.S. should be moving and of the need for the majority of the rest of the world to be moving in the same direction if we are to achieve our national objective. We would move toward economic well being, toward open societies, and toward cooperation between nations; the role we have inherited and have chosen for ourselves for the future is to extend our influence and power to thwart ideologies that are hostile to these aims and to move the world, as best we can, in the direction we prefer. Our ends cannot be achieved and our leadership role cannot be played if some powerful and virulent nation—whether Germany, Japan, Russia or China—is allowed to organize their part of the world according to a philosophy contrary to ours.

In Vietnam, the memorandum said, U.S. forces had "frustrated any Communist design to move into their conventional-warfare 'Stage 3'" (in July, McNamara, in trying to justify the use of U.S. troops, had argued that the Communists had already moved into Stage 3), "but the guerrilla war continues at a high pace, the economy of South Vietnam is deteriorating, and there are no convincing indications that the South Vietnamese body-politic is reviving." Pacification "continues to make little, if any, progress."

With respect to negotiations, the question might soon be faced as to whether the U.S. would be willing to settle for a "compromise" solution. But the U.S. "may already have passed the Y in the road:

---

caused them to cut themselves off—sometimes needlessly—from the other elements of the mission. . . . The challenge presented by the Lansdale group is to prevent their efforts from flying off in all directions; to encourage them to become more explicitly members of a team. . . ."

Lansdale, Kissinger added, while "in theory" responsible for planning and coordinating, was not well suited by temperament or by his position in the Mission bureaucracy to be the chief executive officer, but he could and should play an important role in planning. In order to achieve better coordination, Kissinger proposed that a Program Review Committee should be established, chaired by Deputy Ambassador Porter. Lansdale should be a member, and should be the committee's principal contact with the South Vietnamese Government.

[20] Johnson Library, NSF Country File, Vietnam.

Our course of action has been and is increasingly becoming inconsistent with any design to settle, through negotiations or otherwise, for a compromise solution—especially one involving Communists in the Saigon government and the consequent high risk of quick Communist take-over."

After discussing three alternative courses of action,[21] the memorandum stated a preference for the third of these, which provided for a "hard-line" pause (i.e., the U.S. would resume bombing unless the Communists were moving toward specific concessions that could lead to a "favorable outcome" to the war), after which, if the Communists were not responsive, ROLLING THUNDER would then gradually intensify and Phase II forces would be deployed.[22] A pause was justified, the memorandum said, because there was a "finite chance" that it could lead to reduced Communist activity and possibly to negotiations, and because it would be "a prerequisite to U.S. public and international acceptance of the stern actions implicit in the evolving ROLLING THUNDER and Phase II." For the same reason, increased bombing should precede Phase II troop deployment.

In addition, the memorandum said that in Laos the U.S. might soon have to expand air attacks as well as launching large-scale ground operations. Moreover, if Phase II did not succeed in bringing the insurgency in South Vietnam under control, in Phase III the U.S. might have to erect a 175-mile barrier along the 17th parallel from the Gulf of Tonkin to the border of Thailand.

The McNamara/McNaughton memorandum cautioned, however, that even these additional actions might not bring the war to a successful conclusion:

> . . . the odds are even that the DRV/VC will hang on doggedly, effectively matching us man-for-man (taking into account the lop-sided guerrilla war ratio advantage), while our efforts may not push the South Vietnamese over the crest of the hill, so that the snowball begins to roll our way. *That is, the odds are even that, despite our efforts, we will be faced in early 1967 with stagnation at a higher level and with a need to decide whether to deploy Phase III forces, probably in Laos as well as in South Vietnam.* (emphasis added)

On November 6, 1965, the President met with McNamara, Ball, McGeorge Bundy, William Bundy, Thompson, Raborn and General Wheeler. Clark Clifford was also present. Rusk did not attend.[23] Although the President apparently had not been sent a copy of the

---

21 "COURSE A: 'Soft-line' Pause, then feel way re RT [ROLLING THUNDER] and force levels toward a 'compromise outcome'" "COURSE B: No pause, with evolving RT, with no Phase II. This is a continuation of the present evolving course of action." "COURSE C: 'Hard-line' pause, then evolving RT with Phase II."

22 In his memorandum for the President on July 20 recommending that Westmoreland's 44-battalion request be approved, McNamara suggested that, after deploying ground forces and continued bombing of the North, the U.S. should consider, as part of its diplomatic effort, a six-eight week bombing pause. See pt. III of this study, p. 384.

23 Clifford had just returned from a trip to Asia, which he presumably took at the President's request, to gather more information on the situation. According to a letter on November 9 to William Bundy from Consul General Rice in Hong Kong, one of those he consulted, "Mr. Clifford said the President spends much of his time on Vietnam, and feels forced to make a great many decisions on the basis of inadequate information. What we lack and what he wants, despite the difficulties, is hard intelligence. . . ." U.S. Department of State, Lot File 85 D 240 (William Bundy Papers).

McNamara memorandum,[24] according to William Bundy it served as the basis for the meeting.[25] The discussion centered on the proposal for a bombing pause. Wheeler "argued fervently against the pause, on the military ground that Hanoi could take advantage of it greatly to increase its infiltration, and on the broader ground that Hanoi would draw the conclusion that America will was not firm."[26] Clifford was also strongly opposed, saying a pause would be considered to be a sign of U.S. weakness. Instead, he proposed a speech by the President on the U.S. view of a peaceful settlement, to which the North Vietnamese would be urged to respond. Rusk's position, stated a few days later in a redrafted version of McNamara's November 3 memorandum, was that he, too, was opposed to a pause.

Others, particularly McGeorge Bundy, thought that the proposed speech by the President would not be convincing without a pause.

The President apparently listened to the discussion without stating his own views. In his memoirs he notes that his first reaction to McNamara's memorandum was one of "deep skepticism. The May pause had failed, and I thought that Hanoi would probably view a new cessation in bombing as a sign of weakness."[27]

On November 9, Deputy Under Secretary of State U. Alexis Johnson (who had recently returned from serving as Deputy Ambassador in Saigon) redrafted the McNamara memorandum.[28] Johnson's version generally followed the same line of reasoning as McNamara's, but it also included Rusk's views. (Contrary to some of the opinions expressed earlier, including Rusk's, Johnson's memorandum concluded that, rather than waging a guerrilla war, the Communists were still planning to move toward a Stage III conventional war.) The Communists, the memorandum argued, "can now have no hope of victory. A large part of our task is to reinforce this conviction and not only to consult our own fears but also to weight *[sic]* the fears of the other side in drawing up our balance. A stalemate can have no more attraction for them than it has for us. Our determination and our will is certainly not less than theirs."

There were, the Johnson memorandum said, three alternative courses of action: "FIRST COURSE: No pause, with continuing or evolving Rolling Thunder and with no substantial further deployments to South Vietnam." (This course could prevent a Communist victory, but could lead to a stalemate.) "SECOND COURSE: Pause, extrapolated [increased] Rolling Thunder, and additional deployment." (McNamara, the memorandum said, would recommend this alternative, provided the pause were "hard-line.")[29] "THIRD

---

[24] On November 9, the memorandum was sent to the President, who was then in Texas. See McGeorge Bundy's cover memorandum of that date, Johnson Library, NSF Country File, Vietnam.

[25] William Bundy MS, ch. 33, p. 5.

[26] *Ibid.* This description is based on William Bundy's notes, in his possession, which may be the only record of the meeting.

[27] Johnson, *The Vantage Point,* p. 234.

[28] A copy of U. Alexis Johnson's "Courses of Action in Vietnam," Nov. 9, 1967, is in the Department of State, Lot File 74 D 272.

[29] These, the Johnson memorandum said, were McNamara's reasons for supporting a pause: "(a) It would offer Hanoi and the Viet Cong a chance to move toward a solution if they should be so inclined, removing the psychological barrier of continued bombing and permitting the Soviets and others to bring moderating arguments to bear;

COURSE: No pause, continuing Rolling Thunder at present levels, and gradual Phase II deployments." "Essentially this course of action is designed to maintain momentum in the South so that the South Vietnamese morale and performance can be improved. In essence, it is designed to 'play for the breaks' (as we did in the Berlin blockade and Korea) without actions that would bring the situation prematurely to a head." This third course, the memorandum added, was Rusk's preference.

"As between the SECOND and THIRD COURSES," the memorandum said, "the SECOND COURSE may offer us—if it were to work out favorably—a somewhat greater chance of an acceptable outcome by the end of 1966. On the other hand, with the political dangers of an immediate pause, and the uncertainty and possible widening of the war involved in the latter stage of the extrapolated Rolling Thunder program, the SECOND COURSE would also involve significantly greater chances of either an adverse development in the South or a wider war.

"The THIRD COURSE would give us every reasonable chance of moving ahead in the South before we had to take the critical and difficult actions involved in a pause and a substantially intensified Rolling Thunder program. It would clearly be slower, but it might in the end be surer, particularly in light of the time needed to develop a more solid and effective political structure in the South."

Whichever course of action was adopted, the State Department memorandum added, "maximum effort must be given now and for an extended period to the political, economic and psychological efforts without which South Vietnam will never be made into a workable and reasonably stable non-Communist nation able to cope with the Viet Cong apparatus."

Unlike McNamara's draft, the State Department memorandum did not predict that the U.S. would be faced with "stagnation in early 1967 at a higher level," although it, too, stated that none of the alternatives offered "positive assurance of success." Rather, it said that, as a result of matching efforts by the Communists, there could be by late 1966 or early 1967 pressure to increase U.S. forces, as well as great pressure to invade the North or bomb cities.

On the same day (November 9) the State Department sent its memorandum to the President, McNaughton commented on it in a memorandum to McNamara.[30] He said that the State Department

"(b) It would demonstrate to domestic and international critics that we had indeed made every effort for a peaceful settlement before proceeding to intensified actions, notably the latter stages of the extrapolated Rolling Thunder program;

"(c) It would probably tend to reduce the dangers of escalation after we had resumed the bombing, at least insofar as the Soviets were concerned;

"(d) It would set the stage for another pause, perhaps in late 1966, which might produce a settlement."

Rusk, on the other hand, was opposed to a pause at that time. These, the Johnson memorandum said, were his reasons:

"The Secretary of State believes that a pause should be undertaken only when and if the chances were significantly greater than they now appear that Hanoi would respond by reciprocal actions leading in the direction of a peaceful settlement. He further believes that, from the standpoint of international and domestic opinion, a pause might become an overriding requirement only if we were about to reach the advanced stages of an extrapolated Rolling Thunder program involving extensive air operations in the Hanoi/Haiphong area. Since the Secretary of State believes that such advanced stages are not in themselves desirable until the tide in the South is more favorable, he does not feel that, even accepting the point of view of the Secretary of Defense, there is now any international requirement to consider a 'Pause.'"

[30] Johnson Library, NSF Country File, Vietnam.

memorandum was not "substantially different" than McNamara's. After enumerating and discussing the major differences, McNaughton added his own views. He said he thought the State Department had a "good point in their opposition to 'extrapolating' ROLLING THUNDER," but he thought State was wrong in opposing a pause, adding: "I hate to miss the small chance it offers to turn this thing around."

"Both papers," McNaughton said, "set the goals unrealistically high. . . ." Moreover, "neither memo gives adequate emphasis to what Phases III and IV[31] are likely to look like ('occupation' of South Vietnam, 'quarantine' of Indo-China, pressures to invade North Vietnam, war costs at a rate equal to 10–20 times the GNP of the people being fought for, etc.) and the odds that we will have a Phase III and a Phase IV (50–70%). . . ." Finally, McNaughton said, "neither memo spells out a vigorous 'diplomatic offensive' to accompany the military actions."

On the morning and afternoon of November 11, 1965, the President met in Texas with Rusk, McNamara, Ball, and McGeorge Bundy. Rostow, Clifford and Moyers were also there and may have been present for at least part of the discussion. On the day of the meeting, McGeorge Bundy sent a memorandum to the President urging that the meeting be held and explaining the various points of views.[32] There tended, he said, to be agreement among principal advisers on the need to deploy Phase II troops and to defer decisions on increased bombing. There was disagreement, however, on the proposal for a pause. McNamara was in favor, but Rusk and McGeorge Bundy were opposed "until we get some signal from someone that a pause would have results in matching action by Hanoi." There was also the division, noted earlier, between Lodge and Goldberg on the question of negotiations.

"A still deeper question," Bundy told the President, "upon which McNamara has focused attention in recent discussions is the question of our underlying purpose in Vietnam. Are we seeking a negotiated solution after which the superior political skill of the Communists would eventually produce a Commie takeover?[33] Or are we determined to do all that is necessary to establish and sustain a genuinely non-Communist South Vietnam? All three of us [Rusk, McNamara, McGeorge Bundy] incline to the latter position, but it is clear that its costs continue to grow, and it is still more clear that only the President can decide it."

On the agenda which he prepared for the meeting, McGeorge Bundy listed each of these items as issues to be discussed, conclud-

---

[31] This is a reference to McNamara's July 1965 report to the President in which he projected a two and possibly a three phase plan of U.S. operations. See pt. III of this study, pp. 384–385.

[32] Johnson Library, NSF Memos to the President—McGeorge Bundy.

[33] Judging, among other things, by McGeorge Bundy's phraseology, U.S. officials had little hope at that time for negotiating an acceptable end to the war. To prepare, however, for possible indication of interest by the Communists in negotiations or in an armistice, the State Department's Policy Planning Council, headed by Walt W. Rostow, produced a long paper on "A Settlement in Vietnam," Nov. 2, 1965. (There is a copy in the Department of State, Lot File 74 D 272.) Drafted by Col. Robert H. Ginsburgh, an Air Force officer on detail to the Council, who was serving as Rostow's deputy, and known as the Ginsburgh Report, the paper, after discussing objectives and assumptions, covered a number of aspects, including such "preliminary issues" as options for holding a conference and such questions as location and representation, following which it covered key issues and alternative U.S. positions, including "defining cessation of hostilities," "political arrangements in South Vietnam," relations between the North and the South, compliance, elections, etc.

ing with, "When should we begin additional consultation with Congress—or is such consultation needed?"[34] "In the main," he said, "we are not looking for major decisions but for guidance in further planning."

The only known notes of the meeting of November 11 are the very abbreviated handwritten notes of McGeorge Bundy, which indicate that there was a discussion of Phase II and of a bombing pause.[35] Although the notes are fragmentary, it would appear that at that stage the President was in favor of a pause "about Thanksgiving"—"60–40 for it." "Preparatory to knocking Hell out of 'em," he said, "we're gonna deliver a [words omitted in original notes] those who want a pause."[36]

More Opposition—More Support

During the fall of 1965, there was increasing opposition to the war among those elements of the public who, for one reason or another, did not approve of the role being played by the U.S. On October 15, on what was called the International Day of Protest Against the War in Vietnam, there were teach-ins and demonstrations against the war and the draft in many parts of the country led by the National Coordinating Committee to End the War in Vietnam, the confederation of antiwar groups that had been established in August. (It was announced that same day that the draft quota for December would be 45,224, compared to 36,450 for November and 17,000 the previous July.) These demonstrations, the largest of which was sponsored by the Vietnam Day Committee, Berkeley, California, were denounced by many Members of Congress, including Democratic and Republican leaders. House Democratic Majority Leader Carl Albert (D/Okla.), referring to the "misguided, if not, in the case of some participants in teach-ins and other demonstrations, subversive acts which almost amount to treason," said, "I believe the country and the world should know that not only the leadership but also the Congress is united in supporting the President and the action he has taken. . . ." House Republican leader Gerald Ford agreed, and warned that the demonstrations could result in Communist miscalculations based on a perceived lack of unity in the United States.[37] Senate Democratic Leader Mike Mansfield said that the demonstrators were undermining the President's efforts to achieve a negotiated settlement, and that the demonstrators, "who show a sense of utter irresponsibility and lack of respect, who openly flaunt disobeying the law," were furnishing "fodder to Hanoi, to Peiping, and to the Vietcong." Senate Republican Leader Dirksen called the demonstrators "craven souls," "wailing, quailing, protesting young men," who had for-

[34] Johnson Library, NSF Memos to the President—McGeorge Bundy.

[35] Johnson Library, Papers of McGeorge Bundy, Notes on Vietnam.

[36] In these notes, as is frequently the case with McGeorge Bundy's handwritten notes of meetings, words which were not necessary to convey the essence of a comment were omitted. These quotations are from an undated page which was, according to the Johnson Library, "filed adjacent to material dated November 11 and November 12, 1965." Based on several scraps of evidence—the reference to Thanksgiving and the fact that the President and his advisers did not meet again to discuss Vietnam prior to Thanksgiving, the similarity of numbers in Bundy's doodles on this sheet and on the page of notes dated November 11, and the reference to "ICY" on this sheet as well as on the agenda for the meeting—it is probable that this undated, unnumbered page is the second page of the notes of the November 11 meeting.

[37] These quotations are from *CR*, vol. 111, Oct. 15, 18, 19, 22, 1965.

gotten the role of their country in defending the "cause of freedom." Senator Richard B. Russell, Democrat of Georgia, chairman of the Armed Services Committee, said that the protests would lengthen the war: "Every protest will cause the Communists to believe they can win if they hold on a little longer." He said that he had opposed U.S. involvement in Vietnam, but that the U.S. was committed. "Our flag is committed, our national honor is committed, our prestige is committed, and our whole power for the maintenance of world peace and avoidance of a nuclear war is laid squarely on the line in Vietnam."

Other Senators joined in condemning the demonstrations, including Republican Leaders Leverett Saltonstall of Massachusetts and Thomas H. Kuchel of California, conservative Democrat Frank Lausche, and liberal Democrat William B. Proxmire of Wisconsin. Kuchel praised the announcement that day (October 18) by the Justice Department that it was investigating the demonstrations to see if there were any Communist elements involved. "what has gone on," Kuchel said, "sows the seeds of treason." Lausche said "these demonstrations are the product of Communist leadership," adding:

> Long-whiskered beatniks, dirty in clothes, worn down, seemingly, by a willingness to look like a beatnik, are the ones who are in the vanguard.
>
> They are not entitled to our respect. In my judgment most of them are the antithesis of what a real patriot is. They do not have the backbone or courage to stand up for their country. . . . They are interfering with the lives of genuine American citizens, and with the security of our Nation.

Proxmire, a strong supporter of the administration's position in 1965 who later opposed the war, said that while he believed in the right of protest, the demonstrators were "preventing peace" by leading the Communists to believe that the American public was opposed to the war and would not support continued U.S. involvement. "If these peace marchers want peace," Proxmire declared, "the best contribution they can make is to address their plea to the Communists."

Proxmire inserted in the *Congressional Record* a column by James Reston of the *New York Times* on "The Stupidity of Intelligence," in which Reston took a similar position. The demonstrators, Reston said, "are inadvertently working against all the things they want, and creating all the things they fear the most. They are not promoting peace but postponing it. They are not persuading the President or the Congress to end the war, but deceiving Ho Chi Minh and General Giap into prolonging it. They are not proving the superior wisdom of the university community, but unfortunately bringing it into serious question."

Reston added that many people in the Washington press corps and the Washington political community had supported the student protests earlier in 1965, when President Johnson "was stubbornly refusing to define his war aims in Vietnam, and rejecting all thought of a negotiated settlement . . . but they are now out of date. They are making news, but they are not making sense." "The problem of peace," Reston said, "now lies not in Washington but in Hanoi. . . ."[38]

A number of Members of Congress charged that the Communists were manipulating the antiwar movement and the October demonstrations. One of the foremost of these was Senator Thomas Dodd, an ally of the President, and vice chairman of the Internal Security Subcommittee of the Senate Judiciary Committee, whose subcommittee staff prepared a document on "The Anti-Vietnam Agitation and the Teach-in Movement: The Problem of Communist Infiltration and Exploitation."[39] "I have been asked," Dodd said, "what evidence there is that the anti-Vietnam agitation and the teach-in movement have been infiltrated and are being manipulated by the Communists. There are a number of facts, all of them contained in the study, which, taken together, would, I believe, convince any reasonable person that this is so."[40]

The Judiciary subcommittee staff study concluded that while "the great majority" of those involved in demonstrations and teach-ins were "loyal Americans," control of the antiwar movement had "clearly passed from the hands of the moderate elements who may have controlled it at one time, into the hands of Communists and extremist elements who are openly sympathetic to the Vietcong and openly hostile to the United States, and who call for massive civil disobedience, including the burning of draft cards and the stopping of troop trains. This is particularly true of the national Vietnam protest movement scheduled for October 15–16."

Senator Jacob K. Javits a liberal Republican from New York, who had tried unsuccessfully to get the President, before he sent large-scale U.S. forces to Vietnam, to ask Congress to authorize that action,[41] said that he supported the President's Vietnam policy, and that while he defended the right to protest, he also supported "the right to expose Communist influences in the demonstrations. . . ."[42]

The only congressional support for the October demonstrations came from those few Members of Congress who had openly opposed the administration's position on Vietnam, with Senator Morse once again in the forefront. "What America needs to hear," Morse declared, "is the tramp, tramp, tramp of marching feet, in community after community, across the length and breadth of this land, in protest against the administration's unconstitutional and illegal war in South Vietnam." Morse did not condone unlawful protests, and he condemned draft evasion and draft card burning, even though, as he said, "jungle law is usually met by more jungle law." "It can hardly be wondered at that an administration that engages in war

---

[38] *New York Times*, Oct. 17, 1965.

In August 1965 Reston went to South Vietnam to do a series of articles on the war, and according to a report to the President from Bill Moyers on a luncheon with Reston several weeks later, "his trip convinced him that contrary to his original conviction, we can transport power to the far corner of the earth and apply it effectively; he was impressed with the efficiency and ingenuity of our troops and the wise use of our power which is being applied out there." Johnson Library, Office of the President File, Moyers to the President, Sept. 21, 1965.

[39] This subcommittee print was subsequently reprinted as S. Doc. 89–72.

[40] *CR*, vol. 111, p. 27113.

[41] See citations to Javits' effort in pt. III of this study.

[42] *CR*, vol. 111, p. 28175.

in violation of the means outlined by the Constitution is met with protests taking the form of violation of the draft laws."[43]

Meanwhile, in the Senate Foreign Relations Committee there was very little activity with respect to the war. During the period between July 1965, when the President announced his decision to send large-scale forces, and October 23, when Congress adjourned for the year, the committee held only two meetings during which Vietnam was discussed, and then only peripherally. On September 23, the committee met to consider the appointment of U. Alexis Johnson to his post as Deputy Under Secretary of State for Political Affairs.[44] During the hearing, Johnson was asked by Fulbright "how this struggle can ever be resolved in any way." Johnson replied that he thought it could and would be resolved by "simply fading away."

> My feeling is that if the North decides that at least for the time being it is not a winning road that they may well pull back. I would never say they will pull back permanently any more than they do any place, but they might well decide to withdraw the forces that they have there and at least stop the military phase of this. I think this is going to take some time. I do not think they have come to the conclusion yet that they are required to take this course of action. But the actions that we are now taking, I think that in a foreseeable period of time, I would say within the next year, it is entirely possible that they will do this.

If the war ended in this fashion, Johnson added, rather than from a treaty or a conference, "In some ways this makes it easier for them, and from our standpoint I think would be a relatively satisfactory outcome. . . . I feel that the return to the principles, if you will, of the 1954 [Geneva] settlement is the best possible outcome."

U. Alexis Johnson stressed the importance of forcing the Communists to back down in Vietnam. If there were a Communist victory, he said, "it is going to result in an enormous increase in prestige . . . [for] every Communist party around the world, and we will be finding a reflection of this in Africa, Latin America, and we will be paying a much heavier price over the next generation than we would for the cost of making the stand here at this time."[45]

On October 13, 1965 Secretary Rusk, in testimony before the Foreign Relations Committee on the general world situation, said that U.S. was "in here [Vietnam] for another few weeks and months to find out where, when and how and where the break is coming that will move this matter toward peace."[46] There had been contacts with the North Vietnamese, he said, but these had not resulted in what he called the "critical indication from the north that they are prepared to stop this operation in the south."

Protests against the war increased during November 1965. Washington officials and the public at large were shocked by inci-

---

[43] *Ibid.*, pp. 27386–27387.

[44] U.S. Congress, Senate, Committee on Foreign Relations, *Executive Sessions of the Senate Foreign Relations Committee* (Historical Series), 1965, vol. XVII (Washington, D.C.: U.S. Govt. Print. Off., 1990), pp. 1152–1153.

[45] *Ibid.*, p. 1155.

[46] *Ibid.*, p. 1220. In this published version of the hearing, the word "two" appears in place of the word "few," which was in the stenographic version of the hearing. Use of the word "two" is apparently a misprint.

dents on November 2 when a Quaker war resister, Norman B. Morrison, 32, of Baltimore, Maryland, burned himself to death at the Pentagon to protest the war, and on November 10, when another war resister, Robert Allen La Porte, 22, a Catholic, died of burns from attempted self-immolation at the United Nations.[47]

On November 27, an estimated 20,000–35,000 staged a "March on Washington for Peace in Vietnam." The march was called by the Committee for a Sane Nuclear Policy (SANE), whose political action director, Sanford Gottlieb, one of the most active antiwar organizers during the 1960s and 1970s, was the march chairman. The National Coordinating Committee to End the War in Vietnam and SDS were also involved, and various other groups, especially Women Strike for Peace, were among the sponsors.[48]

Unlike the SDS-sponsored march in the spring of 1965 or the one in August led by the peace groups, the November march was designed to appear to be more moderate in order to make the antiwar movement more appealing to the public. There was no march, as such, through Washington, nor was there any planned civil disobedience. Speakers were carefully selected. Prior to the march, its leaders discussed it with NSC Aide Chester Cooper, who said that if the leaders of the march wanted to help bring about peace talks they should take their case to the North Vietnamese, the Russians and the Chinese.[49] They agreed to do so, and a few days later the co-chairmen of SANE, Dr. Benjamin Spock and Professor H. Stuart Hughes of Harvard University, sent Ho Chi Minh a cable stating that SANE was sponsoring the march, and urging him to accept U.S. offers for negotiations. The cable added: "Demonstrations will continue but will not lead to a U.S. pullout."[50]

Of the speeches at the November march, the one that received the warmest reception was given by Carl Oglesby, the new SDS president, who spoke on "Liberation and the Corporate State." Oglesby, 30, a writer, had just resigned as head of the technical publications department at the Aerospace Systems Division of the Bendix Corporation (while at Bendix he was also a part-time student at the University of Michigan, where he became involved with the first teach-in). The U.S. Government, Oglesby said, had been intervening in revolutionary situations in other countries, including Vietnam, in defense of private corporate interests, and American "corporate liberals" were responsible:[51]

---

[47] *New York Times,* Nov. 3 and 10, 1965. For background stories on the two men see November 7 and 11. McNamara later said about Morrison, who "wasn't 40 feet away from my window," that his death "was a personal tragedy for me." *Washington Post,* May 10, 1984, feature story by Paul Hendrickson.

[48] For descriptions see Kirkpatrick Sale, *SDS* (New York: Random House, 1972), pp. 242–244, Powers, *The War at Home,* pp. 92–94, Milton S. Katz, *Ban the Bomb, A History of SANE, the Committee for a Sane Nuclear Policy, 1957–1985* (Westport, Conn.: Greenwood Press, 1986), pp. 97–99, and Zaroulis and Sullivan, *Who Spoke Up?* pp. 63–66. For a discussion of related trends of thought about the war among the American "intellectual left" during the summer and fall of 1965, see Sandy Vogelgesang, *The Long Dark Night of the Soul: The American Intellectual Left and the Vietnam War* (New York: Harper and Row, 1974), pp. 93–102.

One of the speakers at the march was Representative George E. Brown, Jr. (D/Calif.), whose speech was later reprinted in *CR,* vol. 112, pp. 11881–11882.

[49] Johnson Library, Office Files of Harry McPherson, Cooper Memorandum to McGeorge Bundy, Oct. 26, 1965.

[50] *New York Times,* Oct. 29, 1965.

[51] From the text in Massimo Teodori (ed.), *The New Left: A Documentary History* (Indianapolis: Bobbs-Merrill, 1969), pp. 182–188. For a more complete statement of Oglesby's views see Carl Oglesby and Richard Schaull, *Containment and Change* (New York: Macmillan, 1971). For

Continued

> We are here again to protest against a growing war. Since it is a very bad war, we acquire the habit of thinking that it must be caused by very bad men. But we only conceal reality, I think, to denounce on such grounds the menacing coalition of industrial and military power, or the brutality of the blitzkrieg we are waging against Vietnam, or the ominous signs around us that heresy may soon no longer be permitted. We must simply observe, and quite plainly say, that this coalition, this blitzkrieg, and this demand for acquiescence are creatures, all of them, of a government that since 1932 has considered itself to be fundamentally *liberal.*
>
> The original commitment in Vietnam was made by President Truman, a mainstream liberal. It was seconded by President Eisenhower, a moderate liberal. It was intensified by the late President Kennedy, a flaming liberal. Think of the men who now engineer that war—those who study the maps, give the commands, push the buttons, and tally the dead: Bundy, McNamara, Rusk, Lodge, Goldberg, the President himself.
>
> They are not moral monsters.
>
> They are all honorable men.
>
> They are all liberals. . . .
>
> Revolutions do not take place in velvet boxes. They never have. It is only the poets who make them lovely. What the National Liberation Front is fighting in Vietnam is a complex and vicious war. This war is also a revolution, as honest a revolution as you can find any where in history. And this is a fact which all our intricate official denials will never change.
>
> But it doesn't make any difference to our leaders any way. Their aim in Vietnam is really much simpler than this implies. It is to safeguard what they take to be American interests around the world against revolutions or revolutionary change which they always call Communism—as if that were that.

"[I]f your commitment to human value is unconditional," Oglesby said, noting that he was speaking to the "human liberals," "then disabuse yourselves of the notion that statements can be written, or that interviews with the mighty will bring change if only the mighty can be reached, or that marches will bring change if only we can make them massive enough, or that policy proposals will bring only change if only we can make them responsible enough. We are dealing now with a colossus that does not want to be changed. It will not change itself. It will not cooperate with those who want to change it. Those allies of ours in the Government—are they really our allies? If they *are,* then they don't need advice, they need *constituencies;* they don't need study groups, they need a *movement.* And if they are not, then all the more reason for building that movement with a most relentless conviction."

The response of the President and his associates to the demonstrations in October as well as the march on Washington in November was to maintain official silence while taking a number of steps to gather intelligence on and to discredit the antiwar movement. These counteractions took various forms. In the State De-

---

Oglesby's description of his involvement in antiwar activities see Morrison and Morrison, *From Camelot to Kent State,* cited above, pp. 297–307.

partment, U.S. posts abroad were asked to notify Washington of all communications to individuals and groups in other countries from the Vietnam Day Committee in Berkeley. It was possible, the message said, that upon learning of such communications, private groups in the U.S. might want to send messages supporting U.S. policy.[52] "Opposition to U.S. Vietnam policy," the message added, "comprises small minority in U.S. and represents in large part student energies diverted from other reform or protest movements."

In addition to State Department reports from its overseas Missions, information on antiwar activists was being gathered by the FBI, the CIA and the National Security Agency from surreptitious intercepts of private communications.[53]

Information on antiwar activities was also being gathered through FBI infiltration of the groups involved; surreptitious warrantless entries into homes or offices by the FBI and the CIA ("black bag jobs"), either to install microphones or to procure information at the scene; surreptitious warrantless electronic surveil-

---

[52] U.S. Department of State, Central File, Pol 27 Viet S, Circular Telegram 585, Oct. 8, 1965. There was some discussion in the State Department and at the White House of invoking the Logan Act (62 Stat. 744), passed in 1799, which prohibits citizens, without U.S. authority, from directly or indirectly engaging in "correspondence or intercourse with any foreign government or any office or agent thereof, with intent to influence the measures or conduct of any foreign government or of any office or agent thereof, in relation to any disputes or controversies with the United States, or to defeat the measures of the United States. . . ." The Department of State's Legal Adviser, Leonard Meeker, advised against such a move. (A copy of Meeker's memorandum to Under Secretary Ball, "American Student Activities Directed Against United States Policy on Vietnam," Oct. 18, 1965, is in the Department of State Central File, Pol 27 Viet S.) Noting that there had never been a conviction under the Act, he said, "Both legal and constitutional considerations may stand in the way of invoking the Logan Act successfully." In order to apply criminal sanctions to those responsible it would be necessary for Congress to broaden the act. Such a proposal, however, "would provoke strong opposition in Congress and would almost certainly be declared unconstitutional if tested in the courts." A test case, moreover, might result in the entire act being declared unconstitutional, thus depriving the Government of the benefits of the act. "As it stands now, and without having ever been tested by a prosecution, the Logan Act has a certain value to the Government. It has, for example, apparently prevented Dr. Martin Luther King [Jr.] from going through with his announced intention to write [letters urging opposition to the war] to the governments of foreign countries." Meeker concluded: "To my mind, the strongest and best approach to criticism of our policies is to meet that criticism with informed and reasoned answers, to take account of criticism that is well founded, to expose that which is fallacious, and to continue to carry out energetically the foreign and military policies on which the nation has decided in the exercise of its constitutional processes."

[53] See the description of these programs in U.S. Congress, Senate Select Committee to Study Governmental Operations With Respect to Intelligence Activities, Final Report, Book II, *Intelligence Activities and the Rights of Americans*, S. Rept. 94–755, April 26, 1976, 94th Cong., 2d sess. (Washington, D.C.: U.S. Govt. Print. Off., 1976), p. 6 and *passim* (hereafter this will be referred to as Final Report, Book II of the Senate Select Committee to Study Intelligence Activities.

According to this report, there were also a number of covert government activities designed to intimidate and discredit individuals and groups opposing the war. In the FBI, the principal agency engaged in domestic covert action against the antiwar movement, this was called COINTELPRO—counterintelligence program. COINTELPRO tactics included (*ibid.*, pp. 10–11):

"—Anonymously attacking the political beliefs of targets in order to induce their employers to fire them;

"—Anonymously mailing letters to the spouses of intelligence targets for the purpose of destroying their marriages;

"—Obtaining from IRS the tax returns of a target and then attempting to provoke an IRS investigation for the express purpose of deterring a protest leader from attending the [1968] Democratic National Convention;

"—Falsely and anonymously labeling as Government informants members of groups known to be violent, thereby exposing the falsely labelled member to expulsion or physical attack;

"—Pursuant to instructions to use 'misinformation' to disrupt demonstrations, employing such means as broadcasting fake orders on the same citizens band radio frequency used by demonstration marshalls to attempt to control demonstrations, and duplicating and falsely filling out forms soliciting housing for persons coming to a demonstration, thereby causing 'long and useless journeys to locate these addresses';

"—Sending an anonymous letter to the leader of a Chicago street gang (described as 'violence-prone') stating that the Black Panthers were supposed to have 'a hit out for you.' The letter was suggested because it 'may intensify . . . animosity' and cause the street gang leader to 'take retaliatory action.'"

lance of individuals and groups by microphones, telephone wiretaps or other methods; mail opening; the use of informants; the collection of information from public sources, including the media, public meetings, and published materials.[54] In addition, the military services, particularly the Army, were conducting their own surveillance of antiwar activities.[55]

After an antiwar demonstration in Washington in April 1965, President Johnson requested information from the FBI on whether the Communists had played a role. He also asked the FBI to begin sending information to the White House on individual critics of the war, especially Members of Congress who actively opposed the war.[56] In May, Attorney General Nicholas deB. Katzenbach approved an FBI wiretap on the telephones of the Students for a Democratic Society (SDS), which had sponsored the April demonstration.[57]

One of the principal targets of the covert action program, both for his civil rights and his antiwar activities, was Dr. Martin Luther King, Jr. Information was gathered in part by wiretaps on King's telephones at his home and office, and those of his associates, as well as by microphone recordings in hotel rooms.[58] This information was then sent to the White House, and some of it was made available to selected journalists.

Haynes Johnson, a reporter for the *Washington Post,* later described his experience:[59]

> In late 1965 or early 1966 I received a call from a top aide of FBI Director J. Edgar Hoover. This person had been helpful earlier in stories about the civil rights struggles in the South and especially about FBI knowledge of leaders of the Ku Klux Klan there. He asked if I could drop by his office in the Justice Department, near Hoover's suite, where the FBI was housed then.
>
> When I arrived, shortly before noon, I was shown a pile of documents lying on a table before a couch. I was welcome to take my time and read through them, making notes, but under a stipulation that the meeting then occurring "never took place." The aide then left me alone with the documents.
>
> They were about the Rev. Martin Luther King, Jr. After I finished going through them, another FBI aide escorted me to the elevator. He told me that anything I could write to expose King for what he was would be a great service to the American people. In other words, discredit him.

---

[54] All of these methods are discussed in *ibid.* The principal FBI program under which information was gathered on antiwar activities was COMINFIL—Communist Infiltration. See *ibid.*, pp. 48 ff. and pp. 81–82.

[55] See *ibid.*, pp. 77, 84.

[56] See pt. III of this study, pp. 224–225.

[57] *Ibid.*

[58] See Final Report, Book II of the Senate Select Committee to Study Intelligence Activities, p. 11, 272–277, and the case study of the FBI campaign against King, pp. 79–185, in U.S. Congress, Senate, Select Committee to Study Governmental Operations With Respect to Intelligence Activities, Final Report, Book III, *Supplemetary Detailed Staff Reports on Intelligence Activities and the Rights of Americans*, S. Rept. 94–755, April 23, 1976 (Washington, D.C.: U.S. Govt. Print. Off., 1976) (hereafter this will be referred to as Final Report, Book III of the Senate Select Committee to Study Intelligence Activities). Also useful is David J. Garrow, *The FBI and Martin Luther King, Jr.* (New York: W. W. Norton, 1981).

[59] *Washington Post,* Oct. 16, 1983.

The material I had seen consisted of raw, and no doubt selective, FBI files. They were filled with accounts of surveillance and supposition, from anonymous sources, with allusions to communist contacts, communist associations, communist penetration. There were also, as I remember, materials allegedly linking King and the American antiwar movement to communist control and associations with communist front groups around the world.

This was at a time when King, who won the Nobel Peace Prize a year before, had begun to take a strong public position against our expanding combat role in Vietnam. His criticism of U.S. troops being in Vietnam came amid intensifying dissent about the war. Influential politicians and public figures were beginning to question—and directly challenge—President Lyndon B. Johnson's policies with a force that eventually led to his departure from the White House.

Aside from hearsay, gossip, and anonymous allegations, I saw nothing in the FBI materials about King that would warrant publishing a story. The real story was the campaign to destroy King's public credibility through selective leaks to the press. For, as it quickly became known, that and similar material were being peddled vigorously by the FBI to other Washington reporters. . . .

Judging by a Gallup poll taken in late October 1965, the efforts being made to characterize antiwar demonstrations as Communist-influenced were achieving some success:[60]

"To what extent, if any, have the communists been involved in the demonstrations over Vietnam—a lot, some, to a minor extent, or not at all?"

[In percent]

A lot	58
Some	20
Minor	8
Not at all	4
Don't know	10

In a survey several weeks later, Harris also found support, especially among less-educated respondents, for the concept of Communist influence:[61]

[In percent]

	Total Nation	*Grade School*	*High School*	*College*
Just Demonstrating against something	34	27	34	30
Tool of Communists	26	36	27	20
Trying to avoid draft	14	16	16	5
Moral opposition to war	14	10	14	20
Think Vietnam war wrong	11	9	9	15
Not sure	1	2	....	1

Harris also found that while a majority believed in the right to demonstrate, a large number of respondents believed the public did not have the right to demonstrate against the war:

[60] George Gallup, *The Gallup Poll: Public Opinion, 1935–1971,* vol. 3, p. 1971. Responses are broken down by sex, race, education, etc. in *Vietnam War, A Compilation: 1964–1990,* cited above, vol. 1, no pagination.
[61] *Washington Post,* Dec. 13, 1965.

[In percent]

	Have Right	Don't Have Right	Not Sure
Nationwide	59	[1] 32	9
By education:			
Grade school or less	40	41	19
High School	59	35	6
College	81	16	3

[1] Of the 32 percent who believed there was no right to demonstrate against the war, the reasons given were: "Subversive, revolutionary: 10 percent; Matter for Government to decide: 9 percent; Demonstrations unlawful: 5 percent; Comforts enemy: 4 percent; Upsets our soldiers: 4 percent."

During October-December 1965, public opinion polls reported that support for U.S. policy in Vietnam had increased. These were the results of a question asked in a Gallup Poll reported on November 21 (earlier figures are given for comparison):[62]

"Some people think we should not have become involved with our military forces in Southeast Asia, while others think we should have. What is your opinion?"

[In percent]

	Nov. 21, 1965	May 16, 1965	Jan. 31, 1965
Should have	64	52	50
Should not	21	26	28
No opinion	15	22	22

According to a Harris Survey reported on December 6, 1965, "The overwhelming majority of the American people—71 percent—are prepared to continue the fighting in Vietnam until the United States can negotiate a settlement on its own terms."[63]

"In Vietnam, should the United States stop fighting now and negotiate but keep our troops there, or should we pull out our troops and then negotiate, or should we keep on fighting until we can negotiate on our own terms?"

[In percent]

Keep fighting	71
Stop fighting now	13
Pull out troops	4
Not sure	12

In the White House, trends in public opinion were being monitored by Fred Panzer and reported to Moyers and the President by Panzer or Moyers' assistant, Hayes Redmon. Throughout Johnson's Presidency, direct contacts were maintained with the Harris and Gallup organizations, and Harris was frequently asked to advise the White House on public attitudes.

On December 27, 1965, Redmon sent Moyers a six-page memorandum summarizing and interpreting recent public opinion data.[64] (It is not known whether the President saw the memorandum.) These were Redmon's conclusions:

—The public has supported our military build up.

---

[62] Gallup, *The Gallup Poll,* vol. 3, p. 1971. Figures for the polls of May 16 and January 31 are from the Gallup Poll, as cited in pt. III of this study, p. 273. Responses for the November 21 poll are broken down by sex, race, education, etc. in *Vietnam War, A Compilation: 1964–1990,* cited above, vol. 1, no pagination.

[63] *Washington Post,* Dec. 6, 1965.

[64] Johnson Library, Office Files of Fred Panzer, memorandum for Bill Moyers from Hayes Redmon, "Public Opinion and Vietnam," Dec. 27, 1965.

—They have done so because they think it will bring a peaceful solution nearer.

—They not only overwhelmingly want, but expect a negotiated settlement.

—A majority does not now believe we are sufficiently active in seeking negotiations.

—To maintain public support we need a series of moves—preferably dramatic—to assure them that we are active in the pursuit of peace. They will not support just sitting back and waiting for Hanoi to ring.

—Finally, it would be a serious mistake to talk about winning a "victory" in Vietnam. The door must always be left open to the compromise solution the American public is anticipating and will support.

"The great danger," Redmon said, is that the public would become frustrated over the failure to negotiate a peaceful settlement, and he noted that there were signs that frustration was beginning to set in.

Although public opinion polls indicated broad support for U.S. policy in Vietnam and for the use of American forces in the war, this support was not being taken for granted by the President and his staff. With the mid-term congressional elections less than a year away, and with the costs and casualties of the war increasing rapidly, various moves were being planned or put into effect to bolster public support. In August 1965, as noted earlier, an interdepartmental Public Affairs Policy Committee, chaired by McGeorge Bundy, was established to promote the dissemination of information and to create public support for the war. The committee had no operating responsibilities, however, and the members of the White House staff who were involved in public affairs activities, principally Chester Cooper, as well as Valenti, Moyers, and Cater, had many other responsibilities. The result was a lack of action.

In a memorandum, "Vietnam, The American People, and Us," to Bundy, Moyers, Valenti and Cater on December 14, Cooper stressed the need for a full-time staff for public affairs operations related to the war.[65] Polls, he said, gave the President "high marks," on Vietnam, "but I have a vague feeling that this support may be more superficial than it is deep and committed (many people probably do not even understand what it is that they are supporting.)" The challenge, Cooper said, "is to sustain and nourish this support through hostilities with its high casualties, negotiations with its frustrations, settlement with its inevitable compromises, and reconstruction with its high costs." "Do we have the means at hand to do this? I am not sure; 'Establishment Committees' are only of peripheral help; groups like the Friends of Vietnam are too small to make much of an impact. In the last analysis, I think we must tackle this one ourselves—through direct, timely, and candid official communication with the American People."

During November 1965, in an effort to help maintain strong public support for the war, a report prepared by several persons, most of whom were closely identified with U.S. Government activities in

[65] Johnson Library, C.F. ND 19/CO 312.

Vietnam, and signed by a number of prominent Americans, was issued by Freedom House.[66] Among the signers were Richard Nixon, Dean Acheson, Lucius D. Clay, James Conant, and Douglas Dillon. It said in part, "This is no longer merely a question for domestic debate over national policy. Across the world, friend and foe alike are watching intently to gauge the strength of our national purpose. The consensus, which is clear to all experienced observers, must not be obscured by the behavior of a small segment of our population. They have a right to be heard, but they impose on the rest of us the obligation to make unmistakably clear the nation's firm commitment. . . . Only when the essential unity that exists . . . is hammered home will the aggressors consider withdrawal. . . ."

On December 10, 1965, similar support came from a group of academicians organized by Wesley R. Fishel of Michigan State University, (the chairman of the American Friends of Vietnam, and formerly head of the Michigan State University Group in Vietnam), consisting of 190 faculty members from Harvard University, Yale University, and 15 other institutions in New England. Those who signed the statement, most of them social scientists, (including Samuel Beer of Harvard University and John P. Roche of Brandeis University, both former presidents of the liberal organization, Americans for Democratic Action, which had opposed expansion of the war), said that they supported debate about the war, but were concerned that the tactics of a "small minority of the intellectual community" which opposed U.S. policy could prolong the war by causing the Communists to underestimate American resolve.[67]

On December 15, 1965, the AFL-CIO in its annual meeting also approved a resolution strongly supporting U.S. efforts in Vietnam.[68]

The Battle of Ia Drang, November 1965

The first major battle between U.S. and Communist main force units occurred in mid-November 1965 in the Ia Drang Valley in Pleiku Province, where the 1st Cavalry Division had been deployed in late summer to guard against possible moves by North Vietnamese regiments to enter South Vietnam from Cambodia, capture Pleiku, and then launch an attack that would cut through that narrow neck of Vietnam and split the country. Although it is not clear

---

[66] *New York Times,* Nov. 29, 1965, which said that the report was written by George Field, executive director of Freedom House, Frank R. Barnett, president of the National Strategy Information Center, Leo Cherne, executive director of the Research Institute of America (also chairman of the board of Freedom House), Frank R. Trager, a professor at New York University, and William vanden Heuvel, president of the International Rescue Committee. When Field held a press conference to announce the report he said about those who marched in Washington November 27: "In the main we would characterize Saturday's marchers in Washington as the same sort of people as those decent people of England who cheered loudest when Neville Chamberlain returned from Munich and brought home his peace pact with the Nazis."

Freedom House officials, as well as persons from a public relations firm which they were using, were actively consulting with the staff of the State Department's Far East Bureau as well as with the White House on their plans, including the need for some assistance with funding. See the Nov. 27, 1965 memorandum from Jonathan Moore, an assistant to William Bundy, Johnson Library, NSF Country File, Vietnam.

[67] *New York Times,* Dec. 10, 1965. Other signers were Henry Kissinger and Morton Halperin of Harvard University, Harold Isaacs, Max Millikan, Myron Weiner of the Massachusetts Institute of Technology, and Guenter Lewy of the University of Massachusetts, who later published a study which generally defended the U.S. role in the war: *America in Vietnam,* cited earlier. For additional information about Fishel's role see pts. I, II and III of this study.

[68] *New York Times,* Dec. 16, 1965.

whether Communist forces were undertaking such an offensive, or whether they were primarily testing the will and methods of American forces, or both, two regiments of North Vietnamese troops, which had moved into the area of the Ia Drang Valley in September-October 1965, fought elements of the 1st Cavalry Division in a series of battles in which 1,200–3,000 North Vietnamese and 300 Americans were killed.

This engagement was hailed by U.S. officials as a victory for American forces and a demonstration of the effectiveness of Westmoreland's strategy and tactics.[69] After an extensive review, however, Army Chief of Staff General Johnson questioned whether the 1st Cavalry Division had been as successful as it had claimed to be. In a cable to Westmoreland he said: "Final dispositions of PAVN ["People's Army of Vietnam"—North Vietnam] units indicates to me that they had repositioned themselves to pounce upon the Cavalry. In contrast, the picture painted by the Cavalry is that the PAVN were driven from the battlefield." "I now have some

---

[69] According to Lt. Gen. Harry W. O. Kinnard, Commander of the 1st Cavalry Division, Ia Drang was a victory for the concept that U.S. forces could successfully conduct such "spoiling attacks" on the enemy on a battlefield of the enemy's choice, and represented, therefore, a "decisive benchmark in the war in South Vietnam." It was, he said, a "turning point; no longer would the enemy call the tune." Kinnard, "A Victory in Ia Drang: The Triumph of a Concept," *Army*, 17 (September 1967), p. 72. See also Westmoreland, *A Soldier Reports*, pp. 156–158; Ulysses S. G. Sharp and William C. Westmoreland, *Report on Operations in Vietnam* (Washington, D.C.: U.S. Govt. Print. Off., 1967), pp. 98–99; J. D. Coleman, *Pleiku: The Dawn of Helicopter Warfare in Vietnam* (New York: St. Martin's Press, 1988). For a vivid description of the ferocity of the fighting at Ia Drang, see the article by one of the participants, Army Specialist Jack P. Smith, son of TV commentator Howard K. Smith, "Death in the Ia Drang Valley," *Saturday Evening Post*, Jan. 28, 1967.

For other studies see John A. Cash, "Fight at Ia Drang, 14–16 November 1965," in *Seven Firefights in Vietnam*, by John Albright, et. al. (Washington, D.C.: U.S. Govt. Print. Off., 1973); George C. Herring, "The 1st Cavalry and the Ia Drang Valley, 18 October-24 November 1965," pp. 300–403 in *America's First Battles, 1776–1965*, Charles E. Heller and William A. Stofft (eds.) (Lawrence, Kansas: Univ. Press of Kansas, 1986); Lt. Gen. Harold G. Moore and Joseph Galloway, *We Were Soldiers Once . . . And Young: Ia Drang, The Battle that Changed the War in Vietnam* (New York: Random House, 1992).

In his study of the war, *Summons of the Trumpet: U.S.—Vietnam in Perspective* (San Rafael, Calif.: Presidio Press, 1978), pp. 102–103 Dave Richard Palmer, an Army officer and military analyst, has conveyed the somewhat intangible nature of the victory at Ia Drang, along with his feeling that it was, for the moment at least, a defeat for the enemy:

"Victory in Vietnam was hard to measure. There were no rubble-crested ridges on which to plant a flag, no great cities to liberate, no surrendered armies. As the troopers of the 1st Cavalry Division choppered out of the Ia Drang valley heading for other battles, they left behind no occupying force. Their nearly three hundred dead had already been evacuated. Except for a number of felled trees the jungle appeared untouched. After a few rains even the scars would disappear. And surely the enemy would come back. But the outcome of the fighting along the Ia Drang and under the Chu Pong [mountains] was a victory in every sense of the word. On the strategic scale, a brilliant spoiling attack had completely derailed Hanoi's hopes of earning a decisive victory before full American might could be deployed to South Vietnam. Moreover, in a head-on clash between an American and a North Vietnamese division on the enemy's chosen ground, the NVA [North Vietnamese Army] unit had been sent reeling in defeat. For the moment, at least, an adverse tide had been reversed."

Palmer suggested, however, that while the battle may have been a victory for U.S. forces, it was also a sign of more difficult things to come (*ibid.*, p. 97):

"After ten days in the crucible of combat, the airmobile division had demonstrated its inherent superiority over the field front in terms of firepower and mobility. Portents of a dangerous weakness had cropped up as well, but in the flush of success Americans discounted it. Once on the ground and out of their helicopters, U.S. units were for all intents and purposes immobilized. NVA [North Vietnamese Army] units maneuvered, attacked, broke contact, withdrew, sidestepped, and continued their march; Americans dug in, defended, and watched the enemy fade away to fight again. If the enemy chose to fight, a battle ensued and the Americans, with far greater firepower from air and artillery, were almost sure to inflict disproportionately severe casualties; if the enemy chose not to close, the cavalry men seemed unable to force a fight. In other words, Americans had almost as little foot mobility as their foe had helicopter mobility."

rather serious doubts about this," he said, adding that Deputy Chief of Staff Creighton Abrams agreed.[70]

A few weeks after the battle, Army Chief of Staff Johnson went to Vietnam to assess the situation, particularly the results of the large-unit search-and-destroy operations being employed by Westmoreland. (Although Johnson had acquiesced in the field commander's primacy in directing forces under his command, he was known as a critic of Westmoreland's strategy, preferring instead an anti-infiltration cordon across the top of South Vietnam combined with "a lot of scouting and patrolling activity by quite small units with the capacity to reinforce quickly.")[71] Reportedly, he heard considerable criticism of Westmoreland's strategy, including a report from Gen. Harry W. O. Kinnard, Commander of the 1st Cavalry Division, who said that after the battle he had pled with Westmoreland to "Use their [North Vietnamese] tactics. Put us in Thailand and have us interdict the Ho Chi Minh trail. Seal off the battlefield."[72]

When General Johnson asked a group of colonels whether Westmoreland's large-unit search-and-destroy operations were working, a number of them said that they were not; that, in the words of one of them, "We just didn't think we could do the job the way we were doing it."[73]

In another session, junior officers from the 1st Infantry Division told Johnson that large units could not effectively engage the enemy; that small units constantly moving and patrolling would be more effective. Johnson is said to have replied that although he agreed with their philosophy, he rejected their ideas "since we were not going to be able to respond to the public outcry in the United States about the casualties that might result."[74]

Some military leaders and strategists have since argued that the battle at Ia Drang reinforced the mistaken idea that this was the kind of war the U.S. could and should fight. According to Col. Harry G. Summers, Jr. (U.S. Army, Ret.), "Our initial victory [Ia Drang], lulled us into the delusion that no matter what we did, we couldn't lose." He contends that rather than continuing to seek out the Communists in the south, and to use American forces as part of the counterinsurgency and pacification programs, the U.S. should have used its forces to prevent infiltration from North Vietnam into the south, thus choking off the insurgency by "sealing off" South Vietnam from North Vietnam.[75]

Andrew Krepinevich contends that, for the Army, the battle of Ia Drang represented "the successful application of the attrition strategy. Here were large enemy formations willing to go toe to toe with the Americans, and their big units were being smashed by the Army's firepower and high-tech mobility. Standard operations were working; therefore, no alternative strategies need to be explored." It was, he said, the "validation" of "the Army concept of war, [which] is, basically, the Army's perception of how wars *ought* to

---

[70] CMH, Westmoreland Papers, Message Files, Johnson to Westmoreland, WDC 1253, Jan. 29, 1966.

[71] See pt. III of this study, p. 169.

[72] Perry, *Four Stars*, p. 157.

[73] *Ibid.*

[74] Krepinevich, *The Army and Vietnam*, pp. 171–172.

[75] Harry G. Summers, Jr., "The Bitter Triumph of Ia Drang," *American Heritage*, 35 (February-March 1984), pp. 50–58, at 58.

be waged and is reflected in the way the Army organizes and trains its troops for battle."[76] (emphasis in original) ("The characteristics of the Army Concept are two: a focus on mid-intensity, or conventional, war and a reliance on high volumes of firepower to minimize casualties—in effect the substitution of material costs at every available opportunity to avoid payment in blood.")[77]

"Unfortunately," Krepinevich says, "General Westmoreland and the MACV staff overlooked three important facts. First, it was the NVA that initiated the battle, not the 1st Cavalry Division. Second, the Communists had chosen to operate in large units on this occasion. As subsequent events over the next three years would prove, the Americans could neither force the Communists to fight, nor force them to operate in large formations that were vulnerable to U.S. firepower. . . . Third, MACV ignored unpleasant facts regarding the results of other search-and-destroy operations," namely, the lack of contact resulting from the refusal of the Communists "to fight on the American terms." This was exemplified, Krepinevich says, by the five search-and-destroy missions carried out in the area north of Saigon during June-November 1965, where "Few of the enemy were killed and little of lasting value was accomplished."[78]

A Call for More Troops

Shortly after General DePuy's presentation of Phase II plans in late October 1965, the JCS completed a memorandum for the Secretary of Defense on "Future Operations and Force Deployments with Respect to the War in Vietnam," November 10, 1965, stating the needs and goals of Phase II.[79] Having failed to get civilian approval of their earlier paper "Concept for Vietnam," August 27, 1965, the Chiefs requested approval of this new memorandum, which they said was "an extension of and supports the overall concept for the conduct of the war" set forth in the earlier memorandum.

Phase I, the new memorandum said, "was designed to stop losing the war." Phase II "is the phase needed to start winning it."

> There is now a clear and unmistakable surge of confidence and enthusiasm in South Vietnam which apparently stems from the presence and the performance of U.S. forces. Over the past two years it has been realized how difficult it is to engender this optimism and faith in the future among a war-weary people desperately hoping for a quick end to all the violence. The Vietnamese are beginning to gain some hope of getting security as a result of the U.S. forces commitment. This hope is a fragile thing and is easily lost. If the current efforts are ever permitted to bog down and if the present trend is reversed, the most important ingredient required for victory will have been lost, i.e., the faith and commitment of millions of loyal Viet-

---

[76] Krepinevich, p. 169.

[77] *Ibid.*, p. 5.

[78] Andrew Krepinevich, "Vietnam: Evaluating the Ground War, 1965–1968," a paper presented at the Fourteenth Military History Symposium, U.S. Air Force Academy, October 1990, printed in *An American Dilemma: Vietnam, 1964–1973*, Dennis E. Showalter and John G. Albert (eds.) vol. I of the Military History Symposium Series of the United States Air Force Academy, Carl W. Reddel (series ed.) (Chicago, Ill.: Imprint, 1993), pp. 87–108.

[79] Johnson Library, NSF Country File, Vietnam, JCSM–811–65, Nov. 10, 1965.

namese people. Therefore, a plateau of effort would be dangerous. If the military effort stalls, U.S. political vulnerability will become obvious and the real battle for SVN may well be lost.[80]

For Phase II, the Chiefs requested an additional 113,000 troops as well as 26,000 more for other areas of the Western Pacific to provide support for U.S. forces in Vietnam. Once again, the JCS also requested approval of a much stronger air war against North Vietnam, beginning with an "immediate sharp blow against a significant group of POL facilities and electrical power installations to reduce materially enemy military capabilities."[81] This would be followed by an intensified and accelerated program of airstrikes, including military targets in the Hanoi-Haiphong area, as well as the mining of major harbors. While recognizing that bombing had achieved only limited success,[82] the Chiefs argued that only by modifying or lifting some of the existing constraints could air power be made more effective: "Now required is an immediate and sharply accelerated program which will leave no doubt that the U.S. intends to win and to achieve a level of destruction which they [the North Vietnamese] will not be able to overcome."

The JCS also discussed the concept of operations for waging the war. U.S. forces, they said, with some help from South Vietnamese forces, would continue to be responsible for operations against Communist forces and bases outside the secure areas, while the bulk of South Vietnamese forces would be used for pacification. When the Communists were operating in large units, U.S. forces would seek to "find, fix, and destroy them." When they dispersed and engaged in small-scale guerrilla actions, U.S. forces would place more emphasis on clearing and securing, and on civic action operations.

General Taylor was reported to have questioned the JCS's "static defense" conception of the role of South Vietnamese forces, which he said was a "mistake from the point of view of GVN psychology and U.S. domestic opinion." He suggested instead that the JCS statement should provide that "In the assignment of ground force missions, every effort will be made to avoid the impression and the fact that U.S. forces are taking over the bulk of the heavy fighting and thereby providing a shield for GVN forces to engage in less hazardous operations."[83] Both Ulysses S. Grant Sharp, Jr., Com-

---

[80] JCSM–811–65, p. C–16.

[81] In a separate memorandum to McNamara that day (Nov. 10, 1965), JCSM–810–65, "Air Operations Against the North Vietnam POL System," same location, the Chiefs recommended that the U.S. bomb major POL storage facilities, beginning with those in Haiphong and continuing with others in Hanoi and seven other locations. "Attack of this system," the memorandum stated, "would be more damaging to the DRV capability to move war-supporting resources within country and along the infiltration routes to SVN than an attack against any other single target system."

[82] JCSM–811–65 agreed in large part with intelligence findings on the results of the existing program of bombing, saying that, (p. A–A–2):

"a. The morale of the populace seems to be standing up fairly well despite the air strikes although increasing signs of apprehension and concern for safety are appearing.

"b. The capability of the armed forces of the DRV has not been diminished to an appreciable degree other than their capability for overt aggression.

"c. Infiltration of men and materials through Laos has not been reduced below that required to support the VC/PAVN at present levels of activity. It has, however, been made more difficult.

"d. There have been no indications that US/GVN air strikes have brought the DRV leadership any closer to a willingness to abandon their support and direction of the insurgency."

[83] CMH, Westmoreland Papers, Message Files, JCS 4500–65, Nov. 20, 1965.

mander in Chief, Pacific (CINCPAC) and Westmoreland agreed with Taylor's suggestion. Sharp said: "the heart of the offensive program is a combined US/RVNAF effort, coupled with a significant number of unilateral GVN actions. Any other arrangement would result in our fighting their war for them."[84]

The South Vietnamese, however, seemed quite willing to let U.S. troops assume the principal combat role, and, as Jeffrey J. Clarke has written, "A major part of the war in Southeast Asia had thus become Americanized by the end of 1965. . . . Despite protestations to the contrary, two different wars were now under way in South Vietnam: the 'big battalion,' or conventional war, carried out by American military forces through a strategy of attrition, and the 'other war,' pursued by the South Vietnamese through the strategy of pacification." "American attention," he adds, "both inside and outside the government, quickly became riveted to the first while the second slowly faded into the background."[85]

In response to the November 10 JCS memorandum, McNamara said that he would consider the Chiefs' recommendations in connection with other decisions on U.S. military activities in South Vietnam.[86] He also arranged for Wheeler to see the President in order to explain the JCS position. As he told Ball a few days later, "The Chiefs have been coming to a boiling point on bombing Haiphong . . . [and] it would be wise to insure the Chiefs' views got to the President. . . ." The President asked Wheeler to present a joint recommendation with McNamara.

After Wheeler's meeting with the President, McNamara saw the President and explained that the program of bombing proposed by Wheeler was scheduled to be considered in February 1966. He told the President he was not prepared to recommend it at that time, adding that the State Department was strongly opposed and he thought McGeorge Bundy "leaned against it."[87]

McNamara Expresses Doubts After a Trip to Vietnam

By mid-November 1965, there appeared to be a consensus among U.S. officials in Saigon that, rather than waging primarily a guerrilla war, the Communists were continuing to strengthen their

---

[84] Same location, Sharp to Wheeler, IN NO: 9529, Nov. 23, 1965, and MAC 5875, Nov. 21, 1965.

[85] Jeffrey J. Clarke, *Advice and Support: The Final Years, 1965–1973* (Washington, D.C.: U.S. Govt. Print. Off., 1988), p. 124. Clark's study is one of the volumes in the series on the United States Army in Vietnam being prepared by the U.S. Army's Center of Military History.

The use of U.S. troops as the principal combat forces and the relegation of Vietnamese troops to pacification, as Herbert Y. Schandler has said, had broader implications for the role of the U.S. in the war, especially with respect to helping the South Vietnamese to defend themselves in the future:

"The build-up of U.S. forces and their use in an offensive role throughout Vietnam was an explicit expression of U.S. loss of confidence in the South Vietnamese Armed Forces (RVNAF) and a corresponding willingness on the part of U.S. commanders to take over the major part of the war effort in 1965–67.

"The paradox arose of the Americans fighting on behalf of an army (and a government) that they treated with disdain, even contempt. The South Vietnamese were dealt with as if they really were irrelevant. Thus, there grew a naked contradiction between the political objectives of the war—an independent self-sufficient South Vietnam—and the U.S. neglect of the South Vietnamese government and army in the formulation of American war strategy during the 1965–1967 build-up phases." Schandler, "America and Vietnam: The Failure of Strategy, 1964–67," in *Vietnam as History*, Peter Braestrup ed., cited above, p. 29.

[86] Johnson Library, Warnke Papers, McNaughton Files, "JCS Policy Statements Concerning Operations in Southeast Asia."

[87] Johnson Library, Papers of George Ball, "Presidential Telecons, telecon of conversation between Ball and McNamara, Nov. 23, 1965.

forces in South Vietnam, including greater infiltration of troops from the North, in order to achieve a strategic balance with U.S. forces as a prelude to a general counteroffensive. In an "Estimate of Viet Cong Situation," the U.S. Mission's Intelligence Committee concluded that, "The Communists may calculate that this alternative, combined with extensive terrorism—a course which proved successful against the French—offers the best prospects for wearing down the will and determination of the U.S. to continue the war," and that they would not revert to a lesser level of insurgency or seek negotiations unless this course proved unsuccessful.[88]

On November 23, Westmoreland said that, based on estimates of increasing infiltration of North Vietnamese forces, he would need a larger number of forces in Phase II than had been anticipated.[89] At a minimum, he would need 25,000 more U.S. troops (and 23,000 Korean), and preferably 41,500 U.S. troops (and 23,000 Korean). The additional 41,500 would increase the Phase II requirement of additional U.S. forces to 154,000, compared to the July 1965 estimate of 100,000 and the October and November estimates of 110,000–115,000. A few days later, however, the estimate of the number of forces needed for Phase II was increased to 200,000. According to William Bundy, "It was a drastic step-up, shattering at one blow the scale and force planning that had entered into the President's final decision of July, even putting in doubt the decision not to call the Reserves."[90] (This new estimate, with the increase which had already occurred in Phase I forces from the original 175,000 to 210,000, would increase the Phase II total to 410,000, in contrast to the original estimate of 275,000.)

Even before Westmoreland's message of November 23 was received in Washington, McNamara had decided that he needed to go to Vietnam to assess the situation personally. In a telephone conversation with Ball, McNamara explained that his reason for going was the need to decide on Phase II forces: "We should put the troop strength and financial requirements into our budget; and, assuming the President does not want to make a firm commitment to the end of Phase II, we should begin shipping the troops in the battalion against that schedule in January, without commitment to go beyond a month—unless the President wants to make a stronger recommendation." Ball said that this was his interpretation.[91] As will be seen, McNamara and Ball correctly perceived the President's preference not to make a decision on Phase II troops at that time and to decide the issue in the *ad hoc,* incremental fashion that McNamara proposed.

During the ensuing meetings in Saigon on November 28–29 with Lodge, Westmoreland and Admiral Sharp (CINCPAC), McNamara emphasized the need to increase U.S. covert operations against the Ho Chi Minh Trail in Laos. He also emphasized the need for a greater contribution by the South Vietnamese, saying that "he would approve whatever related requirements were developed to

---

[88] U.S. Department of State, Central File, Pol 27 Viet S, 4-part cable, Saigon to Washington 1677, Nov. 11, 1965.

[89] CMH, Westmoreland Papers, Message Files, Westmoreland to CINCPAC 41485, Nov. 23, 1965.

[90] William Bundy MS, ch. 33, p. 10.

[91] Johnson Library, Papers of George Ball, "Presidential Telecons," telecon of conversation between Ball and McNamara, Nov. 23, 1965.

ensure that RVN [Republican of Vietnam] manpower and US money substitute for US blood even at the expense of continued GVN [Government of Vietnam] economic difficulty."[92]

The question was again raised of establishing an anti-infiltration barrier across South Vietnam near the DMZ and then across Laos (approximately 180 miles). Westmoreland's staff responded that this would be feasible, but that it would take one to two years and would require at least four and a half divisions plus support troops (a total of at least 100,000–150,000 men), and that "it does not appear, under any circumstances, to represent the most profitable use of available resources."

After returning from Vietnam, McNamara sent a memorandum to the President on November 30, 1965, supplementing his memorandum of November 3.[93] There were two alternatives, he said: either work toward a "compromise solution . . . and hold further deployments to a minimum," or "stick with our stated objectives and with the war, and provide what it takes in men and materiel." He did not say which alternative he preferred. If the decision were made to stick with the war, he said he would recommend sending substantial additional troops—raising the total to as high as 74 combat battalions (400,000 men counting logistical forces) by the end of 1966, and possibly adding 200,000 or more in 1967. Under this alternative he said he would also recommend gradually increasing the bombing of the North as well as mining the harbors, but he noted that General Wheeler and Admiral Sharp preferred a higher rate and intensity of bombing. He also again recommended a bombing pause prior to taking the additional military steps. In conclusion, he stated, "We should be aware that the deployments of the kind I have recommended will not guarantee success." And, he added, "U.S. killed-in-action can be expected to reach 1000 a month, and the odds are even that we will be faced in early 1967 with a 'no-decision' at an even higher level."

McNamara's report on the political situation was also discouraging: "The Ky 'government of generals' is surviving, but not acquiring wide support or generating actions; pacification is thoroughly stalled, with no guarantee that security anywhere is permanent and no indication that able and willing leadership will emerge in the absence of that permanent security." Ky, McNamara said, estimated that his government controlled only about 25 percent of the population.

McNamara's visit is said to have been the point at which he underwent "a change from overflowing confidence to grave doubts":[94]

> On this visit he found that American forces were performing well. But he also discovered that despite our new deployments, despite the tremendous military assistance and training programs for the South Vietnamese Army, despite the use of B–52s against enemy bases in South Vietnam and the intensified bombing of North Vietnam, the Communists were increasing the scale and intensity of their military operations; Hanoi's

---

[92] Memorandum for the Record, MACJ03, Dec. 1, 1965, "Summary of Major Points Covered During 28–29 November 1965 Meetings with Secretary of Defense," from microfilm of COMUSMACV records, U.S. Army Military History Institute, Carlisle Barracks, Pa.

[93] Johnson Library, NSF Country File, Vietnam.

[94] Chester L. Cooper, *The Lost Crusade* (New York: Dodd, Mead, 1970), p. 288.

> forces in South Vietnam had expanded, and Communist military equipment and supplies continued to flow down from the North. McNamara sounded grim as he left Saigon. He told the press that the Viet Cong action "expressed a determination to carry on the conflict which can lead to only one conclusion—that it will be a long war."

"Robert McNamara," concludes Deborah Shapley, "looked into the abyss and saw three years of war leading only to stalemate, and he warned the President. He went through the motions of considering compromise but rejected this course. He saw his miscalculation but stuck with the war that winter; he was committed to it, politically, publicly, and emotionally. Giving up was not in his program or his temperament. And he believed the cause was just."[95]

In a very private meeting about a month later (January 6, 1966) with a small group of friends and former associates in the Kennedy administration who were also allies of Senator Robert F. Kennedy (D/N.Y.), McNamara, without President Johnson's knowledge, expressed some of these doubts. The meeting was held at the Georgetown home of Arthur M. Schlesinger, Jr., and was attended by John Kenneth Galbraith, Carl Kaysen, and Richard N. Goodwin.[96] According to Schlesinger, "McNamara told us that he did not regard a military solution as possible. His objective, he said, was 'withdrawal with honor.'" Schlesinger says he noted in his journal that McNamara, who, he says, requested the meeting, "'seemed deeply oppressed and concerned at the prospect of indefinite escalation. Our impression was that he feared the resumption of bombing [there was a bombing pause in effect at the time] might well put us on the slippery slide.'"[97]

In a revision of his November 30 memorandum which he sent to the President on December 7, 1965, McNamara, who did not mention, as he had in his November 30 memorandum, the alternative of seeking a compromise solution, concluded as follows:

> If the U.S. were willing to commit enough forces—perhaps 600,000 men or more—we could ultimately prevent the DRV/VC from sustaining the conflict at a significant level. When this point was reached, however, the question of Chinese intervention would become critical. (We are generally agreed that the Chinese Communists will intervene with combat forces to prevent destruction of the Communist regime in the DRV. It is less clear whether they would intervene to prevent a DRV/VC defeat in the South.) The intelligence estimate is that the chances are a little better than even that, at this stage, Hanoi

---

[95] Deborah Shapley, *Promise and Power: The Life and Times of Robert McNamara* (Boston: Little, Brown, 1993), p. 359. For McNamara's explanation to Shapley of his reasons for continuing to support the war see pp. 359–361.

[96] Schlesinger was a former professor at Harvard University who had been a White House adviser to Kennedy and then became a professor at the City University of New York; John Kenneth Galbraith was a professor at Harvard University who had been U.S. Ambassador to India under Kennedy but was also on good terms with Lyndon Johnson; Carl Kaysen, also formerly of Harvard University, had been on the NSC staff under Kennedy and later became head of the Institute for Advanced Study in Princeton, N. J.; Richard Goodwin, a Harvard-educated lawyer and writer, had been a speech writer for both Kennedy and Lyndon Johnson, and had drafted Johnson's July 28 announcement of the decision to send large-scale U.S. forces. He left the White House in the fall of 1965.

[97] Arthur M. Schlesinger, Jr., *Robert Kennedy and His Times* (Boston: Houghton Mifflin, 1978), pp. 734–735.

> and Peiping would choose to reduce the effort in the South and try to salvage their resources for another day; but there is an almost equal chance that they would enlarge the war and bring in large numbers of Chinese forces (they have made certain preparations which could point in this direction).
>
> It follows, therefore, that the odds are about even that, even with the recommended deployments, we will be faced in early 1967 with a military standoff at a much higher level, with pacification still stalled, and with any prospect of military success marred by the chances of an active Chinese intervention.[98]

In the revised memorandum there was also a section on budget recommendations. In the January 1966 supplemental appropriations request to Congress, the memorandum said, the Department of Defense would need an additional $11 billion to pay for the war through June 30, 1966.[99] For Fiscal Year 1967 (July 1, 1966-June 30, 1967), another $9.8 billion should be requested. (As will be seen, while he recommended a request of $9.8 billion, McNamara told the President that the real cost would be $15–17 billion.)

These estimates of military costs, McNamara said in his memorandum, "are based on the premise that the war will end by June 30, 1967. As time passes and as actions must be taken to cover war costs beyond that date, additional obligational authority will have to be sought. Thus, it may be necessary to go back to the Congress in June or July 1966 for an amendment to the FY 1967 authorization and appropriations to take account of those added costs." (As will be seen, this gross underestimation of the cost for FY 1967, on the assumption that the war would end by June 30, 1967, created a furor in Congress, especially among the Republicans.)

President Johnson's reaction to McNamara's report is not known. He does not appear to have acted on it directly, although he did approve budgetary requests to cover increased costs of the war in 1966 and 1967. But he doubtless pondered the dilemma facing the United States in Vietnam, having been told by McNamara that a force of 600,000 or more Americans might eventually be needed, with no assurance that even then there would be anything better than a higher level of stalemate. He had, of course, been warned that this could happen, not only by Ball, Clifford, and others in the Executive and in Congress, but by the Intelligence Community, which had consistently predicted that increases in U.S. forces would be matched by the Communists. But he had never been given such a pessimistic accounting by McNamara. Only three and a half months earlier, it was McNamara who had asserted with his customary assurance that U.S. forces could fight a guerrilla war, and had predicted that the proposed plan had "a good chance of achieving an acceptable outcome within a reasonable time."

On December 14, 1965, the Intelligence Community once again predicted that if the U.S. increased its forces (Phase II), the Communists would respond by increasing their own. A Special National

---

[98] *PP*, Gravel ed., vol. IV, p. 624. In the Johnson Library, NSF Country File, Vietnam, there is a copy of a draft of this memorandum, "Military and Political Actions Recommended for South Vietnam," dated Dec. 4, 1965.

[99] In August, 1965, a $1.7 billion supplemental appropriation for Vietnam had been requested and approved, and at the time it was predicted that there would be a request in January 1966 for another $10–12 billion.

Intelligence Estimate, (10–12–65, "Probable Communist Reactions to a U.S. Course of Action"), that tended to confirm McNamara's growing pessimism about the efficacy of military means, concluded:[100]

> [P]ressures applied to North Vietnam thus far have not changed Hanoi's determination to prosecute the war in South Vietnam. These pressures include the US buildup in the South and its attendant successes, the present bombing program in the North, and the apparent intention of the US to double its combat strength and to expand the scope of the bombings. Hanoi, however, apparently believes that present US and GVN programs have not brought about any decisive change in the military situation and that contemplated programs can be prevented from doing so. In other words, it believes that in the long run it can still prevail. Unless and until this belief is altered, it appears unlikely that there will be any change in Hanoi's posture. . . .
>
> Hanoi apparently calculates that it can support sufficient forces in South Vietnam, and endure air attacks in North Vietnam, long enough to test US resolve to fight a bitter, unpopular, and inconclusive war on inhospitable terrain. Having balanced all the factors which would go into such a calculation—the present situation, the aid which it can expect from each of its major allies, US intentions and capabilities, GVN capabilities, PAVN/VC capabilities and the situation in the DRV itself—Hanoi has apparently concluded that it can carry on well into 1966 before such a decision must be reconsidered.

The estimate also concluded:

> It does not appear . . . that the air attacks, even if extended and increased, will be a conclusive factor within the next six to nine months in determining North Vietnamese policy on the war in South Vietnam. The North Vietnamese have so far been able to continue supplying their forces in South Vietnam despite disruption of the transportation links by bombing. . . .
>
> By continuing to infiltrate men and materiel at a substantial pace in 1966, Hanoi apparently hopes, at the minimum, to create a stalemate in the fighting in South Vietnam before the pressures of the bombing on the North and the interdiction of supply lines to the South become too costly to bear. The regime probably hopes that if it can prove to the US that a second phase commitment of American combat troops will not conclusively turn the tide, US resolve will weaken and Washington will be ready to make some major concessions in its policy. Hanoi is doubtless counting on heavy US casualties to spur strong domestic opposition to American policy. The North Vietnamese will also be hoping for a new coup in Saigon or some other unforeseeable development to weaken the US position. . . .
>
> If the US buildup in South Vietnam over the next year is successful in turning the course of the fighting decisively against the insurgents, the chances appear better than even that the Communists would be more likely to take the form of

[100] Johnson Library, NSF Country File, Vietnam.

a de facto termination of the fighting than a negotiated settlement.

In December 1965, the Central Committee of the North Vietnamese Communist Party agreed on a resolution calling for resistance to American forces which signalled the determination of the Communists to respond to the U.S. buildup by increasing their own efforts. According to a study published after the war under Vietnamese Government auspices, "the Central Committee set forth the following slogan: 'Endeavor to limit the enemy's war and defeat the enemy in that limited war, inflict heavy casualties on them, and force them to become bogged down and heavily defeated. If that is done we are certain to win a decisive victory in the South.'"

Based on this, the study said, "Our strategic motto was to fight a protracted war and rely primarily on our own strength, while also, on the basis of waging a protracted war, going all-out to highly concentrate the forces of both regions in order to take advantage of the opportunity in order to win a decisive victory on the southern battlefield in a relatively short period of time. At the same time, we still had to prepare to defeat the enemy in the event that the war was prolonged and was extended to the entire nation."

The study added: "We also had to try to win international sympathy, support, and aid, a factor which would contribute decisively to our people's victory. Therefore we had to carry out a diplomatic struggle."[101]

---

[101] War Experiences Recapitulation Committee of the High-Level Military Institute, *The Anti-U.S. Resistance War for National Salvation, 1954–1975,* p. 85. There is a useful analysis of the resolution by William J. Duiker (who had served in Vietnam in the 1960s while in the U.S. Foreign Service), *The Communist Road to Power in Vietnam* (Boulder, Colo.: Westview Press, 1981), pp. 242–244. According to Duiker, the resolution reflected the views of Communist party leaders Le Duan and the commander of Communist forces in the South, Gen. Nguyen Chi Thanh, both of whom advocated an aggressive policy in the South. Philip B. Davidson, *Vietnam at War,* pp. 362–366, says that at the time there was a controversy between Thanh and Le Duan, on the one hand, and Gen. Vo Nguyen Giap, Defense Minister of North Vietnam (who had commanded the forces which defeated the French in the decisive battle of Dienbienphu in 1954) and Truong Chinh on the other. "Thanh and Le Duan argued for a largely conventional war of Main Force units, while Giap's concept emphasized small-unit and guerrilla tactics while holding the Main Force units in reserve."

For a useful presentation of the Communist debate over strategy in the 1965–1968 period, see James J. Wirtz, *The Tet Offensive: Intelligence Failure in War* (Ithaca, N.Y.: Cornell Univ. Press, 1991), ch. 1.

CHAPTER 4

THE BOMBING PAUSE DECISION

Among the President's principal advisers, with the exception of Ball, there was unanimous agreement that the United States should continue to prosecute the war rather than seeking a compromise solution, and that Phase II forces should be approved as recommended by McNamara. They also recognized, however, that an increase of this magnitude would probably produce stronger criticism at home and abroad, and that before increasing its forces the U.S. should make a serious attempt to negotiate an end to the fighting.

There were also the questions of whether to seek further approval of Congress before undertaking such a major expansion of the U.S. commitment to Vietnam, and, should there be a bombing pause, of resuming and increasing the bombing of North Vietnam after the pause. In notes that McGeorge Bundy jotted down on or about November 30, 1965, apparently from a telephone conversation with the President, Bundy posed the question: "What would happen at the end [of the pause]? What troubles P [President] most [is] how do we constitutionally and properly recommit."[1]

On the issue of the bombing pause, the President and his advisers doubted whether it would result in negotiations, although McNamara thought that it could be the beginning of a negotiating process. Even Ball doubted whether a pause would result in negotiations, and said later that he supported it because he hoped it would "break the rhythm of escalation."[2]

William Bundy says, "I myself would never have thought that the bombing pause had more than a fifty percent chance of resulting in a negotiating process." "One of my deepest regrets," he adds, "is that I never really probed on Bob McNamara's optimistic view of negotiations, or shared with him fully my view that they were likely to be extremely unproductive or difficult for a very long time before anything happened from them. Right through to 1967, one can see in his attitude a much more rosy—and I think unrealistic—view of what they would accomplish or whether they would even be conducted in anything resembling good faith."[3]

There was considerable concern that a pause might signal weakness and indecision, and might encourage the Communists to continue fighting. The offsetting factor, and the one that became decisive, was that a pause would help to establish the *bona fide* interest of the U.S. in a settlement, thus making escalation more ac-

[1] Johnson Library, McGeorge Bundy Notes on Vietnam, undated notes, but according to the Johnson Library notation "filed adjacent to material" for Nov. 30, 1965. On December 1, according to the President's Daily Diary, the President talked by phone with McGeorge Bundy, who was present in Rusk's office at the time.

[2] George W. Ball, *The Past Has Another Pattern: Memoirs* (New York: Norton, 1983), p. 404.

[3] Communication to the author from William Bundy, July 1993.

ceptable at home and abroad. As stated in a subsequent Department of State paper on what the press could be told, the following could be used as "very deep background or off the record": "This effort [bombing pause] is the necessary peace punch to go with the military punch which is coming in January. We face a big budget, larger reinforcements, and possibly other drastic measures in the field of taxes and controls. The President cannot ask the American people to join in united support of hard measures until we have given complete proof of our determination to move toward peace."[4]

As noted, Rusk was initially opposed to a pause, believing that it should be considered only when, as a result of continued diplomatic probing, there were "firm indications of a response by specific and acceptable actions on the part of Hanoi."[5]

As for McNamara, according to a memorandum on November 17 to the President from Ball stating the positions of McNamara and Rusk and summarizing the arguments for and against a pause, McNamara believed that a pause could "lay a foundation especially in the minds of the American people and of our allies, for the increased U.S. deployments, casualties, costs and risks that are in prospect." McNamara also believed, Ball said, "that a pause now has a bare chance of starting a chain reaction toward a settlement.

---

[4] U.S. Department of State, Central File, Pol 27 Viet S, "Outline of U.S. Public Position During a Suspension of Bombing," Dec. 18, 1965.

[5] See the November 17 memorandum of George Ball attached to a memorandum on Nov. 17, 1965 from McGeorge Bundy to the President, Johnson Library, NSF Memos to the President—McGeorge Bundy. In the Johnson Library (NSF Country File, Vietnam), there is a draft memorandum to the President, "A Pause," Nov. 30, 1965, drafted by William Bundy, which was apparently intended to be a statement of the State Department's position. This had been in preparation for several weeks (in the same location there is a third draft of the memorandum dated November 14). William Bundy's memorandum discussed the basic elements of a pause, a scenario of action, and pros and cons. It suggested that the pause last one month, but that bombing be resumed prior to that time "if Hanoi clearly rejected the pause or was taking significant additional military actions which we detected." "In the absence of such development, we would play out the full four weeks but would expect to resume unless Hanoi by that time had taken significant responsive action. Above all, we would resist continuing the pause in return for mere negotiating gestures. In other words, the proposal is clearly for what has been sometimes described as a 'hard-line pause.'"

Principal arguments for a pause, according to the memorandum, were:

"1. A pause could lead to either successful negotiations or a tapering off of military action in South Vietnam. Although the odds of this happening at this time may be long, the stake is high enough to justify the risks involved. It seems quite clear that the other side does not believe it can agree to negotiations or to a cessation of military action while the bombing continues and we cannot know whether or not they desire a settlement until we try them out by a pause. . . .

"2. The President's offer of unconditional negotiations greatly strengthened our position throughout the world. A pause can have a similar effect by taking away from the other side the one valid argument they have against negotiations. . . .

"3. American casualties are mounting and further involvement appears likely. A pause can demonstrate that the President has taken every possible means to find a peaceful solution and obtain domestic support for the further actions that we will have to take. . . .

"4. There are already signs of dissension between Moscow, Peking, Hanoi and the Viet Cong. The pause is certain to stimulate further dissension on the other side and add to the strains in the Communist camp as they argue about how to deal with it.

"5. A pause could reduce the likelihood of further Soviet involvement. It would not only help to convince Moscow that we genuinely desire a settlement but would also decrease the ability of Hanoi or Peking to bring pressure upon the Soviet Union for escalating their support."

Principal arguments against a pause included:

"1. . . . there is no indication whatever from Hanoi that a pause would lead to meaningful negotiations or actions. [There is] . . . a very small chance that a pause would produce a constructive response.

"2. . . . a unilateral pause at this time would give Hanoi an excellent chance to interpose obstacles to our resumption of bombing and to demoralize South Vietnam by indefinitely dangling before us (and the world) the prospect of negotiations with no intent of reaching an acceptable settlement.

"3. There is a danger that . . . Hanoi may misread a pause at this time as indicating that we are giving way to international and domestic pressures to stop the bombing of North Vietnam and that our resolve with respect to South Vietnam is thus weakening."

He thinks that, before intensifying the military confrontation and risks in Vietnam, the United States should make every effort to back the DRV/VC down by other means." Furthermore, he believed that a pause, even if it did not result in negotiations, could contribute toward the process of an eventual settlement.[6]

As McGeorge Bundy described the positions of McNamara and Rusk in a memorandum to the President on November 17 accompanying Ball's memorandum, "The man who has to present next year's defense budget will want to have made a last full try. The man [Rusk] who has to cope with an effort by the Communists to embarrass us by ambiguous responses to a pause tends to be against it."[7] "My own judgment," Bundy said, "is marginally against the pause, perhaps because I am more concerned with the diplomatic aspects than with the military budget. But I also have some feeling that if we pause, we may seem to admit that our bombing is the cause of the trouble, and this is simply not so."

The President's own position is not clear. Earlier, as noted, he seemed to favor a pause, but by late November he appears to have had second thoughts. In a memorandum to the President on November 27, McGeorge Bundy said that McNamara and he "have the impression that your mind is settling against a pause," but he told the President that the arguments for a pause were substantially stronger and that he (Bundy) and McNamara believed that the matter "is too important to be decided without making sure that the question has been explored to your satisfaction."[8] Bundy said that a pause should be "very hard-nosed." "[W]e should expect," he added, "that it will not lead to negotiations, but it will strengthen your hand both at home and abroad as a determined man of peace facing a very tough course in 1966."

One of the considerations cited by McGeorge Bundy was "growing evidence that we can count on quiet but strong Soviet diplomatic support in pushing Hanoi toward the conference table during another pause." In part, this judgment was based on a discussion between Bundy and the Russian Ambassador to the U.S., Anatoly Dobrynin, on November 24, in which Dobrynin said that if the U.S. stopped bombing for two or three weeks the Soviet Union would try to persuade the North Vietnamese to respond constructively to the pause. According to William Bundy, Dobrynin's statement, which became "one of the critical factors" in the pause debate and a "very important part of the gradual change to accepting the idea of the pause," "was that of an earnest plea that the United States take such action."[9]

Another reason for a pause, McGeorge Bundy said in his November 27 memorandum to the President, was to forestall moves by other countries to undertake diplomatic initiatives which the U.S. might not welcome. One of these, he said, was "some new Vietnam

---

[6] Ball memorandum of November 17, cited above.
[7] McGeorge Bundy memorandum of November 17.
[8] Johnson Library, NSF Memos to the President—McGeorge Bundy.
[9] William Bundy MS, ch. 33, p. 18, and communication to the author, July 1993.

On December 8, Rusk and Llewellyn Thompson met with Dobrynin, and during the conversation they asked him what the U.S.S.R. would do if the U.S. stopped the bombing of North Vietnam. Dobrynin replied that "stopping the bombing would create a better atmosphere. He could not give any undertaking as to what would happen but the Soviet Union would not try to influence North Vietnam while they were being bombed." Johnson Library, NSF Memos to the President—McGeorge Bundy, Memorandum of Conversation, Dec. 8, 1965, prepared by Thompson.

gambit" which the British Prime Minister was said to be thinking of suggesting when he visited Washington later in the month. "We will spike his guns and those of everyone else like him if we have a pause in effect at the time of his visit."

A pause could also prove useful in relation to the new budget request which the President was preparing to send to Congress in January 1966. By pausing, the U.S., would be seen as having genuinely reasonable and peaceful intentions, and if it were decided that bombing had to be resumed and the war escalated there might be less criticism of these actions and greater support in Congress for the new request.

After McNamara returned from Vietnam and submitted his report to the President (who was in Texas) on November 30, there were intensive discussions among the President's advisers, followed by a revised report on December 3, 1965 and a final version on December 7. At a meeting on November 30 of Rusk, McNamara, McGeorge Bundy, Ball, Vance, U. Alexis Johnson, William Bundy, and McNaughton, McNamara presented his findings. According to McGeorge Bundy's brief, informal notes of the meeting, McNamara characterized the situation as "a tremendous U.S. force on a bowl of jelly." Pacification was "not working at all," he said, and desertion rates from the South Vietnamese Armed Forces were "very, very high." [10]

On December 2, McNamara told McGeorge Bundy that the more he thought about the problem the more convinced he was that the U.S. should not limit its actions to military increases, but "*must* have some form of political action:—a pause, or a ceasefire, or action by the United Nations." (emphasis in original) [11]

On the morning of December 3, there was another meeting attended by Rusk, McNamara, McGeorge Bundy, Ball, William Bundy and U. Alexis Johnson. McGeorge Bundy, who had talked to him before the meeting, said that the President (who was still in Texas) wanted a full package of proposals, including Phase II, the pause, diplomatic moves, and consultation with Congress as well as the possibility of a congressional resolution.[12] On the pause, the unattributed comment of one of those present was that the President saw "great difficulties: we'd lose support." McNamara said that the pause had not been analyzed, nor had it been "played out Red and Blue" (i.e., by a Defense Department politico-military [war] game). Referring to a deployment rate of 15,000 U.S. troops a month in Phase II, he asked, "Do we want a war with China?"

At another meeting that afternoon (attended also by Vance), the group resumed discussion of whether and when China would enter the war if the U.S. increased its forces. McNamara and Rusk were concerned about such a possibility. McGeorge Bundy said he agreed with U. Alexis Johnson that the Chinese "would not fight for South Vietnam but only for what they regard as the survival of North Vietnam." [13]

---

[10] Johnson Library, McGeorge Bundy Notes on Vietnam.

[11] *Ibid.*

[12] *Ibid.*

[13] Johnson Library, NSF Memos to the President—McGeorge Bundy, Memorandum to the President at the Ranch, Dec. 3, 1965.

On the question of bombing, McNamara commented, "We can get qualified experts to say that bombing the North doesn't help militarily. You can't stop 200 tons [of infiltrated supplies] a day by bombing." [14]

Later that day (December 3), McGeorge Bundy reported to the President that discussions at the two meetings "confirm the judgment that we shall almost surely wish to proceed energetically on Westmoreland's course in South Vietnam. Thus all of us believe that we should accept for planning purposes additional deployments averaging fifteen thousand a month over the next year. It does not follow that we should announce a large lump sum increase anytime soon. Indeed our preliminary judgment is that steady increase of pressure on the ground should be as undramatic as possible. . . ." "The open question," he said, "is the pause." "[W]e think the international advantages outweigh the international traps. We also think that firm and steady action in the south, together with public awareness of Chinese Communist danger, should keep most Americans in line with any decision you take on this matter." [15]

There was another meeting of Presidential advisers on December 4 at which the group considered the question of what North Vietnamese reactions would be judged satisfactory in deciding whether to continue a pause, and, conversely, what would prompt the U.S. to resume bombing.[16] Unlike earlier discussions of this subject, where it was argued by Rusk, particularly, that the North Vietnamese would have to demonstrate by their actions in withdrawing forces and ceasing violence in the South that they were serious about negotiating, at this meeting it was agreed that if the Communists said they would negotiate the U.S. "would be virtually compelled to continue the pause. . . . In other words, not only should the messages to Hanoi in any new pause not specifically require military reductions, but it should be recognized that we could get into a situation where the acceptance of negotiations in fact caused a substantial extension of the pause."

On December 6, there was a meeting of Rusk, McNamara, McGeorge Bundy, Ball, Vance, U. Alexis Johnson, William Bundy, McNaughton, Wheeler, Raborn and Clark Clifford.[17] After a brief presentation of the current and proposed military and nonmilitary programs, Clifford said he "wonders where the Hell we are going—further and further in with no prospect of a return." He was "sure" that the U.S. "*must do the job,*" but could it be done by "less costly means?" "Can't we use air power and hold in *defensive positions* on [the] ground without 600,000 ground *troops in jungle war*?" He was in favor of trying to "get the benefit of pause without pausing," adding, "This is the time to negotiate . . . one all-out effort with

---

[14] *Ibid.*

[15] *Ibid.*

[16] Notes on this meeting by William Bundy, which are in his possession, were used in his description, ch. 3, pp. 20–21 of his manuscript. He does not state who specifically attended the meeting. McGeorge Bundy also took a few notes on the meeting, but they are too cursory to be useful.

[17] Johnson Library, McGeorge Bundy Notes on Vietnam. There are also sketchy notes dated December 5 which apparently are Bundy's own summary of the questions to be answered in a presentation to the President, and a similar set of notes on December 6.

some indication that it *is* a last minute effort." (emphases in original)

General Wheeler replied that the U.S. was taking the initiative and was "pouring it on" in South Vietnam. He was opposed to a pause: "any substantial pause will allow them to repair and move. We've paid price once in planes and pilots; we'd have to pay it again. Violent reaction is possible in our own public. The other side will get a wrong signal. Once you stop it's hard to start again, and you could shake GVN to its toenails."

On December 7, 1965, Rusk, McNamara, and McGeorge Bundy met with the President in Texas.[18] The President began by emphasizing the need for more non-military action by more senior U.S. officials with "rank and energy"—an indirect reference to Lansdale, among others. McNamara responded by referring to Lansdale as "a bunch of hot air—a good talker—use him on the Hill [Capitol Hill]."[19]

"What is the best course?" the President asked, "we mustn't take off into the wild blue yonder. I don't want to take off till I know I can get back." "What makes it tough: I've had little real sympathy with Fulbright but I don't see any light down that barrel [escalation]. We're getting deeper and deeper in. 'I bogged my car down. I don't want a bulldozer to come and get me.'" "Where we were when I came in," he said, "I'd trade back to where we were." But he added: "If I have to decide this morning, full steam ahead."

Rusk replied that the "middle choice is still right—as against the alternatives." (There is no explanation of this comment, but presumably Rusk was referring to a continuation of the U.S. course of action without moving toward a compromise that might undermine U.S. policy and goals, on the one hand, or extreme military action on the other.)

The President asked Rusk whether the Communists were "getting ready for a peace offer." Rusk replied, "Not yet." McNamara said that they appeared to be escalating.

The President then turned to the bombing pause proposal: "Is there any chance?" he asked. McNamara and McGeorge Bundy replied that there was "some." McNamara said he would not have proposed a pause "if he didn't think we could manipulate it all." "We ought to probe [diplomatically]," he added, and the President replied: "We tried that, every which way, all over the world with our shirttail out . . . we were prayin' to negotiate." "We don't have

---

[18] The only known notes on this meeting are those by McGeorge Bundy, same location. See also memoranda from McGeorge Bundy to the President on December 4, and 6. A copy of the December 4 memorandum is in the Johnson Library, NSF Memos to the President—McGeorge Bundy. The memorandum of December 6, to which are attached copies of a December 6 memorandum by William Bundy on the pause, as well as suggested points for a Presidential statement, a draft of questions and answers, and the draft of a Presidential speech at the U.N., is in the Department of State, Central File, Pol 27 Viet S. In the same location there is a letter on December 4 to the President from Arthur Goldberg, U.S. Ambassador to the U.N., explaining his reasons for supporting a pause.

Maxwell Taylor was opposed to a pause, and in a memorandum to McNamara on December 6, (Johnson Library, NSF Country File, Vietnam) he said that during his travels since becoming a Presidential consultant on Vietnam in August 1965, he had become impressed with the need for better public information on the war. Referring to a statement on December 4 from the National Council of Churches advocating not just a bombing pause but a cease-fire, he said that, rather than a pause, he would prefer a "carefully reasoned" statement by a senior U.S. official which would attempt to answer some of the major questions about U.S. policy.

[19] For his part, Lansdale thought McNamara did not understand the nature of the problem in Vietnam. See pt. II of this study, pp. 107.

much of a leadership," he added, apparently referring to Congress. Rusk commented that there was a chance of getting the support of Fulbright and the Kennedys "if we convince them we're willing to make peace." The President said he did not think so. McNamara: "Won't get Fulbright. He wants to let Commies [Communists] in." The President: "Won't get Mansfield either."[20]

The President, saying he wondered "where the moderates went," told his advisers that they should consult with Mansfield, Dirksen, Robert Kennedy and Russell "before we go over board." "We're spending too much time with cry babies," he added. "I think we'll be spending more time defending ourselves from the hawks than from the doves—the hawks will be with you longer."[21]

On December 9, McGeorge Bundy sent the President a summary of the congressional talks. Almost all of those contacted—Democrats and Republicans—favored a bombing pause, increased U.S. military action (including bombing) if necessary to "win," and a congressional resolution supporting such action.[22] There was also a general feeling among those contacted that the public did not understand the war and was uncertain where it was leading and whether an expansion of U.S. action would make a difference.[23]

---

[20] This section, beginning with Rusk's comments about Fulbright and the Kennedys, is in someone else's handwriting on the note paper on which McGeorge Bundy had been making notes.

[21] In his memoirs, Lyndon Johnson refers to the meeting of December 7, but does not mention any of the above points. He says that after listening to the case for a pause he told his advisers that he was deeply troubled by the prospect that if the North Vietnamese did not make a positive response it might be difficult to resume bombing. His advisers, he says, replied that this would not be a serious problem, and, he adds: "As it turned out, of course, we received little credit for stopping the bombing and heavy criticism for renewing it." *The Vantage Point*, p. 235.

[22] Bundy also had a congressional resolution drafted. A draft prepared on December 6 provided for reaffirming the Gulf of Tonkin Resolution and the U.S. commitment to unconditional negotiations. It declared, as had the Gulf of Tonkin Resolution, that the U.S. was prepared, "as the President determines, to take all military action, including the use of armed force." But it provided also that "the President is authorized to take such action against the Communist regime in North Vietnam as the continued and belligerent aggression of that regime makes necessary." Moreover, it provided for authority to call up the Reserves in support of military action. (This draft of December 6 is located in the Johnson Library, NSF Country File, Vietnam. There are no notations to indicate where or by whom it was drafted.)

On December 17, the State Department's Legal Adviser, Leonard Meeker, sent McGeorge Bundy drafts of two alternative congressional resolutions. (Meeker's memorandum and the alternative drafts are also in the Johnson Library, NSF Country File, Vietnam.) In a cover memorandum he noted that "*A* emphasizes peaceful settlement rather more than *B*." Both versions provided that the U.S. would continue to make "every possible effort to bring about a just and enduring peace in Southeast Asia," and that Congress "approves and supports the proposal of the President for unconditional negotiations. . . ." Both stated that the U.S. was "prepared . . . to take all necessary military action, as the President determines, to bring the aggression to an end," but neither contained a specific reference to action against North Vietnam.

Both versions contained a very specific provision authorizing the President to call up the Reserves and to extend tours of duty of those already on active duty.

In the introductory, "whereas" section of the draft of December 6 and in both drafts of December 17, there is language noting that the U.S. had made a "further effort" to promote a settlement of the war by suspending air attacks against North Vietnam. This, as Meeker noted in his cover memorandum, was included "on the assumption of a pause in effect when Congress is considering the Joint Resolution." This would suggest that at the time the drafts were prepared there was the expectation that action by Congress would occur during January 1966 if the President decided to request a resolution. Although the President appears not to have agreed to a schedule for the pause, his advisers generally assumed that it would last until the end of January, although there were some, including Ball, who were working on extending it.

[23] For McGeorge Bundy's report on congressional talks see his memorandum to the President on Dec. 9, 1965, with an attached memorandum from McNamara on his telephone calls to Members, Johnson Library, NSF Memos to the President—McGeorge Bundy. Those contacted were Senators John J. Sparkman (D/Ala.), Frank Church (D/Idaho), John O. Pastore (D/R.I.), A. S. Mike Monroney (D/Okla.), Warren G. Magnuson (D/Wash.), Sam J. Ervin, Jr., (D/N.C.), Robert Kennedy (D/N.Y.), Leverett Saltonstall (R/Mass.), Thomas H. Kuchel (R/Calif.), and Jacob K. Javits (R/N.Y.), Speaker John W. McCormack (D/Mass.), and Representatives F. Edward Hébert

Continued

Senator Mansfield, the majority leader and a member of the Foreign Relations Committee, who had been active and influential in the shaping of U.S. policy toward Vietnam for many years,[24] was contacted in Asia where he and several other Senators were on a study trip. He replied that he had been opposed to bombing, but doubted whether a pause would be fruitful, especially if it were intended as preparation for escalation. If it were undertaken, he said, there should be other U.S. initiatives, perhaps including a cease-fire of about a month.[25]

There is no information as to whether an attempt was made to contact Senator Fulbright, who had already suggested publicly the desirability of a pause.[26]

On December 17, 1965, the President met in Washington from 9:41 a.m. to 11:04 a.m. with his principal advisers. Present were Rusk, McNamara, McGeorge Bundy and Ball. Valenti and Moyers also attended. The President said to the group, "I'm willing to take any gamble on stopping the bombing if I think I've got some hope for something happening. We must evaluate this carefully. You have no idea of how much I've talked to the Fulbrights and Lippmanns. They're not coming aboard.[27] McNamara responded: "We will increase bombing. It is inevitable. We must step up our attacks. . . . There is no way to stop bombing in the North except as part of a political move."

Ball said he thought the bombing of the north was having a negative effect. The resistance of the North Vietnamese was hardening, and they were being driven into greater dependency on China. Russia was being "boxed in." Negotiations were more difficult, rather than easier. He recommended stopping the bombing but redoubling military action in the south.

McNamara said, "We just don't know if we are hurting the North Vietnamese or the Chinese." "We may be able to hurt them enough with our 400,000 men to make them behave differently." But, again indicating his growing qualms about U.S. policy, he added, "If we don't, what should we do? We shouldn't be doing anything that has a one-in-three chance. Perhaps a cease-fire in place." McGeorge Bundy replied, "Not now. It takes time." Rusk said, "It could cause the dissolution of South Vietnam." McNamara repeated, "Our mili-

---

(D/La.), Gerald R. Ford (R/Mich.) and Leslie C. Arends (R/Ill.). Calls were made to about an equal number of others, but Congress had adjourned and they were unavailable.

[24] See pts. I-III of this study.

[25] U.S. Department of State, Central File, Pol 27 Viet S, Washington to Hong Kong 762, Dec. 9, 1965, and Manila to Washington 1132, Dec. 10, 1965.

Presidential assistant Joe Califano preferred a cease-fire, with an accompanying diplomatic gesture, to a pause. (See his memorandum to the President on Dec. 13, 1965, Johnson Library, C.F. ND 19/CO 312.) The President, through Moyers, asked McGeorge Bundy to consider the idea. After meeting with Califano and Moyers, Bundy sent a memorandum to the President on December 14 in which he discussed the advantages and disadvantages of that alternative, but concluded that a pause—which he said was strongly favored by Rusk and McNamara and all of their senior staff—was preferable. Johnson Library, NSF Memos to the President—McGeorge Bundy.

[26] *New York Times*, Oct. 25, 1965.

[27] Notes of this meeting by Jack Valenti are in the Johnson Library, Meetings Notes File. Jack Valenti used the notes almost verbatim in his book, *A Very Human President* (New York: W. W. Norton, 1975), but he occasionally added as well as omitted material. In the quotation given here, for example, he added in his book: "'but we must listen to what they are saying.'"

It should also be mentioned that of the deletions made in 1982 by the executive branch when it released these notes, almost all of those portions which were deleted had already been printed in Valenti's book in 1975.

McGeorge Bundy also kept brief notes, which are in his papers at the Johnson Library, Notes on Vietnam, but they do not add to Valenti's account of this meeting.

tary has one-in-three success orders," to which Bundy replied, "I'm more optimistic. Our military is hurting them." "That [cease-fire in place] has some appeal to me," the President replied. "The problem is the Chiefs go through the roof when we mention this pause." McNamara: "I can take on the Chiefs. . . . We decide what we want and impose it on them. They see this as a total military problem—nothing will change their views."

The President said, "I don't think you can sell the American people on the merits of stopping the bombing," but said he thought the administration had an obligation to the public to try to persuade the Communists that the U.S. wanted peace. "Let's put off bombing until we can talk to others." He added: "Let McNamara say to the Chiefs: We've got a heavy budget, tax bill, controls, danger of inflation, kill this great society. With all these things, we've got to make sure the diplomats can talk." He suggested the period from December 22 through January 22.

"They are right," the President said (he did not specify, but appears to have been referring to the Communists), "the weakest chink in our armor is public opinion. Our people won't stand firm—and will bring down the Government." "We're going to suffer political losses. Every President does in off [nonelection] years. But it is because of damn fool liberals who are crying about poverty (which funds I doubled in one year)."

Later that day, the President met for an hour with General Wheeler.[28]

The next day, December 18, 1965, the President met from 12:34 p.m. to 2:19 p.m., and from 3:10 p.m. to 5:10 p.m. with Rusk, McNamara, McGeorge Bundy, Ball and U. Alexis Johnson, who were joined by Supreme Court Justice Abe Fortas and Clark Clifford.[29] Valenti and Moyers also were present. The President said he had talked to General Wheeler, Chairman of the JCS, who presented all of the reasons why the JCS was opposed to a pause, and that he could understand better what McNamara was "living with." "The military," he said, "say a month's pause would undo all we've done." "That's baloney," McNamara said, "and I can prove it." The President replied: "I don't think so. I disagree. I think it contains serious military risks."

The timing of the pause was discussed, and McGeorge Bundy commented, among other things: "Christmas time is a good time psychologically—also get it started before Congress comes back."

The President asked Rusk what he thought of a pause. Rusk replied: "First, there is the underlying question of the American people. They are isolationists at heart. I am convinced the people will do what has to be done in a war situation if they are convinced there is no alternative. You must think about the morale of the American people if the other side keeps pushing. We must be able to say that *all* has been done." (emphasis in original) "Second, it's

---

[28] There are no known notes on the meeting.

[29] Valenti notes in the Johnson Library, Meetings Notes File. McGeorge Bundy also kept brief, cursory notes on the meeting, located in his papers in the Johnson Library, Notes on Vietnam, which do not add to Valenti's account of the meeting.

In preparation for the meeting, the State Department prepared on December 18 five draft papers; 1. an outline of the U.S. public position (cited above), 2. a cable to Lodge, 3. a scenario of diplomatic action, 4. a statement for Rusk or Thompson to give to Dobrynin, 5. a circular cable to be sent to selected U.S. Embassies. Copies of these are in the Johnson Library, NSF Country File, Vietnam.

our deepest national purpose to achieve our goal by peace not war. If there is one chance in ten or twenty a step of this sort could lead to a settlement on the Geneva agreements and 17th parallel, I would take it. One chance in twenty is my guess."

Rusk also thought a pause would give the Russians a chance to "start a movement toward peace." "Try to create a heavy obligation on the Russian's part to settle. If we pause, they will owe us something."

A "minor point," Rusk said, would be to "make sure the world knows that the U.S. is not the obstacle to peace."

One of Rusk's concerns, however, was that the pause might fail, which would "bring pressure to go all out to get it settled," to which the President replied: "That is the most dangerous aspect. Don't we know a pause will fail? If we are in worse shape then, won't we be bringing a deadly crisis on ourselves? The Republicans are looking for an exit. When we suffer reverses, it will be attributable to this. The support we have will be weak as dishwater."

McNamara, asked for his comments, said that the Russians were not applying maximum pressure on the North Vietnamese. "Have they ever applied pressure?" the President asked. "Yes, during the pause in May," Rusk replied. "Our first pause [May 1965]," McNamara responded, "was a propaganda effort. It was a propaganda effort—not for the Soviets to help."

"Military solution to problem is not certain," McNamara said, "—one out of three or one in two. Ultimately we must find alternative solution—must find diplomatic solution." The President: "Then, no matter what we do in military field there is no sure victory." McNamara: "That's right. We have been too optimistic." Rusk: "I'm more optimistic, but I can't prove it."

McNamara emphasized the need to use a bombing pause as one way of moving toward a settlement of the war: "Our military action approach is an unacceptable way to successful conclusion. . . . This seems a contradiction. I come to you for a huge increase in Vietnam—400,000 men. But at the same time it may lead to escalation and undesirable results. I suggest we look now at other alternatives." He went on to challenge the objections to a pause, including the argument that if the pause failed there would be pressure to escalate. "Republicans," he said, "don't dare suggest we bomb cities. P.O.L.? [petroleum, oil, lubricants] I will recommend we bomb them too. Mine Haiphong Harbor? I will suggest this later myself. Three to six months from now we will have to do this." "But danger is Russian reaction. It will be less if we have pause."

McGeorge Bundy said he agreed with McNamara that settlement "must be political." "This will be form of diplomatic initiative," he added.

Fortas and Clifford were opposed to the pause.[30] Public reaction, Fortas said, would be negative. "What they really want is cessation of hostilities . . . 'Anytime there is evidence of lack of certainty on the government's part, it leads to negative thinking in the public

---

[30] "Johnson knew exactly what Fortas would say and do. After all, they had enjoyed a three-hour intimate White House dinner the night before, which followed an hour-long meeting during the day. Johnson knew that the justice was prepared to support him to hell and back. And that was precisely why he was invited." Bruce Allen Murphy, *Fortas: The Rise and Ruin of A Supreme Court Justice* (New York: William Morrow, 1988), p. 243.

mind. It will cause people to worry about depth of conviction in government objective.'" He, too, thought that if the pause failed there would be new pressures for escalation, as well as greater difficulty in conducting future negotiations. He also thought that an action of the kind being considered would be "too little to get the Soviets to do anything."[31]

Clifford said he thought the Communists assumed that the U.S., like France, would tire of the fight and withdraw. Until they were convinced that this was not going to happen and that they would have nothing to gain by continuing to fight, they would not, in his opinion, be seriously interested in negotiating.[32]

McNamara persisted: "Should we pursue military estimate of 50-50 chance of victory—or what should we do?" "If we put in 400,000 men, what will they [the Communists] do? They will match us."

McGeorge Bundy again expressed his feeling that the situation was not as difficult as McNamara contended, and Rusk said he thought the U.S. could be in a more favorable position in a year or two: "I think the other side is hurting just as we are hurting."

Rusk said to McNamara, "I presume you don't think we can put [on] a greatly increased offensive?" McNamara replied, "No. We are increasing but so are the Viet Cong."

Having heard the discussion, the President, according to Valenti, stood up, "looked solemnly at the men around the table. Then he casually addressed McNamara. 'We'll take the pause.' With a slight wave of the hand, he strode from the room."[33]

The following day (December 19), Rusk sent a memorandum to the President, who had apparently requested it during the meeting, discussing the possibility of diplomatic action.[34] The U.S., Rusk said, had made its position clear, but to no avail. "We see no serious possibility of immediate diplomatic progress of a *public* nature unless we are prepared to change the conditions under which public diplomatic action could be undertaken. The principal change of condition available to us would be a pause in the bombing." Private discussions with the U.S.S.R., Hungary, Yugoslavia and others should continue, he added, "to make sure that at least the Eastern

---

[31] Although Fortas was opposed to the pause, he apparently had doubts about U.S. involvement in the war. On Jan. 7, 1966, during the pause, he sent the President a memorandum suggesting the possibility of a U.S. offer, through the United Nations, to accept a cease-fire, followed by early U.S. withdrawal. He said that although this might ultimately result in Communist domination of Southeast Asia, "it is possible that we can deal with the long-range, with future problems, more advantageously if we are *out* of Viet Nam than if we are there, engaged in what appears to be a long war of dubious extent and debatable outcome." (emphasis in original) Laura Kalman, *Abe Fortas* (New Haven, Conn. Yale Univ. Press, 1990), p. 297 from the Fortas papers.

[32] When Clifford finished his statement the President handed him a note, as follows: "Magnificent. To sum up—as Abraham Lincoln said—'You can't fertilize a field by farting thru the fence.'" Clark M. Clifford and Richard C. Holbrooke, *Counsel to the President* (New York: Random House, 1991), p. 436. This note is in the Johnson Library, Clifford Papers, Handwritten Notes.

David L. DiLeo, *George Ball, Vietnam and the Rethinking of Containment* (Chapel Hill: Univ. of North Carolina Press, 1991), p. 118, a useful if somewhat hagiographic study, errs in stating that Clifford joined Ball in opposing the bombing pause.

[33] Valenti, *A Very Human President*, p. 240.

[34] Rusk's memorandum, with a cover note from McGeorge Bundy of Dec. 19, 1965, is in the Department of State, Central File, Pol 27 Viet S.

In November 1965, the State Department and the Arms Control and Disarmament Agency began issuing a "Weekly Report Concerning Negotiations on Vietnam." This report, which was continued at least through Sept. 9, 1966, contained a summary of information on negotiating activity obtained from the U.S. and other government sources, newspapers and radio broadcasts. Copies are located in the Department of State, Central File, Pol 27 Viet S.

European Communists fully understand our position and understand that Hanoi's insistence upon their four points (amounting to victory in South Vietnam) is the central obstacle to peace." (emphasis in original)

"The central point," Rusk concluded, "is that diplomacy cannot produce miracles if Hanoi remains determined to seize South Vietnam. . . . In this instance diplomacy is working within the limitations imposed by Hanoi's objectives in South Vietnam, which are still in fundamental conflict with our own, and Hanoi's continuing hope that they can somehow succeed on the battlefield."

On December 21, Ambassador Lodge sent a memorandum to General Wheeler commenting on the proposed pause.[35] (It is not known why Lodge would have sent such a memorandum to Wheeler out of State Department channels.) He said that the proposal "rests on some fundamental misconceptions as to the real nature of communist governments and would, if carried out, tend to defeat its own purpose . . . [it] will lead the communists away from negotiations because it will be interpreted by them as being a sign of weakness and indecision." The Communists, he said, "can only be induced to follow a certain course by the application of pressure. . . . The way to end this war, therefore, is by the application of U.S. influence and U.S. force. If talks should ever begin, they must be held to the accompaniment of the application of force or else they are foredoomed to failure."

"Indefinite cessation of bombing without cessation of the Viet Cong aggression," Lodge said, "would leave the Viet Cong free to devastate the South with impunity while we tie our hands down in the North." Moreover, it would "collapse morale" in the South Vietnamese Army and would "bring about the collapse of the government or its determined opposition."

"Cessation of bombing," Lodge added, "should be equated with withdrawal of North Vietnamese units through international checkpoints to the North; unimpeded access of the GVN to any part of its territory; a significant reduction of incidents; cessation of infiltration of men and materiel; and an agreement that at any talks which would be held the matter of an inspection system and enforcement devices should be the first item on the agenda."

On December 21, at a brief meeting from 12:25 p.m. to 1:00 p.m. with Rusk, McNamara, McGeorge Bundy, Ball and U. Alexis Johnson (Valenti was also present), the President again indicated his doubts about a pause:[36]

> 1. Once we take our step, we could have serious problems to resume bombing.
>
> 2. The danger is that it conveys the wrong signal—and I think it does.
>
> If men we rely on to fight for us feel as strongly as they do—as Lodge does—I'd hate to have them at odds with us.

A pause, he said "is more a sign of weakness than anything else. All we'll get is distrust from our allies, despair from the troops, and disgruntled generals.

[35] Massachusetts Historical Society, Lodge Papers.

[36] Valenti's notes are in the Johnson Library, Meetings Notes File. McGeorge Bundy's very brief notes are in his papers, Notes on Vietnam.

"Hanoi and Peking tell us we're weak—won't do anything if we pause. If we suffer a severe reverse as a result of this, we'd never explain it. . . . I want more evidence from the Russians before I override Taylor and Wheeler et al."

The group discussed how a pause could and should be announced and how long it should last. The President was not inclined to announce a pause, and it apparently was not clear whether he even intended to have one. He favored announcing only the 30-hour cease-fire that the U.S. and the South Vietnamese had agreed upon; then, McGeorge Bundy said, the U.S. could continue the pause without making any announcement, and could decide when to resume bombing. Rusk, on the other hand, with the support of U. Alexis Johnson, Llewellyn Thompson and William Bundy, was in favor of a long pause (about one month) which would be announced in advance in order to provide enough time for the Russians and others to try to initiate negotiations.

The meeting of December 21 ended without agreement on a pause.

On December 22, the U.S. and South Vietnam announced that there would be a 30-hour cease-fire, including bombing of the North, until December 25, but that hostilities would not be resumed unless the Communists compelled such a move.[37]

On December 21, the President returned to Texas, "leaving his subordinates," according to William Bundy, "feeling that he had either decided against a serious bombing pause, or was waiting to see whether something came of the ceasefire."[38]

---

[37] On December 24, a joint State-Defense cable to Saigon explaining the terms of the cease-fire stated that U.S. forces would not respond to minor incidents and that the responsibility for renewing hostilities would fall on the Communists. See U.S. Department of State, Central File, Pol 27 Viet S, Washington to Saigon 1786, Dec. 24, 1965.

[38] William Bundy MS, ch. 33, pp. 31–32.

On December 23, following a conversation between Rusk and Bill Moyers, several officials in the State Department were asked by Rusk to suggest new diplomatic initiatives that could be taken in Vietnam. The following is a very brief summary of their views (the papers of all but Rostow are in the Department of State, Central File, Pol 27 Viet S; Rostow's reply of December 23 is in Lot File 70 D 48 attached to a memorandum of December 27 from the Executive Secretary Benjamin H. Read, to Rusk):

U. Alexis Johnson: "[O]ur best negotiating initiative at this time would be no further initiative. The fundamental problem of this war is influencing the *will* of Hanoi. I am convinced that any further negotiating move on our part would persuade them that our action was primarily dictated by our concern over domestic and international pressures against us, and thus that we are more anxious than they to find a compromise solution." This, he said, would encourage the Communists to press on in the belief that the U.S. would not be able to fight a protracted war.

William Bundy: The U.S. might develop a list of points, comparable to the Communists' Four Points declaration of May 1965, which might be used as a basis for negotiating. (*Note:* This may have been the genesis of the idea that led in January 1966 to the U.S. 14-point declaration—see below.) He also suggested that bombing could be adjusted to the pace of Communist military activity, thus possibly leading to a progressive de-escalation of hostilities.

Leonard Meeker (State Department Legal Adviser): escalation would not lead to negotiations, and it would be better to undertake a political and diplomatic offensive, beginning with an armistice (cease-fire) for 30 days which would be followed by a peace conference. (*Author's note:* This summary does not do justice to Meeker's very thoughtful paper.)

W. W. Rostow's paper, which he sent directly to the President on December 23 at the suggestion of Jack Valenti, is broader than those summarized above; (conceivably, once it was submitted, the other three may have been asked to state their views on diplomatic initiatives). On the subject of negotiations, he proposed establishing contact with a North Vietnamese representative to see if they wanted to talk. If this was not successful, the U.S. should systematically bomb oil refineries and storage as well as power plants in the Hanoi-Haiphong area. This, he said, might induce the North Vietnamese to negotiate, adding that the U.S. had "an enormous stake at home and abroad in forcing an early, rather than late, ending to the war in Vietnam." He also suggested that the U.S. should assist in building a new, broadly-based political party in South Vietnam to help overcome what he called "the central political weakness in the developing nations"—lack of the national political discipline necessary to govern.

During this period, Bundy says, the President appeared to be very agitated.[39] "On all sides the subject [a bombing pause] was in the air, a fact which in itself drove the President to several outbursts that his staff were leaking. Quite surely this was not so; the planning papers were narrowly held, and the advocates of a pause, above all, knew that leaks in friendly quarters would affect the President in a harshly negative direction. Perhaps, as sometimes seemed to be the case, Lyndon Johnson could not take in that people outside the government could sense the policy possibilities about as well as those inside it. More likely, in this instance, he lashed out at his subordinates because he could not hit at the wider sources of the pressures beating on him. The problem was 'fencing him in,' and he hated being fenced in."

Bundy also notes that the President was developing a very closed and personal system of making decisions. Partly as a result of "his innate preference for keeping his subordinates both guessing and familiar only with a part of the picture" the President, Bundy says, was often "a complete mystery to subordinates at my level . . . and so far as I can tell as much of a mystery to his Secretaries of State and Defense"—and "by December [1965] it was almost impossible to tell how he was reacting and how he might decide to act." The development of this more personal system of making decisions on the war was due also, Bundy suggests, to the pressures which the war was creating for the President: "The war, it is not unfair to say, was beginning to get to him."[40]

The Pause Begins

On December 26, 1965, U.S. forces resumed operations in South Vietnam, but the President allowed the bombing pause to remain in effect. Meanwhile, Rusk sought to determine whether there was going to be any significant response to the pause from the Communists.[41] The next day, after talking by telephone with the President, McGeorge Bundy telephoned Rusk at the President's direction "to urge him to get on every diplomatic wire and tell people that there has been no noise over North Vietnam for four days and that we certainly would like to know if anyone has heard any signal of any sort that this lack of action has done any good."[42] After the conversation, Bundy reported to the President that Rusk was "very resistant indeed" and that he (Rusk), Thompson, U. Alexis Johnson and William Bundy "all think that we cannot get diplomatic mileage this way." "They really would prefer to resume bombing right away and have a longer pause later on, with advance notice to the Russians, as they initially recommended last week." Bundy said that he then "gently tried to say" to Rusk that there had been a pause of four days, and "the question was what use we could make of it if we continued for another period of up to a week," but that Rusk "continued to resist my suggestion." "I

[39] William Bundy MS, ch. 33, pp. 27–28.

[40] *Ibid.*, pp. 35–36. See also William Bundy's observations in his article, "The National Security Process," *International Security*, 7 (Winter 1982), pp. 94–109 at 100–101.

[41] For these efforts, see William Bundy MS, ch. 33, pp. 32–35.

[42] Johnson Library, NSF Memos to the President—McGeorge Bundy, Memorandum to the President from Bundy, Dec. 27, 1965.

do not feel," Bundy told the President, "that I should make further diplomatic contacts tonight behind his back."

Bundy concluded by suggesting to the President that if he decided—"as I myself hope you may"—to continue the pause for several more days, he might want to speak to Rusk about making a concerted effort to explore possible interest on the part of the Communists.[43]

The President, probably after receiving McGeorge Bundy's report on his conversation with Rusk, called Bundy and asked him when bombing was scheduled to begin again. Chester Cooper, who was present in the room, says that during the telephone call he was asked by Bundy whether he had seen any orders, and Cooper said he had not. Bundy told the President that he would check with McNamara. After calling McNamara, who also said that he had not seen any orders, and who agreed with Bundy's suggestion of extending the pause at least through New Year's Day, Bundy reported this to the President.

Shapley says that on that same day (December 27) McNamara flew from Colorado, where he was vacationing, to Texas, where he had dinner with the President and then talked with him from 8:05 p.m. to 10:55 p.m. There is no record of that conversation, but Shapley speculates that McNamara "took advantage of the absence of Dean Rusk . . . to work on Johnson to continue the ban on bombing and to make a major diplomatic effort toward Hanoi." That night, she adds, the President made dozens of phone calls after deciding to begin the "peace offensive," as it was called.[44]

Late that night (December 27), according to Cooper's account, "The two Bundy brothers were summoned from a Debutante Ball. Clad in white tie and tails, they went to the State Department and, together with Secretary Rusk, dispatched the orders extending the pause *sine-die* [without a specific termination date]."[45]

Why did the President decide to approve an extended bombing pause? William Bundy says that it was in part because Johnson wanted peace, and that (Bundy was told later) "Christmas spent in part with younger people who might be called to war had a real effect on his attitudes." But beyond his personal desires, the President, Bundy says,[46]

> was a practical man trying to figure out a way to meet his twin objectives of carrying the war through successfully and of launching the Great Society. Here, the over-riding practical calculation was whether a frontal confrontation with Congress, laying all the cards face up, would be helpful, or the reverse.

[43]That same day, (December 27), probably before telling the President about his talk with Rusk, McGeorge Bundy had sent a memorandum to the President (same location, "Further Notes on Bombing the North,") reporting that in a meeting on Vietnam that afternoon with a group of public affairs officers—probably the committee set up earlier by the White House—all of them had agreed that if the pause was going to continue for another day or so it should then go on for long enough "to be a real answer to our critics." Moreover, he said, Bill Moyers had told him that since the pause had gone on for three days, it should be extended through New Year's Day. Also, General Taylor "now feels very strongly that since we have endured three days of pause, we might as well go on for long enough to take the starch out of the idea once and for all." Taylor said that if the pause were extended he would explain to Westmoreland and Sharp the importance of doing so "from the point of view of proving to the American public that we have left no door to peace untried." Taylor, Bundy said, "does not think the military cost is great. He thinks the political reward of a solid pause is worth it at this stage."

[44]Shapley, *Promise and Power*, p. 364.

[45]Cooper, *The Lost Crusade*, pp. 291–292.

[46]William Bundy MS, ch. 33, pp. 36–37.

I am sure he concluded that such a confrontation would be a disaster, more likely for the Great Society than for the war, and was looking for any way to avoid having the pressures build up for it. From this, it is only a short speculative step to the conclusion that a key factor on the bombing pause may have been its impact in pre-empting attention through the January period, when Congress and the country would again be focused on the new war on which the country was embarked [Phase II]. With the pause to the fore, the President must surely have thought, there would be enough uncertainty to forestall the demands so clearly latent in December, that Congress take a hard look at the war and take some new authorizing action.

The President was also aware of the results of a Harris Survey in late December 1965, published on January 3, 1966, which indicated that there was strong public support for a temporary ceasefire or a pause in bombing to test the interest of the Communists in negotiating.[47] Nationwide, 73 percent favored a temporary ceasefire (20 percent were opposed, 7 percent not sure); 59 percent favored a pause in bombing (33 percent were opposed and 8 percent not sure). Respondents were also asked whether, if the Communists did not agree to negotiate, they would favor or oppose "all-out U.S. bombings of every part of Vietnam," and the response was 61 percent in favor, 22 percent opposed, and 17 percent not sure.

In a poll by Gallup for CBS News taken at about the same time the question was asked: "Which do you think is more likely to bring about a peaceful settlement in Vietnam—to stop bombing temporarily to show that we really want peace, or to increase our bombing to show that we mean business?" The response was: stop bombing temporarily, 21 percent; increase bombing, 58 percent; no opinion, 21 percent.[48]

Juxtaposing the results of this Gallup Poll and the Harris Survey on January 3, it would appear that a majority of the public was willing to try a bombing pause, but, by about the same percentage, doubted whether, as a way to achieve a peaceful settlement, it would be as effective as increased bombing. (There may, of course, have been other factors, such as the wording of the questions and the period of time during which the polls were taken, especially in relation to the President's announcement of a pause.)

The U.S. Mission in Saigon was notified of the reasons for the extended pause, code-named Operation PINTA.[49] Lodge was told by Rusk that Washington policymakers did not expect North Vietnamese to respond "in any significant way," but that Communist propaganda "should be tested and exposed." There was, however, some hope that a pause could help to "drive rift between Communist powers and between Hanoi and the NLF." A major factor, the cable stated, was the decision to deploy Phase II forces: "The prospect of large scale reinforcement in men and defense budget increases of some twenty billions for next eighteen month period requires solid

---

[47] *Washington Post,* Jan. 3, 1966.

[48] CBS News Press Release, Dec. 14, 1965, in author's files.

[49] U.S. Department of State, Central File, Pol 27 Viet S, Washington to Saigon 1805, Dec. 28, 1965. A similar message was sent by McNamara to Westmoreland, Secdef 5041–65, Dec. 29, 1965, CMH, Westmoreland Papers. Westmoreland was told to divert to Laos (the infiltration route along the Ho Chi Minh Trail) all bombing missions that otherwise would have been carried out over North Vietnam. Secdef 5039–65, Dec. 28, 1965, same location.

preparation of American public. A crucial element will be clear demonstration that we have explored fully every alternative but that aggressor has left us no choice." (On the same day as the cable from Washington, Lodge, probably after receiving it, talked with Westmoreland about the war. According to the account in his diary, Westmoreland told Lodge—and noted in the diary that Lodge agreed with his comments—"that unless we escalated to the point where all weapons available to us were used against the enemy I foresaw an extended war of attrition. This I thought we could win since our troops should always be fresh because of the one year tour, and with our firepower and mobility I did not believe the VC and North Vietnamese could afford to sustain the heavy losses that would probably be theirs. However, I made the point that this was going to create some political difficulties because it is inevitable that the American people would clamor for a quick victory which would be difficult to achieve without major escalation.")[50]

Simultaneously with his decision to extend the pause, the President launched an intensive diplomatic campaign to publicize the bombing pause and to emphasize U.S. willingness to negotiate. Vice President Humphrey went to Japan, Harriman visited ten countries, McGeorge Bundy went to Canada, Goldberg visited Rome and the Vatican as well as Paris, Assistant Secretary of State for African Affairs, G. Mennan Williams, went to 14 African countries, and Assistant Secretary of State for Latin America, Thomas Mann, went to Mexico City. In all, special U.S. emissaries were sent to 34 governments. A message was also sent to the North Vietnamese through their consulate in Rangoon, Burma, inviting them to reciprocate "by making a serious contribution to peace."[51]

In a telephone conversation with Harriman on December 28, the President said "we don't have much confidence that much will come out of this [the peace offensive] but that is no reason not to try. . . . I think with your friends Fulbright, Scotty Reston, Mansfield, Arthur Krock and the *New York Times,* all these people thinking there could be peace if we were only willing to have peace, we ought to give it the old college try."[52]

That same day the President also telephoned Ball, who apparently had been made responsible for coordinating the "peace offensive," to urge him to act resolutely. According to notes of the conversation, taken by Ball's secretary who was monitoring the call,[53]

> Pres asked Ball to give him the gist *[sic]* of what was being transmitted. President told Ball he wanted him here because he was inspiring, stimulating and "shoving" just as he had on

---

[50] CMH, Westmoreland Papers, History File, Notes for Dec. 29, 1965. In a cable on December 27 to Wheeler, which Wheeler sent to the White House (CJCS 271559Z), a copy of which is in the Department of State, Central File, Pol 27 Viet S, Westmoreland said that he considered the resumption of bombing "essential." "Our only hope of a major impact on the ability of the DRV to support the war in Vietnam is continuous air attack over the entire length of their LOCs from the Chinese border to South Vietnam, and within South Vietnam."

[51] See the description in Thies, *When Governments Collide,* pp. 116–121. For documentation, see George C. Herring, *The Secret Diplomacy of the Vietnam War: The Negotiating Volumes of the Pentagon Papers* (Austin: Univ. of Texas Press, 1983).

William Bundy says that Harriman's visit to Poland was "by far the most serious part of the effort. The Poles at that time were close both to Hanoi and to Moscow, and Averell made a particular effort there . . . that to me was the real focus and the rest was a good deal of chaff." (Communication from William Bundy to the author, July 1993.)

[52] Library of Congress, Harriman Papers, Telephone Memcons.

[53] Johnson Library, Papers of George Ball, "Presidential Telecons."

two or three other occasions in this field. Pres said even if all this [peace offensive] comes to naught he would feel better. He said he had to survive this thing. He has 3 more years to go and he said he wanted Ball sitting at the bridge calling the signals and he is not to let "them" talk him out of "it." Pres told Ball to get his Dutch toes in concrete and is to say "this is what the man (the Pres) wants and I am here to shove."

After Ball reported to the President on the steps being taken, with accompanying comments and suggestions by the President, the conversation ended with this injunction by the President: "Pres said he was depending on Ball as his lawyer and his devil's advocate. Pres said Ball was not to let 'them' talk him out of anything. Pres said Ball should stay right on it until we are sure we have bled it for all it is worth."

On December 29, Rusk held a press conference in which he urged the North Vietnamese to respond constructively to the pause and offered a new U.S. formulation of 14 negotiating points (which he had personally drafted), as follows:[54]

1. The Geneva Agreements of 1954 and 1962 are an adequate basis for peace in Southeast Asia;
2. We would welcome a conference on Southeast Asia or on any part thereof;
3. We would welcome "negotiations without pre-conditions," as the 17 nations put it; [this referred to a proposal of the 17 "non-committed" nations of which India was one of the principal leaders].
4. We would welcome unconditional discussions, as President Johnson put it;
5. A cessation of hostilities could be the first order of business at a conference or could be the subject of preliminary discussions;
6. Hanoi's four points could be discussed along with other points which others might wish to propose;
7. We want no U.S. bases in Southeast Asia;
8. We do not desire to retain U.S. troops in South Viet-Nam after peace is assured;
9. We support free elections in South Viet-Nam to give the South Vietnamese a government of their own choice;
10. The questions of reunification of Viet-Nam should be determined by the Vietnamese through their own free decision;
11. The countries of Southeast Asia can be non-aligned or neutral if that be their option;
12. We would much prefer to use our resources for the economic reconstruction of Southeast Asia than in war. If there is peace, North Viet-Nam could participate in a regional effort to

[54] *Department of State Bulletin,* Jan. 17 and Feb. 14, 1966. See also David Kraslow and Stuart H. Loory, *The Secret Search for Peace in Vietnam* (New York: Random House, 1968), pp. 137 ff.

Chester Cooper commented later (*The Lost Crusade,* p. 296) that, "where finely tooled instruments were required, we used a sledgehammer. Where confidential and careful advance work were necessary, we proceeded with the subtlety of a Fourth of July parade. Where a dramatic, surprise proposal may have stirred Hanoi's interest, we made a public spectacle of every melodramatic move. Instead of maximizing the effect of our fourteen-point peace package, we buried it in the razzmatazz of sudden, noisy, and florid VIP trips. In short, the President was acting like a ringmaster of a three-ring circus, rather than as the focal point of a carefully worked out exercise in diplomacy."

which we would be prepared to contribute at least one billion dollars;

13. The President has said "The Viet Cong would not have difficulty being represented and having their views represented if for a moment Hanoi decided she wants to cease aggression. I don't think that would be an insurmountable problem."

14. We have said publicly and privately that we could stop the bombing of North Viet-Nam as a step toward peace although there has not been the slightest hint or suggestion from the other side as to what they would do if the bombing stopped.[55]

On December 30, the President, who was in Texas, called Ball to suggest that he should talk to Fulbright, Mansfield and

---

[55] In a cable to Lodge on Jan. 1, 1966, which he drafted personally, Rusk discussed his own view on the question of negotiations (U.S. Department of State, Central File, Pol 27 Viet S, Washington to Saigon 1865, Jan. 2, 1966):

"At heart of problem remains Hanoi's determination to grab South Viet-Nam by force. If that changes, other problems would begin to fall into place; until it does change I am not too much interested in shadow boxing on side issues. We have put forward publicly about all we have to offer for a peace basket. Hanoi's only contribution is their four points, the third of which is what the fighting is all about. [The four points were North Vietnam's statement of principles for a political settlement. (See pt. III of this study, p. 218.) The third point provided that the internal affairs of South Vietnam would have to be settled by the South Vietnamese "in accordance with the program of the South Vietnam National Front for Liberation."]

"If we get to negotiations, I am tempted by the possibility of a QUOTE conference in absentia UNQUOTE where the two co-chairmen would be the only ones to sit at a table to try to find a peaceful solution. An alternative would be for the three ICC nations to attempt the same role. Such middlemen would have to get the agreement of, as a minimum, the Governments of South Viet-Nam, the United States and Hanoi. Each co-chairman would be free to consult anybody, including Adam's off ox, if he wished to, but peace would have to satisfy the essential three. On this basis there would be no conference table to quarrel about. I doubt that Soviets would take on such a burden, but I would appreciate your reaction."

Lodge replied on January 4 (same location, Saigon to Washington 2376, Jan. 4, 1966):

"1. I have been mulling over your . . . suggestion of a 'conference in absentia' where the two co-chairmen would be the only ones to sit at the table to try to find a peaceful solution.

"2. I do not think we can get much good out of this and we might get a good deal of embarrassment. I doubt whether the Soviets would, or even could, take on such a burden. Soviet influence in Hanoi is very slight.

"3. Neither do I think the British could produce very much. [Prime Minister Harold] Wilson and [Foreign Secretary Michael James] Stewart appear to be simply coping with pressures and if they have made any kind of a successful effort to educate public opinion on the realities of the Vietnamese situation, it has certainly escaped me.

"4. About the most that could be expected out of a meeting of this kind would be an attempt to 'put the monkey on somebody else's back' as regards whose fault it is that we haven't got peace. It is absolutely impossible to embarrass the Communists by this kind of tactic. They are indifferent to human life and are intent on conquest. We prize human life and deeply want peace. It is thus very easy to create embarrassment for ourselves. This activity has an unreality about it which is bound further to encourage the type of wishful and unrealistic thinking which seems to be plaguing some people at home.

"5. The alternative idea of having the ICC nations attempt the same thing suffers from similar drawbacks. Hanoi does not appear to trust the Poles; the Canadians, [security deletion] are under heavy domestic pressure and the Indians may have many handicaps.

"6. Nor do I like the idea of reconvening of the Geneva Conference powers. Such a meeting would be filled with representatives of government who either are like the British in that they are motivated by wishful thinking, or like the [security deletion] Chinese Communists who actively want us to fail. We could get into horrible and unnecessary complications.

"7. I still come back to the conclusion that if the time comes when talks are in order that they should be between North and South Viet-Nam with the United States participating on all matters involving the American presence.

"8. Much of this talk of negotiations reminds me of a man with smallpox trying to cure it by putting coldcream on his face. I see no real substance in any of it. The truth is the Communists think they can win. They will not think otherwise until we have done three things: A. Really punish them in the North; B. Decisively defeat the North Vietnamese Army; and C. Show them that we can over come them when it comes to rooting out the terrorists and . . . rebuilding the political structure in the countryside. As soon as we have done these three things, they will then try to win at the conference table what they could not do on the battlefield, but—alas!—this prospect is not immediately in sight. I am confident that we can make very big strides in 1966. Until that time, most of this talk is a 'brutum fulmen.'"

Hickenlooper about the pause. This is the transcript of the conversation made by Ball's secretary:[56]

> Pres said he thought Ball should give some serious thought to getting away a few hours and flying down to talk to Fulbright. Pres said Ball was first to explain to Fulbright that the stories about his not being invited to the WH had no basis and were nonsense. Pres said there was no custom where the head of the For. Relations Committee had to be invited to all the WH functions. Pres said they had checked the records and found that Fulbright had been invited to the WH at least three times more than anybody else. . . . Pres said Ball should tell Fulbright that he (the President) had been laughing about most of this bunk and that he thought most of it was coming from Marcy. Re VN Ball should point out that this is what Fulbright has been saying and the Pres is trying to show our real feelings in the matter and our attempt to do so is not because we are in a panic. Ball should tell him that Bundy talked to Pearson [Lester Pearson, Prime Minister of Canada]; Pres talked to Erhard [Ludwig Erhard, Chancellor of West Germany]; Bruce talked to Wilson [Harold Wilson, Prime Minister of Great Britain]. This is just reiteration of our points and our feelings. It is just an execution of what Fulbright has talked about. Ball should try to make it a Fulbright proposal.
>
> President thought Ball should do the same thing with Mansfield. Ball should say the President had thought it over carefully and thought he should try for peace. Goldberg and Harriman do not have any great hope but in effect are doing what Mansfield has said. Pres said Ball should do this if he has someone in the Dept who could take over for him. Ball said that [U. Alexis] Johnson was backstopping him. Pres said this was fine if he had enough initiative to go on through. Ball said that Dirksen was also in Florida. Pres said Ball should tell Fulbright, Mansfield, and Dirksen not to tell anyone that he is coming down.
>
> Ball mentioned Hickenlooper. Pres said he should be talked to. Pres said Hickenlooper says he does not know enough. Ball should emphasize that this is just a continuation of what the President has said—starting in Baltimore. Ball should not let Hickenlooper think we are retreating. Re the bombing nothing much could be gained by bombing during Holy Week; the weather is not good; and we are just telling everybody about our position.[57]

---

[56] Johnson Library, Papers of George Ball, "Presidential Telecons."

[57] Ball made appointments to see Fulbright, Mansfield and Dirksen, but there is no known record of those meetings.

A few minutes after his call on December 30, the President called Ball again to express his concern about the strained relationship between the U.S. and Cambodia, and his hope that Mansfield could remedy the situation. This is the transcription of the conversation (same location):

"Pres said he had been worried about the Cambodian situation for some time—our harassing their border. Pres said Ball in talking to Mansfield should ask him to tell Sihanouk that he had reported to the President and the President reciprocated Sihanouk's good wishes. He is to tell Sihanouk that we are very anxious to have no border disturbances and we wish he would make a study of these raids that are being initiated within his borders so that our people would not pursue them.

"Ball said he would see what we could get back to Sihanouk. Pres said we should put it on Sihanouk that he should stop these raids from being initiated and that we don't want to go across his borders. Pres said Mansfield is Sihanouk's biggest sponsor and he is a hero to Mans-

On January 3, 1966, the President met with his advisers from 12:55 p.m. to 2:35 p.m. to evaluate the results of diplomatic discussions.[58] Rusk reported that the State Department had been in touch with all 113 of the nations of the world, and that "the general reaction was good." The President asked Rusk, "Do you see anything from any of these conversations that would be encouraging?" Rusk replied, "Not yet." He added that it was too early to assess the results of possible Russian influence with the North Vietnamese, and he asked the President whether he saw any problem in continuing the pause. The President replied: "I see lots of problems, but we should continue."

McNamara and McGeorge Bundy, as well as Ball, said that the pause had been useful. Bundy said, "For the first time we have made headway with the *New York Times.*" Rusk added, "I told Reston [*New York Times* columnist] that no matter how long we stopped bombing it will never be long enough for the *Times.*" Ball said he thought the pause was disarming administration critics in Congress. Rusk reported that several Democratic and Republican congressional leaders who had been contacted were relaxed about letting the pause continue for a while. He specifically mentioned Speaker John W. McCormack (D/Mass.), Senator Hickenlooper, and Representative Frances P. Bolton (R/Ohio), adding that Ball had talked to Senators Mansfield, Dirksen and Fulbright. (The implication was that the latter three also were relaxed about the pause. In Dirksen's case, as will be seen, he was taking the public position that the U.S. should apply greater military pressure.)

The President said he believed that the pause should continue for several more days. He, too, saw some hope in some of the diplomatic discussions, but he added, "Our big problem will be they'll let us stew in our own juice. Then we'll stew in theirs. This will be a bad week, a bad month."

On January 5, there was an NSC meeting from 5:45 p.m. to 6:30 p.m. attended by the President, the Vice President, Rusk, McNamara, McGeorge Bundy, Ball, Raborn, Helms, Wheeler, Goldberg, Fowler and Marks to review the diplomatic situation.[59] Valenti, Moyers and Bromley Smith also attended. Vice President Humphrey reported on the trip he had just completed to four countries in Asia where, he said, the U.S. diplomatic efforts were supported but there were doubts that they would produce any results. USIA Director Marks gave a similar report on the world press reaction. Secretary of State Rusk, after summarizing what was being done to contact other countries, said that if the peace offensive failed and the U.S. resumed bombing, "we will lose the support of almost all those who now support us. . . . Our position will erode here if

field. Mansfield should tell Sihanouk that he gave a full three hour report to the President and told him how great Sihanouk is. We should try in this way to get a little closer to Sihanouk."

[58] Valenti's notes of the meeting are in the Johnson Library, Meetings Notes File. Prior to the meeting, McGeorge Bundy sent the President a memorandum, "The Peace Offensive—where we are today," Jan. 3, 1966, (Memos to the President—McGeorge Bundy), summarizing what had been done. There was also a cable to a number of U.S. diplomatic posts from Rusk, drafted by William Bundy, reporting on the diplomatic moves which were underway. Department of State, Central File, Pol 27 Viet S, Washington Circular Telegram 1260, Jan. 3, 1966.

[59] Johnson Library, NSC Meetings File, Bromley Smith notes of the 555th NSC meeting, Jan. 5, 1966.

we wait much longer to resume the bombing but abroad we will lose support if we resume."

The President said that the U.S. was in a "difficult position but it is a much better position than if we had not responded to the urging that we hold off bombing to see whether this would lead to peace. . . . We have a better basis to call on the U.S. people not only for their sons, but also their treasure. Americans feel better if they know we have gone the last mile even if we have had grave doubts about doing so. The basis for a supplemental budget to pay the increased costs of the war has been laid. . . . We are following a course to unite our people and make possible a follow through."

In cables from Saigon, Lodge said he understood why the President, for reasons of domestic and international opinion, had launched the peace offensive, but the pause, he said, was adversely affecting the situation in South Vietnam and bombing should be resumed.[60] Lodge added that, based on his own extensive political experience, he believed that an effort should be made to educate the American public to the nature of the struggle in which the U.S. was engaged in Vietnam. "[T]his Chinese Communist Imperialism, which manifests itself in so many subtle and disguised forms, is something with which we are going to have to live year in and year out." If the public could become accustomed to that idea, he said, "it will stand casualties better and will not be as impatient because quick results have not been achieved."

In a cable a few days later, Lodge said that he had not meant to appear unaware that the public would not support year in and year out a "hot war" involving substantial casualties.[61] With this in mind, he said, the military side of the Vietnam conflict would have to "have its back broken within the year 1966." Pacification, however, would take longer. He recommended, therefore, "that in this new war, which the North Vietnamese have inflicted on us and the South Vietnamese by bringing in NVN troops, we take extremely drastic action against everything that pertains to North Vietnam, wherever, it may be, so as completely and rapidly to neutralize and render harmless their military potential; and in South Vietnam, continue to help the pacification-countryside-rebuilding-uplift program (which would not involve substantial American casualties) but which could go on for several years and which, I hope, the American public could learn to live with."

Rusk personally drafted a cable to Lodge explaining the peace offensive in which he said, among other things:[62]

> The President is fully aware of the gravity of this present period. He is now saying to the other side "fish or cut bait" on the matter of peace. Obviously if the present effort does not succeed in pushing Hanoi back from aggression, tension will be higher and the situation will be more dangerous than before. I am convinced that the American people will do what has to be done if the issues are clarified and that they know that the honorable alternatives have been exhausted. My prayer is that somehow Hanoi and Peiping will understand in time that they

[60] U.S. Department of State, Central File, Pol 27 Viet S, Saigon to Washington 2399, Jan. 5, 1966.

[61] Same location, Saigon to Washington 2514, Jan. 13, 1966.

[62] Same location, Washington to Saigon 1936, Jan. 7, 1966.

must not underestimate the President and the American people.

No one knows better than you and I that Lyndon Johnson understands power and its use. He is now gathering his political forces at home and abroad. He is not going to give away South Vietnam and he is not going to fail to meet the commitment of the U.S. Indeed, if I were a leader in Hanoi and not prepared for peace, I would be a very worried man.

Lodge replied, in part: "If American opinion is steadfast we cannot lose here; and if it is not, we cannot win."[63]

On January 10, 1966, the President met from 1:10 p.m. to 2:10 p.m. with Rusk, McNamara, Ball, McGeorge Bundy, Wheeler, Taylor, and Helms. Moyers and Valenti were also present.[64] Rusk reported on diplomatic contacts. Taylor said that the pause had shown U.S. sincerity, but its value was wearing off. The President suggested resumption of bombing in a few days. Rusk commented that politically there was no advantage to bombing before the Tet holidays (the end of January) and suspending again for Tet. McNamara said that militarily there would be no disadvantage in waiting until after Tet, but General Wheeler took issue with this, saying, "Every day makes a difference." McGeorge Bundy argued that before resuming the U.S. should publicize the way in which the Communists had taken advantage of the pause to strengthen their military position.

Rusk raised the question of briefing congressional leaders, and the President's reaction was that rather than having a briefing at the White House, it might be better for Rusk, McNamara and others "to appear at as many [congressional] hearings as possible and give them something to have to chew on before their mind hardens—to lay our case before them." Rusk suggested having a luncheon—presumably at the State Department—for congressional leaders and the leadership of committees, and the President agreed.

On January 11, the President met from 1:05 p.m. to 2:05 p.m. with McNamara, Ball, McGeorge Bundy, U. Alexis Johnson, William Bundy, and with David E. Bell, Administrator of the Agency for International Development (which provided funds for pacification activities), who had just returned from a trip to South Vietnam.[65] Bell said that the major problem was pacification. The President said he surmised that pacification had gone backwards. Bell replied that it might have, but not much, but that top AID officials in the field were worried about the situation. "Don't think there's a single area pacified," McNamara said.

Opinion in Congress on Escalating the War

During the White House meeting on January 11, the discussion turned to Congress, where Ball had testified that morning before the House Foreign Affairs Committee. According to Ball, "it's not the same committee I knew before. . . . This had been Gung Ho committee but now they are softer—looking for a way out. . . .

---

[63] Same location, Saigon to Washington 2446, Jan. 8, 1966.

[64] Johnson Library, Meetings Notes File, Valenti notes of meeting of Jan. 10, 1966.

[65] Valenti's notes of the meeting of January 11 are in the same location. A copy of Bell's memorandum of January 19 to the President on his trip, "Non-Military aspects of the effort in Vietnam—January 1966," is in the Johnson Library, NSF NSC History.

They have no solutions—just deeply troubled." The President replied: "I think it is going to get worse. Vietnam is number one thing on their mind. But when you get to specifics they wind up doing the same thing. Don't think the polls are far wrong—55-45. Senate will be worse than House. Must ride out the waves created by 100 experts who visited there."[66]

That same day, January 11, 1966, the Senate Foreign Relations Committee met in executive session to hear a report from Senators Mansfield and George D. Aiken (R/Vt.) on a trip which they, accompanied by Senators Edmund S. Muskie (D/Maine), Daniel K. Inouye (D/Hawaii) and J. Caleb Boggs (R/Del.), had made to Asia, including Vietnam, in December 1965. In his report on the trip, Mansfield said that although "considerable ground has been lost" since his last trip to Vietnam in 1962, the U.S. had succeeded in the past year in "preventing a collapse" of the Government of South Vietnam.[67] "We have not reversed the situation; we have managed to blunt the Viet Cong drive and to hold the situation against further reversals." Additional U.S. forces would be needed, however, and "it is not too early to begin to contemplate the need for a total of upwards of 700,000." "A realistic reckoning . . . would be that there will have to be many defeats of the enemy and years of attrition before a military conclusion may be expected. And the realistic requirement had better be seen not as 170,000 men or 300,000 men or even double that figure but, rather, as an open-end requirement of unpredictable dimensions. It is time not only to disabuse ourselves of any notions, if there are any left, that we can compel the North Vietnamese to 'leave their neighbors alone' at small cost to ourselves and in short order."

Mansfield questioned the assumption that stronger military action was a prerequisite for negotiations, pointing out that the Communists could and probably would increase their manpower in proportion to increased U.S. strength. Moreover, he said, "In my judgment this struggle will go on, at least, as long as North Vietnam wants it to go on and has the means to pursue it."

Mansfield concluded by suggesting that rather than expanding the war, the U.S. should consider defending and holding only those areas then held by the South Vietnamese Government, or an even more limited area on the coast, pending negotiations. But he recognized the problems presented by this approach. "This is a conflict," he said, "in which all the choices open to us are bad choices. We stand to lose in Viet Nam by restraint; but we stand to lose far more at home and throughout the world by the pursuit of an elusive and ephemeral objective in Vietnam."[68]

On January 12, Ball also testified in executive session before the Senate Foreign Relations Committee, and before the hearing, the President telephoned him to ask for a summary of "what is bothering them." He told Ball to tell the committee that "the White House

---

[66] The reference to "100 experts" was the President's way of characterizing congressional visitors to Vietnam during this period.

[67] These quotations are from Mansfield's personal, confidential report to the President, "Vietnam: The Situation and Outlook," which was published in April 1973 in Senate Document 93–11. A modified public version of the report in the name of all of the members of the group, "The Viet Nam Conflict: The Substance and the Shadow," was published as a committee print by the Foreign Relations Committee in January 1966.

[68] In the Department of State, Lot File 70 D 102, there are memoranda of conversation of the meetings of Mansfield's group with Ky, Thieu, and Foreign Minister Tran Van Do.

door is open for any of their suggestions. Stress the point of putting the solution up to them. We don't want to destroy the morale of our people. If they can give us a program, we would be glad to consider it . . . B [Ball] should stress this point."[69]

That afternoon the President telephoned Ball to ask him about the hearing. Ball replied that the members of the committee were "troubled," but were not unfriendly and were sympathetic to the President's problems. "So far as the general tone is concerned, B [Ball] didn't get the same feeling that he had before the House Committee of an undercurrent of criticism. Their problem is they don't know how to talk to their constituents. They don't know whether we see the light for a permanent advantage for the U.S. at the end of the road. They are not convinced there is a way out." The President asked about Fulbright. "B replied that he took his familiar line—he didn't see where we were going and why the commitment."

During the meeting of the Foreign Relations Committee on January 11 at which Mansfield and Aiken presented their report, several members, including Fulbright and Hickenlooper, expressed the need for developing a better understanding of U.S. objectives, and Fulbright, by prearrangement with Hickenlooper, wondered whether the President might be asked to meet with the committee for that purpose. Fulbright asked Mansfield if he would ask the President to do so. Mansfield said he would think about it.[70]

There was also some discussion of the possibility of holding public hearings on Vietnam. Mansfield said he would prefer holding closed hearings.

In his telephone conversation with the President after his testimony on January 12, Ball reported that a Senator had told him about the request for a meeting of the committee with the President. This would not be desirable, Ball told the President "because it would lead to every other committee wanting to do the same thing." The President agreed.[71]

It is not known whether Mansfield asked the President to meet with the Foreign Relations Committee. (In the telephone conversation on January 12, Ball told the President that Mansfield "had not promised it to them and B knows he [Mansfield] will protect the President on it.") Mansfield did ask him to meet with Fulbright, but the President did not do so. However, as Rusk had suggested in the meeting with the President on January 10, there was a luncheon at the State Department on January 13 attended by congressional leaders and senior committee members, including Fulbright and Hickenlooper, at which Ball (Rusk was away) and McNamara discussed Vietnam.[72]

---

[69] Johnson Library, Papers of George Ball, "Presidential Telecons."

[70] U.S. Congress, Senate, Committee on Foreign Relations, *Executive Sessions of the Senate Foreign Relations Committee* (Historical Series), 1966, Vol. XVIII (Washington, D.C.: U.S. Govt. Print. Off., 1993), p. 36.

[71] Johnson Library, Papers of George Ball, "Presidential Telecons."

[72] See Ball's report to the President (included in the President's "Evening Reading" for Jan. 13, 1966), located in the Department of State, Lot File 74 D 164.

Others may have played a role in helping to bring about the meeting at the State Department. On January 10, the day before the idea of a meeting was broached in both the Foreign Relations Committee and the President's discussion with his advisers, Carl Marcy, chief of staff of the committee, reported to Senator Fulbright that at a luncheon that day with James Reston of the *New York Times*, Reston had proposed that a meeting be arranged between the President and

Continued

U.N. Ambassador Goldberg was also asked to talk to leading Members of Congress, and on January 15 he gave the President and the State Department a report on those he had been able to see: [73]

> Senator Fulbright—highly approving of the President's peace initiative and anxious to "make up" with the President. He is obviously disturbed about the recent flurry of stories that he and the President have had a falling-out.
>
> Senators Mansfield and Aiken—enthusiastic about the peace initiative, gravely concerned about the future events in Vietnam, anxious that sufficient time be allowed for the peace moves to germinate and concerned and troubled about any escalation of the Vietnam war.
>
> Senators [Frank] Church [D/Idaho] and [George S.] McGovern [D/S. Dak]—similarly highly approving of the President's recent actions and largely sharing Senators Mansfield and Aiken's views.
>
> Senator Symington—was ambivalent; on one hand, favoring withdrawal and on the other hand all-out war. I tried to point out to him that neither view was practicable or justified.
>
> Senator Dirksen—on the whole sympathetic to the President's actions, but in turn asking for sympathy if to keep his own forces in line he was compelled from time to time to make "Republican" noises.
>
> Senator Hickenlooper—very much interested in the account of the peace initiatives, not expressly disapproving, but as always extremely doubtful about anyone's intentions in the Communist world.
>
> Chairman [Thomas E.] Morgan [D/Pa.]—enthusiastic about the President's leadership and warmly appreciative of being briefed. [Morgan was chairman of the House Foreign Affairs Committee.]

During this period in mid-January 1966, at a time when Congress continued to be generally supportive of U.S. policy, a number of Members of the House and Senate voiced their support for the

---

leading Senate critics of the war. At about the same time, Assistant Secretary of State for Congressional Relations, Douglas MacArthur II, reported a similar conversation with Reston. (For Marcy's report, see his chron file in the papers of the Foreign Relations Committee at the National Archives. MacArthur's report is in the Department of State, Lot File 74 D 164, under the category "Press Contacts 1966.")

Reston, who told Marcy he was opposed to escalating the war, and who also wanted Congress to play a stronger role in the war and was worried about the effect on U.S. foreign policy of the schism between the President and Fulbright, suggested to both Marcy and MacArthur that the President should see more of Fulbright, and should also make an effort, in an informal setting, to discuss Vietnam with some of the senior Members of the Senate. In addition to Fulbright, Reston mentioned Mansfield, Aiken, Russell, and Eugene J. McCarthy (D/Minn.).

Marcy who was also opposed to escalation, sent Fulbright a brief memorandum on January 10 (which is also in his chron file), in which he argued that the bombing pause was the "last clear chance to stop short of unlimited escalation" and that the U.S. should decide to withdraw under U.N. auspices rather than to escalate. Moreover, only by ending the war, he said, could the Democrats win the elections in 1966 and 1968.

On January 21, Marcy prepared an expanded and amended version of this memorandum in which he concluded that neither escalation nor precipitate withdrawal would serve U.S. world interests. He proposed that in addition to a public proposal to the U.N. the U.S. should also make a private proposal to the U.S.S.R. that it would accept a coalition government in South Vietnam which would include the Communists, followed by an election under the auspices of a reconvened Geneva conference. If the Russians showed interest in this proposal, the conference could work out the details of such a settlement. (A copy of the memorandum is in Marcy's Chron File.)

[73] Johnson Library, C.F. ND 19/CO 312, letter from Goldberg to the President.

bombing pause and their opposition to escalation of the war. On January 26, Senator John Sherman Cooper (R/Ky.), who had briefly visited Vietnam during a trip to the Far East in December, called on the President to continue his peace offensive. "Negotiations, not escalation, should be the dominant theme of our activity now," Cooper declared. He added that the U.S. might have to escalate, but that efforts should first be made to negotiate an end to the war. He suggested a cease-fire of 3 to 5 years, supervised and enforced by the U.N., after which there would be national elections pursuant to the 1954 Geneva Agreement.

Cooper also suggested that the "Vietcong" be included in negotiations, "because it is obvious that neither negotiations nor a settlement are possible without their inclusion."[74]

> This is essentially a political and not a military conflict. It is a battle in Vietnam for the hearts and minds of the Vietnamese. It must be limited to Vietnam, and be fought by the Vietnamese if we are to have any realistic hope of an acceptable settlement. . . . It is crucial that the war in Vietnam not be allowed to escalate further. Now is the time to make every conscientious effort to deescalate the conflict. For in escalation there is no practical hope of achieving our aims in that unfortunate country and a very real possibility of an Asianwide war in which America would waste her resources and young men in a slaughter that could achieve nothing but these desperate conditions of chaos ideal for the spread of communism.

On January 19, Senator Morse made a long speech in the Senate in which he repeated many of the points he had made previously, and again urged that the U.S. take the Vietnam problem to the United Nations.[75]

On January 20, Senator McGovern, who had visited Vietnam during December, said in a Senate speech that efforts to negotiate an end to the war should continue, and that U.S. forces should maintain their present positions rather than undertaking new offensives.[76] Bombing, which had not been effective, should continue to be suspended. This was McGovern's conclusion:

> The war in Vietnam will either begin to move this year toward a peaceful resolution—however slow and uncertain the road—or it will degenerate into a deepening morass that may claim the lives of our sons and the sons of Asia for years to come. A major war in the Asian mainland could exhaust America's blood and treasure for all our days and in the end create conditions of bitterness and despair that would curse us for a

---

[74] *CR*, vol. 112, pp. 1246–1247.

[75] *Ibid.*, pp. 662–670. In the course of Morse's remarks, he referred to U.S. pressure on the Philippines to contribute troops to Vietnam, saying that any such troops would be "mercenaries," and that Asian countries contributing forces in return for increased foreign aid were not allies, but "dependencies of the American Treasury." On Feb. 3, 1966, in a memorandum classified "Secret," McGeorge Bundy sent President Johnson a paper from the foreign aid agency (Agency for International Development) requesting approval of a commitment to make a $15 million loan to Korea "as part of the deal," Bundy said, "to get another Korean division and brigade into Vietnam." He added, "The loan commitment is $5 million higher than we would probably make in normal course, but it is much cheaper than any of the items on the long list the Koreans requested. Moreover, [Chung Hee] Park [President of Korea] must show that he has got something from us if he is to sell his electorate on the idea of [a] second division." Johnson Library, NSC Staff File, James Thomson.

[76] *CR*, vol. 112, pp. 775 ff.

generation. I believe that preventing that war is the most urgent task of statesmanship of the next 10 or more years.

Also on January 20, Senator Javits, who had supported the administration's Vietnam policy (even though he had, beginning in the spring of 1965, also urged the President to request a new resolution of authorization and approval from Congress), sent a memorandum to the President reporting on his recent trip to Vietnam. Javits said he was convinced that the U.S. could win a military victory, by which he referred to making the coastal areas, including Saigon, militarily secure. U.S. operations, he said, should be confined to that objective in order to avoid a "bottomless Asia land war." But he was concerned about the task of building a democratic nation after winning a military victory, and critical of the political, social and economic programs efforts which were underway. He recommended that they be expanded "dramatically" and be put under a single director. He also urged the President to take steps "to prepare the American people, and Congress, for the difficult decisions and commitments we will have to make in the years to come in Asia. The Vietnam conflict must be placed in perspective as being just the beginning of the battle for Asia, and we must be ready to journey down a very long road in Asia, all tied to our national interests and to the survival of freedom." [77]

On January 21, a large group of Democrats in the House of Representatives, mostly liberals, led by Brock Adams (D/Wash.), sent a letter to the President expressing support for his diplomatic efforts to end the war and urging him to seek a U.N. cease-fire.[78] In only four hours, Adams and his colleagues got 77 Members of the House to sign the letter.[79]

During January 1966, in addition to growing congressional criticism of the war, there were calls for stronger military action. On

---

[77] A copy of the memorandum is in Javits' papers at the Library of the State University of New York at Stony Brook. Javits made a public report on his trip in a speech in the Senate on Jan. 28, 1966.

[78] When the letter arrived at the White House, Henry Wilson the congressional liaison officer who was responsible for relations with the House of Representatives, and McGeorge Bundy talked to Representative Morris K. Udall (D/Ariz.), one of the more prominent signers, about certain points in the text of the letter which they thought should be changed, but by then the letter had been released to the press. In a memorandum to the President that day (January 21), reporting on this, Bundy concluded: "My own impression is that as we get to the point of decision, we should pick out half a dozen of the stronger and more reasonable members of this group and see if we can get them in position to give firm approval to the necessary resumption [of bombing]." Johnson Library, NSF Memos to the President—McGeorge Bundy.

[79] For the text of the letter and Johnson's reply, see *CR*, vol. 112, pp. 897–898. Signers were: Brock Adams (Wash.), Joseph P. Addabbo (N.Y.), Thomas L. Ashley (Ohio), Jonathan B. Bingham (N.Y.), John A. Blatnik (Minn.), Edward P. Boland (Mass), John Brademas (Ind.), George Brown, (Calif.), James A. Byrne (Pa.), Ronald Brooks Cameron (Calif.), Jeffrey Cohelan (Calif.), James C. Corman (Calif.), Winfield K. Denton (Ind.), John G. Dow (N.Y.), Ken W. Dyal (Calif.), Don Edwards (Calif.), Leonard Farbstein (N.Y.), Donald M. Fraser (Minn.), Samuel N. Friedel (Md.), Richard H. Fulton (Tenn.), Robert N. Giaimo (Conn.), Jacob H. Gilbert (N.Y.), John J. Gilligan (Ohio), Henry B. Gonzalez (Tex.), Bernard F. Grabowski (Conn.), George W. Grider (Tenn.), Martha W. Griffiths (Mich.), Harlan Hagen (Calif.), William D. Hathaway (Maine), Augustus F. Hawkins (Calif.), Ken Hechler (W. Va.), Floyd V. Hicks (Wash.), Chet Holifield (Calif.), Elmer J. Holland (Pa.), Andrew Jacobs, Jr., (Ind.), Harold T. Johnson (Calif.), Joseph E. Karth (Minn.), James Kee (W. Va.), Paul J. Krebs (N.J.), Robert L. Leggett (Calif.), Clarence D. Long (Md.), Rodney M. Love (Ohio), Richard D. McCarthy (N.Y.), Harris B. McDowell, Jr., (Del.), James A. Mackay (Ga.), John C. Mackie (Mich.), Ray J. Madden (Ind.), Lloyd Meeds (Wash.), George P. Miller (Calif.), William S. Moorhead (Pa.), John E. Moss (Calif.), Lucien N. Nedzi (Mich.), Barratt O'Hara (Ill.), James G. O'Hara (Mich.), Alec G. Olson (Minn.), John A. Race (Wis.), Rolland Redlin (N. Dak.), Thomas M. Rees (Calif.), Henry S. Reuss (Wis.), George M. Rhodes (Pa.), Benjamin S. Rosenthal (N.Y.), Edward R. Roybal (Calif.), Herbert Tenzer (N.Y.), Frank Thompson, Jr. (N.J.), Paul H. Todd, Jr., (Mich.), John V. Tunney (Calif.), Morris Udall (Ariz.), Weston E. Vivian (Mich.), Charles L. Weltner (Ga.), Lester L. Wolff (N.Y.).

January 7, Senate Republican Leader Dirksen was reported to have said in a press conference that the U.S. should blockade North Vietnam, especially Haiphong, and should achieve a complete military victory before entering peace negotiations. A few days later, however, he tempered this with the warning that bombing urban centers, especially Hanoi and Haiphong, could result in terrorist attacks or sabotage against Saigon.[80]

In a telephone call from the President on the day of Dirksen's latter statement, Ball asked the President "what magic he had worked on Dirksen." The President replied that Dirksen had called him to say that the reporter who had written the story about the press conference had misquoted him. Dirksen said that he "would be the first to inform the Pres." He said he had some "political things this year," but those did not "take precedence over his country." The President told Ball that Dirksen had then met with him for a couple of hours, and had issued his follow-up statement. He said he had not told anyone of the meeting, except for McNamara, who was "surprised to find him [Dirksen] on board." As for his "magic," the President said "he finds you have to be humble; you have to say you are gloomy about the situation and you feel bad about these things. Although we don't have the answers we can't communicate this gloominess to our boys there."[81]

In a Republican "state of the union" message a few days later Dirksen declared:[82]

> Let us be crystal clear. Viet Nam is not our war. But we pledged ourselves to help a small nation. Our word was given. We are there to keep our word. . . . To retreat and get out would be deemed a confession that we are a paper tiger. . . . To forsake our pledges would shatter confidence in us and further diminish our prestige. . . . To negotiate from weakness would mean defeat before we ever reached the negotiation table.
>
> Is there then a rational course to follow? I believe so. Let the peace efforts continue. Who can object to any honorable effort to secure peace where young blood is involved? Let the military effort continue. It demonstrates our determination to keep our word. Let it be intensified if necessary as sound military judgment dictates. There is, after all, no substitute for victory.

On January 20, Democratic Representative Robert L. F. Sikes of Florida, chairman of the House Military Appropriations Subcommittee, reporting on a trip he had made to Vietnam, said that a build up in U.S. forces was necessary in order to take the initiative and win the war.[83] If the peace offensive failed, he added, there should also be increased bombing of North Vietnam.

On January 24, Senator Russell, the Democratic chairman of the Armed Services Committee, while repeating his advice in 1954 against becoming involved in the war, and warning that "few other problems have so much potential for disaster to our Nation and to the world," declared: "I believe we must decide whether or not we are willing to take the action necessary to win the war in Vietnam

[80] *New York Times*, Jan. 8, 12, 1966.
[81] Johnson Library, Papers of George Ball, "Presidential Telecons," Jan. 12, 1966.
[82] *New York Times*, Jan. 18, 1966.
[83] *CR*, vol. 112, p. 865.

and bring a conclusion to our commitment. The only other alternative I can see is to pull out—and this the overwhelming majority of Americans are not prepared to do."[84]

Senator Stennis, ranking Democrat on the Armed Services Committee, took a similar position. He, too, had opposed U.S. involvement in Vietnam, but once the U.S. was committed he favored using the force necessary to win. In order to do this, he said in a speech on January 29, there should be fewer restrictions on bombing and more troops, adding, "While I am not a military strategist, I would not be surprised if we were ultimately required to commit 600,000 men to the battle. . . ."[85]

Senator Symington, a member of both the Foreign Relations and the Armed Services Committees, said in a Senate speech on January 25 reporting on his recent trip to Southeast Asia that the U.S. had to decide to "move forward," using greater force, or "move out."[86]

> If South Vietnam is not the right place to defend the free world against totalitarian aggression, we should retire from that country on the best terms possible. This would probably result in a Communist takeover of additional countries and

---

[84] *Ibid.*, pp. 965–966.

[85] The text of Stennis' speech was reprinted at pp. 714–718 of the hearings conducted by the U.S. Congress, Senate, Committee on Foreign Relations, *Supplemental Foreign Assistance Fiscal Year 1966—Vietnam*, 89th Cong., 2d sess. (Washington, D.C.: U.S. Govt. Print. Off., 1966).

[86] *CR*, vol. 112, p. 1305. Symington, who had been Secretary of the Air Force in the Truman administration, and was known as a champion of airpower, advocated increased bombing of North Vietnam. While on his trip to Southeast Asia he met on Jan. 4, 1966, with William Sullivan, U.S. Ambassador to Laos. He asked Sullivan for a review of U.S. air action against infiltration routes in Laos, and after Sullivan's description, Symington, according to a cable from Sullivan to Washington on January 5 (U. S., Department of State, Central File, Pol 27 Viet S, Vientiane to Washington 713), "pronounced this [a] shocking waste of air power and said it was a crime to use high-priced, high-powered jets to 'beat the bushes' in Southern Laos." He asked Sullivan whether this was interdicting infiltration. Sullivan replied that "at best we were causing enemy some harassment." Symington then said he understood that three divisions of U.S. troops would be required to interdict the Ho Chi Minh Trail. Should these be requested? Sullivan replied that it would probably require more, and he doubted whether ground forces were the answer. Symington asked whether, instead of bombing in Laos, the U.S. should " 'knock out fuel storage areas, power plants, Port of Haiphong, and hit dams and levees which would flood countryside in North Vietnam.' " Sullivan replied that many of these targets had been hit, and he wondered what the effect of heavier bombing would be on infiltration. "Our experience in Laos suggested that a fuel storage area, once destroyed, would reappear in the form of 50-gallon drums scattered under trees and in caves. It would cause North Vietnam much more work, but would not seriously degrade their ability to get fuel. Power plants would either be replaced by small generators or else products they nourished would be provided by China and Russia. As for dams, I doubted there were many available and busting levees on the Red River would make sense only in July and August, when the river was in flood. Breaking up the port of Haiphong would be a serious blow, but it would just mean that cargo would come in by small coastal vessels transhipping out of Port Wallut and elsewhere in South China. It would, furthermore, place North Vietnam completely in Chicom hands by excluding Soviet shipping."

"My comments obviously pained the Senator," Sullivan reported, "who said that 'everybody else' he had talked to on this trip agreed with him that air strikes such as he proposed would 'take North Vietnam out of the war.' "

Symington also said he understood that Sullivan favored a U.S. amphibious operation at Vinh in North Vietnam. (For an explanation, see below, p. 193.) Sullivan explained why he had proposed such an operation, and Symington wondered whether Sullivan would favor increased bombing in the North "to support 'my invasion.'" Sullivan replied that this was a matter for the military to study.

Sullivan concluded his cable by suggesting that it would be helpful to provide Symington with information on the targets that were available for increased bombing. "Since he [Symington] categorically says that he does not favor 'bombing North Vietnam back to the stone age,' he presumably proposed a fairly limited campaign, with, I fear, limited results."

On the day the cable was received in Washington (January 5), McGeorge Bundy sent a copy to the President with a note saying, "You may be interested in Symington's views as expressed to Bill Sullivan. It may be that we ought to try to talk to him [Symington] before he starts to say this sort of thing in public. He doesn't much like being muzzled by the White House, but he has played ball with us before." Johnson Library, NSF Memos to the President—McGeorge Bundy. It is not known whether this recommendation was acted upon.

> would damage seriously the world position and status of the United States. That would be the price, but it would not be catastrophic.
>
> If South Vietnam is the right place to defend the free world against totalitarian aggression, however, then that fact should be recognized in more practical fashion. We cannot continue indefinitely the plans and programs incident to the current holding operations.

On January 24, Rusk testified in an executive session of the Senate Foreign Relations Committee on the general subject of the world situation. At the meeting there was considerable discussion of Vietnam, especially whether Congress would be consulted if the President resumed bombing and stepped up the war. Fulbright reminded Rusk that the committee had been assured that it would be consulted before any major decisions were made to escalate. Rusk replied, as he had in May 1965, "The President has the question of consultation in front of him. . . . I will have to talk to him specifically about that." Others, including Joseph S. Clark (D/Pa.), John J. Williams (R/Del.), Claiborne Pell (D/R.I.), and Clifford P. Case (R/N.J.), agreed that the committee should be consulted before new major decisions were made.[87] Senator Williams objected to the administration's practice of consulting congressional party leaders rather than the committee when making such decisions.

During the meeting, Fulbright also raised the question of the U.S. position with respect to the National Liberation Front. Rusk's reply was that the NLF was only one of many groups in South Vietnam whose views could be taken into account.[88]

In a memorandum to the President on January 24, Rusk summarized his meeting with the Committee, where, he said, "the atmosphere was frankly more friendly and less critical than I expected."[89] The question of consultation, Rusk said, "was perhaps the single matter most concerning the members." "There was general agreement that we were right in not declaring war, but all felt we should bring the Congress in on major decisions." "I came away," he concluded, "with the impression that what most of the members wanted was a chance to sit down with you on a give-and-take discussion basis rather than for formal presentations and disclosures of pending decisions. While I am aware of the great difficulty of doing this with this Committee as a whole, given the several other Committees in both Houses, who would consider themselves entitled to equal treatment, I do feel that the time is perhaps ripe for us to take another look at the problem of Presidential consultation."

---

[87] U.S. Congress, Senate, Committee on Foreign Relations, *Executive Sessions of the Senate Foreign Relations Committee* (Historical Series), 1966, vol. XVIII (Washington, D.C.: U.S. Govt. Print. Off., 1993), pp. 139, 163, 166, 174, 182.

[88] *Ibid.*, pp. 139–140. On Jan. 11, 1965, Norvill Jones, formerly a member of Fulbright's staff who joined the Foreign Relations Committee staff in 1965, had sent Fulbright a memorandum on Vietnam in which he stated in part: "Unless there is recognition both by us and the South Vietnamese that the NLF is a political fact of life and must be brought into the government, there is little hope that negotiations will take place." (National Archives, RG 46, Papers of the Committee on Foreign Relations, "Memorandum on Vietnam.") As noted above, the committee's chief of staff, Carl Marcy, had also proposed that the U.S. should agree to a coalition government.

[89] Johnson Library, NSF NSC History.

In his memorandum to the President, Rusk mentioned also a query by Symington, based on the question which Symington had asked during his trip as to whether the Chinese would be likely to intervene if the U.S. bombed Hanoi or Haiphong or if U.S. forces were to land in North Vietnam at Vinh. Symington, Rusk said, commented that the response of many Americans during his trip had been that the Chinese would not intervene. Rusk replied "that while it is difficult to predict with certainty what the Chinese would do, in my judgment such action would increase the chances of Chinese Communist intervention." "Several questions of a similar vein," Rusk added, "brought a reasonable degree of consensus on my statement that our present general course of measured action was ultimately less likely to provoke a nuclear war than either of the major alternatives of either abandoning Vietnam or a major escalation on our part."

In a press conference after the committee meeting, Fulbright called for the administration to consult with the Foreign Relations Committee before the President made a decision to resume bombing, noting that Rusk had said that this would be up to the President.

Fulbright also said that the U.S. should recognize the National Liberation Front as a "proper party" in negotiations, and that failure to do so might impede the negotiating process.[90]

That same day (January 24), Rusk also met in executive session with the House Foreign Affairs Committee. In a memorandum to the President he reported that, "The atmosphere was friendly and generally indicated support of the Administration and, at times, almost gleeful opposition to the position of the Chairman of the Foreign Relations Committee. . . ."[91] Of the 25 members of the committee who were present, Rusk said, 15 expressed opinions on the subject of a resumption of bombing, and of those 12 were clearly in favor. The chairman and ranking Democratic member asked about plans for consultation with the Senate Foreign Relations Committee pursuant to Fulbright's request, and expressed the hope that the House would get equal treatment. Rusk replied that the President would be consulting congressional leaders, and that he would report to the President the views of the members of the House committee.

Summarizing the meeting with the House Foreign Affairs Committee, Rusk said in his memorandum to the President: "While it is clear from what the Congressmen said that the large majority of their constituents go along with what we are doing in Vietnam, they indicated that there was, in some cases, increasing sentiment that if the other side would not come to the Conference Table, we should increase our action altogether."

That afternoon (January 24), from 4:35 p.m. to 5:46 p.m., the President met with Democratic congressional leaders: Speaker McCormack, Majority Leader Albert and Majority Whip Hale Boggs (D/La.), and, from the Senate, Majority Leader Mansfield and Majority Whip Russell B. Long (D/La.). Also present were McGeorge

---

[90] *Washington Post*, Jan. 25, 1966. A similar position had been taken earlier in January by Senators Church and McGovern (*New York Times*, Jan. 6, 1966) and was subsequently taken in February by Senators Abraham A. Ribicoff (D/Conn.) and Javits.

[91] A copy of Rusk's memorandum is in the Johnson Library NSF NSC History.

Bundy, Valenti, Lawrence O'Brien (Postmaster General who had been head of congressional liaison in the White House), and several other White House staff members involved in congressional relations. After a long presentation by the President and then by Bundy, there were comments by some of the leaders. Mansfield referred to the desire of the Foreign Relations Committee for a meeting with the President, and again expressed his opposition to a resumption of bombing. There was, he said, "no other avenue. You've used them all . . . I'd think most seriously before final decision is made."[92] The President: "Any time they want to talk we'll talk." Senator Mansfield: "While they've been building up [during the pause] so have we." "It's not just South Vietnam and North Vietnam. It's China—China has been conquered but always conquers the conqueror." The President: "30 days [the length of the pause]—no good comes from it. We got only their answer that the public position is their real position. We've gone for a year in a delicate balance. Hanoi thinks we're weak—they're not about to give way." "We never did have much hope," he added, "but we *did* try." (emphasis in original) Boggs cautioned against the effects on public opinion of an indefinite pause. Speaker McCormack said that as a result of the pause "From now on you'll look weak." Long commented: "This is your decision. Congress can appropriate—can't fight the war." He added that the Communists would "give you nothing at the conference table that you can't get on the battlefield."

After the meeting with Democratic leaders the President met from 6:30 p.m. to 7:34 p.m. with Rusk, McNamara, McGeorge Bundy, Taylor, and Valenti.[93] Rusk reported on his meeting with the committee, and again urged the President to see Fulbright. If he did, Rusk added, the committee "would have no serious problem. . . ."[94] The President did not respond directly, but said, referring to his meeting with Democratic leaders, "Today we had five leaders—four for us and Mansfield against us." He added: "In the House we'd get Ford, [Leslie C.] Arends [R/Ill.], and [George H.] Mahon [D/Tex.]. Don't know about [Frank T.] Bow [R/Ohio]. [L. Mendel] Rivers [D/S.C.] and [William H.] Bates [R/Mass.] are with us. We'll lose only Fulbright and Mansfield." Turning to the question of announcing resumption of bombing, he said, "I think we ought to—quietly—visit with Dirksen and see how he feels. Quietly talk to a couple of Republicans in the House. Then next morning, meet with leadership, when I'm ready to go—so they can't leak anything. . . . Why don't we tell the leaders that if we continue to get pictures of supplies coming down, we must stop them. It will make it difficult for Fulbright to argue against this. I won't say

[92] This and other quotations used here are from cursory handwritten notes by McGeorge Bundy, the only known notes of the meeting. Johnson Library, McGeorge Bundy Papers, Notes on Vietnam.

[93] Johnson Library, Meetings Notes File, Valenti notes of meeting of Jan. 24, 1966.

[94] On Jan. 19, 1966, Valenti talked by telephone with Fulbright, and in a memorandum to the President he reported:

"I also told the Senator that mischief makers in Washington were trying to promote a fight between the President and the Chairman of the Foreign Relations Committee but that the larger problems facing our Nation could not tolerate any regard for these fight promoters. Fulbright responded enthusiastically by saying that newsmen have been trying desperately to spotlight so-called breaks between him and the President simply because they haven't anything else to write about. But Fulbright said he certainly wasn't going to let these newsmen influence him and he intends to cooperate with the President." Johnson Library WHCF, Ex FG 431/F.

anything specific, but I will say I can't wait forever for these supplies to come down."

Rusk replied: "If you are going to see Dirksen, I urge you to see Fulbright and Hickenlooper before you make a decision." Once again, the notes of the meeting do not indicate that the President replied to or paid any heed to this suggestion.

Rusk also referred to Fulbright's comments to the press about a coalition government after the Foreign Relations Committee hearing, adding: "Tragedy about situation is that Fulbright's statement urging extending the pause and recognizing the Viet Cong. *Times* [*New York Times*] will pick it up and applaud it," to which McGeorge Bundy said: "And denounce us for smothering debate."

Despite Rusk's recommendation, the President not only did not meet with Fulbright (it is not known whether he met with Dirksen) but he deliberately snubbed Fulbright in a meeting the following day (January 25) attended by congressional leaders and principal members of key committees of the Senate and House that was held at the White House from 5:30 p.m. to 7:40 p.m.[95] Only Mansfield and Fulbright spoke against the resumption of bombing and increased military action, but, judging by other comments, it seems that the increasing cost of the war, rising casualties, and the prospect of a protracted conflict were preying on the minds of most of the Members even as they supported the President.

Among the Republicans, Dirksen said, "[L]et's do what is necessary to win. I don't believe you have any other choice. I believe the country will support you." Saltonstall said, "if we have our boys there, we have to go forward with bombing. . . . You must give our boys full support." Ford said, "If your advisers say bombing is necessary—I'm for it." Arends, Bates and Bow, as the President had predicted, agreed that bombing should be resumed. Hickenlooper said, "If only Vietnam was concerned, I'd get out. But we are confronting the Communist world. Either get out or lick them." This prompted Fulbright to say, "If we follow Hickenlooper's advice, it will get us into world war III."

Most of the Democratic leaders also urged the President to escalate the war. Russell said:

> This is the most frustrating experience of my life. I didn't want to get in there, but we are there. . . . We are prepared to fight a war. We are *not* fighting. (emphasis in original)
>
> I think we have gone too far in this lull—although I recognize the reason. This pause has cost you militarily. We are going to lose a lot of boys as a result—casualties of our care for peace.
>
> For God's sake, don't start the bombing halfway. Let them know they are in a war. We killed civilians in World War II and nobody opposed. I'd rather kill them than have American boys die. Please, Mr. President, don't get one foot back in it. Go all the way.

---

[95] Johnson Library, Meetings Notes File, Valenti's notes of meeting of President with congressional leaders, Jan. 25, 1966. McGeorge Bundy also took notes, which are in his papers in the Johnson Library.

Russell added: "the problem is, not to fight this war with one hand behind us. The American people won't stand for it. This is an unpopular war but the people want us to win."

Speaker McCormack, House Majority Leader Albert, House Majority Whip Boggs, Senate Majority Whip Long, House Foreign Affairs Committee Chairman Morgan, House Armed Service Committee Chairman Rivers, House Appropriations Committee Chairman Mahon, and Senate Appropriations Committee Chairman Carl Hayden (D/Ariz.) all agreed on the need to resume bombing and to apply additional military force.

Of those present at the meeting, the only dissent came from Mansfield and Fulbright. Mansfield said the pause should be continued. "We have little to lose by lull. Time is on the side of the enemy. Best chance of getting to peace table is to minimize our military action."

Fulbright said he agreed with Mansfield. He said the U.S. should play for time while trying to negotiate a way out.

When Fulbright began to speak, the President "coolly turned to Secretary of State Dean Rusk, at his immediate right, and engaged him in animated conversation until Fulbright had finished."[96]

The President then asked McNamara to reply to Mansfield and Fulbright. McNamara did so by asking what level of military activity should be continued in order to achieve a negotiated settlement, and making the point that such continued actions were "levers to negotiations." "If we adopt the [Gen. James M.] Gavin line [an enclave strategy] the initiative would pass to the VC. The balance of opinion is that minimal military action would be costly—and not lead to peace."

As the meeting ended, the President said, "Appreciate your views. Will take whatever action is necessary. I always keep your [Gulf of Tonkin] resolution in mind. I know you can take it away from me any time you want and I can't veto." Senator Saltonstall replied, "Keep that resolution in your pocket. We won't take it away from you."

While soliciting the views of Democratic leaders, the President also had his congressional liaison staff, supplemented by other White House staff members, conduct a survey of the attitudes of most of the Democrats in the House and about half of those in the Senate. The views of 251 (out of 295) House Democrats were summarized in a report to the President on January 21, 1966, from Henry Hall Wilson, White House liaison to the House of Representatives, and the views of the Senators were summarized in a report to the President on January 25 by Mike Manatos, White House liaison to the Senate. Wilson said that in all but nine of 251 districts "majority sentiment is reported as backing your policy in Vietnam . . . but most districts reported a lot of uneasy people."[97]

Manatos said that, "Without exception, the 19 Democratic Senators who are running for reelection this year expressed unanimous support of their constituents and themselves for your policies on

---

[96] Neil MacNeil, *Dirksen: Portrait of a Public Man* (New York: World, 1970), p. 275. See also the *Washington Post*, Jan. 30, 1966.

[97] Jean P. Lewis, "President Johnson Surveys the Congress," a paper prepared for the Senior Seminar in History, Georgetown University, May 1990, 186 pp., at p. 16. Lewis was a member of the White House Congressional Liaison Staff, 1961–1968. Her paper won a gold medal prize in history.

Vietnam and your handling of the problem. This also held true for additional 12 contacted—total 31."[98]

Thus, Jean Lewis concludes:[99]

> *The results of the January survey were to demonstrate to the President that the great majority of the Congress and of the American public believed that his course of action was the right one, that he need have no worry about the fate of the supplemental request* [a request submitted by the President in January, 1966 for additional funds for the war for the remainder of fiscal year 1966] *or the support of the Congress and the people. His efforts to bring about a peaceful settlement were appreciated, but if they failed—the Congress and the American people would support his actions.* (emphasis in original)

The Decision to Resume Bombing

During the middle of January 1966 the debate on the bombing pause and on the course of U.S. policy continued in the executive branch. On January 8, 1966, the JCS said in a memorandum to McNamara that the pause placed U.S. forces "under serious and progressively increasing military disadvantage, that it had weakened U.S. bargaining power, that it could lead to misinterpretation of U.S. intentions, and that it should be lifted.[100] On January 12, Admiral Sharp urged resumption of bombing, and proposed that ROLLING THUNDER be broadened to include interdiction of lines of communication from China, closing the North Vietnamese ports, destruction of POL and electric power facilities as well as large military facilities. (By the end of 1965, the 94 major target list of April 1964 which had been used for ROLLING THUNDER operations had expanded to a list of 236.)[101] Such an intensified bombing campaign, he said, "will bring the enemy to the conference table or cause the insurgency to wither from lack of support. The alternative appears to be a long and costly counterinsurgency—costly in U.S. and GVN lives and material resources."[102]

On January 18, the Joint Chiefs recommended an intensified bombing effort, generally along the lines recommended by Sharp, based on the air war plan first proposed by the JCS on November 23, 1964. This would begin with a "sharp blow," followed by "uninterrupted increasing pressure" to close North Vietnamese ports, interdict land lines-of-communication from China, attack the POL system, destroy large military facilities in North Vietnam, disrupt electric power, attack airfields where operations were being conducted that interfered with the U.S. air war, and attack targets closer to Hanoi and Haiphong as well as closer to the Chinese border.[103]

In a paper prepared for McNamara by McNaughton on the same day (January 18) it was estimated that, despite interdiction, the North Vietnamese were capable of infiltrating 4,500 men a month

[98] *Ibid.*, p. 34, from memorandum for the President from Mike Manatos, Jan. 25, 1966, Johnson Library, Diary Backup for January 25.

[99] *Ibid.*, p. 17.

[100] JCSM–16–66, Jan. 8, 1966, a copy of which was sent to Rusk by McNamara on Jan. 19, 1966 and is in the Department of State Central File, Pol 27 Viet S.

[101] *PP*, Gravel ed., vol. IV, p. 29.

[102] *Ibid.*, p. 40, from CINCPAC 120205Z, Jan. 12, 1966.

[103] *Ibid.*, pp. 41–42, from JCSM–41–66, Jan. 18, 1966.

and between 50 and 300 tons of supplies a day, depending on the season,[104] against current needs of only 20 tons a day to sustain 1964 levels of activity or 80 tons a day to sustain "light combat." Heavier bombing could reduce supplies to an estimated 50 tons a day (McNaughton noted that this estimate was "without convincing back-up"), and with the anticipated daily requirement of 140 tons a day by an increased year-end level of 155 Communist battalions operating in South Vietnam this would leave a shortfall of about 90 tons a day. Thus, the paper concluded, "since the Communists are not likely to be willing to talk very soon and since it is possible that the interdiction program will be critical in keeping the Communist effort in South Vietnam within manageable proportions," the U.S. should expand anti-infiltration bombing along the lines proposed by the military, including bombing of POL (petroleum, oil, lubricants) and power plants. In addition, the U.S. should mine North Vietnamese ports. (In a second paper on January 19, "Some Paragraphs on Vietnam," the proposed bombing of ports was omitted.)[105] "Also considered," the memorandum stated, "should be a Barrier across Vietnam and Laos south of the 17th Parallel and a Barrier across Vietnam to Cambodia cutting off VC supplies from the Delta. A Barrier across North Vietnam and Laos at Vinh has some appeal but involves, as compared with alternatives, excessive risks of escalation." McNaughton also proposed a study "to see whether most of the benefits of the interdiction campaign can be achieved by a Laos-SVN barrier or by a bombing program which is limited to the Laos-SVN border area of North Vietnam, to Laos and/or to South Vietnam. . . . The objective here is to find a way to maintain a ceiling on potential communist military activity in the South with the least political cost and with the least interference with North Vietnam willingness to negotiate."

This was McNamara's reply to the JCS paper of January 18:[106] "I have reviewed the proposals of the JCS expressed in JCSM–41–66. . . . Since you [Wheeler] were present at the White House deliberations and are aware of the several options exhaustively reviewed prior to the Presidential decision to resume the bombing of NVN, I will not attempt to comment on the specific proposals of the JCS in this memorandum. The JCS views will continue to receive full consideration in the further development of the ROLLING THUNDER program."

On January 24, McNamara sent a memorandum to the President, "The Military Outlook in South Vietnam," in which he renewed his earlier request (which had not been acted upon) for the deployment of an additional 200,000 U.S. troops (Phase II) in 1966. He also recommended heavier bombing of North Vietnam and a continuation of the increased bombing of Laos,[107] but he did not recommend the much heavier "fast escalation" bombing which the Joint Chiefs had requested and which McNaughton had initially proposed on January 18. In the memorandum and in meetings with the President on January 22 and 26, as will be seen, McNamara

---

[104] Johnson Library, Warnke Papers, McNaughton Files, "Some Observations about Bombing North Vietnam," Jan. 18, 1966, 2nd Draft.

[105] *PP*, Gravel ed., vol. IV, p. 48.

[106] "JCS Policy Statements Concerning Operations in South Vietnam," *op. cit.*

[107] *Ibid.*, pp. 49–51. See p. 177 below for more details on McNamara's January 24 memorandum.

took the position that the results of interdiction through bombing had been overestimated and that, even with heavier bombing of the North and Laos and increased ground combat in South Vietnam, by the end of 1966 there would be a continued stalemate at a higher level of forces and casualties. He said, however, as McNaughton's draft had argued, that resumption and intensification of bombing were necessary to prevent even higher levels of infiltration and to avoid sending the "wrong signal" to the Communists, i.e., that the U.S. was not prepared to defend its interests in Southeast Asia.

In the State Department, Rusk, although strongly opposed to the way in which the pause had been handled, agreed that the U.S. should resume bombing in order to avoid sending the wrong signal. William Bundy also supported resumption, but he did not favor "fast escalation." "For a period of two-three weeks at least," Bundy said in a memorandum on January 15, 1966,[108] "while the world is digesting and assessing the pause, we should do as little as possible to lend fuel to the charge—which will doubtless be the main theme of Communist propaganda—that the pause was intended all along merely as a prelude to more drastic action."

There were a number of others in the State Department, however, who opposed resumption or argued for additional time in which to seek negotiations. These included Ball, Thompson, Harriman, Goldberg, Legal Adviser Leonard Meeker, and Joseph Sisco (Assistant Secretary of State for International Organization Affairs—which included responsibility for the U.N.). Ball and Meeker, along with China specialists Allen S. Whiting and Edmund E. Rice, favored a complete cessation of the bombing of North Vietnam.[109]

A leading State Department specialist on the U.S.S.R. and Communist affairs, Charles E. Bohlen, then U.S. Ambassador to France, also questioned the continuation of bombing. In a personal letter to Llewellyn Thompson on January 31, 1966, he said, "What bothers me is the possibility that there are some people in the United States government who believe that bombing of North Vietnam will induce or force Hanoi to the conference table. I feel this is a very fallacious argument since it seems to me that all Communist history shows that they will never yield to external pressure of this kind."[110]

The general argument in favor of extending the pause was that not enough time had been allowed for exploring possible interest in negotiations; that there would be strong opposition in the United States and in other countries if the U.S. were to resume bombing before further testing of diplomatic possibilities and in the absence of new evidence of Communist escalation and, related to this, that the Communists should be made to bear the responsibility for escalation; and, finally, that resumption was not militarily necessary.

---

[108] "Scenario for Possible Resumption of Bombing," Johnson Library, Warnke Papers, McNaughton Files.

[109] For Ball, see his memorandum to the President "Should We Resume Bombing?" Jan. 20, 1966, in the Department of State, Lot File 74 D 272, and his statements in meetings with the President cited below. See also Meeker's memorandum to Rusk, "Length of the Pause," Jan. 22, 1966, same location; Rice's letter to William Bundy, Jan. 11, 1966, same location; and Whiting's notes, which Chester Cooper sent with a memorandum to McGeorge Bundy on January 24, Johnson Library, NSF NSC History.

[110] Charles E. Bohlen, *Witness to History* (New York: W. W. Norton, 1973), p. 524.

The argument for a complete cessation, which was cogently expressed in a memorandum from Ball to the President on January 20,[111] was that bombing had accomplished its objective of raising morale in the South but had not succeeded and could not succeed in accomplishing the other two original objectives of compelling the North to cease its support of the war and of interdicting infiltration. "There is no evidence," Ball said, "that bombing has so far had any appreciable effect in weakening the determination of Ho Chi Minh and his colleagues. Whatever evidence there is points in the opposite direction—toward a hardened line and fierce determination." On the question of interdiction, he said, "The evidence is clear that we cannot—by using any amount of air [power] against North Vietnam—reduce the flow of men and materiel to the South below the level required to maintain increasing fighting strength for the Viet Cong." He said that at that time Communist forces needed only 12 tons a day, and would not need more than 165 tons a day even with sizeable force increases and more intensive combat. (He apparently did not agree with McNaughton's estimate that with an expanded program the U.S. could interdict all but 50 tons a day.) In the early 1950s, Ball said, the Communists had demonstrated that one man with a bicycle could move 500 pounds of supplies, and that at the time as many as 50,000 men had been employed for that purpose.

Ball also argued that continued or increased bombing of North Vietnam could make the North Vietnamese more dependent on China and the U.S.S.R., who in turn could increase their pressure on North Vietnam. It could also lead to a direct confrontation between the U.S. and China and possibly the Soviet Union.

Several days later (January 25), Ball invoked the fear of a war with China as his final argument against resumption of bombing. It was his "strong conviction," he said in a memorandum to the President, *"that sustained bombing of North Vietnam will more than likely lead us into war with Red China—probably in six to nine months."* (emphasis in original)[112] "Our philosophy of bombing," Ball said, "requires gradual escalation. Admittedly, we have never had a generally agreed rationale for bombing North Vietnam. But the inarticulate major premise has always been that bombing will somehow, some day, and in some manner, create pressure on Hanoi to stop the war. This is accepted as an article of faith, not only by the military who have planning and operational responsibilities, but by most civilian advocates of bombing in the Administration." In order for bombing to achieve this result, he said, the U.S., as it had since bombing began, would increasingly have to bomb vital and sensitive targets, and this could lead to increased Chinese intervention and to an eventual clash between the U.S. and China.

The U.S., Ball added, ran the risk of miscalculating the point at which China might enter the Vietnam war, just as it had in the

[111] "Should We Resume Bombing?" cited above.

[112] Ball's memorandum, "The Resumption of Bombing Poses Grave Danger of Precipitating a War with China," is in the Department of State, Lot File 74 D 272. A paper which Whiting sent to Ball on January 24, "China Prepares for War," is in the same location, as is a memorandum from Meeker, "Resumption of Bombing and Escalation," Jan. 25, 1966, which, among other things, argued that resumption of bombing could lead to Chinese intervention and to a U.S. war with China.

Korean war.[113] He quoted the Special National Intelligence Estimate of December 14, 1965,[114] "that the chances are about even that the Chinese, if requested by the DRV, would permit DRV aircraft to intervene from Chinese bases, or would even do so with their own aircraft in the event of continued U.S. air attacks near the Chinese border. They would not expect any of these measures, of themselves, to repel the U.S. attacks militarily, but would hope to make our operations increasingly costly and possibly deter further U.S. escalation while running high but acceptable risks of being bombed themselves." If the U.S. then attacked Chinese air bases, Ball said, again citing the SNIE, it was likely that China would intervene in Vietnam with its ground forces.

In his memoirs, Ball says: "Today—with the wisdom of hindsight—it is clear that I overestimated the prospect of Chinese intervention. But President Johnson was deeply preoccupied with the China menace and the more I emphasized it, the stronger was my case for cutting our losses." [115]

Although Ball may now feel that he overestimated the "prospect" of Chinese intervention, it is also clear that the Chinese, as Whiting warned, were preparing to defend themselves against the Americans, and, if need be, to send their forces into Vietnam. The President, therefore, seems to have had good reason to be "preoccupied with the Chinese menace."

In the White House, McGeorge Bundy, who had originally appeared to be opposed to a pause but had become one of its principal advocates, was in favor of resumption, even though he believed that the bombing of North Vietnam was of secondary importance to pacification in South Vietnam.[116] In a memorandum to the President on January 24 in which he discussed the "pros and cons of immediate resumption of the bombing," [117] he said, among other things, "I think this question narrows to one of timing. The arguments for a complete end to the bombing are unacceptable, and no one wants to bomb Hanoi tomorrow morning."

As the President and his advisers prepared to discuss plans for ending the pause, the Board of National Estimates (the interagency intelligence board under the chairmanship of the CIA) issued a special memorandum estimating the effects of bombing of some of the more sensitive targets, such as airfields, POL, power plants, or mining Haiphong and other harbors. None of these attacks, the

---

[113] In the papers that he prepared for Ball, cited above, Whiting pointed out that China "has steadily increased its covert cooperation [with North Vietnam] in the form of regular army engineering units in North Vietnam, joint air defense developments including sending Chinese Communist fighters over North Vietnam both in practice and active firing against U.S. aircraft, and is improving both sea and land communications routes to North Vietnam." Over half of the Chinese jet fighter force of MiG–19s and a third of the force of MiG–21s were positioned in South and Southeast China, and China was "rushing to completion three new airfields to supplement the five already capable of supporting jets over North Vietnam." "In sum," Whiting said, "the regime has not instituted any crash programs of civil defense or evidenced any panic in undertaking contingency preparations against the eventuality of U.S. attacks. However, it has alerted its elite political and military groups to the sensed imminence of conflict with the U.S., related this conflict to the Vietnam war, and undertaken appropriate air deployments and construction efforts in South China, the area most immediately threatened by escalation. At the same time Peking has acted carefully but deliberately to increase its commitment of gradual air power to assist in the defense of North Vietnam."

[114] SNIE 10–12–65, "Probable Communist Reactions to a U.S. Course of Action," cited above.

[115] Ball, *The Past Has Another Pattern*, p. 406.

[116] See his memorandum to the President on Jan. 11, 1966, Johnson Library, NSF Memos to the President—McGeorge Bundy.

[117] Same location.

memorandum stated, as had a previous estimate in December, "would, in itself, have a critical impact on the combat activity of the Communist forces in South Vietnam."[118]

With respect to the bombing pause itself, the Office of Current Intelligence of the CIA reported on January 18, in a memorandum which Director Raborn sent to Valenti in the White House, that the North Vietnamese "apparently regard the current standdown in air attacks on the DRV mainly as a welcome respite during which to repair bomb damage and to make further preparations for the support of Communist military operations in South Vietnam. They have launched a vigorous propaganda campaign intended to discredit the U.S. peace initiatives, and have in fact stiffened their stated terms for an end to the war since the bombing lull began. On the diplomatic front they are attempting to encourage a continuation of the bombing cessation while carefully refraining from any commitment to begin negotiations in return. . . . Hanoi apparently believes that continued military pressure on the allied force in South Vietnam is currently the best Communist course of action."[119]

On January 20, in preparation for resuming bombing, the President met from 5:54 p.m. to 6:31 p.m. with Rusk, McNamara, McGeorge Bundy, and Ball. Because of his role in the negotiating process, Harriman also attended. Moyers and Valenti from the White House staff were also present. The President told McNamara he wanted from the military a plan for military action, and he told Rusk to tell the press that there had been no response to the pause and that "'the peace jig is up.'"[120]

Later that day (January 20) McGeorge Bundy had lunch with journalist Walter Lippmann and sent a memorandum to the President reporting on the conversation.[121] Lippmann, he said, was not surprised to learn that the peace offensive had not been successful, "Lippmann and I," he added, "discovered, as usual, that we have radically different views of the reality of the situation there. He says he genuinely believes it is a civil war, and that it was not started by Hanoi. I told him I was quite sure that the members of the Politburo in Hanoi would tell him different if they were frank. I said he was saying what French intellectuals said, and I thought

---

[118] Quoted by Ball in his memorandum of January 25, cited above.

[119] Johnson Library, C.F. ND 19/CO 312.

[120] Johnson Library, Meetings Notes File, Valenti notes of the meeting of January 20.

[121] Johnson Library, NSF Memos to the President—McGeorge Bundy.

In an article published on Jan. 17, 1966, Lippmann said that President Johnson was confronted with, "in the President's own words, 'hard decisions.'" *Newsweek*, Jan. 17, 1966. See also Lippmann's columns in the *Washington Post* for Dec. 21 and 28, 1965, and Jan. 4 and 6, 1966. "At bottom," Lippmann said, "the President has to choose between a bigger war and an unattractive peace. He must decide either to launch a big American war in Asia, a war which could easily be bigger than the Korean war because it could so quickly involve both China and the Soviet Union, or to cut our losses by reducing his political and military objectives.

"The hard decision the President has to make is whether he can accept the political and psychological risks of dealing with Vietnam as General Eisenhower dealt with Korea and as General de Gaulle dealt with North Africa. For President Johnson will have to pay a heavy price for the historical mistake of involving the United States in a land war against Asians in Asia. The alternative to paying a price for peace is to pay the enormous price of a great war which threatens to expand into a world war.

"The President has made it quite clear that he realizes the hard choice which is before him. Naturally enough, he is looking for some easier way out of his dilemma. If only he could find one. But by his decisions in 1964, he rejected the warning by men in a position to know that there was not much time left to negotiate an arrangement. He had come very near to locking and bolting the door. He has raised the stakes so high that easy solutions are most improbable and only the hard choices remain."

the evidence went the other way. He asked for such evidence, and I am going to try to assemble some material for him."

Bundy continued:

> Our other basic difference, of course, is on the question whether the U.S. can and should operate on the ground in Asia. Walter says Korea is an exception and that in Vietnam it simply won't work. He quotes MacArthur on his side of the argument. He thinks the best answer is to let the place go Communist as gracefully as possible. He seldom is quite so candid in public. I told him that he was looking at our troubles and not the troubles of the enemy, and that there was a good deal of evidence that the Viet Cong were hurting and that the balance was less unfavorable than he assumed. He asked if I could give him such evidence, and again I said I would see what I could do.

On January 22, the President met from 12:00 noon to 2:12 p.m. with Rusk, McNamara, McGeorge Bundy, Ball, William Bundy, Helms, Harriman, Taylor, Raborn, Llewellyn Thompson, Goldberg and Valenti.[122] That morning, McGeorge Bundy sent the President a memorandum in which he discussed what needed to be taken up at the meeting, especially what steps should be taken to prepare for resumption of bombing. One of these was congressional consultation. He recommended that the President make clear, through such mechanisms as his weekly meeting with Democratic leaders, that the pause had failed, but he also suggested that there should not be any "formal consultation" with Congress.[123]

Except for Ball, Goldberg and Harriman, there was general agreement that bombing should be resumed. The President said that if the Communists had responded the pause could have been continued. "I'm of the mind to continue it anyway," he added, "but we've had no indication of any success at all. We can't impose hardships on our soldiers much longer."

The President also observed, "If we go back in, the pressure will be on us to go further." (This may have been what he was thinking about when he spoke of continuing the pause.)

Ball briefly summarized the dangers of a war with China which he discussed in the memorandum that he completed and sent to the President the following day.

That same day (January 22), a memorandum on "Public Opinion Regarding Bombing of North Vietnam" was sent to the White House by Lloyd Free of the Research Council, a public opinion policy research organization which apparently had been commissioned to undertake the poll.[124] Using the facilities of the Gallup Poll organization, Free, on the basis of interviews conducted during the previous two days, concluded that the public was "divided, confused and unclear about most aspects of the question of whether to start bombing North again"—whether bombing would weaken or strengthen the will to fight of the people of North Vietnam, wheth-

[122] Johnson Library, Meetings Notes File, Jack Valenti notes of the meeting on Jan. 22, 1966. In McGeorge Bundy's papers, Notes on Vietnam, there are also brief, cursory notes which he took of the meeting. William Bundy also took brief notes, which are in his personal papers.

[123] Johnson Library, NSF Memos to the President—McGeorge Bundy.

[124] Johnson Library, Office Files of Fred Panzer, "Public Opinion Regarding Bombing of North Vietnam," the Research Council, Princeton, N.J., Jan. 22, 1966.

er bombing would cause other "free world" countries to agree less or more with U.S. policy, whether bombing, if it were stepped up over time, would or would not tend to cause China to enter the war. On the major question, whether, all things considered, the U.S. should resume bombing, Free's survey found that 42 percent thought that the U.S. should hold off the resumption of bombing "so as not to spoil" any negotiating opportunity, 44 percent favored resumption, and 14 percent did not know. "In sum," Free reported, "there appears to be no public mandate either for continuing the pause in the bombing or for starting bombing again."

From January 26–30, 1966, the President met daily with his advisers.[125] From the available notes of these meetings, he appears to have been dubious about the military benefits of bombing the North, but he also restated his belief that the pause had been a mistake and his feeling that bombing had to be resumed. He expressed concern about pressures to use greater force after bombing was resumed, and appeared fearful that the advocates of that position were gaining strength. On the other hand, while he obviously chafed under the criticism of Fulbright, Mansfield and others, he did not want to appear to be yielding to their recommendation that the bombing pause be extended, and this seems to have reinforced his determination to resume bombing.

At the meeting on January 26 of the President with Rusk, McNamara, McGeorge Bundy, Ball, Raborn, Valenti and Moyers, from 1:25 p.m. to 1:50 p.m. and then from 2:00 p.m. to 3:00 p.m. at which the timing of a decision to resume bombing was considered,[126] there was a discussion of the views of various Senators. The President said, "Each time they [Senate critics] will bring up something to delay us. John Sherman Cooper wants to wait. I asked him if he could deliver VC if I gave him more time. He couldn't answer." The President added, "If you understand Fulbright he wants us to get out. Mansfield wants us to hunker up." "Mansfield's got that Montana water: we want peace. Like that Minnesota water." [127]

Rusk said he was "disturbed as much by other statements," by which he meant congressional demands for stronger action, as he was by the position of Mansfield and Fulbright. The President agreed. Rusk added, "No one can look you in the eye and tell you where we are going if we don't get peace."

There was discussion of Fulbright's position, and Johnson's comment was "I don't want to be in Asia," but the U.S. could not "tuck our tails and run."

McNamara, repeating his feeling the bombing had not been effective in cutting off supplies, said he was also worried about pressure from the "heavier bombing boys."

The President asked "How do you answer Ball's memo on China?" and McNamara replied: "I believe we can tell China we do

---

[125] Valenti's notes of these six meetings (two on January 29) are in the Johnson Library, Meetings Notes File. (There is no mention of the meetings in Valenti's book.)

There are also brief handwritten notes by McGeorge Bundy of the meetings of January 26, 27, and 28 in his papers, Notes on Vietnam, at the Johnson Library.

[126] According to the President's Daily Diary, on the morning of January 26 the President telephoned Justice Fortas to discuss the resumption of bombing.

[127] The quotations beginning "Mansfield's got. . . ." are from McGeorge Bundy's notes of the January 26 meeting. "Minnesota water" was an allusion to Vice President Humphrey.

not intend to destroy the political institutions in North Vietnam." Ball said: "What we need is a philosophy of the bombing. We don't have any now." McNamara said he disagreed, but the notes of the meeting do not contain any further comment by him on Ball's point.

McNamara said that he had to leave the meeting early to testify before a congressional committee, to which the President responded: "There is something wrong with our system when our leaders are testifying instead of thinking about the war."

The next day (January 27), the President received a letter from 15 liberal to moderate Democratic Senators led by Senator Vance Hartke (D/Ind.), opposing the resumption of bombing.[128] The letter, which did not include such other dissenting Democrats as Mansfield, Fulbright, Pell, Albert Gore (Tennessee), Moss, Joseph D. Tydings (Maryland), Philip A. Hart (Michigan), Jennings Randolph (West Virginia) or either of the Kennedys, Robert of New York or Edward of Massachusetts, was the first organized, open challenge to the President from Senate Democrats and, judging by his response, the President did not consider it to be a constructive expression of dissent.

The letter from the Democratic Senators read:

> As members of the senate, we take this occasion to express our general agreement with recent statements of the Majority Leader, Mr. Mansfield, the senior member of the Republican party, Mr. Aiken; and the Chairman of the Committee on Foreign Relations, Mr. Fulbright, which relate to whether the national interest of the United States would be served by renewal of the bombing of North Vietnam at this time.
>
> Senator Fulbright said on January 27 that he was opposed to the resumption of the bombing of North Vietnam by United States forces "for the foreseeable future"; Senator Mansfield said that there should be an "indefinite suspension" of these bombings; and Senator Aiken endorsed the foregoing views by stating, "bombing should be suspended until it becomes perfectly clear that the Communist nations intend to fight the war to the finish."
>
> We believe we understand in some small degree the agony you must suffer when called upon by our constitutional system to make judgments which may involve war or peace. We believe you should have our collective judgment before you when you make your decision.[129]

---

[128] Johnson Library, NSF Country File, Vietnam. The fifteen Senators were: E. L. Bartlett (Alaska), Quentin N. Burdick (N. Dak.), Frank Church (Idaho), Joseph Clark (Pa.), Ernest Gruening (Alaska), Vance Hartke (Ind.), Eugene McCarthy (Minn.), George McGovern (S. Dak.), Lee Metcalf (Mont.), Wayne Morse (Ore.), Gaylord Nelson (Wisc.), Maurine B. Neuberger (Ore.), William Proxmire (Wisc.), Harrison A. Williams, Jr. (N.J.), and Stephen M. Young (Ohio). Frank Moss (Utah), who was overseas at the time, said he supported the proposals made by the group. *Washington Post*, Jan. 29, 1966. The letter was reported to have been drafted by Hartke, McCarthy, McGovern, Burdick, Metcalf, and Moss. *New York Times*, Jan. 28, 1966.

[129] On Feb. 4, 1966, Harriman sent a memorandum to McGeorge Bundy reporting on his conversation with Hartke and three other Senators who signed the letter (Library of Congress, Harriman Papers, Subject File, McGeorge Bundy Papers):

"You will recall that I saw four of the six Senators mentioned in the *Times* January 27 as being opposed to resumption of bombing. Gene McCarthy, George McGovern, Quentin Burdick, and Vance Hartke came to my house for a drink. The other two were out of town.

"We had a good talk, lasting an hour and a half. Unfortunately, the Senators had already sent their letter to the President that same afternoon, urging a continuation of the pause. Therefore, they were somewhat on the defensive.

According to Senator Eugene J. McCarthy (D/Minn.), one of the signers, "The letter to the President did not reflect the full measure of anti-bombing sentiment in the Senate at that time. . . . In my judgment, at that time about one-third of the full Senate, a substantial percentage, and probably a majority of the Foreign Relations Committee, opposed resumption of the bombing. If only one-third were speaking out, I sensed that perhaps another third shared our position." McCarthy also noted that Republican Senators were not asked to sign the letter, which was viewed as a "Democratic responsibility." [130]

This was President Johnson's answer to the letter: [131]

> Dear Senator Hartke:
>
> I write to acknowledge your letter of January 27, in which a group of Senators join you. I am glad to have this expression of opinion.
>
> I continue to be guided in these matters by the resolution of the Congress approved on August 10, 1965—Public Law 88–408—[Gulf of Tonkin Resolution] by a vote of 504 to 2. My views of the present situation remain as stated in my recent reply to a group of Members of the House, of which I enclose a copy.

According to Senator McCarthy, "Members of the Senate were offended on two counts: one, the use of the Tonkin Gulf Resolution as an answer to their serious questioning; and second, the use of a letter to the House of Representatives as an answer to the Senate challenge, since this reflected upon the constitutional responsibility for foreign policy which is quite specifically vested in the Senate." [132]

"In the discussion it became evident that one of their principal concerns was that if bombing in North Viet-Nam was resumed, the pressures from the Joint Chiefs of Staff and the vocal members of the Armed Services Committee would be so great that it would be impossible for the President to prevent escalation of bombing to a point which would bring on a confrontation with Red China.

"I admitted that these pressures from the extremists would exist, but that I had been through the same situation with President Truman. He had resisted them even to the point of firing General MacArthur, and I expressed the same confidence in President Johnson.

"I told them I thought that the resumption of bombing was unavoidable as we had not had a favorable response from Hanoi, and that if their concern was over escalation, I asked whether it would not be better for them to reserve their energies to support the President in resisting the extreme pressures, rather than oppose the President in resumption.

"I felt that Gene McCarthy particularly was impressed and he indicated that he wanted to support the President, but didn't fully understand what was in the President's mind.

"I feel that it would be well worth while for the President to invite Gene down and discuss the problem with him. I am inclined to believe that he could get Gene to be a good balance against some of the more aggressive hawks.

"George McGovern appeared so disturbed by the outlook that he was in a Walter Lippmann mood. I gathered Quentin Burdick was somewhat more balanced and open-minded. Hartke was all over the lot and impossible to pin down.

"I had the impression that Gene McCarthy could be persuaded to take leadership in supporting the President's policies."

[130] Eugene J. McCarthy, *The Year of the People* (Garden City, N.Y.: Doubleday, 1969), pp. 23–24.

[131] *Public Papers of the Presidents,* Lyndon B. Johnson, 1966, p. 112. In a memorandum to the President on January 28, Mike Manatos, White House liaison to the Senate, said that Mansfield told him "that not only did the group [Senators who signed the letter] not solicit his advice but that they purposely avoided him—that when he found out about the letter, which was after it was circulated and signed, he told them this was not the proper approach to the matter. He suggested, however, that your handling of the letter was perfectly proper—that you said the only thing you could have said—and his advice is that you drop the matter . . . Mansfield has been assured that there will be no follow-up of the letter. . . ." Cited by Lewis, "President Johnson Surveys the Congress," *op. cit.*, p. 41.

[132] McCarthy, *The Year of the People,* p. 26.

"During the next few days," McCarthy added, "there was much discussion of the matter in the corridors and cloakroom," and various officials visited Members of the Senate to explain the administration's position.[133]

The action of Hartke, who had been a stalwart supporter of the President and had not previously become involved in the controversy over the war, was a personal affront to the President, as reported by Rowland Evans and Robert Novak:[134]

> When another Democratic Senator delivered a speech about Vietnam, Johnson telephoned to congratulate him on a constructive suggestion, and gratuitously remarked that he was "not like that [obscenity] Hartke." Later, when Hartke took a group of Indiana party workers on a tour of the White House, the President made it his business not to greet them and, through Bill Moyers, publicly referred to Hartke as "obstreperous." Presidential resentment of Hartke extended to the Department of Agriculture, which refused to reappoint Hartke's men to the agricultural stabilization committees in Indiana. All this was part of the exercise of power. Making an example of Hartke might be a warning to others.

Evans and Novak also reported that as discontent about the war spread in the Senate, the President sought to build a new "Johnson Network" of Senators who would support him on Vietnam:[135]

> Gale [W.] McGee [Democrat] of Wyoming (who would soon become the president's leading spokesman on the Foreign Relations Committee), Birch Bayh [Democrat] of Indiana, and Fred [R.] Harris [Democrat] of Oklahoma. They replaced the Hartkes, Fulbrights, and Mansfields at informal suppers at the White House.
>
> So did Senator Paul [H.] Douglas [Democrat] of Illinois, whose crusading liberalism had so often been mocked and foiled by Majority Leader Johnson. Douglas, a hard-line anti-Communist, had suddenly become a friend in need for President Johnson. He backed him on Vietnam, and did so at the cost of some of his liberal supporters in an election year. Douglas became a guest at the LBJ Ranch as the President recuperated from his gall bladder operation and was told by Johnson his election to a fourth term in the Senate was the most important political necessity of 1966. Having lost his old allies, Johnson embraced an old enemy.

At a meeting from 6:20 p.m. to 8:20 p.m. on January 27, 1966, the day of the Hartke letter, which was attended by Rusk, McNamara, McGeorge Bundy, General Wheeler, Valenti and Moyers, the President again asked his advisers for their views on resumption

---

[133] *Ibid.*, pp. 26–27. On the day the letter from the 15 Senators was sent to the President, Senator McCarthy made a brief speech in the Senate, his first on the war, in which he called for a national debate on the war. *CR*, vol. 112, p. 1234. It was not like other wars, he said, in which the American people had been able to make a "full moral commitment" to the achievement of U.S. objectives. "The serious problem today is that we are called upon to make a kind of moral commitment to an objective or to a set of purposes which we do not clearly understand." The bombing of North Vietnam, he added, which had not been successful either militarily or diplomatically, was a case in point. The success of bombing, military or diplomatic, had not been demonstrated.

[134] Rowland Evans and Robert D. Novak, *Lyndon B. Johnson: The Exercise of Power* (New York: New American Library, 1966), pp. 564–565.

[135] *Ibid.*

of bombing. Rusk recommended resuming, but said that bombing policy should be kept under firm control because of the risk of Chinese intervention. He added that some of the senior officers in the State Department (he mentioned Ball and Thompson) wanted more time to explore possible negotiations. The President asked whether Goldberg, one of those who advocated an extension, wanted to pull out. "No," replied Rusk, "He wants to compromise it out." [136] "But the only way to get a fellow to talk to you," the President said, "is to show strength. . . . I think if you stop bombing they will go for something else. If you let them run you out of the front yard, they'll run you out of the house. I don't want war with Russia or China. I feel less comfortable tonight than I felt last night. I don't want to back out—and look like I'm reacting to the Fulbrights. We must realize the price we pay for going back in. We will lose a good part of the Senate." He added "I thought of chucking that resolution [the Gulf of Tonkin Resolution] back to them." He also asked, "Do we want to take on the Senators—or let others take them on?" McNamara replied, "I think the longer we delay the more controversy we produce." Failure to resume bombing, he said, would polarize public opinion in the United States.

McNamara agreed with Rusk that the U.S. must seek "at all costs" to avoid war with China.

McGeorge Bundy made the point that "All estimators say that cessation will strengthen the will of the enemy."

Speaking of the Senate, the President said, "We don't have anyone defending us." McGeorge Bundy replied, "Yes, that's right, and we don't have anyone of stature." "Douglas [Senator Paul Douglas] could do it," the President said. "He's got the standing to do it."

During the meeting the President asked a number of questions, including: "Do you think our failure to bomb the North will materially affect the balance out there?" "What are we cutting off?. . . We really pay a price if we are not getting a pay off." The replies were that bombing was "costing them," but there was no guarantee that it would reduce Communist operations in the South. The President: "Did we make a mistake to start to bomb in the North?" McNamara: "No." The President: "Suppose we would not announce a resumption. We would keep the nations off us. Can we take this same firepower and use it in the South?" McNamara: "We don't need them in the South. . . . We cannot use the same firepower elsewhere."

The President also asked about the position of Senator Robert Kennedy. McNamara replied that Kennedy had said "The burden of proof [on resumption] is on us." "What will he say when we resume," the President asked. McNamara said he did not know, but that he would be seeing Kennedy on Saturday.[137] The President added: "I think we'll carry a big burden when [we] resume with the Senate, peace lovers, Ministers, etc."

---

[136] For Goldberg's views see the memorandum from McGeorge Bundy to the President, "Views of Arthur Goldberg," Jan. 27, 1966, Johnson Library, NSF Memos to the President—McGeorge Bundy.

[137] The White House evidently had heard that Senator Edward Kennedy was considering a speech advocating an extension of the pause, and on January 26 McGeorge Bundy had telephoned him to try to convince him not to do so. McGeorge Bundy memorandum to the President, "Phone Conversation with Ted Kennedy," Jan. 26, 1966, same location.

On January 31, when bombing was resumed, Robert Kennedy warned that bombing was not the answer and that the decision to resume could lead to an escalation of bombing that could result in "catastrophe for mankind."[138] Moreover, U.S. objectives could be gained, he argued, only by pacification programs in "education, land reform, public health, political participation and . . . honest administration" that would inspire the people of South Vietnam.

In a meeting on January 28, from 1:20 p.m. to 3:45 p.m. attended by the President, the Vice President, Rusk, McNamara, McGeorge Bundy, Ball, William Bundy, Goldberg, Harriman, Wheeler, Marks, and Valenti, as well as by Wise Men McCloy, Dulles, Dean and Clifford, the President told the four Wise Men, "Because of [the] large range of judgment and experience you have, I want your evaluation of this." "I see each day serious difficulties, mounting of pressure," he said. "It may result in deep divisions in our government." He added: "A year ago, by 504–2 the Congress told the President to do what was necessary in Vietnam. Today they [the opposition] could muster probably 40 votes."[139]

McGeorge Bundy explained that, "While we did not expect any serious response to the pause, we have no answer—only nibbles of an undefined source to confuse the record." Meanwhile, he said, the North was continuing to supply Communist forces in the South.

McNamara reported on the military situation. He was asked by Arthur Dean what kind of bombing should be undertaken if there were a resumption, as well as whether the U.S. should mine the harbor at Haiphong. McNamara replied that bombing of industrial targets such as POL and power plants was not as important as bombing infiltration routes, and that mining the Haiphong harbor would cut off petroleum supplies, but "don't know if we would markedly cut down supplies to the South." McNamara said he did not think bombing could affect the "will" of the North Vietnamese. Pressure on the Communists in the South, however, could induce them to negotiate, and regardless of bombing there was a need for more U.S. forces—"A chance," he said, "the doubling our force over a period of six months might be sufficient to break their will." McCloy asked whether this would bring about "pacification." McNamara replied, "No, this can't make peace until Vietnam has organized a pacification effort." He added that he favored resumption of bombing because "the American people will not long support a government which will not support, by bombing, 400,000 troops there," nor would the South Vietnamese understand. Failure to resume, he said, also would send the "wrong signal to Hanoi, China," which would interpret cessation as weakness.

General Wheeler agreed, but emphasized that bombing was useful in interdicting supplies. The President asked General Wheeler whether infiltration of troops from the North had increased during the pause. Wheeler said he did not know. "I think so. But can't tell."

Wheeler also said, "Within the next two years we ought to get favorable results."

---

[138] *CR*, vol. 112, p. 1602.

[139] Johnson Library, Meetings Notes File, Valenti notes of meeting of Jan. 28, 1966. William Bundy also took brief notes, which are in his personal papers.

General Taylor commented, "I don't think Hanoi will ever come forward unless our home front is strengthened. It works against all our efforts in the war." The President: "Our enemy gets great encouragement from the opposition voices here. Is that right?" "Yes, it's true," Taylor replied. "Hanoi lives in another world."

The four Wise Men who were present at the meeting endorsed a decision to use greater force, including the resumption of bombing. McCloy said the pause had helped at home, but "General impression abroad is that we overdid it. Hasn't been conducive to bringing about talks—we've been too excited, too panicky—an indication of weakness to the enemy." Dean added, "If you don't [resume] American people won't support you—and casualties will rise." Allen Dulles agreed. So did Clifford, who said: "Only way to get out of Vietnam is to persuade Hanoi we are too brave to be frightened and too strong to be defeated. We must persuade them we cannot lose—and they will never talk until they are so convinced. U.S. attitude is misunderstood in Hanoi. They hear Senators and protests and they are convinced we are losing the support of our people." Clifford said that the U.S. should increase military pressure "to the point where the North Vietnamese people wonder if it is all worth it."[140]

Goldberg, however, disagreed. He said the pause had strengthened the U.S. position, especially in the Communist world, and he recommended that out of deference to world opinion, as well as for the good it might do with congressional critics, the pause should be continued for a short period. Vice President Humphrey replied, "The Congress is without leadership. We must take a firm position. The longer you delay, Congress will run all over the lot."

Wise Man Robert Lovett, who was unable to attend the meeting, told McGeorge Bundy that he was opposed to becoming involved in Vietnam and opposed to the pause, but that once involved the U.S. had to support its forces and apply enough pressure on the Communists to compel them to negotiate. In addition to resumption of bombing, he favored a "friendly blockade" of North Vietnam.[141]

The President concluded the meeting by saying: "I am not happy about Vietnam but we cannot run out—we have to resume bombing."[142]

---

[140] In Clark Clifford's papers in the Johnson Library, Pencilled Notes, there is an outline of the points he apparently intended to make at the meeting, which includes those views cited here.

[141] McGeorge Bundy memorandum to the President, Jan. 26, 1966, in Department of State Central File, Pol 27 Viet S. In McGeorge Bundy's papers in the Johnson Library there are handwritten notes of his conversation with Lovett.

[142] Moyers, who had become very close to the President but may have been having some doubts about the war, sent the President the following memorandum on January 28 (Johnson Library, C.F. ND 19/CO 312):

"You will recall the intelligence summary I showed you this morning. Its major conclusions were, that despite the many and complex pressures on Hanoi *not* to negotiate, a decision by them to negotiate, 'is clearly under consideration.' Further, the report stated the belief, 'that Hanoi does not yet want to close the door to negotiation.' I believe sending Bill Douglas [Supreme Court Justice William O. Douglas] to Hanoi would provide a crucial test of their sentiments.

"First, the very fact that they accept his coming is hopeful. It will mean to the world that it is up to them to say something constructive. It will dramatically demonstrate that you are indeed sincere in going any place, anytime, to talk with anyone. The pressures on Hanoi to negotiate reasonably would be immense. Their failure to do so would be damning—not only abroad but especially at home. It would take a lot of steam out of the noisy group on the Hill.

"Finally, his trip would be the perfect play-out of the peace offensive. It would be your personal, dramatic capstone to the whole effort—and you just might pull the rabbit out of the hat."

On the following day, January 29, the President met from 11:35 a.m. to 12:40 p.m. with Rusk, McNamara, McGeorge Bundy, General Wheeler, Moyers, and Valenti.[143] Rusk reported that Thompson was in favor of resumption to avoid giving the North Vietnamese the wrong signal—combined, he added, with the wrong signal being given by the dissent of Fulbright and other Senators. Ball, Rusk said, wanted more time. McNamara said he believed that the U.S. should resume.

The President said he had picked five men across the country and had asked their opinion about resuming. "One man said, 'have you and Rusk gone crazy—you've been sitting around doing nothing.'" He also talked to Justice Fortas, and "Net effect of what he said was that whole Communist world was working to prolong the pause." Rusk replied: "If that's their object, the Communists have been stupid."

Referring to the letters from the 15 Senators and 77 Representatives, the President said that there were "problems with Senate and 76 in the House," and that he did not think military plans should be discussed with the Senate. Once again he expressed concern about those who "want to go after it" and use greater force. McNamara agreed. "That worries me, too. We must not add fuel to the fires. . . ."

The group talked about going to the U.N. with a report on the pause and a resolution affirming the decision to resume bombing. Rusk said that if such a resolution were offered and vetoed, "Morse will say the UN has rejected us—and we ought to get out of South Vietnam." "Morse" the President observed, "will go to repeal the [Gulf of Tonkin] resolution." Rusk added that if the U.S. reported to the Security Council, "that would mute Morse."

The President emphasized the need to take "maximum initiative" in peace efforts. "We have to demonstrate to the people that we are not Barry Goldwater [Barry M. Goldwater, former U.S. Senator and Republican nominee for President, 1964] but we must make it clear that our military program will go forward vigorously. . . . We have to keep shoving on peace. I want Wheeler to have some running room. Rusk has got to keep moving on peace—let's keep Goldberg busy on peace resolution."

After this meeting ended, the President met from 12:40 p.m. to 1:15 p.m. with the Vice President, Rusk, Goldberg, McGeorge Bundy, Moyers and Valenti to discuss possible peace initiatives in the U.N.[144] The President said: "I was against the first pause, and the second pause. It has created a situation of doubt." He added, however, that he wanted to explore every possible avenue to peace. "I want the diplomats to keep moving. . . . I've played out my pause—not from 115 countries have I gotten anything. I want you men to evolve for me political and peace moves—initiatives of my own. . . . Because I certify that the Fulbrights and the Morses will be under the table and the hard liners will take over—unless we take initiatives."

In an interview several years later, Rusk said that President Johnson's "disappointment in that thirty-seven day bombing pause

[143] Johnson Library, Meetings Notes File, Valenti notes of meeting of Jan. 29, 1966.
[144] Valenti notes, same location.

made a lasting imprint on him, because he was very skeptical from that time onward that anything could be done by way of peace initiatives and probings, and bombing halts, and things of that sort. . . . But it was a calculated risk and a calculated possibility and those of us who recommended it felt that it was worth the try since no great damage was done on the military side. . . ."[145]

On Sunday, January 30, 1966, the President held a meeting of the National Security Council from 12:15 p.m. to 2:25 p.m.[146] Present were Rusk, McNamara, McGeorge Bundy, Vance, William Bundy, Wheeler, Goldberg, Raborn, Helms, Fowler, and Marks. The Joint Chiefs of Staff also attended, along with Moyers, Califano, Valenti and Bromley Smith. CIA Director Raborn reported that, in anticipation of U.S. resumption of bombing, the North Vietnamese had improved their air defenses, and that there had been heavy infiltration of North Vietnamese forces. He also noted that Chinese forces were moving up to the border. Rusk and Goldberg reported that there had not been any diplomatic progress.

The President asked Army Chief of Staff Gen. Harold Johnson what help he most needed. General Johnson replied, "A surge of additional troops into Vietnam. We need to double the number now and then triple the number later. We should call up the reserves and go into mobilization to get the needed U.S. manpower. This involves declaring a national emergency here and in Vietnam." "The bombing must be resumed at once," he added, "to hold down infiltration." All of the other members of the Joint Chiefs agreed that bombing should be resumed. Gen. John P. McConnell, Chief of Staff of the Air Force, was critical of the restrictions placed on the Air Force, saying: "We should lift these restrictions and we would then get results."

On that same day (January 30), Ball gave a stout defense of U.S. policy toward Vietnam in a speech at Northwestern University that had been prepared by the State Department as a basic statement of the U.S. position.[147] This prompted a response from Senator Morse, who commented on Ball's reputation as the Department of State's "leading dove," and said that as a result of the speech "he looks more to me like a dove in hawk's feathers, unless he is a pigeon."[148]

It is of interest to note the President's reaction to one section of Ball's speech when the text of the speech was given to him in draft on January 28 for his approval, having been cleared by McGeorge Bundy, and presumably also by Rusk. In this section, Ball discussed the question of recognizing the National Liberation Front and of including the NLF in negotiations. This idea was strongly rejected in Ball's draft, which said in part, "Yet to recognize the National Liberation Front in such a capacity would do violence to the truth and betray the very people whose liberty we are fighting

---

[145] Johnson Library, Dean Rusk, Oral History Interview II, Sept. 26, 1969, p. 30.

[146] Johnson Library, NSF NSC Meetings File, Bromley Smith notes on 556th meeting of the NSC, Jan. 30, 1966 (the notes erroneously give January 29 as the date). There are also notes by Valenti in the Meeting Notes File.

[147] For the text see the *Washington Post*, Feb. 6, 1966.

[148] *CR*, vol. 112, p. 2067.

In an interview on February 22, 1966 with historian Henry Graff, Ball said, "As far as we are concerned today, we haven't got any options. . . . The one thing we have to do is to win this damned war. . . ." Henry Graff, *The Tuesday Cabinet: Deliberation and Decision on Peace and War Under Lyndon B. Johnson* (Englewood Cliffs, N.J.: Prentice Hall, 1970), p. 73.

to secure. The National Liberation Front is not a political entity expressing the will of the people of South Vietnam—or any substantial element of the South Vietnamese population." When President Johnson reviewed the speech and returned the draft to Bundy he wrote by hand, "Do we want to here refuse NLF?"[149] In the final version of the speech Ball's original language remained unchanged, however, so apparently the President did not press his point or was talked out of it by his advisers. His reaction to the statement in the speech draft would suggest, however, that he, like his old friend and colleague Fulbright, was sensitive to the possibility that the U.S. might have reason to modify its position vis-à-vis the NLF.

Reactions to Resumption of Bombing

On January 31, 1966, President Johnson announced that the U.S. would resume the bombing of North Vietnam.[150] As a part of its continuing pursuit of peace, the U.S., he said, would also ask for consideration of the Vietnam situation by the U.N. Security Council.[151]

"Accordingly," James Reston of the *New York Times* wrote, "Mr. Johnson traveled a familiar path. He gave both extremes in the debate half of what they wanted: limited bombing for the hawks and a gesture toward the United Nations for the doves."[152] Reston added that the President was evidently preparing to increase U.S. military activities in Vietnam. "What the President has said, in effect, is that the objective of the American force in Vietnam is to break the fighting will and power of the enemy, and even the most conservative general officers here think the United States force in Vietnam will have to go well above half a million if the strategy of searching out and destroying the enemy is even to have a chance, let alone succeed."

When he made the announcement, the President obliquely asserted his authority to act without congressional advice or action, and, indeed, worded his statement to make it clear that he did not think Congress had any responsibility for such matters: "As constitutional Commander in Chief, I have, as I must, given proper

---

[149] Johnson Library, NSF Country File, Vietnam.

[150] *Public Papers of the Presidents,* Lyndon B. Johnson, 1966, pp. 114–115. In making this decision, the President deferred any increase in the level of bombing or attacks on new targets.

[151] See Rusk's memorandum to the President, "Bringing Vietnam to the Security Council," Jan. 29, 1966, Johnson Library, NSF Memos to the President—McGeorge Bundy.

In a subsequent memorandum, the State Department summarized the results of the U.S. effort to get the U.N. Security Council to consider the Vietnam issue ("U.S. Efforts to Obtain U.N. Action on Vietnam," inserted in *CR,* vol. 112, p. 13418):

"On January 31, 1966 the United States again requested an urgent meeting of the Council to consider the situation in Viet-Nam. The Council met to consider the question of Viet-Nam on February 1 and 2. After considerable debate, during which inscription of the item on the Security Council's agenda met with strong resistance, the Council voted 9 in favor, 2 opposed (U.S.S.R., Bulgaria), with 4 abstentions (France, Mali, Nigeria, Uganda) to inscribe the item. This bare majority was possible only on the informal understanding that the Council, instead of proceeding immediately to a substantive debate, would adjourn for consultations. The results of the consultations were summarized by the Council's President in late February. He noted three main points:

"a. It was 'impossible to reach agreement on a proper course of action for the Council to follow';

"b. There was 'a general feeling' that no further debate should be held at the time; and

"c. There was a 'certain degree of common feeling' on two points: concern and anxiety over the continuation of hostilities and a strong desire for their early cessation; and a feeling that an end to the conflict should be sought 'through negotiations in an appropriate forum in order to work out the implementation of the Geneva Accords.'"

[152] *New York Times,* Feb. 1, 1966.

weight to the judgment of those—all of those—who have any responsibility for counseling with me or sharing with me the burdensome decisions that I am called upon to make: the distinguished Secretary of State, the Secretary of Defense, my national security adviser, and America's professional military men, represented by the Joint Chiefs of Staff."

In Congress, as expected, reaction was mixed. One of the most notable speeches was made by Senator Aiken, the senior Republican in the Senate and a senior member of the Foreign Relations Committee, who had opposed escalation of the war. "Since we have passed the point of no return," he said, "we should take a good, hard look at the situation as it is today. . . . From now on our number one concern must be the preservation of the United States and its institutions . . . we must be prepared for the worst—and without delay." In order to fight the war successfully, he said, there would have to be increased taxes and "universal conscription." [153] He continued:

> Besides increased taxation and conscription, we must be prepared to accept the concentration of powers and restrictions on our liberties which inevitably accompany any major war.
>
> We must be prepared to accept these controls for an indefinite number of years.
>
> Are we ready to accept a system of priorities—price controls and wage controls?
>
> What about ration cards?
>
> Are we prepared to control hoarding which may already be underway?
>
> Are our shelters adequate to insure the perpetuation of at least a part of our population in the event of a nuclear war?
>
> Have we the facilities necessary for the control of sabotage, subversion, riots, and criminal law violations?
>
> We do not like to contemplate these things; yet they must be considered and acted upon unless the danger is far less than it now appears.
>
> This time we cannot wait until catastrophe strikes.
>
> So long as there is the slightest chance for peace, we should pursue it, even while preparing for the worst, but we must prepare.
>
> Since the Vietnam war began to escalate rapidly 3 years ago, I have repeatedly tried to make clear my belief that a major war would have disastrous results for the United States either militarily or in the loss of personal liberty at home.
>
> Although I have at all times recognized the responsibilities of the United States to the people of South Vietnam, I never for an instant regarded my vote for the concurrent resolution of August 1964 as a vote to give the President authority to wage war at will in southeast Asia.
>
> I opposed as strongly as I could the start of a new war in North Vietnam.
>
> And I believe the President has erred in taking new steps which may lead to a cataclysmic world conflict.

[153] For congressional comments, including those cited here, see *CR*, vol. 112, pp. 1553 ff.

> It appears, however, that my voice has been ineffective and that the President has decided to take such steps.
>
> The most that is left to me now is the hope that the President is right and that I have been wrong.

Aiken concluded:

> If, through the renewed action for which he assumes responsibility, the war can be brought to a quick and satisfactory ending, I will gladly admit the error of my judgment and be among the first to render him acclaim.
>
> To this end, it is my purpose to support his request for higher taxes and for such controls over the American economy as may seem necessary to hold our losses to a minimum and to enhance the prospects for ultimate victory.
>
> To divide our Nation in this time of crisis would be to court certain disaster.

Morse, who had repeatedly urged the use of the U.N. to resolve the Vietnam dispute, praised the decision to take it to the U.N., as did a conservative Republican, Senator Norris Cotton of New Hampshire, who said:

> [T]his must not be purely an American war. So long as the nations of Asia can be given the impression that it is the white man fighting against the yellow man—even though there may be some yellow men on our side—just so long will the nations of Asia who, however they may feel in their minds about communism and the principles involved, in their hearts will find sympathy to be with their own race, against the white man, who has been exploiting them for so many generations. . . . This war must cease to be an American war. The peace that follows must not be an American peace, to be enforced unilaterally by this country and having frontiers in Asia patrolled by American boys.

Republican congressional leaders agreed with the President's actions. Senate Republican Leader Dirksen, who apparently had discussed the matter with the President, spoke in favor of the decision to renew bombing, and afterwards told Valenti that his "mission was accomplished," [154] i.e., that he had spoken in favor of the decision as he apparently had been asked to do. Ford and Laird, however, continued to take advantage of what they thought was a potent political issue. Republican Party strategists were reported to believe that "divisions within the Democratic party and the prospect of an expanding land war in Vietnam may be giving them a winning political issue against President Johnson. They believe the country may eventually turn against a President whose party does not fully support him and whose war policy may produce long casualty lists without military victory or a negotiated settlement. To take political advantage of this, the Republican leaders are pulling back from direct criticism of the Johnson policy and are de-emphasizing their former 'hard line' on how the war should be conducted. . . . The net effect, these leaders hope, will be to con-

[154] Terry Dietz, *Republicans and Vietnam, 1961–1966* (New York: Greenwood Press, 1986), p. 151.

centrate political as well as constitutional responsibility for the war squarely on the President."[155]

A speech by Laird in the House on January 31, 1966, was apparently part of this plan of action.[156] He began by referring to the "public relations campaign" which he said the White House was conducting for resumption of bombing, and went on to say that he was concerned about the conduct of the war: "[A]bout the unexplained shifts of policy, the starting and stopping of bombing in the North, the failure to make any real progress after the commitment of 200,000 American troops, the uncertainty about our objectives, the failure to divulge information which those who sacrifice in this war have a right to be told and the gap between what they are told and reality." Congress, he said, could not even give adequate advice to the President because of a lack of information.

Laird, using the argument of a Democrat to make his case against the Democrats, cited the Mansfield report, which he said, if true, was a "stinging indictment" of the administration. Yet, he added, there had been no comment on it by the administration.

Both Laird and Ford said that the Presidents should clarify U.S. objectives in Vietnam, and that there should be a debate in Congress, perhaps even a new congressional resolution on Vietnam.

The public, which had favored a bombing pause (59 percent in favor, 33 percent against, 8 percent not sure),[157] also supported a resumption of bombing. According to a Harris Survey reported on January 30, 1966, the day before bombing was resumed, if the peace offensive failed, "the vast majority of Americans would support an immediate escalation of the war—including all-out bombings of North Vietnam and increasing U.S. troop commitments to 500,000 men."

"The temper of American public opinion might be described as hesitantly but determinedly militant if acceptable peace cannot be negotiated."[158]

Noting that before the pause began 39 percent of the public had favored increased bombing, the survey reported that 61 percent would be in favor of "all-out bombings" if the Communists refused to negotiate:

> *"Despite the pause in bombings of North Vietnam and the ceasefire, suppose the communists refuse to sit down and talk peace. Would you then favor or oppose all-out U.S. bombings of every part of North Vietnam?"*

[In percent]

Favor	61
Oppose	17
Not Sure	22

These were the responses to the question about increasing the number of U.S. troops:[159]

---

[155] *New York Times,* Feb. 2, 1966.
[156] *CR,* vol. 112, pp. 1564–1566.
[157] See Harris Survey, p. 128 above.
[158] *Washington Post,* Jan. 31, 1966.
[159] The phrase "if that meant the war might be shortened" may have increased the percentage of those who responded in favor of a troop increase. In another poll taken at about the same time which did not contain such wording, the percentage was much lower—45 percent said that they would be willing to continue the war if 500,000 troops were required. See Sidney Verba, Richard A. Brody, Edwin B. Parker, Norman H. Nie, Nelson W. Polsby, Paul Ekman, and Gor-

Continued

"We now have 250,000 U.S. troops in Vietnam, and about 100 Americans are now being killed here [sic] *every week. Would you favor our increasing the number of U.S. troops to 500,000—with higher losses of life—if that meant the war might be shortened or would you be against such a big increase in U.S. troops?"*

[In percent]

Favor	60
Oppose	25
Not Sure	15

The small antiwar element of the public reacted very unfavorably to the resumption of bombing.[160] In New York City on February 1, 1966 there was a 24-hour silent vigil at the U.N. followed by a march of about 1,000 demonstrators to Times Square, where many of the marchers engaged in a sit-down that snarled rush hour traffic.[161] This followed a month-long series of efforts by antiwar groups to support the peace offensive and to oppose resumption of bombing and escalation of the war.

On January 6, the militant civil rights group, the Student Nonviolent Coordinating Committee (SNCC), headed by James Forman, issued a statement saying that the U.S. was following an "aggressive policy in violation of international law" in Vietnam, and that SNCC supported those men "who are unwilling to respond to the military draft which would compel them to contribute their lives to U.S. aggression in the name of the 'freedom' we find so false in this country."[162] The more moderate National Association for the Advancement of Colored People, headed by Roy Wilkins, a friend and supporter of President Johnson, disagreed with SNCC, but Dr. Martin Luther King, Jr. and Floyd B. McKissick, national director of CORE (Congress of Racial Equality), supported SNCC's position. In a related development, Julian Bond, director of communications for SNCC, who had just been elected to the Georgia House of Representatives, was alleged to have engaged in "disorderly conduct" for having advocated violation of the draft, and was denied his seat in the legislature by a vote of 184–12, a decision later reversed by a federal court. (The 12 votes in his favor, 6 black, and 6 white, were from Fulton County (Atlanta), Bond's home.)[163]

Many religious groups were also actively supporting the peace offensive and opposing escalation of the war. On January 15, 1966, the Synagogue Council of America, representing the three main branches of American Judaism, called on President Johnson not to escalate the war if the peace offensive failed.[164] The National Emergency Committee of Clergy Concerned about Vietnam, an interfaith effort organized in New York in January 1966, urged the President to extend the bombing pause and not to escalate the

---

don S. Black, "Public Opinion and the War in Vietnam," *American Political Science Review,* 61 (June 1967), pp. 317–333 at 320n.

[160] On Feb. 4, 1966, the *New York Times* reported that congressional mail was generally opposed to resumption of bombing, but it also reported that, according to an informal survey it had conducted in each region of the country, the general public supported the President's decision to resume bombing.

[161] *Ibid.,* Feb. 1, 2, 1966.

[162] *Black Protest, History, Documents and Analyses 1619 to the Present,* edited with introduction and commentary by Joanne Grant (Greenwich, Conn.: Fawcett, 1968), p. 417.

[163] *New York Times,* Jan. 7, 9, 11, 1966.

[164] *Ibid.,* Jan. 16, 1966.

war.[165] Those active in organizing the group, which later became known as Clergy and Laymen Concerned About Vietnam, included William Sloane Coffin, Protestant chaplain at Yale University; John C. Bennett, president of the Union Theological Seminary; Richard Neuhaus, a Lutheran pastor; Abraham Herchel, a professor at the Jewish Theological Seminary; Harold Bosley, a Methodist minister; Maurice Eisendrath, president of the Union of American Hebrew Congregations and Balfour Brickner, director of the Union's interfaith activities; David Hunter, deputy general secretary of the National Council of Churches; and Father Donald Campion, former editor of the Catholic journal, *America*. (At the time the group was organized, Daniel Berrigan, a Jesuit priest who strongly opposed the war, had been prohibited by his religious order from antiwar activities and had been transferred to Latin America. After a number of protests by Catholics and non-Catholics, including several hundred young Jesuits who threatened to leave the order, he was returned from Latin American and subsequently became active in Concerned Clergy.) By the end of January, the committee consisted of 40 prominent clergymen, including Martin Luther King, Jr. and Robert McAfee Brown, a prominent theologian on the faculty of Stanford University.[166]

A few days later, a statement criticizing the Concerned Clergy and supporting the Johnson administration was issued by a group headed by Dr. Charles Wesley Lowry, president and founder of the Foundation for Religious Action in the Social and Civic Order, and signed, among others by Rabbi Norman Gerstenfeld of the Washington Hebrew Congregation; Dr. George N. Shuster, assistant to the president of Notre Dame University and former president of Hunter College; Kenneth D. Wells, president of Freedom Foundation; and retired Gen. Albert C. Wedemeyer.[167]

Although college and university students were less active at the time because of examinations and vacations, the student-led committee that was coordinating antiwar activities—the National Coordinating Committee to End the War in Vietnam—held a national meeting during the January peace offensive, and, among other things, voted 38–25 against immediate withdrawal of U.S. forces from Vietnam. This action, which reportedly was taken because of concern about the loss of public support for ending the war if the committee approved immediate withdrawal, was indicative of the state of affairs at the time. Although there was strong support for immediate withdrawal, the majority of the members of the committee correctly perceived that the public was not prepared to take such a step, especially during the peace offensive.

Likewise, the administration took a moderate stance in the case of three Americans who went to North Vietnam in December 1965 at the invitation of the North Vietnamese and without U.S. permission, and did not prosecute them, allegedly because such action could adversely affect the U.S. peace offensive. The three were: Herbert Aptheker, director of the American Institute for Marxist

---

[165] *Ibid.*, Jan. 19, 1966.

[166] On the organization and activities of the Concerned Clergy, see Mitchell K. Hall, *Because of Their Faith: CALCAV and Religious Opposition to the Vietnam War* (New York: Columbia Univ. Press, 1990), and William Sloane Coffin, *Once to Every Man* (New York: Atheneum, 1977). On Berrigan's role, see Hall, pp. 14–15.

[167] *New York Times*, Jan. 30, 1966.

Studies, Staughton Lynd of the Yale University history faculty, and Thomas Hayden, a political activist who had been the first president of the SDS. The purpose of their trip was to explore peace possibilities with the North Vietnamese. Upon their return, they said very little except that they were hopeful about peace. Their offer to testify on their trip was declined by the Foreign Relations Committee.[168]

Although the President himself had warned that increasing public opposition could bring down the government and with it the end of U.S. involvement in the war, he continued to be worried about the more militant elements in Congress and among the public which wanted to take stronger military action in Vietnam. Politically, he felt he needed Republican support to offset increasing criticism from his own party in Congress, as well as to withstand pressure to escalate the war from some of the Republicans and conservative Democrats. Thus, instead of trying to appeal to Fulbright, as Rusk, Mansfield and others wanted him to do, he intensified his courtship of the Republicans, especially Dirksen. Mansfield continued to urge Johnson to get together with Fulbright, and following a meeting on foreign aid legislation at the White House on January 31, 1966, he told a White House assistant that he was pleased to see Johnson talking to Fulbright at the meeting. In a memorandum to the President reporting his conversation with Mansfield the assistant said:[169]

> Mansfield believes much could be accomplished if you were to have Fulbright in for breakfast—just the two of you. Mansfield gives me the impression that Fulbright wants to see you alone and assure you of his desire to cooperate but that he feels it is not proper for him to ask the President.
>
> Mansfield made the statement that Fulbright all along has acted in the belief that he was being helpful and that Fulbright is rather concerned that the press has been interpreting his statements as aimed at being harmful to you. All in all Mansfield thinks that if you were to take a few minutes over breakfast some morning it could be a very rewarding occasion.

The President did not act on this advice. A few days later, the Foreign Relations Committee, chaired by Fulbright, opened the first public congressional inquiry into the Vietnam war.

---

[168] *Ibid.*, Dec. 28, 1965, and Jan 10, 11, 1966. For a report on the trip see Staughton Lynd, *The Other Side* (New York: New American Library, 1966).

The State Department agreed to meet with Lynd. For a memorandum of conversation, in which Lynd discussed at length the observations of the North Vietnamese about negotiations, see the State Department's Lot File 74 D 272, "Conversation with Professor Staughton Lynd," Jan. 13, 1966, prepared by James F. Leonard.

[169] Johnson Library, WHCF, Mansfield.

CHAPTER 5

NO END IN SIGHT

In his State of the Union Message on January 12, 1966, President Johnson said that the Vietnam war "just must be the center of our concerns." The U.S., he said, was strong enough both to fight the war and to build the Great Society, but he admitted that because of the war "we cannot do all that we should, or all that we would like to do." [1]

"Tonight the cup of peril is full in Vietnam," the President said, adding, however, "The enemy is no longer close to victory. Time is no longer on his side. There is no cause to doubt the American commitment."

He continued:

> As the assault mounted, our choice gradually became clear. We could leave, abandoning South Vietnam to its attackers and to certain conquest, or we could stay and fight beside the people of South Vietnam.
>
> We stayed.
>
> And we will stay until aggression has stopped.
>
> We will stay because a just nation cannot leave to the cruelties of its enemies a people who have staked their lives and independence on America's solemn pledge—a pledge which has grown through the commitments of three American Presidents.
>
> We will stay because in Asia and around the world are countries whose independence rests, in large measure, on confidence in America's word and in America's protection. To yield to force in Vietnam would weaken that confidence, would undermine the independence of many lands, and would whet the appetite of aggression. We would have to fight in one land, and then we would have to fight in another—or abandon much of Asia to the domination of Communists.
>
> And we do not intend to abandon Asia to conquest.

"The days may become months," he said, "and the months may become years, but we will stay as long as aggression commands us to battle."

In early January, Secretary of State Rusk personally drafted the following cable to Ambassador Lodge, marked "Literally Eyes Only for the Ambassador" (to be seen by no one else):

> In the middle of the night recently, I suddenly realized that the additions to our Defense Budget for the next 18 months because of Vietnam will amount to some $120,000 per Viet Cong. I recalled that our aid to Greece amounted to $50,000 per guerrilla and that we wondered afterward whether we could have

[1] *Public Papers of the Presidents,* Lyndon B. Johnson, 1966, pp. 3–12. In his address the President also reported on the diplomatic efforts made during the bombing pause.

proceeded on a better basis had we started with that concept of available resources. Does the prospect of $120,000 per guerrilla suggest any new lines of thinking about techniques in getting at the fellows? At that rate, they could enjoy the Riviera for many years.[2]

These somewhat puckish observations were also a serious commentary on the predicament facing the United States in Vietnam. From the diplomatic standpoint, it appeared that the Communists did not intend to bargain for peace, believing that the U.S. could be forced to withdraw after an inconclusive conflict increasingly costly in men and money. Militarily, "graduated pressure" through ROLLING THUNDER had failed to compel the Communists to accede,[3] and their response to Westmoreland's plan, to force them through attrition to yield when their losses on the ground reached the "crossover point" (losses exceeding replacements), was to resort to guerrilla tactics and to engage selectively in main-force combat, thereby avoiding heavy casualties.

Moreover, predictions by U.S. military leaders in July 1965 that the Communists could not keep pace with the buildup in U.S. and South Vietnamese forces, and would therefore be progressively outmatched militarily, were proving incorrect. By early 1966 there were an estimated 200,000 Communist troops, regulars and irregulars, in the South, compared to about 100,000 a year before and 153,000 in July 1965.[4] On March 30, 1966, McNamara told a congressional committee that the Communists had 105 infantry (maneuver) battalions at the end of 1965, compared to 65–72 in July of 1965, and would have 155 by the end of 1966—a rate of growth twice that of U.S. and South Vietnamese forces.[5]

It was apparent that, rather than being "won," the war, as McNamara had predicted in his November 1965 report, was becoming stalemated at a higher level of costs and casualties.

During January 1966, McNaughton was privately predicting that as many as one million U.S. troops might be needed to "win."[6]

Likewise, the political situation in South Vietnam, although stabilized somewhat by the endurance of the Ky-Thieu government, did not appear, from the American perspective, to be improving satisfactorily.[7] As McNamara said at a meeting on November 30, 1965, the situation was one of "a tremendous U.S. force on a bowl

---

[2] U.S. Department of State, Central File, Pol 27 Viet S, Washington to Saigon 1935, Jan. 7, 1966. Rusk was whistling a different tune from the meeting with the President on Sept. 9, 1964 when he mentioned the $50,000 it cost per guerrilla in Greece, and said, according to the meeting notes, which indicate that the President and McNamara felt the same way, that it would be "worth any amount to win" in Vietnam. See pt. III of this study, p. 15.

[3] For a good discussion of the results of ROLLING THUNDER during 1965, see *PP,* Gravel ed., vol. IV, pp. 53–58.

[4] U.S. Congress, House, Committee on Armed Services, *Hearings before the House Armed Services Committee on Supplemental Authorization for Vietnam, Fiscal Year 1966,* 89th Cong., 2d sess. (Washington, D.C.: U.S. Govt. Print. Off., 1966), p. 4977.

[5] U.S. Congress, House, Committee on Foreign Affairs, *Foreign Assistance Act of 1966,* Hearings, 89th Cong., 2d sess. (Washington, D.C.: U.S. Govt. Print. Off., 1966), p. 325.

[6] Leslie H. Gelb and Richard K. Betts, *The Irony of Vietnam: The System Worked* (Washington, D.C.: Brookings Institution, 1979), p. 147.

[7] In an effort to obtain information on the attitudes of the South Vietnamese public, the White House commissioned an opinion survey in South Vietnam in the fall of 1965 by the American pollster, Oliver Quayle. A cross-section, which was said to represent 82 percent of the public, was interviewed by Quayle and Company, working with a South Vietnamese public opinion polling group. The results of what was called the TOLEDO project were submitted to the White House, where Hayes Redmon summarized the findings for the President. Quayle's three-volume report is in the Johnson Library, NSF Country File, Vietnam.

of jelly." In a report prepared for McGeorge Bundy on January 7, 1966, NSC staff members James Thomson and Donald W. Ropa said, among other things, that while there had been greater political stability, due in part to a stronger U.S. commitment, the government had been "notably unsuccessful in developing significant popular enthusiasm or positive political support," and "ambitious programs of political, social and economic reforms have made only marginal headway."[8] Pacification, the report said, had made "very little tangible progress" during 1965.

In testimony before the Senate Armed Services Committee in January 1966 McNamara said that there was less control of the countryside than there had been a year before, and considerably less than two years before. Senator Russell: "we are not winning much, are we?" General McConnell, Air Force Chief of Staff: "No, sir, we are not winning."[9]

There were also new signs that, as feared by some U.S. officials, the greatly increased role of the U.S. was having an adverse effect on the ability and the inclination of the South Vietnamese to defend and build their own country. In the *Far Eastern Economic Review,* for December 23, 1965, Dr. Ton That Thien, an academician and editor of an English-language newspaper in Saigon whose views were respected by the Americans, argued that the U.S. was making major decisions "without even lip service paid to prior consultations with the Vietnamese government. . . ." "What is there left" he asked, "for the Vietnamese nationalists to fight for?"

Roy Wehrle, the highly regarded economic counselor of the U.S. Mission, sent the article to Ambassador Lodge on January 10, 1966 with a memorandum in which he said: "Obviously, our efforts here cannot succeed if the Vietnamese adopt in general the attitude that to strive for their country any further is futile."[10]

For their part, the Vietnamese Communists had reaffirmed their determination to prosecute the war. In a December 1965 meeting, the Party's Central Committee adopted a resolution on the strategy to be used in response to the new U.S. role in the war.[11] Anticipating that the U.S. might increase its forces to 300,000–400,000, and increase its attacks in the South as well as the air war against the North, the Central Committee took the position that, no matter what the circumstances, the U.S. would be defeated in two years and forced to withdraw after 60,000 U.S. troops had been killed and 1,000 U.S. aircraft had been shot down. The resolution also said that the war could end in a negotiated settlement, but only on the condition that the Communists would achieve "complete victory."

---

[8] Johnson Library, NSF Country File, Vietnam.

[9] U.S. Congress, Senate, Committee on Armed Services and the Subcommittee on Department of Defense of the Committee on Appropriations, *Supplemental Military Procurement and Construction Authorizations, Fiscal Year 1966,* Hearings on S. 2791 and S. 2792, 89th Cong., 2d sess. (Washington, D.C.: U.S. Govt. Print. Off., 1966), pp. 339, 350.

[10] CMH, Westmoreland Papers, History File.

[11] War Experience Recapitulation Committee of the High-Level Military Institute, *The Anti-U.S. Resistance War for National Salvation,* pp. 83–86; and "Communist Strategy as Reflected in Lao Dong Party and COSVN Resolutions," SRAP 1569 (1967), p. 3, cited in Chester L. Cooper, Judith E. Corson, Laurence J. Legere, David E. Lockwood and Donald M. Weller, *The American Experience with Pacification in Vietnam,* 3 Vols., prepared by the Institute for Defense Analyses for the Advanced Research Projects Agency, Report R–185, March 1972, vol. II, p. 16.

After analyzing U.S. strengths and weaknesses,[12] the resolution further stated that Communist strategy would be to fight a protracted war, but one also aimed at winning a decisive victory in the South in a relatively short period of time by inflicting heavy casualties on American and South Vietnamese forces.

At the same time, the resolution stated, there would have to be a "diplomatic struggle" through which to gain international sympathy, support and assistance.

Finally, the resolution called for "mobilizing the entire nation to resolutely defeat the war of aggression of the U.S. imperialists." "The present mission of opposing the U.S. for national salvation is clearly a sacred mission of our nation and our people in both the South and the North. . . . [we must] have a strong fighting spirit, extraordinary courage, a heroic spirit, and determination to move mountains and fill in the seas, to overcome all obstacles, fulfill all missions, and defeat all enemies."

Signs of Public Impatience and Declining Confidence in the President

In a report on February 28, 1966, of a public opinion survey taken earlier in the month, Louis Harris concluded: "There is 'consensus' in the country today on one point about the Vietnam war: The American people long for an honorable end to hostilities, but by 2 to 1 they believe we have to stay and see it through."[13] Harris also reported that, "More and more the American people are becoming split between those who favor an all-out military effort to shorten the war and those who prefer negotiations to the risk of escalation." He estimated that 16 percent of the population ("hawks") favored all-out war and 10 percent ("doves,") preferred negotiations, but that "If there is a movement of opinion in the country it is toward seeking a military solution to what is generally regarded as a frustrating stalemate."[14]

---

[12] "The carrying out of a passive, unjust war prevented the U.S. from using all of their economic and military strength. The will to fight of the U.S. soldiers was very weak. The U.S. strategy wavered between offense and defense, between holding land and moving around. Its rear area was far away and supply was difficult, and the fighting was not appropriate to the training, organization, and equipment of the U.S. forces, who were forced to fight in the way dictated by the opposition." *The Anti-U.S. Resistance War for National Salvation*, p. 84.

[13] *Washington Post*, Feb. 28, 1966.

[14] In the February 1966 Harris survey respondents were asked to indicate which of the following statements they agreed with most:

"(1) I disagree with present policy; we are not going far enough. We should go further, such as carrying the war more into North Vietnam.

"(2) I agree with what we are doing but we should increase our military effort to win a clear military victory.

"(3) I agree with what we are doing, but we should do more to bring about negotiations, such as a cease-fire.

"(4) I disagree with present policy; we shouldn't be there. We shouldn't be bombing North Vietnam and should pull our troops out now."

The responses were as follows:

[In percent]

Disagree, carry war more to North	16
Agree, but increase military effort	33
Agree, but do more to negotiate	34
Disagree, pull out	9
Not sure	8

The White House interpreted the February 1966 Harris Survey to mean that support for the war fell whenever U.S. military pressure was lessened, and that increased opposition to the war and loss of support for the President's handling of it came primarily from those who favored

The President and his associates were fully apprised of Harris' findings in advance of their publication, and at White House meetings on February 19 and 26, 1966 the conclusions of the poll were mentioned. Moyers, who read aloud the poll results in the second of these meetings, commented that the administration was ". . . being criticized from both ends. President is either not moving strong enough or too strong." He added that the poll revealed the "first signs of American impatience with long war."[15] There are no recorded comments by other participants in the meeting.

The February 1966 Harris Survey, as well as a Gallup poll taken at about the same time, also showed a sudden and substantial decline in the public's confidence in the President's handling of the war. In the first six weeks of 1966, according to Harris, approval dropped from 63 percent to 49 percent, the lowest since January 1965 (when it was 41 percent). (The public's approval of the President's overall performance dropped from 67 to 62 percent.)[16]

From the Gallup and Harris polls taken at the time, it is difficult to ascertain what course of action the public preferred, if, indeed, a clear preference is ascertainable. Generally, the public supported the war and was willing to support some further escalation, while rejecting alternatives that would involve a sudden withdrawal of U.S. forces or abandonment of commitments. But there was also strong support for a negotiated settlement. According to a study by the National Opinion Research Center,[17] "88 percent of the public would be willing to "negotiate with the Vietcong," 54 percent would "hold free elections even if the Vietcong might win," 52 percent would "allow a coalition government including the Vietcong," and 70 percent would approve of a truce negotiated by the U.N.[18] The

---

stronger military action. (*New York Times,* Mar. 10, 1966.) Sidney Verba, et al., "Public Opinion and the War in Vietnam," cited above, disagree with this interpretation, pointing out that a counter-trend reported in another Harris survey in April suggests that the results reported in February were temporary.

[15] Johnson Library, Meetings Notes File, Valenti notes of meeting on Feb. 26, 1966.

[16] For the Gallup Poll, see the *New York Times,* Mar. 10, 1966. According to Gallup, support for the President's handling of the war in this same period declined from 56 percent to 50. The difference in the figures in the two polls may be largely accounted for by Gallup's use of a third, "no opinion" category, whereas Harris grouped opinions into two categories.

[17] Sidney Verba, et al., "Public Opinion and the War in Vietnam," cited above. This article was based on a nationwide poll taken by the National Opinion Research Center of Chicago in late February and early March 1966, as reported in *Public Opinion and the War in Vietnam* (Stanford, Calif.: Institute of Political Studies at Stanford Univ., Mar. 15, 1966).

These were the results of a question concerning alternative courses of military action (p. 328): *"Suppose you had to choose among continuing the present situation indefinitely, fighting a major war with hundreds of thousands of casualties, or a withdrawal of American troops leading to an eventual Communist takeover. Which would you choose?"* The responses were:

"19% Withdraw, allow Communist takeover
"43% Continue present situation indefinitely
"23% Fight major war
" 9% No opinion"

The tendentious wording—"leading to a Communist takeover"—in this question may have affected its results. As Mueller has pointed out (*War, Presidents and Public Opinion,* p. 100), whenever the "Communist" issue was raised by the wording of a question in public opinion polls on the war, the result was to raise substantially the level of respondents' support for the war.

Respondents were also asked (p. 320 n) whether they would be willing to continue the fight in Vietnam given certain changes in U.S. policy in response to the situation. These were the responses: "bombing of military targets in North Vietnam (77% approved), 200,000 troops in Vietnam (61% approved) [it is not clear why these two questions were asked—the U.S. was already bombing military targets in North Vietnam, and there were already 200,000 U.S. troops in South Vietnam], . . . 500,000 troops (45%), all-out mobilization (40%) . . . fighting the Chinese in Vietnam (56%), fighting the Chinese in China (32%), fighting an atomic war with China (29%), and fighting an atomic war with Russia (22%)."

[18] Other responses to questions about de-escalation and negotiations were as follows (p. 321 n): "approval of a withdrawal from Vietnam even if it meant a Communist takeover in Laos

Continued

study concluded that the public was "relatively permissive," and would support a settlement involving a "willingness to deal with the Vietcong that goes beyond present administration policy."[19]

Approval of the Deployment of Phase II Forces

In July 1965, when the President approved the deployment of large-scale U.S. forces to Vietnam, U.S. military leaders estimated that Phase I ("strategic defense") of the proposed plan for fighting the war, under which 175,000 U.S. forces along with South Vietnamese and other forces would reverse the losing trend, would be completed by the end of 1965. This would be followed by Phase II ("strategic offense") during the first six months of 1966, involving 275,000–300,000 U.S. forces. If necessary, there would then be a third phase, requiring an estimated one and a half years, following the completion of the second phase in July 1966, during which the remaining enemy forces would be defeated. An unspecified number of additional U.S. forces would be required for Phase III. By October 1965, however, the military had substantially altered these original estimates. Phase I, rather than being completed in six months, would take at least another year, and Phase I forces would need to be increased to 325,000 during 1966. By November 30, 1965, when McNamara reported on his trip to Vietnam, the estimated number of troops needed during Phase I in 1966 had jumped from 325,000 to 400,000. By early February 1966, the figure had increased to 429,000 (102 maneuver battalions, 79 of which would be American). Even if it were to be assumed that in the making of the original decision the figures and the timetable were tailored to some degree to the political-bureaucratic situation and did not reflect the more realistic assumptions of military leaders,[20] increases and changes of this magnitude would give pause to any policymaker, as they doubtless did to Lyndon Johnson.

It could be argued, of course, that the President recognized when he approved large-scale forces in July 1965 that Phase I would take many more men and months of effort than were called for in the military operations plan, and that the war would be long and costly, but felt that he had no choice but to act as he did. It could even be argued that the President, feeling that he had no choice, approved the use of large-scale forces with the expectation that the war might not be won and might even cost him his Presidency in the belief that it was the only way he could satisfy the demand for greater U.S. involvement while allowing time for the creation of the legislative framework for the Great Society.

Even though the military had estimated that Phase I would not be completed until the end of 1966, they had requested in October

---

and Thailand as well as Vietnam (13% approve) . . . immediate withdrawal (15%), letting Vietcong eventually gain control (28%), gradual withdrawal while letting Vietnamese work out their own problems (39%) . . . agreeing to a UN-supervised truce (69%)."

[19] The Harris Survey in February 1966 found that the public also generally supported the government's efforts to keep the war limited. Harris reported that, "By 2 to 1, public opinion now would sanction a naval blockade imposed on North Vietnam ports. But by 4 to 3, the American people oppose bombing Hanoi, by 5 to 1 are against bombing population centers in North Vietnam, by 7 to 1 believe it is wrong to bomb the Chinese mainland, by 9 to 1 oppose the use of atomic ground weapons and by 11 to 1 are against dropping atom bombs on China." *Washington Post,* Mar. 7, 1966.

[20] It will be recalled that the U.S. Army Chief of Staff told the President in March 1965 that to win would take 500,000 men and five years. See pt. III of this study, p. 166.

1965 the deployment of the additional forces scheduled for Phase II, and McNamara had so recommended in memoranda to the President in November and again in December. The President did not act on these requests. On January 24, 1966, McNamara resubmitted the December request in slightly revised form.[21] With respect to the resumption of bombing, as noted, he did not recommend the heavy "fast track" increase proposed by the military. Instead, he recommended that airstrikes against North Vietnam be increased gradually to 4,000 monthly, compared to an average of 3,000 or less per month during the second half of 1965, and to 4,500 monthly against Laos compared to 511 per month in June 1965 and 3,047 in December. (During the bombing pause in December, airstrikes were diverted from North Vietnam to Laos.) He repeated, however, the estimate in his December 7 memo that the North Vietnamese, while suffering from air attacks, would still be capable of sending large numbers of forces to the South and of sending more than enough supplies to sustain Communist military activity in the South at a "light combat" level. (It was estimated, according to the memorandum, that 140 tons a day would be needed to sustain light combat by the estimated 150 Communist battalions fighting in the South by the end of 1966, and that the North Vietnamese would be capable, despite U.S. air attacks, of supplying 200 tons a day.) Nevertheless, McNamara added, in an apparent justification for the increased level of bombing,

> the increased program probably will not put a tight ceiling on the enemy's activities in South Vietnam, but probably will reduce the flow of supplies to the point where the enemy receives too little for full flexibility and for frequent oppressive actions, too little to defend themselves as often against aggressive US/GVN forces, and too little to permit Hanoi to continue to deploy forces with complete confidence that they can be supplied.
>
> Furthermore, as very important by-products, the program will keep the pressure on North Vietnam—to condition them toward negotiations and an acceptable end to the war—and will maintain the morale of our South Vietnam allies.

With respect to troops, McNamara recommended in his January 24 memorandum that 367,800 U.S. troops be deployed by the end of 1966. He did not recommend the mobilization and callup of Reserves proposed by General Johnson.[22] After citing Westmoreland's

---

[21] Johnson Library, Warnke Papers, McNaughton Files, "The Military Outlook in South Vietnam," Jan. 24, 1966.

[22] One of the major problems with respect to Phase II was the limit on the number of troops that could be deployed to Vietnam without excessively drawing down U.S. forces needed in other areas, calling up Reserve forces, or increasing the draft. In his January 24 memorandum, McNamara told the President that the position of JCS was that in order to deploy expeditiously the number of troops requested by CINCPAC and MACV there would have to be a selective call-up of Reserves and a selective extension of terms of service of existing personnel. For reasons which he considered compelling, the President did not want to call the Reserves. On the other hand, if he did not accede to the military's requests he risked alienating them and their supporters by appearing to balk at taking the necessary military action to "win." This could produce a reaction that could greatly complicate the task of fighting the war and of keeping it limited. It could also exacerbate attacks on the President's domestic programs.

For a discussion of the factors involved in the decision not to call the Reserves, and criticism of the President for not doing so, see Stuckey and Pistorius, "Mobilization for the Vietnam War," pp. 27–38 and Richard B. Crossland and James T. Currie, *Twice the Citizen: A History of the United States Army Reserve, 1908–1983* (Washington, D.C.: Office of the Chief, Army Reserve,

Continued

estimates of what should and would be accomplished by augmented U.S. forces, McNamara said that there could be "a snow-balling in our favor before December." "On the other hand," he said, "if the enemy force build-up is as predicted and if attrition of that force and of its supplies fall short, we could find ourselves 'behind the power curve' going into 1967; we could be faced with the requirement to deploy at least an additional 3-division corps (27 battalions) in 1967. . . . Even though the Communists will continue to suffer heavily from our ground and air action, we expect them, upon learning of any U.S. intentions to augment its forces, to boost their own commitments and to test U.S. capabilities and will to persevere at a higher level of conflict and casualties (U.S. killed-in-action with the recommended deployments can be expected to reach 1,000 a month)."

"If the US were willing to commit enough forces," McNamara said, using language from his December 7, 1965 version of the request "—perhaps 600,000 men or more—we could probably ultimately prevent the DRV/VC from sustaining the conflict at a significant level. When this point was reached, however, the question of Chinese intervention would become critical."

McNamara concluded the January 24 statement of the request for Phase II forces with language that also had been used in the December 7 version: "It follows, therefore, that the odds are about even that, even with the recommended deployments, we will be faced in early 1967 with a military stand-off at a much higher level, with pacification hardly underway and with the requirement for the development of still more U.S. forces."[23]

McNamara's January 24 memorandum requesting Phase II forces seemed to assume that the President had already approved the request.[24] Subsequently, however, as will be seen, McNamara told Defense Department officials and the JCS that a decision had not been made. Was McNamara presumptuous in appearing to assume in his memorandum that the decision had been made? This is unlikely, given his style of operating in close harmony with the President and in formulating his memorandum to the President in accordance with the President's express wishes. A more likely explanation is that the President had led McNamara and other close advisers to believe that he would approve Phase II forces—Phase II was, after all, a continuation of the plan agreed upon earlier—

1984). The use of Reserves had been proposed by McNamara, acting on recommendations from the military, in July 1965, as part of his report to the President on the question of sending large-scale U.S. forces to Vietnam. But the President, partly on the basis of discussions with key Members of Congress, did not approve the proposal. (See pt. III of this study, pp. 384, 417.) There were various reasons for this decision and for the President's continued resistance to the idea until the spring of 1968, when he finally agreed, under special circumstances, to call up a small number of Reserves. The major reason was that he wanted to keep the war from adversely affecting his domestic legislative program. Under the law (10 USC 673) up to 1,000,000 reservists could be on active duty, called involuntarily, each for a period of two years, but he would have to declare a national emergency in order to do so and thereby risk heightening congressional and public concern about the war. Alternatively, he could request congressional approval of a call-up, but this could have the same effect, as well as providing opponents of the war with an opening for debate. Congress might also impose time or other restrictions on the use of such forces, as it did in a case several years earlier involving a crisis over Berlin. In addition, a Reserve call-up could create adverse political effects as a result of the disruption of the lives of reservists.

As will be seen, in late 1966 Congress removed the 1,000,000 limit.

[23] The earlier language had stated "with pacification still stalled, and with the prospect of military success marred by the chances of an active Chinese intervention."

[24] See *PP*, Gravel ed., vol. 4, p. 49.

but that, for various reasons, he was refraining from taking more explicit, formal action on the request. For one thing, he apparently was concerned about possible reactions if it were to become known that he had approved such a large increase in U.S. forces, especially so soon after the bombing halt and the "peace offensive" and at a time when the U.N., at the initiative of the United States, was considering the Vietnam problem. Another major reason was the need, before deploying Phase II forces, to reach an agreement with U.S. military leaders on the manpower problem.

It also seems likely that the President was not certain in his own mind about the course of U.S. action and was not prepared at the time to take final action on the request. Changes in the military timetable, together with McNamara's change of mind and his predictions that military force would lead to a stalemate at a higher level, probably also contributed to the President's restraint.

It will be recalled that in meetings in December 1965 the President had expressed some of these concerns. On December 7, in a meeting with Rusk, McNamara and McGeorge Bundy, he said that although he had little sympathy for Fulbright's position, he did not hold out much hope for a military solution, and that he would gladly "trade back to where we were" when he became President. In a meeting on December 18, McNamara said that a military solution to the problem would have only a one in two or one in three chance of succeeding, and that the U.S. would have to find a diplomatic solution. The President responded: "Then, no matter what we do in [the] military field there is no sure victory," and McNamara replied: "That's right. We have been too optimistic." Rusk said he was more optimistic than McNamara. McGeorge Bundy said he agreed with McNamara that the eventual settlement would have to be "political," but he, too, thought McNamara was being too pessimistic.

The President's ambivalence increased after the bombing pause and peace offensive failed to elicit any positive responses. In an interview several years later Bill Moyers was asked, "When did the feeling emerge that we were into something that we couldn't get out of and that hadn't brought the results we'd hoped for?" He replied: "I think by early 1966. After the failure of the peace offensive—the thirty-seven-day bombing pause, the expeditions overseas, the private messages to Hanoi—after all that came to no good end, I believed the President began to expect the worst. More and more he would talk about a long war with no end in sight. He kept pushing for action on domestic legislation because he realized that time would run out as the costs of the war rose."[25]

Although the President was hesitant, he finally gave limited, tentative approval to the deployment of Phase II forces during a Conference in Honolulu on February 5–8, 1966. The form and manner of this decision appeared to confirm the President's uncertainty about the course of action that was being implemented, as well as his desire, for the various reasons mentioned above, to keep the decision from appearing to be a decision. And, indeed, there is no evidence that there was further Presidential action or a "decision" as such authorizing Phase II forces. Apparently the deployments were

---

[25] "Bill Moyers Talks About the War and LBJ, An Interview," in Robert Manning and Michael Janeway, *Who We Are: An Atlantic Chronicle of the United States and Vietnam* (Boston: Little Brown, 1969), pp. 261 ff at p. 269.

permitted to be made by McNamara with the consent of the President but without the President himself being openly or directly involved.

Westmoreland said that in his private talks with President Johnson during the conference the President "seemed intense, perturbed, uncertain how to proceed with the Vietnam problem, torn by the apparent magnitude of it."[26]

At the conference, Westmoreland met with McNamara, who, probably after talking to the President, said "that we would go for" the number of forces that had been requested by Westmoreland.[27] Westmoreland also met with the President, who asked him how many troops he needed. Westmoreland, replied that he needed twice the number he had, and that he would discuss the matter with McNamara.[28] This led to an agreement at the conference between McNamara and the military on an increase to 429,000 U.S. troops (the U.S. part of the 102 maneuver battalions) by the end of the year, as well as specified increases in U.S. airstrikes, third-country forces, and South Vietnamese forces based on the following statement of missions and objectives:[29]

Expand the offensive actions of such forces while providing essential defense.

The South Vietnamese, U.S. and third-country forces, in coordination will:

1. Defend military bases, political and population centers and food-producing areas now under government control.

2. Open and secure lines of communications required to support military operations and for essential support of the civilian population.

3. Conduct clearing and securing operations to provide military security in the four selected high priority national construction areas.

4. Conduct intensified offensive operations against major VC/PAVN forces, bases and lines of communications—almost doubling the number of battalion-months of offensive operations from 40 to 75 a month.

5. Increase the level of attack on the infiltration routes through Laos and North Vietnam by more than 60 per cent—5,400 to 9,000 attack sorties a month.

Achieve the following results in 1966:

1. Increase the population in secure areas to 60 per cent from 50 per cent.

---

[26] Westmoreland, *A Soldier Reports,* p. 159.

[27] National Archives, Westmoreland-CBS Papers, from "General Westmoreland's Historical Briefing, 16 Feb. 1966."

[28] *Ibid.*

[29] Johnson Library, Warnke Papers, McNaughton Files. Gen. Douglas Kinnard, who served in Vietnam, says that the task assigned to Westmoreland by the Bundy-McNaughton paper, "was not only a big task but, also, in more than one way, a fuzzy one. How, for instance, do you destroy a base area when it might be occupied again? What does 40 to 50 percent mean in such a context?" Kinnard, "The 'Strategy' of the War in South Vietnam," in *Vietnam in Remission,* James F. Veninga and Harry A. Wilmer (eds.) (College Station, Texas: Texas A & M Press, 1985), pp. 19–32, at p. 23.

Kinnard adds: "In 1974, when I surveyed the general officers who had commanded in Vietnam, I asked: 'How clear were the objectives of the war?' . . . In responding to the question, almost 70 percent of the generals said that they were uncertain of the war's objectives. While it seems possible for 70 percent of the privates in a war to be unsure of the objectives, how is it possible for 70 percent of the generals not to understand the objectives? To me, this mirrors a deep-seated strategic failure: the inability of policymakers to frame tangible, obtainable goals."

2. Increase the critical roads and railroads open for use to 50 per cent from 20 per cent.

3. Increase the destruction of VC/PAVN base areas to 40–50 per cent from 10–20 per cent.

4. Ensure the defense of all military bases, political and population centers and food-producing areas now under government control.

5. Military security needed for pacification of the four selected high-priority areas—increasing the pacified population in those areas by 235,000.

6. Attrite, by year's end, VC/PAVN forces at a rate as high as their capability to put men into the field [the "cross-over point"].

It is not clear why, having requested 367,800 U.S. troops on January 24, McNamara should have agreed to 429,000 on February 10. The answer probably lies in a footnote to the earlier figure in the January 24 report that it would "rise substantially above this if estimates of CINCPAC are accepted."

In the February 10 memorandum it was also noted that the approved figure of 429,000 was 20,000 less than the latest request of Westmoreland.

In a meeting of Defense and JCS officials in Washington on February 9, 1966, McNamara, reporting on the Honolulu meeting, summarized the status of action on the request for Phase II forces. He said that it was "simply not possible yet to decide" about the level of troop deployment or whether there would be a Reserve call-up, but he added that Defense and military officials should "assume and act to deploy" forces according to Phase II plans, and that they should "assume and act on the basis that we are authorized to deploy up to 260,000 personnel through March 31, 1966," and that if more were needed they should be requested.[30] "This contemplates," he said, "the deployment by the end of the year of 102 combat maneuver battalions (including third country forces) and related forces amounting to 429,000 U.S. military personnel"—the level of forces planned for Phase II.

McNamara also explained some of the issues involved in deciding whether to call up the Reserves:

> the political aspects of a Reserve call-up are extremely delicate. There are several strong bodies of opinion at work in the country. . . . One school of thought . . . is that this country is over extended economically and that we cannot afford to do what we are doing. Another school of thought feels that we plain should not be there at all, whether or not we can afford it. A third school of thought is that although we are rightly there, the war is being mismanaged so that we are heading straight toward war with China. Furthermore, there is no question but that the economy of this country is beginning to run near or at its capacity with the resulting probability of a shortage of certain skills and materiel. If this continues we may be facing wage and price controls, excess profits taxes,

---

[30] *PP*, Gravel ed., vol. IV, p. 312, memorandum of the meeting on Feb. 9, 1966 of the Secretary of Defense and Department of Defense and military officials.

etc., all of which will add fuel to the fire of those who say we cannot afford this.

"With all these conflicting pressures," McNamara said, "it is a very delicate and difficult task for the Administration to mobilize and maintain the required support in this country to carry on the war properly. The point of all this is to emphasize that a call-up of the Reserves presents extremely serious problems in many areas and a decision cannot be made today."

General Johnson, Army Chief of Staff, stressing the need for a call-up, responded that it might be an important factor in demonstrating U.S. determination to win the war. Call-ups, he said, also tended to help unify public opinion by involving more citizens in the support of a war. Moreover, there was a need to consider the degree to which the U.S. was becoming involved in a program of containing the Chinese Communists along the southern border of China, and the potential manpower requirements that this might entail.[31]

Several weeks later, McNamara accepted a JCS proposal to deploy the additional troops by July 1967 rather than by the end of 1966.[32]

Efforts to Strengthen Pacification and Political Development

Faced with apparent lack of progress in "winning" the war or in negotiating a settlement, U.S. policymakers were confronted with the need to improve existing programs as well as to find better ways of achieving U.S. objectives—to develop, in Rusk's words, "new lines of thinking about techniques in getting at the fellows," as well as the internal strength and security necessary for self-government and self-defense.

There was general agreement that the ultimate success of military operations in achieving U.S. objectives depended upon effective pacification. Only when the rural areas were made secure would it be possible to have a stable and self-sustaining political community. This, of course, had been Lodge's approach, and after he returned to Vietnam in August 1965, the U.S. Mission gave priority to "rural development" ("rural construction") programs, while the CIA increased the training of local paramilitary cadres to provide better security in local areas.[33]

Lodge's selection of Lansdale as his assistant, with general responsibility for creating a "peoples' force"—"competitive political movement," had led to a series of interpersonal and interagency rivalries and antagonisms, however, and after several months Lansdale felt compelled to ask Lodge for some clarification of his

[31] *Ibid.*, p. 314.

[32] JCSM–218–66, Apr. 4, 1966.

[33] Under the guidance and assistance of the CIA, with additional help from AID, the new Vietnamese Ministry of Rural Construction, established in September 1965, launched a "revolutionary development" (RD) program in late 1965. With the help of local security forces consisting of small CIA-trained RD armed teams, (so-called PATs—People's Action Teams—which the CIA had begun to develop in 1964) supplemented by a new Police Field Force (PFF), also trained by the CIA, the ministry initiated a "New Life Development Program" to win the support of the rural population. For an explanation of the development and purpose of the RD armed teams (PATs), see the memoir by Peer de Silva, CIA Station Chief in Vietnam in 1964–66, *sub rosa* (New York: Times Books, 1978), pp. 221–280 *passim*.

role. In a memorandum to Lodge on December 2, 1965, "Role of S.L.O.," Lansdale said that there were three main problem areas:[34]

> One. U.S. permission and support in doing the constructive political work which the GVN and other Vietnamese are begging us to do.
>
> Two. A clear definition of what SLO can do, realistically, in the Vietnamese pacification program.
>
> Three. How can we help you personally in solving non-recurrent contingency problems, from our unorthodox status, without creating antagonism from responsible people in regularly established U.S. agencies?

With respect to the first problem area, Lansdale noted that various Vietnamese leaders had been asking him for help in dealing with their fellow Vietnamese, but that the Mission messages to Washington in each case had cautioned against taking action on the request, and that he "had no inkling of what Washington thinks about these requests." (In the margin next to the comment about Vietnamese asking for help, Lodge wrote: "Very involved questions, and given their national characteristics, extremely delicate position for official Americans to be in.") Lansdale said that, in view of the "obvious resentment of such a role for me on the part of U.S. Mission people," he had hesitated to undertake "such delicate work, with any expectation of success, if responsible Americans are crowding me every inch of the way." "I sympathize with their feelings," he said, "but also believe that perhaps the U.S. cannot afford the luxury of such feelings in a war where winning goes to those who take necessary risks." (In the margin, Lodge wrote: "2 political sections?"—a reference to the friction between Lansdale and his team and Habib, the Embassy's political officer, and the staff of the Political Section.) "Maybe my main usefulness today," he added, "would be simply that of bringing Vietnamese together, overcoming their suspicions of one another. The good Lord knows, they are so split up into rivalries and jealousies that somebody or something has to bring them together into enough unity to save themselves."

The second problem was the direction and management of the U.S. role in pacification. "Much to my surprise and amazement," Lansdale told Lodge, "I find that a number of Americans believe that my function in Vietnam is to provide the directing management on the U.S. side for this whole pacification program—with no other resources than my wits and a title. . . ." (In the margin, Lodge wrote: "*My* job." He also noted: "They should not think this. SLO work is coordinating, spurring on Vietnamese, while OSA and USOM provide and apply wherewithal, training, etc.") (emphasis in original)

The third problem, Lansdale said, was organizational: How could his unconventional, unorthodox operation perform its role in harmony with the "regularly established" organizations (State, Defense, AID)? "A large percentage of our time and energies are spent in coordination just to preserve some measure of harmony, and still meet some of the crash deadlines required to serve you in timely

[34] Massachusetts Historical Society, Lodge Papers. S.L.O. (Special Liaison Office) was the designation given to Lansdale and his team.

and meaningful fashion." No one in SLO "has time or use for the questionable sport of bureaucratic and jurisdictional infighting. . . ." Yet, "We have no clearly defined mission that has been accepted by the U.S. organizations in Vietnam, even though some of the officials in the parent organizations in Washington are hopeful that some magical miracle can be pulled off." (In the margin next to the observation about not having a clearly defined mission, Lodge noted: "You have." In the opposite margin he wrote: "If you succeed you will.")

Lodge responded to Lansdale's memorandum by giving him authority to deal with the various Vietnamese groups "'as they approach' you as regards Rural Construction-Pacification," but told him that "there must be no free-wheeling political maneuvering or stirring up of any special interest groups which could in the slightest degree support a change of Government."[35]

On December 15, 1965, Lodge sent Lansdale a memorandum, "Roles of Different U.S. Agencies in the Three Phases of Rural Construction, that is, Military Clearing, Pacification and Development," in which he sought to clarify the role of Lansdale and his team.[36] Referring to Lansdale as the "principal coordinator for the mission and principal contact point with the GVN in the fields of pacification and development," Lodge said that he considered pacification to be primarily a civilian effort, and that the two principal U.S. civilian agencies, USOM (U.S. Overseas Mission—the term used for the AID staff in Saigon) and the CIA (referred to as OSA—Office of Special Activities) were to be considered the principal operating agencies which Lansdale should use in implementing his role. According to the memorandum, the military (MACV) were not to be considered an operating agency, although they would continue to provide to Lansdale's office "such support as you [Lansdale] may deem necessary to further our effort in this field."

Westmoreland, who was on a trip to CINCPAC headquarters in Hawaii, was told about the memorandum by his Chief of Staff, General Rosson, who said that this would be "extremely injurious to the U.S. effort in Vietnam," and sent him the text of a memorandum to send to Lodge in opposition to the plan.[37] (Among other things, Lodge's plan would have involved the transfer from MACV to USOM/OSA of military personnel who were assigned to pacification.)[38] As suggested, Westmoreland sent the memorandum to Lodge.

In response to Westmoreland, Lodge stated that there was nothing in his directive that would affect the military's role in support of pacification, and that the purpose of the directive was to reduce the number of U.S. Mission contacts with the Rural Reconstruction

---

[35] Massachusetts Historical Society, Lodge Papers, memoranda from Lodge to Lansdale, Dec. 7 and 13, 1965.

[36] Same location. See this same location for a memorandum on December 16 from Lansdale to the members of the U.S. Mission Council in which he asked for their support in getting the information needed to carry out his assignment, and suggested a meeting to work out staffing arrangements.

[37] For the text of Rosson's proposal see CMH, Westmoreland Papers, Message Files, General Rosson to General Westmoreland, MAC 6481, Dec. 16, 1965, and for the cable from Westmoreland to Lodge, see, in the same location, HWA 3420, Dec. 17, 1965.

[38] See Lansdale's memorandum of December 16 on steps to implement Lodge's memorandum of December 15, the text of which is in Rosson's cable cited above.

Ministry "and to place emphasis on the primary civilian, political and social aspect of the rural reconstruction effort."[39]

In a subsequent discussion with Lodge and Porter, as well as a cable to Washington in which he explained MACV's position, Westmoreland argued that there needed to be "complete integration" of all U.S. programs, military and civilian, that were involved in pacification. Moreover, pacification could not be handled by a single element or agency of the U.S. Mission; rather it required a coordinating committee which, Westmoreland proposed, should operate under the direction of Deputy Ambassador Porter.[40]

In his discussion with Lodge and Porter and in the cable to Washington, Westmoreland objected to the designation of Lansdale as pacification coordinator. According to the "talking paper" prepared for Westmoreland's use at the meeting, Lansdale was "well known for his dislike of bureaucratic machinery . . . [and] should not be given the responsibility for the day to day coordination of any major programs. He is simply not disposed to accept such responsibilities nor do I believe his group has the depth or the strength to do so." Lansdale's ability, and the scope and direction of his activities, the briefing paper and the cable stated, were in the area of "political action," which the cable stated was "a very useful function for which General Lansdale has incomparable talents."

When AID Administrator David Bell returned in early January 1966 from a trip to Vietnam, he told the President and his NSC advisers in a meeting on January 11 that the "Number one problem is rural pacification."[41] It was a difficult problem, Bell said. "Must restore some kind of government system that serves the people. A new spirit is needed. Is not being done now. Some areas are thoroughly pacified but have always been historically." Bell also said that the South Vietnamese Army could no longer "clean any area; must have our troops. But even so can't hold it." The President said, "Gather pacification has gone backwards." Bell replied, "Possibly—though not much." McNamara commented, "Don't think there is a single area pacified."

Bell added that part of the difficulty was inadequate coordination of pacification activities, and said that there seemed to be general agreement among top U.S. officials in Saigon that Lodge's deputy, William Porter, should be appointed coordinator.

Bell also reported that the U.S. Mission was going to concentrate on pacifying four priority areas. "If they accomplish this," Bell said, "they will have affected 1/20 or 1/10 of rural population but it will be first time this has happened." The "key question," he added, was "can we get even this little done. Will take 80 man teams to go into each hamlet and village and stay for months at a time. . . . Takes heavy volume of VN manpower to do this. Strong back-up needed also—(AID, CIA, USIA etc.)."

---

[39] CMH, Westmoreland Papers, Message Files, Lodge to Westmoreland, SGN 1579, Dec. 17, 1965.

[40] For the briefing paper prepared for Westmoreland's discussion with Lodge, see CMH, Westmoreland Papers, History File, for Dec. 26, 1965. For the MACV cable to Washington see Message Files, MACV 0117, Jan. 7, 1966.

[41] Johnson Library, Meetings Notes File. A copy of Bell's report, "Non-Military Aspects of the Effort in Vietnam—January 1966," is in the NSF Country File, Vietnam.

On January 8–11, 1966, a meeting of officials from all affected agencies and departments, including Porter, Lansdale and other U.S. personnel in Vietnam, was held at Airlie House near Warrenton, Virginia, to discuss the situation in Vietnam generally, and, more specifically, how pacification could be augmented and made more effective. At the first meeting of the group, Leonard Unger, William Bundy's deputy, who was co-chairman of the conference with Porter, said that in addition to considering such matters as the allocation of resources, the purpose of the meeting was to agree upon a "concept" for pacification which could serve as the "concept on how the U.S. Government handles wars of national liberation."[42]

At the end of its four-day meeting, the group, according to a report prepared by Unger, reached these general conclusions about the situation in Vietnam:[43]

> a) the military situation although not critical nevertheless continues grave in Vietnam with a prospect under the present strategy of several years' more fighting at least in the current scale before the GVN will be in a position to exercise effective control over substantially all of South Vietnam except over Viet Cong base areas;
>
> b) there have been some instances of weakening Viet Cong morale, but the Viet Cong, buttressed by continuing infiltration from the North, continue to be a dangerous and effective fighting force;
>
> c) the Ky Government continues in relative stability with its collegial division of responsibility, is willing and in a limited degree able to take certain measures long considered necessary to improve the domestic and international position but remains fragile and is failing to live up to its "revolutionary" billing as originally presented by Prime Minister Ky or to produce a fighting force appreciably larger or more aggressive than earlier.

The group recommended that existing U.S. politico-military strategy should be reviewed to determine, among other things, the comparative advantages of using allied forces defensively, or for securing (clear-and-hold), or offensively (search-and-destroy), as well as the question of how forces should be allocated between the task of defending pacified areas, on the one hand, and, on the other, the reduction of infiltration and "denial of base areas to the enemy."

With respect to pacification, the group agreed that priority should be given to the four National Priority Areas that had been so designated—Hop Tac (in III Corps), the area around Saigon, which was given the highest priority; Danang (I Corps); Qui Nhon (II Corps); and Can Tho (IV Corps) in the delta.[44] According to the report, "There was a conclusion that the designation of priority rural construction areas for 1966 was important and that the modest goals set for these areas were realistic. However, it was emphasized that the contrast between the massive input of U.S. resources

42 U.S. Department of State, Lot File 69 D 67, Minutes of the Warrenton Meeting.

43 Johnson Library, NSF Country File, Vietnam, "Warrenton Meeting on Vietnam, January 8–11, 1966."

44 See map on p. XVI above for location of corps areas.

and the modest priority goals made success in those areas imperative."[45]

The group also discussed at length the organizational arrangements for the pacification program, both in Washington and in Saigon. Although each agency involved was concerned about protecting its own interests, there was "widespread recognition of the need to provide within the US mission a single form of operational control and management over the full range of the pertinent US efforts in order to gear all such US activities and resources effectively into implementation of the rural construction concept."[46]

There was also considerable discussion of the need to apply pressure on the South Vietnamese to get them to "adopt or vigorously pursue" policies and programs favored by the U.S. The group agreed that, "In principle the U.S., by paying attention to form, should take care to maintain the full appearance of GVN independence, but in view of the U.S. involvement and commitment in South Vietnam, it may be necessary to exert considerable pressure. Ambassador Lodge and the Saigon Mission will have to be the judge of how pressure, persuasion and manipulation are managed in any specific case." Moreover—and here it is of interest to note the skepticism among these key officials—"Some of the participants believe that unless this basic issue—the U.S. ability to influence the GVN—is resolved satisfactorily, *our already questionable chances of success* in South Vietnam will be significantly reduced."[47] (emphasis added)

After the meeting, Lansdale sent a personal letter to Lodge in which he said that there had been heavy emphasis on the need for "strong, firm management" of the U.S. pacification effort. "In Chet [Chester] Cooper's words, what the U.S. needs is a man with 'crunch' to give the orders. . . . I gathered that I am sadly lacking in 'crunch,' but the others have it." He said that Porter would probably be made the coordinator, adding: "This is worth serious consideration, if you can get somebody to run all the other chores that you need somebody to do in that big, sprawling U.S. establishment."[48]

The meeting at Airlie House was followed in early February 1966, as will be seen, by a conference in Honolulu between President Johnson and the South Vietnamese leaders which dealt primarily with nonmilitary activities. Shortly after the conference, the President announced that he was appointing Porter as the coordinator of the U.S. part of the pacification program, and soon thereafter he appointed Robert Komer, who had been serving as McGeorge Bundy's deputy, to be the Washington coordinator for

---

[45] *Ibid.*, Annex D. The *Pentagon Papers* points out that, despite being considered "imperative" to meet, the 1966 goals for the four areas were not met. *PP*, Gravel ed., vol. II, p. 540.

[46] "Warrenton Meeting on Vietnam," Annex D. For a summary of the views of the various agencies, see *PP*, Gravel ed., vol. II, pp. 541–542.

[47] As a part of its effort to improve the pacification program, the U.S. Government was also looking into the possibility of encouraging the defection of specific individual members of the National Liberation Front. (U.S. Department of State, Central File, Pol 27 Viet S, Washington to Saigon 2534, Feb. 25, 1966.) Lansdale was asked to see what he could do.

In the hope of prompting the South Vietnamese Government to make more of an effort toward that end, Lodge raised the subject of NLF defections with Thieu and with Foreign Minister Tran Van Do, whose reaction was that it was "absolutely out of the question to detach any individuals and make anything out of it, because the grip of Hanoi is so strong that there would be immediate assassination." Same location, Saigon to Washington 3202, Mar. 4, 1966.

[48] Massachusetts Historical Society, Lodge Papers, Lansdale letter to Lodge, Jan. 11, 1966.

pacification activities.[49] Under this new arrangement, Lansdale would continue to be the principal liaison officer with the South Vietnamese and, with his team, would also continue to be involved in establishing and maintaining relationships with South Vietnamese government officials and other leaders. These moves were engineered by McGeorge Bundy, McNamara and Ball with support from Bell and Westmoreland.[50]

Could the War Be Waged More Effectively?

With respect to military programs, the consensus in early 1966 among the President and his principal advisers was that ROLLING THUNDER should continue and that additional U.S. ground forces would have to be deployed.[51] ROLLING THUNDER should continue despite its shortcomings because otherwise, as McNamara said in arguing for resumption, the North Vietnamese would assume that "their cause was right" and that the U.S. was losing its will to fight. In addition, as he also said—and this appears to have been his principal reason for supporting resumption of bombing—the American people would not "long support a government which will not support by bombing 400,000 troops there." At the same time, McNamara emphasized that he did not think bombing could affect the "will" of the North Vietnamese, and that while it could reduce the infiltration of men and supplies it could not prevent the North Vietnamese from providing necessary assistance to the Communists in the South.[52]

McNamara's position was supported by the Intelligence Community which, in two estimates in early February 1966, took the position that U.S. bombing had not prevented and could not prevent infiltration of men and supplies, and that even if the U.S. mounted a major assault there could still be "substantially greater" infiltra-

---

[49] For this and subsequent efforts to reorganize the pacification program see the monograph by Scoville, *Reorganizing for Pacification Support,* published by the Center of Military History, U.S. Army (Washington, D.C.: U.S. Govt. Print. Off., 1982).

[50] On January 13, Porter met with McGeorge Bundy, McNamara and Ball to discuss the reorganization. (Scoville, *Reorganizing for Pacification Support,* p. 20.) On January 17, Porter met with the President. Before the meeting, McGeorge Bundy sent a memorandum to the President saying that he, Bell, Ball and McNamara all "strongly agree" that Porter should be made the coordinator. Johnson Library, NSF Country File, Vietnam.

Lodge was opposed to changing the existing system. In a memorandum to the President on Feb. 16, 1966, suggesting the appointment of a Washington coordinator for pacification, McGeorge Bundy summarized at some length the strengths and weaknesses of Lodge, and concluded that Lodge was the "very model of a man who needs staff support." Johnson Library, NSF Memos to the President—McGeorge Bundy.

[51] In late January, U.S. Ambassadors and military leaders in the Pacific (SEACOORD) met to discuss the war, especially anticipated Communist moves during 1966. In their report to Washington they stated that they expected to see the Communists shift their strategy from attempting to control the highlands to concentrating on gaining control of the area just south of the demilitarized zone. (U.S. Department of State, Central File, Pol 27 Viet S, Bangkok to Washington 1470, Jan. 25, 1966.) The enemy's motivation for this, they said, was "largely political, in his hope to precipitate an equivalent of Dienbienphu by taking significant territory, which we would have great difficulty in wrestling back. Enemy would hope that this development would deliver such a blow to our public opinion and to our will to continue that we would be prepared to accept NVN peace terms."

With respect to U.S. operations, the group recommended bombing of new targets, including the port of Haiphong, POL facilities, and power plants. While this would not have an immediate, dramatic effect, its cumulative effect on reducing infiltration would be significant. In addition, the group recommended that U.S. forces continue efforts to destroy Communist forces: "We believe that if we can demonstrably increase enemy casualties well over and above his abilities to replace them if we can significantly hamper his logistics system, and if we can prevent his seizure of any major new territorial gains, then we may effectively break his will to continue. If such a development could be combined with genuine pacification progress we might expect a rather rapid disintegration of the enemy's campaign in 1967."

[52] *PP,* Gravel ed., vol. IV, p. 49.

tion than in 1965.[53] However, a major assault "would almost certainly set a limit to the expansion of PAVN and VC mainforce units and activities in South Vietnam. There are too many uncertainties to permit an estimate of just where that limit would be set."[54]

On February 19, 1966, the JCS again recommended the use of ROLLING THUNDER to achieve "maximum shock effect" on the North Vietnamese.[55]

With respect to ground troops, a doubling of U.S. forces—from 200,000 to about 400,000—"might be sufficient," according to McNamara, "to break their [the Communists'] will."

By early 1966, there were approximately 200,000 American troops in South Vietnam, and in January-February the U.S. command commenced major search-and-destroy missions—Operation MASHER/WHITE WING, conducted by the 1st Cavalry Division in Binh Dinh Province, and Operation DOUBLE EAGLE, conducted by several Marine battalions in Quang Ngai Province.[56] The results of both operations were considered disappointing.[57] Except for a brief encounter at the beginning of MASHER/WHITE WING, weeks of searching produced only minor contacts with the enemy. Main-line enemy units known to be in the area had apparently been forewarned and had left before the operations began.

MASHER/WHITE WING was also further proof of the potentially adverse effects of large-unit military operations on the pacification program. In a month and a half, 132,000 rounds of artillery were fired—1,000 rounds for every estimated enemy fatality. This "lavish use of firepower" by the Army, Krepinevich says, produced a number of refugees, and the 1st Cavalry Division "moved on to other operations, having improved pacification not a whit while

---

[53] See SNIE 10-1-66, Feb. 4, 1966, "Possible Effects of a Proposed U.S. Course of Action on DRV Capability to Support the Insurgency in South Vietnam," and a memorandum from the Office of National Estimates, Feb. 11, 1966, "Possible Effects of Various Programs of Air Attacks Against the DRV." Both are in the Johnson Library, the former in NSF Country File, Vietnam, and the latter in NSF Memos to the President—McGeorge Bundy.

[54] SNIE 10-1-66, p. 4.

[55] *PP*, Gravel ed., vol. IV, p. 75, JCSM 113-66. For a more complete account of the debate in the administration on intensifying bombing, see *ibid.*, pp. 58 ff.

[56] MASHER was renamed WHITE WING after President Johnson reacted to the use of the word "masher." On February 1, Westmoreland received this cable from Wheeler (CMH, Westmoreland Papers, Message Files, JCS 460-66, Feb. 1, 1966):

"I have been quietly approached by McGeorge Bundy with the request that, in view of heated discussion of Vietnamese operations to be expected in the Security Council of the U.N. and in the Congress, we choose neutral designations for our combat operations in South Vietnam. He cited 'MASHER' as the type of designation which should be avoided. I told him that most names used are quite innocuous and gave several examples such as 'MALLARD' etc. He agreed that the nomenclature generally used is in line with his request and asked if I could, without putting a lot of directives on paper, see that all operational names are of like nature. I assured him that I could.

"Since I am sure that guidance of this character will cause you no difficulty, I have no hesitancy in asking you to comply. In this connection, and in contravention of an earlier directive from me, I suggest that at some convenient break in MASHER its designation be changed to some innocuous term upon which even the most biased person cannot seize as the theme of a public speech."

[57] See Krepinevich, *The Army and Vietnam*, p. 222, and Stanton, *The Rise and Fall of an American Army*, p. 111.

One account of MASHER/WHITE WING describes it as a "dream operation, fine line-up of commanders, plenty of support, determined execution, and the enemy got away." John Prados, "White Wing to Pershing: The Failure of Large-Unit War," *Veteran* (April 1989).

According to Marine Lt. Gen. Victor H. Krulak, then the Commanding General of the Marines in the Pacific, both operations failed because the Communists had been forewarned. He also lamented the fact that "both operations taught the people in the area that the Marines 'would come in, comb the area and disappear; whereupon the VC would resurface and resume control.'" Jack Shulimson, *U.S. Marines in Vietnam, An Expanding War, 1966, Marine Corps History and Museums Division* (Washington, D.C.: U.S. Govt. Print. Off., 1982), p. 36.

alienating thousands of homeless victims, who, as refugees, had to start their lives over again from scratch."[58]

Despite this additional evidence that, in response to large-unit search-and-destroy missions, Communist forces were going to continue employing a strategy of guerrilla warfare, there was little inclination in Washington, and less in Saigon, to re-examine U.S. strategy and military operations. After the initial period of questioning in September-October 1965, U.S. officials had closed ranks, especially after the purported success in the battle at Ia Drang, and seemed determined to persevere in the chosen course of attempting to "win" by applying force through bombing and attrition by ground warfare.

There was considerable dissatisfaction, however, with the way in which the war was being fought and with the results of U.S. military actions. A major concern with respect to the success of U.S. ground combat operations in the South was the increasing infiltration of men and supplies from the North. Unless this could be better controlled the strategy of attrition could not succeed in reaching the "cross-over point" at which the rate of attrition exceeded replacement. And until this point was reached—and it presumably would become apparent to the Communists that they would have to find a way to end a war they were not winning—the U.S. would be faced with having to escalate the war, as McNamara had warned, to higher levels of stalemate.[59]

One of the proposals for more effective control of infiltration was to increase the bombing of infiltration-related targets in North Vietnam and to add new targets. This, as noted above, was rec-

[58] Krepinevich, p. 223.

[59] The importance of controlling infiltration had been stressed in the JCS (Goodpaster) study in July 1965, prepared at McNamara's request, which examined whether the U.S. would win "if we do everything we can." The study concluded that the U.S. could win, based on certain assumptions and on "aggressive exploitation of superior military force." One of the assumptions was that the restrictions on U.S. forces would not exceed the following: "(1) No land invasion of NVN by US/SVN Forces; (2) No use of nuclear weapons or chemical weapons; (3) No mass bombing of population per se." (See pt. III of this study, p. 361.) These restrictions, it should be noted, did not bar the use of U.S. forces in Laos and Cambodia.

One of the four principal lines of action for U.S. and South Vietnamese forces that were proposed by the study was "Action against infiltration routes." "The maximum objective," the study stated, "is physically to halt the infiltration of men and supplies moving into SVN. At a minimum, curtailment of the flow should be such as, in conjunction with other lines of action, to permit containment of the insurgency in SVN." Such action would consist of a "full scale air campaign" against North Vietnam, including the mining and bombing of ports, interdiction of men and supplies entering South Vietnam through bombing "and/or establishment of some type of anti-infiltration barrier" using either electronic means, or troops, or both, and raising the intensity of combat to the point where the Communists would be forced to consume greater amounts of material than could be sustained by infiltration.

The control of infiltration had also been emphasized in the August 1965 paper of the JCS, "Concept for Vietnam," in which the military proposed a strategic plan for the U.S. According to the paper, "The physical capability of the DRV to move men and supplies through the Laos Corridor, down the coastline, across the demilitarized zone, and through Cambodia must be reduced to the maximum practical extent by land, naval, and air action in these areas and against infiltration connected targets." (From JCSM–652–65, Aug. 27, 1965, cited above.)

In late November, 1965, in McNamara's meeting in Saigon with Lodge, Westmoreland and Sharp, the question of taking additional steps to control infiltration was considered, prompted in part by Westmoreland's claim that because of increased infiltration of North Vietnamese military personnel, the U.S. needed more forces than originally anticipated. At the meeting, McNamara said that there needed to be increased U.S. covert operations in Laos against the Ho Chi Minh Trail.

Control of infiltration was also a principal issue in the discussion at Honolulu in February 1966. It was agreed that U.S. bombing of infiltration routes in Laos and North Vietnam would be increased by more than 60 percent as one of the steps taken to achieve the cross-over point by the end of 1966. See below.

ommended by the JCS in early 1966,[60] as well as by U.S. Ambassadors and military chiefs in the Southeast Asia region—SEACOORD—at a meeting in late January, 1966.

Another proposal for interdicting infiltration was to establish a cordon across the northern and western borders of South Vietnam.[61] This proposal took various forms, but the general idea was to deploy U.S. forces along the demilitarized zone from the Gulf of Tonkin to the border of Laos and across the panhandle of Laos to the border of Thailand.

The question of a cordon was raised in McNamara's meeting in Saigon in November 1965 with Lodge and Westmoreland. Westmoreland's staff responded that this would take one to two years to become operational, and would require at least four and a half divisions plus support troops—a total of 150,000–200,000 men—and that, "it does not appear, under any circumstances, to represent the most profitable use of available resources."

In early 1966 the idea was once again proposed by General Westmoreland at the suggestion of one of his commanders, and a plan was developed but was not approved.[62]

Associated with the problem of infiltration was the problem of the "sanctuaries"—the use by the Communists of territory in Laos and Cambodia, both of which had long borders with South Vietnam, for the transport and storage of military supplies and as a refuge and base for Communist forces operating in the vicinity of the border. Because both countries were "neutral," and because the U.S. was seeking to avoid an expansion of the war, proposals for incursions into Laos or Cambodia had generally been met with a deaf ear in Washington with the exception of small, selected covert cross-border operations into Laos and, at a later time, into Cambodia.[63]

William Sullivan, U.S. Ambassador to Laos at the time, says that he "was summoned to Washington every six months" by President Johnson and "told to keep U.S. military operations [in Laos] to a minimum." "'President Johnson,'" he adds, "'became increasingly disillusioned with the military as the war in Vietnam dragged on. He felt he had been dragged into an unending conflict after being assured that victory would be quick and relatively easy. He did not

---

[60] In addition to the February 19 JCS memorandum mentioned above, similar recommendations were made in JCSM–130–66, Mar. 1, 1966, and JCSM–153–66, Mar. 10, 1966. See *PP*, Gravel ed., vol. IV, p. 76.

[61] See pt. III of this study, pp. 163–166, and pp. 107 above.

[62] Westmoreland, *A Soldier Reports*, pp. 271–272. For the 1966 proposal see CMH, Westmoreland Papers, Message Files, CINCPAC to COMUSMACV 220233Z, January 1966, and COMUSMACV to CINCPAC 0907, Feb. 2, 1966. The 1966 plan was revived in 1968 in the form of the EL PASO plan, but that too was not approved.

[63] There was, however, a major operation underway in Laos using local tribesmen for attacks on infiltration routes, supported and supplemented by U.S. bombing from bases in South Vietnam and Thailand and from carriers in the Gulf of Tonkin. STEEL TIGER and TIGER HOUND were the code names given to these air operations against Communist infiltration routes in Laos. Earlier and more limited U.S. air operations over Laos were coded-named YANKEE TEAM and BARREL ROLL. STEEL TIGER, which began in April 1965, covered the area in Laos from the 17th parallel (the demilitarized zone boundary between North and South Vietnam), northward to the area of the Mu Gia Pass where the Ho Chi Minh Trail entered Laos from North Vietnam. TIGER HOUND, which began in December 1965, covered the area in Laos from the 17th parallel south to the Cambodian border.

want to be similarly dragged into bigger and bigger adventures in Laos.'"[64]

The covert cross-border operations, called SHINING BRASS (which became PRAIRIE FIRE in 1966), which began in late 1965 along the Ho Chi Minh Trail in the Panhandle of Laos, consisted of small teams of American and Vietnamese, usually mountain tribesmen (Montagnards), which engaged in a wide variety of tasks including reconnoitering infiltration routes, locating targets for U.S. airstrikes and selectively attacking other targets, and capturing prisoners.[65] There was considerable opposition from the State Department to actions that would violate the Geneva Accords with respect to the neutrality of Laos, and very strict limits were placed on SHINING BRASS. In the beginning, cross-border teams could only operate to a depth of 20 kilometers in Laos, could only cross in two areas, and could cross only by foot. These restrictions were circumvented to a certain extent—helicopters were used from the beginning, and maps were chosen that showed the border the furthest west.

Ambassador Sullivan, who had full responsibility for all U.S. operations, military and nonmilitary, and who tussled constantly with General Westmoreland and Admiral Sharp (CINCPAC) over their desire to expand military operations in Laos—both bombing and cross-border operations—had agreed reluctantly and with reservations to limited cross-border ground reconnaissance from South Vietnam.[66] In a cable to William Bundy on January 3, 1966, however, Sullivan said, "I find the role I have to play in this exercise [SHINING BRASS] particularly galling. This is essentially an Eagle Scout program devised by some extremely well-motivated and brave young men. However, except for Max Taylor, nobody in the U.S. military establishment has ever seemed willing to tell them that the program is not militarily worth the price."[67]

In a cable on December 9, 1965 to CINCPAC and Washington, Westmoreland urged that action be taken against Communist operations in Cambodia, saying, "It is perfectly clear to us that the border areas of Cambodia now contain motorable infiltration routes, command center, base, training and supply areas along the pattern of the long development of a similar nature in Laos." He asked for authority to conduct air and ground reconnaissance as well as artillery and airstrikes and ground attacks against Communist forces using Cambodia as a sanctuary.[68]

The response of the State Department was that, as previously authorized, U.S. forces could, in self-defense, conduct very limited

[64] Quoted by Timothy N. Castle in his excellent study, *At War in the Shadow of Vietnam: U.S. Military Aid to the Royal Lao Government, 1955–1975* (New York: Columbia Univ. Press, 1993), p. 93.

[65] These cross-border operations, which were run by the group established in 1964 to conduct clandestine operations against North Vietnam—the Studies and Observation Group (SOG)—were authorized by Operations Plan (OPLAN) 35, approved in September 1965. There is very little information available on U.S. special operations in Vietnam. There is a brief account in General Westmoreland's memoirs (*A Soldier Reports*, pp. 106–109). See also Terrence Maitland and Peter McInerney, *A Contagion of War*, pp. 119–135, a volume in the series, *The Vietnam Experience* (Boston: Boston Publishing Co., 1983). There is also an account in Kevin M. Generous, *Vietnam: The Secret War* (London: Bison Books, 1985).

[66] See U.S. Department of State, Central File, Pol 27 Viet S, Vientiane to Washington 142, Aug. 9, 1965.

[67] Same location, Vientiane to Washington 703, Jan. 3, 1966.

[68] Same location, COMUSMACV (MACJ3) 43199 to CINCPAC and Washington, Dec. 9. 1965.

air and ground attacks across the Cambodian border, but Westmoreland's request for ground reconnaissance was denied.[69] "Such action might readily be picked up and would not have clear self-defense justification of other actions contemplated by form of authority."[70]

A Proposal for Invading and Holding the Southern Part of North Vietnam

Since the beginning of active U.S. involvement in the Vietnam war, there had been numerous proposals for invading North Vietnam, and U.S. contingency plans had provided for such action in the event of an invasion of South Vietnam by the North Vietnamese, or by China, or by the Chinese and the North Vietnamese.[71] Among the proposals were some that called for sending U.S. forces into the southern part of North Vietnam in the area south of Vinh and establishing a defensive line across that narrow part of the country as a way of gaining better control of infiltration, as well as holding the area hostage in order to get the North Vietnamese to agree to end the war.

One of the principal proponents of this strategy was Walt W. Rostow, who first suggested it to President Kennedy in June 1961.[72] Another proponent was William Sullivan, U.S. Ambassador to Laos, 1964–1968, who says that he first learned of the idea from General Lyman Lemnitzer in 1961.[73] In a cable to Washington on December 15, 1965, Sullivan proposed that U.S. forces, with air and sea cover, land in North Vietnam near Vinh, establish a defen-

---

[69] The existing authorization had been given in a cable to Lodge on Nov. 20, 1965, as follows: "authority to US/GVN units to return fire, to eliminate fire coming from Cambodia, and to maneuver into Cambodia territory as necessary to defend selves while actively engaged in combat with PAVN/VC units. This authority includes artillery and close air support operations against enemy units as long as such units are actually engaged with US or GVN forces. It excludes authority to engage Cambodia forces, if encountered, except in self-defense, to conduct tactical air or artillery operations against populated Cambodia areas, or to attack Cambodian base areas other than in circumstances when justification of self-defense exists in terms of continuing engagement and direct threat to GVN or US forces." Johnson Library, NSF Country File, Vietnam, Washington to Saigon 1399, Nov. 10, 1965.

[70] Same location, Washington to Saigon 1634, Dec. 11, 1965. For a JCS cable on the ground rules for operations involving Cambodia, see U.S. Department of State, Central Files, Pol 27 Viet S, JCS 8706, Dec. 15, 1965, JCS to MACV, a copy of which was sent to the State Department.

On Feb. 1, 1966, Westmoreland asked for authority to train and equip reconnaissance teams in preparation for possible use in Cambodia. National Archives, Westmoreland-CBS Papers, COMUSMACV (MACJ3) 03170, Feb. 1, 1966. By 1967, SOG's Oplan 35 was permitted to send cross-border teams into Cambodia in Operation DANIEL BOONE (later called SALEM HOUSE). Between 1965 and 1973, SOG conducted some 3,000 cross-border missions into Laos and Cambodia, at a cost of 103 Americans killed in action—76 in Laos and 27 in Cambodia. *A Contagion of War*, pp. 134–135.

[71] See Krepinevich, *The Army and Vietnam*, p. 261.

[72] Walt W. Rostow, *A Diffusion of Power* (New York: Macmillan, 1972), p. 286. Rostow says that he "placed an exceedingly high priority on closing off the infiltration trails . . . I was skeptical that Vietnam could be saved, except at a prohibitive cost, if the Vietnamese frontier remained open to infiltration . . . I deeply feared the consequences of a strategy which permitted continued infiltration and which dealt only with its disruptive consequences. I felt it would tempt Hanoi to persist; the struggle would be protracted; and, at some time, if the situation disintegrated, the United States would intervene convulsively, as it had done late in the other great military crises of the twentieth century."

Rostow proposed a "direct attack on North Vietnam sufficiently costly to induce Hanoi to end its war against South Vietnam. I had in mind not only the possibility of air action but, after a suitable program of diplomatic warnings, moving forces into North Vietnam itself—not in the area around Hanoi, but north of the DMZ, perhaps as far as Vinh." "The holding of a portion of North Vietnam," Rostow said, "would permit certain of the supply routes to South Vietnam to be cut directly from within. More important, it would constitute a serious hostage for North Vietnamese actions in Laos and South Vietnam."

[73] U.S. Department of State, Central File, Pol 27 Viet S, Vientiane to Washington 651, Dec. 15, 1965.

sive line from there to the border of Laos, and remain in that position until the North Vietnamese agreed to negotiate. In his cable Sullivan said, "By seizing and holding a piece of DRV territory, by emphasizing that we are doing it in order to throttle infiltration, and by making clear that we are willing to give it back when the eventual guaranteed political settlement is reached, we should have our equivalent [to Communist terror in South Vietnam] in spades." Sullivan proposed, further, that the U.S. should notify the Chinese of American intentions, and should assure them that U.S. forces would not move further north where they might be considered a threat to Chinese interests.

In the cable, Sullivan said that infiltration was increasing, and that maximum interdiction must be achieved "if we are to have any hope of approaching isolation of the highlands battlefield in South Vietnam." SHINING BRASS could, at best, harass the Communists, and proposals for deploying U.S. forces across South Vietnam in the area south of the demilitarized zone "would do nothing more than spread a picket of men along horrendous terrain, and expose them in any one location to the bloodletting of concentrated enemy attacks at places and times of the enemy's choosing."

Sullivan said that he had heard of Westmoreland's request for the deployment of additional U.S. troops, and he thought that such a move would result in the infiltration of additional North Vietnamese forces. "I wonder," he asked, "where we believe this constant reciprocal escalation of manpower will lead." His proposal for an invasion, he said, would provide an alternative to this pattern of escalation and to the deployment of an increasing number of U.S. forces in the countryside of South Vietnam to fight inconclusive battles against an elusive enemy.

On December 16, Sullivan again cabled Washington, saying he had just learned that on December 3 a paper had been drafted in Washington by Unger for William Bundy discussing the possibility of an invasion, and he wondered whether it was still being considered.[74] On December 27,[75] Bundy replied that such a paper had been written, but that its conclusions were that an invasion of North Vietnam would raise unacceptable political problems and would be of little value militarily.[76]

---

[74] U.S. Department of State, Central File, Pol 27 Viet S, Vientiane to Washington (number unknown), Dec. 16, 1965.

[75] Same location, Washington to Vientiane 687, Dec. 27, 1965.

[76] These cables are in the same location. The Unger paper, "Political Implications of U.S. Military Action to Seal off the Narrow Southern Neck of North Vietnam in Order to Stop the Flow of Men and Materiel into South Vietnam," is in Lot File 85 D 240 (William Bundy Papers). This is the text of the Unger/Bundy paper:

"To interdict overland passage from North to South Viet-Nam at its source, it would be essential to hold a line approximately at parallel No. 20. It might in fact also be necessary to move northward along the mountain chain to just south of Vinh in order to hold the Nape Pass (Col de keo Neua) unless traffic on Route 8 could be interdicted on the Laotian side of the frontier. It is assumed that such an operation could best be accomplished by a combination of airbourne and amphibious actions rather than by an overland push through the demilitarized zone.

"Such a course of action recommends itself in that it would require the holding of a fairly short line which could be served by sea and it would go to the source of the problem both geographically and politically.

"Politically such an action could be justified on the grounds that we have justified our actions in South Viet-Nam and Laos to date, i.e. that it is North Viet-Nam which has mounted the aggression against the south and that we are justified in obstructing North Viet-Nam's further nourishment of the rebellion. We could also call attention once again to North Viet-Nam's violations of the '54 and '62 Accords through its use of the territory of Laos. To those countries which wholeheartedly support our present action in Viet-Nam and to domestic groups which think in

Rusk directed William Bundy to circulate Sullivan's proposals to U.S. Embassies in several countries, and according to Sullivan, "All of them, moved by the conventional wisdom of our Korean experience, expressed the conviction that China would send forces into North Vietnam if U.S. forces landed at Vinh."[77]

From his China intelligence post in Hong Kong, Edmund Rice reported that he and his colleagues had talked to Sullivan, and that out of seven political officers (State and CIA) and three military liaison officers present for the meeting, all three members of the China Mainland Section and two of the three military officers thought that such an operation would trigger a major Chinese military reaction. (The third military officer reserved opinion, but thought it would be the height of folly to assume that China would not react militarily.) Of the four remaining political officers, one agreed that the Chinese would act, two did not express an opinion, and one thought that the idea was preferable to totally destructive bombing of the North, which he thought would cause the Chinese to intervene.[78]

---

similar terms and which feel that we have not acted with sufficient strength and determination, our moving into southern North Viet-Nam would be greeted with enthusiasm.

"On the other hand there is no question but that such a move would immediately and basically change the complexion of the current struggle in Viet-Nam. However much we might insist that we were taking a limited action intended only to stop infiltration and required because of the apparent impossibility of stopping the flow farther from the source, our action would be branded and widely accepted as an attack on North Viet-Nam. We have thus far insisted quite credibly that we were not aiming to destroy North Vietnam or to overturn its regime but this position would promptly evaporate. In fact it is hard to see how, from a military point of view, we could limit the operation to the geographical bounds mentioned above and it seems almost inevitable that we would find ourselves moving continuously farther northward in order to avoid being pushed back into the sea.

"Politically the most immediate consequence would be the prompt rallying of the DRV's Communist allies to its defense. It seems inevitable that Communist China would have to move militarily in support of the DRV with massive forces, lest this adjacent geographically and dependent ally fall into hostile hands. Failure to move in these circumstances would certainly destroy the image Communist China has been seeking to build for itself of being the supporter of national liberation wars and the friend and defender of those threatened by Western imperialism. Moreover, these circumstances would also be such as to cause North Viet-Nam to put aside its considerable distaste for letting Chinese military enter its territory because of the greater evil it would otherwise face.

"Once China decided the die was cast it is hard to know what limits it would place on its actions. While it would presumably continue to be the Chinese hope to keep the war off its own territory, it nevertheless seems likely that the Chinese would feel free to involve Laos and perhaps launch a diversionary threat toward or into Thailand.

"Our moving into North Viet-Nam could also be counted upon to bring the Russians into much more direct action in defense of the DRV and to force a trend toward greater cooperation, even if only superficially, between the Russians and the Chinese. Facing the common danger it seems likely that both powers would be obliged to appear before the lesser members of their bloc to be working loyally together in the common cause. Under these circumstances we could expect any trend toward better US-Soviet relations to come promptly to an end, although it seems unlikely that the hostile situation would find any military expression outside Southeast Asia.

"The uncommitted world and many of our friends who already have serious doubts about our action in Viet-Nam would launch the sharpest criticism of our action, and this might well include not only the Indians, French, Scandinavians, but possibly also the British and Canadians. Thus our position in international forums and bodies such as the UN would be difficult and probably foreclose any kind of a collective action even of a relatively mild nature against the Chinese Communists.

"In conclusion it would appear that US action in southern North Viet-Nam should be avoided unless we have reached the conclusion that infiltration of the south must absolutely be cut off and that we are prepared for a war with Communist China (and the USSR?) and are ready to place ourselves in a much weaker position internationally speaking."

[77] Letter to the author from William Sullivan, July 24, 1986.

[78] U.S. Department of State, Central File, Pol 27 Viet S, Hong Kong to Washington 1179, Dec. 21, 1965. In a cable on Jan. 19, 1966, Tokyo to Washington 2515 (same location), the U.S. Ambassador to Japan, Edwin O. Reischauer, a Far Eastern specialist on leave from Harvard University, said he agreed with Sullivan's arguments against bombing population centers or establishing an anti-infiltration line across the northern part of South Vietnam. But he said he also agreed with Rice that a landing at Vinh would entail "unacceptable risks." "As we learned from

Continued

Rice also doubted whether Sullivan's proposal would help negotiations. He expressed concern about the danger of ". . . seeking farther and farther afield the answer to problems which can be solved only in South Vietnam itself. Our biggest problem, it seems to me, is that the U.S. and ARVN troops can go pretty much anywhere they please there, like a boat through a sea of people, but then the waters close in after our passage leaving the situation too much as it was before." "With Viet Cong units operating from nearby strong holds even in the suburbs of Saigon itself," Rice said, "it seems to me the most urgent problem is helping create a GVN ability to control the population at least in areas our military forces can jointly dominate." "[W]e could extend our military forces beyond South Vietnam," he added, "with no better results than proportionately to increase our problems and dissipate our efforts."

There was also opposition to Sullivan's proposal from the Department of State's Russian experts, including the Ambassador to the U.S.S.R., Foy Kohler, and Llewellyn Thompson. In a letter from Moscow on February 3, 1966, Kohler said, "I believe the Soviets would feel compelled to take direct action to counter such a United States move and would risk the dangers involved in supplying the DRV with means of counter-attack, e.g. aircraft for raids on South Vietnamese cities or United States bases, heavy ground equipment, etc., as well as personnel to operate sophisticated weaponry, which DRV soldiers are unable to handle." Moreover, Kohler said, "While the Soviets would clearly not relish a secondary role to Peking, we believe they would feel they had no choice but to back up a Chinese attempt to repulse such a move. We assume, along with Hong Kong [Rice], that the Chinese would respond in force to an amphibious invasion of the DRV. To do otherwise would contradict Maoist aspirations to leadership of world revolutionary forces, ignore the threat to their own security, and provide the Kremlin with an overpowering weapon in the Sino-Soviet dispute. The landing at Vinh would thus, in our view, mean following a strategy of seeking an early showdown with the Chinese."[79]

Sullivan does not recall receiving support for his proposal from any military quarters. "I was a minority of one," he writes.[80] He also doubts whether his proposal was ever put before the President or discussed with Congress.[81] However, as noted earlier, at least one Member of Congress knew about the proposal. On January 4, 1966, Sullivan met with Senator Stuart Symington, who said that he had heard of Sullivan's proposal. Sullivan discussed the plan with Symington and reported to Washington that he had done so. A copy of the cable was sent by McGeorge Bundy to the President,

---

the Korean War, the Chicoms are extremely sensitive to actions in their immediate border areas, and I believe U.S. ground operations anywhere in North Vietnam would probably trigger a Chicom response of the sort we are trying to avoid." He added that a U.S. invasion of North Vietnam would be much more damaging to the U.S. in its relations with Japan than the bombing of cities or the line across South Vietnam. "The real need," Reischauer said, "is for a political answer in the South, not the spread of military operations to other areas."

[79] U.S. Department of State, Central File, Pol 27 Viet S, excerpts from a letter from Kohler to Thompson, Feb. 3, 1966, attached to a letter from Thompson to Rice, Feb. 9, 1966 in which Thompson, without commenting further on the matter, said he thought Rice would find Kohler's comments interesting.

[80] Letter to the author from Sullivan, cited above.

[81] *Ibid.*

who, if he read it, which he probably did, would also have learned of Sullivan's idea.[82]

Although there may not have been support from the military for Sullivan's proposal, Westmoreland, who had decided in January 1966 that the Communists had changed their strategy from one of dividing the country in half through the highlands to one of taking control of the two northernmost provinces in I Corps (Quang Tri and Thua Thien), requested CINCPAC in late January 1966 to have the Seventh Fleet prepare a plan for an amphibious landing "immediately south of the DMZ or to the north" which could be carried out if there was a threat to these provinces from the North Vietnamese Army.[83]

At about the same time, Lodge, in his weekly cable to the President, pointed out that the North Vietnamese, feeling that they were not threatened by invasion, were sending large numbers of forces to the South. To counter this, he suggested the possibility of taking some action "which would make Hanoi think we were planning an invasion."[84]

There is no record that Sullivan's idea received more than passing attention in the State Department or elsewhere in the Government. Opposition from Chinese and Russian experts was probably enough to quash any notion that an invasion of the North could help in winning the war.

In an interview some years later, Sullivan said that the opinion of the experts was "'absolutely not—the Chinese would come in.'" "Well," he continued, "that's the lesson that we learned in Korea which was being applied—last war's lesson to this war. I don't think in this instance they would have come in, but I didn't have the means to override the views of all the China experts and all the Soviet experts."[85]

There was also potential opposition from at least one very influential Member of Congress. Although he may not have been apprised of Sullivan's proposal, and may have been directing his comment to the question of an invasion for offensive purposes rather than the establishment of a defensive line across the southern part of the country, Senator Russell, chairman of the Armed Services Committee, while favoring increased bombing and the mining of ports, said that he was strongly opposed to an invasion of North Vietnam by U.S. forces.[86]

The Marine Corps Dissents from Westmoreland's Strategy

In late 1965-early 1966, as U.S. forces conducted major search-and-destroy missions under Westmoreland's "attrition strategy," there were also two serious challenges from within the military to prevailing military doctrines and practice. The first came from the Marine Corps and the second from within the Army.

Leaders of the Marine Corps, including its three highest ranking officers—Gen. Wallace M. Greene, Jr., Commandant, Lt. Gen. Victor H. Krulak, Commander of the Fleet Marine Force in the Pacific

[82] See p. 142 above.
[83] CMH, Westmoreland Papers, History File, entry for Jan. 21, 1966.
[84] U.S. Department of State, Central File, Pol 27 Viet S, Saigon to Washington 3159, Mar. 2, 1966.
[85] CRS Interview with William Sullivan, July 31, 1980.
[86] *CR*, vol. 112, p. 4717.

and Maj. Gen. Lewis Walt, Commander of Marine forces in Vietnam—disagreed strongly with General Westmoreland about placing primary emphasis on large mobile operations in less-populated areas. According to General Krulak, "The Marines saw the MACV idea as flawed. It would leave the population and the wealth of the land largely uncovered, it would engage the enemy in the hinterland where circumstances favored him, and it would generate very large U.S. manpower requirements. And something else—the American's conduct of search and destroy operations would be hampered by the fact that, more often than not, the enemy would know in advance what we were going to do."[87] Rather, the Marines argued that the emphasis should be on small-unit operations designed to protect the people in the more populous areas against Communist guerrillas, combined with action against larger Communist forces as needed or when there was the opportunity for such action on terms favorable to U.S. forces. They also believed that a greater effort should be made in the air war to prevent infiltration of supplies to the South by mining and destroying docking and transportation facilities in North Vietnamese ports.

Having failed to make any headway with Westmoreland, General Krulak, after getting approval and encouragement from General Greene and from Admiral Sharp (CINCPAC), took the Marines' case directly to McNamara, with whom he had worked in an earlier capacity as Special Assistant for Counterinsurgency. In a paper which he personally presented to McNamara in January 1966, Krulak argued that attrition was "the route to defeat."[88] "I saw what was happening as wasteful of American lives, promising a protracted strength-sapping battle with small likelihood of a successful outcome." The Communists, he said, referring to the Ia Drang battle, were "seeking to attrit U.S. forces through the process of violent, close-quarters combat which tends to diminish the effectiveness of our supporting areas . . ." believing that, in time, they could force the U.S. to withdraw as a result of public reaction to the seeming futile losses resulting from attrition. "Obviously we had become involved in a self-punishing, self-defeating cycle brought on by a faulty attritional strategy. Thus, our self-declared victories in the search-and-destroy operations were not relevant to the total outcome of the war. Things were bad and bound to get worse unless our strategy was altered."

Attrition, Krulak said, was "peripheral," the main struggle being for the loyalty and support of the people—"these simple, provincial people who are the battlefield on which the war must be fought." "The conflict between the North Vietnamese/hardcore Vietcong, on the one hand, and the U.S. on the other, could move to another planet today and we would not have won the war. On the other hand, if the subversion and guerrilla efforts were to disappear, the war would soon collapse, as the enemy would be denied food, sanc-

---

[87] Victor H. Krulak, Lieutenant General, (U.S. Marine Corps, Ret.), *First to Fight: An Inside View of the U.S. Marine Corps* (Annapolis, Md.: Naval Institute Press, 1984), p. 198. For Westmoreland's criticism of the Marines for what he considered their tactical shortcomings in not leaving their beachheads to conduct search-and-destroy missions, see his memoir, *A Soldier Reports*, pp. 164–166.

[88] Krulak, *First to Fight*, p. 198. A copy of his paper, "A Strategic Appraisal, Vietnam," December, 1965, was kindly provided by General Krulak to the author. For the sake of brevity, quotations used here are from Krulak's summary of the paper in his book.

tuary and intelligence." "The Vietnamese people are the prize," he said.[89]

In conclusion, Krulak made these recommendations:

> Shift the thrust of our effort to the task of delivering the people from guerrilla oppression, and to protecting them thereafter; meanwhile seeking out and attacking the main force elements when the odds can be made overwhelmingly in our favor.[90]
>
> Address our attritional efforts primarily to the source of North Vietnamese material introduction, fabrication and distribution;—destroy the port areas, mine the ports, destroy the rail lines, destroy power, fuel and heavy industry. . . .
>
> Put the full weight of our effort into bringing all applicable resources—U.S. and Vietnamese—into the pacification process. . . . Increase the level of medical assistance. . . . Increase the level of Popular Forces training. . . . Direct the conduct of comprehensive military civic action programs.
>
> Press the Vietnamese Government to move immediately into a major land reform program. . . .

When he met with McNamara, Krulak gave him the paper and explained it in detail. McNamara, with his penchant for quantification, is said to have taken note of Krulak's statistics. He also told Krulak that he should talk to the President, but he did not volunteer to arrange such a meeting.[91]

In response to Krulak's recommendation for bombing the ports, McNamara defended the use of graduated pressure in the air war, and told Krulak that he should discuss the matter with Harriman. McNamara knew that Harriman would react negatively to the recommendation for bombing North Vietnamese ports, and that Harriman might help to convince Krulak not to press his case.

Krulak met with Harriman, who criticized the recommendation for bombing the ports, saying, "'Do you want a war with the Soviet Union or the Chinese?'" Krulak said he did not, but that the North Vietnamese hated the Chinese and that Russians would not start a war with the United States over incidents occurring in Indochina.

McNamara apparently did not follow up on his comment that Krulak should see the President, if, indeed, he intended to follow up but this was done by General Greene, and the meeting finally was held on August 1, 1966. It lasted 40 minutes, and ended abruptly when Krulak mentioned the mining and bombing of North Vietnamese ports. At that point, according to Krulak, "Mr. Johnson got to his feet, put his arm around my shoulder, and propelled me firmly toward the door."[92]

In May 1966, Krulak met again with McNamara, who said that the program recommended by the Marines would require too many men and too much time. Krulak responded by sending McNamara

---

[89] In his paper, Krulak added that "attrition alone cannot win the war, either by destroying the war machine or by applying graduated pressure to break the enemy's will. . . . The Vietnam conflict ultimately has to be decided among the people in the villages of South Vietnam."

[90] In his paper, Krulak added: "we must not engage in an attritional contest with the hard-core just for the sake of attrition; nor should we react to Viet Cong initiatives or seek them out just to do battle. The attritional ratio under these circumstances is not going to favor us, and this form of competition has little to do with who ultimately wins anyhow."

[91] Sheehan, *A Bright Shining Lie*, p. 632.

[92] Krulak, *First to Fight*, p. 202.

a long letter explaining his position in which he argued, among other things, that the results being achieved in areas where the Marines were applying their concept, although more difficult to quantify, was a better indicator of progress than body counts. "The raw figure of VC killed," he said, "can be a dubious index of success since, if their killing is accompanied by devastation of friendly areas, we may end up having done more harm than good."[93]

Meanwhile, General Greene's staff had conducted a study that confirmed Krulak's statistical analysis of the results of attrition, but when Greene made the case for the Marine's concept of a more effective strategy in meetings of the JCS, he apparently failed to convert the other members.

During a trip to South Vietnam in August 1966, Greene argued with Westmoreland about the way the war was being fought. "[H]e pointed out to Westmoreland that the tactics of attrition made no more sense than the strategy. He had read the report of an Army unit fighting its way to the top of a jungle ridge only to have to fight its way back down again. This was not a sound expenditure of American soldiers, Greene said."[94]

Even though they were constantly exhorted by Westmoreland and his staff to get out of their beachheads and to conduct search-and-destroy missions, the Marines, while trying to satisfy the Army, managed also to conduct in their own area of operations a small-unit counterguerrilla war involving "combined action platoons" (CAPs) typically consisting of a South Vietnamese Popular Forces platoon of 35 men together with 14 U.S. Marines and one U.S. Navy hospital corpsman. The leader of each combined group was a U.S. Marine noncommissioned officer. The first of these platoons had been established in the summer of 1965, and by the end of 1966 there were 57. (Eventually, 114 were established.)[95] The primary role of the CAP was to help provide local security by seeking to destroy the Communist network (infrastructure) in villages and hamlets. Civic action was also emphasized.[96]

Although there have been few studies of the CAP experience,[97] this method of fighting the war generally has been given high marks. Blaufarb, for example, calls the CAP Program "the kind of tactics which, if used on a wider scale, could have made a vast difference in the war for the countryside."[98] Krepinevich says that according to studies made at the time, the CAPs produced results—only one CAP was ever overrun—at a casualty rate one-half that of search-and-destroy units.[99]

General Westmoreland and the U.S. Army Command, however, felt that the CAPs were a diversion from the principal mission of

[93] Quoted by Sheehan, *A Bright Shining Lie*, p. 636.

[94] *Ibid.*, p. 639.

[95] See Shulimson, *U.S. Marines in Vietnam: An Expanding War, 1966*, pp. 239–245, Blaufarb, *The Counterinsurgency Era*, pp. 256–258, and William R. Corson, *The Betrayal* (New York: W. W. Norton, 1968), pp. 174–198. Corson, then a lieutenant colonel in the Marines, was in charge of the CAP program in 1967–1968.

[96] For an absorbing account of the CAP in the village of Binh Nghia in Quang Ngai province, see F. J. West, Jr., *The Village* (New York: Harper and Row, 1972).

[97] A three-volume study of pacification prepared for the military in 1972, for example, while mentioning its usefulness, gave the CAP program only passing attention. (Cooper, *et. al.*, *The American Experience with Pacification in Vietnam*, cited above, vol. II, pp. 72–75.) MATs, a similar program initiated by the Army (see below) was not even cited.

[98] Blaufarb, *The Counterinsurgency Era*, pp. 257–258.

[99] Krepinevich, *The Army and Vietnam*, pp. 174, 175.

fighting main-force units, and "opposed expanding the CAP concept to the other corps zones, believing that it would drain the strength of maneuver battalions [even though in all of the 114 CAP units there were only 2,000 U.S. personnel], duplicate the advisory effort, and make the territories [rural population] dependent on American support."[100]

Although Westmoreland and his associates opposed the CAP program, they eventually created a similar program, Mobile Advisory Teams (MATs), several hundred of which were organized in 1967 following the creation of CORDS (Civil Operations and Revolutionary Development Support) and the transfer of all U.S. pacification activities to Westmoreland's command. MATs were small (five-man) teams assigned to train and advise local South Vietnamese Regional and Popular Force units garrisoned in the villages. In practice, these U.S. Army teams, like the Marines' CAPs, tended to play more of a leadership than an advisory role in helping local forces to provide security for the villages.[101]

Dissent Within the Army: The PROVN Report

The other major challenge from within the military to prevailing military doctrine and practice occurred in the Army where, in certain quarters, there was opposition to Westmoreland's choice of strategy and tactics, especially among the young majors and lieutenant colonels who had served as advisers in Vietnam. In July 1965, the Chief of Staff of the Army, General Harold Johnson, who had criticized Westmoreland and his staff for developing a conventional plan for using U.S. forces that did not adequately take into account the unconventional nature of the war in Vietnam,[102] commissioned a study to develop "new sources of action to be taken in South Vietnam by the United States and its allies, which will, in conjunction with current actions, modified as necessary, lead in due time to successful accomplishment of U.S. aims and objectives."[103]

---

[100] Clarke, *Advice and Support: The Final Years, 1965–1973,* p. 181. In his memoirs, *A Soldier Reports,* p. 166, Westmoreland says that although the Marines "achieved some noteworthy results" with the CAP program, "I simply had not enough numbers to put a squad of Americans in every village and hamlet; that would have been fragmenting resources and exposing them to defeat in detail." Krepinevich maintains (*The Army and Vietnam,* pp. 175–176) that Westmoreland's argument is not supported by the facts: "First, it was not necessary to place army squads in every village simultaneously; indeed, the 'oil spot' principle called for gradual expansion outward from selected areas. Westmoreland's argument is more reflective of the Army's impatience with quick results in a conflict environment that would not produce them. Second, even if encadrement of every village and hamlet had been the requirement, a 1967 DOD [Department of Defense] report found that it could be met by utilizing 167,000 U.S. troops, far fewer than the 550,000 eventually assigned to South Vietnam." Within the 550,000 ceiling, Krepinevich says, there could have been a CAP force together with several army divisions to counter any moves by major Communist forces, and "Casualties would have been minimized, and population security enhanced."

[101] For a compelling case study, see David Donovan (a pseudonym), *Once A Warrior King* (New York: McGraw-Hill, 1985).

See also Thomas John Ferguson, "American Perceptions of the Vietnam War in Popular Literature: An Interpretation by a Professional Soldier," PhD dissertation (Univ. of Hawaii, 1988). Ferguson, at the time a lieutenant colonel in the Army, served with the 25th Division in Vietnam in 1966–1967.

For a discussion of MATs, see also Clarke, *Advice and Support: The Final Years, 1965–1973,* pp. 236–239, 510–511, and Stuart A. Herrington, *Silence Was a Weapon: The Vietnam War in the Villages, A Personal Perspective* (Novato, Calif.: Presidio Press, 1982).

[102] For General Johnson's views, see part III of this study, pp. 169–170, 358–359.

[103] *PP,* Gravel ed., vol. II, p. 576, from the directive's statement of the purpose of the study. Bergerud, *The Dynamics of Defeat,* p. 81, commenting on the origin of the study, states, without giving a source, that General Johnson had lunch with Bernard Fall, who challenged some of the "basic demographic facts" on Vietnam that General Johnson had been given by his staff.

Continued

General Johnson, who was known as a strong proponent of counterinsurgency,[104] favored an anti-infiltration cordon across the top of South Vietnam combined with "a lot of scouting and patrolling type of activity by quite small units with the capacity to reinforce quickly."[105] But, his views were not widely supported in the Army, and, consistent with military practice, he deferred to the field commander on strategy and tactics.

As the following incident suggests, General Johnson also appears to have assumed that such small-unit operations would involve higher U.S. casualties, and therefore would be less acceptable to the American public than the large-unit operations. (Ironically, the opposite appears to have been true—small-unit operations involved less casualties by comparison to those of larger units.)[106] On a visit to Vietnam in December 1965, General Johnson met with some junior officers of the 1st Infantry Division, who told him that rather than large-unit missions, it would be more effective to have small units constantly moving and patrolling. General Johnson is said to have told the officers that although he agreed with their philosophy, he could not support their ideas. He was quoted as saying that the reason for this was that "we were not going to be able to respond to the public outcry in the United States about the casualties that might result."[107]

By commissioning the study of new sources of action, and by appointing to the Special Study Group some of the best of the younger officers who were also staunch supporters of counterinsurgency, General Johnson may have been hopeful, however, of developing a counterinsurgency alternative to Westmoreland's strategy and tactics. When he met with the study group, General Johnson told them that he wanted a program for the long-term pacification of Vietnam, even if it took 50 years for it to be effective.[108]

The study group consisted of the following members: Col. Thomas J. Hanifen (Armor), the leader of the group, Lt. Col. Charles E. Spragins (Infantry), Lt. Col. Donald S. Marshall (Civil Affairs), Lt. Col. Harry H. Jackson (Infantry), Lt. Col. Harris Emmons (Army Intelligence & Security), Lt. Col. Volney F. Warner (Infantry), Lt. Col. Daniel F. Schungel (Infantry), Maj. Anne M. Doering (Women's Army Corps), Maj. Arthur E. Brown, Jr. (Infantry), Maj. Ames S. Albro (Corps of Engineers), Maj. John D. Granger (Military Police Corps). Emmons and Doering studied intelligence gathering. Marshall, an anthropologist, studied the U.S. advisory effort in the provinces. Warner developed a long questionnaire with which he studied the attitudes and experience of over 400 former U.S. provisional advisers, especially the question of how the U.S. could apply

---

According to Bergerud, "After later examining these discrepancies and learning that Fall was correct in each case, Johnson realized that many basic statistics and matters of factual detail concerning Vietnam were unknown to Army personnel. More importantly, he concluded that the Army had no coherent picture of the essential problems faced in Vietnam and consequently lacked a long-term program of action."

[104] According to General DePuy, "HK [Johnson] was a counterinsurgency man 100 percent." See part III of this study, p. 170.

[105] Interview (one of a series) with Gen. Harold K. Johnson, May 21, 1974, Senior Officer Oral History Program, U.S. Army Military History Institute, Carlisle Barracks, Pa.

[106] Krepinevich, *The Army and Vietnam,* p. 174.

[107] *Ibid.*, pp. 171–172.

[108] Interview with Gen. Volney F. Warner (U.S. Army, Ret.), 1983, Senior Officer Oral History Program, U.S. Army Military History Institute, Carlisle Barracks, Pa.

"leverage." Brown studied the history of the Vietnamese. Schungel worked on the military aspects of the study.

One of the more forceful members of the group was Lt. Col. Warner, who had been an advisor in Kien Giang Province (in the delta south of Saigon, where the Communists were well-entrenched) in 1963–1964. Based on that experience, he became convinced that the war was a civil war, a political war, and could not be won by the use of American forces. The problem, he said in an interview some years later, was not "communism." In the delta "They didn't know communism from any other damn thing in the world, and couldn't care less. All they wanted to do was eat, stay alive and hope the province chief would leave them alone."[109] The problem was to develop a government that would be acceptable to the people, and an army that cared for and helped the people. He said he was "terribly disturbed down in the Delta thinking about how screwed up MACV was, and how lousy the Vietnamese military were, and how we were carrying their war for them. They didn't give a damn about their own people. I watched a few situations where they surrounded a town, shot artillery into it and then ran the bag carrier in to pick up the money raised by the villagers so as to avoid a second shelling. . . . My statement as a major [his rank as an adviser] was that had I been Vietnamese, I would have been a Viet Cong. The reason I said that was because of my year in the Delta watching the maltreatment of the peasants by what passed as a legitimate government at the provincial and district level. It was just incredible to me, that the South Vietnamese would expect that anybody would support them, with the killing, and with the bagmen going around paying a district chief by giving him 50 percent of what they collected in the way of taxes in the villages, principally by the use of military force."

Warner said he was opposed to the use of U.S. forces "on the basis that the Vietnamese hadn't done sufficiently well on their own," and he opposed the bombing of the North because "no amount of bombing in the North could bring an effective government into being in the South. That was the fundamental problem. . . ."

"Many other of the province advisor types," Warner said, "had a sensing, resulting from their rice paddy existence, that was quite different from those who were arguing for a military solution and going over with U.S. troops to solve it. There was constant harassment [in the Pentagon] back and forth between the two factions." "We were trying to get the 'other side' of the war—pacification—into everybody's consciousness with an intensity that no one else had pursued before. We argued vehemently with General Taylor about the bombing in the North. We later fought with [W. W.] Rostow's guidance as he asked us for gold nuggets to show a success, and instead we had 10,000 clods that showed failure."[110]

---

[109] *Ibid.*

[110] In a speech in 1986, General Warner summarized his conclusions about Vietnam (statement in author's possession, provided by General Warner and quoted with his permission):

"1. Our truly most pernicious problem was the government of South Vietnam. No amount of iron bombs dropped on the North could ever bring into being an effective government in the South.

Continued

On March 14, 1966, eight months after it had been created by General Johnson, the Army's Special Study Group completed its report, "A Program for the Pacification and Long-Term Development of South Vietnam" (PROVN),[111] a 900-page, two volume analysis of the situation and a "Blueprint for National Action," utilizing interviews with participants and studies by various consultants. Of all of the studies and reports prepared in or for the U.S. Government during the war, it was one of the most important. But it was also one of the most sensitive and controversial. General Johnson said in an interview in 1970 that it was "the only good study that has been done," but that, given its nature and conclusions, "It took a lot of maneuvering around to get it what I would call on the street."[112]

It is little wonder that the report should have been considered sensitive for it was highly critical of the way in which the war was being fought, and it concluded that time was running out for the Army to shift from a military response to one in which the central concern would be the development of popular support for the government. Noting that the situation had "seriously deteriorated," and that the Government of South Vietnam controlled less than 10 percent of its territory and 25 percent of its population, the study group said that, "Steps taken in 1966 may either ensure eventual success or reinforce the present trend to win battles but lose the war."[113]

"Present U.S. military actions," the report declared, "are inconsistent with that fundamental counterinsurgency doctrine which establishes winning popular allegiance as the ultimate goal. While conceptually recognizing the total problem in our literature, Americans appear to draw back from its complexity in practice and gravitate toward a faulty premise for its resolution—military destruction of the VC. Frustrated by our inability to find the 'method' to cope with conflict of this nature we have resorted to methods employed in wars of the past to address almost exclusively the battle's military dimension."[114]

"2. For the U.S. to do what needed to be done politically in South Vietnam would have required its virtual colonialization—an effort for which the French had just been repudiated and driven from the country. . . .

"3. When it became apparent in 1965 that, despite the best efforts of the U.S. Advisory Team, the South Vietnamese were losing the war for their people, we should have withdrawn, without further U.S. military involvement

"4. There never was a time in the war when U.S. forces could have won militarily in South Vietnam.

"5. However, since we did decide to deploy U.S. forces to fight the war against the North Vietnamese regular forces, we should have carried it to the North on the ground in order to win. (And here there is admittedly a serious question as to what win would mean. Once the war was over, someone would still have to govern SVN!)

"6. To blame the U.S. military for the unfavorable outcome of Vietnam is fundamentally wrong. The decision to make war is a political decision not a military one. However, once the decision to fight is made and the battle is joined there is no reason to fight it any less well because the political decision was a poor one!

"So in summary, we reaped the worst of all decisions, failing in the advisory effort we deployed U.S. forces only in the South to accomplish wholly unattainable objectives, then publicly blamed our soldiers! (emphasis in original)

[111] The PROVN Report, which was declassified at the request of the author, is in CMH, Westmoreland Papers. The second volume of the report consists of a number of annexes, including studies prepared for the group.

[112] CMH, Department of the Army Interview with General Johnson, Nov. 20, 1970, conducted by Charles B. MacDonald and Charles von Luttichau.

[113] PROVN Report, vol. I, Resume, p. 31.

[114] *Ibid.*, p. 53.

"PROVN," on the other hand, "contends that people—Vietnamese and Americans . . . constitute the strategic determinants of today's conflict. . . . This fact, too often mouthed without real understanding in the now trite phrase 'winning the hearts and minds of people,' must guide all of our future actions. . . . The current battles for the villages of South Vietnam may well prove to be one of the most important and decisive conflicts in world history. PROVN focuses on this central battle; all other military aspects of the war are secondary."[115]

"Rural construction [pacification] must be designated unequivocally as the major US-GVN effort," the report said. This would require the preponderance of South Vietnamese military and paramilitary forces, which "must be associated and intermingled with the people on a long-term basis. Their capacity to establish and maintain public order and stability must be physically and continuously credible. The key to achieving such security lies in the conduct of effective area saturation tactics, in and around populated areas, which deny VC encroachment opportunities."[116]

The role of U.S. forces, together with some Vietnamese units, should be to assist with pacification by attacking Communist base areas in South Vietnam as well as lines of communication in South Vietnam, Laos and Cambodia.[117] Ground forces should be used more extensively in the areas of major points of entry into South Vietnam from Laos and across the demilitarized zone, and special forces should conduct covert raids into Laos. If these efforts did not adequately control infiltration, U.S. forces should conduct the necessary operations against the Ho Chi Minh Trail in Laos, and possibly in Cambodia as well, and preparations should be made to occupy and defend a line along the demilitarized zone from the Tonkin Gulf into Laos.

Moreover, the report said, diplomatic and military actions should be taken to "eliminate" the use of Laos and Cambodia as sanctuaries ("safe havens") by Communist forces. Laos should be asked for permission for U.S. forces to undertake such operations in Laos, or to allow or acquiesce in "hot pursuit" across the border. Cambodia should be asked to close its borders with South Vietnam, and to seal the port of Sihanoukville (where Communist supplies were being received), and U.S. forces could then engage in "hot pursuit" of Communist forces withdrawing from South Vietnam to their safe havens across the Cambodian border.[118]

The report emphasized, however, that U.S. and South Vietnamese military operations should adopt "selective warfare . . . as a cardinal principle in order to avoid elimination of the population through unwise application of military force and troop misconduct." The following rules were stated as a "minimum": "(1) No unobserved [H and I—harassment and interdiction] artillery fire in populated areas. (2) No fighter-bomber strikes in populated areas unless they are in support of a friendly unit in contact. (3) 'Scorched earth' measures are appropriate for VC base areas and war zones but must not be taken in contested areas. (4) Troop con-

[115] *Ibid.*, p. 100.
[116] *Ibid.*, pp. 65, 69.
[117] *Ibid.*, ch. 5, pp. 13 ff.
[118] *Ibid.*, ch. 5, pp. 11–15.

duct is a command responsibility; there must be no misconduct toward noncombatants. (5) Excessive speed must be avoided, especially on roads and in towns where there are many pedestrians. (6) GVN troops must not be used as tax collectors."[119]

The success of both military efforts and pacification programs, the report said, depended upon achieving a "viable government." It described the existing Government of Vietnam as being "without a popular mandate":

> It seized power through the imposition of military force and retains control by the exercise of this same power factor—buttressed now by unequivocal US support. Governmental policies are formulated by a committee whose personal interests frequently prevail over national interests. Provinces of reform are anticipated by GVN spokesmen who have no genuine interest in bringing social reform to the people. Translation of these promises into action, however, is dependent upon a self-oriented, corrupt bureaucracy which is not engrossed in the public, particularly in the peasant. . . .
>
> Under the present US program of assistance to SVN, governmental efficacy and effectiveness continues to decrease. Massive injections of US combat power are not matched by social and political reforms. A "fight now—reform later" concept prevails.[120]

The study group argued that in order to achieve the necessary reforms and to create a viable government supported by the people, the United States, despite its reluctance to become involved in the country's internal affairs, would have to intervene actively in the government and politics of South Vietnam: "We must be prepared," the report stated, "to recognize, to accept and to play a new role in this conflict. In broadest possible perspective, Americans will have to perform as social innovators in order to respond fully to the GVN's intrinsic needs for assistance. . . . If we lose in Vietnam, we pay the price no matter how carefully American officials rationalize the need to respect Vietnamese sovereignty. . . . While considerations of Vietnamese sovereignty are important, these considerations should not become an obstacle to the achievement of US national objectives. Standing on this outdated diplomatic principle can result in military defeat."[121]

In the case of some "selected critical programs" proposed by the U.S., the U.S. "must be prepared" to execute such programs unilaterally should the Government of South Vietnam prove unwilling or unable to do so.[122]

"The US support effort," the report contended, "should be geared to influence *any* Vietnamese leader—at *any* political level and within *any* organizational structure—to contribute to the achievement of responsive government. . . . The US must engage in a systematic effort to stimulate, foster and guide the growth of fundamental

---

[119] *Ibid.*, ch. 5, pp. 19–20.
[120] *Ibid.*, p. 76 of Resume.
[121] *Ibid.*, pp. 54–55 of Resume and p. 9 of ch. 3.
[122] *Ibid.*, p. 189 of Resume. It will be recalled that John Paul Vann and Daniel Ellsberg made similar suggestions for U.S. intervention in the process of government in South Vietnam.

political institutions and responsible behavior."[123] (emphases in original) Long-range objectives should be:[124]

(1) A stable government with fully institutionalized arrangements for changing leadership.

(2) Active, constructive political parties with broad-based membership.

(3) National assembly fully established as legislative branch of government.

(4) Free elections at all echelons.

(5) A professional, service-oriented civil service.

(6) A modernized legal system.

(7) Full support of political institutions by all sections of society.

(8) Integration of minority groups into society.

(9) A professional diplomatic corps.

(10) Active participation in the community of Free Nations.

To provide the U.S. staff for carrying out this far-reaching plan to apply Western democratic concepts and principles to a country with a very different social and political tradition, the study group recommended, among other things, that 43 American lieutenant colonels and colonels, drawn in part from those who had already served as advisers, be selected as "sector advisers" to the Government of South Vietnam.[125] "At present," the report said, "the US is not well prepared to assist the passage of the Vietnamese people through a social revolution even they themselves cannot fully understand. However, those major ideas, ideals, value and attitudes that contribute to any modern cohesive society can be identified. Moreover, the subtle techniques of transferring them to a foreign counterpart can be learned and employed by US representatives."[126]

Finally, the Army study group was optimistic that, in the long-run, the PROVN plan would be successful not only in helping the South Vietnamese to become independent, non-Communist and self-governing, but in building a nation that would meet the standards that the study group considered to be desirable. This, the report said, referring to General Johnson's admonition to devise a plan that would be effective even if it took 50 years, could be done "in less than 50 years."

> In less than 50 years, SVN should have effectively integrated its significant minority groups into the fabric of its society. The government should be basically democratic with firmly established political institutions capable of withstanding crises and allowing for the legal and peaceful transfer of political power. Economically, SVN should have passed the take-off point to self-sustaining growth. A somewhat smaller, well-equipped and well trained military establishment, backed by regional and

[123] *Ibid.*, p. 56 of Resume and p. 63 of ch. 3.
[124] *Ibid.*, ch. 3, p. 62.
[125] *Ibid.*, ch. 2–45.
[126] *Ibid.*, p. 55 of Resume.

international security guarantees, should be able to ensure national security.[127]

Throughout this long-range period of development, the report added, "the U.S. presence should be minimal." [128]

After the PROVN Report was produced, those who had reason to resist its conclusions took steps to control its distribution and to minimize its impact on existing policy and practice. And although some of the conclusions and 140 specific recommendations of the report were eventually implemented, at least in part, the effort to prevent the report from having any major effects on the way the war was being fought was very successful.[129] The security classification of the report was upgraded from secret to top secret to reduce its circulation and to inhibit possible divulgence of its contents. Distribution of the report outside the Department of Defense was not authorized, and the JCS distributed copies inside the Department only on a very limited "need-to-know" basis, with the proviso that the report did not necessarily represent its views. Army officials were forbidden to discuss even the existence of the report outside the Pentagon.

These steps were followed by a recommendation from Westmoreland and his staff, approved in Washington, that the report be "reduced primarily to a conceptual document," rather than a study that could become the basis for action.[130] MACV called the report "an excellent overall approach in developing organization, concepts, and policies to defeat communist insurgency in South Vietnam," and recommended that the report be submitted to the National Security Council "for use in developing concepts, policies, and actions to improve the effectiveness of the American effort in Vietnam." [131]

MACV avoided commenting on the report's criticism of U.S. military operations, focusing instead on the recommendation for greater U.S. involvement in influencing the politics and Government of South Vietnam. It agreed with the recommendation, but took the position that there was "great danger that the extent of involvement envisioned could become too great," that the South Vietnamese would "resent too great involvement," and that "US manipulations could easily become an American takeover justified by US compulsion to 'get the job done.'" "Such tendencies must be resisted. . . . Our goals cannot be achieved by Vietnamese leaders who are identified as US puppets. The US will must be asserted, but we cannot afford to overwhelm the structure we are attempting to develop."

127 When the authors of the PROVN study briefed the JCS, Lt. Col. Donald Marshall was reported to have said that "We needed fifty years to do what we wanted to do in Vietnam. We had to change the Vietnamese national character, and that would take, at a minimum, three generations." Quoted in Maitland and McInerney, *A Contagion of War,* p. 60.

128 PROVN Report, p. 9, of Resume.

129 According to Krepinevich, *The Army and Vietnam,* p. 182, the Army suppressed the PROVN Report, and, "despite Westmoreland's claims that MACV had responded to the PROVN study, the second half of 1966 saw MACV utilize its maneuver battalions almost exclusively in search-and-destroy operations."

130 CMH, MACV to CINCPAC, MACV 18244, May 27, 1966 and *PP,* Gravel ed., vol. II, p. 576.

131 It has been suggested by an Army historian that the MACV cable did not necessarily represent Westmoreland's views: "Drafted by junior staff officers who were more sympathetic to PROVN than were Westmoreland and senior members of his staff, the message was phrased to be as favorable as possible while not inviting Westmoreland's contingent rejection." Scoville, *Reorganizing for Pacification Support,* p. 29 n, based on an interview by Scoville.

For very insightful comments on the reaction of Westmoreland and his staff, see Bergerud, *The Dynamics of Defeat,* pp. 111 ff.

It is not known whether the PROVN Report was sent to the White House or the State Department or whether the President even knew of its existence.[132] It does not appear to have been presented to the NSC. At some unknown point, NSC staff member Robert Komer, who was named by the President in the spring of 1966 to be Washington Coordinator for Pacification, got a copy of the report, and, as will be seen, attempted to carry out some of its recommendations.

It is not clear what role, if any, McNamara and other civilians in the Defense Department had in the preparation of and response to the report. McNamara, as well as the Secretary of the Army, were briefed on the complete report, but neither official appears to have taken any action.[133]

Nor did the JCS take any action beyond "staffing" the report (reviewing it for the purpose of organizing plans for its implementation.)[134]

There was a briefing on the report for the U.S. Mission Council in Saigon on August 8, 1966, almost five months after the report was issued. General John C. F. Tillson, Jr. gave the Army's presentation, the focus of which was on the military support provided by U.S. and South Vietnamese forces for the pacification program, and the lack of support by the South Vietnamese Army.[135] He did not discuss the major conclusion of the PROVN Report that existing U.S. military operations—large search-and-destroy missions together with bombing and shelling—were "inconsistent with the goal of winning popular allegiance" and were "secondary" to the goal of protecting the people and providing security for the villages.

After Tillson's presentation, Ambassador Lodge gave this summary of the MACV position:

> We are recognizing that this war is a political struggle with violent military and terroristic overtones. This means that we must be successful in both the conventional military and in the unconventional guerrilla/terroristic areas. If we are not successful in both of these areas, Hanoi will never give up but will find some way of sliding back to "Phase One" activities consisting primarily of clandestine guerrilla activities. The proposed primary mission of ARVN is to engage in pacification activities, to support district and village chiefs in the establishment of law and order. This encompasses the activities of police force and the RF [Regional Forces] and PF [Popular Forces]. Some elite ARVN units will still remain to fight the VC main force and NVA elements. In the pacification area, much greater stress will be placed on ARVN small units operating at night. There must be an attitudinal change on the part of ARVN toward the peasants. All of these the Vietnamese will have to do for themselves. If we are criticized that we are carrying the brunt of the fight, we will explain that we are creating the opportunity for ARVN to do the pacification job themselves, with-

[132] According to the archivists at the Johnson Library, who conducted a search at the author's request, Johnson's files do not contain a copy of the PROVN Report or any papers dealing with the report.

[133] Lt. Col. Marshall, one of the authors of PROVN, attributes McNamara's lack of support to an "inadequate briefing." Scoville, *Reorganizing for Pacification Support,* p. 29 n.

[134] This information is derived from CMH files on the PROVN Report.

[135] CMH, Minutes of the Mission Council Meeting of Aug. 8, 1966.

out which the war cannot be brought to a successful conclusion.

General Westmoreland said that this was a "succinct summary of the MACV concept."

In Washington, General Abrams, the Vice Chief of Staff of the Army, after reading a newspaper article on the subject of the U.S. Army's operations in Vietnam and a statement by General Krulak of the Marine Corps' view of how the war could be won, raised the question "Quite apart from parochialism, do we have any succinct statement of what the Army's strategy is on how to win in South Vietnam?" In response, DCSOPS (Deputy Chief of Staff for Military Operations), Gen. Vernon Mock, said in a memorandum to Abrams on August 31, 1966, that the PROVN Report "represents a succinct statement, not of what our national strategy is, but of what it should be in order to win in Vietnam."[136] In the DCSOPS characterization of the report, however, as well as in an Army summary of the report which was included with the DCSOPS memorandum, some of the major findings of the report were avoided. Instead, the report was characterized as providing for "a major offensive along three mutually supporting axes—eliminating armed Communists, increasing the effective performance of the SVN and conducting an effective combined US-GVN Revolutionary Development program." With the summary of PROVN, Mock's office also sent to Abrams a summary of the JCS memorandum of August 1965, "Concept for Vietnam," recommending the military measures that the U.S. should take in Vietnam.[137]

In response to Abrams, DCSOPS went even further in seeking to diminish the significance of the PROVN Report and to brush aside its conclusions. According to the DSCOPS memorandum, two papers—the JCS military strategy proposal "Concept for Vietnam" and the PROVN Report—"are not, with minor exceptions, incompatible. The major military issues in SVN are not conflicts concerning a strategy of how to win, but conflicts concerning the relative priority of military and non-military tasks to be performed, and conflicts over the type of military operations best suited for their accomplishment."

Mock's office also sent to Abrams a copy of the MACV briefing to the Mission Council on August 8, noting that it gave "first priority" to search and destroy operations against major VC/NVA forces. . . ."

Although the official position of DCSOPS was that the PROVN Report was a good statement of what U.S. strategy should be, Warner reported in a later interview that General Mock himself had a very different reaction:[138]

> When we tried to get the DCSOPS, General Mock, to approve it [the PROVN Report] we had a very difficult session. He read it, we briefed him on it, and since it was so controversial, he said, "I'll not sign it. If you want it signed, you can get one of the cleaning ladies to sign it in the hallway early in the morning." It was a fascinating discussion, and we began to

---

[136] General Mock's memorandum with enclosures is at CMH.

[137] This, it will be recalled, was the proposal that was not acted upon by McNamara.

[138] Interview with General Warner, cited above.

argue with him until General [Donn R.] Pepke finally told us, with a note that he passed, to both General [Robert B.] Spragins [then a colonel] and myself, to "shut up." But, we were very distressed with General Mock. Having worked with him before as an action officer, it wasn't unusual for him to say, "All right, Warner, I don't understand it, and I don't want you to explain it, but I'll advise you that when we get in to see the Chief, if he doesn't agree with it I'm going to cut you off and say that I didn't agree with it either. So, if you're willing to present it on those ground rules, go at it." So at least you knew where you were, but you didn't always have his support. We were going through this same litany on this study.

Although Westmoreland and his associates, as well as Army and other military officials in Washington, were quite successful in their opposition to the PROVN Report, a number of the recommendations were implemented subsequently, in part because of the quiet support of Army Chief of Staff General Johnson and others on the Army general staff who, while apparently disagreeing with various aspects of the report, "were brilliant enough"—in Warner's words—"to decide to put us [those who had worked on the report] in key positions throughout the Defense Department and give us an opportunity to put into action . . . the recommendations of the study." These included Warner, Granger, Spragins, Brown, Schungel, Marshall, all of whom, Warner, says, "were pretty well plugged into the system, with the challenge that although our recommendations weren't officially accepted, we would have an action format that might drive the system." Thus, Warner, who was assigned to ODCSOPS, says that he "had a lot of fun in ODCSOPS . . . in trying to counterbalance the 'go get 'em guys'—George Patton, Frank Blazey, Dick Kotite."[139]

In 1967, Warner volunteered for an assignment to the pacification staff in the White House. "I spent a lot of time," Warner said in the interview, "trying to get the White House to ask the JCS for solutions that we [PROVN] had, that would, in turn, force them to jam it through the JCS system and OSD [Office of the Secretary of Defense] for a decision, whether they liked it or not. . . . We had come up with a mechanism that was viable, and Komer was our champion! We were trying to get the 'other side' of the war—pacification—into everybody's consciousness with an intensity that no one else had pursued before."[140]

In an interview in 1970, General Johnson said that the PROVN Report was "basically the blueprint for what we're doing in Viet-

[139] At that time, George S. Patton, Frank E. Blazey, and Richard S. Kotite, were lieutenant colonels in ODCSOPS. Patton later became a major general, and Blazey and Kotite became brigadier generals.

[140] *Ibid.* In 1969, Warner, resuming his regular Army career with the knowledge that his future depended on having a command assignment during the war, returned to Vietnam as the Commander of the 3d Brigade, 4th Infantry Division. "I sought the brigade out," he said later, "but I knew that there was not a prayer in hell . . . that whatever that brigade did would be relevant to the war as I knew it. So, I had a crisis of conscience. I was over there in Vietnam, obviously responsible for people who might get killed, trying to fight a war that couldn't be won. . . . I reconciled that in my conscience by saying, "Once the battle is joined, then there's no reason whatsoever to fight it any less well! You'd better win it. Whether you should have joined it or not is not an issue that a soldier resolves."

nam now. . . . Despite the lack of an endorsement, the ideas in there were . . . in large measure adopted."[141]

[141] CMH, 1990 Interview with General Harold K. Johnson, cited above. A report in early 1967 stated that of the 140 recommendations in the PROVN Report, 53 had been implemented and 45 had been partially implemented. CMH, a report by Col. Robert M. Montague, Jr., Mar. 2, 1967.

CHAPTER 6

CONGRESSIONAL DISCONTENT

By early 1966, the congressional consensus on Vietnam policy was beginning to break down, not because of opposition from the minority, the Republicans, but because of dissent within the President's own Democratic Party, which was then the majority party in both Houses of Congress. In addition to the Democratic leader of the Senate (Mansfield) and the Democratic chairman of the Foreign Relations Committee (Fulbright), both powerful positions, there were at least 26 other Democratic Senators who had expressed concern about the escalation of the war. (At the time there were 67 Democrats in the Senate out of 100 seats.) In the House of Representatives, among the younger, more liberal Democrats, many of whom had been elected for the first time in 1964 (when the Democrats gained 70 new seats in the House of Representatives, giving President Johnson the support he needed for the Great Society program), there was increasing concern about the war and the course of U.S. policy. This feeling was so intense and widespread that, as noted, a letter to the President on the subject in January 1966 was signed by 77 Democrats in only four hours (at the time, there were 295 Democrats in the House of Representatives out of 435 seats), despite the fact that the Speaker of the House, John McCormack, was strongly in favor of the war and was supported by the other Democratic leaders of the House.

In the realignment of congressional views that was occurring, the liberals and some moderates of both parties, most of whom had previously supported an active foreign policy, were becoming doubtful about U.S. policy in Vietnam, especially the heavy reliance on conventional military force. On the other hand, the more conservative members of both parties, some of whom had been very reluctant to have the U.S. become involved in Vietnam, continued to support the President but were concerned about the lack of results and favored stronger military action.

Complicating the situation even further was the fact that the liberals and moderates, especially among the Democrats, while opposing the President on Vietnam, were the principal supporters of his Great Society program, whereas many of the conservatives used the need to intensify the war as an argument against increasing expenditures on domestic programs. Thus, to maintain support for the war, as well as to try to avoid having the war used as a way of attacking domestic programs, the President felt the need to court the Republicans and conservative Democrats. At the same time, he knew that if he neglected the Democrats, especially the liberals, he would risk serious setbacks to the Great Society.

This combination of factors created a number of problems for the implementation of U.S. policy toward Vietnam (and, of course, for domestic policy), one of the most basic of which concerned the cost of the war and the making of politically sensitive decisions about taxation.

The Decision Not to Request a Tax Increase or a New Congressional Resolution

When he decided in July 1965 to send large-scale forces to Vietnam, the President rejected the advice of McNamara and others that there should be a tax increase. He told McNamara that Congress would not approve new taxes for the war, and, furthermore, that such a request would be used as a way of attacking domestic programs. He was reported to have said: "in the course of the debate they'll say: 'You see, we've been telling you so. You can't have guns and butter, and we're going to have guns.'"[1] At that time the President was also very reluctant, at least in part for the same reason, to request new appropriations for the expanded American role in the war. He preferred, as he told a meeting of congressional leaders on July 27, 1965, to request only a small amount and to defer the remainder until January 1966—"to give you the story now and the bill later." There was a chance, the President said, that in the interim the Communists might show some interest in negotiating. Both the President and the leaders, who generally seemed to agree with his proposal, knew, however, that they were—as the President told several of his advisers after the meeting—merely "postponing the agony" involved in requesting additional funds.[2]

The efforts by the President to maintain support for both guns and butter were alluded to in a telephone conversation on November 18 between Secretary of the Treasury Henry Fowler and White House Press Secretary Bill Moyers concerning a speech Fowler proposed to make to a business group. Moyers said he had shown the draft to the President, who thought it was "a little too hard on the Vietnam situation." Fowler replied that he had "tried to avoid saying that there was a war on," but he added, "that is the only psychological ribbon on which we can fight a lot of these things." Moyers responded that "he is saying himself that we can have both guns and butter," and that the speech "might draw doubts to the fact that he can't have both . . . what the President doesn't want to do is say to business community that we have declared war in Vietnam."[3]

Budget Director Charles L. Schultze, according to Shapley, has another explanation for Johnson's desire to avoid the impression that the U.S. was involved in a major war: "The President avoided asking for a major tax increase because he feared the generals, Schultze explains. 'He couldn't have gotten a tax increase on economic grounds alone; you can't sell Congress on tax hikes. He could have gotten it by wrapping himself in the flag and declared Hanoi despicable and sought wage and price controls and called on the National Guard. I recall Joe [Henry] Fowler telling him, Mr. President, if you make it a war tax you'll get it. But—people forget

[1] See pt. III of this study, p. 389.
[2] *Ibid.*, pp. 427–429.
[3] Johnson Library, Papers of Henry H. Fowler, "Notes of Telephone Conversation, Nov. 18, 1965.

this—Johnson at that time was a dove. He knew that to get a tax hike he'd have to call it a war. As Toynbee says, it's easy as hell to get a democracy to hate somebody. He literally was afraid he'd lose control.'"[4]

By December 1965, as the time approached for returning to Congress for the additional funds needed to finance the war until June 30, 1966, as well as new funds for the following year, the President was faced with increasing inflation resulting from expenditures for the war and the apparent need for a tax increase to help to control excessive demand in the economy. His three principal economic and financial advisers—the "Troika"—Gardner Ackley, Chairman of the Council of Economic Advisers, Charles Schultze, Director of the Bureau of the Budget (which was transformed into the Office of Management and Budget a few years later), and Secretary Fowler, said that a tax increase was or would be needed shortly. Ackley urged him to propose "a significant tax increase" to prevent "an intolerable degree of inflationary pressure."[5] In a memorandum to the President, Ackley said that from an economic standpoint this should be done "as soon as possible," but that "tactically, it may only be feasible to propose higher taxes later in the year." Schultze and Fowler also favored a tax increase but apparently thought that it should be postponed until later in the year.

On December 22, Fowler conferred in Little Rock, Arkansas, with Representative Wilbur D. Mills, chairman of the House Ways and Means Committee, without whose support it would have been extremely difficult if not impossible to pass a tax increase.[6] Mills took the position that civilian expenditures in the budget for the 1967 fiscal year (July 1, 1966-June 30, 1967) that was to be sent to Congress in January 1966 should not exceed those of fiscal year 1966. To keep the budget as low as possible he also suggested that "The full impact of Viet Nam expenditures should not be put in the fiscal

---

[4] Shapley, *Promise and Power,* p. 373. Hammond, *LBJ and the Presidential Management of Foreign Relations,* p. 191, observes that the "middle course" which Johnson had chosen to follow in fighting the war "placed Johnson in a delicate position, between his generals (and admirals), who were frustrated by not being given a clear mission and the freedom to accomplish it without interference, and a public that could become aroused and impatient for results. . . . Johnson, faced the situation of managing an American general, Westmoreland, who was leading American troops in a distant land against a foreign enemy, a situation fraught with potential political trouble because of the prospect of American military leaders' using the Congress as a forum for venting the usual frustrations of field commanders with insufficient resources to accomplish the assigned mission."

[5] Memoranda to the President from Gardner Ackley, Dec. 17 and 27, 1965, cited in Donald F. Kettl, "The Economic Education of Lyndon Johnson: Guns, Butter, and Taxes," in Robert A. Divine (ed.), *The Johnson Years,* Vol. 2 (Lawrence, Kansas: Univ. Press of Kansas, 1987), pp. 54–78 at 59. The December 17 memorandum is in the Johnson Library, Ex/FI4, and the December 27 memorandum is in C.F. FI4.

See also Allen J. Matusow, *The Unraveling of America: A History of Liberalism in the 1960s* (New York: Harper Collins, 1984), pp. 159–160, Ronald F. King, "The President and Fiscal Policy in 1966: The Year Taxes Were Not Raised," *Polity,* 17 (Summer 1985), pp. 685–714.

According to former Secretary of the Treasury Douglas Dillon, he wrote to the President in February 1966 urging him to request a tax increase "that was needed if we were to continue with both policies [the war and the Great Society] and avoid the onset of inflation that would otherwise ensue." (Letter from Douglas Dillon to Professor Fred Greenstein, Princeton University, Nov. 29, 1989, used with permission of Mr. Dillon and Professor Greenstein.) "Unfortunately, the President did not even bother to acknowledge my letter, and history bears witness to the damage inflicted by the inflation which ensued and for which President Johnson bears the chief responsibility." (*Ibid.*) After a search conducted at the author's request, the archivists at the Johnson Library have not been able to find Dillon's letter.

[6] Fowler's memorandum to the President on December 29, 1965, summarizing the meeting, is in the Johnson Library, C.F. FI2. See also Edwin C. Hargrove and Samuel A. Morley (eds.), *The President and the Council of Economic Advisers, Interviews with CEA Chairmen* (Boulder, Colo.: Westview Press, 1984), pp. 250–251, 303, and Lawrence C. Pierce, *The Politics of Fiscal Policy Formation* (Pacific Palisades, Calif.: Goodyear, 1971), p. 190.

1967 budget." The budget "will have to reflect the current rate of expenditures for the war, but it need not do more than that—who knows what the future level of Viet Nam expenditures will be. . . . The President may want to submit a supplemental request for fiscal 1967 in May or June 1966, or even September 1966, or perhaps not until 1967—who can tell now." "Play the game carefully," Mills added, "the Republicans will certainly be playing the game with great care. Cover our present rate of Viet Nam spending, but no more."[7]

On the question of new taxes to pay for the war, Mills said he "'wouldn't do it in 1966 if the budget doesn't show any more imbalance than we are talking about.'" (The notes of the meeting do not indicate what amount was being discussed.) But, he added, "we must seriously think about a tax increase in 1967 if the acceleration in expenditures continues." If Congress were asked for new taxes in 1966, he said, "The Republicans, and some Democrats, and liberals, would start tearing at the budget instead."

For his part, President Johnson apparently was determined, if necessary, to accept the economic effects of increased expenditures without a compensating tax increase. Ackley was asked in a later interview whether the President was prepared to fight the war "at the cost of inflation and economic disrepair," and he replied: "He was certainly prepared to accept that, yes."[8]

Faced with a projection by McNamara that the war would cost $15–17 billion in fiscal year 1967, the President, referring to the larger budget that would result from including the full amount said in a conversation with McGeorge Bundy on December 3, 1965, "My 70 young congressmen can't take it." "You don't want a January number," he said, by which he probably meant that the January budget request should not contain the full amount estimated by McNamara. "I'd much rather go for a 10 Billion supplemental."[9]

On December 27, 1965, Schultze sent the President a memorandum in which, based on the President's position and on the advice from Mills, he proposed including in the fiscal year 1967 budget only a part of the anticipated cost of the war for that year.[10] Rather

---

[7] When the Council of Economic Advisers was told by the President that a tax increase would not be approved by Congress, the members of the Council apparently agreed that the President should not make the request. According to one of the members, "After much deliberation, we told him [the President] that it would probably be better not to ask for it, that from the psychological standpoint, the costs of a loss of faith in the 'new economics' would be less than the costs of a loss of confidence in the financial markets at home and abroad arising out of the president's inability to get such a request enacted." Pierce, *The Politics of Fiscal Policy Formation,* p. 122.

[8] Hargrove and Morley, *The President and the Council of Economic Advisers,* p. 254. In his memoirs, the President took the position that, "all the indicators suggested strongly that in terms of its effect on the American economy the cost of a limited war in Vietnam could, for the time being, be kept manageable." Johnson, *The Vantage Point,* p. 325.

See also Hammond's analysis, "Hubris and Keynesian Expansionism," pp. 201 ff. of *LBJ and the Presidential of Foreign Relations.* He argues that major U.S. military expansions after World War II had occurred "largely without reference to American resource limits," but that when Johnson became President the economy was "running at full employment, with virtually no slack in it," and that Vietnam therefore "should have posed the resource-constrained question . . . How important to the United States was the survival of South Vietnam. . . ." "[T]he idea that the U.S. economy . . . could, with proper management, be pushed to higher productivity levels by demand-side government." Hammond says, "softened choice and underwrote *hubris.*"

[9] Johnson Library, Papers of McGeorge Bundy, Notes on Vietnam, Dec. 3, 1965. The President apparently thought that it would be helpful politically to have a national budget and a Vietnam budget by which to separate Vietnam from other government expenditures, and he seems to have thought that this could be accomplished to some degree by using supplemental budget requests, rather than the regular budget, as the vehicle for funds for Vietnam.

[10] Johnson Library, C.F. FI4, Memorandum for the President from Charles L. Schultze, "1967 Budgetary and Fiscal Policy," Dec. 27, 1965.

than requesting the full amount—which he estimated at $16-18 billion—the budget would provide for $10 billion. If the fighting continued, however, there would be a request in May or June 1966 for supplemental funds of $6-8 billion as well as a request for increased taxes on personal and corporate incomes of approximately $5 billion.

In order to use this two-step approach while remaining within the requirements of the Budget and Accounting Act, however, a way had to be found to limit the estimated cost of the war. The answer was found in an act of budgetary legerdemain by which it was assumed that the war would end and defense expenditures would return to their pre-Vietnam level by December 1966, thus reducing the cost of the war during the 1967 fiscal year. (The argument was that if the war were being concluded, U.S. costs would begin to decline.) As justification, it was argued that it was difficult at that stage to estimate how long the war would last or how much it would cost, and that it would be preferable to fund it in increments, at least until better estimates could be made.[11]

The advantages of the "two-stage" strategy, Schultze said in his memorandum, were that "*the general tax increase* required to hold down inflationary pressure would be *directly tied to a supplemental Vietnam request,*" and that "it would *not be linked to overexpansion in Great Society program expenditures.*" [emphases in original] "Nothing can prevent Congress from trying to pare Great Society appropriations below your budget request," he said, "but the 'two-stage' strategy should minimize the danger." It would also enable the President to argue that the 1967 budget deficit was the lowest since 1960.

Having devised the logic to justify avoiding either a tax increase or the full amount of appropriations needed for the war, the President sent to Congress in January 1966 a request for a budget of $112.8 billion for Fiscal Year 1967, which included $58.3 billion for defense (of which $10 billion was for the cost of the war).[12] A small, token tax increase was also requested. The new budget, the President said, following Schultze's advice, would produce the lowest deficit in seven years. (At the time this argument was made—January 1966—the deficit for FY 1967 was estimated at $1.8 billion. As the cost of the war soared during the following fiscal year from the estimated $10 billion for FY 1967 to an actual expenditure of at least $20 billion, the FY 1967 deficit rose from the estimated $1.8 billion to an actual $9.8 billion.)

---

[11] For this and other arguments, see Ackley's December 27 memorandum, cited above. According to Adam Yarmolinsky, a special assistant to McNamara at the time, there was a meeting at the Pentagon at which McNamara said, ". . . we're going to go on the assumption, and it's a purely arbitrary assumption, that the war will be over by a specified date . . . we have no idea when the war is going to be over, but we have to have an assumption from which to do the budgeting. And as long as we make the assumption explicit, we aren't doing anything unrealistic." CRS Interview with Adam Yarmolinsky, Jan. 27, 1978.

[12] In a later conversation with Doris Kearns, former President Johnson defended this position, saying, "'When he [McNamara] told the Congress that he was assuming for political purposes that the war would be over by June 30, 1967, it was not a lie; it was simply the most efficient way to plan the military budget and enforce the requirement on the Joint Chiefs of Staff that they were not to receive one nickel without a plan. And moving step by step was not only the best way to plan the budget; it was the best way to save the Great Society.'" Doris Kearns, *Lyndon Johnson and the American Dream,* p. 298.

In his budget message President Johnson said:[13]

> We are a rich nation and can afford to make progress at home while meeting obligations abroad—in fact, we can afford no other course if we are to remain strong. For this reason, I have not halted progress in the new and vital Great Society programs in order to finance the costs of our efforts in Southeast Asia. . . . a truly Great society looks beyond its own borders. The freedom, health, and prosperity of all mankind are its proper concern.

He added:

> No one can firmly predict the course of events in Southeast Asia. They depend not only upon our own actions but upon those of our adversaries. As a consequence, ultimate budgetary requirements could be either higher or lower than amounts I am now requesting. . . . Should our efforts to find peace in Vietnam prevail, we can rapidly adjust the budget to make even faster progress in the use of these new programs for the solution of our domestic problems. If, on the other hand, events in Southeast Asia so develop that additional funds are required, I will not hesitate to request the necessary sums. Should that contingency arise, or should unforeseen inflationary pressures develop, I will propose such fiscal actions as are appropriate to maintain economic stability.

In an interview some years later, William Bundy said that, "Beginning with the budget presentation in January 1966, he [President Johnson] engaged in a fudging of the figures. He did this, I am sure, primarily for the sake of getting approval of the major appropriations to carry out the Great Society domestic programs that had been approved in 1965. . . ."[14] Bundy added:

> The Executive was not being candid, at least until the fall of 1966, and the Congress was not doing more than sporadic questioning . . . and only when the costs of the war were brought home, which was roughly beginning in the late summer and fall of 1966, then the Senate did start to react, and the whole matter . . . came to a head in the wholesale cuts in the Great Society appropriations in the spring of 1968. The President was trying to hold off that pressure and get his programs launched, and this created a degree of lack of candor that cast a shadow over the relationship with the Congress. It certainly was a major factor in the President's unwillingness to have a great debate in early 1966. . . .

In response to a question in a later interview as to whether the President's economic advisers knew that the budget request would not cover the cost of the war in fiscal year 1967, Ackley said: "I believe it is frequently assumed that at this period the Council of Economic Advisers and perhaps other people were misinformed about some of the facts, or what were later to emerge as facts, about the size of prospective government expenditures, and that their advice was handicapped by lack of understanding of what the real questions were. I would like to try very hard to disillusion any-

---

[13] Bureau of the Budget, *The Budget of the United States Government for the Fiscal Year Ending June 30, 1967* (Washington, D.C.: U.S. Govt. Print. Off., 1966).

[14] CRS Interview with William Bundy, Aug. 3, 1978.

body who believes that. . . . We knew what numbers were being talked about, and we also knew very well that, whatever those numbers, they weren't nearly big enough in terms of what was going to happen to defense expenditures."[15]

The budgetary problem also seems to have been a major reason for the lack of action on a new congressional resolution on the war.[16] It will be recalled that in December 1965, as the President and his advisers considered the request of the military for more forces and stronger military action, there was some discussion of asking Congress to reaffirm its support for U.S. policy and for the course of action being taken by the President. The text of a new resolution was drafted in the State Department, and at the President's direction key Members of Congress were asked for their opinion. Almost all of those consulted thought that a new resolution would be desirable. In February 1966, however, the idea apparently was abandoned. Although there was no question that Congress would overwhelmingly pass such a resolution, congressional opposition to the war had increased to the point that such a request, especially in view of the requests for additional funds, would be apt to produce a major debate on the war that could adversely affect the public and congressional support needed for the war as well as the President's domestic legislation. Meanwhile, as will be seen, pressure for passage of a new resolution was mounting among Senate critics of the war.

How did the public feel about domestic economic effects of continuing to fight the war? There are very few available data, but from one study in late February-early March 1966 it would appear that, while supporting the war, the public did not approve of the domestic costs that might become involved: "Approval for 'increasing taxes at home' was 31% and disapproval 66%. 'Putting government controls over wages and prices' got 41% approval and 53% disapproval. 'Reducing aid to education' got 19% approval and 79% disapproval. 'Spending less money for the War on Poverty' received approval from 46% and disapproval from 51%. 'Reducing the Medicare program' received 28% approval and 65% disapproval."[17]

January 1966: The President Requests Supplemental Funds

On January 19, 1966, several days before he submitted his annual budget recommendations requesting $10 billion for the war for FY 1967 (July 1, 1966–June 30, 1967), the President asked Congress for $12.7 billion in supplemental funds for Vietnam for FY 1966 (the fiscal year then in progress, which ended on June 30, 1966), $12.3 billion for military costs and about $400 million for

[15] Hargrove and Morley, *The President and the Council of Economic Advisers,* p. 248. The President's action in requesting in his FY 1967 budget only half of the funds actually required for the cost of the war during that year led to considerable congressional criticism. See, for example, U.S. Congress, Joint Economic Committee, *The 1967 Economic Report of the President,* Hearings on February 2, 3, and 6, 1967, Pt. 1, 90th Cong., 1st sess. (Washington, D.C.: U.S. Govt. Print. Off., 1967), *passim,* and *Economic Effect of Vietnam Spending,* Hearings on April 24, 25, 26, 27, 1967, Pt. 1 (Washington, D.C.: U.S. Govt. Print. Off., 1967), *passim,* especially testimony by Senator Stennis on pp. 70 ff. See also the report of the Joint Economic Committee on *Economic Report of the President,* S. Rept. 90–73, Hearings on March 17, 1967 (Washington, D.C.: U.S. Govt. Print. Off., 1967).

[16] See William Bundy's MS, ch. 33, pp. 25–27.

[17] Sidney Verba, et. al., "Public Opinion and the War in Vietnam," cited above, p. 321 n.

foreign aid.[18] bringing the total for FY 1966 (including the $1.7 billion supplemental approved in September 1965) to almost $15 billion. The President reminded Congress that it had approved U.S. participation in the war. Referring to the Gulf of Tonkin Resolution, he said: "It is in the letter and spirit of the Resolution that I request this supplementary appropriation. While that Resolution remains in force, and until its obligations are discharged, we must persevere."

On January 20, the day after the President's request was sent to Congress, the Senate Armed Services Committee and the Defense Department Subcommittee of the Senate Appropriations Committee began joint hearings on a bill to authorize the military portion of the request.[19] (Senator Russell was chairman of both the Armed Services Committee and the Defense Appropriations Subcommittee.) A few days later, the House Armed Services Committee began hearings on the same legislation.[20]

In both Senate and House hearings there was strong support for the President and for the request for additional funds for military activities in Vietnam. Many members of both committees also voiced concern, however, about U.S. strategy, and there was considerable support for heavier bombing of North Vietnam as well as action to close the port at Haiphong.[21]

Related to this was the general feeling in both committees, noted earlier, that the U.S. public would not support a long, costly, inconclusive war, especially one being waged for purposes that were not clearly understood and accepted. In the words of House Armed Services Committee Chairman Rivers:[22]

> This war is getting very unpopular the way we are conducting it. These sanctuaries, all these things—Haiphong—the American people just don't believe in waiting and waiting and waiting; this is a Communist game. That wouldn't faze the Communists to wait 10 years over in Vietnam. They would wait 100 years. That is their business. And furthermore they are orientals, add another 100 years for orientals, they will wait you out. The American people want this thing over yesterday.
>
> You get out in the crossroads and the grassroots, this thing is getting hard to take. . . . The American people are not going to take a long-drawn out war; they just aren't going to do it.

---

[18] *Public Papers of the Presidents,* Lyndon B. Johnson, 1966, pp. 32–33.

[19] U.S. Congress, Senate, Committee on Armed Services and the Subcommittee on Department of Defense of the Committee on Appropriations, *Supplemental Military Procurement and Construction Authorizations, Fiscal Year 1966,* cited above. The bill in question (there were actually two, but they were treated as one) provided authorization of $4.8 billion for military construction and procurement (the remainder of the $12.3 billion military portion of the request had already been authorized).

[20] Hearings before the House Committee on Armed Services, *Supplemental Authorization for Vietnam, Fiscal Year 1966,* cited above.

[21] On U.S. strategy, see the House hearings, (pages for the entire hearing were 4875–5252 in the House Armed Services Committee's cumulative numbering for all of its hearings in that Congress), pp. 4902, 4930, 4942, 4947, 4965, 4973, 5167, and the Senate hearings, pp. 39, 112, 149, 154, 160, 173, 200, 259, 264, 281, 297, 314, 318, 348, 353, 361.

[22] House hearings, pp. 5167–5168.

Senate Armed Services Committee Chairman Russell again expressed a similar view:[23]

> Chairman Russell. [U]nder our system public opinion doesn't control or direct the war, but it has a great deal to do with the support of a war. I don't think any reason has yet been given, that is satisfactory to the masses of the American people, as to why we don't close the harbor of Haiphong.
>
> Senator Symington. Amen.
>
> Chairman Russell. And knock out those petroleum dumps. I know that in the correspondence I get, that is causing more trouble than any other one thing, and if any public demand grows to get out of Vietnam, it is not going to be for fear of the Chinese or for fear of Russia. It is going to be because they feel our people are being made to fight out there under conditions that could be improved by a relatively simple operation. Nobody wants to kill all the civilians in Hanoi or Haiphong, but I think people would feel a great deal better about the war if this action were taken there. . . .

In response to comments by members of the House Armed Services Committee about public morale, Secretary of Defense McNamara said that "patience will be the key to success." He said he could not estimate how long the war would last, but that it would take a "long time." He added that he regretted the phrasing of his statement in October 1963 in which he reported his and Taylor's conclusion that the "major part of the U.S. military task can be completed by the end of 1965. . . ."[24]

Although McNamara declined to estimate how long the war would last, General Wheeler, Chairman of the JCS, testified that during 1966 "we should see substantial progress made toward achieving our objective in South Vietnam."[25]

McNamara emphasized that U.S. objectives were limited: "The objectives are not to destroy or to overthrow the Communist government of China, or the Communist government of North Vietnam. They are limited to the destruction of the insurrection and aggression directed by North Vietnam against the political institutions of South Vietnam."[26] As several members of the House committee explained, however, it was difficult for the public to understand such a limited objective, even after the Korean experience.

In the Senate Armed Services Committee, Senator Sam Ervin's reaction was that because "people are dying unlimitedly in a limited war," the U.S. should put the "shortest time limit on winning." He and several others on the committee felt that there should be heavier bombing of the North to force the North Vietnamese to cease supporting the insurgency in the South. Senator Symington was particularly vocal on the subject. "They [the administration] have taken the Air Force, put it in the ring, said make a good fight, then tied one of its arms, then criticized it." He said the U.S.

---

[23] U.S. Congress, Senate, Committee on Armed Services and the Subcommittee on Department of Defense of the Committee on Appropriations, *Military Procurement Authorizations for Fiscal Year 1967,* Hearings, 89th Cong., 2d sess. (Washington, D.C.: U.S. Govt. Print. Off., 1966), p. 314. For Russell's comments on the same subject during January 1966, see above.

[24] Hearings before the House Committee on Armed Services, *Supplemental Authorization for Vietnam, Fiscal Year 1966,* pp. 5008–5010.

[25] *Ibid.*, p. 4952.

[26] *Ibid.*, p. 4903.

should "start serious bombing . . . [and] take out meaningful military targets, such as harbors, oil. . . ." "[W]e either ought to go on with it or get out," he added. McNamara replied, as he did to others during the Senate and House hearings, that strategic bombing of the kind recommended by Symington would not be effective in influencing the war in the South. "[W]e could take out all of their power systems, all of their oil, all of their harbors, destroy their dams and they could still carry on the infiltration of the men and equipment necessary to support some level of operations in the South." Symington disagreed, saying: "You turn loose the Naval air and Air Force air of this country against North Vietnamese military targets and you are going to have a changing situation in South Vietnam."[27]

General Wheeler explained that there was "no industrial target system, per se—the destruction of which would have any direct effect on the war."[28]

Although he took the position that strategic bombing of the North would not prevent men and supplies from being sent to the South, McNamara testified that he "strongly" believed in the bombing of North Vietnam as a way of influencing the "will" of the North to continue supporting the insurgency. "We haven't reached that point yet," he added. "I cannot guarantee to you that the bombing will be a major factor when we do reach it, but I think it may be."[29]

In the hearings of the House Armed Services Committee there were also a number of questions about the administration's assumption in the FY 1967 budget that the war would end by June 30, 1967. One member of the committee called it "a bookkeeping game, which is not fair to the American people," and McNamara replied, "I say you are absolutely wrong, and the implication is absolutely unfounded."[30] He added that the same practice had prevailed in the Korean war. The Senate committee generally ignored the issue, however, and neither committee undertook to challenge the administration on the validity of the assumption.

The Foreign Relations Committee Holds Hearings on the Supplemental and on the War

Shortly after the Senate Armed Services Committee began hearings on the military portion of the President's request for $12.7 billion in supplemental funds, the Senate Foreign Relations Committee began its hearings on January 28, 1966 on the $400 million foreign aid portion of that request, with Rusk as the principal witness.[31]

For several weeks, Fulbright had been discussing with the staff and with other members of the committee the need for public hearings on Vietnam. On December 23, 1965, based on Fulbright's own conclusions, the staff had proposed such hearings in a memoran-

---

[27] Senate hearings on supplemental authorization for FY 1966, pp. 153–154, cited above.

[28] House hearings, p. 4909.

[29] *Ibid.*, p. 4935.

[30] *Ibid.*, p. 4957.

[31] On January 26, Rusk had testified on the foreign aid portion of the supplemental request before the House Foreign Affairs Committee. It was a brief hearing with almost no substantive discussion. See U.S. Congress, House, Committee on Foreign Affairs, *Supplemental Foreign Assistance Authorization Fiscal Year 1966*, 89th Cong., 2d sess. (Washington, D.C.: U.S. Govt. Print. Off., 1966).

dum written by Seth Tillman and sent to Fulbright by Pat Holt, acting staff director, which said that "carefully prepared public hearings could have a valuable educational effect for both the Congress and the public."[32] According to the memorandum,

> Public hearings on Vietnam are not only *appropriate* for the Foreign Relations Committee but can even be regarded as a Committee *responsibility*. It has been suggested, by Walter Lippmann for example, that one of the reasons for the student protest movement has been the absence of significant debate on United States foreign policy on the official level, which is to say, in Congress. The staff is divided on the validity of this thesis, but if there is something in it, then the proposed hearings might serve to help curb irresponsible expressions of protest by bringing the debate to an official forum where all major tendencies of opinion could receive a fair hearing. [emphases in original]

The committee staff recommended that before raising the question of hearings with the full committee, Fulbright should discuss the idea informally with the two senior Republicans, Hickenlooper and Aiken, as well as with Majority Leader Mansfield, who was also on the committee.

As recommended, Fulbright discussed the idea with others on the committee, and then raised it at the closed meeting of the committee on January 11, 1966, at which Mansfield and Aiken reported on their trip to Vietnam. After their report, Fulbright said he thought a further discussion of U.S. policy and objectives in Vietnam would be useful, and asked the members what they would think of having open, public hearings on the subject. The reaction of Hickenlooper and Mansfield was that it would be better to have closed meetings at which the views of members could be expressed more freely and frankly.

Several Senators who were not on the committee but were concerned about the war met with Fulbright on Saturday, January 29, 1966 to urge that public hearings be held. On February 1, 10 of the 15 Senators who had signed the (Hartke) letter to the President opposing the resumption of bombing met privately with Fulbright, and together they agreed to try to force the administration into a thorough discussion of U.S. policy toward Vietnam.[33]

On February 3, the Foreign Relations Committee met in closed session and agreed to have public hearings, leaving the selection of witnesses to Fulbright and to Hickenlooper (who was still opposed to public sessions). "The genesis of this decision," the *New York Times* reported, "was a growing feeling among many Senators, . . . that while President Johnson wants their 'consent' on any moves

---

[32] This memorandum is in the papers of the Committee on Foreign Relations, National Archives, RG 46.

On January 27, Tillman sent Fulbright a policy memorandum on the war in which he discussed the difficulty of intervening in a country in which a nationalist movement also happened to be a Communist movement. He also discussed the origins of the war and Eisenhower's decision not to intervene with U.S. forces. He concluded that the U.S. should commit itself to withdrawal after a period of several years, and should agree to accept the outcome of internationally supervised elections. He proposed that the U.S. should ask the U.S.S.R., in its capacity as co-chairman of the 1954 Geneva Conference, to reconvene the Conference for the purpose of settling the war, and that the U.S. should accept the decisions reached at the Conference. Tillman's memorandum is in the same location.

[33] *New York Times*, Feb. 2, 1966.

he may decide to make, he does not want their 'advice.' This feeling reached the boiling point last week after the Senators had urged that the pause in the bombing of North Vietnam be continued and had questioned the increasing involvement of United States ground forces [the letter from the 15 Senators]. In reply to the Senators, Mr. Johnson and Secretary of State Dean Rusk both cited the Gulf of Tonkin Resolution of 1964." [34]

In advance of the January 28 hearing, the State Department had balked at having Rusk testify publicly, and Rusk's congressional liaison chief, Douglas MacArthur II, a veteran Foreign Service Officer and former Ambassador who had worked on Vietnam in the early 1950s while serving as the counselor of the State Department under John Foster Dulles, pressed the committee staff to keep the hearing closed. According to a memorandum to Fulbright from Carl Marcy, chief of staff of the Foreign Relations Committee: [35]

> Doug MacArthur telephoned me late Thursday to raise hell in an ungentlemanly way about my suggestion that Mr. Rusk should testify next Thursday on the Supplemental in Open Session. He said we are not trying "to make Brownie points" and that it should be decided "at a higher level" whether Mr. Rusk would be able to testify on this suggestion, "since we are at war," in open session. I told MacArthur that I thought I was representing the views of a number of Committee Members in suggesting that Rusk testify in Open Session. I said further that, if it was going to be decided "at a higher level," [the President] the higher level should communicate this directly to Senator Fulbright.
>
> If you are called on this subject, it might be a good idea if you decide not to acquiesce to the Administration's request for an Executive Session, to sound out the Committee at its business meeting on Tuesday morning.
>
> MacArthur said that "all of the other Committees are receiving this testimony in Executive Session."

The hearing on January 28, which, despite the State Department's objection, was held in open session at the insistence of the committee, was long and intense. According to one observer, Rusk was "battered by questions," not on foreign aid, or even on the request for more foreign aid funds for Vietnam, but on the subject of U.S. involvement in Vietnam.[36] Most of the members of the committee were present (Mansfield was not), and participated actively in the questioning. Felix Belair, the *New York Times* reporter who had covered Capitol Hill for many years, commented: "Rarely has a Secretary of State been put through such a cross-examination by virtually all 19 members of the Senate committee." [37]

Fulbright told Rusk: [38] "I have been in the Congress quite a long time, and I do not recall any issue since I have been here where there has been so much apprehension concerning a military involvement. . . . It seems to me that something is wrong or there would not be such great dissent, evidenced by teach-ins, articles

---

[34] *New York Times*, Feb. 4, 1966.
[35] University of Arkansas, Fulbright Papers, series 48, box 16.
[36] *Washington Post*, Jan. 28, 1966.
[37] *New York Times*, Jan. 29, 1966.
[38] *Supplemental Foreign Assistance Fiscal Year 1966—Vietnam.*

and speeches by various responsible people." "I am perfectly willing," he added, "to admit at the proper time that I made a mistake. Perhaps it is impossible for a great nation to do that, too. I do not know. But I think there have been many cases of where great nations have drawn back from commitments which they came to believe were wrong."

Rusk took the position that the U.S. had a "clear and direct commitment to the security of South Vietnam against external attack," and that "The integrity of our commitments is absolutely essential to the preservation of peace right around the globe." "At stake also," he said, "is the still broader question whether aggression is to be permitted, once again, to succeed. We know from painful experience that aggression feeds on aggression. . . . If the bellicose doctrines of the Asian Communists should reap a substantial reward, the outlook for peace in this world would be grim indeed."[39]

Fulbright said that neither he nor most of the members of the committee expected at the time of the Gulf of Tonkin Resolution in 1964 that the war would develop as it had. Rusk countered by saying that the policy expressed by that resolution had existed for many years, and was expressed previously in the Southeast Asia Treaty (SEATO) of 1955. "I am a little concerned," Rusk added, "that formal acts of the Government over a period of years in a variety of ways would appear to catch people by surprise at the moment when things begin to get difficult. I would hope that the Senate would not ratify an alliance if it did not intend that alliance to be taken seriously." Fulbright replied: "We have a difference of view of what that alliance means, you see. That is what has developed, I think."

Fulbright asked Rusk, "Don't you think we ought to understand what we are in for, and that the Congress should give its further approval of this changed situation?" Rusk replied that this was "a matter for consideration between the executive and legislative branches," but declined to be more specific. He was asked whether, by voting for the pending request for supplemental funds for Vietnam for the remainder of FY 1966, Congress would be voting for "approval of an all-out war," and when he answered vaguely that "the Executive and Congress must at all times move together on these matters," Fulbright interrupted to say that the answer was not responsive. "With a weary grin," according to the *New York Times,* Rusk replied that he was "aware of this," and that "I will have to take it under advisement."[40]

Other Democratic members of the committee indicated their concern about the U.S. role in Vietnam, especially Senators Morse,

[39] Despite the contention of Rusk and others in the Kennedy and Johnson administrations, as well as some scholars in later years, that the Truman Doctrine was designed to elicit congressional and public support for aid to Greece and Turkey, and was not intended to be general policy, Rusk began his testimony by quoting Truman's statement about supporting free peoples, saying, "That is the policy we are applying in Vietnam in connection with specific commitments which we have taken in regard to that country." *Supplemental Foreign Assistance Fiscal Year 1966—Vietnam,* p. 2. Rusk made the same statement in his testimony before the House Foreign Affairs Committee on January 26 on the supplemental appropriation request.

The full sentence from Truman's 1947 address to Congress was: "I believe that it must be the policy of the United States to support free peoples who are resisting attempted subjugation by armed minorities or by outside pressures." For a further discussion, see ch. 1 of pt. I of this study.

[40] *Supplemental Foreign Assistance Fiscal Year 1966—Vietnam,* pp. 50–51, 61 and *New York Times,* Jan. 29, 1966.

Gore, Church, Clark, Pell, and McCarthy, but the Republicans, while asking questions about the request for additional funds, avoided getting involved in what they obviously viewed as a dispute among the Democrats. In addition, the six Republicans on the committee, with the possible exception of Aiken, supported the administration's position at that stage, as did four of the 13 Democrats—Senators Long, Lausche, Symington, and Dodd.

Morse declined to question Rusk, saying that he was going to propose a complete review of the Vietnam situation and would save his questions for that occasion. (The next day, Morse introduced a resolution in the Senate calling on the Foreign Relations Committee to conduct such an investigation. He also introduced a resolution to repeal the Gulf of Tonkin Resolution.)[41]

Church said: "I do not think, in the face of the actuality of war, Congress is going to repeal the war. There is very little to do but support the American boys who are committed there with such funds as may be required." The real question, he said, was where U.S. policy was leading, and he told Rusk, "as I have listened to your explanations this morning, I gather that whenever a revolution occurs against an established government, and that revolution, as most will doubtlessly be, is infiltrated by Communists, that the United States will intervene, if necessary, to prevent a Communist success." Rusk replied that the U.S. was not opposed to change, and was supporting "very sweeping revolutions" in such places as Latin America, but that there was "a fundamental difference between the kind of revolution which the Communists call their wars of national liberation, and the kind of revolution which is congenial to our own experience, and fits into the aspirations of ordinary men and women right around the world." Church responded: "The question I think facing this country is how we can best cope with the likelihood of revolt in the underdeveloped world in the years ahead, and I have very serious doubt that American military intervention will often be the proper decision."[42]

---

[41] For Morse's speech, see *CR*, vol. 112, pp. 1506 ff. On February 3, Morse, in another long speech in the Senate, questioned the administration's argument that U.S. actions in Vietnam were covered by the Southeast Asia Treaty. See *ibid.*, pp. 2064–2067.

[42] *Supplemental Foreign Assistance Fiscal Year 1966—Vietnam*, pp. 73–75.

At about this same point in early 1966, the Clement J. Zablocki (D/Wisc.) subcommittee (Far East and the Pacific) of the House Foreign Affairs Committee held a brief set of hearings on U.S. policy towards Asia at which several academic experts testified. U.S. Congress, House, Committee on Foreign Affairs, *United States Policy Toward Asia,* Hearings before the Subcommittee on the Far East and the Pacific of the Committee on Foreign Affairs, 89th Cong., 2d sess. (Washington, D.C.: U.S. Govt. Print. Off., 1966). The report on these hearings was issued as a subcommittee print and was subsequently reprinted as H. Doc. 89–488. One of the witnesses was Thomas C. Schelling of Harvard University, a well-known strategist who had been an exponent of theories of coercion and an advocate of the use of graduated pressure on North Vietnam. In the hearing on Jan. 27, 1966, Schelling reiterated his support for the administration's Vietnam policy, which he said was "an extraordinary demonstration of firmness combined with restraint." He also stressed the importance of communicating to China, through U.S. actions in Vietnam, the resolve of the United States to stand firm in Asia, adding, "I even think one could go so far as to say that it would be a disservice to the Communist Chinese for us to behave in Vietnam in a way that induces them to think we shall not react in the future when in fact we shall."

Schelling justified the bombing of North Vietnam not only in terms of its coercive effect on the North Vietnamese, but in communicating with China: "The bombing of North Vietnam may well have communicated to Communist China that there is at least one kind of war that they may have to consider, in which their manpower advantage would not be a decisive one, a war that would not be so horrendously thermonuclear that the United States would necessarily, and perhaps wisely, shrink from it." "In many respects," Schelling added, "the American military credibility in southeast Asia goes beyond the question of whether we can achieve our Vietnamese objectives and has to do with whether the Chinese can be made, and the North Vietnamese

After this preliminary hearing on January 28 and after deciding on February 3 to hold public hearings, the Foreign Relations Committee met on February 4 for the first of five such hearings on Vietnam.

Because of the growing controversy over the war, the prominence of the Foreign Relations Committee, and the publicity generated by the anticipated confrontation of Fulbright and others on the committee with the administration, the February 4 hearing attracted extraordinary media and public attention. All three commercial television networks gave complete "gavel-to-gavel" live coverage, and the press tables were crowded with reporters.[43] The large committee room was packed with spectators, with lines of others waiting in the hall to get a seat. It was the first time in the history of national television that the networks had provided such a public forum. As David Halberstam so aptly described the significance of the hearings and of the television coverage,[44]

> They ended more than a generation of assumed executive branch omniscience in foreign policy, and congressional acquiescence to that omniscience. They came almost a year after the combat commitment to Vietnam had begun; up until then, the national media, in particular the television networks, had belonged exclusively to the executive branch. There had not been

---

can be made, to regret, or at least not to want to repeat, the kind of thing that caused this American reaction."

Schelling said he was also concerned that if the United States "lets itself lose in South Vietnam in a way that doesn't show at least that we tried, within the limits of decency and the concern for a peace, here at home we may become fed up with a large, important part of the world and rationalize for ourselves a kind of isolationism that may not only extend to losing interest in military credibility, but may even extend to displaying reduced interest in the more important [economic] developmental kinds of things. . . ." He added this remarkable statement, suggesting that success in Vietnam was critical for U.S. self-confidence: "The great danger if all Asia goes Communist is really exclusion of the United States and what we call Western civilization from a large part of the world that is poor and colored and potentially hostile. The worst aspects of that exclusion are not military but are social, political, spiritual, philosophical, and have to do with the kind of world that we would like to help build and with the fact that a country like the United States probably cannot maintain self-confidence if just about the greatest thing it ever attempted, namely to create the basis for decency and prosperity and democratic government in the underdeveloped world had to be acknowledged as a failure or as an attempt that we wouldn't try again."

On Feb. 1, 1966, Roger Hilsman, a professor at Columbia University and former Assistant Secretary for the Far East in the Kennedy administration, testified before Zablocki's subcommittee that "The United States should not—and cannot—desert them [the South Vietnamese]. To do so would be to turn our backs on everything our country stands for." He said he was "heartily in favor of the decision to send U.S. ground forces to Vietnam, and of giving the Vietnamese military and economic support to the extent of our capability." He urged, however, that military measures be put into a "political context," and said, "If we over-Americanize the struggle in Vietnam, if we get out front and make of it an American war, then no matter how thoroughly we pulverize the Vietcong the struggle itself will have been lost in a political sense. . . ." He added that bombing the North was a mistake, and that he favored an enclave strategy for U.S. forces, saying: "We should 'deescalate' the struggle in Vietnam; we should 'demilitarize' it; and we should 'de-Americanize' it." Although the prospects were "grim," the only hope was to "turn our whole perspective upside down. We should recognize that the heart of the struggle in Vietnam is to win the allegiance of the people away from the Vietcong. . . . This means subordinating military measures to a political program and accepting the idea that Vietnam will be a 10- to 15-year struggle, at least, and behaving accordingly."

A few weeks later, Zablocki went to Vietnam, and in his report on the trip he drew from the disparate advice he had been getting from witnesses in the hearings. He recommended heavier bombing of the north, including petroleum, airfields, and power plants, but he also said, "We must begin to concentrate to a greater degree than we have in the past on the psychological aspects of the struggle in Vietnam. A sense of national identity, an allegiance to the central government, and a greater will to fight needs to be instilled, or stimulated, among the population." U.S. Congress, House, Committee on Foreign Affairs, Committee Print, Mar. 17, 1966, 89th cong., 2d sess. (Washington, D.C.: U.S. Govt. Print. Off., 1966).

[43] For the decision by CBS to televise the hearings, see Halberstam, *The Powers That Be*, pp. 504–505.

[44] *Ibid.*, p. 492.

a declaration of war, there was not a national emergency, but there was presidential action, and with presidential action, governmental consensus, and that, for the networks and much of the print press, was good enough; they had accepted, with very little questioning and debate, the President's case for military intervention in Vietnam.

The witness on February 4, the first day of the hearings, was the Administrator of the foreign aid program (Agency for International Development, AID), David Bell, who was questioned at length on foreign aid to Vietnam. On most of the more general policy questions, especially those concerning military matters, he declined to express an opinion, saying that these would have to be answered by others.

Unbenownst to the committee, the FBI, at the direction of the President, was monitoring the hearings for the purpose of preparing a memorandum for the President comparing statements of Senators Fulbright and Morse, in particular, with "the Communist Party line."[45] Several weeks later, the President met with FBI Assistant Director Cartha ("Deke") DeLoach, and told him that he wanted the FBI to monitor and to report the contacts made between foreign Embassies, especially the Soviet Union, and Members of Congress and prominent citizens. According to DeLoach's report of the meeting, "The President stated he strongly felt that much of this protest concerning his Vietnam policy, particularly the hearings in the Senate, had been generated by [certain foreign officials]."[46] The President, DeLoach added, said that there was a nucleus of six Senators who opposed the war: Fulbright, Morse, Robert Kennedy, Gruening, Clark and Aiken, all of whom, he said, had been to the Russian Embassy or met with the Ambassador. DeLoach reported the President as saying also that Fulbright and Morse were under the control of the Russians. The President further said, according to DeLoach, that Fulbright "doesn't know what the smell of cartridge is—he's a narrow-minded egotist who is attempting to run the country." Robert Kennedy, he said, was trying to discredit him and to strengthen his own position.

---

[45] Final Report, Book II of the Senate Select Committee to Study Intelligence Activities, p. 229 and Final Report, Book III of the Senate Select Committee to Study Intelligence Activities), p. 489. Reportedly, a top, unnamed FBI official stated, "We felt that it [monitoring the hearings and preparing the report] was beyond the jurisdiction of the FBI, but obviously Mr. Hoover felt that this was a request by the President and he desired it to be done." On Feb. 24, 1966, Hoover sent the requested memorandum to the President. In the memorandum, Hoover said that there was no indication that the Communist Party had provided materials to members of the Foreign Relations Committee. See Athan G. Theoharis, *Spying on Americans: Political Surveillance from Hoover to the Huston Plan* (Philadelphia, Pa.: Temple Univ. Press, 1978), p. 177.

[46] Theoharis, *Spying on Americans*, p. 177. The meeting of the President with DeLoach was held on Mar. 14, 1966. The names of the officials were deleted by the FBI when the report was released for public use.

On Mar. 22, 1966, the FBI sent the White House a 67-page list of the contacts of Members of Congress with the designated foreign Embassies during the period July 1, 1965-Mar. 17, 1966. A second survey of congressional staff contacts was sent on May 13, 1966, and biweekly reports were then sent to the White House until the end of the Johnson Presidency in 1969. *Ibid.*, 178.

After receiving two memoranda from the FBI that were sent on FBI letterhead stationary and signed by Director J. Edgar Hoover, the White House told Hoover that in such matters of "extreme secrecy," the report to the White House should be "a blind-type memorandum which bore no government watermarks or no letterhead signifying the source of the memorandum." *From the Secret Files of J. Edgar Hoover*, edited with commentary by Athan Theoharis (Chicago: Ivan R. Dee, 1991), p. 236, from the text of a memorandum from Assistant Director DeLoach to Associate Director Clyde Tolson, Mar. 1, 1966.

On March 7, 1966, the day before the Senate Foreign Relations Committee held hearings on U.S. policy toward China, DeLoach sent the following memorandum to Associate Director Clyde Tolson:[47]

> Pursuant to instructions, I saw [Minority Leader] Senator [Everett] Dirksen . . . [who] was advised that it would be appreciated if our entire conversation could be maintained in strict confidence. He agreed to this.
>
> I told Senator Dirksen that I was seeing him at the specific request of the President to the FBI. [Four lines withheld on national security grounds.]
>
> Senator Dirksen was advised that [four paragraphs withheld on national security grounds], but refers to information concerning Senators J. William Fulbright and Wayne Morse]. . . .
>
> Senator Dirksen mentioned that he was not aware of all the entanglements involving Senators Fulbright and Morse; however, he felt that both men were deeply involved and very much obligated to communist interests. He stated the information he had been furnished by me, if known to the American public, could obviously ruin Senator Morse. . . .
>
> Senator Dirksen mentioned that Senator Fulbright had now initiated hearings concerning Red China. He stated that obviously Fulbright had been instructed to do this by certain contacts.
>
> Senator Dirksen asked if the information furnished above would be given to any other senators. I told him that [Republican] Senator [Bourke] Hickenlooper was to be advised [and was on March 8]: however, this was the only additional person who would receive this information. . . .
>
> If the Director has no objections, I will advise Marvin Watson verbally of the facts.
>
> [Hoover's handwritten notation: "O.K. but after doing so prepare memo of action taken."]

Later in March, DeLoach told FBI Director Hoover that the President was going to set up a network television appearance for Hoover, and that he wanted Hoover to mention the contacts between Members of Congress and the Russian Embassy and to refer to the control of the Embassy over Fulbright and Morse.[48]

The White House staff also asked the State Department's Office of Intelligence and Research, headed by former Humphrey aide Thomas Hughes, for a political dossier on Fulbright and other critics. Hughes refused, saying it was improper, and Ball counter-

---

[47] Athan G. Theoharis, *From the Secret Files of J. Edgar Hoover,* pp. 237–238. Bracketed material was added by Theoharis.

[48] William C. Sullivan with Bill Brown, *The Bureau* (New York: W. W. Norton, 1979), p. 65. According to Sullivan, who was then an assistant director of the FBI, "Johnson didn't limit his paranoia to senators and congressmen with possible Soviet connections, though. He wanted the FBI to keep an eye on every senator and congressman who opposed his policies, whether they were Republicans or Democrats, whether they leaned to the left or to the right. He wanted anything our agents could dig up on them that might prove embarrassing or politically damaging. He leaked the information we sent him on Republicans to the press himself, but he was reluctant to attack members of his own party and supplied whatever damaging information he had on the Democrats to Everett Dirksen, the leading Republican in the Senate." *Ibid.*

manded the White House request. Fulbright was informed of the incident in a memorandum from Marcy on February 22.[49]

In another move to blunt the opposition of the President's two most worrisome critics—Fulbright and columnist Walter Lippmann—Ambassador Lodge invited each one to come to Vietnam for a visit. (McGeorge Bundy was kept informed of the invitations and the responses.) Both men declined. Fulbright said that his committee was holding hearings. Lippmann replied, "If I were 25 years younger, I would be tempted to accept, if only to say when I got home that I had been there. But I would not expect to find out anything more than the stream of visiting journalists and VIPs bring back with them." [50]

The Honolulu Conference and Vice President Humphrey's Trip

In mid-morning on February 4, the telecast of the Foreign Relations Committee hearing was interrupted by a news report that President Johnson was leaving the next day for a meeting with Vietnamese leaders in Honolulu. Although at least one member of the President's staff had recommended that such a meeting be held, this sudden decision was apparently prompted by a desire to draw attention from the hearings.[51] To downplay the escalation of U.S. military activities, the President also directed that the Honolulu meeting be centered on political, economic and social matters—the "other war."

After the meeting, which was held on February 6–8, 1966, a final communique, "The Declaration of Honolulu," was issued.[52] Written

---

[49] See Thomas L. Hughes' article in *Secrecy and Foreign Policy,* "The Power to Spend and the Power to Listen: Reflections on Bureaucratic Politics and a Recommendation on Information Flows," Thomas M. Franck and Edward Weisbend (eds.) (New York: Oxford Univ. Press, 1974). Marcy learned of the request from sources in the State Department and passed along the information to Fulbright. National Archives, Papers of the Committee on Foreign Relations, RG 46, Marcy Chron File, Marcy to Fulbright, Feb. 22, 1966.

[50] U.S. Department of State, Central File, Pol 27 Viet S, Saigon to Washington 2777 and 2778, Feb. 2, 1966, 2793, February 3, and Washington to Saigon 2224, February 2, and 2308, February 9.

[51] See the *Washington Post,* Feb. 6, 1966, and Evans and Novak, *Lyndon B. Johnson: The Exercise of Power,* p. 593.

In a memorandum to the President on Jan. 31, 1966, as the bombing pause ended, Valenti suggested several additional "peace moves," one of which was that the President should meet in Honolulu with South Vietnamese leaders and Westmoreland to get a report on the military situation, but, "most important the President could appear with Minister Ky and stress the political economic and social future of South Vietnam once the fighting has stopped. . . . Moreover, it would be very helpful for the world to see the cordial relations between Ky and the President and the combined faith in the kind of world that can be built without fighting in South Vietnam." Johnson Library, NSF NSC History.

[52] American officials attending the meeting included Rusk, McNamara, Lodge, Westmoreland, McGeorge Bundy, Secretary of Agriculture Orville L. Freeman, Secretary of Health, Education and Welfare John W. Gardner, and AID Director Bell. For the text of the Declaration of Honolulu see *Public Papers of the Presidents,* Lyndon B. Johnson, 1966, pp. 153–155. For documents dealing with the Conference see the Johnson Library, NSF NSC History, Box 44; International Meetings and Travel, boxes 1–2; Diary Backup, box 28. There are also documents on the conference in the Department of State, Lot File 72 D 207.

In the Department of State, Central File, Pol 27 Viet S, there is an airgram from Saigon to Washington, A2254, Feb. 18, 1966, sent during the Honolulu Conference, that contains a summary report of the meeting on Feb. 7, 1966 of the U.S.-South Vietnamese Reconstruction Working Group.

In the Department of State, Lot File 74 D 272, there is a memorandum on Feb. 16, 1966 from Bill Moyers to U. Alexis Johnson summarizing the major aspects of a private meeting between President Johnson and Ky and Thieu on February 7, as follows:

"1. The principals agreed that their economists would study again the question of the exchange rate and make recommendations for resolving the issue;

"2. The President pressed Ky and Thieu to implement the measures designed to improve the economic stabilization of SVN. Ky agreed to announce some of the measures 'upon my return and no later than next week.'

by the Americans on the plane to Honolulu, it was basically an American document emphasizing the need for economic, political and social reform, the holding of elections, and a program of welcoming Communist defectors, the "Open Arms" or Chieu Hoi program—an agenda quite similar to that proposed by Ball and Acheson in May of 1965.[53]

"3. Ky said he intends to split the Ministry of Economics into a Ministry of Trade and a Ministry of Industrialization in order to weaken the present Ministry which 'has too much power and is prone to corruption.'

"4. The President urged stronger support of the 'Open Arms' [Chieu Hoi] program and Ky and Thieu agreed to place greater emphasis on it.

"5. The President strongly urged Ky to urge the defection of 'three or four' prominent VC or VC supporters and use them on radio for propaganda and psychological purposes. He pressed Ky and Thieu to develop better contacts with the VC in order to gain increased understanding of the movement.

"6. President stressed specific implementation of economic, social, and political steps agreed upon during Bell's visit to Saigon in January and at the Honolulu Conference.

"7. The President urged a strong program aimed at the 'very young members of the VC.'

"8. The President told Ky and Thieu they should study more carefully and consistently the criticisms and policies of anti-Vietnam Americans, including 'journals like the *New York Times* and members of the Foreign Relations Committee.' The President said: 'You need to know what our pressures are just as we need to know what yours are.'

"9. The President and the Secretary of State made strong appeals that 'we all should list those reasons we think Hanoi believes it will win, and go after them one by one to change their minds about the prospects of succeeding.'

"10. The President urged further internal reforms in the South Vietnamese military. He urged Ky to spend more time in the countryside 'acting like a politician instead of just a general.'"

[53] See pt. III of this study, p. 259.

During the conference, at a meeting between South Vietnamese and U.S. diplomatic officials, Rusk asked Foreign Minister Tran Van Do what his government was doing "toward building democratic processes." After explaining the plan for establishing a National Council ("Democracy Building Council") and drafting a constitution, the Foreign Minister observed that "there was a great need to educate the Vietnamese people politically step by step." Time was needed, he said, to "develop a political atmosphere for organized politics." The constitution, drafted by the Council, would help to prepare the way for subsequent elections by providing an opportunity for political discussions. There were 50 parties, "and before elections could be held it would be necessary to reorganize the political system." This response did not find favor with the Americans, however, and Secretary Rusk "said that it was important for the Government not to indicate any lack of confidence in the people of South Vietnam. It was important internally and internationally. There was no greater strength than saying that the people would be asked to choose. Power has to come from the people. This is a great weakness in South Vietnam and it gives a great deal of difficulty internationally." U.S. Department of State, Lot File 70 D 102, Memorandum of Conversation, Diplomatic Track Working Group, Honolulu Conference, Feb. 7, 1966.

W. W. Rostow, the Counselor of the State Department and Chairman of its Policy Planning Council, who replaced McGeorge Bundy as the President's National Security Adviser on Apr. 1, 1966, was deeply interested in the political development of South Vietnam. (While on the faculty at MIT in the 1950s he had done considerable work on the question of economic development as a central aspect of "nation building.") When large-scale U.S. forces began to be deployed in August 1965, Rostow had proposed in a memorandum on "Politics and Victory in South Vietnam" that the U.S. needed to "turn to the problem of the political life of South Vietnam with a seriousness which matches that now accorded to military and diplomatic aspects of the crisis. . . ." One of his proposals was the establishment of a large, national political party in South Vietnam—a "modern revolutionary party" that would seek to include all of the major groups in the society, and that could "focus the authentic nationalism which suffuses the country with an instrument capable of coping with Communist organizational techniques."

On December 30, 1965, Rostow presented his ideas on the political development of South Vietnam to a meeting of the Planning Group—the informal interdepartmental group representing the departments and agencies in the national security area that met irregularly to consider important current issues, proposals, etc. On Jan. 21, 1966, he sent a copy of his presentation to Lodge, with a letter expressing the hope that Lodge, with the help of Lansdale and with advice from an academic specialist such as Lucian Pye (MIT), could explore the establishment of a national political party, not only to mobilize the non-Communist elements in the country, but to prepare for the eventuality, as a result of negotiations, of elections in the South in which the National Liberation Front would be allowed to participate. (Rostow's letter to Lodge and his appended statement of Dec. 30, 1965, are in the Department of State, Lot File 70 D 207.)

On January 14, Rostow sent a memorandum to Ball, at the time the Acting Secretary of State, in which he discussed these ideas, saying that it was "urgent" for the U.S. to press the South Vietnamese to take these new political initiatives: "[W]e must force the pace in Saigon of political consolidation and initiative on a wide front, at highest priority and sensitivity." Department of State, Lot File 72 D 139.

Continued

From the standpoint of the U.S. Government policy and operations, the significance of the Honolulu Conference was its emphasis on nonmilitary programs. For the first time, President Johnson took a strong public stand on the need for "pacification," and, as the *Pentagon Papers* say,[54] "the President's pledge on behalf of the U.S. Government to the pacification effort began a new period for the U.S. Government in Vietnam. From Honolulu on it was open and unmistakable U.S. policy to support Pacification and the 'other war,' and those who saw these activities as unimportant or secondary had to submerge their sentiments under a cloud of rhetoric."[55]

For a brief period, the impetus created by the conference also had a minor impact on the policymaking system. Beginning with a meeting on Saturday, February 26, from 12:45 to 2:16 p.m. of the President and a number of advisers involved in the conference,[56] meetings of the group, called the President's Vietnam Group, were held every Saturday for several weeks, with and without the President.[57] The apparent purpose of the group was to provide a way by which representatives of the various agencies of the government involved in the "other war" could meet regularly with the President to discuss implementation of U.S. nonmilitary programs. At this first meeting, the President said that the group "might meet every Saturday for an hour and also during the week, depending on whether the Secretary of State and the Secretary of Defense felt a meeting would be useful."[58]

During the first meeting, the discussion ranged over a number of subjects, including appointment of a "czar" to coordinate the Washington end of the "other war" as well as a czar for Saigon. The President said that a Washington czar would be picked in a few days (Komer was named). Economist Robert Nathan was suggested for Saigon, and the President asked the Vice President to approach Nathan about taking the job (no one was named).

Rostow, also proposed that, in preparation for the development of a constitution, the U.S. should provide the South Vietnamese with material on "the political experiences of other developing countries," as well as encouraging visits to those countries. See his memorandum of Jan. 20, 1966, to Leonard Unger, a copy of which was attached to his letter to Lodge.

On Feb. 21, 1966, Rostow sent a memorandum to Rusk as well as to the President in which he recommended a program for "Putting the Democracy Building Council on the Road." (Department of State, Lot File 70 D 207.) Once the Council was appointed to draft the constitution and the electoral law, he said, the Vietnamese Government should send the members on 3-4 day visits to several developing countries (he suggested Korea, Japan, Mexico, Venezuela, Tunisia, Tanzania or Kenya, Turkey, India, and Pakistan, to study their constitutions, electoral laws and political party organization.

In the weeks that followed there were numerous communications back and forth between Washington and the U.S. Mission in Saigon on the subject of political development in South Vietnam, especially in relation to the election of a Constituent Assembly and the drafting of a constitution. Issues being considered included the formation of political parties, rules for the election—particularly the sensitive question of who should not be allowed to vote or stand for election, provisions in the constitution concerning the structure of the new government, what the role of the U.S. should be during the election and U.S. relationships with candidates. A major issue was how the U.S. could exercise its influences without being branded "colonialist." The cables from Washington and from Saigon are in the Department of State, Central File, Pol 27 Viet S, and in the Johnson Library, NSF Country File, Vietnam. For a good sampling see Washington to Saigon 3044, Apr. 9, 1967; 3080, April 13; 3119, April 18; 3230 April 27; 3249, April 29; 3268, April 30, and the replies from Saigon cited therein.

[54] *PP*, Gravel ed., vol. II, p. 554.

[55] The best discussion of the Honolulu Conference is in *ibid.*, pp. 548–554. See also *The Vantage Point*, pp. 242–245.

[56] Johnson Library, NSF Files of Bromley K. Smith, notes by Smith on the meeting of Feb. 26, 1966. Attending were the President, the Vice President, Rusk, McNamara, McGeorge Bundy, Vance, General Wheeler, U. Alexis Johnson, Raborn, Helms, Unger, Rostow, Marks, Gaud, and from the White House and NSC staffs Komer, Moyers, Valenti and Bromley Smith.

[57] See Herring, *LBJ and Vietnam*, p. 12.

[58] Smith notes of the meeting, cited above.

The group also discussed a suggestion by the President that an Asian Task Force be organized to consider the potentialities of the area and to recommend solutions to some of its problems, saying that "He thought we should direct intense public attention to Asia such as was done in the civil rights issue." "He added that there were not enough dreams in the foreign field." [59]

After a short time, however, the group stopped meeting, whether because of its composition or size or lack of leadership, or, more likely, because of a lack of purpose, especially after Komer was put in charge of the Washington end of nonmilitary activities.

There were mixed reports of the effects of the Honolulu Conference on attitudes in South Vietnam. The French journalist, Jean Lacoutre, warned of resentment: [60]

> the Honolulu meeting exposed the nearly total failure of a great Western power to understand public opinion in a small country, where feelings of oppression and resentment have been smoldering for years. In organizing the conference Washington had hoped not only to strengthen Ky's position but to encourage him to be more flexible politically and to undertake social reforms. However so far as most Vietnamese were concerned, Washington had already shown unprecedented contempt for their country by imposing Premier Ky on them in the first place; to them, the meeting was no more than a summons from a foreign general to a cocky lieutenant—a glaring example of Saigon's "abject" dependence on Washington. The following week [Buddhist leader] Tri Quang warned an American visitor that a wave of anti-American agitation was sure to follow.

Ambassador Lodge, on the other hand, was exultant: [61]

> Among less sophisticated Vietnamese . . . the dominant attitude appeared to be one of national pride, because the Vietnamese sat as equals with the leader of the world's most powerful nation. . . .
>
> Among the sophisticated but generally non-political Vietnamese . . . there was a feeling that the Honolulu Conference, by the mere fact that it was held, somehow meant that the war in Vietnam was destined for an early end. . . .
>
> Among the better-informed Vietnamese . . . there was a strong reaction that the non-military aspect of the war . . . had at last gotten the attention it deserved and that as a result of the meeting new social welfare and economic development programs could be expected.

As the Honolulu meeting ended, and the U.S. group headed for home, President Johnson continued to stage-manage the administration's efforts to dominate the news and to put the best possible face on the situation in Vietnam. He told Vice President Humphrey to meet him in Los Angeles, where some of the returning U.S. officials and staff would join Humphrey, who would then proceed to

---

[59] *Ibid.*

[60] Jean Lacoutre, "Vietnam: The Turning Point," *New York Review of Books,* May 12, 1966.

[61] U.S. Department of State, Central File, Pol 27 Viet S, Saigon to Washington 2985, Feb. 16, 1966.

Honolulu to fly with the Vietnamese back to Saigon. After a brief visit there, Humphrey would visit other Asian countries.[62]

Humphrey, back in the good graces of the President after being shunned for a year for questioning U.S. bombing of North Vietnam and greater U.S. military involvement in the war, did his best to prove his loyalty, but his zeal led to increased concern in Congress about the potential commitments made at Honolulu. In a television interview he said that the Honolulu Declaration was a "pledge to ourselves and to posterity to defeat aggression, to defeat social misery, to build viable, free political institutions and to achieve peace. . . . I think it has as much significance for the future of Asia as the Atlantic Charter had for the future of Europe." Asked if it represented a "Johnson Doctrine" for Asia, he said that it did. In a statement that caused tremors on Capitol Hill, he added: "I think there is a tremendous new opening here for realizing the dream of the Great Society in the great area of Asia, not just here at home."[63]

A long report was drafted for the Vice President to give to the President, during the preparation of which Jack Valenti is said to have exhorted the drafters to be optimistic: "The President wants optimism; the President wants optimism."[64]

Although there does not appear to have been a final report, the draft prepared for Humphrey by some of those who accompanied him as well as a draft which his office submitted to the White House on February 25, if not "optimistic" were at least strongly affirmative.[65] The draft sent to the White House asserted that the tide of battle was changing, and that allied forces had the initiative. However, the struggle would be "long, tough and costly. It will test the moral fiber and the resources of our country. But, despite formidable obstacles, we *can* achieve our objective in South Vietnam." (emphasis in original) The "key to the war's outcome lies in the villages," it said. "The prospects for success in the military field are improved by a growing appreciation among Vietnamese leaders that resistance to Communist-backed aggression can ultimately succeed only if accompanied by a social revolution which brings health and hope, food and education, to the mass of the people."

"No one with whom I talked in Asia," the draft said, "foresaw an easy solution . . . [or] a speedy end to the trouble. Almost without exception those with whom I talked were convinced that the menace and the presence of aggression is real. Yet they were convinced that through the coordinated action of men and nations, aggression could be defeated in Vietnam—and social revolution could be accomplished. To stand aside, to turn back, or to think it will all go

---

[62] For Humphrey's description of the trip see his *The Education of a Public Man,* Norman Sherman (ed.) (Garden City, N.Y.: Doubleday, 1976), pp. 329–338. The memoir of Humphrey by his close friend and physician, Dr. Edgar Berman, *Hubert* (New York: G. P. Putnam Sons, 1979) also contains (pp. 106–114) interesting and revealing comments on the trip.

[63] CBS Television Interview with Humphrey, Apr. 19, 1966, quoted in the *Wall Street Journal,* Apr. 20, 1966; *The Education of a Public Man,* p. 330.

[64] CRS Interview with Humphrey's assistant, John E. Rielly, Mar. 29, 1979.

[65] For the draft prepared for Humphrey's use see U.S. Department of State, Lot File 74 D 272, and for the draft sent to McGeorge Bundy by Humphrey's administrative assistant, William Connell, on February 25, see the Johnson Library, NSF Name File, Vice President. In a note to Bundy, Connell said that the draft, entitled "Vice President's Report to the President, February 25, 1966," had not been cleared by the Vice President. No other copy of this or any subsequent version of this report has been found at the Johnson Library. The White House did not make public a report from Humphrey. Instead, it released a brief summary.

away if we retreat, would be in the view of Asia's leaders, a disaster to the hopes of men who value freedom." "It is in Vietnam," the report added, "that the full brunt of Communist aggression is now being borne. It is there we see the unfolding of the doctrine of 'wars of national liberation. . . .' If the Communists are forced back in Vietnam, beaten on both the battlefield and in the village, then the so-called war of national liberation as an instrument of fear and force will be discredited. It will be possible then to look realistically to an Asia expanding in freedom and economic progress. That is why Vietnam is so crucial to the destiny of so many countries, large and small, whose aim is to lead their own life in their own way."

From his National Security Assistant, McGeorge Bundy, who also accompanied the Vice President for part of his trip, the President got considerable "optimism." In a memorandum sent to the White House from Saigon on February 11, Bundy told the President: "The general atmosphere here is enormously better than it was a year ago. There is a long and tough job ahead, but the Mansfield report is just plain wrong and we believe there can be a Humphrey report which proves it."[66] On February 15, while flying back to Washington, Bundy outlined a memorandum to the President, Rusk and McNamara in which he noted: "The change from 1965. Fantastic." Despite the fact that the task would be "long and slow," it was "enormously worth doing—and believed worth doing."[67]

On February 24, 1966, after Humphrey returned to Washington, the President and the Vice President met with congressional leaders at 8:00 a.m. Present were, from the House, the Speaker, Albert, Boggs, and Republicans Ford and Arends, and from the Senate, Democrats Long and Smathers of Florida (Mansfield was in Florida recovering from an illness), and Republicans Dirksen and Kuchel. According to White House notes of the meeting, Humphrey told the group that U.S. objectives were being achieved, but "No one saw easy solution. No one predicted speedy end. Aggression can be defeated, subversion could be stopped, social revolution can be started. . . . Tide of battle has turned in Vietnam. We need to understand that this battle can be won."[68]

The President, with the hearings of the Foreign Relations Committee obviously in mind, spoke to the leaders about the need to resist Communist aggression, referring to the Southeast Asia Treaty, which he pointed out, had been approved by the Senate 82–1. He also said he had gone to Congress with the Gulf of Tonkin Resolution because he wanted Congress to join in preventing aggression, adding, "I intend to carry out the resolution. If you choose, you can repeal the resolution. I think I have the authority without the resolution." Speaker McCormack replied, "Resolution repeal wouldn't get to first base," House Republican Leader Ford said he agreed, but he thought it would be a good idea to have a vote on repealing the resolution so that a current vote could be registered

[66] Johnson Library, NSF Memos to the President—McGeorge Bundy.

[67] Johnson Library, Papers of McGeorge Bundy, Notes on Vietnam. See the same source for an outline by McGeorge Bundy of an answer to the "Lippmann thesis," also prepared on February 15 on the flight from Asia to Washington.

[68] Johnson Library, Meetings Notes File. There are also notes by Bromley Smith, NSF Files of Bromley Smith. The description here draws from both sets of notes.

on U.S. policy. Senate Republican Leader Dirksen said, "Repeal wouldn't get four votes."

The President added, "[I] can't understand why Americans who dissent can't do their dissenting in private. Once we are committed to a program of action, there never has been public dissent. . . . Our men understand why we are in Vietnam even if our Senators can't."

He also brought up the subject of the National Liberation Front,[69] saying,

> Government in Vietnam could not survive if VC were brought into Government. What Hanoi wants is for us to meet their conditions. They have made no concessions whatsoever. We want peace. They want conflict. They regard us as weak. Therefore, they think they will win. To treat VC, who are murderers and assassins, as legitimate government would disintegrate all that we have in Vietnam.

When the meeting adjourned, the President, the Vice President, Rusk, and McNamara, as well as the congressional leaders who had attended, met with members of the Foreign Relations and Foreign Affairs Committees and the Senate and House Armed Services and Appropriations Committees.[70] The President also invited the entire Congress to the White House, in four groups, to hear Humphrey's report. After one of these meetings, a very respected liberal Republican in the House, Charles McC. Mathias, Jr. (Maryland), who supported the administration on the war, confided to a State Department official that the President's credibility with Congress had been affected after denials in the meeting that there would be substantial troop increases in the near future, followed by an announcement a few days later that 20,000 more U.S. troops were being deployed. This, Mathias said, "had created considerable disillusionment on Capitol Hill among members of Congress who had attended the White House briefing and in particular it had raised the question of the credibility of the Administration." He said that a number of Members of Congress felt that it would have been better to have had no briefing at the White House rather than to have one at which the Members had been misled about the fact that in a matter of only a few days 20,000 additional troops had been on their way. "If the President had frankly said they would have to send more troops it would have been understood, although not necessarily welcomed, and the credibility and overall impact of the briefing would have been much greater and would have been sustained."[71]

Humphrey was also asked to testify before the Foreign Relations Committee. He told Fulbright that he would, but the President vetoed the idea, saying that no Vice President had ever testified before a congressional committee. After considerable discussion, it was agreed that Humphrey could meet with the committee informally and on his own accord.

---

[69] In part, at least, the President raised this subject in response to a speech by Senator Robert Kennedy on February 19. See below.

[70] In the Johnson Library, Congressional Briefings Notes, there is a transcript of the meeting of February 24.

[71] U.S. Department of State, Central File, Pol 27 Viet S, Memorandum from Douglas MacArthur II to Rusk, Mar. 8, 1966.

The meeting of the committee with Humphrey, which was held in Mansfield's office on March 2, 1966,[72] resulted in a bitter encounter between Fulbright and Humphrey in which Fulbright questioned him so sharply that Humphrey is said to have begun to cry.[73] The two men were old friends and, on many occasions, allies, and Humphrey had been a member of the committee for many years before being elected Vice President. But the tensions between Fulbright and the administration over Vietnam policy had become so strong that these personal and political ties were not enough to prevent a clash between the two men representing the two branches of government.

Fulbright's questions centered on two points: The nature of a pledge of U.S. assistance that Humphrey gave to Thailand, which Fulbright feared might lead to deployment of U.S. forces, and the question as to whether the U.S. should include the National Liberation Front in negotiations. Humphrey took the administration's position that the NLF did not constitute a government.

As the meeting ended, Fulbright and others thanked Humphrey and told him they were not trying to be critical of him. Fulbright said, "You know we all love you." The committee obviously did not hold Humphrey responsible. He was merely the scapegoat for criticism directed at the President.

Halberstam described the prevailing mood as the President, faced with growing skepticism and opposition in Congress and the public, began to show his frustration:[74]

> The Senate was beginning to rise up; he knew that and he knew why—it was that damn Fulbright. He knew what Fulbright was up to, he said; even a blind hog can find an acorn once in a while. So by early 1966, attitudes in the White House had become frozen. One could stay viable only by proclaiming faith and swallowing doubts. The price was high; it was very hard to bring doubts and reality to Johnson without losing access. The reasonable had become unreasonable; the rational, irrational. The deeper we were in, the more the outcry in the country, in the senate and in the press, the more Johnson hunkered down, isolated himself from reality. What had begun as a credibility gap became something far more perilous, a reality gap. He had a sense that everything he had wanted for his domestic program, his offering to history, was slipping away, and the knowledge of this made him angrier and touchier than ever; if you could not control events, you could at least try and control the version of them.

Among those who were concerned about the consequences of the break between Johnson and Fulbright there continued to be attempts at a reconciliation. In late February 1966, this possibility was discussed during a dinner party at Fulbright's house attended, among others, by his nephew, Kenneth S. F. Teasdale, an attorney from St. Louis, Missouri who had succeeded Harry C. McPherson,

---

[72] U.S. Congress, Senate, Committee on Foreign Relations, *Executive Sessions of the Senate Foreign Relations Committee* (Historical Series), 1966, vol. XVIII (Washington, D.C.: U.S. Govt. Print. Off., 1993), pp. 411–467 passim.

[73] CRS Interview with Chester Cooper, Apr. 10, 1979. Cooper accompanied Humphrey on his trip to Asia and to the committee hearing.

[74] David Halberstam, *The Best and the Brightest* (New York: Random House, 1972), pp. 623–624.

Jr., as counsel to the Senate Democratic Policy Committee. Teasdale wrote to McPherson, Counsel to President Johnson, saying, "Contrary to appearances at this time, I believe that it may be possible, with very careful planning, to reconcile the differences between the Administration and the Senator. His views actually are different in some degree from those which have appeared to be his, up until this time. He has refrained from expressing them because of several very good reasons, which you or I did not give him credit for. In addition, he bares *[sic]* absolutely no personal feeling in the matter toward the President, and is, on the contrary, sorry that personal feelings appear to have entered into the problem, making it still more difficult to resolve."[75]

On March 2, McPherson sent the President a memorandum quoting this excerpt from the letter, which he prefaced with the statement, "For what it's worth. . . ." The President returned the memorandum to McPherson with a handwritten notation: "Pursue this."

McPherson then sent to Bill Moyers, who had been closely involved in discussions about a possible reconciliation, a copy of another letter he had received from Teasdale suggesting the steps that could be taken to bring about a face-to-face meeting between Johnson and Fulbright. Enclosed was a copy of a letter from Teasdale to his aunt, Fulbright's wife, summarizing the ideas on U.S. policy toward Vietnam which were expressed by Fulbright at the dinner.

In the letter to his aunt on February 28, Teasdale gave this summary of the "ABC's" of the Senator's position:

> a. The policy which ought to be ultimately followed by the U.S. in Southeast Asia is one in which Vietnam, Laos, Thailand (and perhaps some other places) would become neutral in character which neutrality would be guaranteed by some sort of international control, perhaps, for example, the U.N. Neither the U.S. nor Communist China would remain physically present in that section of the world.
>
> b. It would be necessary for this state of affairs to be arrived at by negotiations between the U.S., China, and North Vietnam. These negotiations cannot be brought about unless China and North Vietnam are made willing to negotiate. This seems most likely to be brought about by,
>
> c. The establishment of fortified bases which have the appearance of a permanent character at several places in South Vietnam. The perimeters of these bases could be gradually expanded to cover more and more area as the surrounding ground was pacified. Within these protected provinces social and economic political experimentation could go on in a meaningful way without disruption and communist interference. No further escalation of the war would take place, and in fact, our offensive exercises should be considerably reduced. However, it would be understood that forays would be made out into the surrounding country, in order to prevent undue communist concentration, etc. This is, I gather, entirely constant with

[75] This letter and other documents cited here are in the Johnson Library, Office Files of Harry McPherson.

General Gavin's and Ambassador [George F.] Kennan's testimony before the Committee.

In his letter to McPherson, Teasdale, referring to the summary of Fulbright's position, said that if the President were to agree with the policy stated in points (a) and (b), the remaining disagreement between the President and Fulbright would be on the question of means—point (c)—which could be the subject of discussion between the two men.

The letter continued:

> I believe that almost any excuse that we could contrive which would lead to a face-to-face visit, in which the President would agree to let personal feelings be bygones, would accomplish a very great deal; either agreement, perhaps on some course to be followed, or if not, possibly at least a closer understanding of each other's position, a drawing closer together of each other's position and consequently, less complaints on the part of Senator Fulbright. The sooner that his complaints can be quieted, the better for the country.
>
> Do not mistake me, there is much support for what he says, at least out this way, but if he and the President could be brought to agreement or at least to a less bitter disagreement, it would go far to unite the country, which should be achieved at all costs as soon as possible for obvious domestic and international political reasons.

Teasdale added that Fulbright was "extremely concerned about making these views known. He has been told by some people that any view that he might have would be rejected by the President automatically, simply because the Senator had it."

In his memorandum to Moyers, McPherson asked him to look over the letters, adding, "If there is common ground here, it is mighty skinny." Moyers returned the memorandum and letters to McPherson with a handwritten note, in which, in effect, he dismissed the Teasdale approach: "We have been trying, through other personal channels, to effect a reconciliation of sorts—and this effort continues."

The Foreign Relations Committee Continues Its Hearings

After David Bell's testimony on February 4, the hearings of the Senate Foreign Relations Committee on the supplemental foreign assistance bill resumed on February 8—the final day of the Honolulu Conference—with retired Gen. James Gavin, followed by retired Ambassador George Kennan on February 10, retired Gen. Maxwell Taylor on February 17, and Secretary Rusk on February 18. The hearings continued to be televised, and were considered by media news executives to be so important that the decision of CBS to show "I Love Lucy" and "The Real McCoys" reruns rather than to televise the February 10 hearing with Kennan helped to precipitate the resignation on February 15 of Fred Friendly as president of the CBS News Division after Frank Stanton, president of CBS and a friend and supporter of President Johnson, made the decision against Friendly's advice.[76]

Gavin, who, while serving as head of the Army's Division of Plans, had been involved in the 1954 consideration of using U.S. forces in Vietnam, and while Ambassador to France in 1961 had helped President Kennedy negotiate with Souvanna Phouma for the neutrality of Laos, testified in favor of limiting U.S. commitments to Vietnam. He recommended that the U.S. cease bombing of the North, and limit the number and use of ground forces. As General Taylor had proposed a year before, Gavin suggested that the U.S. hold several enclaves on the coast of Vietnam and avoid escalating "at the initiative of the enemy." "What I want is to see my Nation act restrained and wisely and . . . we'll win around the periphery with each confrontation. I think we are doing quite well in Vietnam. I worry about going further. Whether or not we win a so-called war of liberation vis-a-vis the Chinese doesn't worry me half as much as all the other things that could happen with us. . . ."[77]

Gavin said that in proposing enclaves he was not suggesting that U.S. forces should stay in those positions, but "just to use them to get out, that's all. We are getting out. We're not staying there any longer. It was stupid to stay there."

Gavin reported that in late January 1966 he was invited to the Pentagon by McNamara. Joined by Vance and General Wheeler, they talked about Gavin's point of view.[78] According to Gavin, McNamara was not sympathetic:[79]

> He [McNamara] said, "I'm not going to worry about getting out. I want to know how you're going to fight when you're over there." I said, "Well, we shouldn't be there." It was a standoff. I remember as I left his office, I turned, I had my hand on the door, and I said, "I wouldn't be in your position for anything." Because he was recommending staying. And I could tell him without any doubt on my part, "You're going to get murdered if you stay there. Your troops, you'll have to keep reinforcing them and reinforcing them. You've got to get out."

---

[76] See Halberstam, *The Powers That Be,* pp. 505–506, and the *New York Times* and the *Washington Post,* Feb. 16, 1966. The coverage of these hearings by the three commercial TV networks was, next to the Watergate hearings in 1973, the longest such telecasting of any congressional hearings between 1960 and 1976. A total of 119:18 hours were telecast, 22:36 by ABC, 27:33 by CBS, and 69:09 by NBC. The source of these figures, provided by the networks, is Steve Rutkus, "Television Network News Coverage of Senate Committees," U.S. Congress, Senate, Temporary Select Committee to Study the Senate Committee System, *Operations of the Senate Committee System: Staffing, Scheduling, Communications, Procedures, and Special Functions,* Appendix to the Second Report, Committee Print, 95th Cong., 1st sess. (Washington, D.C.: U.S. Govt. Print. Off., 1977), p. 88.

[77] *Supplemental Foreign Assistance Fiscal Year 1966—Vietnam,* p. 246. Gen. Matthew B. Ridgway supported Gavin's position. See Ridgway's article, "Pull-out, All-out, or Stand Fast in Vietnam?" in *Look* magazine, Apr. 5, 1966. For a strong endorsement of the administration's position, see the lengthy editorial in *Life* magazine, Feb. 25, 1966, by Hedley Donovan, editor in chief.

[78] See the *New York Times,* Jan. 28, 1966.

[79] CRS Interview with James Gavin, Oct. 11, 1978.

Gavin's position was strongly attacked by General Taylor, as will be seen, and by the JCS. In response to a memorandum from McNamara, the Chiefs said that "By forfeiting the initiative, abandoning solid negotiation leverage, conceding large land areas to the enemy, and alienating the GVN and other friendly governments, the 'enclave' strategy, in effect, abandons national objectives. The military consequences would . . . lead to US/GVN defeat in SVN or ultimate U.S. abandonment of Southeast Asia."[80]

In addition to criticism from McNamara, Wheeler, and others at the Pentagon, Gavin's proposal was strongly criticized by many members of the Senate and House Armed Services Committees, whose attitude was typified by Chairman Russell's comment at the Senate hearings on the military portion of the FY 1966 supplemental:[81]

> The Gavin theory, if carried out, would be an absolutely interminable stalemate not only of unknown duration but nobody knows how many people it would take to hold those enclaves for any period of time. Really, that would be the worst kind of Maginot line concept, getting in those fortified areas on the coast. . . . could [we] possibly ever win the war sitting there on the coast?

In an interview some years later, General Gavin stated that several months after he took his stand on the war, the Internal Revenue Service began an extensive audit of his tax returns for the several preceding years. He believed this action was initiated by President Johnson, who, he said, was retaliating against him because of his opposition.[82]

Although it may not be possible to substantiate General Gavin's contention about his tax returns—relevant government documents may have been destroyed—a later inquiry revealed that the government was using tax information in this fashion against individuals and groups who expressed opposition to U.S. policy in Vietnam. This illegal activity was carried out by the FBI and, to a lesser extent, the CIA, with the cooperation of the Internal Revenue Service, under general mandates from the White House and the Justice Department to suppress antiwar activity.[83]

As the hearings of the Foreign Relations Committee continued on February 10, George Kennan, a prominent former Foreign Service Officer who had achieved fame as the author of the "containment" policy,[84] (among other things, he had served as the Director of the State Department Policy Planning Staff and as U.S. Ambassador to the Soviet Union and Yugoslavia), testified that the U.S. should limit its military role in Vietnam, and find a way to negotiate a withdrawal that would not do "inordinate damage" to U.S. prestige

---

[80] Johnson Library, NSF Country File, Vietnam, JCSM–76–66, Feb. 3, 1966.

[81] Senate hearings on *Supplemental Military Procurement and Construction Authorizations, Fiscal Year 1966*, cited above, pp. 275–276. See also pp. 149, 281. For McNamara's comment see p. 1.

[82] CRS Interview with James Gavin, Oct. 11, 1978.

[83] Final Report, Book II of the Senate Select Committee to Study Intelligence Activities, pp. 93–96, and Book III of the Senate Select Committee to Study Intelligence Activities (Staff Reports), "The Internal Revenue Service: An Intelligence Resource and Collector," pp. 835–920. According to the latter report, p. 847, n. 9, all IRS records of the disclosure of information to the FBI prior to 1968 were destroyed in about 1972 in a "space-saving drive."

[84] See pt. I of this study, pp. 27–28.

or the stability of Southeast Asia. Kennan questioned how much of a commitment the U.S. had to defend South Vietnam, and how the commitment had been made.[85]

After the Gavin and Kennan hearings, Senator Russell Long, the Democratic whip then serving as acting majority leader in Mansfield's absence, and one of the President's principal spokesmen in the Senate, especially on political questions, made a speech in the Senate on February 16 in which he attacked "these advocates of retreat, defeat, surrender, and national dishonor . . . [who] went before a television network suggesting that this Nation was not committed to fighting aggression in this area."[86] He was referring to Senators who had questioned, during the hearings, whether the U.S. was committed to fight in Vietnam, and the basis for such a commitment, and he added:

> when the Nation is committed and our men are fighting in the field, we have a responsibility not to do things that will divide and confuse the People and prolong the war. The information I am getting and it is coming from very high sources in the Government—is that one of the greatest difficulties in bringing the war to an end is that every time a Senator suggests that we retreat and accept defeat or surrender, that word goes right back to Hanoi, Ho Chi Minh, and the powers at Peiping. . . . I maintain that speeches on the floor of the Senate and on television, advocating that our boys not fight for their country, and that the people back off from the effort to help their country, handcuff our fighting men and to hold our country down when the going gets tough, do nothing but encourage the Communists to continue the war.[87]

On February 17, 1966, General Taylor, former U.S. Ambassador to Vietnam, who at the time was a consultant to the President, testified before the Foreign Relations Committee on behalf of the administration's position, and emphatically rejected Gavin's enclave proposal. Taylor also spoke sharply to the committee about the adverse effects of domestic dissent, saying that the Communists "have not forgotten that the Vietminh won more in Paris than in Dienbienphu and believe that the Vietcong may be as fortunate in Washington. They doubt the will of the American public to con-

---

[85] Many years earlier, Kennan had directly contributed to the U.S. decision to support French reoccupation of Indochina after World War II and to oppose the independence movement led by Ho Chi Minh and the Vietminh. In September 1945, as the French were forcibly reoccupying Vietnam, and the Far East Division of the State Department was trying to work out a solution that would avoid a reinstatement of the old colonialist system, Kennan, then in the U.S. Embassy in Moscow, advised Washington that although the Russians probably would not intervene directly in Indochina, they wanted to bar French and other Western countries from exercising power in the area in order to leave it "completely open to Communist penetration." This cable was instrumental in the successful effort by the Europeanists in the State Department to support French reoccupation of Indochina. See ch. 1 of pt. I of this study for further details.

See also Walter L. Hixson, *George F. Kennan: Cold War Iconoclast* (New York: Columbia Univ. Press, 1989), pp. 227–238. According to Hixson (p. 222), "Kennan was among the leading State Department advocates of containment [of communism] across the 'great crescent' of Asia in the early cold war and he viewed the preservation of noncommunist regimes in Indochina as vital to ensuring the economic recovery and Western orientation of Japan." Vietnam, Hixson says (p. 238), "unearthed all the contradictions of containment and found Kennan unable to recommend a consistent approach to the war. He called on the United States to hold the line in Vietnam to avoid a prestige defeat even as he admitted the hopelessness of the U.S. position there. . . . Torn by conflicting emotions, Kennan found his way out only when he threw in the towel on the whole enterprise and called [in 1969] for a unilateral American withdrawal."

[86] *CR*, vol. 112, p. 3041.

[87] For responses by Gruening, Gore, and McGovern, see *ibid.*, pp. 3041–3043.

tinue the conflict indefinitely."[88] Senator Case of New Jersey, a liberal Republican who supported the war, took issue with this, saying he was "troubled by any suggestion that any question raised is weakening American efforts abroad . . . the only basis on which a democracy can demonstrate its determination is first understanding what the policy is all about. . . . [T]he experiences we have had over the last few years," Case added, "are not such in many cases as to make us completely easy with just a rather calm assurance to 'trust us.'"[89]

Senator Morse said, "You know we are engaged in historic debate in this country. There are honest differences of opinion. I happen to hold to the point of view that it isn't going to be too long before the American people repudiate our war in southeast Asia."

This sharp exchange with Taylor followed:[90]

> General Taylor. That, of course, is good news to Hanoi, Senator.
>
> Senator Morse. I know that that is the smear artist—that you militarists give to those of us who have honest differences of opinion with you. But I don't intend to get down in the gutter with you and engage in that kind of debate, General. I am simply saying that in my judgment the President of the United States is already losing the people of this country by the millions in connection with this war in southeast Asia. All I am asking is if the people decide that this war should be stopped in southeast Asia, are you going to take the position that is weakness on the homefront in a democracy?
>
> General Taylor. I would feel that our people were badly misguided and did not understand the consequences of such a disaster.
>
> Senator Morse. Well, we agree on one thing, that they can be badly misguided. You and the President in my judgment have been misguiding them for a long time in this war.

Morse's comments were applauded by the spectators in the committee room, and Fulbright reminded the audience that the rules forbade demonstrations.

After the hearing, Taylor received this note from Bill Moyers:[91] "The President was very proud of you, and less importantly, so were all of us who believe we must carry forward the pursuit of our policy in Southeast Asia."

The televised hearing with Rusk was held on February 18. Fulbright announced that McNamara had declined to testify in public session. (McNamara eventually did so on April 20, 1966 and that hearing was also televised, as was a subsequent hearing on May 10, 1966 at which Rusk and Bell testified.) In his opening statement, which was one of the clearest and most cogent presentations of the administration's case during the entire war, Rusk emphasized that a war of aggression was being waged by the Communists

---

[88] *Supplemental Foreign Assistance Fiscal Year 1966—Vietnam,* p. 438.
[89] *Ibid.*, p. 530.
[90] *Ibid.*, pp. 454–455.
[91] John M. Taylor, *General Maxwell Taylor, The Sword and the Pen* (New York: Doubleday, 1989), p. 335.

of North Vietnam against the people of South Vietnam.[92] U.S. forces were sent to South Vietnam, he added, because South Vietnam "has, under the language of the SEATO Treaty, been the victim of aggression by means of armed attack." Quoting the provision in article IV of the treaty, which stated, "each party recognizes that aggression by means of armed attack . . . would endanger its own peace and safety, and agrees that it will in that event act to meet the common danger . . ." he said that the treaty, together with the mutual security pact which the U.S. had with Vietnam, committed the United States to defend South Vietnam against such armed attack. He also pointed out that the Southeast Asia Treaty had been ratified 82–1 by the Senate. Following these comments, several members of the committee disagreed with Rusk's interpretation of U.S. obligations under the Southeast Asia Treaty. (Mansfield, who had been one of two Senators on the U.S. delegation, and had signed the treaty, did not attend this hearing.)[93]

After also reviewing U.S. goals in Vietnam and efforts to negotiate an end to the war, Rusk concluded his testimony by stating what he called "certain simple points which are at the heart of the problem and at the heart of U.S. policy in South Vietnam":

> 1. The elementary fact is that there is an aggression in the form of an armed attack by North Vietnam against South Vietnam.
> 2. The United States has commitments to assist South Vietnam to repel this aggression.
> 3. Our commitments to South Vietnam were not taken in isolation but are part of a systematic effort in the postwar period to assure a stable peace.
> 4. The issue in southeast Asia becomes worldwide because we must make clear that the United States keeps its word wherever it is pledged.
> 5. No nation is more interested in peace in southeast Asia or elsewhere than is the United States. If the armed attack against South Vietnam is brought to an end, peace can come very quickly. Every channel or forum for contact, discussion, or negotiation will remain active in order that no possibility for peace may be overlooked.

Although most of the members of the committee attended the Rusk hearing, the questioning in this open, public session, as might be expected, was generally more hortatory than it usually is in executive (closed) sessions where the public and the press are excluded. Gale McGee, a member of the committee at two different times, gave this explanation of the differences:[94]

> Number one, when we were on T.V. some Senators on the committee were more belligerent—let's say more ham, obviously pitching for the constituent vote than they were when we were in executive session with the same witness in committee

[92] Rusk's statement is in *Supplemental Foreign Assistance Fiscal Year 1966—Vietnam,* pp. 563–576.

[93] Nicholas Katzenbach, then Attorney General, who became Under Secretary of State when George Ball resigned in the fall of 1966, said in an interview several years later that he disagreed emphatically with Rusk's interpretation of SEATO, and argued that he should not use it as a basis for justifying and defending U.S. military operations in Vietnam. (CRS Interview with Nicholas Katzenbach, Nov. 7, 1978.)

[94] Johnson Library, Gale McGee Oral History, Oct. 1969.

chambers without T.V. Nearly every one of the members of the committee in executive session were gentlemen, they kept their voices in low key, they expressed disagreement; but they asked the tough questions that ought to be asked of a Secretary of State or Secretary of Defense, none of this smarty business or these perorations about the dying boys on the battle field in Viet Nam and this sort of thing. That was the distinct difference between the two circumstances.

The second difference was that when we were on T.V. nearly all members of the committee would show up in order to get his free time. If you had an executive session it was desperately difficult even to get a quorum in order to have a vote on the committee. If you didn't have a T.V. camera there, the numbers of the committee members that refused to show was a disturbing factor.

Many of the questions which Rusk was asked by members of the committee were of the type described by McGee, but there were several comments which touched on significant issues. One of these was the statement by Senator Clifford Case concerning the meaning of the 1964 Gulf of Tonkin Resolution. Case, who had been a supporter of the war and of the President's handling of it, said:[95]

> I don't think it [the resolution] should be taken for more than an expression of confidence in the President in the immediate situation, and not a power of attorney irrevocably delegating all of the congressional authority to the President for whatever period the President may see fit. . . . Among other things it means constant consultation. . . . We are trying to find an effective substitute for the "declaration of war" provision in the Constitution, and it seems to me the only real substitute is the practical one of working together continuously and certainly when matters begin to change or turn or assume a different course.

Rusk replied that there had been more consultation on Vietnam than on any other issue he could recall, adding, "there is no inclination, Senator, to take the view that the Congress at that point abdicated its responsibility. The President and the Secretary of State and indeed our military men in the field want to proceed on the basis of a national policy in which the Congress participates fully." Rusk said there had been "consultation with some of the leadership about whether a new resolution is required. There has been, I think, some divided counsel on that matter, but nevertheless the issue is in front of you in the votes to be taken in the Senate, in the Congress, in connection with these supplemental appropriations requests."

Rusk said that if Congress was in doubt, the matter should be put to a vote, adding,

> But if I may say so, Senator—and I am not now pointing a finger at you at all—if I may say so, I would hope that, before the votes are taken, the Members of the Congress, of the House and the Senate, would go into a quiet corner and think very long and deeply about what we have been through for the

---

[95] *Supplemental Foreign Assistance Fiscal Year 1966—Vietnam,* p. 618.

last three decades, four decades, and on what basis we have any chance whatever to organize the peace in the world—on what basis can we build a peace—and then decide which vote is a vote for war and which vote is a vote for peace.[96]

---

[96] Rusk also stated in the hearing that the administration was filing with the committee a legal memorandum on U.S. participation in the war. This, which was sent to the committee a few days later, was the so-called "Meeker Memorandum" (Leonard Meeker was State's Legal Adviser), entitled, "The Legality of United States Participation in the Defense of Viet-Nam." (For the text, see *Department of State Bulletin*, Mar. 28, 1966, and for further discussion, see ch. 5 of pt. II of this study and ch. 1 above.)

Several weeks earlier, (Jan. 25, 1966) a group of lawyers and professors of law, calling themselves the Lawyers Committee on American Policy Towards Vietnam, had written to the President stating their opposition to the war, and enclosing a memorandum of law. (For the text of the letter and the memorandum see *CR*, vol. 112, pp. 4166–4173.) The letter stated, among other things: "Our committee has reached the regrettable but inescapable conclusion that the actions of the United States in Vietnam contravene the essential provisions of the United Nations Charter, to which we are bound by treaty; violate the Geneva accords, which we are pledged to observe; are not sanctioned by the treaty creating the Southeast Asia Treaty Organization; and violate our own Constitution and the checks and balances which is at the heart of it, by the prosecution of the war in Vietnam without a congressional declaration of war." The Lawyers Committee favored a cessation of bombing, a cease-fire, and negotiations which would include the National Liberation Front.

The White House asked the Justice Department to comment on the memorandum from the Lawyers Committee, and on February 19 Attorney General Katzenbach sent the President a memorandum on the subject in which, after examining briefly each of the contentions, he concluded: "In sum, the memorandum seems to me to be based on a blatant misreading of the facts, the relevant history and the law." He said he did not make a detailed analysis of the memorandum because it was "so completely indefensible that I did not want to dignify it by a long, scholarly rebuttal." In a cover memorandum, Katzenbach said he thought it would be preferable to arrange, as the White House was then planning to do, for a reply to come from legal scholars rather than just from the government. Johnson Library, Ex ND 19/CO 312, Memorandum (with attachment) for the President from Katzenbach, Feb. 19, 1966.

On Feb. 5, 1966, White House Counsel Harry McPherson, wrote to Prof. Neill H. Alford, Jr., University of Virginia School of Law, who had agreed, along with Prof. Myres S. McDougal of the Yale Law School, to enlist other scholars, suggesting that the group send a letter to the President stating its views in support of the administration's position. Johnson Library, Office Files of Harry McPherson, Vietnam, 1966. McPherson said, "It would be desirable, though not essential, to reject the position expressed in the Lawyers' Committee letter." He urged the group to act quickly because of the imminence of the Foreign Relations Committee hearings on Vietnam. The letter, signed by Alford and McDougal, as well as by two professors of law at Harvard University and one at the University of Michigan, was sent to the President on Feb. 14, 1966. For the text see *CR*, vol. 112, p. 3843. It took issue with the analysis and the conclusions of the Lawyers Committee, and stated, "the legal position of the United States in South Vietnam is clearly defensible. It would, in fact, seem the legal position most compatible with protecting the genuine self-determination of the peoples of South Vietnam." Again at White House urging, the McDougal group prepared a memorandum of law stating its position on the legality of the war, "The Lawfulness of United States Assistance to the Republic of Vietnam." Prepared by McDougal, John Norton Moore of the University of Virginia Law School, and James L. Underwood of the University of South Carolina College of Law, it was issued in May 1966 and distributed by the American Bar Association to each Member of Congress. By request, Javits put excerpts from the study in the *Congressional Record*. See vol. 112, pp. 13870–13874. The full text was inserted by Senator Russell Long on pp. 15519–15567.

A somewhat shorter version of the McDougal group's memorandum appeared under John Norton Moore's name in the January 1967 issue of the *American Journal of International Law*, pp. 1–34.

For a detailed reply to the McDougal group by the Lawyers Committee on American Policy Towards Vietnam, see *Vietnam and International Law: An Analysis of the Legality of the U.S. Military Involvement* (New York: O'Hare, 1967), prepared by the Consultative Council of the Lawyers Committee, consisting of Richard A. Falk, chairman, John H. E. Fried, who drafted the study, Richard J. Barnet, Wallace McClure, Hans Morgenthau, John H. Herz, Saul H. Mendlovitz, William C. Rice, Stanley Hoffmann, Richard S. Miller, and Quincy Wright.

Several months earlier, the White House had organized a similar rebuttal to a memorandum of law from the Lawyers Committee issued in September 1965. (For the text of the Lawyers Committee memorandum see *CR*, vol. 111, pp. 24902–24910.) McPherson arranged for E. Ernest Goldstein, a professor of law at the University of Texas, to draft a statement to the President, signed by Goldstein and 30 other professors of international law including Alford and McDougal, defending the lawfulness of the U.S. role in Vietnam. For the text of the press release issued by the group of 31 on Nov. 23, 1965, see Johnson Library, Office Files of Harry McPherson, Vietnam, 1966.

The White House also was involved in passage by the House of Delegates of the American Bar Association, by a vote of 279–0, of a resolution on Feb. 21, 1966, which stated: "The position of the United States in Vietnam is legal under international law and is in accordance with the Charter of the United Nations and the Southeast Asia Treaty." Eberhard P. Deutsch, chairman of the ABA Committee in which the resolution originated, subsequently stated his views on the

Several members of the committee took issue with Rusk, while others agreed with him, but the principal exchange, as the hearing came to an end, was between Rusk and Fulbright. Although both men were very controlled, it was a dramatic moment, and it highlighted the profound differences that had arisen between Fulbright, and others like him in the Congress, and the President and his associates.[97] It also exemplified the deep feelings on both sides, and the antagonism that had developed between people of the same political persuasion over an issue on which they had once been united. As such, it was a microcosm of the differences of opinion and disagreements that were developing in the country as a whole with respect to Vietnam, which would divide the American people in the months ahead as they probably had not been divided since the Civil War.

Fulbright said that the war had begun as a "war of liberation from French rule"; that it was "more in the nature of a civil war in which outside parties have become involved" than a war of aggression from outside. With respect to negotiations, he said he did not see in the U.S. position any willingness to compromise. Yet he thought compromise was essential, and the conflict was not one "that warrants a vast escalation, a vast expenditure of money and many thousands of deaths. I think it is not that kind of a vital interest. . . . I also think that the great countries, especially this country, is quite strong enough to engage in a compromise without losing its standing in the world and without losing its prestige as a great nation. On the contrary, I think it would be one of the greatest victories for us in our prestige if we could be ingenious enough and magnanimous enough to bring about some kind of a settlement of this particular struggle."

Rusk, who had said to Fulbright a few minutes earlier, "Senator, do you have any doubts about the good faith and the credibility of the other side here in this situation?" responded: "Mr. Chairman, we wouldn't have much of a debate between us on the question of compromising and a settlement, but we can't get anybody into the discussions for the purpose of talking about it."

> The Chairman. I think there is something wrong with our approach. . . .
>
> Secretary Rusk. Senator, is it just possible that there is something wrong with them [the Communists]?
>
> The Chairman. Yes, there is a lot wrong with them. They are very primitive, difficult, poor people who have been fighting for

---

subject in "The Legality of the United States Position in Vietnam," *American Bar Association Journal,* May 1966. According to the *New York Times,* Feb. 22, 1966, Deutsch's sponsorship of the resolution was prompted by Senator Russell Long, from Deutsch's own state of Louisiana.

(A note to McGeorge Bundy from Chester Cooper on the day that the resolution was passed, to which Cooper attached a copy of the wire service story on the ABA action, stated: "Mac—You should know that Morris [Morris Liebman] (one of my tame clients) was instrumental in pushing this through." Liebman, a Chicago attorney, one of the Wise Men, strongly supported the war and was very active in helping the White House organize public support activities.) Senator Morse, a former professor of law and law school dean, responded: ". . . apparently what the American Bar Association needs is a freshman refresher course on both international law and constitutional law." *CR,* vol. 112, p. 3561.

For a rejoinder to Deutsch's article, see William L. Standard, "U.S. Intervention in Vietnam is Not Legal," *American Bar Association Journal,* July 1966. Standard was chairman of the Lawyers Committee on American Policy Towards Vietnam.

[97] See *Supplemental Foreign Assistance Fiscal Year 1966—Vietnam,* pp. 650 ff.

20 years and I don't understand myself why they can continue to fight, but they do.

Secretary Rusk. And they want to take over South Vietnam by force.

On March 3, the Foreign Relations Committee met in executive sessions to hear McNamara, who had refused to appear in open session. Perhaps the most interesting and significant exchange occurred when Fulbright asked McNamara what would happen if the Communists did not desist, adding, "They haven't given up for 20 years." McNamara replied:[98]

> Nor have they been facing for 20 years the force that we are presently applying to them, Mr. Chairman. Nor have they been paying for 20 years the price they are presently paying in casualties. I think it is quite clear they have not decided to give up yet. I think it is quite clear they will probably expand their forces. I think if they do, we must continue to expand ours. If they do . . . we will exact an increasing toll from them. There will come a time when they will be unable to increase their forces further.

Fulbright replied by questioning whether the Vietnamese Communists were limited in manpower in view of the large number of Chinese forces that were available to back them up, but McNamara, contrary to his advice to the President that increased forces would lead to a "military standoff at a higher level," stuck to his position that there would come a time at which the Vietnamese Communists would, in effect, sue for peace. By taking this position he was making the same argument the military Chiefs had made in July 1965, and continued to make, that, through attrition, U.S. military superiority would eventually force the Communists to accept a compromise settlement.

What did the Senate Foreign Relations Committee's Vietnam hearings accomplish? In Congress itself, the hearings do not seem to have made much of an impression.[99] In the executive branch, the principal effect appears to have been one of drawing the lines of political battle even tighter and stimulating the President and his associates to take additional steps to counteract congressional critics.[100] McGeorge Bundy commented later that the hearings were

---

[98] U.S. Congress, Senate, Committee on Foreign Relations, *Executive Sessions of the Senate Foreign Relations Committee* (Historical Series), 1966, vol. XVIII (Washington, D.C.: U.S. Govt. Print. Off., 1993), pp. 499–500.

[99] This conclusion is based primarily on CRS interviews with a number of Members and staff of the Senate and the House who were in office at the time.

[100] Lodge tried to create the impression that the hearings had hurt U.S. morale. Westmoreland, who was asked for his comments, told Lodge that although the hearings may have adversely affected public opinion in the U.S. and provided propaganda for the Communists, they had "little or no effect on troop morale." (CMH, Westmoreland Papers, History File, Memorandum from Westmoreland to Lodge, Feb. 22, 1966.) Lodge then visited the First Cavalry Division, and reported to the President that at lunch with some of the officers the conversation was "somewhat as follows (U.S. Department of State, Central File, Pol 27 Viet S, Saigon 3075, to Washington, Feb. 23, 1966):

"How many at home realize how difficult it is to explain why the Foreign Relations Committee is holding public hearings which are devoted to attacking U.S. policy in Viet-Nam—and doing so long after the fact of aggression has been clearly established and while American troops are in combat?

"We here who circulate constantly among Americans, civilians and military, do not meet anyone who can understand why this public attack is going on. The aggression having been clearly and flagrantly committed; the decision having been carefully reached to ward off the aggression; and American troops being actually in combat, it seems to everyone we see, American and foreigner alike, that organized public criticism from Congress should cease.

"badly handled on both sides. I don't think that the Fulbright hearings were really trying to propose an alternative policy, and I think the administration was stonewalling . . . telling as little as they could get away with. . . ."[101]

The public effect of the hearings, however, while difficult to gauge, apparently was significant. According to Norvill Jones, the hearings "really struck a responsive cord," and produced a "torrent" of mail (something on the order of 25,000 letters, with a favorable ratio of 6 or 7 to 1).[102]

Senator Claiborne Pell, Democrat of Rhode Island and a member (and later chairman) of the committee, believes that the hearings "made peace a respectable word and showed that disagreement is respectable, too. If such a group of respectable stuffed shirts as the Senate Foreign Relations Committee could question this war, it gave other people courage to question it." "I really think," Pell added, "that our Committee was more responsible than any other single individual or body of individuals for turning public opinion around on that war."[103]

According to Senator Frank Church, Democrat from Idaho and a member (and later chairman) of the committee, the hearings brought the Foreign Relations Committee "to the fore in considering the policy questions that related to the war," and caused the President to pay it more heed, as well as enabling the committee to provide better leadership to the public.[104] "As long as the Committee conducted executive sessions behind closed doors," Church said, "it was really the captive of the President and the State Department. . . . I remember the immediate reaction at the White House when Senator Fulbright commenced the public hearings. It was only at that point that the President really began to take the Committee seriously."

As far as the public was concerned, Church said, "the general resistance to the war and the debate itself over the war began to spread in the country . . . if we had not gone out from behind closed doors, this never would have happened."

For some of the more prominent critics, like General Gavin, the hearings provided reassurance and support. As Gavin said later, "When you get into a predicament like that, you get shot at from all directions, friend and foe. And Congress is in a position to help you."[105]

From the perspective of the White House, as George E. Reedy, Jr., President Johnson's long-time aide, pointed out in a perceptive memorandum to the President on February 17, 1966, the effect of the hearings was to deepen ideological differences and to force people to choose sides at a time when the President needed flexibility to take the necessary steps to end the war.[106] The "situation is not helped," Reedy said, "by the unanimity among the President's advisors. This is an honest unanimity but to the public it presents the

---

"Indeed, it is hard to explain why the very prominent and distinguished Americans responsible for this are not doing their talking and inquiring in private."

[101] CRS Interview with McGeorge Bundy, Jan. 8, 1979.

[102] Author's telephone conversation with Norvill Jones, July 12, 1993.

[103] CRS Interview with Claiborne Pell, Jan. 24, 1979.

[104] Johnson Library, Frank Church Oral History.

[105] CRS Interview with James Gavin, Oct. 11, 1978.

[106] Johnson Library, WHCF, Ex/CO 312.

picture of a President who is listening only to advice from a group of men who are so deeply involved themselves in an enterprise that they have no alternative other than to agree with him. It would, of course, be foolish to create an artificial discord among competent and conscientious men where it does not, in fact, exist. But it would be reassuring to the public if it were thought that the President was giving a real audience to the more respectable and responsible voices of dissent."

Reedy said that the Senate testimony of Gavin and Kennan was "an excellent example of men being placed in categories of opinion which they do not really hold." He pointed out that both men were taking a moderate position of questioning whether U.S. operations in Vietnam were being conducted in a way that was consistent with U.S. world strategy; yet they had "become the darlings of the 'doves'. . . ." He said that they might be making a good point, or at least one that was worth listening to, and that "It would have a good effect upon the country if the President were to invite Gavin and Kennan to the White House for a quiet, but lengthy and thorough, luncheon conference" that might result in continuing contacts with the two men.

Although the President had taken the position in a news conference on February 11, possibly at Reedy's urging, that there did not appear to be any important differences between what Gavin and Kennan were recommending and what the administration was doing, he did not act on Reedy's advice that the two men be invited to the White House for a discussion.[107]

There are almost no polling data on public reaction to the hearings of the Foreign Relations Committee. A survey by Louis Harris suggests that the hearings may have contributed to better public understanding of U.S. objectives in Asia, which is, of course, what the committee hoped to achieve, but may also have been confusing or harmful. Harris' survey, made after the Vietnam hearings in February and hearings on China conducted by the committee in March and April, asked whether the respondents had heard of the hearings, and, if so, whether the hearings had *"helped people such as yourself to better understand the war in Vietnam, have they confused things, have they set back American unity or have they not made much difference one way or the other?"* Only 37 percent of those polled said that they had followed the hearings.[108] Of these, the following were the percentages for each answer:

[In percent]

Helped Understanding	46
Confused Things	23
Set Back Unity	9
Not Much Difference	16
Not Sure	6

[107] For the February 11 news conference statement see *Public Papers of the Presidents,* Lyndon B. Johnson, 1966, p. 173.

The President appeared even less interested in Mansfield's views. When the White House liaison with the Senate, Mike Manatos, was told by the President to discuss a matter with Mansfield, he reported in a memo to the President on February 10 that he had done so, and that while he was in Mansfield's office he happened to pick up the February 14 issue of *Newsweek,* and found underlined the following quote from the President: "Mike is a cross between Jeanette Rankin and Burton K. Wheeler [two well-known "isolationist" Members of Congress from Montana at the time of the Second World War], and I don't need advice from either of them." Johnson Library, WHCF, Name File, Mansfield.

[108] *Washington Post,* June 14, 1966.

Although 46 percent of the 37 percent that had heard of the hearings thought they had "helped understanding," a total of 32 percent thought the hearings had either been confusing or harmful, and a total of 48 percent (23 percent plus 9 percent plus the 16 percent "not much difference") thought the hearings had not made much difference, had not been helpful, or had been harmful.

A similar assessment was made by former White House speechwriter Richard Goodwin, who had resigned in the fall of 1965, attended the meeting with McNamara at Schlesinger's house in January, 1966, and would later become very critical of Johnson and the war. In a telephone call to Presidential Assistant Joe Califano on February 18, the day of Rusk's testimony before the Senate Foreign Relations Committee, Goodwin said, according to Califano's memorandum to the President, that "everywhere he speaks, he runs into deep concern about the situation in Vietnam. He said he is personally and firmly convinced that you are pursuing the correct course, but that the Fulbright hearings particularly are doing a tremendous amount to confuse the American people. He recommended that you make a simple and clear statement, in some detail, on television to the American people about what is going on in Vietnam and what we are trying to do there." [109]

The Senate Rejects Repeal of the Gulf of Tonkin Resolution

During the latter part of January and early February 1966, as a new escalation of the war appeared imminent, there was a growing interest among some Members of the Senate, especially on the Foreign Relations Committee, in a new congressional resolution that would augment or replace the Gulf of Tonkin Resolution. On January 29, Morse introduced an amendment to repeal the Gulf of Tonkin Resolution. On January 31, Carl Marcy, chief of staff of the Foreign Relations Committee, sent a memorandum to committee staff members Norvill Jones and James Lowenstein saying that Chairman Fulbright wanted to have a draft of a resolution or an amendment to the Vietnam supplemental appropriations bill "which would be a positive statement of what we are for and by implication, therefore, would replace the Southeast Asia [Gulf of Tonkin] Resolution." According to Marcy, Fulbright said that "He would hope to get 20 to 30 votes for this. . . ." [110]

On February 2, Javits and Randolph again proposed that Congress replace the Gulf of Tonkin Resolution with a resolution specifically approving the waging of a large-scale war, as well as more specifically stating U.S. goals and objectives.[111]

On February 10, Marcy prepared the text of four alternative amendments to the Vietnam supplemental appropriations bill, as follows: [112]

> 1. It is the sense of the Congress that the interests of the United States will be served by continuous efforts on the part of this and other governments to promote negotiations leading

[109] Johnson Library, Ex ND 19/CO 312, Memorandum to the President from Califano, 9:00 p.m. Saturday, Feb. 19, 1966.

[110] National Archives, RG 46, Papers of the Foreign Relations Committee, Marcy Chron File.

[111] *CR*, vol. 112, pp. 1892 ff. See also Javits' subsequent remarks on pp. 3885 ff. and pp. 4374 ff. For a more detailed discussion of the Javits-Randolph proposal, see pt. III of this study.

[112] Marcy Chron File.

to a termination of hostilities in Vietnam on the basis of self-determination and independence.

2. Notwithstanding any other provision of law, or resolution, it is the sense of the Congress that the commitment of substantial additional American military forces to Vietnam should not be undertaken without further action by the Congress.

3. Nothing in this Act shall be construed as either approval or disapproval of past U.S. policy in Vietnam (or as indicating a desire on the part of the U.S. to expand hostilities in Vietnam).

4. Nothing in this Act shall be construed as indicating a desire on the part of the United States to expand hostilities in Vietnam (or to commit additional American forces to action there).

On February 18, Marcy told White House Senate Liaison Mike Manatos that, as Manatos said in a memorandum to the President, a majority of the members of the Foreign Relations Committee wanted some kind of "'sense of committee' language expressing fear of escalation. Apparently the 600,000-men figure is worrysome. Marcy said he 'can't tell' now whether General Taylor and Secretary Rusk succeeded in allaying those fears."[113] (The 600,000 figure was used by Stennis in a speech on January 29, 1966.)

On February 16, 1966, the Senate began debate on the bill that had been reported unanimously from the Armed Services Committee to authorize appropriations for the military portion of the $12.7 billion supplemental for Vietnam for the remainder of FY 1966.[114] For two weeks the critics talked—Gore, Hartke, Church, Young (Ohio), Gruening, Morse, and Clark, with Pell, Lee Metcalf (D/Mont.) and Fulbright adding occasional comments—while Russell, who was in charge of the bill as chairman of the Armed Services Committee, and Long, who, as the acting majority leader, was carrying the administration's case, warned, among other things, that the delay in approving the new funds could help the enemy and cost U.S. lives. Russell and Long were supported by various Republicans, including Dirksen, Hugh Scott (Pennsylvania), John G. Tower (Texas) and Jack Miller (Iowa), and by several Democrats, including McGee (Wyoming), Monroney (Oklahoma), and Smathers (Florida), as well as by a number of other Democrats and Republicans on the Senate Armed Services Committee. Symington, the only Senator on both Armed Services and Foreign Relations, actively supported Russell's position.

Russell argued that the supplemental military authorization bill did not involve policy; its sole purpose was to assist U.S. forces fighting in the field. Thus, he said, a vote for the bill would not be a vote for or against U.S. policy in Vietnam: "Nothing in this legislation can properly be considered as determining foreign policy, as ratifying decisions made in the past or as endorsing new commitments. . . . It involves more the throwing of a rope to a man in the water. We may have cause to question how he got there, but he is there, he is a human being, he is our friend, and a member of our family and, therefore, if we have a rope and do not throw

[113] Johnson Library, WHCF, Ex., Manatos Memorandum for the President, Feb. 18, 1966.
[114] For the debate, see *CR*, vol. 112, pp. 3135–4404, *passim*.

it to him to enable him to assist himself out of the water, this would be a callow and heartless attitude for us to take."

Russell's position that a vote for the bill would not be a vote to approve the war was carefully calculated to give critics of the war a justification for voting for the bill while continuing to oppose the war, and most of them did, saying that they were not approving the war and that they reserved the right to disapprove subsequent requests or actions of the Executive.[115]

On February 21, Rusk had lunch with four of the "problem Senators," as he called them, on the Foreign Relations Committee: Case (who still publicly supported the war), Church, Clark and Pell. In a memorandum to the President for his "night reading," Rusk reported that none of the four favored a precipitate U.S. withdrawal, but they all opposed increasing U.S. forces, and were concerned about the report that 600,000 troops would be needed. They recommended that the President hold a private briefing for the Foreign Relations Committee "so that they would have a firm understanding of both prospects and intentions in Vietnam."[116]

In meetings on February 19, 22, and 26, 1966, the President and his advisers discussed how to handle the situation in the Senate, especially the question of a resolution. The meeting on February 19, from 10:04 a.m. to 1:34 p.m. was attended by the President, Rusk, McNamara, McGeorge Bundy, Ball, Vance, Raborn, Wheeler, Moyers and Marvin Watson. The President referred to Stennis' 600,000 figure, saying, "Real source of our trouble is Stennis. The wild figures in the papers come from him and that's what scares Mansfield and Fulbright."[117] Turning to McNamara he said, "The problem is that he [Stennis] gets our figures." McNamara replied, "We have *not* indicated our plans." (emphasis in original) The President: "The real plans do get to Stennis, and let's try to prevent it."

"Maybe we consult with 'em too much," the President commented—"that and the press may be the root of our trouble." Fulbright he noted (referring to the Foreign Relations Committee hearings), "got a surprisingly favorable press." But "those people [Senate critics] are going to be unhappy no matter what you do."

Turning to the question of Senate action on a resolution he said, "You could lose the Senate—depends how the vote goes." Part of the problem was with the Democratic leadership. Mansfield did not work well with Russell Long and was trying to "hand the mantle" of the whip's job to Muskie.

In terms of the administration's strategy, the Morse amendment, the President said—singling it out because he assumed that it would get the least support—"is the one to press."

"We brought this [increasing criticism and opposition in the Senate] on ourselves. The pause has done this to us. The more you re-

[115] "Reservationists," Morse had scornfully called those who used the same justification the previous May in voting for the $700 million supplemental for Vietnam. He, too, had voted for the $1.7 billion supplemental in August 1965, however, arguing that U.S. forces had to be adequate provisioned.

[116] U.S. Department of State, Lot File 74 D 164. The "night" or "evening" reading file, which was compiled by the President's staff in late afternoon, consisted of reports from government departments and other materials.

[117] These quotations are from McGeorge Bundy's handwritten papers in the Johnson Library, Notes on Vietnam. They are the only known notes of the meeting.

spond to it [pressure to pause or otherwise deescalate] the deeper in you're going to get."

During the meeting, one of the President's secretaries brought him an announcement of a speech that had just been made by Senator Robert Kennedy in which he said that in the interest of getting a negotiated settlement the U.S. should accept the need to give the National Liberation Front a share of power and responsibility in South Vietnam. Kennedy suggested the possibility of a "compromise government." [118]

At the White House meeting on February 22 from 11:45 a.m. to 1:36 p.m., attended by the President, Rusk, McNamara, McGeorge Bundy, Ball, Vance, Taylor, General Wheeler, Admiral Raborn, Helms, Walt Rostow (who would soon be named to succeed Bundy as the President's National Security Adviser), Moyers, Komer, Bromley Smith, as well as Clifford, the discussion centered on the question of whether the administration should propose a new or revised congressional resolution.[119] There was strong opposition. Rusk said he was against such a move except as a way "to beat Morse." McNamara was also opposed, as was Clifford. Ball said that they could "do nothing and ride it out," but if they did "the country will stay in an uproar," or they could propose several modifications in the preamble clause and operational provisions of the Gulf of Tonkin Resolution.[120] The notes do not indicate what position, if any, the President took on the question.

Although this was not mentioned in the notes, CIA Deputy Director Helms apparently pointed out during the meeting that if, in voting on a resolution, there were a number of congressional votes against the administration's position, this could help to give to the North Vietnamese the impression that weakening domestic support would eventually cause the U.S. to withdraw. In a memorandum

---

[118] *CR*, vol. 112, p. 5169. "Any negotiated settlement," Kennedy said, "must accept the fact that there are discontented elements in South Vietnam, Communist and non-Communist, who desire to change the existing political and economic system of the country. There are three things you can do with such groups: kill or repress them, turn the country over to them, or admit them to a share of power and responsibility. The first two are now possible only through force of arms. The last—to admit them to a share of power and responsibility is at the heart of the hope for a negotiated settlement." Kennedy's proposal was praised by various Democrats in Congress and by some elements of the press. See *ibid.*, pp. 4598 ff.; *New York Times*, Feb. 22 and 27, 1966; and Walter Lippmann's column in the *Washington Post*, Feb. 22, 1966. The administration was sharply critical of the idea, and Kennedy's position was attacked by McGeorge Bundy and George Ball, and by Vice President Humphrey, who said it would be like "putting a fox in a chicken coop." *New York Times*, Feb. 21, 1966.

On March 1, the House Republican Policy Committee issued a statement repeating some of Humphrey's comments and calling on the President to disavow Kennedy. Republicans, the statement said, were united behind the war, but divisions in the Democratic Party were "prolonging the war, undermining the morale of our fighting men, and encouraging the Communist aggressor." *CR*, vol. 112, p. 4596.

[119] The only known notes of the meeting are the sketchy handwritten notes of McGeorge Bundy, quoted here, which are in his papers in the Johnson Library, Notes on Vietnam.

In preparation for the meeting, the State Department Legal Adviser's office once again drafted a congressional resolution. (See the memorandum from Meeker to Ball, Feb. 21, 1966, in the State Department Lot File 74 D 272.) Although it was based primarily on the 1964 Gulf of Tonkin Resolution, several new paragraphs were added to provide, according to the cover memorandum, "some additional elements designed to have a reassuring and unifying effect on members of Congress who have expressed some disagreements or reservations about the Administration's course." One new paragraph declared congressional support for "the determination of the President to continue to exert every effort and to explore every avenue that might lead to a just and lasting peace in Southeast Asia." Another provided: "The Congress considers that close consultation should be continued between the Congress and the Executive Branch concerning developments in the situation in Southeast Asia including any major decisions on the conduct of hostilities and on efforts to achieve a peaceful settlement of the conflict."

[120] Ball was probably referring to the modifications proposed by Meeker in his draft resolution of February 21, cited above.

the next day (February 23) to Moyers, Helms elaborated on this point:[121] "It is understandably difficult to specify how many 'anti' votes would strengthen the North Vietnamese Government in its consistent belief that domestic pressure is going to force the President to stand down the war and bring about an outcome similar to that which occurred with France in 1954. Nevertheless I think it likely that as many as twenty votes against a new resolution would be interpreted as a significant erosion of the Administration's public backing in the United States." "I send this note to you," Helms added, "because it would seem to reinforce the recommendations yesterday of Messrs. Rusk, McNamara, and Clifford."

In the meeting on February 26, the President was asked about his position on whether to seek a congressional resolution supporting the administration's policy in Vietnam, and he replied that "nothing more need be done now."[122]

With respect to the motions pending in the Senate, the group agreed that Morse's motion should be allowed to be voted on, but that Russell's motion to reaffirm the Gulf of Tonkin Resolution should not be.

The President also discussed the state of public support for the administration's Vietnam policy, citing a Harris survey which he said indicated "that the extremists consisted of about ten percent doves and sixteen percent hawks." He added that he thought the rising cost of living was a "major element in determining public attitudes."

On February 28, as the debate ended on the bill providing for the military part of the supplemental request and the Senate prepared to vote on amendments, there was a meeting of Democratic Senators who were opposed to the war to consider a possible "sense of Congress" amendment. The purpose and contents of such an amendment were set forth in a memorandum, "Points to Make on Sense of Congress Amendment," prepared for the meeting by Norvill Jones, formerly an assistant to Fulbright, who was a professional staff member on the Foreign Relations Committee staff:[123]

> 1. The Administration will use the vote on this [bill] as a vote of approval for its policies, and as evidence of a further "commitment" to Vietnam.
>
> 2. The "snowballing" effect of what the Administration says are Congressional votes of approval can be stopped or slowed down by a "sense of Congress" rider.
>
> 3. Through the recent hearings the public has been made more aware of the dangers of the Vietnam conflict expanding into a war with China and Russia. This issue must continue to be emphasized through every means possible.

---

[121] Johnson Library, C.F. ND 19/CO 312.

[122] Johnson Library, NSF Files of Bromley Smith, notes of meeting on Vietnam Feb. 26, 1966. The meeting, at which follow-up on some of the matters discussed in Honolulu was also discussed, was attended by the President, the Vice President, Rusk, McNamara, McGeorge Bundy, Vance, U. Alexis Johnson, Wheeler, Raborn, Helms, Marks, Gaud, Unger, Rostow, and White House and NSC staff members Moyers, Komer, Valenti, and Bromley Smith. After the meeting, which lasted from 12:45 p.m. to 2:15 p.m., the President met with the Vice President, Rusk, McNamara and McGeorge Bundy from 2:16 p.m. to 2:50 p.m. There are no known notes of this latter meeting.

[123] National Archives, RG 46, Papers of the Committee on Foreign Relations.

4. We do not want to be in a position of blocking the bill but only in delaying it to permit considerable debate which can be continued with the aid supplemental.

5. There is no urgency on this bill—it is to buy long lead time items such as planes and for construction of bases. It does not contain any funds for direct troop support.

6. The Administration has slowly and steadily by increments committed the nation to a major war—in the process deceiving both the Congress and the Public about what was happening.

7. Congress has a responsibility to focus attention on the question of a declaration of war. The Administration is anxious to avoid this issue. Debate on this point is the only way that the seriousness of the situation can be driven home to the American people.

8. The Senate will be forced to vote on a policy statement whether it wants to or not and it is important that strategy be planned in recognition of this fact.

(a) Senator Morse will offer an amendment to rescind the Southeast Asia Resolution.

(b) Senator Russell will offer as a substitute a reaffirmation of the resolution.

(c) The planning should be in terms of what is feasible within these extremes.

The suggested sense of Congress amendment, according to the statement, would make three main points:

(a) Congress will support our boys in Vietnam.

(b) Congress favors a negotiated settlement and does not want to widen the war.

(c) The President should not expand the war without asking for a declaration of war.

The memorandum went on to say, "In order to avoid putting Senators in a position of choosing between Fulbright and Johnson, it may be advisable to have the amendment offered by a Senator who has not been publicly identified as anti-Administration on Vietnam." In addition, the memorandum suggested the possibility of having another amendment offered that would be less extreme than Morse's but more extreme than the proposed compromise amendment, "to make this one look even more reasonable (one urging Viet Cong be parties to negotiations, etc.)."

The meeting was attended by 12 Democratic Senators who were critical of the war, primarily those who had signed the letter to the President in January. Present were: Gore, Young (Ohio), McCarthy, McGovern, Gruening, Morse, Clark, Bartlett, Burdick, Moss, Fulbright and Robert Kennedy. Reportedly, the group first tried to persuade Morse not to call up his amendment to repeal the Gulf of Tonkin Resolution. Morse refused to do so, saying he had made commitments that he intended to keep. The group reportedly then discussed a compromise amendment, as described in the memorandum prepared by Jones. Even though several weeks earlier he had proposed such a move, Fulbright opposed the idea of an amendment of any kind, saying that it would get only 15 or 16 votes and that the administration could then claim a great victory. (When he had first proposed such an amendment he had said that he expected it would get 20–30 votes.) McCarthy argued that 15 votes would be better than not having a vote. "We've got a wild man in the White House," he was reported as saying, "and we are going to have to treat him as such." Gore was also concerned. "He described the President as a 'desperate man who was likely to get us into war with China, and we have got to prevent it. We all like the President, but we've got to stop him!'" Robert Kennedy agreed that a new resolution would be desirable, but also agreed with Fulbright that getting only 15 votes would be a defeat.[124]

The critics decided not to offer a compromise amendment. Instead, Mansfield, Fulbright and Russell then worked out an agreement by which Morse's proposal would be tabled, thus avoiding a direct vote on the proposal itself, in return for which Russell's proposed reaffirmation of the Gulf of Tonkin Resolution would not be offered.[125]

The Senate proceeded to act on Morse's amendment to repeal the Gulf of Tonkin Resolution. When he called it up the next day (March 1), Morse argued that the President was getting ready to send thousands of additional troops to Vietnam, and that Congress must stop the escalation, and should begin by repealing the Gulf of Tonkin Resolution. Russell disagreed. He noted that he had opposed the original decision to send military aid and advisers to Vietnam, and that he was "not now in favor of intervention throughout the entire world. By instinct and inclination, I must confess that I am an isolationist. I do not believe that the might and power of the United States can bring about the millennium." He added that he was "a congressional man. I have stood here for more than 32 years and deplored—almost wept over—the slow erosion of congressional power. . . ." But he said he could not "plead ignorance." He had known that the Gulf of Tonkin Resolution conferred "a very great grant of power." As for the pending bill, it was necessary for the support of U.S. forces. "I am going to throw the rope," he declared.

Russell also said that he would interpret a vote against repeal of the Gulf of Tonkin Resolution as reaffirmation of the resolution. Javits disagreed, but asserted that the President had the "constitutional authority . . . to intercede in Vietnam or any place with the Armed Forces of the United States where the interests of the United States are in such imminent danger." The Gulf of Tonkin Resolution, he added, "was not juridically necessary and it has no juridical force. But in terms of policy it is critically important. It committed us to Presidential policy as of that time." If Congress felt that the President had abused his constitutional power, he said, Congress had a remedy: "deny him the money."

Fulbright said it was unfortunate that Morse's proposal was forcing "a decision on the floor as to whether the Senate should reaffirm policies which I do not wish to reaffirm. . . ." He thought the vote on the Gulf of Tonkin Resolution should be delayed "to a better day so we can make the decision under more favorable circumstances . . . where the matter of our involvement in Vietnam as a matter of national policy can be discussed as freely as possible

---

[124] This account of the February 28 meeting is based on the "Washington Merry-Go-Round" column by Drew Pearson, *Washington Post*, Mar. 10, 1966.

[125] *New York Times*, Mar. 1, 1966.

and without being intertwined into our flag. . . . It makes it very difficult, really, for us to discuss a matter of high policy under these circumstances." He went on to say that Morse did not have the votes to pass the amendment. "I like to argue theory in other forums, but in the Senate we have to recognize the facts and vote accordingly on an issue which could if pressed have the effect of reaffirming a policy I do not wish to reaffirm. This may not be a very gallant or straightforward way in ordinary business, but in politics, I believe it is perfectly logical and necessary, certainly in this instance."

Mansfield then moved to table Morse's amendment, saying that it was "inappropriate and inadvisable in connection with this bill at this time. . . . We are in too deep now. The situation is one of the utmost delicacy and the risk of misinterpretation is very great."

On the motion to table, of the 97 Senators (of the 100 Members of the Senate) present and voting, 92 voted to table, thus killing the amendment, and 5—Morse and Gruening, joined by Fulbright, McCarthy, and Young (Ohio), voted not to table.[126]

Gruening then called up an amendment, co-sponsored by Morse, to provide that no draftee could be sent to Vietnam involuntarily without action by Congress. This was tabled 94–2, with Gruening and Morse in opposition.

On March 1, 1966, the military supplemental bill was passed by the Senate by a vote of 93–2, with Gruening and Morse voting no.

Nelson and McGovern, both of whom were very critical of the war, voted to table the two amendments and voted for the bill.[127] Nelson said he voted against repealing the Gulf of Tonkin Resolution because he did not think it was in the national interest to withdraw that commitment. He also did not think the commitment should be broadened, however.

McGovern said he voted for the military supplemental because although he had opposed the war, ". . . since we have sent 300,000 men to southeast Asia, we have no practical alternative now except to provide them with the equipment they need to survive."

McCarthy said that although he voted against tabling the Morse amendment, he would also have voted against the amendment itself if it had been put to a direct vote, as well as against any

---

[126] For the vote, see *CR*, vol. 112, p. 4404. Of the three Senators who were not present, two said that they would have voted to table. The third—Church—did not indicate how he would have voted.

[127] At noon that day (March 1), before the vote occurred, George Ball had lunch with Senators McGovern, Clark, Ribicoff and Tydings at McGovern's request. In a memorandum on March 1 to the President, Ball said that he indicated his support for U.S. policy in Vietnam, and asked the "dissenting Senators," as he said they described themselves, to suggest alternatives. "Their only suggestion," he said, "was that we follow a 'Gavin-Kennan' policy which they defined as 'staying where we are with what we have on the ground.'" He said he argued that this was "totally unrealistic," and went on to explain why, as well as to respond to several questions. U.S. Department of State, Lot File 74 D 272.

The next day (March 2), Ball had lunch with Walter Lippmann, a neighbor and close friend, and argued strenuously that Lippmann should cease attacking the President's policy. Ball said he thought that if Johnson had been elected in 1960 it was "highly likely" that the U.S. would have followed a different course, but that the time had come to stop giving encouragement to the Communists by "philosophical argument that had no practical effect except to prolong the fighting." He told Lippmann that he (Ball) "was now persuaded that with more than 200,000 men in South Vietnam and several thousand casualties we had no option but to carry on the war until we had achieved our political objectives." U.S. Department of State, Central File, Pol 27 Viet S, memorandum from Ball to the President, Mar. 3, 1966.

amendment proposal to reconfirm the Gulf of Tonkin Resolution. He was critical of the practice of passing resolutions:

> If we are to allow this practice to grow and establish precedents whereby resolutions of this kind begin to take on strength of their own, the only logical conclusion is that, first, the constitutional powers which Presidents have exercised since the country was founded are being challenged, and perhaps even undermined.
>
> Second. There is danger in this kind of resolution that there may be a growth of tradition and the establishment of precedents of power in the Congress which it does not possess and which is not provided for under the Constitution.
>
> Third. There is danger that resolutions of this kind will be turned against Congress in order to prevent criticism or discredit critics. Whether the attempt would be successful or not is an open question, but if we are concerned about protecting the constitutional powers of the President, if we are concerned with not making the Senate into a kind of garden club which passes resolutions with reference to Presidential powers, and if we are concerned perhaps with the freedom of this body to carry out its own constitutional responsibilities in the field of foreign policy, resolutions of this kind should not be approved in the future.

As debate on the bill ended, Fulbright, seeking in part to reply to the argument that critics had not offered an alternative, made a major speech in which he proposed a plan for the neutralization of Southeast Asia under which both the U.S. and China would withdraw their military power from the region.[128] Noting that "the practical choice before us is between a policy of accelerated war . . . and a policy of deescalation aimed at negotiation and an accommodation between the parties to the South Vietnamese civil war," he said: "Unless we are prepared to fight a general war to eliminate the effects of Chinese power in all of Southeast Asia, we have no alternative but to seek a general accommodation." Fulbright said he doubted whether the Chinese would agree to an accommodation in view of the growing American military effort, which the Chinese might assume would lead to declining support at home and to U.S. withdrawal from the region. China might be induced to accept accommodation, however, if confronted with the "prospect which she most fears" of permanent U.S. military bases on its periphery consisting of enclaves on the coast or inland where appropriate, as General Gavin had recommended during the hearings, which could be held with little cost or loss of lives and thus could be more easily justified to the American public.

On March 19, Fulbright wrote to the President to suggest that consideration be given to such a plan.

Congress Approves Supplemental Funds for Vietnam

On March 1, 1966, the same day that the Senate passed the supplemental military authorization, the bill was passed also by the House, 393–4, with four liberal Democrats—George E. Brown (Calif.), Phillip Burton (Calif.), John Conyers, Jr. (Mich.), and Wil-

[128] *CR*, vol. 112, pp. 4379 ff., and the *New York Times*, Mar. 2, 1966.

liam Fitts Ryan (N.Y.) voting no. Once again, those in charge of the bill said it was not a vote on policy, thus enabling most critics of the war to declare that they were voting for the bill because of the need to support U.S. forces, and were not approving an expansion of the war.[129]

Meanwhile, the House had passed on February 24 the bill authorizing the foreign aid portion of the supplemental request. The vote was 350–27. Brown was the only critic of the war who voted against the bill. The other 26 votes in opposition came from some of the conservatives who opposed the foreign aid program. Some Members who were opposed to the war said they supported the bill because it provided funds for the "other war," which most of them strongly supported.[130]

On March 8, 1966, the Senate Foreign Relations Committee reported the same foreign aid portion of the supplemental request, with only Morse voting no.[131] In "marking up" the bill the commit-

---

[129] At least 78 of these, all Democrats, and almost all liberals, signed a statement to this effect. See *CR*, vol. 112, p. 4431. House discussion of the bill is on pp. 4427–4475.

[130] For House proceedings on the bill see *ibid.*, pp. 4001–4037.

[131] S. Rept. 98–1060. On February 23, Marcy sent a memorandum to Fulbright in which he posed several questions for the Committee's consideration. (National Archives, RG 46, Marcy Chron File.) He asked what the committee's views were on the situation in Vietnam as a result of the hearings, whether there was majority agreement "on the delicate expression of any policy conclusion?" and whether the committee had any preference for expressing its views through an amendment to the policy statement in the bill, a sense of Congress resolution, or supplemental views in the committee report.

With his memorandum Marcy sent Fulbright the text of a suggested statement of supplemental views which could be used in the committee report, the principal provisions of which were as follows:

"In its public hearings which examined the political and military implications of U.S. involvement in Vietnam, the Committee was deeply conscious of its limitations. It did not wish to request in public sessions the revelation of information which might be helpful to the other side. It did not wish to convey any implication that it was involved in tactical detail and trying to run the war. Nevertheless, the Committee felt that it was imperative to examine tactical decisions which had outrun tactics and become matters of the utmost policy significance.

"The Committee concedes that the sending of 20,000 men to Vietnam as had occurred at the time of the Southeast Asia resolution might be viewed as a proper tactical decision for the Commander-in-chief. But when that number increased ten-fold, to 200,000, significant new foreign policy questions were raised. . . .

"We believe that the following conclusions based upon the hearings of the Committee on Foreign Relations are proper statements falling within our constitutional obligation to advise the President in the conduct of foreign policy. (These propositions range roughly from those upon which there is the clearest agreement to those of questionable acceptability).

"1. It is unfortunate that the United States has become so deeply involved militarily in Vietnam.

"2. The investment of over $2 billion in AID funds since 1954 has shown very slim, if any, results in building a viable economy or political unity.

"3. While to some extent U.S. aid shortcomings are attributable to Vietcong activity, much is attributable to inconsistent policies and poor administration.

"4. The Vietnamese Government has not been, and shows little likelihood in the near future of being, broadly representative of the people under its control.

"5. American troops should not become involved in a "land war" in Asia. The involvement of much more than 200,000 men begins to assume that nature and should not be undertaken without the specific approval of the Congress as required by Article I, Section 8, paragraph 11 of the Constitution.

"6. The United States should do all within its power to avoid war with North Vietnam or China.

"7. If either of these eventualities should occur, there would be serious likelihood that the demand on American forces for the use of nuclear weapons would be irresistible, and the consequences of such acts upon world opinion could be catastrophic.

"8. The concept heard in some quarters that China must be destroyed now or later is rejected.

"9. The integrity, loyalty, and devotion of presidential advisers on U.S. policies in Vietnam is not questioned. There is doubt, however, whether their past judgments have been valid and it is believed that they have become so committed to the present course of action as to impair their objectivity in passing judgment as to the domestic and international consequences of continuation of the present course of action.

"10. The United States wants no permanent base or bases in Southeast Asia.

"11. In our opinion, the majority of the American people are not convinced that the interests of the United States—whether those interests are defined as 'defending freedom,' 'resisting com-

tee defeated two Vietnam-related amendments. The first, by Fulbright, provided that U.S. assistance of any kind to another country was "not to be construed as a commitment to use armed forces of the United States for the defense of such country." Fulbright offered it after becoming concerned—partly as a result of Rusk's testimony on January 24, in which he cited foreign aid commitments as one element of U.S. commitments to Vietnam—that foreign aid commitments were being used as an entering wedge for U.S. involvement, thus setting the stage for military intervention.[132] There was a long discussion of the amendment at an executive session of the committee on March 7. Hickenlooper, the senior Republican, was strongly opposed to any Vietnam-related amendment that might appear to represent weakness on the American side. He said that the administration had already made too many concessions, and that the U.S. had to avoid giving the impression that it was weary of the war. A number of other members expressed their fear that if the committee voted to include the amendment in the bill and it was subsequently defeated in the Senate, the President could claim another victory over Congress. It was also argued that such a defeat could enable the executive branch to make the opposite claim, namely, that foreign aid commitments *could* be construed as a basis for committing the Armed Forces. The alternative, suggested by Pell, of putting the language in the committee report rather than in the bill, was also discussed at some length before being rejected.

The vote on Fulbright's amendment was 6–13, with Fulbright, Morse, Gore, Church, Clark, and Pell voting for it, and Sparkman, Mansfield, Hickenlooper, Aiken, Long, Lausche, Symington, Dodd, McCarthy, Frank Carlson (R/Kan.), Williams (Del.), Karl E. Mundt (R/S. Dak.), and Case voting no.[133] (As will be seen, however, a modified version of Fulbright's amendment was subsequently approved and became law.)

---

munism,' or 'opposing aggression'—are sufficiently involved in the war in Vietnam to justify further U.S. unilateral expansion of military effort there—considering the price to be paid in domestic programs and in the weakening of U.S. influence and power elsewhere in the world.

"12. This position might be changed if the 42 military allies of the United States—or even half of them—would supply token forces of 1000 men each. There would then be convincing evidence that other nations view the war in Vietnam as of significance to their own security and in defense of freedom. This is not now the case.

"13. Not more than a dozen nations the world over agree as a matter of public government policy that, as the President said in Hawaii, 'if we allow the Communists to win in Vietnam it will become easier and more appetizing for them to take over other countries in other parts of the world.' And if we do not stop the Communists here, 'we will have to fight again someplace else. . . .'

"14. The United States should maintain (but not increase) its present strength in Vietnam but express its willingness to withdraw when the following conditions have been met:

"a. There is in existence in South Vietnam a coalition government which is reasonably representative of various groups having their residence in South Vietnam—the existence of such a Government being determined by the Control Commission or some other international body;

"b. There is assurance that the basic human rights of minority groups shall not be violated;

"c. North Vietnam undertakes to honor the territorial integrity of South Vietnam until a referendum under the auspices of an appropriate international body shall determine the issue.

"15. If the independence of South Vietnam as a neutral nation is assured, the United States would be ready to assist that nation to recover from the effects of the last twenty years of war."

This statement was not used in the Foreign Relations Committee report.

[132] See Senate Foreign Relations Committee hearings on *Supplemental Foreign Assistance Fiscal Year 1966—Vietnam,* p. 581, cited above.

[133] U.S. Congress, Senate, Committee on Foreign Relations, *Executive Sessions of the Senate Foreign Relations Committee* (Historical Series), 1966, vol. XVIII (Washington, D.C.: U.S. Govt. Print. Off., 1993), pp. 609–641 passim.

Church then offered an amendment on behalf of McGovern, who was not a member of the committee, to provide that passage of the bill "shall not be construed as a ratification" of previous or future U.S. decisions on Vietnam. The amendment also expressed the sense of Congress, as the Javits-Randolph amendment also did, that the U.S. should seek to minimize military involvement in favor of the "other war." The McGovern amendment was defeated 5–14, with only Pell switching from the earlier vote on the Fulbright amendment.

The administration had opposed both amendments. A letter from Rusk to Fulbright on March 6 stated that the President had been acting "fully within his constitutional powers and in consonance with purposes jointly declared by the executive and legislative branches." Rusk cited the Gulf of Tonkin Resolution as well as the 92–5 vote on Morse's repeal amendment. "Under these circumstances," the letter continued, both amendments "would create confusion in the minds of our friends, make our enemies more obdurate and militate against the interests" of the U.S. American forces, he said, needed the "unqualified support of their government," and it was essential for Congress and the President to be united.[134]

According to press reports, Rusk's letter irritated some members of the committee, and Eugene McCarthy "grew red in the face with anger as he expostulated against the letter and the implication that a vote for either amendment was equivalent to nonsupport of the United States troops and comfort to the enemy."[135]

In its report on the Vietnam supplemental foreign aid bill, the Foreign Relations Committee expressed the hope that the funds would be effective in supporting the "other war," but it was skeptical that this would be the case:[136]

> The committee finds little room for encouragement under existing circumstances about the prospects for our aid being effective in molding sound economic and social developments leading to a better way of life for the people of South Vietnam. Until the military situation improves, our aid program is likely to be little more than a holding operation, keeping the wolves of rampant inflation away from the door, and providing relief where needed. The committee hopes that the officials of the South Vietnamese Government will vigorously pursue a program of economic and social reforms as pledged in the Declaration of Honolulu. This committee will remain skeptical until words are matched with measurable deeds.

In supplemental views, Church and Clark, explaining their support for the McGovern amendment, which Church had offered, said that evidence presented to the committee raised questions about U.S. involvement in Southeast Asia and demonstrated that it was having an adverse effect on other U.S. foreign policy interests as well as on domestic interests.

---

[134] U.S. Department of State, Lot File 70 D 207, letter from Rusk to Fulbright, Mar. 6, 1966.
[135] *New York Times*, Mar. 8, 1966.
[136] S. Rept. 98–1060.

Senate debate on the supplemental foreign aid bill on March 10, 1966, was brief and perfunctory, and the bill was passed, 82–2, with Morse and Gruening voting no.[137]

Passage by Congress of the two supplemental authorization bills (military aid and foreign aid) cleared the way for Congress to pass the third bill—the supplemental appropriations bill itself—required for approval of the $12.7 billion supplemental request for Vietnam for the remainder of FY 1966. This was passed by the House on March 15, 1966 after a number of speeches but very little substantive debate. No amendments were offered. The House vote was almost identical to the vote on the military bill on February 24—389 to 3, with Burton (Calif.), Conyers, and Ryan voting no. Brown of California, who had voted no on the military and foreign aid authorization bills, was absent.[138]

There was somewhat more of a policy discussion when the Senate debated the bill, but Senate critics of the war generally conceded that the new funds were necessary for the support of American forces.

Once again, Russell warned that the public would not support a long, inconclusive war:

> I do not think we can afford to let this war drift on and on as it is now. Search-and-destroy tactics may, after 10 or 12 years, bring the Vietcong to their knees; but the American people are going to be very unhappy about it. . . .
>
> It is going to be necessary to have a change of policy in some direction in the very near future, in my opinion, or this war will assume political proportions that will absolutely force it upon any man who has to go before the electorate of this country and seek public office.

Russell repeated that the U.S. should close the port at Haiphong, and through this and other steps seek to force the North Vietnamese to negotiate. Symington agreed. McGovern and others questioned whether such a move would achieve the desired result.

The Senate passed the supplemental appropriations bill, on March 22, 1966, 87–2, with Morse and Gruening voting no.[139]

Thus, Congress approved the entire FY 1966 $12.7 billion supplemental request for Vietnam with only a few votes in opposition and without any policy amendments. It was clear that although there were 25-30 Senators and 100 or more Representatives who were opposed to the war, or at least to the way in which it was being conducted, the President and his allies in Congress, both Democrats and Republicans, were still firmly in control of the legislative situation. It was also clear, however, that Congress was becoming more divided on the war, and that the unity represented by the virtually unanimous approval of the supplemental appropriation was more apparent than real.

---

[137] *CR*, vol. 112, p. 5563.

[138] For House proceedings on the bill see *ibid.*, pp. 5802–5823. For hearings by the House Appropriations Committee on Jan. 26 and 28, 1966 on the supplemental appropriations bill see *Supplemental Defense Appropriations for 1966*, 89th Cong., 2d sess. (Washington, D.C.: U.S. Govt. Print. Off., 1966). During testimony by McNamara and Wheeler, several senior Democrats and Republicans on the committee, noting public concern, questioned what the plans were for winning the war and why the early predictions of success had not been accurate.

[139] For the Senate proceedings see *CR*, vol. 112, pp. 6389–6419, 6441–6462.

Hearings on China

On March 8, 1966, the day after it reported the foreign aid bill, the Senate Foreign Relations Committee began seven days of open hearings on U.S. policy toward China.[140] The announced purpose of the hearings was "education"—to provide a forum for experts to testify concerning U.S. policy toward China, including policy alternatives. The real but unannounced purpose was to continue and to broaden the Vietnam hearings.

The idea for the hearings originated in a meeting between Senator Fulbright and Allen Whiting who, as noted earlier, was one of the principal China experts in the State Department. Whiting was opposed to the war and was quite concerned about Chinese intervention, and he had decided that he would have to resign after a final trip to South Vietnam. Before going, he talked privately to Max Frankel of the *New York Times,* who talked to James Reston. Frankel then asked Whiting to have lunch, at which he told him that Reston said that he would arrange for Whiting to talk to Fulbright in complete confidence. Whiting agreed, and he and Fulbright met. Fulbright said that he had no access to the President but that he could hold hearings. He suggested that they should be held on China rather than on Vietnam, and asked for Whiting's advice on format and witnesses. They agreed that the hearings would be held while Whiting was on his trip in order to avoid implicating Whiting.[141]

During the hearings, Fulbright and others on the committee, in addition to questioning the witnesses about China, asked a number of questions about the Vietnam war, about Chinese attitudes and policy toward the war and toward the North Vietnamese, possible Chinese interventions in the war, and how the U.S. could influence the role of China in relation to the war. There was general agreement among the witnesses and members of the committee (the few who attended and commented) that the Chinese Communists posed a threat to countries of Asia, especially Southeast Asia, and must be "contained"—quite a different note than the dissenting testimony in the earlier Vietnam hearings. It was also generally agreed, with various shades of difference among witnesses and among members of the committee, that it was vital for the U.S. to help maintain the "power balance" of Asia, and that its effort to prevent the Communists from taking control of South Vietnam was an essential aspect of that objective. Most of the witnesses shared Fulbright's (and Whiting's) concern about the war and about a possible war with China, but very little hope was expressed for Fulbright's proposal for the neutralization of Southeast Asia. Some of the witnesses saw scant hope for a change in China's policy or what they considered to be its expansionist tendencies, but most witnesses and members of the committee seemed to agree, as Prof. John K. Fairbank recommended, that the U.S. should move from a position of trying to isolate China to one of "motivating" the Chinese toward an "acceptance of the international world" and "par-

---

[140] U.S. Congress, Senate, Committee on Foreign Relations, *U.S. Policy With Respect to Mainland China,* Hearings on March 8, 10, 16, 18, 21, 28, 30, 1966, 89th Cong., 2d sess. (Washington, D.C.: U.S. Govt. Print. Off., 1966).

[141] This information was provided by Allen Whiting and is used with his permission.

ticipation in the world scene."[142] Fairbank added, however, that at the same time there had to be "a cognate attitude of firmness backed by force." "Military containment on the Korean border, in the Taiwan Straits, and somehow in Vietnam cannot soon be abandoned and may have to be maintained for some time."

On March 23, 1966, as the China hearings were concluding, Marcy sent Chairman Fulbright the following memorandum discussing the steps that the committee might take to continue to focus attention on the war:[143]

> Senator:
>
> My thinking on the future role of the Committee runs along these lines:
>
> 1. There are two points to Committee hearings on non-legislative subjects;
>
>   a. to educate the public, or
>
>   b. to get the Administration to do something, or both.
>
> 2. In both instances publicity is the crucial feature.
>
> 3. When the Committee is active in foreign policy, it is competing with the President for publicity. He can command radio, TV, the press, and has his own publications. (For example, State Department publications on Vietnam include only the statements of Rusk and Taylor, not Gavin or Kennan).
>
> 4. The Vietnam and China hearings have put the Committee back in the limelight. This is a consequence of the caliber of the witnesses and, more important, the fact that the majority of the Committee disagrees with the fundamentals of our policies.
>
> 5. Where does the Committee go from here? Here are the possibilities:
>
>   a. Subside; moving gently to some other subject of a less controversial nature. Non-proliferation; Disarmament; NATO.
>
>   b. Go back to the regular order; i.e., Foreign Aid. This will provide a qualified easing out of the present subjects, but I suspect that Rusk, Bell and McNamara will be questioned about Vietnam and commitments regardless of their aid testimony.
>
>   c. Return to the subject of Vietnam and Southeast Asia on the theory that now, with background on China, the Committee might look again to the nature of the war in Vietnam. If the Committee were to move back into this subject with Goldwater, LeMay, Nixon and similar witnesses, the publicity process would be rejuvenated and there might be some interesting educational fall out. Vietnam, which tragically is now moving to the back pages at the time casualties are rising, would be in the forefront again.
>
> 6. I am inclined to think that the non-proliferation course spins the wheels until we have made some settlement in Vietnam and while this would be important it would be a waste of Committee time and energy.

[142] *U.S. Policy with Respect to Mainland China,* p. 107.

[143] National Archives, RG 46, Papers of the Senate Foreign Relations Committee, Marcy Chron File.

> To proceed with hearings on Foreign Aid—upon which course we are now tentatively embarked—would be a compromise between the two positions.
>
> The third course, to come back to Vietnam, would be politically dangerous but it would keep the Committee in the midst of the crucial decisions relating to war and peace. I am inclined to think that with all its dangers, this is the role the Committee should try to play.

Although the committee did not hold further hearings on the subject of Vietnam, it continued to provide a forum for raising questions about Vietnam during hearings on foreign aid and other subjects. In addition, of course, Fulbright and other members of the committee continued to speak out. While Marcy's hopes were not realized, it may have been unrealistic to think that the committee could have remained in the limelight. The 1966 hearings gained attention and extensive television coverage because they were the first open inquiry by Congress into Vietnam policy, because they featured the split between the President and the chairman of the Foreign Relations Committee, and because they focused attention on the war and its problems at a time when the public was beginning to be aware and interested.[144]

[144] Another reason for not acting on Marcy's suggestion to return to Vietnam was the feeling on the part of those on the committee who were opposed to the war that the committee should "not move too fast . . . get too far ahead of the rest of Congress." There was concern that the committee's role and influence might be weakened if it were perceived as getting "too far out in left field." Author's telephone conversation with Norvill Jones, July 12, 1993.

CHAPTER 7

WHIRLWIND: THE BUDDHIST PROTEST, SPRING 1966

Beginning in March 1966, and continuing until mid-June, there were serious political disturbances in South Vietnam, so serious that for a time the future of the existing government (the military Directorate, or "Directory") appeared very doubtful, and American policymakers began to consider alternative courses of action if the situation became more critical.[1] As President Johnson said in his memoirs, "Our deepest worry at that time was not the military threat of the Communists, but the prospect of another major political crisis in South Vietnam."[2]

Following the Honolulu Conference in early February, at which the U.S. indicated its continued strong support for Premier Ky and Chief of State Thieu, Buddhist leaders and others who were opposed to the military junta and wanted the war ended began to agitate for changes in the government—the so-called "Struggle Movement."[3] The U.S. Government was fully apprised of these developments. John Negroponte, a CIA officer serving as Second Secretary of the U.S. Embassy in Saigon, reported that on February 25, in a conversation which he arranged, the more moderate of the two principal Buddhist leaders, Tam Chau, chairman of the Institute for the Propagation of the Buddhist Faith (the other principal leader was Tri Quang),[4] expressed concern about the political situation

---

[1] For detailed information on these events see the *New York Times*. Also useful are Fitzgerald, *Fire in the Lake*, George McT. Kahin, *Intervention: How America Became Involved in Vietnam* (New York: Knopf, 1986), and Robert Shaplen, *The Road from War, Vietnam 1965–1970* (New York: Harper and Row, 1970). See also the *Pentagon Papers*, Gravel ed., vols. II and IV. For the role of the U.S. military in the crisis see Clarke, *Advice and Support*, Shulimson, *U.S. Marines in Vietnam, An Expanding War, 1966*, and Hammond, *Public Affairs: The Military and the Media, 1962–1968*, Westmoreland, *A Soldier Reports*, pp. 169–176, and Gen. Lewis W. Walt, *Strange War, Strange Strategy: A General's Report on Vietnam* (New York: Funk and Wagnalls, 1970).

In the State Department Central File, Pol 27 Viet S there are numerous "situation reports" which the U.S. Embassy in Saigon cabled to Washington several times a day during the more critical points in April and May. There is also a detailed 82-page daily account, "The March-June 1966 Political Crisis in South Vietnam and Its Effects on Military Operations," prepared by Don M. Larrimore, Military History Branch, Office of the Secretary, Joint Staff, MACV.

[2] Johnson, *The Vantage Point*, p. 246.

[3] For one explanation of the movement by Americans with extensive experience in Vietnam, see Don Luce and John Sommer, *Viet Nam—The Unheard Voices* (Ithaca, N.Y.: Cornell Univ. Press, 1969) pp. 120–137. Luce had been the director of the International Voluntary Services teams in South Vietnam, a project similar to the Peace Corps. In the summer of 1967, he resigned in protest against the war.

For an explanation of Buddhism and Buddhist views of the war by a monk who was known as a scholar and a poet, see Thich Nhat Hanh, *Vietnam: Lotus in a Sea of Fire* (New York: Hill and Wang, 1967). In a foreword, Catholic philosopher Thomas Merton says that "While many of his countrymen are divided and find themselves, through choice or through compulsion, supporting the Saigon government and the Americans, or formally and explicitly committed to Communism, Nhat Hanh speaks for the vast majority who know little of politics but who seek to preserve something of Vietnam's traditional identity as an Asian and largely Buddhist culture. Above all, they want to *live* and see an end to a brutal and useless war." (emphasis in original)

[4] *New York Times* referred to the institute with which Tam Chau was associated as the "Buddhist Institute of Secular Affairs." Tri Quang was secretary general of the High Council of the

Continued

and the growing uneasiness among Buddhists about the Ky government. "Chau remarked gloomily that the political situation is going from bad to worse. Corruption increases every day and the masses, preoccupied with the rising cost of living, are 'fed up.'" Moreover, recent appointments of Catholics to the Cabinet had given rise to new concerns among the Buddhists that the government was reverting to some of the objectionable political practices of the Diem era.[5]

In a report on March 2 covering developments during the previous week, the CIA stated: "Despite the Ky Government's efforts to sustain the momentum generated in the wake of the Honolulu conference, there have been further indications of a hardening attitude in some circles toward the character and performance of the military regime. These signs were particularly evident during the past week in Buddhist circles, which have reacted negatively to Ky's cabinet reorganization, and among certain political and intellectual circles which appear skeptical of the government's willingness and ability to carry out reforms in the political, economic and social fields. . . . According to a fairly reliable journalist, a group of prominent Saigon politicians, including former Deputy Premier Tran Van Tuyen and possibly current Foreign Minister Tran Van Do, are working on plans for a new government with support from unidentified young Saigon intellectuals. Tuyen is alleged to have told the group presently that he expected peace and neutralization of South Vietnam in about six months."[6]

On March 9, Ambassador Lodge received a telephone call from Ky's office asking him to come immediately for a meeting with the Premier. At the meeting, Ky spoke of the problem he was having with one of the members of the Directorate, General Nguyen Chanh Thi, commander of South Vietnamese forces in I Corp in central Vietnam. Thi, considered to be Ky's most powerful rival, was known to have strong political support, especially in his native central Vietnam. (In the summer of 1965, he had been chosen by

---

United Buddhist Association and president of the Association of Buddhist Monks in Central Vietnam and of the General Association of Buddhist Monks. (The *New York Times* referred to Tri Quang as leader of the "Institute of Religious Affairs of the United Buddhist Church.")

Of the 15 million people in South Vietnam, 1.5 million were Christian, largely Catholic. Most of the remaining 13.5 million were nominally Buddhist, but it was estimated that 6 million of these were "practicing" Buddhists. Most of the Buddhists were indigenous southerners, whereas most of the Catholics were refugees from North Vietnam. The Government of South Vietnam had been dominated by the Catholics, beginning with Ngo Dinh Diem in 1954. Ky was a nominal Buddhist; Thieu was a Catholic.

[5] For Negroponte's report see U.S. Department of State, Central File, Pol 27 Viet S, Airgram A505 from Saigon to Washington, Mar. 1, 1966.

A memorandum on Mar. 19, 1966 by the State Department's Bureau of Intelligence and Research gave a succinct summary of the position of the Buddhists (Johnson Library, NSF Country File, Vietnam):

"Buddhist demands reflect longstanding grievances against the Ky-Thieu leadership which is felt to have moved too slowly and grudgingly to legalize its status, hold national elections, and, return the reins of government to elected officials—in general reversing rather than furthering the 1963 revolution. Although advanced particularly by Tri Quang and his Buddhist and student followers, these views appear to be widely shared among other Buddhists, students, intellectuals, and out-politicians. Many of these critics are almost certainly motivated by personal and political ambitions and by their basic antipathy to almost any conceivable government. But many others regard 'the revolution,' however vague their understanding of even its broad outlines, as the only means of achieving any degree of political stability and national unity in the face of the Communist insurgency. Legalization of the government, therefore, has become an issue synonymous with stabilization among an increasingly large sector of the politically articulate elements of Vietnamese society."

[6] Johnson Library, NSF Country File, Vietnam, CIA Weekly Report on *The Situation in South Vietnam*, Mar. 2, 1966, OCI No. 0364/66. The report did not identify the "fairly reliable journalist."

the other members of the Directorate to be Premier, but, knowing that he would be opposed by the Americans, partly because of his close ties to the Buddhists, he declined the job, and Ky, a nominal Buddhist, was selected.)

Ky told Lodge that Thi was "becoming more and more difficult. His judgment was poor, he had delusions of grandeur, he did none of the things that were expected of him. . . . He was deliberately insubordinate." With Thi controlling one-fourth of the country, Ky said, "Vietnam could not really call itself a nation."

Ky asked Lodge for advice about removing Thi, saying that at a meeting earlier that day other members of the junta had favored removal. He added that he could not continue as Premier unless this was done. Lodge replied that, as U.S. Ambassador, he could not comment, but speaking unofficially and as a friend he thought Ky should plan his moves carefully and should document his case against Thi before acting.

In his unpublished "Viet-Nam Memoir," Lodge said that after talking with Ky he consulted with members of the U.S. Mission Council, and that "everyone agreed that there might be trouble but that if Ky was determined to go ahead with his move against Thi, we should not thwart him."[7]

In his "Flash" cable to Washington reporting on the conversation with Ky, Lodge said that he was sympathetic with Ky's view that his orders should be carried out, but he hoped that Ky would reconsider the decision to remove Thi.[8]

The State Department responded that same day with a forceful "Flash" cable stating its deep concern about the possible consequences of Thi's removal.[9] Lodge's report, it said, had "quite frankly taken us completely by surprise since we were aware of no recent indication that Thi was not cooperating with government at least in his usual somewhat autonomous fashion." "We must make clear our deep concern . . . over any actions that would weaken or bring down the present government and with it the military and development efforts which have been so laboriously brought to at least beginning of hopeful stage." Rather than removing Thi, the cable suggested that the other generals call him in for a "Dutch uncle" talk that might make him more cooperative, and would at least allow time to prepare the groundwork with the Buddhists and the students for his removal.

Rusk's cable to Lodge concluded:

> Realize this is uniquely problem which must be decided in Saigon but I know you realize depth and gravity of US commitment and how disastrous it would be to everything we are trying to do there and our efforts here to support it if there should develop a split in GVN.

After receiving Washington's reply, Lodge met again with Ky and urged him not to remove Thi unless he could be sure of success. Ky, supported by Thieu, told Lodge that Thi could be removed

---

[7] Massachusetts Historical Society, Lodge Papers, "Vietnam Memoir," cited above, pt. IV, ch. III, p. 5.

[8] This cable, Saigon to Washington 3260, Mar. 9, 1966, which the author did not find in the State Department files, was obtained from CMH, Westmoreland Papers, History File.

[9] Same location, Washington to Saigon 2653, Mar. 9, 1966.

without difficulty.[10] In a memorandum to President Johnson reporting on these developments, NSC Executive Secretary Bromley Smith said that *"Ambassador Lodge appears to have done everything he can to assure that a coup does not result from the confrontation of the two Generals."* (emphasis in original)[11]

Anti-Government Protests Begin in Central Vietnam and Saigon

On March 10, the Military Directorate voted unanimously to remove Thi (who was present and dutifully voted for his own dismissal), and to expel him from the country for four months. Thi told his U.S. military adviser, Jasper Wilson, that he did not want to leave the country. Wilson advised him to "go gracefully."[12] Ky then asked the U.S. for help in getting Thi to leave, and, at the request of Lodge, Westmoreland issued an invitation for Thi to go to the United States for "medical treatment" of an alleged sinus condition.[13]

At the news of Thi's removal, Buddhist demonstrations in support of Thi began in Danang, Hue and other parts of I Corps. In a cable to the President, Lodge said that the Buddhists "obviously read the new political situation in I Corps as an opportunity to bring pressure on the government hoping either to transform it into a creature subject to their will or to replace it with a government to their liking."[14] "The U.S. Mission," Lodge added, "is leaving no stone unturned and [we] are in contact at virtually all points. I have a card to play in my relations with the two Buddhist leaders, Tri Quang and Tam Chau, and am studying how best to do it."

The Buddhists called for the resignation of Ky and Thieu and the election of a civilian government and a representative assembly. They also criticized the role of the United States. "These students and intellectuals," according to an article by Neil Sheehan in the *New York Times*, April 24, 1966, "fear that traditional Vietnamese society will not survive the American cultural and economic impact. They see the United States as a neo-imperialist power that is gradually eroding South Vietnam's independence with its military might."

Contributing to the discontent, Sheehan reported, was the severe inflation in South Vietnam brought about by the war and by U.S. expenditures, despite a large U.S. commodity import program designed, in part, to keep inflation under control. "Many Vietnamese find it necessary to put their wives or daughters to work as bar girls or peddle them to American servicemen as mistresses to increase the family income." Vietnamese, Sheehan said, had trouble getting taxis or housing in Saigon because of the greater wealth of the Americans. "Cartoons in Vietnamese newspapers," he added, "portray 'the new social structure' that has developed from the American influx. At the top of the social pyramid are the bar girls,

---

[10] Johnson Library, NSF Country File, Vietnam, Memorandum for the President from Bromley Smith, Mar. 9, 1966.

[11] *Ibid.*

[12] *PP*, Gravel ed., vol. II, p. 370.

[13] See CMH, Westmoreland Papers, Message Files, MACV 2223, Mar. 19, 1966.

[14] U.S. Department of State, Central File, Pol 27 Viet S, Saigon to Washington 3352, Mar. 16, 1966.

below them come the prostitutes, then the pimps and bar owners and finally the taxi drivers."

Sheehan also noted the traditional xenophobia and racial prejudice of the Vietnamese. "'We Vietnamese,' one Saigon intellectual said, 'are somewhat xenophobe. We don't like foreigners, any kind of foreigners, so you shouldn't be surprised that we don't like you.'" "'Don't forget,' a Vietnamese said, 'that we sometimes still call you "crooked noses" and you look to us like big, uncouth oafs.'"

On March 11, the day after it was announced that the decision had been made to remove Thi, President Johnson held a meeting with his senior advisers from 12:35 p.m. to 1:30 p.m., during which, following a discussion of the latest military developments, there was a very brief discussion of the Thi decision. Present were the President, Rusk, McNamara, Ball, Vance, General Wheeler, General Goodpaster, General Taylor, Secretary of Health, Education and Welfare John Gardner, who was preparing to leave for a trip to South Vietnam, Raborn and Helms from the CIA, Leonard Marks, Director of the U.S. Information Agency, David Bell, Director of AID, and Komer, Valenti and Bromley Smith from the NSC and White House staffs. McNamara introduced the subject, saying that Thi had been removed, but that the situation was "under control, looks as though it's coming out all right. I believe he'll come out."[15] The President asked, "Do our people want him to leave?" McNamara replied: "I do," and Taylor added: "He's a bad character and good riddance." Wheeler said: "General Walt got on well with him. But a conniver. Hard to keep eye on him."

Rather than being under control, the situation grew more serious as protests increased and the dissidents took control of Danang and Hue. Ky and Thieu, with advice from the Americans, delayed Thi's departure for the United States; instead, he was asked to appear in Danang and to indicate publicly that he accepted the action of the Directorate as being in the best interest of the country.[16] The U.S., while taking the position that it would not use its military forces except against the Communists, transmitted to Ky, primarily through the CIA, information on "insurrectionist elements" involved in the protests, in the hope that this would lead to the arrests of those leaders and thus to the undermining of the Struggle Movement.[17]

On March 16, President Johnson, who had become concerned about the situation, sent the following message to Lodge (drafted by Unger):[18]

> We must find way to make Buddhists understand that, with profound US involvement in defense their country against Viet Cong take-over, to say nothing of deep commitment their own government and armed forces, this is not the time to overturn everything and set back efforts now beginning to show results.

---

[15] Johnson Library, Meetings Notes File, Valenti notes of meeting on Mar. 11, 1966.

[16] U.S. Department of State, Central File, Pol 27 Viet S, Saigon to Washington 3381, Mar. 17, 1966, and CMH, Westmoreland Papers, Message Files, Westmoreland to Wheeler, MAC 2119, Mar. 16, 1966.

[17] CMH, Westmoreland Papers, Message Files, Westmoreland to General Walt (Commander of U.S. Marine Corps forces in I Corps), MAC 2019, Mar. 12, 1966.

[18] Johnson Library, NSF Country File, Vietnam, Washington to Saigon 2736, Mar. 16, 1966. In a note to the President at 6:25 p.m. that day, which accompanied the text of the cable, Bromley Smith said, "Your views on current destructive Buddhist activities in South Vietnam were sent this afternoon to Ambassador Lodge to pass on to Buddhist leaders." Same location.

> Furthermore US, as well as Ky Government, has also pledged itself to economic and social progress which Buddhists are also insisting upon but these things cannot be achieved overnight and certainly would not be achieved at all if the Viet Cong were to win out. Moreover, their achievement can only be delayed, not hastened, by starting over again with a new government. Buddhists must be told in fact that our possibilities of continuing to help the Vietnamese to defend themselves and develop their country depends heavily on their readiness also to put aside differences among themselves and work together.
>
> In your discretion you are authorized to convey or have conveyed to Tri Quang and such other Buddhist Institute and lay leaders as you consider desirable the President's considered view that, if they persist in their present irresponsible and destructive course, not only will they lose the US public and official sympathy that they have heretofore had, but they may well bring about a situation of chaos and anarchy in which USG [U.S. Government] support to Viet-Nam could no longer be effective. The President hopes that they will most deeply reflect on this, not only as patriotic Vietnamese interested in the future of their country but also as religious leaders interested in the future of their believers and the religious beliefs for which they stand.

The next day (March 17), Lodge met for two hours with Tri Quang, who said that the Buddhists wanted three things: "(1) That the Americans avoid giving the impression that they are opposed to legal government. (2) That the impression that the generals can make a coup at any time be corrected. (3) Popular participation in government."[19] The Buddhists, he said, did not want a coup or a sudden change of government. "They want to quicken the process of democracy and convene a national convention [to elect a Prime Minister and write a constitution] at the earliest possible date. They do not want the country to be governed by the military."

Lodge, as requested, told Tri Quang of the President's views on the disturbances, and argued that a change of government at that time "would make Vietnam seem to the rest of the world unfit for self-government. It would even appear crazy." Tri Quang replied that Ky and Thieu were not capable of carrying out the social reforms agreed to at the Honolulu Conference, but he wanted to assure Lodge "that he harbored neither anti-U.S. feelings, nor the desire to allow the Vietnamese Communists to participate in the government here."

Lodge concluded his cable with the comment, "Tri Quang is brilliant, dynamic, deeply interested in politics, totally ignorant of democratic methods, with a desire for debate and demagoguery. It is hard to tell how much he believes the bunch of specious arguments he gave me. I believe he will reflect on what I said, but he appears quite determined to pursue his course for the time being."

Later that day (March 17), Bui Diem, assistant to Ky, called the U.S. Embassy political officer, Philip C. Habib, to report that Thieu and Ky were considering two plans in response to the pressure from the Buddhists. One would provide for creating a "Democracy

---

[19] Same location, Saigon to Washington 3371, Mar. 17, 1966.

Building Council" of 100 people. The other would provide for convening a Constituent Assembly in August or September to write the constitution. Diem said he preferred the latter, as did Thieu, but that Ky had not yet decided.[20]

While Lodge was meeting with Tri Quang, Buddhist leader Tam Chau was meeting with Thieu and Ky to present the Buddhists' "final demands." After his meeting with Lodge (as well as the discussion between Bui Diem and Habib), Tri Quang telephoned an Embassy official to report that in the meeting with Chau, Thieu and Ky had promised that they would announce on March 18 a plan to convene a Constituent Assembly later in the year. If this promise was kept, Tri Quang said, the political situation in central Vietnam would return to normal.[21]

In its reply, the State Department agreed that either of the two plans being considered was acceptable, even though both plans "take us more rapidly than we had envisaged down road with many pitfalls."[22] The Department also agreed that the plan for a Constituent Assembly (or Constitutional Assembly) was preferable, partly because it would "buy more time for careful preparation" than would the proposed council.

On March 18, the State Department sent Lodge a message, drafted by Unger, that expanded on the position taken in the March 17 cable:[23] "We are deeply concerned that situation South Vietnam heading toward GVN/Buddhist confrontation which can only be harmful to our collective interests and, based on past experience, probably end disastrously for present government." There appeared to be two possible courses of action, the cable said, that might avoid such a confrontation while also avoiding the "slippery slope of excessive concessions to Buddhists." The first of these would be to take a firm stand against the protests while at the same time offering to discuss common interests in elections and a return to civilian government. "Believe this may be soundest line to pursue," the cable said, "but calls for great skill and behind the scenes management." It would also succeed only if "responsible Buddhists are split off from Tri Quang who of course will oppose Government posture such as we have just described." Opposition from Tri Quang would probably lead to increasing disorder, especially in central Vietnam. "Under these circumstances," the cable said, "we wonder how long Directorate solidarity will last and we see as likely consequence upsetting of present Government, new period of military disunity, and Buddhist-Catholic confrontation."

The second course of action would be to mollify the opposition by holding a constitutional convention in August or September of 1966. (In January, the South Vietnamese Government had stated that it was going to call such a convention.)

If, as appeared likely, the government chose the first course of action, it was essential, the cable said, that "they have brought to their attention in strongest terms necessity for charting and following course which has some chance of success and avoids head-on collision with organized Buddhists. In particular believe we must

[20] Same location, Saigon to Washington 3382, Mar. 17, 1966.
[21] *Ibid.*
[22] Same location, Washington to Saigon 2745, Mar. 17, 1966.
[23] Same location, Washington to Saigon 2764, Mar. 18, 1966.

convey to Thieu and Ky the point that their early judgment on ease with which Thi could be removed was not correct and that they must accept responsibility for their decision and exercise real skill and statesmanship to resolve present situation."

In a "literally eyes only" cable to Lodge on March 22, Rusk, who drafted it himself, told Lodge that he appreciated his efforts to "settle down our various South Vietnamese friends and to keep them working together against the Viet Cong." "I cannot overestimate the importance," Rusk said, "of both the fact and appearance of solidarity among the principal South Vietnamese groups in this situation. Quite frankly, another round of dissension, turmoil and disunity would be more than the flesh and spirit can bear."[24]

On March 22, Lodge, after consulting with his associates, met with Ky. He advised Ky to complete the selection of the members of the Constitutional Convention and to announce the convention and those who would attend.[25]

On March 23, in his regular weekly cable to the President, Lodge reported that "From the standpoint of the ability of the government of Vietnam to influence events and promote stability, last week was bad and so is this week. . . . I worry lest the Directorate may be coming apart."[26]

> We are at the stage here when everything you try to grab is like quicksilver. Moreover, as the Buddhists go further, the chances of Catholics and Northerners (Cochinchinese) getting going increases and instead of the delicate balance we have had for 8 months, the scales will start wildly clashing up and down.
>
> So now I find myself thinking the same thoughts that I was thinking in October 1963, that is: "What can be done without a civil government?" I think it is clear that military operations could go on for quite a while, but everything which requires forward planning, such as "Revolutionary Development," would start grinding down.

The North Vietnamese, Lodge said, were counting on the fragility of the South Vietnamese Government to weaken American support for the war, "and if I were advising them, I would advise them to do just what they are doing to encourage the national divisiveness in South Vietnam."

The attitudes of the Buddhists, Lodge said, "undoubtedly reflects Communist advice, carefully planted among Buddhist priests, who think themselves very clever but who actually are lacking in knowledge of the world."

Westmoreland and his associates generally agreed with Lodge's position, even though they had been displeased with the removal of Thi, but they argued for stronger action. Westmoreland thought that protesting students should be drafted,[27] and his deputy, Lt. Gen. John A. Heintges, told Westmoreland in a memorandum on March 23 that he thought it was "a crying shame to let the students up there get away with their anti-government and anti-U.S.

[24] U.S. Department of State, Central File, Pol 27 Viet S, Washington to Saigon 2793, Mar. 22, 1966.
[25] Johnson Library, NSF Country File, Vietnam, Saigon to Washington 3463, Mar. 23, 1966.
[26] Same Location. Saigon to Washington 3467, Mar. 23, 1966.
[27] Clarke, *Advice and Support: The Final Years,* p. 130.

activities."[28] Heintges said he was afraid that the situation was getting out of hand. He thought that Lodge and other U.S. political officers were not being firm enough, and that if the students would not listen to reason, the government should "step in with firm hand and straighten the students out." Agreeing with Westmoreland that the protests were Communist-inspired, he said: "I think these young punks up there are doing as much damage to the overall course in this country as the VC. . . ." "I am afraid," Heintges concluded, "that if something positive is not done soon our people back home are going to get their dander up and want to wash their hands of this mess over here."

On March 24, Lodge, on Westmoreland's recommendation, telephoned Ky to report the latest U.S. casualty figures (228 killed and 850 wounded between March 1 and 23), and told Ky that "we were paying this price in blood, while all this disorder was going on in Hue and Danang. We were not making these figures public, but he should realize what a very bad effect indeed this would have on U.S. opinion."[29]

That night in Washington, President Johnson called the White House Situation Room at midnight and again at 6:30 a.m. to inquire about developments in Vietnam.[30]

On March 25, Ky announced that there would be a Constituent Assembly, renamed the Constitutional Preparatory Commission, and that it would complete its work in two months, after which there would be elections by the end of the year. This action seemed to have little if any effect on the protests, however, which grew more intense the following day.

On March 29, Ky told Lodge that he and the other members of the Directorate wanted to use force against the protesters. Lodge, who had been urging the Vietnamese to take action to restore order, agreed on the need for action, but in his weekly report to the President on March 30 he said that "to me, as a typically impatient American who naturally wants action most of the things he [Ky] says come about a week too late. . . . Also, one always wonders whenever a Vietnamese says something intelligent and true, whether he is in any way able to do anything about it."[31]

On March 30, the State Department sent two cables to Lodge expressing the growing concern of Washington policymakers about the situation. Rusk himself drafted the first, in which he said, "We are deeply distressed by the seeming unwillingness or inability of the South Vietnamese to put aside their lesser quarrels in the interest of meeting the threat from the Viet Cong. . . . We face the fact that we ourselves cannot succeed except in support of the South Vietnamese. Unless they are able to mobilize reasonable solidarity, the prospects are very grim."[32] Rusk said that he assumed Lodge had done all that he could to impress upon Tri Quang and

[28] CMH, Westmoreland Papers, History File.

[29] U.S. Department of State, Central File, Pol 27 Viet S, Saigon to Washington 3483, Mar. 24, 1966.

[30] Johnson Library, NSF Country File, Vietnam, Memorandum to Komer from Art McCafferty, Mar. 24, 1966.

[31] U.S. Department of State, Central File, Pol 27 Viet S, Saigon to Washington 3589, Mar. 30, 1966.

[32] Johnson Library, NSF Country File, Vietnam, Washington to Saigon 2884, Mar 30, 1966.

the other Buddhist leaders "the importance of putting first things first."

Later that same day a second cable, drafted by Robert Miller, the officer in charge of the Vietnam desk in the Far East Bureau, declared that "situation seems to be going from bad to worse without any indication that GVN has any clear idea of how to deal with it. In our view, longer this continues, GVN has fewer chances to stem tide. . . ."[33] The cable proposed several steps that could be taken:

> 1. You should urge GVN consider isolating and identifying any Communist agitators in Hue and Danang struggle movements, and arresting those with solid evidence of VC connections.
>
> 2. Similarly urge GVN consider meting out military discipline to key military personnel supporting struggle movement, or at least transporting additional single leaders to boondocks somewhere; could same be done with any civil service ringleaders?
>
> 3. Cannot GVN neutralize . . . media equipment being used by struggle forces? . . .
>
> 4. If GVN unable to obtain consensus for democracy building plan, could it as alternative call conference of key figures in drama [Buddhist and Catholic leaders] to hammer out solution in one room followed immediately by joint announcement. . . .

In addition, the message suggested the possibility of a joint public statement by the U.S. and the Government of South Vietnam which, among other things, would state that anti-U.S. statements were undermining efforts to win the war and were causing the U.S. public to question the war.

On March 31, Lodge replied to Rusk's cable.[34] "Tri Quang," Lodge said, "refuses to listen." Another talk would not be helpful. "On the contrary, he [Tri Quang] has made it clear in conversations with others, including Embassy officers, that he looks on his use of the anti-American theme as a deliberate device to bring pressure on the South Vietnamese. . . . He has embarked on a course deliberately designed not only to bring down the Government, but to have its replacement substantially subject to his control. . . . He will have to be taken care of by Vietnamese, in a Vietnamese way. This may involve either a compromise, or a gesture with a measure of force, or just plain force."

On April 2, in preparation for a White House meeting that day, William Bundy drafted a memorandum for Rusk to send to the President.[35] Reports received in Washington, the memorandum said, "further reinforce the picture that Hue and Danang are now virtually out of control and that the themes of the so-called 'struggle' movement are spreading to other areas in a significant fashion. . . . The only bright spots are that Saigon has remained under control and that Ky and the government apparently have

---

[33] U.S. Department of State, Central File, Pol 27 Viet S, Washington to Saigon 2893, Mar. 30, 1966.

[34] Johnson Library, NSF Country File, Vietnam, Saigon to Washington 3614, Mar. 31, 1966.

[35] A copy of the memorandum of Apr. 2, 1966, on which Rusk noted, "Not used except orally," is in the Department of State, Lot File 85 D 240 (William Bundy Papers). A copy in the Johnson Library, NSF Country File, Vietnam, does not have Rusk's notation.

considerable latent support in the southern part of South Vietnam and to some degree in the central areas."

The memorandum listed several possible actions that could be taken. These included the immediate appointment of a group to draft the new constitution, the appointment of a new commander for I Corps who would be acceptable to Buddhists (General Duong Van "Big" Minh, who headed the Post-Diem government, was suggested), a possible "deal" with Thi to give him a "major Saigon role" and thus partially satisfy the protesters, and a "facelifting for the Directorate under which Ky would be replaced, senior civilians would be appointed to the Cabinet, and the relationship of the Cabinet and the Directorate would be defined. According to the memorandum, however, "even this program, applied immediately, would have no assurance of success. The plain fact is that Thieu and Ky have been drastically weakened by their inability to cope with the crisis, and we must still be prepared for the worst, namely a complete change of government."

The only alternative, Bundy's memorandum concluded, with "any possibility of success," would be "some such figure as General Minh, who is military but also commands a wide civilian following. From here, we do not see any civilian, nor do we believe that Thi could be installed without setting off drastic counteraction from other elements such as the Catholics."

In Saigon on April 2, after a meeting with his associates, Lodge said in a cable to Washington that "Disorder in Hue, and threats of similar loss of control elsewhere, have brought the Government to a point where firm decisions and necessary action can no longer wait."[36] Ky, Lodge said, had not taken any significant steps to restore order, but had stated that he would take drastic action if a peaceful solution could not be reached in two days.

Firm action by the government, Lodge said, would require an immediate announcement of the program for drafting the constitution and holding elections, coupled with the use of South Vietnamese forces to restore order in the Hue/Danang area. Furthermore, leaders of the Struggle Movement, as well as military and civilian government personnel who had played key roles in the protests, should be arrested.

Lodge said that, if asked, the U.S. should agree to transport South Vietnamese forces to Danang/Hue, but all other U.S. personnel should continue to avoid becoming involved in the dispute. If Ky asked for help, the U.S., before agreeing, should review the plan for using troops in order to make sure that it "was adequate," and should refuse to provide assistance if it was not.

In addition, the cable reported that Lodge and his associates had discussed the idea of a citizen's committee of senior leaders from various parts of the country that could declare its support for the government and assist with the process of preparing for a constitution and elections. (Unlike the State Department proposal of March 30 for a meeting of key protest figures, this committee would not include religious leaders.) But the cable added that it would not be possible to organize and get such a group to act in the near future. Moreover, the Ky government might not be willing to "trust its own

[36] Johnson Library, NSF Country File, Vietnam, Saigon to Washington 3672, Apr. 2, 1966.

future" to a group that might not be fully supportive of the government's position.

In view of the possible demise of the Ky government, however, Lodge said that the U.S. needed to have a contingency plan that would provide, among other things, for "an effort to rally the widest possible support from responsible elements to devise a transitional solution which would preserve a Government and devise a solution of longer life."

Lodge's cable apparently arrived in Washington at 12:50 p.m. on April 2 and was delivered to Rusk at 12:53 p.m., possibly in time for him to read it prior to a 1:00 p.m. luncheon meeting with the President.[37]

At the luncheon meeting held from 1:00 p.m. to about 2:20 p.m. with Rusk, McNamara, Rostow, Moyers and Valenti,[38] the President told the group that "every effort" should be made to preserve Ky if possible. "But be ready to make terrible choice. Perhaps take a stand in Thailand—or take someone else other than Ky." "Prepare fallback position," he added. "Involves talking to Buddhists and if necessary, get out of I Corps and even Vietnam." McNamara said he thought "we ought to get rid of Tri Quang." Lodge, he said, "ought to have it out with Tri Quang. Quang needs to know what situation is and how prepared we are to clear out of I Corps area. We need to know if Quang really wants us out—for if he does, we better get out now. But . . . Quang believes that we are committed."

The President said that Lodge should be told to talk to Tri Quang and to "get tough with him."

Later that day (April 2), Rusk, in a message he personally drafted, cabled Lodge the results of the meeting with the President:[39]

> It seems to us that Tri Quang (and apparently also Thi) is taking for granted that the US commitment in South Viet-Nam is such that we are stuck with continued support regardless of what he and his "struggle front" might do. If possible he should be disabused of thinking that US is a satellite or that the lives of Americans are at his disposal in the pursuit of his personal ambitions. The elementary fact is that if the US is to persist in South Viet-Nam it must have something to support. A minimum requirement is solidarity among all major elements of South Vietnamese against what Hanoi and Liberation Front are trying to do. We see advantage here in your again having candid and entirely personal talk with Tri Quang to force him to disclose fully his attitude toward Hanoi and Liberation Front, and to disabuse him of idea that the American commitment will tolerate division or discord from within or will permit Communist leaders or sympathizers to achieve their purposes through our leniency.

"Our interest," Rusk added, "is that Directorate continue with present assignments of such individuals as Thieu and Ky, and get the job done while moving toward a democratically selected civilian government at the earliest possible date. . . . So far as we can see

[37] The times are noted on the copy of the cable in the Johnson Library.
[38] Johnson Library, Meetings Notes File, Valenti notes of the meeting of Apr. 2, 1966.
[39] Johnson Library, NSF Country File, Vietnam, Washington to Saigon 2950, Apr. 2, 1966.

there is no alternative to firm and effective movement to restore order in First Corps Area, accompanied by most imaginative political steps possible." He added, however, that thought was being given to "major contingencies," and he assumed that Lodge and his associates were doing likewise. "The President," he added, "would like to have your personal views on major alternatives should present track fail."

In another cable, drafted by William Bundy (and cleared by Rusk personally), based on Bundy's memorandum earlier that day, the State Department suggested that Big Minh or General Tran Van Don, who, like Minh, had been a key figure in the Diem coup in 1963 and a member of the junta that replaced Diem, could be considered to replace the ineffectual I Corps commander.[40]

In his reply to the two cables Lodge said that Tri Quang's actions were "totally consistent with Communist aims" and that the Communists were exploiting the protests.[41] He was concerned that if the Struggle Movement succeeded in taking over the government, it "could lead Vietnam into unknown waters, not excluding French-backed neutralism and Hanoi take-over." With respect to alternatives, if Ky were to step down, Lodge said, the best alternative might be to replace him with another member of the Directorate, preferably General Phan Xuan Chieu, Ky's chief political adviser and the third-ranking member of the government. Other possible candidates, Lodge said, would be the two suggested by Bundy for I Corps commander—Big Minh and Don.

An Abortive Effort to Suppress the Disturbances in Danang

By April 4, the situation had become so acute that the Ky government felt compelled to act. It was announced that Danang had been taken over by the Communists and that the government would use force to rectify the situation. At the same time, it was announced that a "National Political Congress" of representatives from various groups, including Buddhists, would be formed to suggest ways and means for moving toward a representative government.[42]

Lodge then met with Ky, and cabled Washington that Ky had asked for U.S. planes to airlift troops, and that he had approved the request.[43]

This news prompted a meeting from 7:10 p.m. to 8:42 p.m. on April 4 of the President, the Vice President, Rusk, McNamara, Rostow, General Taylor, William Bundy, Jack Valenti, as well as Justice Fortas[44] to discuss the situation and to consider drafts of

---

[40] Same location, Washington to Saigon 2948, Apr. 2, 1966.

[41] U.S. Department of State, Central File, Pol 27 Viet S, Saigon to Washington 3699, Apr. 4, 1966.

[42] Johnson Library, NSF Country File, Vietnam, Saigon to Washington 3698, Apr. 4, 1966.

[43] *Ibid.* For additional information on the plans for the National Political Congress and the reactions of the Buddhists to the idea, see Lodge's weekly report to the President, Department of State, Central File, Pol 27 Viet S, Saigon to Washington 3922, Apr. 12, 1966.

[44] Johnson Library, Meetings Notes File, Valenti notes of the meeting on Apr. 4, 1966.

Prior to the White House meeting, there was a meeting at the State Department at 3:00 p.m. of senior officials from State, Defense, the White House and the CIA. (For a "Checklist of Questions on Vietnam" prepared for the State Department meeting by William Bundy, with brief notations of the conclusions reached, see the memorandum to W. W. Rostow by D. W. Ropa, Apr. 4, 1966, in the Johnson Library, NSF Country File, Vietnam.) One of those who attended was Allen Whiting, head of the Far East branch of State's Office of Intelligence and Research. He

Continued

cables to Lodge. The President began by saying that "Westmoreland thinks 'prospect of success in Danang'" but that he did not agree. McNamara and Rusk said that they also disagreed.

At the meeting, the President was asked to approve two cables to Lodge. He approved the first, which directed U.S. personnel to refrain from getting involved in the disturbances, saying that it was "important to keep our troops and equipment out of riot area. We don't want to become involved." He said he wondered about the second cable, which discussed alternatives to Ky as well as ways in which the Ky government could meet some of the demands of the protesters. "Appeasement never wins," he said, adding that he was "worried about a constitutional assembly" (one of the matters discussed in the cable) and that he would "rather have someone we can control than a communist takeover at the assembly." Rostow commented that the Ky government had not been "credible." "Why and how?" the President asked. "Ky was going to call a group to draft a constitution," Rostow replied, "and hasn't done so." The President: "What are problems in calling it?" Rostow: "Not getting agreement on a total list." William Bundy added that the Ky government had been working on a list since January (when the announcement was made that a drafting group would be organized).

Vice President Humphrey asked who was in touch with General Thi. "No one really," Bundy replied.

Taylor said that he was "worried about Thi. Tri Quang is back of him and we cannot take a Tri Quang government. He will tear down everything." Rusk responded: "Alternatives are less desirable than what we have now, so we are trying to save what we have."

The President, stressing the "need to do more planning on how to pick a man before he takes over so we won't have to get out when the wrong man gets in," said that "time has come when the alternative is to get out—or do what we need to do to get the government shored up—move in with power and stay there."

The Vice President returned to the subject of Thi, saying that he was "pleasant, Buddhist and clever. Ky is jealous of Thi." "Isn't he [Thi] out of our hands now?" the President asked. The Vice President replied, "I don't know. But we ought not let him get out of our hands. We need to know more about the Buddhists." The President responded: "We need a Garcia-Godoy type—with an adviser by his side." McNamara added: "We need a Bunker in Vietnam." (Garcia-Godoy was President of the Dominican Republic when Ellsworth Bunker was U.S. Ambassador. A year later, Ellsworth Bunker, U.S.

---

had just returned from an 18-day visit to South Vietnam where he found considerable opposition to military rule and a widespread feeling that Ky should be replaced. "Ky will have to go; he cannot provide leadership for Vietnam and can never command the respect of the people. He was not a respected figure to begin with and derives his status only from the U.S. hand on his back." This quotation is from a memorandum to W. W. Rostow from NSC staff member James Thomson, Jr., Apr. 7, 1966, summarizing an account of the trip given on April 7 by Whiting. On April 8, Rostow sent it to the President with a cover note saying that Whiting was "a first rate Far Eastern analyst in State." (Johnson Library, NSF Memos to the President—Walt Rostow. The cover memorandum is attached to another copy of the Thomson memorandum located in NSF Country File, Vietnam. Parts of the copy of the Thomson memorandum in this location were excised when it was released in 1979. The copy in Rostow's file was declassified in full in 1985.)

Whiting also found (again quoting Thomson's summary) that "The Vietnamese have a desperate need for self-respect and dignity—and increasing dependence on the U.S. deprives them of such self-respect and dignity. We can expect inevitable and psychologically necessary flare-ups that are an expression of bottled up resentment along these lines. (They don't feel that they own their country.)"

Ambassador to the Dominican Republic, became Ambassador to South Vietnam, replacing Lodge.)

"The way I see it," the President said, "Ky is gone, the last gasp. Doubt he can pull it off. When he goes, there'll be hell [to pay] in this country. Let's get a government we can appoint and support. We need a tough adviser." Taylor responded: "We can minimize our losses if Ky goes and the Directory stays. We have to take sides this time."

After the meeting, the State Department sent the cables that the President had approved informing Lodge that[45] "Whether or not current GVN effort in Danang produces local solution crisis has clearly come to a head and some political answer must be found as quickly and peacefully as possible," and urging him to have "substantially more contact with GVN and with opposing and other political elements than has hitherto seemed wise either to you or to us." Either Lodge or Negroponte (U.S. Consul General in Hue) should see Tri Quang, and every effort should be made to persuade Buddhist leaders "that present situation represents grave danger of simply handing over country to VC and that they must cease to insist on unrealistic demands."

Contact should also be arranged with General Thi in order to devise a "prompt solution to his future." In the event that he became a "major candidate" to replace Ky, a possibility "we would not be in favor of . . . particularly in view of his close tie with Tri Quang . . . we may have to face up to it and consider how we would handle."

The cable agreed with Lodge's suggestion that a successor to Ky should be chosen from the Directorate, preferably Chieu, and, in a comment that exemplified the dilemma with respect to replacing the military government with civilians, added: "We are at a loss here to suggest any civilian who could really form agreement." The "only name that occurs to us is Pham Quang Dan," (a leader in opposition to Diem in the early 1960s, who at the time was head of a provincial council).

For the present, the important thing was to get action on the formation of the National Political Congress, and Lodge was urged to exert influence on key groups to persuade them that their participation in such an effort was "absolutely vital to preserving government structure."

On April 5, 1966, the Ky government sent two battalions of South Vietnamese Marines, equipped with tanks, to Danang by airlift supplied by the U.S., and Ky himself, along with Deputy Prime Minister (and Minister of Defense) Nguyen Huu Co, Army Chief of Staff Cao Van Vien, and Ky's close associate, Col. Nguyen Ngoc Loan, head of the Military Security Service, went to Danang to take charge of the operation. General Nguyen Van Chuan, who had replaced Thi as Commander of South Vietnamese Forces in I Corps, was opposed to using troops against the dissidents, however, and blocked exits to Danang from the air base to prevent the marines from moving toward the city. At the same time, the commander of the 1st ARVN Division stationed in Hue, General Phan

45 U.S. Department of State, Central File, Pol 27 Viet S, Washington to Saigon 2964 and 2966, Apr. 4. 1966.

Xuan Nhuan, together with other officers from the division, announced his support for the Struggle Movement, and vowed to resist efforts by the government to use force against Hue.

Faced with these developments, Ky returned to Saigon later that day, leaving General Co in charge. That night, all of the principal Buddhist leaders except for Tri Quang met with Ky at his home, where they told Ky that they wanted the government to hold a constitutional assembly within six months. They said they wanted him to stay in office during the transition to a new government (it was not clear what time period they had in mind) because, as reported by Lodge, "they have no confidence in anyone else. The politicians are corrupt. And they don't trust the other generals."[46]

In a memorandum to Rusk that day (April 5), William Bundy said, "My net judgment is that the worst possible outcomes have been avoided, but that Ky essentially capitulated to the combination of local and Buddhist sentiment represented by General Chuan. I would guess that this would seriously damage his position . . . we may save Thieu, but Ky looks pretty far gone." "My own thought for the moment," Bundy added, "is that we might cable Lodge that this would not be too bad, and might point toward a reshuffled Directory with Chieu moving up. . . ."[47]

That same day, the President's new national security adviser, Walt W. Rostow, sent him a memorandum summarizing his views.[48] "If the Vietnamese work their way out of this—and a civil constitution-drafting group is born—we will have passed a great turning point. . . . *Then will be the time to pour it on* and see if we can't force, in the months ahead, a resolution of the conflict. *The strain on our political and economic life and the strain on the South Vietnamese is all but intolerable."* (emphases in original)

On the military side Rostow recommended that the U.S. "impose heavy attrition" on Communist ground forces, harass more effectively their supply lines from the North, and bomb the North more heavily, including attacks on POL (petroleum, oil, lubricants), and attacks on Hanoi "on a precision bombing basis." "It is not, Mr. President, that I'm bloody-minded or a hawk," Rostow said, "But the strain of trying to do the job principally by attrition of main force units places almost intolerable burdens on the political life of our country and on the war-weary South Vietnamese. *We've got to try to shorten this war without doing unwise or desperate things."* (emphasis in original)

On the nonmilitary side, Rostow said, the most urgent need was "to cut the radicals out of the herd by getting the literate, urban leaders—and others—into a hall and around tables talking about the political future." Rural reconstruction was essential, he added, but more effort should be given to "political development: how to keep the Directorate together; the political party clause in the constitution; how to balance majority and minority interests; the formation of a national wide-ranging party, etc."

---

[46] Johnson Library, NSF Country File, Vietnam, Saigon to Washington 3761, Apr. 6, 1966.

On April 5, the President held a luncheon meeting on Vietnam from 1:05 p.m. to 2:25 p.m. with the Vice President, Rusk, McNamara, Taylor, Admiral McDonald (representing the JCS), Rostow, Valenti and Moyers. There apparently are no notes of this meeting.

[47] U.S. Department of State, Lot File 70 D 201.

[48] Johnson Library, NSF Memos to the President—Walt Rostow.

On the morning of April 6, Ky asked Lodge to come to his office. He told Lodge that Co was negotiating with Struggle committee representatives in Danang. The dissidents would be given until midnight to accept the government's terms, and if they did not, Ky said, government troops would move at midnight against Danang. This could produce a clash between the forces on both sides. "'If we decide to do this, it may create trouble. Are you agreed with this procedure?" Lodge replied that the government had to reestablish its authority in Danang. He said he thought Ky had been "very patient," but that if negotiations were not successful, "then ultimately the time of testing could not be avoided."[49]

Although Lodge and Westmoreland supported the government's action in sending forces to Danang, General Walt, Commander of U.S. Marines in I Corps, who had a good relationship with Thi, Dinh and others, was opposed to the use of government troops at Danang, and recommended that they be withdrawn and that the government support Dinh, the Commander of I Corps. This advice was rejected by Westmoreland and by the Directorate.[50]

That afternoon, Ky's assistant, Bui Diem, went to Lodge's office to tell him that after the meeting of Ky and Lodge that morning, Ky had met with Thieu and Vien and it was agreed that, given the opposition of General Chuan to the use of force against the dissidents, the government should first seek a political solution to the problem. The proposal of the Buddhists for holding a Constitutional Assembly within six months was accepted, and Ky sent a letter to Tam Chau saying that this would be done.[51] Lodge told Bui Diem that the Buddhists "will never make a deal that they will stick to," to which he replied, "Yes, but we'll take the wind out of their sails." Lodge retorted that this decision was a "big setback," and that "sooner or later this crisis is going to have to be settled."

In his cable to Washington reporting on the conversation Lodge commented that the plan announced by Ky in his meeting with Lodge that morning had been "in the right direction," and that "one thing seems clear tonight: GVN has a big case of cold feet."[52]

In Washington on Sunday, April 6, 1966, from 5:20 p.m. to 6:10 p.m. President Johnson met with Vice President Humphrey, Rusk, McNamara, Rostow, William Bundy, U. Alexis Johnson, McNaughton, Raborn, Helms, Leonard Marks, Valenti, Moyers, and Bromley Smith. Notes on the discussion were less than one-third of a page double-spaced, as follows:[53]

---

[49] Same location, Saigon to Washington 3755, Apr. 6, 1966.

[50] Shulimson, *U.S. Marines in Vietnam: An Expanding War, 1966*, pp. 84–85.

[51] A copy of a translation of Ky's letter of Apr. 6, 1966 to Tam Chau is in the Johnson Library, NSF Memos to the President—Walt Rostow.

[52] Saigon to Washington 3761, cited above.

[53] Johnson Library, Meetings Notes File, Valenti notes of meeting on Apr. 6, 1966. That night (April 6), Valenti, who was about to leave the White House to become president of the Motion Picture Association of America, drafted the following memorandum to the President (Johnson Library, Office of the President File, Jack Valenti): "A final note, Mr. President. I truly believe we need to find some way out of Vietnam. All that you strive for and believe in, and are accomplishing is in danger, as long as this war goes on. If there were a way out, some hint of the end with honor, I would believe it best to stay there til the bitter conclusion. But there is no reasonable hope. All your military advisors insist you must double your force, and still they give you no prophecy of victory, however shapeless, however mild.

"Without a large scale war in VN, you become a candidate for valid greatness as an all-time great President because all else that you do is magnificent in design and result.

Continued

Rusk: Question whether Lodge should say struggle movement is infected with communists—Rusk opposed.

McNamara: Struggle movement may be too strong to throw off. We don't know much about their objectives. They obviously have strength we didn't know about, and I don't want to go to war against them.

Vice President: Agree with McNamara. Too uncertain to judge who will line up on top.

William Bundy's draft of a cable to Lodge apparently was approved by the President.[54] Judging by the cable it would appear that, contrary to Lodge's position that a second effort should be made to quell the Danang disturbance, by force if necessary, the President and his associates believed that this should be postponed pending the outcomes of political negotiations.[55] Moreover, as the cable explained, "the Danang operation would be unwise unless and until GVN has prepared the way by visible political moves and hopefully by obtaining agreement at least of moderate Buddhist elements led by Tam Chau to such moves."

Washington was also concerned about the effects of having used U.S. planes to transport South Vietnamese forces to Danang:

> We must also bear in mind that our action in supporting Danang operation through airlift, including the decision to send tanks during April 6, have heavily involved USG so that if Danang operations were undertaken and failed—as we believe overwhelmingly likely under present circumstances—it would result not merely in tremendous criticism of USG here and elsewhere but could mean that our whole position within SVN would be gravely damaged and we might be virtually unable to resume any kind of cooperative relation with major elements particularly in I Corps area. We entirely support decision on furnishing this airlift, but fact is that it has involved us with these possible consequences and . . . we simply must be able to show that we have helped to stimulate political programs whether or not Danang operation finally becomes essential.

"Accordingly," the cable concluded "we believe that you should not urge immediate Danang operation at present, but rather that entire focus of your efforts and all levels should be to get political process started."

On April 7, Lodge met with Ky, who said he had received a reply from Tam Chau asking for four things: first, no punishment for government personnel civilian and military who had supported the

"The US public will tolerate small operations (the Congo, post-war Korea, Dominican Republic) but they really can't swallow 250,000–400,000 men engaged in a war without end or hope or ultimate victory.

"If we hold in Thailand—if we keep India and Pakistan independent—if we stand ground over the Asian Pacific—if we can, discreetly, in time, aid the anti-Sukarno govt—and if we can withdraw from Vietnam without losing our courage or our resolve (but only a friendly govt to help) have we really lost? Have we diminished our leadership?

"We can't force people to want to be free. We can only help those who want to help themselves—which is our national policy today." There is no record that Valenti sent this memorandum. The only copy in the file is the handwritten draft.

[54] Two additional cables, one on "public policy on the Communist role" and the other on "further tactical moves," may also have been approved. Drafts of all three are attached to an agenda of the April 6 meeting. Johnson Library, NSF Country File, Vietnam.

[55] Same location, Washington to Saigon 3001, Apr. 6, 1966.

protests; second, release of all persons who had been detained; third, withdrawal of all troops sent to Central Vietnam to quell the protests; and, fourth, a decree ordering that the Constitutional Assembly be convened "within the next two or three days."[56] (Actually, as Lodge discovered when he returned to his office, Tam Chau's letter had stated "in the shortest time," rather than in two or three days.) Ky, Lodge said, was "much perturbed" by the demand for holding the assembly in two or three days, and told Lodge that this proved that the Buddhists were not really in favor of an assembly; that they wanted to overthrow the government. The government, he said, must act to restore order. "If we take no action now, we will have lost Central Vietnam."

Lodge replied that the U.S. worried that the use of force could "lead to bloodshed," and hoped that a political solution could be found.

Ky, repeating that action was necessary, said he was going to give the order that night to airlift two more battalions to Danang.

In a cable to Washington on April 8, Lodge reviewed the situation and suggested possible courses of action.[57] He was very critical of the Buddhists. Their demands, he said, "when stripped of hypocrisy and cant, boil down to a naked grab for power. . . . It is prudent to assume that they actually want to overthrow the government, seize power (through stooges) and are quite willing to risk strong Communist influence." Concessions to the Buddhists, he added, would "put the GVN on a slippery slope without a visible end."

The alternative, which Lodge strongly favored, was for the government to "assert its authority" against the dissidents while moving as rapidly as possible toward a constitutional system. He was very critical of Ky, who he said had "failed to assert the authority of the government, to the point where his own position is now endangered, the unity of the government is severely threatened, and the effectiveness of the armed forces is in question."

There were two possible courses of action, Lodge said. The first would involve the use of force to quell the disturbances, beginning with Danang. "Unfortunately," he said, it was "late" for this course, which could lead to bloodshed and to desperate acts by the Struggle forces that could involve U.S. installations and personnel, and might require additional direct U.S. support. Moreover, it might not succeed quickly enough or at a low enough cost "in terms of pitting Vietnamese against Vietnamese." However, this was the course of action that Ky had proposed, Lodge said.

The second course, which Lodge said he preferred, would be to avoid a direct military clash, and by the "selective application of force to reduce and discourage Buddhist and V.C. originated rebelliousness, meanwhile seeking so-called 'political solution.'" This course of action, he said, could lead to a direct military clash at a later date, "but under less difficult conditions" as a result of the steps taken meanwhile. The "selective application of force," he said, would involve leaving troops in Danang, and seeking to "cordon off" the rebellion in Danang and Hue by controlling transportation and

[56] The cable and a translation of Tam Chau's statement are in the Johnson Library, NSF Memos to the President—Walt Rostow.

[57] Johnson Library, NSF Country File, Vietnam, Saigon to Washington 3817, Apr. 8, 1966.

communications. "Severe" action would be taken against the movement in other parts of the country, especially Saigon, and leaders would be arrested if necessary. At the same time, the government would adhere to the promise of Ky to Buddhist leader Tam Chau to convene a constitutional assembly within six months.

On April 9, Rusk personally drafted a cable for Lodge thanking him for his "fine job."[58] It was very important, Rusk said, for the South Vietnamese Government, despite its lack of control in Hue-Danang, to maintain order in the country. "To me, the simple fact is that the present government must govern until it can turn over to a new government arising from a broadly based constitutional process. It cannot turn over to a non-government."

On April 8, Westmoreland was summoned to meet with Ky and Thieu, who told him that the government was going to "put on a real show of force in Danang." They asked whether U.S. planes could ferry two more battalions to the city, and Westmoreland, by prearrangement with Lodge, said that they would have to ask Lodge who would have to ask Washington. (Knowing that this meant "no," they did not ask Lodge.)

On the night of April 8, the Ky government, using planes from its own air force, airlifted two more battalions of troops to the U.S. airbase at Danang.

In response to a series of questions from JCS Chairman Wheeler on April 8, Westmoreland said that he did not recommend direct military action against the dissidents. The government did not have a well-conceived plan of action, he said, and the operation would probably fail. Moreover, the use of force might give the Buddhists a "'martyr theme' that could be magnified into unmanageable proportions."[59]

He favored the course being followed of "breaking down the opposition by a show of military force coupled with reliance on increasing economics and morale difficulties. . . . Meanwhile, by giving wide publicity to the Government's intention to push ahead with the political Congress and later the constituent assembly, much of the steam is taken out of the opposition campaign."

In his reply to the same questions, Admiral Sharp (CINCPAC) said that if the political solution failed, military action would be necessary. "The confrontation cannot go on indefinitely, since the struggle forces may grow steadily stronger if allowed to coalesce undisturbed. Orientals being what they are we should not be impatient. They may be able to solve this problem without bloodshed."[60]

What Should the U.S. Do?

On April 8, 1966, a small group of officials (the President was in Texas) met to review the situation and to discuss further action by the U.S. The Struggle Movement and its supporters effectively controlled the central part of South Vietnam, and Ky was viewed as having been weakened by his failure to restore order—compounded by the events of April 5 when he backed down on using force at

[58] U.S. Department of State, Central File, Pol 27 Viet S, Washington to Saigon 3035, Apr. 9, 1966.

[59] Wheeler's cable, JCS 1889–66, Apr. 8, 1966, and Westmoreland's reply, MAC 2812, Apr. 9, 1966, are in CMH, Westmoreland Papers, Message Files.

[60] Same location, Sharp to Wheeler, Apr. 10, 1966.

Danang. Moreover, with the notable exception of Lodge, there was considerable reluctance among U.S. policymakers to use force against the Struggle Movement. As McNamara said in the meeting with the President on April 6, "They obviously have strength we didn't know about, and I don't want to go to war against them."[61]

The meeting, which was held at the White House, was attended by subcabinet officers and Presidential aides. According to a message at 9:20 a.m. from Moyers to the President, "The situation in Saigon is disturbing this morning, and I have suggested to Rostow that we have a meeting in the Situation Room beneath the McNamara-Rusk level at 1:00 p.m. to try to pull the parts together, and we'll report back to you after that.[62]

Apparently the group discussed the possibility that the Struggle Movement would succeed in toppling the military government and in taking power. George Carver, a CIA Vietnamese specialist (who became special assistant for Vietnamese Affairs to the Director of the CIA in September 1966), prepared a memorandum on April 11, which he said had been requested at the meeting, which he attended, on the subject, "Consequences of a Buddhist Political Victory in South Vietnam."[63] In the memorandum, Carver emphasized the political strength of the Buddhists and concluded that, despite the problems that the U.S. would have in dealing with a Buddhist government, "the longer-term consequences of a Buddhist victory could turn out very much to our advantage." "[T]here would be," Carver said, "a very sticky and dangerous period of transition during which only U.S. and allied military might would prevent a

---

[61] Among U.S. military leaders there was also considerable concern about the use of force. In part, this was due to their opinion that the Ky government was not prepared to use force effectively, and a fear of the consequences of failure. There was also strong support for General Thi, especially on the part of Major General Walt, Commander of the Third Marine Amphibious Force, headquartered in Danang, who was Thi's American counterpart in I Corps. (See Shulimson, *U.S. Marines in Vietnam, An Expanding War, 1966,* cited above, and Walt's own book, *Strange War, Strange Strategy,* as well as Clarke, *Advice and Support: The Final Years,* and other sources noted above.) The overriding interests of the U.S. military were in avoiding any involvement of American forces and in continuing to fight the war. Thus, they were concerned about the effect of the contest between the government and the dissidents in diverting substantial numbers of personnel of the South Vietnamese Armed Forces from their regular duties, and in reducing, to some degree, U.S. combat operations in the area.

U.S. military officials in South Vietnam were called upon to play an important role in the crisis, especially in serving as intermediaries with South Vietnamese military leaders in gathering intelligence on the situation, and, on several occasions, in preventing clashes between the forces of both sides. (See above sources, and for a good summary see Westmoreland's report to Wheeler, CMH, Westmoreland Papers, Message Files, MAC 2998, Apr. 13, 1966.)

[62] Johnson Library, President's Appointment File, Diary Backup for Apr. 8, 1966. There apparently are no notes from the meeting, nor is there any information as to what the President was told about the results of the meeting.

[63] Johnson Library, NSF Country File, Vietnam. It is not known who received or who read Carver's memorandum.

See also in the same location Carver's 14-page memorandum of April 2, 1966, "The Political Situation in South Vietnam: The Current Crisis, Possible Future Developments, U.S. Options." Among other things, he said that U.S. interests would be adversely affected if the crisis continued for more than a week or two, but added that, while it was essential to re-establish government authority over I Corps, this could not be done by military force. "The government," he said, *"must show concrete forward motion toward the objective of reestablishing civilian rule."* (emphasis in original) "The best way to do that would be to announce promptly the creation of a group to draft a constitution. At the same time, Thi "must be gotten out of I Corps and, preferably, sent abroad for at least a short period of 'medical treatment' to prove that the Directory is capable of making its ruling stick."

It was not essential, Carver said, for Ky to remain as premier, and even though it was "vastly preferable" for the Directory to remain in power, the position and interests of the U.S. could still be preserved if a successor government were publicly dedicated to the objectives of prosecuting a war and building a free Vietnamese nation independent of Communist control."

This memorandum was written for the Director of Central Intelligence and was not circulated in the government. It was sent by Carver to Donald Ropa, a CIA employee working with the NSC, and William Bundy was shown a copy of the draft.

Communist seizure of power. Given the latent popular base that a Buddhist government would have, however, and the organizational talents which the Buddhist leadership has displayed[64] it is not inconceivable that from this shaky beginning there could evolve a uniquely Vietnamese Government which, over the long run, would not only be tolerably effective but would enjoy solid popular support. The road would be rocky indeed, but it could ultimately lead to something approaching genuine political stability."

Although success of the Struggle Movement could cause tension among the military, one of the results of a Buddhist government, Carver said, "given the degree of at least latent support for the Buddhists prevalent throughout the South Vietnamese military establishment (particularly in enlisted and junior officer ranks) . . . might be an even greater degree of unity within the military establishment than now exists and a greater sense of identification between the army and the populace."

Carver said that a Buddhist victory could result in Communist gains during the transition, but that the Buddhists were nationalist and were opposed to Communist domination of the country. "Their long term political objectives are essentially similar to ours, though their tactical behavior often aids the Communist cause."

A Buddhist controlled government, Carver said, would probably consist of an elected assembly that would chose the chief of state and the premier. One likely candidate for chief of state would be General Duong Van "Big" Minh, and a possible choice for premier would be a Buddhist political activist, Bui Tuong Huan, rector of Hue University.

"There is little question," Carver added, "that the Buddhists emotionally resent the present extent of U.S. involvement in Vietnamese affairs and the sheer physical magnitude of the current U.S. presence in Vietnam. . . ." Whether they would want the U.S. to leave soon, "and in a manner which might result in an inevitable Communist victory," remained to be seen, he said. "On balance we believe they would not, even though their short-sightedness might prompt them to act in ways involving the serious risk of producing just this effect."

On April 9, after the President had apparently expressed his opinion that action was needed, Rostow sent a memorandum to Rusk and McNamara, "Breaking Tri Quang's Momentum."[65] He argued that the Ky government did not have the "unity, will, or force" to suppress the protests by force. The U.S., moreover, was not a nation that could use force "to shoot people [Ky had threatened to shoot the mayor of Danang] apparently demanding a constitution and free elections; and we cannot support for long governments that do this." But, he added, the U.S. could use force to suppress protests that would disrupt a representative assembly, and could support a government seeking to do so. "It follows," he said,

[64] Of Tri Quang, who, if the Buddhists took power, would be "at least temporarily the most powerful political figure in South Vietnam," Carver said: "Tri Quang is infinitely complex and uniquely Vietnamese. He is vain, ignores the 'people's' wishes with his own prestige, and thoroughly enjoys playing the game of politics for its own sake. He is nationalistic to the point of xenophobia, a consummate master of the arts of agitation and pressure, and without question the most effective politician now active in South Vietnam."

[65] Rostow's memorandum is in the Johnson Library, NSF Memos to the President—Walt Rostow. On April 11, Rostow, at the suggestion of Valenti and Moyers, sent the memorandum to the President.

"that it may be better to accept a constitutional gathering heavily weighted with provincial and municipal officials, as the Buddhists claim they want, than it is to try first to suppress the disorder in the streets."

This means:

—substantial concessions to the Buddhists formula for a constitutional gathering;

—maintenance of the unity of the Directorate;

—probably—but not necessarily—the replacement of Ky, who has shown guts and some political sensitivity;

—then, at the right moment, a countrywide curfew, backed, if necessary, by U.S. forces, to permit the constitutional group to work.

"The guts of the issue," Rostow said, "is to get enough Buddhists into the convention to give the Directorate—and perhaps us—a credible basis for suppressing disorder." In so doing, the U.S. would need to make compromises. "Some deal with Thi may be a critical element."

On April 9, 1966, there was a meeting of the President's senior advisers at which assignments were made for papers for a review of U.S. options. (There are no known notes of the meeting.) Carver was asked to do a paper arguing for the status quo—option A; Leonard Unger (William Bundy's deputy) would do a paper on the "optimistic" case for continuing but seeking a compromise solution—option B-O; McNaughton would do a paper on the "pessimistic" side—option B-P; and Ball, who was in charge of the review, would do a paper on withdrawal—option C.

Option A, as presented in Carver's paper, provided for continuing present programs and policies, while recognizing that the political contest would result in changes in the political structure of South Vietnam, and that the execution of U.S. policy "will have to be marked by flexibility and considerable capacity for tactical adjustments."[66] Military operations against North Vietnam and against the Ho Chi Minh Trail should be intensified. New targets in North Vietnam should be attacked, including POL, and the harbor at Haiphong should probably be mined.

Because of the disruptive effect of political changes—"at best, we will be in for a situation like that of late 1963"—it was essential during the transition period to block Communist military advances in South Vietnam by the aggressive use of U.S. and other forces.

At the same time, the U.S. should make clear that its continued support was contingent upon "some modicum of responsible political behavior on the part of the Vietnamese," and should, "without intruding in a way that is politically counter-productive," help the South Vietnamese with the development of their political institutions. "[W]e must initiate the Vietnamese in the techniques of developing political institutions such as constitutions and parties . . . but no effort should be made to force their evolution into a mold fashioned in our image."

Carver concluded: "A coldly rational weighing of all operative factors cannot produce a very high estimate of South Vietnam's

[66] Carver's paper, "Option A," which was not dated, is in the Johnson Library, Warnke Papers, McNaughton Files.

chances for developing a stable and effective central government. . . . Events in South Vietnam, however, never have moved in the manner pointed to by tidily logical predictions. . . . Vietnam being Vietnam, there is at least an even chance that the transition to civilian rule will be marked and effected in more or less orderly fashion over a period of two or three months."

Option A would fail, Carver said, if the central government were unable to exercise effective authority; but, if that occurred, the U.S. could disengage "at less net political cost" than if U.S. policy were to be reversed during the existing crisis.

The paper drafted by Unger on the second option, B-O ("O" for optimistic), was based on the assumption that there would be a policy decision to negotiate an end to the war "on terms that preserve South Vietnam intact and in a condition which offers at least a 60–40 chance of its successfully resisting communist attempts at political takeover."[67]

Course B-O provided for military action to be based on strengthening the negotiating posture of the U.S. and the South Vietnamese. Ground operations in the South would continue as planned, but there would be only "modest" increases in U.S. forces as required to continue "modest forward motion" and to respond to new threats from infiltrated forces. Similarly, the air war against North Vietnam would continue but would not be expanded "into areas or against targets which seriously risk bringing Communist China more actively into the conflict." Moreover, there would be no ground action against North Vietnam or air attacks against the Chinese border or the more central parts of Hanoi and Haiphong.

On the nonmilitary side, option B-O provided for increased political development (writing a constitution, holding elections) in order to strengthen the political posture of the South Vietnamese vis-à-vis the Communists.

Option B-O, would also be well received in the United States, where, Unger said, "sentiment today appears overwhelmingly to favor the Government's pursuing negotiations and seeking a peaceful settlement." There would be some criticism by those who supported the war, and if the settlement appeared to "open the door to a communist take-over, it would certainly be condemned by majority opinion."

In conclusion, Unger said, in a comment that could as easily have been made in 1973 when the cease-fire was finally agreed to,

> Our judgment may prove wrong and arrangements that are worked out and appear to be safe enough may lead to the disintegration of noncommunist forces in the South and leave the door wide open for the VC/NLF to take charge, directly or in stages. It appears unlikely this could take place at any early date when the GVN military is still fairly well organized and we would probably still be present at least in some form. Thereafter if this should occur it would probably have to be accepted since there would be little alternative short of what would amount to an invasion by outside forces.

The third option, B–P ("P" for pessimistic), assigned to McNaughton, apparently was not presented in the form of a com-

---

[67] Unger's paper, "Course B-O," is in the same location.

pleted paper, but on April 4, 1966, McNaughton had drafted a paper, "Some Thoughts About Vietnam," in which he stated the case for a pessimistic point of view:[68]

> Cuba II [missile crisis] came out well (1) because our vital interests were at stake and Russia knew it, (2) because we had local military superiority and Russia knew it, and (3) because the equities were on our side and Russia knew it. Berlin 1961–62 came out well despite the fact that the second of these characteristics was missing. Vietnam 1966 is a case in which none of the three characteristics is fully present . . . .
>
> The situation in Vietnam is bad and not getting better. The military situation in one sense is better than it was a year ago: We thwarted the VC hope to achieve a quick victory in 1965; the VC now share the initiative with us (mainly with the U.S., since the ARVN is tired, passive and accommodation-prone). In another sense, the military situation is worse than a year ago: The "temperature" of the war has gone up by a factor of ten. There has been no progress in pacification of the Priority Areas; for one reason or another, "this" year is still the year for preparation and "next" year the year for progress. Ky's "revolution" is stalled. The economy of South Vietnam is in a precarious state; inflation is serious. Corruption of a destabilizing kind (like pre-1948 China not like modern Thailand) is widespread. Government control is confined to enclaves as it was a year ago, with a moribund political infrastructure especially in the rural areas. While the tide of defeatism that was flowing a year ago has been stemmed, the recent riots—not only in I Corps but also in the rest of the country including Saigon, and not only involving civilians but also ARVN soldiers—reveal a rottenness in the fabric that may not be curable within the time with which we have to work . . . .
>
> The best judgment is that, even with full US deployments, we will probably be faced in 1967 with a continued stalemate at a higher level of forces and casualties.

Even if the war were to be "won," McNaughton said, "no one sees the end of the road in South Vietnam. . . ."

> The Communists can be expected to resort to heroic extremes to prevent the government from providing security to the people. While the Communists would have failed, they would still have the power to prevent our success. Only the most rigorous population control could suppress such an insurgency, and all indications are that the people of South Vietnam, under any political leadership that is likely to arise (other than Communist), could not achieve such population control. (Experience indicates that no South Vietnamese government is likely to be able to provide both stability and leadership. The attempt to provide the latter destroys the former.) Thus there is no clear plan for or prospect of "winning the peace" except at a level of violence and of Communist challenge far below the one that is likely to pertain. It follows, among other things, that a substantial number of US forces—several

[68] A copy of McNaughton's paper is in the State Department, Lot File 70 D 207.

divisions—would probably have to remain in Vietnam for a period of years even if our present military efforts succeed.

On April 15, McNaughton drafted an incomplete "first rough draft" of Option B–P, which he described as "maintain present course but accept 'soft' compromise," in which he discussed a "fight-and-compromise" policy of increasing diplomatic probing for a negotiated settlement while continuing to increase military pressure. This was a summary of the plan:[69]

1. Most Important: Change objectives from do-what-it-takes-to-make-the-North-stop-it to do-what-it-takes-to-force-a-GVN/VC-compromise.

2. Recognize that we are on a losing wicket in Vietnam. While the military situation is not going badly, the political situation is in "terminal sickness" and even the military prognosis is of an escalating stalemate.

3. Make a private presidential decision to seize upon the I Corps troubles as the vehicle for disengagement by the United States. Success will require secrecy and completely loyal execution. (Query how to bring Lodge on board and how to deal with Congressional leaders.)

4. Choose between two approaches: (a) Fast ("fed up") withdrawal, and (b) slow ("patch up but squeeze the GVN") approach. The former would be wise only if GVN left-footedness or anti-Americanism becomes extreme.

5. While a new Saigon government is being formed (now), deliver a US "ultimatum" to all interested parties (including Buddhists) that they must shape up or we will ship out. We could either (a) insist now that they compromise with the VC or (b) assume that they will be able to shape up, so that compromise with the VC would come later.

6. Ensure that US civilian and military personnel in Vietnam can be protected.

7. Initiate an effort to re-educate US and world opinion:

a. That our commitment is to support a representative government and people who help themselves (and that the GVN has now shown itself not to be representative and that the people of South Vietnam have demonstrated that they will not help themselves).

b. That the South Vietnamese case is unique—unlike the case of our other "clients" (giving the reasons in detail).

c. That we have more than delivered the goods in blood and treasure in Vietnam—enough to honor our guarantee and enough to cause any aggressor to pause lest an equivalent amount be delivered against him in another case.

8. Consult with key allies—ROK [Republic of Korea], Australians, New Zealanders, Japanese, etc.

9. Continue U.S. aid and deployments to and actions in "cooperative" areas and continue strikes against North Vietnam and Laos *if and only if* solid efforts are being made toward working out a compromise with the VC. [emphasis in original]

---

[69] A copy of Warnke's paper of April 15, together with the summary ("Possible 'Fall Back' Plan" which had been drafted on April 5, 1966), is in the Johnson Library, Warnke Papers, McNaughton Files.

(Of course, if we were surprised by the appearance of a Magsaysay [Ramon Magsaysay, late President of the Philippines], we could change our strategy.) If no such efforts toward compromise are made, stop new deployments, move into a unilateral US ceasefire, and withdraw into enclaves preparatory to departure from Vietnam.

10. Press for an international conference, moves in the UN and an election.

11. Be prepared for serious deterioration in Vietnam, shock in Asia, damage to our influence throughout the world, gloating by the Communists, and political back-lash at home.

12. Take initiatives in Asia and elsewhere to offset and diffuse the issue.

The fourth option (C), presented in a paper, "Cutting our Losses," drafted by George Ball on April 21, 1966, was based on the assumption that the South Vietnamese were not capable of establishing a government that could effectively govern or prosecute the war or govern the country afterward.[70] "Divisions are too old, too deep, and too fundamental. Hatred and jealousies are too intense and the elements of cohesion are too evanescent. The current experimentation with a democratic process is, therefore, far more likely to intensify the power fight than to produce a stable, broadly-based government."

An "effective strategy" for cutting U.S. losses, Ball said, "must focus on making it clear and unambiguous: (a) that the United States has fully met its obligations to the South Vietnamese people and to the world, and (b) that it is the South Vietnamese people who have failed, not us."

Accordingly, the U.S. should take the position:

(a) That the United States is prepared to provide whatever help is necessary to secure independent South Viet-Nam. However, the failure of the South Vietnamese people to create a stable government is making it difficult, if not impossible, to achieve that objective.

(b) Before we commit further forces to South Viet-Nam the South Vietnamese people must demonstrate by deeds that they can achieve the unity necessary for the success of our common objectives.

(c) The United States hopes that if the South Vietnamese people frankly face the realities of their predicament they will achieve the necessary unity; certainly unity must be quickly achieved if the war is to be won.

(d) Pending achievement of a stable government the United States will halt the deployment of additional forces, reduce the level of air attacks on the North, and maintain ground activity at the minimum level required to prevent the substantial improvement of the Viet Cong position.

Ball concluded that there were "no really alternative options open to us. To continue to fight the war with the present mushy political base is . . . both dangerous and futile. . . . On the other hand, we can—if we choose—utilize the resumption of political tur-

[70] A copy of Ball's four-page paper is in the Johnson Library, Warnke Papers, McNaughton Files.

moil in Vietnam [which he predicted would occur in the near future] as the basis for a long overdue show-down with the South Vietnamese people. Either they do what is required to win the war or our own effort becomes pointless."

Maxwell Taylor, who, after returning from Saigon in July 1965, had become a White House consultant on Vietnam, also stated his position in a memorandum to the President, "Current Situation in South Vietnam," April 12, 1966. "While Ky has won good marks for prudence," Taylor said, "he has appeared vacillating on occasion and has certainly not yet shown himself capable of ordering the 'whiff of grapeshot' which may be necessary someday if his government is to survive." Ky was expendable, Taylor added, but Tri Quang must be prevented from overthrowing the Directorate. "In explanation of such a program, the GVN (Ky, for the present) should be encouraged to use the necessary force to restore and maintain order, short of attempting to reimpose government rule by bayonets on Danang-Hue which, for the time being, should be merely contained and isolated." "I feel it in my bones," Taylor said, "that over-reaction at this time either in Washington or Saigon is more dangerous than a continuation of restraint. Hence, I would recommend a prudent use of force within the law against the Buddhists, and an effective isolation of the dissident part of the Center [of the country] while trying to buy off Thi and urging the military to close ranks. In Washington, we should continue to reject the slogan 'take over or get out' which, unfortunately, will gain in advocates if the political situation does not soon stabilize."[71]

Consideration of Options

On April 12–14, 1966, the National Political Congress met in Saigon. In attendance were 92 (115 by the final day) out of 170 handpicked by the government. Dr. Phan Quang Dan, an American favorite, was elected chairman. A Buddhist "observer" from the Institute sat in on the final session, and Tam Chau expressed his support for the government's action in convening the Congress, but other Buddhist leaders continued to rail at the "Ky-Thieu clique" and to demonstrate against the government.[72] On April 14, Thieu signed a decree calling for elections to a Constituent Assembly (constitutional convention) within three to six months, and he and Ky agreed to take certain actions stipulated by the Congress, among which were that the military government would resign as soon as elections for the Assembly were held, the problems in I Corps would be solved by political rather than military means, and no one involved in the demonstrations would be punished.[73] The Buddhists responded by halting their protests.[74] In a speech in Hue, Tri Quang, while continuing to criticize the Ky government and the Americans, urged his listeners to suspend demonstrations and to support the establishment of a national assembly. In what one unnamed American official called a "brilliant political performance," Tri Quang said: "We cannot just demonstrate against the

---

[71] Johnson Library, Memos to the President—Walt Rostow.

[72] U.S. Department of State, Central File, Pol 27 Viet S, Saigon to Washington 3920 and 3985, Apr. 12 and 13, 1966; *New York Times*, Apr. 15, 1966.

[73] *New York Times*, Apr. 14, 1966.

[74] U.S. Department of State, Central File, Pol 27 Viet S, Saigon to Washington 4006, Apr. 15, 1966.

government, from this government to another government, to be betrayed again and again. We would be demonstrating against the government every six months." A National Assembly, he said, could only "betray us to a fixed degree and for a fixed time." [75]

In a cable to Washington on April 16, Lodge discussed the problems facing the South Vietnamese Government as a result of the disturbances and made suggestions for the U.S. Government's position on key issues.[76] There should not be a military campaign against the Danang/Hue area, he said, but there should be "clever police-type" steps taken "to shrink, whittle and subdivide" the leaders of the protests. General Thi should be given a job in the government, but should be removed from his base in I Corps.

"If possible," Lodge said, "there should be little or no change in the Directorate" and the U.S. should work through the Ky government as much as possible. It should also encourage the development of a strong pro-government political party before the end of 1966, and strengthen contacts with political groups and individuals.

"We are now faced with the prospect," Lodge added, "that political forces will be at work in Vietnam in great variety and without clear direction." [77]

In its reply on April 20, drafted by Miller, the State Department replied that it was concerned that the "'current breather' in SVN political crisis is being subjected to increasing strains by maneuverings and acts of violence between struggle and antistruggle forces in I Corps, by increasing doubts expressed by certain Saigon groups of wisdom of going ahead with elections and by tortuous procedure proposed by GVN for drafting electoral law for constituent assembly elections. . . . If current fragile agreement to proceed with constitutional assembly elections is to be prevented from coming apart at the seams, . . . GVN should move rapidly and as far as its still uncertain authority permits to try to stop bickering in I Corps and to urge all groups to cooperate in preparing for forthcoming elections. We also think Mission may have to give GVN behind-the-scenes assistance on this scope." [78] In response later that same day to another cable from Saigon, the State Department (Miller drafting) said that it agreed with Lodge's com-

[75] *New York Times*, Apr. 20, 1966.

[76] Johnson Library, NSF Country File, Vietnam, Saigon to Washington 4033, Apr. 16, 1966. See also Lodge's weekly report to the President, same location, Saigon to Washington 4085, Apr. 20, 1966.

[77] Lodge himself was the subject of some discussion. In a "special annex" to his report to the President of Apr. 19, 1966, after a trip to Vietnam to review the pacification program, Presidential Assistant Robert Komer said, "I think we have a Lodge problem on our hands . . . he (even more than his top people) deeply distrusts the Buddhists and really sees little but a time of political troubles ahead. He fears a neutralist regime is in the cards. Porter, who is thoroughly loyal to him, told me privately before I left that he was most unsure Lodge would have much stomach for all the painful jockeying needed. Porter thinks that we should start thinking now about a replacement." (Johnson Library, NSF Country File, Vietnam.) On his copy of this annex, Komer noted: "The President has only other copy."

Komer, as a way of laying the groundwork for removing Lodge, asked Porter to mention to Lodge his (Komer's) concern about rumors that Lodge would be leaving Vietnam. Several weeks later, Porter did so, and reported to Komer that it had the desired effect. Lodge said that he had no intention of "deserting ship," especially before the November U.S. congressional elections, but that "any man got stale after too long out here," and if the President would be interested in using him in some other diplomatic post he would be "most interested." "In sum," Porter said in his cable, "situation under control and options open." Komer noted by hand on his copy of the cable that he had sent it to the President. Johnson Library, NSF Files of Robert W. Komer, Backchannel Cables Porter-Komer, Saigon to Washington 3959, June 22, 1966.

[78] Johnson Library, NSF Country File, Vietnam, Washington to Saigon 3144, Apr. 20, 1967.

ments to Ky about the "dangers of moving against Thi at this stage . . . we continue to favor bringing Thi back into the fold in some fashion as means for undercutting I Corps dissidents further."[79]

In Washington, where the review of policy options continued, Rostow prepared and circulated on April 14 a list of the various actions which should be considered in connection with developing U.S. strategy for "the next phase."[80] These included a possible statement by the President expressing satisfaction with the moves toward a "constitutional democratic government," but indicating that the continuation of U.S. assistance depended upon efforts by the South Vietnamese to maintain order and to prosecute the war and revolutionary development. For its part, the U.S. should urge the South Vietnamese to study experiences of other countries with political development, and, "in the most discreet way possible," should make available experts to help in drafting the constitution. Moreover, there should be a major effort to gather intelligence on those persons and interests that would be participating in the constitutional convention. "We should crank up a systematic effort which would yield us the same kind of knowledge of the local interests and personalities as we would for a U.S. national political convention."

Rostow also raised the question of increasing the bombing of the North by attacking POL sites, and asked whether increased ground combat in the South was desirable and possible. He also suggested that U.S. policymakers should consider "whether, when, and how we might suggest to the government [of South Vietnam] that they try to open a covert dialogue with the VC and perhaps, when the constitution and party-making process is firmed up, an open invitation to the VC to stop their terror attacks and join in making a democratic nation, including a willingness to have them take part in constitution-making."

To minimize the adverse effect of the situation on Congress and the public, senior officials in Washington were also very active during April, as well as in May and June, in holding "background" sessions with prominent political reporters, especially major newspapers, "in an effort to avoid excessive and alarmist interpretation of the political crisis in Vietnam."[81]

On April 16, three additional memoranda were prepared and circulated among those involved in the policy review, apparently in connection with a meeting of the group that day: "How We Should Move" by Carver, "Scenario" by Unger, and "Politics in Vietnam: A 'Worst' Outcome," by McNaughton.[82] Carver and Unger's papers suggested that the U.S. commitment in South Vietnam should be clarified by emphasizing that it was contingent upon what Carver called the Eisenhower position, namely, the "essential premise" that external help could be effective only if there was adequate internal self-support. This clarification, Carver said, should be publicly and privately presented in order to give the U.S. "maximum

---

[79] Same location, Washington to Saigon 3145, Apr. 20, 1967.

[80] Johnson Library, Warnke Papers, McNaughton Files.

[81] This quotation was used in several of the reports of such meetings which were sent to the White House on a weekly basis by State Department officials, primarily Rusk, Ball, and William Bundy. These are located in the Department of State, Lot File 74 D 164.

[82] All three papers, dated April 16, are in the Johnson Library, Warnke Papers, McNaughton Files.

leverage over our Vietnamese allies and maximum freedom of unilateral action." Once this position was clear, the U.S., depending on the response of the South Vietnamese, could then implement either option A (a continuation of U.S. programs) or option C (withdrawal).

Carver added that, "Domestically and internationally we cannot appear to have initiated a policy reversal." For this reason, there should be a guarded but increasing emphasis on the conditional nature of U.S. aid, "while making it appear that our policy remains what it has always been."

In a set of questions at the conclusion of his paper, Carver asked whether the U.S. should deploy more troops or halt deployment, how the U.S. should approach the South Vietnamese on American demands for improved performance, whether the U.S. should continue seeking to negotiate with the Communists, and whether the U.S. should encourage the South Vietnamese to undertake negotiations.

Unger's scenario was based on the continuation of U.S. programs, but provided also for encouraging the South Vietnamese to "exploit all possible contacts with VC/NLF" to seek a negotiated settlement.

McNaughton's paper on the "worst" outcome dealt with the possible fall of the military government and its replacement by neutralists who would seek to negotiate with the Communists for a cease-fire and a coalition government. After discussing the various possible responses of the United States to such an event, he concluded: "Few of the possible U.S. courses offer any promise of a less-than-disastrous negotiation. . . . When things come to this postulated pass, the United States has little choice but to get out of Vietnam." If forced to withdraw the objectives should be: "minimizing the inevitable loss of face and protecting US forces, allied forces, and those South Vietnamese who appeal to us for political refuge."

On April 21, 1966, as the review of options was being completed and recommendations were being prepared, Rostow, in a memorandum for the President, "Vietnam—the Critical Issues," again argued for increased military action to force an early end to the war.[83] "In Vietnam," he said, "we face an enemy whose main hope is that American political life cannot stand the strains of protracted war and of baffling political turbulence in Vietnam. They are playing us as they did the French in 1953." "Our task is to convince them at the earliest possible moment that they are wrong; and that time is their enemy, not their friend."

"[W]ar-weariness in Vietnam and the domestic strains of the whole affair," Rostow said, "might well cause a break in Saigon or in Washington at some point, if it appears endless. We must, therefore, look to measures which will force a favorable decision in Hanoi now rather than later." These were, he said, to:

1. Increase the cost to Hanoi of continuing the war by hurting them badly around Hanoi-Haiphong.
2. Find a way to block or radically to inhibit the supply roads from Laos.

[83] Johnson Library, NSF Memos to the President—Walt Rostow.

3. Increase sharply the attrition rates against VC-PAVN main force units to the point where they begin to disintegrate.
4. Produce a relatively stable consolidation of anti-Communist political groups.
5. Get inflation under control and steadily build up rural reconstruction in the provinces.

Rostow concluded his memorandum by noting that there would again come a time when the President would speak to the Nation about Vietnam, and he suggested that he might want to speak on the theme, "We are all being tested by this crisis." The American people, Rostow said, "are being tested to understand the nature of the war; to understand the confusing but essentially constructive struggle of a democratic nation to bloom; and, above all, by the fact that the Communists are counting on us to despair and give up." After the speech, there would need to be a campaign to explain the nature of the political development occurring in South Vietnam. "If our people really understand, I believe they would be quite tolerant of the birth pangs."[84]

On April 25, the President met from 6:30 p.m. to 6:48 p.m. with the Vice President, Rusk, McNamara, Ball, William Bundy, Rostow, Raborn, Helms, Komer and Moyers. The principal item on the agenda was the report and recommendations of the Working Group, headed by Ball, that had been examining U.S. options.[85]

The Working Group report, "Basic Choices in Vietnam," dated April 25, which was drafted by William Bundy, said that, "the mere fact that such a crisis could come as close as it already has (and may again) to disastrous civil strife and chaos or could raise, as it also has, the spectre of a government's coming to power which would ask us to leave forces us to look hard at our basic position and policy in South Vietnam. We must now recognize that three contingencies of the utmost gravity are, in some degree, more likely than our previous planning had recognized:

(1) *There may be a state of chaos and total paralysis. . . .*

(2) *There could emerge a government that would seek to end the war on almost any terms and that would ask us to leave, with such broadly based support that we would virtually have to accept or take what seems to most of us the practically impossible alternative of continuing the struggle on our own. . . .*

(3) *The government continues weak and ineffective, especially in its prosecution of the non-military programs that are crucial to eventual success. . . .* (emphases in original)

The members of the Working Group, according to the memorandum, believed that the chances of the first contingency were small—10–15 percent (Ball thought they were "substantively higher"), and less for the second contingency. "All members of the group agree that if either of these contingencies should materialize, we would have virtually no choice but to start withdrawing, and that

[84] On May 1, Rostow sent a memorandum to the President (Johnson Library, NSF Memos to the President—Walt Rostow) proposing a Presidential "fireside chat," "to rally the sound 60% of the country to sweat out the next stage [the political campaign in Vietnam for a constitution and elections] with confidence. . . ."

[85] The final version of the report, with a two-page cover memorandum from Rusk, is in the Department of State, Lot File 70 D 207 (William Bundy Papers).

in these circumstances we would have little bargaining leverage in connection with our presence or withdrawal."

Three options were assessed:[86]

> *Option A:* To continue roughly along present lines, in the hope that the setback is temporary.
>
> *Option B:* To continue roughly along present lines, perhaps with a decrease in the rate of entry of US troops, but moving more actively to stimulate contact between the Saigon government and elements in the Viet Cong. Such contact could either begin with a public call for negotiations by the GVN or with covert tentative feelers. After the rough outlines of the VC position had been determined, the US would then decide on whether to press the GVN to continue negotiations or to support the GVN in its reluctance to accept difficult terms.
>
> *Option C:* To decide now that the chances of bringing about an independent and non-Communist South Vietnam have shrunk to the point where, on an over-all basis, the US effort is no longer warranted. This would mean setting the stage where, at the proper moment, steps can be taken that would probably lead to a disengagement and withdrawal.

All options, the memorandum noted, would involve "indicating more clearly than in the past that our continued support is contingent upon adequate unity and effectiveness on the part of the Vietnamese."

The final part of the report surveyed the "broader factors" involved—relations with allies and with the Soviet Union and China, U.S. public and congressional opinion, and the effect of a U.S. "failure" in Vietnam on the defense of other Asian countries. With respect to the last of these, the report took the position, contrary to McNaughton's argument, that such a failure would probably result eventually in Communist domination of all of Southeast Asia, beginning with Thailand.

This was the report's assessment of the possible public and congressional effects of the political crisis in South Vietnam:

> Within the US, popular and Congressional support for the conflict has been at adequate levels prior to the recent difficulties. This support has certainly been shaken, how much we cannot yet tell. The contingencies of "chaos" and "being asked to leave" would certainly reduce domestic support to the unacceptable level. Moreover, the contingency of continued GVN weakness and moderate political unrest is itself bound to cut down support. As we look a year or two ahead, with a military program that would require further budget costs—with all their implications for taxes and domestic programs—and with steady or probably rising casualties, the war could well become an albatross around the Administration's neck, at least equal to what Korea was for President Truman in 1952. It does not seem likely that the American people will wish to quit under pressure, as the French did, but the scars of a war conducted in an atmosphere of growing malaise and backbiting could be very serious indeed.

---

[86] See the report for a discussion of each option.

The Working Group, with the exception of Ball, did not express a preference for any one option. In a cover memorandum for the President, which probably represented the consensus of the group, Rusk recommended option A—continuing along present lines—but added, in relation to the provision in option B for stimulating contacts between the South Vietnamese and the Communists, that there should be discussions with Lodge about "the possibility of probing individuals or groups in the Viet Cong in an effort to create divisions among them." Rusk, at least, apparently did not favor the stimulation of such contacts for the purpose of negotiations.

Unfortunately, there are no known notes of the meeting of April 25 of the President and his advisers to consider the report of the Working Group except for a one-page memorandum by Rostow which says only that the President decided that, "We shall stay on course and explore with Lodge a cautious Track B"—in other words, he accepted Rusk's recommendation.[87]

On April 27, the State Department sent a cable to Lodge asking for his comments on a memorandum drafted for Unger by Robert Miller, "Political Tactics in Vietnam Over Next Few Months," which had been prepared in conjunction with the review of options.[88] Among the key issues, according to the cable, was whether the existing government would stay in power until the constitution was approved, or whether, as the Buddhists and others argued, it should and would end once the Assembly was elected to draft the constitution. The cable took the position that the government should remain in power, or should resign and be reappointed as an interim government by the Assembly, and should continue in power until a new government was formed under the constitution.

Another key issue was the lack of well-organized and functioning political parties or "fronts." The cable took the position that unless such parties, opposed to the Communists, were organized prior to the elections, "those elections will lead at least to weakness and division and possibly to establishment by VC of foothold through apparently respectable groups under its influence." Although organizing parties and fronts in time for the election might not be possible, the U.S., the cable added, should "influence political process as far as possible in this direction before those elections are held."[89]

That same day (April 27), after a report from Lodge on a meeting of the Directorate (South Vietnamese military leaders), the State Department (Miller drafting) sent a cable to the U.S. Embassy in Saigon expressing concern about what appeared to be a trend on the part of the military toward greater control of the forthcoming election by such means as "permitting only 'tame' personalities to

[87] Johnson Library, NSF Country File, Vietnam, Rostow Memorandum for the Record, Apr. 25, 1966.

[88] The paper is attached to the Working Group Memorandum, source cited above. The cable, Washington to Saigon 3230, Apr. 27, 1966, is in the Department of State Central File, Pol 27 Viet S.

[89] To assist in the formulation of U.S. policy and operations in connection with the forthcoming Constitutional Assembly in South Vietnam, the State Department organized an interdepartmental Political Development Working Group that met from April to December 1966. Unger was chairman, and other participants from State were Miller, William Jorden (public affairs), John Helbe (Vietnam desk), and Louis Sarris (intelligence). Others were Ropa (a CIA officer) from the White House, William E. Colby from the CIA, and Sanford Marlowe from USIA. Summary records of each meeting, the first of which was on Apr. 25, 1966, are in the Department of State, Lot File 70 D 102.) At meetings of the group on April 25, May 2 and May 6, there was discussion of the questions raised by Unger (Miller) in his paper on political tactics.

participate," and "carrying out hasty programs such as police housing to capture important voting blocs." "In our view," the cable said, "this could very rapidly lead to big trouble with Buddhist extremists as well as with other major groups which have expressed themselves in favor of early return to elected civilian government. For this reason, we strongly believe that Directorate must take great pains to share responsibility for decisions on all major election issues with electoral council and to avoid appearance of dictating to council or to groups represented on it." "In short," the cable concluded, "Vietnamese military have got to be made to understand that, while SVN's political development is internal affairs and U.S. will not interfere with it or impose solutions, U.S. cannot let domestic and international support for its massive commitment to SVN be undermined indefinitely by apparently endless political disorder."[90]

In early May, 1966, Lodge was called to Washington for consultation on the issues facing the U.S. in South Vietnam. On May 2, Unger prepared for William Bundy and Rostow a list of issues for discussion with Lodge.[91] These included inflation, elections for the Constitutional Assembly, political parties, the "life of the present government," and military programs. With respect to elections for the Constitutional Assembly, the memorandum stated that, "The President should make it clear to Ambassador Lodge that from the point of view of United States' opinion, to say nothing of international opinion, failure to follow through on this commitment would seriously undermine support of our Vietnam policy." With respect to the "life of the present government," the memorandum took a modified position from that which Unger had suggested in his memorandum of April 27 that the present government should continue after the elections for the Constitutional Assembly, or should be reappointed by the Assembly, and should be replaced only after a general election held after the constitution took effect. Unger's May 2 memorandum argued instead that, "While in the abstract it may seem preferable to seek a continuation of the present government until a new one can be set up under the constitution, politically it may be more realistic and advisable to favor the ceding of authority to the constitutional assembly once elected. That body could either confirm the continuation of the present government as a caretaker until there will be new elections under the constitution, broaden the present government or, a less satisfactory alternative, install an entirely new government."

On May 6, Ky, apparently without consultation with the U.S., announced that his government would remain in power until the election in 1967 of a new government under the constitution.[92]

As a result of this reversal of Ky's earlier position, there were new disturbances, and in a cable on May 13, Porter, acting for Lodge, said that, "The dangers of a confrontation between militant Buddhists and the Directorate-Catholic-Northerners alliance and of the development of anti-American attitudes are already real and present ones." Porter argued that the U.S. could not remain pas-

[90] Johnson Library, NSF Country File, Vietnam, Washington to Saigon 3229, Apr. 27, 1967.
[91] U.S. Department of State, Lot File 70 D 102.
[92] *New York Times*, May 7, 1966. See also U.S. Department of State, Central File, Pol 2 Viet S, Saigon to Washington 4489, May 10, 1966.

sive, and that "we should make up our minds what our interests require and then marshal our assets and direct them in a carefully synchronized and skillfully executed effort to influence the course of events." With respect to the situation in I Corps, the government should reassert its authority, he said, not by a "violent attempt to 'reoccupy' Danang and Hue, but rather a firm persistent and quiet effort with little or no publicity to whittle away at the Buddhist machine in the First Corps. . . ."[93]

On May 10, the National Security Council was convened to consider the situation. Meeting with the President from 5:45 p.m. to 7:32 p.m. were the Vice President, Rusk, McNamara, Ball, Rostow, Lodge (accompanied by Habib and Lansdale), William Bundy, Unger, Vance, McNaughton, General Wheeler, Ambassador Goldberg, Fowler, Raborn and Helms, Marks, William S. Gaud (Deputy Administrator of the Agency for International Development), and White House and NSC staff members Moyers, Valenti, Taylor, Komer, and Bromley Smith.[94]

General Wheeler gave a briefing on the military situation.[95] He also commented on the effect on the military of the political disturbances, saying that they had a "small" effect on U.S. forces but a "larger" effect on South Vietnamese forces. McNamara added: "We hope that heavy pressure by U.S. forces will carry us over the present period."

Lodge analyzed the political situation. "The Saigon Government is now almost paralyzed," he said, "but we will have to learn to work in this atmosphere. . . . The word for the future is evolution rather than stability."

Rusk emphasized the importance of having a "broad based constituent assembly." "It would be a real setback for us," he said, "if this Assembly does not come out of the present political activity in Saigon." "In order to ensure that Saigon will act," he added, "we may have to go so far as to use the threat to get out of Vietnam."

---

[93] Johnson Library, Files of Robert W. Komer, Saigon to Washington 4554, May 13, 1966.

[94] In advance of the meeting a number of papers, with recommendations, were prepared on the subjects to be discussed. (Copies of these and a summary of all of the papers are in the Johnson Library, Meetings Notes File. Material quoted here is from the summary.) Among these were papers drafted by the State Department on the Constitutional Assembly, political parties, and the life of the present government. It was recommended that the U.S. position on the life of the government should be "a flexible position avoiding resolution of the issue now, while continually reappraising the desirability of the present GVN remaining in power during the interim period. . . ." On the Constitutional Assembly, it was recommended that,

"(a) We should do everything possible to see that Assembly election is held as promised by GVN;

"(b) take no position now on role of Assembly beyond its constitution drafting task;

"(c) encourage discussion and political activity to start the process of political party formation;

"(d) encourage formulation of an election law that ensures all noncommunist groups are adequately represented in Assembly—probably through constituencies based on population with multiple representation from each;

"(e) get major non-communist groups to agree before elections on a common body of agreed principles, such as social revolution, progress toward representative government, etc.;

"(f) encourage unity of directorate and promote reconciliation between Generals Ky and Thi;

"(g) encourage candidate qualification language that would disqualify 'agents of a foreign power' or other terms rather than disqualifying 'neutralists' or even 'communists' by those designations;

"(h) provide election experts to Mission, and quietly to the Vietnamese."

On political parties, the recommendation was that besides encouraging an electoral law that would provide for representation of major groups, the U.S. should "actively discourage any effort by Ky to form a government party designed purely to perpetuate himself in power and to exclude the militant Buddhists."

[95] Notes on this 557th NSC meeting were prepared by Bromley Smith, and are in the Johnson Library, NSF NSC Meetings File.

The President concluded the discussion by declaring: "We are committed and we will not be deterred. We must accept the fact that some will always oppose, dissent and criticize. We want results."

On May 12, Lodge met with the Senate Foreign Relations Committee for a discussion, generally very friendly, of the political situation in South Vietnam and U.S. military operations.[96]

Congressional Concern About the Situation in Vietnam

The political situation in South Vietnam during the spring of 1966 troubled many Members of Congress, even those like Senator Russell who were opposed to withdrawing and who thought the U.S. should make more of an effort to win the war.[97] In an interview in late April, Russell, who had been opposed to U.S. intervention in Vietnam, said, "For my part I think a very careful survey should be made in South Vietnam as to what people in the cities really think. If that survey shows that the majority of them are anti-American, I think we should withdraw now, because we can't possibly win if we are fighting an enemy in front of us while the people we are supposed to be helping are against us and want us out of their country." He was asked if it would be "disastrous" for the U.S. to withdraw. No, he said, not if the demonstrations continued, adding, "I don't buy this so-called 'domino' theory. Cambodia and Laos might go, along with South Vietnam, if we left. But I don't think that's any irreplaceable loss. Neither of them has any tremendous military value, either strategic or tactical." Nor did he feel that U.S. withdrawal would result in Communist conquest of neighboring countries, other than possibly Laos or Cambodia, and he noted traditional Vietnamese resistance to the Chinese as an important factor in deterring Chinese Communist influence in Southeast Asia.[98]

Senator Stennis, a conservative Democrat from Mississippi who was the ranking Democrat on the Armed Services Committee (following Russell) and chairman of its Preparedness Subcommittee, took a similar position. Although he supported the war and favored a much stronger military response, he said that if a freely-elected government in South Vietnam were to ask the U.S. to leave, it would have to do so.[99]

Senator Cooper, a moderate Republican from Kentucky, who had visited Vietnam twice in the preceding four months, took a similar position: "[W]e cannot defend people who are not willing to defend

[96] For a transcript of the hearing see U. S. Congress, Senate, Committee on Foreign Relations, *Executive Sessions of the Senate Foreign Relations Committee* (Historical Series), 1966, vol. XVIII (Washington, D.C.: U.S. Govt. Print. Off., 1993), pp. 725–768.

[97] For congressional comment see *CR*, vol. 112, pp. 7635–12104, *passim*.

[98] *U.S. News and World Report*, May 2, 1966. For Russell's opposition to U.S. intervention in Vietnam, see pts. I and III of this study.

In a television interview in 1970 Russell said: "I never thought . . . that French Indo-China, which includes South Vietnam, has any military, political, or economic values that make it worthwhile for us to go in there, even if it were to fall into the hands of the Chinese or the Russians. And I don't think it would fall into the hands of either because the other would challenge them on it and stop it." "Richard Russell: Georgia Giant," transcript of television documentary, pt. 3, February 1970, Cox Broadcasting Co., Atlanta, Georgia quoted by Ziemke, "Senator Richard B. Russell and the 'Lost Cause' in Vietnam, 1954–1968," cited above.

[99] These remarks by Stennis on the American Broadcasting Company's television program, "Issues and Answers," were reported in the *New York Times*, Apr. 18, 1966.

themselves. And a government which cannot gain the support and confidence of the people cannot act for the people."[100]

Others in the Senate, including Javits, Clark, Gore, Proxmire and Thruston B. Morton (R/Ky.), while stressing the importance of avoiding overinvolvement in the internal affairs of South Vietnam, said that an election should be held as soon as possible in order to allow political grievances to be aired and to give South Vietnam a more stable and representative government. Javits, a liberal Republican from New York, took the position that if a government should come into power which was opposed to continuing the war, the U.S. should redeploy its troops to another Asian country or countries where they could be available in the event of Chinese aggression. Although he was opposed to voluntary U.S. withdrawal from Vietnam, it "would be no disgrace" if circumstances required such a move.[101]

Abraham A. Ribicoff (D/Conn.) also favored an election but said in a Senate speech on May 5 that if the election were conducted by the Ky government the Buddhists and others would refuse to participate. Moreover, if the U.S. became too involved, it might end up having to be the guarantor of the outcome. For these reasons, he recommended the use of U.N. observers.[102]

Morse, calling it a "civil war within a civil war," said that "we can scarcely avoid a growing animosity among its people for a foreign military power [the U.S.] that destroys their country in the name of its own national interest." The U.S., he said, was "supporting an immoral and illegal war and involving itself in bloodletting in a country in which it had no right to be in the first place," and the rationale for U.S. action "requires that we remain whether or not there is a government in Saigon worthy of the name." The rebellion would be put down, he added, but this would be done with the help of the Americans. Yet, "the sad fact is that my Government and yours is supporting a tyranny in South Vietnam, a brutal military junta that has not the slightest conception of the meaning of the word freedom."[103]

Mansfield, in a statement in the Senate on April 18, 1966, proposed that, in view of the political instability in South Vietnam, the

---

[100] *CR*, vol. 112, Apr. 13, 1966, p. 8114.

[101] *Ibid.*, Apr. 14, 1966, p. 8153.

[102] *Ibid.*, vol. 112, pp. 8685–8689, 8693, 9922–9925, 10347. Ribicoff was correct: the election was boycotted by some of the Buddhists. In the meantime, however, the Struggle Movement had been suppressed, and, according to Shaplen, "The Buddhists' boycott of the election was no more effective than the Vietcong's threats to attack voters—about thirty five Buddhists running independently were elected, and violence was at a minimum. . . ." *The Road from War*, p. 85.

In a memorandum on May 6 to the President on Ribicoff's proposal, Rostow noted that it did not deal with possible objections of the South Vietnamese Government to such outside observers—a point Rostow said that Porter, U.S. Deputy Ambassador to South Vietnam, had raised when queried about Ribicoff's idea. Rostow concluded: "It is hoped that the Ribicoff proposal will die on grounds of being unreal in view of the position taken by Moscow, Hanoi and Peiping in opposition to any UN action on Vietnam." Johnson Library, NSF Memos to the President—Walt Rostow.

Ribicoff introduced a resolution to express the sense of the Senate that the U.S. should urge the Government of South Vietnam to seek U.N. observers. This was sent to the State Department by the Foreign Relations Committee with a request for comment. In its reply on June 28, 1966, the Department stated that the Government of South Vietnam had made such a request, but that action would probably be blocked by other governments. In that event, the letter said, it was hoped that the South Vietnamese could make other arrangements for observation of the election by "impartial observers." U.S. Department of State, Central File, Pol 27 Viet S, letter to Chairman Fulbright from Assistant Secretary of State Douglas MacArthur II.

[103] *CR*, vol. 112, Apr. 5, 1966, pp. 7635–7637.

U.S. should make a new effort to negotiate an end to the war.[104] He said it was unfortunate that neither the U.N. nor the permanent cochairmen of the Geneva Conferences—the United Kingdom and the U.S.S.R.—had been able to initiate such negotiations, but he thought it might be even more useful for talks to be organized by other countries from the area—Japan, Burma or some other Asian nation—and to occur in the region and among the parties involved: the U.S., the North Vietnamese, the Chinese, and "such elements in South Vietnam as may be essential to the making and keeping of a peaceful settlement. . . ." (The latter language was apparently an oblique reference to the need to include the NLF.)

The importance of negotiating an end to the war, Mansfield said, had been emphasized by the political situation in South Vietnam. Speaking carefully, he referred to "inner conflicts" in South Vietnam, the "recent manifestations" of which underscored the need to avoid "turning the war in Vietnam into one which is, at best, irrelevant to the people of Vietnam and, at worst, one in which their hostility may readily be enlisted against us." "It cannot be said too often," he added, "that . . . our efforts cannot be substituted for the efforts which must come from others on behalf of their own peoples."

The State Department, with White House approval, issued a statement welcoming Mansfield's suggestion, but insisting that the South Vietnamese Government would have to be the sole official representative of South Vietnam.[105]

In a statement on April 20, Senator Claiborne Pell, Democrat of Rhode Island, a member of the Foreign Relations Committee, agreed with Mansfield's suggestion that there should be a conference, and that it should be held in Asia and among opposing parties. He also commented that under the uncertain political situation that existed in South Vietnam, "if conditions should arise that a government comes to power which asks us to leave, let us have the good sense to follow that advice. I hope that we would not have the poor sense to prop up a government, or organize a counter coup in order to avoid just such a contingency."[106]

Senator Frank Church, Democrat of Idaho, another member of the Foreign Relations Committee and a critic of the war, said in a private discussion in London on May 10 with the Prime Minister that he "doubted whether much could be done [to end the war] until Ho understood he could neither drive Americans out of Vietnam nor defeat them."[107] The U.S., Church stated, should attempt to stimulate talks between the Vietnamese themselves. He added that he hoped elections would produce a broader based government that would be willing to enter into such negotiations. If these steps did not prove effective, however, "U.S. would have to continue increase strength in VN until VC suppressed. While this put U.S. in a position establishing protectorate, it preferable to a wider war."

Concerns about the political situation in South Vietnam were also voiced in the House of Representatives, but a special sub-

---

[104] *Ibid.*, pp. 8223–8225.
[105] *New York Times*, Apr. 20, 1966.
[106] *CR*, vol. 112, p. 8611.
[107] U.S. Department of State, Central File, Pol 27 Viet S, London to Washington 5440, May 17, 1966, based on a "cleared memcon provided by [James] Lowenstein, Senate Foreign Relations staffer."

committee of the House Armed Services Committee was optimistic after a trip to Vietnam on April 7–19, 1966:[108]

> American military operations in South Vietnam are proceeding most favorably. . . .
>
> Our forces have met the Vietcong and have mastered them on the field. We have demonstrated, after some painful starts, a typically American ability once again to outguess and outthink the enemy in his own unique brand of warfare. . . .
>
> So successful has been our military progress that the subcommittee believes we are moving steadily toward victory over the Vietcong, provided we can keep infiltration from the north within something like present limits, and provided, too, that we can have reasonable political stability within South Vietnam.

The group, headed by Representative Samuel S. Stratton (D/N.Y.), and including Robert Leggett (D/Calif.), Floyd Hicks (D/Wash.), Charles E. Chamberlain (R/Mich.), and Robert T. Stafford (R/Vt.), said that antigovernment and anti-American demonstrations in Vietnam should not be interpreted as a sign that the Vietnamese were unappreciative of American help or wanted the U.S. to leave. Moreover, "Such sentiment as has been expressed we believe to be limited in location and scope and not representative of the sentiment of the people as a whole." These protests, the subcommittee added, were to be expected in a country where "street demonstrations with violent overtones seem the only way . . . of attracting the attention of public opinion." The mere display of strength on the part of opposing groups, the report contended, was a sign that the war was being won, and that various groups were warming up for the postwar political contest.

The subcommittee, while favoring efforts to establish a political coalition between the military and the major contending groups, and the election of a Constituent Assembly, also concluded that with a "reasonable degree of political stability within South Vietnam" the war could be won despite the political turmoil and "without first solving all the complex political and economic problems which currently face that unhappy country."

The Continuing Tension Between the President and Senator Fulbright

In a series of lectures toward the end of April 1966, Senator Fulbright said, "America is in danger of losing its perspective on what exactly is within the realm of its power and what is beyond it . . . a great nation is peculiarly susceptible to the idea that its power is a sign of God's favor, conferring upon it a special responsibility for other nations—to make them richer and happier and wiser, to remake them, that is, in its own shining image. Power confuses itself with virtue and tends also to take itself for omnipotence. Once imbued with the idea of a mission, a great nation easily assumes that it has the means as well as the duty to do God's work." This attitude results in "the arrogance of power," which he defined as

[108] The subcommittee reported orally to the House Armed Services Committee upon its return in April 1966. These quotations are from its written report, printed in the House Armed Services Committee cumulative series, 89th Cong., pp. 9545–9569.

"the tendency of great nations to equate power with virtue and major responsibilities with a universal mission."[109]

Fulbright also talked about the war in Vietnam and the stated aims of the U.S. "to defeat what is regarded as North Vietnamese aggression, to demonstrate the futility of what the communists call 'wars of national liberation,' and to create conditions under which the South Vietnamese people will be able freely to determine their own future":[110]

> I have not the slightest doubt of the sincerity of the President and the Vice-President and the Secretaries of State and Defense in propounding these aims. What I do doubt, and doubt very much, is the ability of the United States to achieve these aims by the means being used. I do not question the power of our weapons and the efficiency of our logistics; I cannot say these things delight me as they seem to delight some of our officials, but they are certainly impressive. What I do question is the ability of the United States or any other Western nation to go into a small, alien, undeveloped Asian nation and create stability where there is chaos, the will to fight where there is defeatism, democracy where there is no tradition of it, and honest government where corruption is almost a way of life.

"The cause of our difficulties in Southeast Asia," said Fulbright, "is not a deficiency of power but an excess of the wrong kind of power, which results in a feeling of impotence when it fails to achieve its desired ends. We are still acting like Boy Scouts dragging reluctant old ladies across streets they do not want to cross. We are trying to remake Vietnamese society, a task which certainly cannot be accomplished by force and which probably cannot be accomplished by any means available to outsiders."[111]

He concluded:[112]

> Gradually but unmistakably America is showing signs of that arrogance of power which has afflicted, weakened, and in some cases destroyed great nations in the past. In so doing we are not living up to our capacity and promise as a civilized example for the world. The measure of our falling short is the measure of the patriot's duty of dissent.

In another lecture in the series, Fulbright, showing his preference for working within the system, said, in reference to demonstrations by American students, that in the U.S., "soft words are likely to carry more weight than harsh words, and the most effective dissent is dissent expressed in an orderly, which is to say a conservative manner. For these reasons such direct action as the burning of draft cards probably does more to retard than to advance the views of those who take such action. . . . Frustrating though it may be to some Americans, it is nonetheless a fact that in America the messages that get through are those that are sent

---

[109] J. William Fulbright, *The Arrogance of Power* (New York: Random House, 1966), pp. 3, 9. The lectures were also inserted in the *Congressional Record,* and were widely reported in the press.

[110] *The Arrogance of Power,* p. 15.

[111] *Ibid.*

[112] *Ibid.,* p. 22.

through channels, through the slow, cumbersome institutional channels devised by the founding fathers in 1787."[113] He added:

> It is only when the Congress fails to challenge the Executive, when the opposition fails to oppose, when politicians join in a spurious consensus behind controversial policies, and when institutions of learning sacrifice traditional functions to the short-term advantages of association with the government in power, that the campuses and streets and public squares of America are likely to become the forums of a direct and disorderly democracy.

Fulbright proposed that as an alternative to existing U.S. policy toward Vietnam the following steps should be taken:[114]

> (1) The South Vietnamese government should seek peace negotiations with the National Liberation Front. . . .
>
> (2) At the same time as the Saigon government makes direct overtures to the National Liberation Front the United States and South Vietnam together should propose negotiations for a cease-fire among military representatives of four separate negotiating parties: the United States and South Vietnam, North Vietnam and the National Liberation Front. . . .
>
> (3) The United States should terminate its bombing of North Vietnam, add no additional forces in South Vietnam, and reduce the scale of military operations to the maximum extent consistent with the security of American forces while peace initiatives are under way. . . .
>
> (4) The United States should pledge the eventual removal of American military forces from Vietnam.
>
> (5) Negotiations among the four principal belligerents—the United States and South Vietnam, North Vietnam and the National Liberation Front—should be directed toward a cease-fire and plans for self-determination in South Vietnam. . . .
>
> (6) After the principal belligerents have agreed on a cease-fire and plans for self-determination in South Vietnam, an international conference of all interested states should be convened to guarantee the arrangements made by the belligerents and to plan a future referendum on the reunification of North Vietnam and South Vietnam. . . .
>
> (7) In addition to guaranteeing arrangements for self-determination in South Vietnam and planning a referendum on the reunification of North and South Vietnam, the international conference should neutralize South Vietnam and undertake to

---

[113] *Ibid.*, pp. 38–39.

[114] *Ibid.*, pp. 188–196. Each of these recommendations is discussed in detail in the book.

Javits took issue with Fulbright, saying that rather than "arrogance of power," the theme should be the "acceptance of power." "It is my belief," he said, "that our participation in the Vietnam struggle will go a long way toward convincing aggressors that the United States will not abandon those who are attacked." *CR*, vol. 112, pp. 9920–9922.

In a book published five years later, Eugene Rostow, who was Under Secretary of State for Political Affairs at the time of Fulbright's lectures, took issue with Fulbright for defending the role of the U.S. in the Korean war while opposing U.S. involvement in Vietnam. He said, moreover, that Fulbright's analysis lacked a "guiding principle" or consistent "theory of foreign policy." Partly because of this it was impossible, Rostow argued, to discover what interest, if any, Fulbright thought the U.S. had or should have had in Vietnam. Fulbright's eight-point peace proposal, he added, "had already been tried and repeatedly rejected." Eugene Rostow, *Peace in the Balance: The Future of American Foreign Policy* (New York: Simon and Schuster, 1972), ch. 6 *passim.*

negotiate a multilateral agreement for the general neutralization of southeast Asia. . . .

(8) If for any reason an agreement ending the Vietnamese war cannot be reached, the United States should consolidate its forces in highly fortified defensible areas in South Vietnam and keep them there indefinitely.

Apparently, the President thought that "arrogance of power" was directed at him, and at a White House diplomatic reception in early May 1966, which Fulbright attended, he made an oblique reference to the issue. Fulbright then wrote to him on May 9:[115]

. . . I know you cannot possibly have the time to read the full text of all the speeches that are made in these hectic days, so I must assume that someone else who had read part or all of my "Arrogance of Power" speeches gave you a completely wrong impression.

Never at *any* time have I spoken, or even thought, of you in connection with arrogance. My whole theme has been the arrogance of power developed by the nations that became the biggest and most powerful countries of their era. Greece, Rome, Spain, England, Germany, and others lost their pre-eminence because of failure to recognize their limitations, or, as I called it, the arrogance of their power; and my hope is that *this* country, presently the greatest and the most powerful in the world, may learn by the mistakes of its predecessors. I believe that under your leadership we will avoid similar mistakes.

You and I, Mr. President, have the same ultimate interest: the return to peace and security of our country, and I believe that my opposing the views of some of your advisors, who have a different viewpoint from mine, can be of help to you. (emphases in original)

As will be seen, the President did not reply until May 27. Meanwhile, in a speech on May 11, he continued to defend his position: "The exercise of power in this century has meant for all of us in the United States not arrogance but agony. We have used our power not willingly and recklessly ever, but always reluctantly and with restraint."[116]

On May 12, at a Democratic fund-raising dinner in Washington, the argument became more personal as the President taunted his critics, especially Fulbright:[117]

The President began by saying that he was "glad to be here among so many friends—and some members of the Foreign Relations Committee." Embarrassed laughter. "You can say one thing about those [Foreign Relations Committee] hearings," said the President, "but I don't think this is the place to say it." More embarrassment. In a party so deeply split, the sarcasm was resented. Nor was there enthusiasm for the President's summons to all Democratic candidates that night to campaign on a policy of supporting his stand in Vietnam. It was, on the whole, a sour night for both Lyndon Johnson and

---

[115] University of Arkansas, Fulbright Papers, series 2.
[116] *New York Times*, May 12, 1966.
[117] Evans and Novak, *Lyndon B. Johnson: The Exercise of Power*, pp. 572–573. For the text of the speech see *Public Papers of the Presidents*, Lyndon B. Johnson, 1966, pp. 502–505.

his party, and it reflected how useless Johnson's old and tested political weapons were in dealing with the great crisis of Vietnam.

At a Democratic dinner in Chicago on May 17, 1966, the President again attacked his critics. Declaring that "the road ahead is going to be difficult," he said, using an expression that became widely quoted, that there would be some "Nervous Nellies" along the way, but that America would prevail.[118]

On the morning after the President spoke to the Democratic dinner in Washington, White House Counsel Harry McPherson sent him the following memorandum:[119]

> I was disturbed by the speech last night in the Armory. I felt it was harsh, uncompromising, over-militant. It seemed you were trying to beat Fulbright's ears down before an audience of Democrats who, I am told, had earlier applauded him strongly.
>
> The speech does not read as bad as it sounded. The combination of tone, emphasis and frequent glances down at Fulbright made it (for me) wrong. There was nothing of Baltimore or subsequent assurances that we want to negotiate an honorable way out.
>
> If the purpose was only to tell Democrats that the policy line is hard, that is one thing. But most of them know it. Those who agree can only holler yes when it is reiterated. Those who disagree feel further estranged by high-powered shouting. Even in the first group there are those who think Fulbright is a luminary of our Party, although wrong on this issue. I talked to a couple of these who were embarrassed to see him gored like that
>
> Lastly, there was nothing perceptive or careful or restrained in it. Even a political speech by the President ought in my judgment to make some distinctions. I am sure we are not going to fight Uganda if she attacks Ruanda and "oppresses her freedom." Yet the speech sounded that way. Wherever it touched on foreign policy it was militant—if not in language, then in delivery. Nothing about the U.N. Nothing about food or education or health. Nothing about a willingness to talk without conditions. Standing in Viet Nam is the only issue for America.
>
> Mr. President, I am one who believes we are right to stand in Viet Nam. I abhor the kind of vapid sophomoric bitching Fulbright is producing nowadays. But there are questions about Viet Nam, and about our appropriate role in the world, that are extremely difficult for me to resolve—difficult for anyone, I think, who gives them serious attention. They cannot be shouted out of existence.
>
> Churchill rallying Britain in 1940 is not the only posture a wise and strong leader can assume today, especially an American leader with half of the world's power at his disposal. The speeches you make, even on the stump, ought to pay some at-

---

[118] For the text of the speech see *Public Papers of the Presidents,* Lyndon B. Johnson, 1966, pp. 513–520.

[119] Johnson Library, Office of the President File.

tention to the complexity and diversity of the questions America faces. To stand or not to stand is simple. After that nothing is. I hope what you say, and indeed, sir, how you say it, will reflect that; for you set the tone for all who follow your banner.

In a later interview, McPherson said that for several days after sending the memorandum he got the "freeze-out treatment" from the President, and that he was told that his memorandum had a lot to do with Johnson's Nervous Nellies comment in his speech in Chicago. "[H]e [Johnson] was so furious with me," McPherson said later in an interview, "and through me at Fulbright and all these pissers and moaners, that he really let fly with that Nervous Nellies business, which was a political disaster. Had the war been, quote, popular, it would have been just the thing to say. But it wasn't. Everybody felt nervous about it at that time. So, if you're talking about Nervous Nellie, you're talking about me." [120]

In that same interview McPherson made an interesting observation about the President's state of mind at the time, as frustration with the war continued to grow:

> That sense of fury on the part of people, that we were not going ahead and winning the damn thing, that we were permitting ourselves to be bogged down and losing thousands of people, and creating the disruptions on the campus, and so on, and that that seemed to be going indefinitely because we wouldn't take the steps necessary to win the war, get it over with, that, he [the President] always considered, at least he told me he always considered, to be his big problem about Vietnam. And if he had such a perception, truly, then the captious criticism from the left, represented by Fulbright, must have seemed infuriating. You know, "Goddamn It! I'm trying not to go in there with hobnail boots and kill a half a million people in Vietnam in order to win this war. I'm trying to be restrained, and you're telling me that I'm a stupid, brutal President to continue the war at all."

On May 27, the President replied to Fulbright's letter of May 9: [121]

> My hope is that we do learn from the past—including the *recent* past. Your analogies of nations in history which were drunk with their own importance are vivid. I also believe there are some very pertinent recent analogies which are applicable, too—and the most significant, as far as I am concerned, is the analogy of what happens when ambitious and aggressive powers are freely permitted in areas where the peace of the world is delicately balanced, to use direct or indirect force against smaller and weaker states in their path.
>
> We are not called upon to bring our power to bear in every one of the quarrels and crises which erupt in the world. I think we are called upon, by the very nature of things, to act when there is a threat to the larger security. When we also have a commitment entered into as a part of the peace-building efforts of the past, action is even more clearly necessary.

---

[120] CRS Interview with Harry McPherson, Feb. 28, 1979.
[121] Johnson Library, NSF Memos to the President—Walt Rostow.

> I know how you feel about such commitments, but from where I sit it is not an easy thing to take an indifferent attitude toward them, especially—as I have already mentioned—if there is also involved the broader issue of how inaction would affect the overall balance of security in the world.
>
> I also feel strongly, as I hope you realize, about the right of small nations to develop their own political processes without interference from a belligerent nation. And belligerence is no less a reality when it involves the external support of insurgency than it is when it involves armies moving across national boundaries.
>
> South Vietnam, in my opinion, is moving toward a government that will reflect the traditions and values of its people. I do not believe it could do so if we were not willing to contest the effort of others to take it over arbitrarily by force.
>
> These are my views, Bill. They are not textbook abstractions but daily working convictions. In this connection, I am not sure whom you have in mind when you refer to some of my advisers. There are, of course, always differences of nuance and emphasis; but I believe my top diplomatic, military, and economic advisers are more in harmony on this course this Administration is pursuing than has been the case in most other administrations with which I have been familiar over the last thirty-five years. I would be derelict to the people who elected me to this Office if I let anyone else substitute their judgements for mine. I listen to everyone I can, but I must take the responsibility for deciding the policy—not my "advisers." (emphasis in original)

This letter was drafted by Moyers, who had supported the war, but who seems to have been developing some doubts about U.S. policy, and, along with McPherson and others who were concerned about the effect of the friction between Johnson and Fulbright on Democratic politics as well as on foreign policy, was seeking to help improve relations between the two men. The last paragraph of the letter was suggestive of that effort: "While I have seen the leaks from the other end of the avenue [Capitol Hill] about my 'slighting' you at social occasions or other irrelevant matters, I cannot believe that our differences of policy have erased the friendship we have shared so long. I have a fondness for Betty and you that is real. I am sorry that careless people have appeared to paint another picture."

Meanwhile, despite these policy differences, there continued to be indications that the friction between Johnson and Fulbright had not "erased" their friendship or disrupted communication. Several days after Fulbright began his lectures, the President invited him and his wife to accompany him on an overnight trip to Houston, where he was giving a speech to a group of political fund-raisers. Fulbright, who had to decline because of a speech he was making in New York, replied that he was "terribly disappointed" not to be able to make the trip, but hoped that "at some convenient time in the near future we will have a chance for a visit." [122]

[122] University of Arkansas Library, Fulbright Papers, Memorandum to Fulbright from his administrative assistant, Lee Williams, Apr. 25, 1966, and letter to the President from Fulbright, Apr. 26, 1966.

CHAPTER 8

SUPPRESSING THE BUDDHIST PROTEST

Early on May 15, 1966, Ky and the junta ordered South Vietnamese forces to occupy Danang, and within a few hours they took control of most of the city. Dissidents sought refuge in pagodas.

The Commander of South Vietnamese forces in I Corps, Gen. Ton That Dinh, who had replaced General Chuan, objected to this action and was replaced by Gen. Huynh Van Cao. Dinh went to Hue, where he joined Thi and others who were opposed to the government's use of force against the dissidents.

The decision to use troops against the dissidents is said to have been made by Ky and the junta without any consultation with or notice to the Americans.[1]

In a "flash" cable to Porter at 1:29 a.m. on Sunday, May 15, which he drafted, Rusk's reaction was that "It is intolerable that Ky should take such far reaching move as that against Danang without consultation with us." But he added that the "immediate problem is to pick up pieces and prevent a major debacle." "Most urgent need is to insist that principal figures in Danang area (such as Ky, Vien, Dinh, Lam, Nhuan and Thi)[2] agree at once to prevent further fighting among SVN elements pending further discussion of more lasting solution. This may require tough talk with several of them but United States cannot accept this insane bickering." "I cannot emphasize strongly enough that the disarray among South Vietnamese leaders has been rapidly undermining support of American people for war effort. The question 'what are we being asked to support?' is becoming insistent and is becoming more and more difficult to answer."[3]

In an interview several years later, William Bundy commented on the reaction after the news of the move against Danang was received in Washington:[4]

> In the first hours it wasn't at all clear what was going on, and not at all clear whether he [Ky] would succeed. So we were in the position where quite possibly in even a few hours or a

---

[1] Apparently the issue of making U.S. aircraft available to assist with the operation was being considered by the U.S. Mission, judging by a declassified "flash" cable from Washington to Saigon sent to Porter by Rusk at 10:04 p.m. (Washington time) on May 14 which stated "Do not make C–130's [U.S. transports] available without authorization from here." U.S. Department of State, Central File, Pol 27 Viet S, Washington to Saigon 3446, May 14, 1966. It is not known whether or not this matter was raised before or after South Vietnamese forces were sent into Danang.

A U.S. aircraft was used by Ky for his trip to Danang to oversee the operation, but this may have been approved before it was known what he was planning to do. See the "flash" cable (sent at 7:31 a.m.) from State (Bundy) to Porter, same location, Washington to Saigon 3450, May 15, 1966.

[2] Gen. Hoang Xuan Lam was commander of the ARVN 2d Division stationed in I Corps. Thieu had remained in Saigon.

[3] U.S. Department of State, Central File, Pol 27 Viet S, Washington to Saigon 3448, May 15, 1966.

[4] CRS Interview with William Bundy, Sept. 29, 1986.

couple of days or whatever we would be in a position of the government having tried its best shot and having failed, so that you didn't just have a mess and a situation out of control locally, you had a real failure of the government to have any control over the whole northern part of South Vietnam, the whole central Vietnam, and the government would thereby lose enormous prestige and could be destroyed and so on. And I remember a whole group of us being in the operations room around that conference table waiting for the next cable, and I think we were even having a teletype with the Embassy in Saigon, and the question came up, what do we do if there's just no South Vietnamese Government that's of any consequence whatsoever? I remember Cabot [Lodge] there and his saying, "Well, we have to go on, we go on, we just go on." I didn't see how we went on. What are we going to do, have American MPs at every corner in Saigon? Or are we going to take over the mayor's office? I just couldn't picture it. But it's interesting of the cast of mind, because it shows Cabot really did believe you just took over and set up a new government. The rest of us just didn't see how you could do it. We didn't get in a heated argument because it was a hypothetical, and within a few hours it was clear Ky had brought it off, so that it wasn't pursued. . . .

In his memoirs, Ky said that when Lodge returned to Vietnam on May 20 he told Ky, "I'm delighted you took the decision to send in troops. If you hadn't you'd have disappointed me."[5]

At 5:39 a.m. (Washington time) that day (Sunday, May 15), the State Department received a cable from Saigon containing a message from Tri Quang to President Johnson as follows:[6]

Buddhists and people of I Corps have shown their good will by stopping all activities. But morning May 15 the Thieu-Ky group once again brought Marines and Air Force troops to Danang to attack the soldiers and civilians of I Corps, encircling and preparing to attack the main Buddhist places of worship. Arms have been fired, and the people are being oppressed. I urgently appeal to your responsibility to intervene. Respectful thanks.

Later that day, the State Department sent this message to Tri Quang:[7]

U.S. Government is following developments to which you have referred with fullest attention. As you know from a number of conversations with American officials, U.S. Government fully supports the process of political development, including elections for a Constitutional Assembly, which was announced at the close of the National Political Congress in April. It is our sincere hope that the Vietnamese people will be able to carry this political development process through to a successful conclusion, an effort which will obviously require the most constructive cooperation of all groups.

[5] Nguyen Cao Ky, *Twenty Years and Twenty Days* (New York: Stein and Day, 1976), p. 97.

[6] U.S. Department of State, Central File, Pol 27 Viet S, Saigon to Washington 4610, May 15, 1966.

[7] Same location, Washington to Saigon 3453, May 15, 1966.

> We are aware of your concern over the recent events in Danang. The efforts and influence of the U.S. Government will be used to persuade all elements and groups in South Viet Nam to find a resolution to their difficulties and to establish the unity required if South Viet Nam is to maintain its freedom and independence.

At 7:31 a.m., the State and Defense Departments, in a joint "flash" cable drafted by William Bundy and cleared by Rusk, McNamara and Rostow, expressing dismay about the use of troops at Danang, asked for detailed information on the situation, directed that U.S. military advisers should be withdrawn from South Vietnamese forces in I Corps except for those units that were continuing to fight the Communists, urged maximum U.S. contact with South Vietnamese military and civilian leaders in Saigon and I Corps, and encouraged efforts to get "any useful political leaders in Saigon" to seek to influence members of the Directorate toward a compromise that would avoid bloodshed.[8] The cable concluded: "Basic to all of above is that we should not throw our weight in any way behind GVN effort that seems badly planned and ill-advised, likely to drive militant Buddhists and many others into clear opposition which GVN may not be strong or determined enough to handle without compromise or worst outcome of extended bloodshed."

The U.S. Mission replied:[9]

> Fully agree we should not throw our weight behind any GVN effort that seems badly planned and ill advised. We have not done so. Believe however that we should not hasten to pull the rug from under GVN effort however misguided until we have some reading on how it is going to work out . . . we must realize that all eyes will be on us and our reaction. If we move quickly and give impression we are pulling the rug out from under Ky, government will undoubtedly fall and ARVN, which despite revolving door changes in government since November 1, 1963 has remained one reasonably stable unit in government, may be irreparably damaged. Government which will emerge may very well not be "other side" but will probably be the worst sort of jury-rigged affair imaginable. It will in all likelihood be a poorer government, one incapable of waging war and even of making any acceptable sort of peace.

That morning (Sunday, May 15), Porter cabled a report on a meeting in Danang between General Walt, Commander of U.S. Marines in I Corps, who had close relationships with South Vietnamese military commanders in the area, and Premier Ky.[10] "Walt found Ky willing to talk but evasive. He tried hard to pin him down on immediate reason for move against Danang, Ky said it necessary for government to take action as struggle movement had initiated action Saturday night to oppose government. Walt believes fabricated message sent by pre-planning from Danang garrison to Saigon alleging struggle forces trying to take over. Walt unable to obtain evidence of any action by struggle forces Saturday

---

[8] Same location, Washington to Saigon 3450, May 15, 1966.
[9] Same location, Saigon to Washington 4636, May 16, 1966.
[10] Same location, Saigon to Washington 4612, May 15, 1966.

night. Nevertheless on strength of this message Ky said he found it necessary make quick decision."

That afternoon, while, as will be seen, an antiwar march was in progress in Washington, President Johnson met from 2:35 p.m. to about 3:00 p.m. with Rusk, McNamara, William Bundy, Lodge, Rostow, Admiral Raborn, Helms, Taylor, Komer, Unger, U. Alexis Johnson and William Jorden. Philip Habib, who had come to Washington with Lodge, also attended. According to the agenda prepared by Rostow, the subjects to be discussed were: the situation, the proposed text of a press statement, the reply to Tri Quang's message, and further guidance to the U.S. Embassy in Saigon.[11] Unfortunately, there apparently are no notes of the meeting, but it is possible to glean a fairly good idea of what transpired by referring to the cables sent after the meeting to the U.S. Mission in Saigon by the State Department. In these cables, Porter was told by Rusk to see Ky and Thieu and, in addition to gathering more information, to urge them to reaffirm the government's intention to hold the Constitutional Assembly as scheduled.[12] Porter was also instructed to press them for their plans for "achieving solidarity." Direct contact would also be made with Generals Lam and Dinh and General Thi to emphasize the need for solidarity. The point should be made that the "central issue is whether South Vietnamese are going to have their own country to quarrel about or whether Viet Cong and Hanoi will take that country away from them." "It is incomprehensible to us," Rusk said, "that personal rivalries among individuals or temporary differences on political matters should be allowed to paralyze South Vietnam in the face of a common enemy." Once again he warned of an adverse U.S. public reaction: "We must find some way to emphasize privately to all of these leaders, regardless of their differences among themselves, that the American people are becoming fed up with the games they are playing while the American people are being asked to sustain such major burdens to assure that they have a country to quarrel about."[13]

Rusk's comment reflected the reaction in Washington to the news that the Vietnamese were fighting each other. According to the account by Max Frankel in a dispatch from Washington to the *New York Times* on May 16,[14]

> This was a gloomy capital today, bemoaning its helplessness in Vietnam and fearing that the worst in political turmoil there was still to come.
>
> The "hawks" and "doves" alike on Capitol Hill, at the White House, State Department and Pentagon spoke less of the fact of the situation than of their despondency. Most preferred not to say anything for the record, lest their pessimism itself contribute to a further deterioration in Saigon.

---

[11] Johnson Library, NSF Country File, Vietnam. In this file there is a copy of the text of the press guidance statement.

[12] U.S. Department of State, Central File, Pol 27 Viet S, Washington to Saigon 3455, May 15, 1966.

[13] Same location, Washington to Saigon 3470, May 16, 1966. In an effort to make the government's case with Congress and the public, as well as to give emphasis to private diplomatic communications, Rusk also held a press conference on May 17 in which he made some of these same points. (*New York Times*, May 18, 1966). He ended the press conference with the statement, delivered with a "wry smile," that some of the issues being fought over in Vietnam were secondary to the "issue of achieving a safe country about which they can perhaps quarrel at their leisure later on."

[14] *New York Times*, May 17, 1966.

But one Senator characterized the attitude of his colleagues with this remark: "We feel the stuffing has gone out to it."

Senator Symington was reported to have said that he had never felt so discouraged about the situation in Vietnam, which he said "is less clear than it has ever been for me." Senator Jackson said that most of his colleagues were "simply throwing their hands in the air in frustration . . . ." Senator Mansfield, after a meeting of congressional leaders with the President, said that the U.S. had to avoid becoming involved in the dispute, but that if the contending factions did not reconcile their differences, "the prospects of civil war are real and imminent."[15] Senator Cooper said that if the situation continued, "I don't see how we can long make the fight for them." Senator Gore observed that the crisis would adversely effect the war effort as well as plans for elections.

There were statements by a number of others in Congress expressing their concern about the situation and their hope that the crisis would pass and the scheduled election could be held.[16]

On May 16, there was another discussion of the situation in a meeting from 12:20 p.m. to 1:05 p.m. of the President with Rusk, McNamara, Ball, William Bundy, Rostow, McNaughton, Raborn, Helms, David Bell, and Komer, that was also attended by Moyers and Komer's deputy, William Leonhart. From 1:05 p.m. to 1:20 p.m. the President met with Rusk, McNamara, Lodge, Rostow and Moyers. There apparently are no notes of either meeting.

Over the next several days, as the South Vietnamese Government strengthened its hold on Danang, the U.S. became very involved in mediating the situation, especially in trying to work out an agreement between Ky and Thi.[17]

On May 19, in a cable to Porter, Rusk said that it was his hope that, having re-established its authority in Danang, the Government of South Vietnam would be able to bring all of I Corps under its authority while avoiding a full-scale confrontation with the 1st ARVN division (which had largely taken sides with the dissidents). Rusk urged Porter to make every effort to get Ky and Thieu to work out an agreement "which will bring an end to divisions in their country which we can no longer accept."[18]

Later that day, Bundy sent another cable to Porter (drafted by Unger) in which he said that Thi was a "key figure and bringing him and Ky together again ought to make it possible to get political process under way and also further reduce Tri Quang's estimate of his bargaining power."[19] While Thi's administration of I Corps had left something to be desired, Bundy said, "we have learned since his dismissal how much worse situation can become in that area. Therefore we would see no objection if he could be reappointed Commander I Corps as long as this could be done without completely blowing apart the Directorate." Bundy urged Porter to "maintain continuous and heavy pressure" to arrange for a meeting of Ky and Thi, adding: "We have been shaken by events of recent

---

[15] *Ibid.*
[16] See *CR*, pp. 10666–12105 passim.
[17] See, for example, Saigon to Washington 4688 and 4699, May 17, 1966, and 4718, May 18, 1966 in the State Department, Central File, Pol 27 Viet S.
[18] Same location, Washington to Saigon 3524, May 19, 1966.
[19] Same location, Washington to Saigon 3545, May 19, 1966.

days and best way for them to demonstrate their purpose is to bury rivalries and sensitivities, however justified they may be, and do something striking now for their country's good. If this requires Ky to make a forthcoming statement and Thi to swallow his resentment over dismissal, so be it."

On May 20, the President met from 6:06 p.m. to 7:05 p.m. with the Vice President, Rusk, McNamara, Ball, Rostow, Ambassador David K. E. Bruce, former Secretary of State Dean Acheson, and Bill Moyers, and from 7:05 p.m. to about 8:00 p.m. with Rusk, McNamara and Rostow. There apparently are no notes of these meetings, but according to the *New York Times*, "Increasingly discouraging reports from South Vietnam were placed before President Johnson and his principal advisers. . . . The White House meeting was advised that the threat of major violence had grown considerably in the last 24 hours and that there was new doubt that Premier Nguyen Cao Ky could survive the conflict that he had provoked with Buddhist leaders." The story, filed by Max Frankel, added: "The officials here acknowledged that the United States appeared to be lame and helpless, but they said this was preferable to a vigorous effort to force a settlement where none was in sight."[20]

After the meeting, Rusk, who personally drafted the cable, sent a message to Lodge asking for his and Westmoreland's judgment of the situation and recommendations for action:[21]

> Cannot overemphasize the vulnerability of our position here as long as Ky seems to have neither the military power to succeed in establishing government authority in first Corps nor the prospect for a negotiated solution with key leaders or resistance elements. Since major military effort may be beyond his capabilities, we return again to the importance of contacts which might lead to solution of present impasse. You should review recent DEPTELS [Department telegrams] on this subject and consider whether a meeting between Ky and Thi can be worked out or whether a senior official (possibly Porter) should undertake an intermediate role to find a basis on which present situation can be resolved.
>
> We believe that you and Westmoreland should pass the word discreetly that we support the government and must not have any coups or reckless adventures. Present government has itself taken the leadership in initiating a process by which it will stand down in favor of a properly constituted government. There is no successor government in sight which could come in by coup or manipulation that seems to offer any improvement. Therefore all hands should stop maneuvering, get on with the war and give the constitutional process a chance.

A cable that same day (May 20) from Wheeler to Westmoreland (who had just returned to South Vietnam) provided further evidence of the deep concern in Washington about the political disturbances.[22] "In my judgment," Wheeler said, "the effect of the present situation on the public and in the press and in the

---

[20] *New York Times*, May 21, 1966.
[21] Johnson Library, NSF Country File, Vietnam, Washington to Saigon 3568, May 20, 1966.
[22] CMH, Westmoreland Papers, Message Files, CJCS 2837–66, May 20, 1966.

Congress . . . is far more adverse than heretofore. . . . As you know, I am usually pretty much of an optimist. . . . This time, however, I think I can feel the first gusts of the whirlwind generated by the wind sown by the Vietnamese . . . even if we get some semblance of solidarity and common purpose among the contending factions, we must all recognize that we have lost irretrievably and for all time some of the support which until now we have received from the American people. In other words, regardless of what happens of a favorable nature, many people will never again believe that the effort and the sacrifices are worthwhile."

Wheeler's prediction, as will be seen, was quite accurate. Public support for the war dropped sharply during this period and never rebounded to its former level.

Westmoreland replied that although the situation was serious, he thought it had been "blown out of proportion" by the press. The South Vietnamese Government was making "positive headway" in restoring order, and plans were being made for a meeting of Ky and Thi.[23]

On May 20, Tri Quang told a U.S. official at the American consulate in Hue that negotiations with Ky and Thieu were "impossible," because by sending troops to Danang the government had shown that its promises could not be trusted. The only solution, he said, was for Ky and Thieu to step down. This could be done by a coup brought about by a public threat to withhold U.S. assistance to the government unless they did so. When asked who would lead the coup, Tri Quang replied that he had already made known his preference (Tran Van Don).[24]

On May 21, after clashes between government troops and dissidents in Danang, and an attack on a pagoda in which monks and nuns were killed, wounded or arrested, Tri Quang gave the American consulate in Hue a message for President Johnson requesting the end of U.S. assistance to Ky and Thieu and a ban on the use against the Buddhists of tanks and aircraft given to South Vietnam to fight the Communists.[25]

On that same day, President Johnson held a press conference in which he said in an opening statement:[26]

> We are watching the situation in Vietnam very closely. We believe everything possible should be done to bring the various factions to an understanding of the need for unity while the constitutional process is moving forward. . . .
>
> The South Vietnamese are trying to build a nation. They have to do this in the teeth of Communist efforts to take the country over by force. It is a hard and a frustrating job, and there is no easy answer, no instant solution to any of the problems they face.
>
> We are not in Vietnam to dictate what form of government they should have. We have made it abundantly clear that it is our wish to see them increasingly able to manage their own af-

---

[23] Same location, MAC 4070 and 4081, May 22, 1966. Admiral Sharp agreed with Westmoreland. See his message of May 23, DTG 230929Z, in the same location.

[24] U.S. Department of State, Central File, Pol 27 Viet S, Saigon to Washington 4784, May 20, 1966.

[25] Same location, Saigon to Washington 4820, May 21, 1966.

[26] *Public Papers of the Presidents*, Lyndon B. Johnson, 1966, pp. 531 ff.

fairs with the participation of an ever broader share of the population. We regret any diversion from that task and from efforts to defeat the Communist attempt to take over South Vietnam.

Several questions were asked about the political situation in South Vietnam and about U.S. policy, but the President declined to answer, saying only: "The longer we are there, the more sacrifices we make. The more we spend, the more discontent there will be, the more wish and desire there will be to get out. Leading that parade is the President. If you want to feel that it troubles you 100 percent, just double that and make it 200 percent for the President."

Later that day, after a meeting from 4:35 p.m. to 4:55 p.m. of the President with William Bundy and Rostow, the State Department sent a cable (drafted by Bundy/Unger) to Lodge, who had just returned to Saigon, expressing great concern about the situation.[27] "We regard situation as extremely critical," the cable stated, "both in substance and because of press reports tending to exaggerate matters." "[T]he situation now appears to American public to be getting out of hand with U.S. in helpless position." The resolution of the crisis was a "matter of drastic urgency from any standpoint."

"[T]here is no acceptable course," the cable said, "except for GVN leadership and dissidents to find some compromise *modus vivendi* which will stop fighting and demonstrations and permit all efforts to be turned to fighting VC, preparing for elections and bringing inflation under control." In Lodge's discussion with Ky, which the cable said was critically important, he should stress adverse effects on U.S. public support for the war, and the need for "absolute candor" from Ky on his plans, as well as the need for the U.S. to have the opportunity to comment before actions were taken.[28] Further, Lodge should stress the need for Ky to meet with Thi, as well as other dissident generals (Nhuan and Dinh), to seek a *modus vivendi.*

---

[27] U.S. Department of State, Central Files, Pol 27 Viet S, Washington to Saigon 3575, May 21, 1966.

That same day, Saturday, May 21, the President discussed the situation with Justice Fortas by telephone, and Fortas responded with a handwritten memorandum in which he declared:

"a. We've got to make a commitment to success.

"b. We've got to go on the offensive in the propaganda war.

"c. We've got to stir enthusiasm among those who are on our side—including the youngsters subject to the draft."

He said that "if Ky succeeds in Danang" there should be a public statement affirming that the South Vietnamese were committed to achieving success, "And so are we. . . . We cannot and will not permit South Vietnam to be a monument to freedom's defeat—or a franchise to infiltration and subversion." "Our resistance in South Vietnam," Fortas added, "has given courage to the people of Asia, Africa and Latin America to resist the efforts of Communism to take over. Our retreat would be a mortal and savage blow to them."

This memorandum, which is not dated, is in the Johnson Library, NSF Country File, Vietnam, Box 99, where it was incorrectly filed in a folder dated 9/67–10/67. Clearly, the reference to Ky's succeeding at Danang dates the memorandum as having been written in May 1966, not in the period from September to October 1967. Research by the Johnson Library staff now reveals that there was a telephone conversation between Fortas and the President on Saturday May 21, 1966, (in the memorandum Fortas mentioned this), which suggests that the memorandum was written a day or so later.

In his study, *Lyndon Johnson's War*, p. 87, Larry Berman, apparently relying on the Johnson Library's filing of the memorandum, gives it the incorrect date of October 14, 1967. In her study, *Fortas*, p. 248, Kalman also states that the memorandum was written in October 1967.

[28] In a cable earlier that day Lodge had said that he was going to meet with Ky in an attempt—which he did not think would succeed—to find a resolution to the crisis that both sides would accept. Same location, Saigon to Washington 4837, May 21, 1966.

The State Department also told Lodge to explain to Ky the U.S. position vis-à-vis Tri Quang, "making clear that we have confined ourselves to telling Tri Quang issue must be resolved peacefully but are also conveying message to him taking firm line against any threats of attack on our installations." Ky should know, the cable said, that the U.S. was telling Tri Quang that, while it was advising South Vietnamese Government against attacking Buddhist pagodas, it was also stressing to Tri Quang the need for the Buddhists to work out basic issues with the government and to permit the election process to proceed.

The Department also told Lodge that Washington policymakers were

> inclined more and more to believe Directorate as presently constituted cannot expect to maintain degree of acceptance and support required to carry through elections and govern country effectively. At same time, we are quite clear that only leadership that includes respected military men can do the job. While we support Ky and his colleagues fully in the general sense for the time being, we can envisage possibility that broadening of Directorate to include Thi, and perhaps even Don, may become essential measure at some point. A further variant might be inclusion of civilians (such as Quat or even Big Minh) who have held high positions in past [Phan Huey Quat had served in Cabinets in the 1950s; Duong Van "Big" Minh had been chief of state in 1963 after Diem's assassination].

The concluding paragraph of the May 21 cable to Lodge suggests that the subject of considerably stronger U.S. intervention was discussed at the White House meeting that day: "Finally, we would be glad to have your judgment as to whether we ought to move more forcefully and drastically to assert our power in an effort to bring an end to present strife among non-Communist elements. We recognize gravity of such steps but they may become necessary."[29]

On May 23, Rusk held separate meetings at the State Department with leaders of the Senate—Long and Kuchel (Mansfield and Dirksen apparently were not available), Russell, Saltonstall, Fulbright, Hickenlooper, Hayden, Milton R. Young (R/N. Dak.), and of the House—McCormack, Albert, Ford, Arends, Mahon, Frank T. Bow (R/Ohio), Thomas E. Morgan (D/Pa.), Bolton, Rivers and William H. Bates (R/Mass.), to try to assure them that the situation

---

[29] That same day (May 21), JCS Chairman Wheeler cabled Westmoreland for his comments on a plan to ameliorate the situation that would involve the U.S. more directly. (CMH, Westmoreland Papers, Message Files, CJCS 2840–66, May 21, 1966.) Lodge and Westmoreland would personally contact leading government and antigovernment figures, and would tell them that the U.S. "can no longer tolerate the situation caused by the contending parties." They would then arrange for leaders of both sides, to meet, and, after re-emphasizing to the group the dissatisfaction of the U.S. with the situation, they would let the leaders discuss how the dispute could be resolved. In addition, Wheeler said, a U.S. Presidential envoy, perhaps Harriman, accompanied by Wheeler, would go to South Vietnam to give greater emphasis and force to efforts of Lodge and Westmoreland.

Wheeler said that the JCS was also considering ways of bringing greater pressure to bear, including withdrawing all aid and U.S. advisers to I Corps, and having U.S. military units in the area cease offensive operations.

In his reply, Westmoreland rejected these ideas, but said that he and Lodge were already planning to tell the Vietnamese leaders from the government and the Struggle group that the situation was doing "irreparable harm" to their cause. Again he said, "that the whole matter was being blown out of proportion in the minds of authorities in Washington and by the American people because of press reports from a group of reporters on the scene attempting to make a name for themselves and to play a role." (Same location, MAC 4081, May 22, 1966.)

in Vietnam was improving. He gave what was described as a "guardedly optimistic report," saying that, with Danang under government control, the remaining center of protest was Hue, where there were prospects for a settlement. After the meeting, Senator Fulbright commented to reporters that he was not encouraged by Rusk's report.[30] And a State Department memorandum for the President summarizing the two meetings stated that in the meeting with Senate leaders, "There was understandable and deep concern about the internal dispute between different elements in South Vietnam and queries to what the Administration would do if the South Vietnamese went on squabbling with each other instead of uniting to defeat the Communists."[31]

In the meeting with leaders of the House, similar concerns were expressed. "Congressman Bates [the ranking Republican on the House Armed Services Committee, who supported the war], supported by others present, stressed that the American people have been getting progressively more restive in the last three weeks over activities of the South Vietnamese who seem more interested in fighting each other than in facing the Communist enemy and that if this situation does not rapidly improve, there will be an increasing number of Americans who will feel that we should pull out of Vietnam."

Carl Marcy, the chief of staff of the Foreign Relations Committee, was urging Fulbright to try to persuade Mansfield and Russell to set up a meeting with the President at which a few senior Democratic and Republican Senators who were concerned about the war could privately advise him of the need to change the course of U.S. policy. In a memorandum on May 20, 1966, in which he made this suggestion, Marcy proposed that in the meeting the President should be urged to act as follows:

> 1. A radical shift in American policy in Vietnam is required for a number of reasons:
>
> a. Civil disturbance in South Vietnam;
>
> b. Increased U.S. casualties, decreased Vietnamese casualties;
>
> c. Lack of support from abroad;
>
> d. Rising dissatisfaction in U.S. (impact on Congressional election).
>
> e. U.S. commitments are too wide and weakening us.
>
> 2. The shift must be in the direction of lessening U.S. involvement.
>
> 3. Only the President can take the lead. He could make a speech with a tone of "more in sorrow than in anger," making such points as:
>
> a. Three Presidents have tried to help the Vietnamese.
>
> b. The U.S. has almost alone sacrificed blood and treasure.
>
> c. Neither the Vietnamese, the free world, nor the United Nations have apparently understood the magnanimity and generosity and good impulses of our actions.

---

[30] *New York Times*, May 24, 1966.

[31] U.S. Department of State, Lot File 74 D 164, Memorandum "For the President's Evening Reading," May 23, 1966.

d. Under these circumstances, the President is ordering the orderly withdrawal of U.S. forces to designated areas, ceasing the destruction of lives and property and leaving it to the Vietnamese themselves to resolve their problems.

e. The United States will stay in these areas for a period of not to exceed 2 years to provide an area for those who may need refuge, but we hope there will be none.

f. At the end of two years, the U.S. will withdraw completely provided; (1) the U.N. has made arrangements to deal with refugee problems, and (2) the U.S. has not by then been asked to stay by stable representative governments *in the area.* (emphasis in original)

"This may seem pretty wild," Marcy added, "but something along these lines may provide the last clear chance for us to get out and keep our tattered shirts."[32]

On May 22, Marcy sent a copy of the memorandum to Senator Vance Hartke, Democrat of Indiana, with a note suggesting that concerned Senators needed to take the initiative to talk to the President privately about Vietnam along the lines suggested in the memorandum. "Mansfield," he said, "would have to be the leader. (Mansfield, Fulbright, Russell, Cooper, Aiken.)"[33]

The Government Regains Control of Hue

On May 22–23, 1966, the situation in South Vietnam appeared to become even more acute as the Buddhists warned of possible anti-American demonstrations.[34] In a meeting with a U.S. consular official in Hue on May 23, Tri Quang angrily threatened "massive demonstrations" against the Americans after a press conference the previous night in which President Johnson minimized the Struggle Movement and sought to play down the seriousness of the situation.[35] "'Why does Johnson stab us in the back' by such statements," Tri Quang asked, "'deliberately misinterpreting' struggle movement? . . . this means Americans now firmly allied with Thieu and Ky to kill Buddhists of South Vietnam."[36]

By May 24, 1966, all of the dissident forces in Danang had ceased fighting or had surrendered, and the city was under government control. In Hue, however, the situation was becoming even more volatile, and on May 26, as Tri Quang had warned, there was an anti-American demonstration and a group of young Buddhist dissidents burned down the U.S. Information Service Agency (USIA) library.

Meanwhile, some progress was being made in persuading Thi and other leading military supporters of the Struggle Movement to cooperate with the government. A number of discussions were held by Lodge, Westmoreland, and his staff, General Walt and other

---

[32] U.S. National Archives, RG 46, Papers of the Senate Foreign Relations Committee, Marcy Chron File.

[33] Marcy Memorandum to Senator Hartke, same location.

[34] See in the Department of State Central File, Pol 27 Viet S, Saigon to Washington 4843 and 4866, May 22, 1966, for conversations between Embassy officers and Quang Lien and Minh Chau.

[35] *New York Times*, May 23, 1966.

[36] U.S. Department of State, Central File, Pol 27 Viet S, Saigon to Washington 4878, May 23, 1966. For a report on a speech by Tri Quang on Radio Hue on May 23, see, in the same location, Saigon to Washington 4899, May 23, 1966.

U.S. military and civilian officials, with Ky, Thieu, Vien (Chief of Staff), Thi, and Dinh.[37] On May 27, after a preliminary meeting with Westmoreland on May 24, General Thi met with his arch-opponent, General Ky. Ky is said to have offered him a post in the army, and Thi agreed to cooperate in quelling the disturbances.[38] (In the end, Thi, rather than taking another post, accepted Westmoreland's invitation to go to the United States for a medical checkup, and he and his family left South Vietnam for Washington.)[39]

On May 27, General Walt met with General Dinh to try to persuade him to meet with Ky to discuss the situation. Dinh said he intended to stay in Hue, but that he would try to help to ease the situation and to prevent further anti-American actions. He refused to meet with Ky, but said he would meet with Vien, whom he respected.[40] Walt arranged for Dinh and Vien to meet on June 1, and afterwards reported to Westmoreland that the talk had gone well. Dinh asked how he could help the government and stated that although he intended to remain in Hue, he was loyal and would withdraw from any action by government forces in Hue.[41]

In Washington meanwhile, the President, apparently at his request, received from Rostow on May 27 a statement of five policy alternatives for the U.S.—"(1) Withdraw from Vietnam (2) Withdrawal to enclaves, (3) Follow present course, (4) Major escalation: huge ground forces, major expansion of air assault, (5) Maximum non-nuclear effort, North and South: invade North, hit bases in China if used in support, ground forces into panhandle of Laos, etc."—with a listing of the advantages and disadvantages of each.[42] In a cover memorandum to the President, Rostow commented that what the authors of the statement, William Jorden and Col. Robert Ginsburgh, were saying, "in effect, is that we need something more than our present course (Alternative 3) but less than a major escalation (Alternative 4). I agree."[43]

There is no indication that there was any discussion or action on the alternatives paper. A copy was given by the President to Senator Mansfield, who replied with a memorandum to the President on June 13 in which he re-stated the advantages and disadvan-

---

[37] For relevant cables, see, among others, Washington to Saigon 3577 of May 22, 3596 of May 23, 3611 of May 24, 3680 of May 27, Saigon to Washington 4887, 4898 and 4899 of May 23, 4945, 4952, 4963, 4968 and 4977 of May 25, and Westmoreland to Wheeler MAC 4117 of May 23, 4196 and 4197 of May 35, and 4238 of May 26. State Department cables are in the Central File, Pol 27 Viet S, and Westmoreland's cables are in his papers at CMH. For the role played by Westmoreland and his associates see also Clarke, *Advise and Support: The Final Years*, pp. 140–141, and Westmoreland, *A Soldier Reports*, pp. 170 ff. For the role of General Walt, see Shulimson, *U.S. Marines in Vietnam: An Expanding War, 1966*, ch. 5.

[38] U.S. Department of State, Central File, Pol 27 Viet S, Saigon to Washington 5037, May 27, 1966 and 5073, May 28, 1966, and CMH, Westmoreland Papers, Message Files, MAC 4300, May 27, 1966.

[39] It is reported that after arriving in Washington, where they became permanent residents, Thi and his family were given a "substantial allowance," by the U.S. Government, which, according to Kahin, was abruptly terminated after seven years. Kahin, *Intervention*, p. 429.

[40] U.S. Department of State, Central File, Pol 27 Viet S, Saigon to Washington 5024, May 27, 1966.

[41] CMH, Westmoreland Papers, Message Files, Walt to Westmoreland, DTG 010742Z.

[42] Johnson Library, NSF Memos to the President—Walt Rostow, Memorandum from William Jorden (who was in public affairs in the State Department) and Robert Ginsburgh (an Air Force officer who had worked with Rostow on the Policy Planning Council, and subsequently moved to the NSC staff), May 27, 1966. On June 2, Rostow sent the President a shorter version which had been prepared by Jorden. Same location.

[43] Same location, Rostow cover memorandum of June 2 for the statement of alternatives, cited in previous footnote.

tages of alternatives (2) and (3) and said he preferred the alternative of withdrawal to that of enclaves, pointing out that the present course was rapidly leading to major escalation.[44] The best course, he said, would be "one which limits the military involvement as far as possible while placing the emphasis on seeking negotiations."

In a memorandum to the President analyzing Mansfield's reply, Rostow stated:

> It seems to me there are two gut questions here:
>
> (1) Do we want a settlement that is going to leave South Viet Nam independent or do we just want to get out with as much as we can salvage?
>
> (2) If we want meaningful negotiations, which course is more likely to convince Hanoi of our seriousness of purpose; that is, are we trying to convince them they can't win, or are we trying to make it so costly they will call off the aggression?
>
> If we just want to arrange our withdrawal from the scene, then obviously we can "hunker up like a jackass in a hailstorm." We would then get about the kind of settlement we could have had if we had negotiated from the Pusan perimeter in 1950 [the small area around Pusan, Korea, to which South Korean and U.S. troops had been forced to retreat early in the Korean war].
>
> But we would be kidding ourselves if we thought that this kind of posture would really (as the Senator's "advantages" suggest) "'provide a believable U.S. bargaining position for negotiations.'"

In his reply to Mansfield on June 22, written by Rostow, the President made these same points, and concluded:

> Once they [the North Vietnamese] become convinced that we are not weak; that we are not impatient; that we are not going to falter; that they cannot win; that the cost to them of their continued aggression is rising; that their bargaining position at a conference is getting weaker every day—then peace will come, whether at the negotiating table or not. And when that day comes, we shall be a good deal closer than we now are to a shining goal—a world of peace, safety and of promise for people everywhere.

On June 25, 1966, Mansfield replied to the President's letter of June 22, restating his position.[45] On June 30, 1966, the President acknowledged receipt of that letter, but did not comment on it.[46]

In a speech on June 16, Mansfield also proposed that Rusk meet with the Chinese Foreign Minister to seek an end to the war. "Peace in Vietnam and peace in China," he said, "are very closely interrelated, if not, indeed, inseparable." "The question must be asked here as well as in Peking, can there be a turning off from the course of collision and over the road of settlement, before, rather than after, the crash." The White House issued a statement saying that the President welcomed suggestions from Members of Con-

---

[44] Johnson Library, NSF files of Mike Mansfield.
[45] Same location.
[46] Johnson Library, WHCF, ND 19/CO 312.

gress, and that Mansfield's statement would be reviewed by Rusk and others.[47]

In late May, there were at least two meetings of the President with his senior advisers to discuss the situation in Vietnam, one on May 25 from 1:48 p.m. to 4:25 p.m. with Rusk, McNamara, Rostow and Moyers, at which Vietnam was one of the items on the agenda, and the other on May 27 from 1:27 p.m. to about 3:00 p.m. with Rusk, McNamara, Rostow and Komer, but there apparently are no notes of either meeting.[48]

It was proposed, possibly at the meeting on May 27, that McNamara should make another of his trips to review the situation, but this idea was abandoned after Lodge said that such a trip would not be timely and could adversely affect the situation.[49]

McNamara himself apparently opposed further escalation, according to a memorandum of a conversation by Averell Harriman, who said that he saw McNamara on May 28 and that "He [McNamara] hopes for some settlement, and gave me the impression he didn't see any value in escalation. He said he thought a good settlement would be: if North Vietnam would pull its troops out, we should do the same; and establishment of an expanded ICC [International Control Commission] to assure no evasion." "We might stop bombing," McNamara added, "if the North Vietnamese stopped infiltration of men and perhaps supplies."

"He [McNamara] is flexible," Harriman noted, "because it is clear a political settlement, not a military settlement, is the only way to end the fighting."

According to Harriman's notes, McNamara also thought that the U.S. should "let the South Vietnamese decide their own future even if it meant a coalition government with the Viet Cong, which might or might not take over."[50]

---

[47] *New York Times*, June 17, 1966. There is no information as to whether Mansfield's statement was "reviewed" by Rusk and others.

[48] Johnson Library, President's Daily Diary for May 25 and 27, 1966, agenda prepared by Rostow for the meeting on May 25, NSF Memos to the President—Walt Rostow.

[49] U.S. Department of State, Central File, Pol 27 Viet S, Saigon to Washington 5024, May 27, 1966.

[50] Library of Congress, Harriman Papers, Subject File, Vietnam, "Memorandum of Conversation with Secretary McNamara," May 30, 1966, and "Further Notes on Conversation with Secretary McNamara—May 28," June 27, 1966.

On May 25, Stanley Karnow, a veteran journalist then with the *Washington Post*, commented in a story from Saigon:

"Only a few months ago, to question the wisdom of U.S. policy and practice in Vietnam was to invite snarls from most Americans here.

"These Americans, immersed in the blood, tears, toil and sweat of the Vietnam conflict, understandably opposed any talk that smelled of surrender. Today, however, that sense of determination has altered to a perceptible mood of doubt, frustration and even disgust—a mood generated by the complex, confused political strife that has been roiling this country.

"By no means does this feeling signify that Americans here advocate U.S. withdrawal from Vietnam tomorrow. But it has set them to wondering if they can give this situation the patient, persistent involvement it requires.

"More and more, Americans who once considered negotiation a defeatist term, now ruminate aloud on 'how we get off the hook' here."

Writing in *Newsweek* on May 30, 1966, after a trip to Vietnam, Emmet John Hughes, another prominent journalist, commented on "the troubled spirit of the American presence, for all its awesome armor . . . it's hazy elusiveness of purpose and its uneasy vision of the future." The "fatal flaw" in the U.S. role in Vietnam, Hughes said, was the misguided idea that Americans had a "gift for the most elaborate political achievement—the making of a new and free nation."

"It is a debatable theory that the Vietnam conflict has perilously overextended U.S. power *militarily*, for some U.S. presence presumably could stay impregnable for decades. But it is a demonstrable fact that U.S. policy has overextended itself with reckless extravagance *politically*. This involvement is wholly without precedent in American policy. It bears no analogy at all to the defense of Germany or Korea or Greece. For the American undertaking here—and here alone—implies an intent profoundly different from defending free nationhood and repelling ag-

On May 30, Lodge sent a cable to Washington in which he commented on the situation: "The current cynical campaign of huge strikes, letters in blood and suicides which the extremist political bonzes and the 'struggle movement' have now unleashed is obviously a desperate effort to bring maximum pressure on the U.S. to force the Government of Vietnam into conceding to Tri Quang. . . . Their publicity campaign is designed to obfuscate by emotional and irrelevant acts their true goal: the replacement of the present government of Vietnam by one amenable to their manipulation."

Ky, Lodge said, was endeavoring to isolate the more extreme Buddhists, and as he was able to achieve greater success the dissidents would become more desperate and more fanatical, including engaging in more anti-American actions.

If Ky succeeded, a compromise could become possible, but at the time, Lodge said, there was no basis for negotiation and compromise. Tri Quang "is not to be reasoned with" by the South Vietnamese Government or the U.S.

Lodge concluded his cable by urging continued support for the Ky government: "We realize that the 'struggle' publicity campaign

---

gression. Behind the military shield, it means educating a whole people to govern themselves when they have never done so. It means discovering a corps of democratic leaders where it has never existed. It means writing laws and combating poverty. It means inventing new political institutions and fostering new political parties. And far from the simple defense of free nationhood, it means arousing a sturdy sense of nationality in a people who have never been a nation.

"Such a nearly delirious design would require, among many remarkable things, one luxury above all: a vast amount of time. But time is running out in Vietnam." (emphasis in original)

According to Hughes, the choices facing the United States "rather inexorably dissolve toward one. As a wise and sympathetic statesman of Southeast Asia stated to me: 'You are going to leave Vietnam. You are not going to be routed or humiliated: your armadas and your bombers make you the greatest power in the South Pacific. But you are going to leave because the earthbound politics of Vietnam cannot be solved by the airborne cavalry of America."

For a contrary view by another prominent journalist, see Joseph Alsop, "Why We Can Win in Vietnam," *Saturday Evening Post*, June 4, 1966.

There were optimistic reports from persons who supported the U.S. role in the war, especially those who had been closely associated with such U.S. Government activities in the past. One of these was William J. Casey, formerly of the OSS, and later the Director of the CIA in the Reagan administration. In 1966, Casey, who was in private business, was a director of the International Rescue Committee headed by Leon Cherne, which had played an intimate role in Vietnam in support of U.S. Government programs since the Geneva Conference in 1954. In May 1966, Casey went to Vietnam under the auspices of the Rescue Committee. He returned "greatly encouraged," and in a report he said, "We have big problems, we may experience setbacks. We can question the wisdom which got us where we are. But we are there and we must face it." The war, he said, was "primarily a contest to win the allegiance of these people, in showing them that we can help them to a better life. Although lives are being lost, we are primarily engaged in helping a people enter the 20th century. . . . The Viet Cong is a nuisance which must be fended off, somewhat like the malaria-bearing mosquito, in order to get the job done."

Casey's emphasis, like that of the CIA at the time, was on pacification and local security rather than on military escalation. He wanted to avoid a larger war in Asia and was strongly opposed to bombing the populations of Hanoi or Haiphong or mining Haiphong harbor, and he argued, "Don't permit the military pressures or the harassments of the Viet Cong to hold us back from our essential task in Vietnam, which is to help build the nation, create a viable Vietnamese government and help the long-suffering people of that land. That's the only way we will, in the final analysis, win the war and show the Communist powers that the technique of national wars of liberation . . . does not work." Casey's report was reprinted in *CR*, vol. 112, pp. 11967–11969.

In June 1966, Freedom House, another organization with close ties to the U.S. Government, and in which Leo Cherne was also a key official, issued a statement reaffirming its support of U.S. policy in Vietnam, including military restraint (the statement opposed the bombing of cities) and the avoidance of a larger war, as well as the search for a negotiated settlement. The statement said in part that the U.S. should stand firm in Vietnam despite the political situation, and should not allow "hostile forces . . . using public agitation and demonstrations to undermine our position in Vietnam. It added: "Not all the divisive factions are in Saigon. The appearance of division within the United States continues to block our best efforts to achieve a negotiated settlement. Those in positions of leadership—in the Congress as in the Administration, in the universities as in the community—bear a heavy responsibility for establishing a climate in which the hoped-for settlement can be achieved." For a reprint of the statement see *ibid.*, pp. 13765–13766.

makes this extremely difficult to do; nevertheless we should persist."[51]

That same day (May 30), Premier Ky met with Tam Chau, chairman of the Buddhist Institute, who had just returned from several weeks abroad. This was followed by a meeting the next day between six Buddhist leaders from the Institute, including Tam Chau and Thien Minh, and six members of the Directorate, including Ky, Thieu, Co and Cao Van Vien. Ky offered to double the size of the Directorate by the addition of ten civilian members, and reaffirmed the government's intention to proceed as planned with elections. The Buddhist leaders indicated that they would accept these terms and would call off further protests. Vien asked if they could assure the government that Tri Quang would also agree. They replied that he would have to accept any arrangement made by the leaders of the Institute.

In his cable to Washington reporting on this development, Lodge said that when Ky told the U.S. Embassy's political officer about the meetings and the agreement he "spoke of the need to save face on all sides."

Lodge commented that the agreement between the government and the Buddhists "sounds too good to be true, and we will await next steps."[52]

On June 1, violence erupted again in Hue as dissidents burned the U.S. consulate.

At about the same time in Saigon, and prior to a final meeting later that day of the Directorate and Buddhist leaders to complete their agreement, a bomb exploded in an automobile carrying Thien Minh, injuring him seriously. Tri Quang sent a message to President Johnson saying that the U.S. was to blame for the attempted assassination because of its support for Ky and Thieu.[53]

At the meeting of the Directorate and Buddhist leaders, according to information given to Westmoreland by Thieu, the Buddhists argued that while the offer to enlarge the Directorate was acceptable, "the people" were insisting that Ky and Thieu must resign because of their actions, including the latest—the bombing of Thien Minh.[54] According to a conversation between Ky and Habib after the meeting ended, however, Ky asked Tam Chau, "'Do you want me to go or not?'" and Tam Chau replied, "'No, that never had been his intention.'"[55] Whichever version is correct, the statement issued after the meeting by the Buddhists, which expressed agreement with the plan to add civilians to the Directorate and to estab-

---

[51] Johnson Library, NSF Memos to the President—Walt Rostow, typed copy of Saigon to Washington 5124, May 30, 1966.

[52] U.S. Department of State, Central File, Pol 27 Viet S, Saigon to Washington 5163, June 1, 1966.

[53] U.S. Department of State, Central File, Pol 27 Viet S, Saigon to Washington 5224, June 2, 1966. According to Kahin, *Intervention*, pp. 430, 539, the attack on Thien Minh was "generally believed to have been carried out by operatives of Ky's deputy, Colonel Loan." Kahin bases this on Vietnamese and U.S. Embassy sources.

In a conversation with Westmoreland during a meeting on June 1, after the attack on Thien Minh, Thieu ridiculed the Buddhists' statement that "the people" wanted Ky and Thieu to resign. He said that the militant Buddhists were a small minority and did not represent the people. "Thien made a very interesting comment," Westmoreland added in his cable to Wheeler reporting on the conversation. "He said he believed that if Thien Minh and Tri Quang were killed that things would remain quiet." MAC 4474 cited above.

[54] U.S. Department of State, Central File, Pol 27 Viet S, Saigon to Washington 5195, June 1, 1966, and CMH, Westmoreland Papers, Message Files, MAC 4474, June 1, 1966.

[55] Saigon to Washington 5195, cited in previous footnote.

lish an advisory committee—the points included in a separate statement issued by the government, said that agreement had also been reached on the resignation of Ky and Thieu after the addition of the civilians to the Directorate on June 6, but it did not say when they were to resign. The statement also urged Buddhists to cease demonstrating until June 6.[56]

Most militant Buddhists rejected this announcement, and Tri Quang again demanded the resignation of Ky and Thieu and vowed to continue the struggle.

In his weekly personal report to President Johnson on June 1, Lodge blamed the attack on Thien Minh on the Communists, saying "This may mean that the Communists take Ky's 'understanding' with the Buddhists seriously and are moving in as a last desperate means. Burning the Hue consulate may be similar."[57] He went on to comment on the "power-hungry Buddhists," saying that they were, "out to make an effect on the American political scene. . . ." "We have," he added, "gone through a period of demonstrations, agitation, and argumentation. Now I fear that fanatic—if not actually, macabre—stage is about to come. I believe there is a plentiful supply of Buddhists—mystics and mental defectives—ready to burn themselves alive, and men ruthless enough to use them."

The efforts of the militant Buddhists, Lodge said, "is a very much pumped-up, heavily financed, well organized affair. They use many mercenaries for their parades as well as children. We are trying to find out where the money comes from—from the Viet Cong or the French."[58]

Lodge concluded by telling the President: "As the Buddhist uproar grows, I hope you will get deserved satisfaction from the thought that our policy of working through the government . . . is absolutely right."

That same day, June 1, the U.S. received word that General Hoang Xuan Lam, formerly Commander of the ARVN 2d Division who was newly appointed I Corps Commander (he replaced Cao who replaced Dinh who replaced Chuan who replaced Thi—all in the course of two and a half months), was immediately going to take steps to restore order in Hue as a result of the burning of the consulate, rather than, as he had planned, moving in more slowly.[59] The State Department sent a "flash" cable to Lodge saying that such action was of serious concern because of the possibility of undoing the agreement that had just been reached. Lodge was asked to see Ky at once and to tell him of U.S. concern. He should

[56] Saigon to Washington 5524, cited above.

[57] U.S. Department of State, Central File, Pol 27 Viet S, Saigon to Washington 5178, June 1, 1966.

[58] Thieu told Westmoreland that the money came from funds collected by the Buddhists for building pagodas, from some French colonists, or perhaps from some French-oriented Vietnamese. (MAC 4474 cited above.) In a cable to the President on June 15 (Department of State Central File, Pol 27 Viet S, Saigon to Washington 5546) Lodge said he had received "unconfirmed reports that the French have given ten million piasters to Buddhists in Hue and Danang and the same sum to Buddhists in Saigon to support the 'Struggle' Movement, the money having been brought to Vietnam by an unidentified French professor. . . ."

[59] CMH, Westmoreland Papers, Message Files, MAC 4473, June 1, 1966.

also make the point, the cable said, that destruction of U.S. property should not affect the timing of a move to restore order.[60]

Despite the State Department's concern, the movement of troops into Hue was scheduled for the morning of June 2. On the night of June 1, however, General Nhuan, Commander of the ARVN 1st Division, whose sympathies lay with the Struggle Movement, told Tri Quang about the operation, and this led to its being canceled.[61]

On June 3, Tri Quang held a press conference in Hue at which he again called for Ky and Thieu to resign, declaring that "the struggle movement will never tolerate a government which creates a civil war to oppress Buddhism and kill Buddhists."[62] Behind the scenes, however, there were talks between Tri Quang, Thi and Nhuan, in which Thi said he was the personal representative of Ky, about resolving the dispute and ending the demonstrations.[63]

On June 8, with the situation still unresolved, South Vietnamese Government troops moved into Hue. Several hundred Buddhist monks, students and others were arrested and imprisoned. Tri Quang, who had urged citizens not to resist the troops, was arrested. He began a hunger strike and at the end of June he was moved to a clinic in Saigon. Thi, Dinh, Cao, Nhuan and Chuan were brought before a special tribunal, given 60 days of confinement, and retired from service (Dinh was given a dishonorable discharge).[64]

By June 9, Hue was under government control, but it was the 22d of June before active resistance was said to have ended.[65]

On June 26, Tri Quang was interviewed by an American journalist in the clinic in Saigon to which he had been moved. He gave the journalist a letter that he wanted sent to President Johnson, and the journalist gave it to the U.S. Embassy. It read as follows:[66]

> I think it is not necessary to remind you of my excessive confidence in Americans (but if I die, as many have and are now dying because of the oppression of which I spoke, it is because of that excessive confidence); neither do I need to establish again the good will and patience which I have maintained with all my strength; nor is it necessary to refer to the future national assembly which is now suspicious and betrayed and for which no one has any confidence or enthusiasm.

---

[60] U.S. Department of State, Central File, Pol 27 Viet S, Washington to Saigon 3714, June 1, 1966.

[61] CMH, Westmoreland Papers, Message Files, MAC 4508, June 2, 1966. This occurred before Lodge saw Ky on June 2 to communicate to him the State Department's concern. For Lodge's report of that conversation, see U.S. Department of State, Central File, Pol 27 Viet S, Saigon to Washington 5215, June 2, 1966.

[62] U.S. Department of State, Central File, Pol 27 Viet S, Saigon to Washington 5252, June 3, 1966.

[63] See the memorandum for the record on June 2, 1966 by Lt. Col. C. G. Cleveland, "Telephone Discussion with General Platt at 1420 hours, this date," CMH, Westmoreland Papers, History File.

[64] U.S. Department of State, Pol 2 Viet S, Saigon to Washington 819, July 12, 1966.

[65] Kahin, *Intervention*, p. 430 and Fitzgerald, *Fire in the Lake*, pp. 290–291.

[66] U.S. Department of State, Central File, Pol 27 Viet S, Saigon to Washington 5773, June 26, 1966.

> I only say that when the French came to govern my country, there were innumerable people who died without thinking of victory. But they died to alert and activate the will to struggle of my people.
>
> Today the Vietnamese, whether my friends or my enemies, all know that my death is what the Americans are hoping for. But I am determined to do what my forefathers did when faced with a colonial policy like yours, Mr. President.
>
> There is a Vietnamese proverb that says when a bird is about to die its song is both piteous and miraculous. I now use that kind of voice to pray that my country and my faith will soon escape from the policy which I again say I most deeply resent.

In a lengthy report to Rostow on June 11, 1966, Lodge, with his customary optimism and confidence, viewed the suppression of the Buddhist uprising as a successful episode in the building of a "modern nation state."[67] Komer took the same position, arguing that the dissidents were simply jockeying for political power, and that the situation had not been as serious as it may have appeared to be. He said it was not a "popular upheaval," nor was it an "invite" for the U.S. to leave. "It was rather part of the painful process of a young nation at war struggling toward consensus. The military used repression at times, the dissidents used riots and immolations. But it was not *Gotterdammerung*."[68]

Lodge and Komer also emphasized that the crisis had given greater momentum to the drafting of a constitution, the holding of elections, and a return to representative government.

Similar views were expressed by Habib at Westmoreland's commanders' conference on June 5 attended by all of the principal American military commanders in Vietnam. The U.S., Habib said, had "an unhappy role in this crisis, a role of preaching moderation to extremists on both sides. This is a dialogue of the deaf. What we can do is to determine procedures which will give us the least trouble, remembering that there is strength in evolutionary processes. It will be difficult to smooth a path to consensus among the Vietnamese, but we can at least improve the political climate."[69] The U.S., he added, "cannot and will not abandon the government

---

[67] U.S. Department of State, Saigon to Washington 5473, June 11, 1966. In another cable Lodge said: "It would be wonderful if out of all this wreckage, a sober, responsible Buddhist Church might emerge." Johnson Library, NSF Memos to the President—Walt Rostow, Saigon to Washington 5684, June 22, 1966.

According to Lodge, McNamara, while on a trip to Vietnam, told him on Oct. 11, 1966 that he, Rusk and the President "had wanted to compromise with Thi, but that Lodge had been right and they had been wrong. McNamara said that it was now clear that if this had been done there would never have been elections, other cities would have fallen, and the war effort as a whole would have been jeopardized. He said to Lodge: 'You had better nerves than we did.'" Lodge, "Viet-Nam Memoirs," cited above, pt. IV, ch. III, p. 26.

[68] Johnson Library, NSF Files of Robert W. Komer, Memorandum from Komer to Bill Moyers, "Vietnam Press Guidelines," June 2, 1966.

[69] CMH Westmoreland Papers, History File, Memorandum for the Record of June 20, 1966, on the MACV Commanders' Conference of June 5.

in this crisis. Our policy is to limit the visceral, excessive emotional reactions of the government and, at the same time, to back the authority and control of the government over all of South Vietnam. Islands of anarchy are thus unacceptable."

Westmoreland added: "What we are dealing with here is an adolescent nation which, like young men, is radical and schizophrenicly inclined. In a country like this, political turmoil is inevitable. . . ." The danger, he said, was not so much the effect of the crisis in Vietnam itself as the effect on public opinion in the U.S., where it had been "blown up out of all proportion by the press."

In the aftermath of the Buddhist crisis, the United States, which had found itself in a very awkward and difficult situation during the crisis, especially in the case of the abortive effort by the Ky government to use force against Danang without consulting its American ally, took steps to improve its intelligence operations. Among other things, this included further penetration of the South Vietnamese Government through a tap by the CIA in the office of Chief of State Thieu. The "take" from this tap was translated by the CIA Station in Saigon and cabled to Washington where the CIA prepared a "sanitized" version concealing the source of information. These transcripts were then sent to the President and to several of his principal associates. "Two sources said that Johnson himself . . . knew of the tap, and sometimes read the actual transcripts themselves, brooding over the inconstancy of his ally." [70]

Decline in American Public Support

Public support for the war, which had continued at a high level since the summer of 1965, declined sharply during April-June 1966. Moreover, this loss of support was never regained, despite several brief interludes in 1966–67 during which support increased slightly, only to fall even further. This was the trend from the end of 1964 until the beginning of 1972: [71]

[70] Thomas Powers, *The Man Who Kept the Secrets: Richard Helms and the CIA* (New York: Knopf, 1979), p. 185.

[71] Mueller, *War, Presidents and Public Opinion*, p. 56. This analysis, according to Mueller, was based on a combination of the results of polls by Gallup using two different questions: (1) "*In view of the developments since we entered the fighting in Vietnam do you think the U.S. made a mistake sending troops to fight in Vietnam?*" and, (2) "*Some people think we should not have become involved with our military forces in Southeast Asia, while others think we should have. What is your opinion?*" The second question was not asked after November 1965, however, and therefore the trend line shown in the chart for the period after that date is based entirely on the first question.

The first question, the so-called "mistake question," reflects at least two kinds of opinions as to why the use of U.S. forces was a mistake—those who opposed the war, and those who wanted to use greater force. Thus, it is not a reliable guide to antiwar sentiment even though it is useful in indicating the level of support for the war. For a discussion, see pt. III of this study, p. 142.

TRENDS IN SUPPORT FOR THE WAR IN VIETNAM

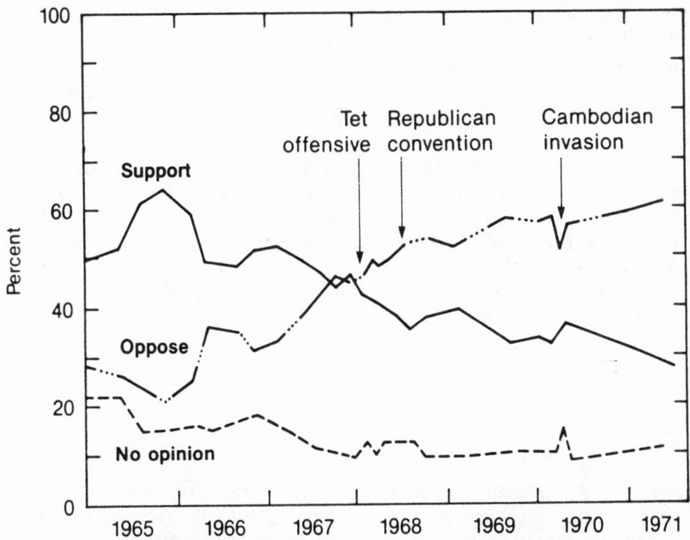

Source: John E. Mueller, *War, Presidents and Public Opinion* (New York: John Wiley and Sons, 1973).

Given the inadequacy of polling data on the war, it would be difficult to attribute the sudden ten-point drop in support between March and May of 1966 to specific causes, but it appears to have resulted from public reaction to the increasing cost of the war in lives and money when measured against the progress being made or foreseen, as well as from the political instability in South Vietnam, which created doubts about whether the Vietnamese wanted U.S. help, or could, in the final analysis, govern themselves effectively.[72]

The decline during the spring of 1966 in support for the war and increase in support for ending the war by withdrawal are also illustrated by the results of a Gallup poll in June 1966 as compared to a similar poll in June of 1965:[73]

> *"Suppose you were asked to vote on the question of continuing the war in Vietnam or withdrawing our troops during the next few months—how would you vote?"*

[72] Mueller, p. 53, noted these reasons for the drop in support: "The Buddhist crisis and the frustrating South Vietnamese political instability of the time . . . undoubtedly affected this change. In addition, the increasing disaffection of prominent American politicians and intellectuals, voiced in the Fulbright hearings of February and March 1966, probably helped to make dissent respectable."

[73] *Washington Post*, June 19, 1966. Responses are broken down by sex, race, education, etc., in *Vietnam War, A Compilation: 1964–1990*, vol. I.

It should be noted that in June 1965 there were many fewer U.S. troops and they had not begun to play a fully active combat role. Thus, casualties were far lighter than in June 1966.

[In percent]

	June 1966	June 1965
Continue	48	66
Withdraw	35	20
No Opinion	17	14

There is additional evidence of this decline, as well as the increase in the trend, noted earlier, toward favoring more extreme measures (withdrawal and escalation), in the Harris Survey conducted in June 1966:[74]

> *"All in all, what do you think we should do about Vietnam? We can follow one of three courses: carry the ground war into North Vietnam at the risk of bringing Red China into the fighting, withdraw our support and troops from South Vietnam or continue to try to hold the line there to prevent the Communists from taking over South Vietnam. Which do you favor?"*

[In percent]

	May 1966	December 1965	September 1965
Withdraw	15	7	25
Hold the line	47	65	49
Carry War to the North	38	28	26

Harris' interpretation of the results of this survey was that, "American public opinion is rising toward increased militancy about the Vietnam war and a 'get it over with' mood. . . . The people show a distaste for what they regard as an indecisive stalemate in which American lives are being spent, but they cannot arrive at any firm conclusion about what should be done to end the war."[75]

A large percentage of the public seems to have continued to believe that the war would end in a compromise solution rather than an "all-out victory," and that efforts should be made to find such a compromise and to avoid escalation. A Gallup Poll conducted toward the end of March 1966 found that 62 percent were in favor, with 18 percent opposed, and 20 percent no opinion, of having the U.S. and North Vietnam withdraw their forces from South Vietnam, on the condition that U.S. ships and planes would stand by to be used if necessary, followed by a U.N.-sponsored vote in North and South Vietnam to determine whether there should be unification.[76]

---

[74] *Washington Post*, June 13, 1966. "No opinion" percentages were not included in the published results of the poll, thereby increasing the percentages of the three alternative answers.

One study concluded: "[F]rom the middle of 1965 until roughly the spring of 1966 . . . Americans were attentive to the administration's justification of United States involvement in Vietnam. In effect, this was the period when most citizens were willing to give the new war policy a chance to work. When the results of this support were not encouraging, restlessness and uncertainty began to set in, in the form of larger numbers who began to say that U.S. involvement in Vietnam was a mistake. . . . At the same time, escalation sentiment was beginning to build up." William L. Lunch and Peter W. Sperlich, "American Public Opinion and the War in Vietnam," *Western Political Quarterly*, 32 (March 1979), pp. 21–44 at p. 30.

Lunch and Sperlich suggest (p. 29) that there were four stages in public reaction to the Vietnam war: "There is first the 'innocence' phase, which starts with the initial polls about Vietnam in 1964 and extends to the 'rally-round-the-flag' phenomenon in mid-1965. The second period might be called the 'permissive majority' phase—it is visible from mid-1965 for nearly a year, until roughly the spring, 1966. The third stage could be called the 'escalation' phase, and it extends from mid-1966 until late 1967 or early 1968. The later period, the 'withdrawal' phase, encompasses most of 1968 and the years that followed, until direct military involvement was terminated in 1973."

[75] *Washington Post*, June 13, 1966.

[76] *The Gallup Poll*, vol. III, p. 2001. For a breakdown by sex, race, education, etc., see *Vietnam War, A Compilation: 1964–1990*, vol. 1.

Further evidence of public dissatisfaction is provided by surveys of attitudes on the President's handling of the war. Beginning in July 1965, with the U.S. decision to send ground forces to Vietnam, until February 1966, the polls showed a high and steady support for the President's performance. According to responses to a question asked by the Harris Survey: *"How would you rate the job President Johnson has done in handling the war in Vietnam—excellent, good, only fair or poor?"* about 65 percent in the late summer of 1965 said he was doing an excellent or good job with the war, while about 35 percent said it was fair or poor. In February 1966, this changed abruptly to a 50–50 split.[77] By June 1966, this had declined to 42 percent excellent or good and 58 percent fair or poor. In July, after increased bombing of North Vietnam, it rebounded to 54 percent excellent or good and 46 percent fair or poor, but by September it had dropped again to 42 percent excellent or good and 58 percent fair or poor, and the downward trend continued for the remainder of Johnson's Presidency.[78]

The following table shows public approval of Johnson's handling of the war during 1965–1968 in response to Gallup's similar question: *"Do you approve or disapprove of the way President Johnson is handling the situation in Vietnam?"* (During 1965, the question was worded as follows: *"Do you approve or disapprove of the way the Johnson Administration is dealing with the situation in Vietnam?")* [79]

PUBLIC APPROVAL OF THE JOHNSON ADMINISTRATION'S HANDLING OF THE VIETNAM WAR

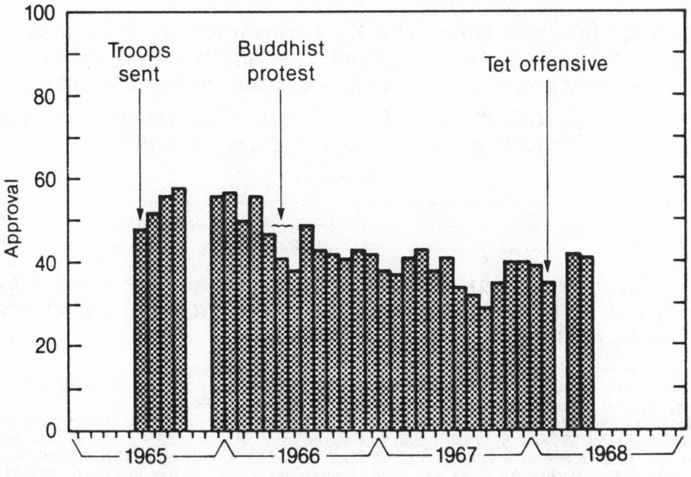

Source: *The Gallup Poll*

[77] *Washington Post,* July 11, 1966.
[78] *Ibid.,* Sept. 11, 1966.
[79] Data are from *The Gallup Poll,* vol. III, except for July 24, 1966, which are from the Gallup press release on that poll. For a breakdown of each poll by sex, race, education, etc., see *Vietnam War, A Compilation: 1964–1990,* vol. 1 cited above.

There are also some polling data on American attitudes toward the political unrest in South Vietnam in the spring of 1966. Following are the responses to three questions asked by Gallup in mid-April:[80]

"Suppose the South Vietnamese start fighting on a big scale among themselves. Do you think we should continue to help them, or should we withdraw our troops?"

[In percent]

Continue to help	28
Withdraw	54
No opinion	18

"If the South Vietnam government decides to stop fighting (discontinue the war), what should the United States do—continue the war by itself, or should we withdraw?"

[In percent]

	April 1966	*August 1965*
Continue to help	16	19
Withdraw	72	63
No Opinion	12	18

"Do you think the South Vietnamese will be able to establish a stable government, or not?"

[In percent]

	April 1966	*January 1965*
Yes	32	25
No	48	42
No Opinion	20	33

In mid-May, just before the Ky government used force to regain control of Danang, Gallup asked two additional questions about American reaction to the political situation in South Vietnam:[81]

"Do you think most of the South Vietnamese want the United States to get out of their country, or not?"

[In percent]

Yes	34
No	38
No Opinion	28

"Suppose a majority of the South Vietnamese wanted us to pull our troops out of Vietnam, do you think we should do so, or not?"

---

[80] *The Gallup Poll,* vol. III, pp. 2007–2008. For a breakdown of each of the three questions by sex, race, education, etc., see *Vietnam War, A Compilation: 1964–1990,* vol. 1.

The State Department sent the results of this survey to Lodge (U.S. Department of State, Central File, Pol 27 Viet S, Washington to Saigon 3553, May 20, 1966) who said in his reply, (same location, Saigon to Washington 4880, May 23, 1966), among other things, that the survey demonstrated "a rather fundamental misunderstanding of the entire situation here. 'Internal squabbling' is an organic part of the war, and is being undertaken as a counterpart to military success and a part of jockeying for position prior to the elections. It is also an integral element of Vietnam's evolution from a tropical, Confucianist, colonial and feudal sectarianism into a modern, centrally organized nation-state." "It is obviously true," he added, "that the Vietnamese are not today ready for self-government. . . . But if we are going to adopt the policy of turning every country that is unfit for self-government over to the Communists, there won't be much of the world left."

[81] *Washington Post,* June 19, 1966. The interviewing dates were May 5–10.

[In percent]

Yes	51
No	33
No opinion	16

In early June 1966, declining public support for the war and confidence in the President's handling of it were noted with concern by Moyers in a memorandum to the President. He reported that conversations with Harris, Gallup and other polling professionals "confirm only one thing: that our standing is down and likely to drop further."[82] There was unanimous agreement, he said, that the major issue was Vietnam, followed by the cost of living. "There is general agreement among all of these men with Lou Harris' comment this morning: 'the people are in a foul mood over Vietnam'. . . .

"The overwhelming sentiment," Moyers added, "is not for the United States to withdraw; it is, rather, 'Why can't we get it over with?'" He continued:

> Gallup and Harris both contend that people, as reflected in the polls, do not understand how a country of our size and power can seemingly make so little progress in Vietnam.
>
> In one word—according to Gallup—the people are "frustrated."
>
> Harris says that the President is on "dead center, satisfying neither side—those who want to get it over with by negotiations, those who want to get it over with by force."

"The problem both Gallup and Harris see," Moyers said, "is that the isolated island in the middle, on which the President is now standing, will shrink smaller and smaller," and that this trend would continue "until there is some movement—either toward a military victory or toward a negotiated settlement." "Their joint recommendation is 'to offer some ray of hope.' Simply 'biting the bullet,' they contend, will not work." "But such a 'ray of hope' must not be what Gallup calls a 'continuance.'" If, Gallup said, the President held out the hope of either negotiations or military success and nothing happened in six months, "'we would be in a more disastrous position with the people than now.'"

Several days earlier, Moyers had sent the President, at his request, a long memorandum on relations with the press, which Moyers said were deteriorating and were producing an adverse effect on public opinion.[83] "In the past three months particularly," Moyers said, "there has grown up between the White House press corps and the White House *an atmosphere of hostility*. . . . In essence, the White House Press Corps has come to believe that we antagonize them deliberately, keep them as uninformed as possible, make their personal lives as difficult as we can, play games with them, are unduly secretive, massage them when we need them and kick them when we don't and generally 'downgrade the profession.'" (emphasis in original)

---

[82] Johnson Library, WHCF, CF PR 16, memorandum for the President from Moyers, June 9, 1966.

[83] Johnson Library, Office Files of Bill Moyers, Memorandum to the President from Moyers, June 6, 1966.

There was some evidence, Moyers said, that the "credibility gap," which he said every President faced, was becoming a "confidence gap."

Moyers, in proposing some steps to remedy the situation, said that he believed good press relations "are as attainable as the upswing I believe will come in public approval of your performance as President." "Just as we do our best to persuade and reason with and even flatter SOBs with whom we have to work in Congress—not because we like them but because we have to deal with them—it seems to me that similar tactics should guide us in dealing with the press."

Among the steps he suggested were to show greater consideration for the press by avoiding, where possible, last-minute announcements of trips, holding frequent press conferences, making answers to questions "more responsive," and holding more televised press conferences. None of these, he concluded, would "make life with the press all peaches and cream. But we can strike a better balance and we can arrest the most disturbing but growing feeling of all—*that we cannot be trusted.*" (emphasis in original)

U.S. Protests Increase

During the spring of 1966, as public doubts about the war continued to grow, the antiwar movement also grew.[84] On March 26, 1966 there was another march against the war in various U.S. and foreign cities during what was again called "Days of International Protest." Organized by the National Coordinating Committee to End the War in Vietnam, and led by SANE, Women Strike for Peace, the Committee for Nonviolent Action (headed by the Reverend A. J. Muste), and the Students for a Democratic Society (SDS), thousands of persons demonstrated in New York (where 20,000–25,000 participated), Boston, Philadelphia, Washington,

[84] As the following graph shows, there was, as could be expected, a direct correlation between disapproval of the war and the numbers of those demonstrating against the war:

SIZE OF ANTIWAR DEMONSTRATIONS AND PERCENTAGE OF ANTIWAR SENTIMENT

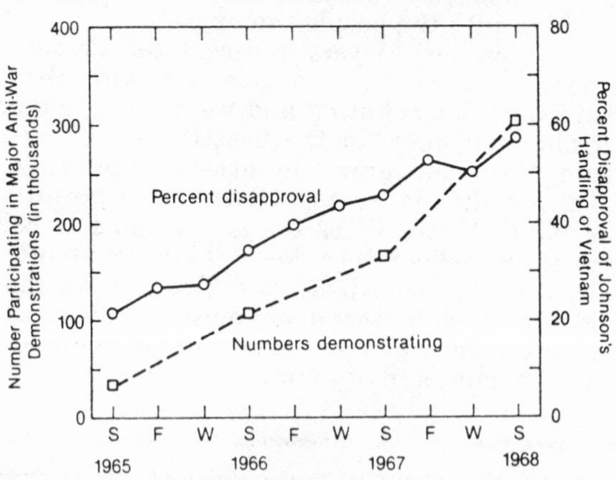

Source: *The Politics of Protest*, Task Force on Violent Aspects of Protest and Confrontation, National Commission on the Causes and Prevention of Violence (New York: Simon and Schuster, 1968), p. 32.

Chicago, Detroit, San Francisco, and Oklahoma City, among others. Abroad, there were demonstrations in Ottowa, London, Oslo, Stockholm, Lyon, and Tokyo.[85]

Prominent American writers, including Lillian Hellman, Irving Howe, John Hersey, Alfred Kazin, Elmer Rice, Louis Untermeyer, and Edmund Wilson, organized the American Writers and Artists Against the War in Vietnam and began holding "read-ins" against the war at colleges and universities, primarily in the northeastern part of the country.[86]

On the campuses, there were demonstrations of various kinds, including fasts. In May 1966, after the Selective Service System announced that deferments from the draft would be based on academic performance, and, for those in the lower half of their class, on relative scores on an examination to be given by the Selective Service System, the first student occupation of college and university administration buildings, led by the SDS, occurred at the University of Chicago, the City College of New York, and the University of Wisconsin, to protest the cooperation of academic authorities with local draft boards.[87]

There were also demonstrations on May 14 at many of the 1,200 centers around the country where the Selective Service draft deferment exams were given to men who were ranked academically in the lower half of their class.

In Washington, on May 15, there was another march against the war led by SANE and Women Strike for Peace, in which 8,000–10,000 took part.[88]

In early June 1966, some students at Amherst College as well as some students and faculty at New York University protested the war by walking out of graduation ceremonies at which Secretary of Defense Robert McNamara received honorary degrees.[89]

On June 5, 6,400 educators and others, including 351 teachers, 324 artists, 272 psychologists, 259 physicians, 203 writers, 142 religious representatives, and 105 scientists and technologists, signed a three-page advertisement in the *New York Times* calling for immediate cessation of U.S. offensive military operations, and an

---

[85] *New York Times*, Mar. 27, 1966. Marxists and Communists also participated, including the W. E. B. DuBois Clubs, which had just been listed by the Justice Department as a subversive organization.

In the middle of April, Muste and five other U.S. pacifists carried their protest to Saigon, where they were harassed by the Ky government, and after a week, when their tourist visas expired, they were forced to leave the country. See *ibid.*, Apr. 20, 22, 1966.

[86] *Ibid.*, Apr. 27, May 4, 1966.

[87] *Ibid.*, May 13, 14, 17, 24, 1966. See also Sale, *SDS*, pp. 253–263. Some colleges and universities were providing information on class standing to local draft boards or to the students themselves. Even when this was being done only by request of the student, and even if the information was given directly to the student, it was argued by protestors that the institution was cooperating with the authorities, and that students who did not choose to take part would be singled out for the draft.

On May 26, 1966, the faculty council at the University of Chicago strongly condemned the student seizure of the administration building, and a referendum conducted by the student government showed that by a vote of 3–1 (924–322, out of a total undergraduate enrollment of 2,400), the general student body supported the university and the faculty. At the same time, the university announced that thereafter, data on grades would go directly to the students rather than to draft boards. *New York Times*, May 27, 1966.

[88] *New York Times* and *Washington Post*, May 16, 1966.

[89] *New York Times*, June 4, 5, 1966.

evaluation of whether U.S. and Vietnamese interests would be best served by U.S. withdrawal.[90]

In early June, the Johnson administration, working through friends in the civil rights movement, succeeded in blocking efforts by more militant elements, led by Floyd McKissick, national director of the Congress of Racial Equality (CORE), to pass an antiwar resolution at a White House Conference on Civil Rights. According to Whitney M. Young, Jr., executive director of the National Urban League, "The people are more concerned about the rat tonight and the job tomorrow than they are about Vietnam. If the alternative were guns or butter then we must cut Vietnam."[91]

In late May and early June, a group was formed to support antiwar candidates in the 1966 congressional elections. It was called the National Conference for New Politics, and its co-chairmen were Dr. Benjamin Spock, Rev. William Sloane Coffin, Julian Bond and Simon Casady, former president of the California Young Democratic Councils, a reform group in the California Democratic Party.[92] Sponsors included Jerome Grossman, a Boston business executive, who was chairman of the Massachusetts Political Action for Peace, Paul Booth, national secretary of the SDS, Stokely Carmichael, new chairman of SNCC, and Dick Gregory, a comedian and political activist.

On June 20, 1966, the Internal Security Subcommittee of the U.S. Senate Judiciary Committee, which had issued a staff study in October 1965 linking antiwar demonstrations to the Communists, issued a subcommittee report, "Communist Youth Programs," based on hearings held on May 17, 18, 1965. Referring especially to the Free Speech movement at the University of California (Berkeley), and antiwar demonstrations there and at the University of Wisconsin, it stated:[93]

> These demonstrations appeared spontaneous at first. But a pattern emerged on campus after campus which made it unmistakably clear that the Communist Party, U.S.A., and its front organizations were playing a key role in organizing them. . . . Student body grievances were either fraudulent, created, stimulated, or exaggerated as a catalytic means of setting off mob explosions. Once aroused, student energies were channeled and directed by

---

[90] *Ibid.*, June 5, 1966. Among the signers were 3,938 persons from 180 colleges and universities, including 190 from Columbia University, 176 from Harvard University, 131 from the University of California at Berkeley. In an article, "Checking Credentials of Vietnam Critics," *National Observer*, Sept. 19, 1966, Rodger Swearingen, a professor of international relations at the University of Southern California, and director of its Research Institute on Communist Strategy and Propaganda, who supported the war, concluded, after analyzing the credentials of the academicians who signed the June 1966 statement as well as those who signed a similar statement on May 9, 1965, that these persons were only a small part of the academic community and should not be considered representative; that the "overwhelming majority" were from fields of study which did not equip them professionally to make such judgments; that few qualified professionals were included; and that the views expressed were not well-founded, realistic, or in the interest of the U.S. or South Vietnam. They were, he said, moral judgments, which should not be "interpreted as meaning that *the* academic community and the members of the professions in the United States do not support their Government's policy in Vietnam." (emphasis in original) In October 1967, Swearingen was one of 109 persons named as members of the Citizens Committee for Peace with Freedom in Vietnam, which had been organized by the White House to support the war. See the *Washington Post*, Oct. 26, 1967.

[91] *New York Times*, June 3, 1966.

[92] *Ibid.*, June 10, 1966. For an advertisement by the group announcing its formation, see *ibid.*, May 22, 1966.

[93] This was a subcommittee print which was not subsequently issued as a committee report. For discussion of the hearings, see p. 91 above.

professionals and their disciples into forums, rallies, protests, resolutions, defiance of law and out-and-out law violations.

Critics in Congress Ponder What to Do

During June 1966, as the political crisis in South Vietnam came to an end and it was apparent that the President was preparing to escalate U.S. military action, some Members of Congress who wanted to bring about a change of policy made a renewed effort to influence the President.

It will be recalled that in late May, Marcy, the chief of staff of the Foreign Relations Committee, had urged Fulbright to try to persuade Mansfield and Russell to arrange a private meeting between the President and a few senior Democratic and Republican Senators for an off-the-record discussion of U.S. policy in Vietnam. Apparently no action was taken on the recommendation.

In a brief memorandum on June 1, Marcy then suggested to Fulbright that he try to get Mansfield to hold a "rump session" of senior Senators (he mentioned Democrats Russell, Stennis, Mansfield, Fulbright, and Republicans Cooper and Aiken) to discuss "the future of this nation in Vietnam." "I think," Marcy said, "this is the most important thing such individuals could be doing now. Somehow the direction the President is taking must be changed and I know of no other method. This would be senatorial advice in the constitutional sense!"[94]

Meanwhile, arrangements were being made for Fulbright and the President to have a private talk about Vietnam. The meeting was requested by Clinton P. Anderson (D/N. Mex.), a respected senior Senator, chairman of the Senate Aeronautics and Space Committee, who was on very good terms with both Fulbright and the President. It is not known why Anderson was the one who requested the meeting. It is unlikely that he made the request without some prompting from persons who were concerned about the Johnson-Fulbright relationship, although Anderson himself was also quite concerned.

The confidential nature of the meeting was apparent in a memorandum to the President on May 27 from Marvin Watson, White House Chief of Staff, saying that Senator Anderson would like to come to the White House "and bring his guest" on June 1.[95] When Anderson arrived with his "guest"—Fulbright—he stayed from 6:20 p.m. until 6:35 p.m., after which he left the room and waited in Marvin Watson's office for the meeting to conclude. At 6:45 p.m., Rostow joined Fulbright and the President. The meeting, which ended at 8:13 p.m., consisted primarily, according to Rostow's notes, of comments by the President on "the options open to him and why the option he has chosen is in the national interest."[96]

---

[94] U.S. National Archives, RG 46, Papers of the Senate Foreign Relations Committee, Marcy Chron File.

[95] Johnson Library, President's Appointment File, Diary Backup for June 1, 1966. Watson's memorandum was sent on the same day that the President replied to Fulbright's letter to the President of May 9 on the "arrogance of power."

[96] Johnson Library, President's Daily Diary for June 1, 1966, notes dictated by Rostow and typed onto that page of the diary. According to another typed note, Senator Anderson, apparently while waiting in Marvin's office "expressed his pleasure that these two men, with whom

Continued

"Senator Fulbright listened, said he wished he could share our confidence that there is an honorable way out; but would keep in touch."

On June 7, 14, and 15, Fulbright was invited to various White House ceremonies. At the close of the ceremony on June 15, according to notes on the President's Daily Diary for that day, "The last person to shake hands with the President was Senator Fulbright, a guest. The President greeted him warmly as an old friend, put his arm around the Senator and talked animately for several seconds."[97]

After the ceremony on June 15, the President met privately with Fulbright from 12:50 p.m. to 1:40 p.m. There are no notes of that meeting, but according to one source, who apparently talked to Fulbright soon afterwards, it was "a highly emotional harangue" in which the President said that the U.S. must win a military victory, and that if the Communists did not relent the U.S. would use its power to force them to do so. Fulbright, according to this account, "had never seen Johnson so insecure, so frenetic. He seemed to be desperately trying to convince himself, as well as his old friend. Fulbright went back to Capitol Hill very troubled. He told members of his staff he was afraid the President was beyond a rational discussion of Vietnam. The Senator feared that while Johnson was in this mood, he was capable of almost any recklessness, including the bombing of China."[98]

At a press conference on June 18, the President made a lengthy statement in which he said, among other things, that he had examined the alternatives, but felt that the U.S. should persist in its present policy:[99]

> In the past few weeks the battle in Vietnam has become more intense. The large forces infiltrated from the North into South Vietnam in recent months are now being engaged—sometimes at their initiative, sometime at ours. The forces of South Vietnam, the United States, and our allies have responded with skill, courage, and effectiveness.
>
> During this period my advisers and I have—almost on a daily basis—continued closely to examine and to scrutinize what the aggressor has been doing and our own course of action.
>
> We have examined the alternatives open to us—including all suggestions from those who have not shared our views.
>
> In the light of the full information available to the President of the United States, we sincerely feel that the national interest requires that we persist in our present policy. That policy is to bring to bear the ground, naval, and air strength required to achieve our objective.
>
> I must observe that this does not mean that we shall not increase our forces or our operations. It is not good national policy publicly to declare to those conducting aggression that

---

he felt so close, had come together for this talk." Apparently there are no other notes of the June 1 meeting.

97 Same location, Notes on the President's Daily Diary for June 15, 1966.

98 Coffin, *Senator Fulbright*, p. 313.

99 *Public Papers of the Presidents*, Lyndon B. Johnson, 1966, pp. 628–629.

there are particular limits on how we shall act to defeat that aggression.

But our objectives remain what they have been:

—to guarantee that infiltration, subversion, and terror mounted and infiltrated from North Vietnam cannot swallow or conquer South Vietnam;

—to permit the people of South Vietnam to select their own government and to build a way of life which conforms to their own traditions and desires.

In meeting this objective, we must also reassure the world that America's agreements, once they are made, are not broken. We are not fighting to remain in South Vietnam, not to hold bases there, not to control the affairs of that people.

We are there to defeat aggression, to permit a young nation to develop its own destiny, to help its people rebuild and create a modern nation even before the guns go silent.

But to these limited objectives we are fully committed.

What are our prospects?

I must frankly tell you that our intelligence indicates that the aggressor presently bases his hopes, we think, more on political differences in Saigon and Washington than on his military capacity in South Vietnam. While we have differences and divisions, I want our men in the field and our people at home to know that our course is resolute, that our conviction is firm, and we shall not be diverted from doing what is necessary in the Nation's interest and the cause of freedom.

Apparently convinced that he had not and could not persuade the President to change the course of U.S. policy, Fulbright considered making a speech proposing a new course of action. In a memorandum on June 18 commenting on a draft that had been prepared, Marcy summarized the proposal as follows:[100]

"Announcement that the United States will support only an elected government in Saigon that will seriously negotiate with the Vietcong and Hanoi for a cease fire;

"Termination of the bombing of North Vietnam and a cessation of additional build-up of United States forces in Vietnam while negotiations are underway between the four principal belligerents;

"Concentration during those negotiations on achieving a cease-fire and creation, first, of procedures for self-determination in South Vietnam, and, second, determination of whether North and South Vietnam can be united by means determined by them;

"The calling of an international conference of interested states to guarantee arrangements for self determination, the neutrality of Vietnam, and to seek to negotiate a multilateral agreement for the general neutralization of Southeast Asia.

"If the steps along the lines I have suggested and which would create conditions under which U.S. forces can be withdrawn cannot be taken, then we must be prepared to make credible our decision to stay in Southeast Asia until a settle-

[100] National Archives, RG 46, Papers of the Senate Foreign Relations Committee, Marcy Chron File, Memorandum to Fulbright from Marcy, June 18, 1966.

ment is reached by reducing our commitment to a level we can and will sustain indefinitely."

Marcy also suggested to Fulbright that he write a personal letter to the President enclosing a draft of a principal part of the speech, with the notation that it would be made in the Senate in the near future. The letter would be given to Moyers, who would be told that if the President wanted "to make these suggestions his own," Fulbright would not propose them publicly. If the President did not agree, Fulbright would then make the speech.

Marcy said that the problem with even this kind of private approach to the President was the reaction of the President's advisers: "They have a vested interest in continuation of the present course and will have a knee-jerk reaction to anything *you* propose. Thus, if you were to send these proposals to the President in the hope that he might accept them, he will consult his advisers and they are likely to respond in the usual fashion—nothing good comes from the Senate Office Building—and will nit-pick it to pieces." (emphasis in original)

Meanwhile, on June 6, following his letter of March 19 on the subject, Fulbright sent the President a copy of the study, *Neutralization in Southeast Asia: Problems and Prospects,* which had been made, at Fulbright's request, by several faculty members at Princeton University. In an accompanying letter, Fulbright said, quoting the study: "[V]iewed as an alternative to the long-term continuation of a large American military presence in South Vietnam, the idea of neutralization merits serious consideration on the part of the United State government. A policy of neutralization, if reasonably successful, would facilitate the achievement of the American objective of permitting countries to fashion their own destinies without massive interference from the outside. . . ."[101] The study, which Fulbright said had been shown in draft to several State Department officers for any advice they might have, suggested that there should be exploratory negotiations, conducted as quietly as possible, "to test existing national policies with regard to Southeast Asia. They might also have positive effects on the attitudes of other nations toward the United States."

The letter was acknowledged in a letter to Fulbright on June 7 from the White House Congressional Liaison staff, and Fulbright's letter was transmitted to Rostow for further action.[102] On June 28, Marcy telephoned Rostow to urge him to arrange for a reply from the President. In a memorandum to Fulbright the next day, Marcy reported on the conversation with Rostow:[103]

> Symptomatic of the approach of the Administration to Southeast Asia is the informal reaction I got yesterday from Walt Rostow to the neutralization study done by Princeton.
>
> He said the study had some useful suggestions and that he was recommending that it be passed on to Mr. Owen of the State Department Planning Council. He said that he would

---

[101] Johnson Library, Files of Walt Rostow, letter from Fulbright to the President, June 6, 1966. There is also a copy of the study in this same file, together with various memoranda concerning the response that should be made to Fulbright's letter.

[102] Same location.

[103] National Archives, RG 46, Papers of the Senate Committee on Foreign Relations, Marcy Chron File, Marcy memorandum to Fulbright, June 29, 1966.

recommend that the President reply to your letter and expressed the hope that the study would not be published at this time. It would be misunderstood abroad and indicate divisions on policy views.

Rostow added that any widespread discussion of the concept of neutralization would lend encouragement to guerrilla bands being formed along the Chinese border—in such places as Northeast Thailand.

After talking with Marcy, Rostow sent a memorandum to the President at 11:30 p.m. that same night, in which he said:[104] "The operational question is: should the Princeton report, prepared at the request of the Senate Foreign Relations Committee, be released to the public? To the Foreign Relations Committee?

"Even in the latter case, it is likely to leak and start an unhelpful discussion.

"An Executive Branch willingness respectfully to study the document seemed to me that best solution, communicated in a letter in which you kept a good arm's length from approving the concept of neutralization."

"I found the job seriously done," Rostow added, but said he questioned whether there could be adequate control to ensure the success of such a plan.

With the memorandum to the President Rostow enclosed a draft of the proposed letter from the President to Fulbright. "Clearly," the Rostow draft concluded, "at this time, the Government cannot back a general scheme of neutralization of Southeast Asia; although, as you know, the principle is accepted in Laos, and we have never had a direct defense pact with South Vietnam." The draft added that it would be "wholly appropriate" for the Policy Planning Council of the State Department to examine the study "along with other long-run concepts for assuring the security and independence of the nations of the region." Finally, the draft stated, as Rostow had told Marcy, that "public discussion of the concept at this stage, sponsored by any branch of the government, would not be in the public interest."

Rather than sending the letter, the President told Moyers to tell Marcy that Rusk would contact Fulbright about the study.[105] It is not known whether Rusk did so, or, if he did, what he and Fulbright talked about.

On June 29, Fulbright invited 16 Democratic and Republican Senators to an informal meeting to discuss the war. The list is indicative of which Members of the Senate could be considered, as of that time, to be opposed to the way the war was being conducted: Democrats Bartlett, Burdick, Church, Clark, Fulbright, Gore, Gruening, Hartke, McCarthy, McGovern, Metcalf, Frank E. Moss (D/Utah), Nelson, Neuberger and Young of Ohio, and Republicans Aiken and Cooper. Mansfield was not invited, nor for some reason, was Morse. In a memorandum to Fulbright reporting that all of those invited were expected to attend except for Gruening and Moss, who would be out of the city, Marcy said:

[104] Same location.

[105] See the handwritten note by Moyers on the face of Rostow's June 28 memorandum to the President.

It is hard to know what might develop in a meeting such as this. However, I think headway would be made if nothing more develops than:

1. An informal exchange of views.
2. Agreement to meet again after the July recess for another informal exchange.
3. The addition of others to the group at a future meeting.
4. Possible discussions with people just back from Vietnam such as Eric Sevareid [CBS].
5. A general understanding that when speeches on the subject of Vietnam are delivered, this group would try to be present.[106]

On July 1, after a speech on June 30 by the President saying "I want to see the alternatives," and a Senate speech on the same day by Russell in which he, too, said that he was waiting for alternatives to be presented, Marcy again recommended to Fulbright that he make the speech proposing a new course of action: "I think that speech, plus the [Princeton] neutralization study, make a pretty credible showing of initiative and search for alternatives. Since the hawks say 'put up or shut up,' maybe you ought to 'put up'—not that I have any hope that you can change the direction of the torrent. But history may make these alternatives look pretty good."[107]

On June 28, 1966, Majority Leader Mansfield held two meetings with Democratic Senators, one with chairmen (or their designated alternates), including Russell and Fulbright, for 1 hour and 45 minutes, and the other for 3 hours with junior Democrats. In a memorandum to the President on June 29 Mansfield summed up the reactions of both groups:[108]

1. There is general support for you among the Members in your overwhelming responsibilities as President;
2. The prompt end to the war is seen as most essential and there is confusion and deep concern that we have not yet found the way to end it, either by extension or contraction of the military effort;
3. There is no sentiment among the Members for an immediate withdrawal;
4. There is a strong conviction that candidates of the Democratic Party will be hurt by the war.

Reproduction here of the major part of the summary of the meeting with chairmen may convey some sense of what senior Demo-

---

[106] National Archives, RG 46, Papers of the Senate Foreign Relations Committee, Memorandum from Marcy to Fulbright, June 29, 1966. There apparently are no notes of the meeting.

[107] Same location, Marcy Chron File, Memorandum to Fulbright from Marcy, July 1, 1966.

[108] Mansfield's cover memo and his separate report on the two meetings are in the Johnson Library, NSF files of Mike Mansfield. Those present at the first meeting were: Richard B. Russell (Ga.), Allen J. Ellender (La.), James O. Eastland (Miss.), John L. McClellan (Ark.), Warren G. Magnuson (Wash.), J. William Fulbright (Ark.), A. Willis Robertson (Va.), Russell B. Long (La.), Clinton P. Anderson (N. Mex.), Ralph W. Yarborough (Tex.), Henry M. Jackson (Wash.), Alan Bible (Nev.), B. Everett Jordan (N.C.), Jennings Randolph (W. Va.), Daniel K. Inouye (Hawaii), John O. Pastore (R.I.), Harrison A. Williams, Jr. (N.J.), and at the second meeting, Birch Bayh (Ind.), Daniel B. Brewster (Md.), George McGovern (S. Dak.), Abraham A. Ribicoff (Conn.), Fred R. Harris (Okla.), Joseph M. Montoya (N. Mex.), Walter F. Mondale (Minn.), Joseph D. Tydings (Md.), Harry F. Byrd (Va.), Lee Metcalf (Mont.), Claiborne Pell (R.I.), Philip A. Hart (Mich.), Edward M. Kennedy (Mass.), Robert F. Kennedy (N.Y.), Ross Bass (Tenn.).

cratic Members of the Senate were thinking and saying privately about the war, as well as the variety and diversity of senatorial ideas on the subject:[109]

Summary of Principal Lines of Thought and Ideas Expressed

A. General Comment

1. We may have gone too far in trying to obtain negotiations last year, even though we want the matter settled honorably at a conference table.
2. We ought not to withdraw unilaterally, but we are in a fix, and it is not clear how we are going to get out of it.
3. To get out in present circumstances would be very destructive of our stature in the world.

B. The War and Policies

1. We already have 400,000 men in the area and the cost will soon reach $2 billion a month.
2. Unless stable government can be had, the war is not going to be won, and the pressure to pull out altogether will increase.
3. Stability of government in Saigon cannot be expected soon, and we make a mistake by emphasizing it. Any government there is going to be a "puppet" for the present. What is involved here is that "this is Communism's last stand" and the problem is to hit the Communists harder while giving whatever puppet government we have in Saigon the economic support it needs.
4. The only moral reason we have for being in Viet Nam is the contention that the South Vietnamese people want us there but have we tried to find out whether this is really so or not—whether, in fact, the people want us?
5. The Secretary of State's theory of the conflict has been that we are facing an aggression pure and simple; it is a wrong theory. We face, in fact, a situation not too different than that faced by the French.
6. Recent broadcasts by Eric Sevareid and Bill Lawrence have been very revealing and suggest we have not, heretofore, been getting a complete and accurate picture of what is happening in Viet Nam.

* * * * * * *

D. Suggestions:

1. If we cannot get a stable government, we should agree to elections and get out as best we can; and sooner rather than later, because it is a very expensive war. It is not dishonorable to have a conference and get out.
2. We must think of our prestige and honor even if the area is not vital in a geographic sense.

[109] Omitted here is a section of the summary, "Other Nations, International Organizations and the War."

The summary of the meeting with junior Members was similar in format and generally similar in substance to the summary of the meeting of chairmen.

3. The Communists are seeking to protract the war in the hopes of U.S. impatience; we must contract the protraction or get out.

4. The question is not to stay in or get out but how to get out.

5. Increased military pressure is necessary. If we back off in Viet Nam, the U.S. public will support no President in any effort to save any part of Southeast Asia.

6. It may not be possible to settle the war by negotiations; both sides would save face if the war just peters out.

7. The bigger the war is expanded, the more it is going to be lengthened; a quick ending by expansion is a fallacy.

8. The way to get negotiations is by calling for a ceasefire and neutralism.

9. The President should get his advice from the Armed Services.

10. The President should call groups of Senators together and tell Rusk and McNamara to be quiet while they talked.

11. Is there not some way in which the U.N. can be brought in?

E. Political Implications

1. The Democratic Party is badly hurt by the war even though individually some Democrats may not be troubled.

2. If war drags on, the Party will suffer badly. People want a decision, by a step-up of the war; they are not interested in casualties. Indeed, it might be a good idea to stop televising what is going on over there.

3. The people are following the President but not with enthusiasm, in part, because they do not understand the importance of the war. There is a lot of worry over why we are there.

4. It is not a major war, but its consequences are being felt by many families in the nation.

5. The war is hampering domestic programs of the Administration.

6. Democrats are badly split in West Virginia; the matter is not an issue in Virginia; the political difficulties among Democrats in New Jersey over the war, as recently reported in the *New York Times,* were vastly over-stated.

7. Viet Nam is worse than Korea and remember what Eisenhower did with the latter.

Although one of the suggestions at the meeting was that "The President should call groups of Senators together and tell Rusk and McNamara to be quiet while they talked," among officials in the executive branch the role of Members of Congress was seen primarily as one of supporting the administration's position by approving funds for the war and by educating and influencing the public. In keeping with this attitude, new efforts were made during the summer of 1966 by the executive branch to involve supportive Members of Congress in promoting and defending U.S. policy toward Vietnam. In June, the White House asked the Defense Department to prepare a summary of the views of those Members (about 100) who had been to Vietnam, after which Defense and White House legislative liaison officers were to begin supplying information to them for their use in making public statements and speeches.[110]

Members of Congress who agreed to speak to public groups were thoroughly briefed in advance. According to Representative Thomas P. O'Neill (D/Mass.), later Speaker of the House, who was one of those who made such speeches on college campuses during this period, executive branch briefers, using material gathered by the FBI and the various intelligence services, "even anticipated the questions that the students were going to ask me because they'd say this was asked at the University of North Carolina, this was asked at Wisconsin, this was asked at Cal, this was asked at Rice. . . ."[111]

In July 1966, the White House arranged for 14 Representatives—10 Democrats and 4 Republicans—who supported the war, all veterans of World War II or the Korean war, to tour Vietnam and then to appear at the White House to report their findings directly to the President.[112]

According to Representative Tim Lee Carter, a conservative from Kentucky who was the senior Republican on the trip, the group, called the "Speaker's Committee," was "supposed to say the war's going on all right, when we got back. I believe that they wanted us to do that."

When the group returned from Vietnam, they were taken by helicopter directly from Andrews Air Force Base to the White House, where the President, joined by Speaker McCormack, met them. The President, Carter said, asked each Member how the war was going, and, with the exception of Carter, they said it was going fine. Carter said he told the President, "No, Mr. President, you're not winning the war."

Carter, who consistently supported appropriations for the war, feeling that U.S. forces had to be adequately supplied, and who subsequently voted against amendments to control the war, said that when he made this comment, "It sort of took him [the President] aback. It shocked him that a Kentuckian, and one from the mountains of eastern Kentucky, would differ with him. But it's the way our people felt. I could sense that from the people of my area." The U.S. should not have become involved in Vietnam, Carter added, but once involved, should have made more of an effort to win the war.

Carter was asked what the President's reaction was. "Well, it was to start with an old story about going over, that it took a long time, that we were there and that we were winning, and if we didn't stay fast in our position and fight that we'd lose the war.

---

[110] Johnson Library, NSF files of Henry Hall Wilson, Vietnam, Memorandum from White House Special Assistant Robert E. Kinter (former president of the National Broadcasting Company), to Deputy Secretary of Defense Vance, June 17, 1966.

[111] CRS Interview with Thomas O'Neill, Dec. 27, 1978.

[112] Those who made the trip were Democrats John M. Murphy of New York, the leader of the group, John J. Gilligan of Ohio, Teno Roncalio of Wyoming, Thomas C. McGrath of New Jersey, James C. Corman of California, William D. Hathaway of Maine, Roman C. Pucinski of Illinois, Basil L. Whitener of North Carolina, Gale Schisler of Illinois, Robert B. Duncan of Oregon, and Republicans Tim Lee Carter of Kentucky, Edward J. Gurney of Florida, Hastings Keith of Massachusetts and John B. Anderson of Illinois. For their statements after the trip see *CR*, vol. 112, pp. 15364–15376, and 16688–16691.

Just sort of the same old chatter that I'd heard for years. I was nice to him, but I didn't back down in what I said."[113]

Representative Carter's subsequent House speech in August 1967, in which he called for withdrawal of U.S. forces from Vietnam, was viewed as a sign of the trend of congressional and public opinion.

Meanwhile, the CIA, doubtless with the knowledge and consent if not at the direction of the White House, continued a practice it had begun some time earlier of sending to congressional critics of the war, like Fulbright, reports from Communist sources, such as items in the Russian newspaper *Pravda,* on the publicity being given by the Communists to congressional criticism.[114]

---

[113] CRS Interview with Tim Lee Carter, Mar. 19, 1979.

[114] See, for example, material sent to Fulbright by the CIA in August 1966, Fulbright Papers, University of Arkansas, series 48, box 43.

CHAPTER 9

THE U.S. ESCALATES MILITARY AND POLITICAL ACTION

In June 1966, having helped the South Vietnamese Government to suppress the Struggle Movement and regain political control over Central Vietnam, the U.S. Government, while continuing to explore various possibilities for a diplomatic settlement, intensified its military and political programs in an effort to hasten the end of the war. Faced with little if any progress in pacification, inconclusive results—and adverse effects on pacification—from ground combat operations,[1] and the failure of ROLLING THUNDER to affect significantly the will of North Vietnam or to achieve the desired interdiction of troops and supplies to the South, U.S. policymakers saw the need for a more vigorous pacification program, bombing of key industrial and transportation targets in the North, and continued expansion of the ground war in the South. Meanwhile, they expected that greater political strength and stability would be achieved by the election in September 1966 of an Assembly to draft a constitution, followed by election of a government in 1967.

The President and his principal advisers, with one exception, appeared to be optimistic about the situation.[2] The one exception (be-

---

[1] At a meeting of McNamara with CINCPAC officials in Honolulu on July 8, 1966, there was a presentation by CINCPAC staff of the progress made in reaching the six goals that had been stipulated during the February 1966 Honolulu Conference. With respect to the first goal—"Attrit, by year's end, VC/NVA forces at a rate as high as their capability to put men into the field"—CINCPAC staff said that "This goal is unlikely to be achieved because of the enemy's demonstrated ability to increase his forces despite losses." With respect to the second goal—"Increase the percentage of VC/NVA base areas denied the VC from 10–20 percent to 40–50 percent"—the staff reported that "This goal can be met if the required force is allocated to this task," but that, if this were done, progress toward other goals, such as attrition of the enemy, might be adversely affected. National Archives, Westmoreland-CBS Papers, CINCPAC to COMUSMACV, 112330Z, July 11, 1966.

At Westmoreland's Commanders' Conference in Saigon on July 24, 1966, the J–3 [operations] staff also reported on progress being made toward achieving the February 1966 Honolulu Conference goals. Base area denial remained unchanged at 15.1 percent. With respect to attrition, "The enemy buildup continues. Despite confirmed losses of 6800, enemy strength increased by [a net figure of] 3500 in June."

J–3 also reported on the level of North Vietnamese infiltration of troops and matériel. There were 152 North Vietnamese combat battalions in the South as of the end of June 1966, with a daily requirement of 132.3 tons of matériel. The North Vietnamese were capable, however, of infiltrating 308 tons of matériel a day. (CMH, Westmoreland Papers, Memorandum for the Record, Aug. 17, 1966, of MACV Commanders' Conference on July 24.) This estimate of 308 tons compares with the earlier estimate of 200 tons made by McNamara six months earlier.

It should also be noted that the estimated requirement of 132.3 tons a day was for what the Army called "light combat," but that during this period the Communists in North Vietnam were engaged primarily in guerrilla warfare, rather than "light combat," and their needs for matériel were much lower than the estimate. In a memorandum to the President in March 1966, McNamara stated that less than 20 percent of enemy matériel requirements had to come through external sources—20–30 tons a day (compared to the MACV estimate of 132.3 for light combat)—and that at this rate the infiltration routes from North to South were being used at only 5 percent of capacity. (Johnson Library, Warnke Papers, McNaughton Files, memorandum from McNamara to the President, "April program of air strikes against North Vietnam and Laos."

[2] In the course of a conversation with the South Vietnamese Foreign Minister, Tran Van Do, during a SEATO Council meeting in Canberra, Australia, at the end of June, Rusk commented

Continued

sides Ball, who had opposed the war from the beginning, and Goldberg, who, as will be seen, was opposed to escalation and favored a negotiated settlement), was the President's own Secretary of Defense, Robert McNamara. Having argued the case for committing large-scale U.S. forces in July 1965, McNamara had become increasingly convinced that a military solution was not possible, and by June of 1966 he was even reported to have taken the position that the U.S. should "get in direct touch" with the North Vietnamese and the National Liberation Front.[3]

Rostow, Lodge and Komer continued to encourage the President about the progress they thought was being made. In a memorandum to the President on June 25, Rostow said: "Mr. President, you can smell it all over: Hanoi's operation, backed by the Chicoms, is no longer being regarded as the wave of the future out there. U.S. power is beginning to be felt. We're not in; but we're moving."[4]

In a cable to the President on June 29, Lodge said that the U.S. would succeed if the American people continued to support the war:[5]

> the greatest danger here is not that the Viet Cong will win; or that a government—Buddhist dominated or otherwise—will emerge and order the Americans out; or that the war will escalate; or that China will intervene. These are the standard nightmares and none can really stand the light of day. Indeed we need not limit ourselves to rejecting nightmares; we can point to some very affirmative achievements, and say:
>
> —that the military side of this war is going well—plenty well enough to keep the main force units off of the backs of the government of Viet-Nam, and thus enable a real start to be made on pacification;
>
> —that with a big assist from us, the Vietnamese are turning their attention to pacification;
>
> —that the government has done bold work in the field of anti-inflation;
>
> —that its overall handling of the political situation once the original blunder had been made was effective and, in some respects, skillful;
>
> —and that if we persist, we are going to succeed.
>
> This means that the real danger—and the only real danger —would be if the American people were to lose heart, and choose to "bring the boys home." This would indeed be the first domino to fall.

On July 1, Komer, the Washington coordinator for pacification activities, said in a memorandum to the President that he had returned from a trip to Vietnam on June 23–29 "both an optimist and a realist":[6]

---

that "the situation has reached the point where North Vietnam cannot succeed. The question is whether Hanoi will make peace or the Chinese Communists will face the question of whether or not to intervene." U.S. Department of State, Central File, Pol 27 Viet S, Memorandum of Conversation, June 28, 1966.

[3] Library of Congress, Harriman Papers, Vietnam Subject File, Harriman "Postscript to Memorandum of Conversation with Secretary McNamara," June 23, 1966.

[4] Johnson Library, NSF Memos to the President—Walt Rostow.

[5] U.S. Department of State, Central File, Pol 27 Viet S, Saigon to Washington 5830, June 29, 1966.

[6] Johnson Library, Warnke Papers, McNaughton Files.

> Optimistic because Westy's spoiling operations are going well; his prudent concern that a monsoon "offensive" is still in the offing is partly offset by abundant evidence that the VC has lost a lot of steam despite the infusion of strength from the north. Optimistic also because our own civil side effort has finally gotten off the ground, and because the GVN [Government of Vietnam] itself has a new wind—born of its success in containing the Buddhist bid for power over the last three months. It is taking pacification more seriously too. Third, we've got the economic situation under better control. In short, the US/GVN effort is greater and more efficient than ever before—though one keeps wondering why it takes so long.
>
> But is all this enough? The more I learn the more I'm sobered by the realization of how much further we may have to go. On the military side, our intelligence is improving but it is still only one in several sweeps that really catches and clobbers a VC main force unit. Nevertheless, Westy sees the VC/NVA as committed to a classical Phase III Maoist strategy rather than reverting to guerrilla war. He thinks they are trying to concentrate in divisional strength in at least 8–10 different areas. Their aim is to tie down our forces by synchronized though widely separated attacks and hopefully to overwhelm us in at least some cases. Westy's counterstrategy is to mount spoiling attacks, hitting the VC first wherever he can pinpoint a concentration. He seems to be keeping them off balance.

The problem, Komer said, was pacification:

> [O]ur military effort against the VC is not yet matched by our pacification and civil side operations. Our greatest weakness is our inability as yet to capitalize on the initiative our own military operations have given us by extending our control over the countryside. We have stopped the erosion of GVN control, but I would judge that we have not really extended our control significantly outside the main towns over the last year. Until we can get rolling on pacification in its widest sense—securing the villages, flushing out the local VC (not just the main force) and giving the peasant both security and hope for a better future—we cannot assure a victory.

By the summer of 1966 it was becoming apparent, however, that public and congressional support for the war was slipping, and that this trend, unless arrested, could result in increasing pressure on the U.S. Government to "win or get out."

One response to this situation would have been to make major personnel changes, and in July 1966 President Johnson apparently considered doing so at the time he replaced Ball, who had resigned and was leaving in September. He asked Rostow about replacing Ball with McNamara, and mentioned also possibly replacing William Bundy with Komer. In a memorandum to the President on July 26, Rostow said that the Rusk-McNamara combination "is in many ways exceedingly attractive."[7] But he recommended against it: "We need Bob McNamara in Defense until we are over the hump in Vietnam; [and] it would be exceedingly difficult for Secretary

[7] Johnson Library, NSF Files of Walt W. Rostow, Memorandum from Rostow to the President, July 26, 1966.

Rusk to appear other than a lame duck, despite Bob's best efforts." Rostow recommended that Ball be replaced by either David Bruce (then Ambassador to Great Britain) or Clark Clifford. He preferred Bruce. Bundy, he said, could be made Ambassador to Great Britain or Deputy Under Secretary of State for Political Affairs, to replace U. Alexis Johnson, who had been appointed Ambassador to Japan. (He added that Foy Kohler, Ambassador to the U.S.S.R., would be the best choice to replace Johnson, but that Kohler could be given another position if Bundy were chosen.)

It is not known what prompted the President to consider making these changes. He may have thought that McNamara's increasing skepticism about the war was a liability in the Defense Department but could be an asset at the State Department. He may also have been concerned about making the State Department more effective. Or he may have thought such changes would help with the problem of public and congressional support for the war, and that new leadership in both State and Defense could energize U.S. policy and programs. Whatever the reasons, there is no indication that the President gave further consideration to the idea. Nicholas Katzenbach, then serving as Attorney General, was appointed to replace Ball, and Kohler replaced U. Alexis Johnson. Rostow's brother, Eugene Rostow, a professor of law at Yale University, was appointed Under Secretary for Political Affairs.

Another response to the decline in support for the war was to improve congressional and public perception of the President's performance, and in June 1966 a group of White House assistants under the chairmanship of Moyers began discussing how that could be done. (Apparently, the President had approved this move after Moyers' earlier memorandum on the need to improve press relations.) At a meeting in the latter part of June to discuss themes for upcoming Presidential speaking engagements, there was general agreement that the President needed to become more active in explaining and promoting his Vietnam policies and programs. As Moyers said, "Need movement—need momentum. Need to get him moving." "He's in a rut. Same meetings each week and frills in Rose Garden."[8] According to Moyers, "All [Presidential assistants] should try to convince him" to hold regular press conferences, to hold other televised sessions, and to make a "major fireside chat." Robert Kintner, former president of the National Broadcasting Company, who had joined the White House staff in the spring of 1966 as an adviser on communications, said that the President needed to go on television. He, too, thought a fireside chat would be desirable.

Douglass Cater, a journalist and speechwriter who handled education and other domestic matters, stressed the need to "humanize him" (the President), and Harry McPherson, White House Counsel, who was also a speechwriter, added: "No humor, no wit. Too much search for consensus." The public, McPherson said, think that the

[8] Johnson Library, Tom Johnson's Notes of Meetings.

Valenti, who had left the White House to become president of the Motion Picture Association of America, also urged the President to make more public appearances, hold more press conferences, avoid showing displeasure with the press, "use humor as a weapon against the polls and the critics," stress peaceful objectives of Vietnam policy, "keep right in front of the public the strong decisiveness and resolution of the President." Johnson Library, Office Files of Jack Valenti, Memorandum to the President from Valenti, Sept. 18, 1966.

President "is boxed in." Rostow agreed: "People think President is driven in a corner. Don't have initiative." There was "no consistent image," he said, and he urged the development of a central theme for the "campaign" (presumably the 1966 congressional election campaign).

The group agreed that the President needed to talk more about Vietnam. Moyers said that in a speech to be given a few days later the President "Needs to be educator. . . . Show them what type of dirty little war out there." Members of the group generally agreed with McPherson that the President should "talk about peace."[9]

In a speech on Vietnam in Omaha, Nebraska, on July 7, which seemed to have been somewhat influenced by this advice, the President began by emphasizing "peace," but devoted most of the speech to a justification of the war and an indirect attack on antiwar dissent in the U.S. The Communists, he said, "sometimes do get encouraged . . . about the dissension in the United States of America. They believe that the political disagreements in Washington, the confusion and doubt in the United States, will hand them a victory on a silver platter in Southeast Asia. Well, if they think that, they are wrong. To those who would try to pressure us or influence us, mislead us or deceive us, I say this afternoon, there can be only one decision in Vietnam, and that is this: We shall see this through. We shall persist. We shall succeed."[10]

On the trip back to Washington from Omaha, Rostow, who had traveled with the President, prepared a memorandum for him in which he said that the Omaha speech (which occurred several days after the U.S. bombed POL sites in North Vietnam), "was a personal breakthrough against the background of your decision to go for POL. . . . I believe the POL bombing and Omaha have caught the nation's attention. Our people sense new determination; new ideas; new hope."

Rostow recommended a campaign to "drive home" each of the themes of the speech:[11]

> —We are fighting aggression; we are confident *(not* optimistic: we don't want to promise too much, too soon); we shall persist; we shall succeed. [emphasis in original]
>
> —We are proud of our skillful, brave, compassionate men fighting in Vietnam; and we shall back them to the hilt.

---

[9] A few weeks later, McPherson sent a memorandum to Moyers on his impressions of attitudes toward the war among persons of middle-to-upper income, mostly Republicans, with whom he had vacationed in Rhode Island. (These included a real estate broker, a retired manufacturer and his wife, and the young head of a Wall Street mutual fund.) *"Nobody,"* he said "was affirmative about Vietnam. It is an extremely unpopular war. . . ." "Many people are simply not satisfied with the official explanations. . . . Feeling no basic empathy with the Vietnamese, people are estranged even further by 1) the inability of the Vietnamese to agree among themselves, 2) reports of their anti-Americanism, 3) reports of their war weariness. . . ." *"Everybody* I talked to at any length," McPherson said, "expressed the strongest wish for peaceful overtures—for cooperation with the Russians, chiefly. To some people the freeze in our relations with the Russians is the worst consequence of the Vietnam war—worse than the casualties or the cost or the confusion." (emphases in original)

McPherson said he thought these comments reflected the attitudes of the "relatively well informed, internationalist middle class," especially of New England and the Middle Atlantic states. "Their support," he said, "is vital, and we don't have much of it right now." (Johnson Library, Office Files of Harry McPherson, memorandum to Bill Moyers from McPherson, Aug. 4, 1966.)

Moyers sent a summary of McPherson's memorandum to the President, noting that McPherson's observations "closely fit what I have been saying." (Johnson Library, Office Files of Bill Moyers, Memorandum to the President from Moyers, Aug. 4, 1966.)

[10] *Public Papers of the Presidents,* Lyndon B. Johnson, 1966, p. 684.

[11] Johnson Library, NSF Memos to the President—Walt Rostow.

—There is a vital free Asia emerging behind our defense of Vietnam.
—There is a vital, modern South Viet Nam emerging.
—Peace. Why we believe that there is a fair prospect of a relatively tranquil era ahead if we see it through in Viet Nam, but only trouble and more war if we bug out.
—Food and Development. This is the real war for all to fight.

"These six Omaha themes," Rostow said, "must be repeated until every newspaper in the county knows them; every knowledgeable citizen, every commentator." Observing that "Repetition is the heart of both politics and teaching," he suggested to the President a series of talks to elaborate each theme. He also suggested that Rusk and McNamara and all other officials in State and Defense should do the same. The President agreed, and Rostow sent a memorandum to Rusk and McNamara saying that the President wished the six themes of the Omaha speech "elaborated and driven home systematically in speeches and statements" by officials of the two departments.[12]

The Increased Application of Military Force

During the period of political unrest in South Vietnam from mid-March to late June, U.S. Army units undertook new search-and-destroy missions—elements of the 1st Infantry Division conducted Operation BIRMINGHAM in Tay Ninh Province (in III Corps on the Cambodian border west of Saigon), elements of the 25th Infantry Division conducted Operation PAUL REVERE in Pleiku Province (in II Corps in Central Vietnam), elements of the 1st Cavalry Division conducted Operation CRAZY HORSE in Binh Dinh Province (next to Pleiku Province), elements of the 1st Infantry Division conducted Operation EL PASO II in Binh Long Province (next to Tay Ninh), and the 1st Brigade of the 101st Airborne Division conducted Operation HAWTHORNE in Kontum Province (next to Pleiku). Because of the unrest in Central Vietnam, where U.S. Marines were stationed, there were no major offensive operations by American or South Vietnamese forces in that region (I Corps) between March and July.[13]

In a cable to the President on June 8, 1966, Lodge commented on the situation:[14]

> I have been hoping that we could get decisive military results within a year. I had based this hope on our considerable military accomplishments in overcoming the main force units of the Viet Cong and large units of the Army of North Vietnam, and in destroying the redoubts in the jungles. But MACV does not think that it can do anything decisive in a year. Their operational plans for the next year, if carried out, would mean that good progress had been achieved, but nothing decisive.

Lodge added: "The best estimate is that 20,000 men of the Army of North Vietnam have come into South Vietnam since January and, as far as I can learn, we can't find them."

[12] U.S. Department of State, Central File, Pol 27 Viet S.
[13] These missions are briefly described by Shelby Stanton in *The Rise and Fall of An American Army*, cited above.
[14] U.S. Department of State, Central File, Pol 27 Viet S, Saigon to Washington 5378, June 8, 1966.

In counterterror, counterguerrilla warfare, the major responsibility for which had been left to the South Vietnamese, there had also been little progress. In a cable to the President on June 22, 1966, Lodge, while speaking approvingly of recent U.S. search-and-destroy missions, said: "we still seem to be having great difficulty in dealing with the Viet Cong's systematic campaign of terror." Noting that local officials were being abducted or killed at about the same rate as in 1965 (70 a month), he said: "I doubt that Hanoi will conclude that it cannot win in South Vietnam as long as they can do so well with local terrorism." [15]

This, of course, valid or not, was the argument being made by the Marines and by the Army officers in the PROVN study: That the war could and would be won by military operations designed to provide greater security to the populace—a mission that large U.S. military units with heavy firepower were not equipped or suited to perform.

As part of a long cable from Lodge to Rostow on June 11, 1966, summarizing the situation in Vietnam, Westmoreland reviewed the military situation and discussed his strategy for the coming months, based on an earlier cable he had sent to CINCPAC on June 5.[16] The enemy, Westmoreland said, had increased its forces in South Vietnam to 267,000, mostly from regular North Vietnamese units that had moved into the South. The principal effort of the enemy in the coming months, he said, would be in the provinces, primarily Kontum, Pleiku and Darlac, adjacent to Communist base areas in the Laos and Cambodian "sanctuaries." [17] In his cable to CINCPAC, Westmoreland explained that "He [the enemy] is capable of achieving only tactical success along the coast line; but, by virtue of the proximity of the Laos and Cambodian sanctuaries, he has the capacity to achieve strategic success in the plateau area." Accordingly, Westmoreland said that his strategy in the highlands would be, "pressing toward the Laos and Cambodian borders in order to gain early warning of enemy buildup and to react against him before he can achieve readiness for offensive actions." [18]

---

[15] Johnson Library, NSF Memos to the President—Walt Rostow, Saigon to Washington 5684, June 22, 1966.

[16] Lodge's cable is in the Department of State Central File, Pol 27 Viet S, Saigon to Washington 5473, June 11, 1966. Westmoreland's cable to Admiral Sharp (CINCPAC), MAC 4612, June 5, 1966, is in CMH, Westmoreland Papers, Message Files.

[17] Plans were being made for U.S. operations in the delta south of Saigon (IV Corps), an area dominated by the Communists who used it for food and new recruits as well as for receiving supplies by sea. For Westmoreland's comments, see his cable to Admiral Sharp (CINCPAC), MAC 3797, May 11, 1966, CMH, Westmoreland Papers, Message Files.

[18] For Westmoreland's comments on forthcoming military operations in other parts of the country, see his cable to CINCPAC, MAC 4612, June 4, 1966, cited above.

As noted, Westmoreland had requested greater authority to conduct cross-border military operations in Cambodia and Laos. In March, 1966, in connection with an operation near the Cambodian border, he requested permission to move U.S. forces into a limited area of Cambodia in order to trap North Vietnamese soldiers who had crossed into South Vietnam. (Westmoreland, *A Soldier Reports*, p. 181.) Although supported by the JCS, this was denied because of "political sensitivity." (CMH, Westmoreland Papers, Message Files, JCS 1710–66, Apr. 1, 1966. Cambodia had broken relations with the U.S. in the spring of 1965, but President Johnson and his civilian advisers wanted to keep the war from spreading, and were seeking a reconciliation with Prime Minister Sihanouk. The U.S. also was supporting Sihanouk's request to the International Control Commission for help in patrolling the border in order to prevent Vietnamese communist forces from operating on Cambodian territory. This effort was being stymied within the Commission, however, by Poland and the U.S.S.R., as well as by the inaction of India.)

On April 26, 1966, after receiving a cable from the U.S. Mission expressing concern about the evidence of increasing use of Cambodian territory by Communist forces fighting in South Vietnam, Rusk and McNamara sent Lodge a joint cable on the subject. It was not in U.S. interest

Continued

On June 28, 1966, the President sent the following memorandum to McNamara (drafted by Rostow) urging faster deployment of U.S. troops to Vietnam:[19]

> As you know, we have been moving our men to Vietnam on a schedule determined by General Westmoreland's requirements.
>
> As I have stated orally several times this year, I should like this schedule to be accelerated as much as possible so that General Westmoreland can feel assured that he has all the men he needs as soon as possible.
>
> Would you meet with the Joint Chiefs and give me at your earliest convenience an indication of what acceleration is possible for the balance of this year.

Intensification of the Air War

While intensifying the ground war in South Vietnam, the U.S., following the resumption of bombing at the end of January, also took steps to intensify the air war against North Vietnam.[20]

Despite consistent intelligence findings that bombing was not achieving its objectives—either that of affecting the will of the North Vietnamese or that of preventing the North from providing necessary men and supplies to Communist forces in the South—there were recommendations for a major escalation in ROLLING

---

at that time, they said, to go beyond the authority already given the military to attack across the border in self-defense. Offensive operations across the border could lead to Cambodia's becoming a belligerent "or otherwise in open collaboration with the VC/NVN." Moreover, "questions of law and of international and domestic opinion also weigh heavily with us. In present circumstances, the political consequences, foreign and domestic, of military operations on Cambodian soil would, in our opinion, be serious and far-reaching, and we regretfully are not optimistic that evidence now available and releasable is such as to bring about any significant shift in the present climate of opinion." (U.S. Department of State, Central File, Pol 27 Viet S, Washington to Saigon 3212, Apr. 26, 1966.) At the time, the "rules of engagement" with respect to Cambodia "prevent immediate pursuit of hostile troops or vessels into Cambodian territory or territorial waters. U.S. land forces are forbidden to enter Cambodia or to fire into Cambodia except with prior Washington approval in each instance, or in emergency situations specifically involving self-defense. Pursuit of hostile aircraft into Cambodia air space is permitted when actually engaged in combat." Johnson Library, Meetings Notes File, Briefing Paper on "Rules of Engagement—Cambodia" for an NSC meeting on May 10, 1966.

In a meeting with the NSC staff in June, 1966, President Johnson asked, according to Rostow, for "proposals to get closer to Sihanouk." (Memorandum from Rostow to Rusk, June 21, 1966, in the files of the Executive Secretariat, Department of State.) James Thomson, a Far East specialist on the NSC staff, who opposed the way the war was being fought, was asked to prepare the memorandum. (The memorandum, "Possible Approaches to the Cambodian Problem," June 14, 1966, is attached to Rostow's memorandum to Rusk on June 21.) Thomson recommended a number of steps to improve relations, saying that better relations would "clearly serve our national interest not only by limiting the Indo-China battlefield but by proving our willingness and ability to pursue a live-and-let-live relationship with a neutral and unaligned Southeast Asian state." Among his proposals were support for an expansion of ICC efforts, a Presidential message to Sihanouk urging renewed diplomatic relations, unofficial visits to Americans to Cambodia and private contacts between diplomats of the two countries. These were listed at the end of the memorandum with spaces for the President to indicate his approval or disapproval. He approved all of them, and added comments indicating his strong support for each one, as well as a comment about the memorandum as a whole: "This is excellent. I'm proud."

Although it was not listed separately for "approval/disapproval," Thomson also proposed that the U.S. should avoid provoking Cambodia: "We should issue firm instructions to keep MACV (and the Pentagon) from further public accusations of unproven Cambodian collusion with the Communists. There is an understandable MACV tendency—with heavy Vietnamese support—to distort and magnify Communist use of Cambodia. We should accept the fact that some border violations will be inevitable in such a war; that although some border officials do encourage such violations, the Cambodian Government so far does not; and that there is a clear net value to us in preventing the expansion of the Vietnam War's battleground to include 66,000 square miles of Cambodia."

For Westmoreland's comments on the effects on U.S. military operations of American policy towards Cambodia, see *A Soldier Reports*, pp. 180–182.

[19] Johnson Library, NSF Memos to the President—Walt Rostow.

[20] In addition to other sources cited below, see Clodfelter, *The Limits of Air Power*, chs. 3, 4.

THUNDER, the principal element of which was to be airstrikes against POL, both storage and distribution facilities and the ports where foreign oil, on which North Vietnam was almost totally dependent, was received. The JCS argued that this would be "more damaging to the DRV capability to move war-supporting resources within country and along infiltration routes to SVN than an attack against any other single target."[21]

Since 1964, the JCS had repeatedly recommended "shock" attacks against North Vietnam but each time there was opposition, especially from the State Department, and the recommendations were not acted upon. The argument against shock attacks and against the bombing of POL were generally that extreme measures were not needed; that bombing of infiltration routes was more effective than attacking transportation facilities and industrial targets; that heavier bombing near populated areas would increase civilian casualties, which in turn could alienate U.S. and world opinion and weaken relations with key allies, such as the British; and that the bombing or mining of ports, as well as increased bombing in the area near the Chinese border, would increase the chances of greater intervention by the U.S.S.R. and China.[22]

On January 18, 1966, during the December 1965-January 1966 bombing pause, the JCS, based on a request from CINCPAC, again recommended a "sharp" blow against the North followed by "uninterrupted increasing pressure" to close the ports, interdict land lines of communication from China, destroy the POL systems, destroy large military facilities, disrupt electric power, and, through attacks on airfields, to destroy the capability of the North Vietnamese Air Force to interfere with U.S. air operations.[23]

In a memorandum prepared for McNamara that same day (January 18), as was noted earlier, McNaughton recommended a bombing program similar to that which CINCPAC had proposed and the JCS had endorsed in which he said, among other things, that "the ingredients of an effective interdiction program must be these: (a) Intensive around-the-clock armed reconnaissance throughout NVN; (b) Destruction of the LOC targets heretofore targeted; (c) Destruction of POL; (d) Destruction of thermal power plants; (e) Closing the ports."[24] On January 25, McNamara sent a memorandum to the President in which he recommended heavier bombing, including around-the-clock armed reconnaissance against lines of communication as well as attacks on POL storage sites, but did not recommend attacking power plants or closing the ports.[25]

On February 19, March 1 and March 10, 1966, the JCS again recommended a bombing program designed to achieve "maximum shock effect."[26]

In early February, 1966, the Board of National Estimates was asked to prepare an intelligence estimate on the effect of such "shock" attacks, assuming that the objective would be the destruc-

---

[21] JCSM-810-65, Nov. 10, 1965, cited in *PP*, Gravel ed., vol. IV, p. 75.

[22] For a good discussion of these and other factors involved in the debate over bombing POL, see *ibid.*, pp. 79-81.

[23] JCSM-41-66, Jan. 18, 1966.

[24] *PP*, Gravel ed., vol. IV, p. 43.

[25] *Ibid.*, pp. 49, 68.

[26] JCSM-113-66, Feb. 19, 1966, JCSM-130-66, Mar. 1, 1966, and JCSM-153-66, Mar. 10, 1966.

tion of POL, electric power plants, and all large military facilities except airfields and surface-to-air missile sites (unless the SAMs seriously interfered with U.S. air operations) as well as the interdiction of land lines of communication from China and throughout North Vietnam. As noted earlier, the Board reported on February 4 that such attacks would not prevent the North from supplying Communist forces in the South at substantially higher levels than in 1965.[27]

On the question of attacking POL, the Board said that while the North would be handicapped by being forced to rely on current imports, the losses from bombing would not cripple the economy or substantially reduce infiltration.[28]

A few weeks later, however, the CIA issued a report that, for the first time, supported the contention of the Air Force and the JCS that a "shock" air attack on North Vietnam might help to win the war.[29] Although the report concluded, as had previous intelligence reports and estimates, that airstrikes on infiltration targets would not significantly block the necessary flow of men and supplies to the South, it also concluded that punitive strikes directed primarily against "the will of the regime as a target system" might, by being more disruptive to the North Vietnamese, affect their desire to continue the war.

According to the report, "Self-imposed restrictions have limited both the choice of targets and the areas to be bombed. Consequently, almost 80 percent of North Vietnam's limited modern, industrial economy, 75 percent of the nation's population and the most lucrative military supply and LOC targets have been effectively insulated from air attack. Moreover, the authorizations for each of the ROLLING THUNDER programs often have imposed additional restrictions, such as limiting the number of strikes against approved fixed targets. The policy decision to avoid suburban casualties to the extent possible has proved to be a major constraint. The overall effect of those area and operational restrictions has been to grant a large measure of immunity to the military, political and economic assets used in Hanoi's support of the war in the South and to insure an ample flow of military supplies from North Vietnam's allies. Among North Vietnam's target systems, not one has been attacked either intensively or extensively enough to provide a critical reduction in national capacity. No target system can be reduced to its critical point under existing rules."[30] Based on the "principle of concentration,"[31] such punitive strikes could include intensive attacks on the rail lines to China, the mining of the

---

[27] SNIE 10–1–66, Feb. 4, 1966, "Possible Effects of a Proposed U.S. Course of Action on DRV Capability to Support the Insurgency in South Vietnam," cited above.

[28] According to SNIE 10–1–66, even if the ports were closed and lines of communication from China were disrupted or cut, the problem of importation of POL "would be surmountable in a comparatively short time, probably a few weeks. . . . Soviet POL could be unloaded from tankers at Chen-chiang in South China, moved thence by rail to the DRV border and from there to the Hanoi area by truck. It could also move from the U.S.S.R. by rail directly across China, or down the coast from Chen-chiang in shallow-draft shipping."

[29] *PP*, Gravel ed., vol. IV, pp. 71–72, CIA, SC No. 1826/66, "The Role of Air Strikes in Attaining Objectives in North Vietnam," March 1966. This document is not in the Johnson Library.

[30] *Ibid.*, p. 72.

[31] *The Pentagon Papers (ibid.*, p. 74) defines "principle of concentration" as that in which "enough of the system could be brought under simultaneous attack to cut through any cushion of excess capacity, and in which a concentrated attack might be able to overwhelm the other side's ability to reconstruct, repair, or disperse its capacity."

ports, and the bombing of POL storage facilities, the Haiphong cement plant, and military barracks and/or supplies facilities, and the bombing of industrial plants, or alternatively, the principal electric power plants.

According to the *Pentagon Papers,* this CIA report strengthened the JCS proposals for increased bombing of the North, and "gave a substantial boost to the proposal to hit the POL targets."[32]

On March 17, Westmoreland submitted a new intelligence assessment which concluded that the enemy was "building up organizationally and materially."[33] Based on this assessment, Westmoreland took the position that "Attainment of maximum damage and disruption in and adjacent to the Laos panhandle [the Ho Chi Minh Trail] by tactical air during the remaining period of good weather [before the Monsoon] becomes an objective of over-riding priority."[34] CINCPAC concurred.[35] Both MACV and CINCPAC also recommended increased bombing of lines of communication and transportation systems in North Vietnam, with priority to be given to the bombing of POL.[36]

On March 29, General Taylor (then an assistant to the President) agreed with Westmoreland's position, saying:[37]

> My own conclusion is that the time has now come to raise significantly the level of pressure on North Viet-Nam by attacking POL stocks, interdicting effectively the two railways linking Hanoi with China and mining Haiphong and the two secondary ports in the area. In the eyes of the Hanoi leaders, the ground war in South Viet-Nam must now appear to be going rather badly and it is important that they receive an equally discouraging impression from the air war. Not until they get a gloomy composite from both is there much hope of bringing them to negotiations. The risks involved in this course of action appear to me to be acceptable and, in my judgment, should be undertaken in view of the probable advantages accruing from a significant increase of pressures on the will of the leaders in North Viet-Nam.

On March 26, the JCS again recommended increased bombing, including strikes on POL.[38]

Toward the end of March 1966, McNamara sent a memorandum to the President drafted by McNaughton that was similar to McNaughton's draft of January 18, endorsing, among other things, the bombing of seven major POL storage facilities, the Haiphong cement plant, and transportation lines between North Vietnam and China.[39] Although McNamara took the position that the proposed

---

[32] *Ibid.* POL facilities, the report said, had a "direct bearing" on the regime's ability to support the war in the South, and were the target system to which the principle of concentration could be best applied.

[33] MACV 8328, Mar. 17, 1966, summarized in Tab C of a memorandum from the Far East Bureau (Unger) of the State Department to Secretary of State Rusk, Mar. 30, 1966, "Increased Military Pressures Against North Vietnam," a copy of which is in the State Department, Lot File 74 D 164.

[34] MAC 8332, Mar. 17, 1966, which is also summarized in the Unger memorandum.

[35] *Ibid.*

[36] *Ibid.*

[37] Johnson Library, NSF Memos to the President—McGeorge Bundy.

[38] *PP,* Gravel ed., vol. IV, p. 87, citing JCSM-189-66 of Mar. 26, 1966.

[39] McNamara Memorandum for the President, "April program of air strikes against North Vietnamese and Laos," cited above.

program "is not expected to get quick results," and pointed out that North Vietnam had large reserves of POL, he also noted that 70–80 percent of the country's storage facilities would be included in the attacks, and that, "The attacks should significantly increase the cost of moving war-supporting materiel southward through the infiltration routes and would cause concern in Hanoi about their ability to support troops in South Vietnam."

McNamara also said that, "in the longer term," such attacks could increase North Vietnam's manpower problem, and, by causing popular disaffection resulting from shortages, might aggravate possible policy differences within the regime.

According to the *Pentagon Papers,* the memorandum was much more forceful than the bombing recommendations McNamara had made in January, but, "one cannot be sure that McNamara expected or wanted the President to approve his recommendations."[40]

At meetings with the President toward the end of March, it was decided, in large part because of the political situation in South Vietnam, to defer action on accelerating the air war. CINCPAC was told, however, to plan for carrying out the new strikes, including POL, during April.[41]

On March 30, the Far East Bureau (FE) of the State Department sent a memorandum to Secretary Rusk, drafted by Unger, making recommendations for a State Department position on the military's request for an intensification of the air war against North Vietnam. FE believed, the memorandum said, that the air war should continue to be directed primarily at interdicting infiltration. Actions against new targets other than those pertaining directly to infiltration should be selective in view of the impact of such new moves on the North Vietnamese. "Our objective," the memorandum said, "continues to be to persuade the powers that be in Hanoi to abandon their efforts against the south and for a time at least, when we are striking a new kind of target which poses a threat to a part of their economy or infrastructure hitherto considered immune [such as POL], we can influence their calculation by one strike practically as much as by 10."[42]

[40] *PP,* Gravel ed., vol. IV, pp. 77–78.
[41] *Ibid.,* p. 79.
[42] FE memorandum to Rusk on March 30, cited above.

FE, the memorandum stated, was opposed to the mining of Haiphong harbor.[43] It was also opposed to attacks on targets in populated areas that might result in large civilian casualties.[44]

In its memorandum to Rusk on March 30, FE said that if the decision were made to intensify bombing, which "presupposes a readiness to increase the risks of Chinese and possibly Soviet responses up to the point of some measure of direct participation," that the central criterion should be to "keep those risks as low as possible

---

[43] Attached to the FE memorandum of March 30 was a copy of a memorandum of March 10 from Unger to Deputy Undersecretary U. Alexis Johnson, "Proposed Mining of Haiphong Harbor," in which FE took the following position:

"The Department has consistently taken the position that mining or blocking the Haiphong harbor would constitute a major escalatory step in the Vietnam conflict, primarily because it would involve third-country shipping and would be considered to go far beyond the measures currently being taken against North Vietnam. Although our diplomatic efforts to remove free world shipping from the North Vietnam trade has been successful to a large extent, some free world shipping (primarily under British flag) is still engaged in the trade. While mining the Haiphong harbor might succeed in removing the remainder of free world shipping from the trade, the possibility of sinking or damaging a free world ship, or wounding free world personnel by an American mine could have serious consequences, particularly with the British.

"Even more serious, however, would be the increased challenge to Communist China and the Soviet Union if one or more communist bloc ships were destroyed by mines. Neither the Chinese nor the Soviets could afford to stop their shipments to North Vietnam and they would undoubtedly feel obliged to take measures of one kind or another leading to their more direct involvement in the conflict. This of course would increase the prospects of direct confrontation between Soviet and Chinese military forces, and U.S. forces, thereby intensifying the dangers of a wider war."

In a memorandum on Feb. 4, 1966, the State Department's Legal Adviser, Leonard Meeker, took the position that although the mining of North Vietnamese harbors was legally justifiable as part of the collective defense action in which the U.S. was engaged, "The real difficulty about a proposal for mining lies in the consequences with respect to Soviet, Chinese, and neutral shipping. The sinking of Soviet and Chinese vessels by mines placed in harbors would be an important factor in escalation and expansion of the whole conflict. Beyond that, there is a very large question whether our action would be sustained if a judicial body were ever to scrutinize it in litigation between the United States and a third country. In Vietnam we have no findings and recommendations from the United Nations Security Council such as we had in Korea. Nor do we have the benefit of any resolution from a competent regional organization, such as we had from the OAS at the time of the Cuba missile crisis. We have simply our own conclusions—those of an interested party—as to facts and law, that North Vietnam is engaged in an armed attack on the South. While this may be enough to sustain U.S. military measures against North Vietnam, it would probably be insufficient in the eyes of an impartial tribunal to justify military actions impinging on third country shipping, unless these could be shown, to the satisfaction of the tribunal, to be directly necessary to the defense of South Vietnam." U.S. Department of State, Central File, Pol 27 Viet S, Memorandum for the Secretary from Leonard Meeker.

[44] The March 30 FE memorandum also commented on two other proposals for action against North Vietnam:

"Vietnamese Ambassador [to the U.S.] Vu Van Thai and Foreign Minister Tran Van Do have raised at various times two other proposals for military action against the north:

"(1) A bombing of dikes and/or watergates early in the season of rising river levels (i.e. the spring) as a means of warning Hanoi of our capability to wreak considerable havoc without in fact seriously endangering life at this time, and

"(2) A feint by Vietnamese craft against the north which would cause Hanoi to immobilize substantial numbers of soldiers on its coast and would also have an unnerving psychological effect.

"The second of these proposals seems to us dangerous in terms of possible provocation of the Chinese and also out of keeping with our stated policy of not threatening the regime in North Vietnam. The first proposal might, if we must continue to intensify still further, have some utility, and a discussion of this possibility is appended at Tab B." Tab B, "Strikes Against Flood Control Dikes in North Vietnam," prepared by the Far East Bureau, stated that "Dr. Do and Ambassador Thai believe this course of action would:

"a. Force the North Vietnamese Government to move quickly to repair the dikes before heavy rains begin, with a strain on manpower (including utilization of military forces) and material resources;

"b. Demonstrate our ability and possible intent to destroy the dike system causing widespread flooding which would have a tremendous psychological effect on the regime and the people of North Vietnam. (We would not in fact contemplate causing such flooding but rather leaving the threat hanging over the Hanoi regime.)"

The FE memorandum further stated that striking the dikes "would move our program away from its close tie to infiltration and would be aimed at applying stronger pressures to persuade Hanoi to desist." "We believe," it said, "we should be prepared to take such action only if as a matter of high policy it is decided such pressures are required." FE suggested to Rusk that McNamara be asked to develop specific plans for bombing the dikes, after which FE would restudy the proposal.

for as long as possible." Based on this criterion, FE proposed that before striking POL facilities the U.S. should restrike or continue striking transportation targets that had been attacked prior to the December 1965 pause, as well as extending the area of armed reconnaissance to the northeast part of North Vietnam, except for the Chinese border areas and the zones around Hanoi and Haiphong.

At the time (spring 1966), these were the limitations on air operations over North Vietnam:[45]

> a. Utmost caution will be exercised in attack of all targets, including those developed by armed recce, to avoid striking populated areas.
>
> b. Collateral damage will be kept to a minimum consistent with the desired objective.
>
> c. The following are *not* authorized targets for attack (unless otherwise directed):
>
> (1) JCS Tgt. 39.21, Yen Phu Army Bks [barracks] NE (now believed to be a leprosarium).
>
> (2) Former JCS Tgt. 38, Vinh Army Bks Central NE, (now designated a population center).
>
> (3) Locks and dams.
>
> (4) Hydroelectric power plants.
>
> (5) Watercraft which are obviously fishing boats or appear to be engaged in fishing.
>
> (6) Clusters of sampans or houseboats in populated areas which are probably homes.
>
> d. Restricted areas in which no attacks of any type are authorized (unless otherwise specifically directed):
>
> (1) Within 30 NM [nautical miles] of center of Hanoi.
>
> (2) Within 10 NM of center of Haiphong.
>
> (3) Zone along CHICOM border 30 NM wide from Laotian border to 106° E, and 25 NM wide from 106° E to Gulf of Tonkin.
>
> e. Flight paths for conducting strikes will not be closer than 20 NM of CHICOM border.
>
> f. Aircraft in immediate pursuit may pursue into restricted target areas, but pursuit must stop at the Chinese communist border.
>
> g. Aircraft in immediate pursuit will not attack SAM [surface-to-air missile] sites within 30 NM of Hanoi or North Vietnam air bases from which attacking aircraft may be operating. (emphasis in original)

On April 14, the JCS, responding to McNamara's earlier request for a study of interdiction of infiltration by bombing, submitted a report on the subject,[46] together with another recommendation for shock attacks, including POL. This, too, was rejected by McNamara, who on the previous day had replied to the earlier JCS recommendation of March 26: "I have received JCSM–189–66 [March 26]. Your recommendations were considered in connection with the

---

[45] Johnson Library, Warnke Papers, McNaughton Files, from CINCPAC Basic Operations Order, April 1966.

[46] "ROLLING THUNDER Study Group Report: Air Operations Against NVN," cited in *PP*, Gravel ed., vol. IV, p. 86.

decision on ROLLING THUNDER 50 [the proposed bombing program for April]."[47]

During April and May, action on the recommended POL attacks continued to be deferred, primarily because of the political situation in South Vietnam. Although very little information is available, another reason for the delay may have been opposition from Rusk and presumably from others in the State Department.[48] On May 10, Rostow sent a memorandum to the President on the bombing of POL in which he said that Rusk believed that POL attacks "will greatly heighten international tensions." Rostow, who was strongly advocating such attacks, said that Rusk's position was "debatable." "Some of us," he said, "believe systematic oil attacks could have a major effect on the military and economic position of North Vietnam."[49]

On May 24, JCS Chairman Wheeler reported to Admiral Sharp (CINCPAC) and Westmoreland that he had talked to McNamara, who said that the "single obstacle" to the approval of POL attacks was the "political turmoil" in South Vietnam.[50]

On June 2, Wheeler told Sharp and Westmoreland that the time for a decision on POL attacks was close at hand, and suggested that in a few days Westmoreland should send a cable asking that the attacks be approved.[51] Westmoreland did so on June 5.[52]

In a cable to Washington on June 8, Lodge also recommended intensification of the air war, arguing that this might help to compensate for lack of progress in the ground war:[53]

> If we are now going as hard and fast as we can go in South Vietnam militarily and cannot get a decisive military result in a year, the question arises as to whether we should not intensify the air attack on North Vietnam—whether we cannot thus bring about strains which will neutralize their army in South Vietnam, in spite of our inability to do it in South Vietnam on the ground within a year.
>
> The reports I get are certainly consistent with the proposition that the Hanoi regime is feeling real pain because of our bombing. If there is this change of feeling in Hanoi—as seems likely—I believe the bombing has had a lot to do with it, al-

---

[47] *Ibid.*, p. 87, from the memorandum from the Secretary of Defense to the Chairman, Joint Chiefs of Staff, "Subject: Air Operations Against North Vietnam," Apr. 13, 1966.

[48] In the State Department Files (Central File, Pol 27 Viet S) there is an eight-page memorandum of May 5, 1966, from George Ball arguing against the bombing of the POL storage at Haiphong. It was based on a 14-page draft on April 28 prepared by D. K. Myers, Pol 27 Viet S file. Briefly, the arguments were that the bombing of POL would not appreciably affect the will of the North Vietnamese or the availability of POL and the movement of troops and supplies to the south; that the bombing of the Haiphong POL facility could lead to greater U.S. escalation in military operations against North Vietnam, which in turn could increase the risks of Chinese intervention; and that the bombing could also adversely affect U.S. relations with the U.S.S.R., the principal supplier of POL to North Vietnam, thus reducing the chances for cooperation from the U.S.S.R. in ending the war, and increasing the prospects of greater assistance by the U.S.S.R. to the North Vietnamese.

[49] Johnson Library, NSF Memos to the President—Rostow. Several days earlier, Rostow had sent a memorandum to Rusk and McNamara over his own name in which he argued that the impact of "systematic and sustained bombing of POL in North Vietnam may be more prompt and direct than conventional intelligence analysis would suggest." He added: "I would underline, however, the adjectives 'systematic and sustained.' If we take this step we must cut clean through the POL system—and hold the cut—if we are looking for decisive results."

[50] CMH, Westmoreland Papers, Message Files, C/JCS 2397-May 66.

[51] Same location, JCS 3086, June 2, 1966.

[52] Same location, MACV 19218, June 5, 1966.

[53] U.S. Department of State, Central File, Pol 27 Viet S, Saigon to Washington 5378, June 8, 1966.

> though ground casualties, of course, play a part. This being true, an intensification of the bombing would be the most effective step we could take to get Hanoi to the negotiating table or—better still—to start "fading away."

On June 8, 1966, the CIA issued a special assessment of the probable results of POL attacks in which it concluded that while they would be costly and would create additional burdens for the regime, "the infiltration of men and supplies into SVN [South Vietnam] can be sustained."[54]

On June 11, the CIA sent the White House a copy of a report on the results of the first year of bombing of North Vietnam. According to the transmittal memorandum, the report concluded that the major effect had been "to force Hanoi to cope with disruption to normal economic activity and to divert manpower in significant numbers to war supporting activities."[55]

The Bombing of POL, June 1966

By the middle of June, as it became clear that the Ky government was in the final stages of suppressing the Buddhist uprising, steps were taken to prepare for Presidential approval of POL attacks. Rostow, at the President's direction, met with two administration officials, Harriman and Goldberg, who were opposed to military escalation, including POL attacks, in an effort to soften their opposition.[56]

---

[54] *PP*, Gravel ed., vol. IV, p. 104, from the CIA memorandum, SC No. 08440/66, "The Effect of Destruction of NVN Petroleum Storage Facilities on the War in SVN, "June 8, 1966.

[55] Johnson Library, NSF Country File, Vietnam, CIA transmittal memorandum of June 11, 1966, attached to memorandum from Rostow to the President, June 16, 1966.

[56] For brief reports by Rostow to the President on Harriman on June 13, 1966, and on Goldberg on June 16, see the Johnson Library, NSF Memos to the President—Walt Rostow. For Goldberg's views on the need to avoid escalation and to negotiate an end to the war, see his letter to the President on May 13, 1966, Department of State, Central File, Pol 27 Viet S.

In June 1966, Goldberg recommended new steps toward a negotiated settlement. After discussing his plan with Ball, William Bundy and Joseph Sisco, Assistant Secretary of State for International Organization Affairs, Goldberg prepared a draft memorandum for the President which he discussed with Rusk, William Bundy and Sisco in a meeting on June 15. (There are apparently no notes of that meeting. A copy of Goldberg's draft memorandum for the President, "New Peace Moves on Vietnam," June 14, 1966 is in the Department of State Central File, Pol 27 Viet S. On April 8, Goldberg had made a similar proposal to the President. See his letter of May 4 to Rusk, with whom he discussed the proposal, Department of State, Central File, Pol 27 Viet S). In the memorandum, Goldberg said that although there were "no signs at this time from the other side that any moves we might make will bring about in the near future either negotiations or an end to the fighting . . . there are compelling reasons for us to make new efforts. The political instability in South Vietnam may ebb and flow, but this in itself makes it important that—alongside our military effort—we make further efforts, with some new feature, to demonstrate our resolve to end the conflict peacefully, particularly as our own elections are drawing near. Secondly, no one can guarantee that military means alone, however effective, will by themselves bring the conflict to a relatively early conclusion; at the same time, we must make clear to friend and foe alike that we do not consider our position so eroded by the political instability in South Vietnam that we are unwilling to run the risks of negotiation. Finally, our policy and objectives in Vietnam need reaffirmation in terms which are so brief and simple that there is no room for misunderstanding or confusion, either at home or abroad."

Goldberg proposed a mutual cessation of hostilities throughout Vietnam and the convening of a Geneva conference for the purpose of "reaffirming and revitalizing the Geneva Agreements of 1954 and 1962." The conference would be attended by those nations that signed the agreements, and "by any interested belligerent group, including the National Liberation Front." After securing new agreements, implemented by effective international supervision, the U.S. would withdraw its forces from South Vietnam.

The "new feature" in this proposal, Goldberg noted in the memorandum, was the provision for the NLF to participate (even though it would do so as a "belligerent group" rather than as a government).

No one could foresee or guarantee the results of such a conference, Goldberg said, but "the extremely difficult circumstances we face with regard to the Vietnamese problem, both here and within South Vietnam, fully warrant our taking the risks involved in the hope of achieving some viable settlement (e.g., as at the 1962 Geneva Conference in Laos)."

There were also conversations with several U.S. allies about the intention to bomb POL. The British opposed the move. In a cable to President Johnson on June 3, Prime Minister Harold Wilson said:[57]

> the possible military benefits that may result from this bombing do not appear to outweigh the political disadvantages that would seem the inevitable consequence. If you and the South Vietnamese Government were conducting a declared war on the conventional pattern . . . this operation would clearly be necessary and right. But since you have made it abundantly

---

Leonard Meeker, the State Department legal adviser also proposed a U.S. peace initiative. In a memorandum to Rusk and Ball on May 12 (Department of State, Central File, Pol 27 Viet S), he said that although a direct approach by the U.S. might not succeed, a third-party effort might produce results. This could be arranged by having a neutral government such as Austria, Ireland or Japan take up the matter with other governments that were not parties to the war. Out of these talks could come a proposal for a cease-fire and a withdrawal of forces supervised by international observers under the direction of these governments. This would be followed by election of a National Assembly in South Vietnam which would organize a provincial government and draft a constitution.

Another proposal was made to the President by W. W. Rostow, after conversations with Gunnar Myrdal, a prominent Swedish economist who was very active in international political circles. Myrdal said that the pressures from the war were isolating the U.S. from the "good people" of Western Europe and many parts of Asia, and that the war was preventing progress in dealing with various international problems. He suggested that the U.S. take the lead in holding a meeting of the four parties to the war: the U.S., the Governments of South Vietnam and North Vietnam, and the National Liberation Front, for the purpose of making arrangements for the U.S. to stop bombing in return for an end to infiltration and for free elections in South Vietnam. Rostow asked Myrdal whether the Swedish Government would be prepared to send troops to monitor the infiltration routes after such an agreement, and Myrdal replied, according to Rostow's memorandum on May 8, 1966 on the conversation which he sent to the President, that "he felt absolutely confident that the Swedish government would be prepared to do this if Hanoi and the U.S. agreed." In an accompanying memorandum on May 8 to the President (same location) Rostow said:

"If we could offer Hanoi and the world a conference of the four fighting forces to stop the bombing and stop infiltration, on a monitored basis, as we take on POL, we have a pretty good package [i.e., a peace proposal to help soften the reaction to an escalation of the war].

"If the Swedish government bought it and offered a regiment, this might stop the imminent defection of Scandinavia on our Viet Nam policy and turn the flank of world opinion.

"The two gut problems are:

"1. Getting Ky aboard before we act.

"2. See if the Swedish government really would accept the responsibility, if asked by Hanoi and Washington—and announce it at the time we made the offer.

"In fact, we might want some Ethiopian, Danish, etc. troops invited, as well as Swedes."

The reaction of the State Department, in a memorandum from William Bundy to Rusk on May 11, was that "we let this one drop." Bundy said that he could not believe that Myrdal, who, according to Ball, had been "increasingly vague and a 'blowhard,'" could speak for the Swedish Government. Moreover, the Swedes were unlikely to offer troops.

On the issues raised in Rostow's memorandum, Bundy said that the proposal would negate U.S. objections to recognizing the NLF as an independent entity and open the door for NLF representatives in the South Vietnamese Government. Moreover, a cessation of bombing was not an issue involving the NLF, and should be negotiated directly with the North Vietnamese. (Rostow's and Bundy's memoranda are in the Department of State, Central File, Pol 27 Viet S.)

Both Lodge and General Taylor commented on the question of negotiations. In a cable to the President on June 10, Lodge took the position that the U.S., in order to enable the North Vietnamese, who he said were "genuinely disturbed by the vigor of our bombing, and genuinely would like to end the war," to "save face," should not talk publicly about negotiations. Rather, "The situation calls for silence and action, the action to consist of steady bombing on the one hand, and a discreet willingness to get into very secret talks on the other." (Johnson Library, NSF Memos to the President—Walt Rostow, Saigon to Washington 5437, June 10, 1966.)

Taylor sent a memorandum to the President on Apr. 27, 1966, "An Assessment and Use of Negotiation Blue Chips," known as the "Blue Chips" memorandum, in which, after enumerating what "chips" each side had, he proposed that, without giving up the principal blue chip—bombing—without equal gain, the U.S. could agree to stop bombing in return for a cessation of "Viet Cong incidents and military operations," both of which were verifiable, whereas he doubted the feasibility of verifying the cessation of infiltration. (Department of State Central File, Pol 27–14 Viet.) Taylor's memorandum is attached to a memorandum from Rostow to Rusk asking the State Department to consider the proposal.

Lodge replied that he would prefer to link the cessation of bombing to the stopping of infiltration, rather than to the cessation of incidents and troop withdrawal, Memorandum to Rostow, June 17, 1966, Department of State, Central File, Pol 27–14, Viet.

[57] Cited in *PP*, Gravel ed., vol. IV, p. 102.

clear—and you know how much we have welcomed and supported this—that your purpose is to achieve a negotiated settlement, and that you are not striving for total military victory in the field, I remain convinced that the bombing of these targets, without producing decisive military advantages, may only increase the difficulty of reaching an eventual settlement. . . .

Wilson added that while the British would continue to support U.S. policy, "the effect on public opinion in this country—and I believe throughout Western Europe—is likely to be such as to reinforce the existing disquiet and criticism that we have to deal with."

In a cable on June 14, after Wilson had apparently made a public statement about the importance of not attacking population centers, and after Rusk and Wilson had talked privately, President Johnson replied that the attack would be against POL installations and would not be an "assault on civilian centers." He said he saw "no way of avoiding such action, given the expansion of the illegal corridor through Laos, the continuing buildup of North Vietnamese forces in South Vietnam, the growing abuse of Cambodia neutrality, and the absence of any indication in Hanoi of a serious interest in peace." "We expect costly fighting during the Monsoon season," he added. "I must do what I can to reduce our casualties at the hands of those who are moving in from the north."[58]

In response to a statement by Wilson to Rusk that if the U.S. bombed POL sites he would feel compelled to state publicly that the British dissociated themselves from that action, Johnson also said in his June 14 cable that he hoped Wilson would not "speak in terms of disassociation." If Wilson did so, however, Johnson said he hoped that the statement would include various clarifications (which he listed), such as the fact that the attack was on POL sites and was not directed against population centers.

There had been some discussion of a visit to Washington by Wilson, and in his cable Johnson suggested that this could be scheduled during the latter part of July. As a result of Wilson's opposition to POL bombing, however, Johnson apparently did not want him to come, and stipulated, according to Rostow, that the visit should take place only on three conditions: "(1) the visit must be very carefully prepared; (2) the Prime Minister, whatever his pressures at home, should not come unless *what he says here in public and in private reinforces your* [the President's] *position on Vietnam;* (3) if this is impossible for him, he must find an excuse for the visit not to take place."[59] (emphasis in original)

On June 29, the day the POL attacks began, Wilson, without including any of the clarifications recommended by Johnson, made a statement in the House of Commons in which he said—despite efforts of his own Foreign Office to get him to speak in a "less forthright" way—that the British noted the POL bombing "with regret," and "feel bound to re-affirm that we must dissociate ourselves from

[58] Johnson Library, NSF Memos to the President—Walt Rostow.

[59] Johnson Library, NSF Country File, Vietnam, Washington to London 1116, July 2, 1966. These three conditions had been suggested to the President by Rostow. See his memorandum to the President, June 17, 1966, in the Johnson Library, NSF Memos to the President—Walt Rostow. In a memorandum to the President on June 2, Rostow had stated: "On balance, I think a Wilson visit is a good idea. But it *must* be publicly focused on NATO and other matters, not Vietnam." (emphasis in original) Same location, NSF Country File, Vietnam.

an action of this kind. . . ."[60] (In a cable on June 23, Wilson had sent word that he planned to reaffirm in his speech the dissociation of the British from the bombing of POL.)[61]

At the same time, Wilson sent a message to Johnson explaining his political situation and how it affected the position he had taken. Johnson replied on July 2, thanking Wilson, but saying, "My problem is not merely political. I must also convince Hanoi that the will of the United States cannot be broken by debate or pressures—at home or from abroad." "We must and will continue," he added, "to apply hard military pressure."[62]

Wilson was preparing to go to Moscow for a meeting with Kosygin, and Johnson said that he hoped Wilson would "canvas all useful [negotiating] possibilities with Kosygin and his colleagues and that your joint responsibilities as co-chairman [of the 1954 Geneva Accords] might lead to some constructive initiative."

On July 3, the State Department suggested to the U.S. Ambassador in London, David K. E. Bruce, that he discuss with Wilson "the need to leave in Washington the sense that the UKG [the Government of the United Kingdom of Great Britain and Northern Ireland] is giving the U.S. full support in Vietnam." Wilson should avoid repeating the statements he had made in Parliament, and "a great deal of the problems could be avoided if he were to express "strongly optimistic views about the progress of free Asia generally."[63]

After seeing Wilson, Bruce replied that Wilson was "absolutely confident he would and could avoid any embarrassment to the President. . . . He is a politician, and, as such, highly sensitive to the other statesmen's concerns."[64]

The meeting between Johnson and Wilson was held in Washington on July 29, 1966. Apparently, the subject of Vietnam was barely mentioned, and Wilson, who observed in his memoirs that he expected to get a "frozen mitt" from Johnson, said he was surprised by Johnson's cordiality.[65]

---

[60] Harold Wilson, *The Labour Government, 1964–1970: A Personal Record* (London: Weidenfeld and Nicolson, 1971), p. 248.

In a cable to Washington on July 12, the U.S. Embassy in London explained Wilson's position. "He [Wilson] has never believed in possibility of clearcut military decisions in VN. He has said that VC cannot themselves win against U.S. military power, but that only possible settlement must be political, getting sides to peace table. He has become increasingly frustrated and defensive that formula for settlement could not be found. He has constantly blamed Hanoi for this failure." (Johnson Library, NSF Country File, United Kingdom, London to Washington 229, July 12, 1966.

The cable also commented on the question of possible dissidence in the Labour Party if Wilson had supported the POL decision or withheld his statement until the results of the bombing were available: "Unrest and concern about Vietnam are not confined to committed, hard-line leftists. Feeling is widespread in party about dangers of situation. Wilson has not invented opposition and cannot ignore its deep emotional drives. In circumstances, with press and television feeding public alarm, even hysteria, when news of bombing broke, it would have shown remarkable restraint if Wilson had remained silent or acquiesced in accomplished fact. It is improbable that he could have supported American action without serious political repercussions here although after fact some Labour supporters wished he had done so."

[61] Johnson Library, NSF Memos to the President—Walt Rostow, London to Washington 6155, June 23, 1966.

[62] Wilson's message to Johnson, CAP 66423, and Johnson's reply on July 2, PRUS001, 1701 Zulu, are in the Johnson Library, NSF Files of Walt Rostow.

[63] Same location, Washington to London 1235, July 3, 1955.

[64] Same location, London to Washington 53, July 4, 1966.

[65] Wilson, *The Labour Government*, p. 248. In a memorandum to the President on July 28 (Johnson Library, President's Appointment File, Diary Backup, July 29, 1966) Rostow gave this report on Wilson's position:

Continued

In preparation for the POL attacks, the NSC met on June 17, 1966 from 6:05 p.m. to 8:00 p.m. In attendance were the President, the Vice President, Rusk, McNamara, Rostow, William Bundy, Goldberg, Raborn, Helms, JCS Acting Chairman Harold Johnson, Fowler, U.S.IA Director Marks, and Moyers, George Christian and Bromley Smith. Ball, although still in the Government, was not present.[66] The President reviewed the reasons for the impending decision to bomb POL: "In general, we should seek, with minimum loss and minimum danger of escalating the war, to achieve the maximum effect on the North Vietnamese. We know that the North Vietnamese are dispersing their POL stocks in an effort to anticipate our bombing. The effect of not disrupting POL shipments to the North Vietnamese forces in the field is to pay a higher price in U.S. casualties. The choice is one of military lives vs. escalation."

Rusk then spoke: "We have an elementary obligation to support our combat troops when they are carrying out an assignment." Moreover, he said, more effective military measures were needed to prevent the erosion of public support. The American people were becoming restless, as the polls showed, and "over time, they may demand a quick end to the war as the price for their continued support." But Rusk also stressed the need to avoid a negative reaction from those elements of the public who would be concerned about civilian casualties, saying, "We must get across to the public that if we widen the bombing program to include POL targets that this does not mean a change in our policy of making every effort to avoid killing civilians."

He also spoke about the international effects of the bombing of POL, saying that "Opinion abroad hopes that no larger military measures will be necessary," and that the attacks "will produce sharp reactions throughout the world. There probably will be attacks on our Embassies. . . . We cannot guess what the Chinese Communist reaction will be. Our guess is that there will be no military reaction from the Chinese Communists or the Soviets. There will be many problems in the UN."

McNamara then spoke:

> Strikes on POL targets have been opposed by me for months. The situation is now changing and the earlier bombing decision must be reconsidered. POL targets are military targets. The military utilization of these targets has been greatly increased. The North Vietnamese dispersion of their POL is lessening our

---

"I asked Dennis Greenhill, an advance party for Wilson's visit, what difference in basic assessment lies behind Wilson's posture on Viet Nam. His reply was, I believe, candid.

"1. He said: Just as the Conservative government in 1961–62 was very jumpy about the Berlin crisis, so the Wilson government fears confrontation in Viet Nam. In both cases they leaned to diminishing the confrontation and looking for a 'political' solution.

"2. He said that we were proved right on the Berlin crisis in 1961–62 although the British kept dragging their feet.

"I wondered aloud what the British government would have had us do about the Cuba missile crisis. He said: 'Thank God you didn't ask.' In this he was joined by John Killick, a British Embassy colleague.

"In short, we are up against an attitude of mind which, in effect, prefers that we take losses in the free world rather than the risks of sharp confrontation.

"I believe this to be an accurate assessment."

[66] Johnson Library, NSF NSC Meetings File, List of Attendees, NSC Meeting, and Summary Notes of the 559th NSC Meeting, June 17, 1966.

Rusk also referred to the need to continue using airpower to coerce the North Vietnamese: "We must try to bring Hanoi to a decision," Rusk said. "There is no evidence of their willingness to talk now."

chance of ever destroying their POL supplies. Military infiltration from the north is up sharply. Consequently, the pressure on their lines of communication has increased. Their POL imports have doubled. The military importance of their POL system is way up and will increase further.

The reasons for attacking POL targets are:

1. Our guess is that such attacks will limit infiltration from North Vietnam.

2. Those North Vietnamese troops in the south will worry about their source of supplies.

3. Pressure will be exerted on the political leaders in Hanoi. This bombing program seems to be the least costly way to tell them of our serious intentions.

"If we do not widen our bombing," McNamara added, "the morale of U.S. troops and of the American people will suffer. People will say: If you consider a POL target a military target, why do you not strike it?"

Speaking for the Joint Chiefs, General Johnson, Army Chief of Staff, said that the Chiefs viewed POL targets as "a first priority." "If the POL targets are hit," he said, "the North Vietnamese will have to find alternative ways of delivering POL. Meanwhile, the dispersion of their petroleum supplies is continuing." The President asked General Johnson what lay ahead in the next 60 days. General Johnson replied: "The North Vietnamese will reinforce the military power they now have and make a drive into central Vietnam—possibly even further south. Hitting the POL targets will hurt them in moving rice and weapons to replace those we have captured. They have to step up the rate of supplies from the north to the south."

Rostow commented that bombing was forcing the North Vietnamese to divert manpower to repair roads and bridges. "The decision is a rational one. Taking out the petroleum supplies sets a ceiling on the capacity of the North Vietnamese to infiltrate men into South Vietnam. A sustained POL offensive will seriously affect the infiltration rate." "Our policy should remain steady and our actions should be cool and professional," he added. "We should not be on the defensive. Our military effort is based on the violation of the Geneva Accords by the North Vietnamese."

Vice President Humphrey also supported the bombing of POL. "I have come around reluctantly," he said, "to accepting the wider bombing program. Not to attack the POL targets would be to contribute to North Vietnamese strength. The strikes will complicate their logistic problems and exert pressure on Hanoi. As to the political consequences, it will play hell. But we should go ahead with the additional strikes, exercising precautions." "We should keep up the punishment we are inflicting on North Vietnam while seeking peace."

Fowler, Raborn, Helms, and Marks also spoke in favor of bombing POL. According to Helms, (Deputy Director of the CIA, who soon became Director), "The petroleum supplies are feeding the meat grinder in South Vietnam and this North Vietnamese military effort will continue unless we take out their petroleum supplies."

William Bundy, who did not express a personal view, observed that the recent meeting of U.S. Ambassadors and military Chiefs in Asia (SEACOORD) recommended the expanded bombing program.

The only person attending the meeting to speak against the bombing of POL was U.N. Ambassador Goldberg, who said that the risk was too great and that the results "will not be what we think." He added:

> The Chinese and Soviet reactions to the headlines reporting the bombing of Hanoi and Haiphong [where POL targets were located] will be a challenge to them to give all aid necessary to make up the loss. . . . The Communist bloc is not going to let this outfit go down the drain. They see the Vietnam war as a confrontation. With minimum risk, they can make up for the damage we do to the North Vietnamese petroleum supplies. In addition, the world reaction will be strongly adverse—even Canada would oppose our action . . . we will be isolating ourselves internationally.

Goldberg added that if POL strikes did not end the war, the reaction in the U.S. would be "very adverse." "The country's mood will turn at election time if the war is still going on. The American people are supporting the President because he is cool and reserved."[67]

The NSC met again five days later, on June 22. Present for the meeting, which was held from 12:30 p.m. to 2:20 p.m., were the President, the Vice President, Rusk, McNamara, Ball, Rostow, William Bundy, Goldberg, Vance, McNaughton, Raborn, Helms, JCS Chairman General Wheeler, Army Chief of Staff General Johnson, Chief of Naval Operations Admiral McDonald, Air Force Chief of Staff General McConnell and Marine Commandant General Greene, Secretary of the Treasury Fowler, USIA Director Marks, and from the White House and NSC staffs General Taylor, Robert Kintner, Bromley Smith and George Christian.[68]

Following a recapitulation by McNamara of the reasons for bombing POL, the President asked General Wheeler a series of questions about military aspects of the attack, concluding with the following:

> *The President:* Suppose your dreams are fulfilled. What are the results?
>
> *General Wheeler:* Over the next 60 to 90 days, this will start to affect the total infiltration effort. It will cost them more. In a very real sense, this is a war of attrition.
>
> *The President:* You have no qualification, no doubt that this is in the national interest?
>
> *General Wheeler:* None whatsoever.
>
> *The President:* People tell me what not to do, what I do wrong. I don't get any alternatives. What might I be asked next? Destroy industry, disregard human life? Suppose I say no, what else would you recommend?

---

[67] The concluding paragraph of the notes of the meeting states: "Each person in the room, during the course of the discussion, indicated approval of the recommendation to strike the recommended POL targets." Based on Goldberg's statement, however, as well as his reiteration on July 22 (see below) of his opposition, the notes may be in error in saying that each person in the room approved of the bombing.

[68] Johnson Library, NSF NSC Meetings File, List of Attendees, NSC Meeting June 22, 1966, and Notes by George Christian of the 560th NSC meeting.

General Wheeler: Mining Haiphong.

The President: Do you think this will involve the Chinese Communists and the Soviets?

General Wheeler: No, Sir.

The President: Are you more sure than MacArthur was?

General Wheeler: This is different. We had ground forces moving to the Yalu.

The President also asked Wheeler whether there would be "retaliatory pressure" from the U.S.S.R. Wheeler replied: "They could stop duty trains in Germany. In 1962 they ran maneuvers in the air corridors in West Berlin."

Rusk commented that Llewellyn Thompson did not believe there was "a danger" from the U.S.S.R.

The President asked General Taylor for his opinion. Taylor said he was optimistic, adding: "I think we have to press hard on all four fronts—economic, political, military and diplomatic. I see a movement upward all the way. We should be escalating. Personally I would mine Haiphong at the same time and get the political flak over with."

The President: "I think that public approval is deteriorating, and that it will continue to go down. Some in Congress are disgusted about the Buddhist uprising and are talking about pulling out." Rusk responded: "The overplay on the Buddhist matter hurt more than anything else."

The President then went around the table asking each of the officials who was present to state his position on bombing POL. With the exception of Goldberg, all agreed. The Vice President said: "I reaffirm my position in favor." Deputy Secretary of Defense Vance said: "Fully agree," as did Rostow. William Bundy said: "I favor the strikes." Ball also agreed, saying: "All things equal, this is a good thing to do, but it does not outweigh disadvantages. . . . I am concerned about increasing the level of violence. I believe we have considerable trouble ahead on the political front. But if we are going to do it, do it now." Raborn said he approved, adding: "we need even more pressure, such as mining." Helms also approved of the bombing, but said that "the most effective thing we can do is mining."

Goldberg said he was still opposed:

> I do not think it will bring them to the conference table. I am the least expert in this room, but I can see these risks:
>
> —More involvement of North Vietnamese in the South.
>
> —No real shortage of supplies (Red China has plenty for them).
>
> —More involvement by the Chinese.
>
> —More involvement by the Soviets. (It is inconceivable that they can let this significant action to pass without reaction of some kind.)
>
> —Attrition of friends abroad and people at home. This would be regarded in the world as a major step and there are bound to be reactions.
>
> What are the alternatives? Don't withdraw. I think we are doing well. Beef up our forces, go after more successes and pressure of that type. Don't convert this to an extension of the war even to Hanoi. It is tough and painful to absorb, but it will

hopefully lead to an agreed solution to let the people in the South alone.

Later that day (June 22), the President held an off-the-record meeting from 5:45 p.m. to 7:10 p.m. with 30 Democratic and Republican Members of Congress (10 Senators and 20 Representatives,) members of the Committees on Armed Services or the Foreign Affairs/Foreign Relations Committees, all of whom had been to South Vietnam.[69] Also present were Rusk, McNamara, JCS Chairman Wheeler, Rostow and George Christian. According to an unpublished account by one of the congressional participants, the President and his associates showed the strain and fatigue brought on by their work on the war. Johnson, the report said, looked "very tired" and nodded occasionally. Rusk also looked tired, "as did McNamara whose eyes lidded over involuntarily from time to time." As the meeting progressed, however, the President became more animated, and, telling the group "We are going to win!" he said:[70]

> More men were going into Viet Nam and people could say that this was wrong or that was wrong, but no one could give him an alternative that was better than what McNamara suggested or what Wheeler suggested. Sam Rayburn [Speaker of the House of Representatives] used to say that if you couldn't rely on the generals, we've wasted an awful lot of money on West Point. If some people thought he was going to waver because they didn't like this policy, they didn't know him. He cited the man who, when LBJ was a boy, heard him say "go to hell" and warned him that it was one thing to tell someone that and another to make him go there. He referred sneeringly to the actions of "some Senators" and said that Hanoi read their remarks more carefully than we did. . . .

The President added that he was trying to do what was "right," and that he was "following his Chiefs' recommendations. . . . He was supporting the commitments that had been made over the years. He got the best men from Harvard and the best men from West Point and asked them what he should do and, when they told him, he went ahead and did it."

Rusk and McNamara also commented, as did some of the Members of Congress who were present. Most congressional comments emphasized the need for the U.S. to be more aggressive in its military efforts, as well as noting that the public expected results and was becoming discontented. Mansfield and Aiken, however, disagreed with the call for a more aggressive policy. Mansfield said that the President knew where he (Mansfield) stood. The President

[69] Those present were Senators George D. Aiken (R/Vt.), Daniel B. Brewster (D/Md.), Daniel K. Inouye (D/Hawaii), Henry M. Jackson (D/Wash.), Gale W. McGee (D/Wyo.), Mike Mansfield (D/Mont.), Jack Miller (R/Iowa), Stuart Symington (D/(Mo.), John G. Tower (R/Tex.) and Stephen M. Young (D/Ohio), and Representatives William G. Bray (R/Ind.), James A. Byrne (D/Pa.), Charles E. Chamberlain (R/N.H.), John C. Culver (D/Iowa), Richard H. Fulton (D/Tenn.), Charles S. Gubser (R/Calif.), Porter Hardy, Jr. (D/Va.), Wayne L. Hays (D/Ohio), Floyd V. Hicks (D/Wash.), Robert L. Leggett (D/Calif.), Harris B. McDowell, Jr. (D/Del.), John S. Monagan (D/Conn.), William T. Murphy (D/Ill.), Philip J. Philbin (D/Mass.), Otis G. Pike (D/N.Y.), Alexander Pirnie (R/N.Y.), Samuel S. Stratton (D/N.Y.), Vernon W. Thomson (R/Wisc.), Charles H. Wilson (D/Calif.), and Clement J. Zablocki (D/Wis.).

[70] This is quoted from unpublished personal recollections of John S. Monagan, a former Democratic Member of Congress from Connecticut, who, as noted, was present at the meeting. It is used with the permission of Mr. Monagan.

replied that the night before he had reread Mansfield's memorandum of June 13.[71]

The POL attacks were launched on June 29, "reportedly with great success."[72] McNamara described the raids as "a superb professional job," and he told Admiral Sharp (CINCPAC) that the President wanted the complete "strangulation" of the POL system.[73]

Reaction to the POL Attacks

Proponents of stronger military action hailed the results of the new airstrikes, while those who questioned the direction of U.S. policy in Vietnam expressed their regret that the war was being escalated. Westmoreland said that allied forces had begun to win the war, and Prime Minister Ky said that as a result of the bombing the war would end in six months with North Vietnam asking for a cease-fire.[74] In Washington, Senator Russell said he approved of the POL attacks. "It seems to me we have exhausted every effort to arrive at negotiations. Any further delay in drying up the sources of supply for the Vietcong and the North Vietnamese troops in the south could only increase the casualty lists of American dead and wounded." Senators Saltonstall and Symington, as well as House Republican Leader Ford, took similar positions.

Senator Mansfield, who was described as being angry, disagreed, saying, "I think it indicates a new stage in the war. I think it will also bring about a greater amount of aid from the Soviet Union and Peking." "The destruction of petrol facilities," he added, "won't deter infiltration. It may slow it down for the time being, but the end result may be increased infiltration and that will make the road to the negotiating table that much more difficult." Senators Fulbright, Robert Kennedy, and Javits, as well as a number of House Democratic liberals, agreed. Senator Aiken said, "in a voice quaking with emotion," "He [President Johnson] is apparently taking the advice of the same people who assured him 18 months ago that a few days bombing of North Vietnam would bring it to its knees and the conference table. They were wrong then. Now McNamara uses the greatly increased infiltration as an excuse for intensifying the war. The President has made a mistake. Instead of lessening the war, it will expand it, and it won't shorten it."[75]

On June 30, 1966, during testimony by Under Secretary of State Ball before the Senate Foreign Relations Committee, Chairman Fulbright called the bombing "one more step toward the ultimate war." This action, he added, "appears to me to mean that the only solution we contemplate is the surrender of North Vietnam as the result of a complete military victory." Ball disagreed. He said that bombing was weakening North Vietnamese morale, and added that

[71] *Ibid.*

[72] *PP*, Gravel ed., vol. IV, p. 106. See also McNamara's press conference on June 29, the transcript of which was in the *New York Times* on June 30, 1966.

[73] *PP*, Gravel ed., vol. IV, pp. 106, 109.

[74] *New York Times*, July 2, 3, 1966.

[75] *Ibid.*, June 30, 1966. For other congressional comments see the *Congressional Record* for June 29 and 30, 1966.

he had "no doubts or reservations" with respect to U.S. policy toward Vietnam.[76]

The day after the hearing, Bill Moyers telephoned Ball to tell him that he thought Ball "had done a wonderful job for the President." Ball replied that he was "very glad to have had a chance to put it on the record that he had no reservations about what the administration was doing." [77]

The reaction of the public was muted. Generally, there was support for the President's decision, consistent with the phenomenon of increased public support for Presidential initiatives.[78] In a poll taken after the POL strikes, the Harris survey found that a substantial percentage of the public approved of the President decision (62 percent in favor, 11 percent opposed, 27 percent no opinion), and that, as noted earlier, support for the President's handling of the war rose from 42 percent in June to 54 percent in July after the bombing.[79] Gallup found that 70 percent approved the POL strikes, 11 percent disapproved, and 19 percent had no opinion.[80]

On July 16, North Vietnam responded to the new air attacks by calling up some of its military Reserves. "The war may last still 5, 10, 20 years or longer," Ho Chi Minh said. "Hanoi, Haiphong and other cities and enterprises may be destroyed, but the Vietnamese people will not be intimidated. Nothing is more precious than independence and freedom." [81]

The U.S.S.R. protested the POL attacks, claiming that bullets from American planes had struck one of their cargo ships in Haiphong harbor. (That ship, incidentally, was carrying some POL for the North Vietnamese.) Intelligence memoranda from the State Department and the CIA discounted the seriousness of this objection, however, and State argued that there was "no qualitative change in the Soviet policy lines already evident for some time: aid, probably increasing in quantity, to North Vietnam; diplomatic and propaganda pressure to get us to desist or at least to deter us from escalation; no initiative toward a peaceful settlement unless and until Hanoi gives a green light; nevertheless keep in touch with us on issues such as outer space and non-proliferation and on selected bilateral problems such as fisheries." [82]

Edmund Rice, the Department of State's chief "China-watcher," reported from Hong Kong on July 23 that, as a consequence of POL strikes, the Chinese appeared to have made new decisions to help North Vietnam. "It would be dangerous," Rice said, "to assume that we could carry measures against the DRV to the point which we could break the will of its regime without Communist China's intervening as it might deem necessary to support the regime—just as a far weaker China intervened to save that of North Korea." [83] Rostow thought that Rice's cable was important enough to be di-

---

[76] *New York Times*, July 1, 1966.

[77] Johnson Library, Papers of George Ball, Presidential Telecons.

[78] See pt. III of this study, p. 72.

[79] *Washington Post*, July 11, 1966.

[80] *Vietnam War, A Compilation: 1964–1990*, vol. 1, cited above.

[81] *New York Times*, July 17, 1966.

[82] Johnson Library, NSF Files of Walt W. Rostow, Memorandum for Rostow from Thomas L. Hughes, Director of Intelligence for the State Department, Aug. 6, 1966, and Memorandum to the President from CIA Director Helms, Aug. 6, 1966.

[83] U.S. Department of State, Central File, Pol 27 Viet S, Hong Kong to Washington, 509, July 23, 1966.

rected to the President, and on July 25 he sent him a copy with a cover memorandum recommending that he read the cable, but pointing out that Rice "was always against bombing in the North"—a not entirely accurate observation.[84]

On August 2, Rostow sent the President intelligence reports of July 29 and August 2 which he said in an accompanying memorandum concerned "indications of the possibility that some Chinese Communist ground force elements may have moved into North Vietnam." The evidence was not conclusive, he said, and there was no cause for alarm. Nevertheless, he had asked Clark Clifford (chairman of the Foreign Intelligence Advisory Board) "quietly to make an assessment of whether our various intelligence collection agencies are making a maximum effort to acquire intelligence on such Chinese Communist ground force movements."[85]

Rostow also sent the President a Special National Intelligence Estimate of August 4, on "Chinese Communist Intentions in the Vietnam Situation" which concluded that China had not changed its basic policy as a result of the POL strikes, but that, as a result of increasing pressure by the U.S. on North Vietnam, the Chinese were increasing their support for North Vietnam and "would almost certainly intervene if North Vietnam were invaded or if the collapse of the Communist regime seemed likely." The SNIE also noted that there were 25,000–40,000 Chinese military personnel in North Vietnam. "More assistance of this nature is almost certain. Beyond this, the Chinese may move some infantry troops into North Vietnam, initially perhaps as security for a base and airfield under construction by the Chinese some 75 miles northwest of Hanoi. . . . Hanoi and Peking may now believe that the time has come to move ahead with plans for greater Chinese support against the contingency of an invasion."[86] The SNIE also noted, as did Rostow in a memorandum to the President on July 25, that the upheaval produced by the "cultural revolution" then occurring in China "would seem to argue against a decision to go to war in Vietnam."

Studies and Reports Indicate Little Progress

Claims by proponents that the POL airstrikes would be successful were short-lived. According to the *Pentagon Papers*,[87]

> It was clear in retrospect that the POL strikes had been a failure. Apart from the possibility of inconveniences, interruptions, and local shortages of a temporary nature, there was no evidence that NVN had at any time been pinched for POL. NVN's dependence on the unloading facilities at Haiphong and large storage sites in the rest of the country had been greatly overestimated. Bulk imports via oceangoing tanker continued at Haiphong despite the great damage to POL docks and storage there. Tankers merely stood offshore and unloaded into barges and other shallow-draft boats, usually at night, and the POL was transported to hundreds of concealed locations along

[84] Johnson Library, NSF Memos to the President—Walt Rostow.
[85] *Ibid.*, Memorandum for the President from Rostow, Aug. 2, 1966.
[86] *Ibid.*, SNIE 13-66, Aug. 4, 1966, attached to cover memorandum from Rostow to the President, August 5.
[87] *PP*, Gravel ed., vol. IV, pp. 110–111.

internal waterways. More POL was also brought in already drummed, convenient for dispersed storage and handling and virtually immune from interdiction.

The difficulties of switching to a much less vulnerable but perfectly workable storage and distribution system, not an unbearable strain when the volume to be handled was not really very great, had also been overestimated. Typically, also, NVN's adaptability and resourcefulness had been greatly underestimated. As early as the summer of 1965, about six months after the initiation of ROLLING THUNDER, NVN had begun to import more POL, build additional small, dispersed, underground tank storage sites, and store more POL in drums along LOCs and at consumption points. It had anticipated the strikes and taken out insurance against them; by the time the strikes came, long after the decision had been telegraphed by open speculation in the public media, NVN was in good position to ride them out.

As the CIA had also predicted, the bombing of POL facilities apparently had little if any effect on the infiltration of men and supplies into the South, and by September 1966 the Defense Department's own Defense Intelligence Agency concurred with the judgment that there was no shortage of POL in North Vietnam after the bombing of the facilities, no evidence of insurmountable transportation problems, no significant economic dislocation, and no weakening of public morale.[88]

McNamara, supported by a study of the results of the bombing of North Vietnam, as will be seen, which was conducted at his request during the summer of 1966 by the JASON Division of the Pentagon's Institute for Defense Analyses, "made no effort to conceal his dissatisfaction and disappointment at the failure of the POL attacks. He pointed out to the Air Force and the Navy the glaring discrepancy between the optimistic estimates of results their pre-strike POL studies had postulated and the actual failure of the raids to significantly decrease infiltration."[89]

It was evident that U.S. military operations, while successful in checking the Communists, were not achieving the kind of progress that had been hoped for and projected. As noted earlier, CINCPAC had concluded by the summer of 1966 that the goal established at Honolulu in February 1966 of reaching the "crossover point" by the end of 1966 (killing the enemy at a rate exceeding replacement) was unattainable as long as the Communists were able to maintain their capability to increase their forces at a rate exceeding attrition and to provide those forces with the necessary supplies.[90]

Moreover, it was clear that, as the U.S. escalated the war so did the Communists, and that, as McNamara had predicted, the higher the level of U.S. military activity, the higher the level of stalemate.

On August 8, the *New York Times* reported that an unnamed source had stated that a study prepared in the Pentagon estimated

---

[88] *Ibid.*, p. 111. According to Clodfelter, a career Air Force officer, "Air commanders grossly miscalculated the value of oil to the Northern war effort." *The Limits of Air Power*, p. 140.

[89] *PP*, Gravel ed., vol. IV, p. 112.

[90] In a cable on Aug. 31, 1966, Lodge stated that Westmoreland believed, however, even in the face of the evidence presented by his own staff in late July, that the crossover point had been reached. (U.S. Department of State, Central File, Pol 27 Viet S, Saigon to Washington 4923, Aug. 31, 1966).

it would take eight years to "win" in Vietnam (bring the insurgency under control), or five years if U.S. forces were increased to 750,000 and there were a partial mobilization and Reserve callup. The source, it turned out, was Gen. Greene, Commandant of the U.S. Marine Corps, who said that while in Vietnam on a trip he had revealed this information to the press in a "deep backgrounder" at the direct "order" of Lodge. "The reaction, Greene later recalled, 'was immediate, explosive and remarkable.' An 'agitated' and 'as usual, profane' Lyndon Johnson, over long-distance telephone, demanded to know 'what in the God-damned hell' Greene meant by making such a statement. The commandant was forced to issue denials, and the White House denied the existence of studies leading to such conclusions."[91]

During this period, President Johnson continued to express optimism, although his carefully chosen rhetoric reflected the fact that, while the Communists were being checked, there was little progress in bringing the war to a conclusion, as well as the fact that in the United States there was declining public support for the war. In mid-August 1966, the President arranged for General Westmoreland, who was in Honolulu for a CINCPAC Conference, to fly to Texas for a meeting with him, after which the President and Westmoreland spoke to the press in an effort to strengthen public confidence and support.

In his statement, the President declared that a "Communist military takeover in South Vietnam" was "impossible" as long as U.S. and other forces were in the field, and said that "the single most important factor now is our will to prosecute the war until the Communists, recognizing the futility of their ambitions, either end the fighting or seek a peaceful settlement." "No one," he added, "can say when this will be or how many men will be needed or how long we must persevere." In conclusion, he said that "The American people must know that there will be no quick victory, but the world must know that we will not quit. . . . when you [Westmoreland] return, tell the men in the field that their determination and their courage in Vietnam will be matched by a dedicated resolve and support here at home."[92]

In mid-July 1966, a report prepared in the U.S. Mission in Saigon by a Priorities Task Force, created in April by Deputy Ambassador Porter at the urging of Komer, provided a clear and compelling statement of the enormous problems facing the U.S. and South Vietnam.[93] From the military standpoint, the report concluded, the

[91] Herring, *LBJ and Vietnam,* p. 50.

[92] *Public Papers of the Presidents,* Lyndon B. Johnson, 1966, pp. 821–822.

[93] Quotations are from the Priorities Task Force Report Summary, *PP,* Gravel ed., vol. II, pp. 580, 582.

According to the *Pentagon Papers (ibid.,* pp. 582–583), the original intent of the study to focus and reduce the number of U.S. programs in South Vietnam was not served by the report: "The Task Force divided all activities in Vietnam into categories of importance, and assigned them priorities in groups. Unfortunately, the divisions were either too vague to be useful or else they designated specific activities, such as agriculture, to such a low position that Washington found the selection unacceptable. . . . It was scarcely a list from which one could assemble a coherent program. Moreover, the list of 16 'highest priority' tasks, was followed by a group of ten 'high priority' tasks—including strengthening provincial governments, autonomous municipal government, better budgetary procedures, better refugee programs, minority programs, and so on. These, in turn, were followed by a nine-point list of 'high priority programs.' Into at least one of the 35 highest, high, or just plain priority programs, one could fit every program and project then being pursued in Vietnam."

war would increase in intensity, but *"decisive military victory for either side is not likely."* (emphasis in original) "The enemy now has a broad span of capability for interfering with progress toward achievement of U.S. objectives. He can simultaneously operate offensively through employment of guerrilla and organized forces at widely separated points throughout the country, thus tying down friendly forces, while concentrating rehearsed surprise attacks in multi-battalion or even multi-regimental strength."

The outlook for pacification was also bleak: "GVN control of the countryside is not now being extended through pacification to any significant degree and pacification in the rural areas cannot be expected to proceed at a rapid rate."

"Politically," the report concluded, "The Vietnamese will continue to face grave problems in creating an effective system of government. Under present conditions we cannot expect a strong GVN to emerge over the planning period [two years], nor can we expect political unity or a broadening of the base of popular support. The increased American presence, rising inflation and an image of considerable corruption are issues which will be increasingly exploited by unfriendly and opportunistic elements. U.S. influence on political events continue to be limited while our responsibility for Vietnam's future is increasing."[94]

Another important study, noted above, was made in the summer of 1966 at the request of McNamara by a group of distinguished scientists working on contract with the JASON division of the Pentagon's Institute for Defense Analyses.[95] The JASON Summer Study, as it was called, was arranged by McNaughton's office with Jerrold Zacharias of the Massachusetts Institute of Technology, Jerome Weisner, also of MIT, and George Kistiakowsky and Carl Kaysen of Harvard University. All four had served as scientific advisers to the government, and Kaysen had been on Kennedy's NSC staff. A group of 47 scientists was recruited for the project. Organized into four working groups, they produced in August of 1966 the following reports: (1) "The Effect of U.S. Bombing in North Vietnam," (2) "VC/NVA Logistics and Manpower," (3) "An Air-Supported Anti-Infiltration Barrier," and (4) "Summary of Results, Conclusions and Recommendations."

The group concluded that the bombing of North Vietnam had made and could only make a small contribution to winning the war. It found, as intelligence studies had found, that bombing had not significantly affected either the will of the North Vietnamese to continue supporting the war in the South or their ability to infil-

[94] One of the recommendations of the Priorities Task Force was that a group should be established by the U.S. Mission in Saigon to study the role and mission of each military, paramilitary, and police and civilian force in South Vietnam. This was done, and the resulting Roles and Missions Report made 81 recommendations, of which 66, according to the *Pentagon Papers,* were acceptable to all of the U.S. agencies represented in Saigon. "But even these 66 were not immediately adopted as basic doctrine. Because of inertia and weariness, rather than deliberate sabotage, the recommendations were never treated as basic policy, and simply were carried out or not depending on the drive and desire of the individual officials." (*PP,* Gravel ed., vol. II, p. 583.) For the reactions to the report of the various U.S. agencies represented in Saigon, see pp. 385–386 and 585–586.

On August 7, Komer produced a lengthy report, "Giving a New Thrust to Pacification," in which he made many of the same observations and recommendations contained in the Priorities Task Force Report and later in the Roles and Missions Study Group Report. See *PP,* Gravel ed., vol. II, pp. 570–575.

[95] The information on the JASON study is derived from *PP,* Gravel ed., vol. IV, pp. 115 ff.

trate the necessary supplies and personnel. Moreover, little would be accomplished by lifting the constraints and by bombing and mining the harbors or otherwise increasing the scope and intensity of the air war.[96]

The group also concluded that, as an alternative to bombing, an anti-infiltration barrier could be established across Vietnam south of the 17th parallel (the demilitarized zone—DMZ). It was this idea which had prompted McNamara, who was disillusioned with bombing, to ask for the JASON study, and, as will be seen, the report from the group served to buttress his case when he decided that the barrier should be built.[97]

Another, and in some ways the most startling of the group's conclusions, though not directly related to the principal objects of the study, was reported to Harriman by Chester Cooper (who, after leaving the White House in the spring, had joined the State Department to work with Harriman on the quest for a negotiated settlement), after he and others from the government met with the JASON group in mid-August:[98] "[T]he study concluded that with very few exceptions our information on communist logistics and manpower was so inexact that it was difficult to come to any conclusions as to the effectiveness of our military policy. It is not an exaggeration to say that the data is so soft that we cannot state with confidence whether we have been doing better or worse militarily over the past year."

Another significant report on the situation in South Vietnam and on the pacification program in particular was made in August 1966 by Professor Henry Kissinger, a member of the faculty at Harvard University and a consultant to the State Department who, it will

---

[96] For a more complete statement of these conclusions see *ibid.*, pp. 116–119.

In the White House, Ginsburgh told Rostow in a memorandum analyzing the JASON bombing study that if the conclusions of the study were accepted, "it would appear that no expansion of the bombing program would be authorized and that the current program might even be cut back. Either would in my opinion be a grievous mistake." Johnson Library, NSF Country File, Vietnam, Ginsburgh Memorandum to Rostow, Sept. 13, 1967.

Ginsburgh commented on several of the major conclusions of the JASON study, even though he said that the report would be "difficult to refute conclusively because it involves many judgments which can not be proven wrong unless an expanded program is authorized." He ended with this statement in response to the JASON group's conclusion that bombing had not affected the will of the North to continue the war:

"I don't know of anyone who argues that the indirect punitive effects of bombing would in themselves prove decisive. It is only one element in the total political, military, economic equation involving in-country and out-of-country actions. Certainly the single most important influence on Hanoi's will to continue the war is most likely to be the course of the war in the South. Nevertheless the bombing of the North must have some effect on the war in the South and the punitive effects in the North must have some influence in measuring the course of the war in the South against costs to the North."

Clodfelter (*The Limits of Airpower*, p. 100), says that Ginsburgh's assessment "typified air commanders' perceptions of Rolling Thunder in September 1966. . . . Ginsburgh's comment indicated the depth of the air leaders' conviction that their bombing doctrine suited the nature of the war. In fact, air commanders had molded the war to suit their doctrine. Most air chiefs viewed the war as a conventional conflict in which the enemy required essential logistical support, not as an infrequently waged guerrilla struggle. Those few who perceived Vietnam as a 'people's war' thought that the North attached great value to its nascent industrial establishment, which included the transportation and POL systems. In like fashion, the air chiefs' emphasis on destroying the 'modern' elements of the Northern state obscured Johnson's negative goals and caused many commanders to dismiss the President's fears of Chinese or Soviet intervention. Air leaders thus proceeded in Vietnam much as their predecessors had in World War II—they aimed to wreck the enemy economy to produce a prostrate foe. They seldom paused to consider whether or not their perception of the war was correct, or if it conformed to that of their political leaders."

[97] *PP*, Gravel ed., vol. II, pp. 120–123.

[98] U.S. Department of State, Lot File 70 D 207, Memorandum from Cooper to Harriman, Aug. 19, 1966.

be recalled, had been sent by the State Department to South Vietnam in the fall of 1965 to study the situation. After another trip in July 1966 at the request of Unger,[99] Kissinger sent a letter to Lodge in which he made several recommendations similar to those of the Priorities Task Force. He also commented on his view of the U.S. effort in South Vietnam:[100]

> I always find it inspiring to visit Vietnam. I can imagine no more vital assignment in today's world. Vietnam has become the hinge of our national effort. If we fail there, I foresee decades of mounting crisis. If we succeed, it will mark a historic turning point in the postwar era. Just as the Cuban-Berlin confrontation may have convinced the Soviets of the futility of seeking political breakdowns by military means, so Vietnam can put an end to Chinese expansionism by the use of threat of force.

Kissinger added that "the process of prevailing will be slow. We are engaged in Vietnam in rebuilding a political structure. In Europe the transition from feudalism to the modern state took three centuries. We must not be impatient if it takes a few years in Vietnam. . . ."

With respect to pacification, Kissinger told Lodge, "Candor compels me to say that I did not find any substantial change in the provinces with the possible exception of Binh Dinh." He also questioned the validity of the system by which villages were classified as pacified, and suggested making a survey of how much taxation was being levied by the Communists. In one province, he said, which was shown on the U.S. maps as being 70 percent pacified, 80 percent of the people were being taxed by the *Communists*. (emphasis in original)

Kissinger gave a more complete report on his findings at a meeting in Washington on August 2, 1966 with Harriman, who requested the meeting.[101] According to Harriman's notes of the meeting, Kissinger "emphasized the conspiratorial atmosphere which he said prevailed throughout South Vietnam. He had never visited a country which was so self-absorbed. . . . To many Vietnamese, conspiracy had become a way of life making political stability that much harder to achieve." "He was also impressed by the amount of backbiting that went on among the Vietnamese and the value they attached to qualities like cleverness and cunning as opposed to attributes like probity and integrity which were esteemed in the Western World."

Kissinger said that despite a short-term improvement in the military situation resulting from the use of U.S. forces, he "had

---

[99] In a letter on July 1, 1966 to Philip Habib, the U.S. Mission's political officer, with a copy to Lodge, Kissinger commented: "The major use of my visit as I see it, in addition to whatever impact it may have on your operations, would be to enable me to speak with some authority in Washington on matters in which the Saigon view might perhaps be discussed as parochial. As you know, my view and that of the Embassy are very close indeed." Massachusetts Historical Society, Lodge Papers.

[100] U.S. Department of State, Lot File 85 D 240 (William Bundy Papers), Kissinger letter to Lodge, Aug. 18, 1966 attached to Kissinger memo to Bundy Aug. 19, 1966. For memoranda on conversations between Kissinger and 11 South Vietnamese political, governmental and religious leaders, see Department of State, Central File, Pol 27 Viet S, Airgram A–41, Saigon to Washington, July 29, 1966.

[101] U.S. Department of State, Central File, Pol 27 Viet S, Harriman Memorandum of Conversation with Kissinger, Aug. 2, 1966.

seen no sign that the Viet Cong's political organization and capacity for guerrilla warfare had been seriously affected by our military operations. . . . The Viet Cong still moved with relative impunity outside the main cities and towns . . . and more often than not . . . could avoid contact [with U.S. forces] when they wanted to." He was also critical of U.S. military strategy: "'The best way to exhaust ourselves is to spend our time chasing main force units near the Cambodian border.'" "Only the Marines," he added, "had learned that the war had to be won against the guerrillas and not against the main force units."

Kissinger also reported, as he had told Lodge, that pacification had made "little progress," and that, in attempting to establish effective civil government, "We tended to confuse charitable activities with political action. The rebuilding of schools and the distribution of emergency food supplies were useful and constructive actions which won friends for us among the villagers. Such activities, however, did little to break the Viet Cong stranglehold on the villages when our forces had departed."

Finally, as was mentioned earlier, Kissinger said he thought that the entire U.S. effort—military, political and economic—should be directed toward "creating a situation favorable to negotiations with the NLF–VC. . . . In practice this would mean (a) re-orienting our military strategy to put antiguerrilla operations before operations against main force units, (b) encouraging the development of a broader political base in Saigon through elections and increased civilian participation in the Government and (c) putting more effort into improvements of civil administration both in Saigon and in the provinces." [102]

---

[102] In an article in *Look* magazine, Aug. 9, 1966, Kissinger explained his views:

"The war in Vietnam is dominated by two factors: Withdrawal would be disastrous, and negotiations are inevitable. . . .

"A victory by a third-class Communist peasant state over the United States must strengthen the most bellicose factions in the internecine Communist struggles around the world. . . .

"A demonstration of American impotence in Asia cannot fail to lessen the credibility of American pledges in other fields. The stability of areas geographically far removed from Vietnam will be basically affected by the outcome there.

"In short, we are no longer fighting in Vietnam only for the Vietnamese. We are also fighting for ourselves and for international stability. . . .

"Negotiations could start only after the enemy had been crushed. But the primary issue in Vietnam is political and psychological, not military.

"What makes the war so complicated is the existence of a Communist 'shadow government,' permeating every aspect of Vietnamese life. A favorable outcome depends on the ability to create a political structure that can command the loyalties of the Vietnamese people. . . .

"Negotiations are likely when Hanoi realizes that its political apparatus in the countryside is being systematically reduced, and that this process will accelerate the longer the war lasts. It follows that the primary goal of military operations should be the creation of secure areas. . . .

"We must understand that political instability in Vietnam reflects the transformation of an essentially feudal structure into a modern state—a process that took centuries in the West. Such a process involves a profound shift of loyalties—a task that would be searing in the best of circumstances, but is compounded by the pressures of civil war. This imposes two requirements on us: (a) We must have compassion for the travail of a society that has been wracked by war for two decades and not use its agony as an alibi for failing in our duty; and (b) we must give special emphasis to building political structures from the ground up. . . ."

CHAPTER 10

NEW EMPHASIS ON A SETTLEMENT

When President Johnson decided in July of 1965 to send large-scale U.S. combat troops to South Vietnam, he said that he had to use both hands—"Bob McNamara for the military response and Dean Rusk for the diplomatic search for a settlement."[1] During the following year, the major emphasis was on the military response, and only when this proved to be inconclusive were steps taken, beginning in the summer of 1966, to organize more effectively the search for a settlement of the war.

At about that same time, the Communists appeared to have become more interested in negotiations. In part, this may have been more apparent than real—rather than an indication of interest, it may have been a tactical move to create the impression of interest. It may also have been caused in part by the internal debate among North Vietnamese strategists. Wallace J. Thies concludes that "by the summer of 1966 there was more interest in negotiations than ever before in Hanoi," and suggests that this was "almost certainly related to a rising tide of discontent over the course of the war in the South . . . at least some of the leadership apparently questioned the wisdom of attempting to stay on the offensive against as formidable an opponent as the Americans."[2]

American efforts to move toward a settlement of the war took two forms. The first, to be discussed subsequently in this chapter, was pacification and political development ("revolutionary development"), which, by strengthening the South Vietnamese Govern-

---

[1] Pt. III of this study, p. 437.

[2] Thies, *When Governments Collide*, pp. 336–337. See also Patrick J. McGarvey, *Visions of Victory: Selected Vietnamese Communist Military Writings, 1964–1968* (Stanford, Calif.: Hoover Institution on War, Revolution and Peace, Stanford Univ., 1969).

There was, in fact, some concern among American officials that the U.S. might be "caught by surprise," as General Taylor said in a memorandum to the President on July 11, 1966, by a Communist proposal for a cease-fire or a proposal to "stop bombing and start talking." Following up on his earlier "Blue Chip" memorandum, Taylor urged the President to have plans prepared for dealing with such a contingency. Johnson Library, NSF Memos to the President—Walt Rostow, Taylor Memorandum to the President, "Preparation for a 'Cessation of Hostilities' in Vietnam," July 11, 1966, attached to a memorandum from Rostow to the President, July 11, 1966.

At the State Department, where efforts to prepare for negotiations had been under way for some time, a paper was drafted in the Far East Bureau on August 10 on "Possible Sequence of Actions Toward a Settlement in Vietnam." (Johnson Library, Warnke Papers, McNaughton Files.) This was discussed in the August 11 meeting of the Negotiations Committee, a group which, as will be seen, was established in early August 1966, to provide a better focus for U.S. efforts to secure a settlement, and the "three-track" approach suggested in the sequence of actions paper became the basis for the "Phase A-Phase B" formula that was adopted several weeks later.

Concern about how the U.S. could and should respond if the Communists proposed a cease-fire also resulted in a decision to hold an interagency politico-military game, SIGMA I–66, in September 1966. Unlike the five previous such games, which dealt with military escalation, it was devoted entirely to the question of deescalation—"the problems which may be encountered if the Communist side does decide to begin talking and stop shooting." Johnson Library, NSF Agency File, JCS, *SIGMA I–66 Final Report*, Joint War Games Agency, JCS, Sept. 1966, p. A–1.

ment and its support by the public could, it was hoped, eventually cause the Communists to "fade away" or to agree to some form of settlement, possibly an internal settlement between the government and the National Liberation Front. The other was a negotiated settlement, which could involve action by the U.N. or through an international conference of some type, or by direct negotiations between the U.S. and North Vietnam.

Efforts to negotiate a settlement had begun in the spring of 1965, after the U.S. began bombing North Vietnam.[3] At that time, operational responsibility for negotiations was assigned to the Far East Bureau (FE) of the State Department. In the fall of 1965, as U.S. troops went into action, there was some concern that the U.S. might be drawn into negotiations before adequate preparations had been made, and at the instigation of Chester Cooper in the NSC staff, Leonard Unger, Deputy Assistant Secretary for the Far East, and others, an interdepartmental group called the "Planning Group" was established to work on the problem. Its first task in October 1965 was to draft a paper that could be used as the basis for the U.S. negotiating position.

The appointment in May 1966 of Averell Harriman to direct the search for a negotiated settlement, together with the energetic actions of Arthur Goldberg, U.S. Ambassador to the United Nations, gave considerable impetus to efforts to give priority to negotiations. Whereas responsibility had been lodged in the Far East Bureau, where it tended to be subordinated to other aspects of U.S. policy toward the war, and in the Planning Group, which lacked operational power and responsibility, the creation of the "Peace Shop," as Harriman's office was referred to, gave new focus, form and bureaucratic status to the enterprise.[4]

In a meeting with Chester Cooper, Harriman's newly appointed assistant who had left the NSC staff in the spring of 1966, Rusk expressed "intense interest" in the search for a negotiated settlement. Commenting on the need for "sensitive experienced people" like Harriman to be working on the problem, he said he "had the feeling that when Hanoi or the NLF was ready to talk peace we would learn about it only through some subtle sign and that we must be neither so 'blind nor deaf' that we cannot see or hear the signal."[5]

One of Harriman's first acts was to establish a "Negotiations Committee," an informal group consisting of Deputy Under Secretary U. Alexis Johnson, William Bundy, or his deputy Leonard Unger (or Bundy's special assistant Daniel I. Davidson), Assistant Secretary for International Organization Affairs Joseph Sisco, Ambassador at Large Llewellyn Thompson, Benjamin Read, Executive Secretary of the Department, Harriman's staff assistants Chester Cooper and Monteagle Stearns, and Rostow or one of his staff from the White House. The group met about once a week in Harriman's

[3] For efforts during the spring and summer of 1965, see, in pt. III of this study, the page numbers for "Negotiations" under the index heading "United States Policy and Planning." For the period between July 1965 and June 1966, *passim*.

For a Canadian initiative involving visits to Hanoi in February and June 1966 by diplomat Chester Ronning, see Herring, *The Secret Diplomacy of the Vietnam War*, pp. 159–207, Thies, *When Governments Collide*, and Kraslow and Loory, *The Secret Search for Peace in Vietnam*.

[4] Cooper, *The Lost Crusade*, p. 309.

[5] U.S. Department of State, Lot File 70 D 207, Cooper Memorandum of Conversation with Rusk, Aug. 23, 1966.

office beginning in early August 1966. According to Read, in addition to its substantive role, the committee had been "set up with part public relations in mind and had more than a casual relation with the 1966 [congressional] elections. . . ."[6]

Several proposals for negotiations had been made in May-June 1966. Ambassador Goldberg suggested a mutual cessation of hostilities leading to agreement at a new Geneva conference on withdrawal of foreign forces and international supervision. Rostow, primarily as part of a "political package" to soften the reaction to the escalation that was to occur when the U.S. bombed POL, suggested to the President a plan to convene a meeting of the U.S., South and North Vietnam, and the National Liberation Front to make arrangements for an end to bombing and to Communist infiltration which would be monitored by an international force. Leonard Meeker, the State Department's Legal Adviser, proposed that a neutral country take the initiative, along with other countries that were not parties to the war, in preparing a cease-fire and the withdrawal of forces supervised by an international force under the direction of these governments.

In late June 1966, William Sullivan, U.S. Ambassador to Laos, made a new and interesting proposal. The North Vietnamese, he said, were "hurting badly and would be interested in seeking some way out of their current predicament." But, he argued, "in the political sense, they cannot do this unless they are provided some assurances with respect to their future . . . their need to have a guarantor of their political and military continuance as a Communist state and of their economic development to a tolerable level of existence." By reducing or ending their support of the war in the South, the North Vietnamese would lose China—which supported the struggle—as their guarantor, and would turn to the U.S.S.R. How, then, could the U.S. interest the U.S.S.R. in assuming the role of "supporting North Vietnamese in a state of peaceful coexistence in Southeast Asia"? Sullivan suggested an indirect, "more oriental" approach by which the U.S. would propose membership in the U.N. of both North and South Vietnam and the use of the U.N. to settle the war.[7]

The U.S. would also propose dual U.N. membership for North and South Korea and "dual reception" in the General Assembly for Communist and Nationalist China. "In other words," Sullivan said, "I would propose wrapping all three of these into one large and rather impressive initiative which would capture public imagination and at the same time give a positive thrust to our inevitable change of policy on the question of Chinese representation."

---

[6] Johnson Library, Interview with Benjamin Read, Jan. 13, 1969.

Notes of some of the meetings of the Negotiations Committee are in the Department of State, Lot File 70 D 207. Others are in the Central File, Pol 27 Viet S or in the Harriman Papers in the Library of Congress. In the same lot file there are weekly reports on "Potential Peace Initiatives" prepared and distributed by Harriman's staff beginning in the fall of 1966.

[7] In his memorandum to the Acting Secretary of State (Ball at that time) on June 29, 1966, (U.S. Department of State Central File, Pol 27 Viet S), Sullivan explained the "by-products" of such a move: "First, it would enable the Soviets and others to recognize the accredited existence in Saigon of a government which is chosen by means acceptable to the membership of the U.N. This absolves them of their responsibility to seek only a Viet Cong dominated government. Secondly, it would address itself to the ultimate goal of unification and stipulate that goal as part of the purpose of membership. Thirdly, it would provide us with a *quid pro quo* against which we could suspend bombing operations in the North. Fourthly, it would be a revival of an old Soviet proposal and therefore presumably difficult for them to ignore."

"This device," Sullivan said, "would bring us for the first time into serious negotiations with the Soviets on the price which they will demand for some initiatives with respect to Vietnam." That price would be membership in the U.N. for East Germany, or possibly some concessions by the U.S. on aspects of the military confrontation of the U.S. and the U.S.S.R. in Europe.

On July 1, 1966, the European Bureau of the State Department (which included the U.S.S.R.) replied to Sullivan's proposal in a memorandum reminiscent of the reply of the European Bureau in 1945 to the Far East Bureau's opposition to a proposal that the U.S. should not object to or seek to block French reoccupation of Indochina.[8] Assistant Secretary of State for Europe, Walter J. Stoessel, Jr., said that Sullivan's proposal was "a non-starter and one we cannot afford, particularly at the risk of paying the price with no return whatsoever."[9] There was no need, he said, for taking such steps to get negotiations started, nor did the U.S. need to pay a price to get the U.S.S.R. to become the guarantor. "This is one of its prime objects today and . . . [it] would seize any opportunity to accomplish it with enthusiasm and alacrity. The resulting political victory for the U.S.S.R. over Communist China, and the consequent reverberations in the international Communist movement as well as within China itself would be worth ten times the price of Soviet assistance in the rehabilitation of North Vietnam."

Stoessel also emphasized the consequences for U.S. relations with Germany, which would feel betrayed by a proposal for U.N. membership for East Germany. Moreover, Stoessel said that the timing of Sullivan's proposal was unfortunate because "Suspicion is rife in Europe that U.S. interests in Asia are greater than those we have in Europe and that we might be willing to sell European security interests for a solution to our problems in the Far East."

It is not known what happened to Sullivan's proposal following this memorandum from the European Bureau, but, given the strength of that opposition, it probably received very little further consideration.[10]

Another proposal was made by Senator Mansfield, who suggested "face-to-face" talks between the U.S. and China to avoid a wider, more destructive war that could leave North and South Vietnam, other Southeast Asian nations, "and regions beyond," "a charnel house amidst smoking, silent ruins." Warning that Chinese participation in the war was likely to increase, he proposed direct contact between Washington and Peking to arrange for a peace conference between the two countries or one that would also include belligerents in the war and other countries of Southeast Asia, "since they all lie in the swath of the war's spreading destruction."[11]

Toward the end of June 1966, Janusz Lewandowski, the Polish representative on the International Control Commission, who had

---

[8] See pt. I of this study, p. 20.

[9] U.S. Department of State, Central File, Pol 27 Viet S, Memorandum to Ambassador Thompson (who was handling Sullivan's proposal for the Secretary of State) from Walter J. Stoessel, Jr., "Ambassador Sullivan's Proposal for an Asian Peace Offensive," July 1, 1966.

[10] Harriman also was critical of Sullivan's proposal. See U.S. Department of State, Lot File 70 D 207, Memorandum of Meeting of Negotiations Committee, Oct. 6, 1966 in Governor Harriman's office.

[11] *Washington Post,* June 17, 1966.

just returned to Saigon from a trip to Hanoi, informed Giovanni D'Orlandi, the Italian Ambassador to South Vietnam, that he had a "very specific peace offer" from the North Vietnamese, who, he said, were open to a "political compromise" to settle the war, and were willing to go "quite a long way" to do so.[12] D'Orlandi passed the information to Lodge, and for the next six months, as will be seen, this possibility, with the code name MARIGOLD, was the subject of intense secret diplomatic activity.

In July 1966, another possible lead developed as a result of a trip to North Vietnam by Jean Sainteny, recently a member of de Gaulle's cabinet, who had been sent by de Gaulle to explore a possible settlement. While in Hanoi, Sainteny met with President Ho Chi Minh and Premier Pham Van Dong, with whom he had established good relations while serving as a French commissioner in Vietnam after World War II. Upon his return, he reported to the U.S. Ambassador to France, Charles Bohlen, that the North Vietnamese might be willing to cease infiltration if the U.S. stopped bombing the North—a reversal of their position. The State Department was "puzzled" and asked Bohlen for clarification.[13]

Based on Sainteny's report, Bohlen said that direct talks with the North Vietnamese appeared to be the most promising way to negotiate. Rostow sent the President a copy of Bohlen's cable, saying, "I would agree that our best chance for making negotiating progress is through very secret talks with Hanoi. This was, as you may recall, Dobryinin's [U.S.S.R. Ambassador to the U.S.] final advice to me in my last talk with him."[14]

In a meeting of the Negotiations Committee on August 18 it was agreed that Henry Kissinger should meet with Sainteny, whom he knew, to seek further clarification of the North Vietnamese position as well as advice on what the U.S. should seek to communicate to the North Vietnamese.[15]

A proposal for an all-Asian peace conference also was attracting some attention in the summer of 1966. The origin of the idea is not clear, but one of its earliest proponents was Charles H. Percy, the Republican nominee for the 1966 U.S. Senate election in Illinois,

---

[12] This account is derived in part from Thies, *When Governments Collide,* pp. 138 ff. and 340 ff. For details, see *The Secret Diplomacy of the Vietnam War,* pp. 210–270. See also Kraslow and Loory, *The Secret Search for Peace in Vietnam,* Allan E. Goodman, *The Lost Peace: America's Search for a Negotiated Settlement of the Vietnam War* (Stanford, Calif.: Hoover Institution Press, 1978), and Cooper, *The Lost Crusade.* Benjamin Read, who was executive secretary of the State Department in 1966, calls the account of MARIGOLD by Kraslow and Loory "depressingly accurate." Johnson Library, Interview with Benjamin Read, Jan. 13, 1969.

[13] U.S. Department of State, Central File, Pol 27 Viet S, Washington to Paris 18844, July 30, 1966. See also follow up cables: Paris to Washington 1535, August 1, and Paris to Washington 1657, August 3, in the same location.

[14] Johnson Library, NSF Memos to the President—Walt Rostow, July 22, 1966.

[15] U.S. Department of State, Lot File 70 D 207, Notes of Meeting of the Negotiations Committee, Aug. 18, 1966. Kissinger met with Sainteny on September 9.

In early 1967, Sainteny was asked by the State Department to return to Hanoi and to seek to establish a preliminary contact between the U.S. and North Vietnamese Governments. This decision was made in a meeting of the Negotiations Committee on Dec. 21, 1966 attended by Harriman, Llewellyn Thompson, William Bundy, Unger, Sisco, William Jorden from the NSC staff, and Chester Cooper, to discuss how the U.S. "negotiating package" that had just been completed could best be communicated to the North Vietnamese. Rostow favored a direct approach, but Harriman felt strongly that this would "smack too much of an ultimatum," and that the best approach would be through an intermediary. He favored asking Sainteny to perform the task, and the other members of the committee agreed. (Same location, Notes of Meeting of the Negotiations Committee, Dec. 21, 1966.)

Cooper then went to Paris to ask Sainteny, who, after checking with de Gaulle, declined to undertake the mission. American officials interpreted this as a sign that de Gaulle wanted to "deliver a political settlement." (See Cooper, *The Lost Crusade,* pp. 348–350.

opposing the Democratic incumbent Paul Douglas. Desiring to offer a constructive alternative to the continuation of a destructive and inconclusive war, as well as an alternative to Douglas' position strongly supporting the war, Percy, with the help of his assistant, Scott Cohen, proposed on July 2, 1966 that the nations of Asia convene a conference to work out a settlement of the conflict. In a later interview, Percy, who defeated Douglas, said that his proposal called for "letting the Asians settle more of their own problems." "The more we leave it to them, the better off we will be . . . we could participate in helping stimulate it, but it should be an *Asian* peace conference to deal with *Asian* problems."[16] (emphasis in original)

The idea gained international recognition when the Foreign Minister of Thailand, Thanat Khoman, during a meeting of Thailand, Malaysia and the Philippines in Bangkok on August 2, 1966, called for an all-Asian conference to be attended by 16 nations, including China and North Korea.[17] Rusk said that the U.S. welcomed the suggestion, but the Chinese denounced it as another move in the "U.S. 'peace talks' fraud," and North Vietnam called it "'shop-worn merchandise' from President Johnson's 'clique,'" and accused the leaders of the three countries of being "subservient to the U.S. Devils.'"[18]

In the Senate, where concern about the war appeared to be increasing, the proposal of Thailand was welcomed by a number of Senators, including Mansfield, Aiken, and Cooper.[19] Conservative Republican Len Jordan of Idaho, who had supported the war, declared that the war was causing death and destruction among the very people the U.S. was endeavoring to save. "Our military efforts have been escalated, he said, but our efforts for peace have not," and more consideration should be given to finding a peaceful solution to the conflict.[20]

The idea that an all-Asian peace conference could offer an alternative to the escalation of the war appealed to leaders of the Republican Party, especially Senator Thruston Morton, chairman of the Senate Republican Campaign Committee, and Thomas Kuchel of California, the Senate Republican whip, as well as to the Republican leadership in the House of Representatives.[21]

On August 23, after a meeting with Republican Senators and at the urging of Senator Morton, Richard Nixon, former Vice President and Republican nominee for President in 1960, who was a leading contender for the Presidential election in 1968, announced his support for an all-Asian peace conference. (Former President

[16] CRS Interview with Senator Charles Percy and his administrative assistant, Scott Cohen, Jan. 31, 1979. Percy later became chairman, and Cohen, chief of staff, of the Senate Foreign Relations Committee.

[17] *New York Times,* Aug. 4, 1966.

[18] *Washington Post,* Aug. 8, 1966, and *New York Times,* Aug. 19, 1966.

[19] *CR,* vol. 112, pp. 18552–18556.

[20] *Ibid.,* p. 19188.

[21] On August 25, the Republican congressional leadership issued a position paper praising the idea of an all-Asia conference, rather than a reconvening of the Geneva Conference: "A peaceful and honorable settlement of the conflict in Vietnam cannot now be originated, formulated or influenced by non-Asia nations. Only under Asian skies, under Asian auspices, under Asian responsibility and guidance can such a move now be made with genuine hope of success." *New York Times,* Aug. 26, 1966.

Eisenhower had also announced his support.) Nixon said that both China and North Vietnam should be invited to attend.[22]

Both Nixon and the Republican congressional leadership, however, said that the war should be supported. Nixon, who said that on the basis of U.S. military commitments the war would last for at least five more years, called for increasing ground forces by 25 percent.[23] He also recommended efforts to convince European allies to cut off shipments of oil and other supplies to North Vietnam, as well as barring U.S. aid to countries trading with the enemy, but he took the position, according to the news account of his remarks, "that the bombing of Hanoi and other important targets would not end the war and could possibly widen it."[24]

President Johnson, in remarks that the *New York Times* said "were designed to blunt a Republican drive in support of an Asian meeting," said on August 24 that he would welcome such a conference.[25]

There was also a possibility that Cambodia could play a peacemaking role. The U.S. planned to send Harriman to meet with Prince Sihanouk in early September, but this was postponed on August 13 by the Cambodians after a border village was bombed by U.S. planes. (The U.S. initially said that the village was in South Vietnam, but then acknowledged that it "might be" in Cambodia.)[26] In late August 1966, French President Charles de Gaulle, who had been urging the U.S. to end the war, paid a state visit to Cambodia where, among other things, he was expected to discuss the war with Sihanouk. Although the relationship between France and the United States was anything but cordial, Secretary of State Rusk expressed hope that the visit could help to convince the Communists to negotiate. Mansfield, who was on very good terms with Sihanouk, also expressed hope that the Cambodians would play a peacemaking role and that de Gaulle and Sihanouk would conduct a "close-up review of the devastating war in Vietnam and the prospects for bringing it to a close."[27]

Mansfield noted that Sihanouk had suggested direct negotiations with the National Liberation Front rather than with the North Vietnamese and/or China.[28] As will be seen, this idea was being carefully explored at that time by U.S. officials. When Rusk was asked in a press conference on August 5 about Sihanouk's suggestion, he deliberately skirted the question, saying that the "problem of contact is not the problem"—that there was "no indication from those

[22] *Washington Post,* Aug. 26, 1966.

[23] *New York Times,* Aug. 26 and Sept. 1, 1966.

[24] *Ibid.,* Sept. 1, 1966.

[25] *Ibid.,* Aug. 25, 1966.

[26] *Ibid.,* Aug. 30, 1966. At a meeting of the Negotiations Committee on August 11, Harriman said that he was "appalled by our delay in publicly expressing regret for the loss of innocent lives in the incidents. Attempts to find technical justification for the strikes did not solve the problem. He and Ambassador [U. Alexis] Johnson agreed that the record was nothing to be proud of. . . ." Library of Congress, Harriman Papers, Vietnam General, Notes of Meeting of Negotiations Committee, Aug. 11, 1966.

[27] *CR,* vol. 112, pp. 21057–21060 and *Washington Post* and *New York Times* for Aug. 30, 1966. In a speech in Cambodia, de Gaulle said that the U.S. must withdraw its forces before negotiations could take place. A military solution, he said, was impossible, and that "while it is unbelievable that the American military display should ever be annihilated in the field, there is, conversely, no chance that the peoples of Asia will submit to the law of foreigners from over the Pacific, whatever their intentions and however powerful their army." *New York Times,* Sept. 1, 1966.

[28] *CR,* vol. 112, p. 18552.

who have the real influence on the other side that they are prepared for serious talks."[29]

Mansfield also urged President Johnson to meet with de Gaulle, after the latter's discussion with Sihanouk, to explore possible peace moves. Senators Aiken and Pell praised Mansfield's suggestion. Fulbright also commended him, but said that the executive branch was not interested in a compromise, "short of surrender." "What can they [Johnson and de Gaulle] meet about if our Government requires surrender?"[30]

If the executive branch was not in a good position to initiate negotiations, would it be possible for Congress to be of assistance? In a memorandum to Fulbright, Mansfield and Aiken on August 15, Carl Marcy, chief of staff of the Foreign Relations Committee, suggested that possibility.[31] "It seems likely," Marcy said, "that the basic Rusk-Rostow policy is for the United States to stay on the continent of Asia. . . . Rusk and Rostow are willing to pay any price to prevent Chinese hegemony from expanding . . . the United States is in Asia to contain Chinese power and its development over the next decade or two. . . . On the chance that the President is not yet fully committed to this course which involves complete victory, he personally, or the Senate, might try to give the other side a chance to talk." The Harriman mission to Cambodia, Marcy added, might have made this possible, but this had been aborted. But there was "another opportunity," namely, that the Senate, which had been invited by Sihanouk to send three Senators to Cambodia for discussions, might aid in allowing the "other side to talk." The Senate, Marcy said, might accept the invitation, and send a delegation headed by Mansfield, Fulbright or Morse, which would have at least the tacit approval of the President. "Its ostensible purpose would be to respond to the Cambodian invitation. The actual purpose, hopefully, however, would be that the presence of the mission in the area might give either the National Liberation Front, or Hanoi, or both, a chance to talk." Neither the Front nor the North Vietnamese, Marcy said, believed officials of the executive branch. "They may not trust Mansfield, Fulbright, or Morse, either—but they are more likely to talk with them with candor than with Administrative officials." "The principal purpose of this course of action," Marcy concluded," would be to get talks started. Failing that, however, the political fallout would be in Johnson's favor; the President's willingness to use such a mission would show that he was doing everything he could to bring peace to Southeast Asia and was trying to take steps that would reestablish a consensus within his own party."

Fulbright's reaction to Marcy's proposal is not known, but he seems, as he said in his exchange with Mansfield about the difficulty of talking without being willing to compromise, to have questioned whether the administration was willing to take the steps necessary to effectuate negotiations. In a meeting luncheon with Fulbright several days after Marcy's proposal, Harriman, who

---

[29] *New York Times*, Aug. 6, 1966.

[30] *Ibid.* During de Gaulle's trip, a spokesman said, in response to Mansfield's suggestion, that there were no plans for such a meeting. *Ibid.*, Sept. 1, 1966.

[31] National Archives, RG 46, Papers of the Committee on Foreign Relations, U.S. Senate, Marcy Chron File.

had been asked, either by Rusk or the President, to arrange the meeting in order to sound out the Senator, asked Fulbright for his opinion on the way to get negotiations going.[32] Fulbright, according to Harriman's report on the conversation, "rather evaded the question," but said that there were two matters preventing discussions: "First was our unwillingness to accept the NLF or VC as full-fledged participants; second, and even more important, Hanoi did not believe that the United States Government had any intention of withdrawing its forces from Vietnam or, in fact, Southeast Asia. He said he himself did not believe that we would in fact withdraw and pointed to the size of our installations in Thailand as well as Vietnam." Harriman replied that the President "had every intention of removing our troops from South Vietnam if the North Vietnamese did likewise."

Harriman, agreeing that North Vietnam doubted the sincerity of the U.S., also made the point that both North Vietnam and the U.S.S.R. "were convinced that the President would be forced by public opinion to change his policies and that we would withdraw as the French did." Fulbright replied that Congress was "more warlike than the President and would force the President to take action which would involve us with China and the Soviet Union."

Exploring the Possibility of Direct Talks Between the South Vietnamese Government and the NLF

The profusion of proposals for negotiations during the summer of 1966 signified the growing concern in the U.S. as well as in other countries that the war was being prolonged at great cost without a resolution. Yet, both the United States and South Vietnam, on the one hand, and North Vietnam supported by the U.S.S.R. and China on the other, appeared to have taken hard and fast positions that allowed little or no room for compromise.

Another and possibly more promising approach would be for the South Vietnamese Government and the Communists in the South (the "Vietcong") to work out a settlement. There were, of course, many pitfalls in this approach as well, but at that time it was regarded by many of those working on the problem as perhaps the most feasible way of ending the conflict. In a Tuesday luncheon meeting with Rusk, McNamara, Rostow and Moyers from 1:24 p.m. to 3:30 p.m. on August 2, 1966, the President directed the State Department to follow up on a report from Lodge of a conversation with Nguyen Dinh Thuan[33] about "possible contacts with the VC" and to tell Lodge to encourage the South Vietnamese Government "to begin to see what contacts can be made covertly with VC." Covert operations should be maximized, he added, and Lodge should tell Ky that "instead of sounding off about going to North [Viet-

---

[32] Library of Congress, Harriman Papers, Fulbright File, Memorandum of Conversation between Harriman and Fulbright, Aug. 24, 1966. Prior to this meeting, William Sullivan, U.S. Ambassador to Laos, who had been Harriman's assistant at the 1962 Geneva Conference, talked with Fulbright on August 10, and reported to Harriman that the discussion was "fairly unproductive," and that he did not think "the Senator wants to be confused with the facts." He said he urged Fulbright to have Harriman come up and talk to him, but that Fulbright did not react to this suggestion. The Senator's staff, he added, said they would try to get the Senator to do so. Same location, note from Chester Cooper to Harriman, Aug. 11, 1966.

[33] Nguyen Dinh Thuan had been a prominent member of the Cabinet of President Diem, and when the U.S. was preparing for a change of leadership after the expected coup against Diem it considered putting Thuan in a newly created post of Prime Minister after the coup.

nam],[34] he ought to launch peace campaign based on Honolulu [Conference of February 1966] where he said: 'Come on over.'"[35]

That same day (August 2), Harriman met with Kissinger, who had just returned from South Vietnam following discussions in his capacity as a consultant for the Far East Bureau of the State Department. Among other things, Kissinger told Harriman that he thought the entire U.S. effort—military, political and economic—should be directed toward "creating a situation favorable to negotiating with the NLF-VC." Such negotiations, he said, "offered a greater chance of success" than international negotiations or direct negotiations with the North Vietnamese.[36]

Later that day, Harriman's Negotiations Committee agreed that a message should be sent to Lodge "exploring the possibilities and problems of secret GVN talks with the NLF-VC," and telling Lodge that this should be considered a "top priority requirement."[37] (It would appear, although this is not clear, that the Committee had been informed that the President, as noted above, had directed the dispatch of such a message in the luncheon meeting earlier that day.) Committee members who were present—Harriman, U. Alexis Johnson, Llewellyn Thompson and Unger—agreed that there would be considerable resistance, both from the Government of South Vietnam and the U.S. Embassy in Saigon, to the idea of negotiating with the NLF/VC.

Two cables, drafted by Unger and approved personally by Rusk, were then sent to Lodge. The first dealt with the question of covert negotiations and the second with an overt internal political program for the Government of South Vietnam.[38] The first cable advised that several reports from Saigon had "raised intense interest here at high levels in possibility of generating GVN initiatives to foment divisions among VC/NLF, stimulate increasing scale of defections and ultimately pave way to GVN-VC/NLF talks to work out negotiated solutions to Vietnam conflict on favorable terms," and asked Lodge to take action on the matter. (A program for encouraging Communists to defect—Chieu Hoi [Open Arms]—had existed for some time, but its success had been uneven and there had

---

[34] In an interview cited in *U.S. News and World Report*, July 25, 1966, Ky was quoted as saying that he thought that if the North Vietnamese persisted in its "aggression," an invasion of North Vietnam would become necessary in order to win the war.

[35] Johnson Library, Files of Walt W. Rostow, Meetings with the President, "Notes on a telephone conversation [with Benjamin Read, Executive Secretary of the Department of State] on August 2, 1966 re Lunch meeting with President."

On July 30, William Jorden, a member of the NSC staff, had prepared a memorandum for Rostow, apparently at his request, on "The Viet Cong and Liberation Front," which argued that they should be treated as a "target of opportunity" rather than "ignored politically or destroyed militarily." Covertly, Jorden said, "we should be trying by every possible means to promote high-level defections from the VC and the Front." Overtly, Ky should make a "major appeal to the VC." Rostow sent Jorden's memorandum to William Bundy with a memorandum stating that, "It is for you, if it is helpful—not for further circulation." U.S. Department of State, Lot File 70 D 207.

[36] U.S. Department of State, Central File, Pol 27 Viet S, Memorandum of Harriman-Kissinger Conversation, Aug. 2, 1966. In a meeting of the Negotiations Committee on Aug. 18, 1966, William Bundy said that Kissinger had found Thieu and Gen. Cao Van Vien, Chief of the Joint General Staff, "negative" about the value of contacts with the Communists. Foreign Minister Tran Van Do, Bundy said, was "less rigid and had told Kissinger that contacts between GVN officials in Paris and resident Vietnamese 'neutralists' had been undertaken at Do's initiative." U.S. Department of State, Lot File 70 D 207, Notes of Meeting of Negotiations Committee, Aug. 18, 1966.

[37] U.S. Department of State, Lot File 70 D 207, Notes of Meeting of the Negotiations Committee, Aug. 2, 1966.

[38] The two cables, Washington to Saigon 21944, Aug. 4, 1966 and 23182, Aug. 5, 1966, are in the Department of State Central File, Pol 27 Viet S.

not been any high-level defectors. At the Honolulu Conference in February 1966 it was agreed that greater emphasis would be given to Chieu Hoi, and in a private meeting President Johnson urged Ky and Thieu to seek to get three or four prominent Communists to defect and to use them for propaganda purposes. He also urged them to develop better contact with the Communists "in order to gain increased understanding of the movement." Lansdale was given the assignment of seeking to secure the defection of members of the NLF, but when Lodge raised the subject with Thieu and Foreign Minister Tran Van Do, their reaction was that this was out of the question—that it would result in assassination of those seeking to defect. In late May, Lansdale reported to William Bundy that his effort to secure defections was blocked by the political turmoil that ensued after the dismissal of General Thi. "The GVN side," Lansdale said, "simply looked too shaky and unattractive to woo significant folks over to it." "There will be much better odds," he added, "for a gamble by folks on the other side once our side gets on a sound political footing."[39]

The second cable from the State Department to Lodge discussed an overt "national reconciliation" program to encourage Communists to surrender and to be given amnesty and the right to participate in politics. This, it suggested, could be launched by a national proclamation in late September or in October 1966 which, in addition to offering amnesty and participation in political life, would announce phased withdrawal of foreign forces as security was re-established, together with talks between North and South Vietnam on such matters as trade and reunification.

In his reply to the first cable from the State Department, Lodge said that the U.S. Mission was attempting to set up a test program in one province to determine whether certain incentives would induce "high level NLF-VC defections."[40] These would include "Substantial cash awards to families to enable such high-level defectors to 'reconstitute their lives'; and assurances that their status as officials will be recognized if they come over, that they will not be herded into ordinary Chieu Hoi centers or prisons, that they and their families will not be maltreated; and that they will be permitted to resume their professions if they have them, provided they maintain correct attitudes toward GVN."

With respect to the overt program of national reconciliation, which was hoped might lead to a settlement of the war, Lodge said that given the attitude of the South Vietnamese military junta that the way to end the war was to "win" it, such an approach could

---

[39] U.S. Department of State, Central File, Pol 27 Viet S, Letter to William Bundy from Edward Lansdale, May 27, 1966.

[40] Same location, Saigon to Washington 2818, Aug. 6, 1966. Lodge also reported that Lansdale had been approached by an intermediary and asked to meet with the uncle of Nguyen Huu Tho, the chairman of the NLF, who, for family reasons, was said to be anxious to induce Tho to defect. The meeting was held, and Lodge reported that word had apparently been sent to Tho. Rusk responded immediately with a "Literally Eyes Only" cable to Lodge saying that the State Department had information from "an interested Viet Cong source in Europe" that Tho might be inclined to defect, and that "A defection by some of the key Liberation Front leaders could be worth many battalions to us and could greatly stimulate Chieu Hoi among rank and file." "I'm sure you know," Rusk told Lodge, "that funds in any amount will be provided if silver bullets will help." (Same location, Washington to Saigon 23355, Aug. 7, 1966.) Lodge replied that arrangements had been made for the uncle to meet with Tho, and told Rusk he would keep Washington informed. (Johnson Library, NSF Memos to the President—Walt Rostow, Saigon to Washington 3038, Aug. 9, 1966.) In the end, the contact proved fruitless and Tho did not defect.

best be undertaken by meeting with the generals, and, through an "educational process," to induce their support.[41] The State Department replied that it agreed with Lodge's suggestion of such a dialogue.[42]

On August 18, 1966, Harriman, with the approval of members of the Negotiations Committee, sent the President and Secretary Rusk a memorandum reporting on steps being taken to effect a settlement internally: "As a result of previous considerations, and particularly Henry Kissinger's talks in Vietnam, we have begun to take several steps looking toward possible eventual reconciliation between substantial elements of the Viet Cong and the GVN."[43] "Our targets," he said, "are the noncommunist VC. There is not much hope of influencing the hard core communists who are a part of Ho Chi Minh's party apparatus."

Harriman said that action was being taken in three areas:

(1) Efforts to increase defection, including the higher echelons;

(2) Consideration of ways and means to create divisions within the NLF or VC;

(3) Development of conditions which might eventually lead to negotiations between the GVN and NLF.

In the weeks that followed, Harriman and the Negotiations Committee continued to work on the question of negotiations between the South Vietnamese and the NLF. In a memorandum on August 29 drafted for Rusk to send to the President, they proposed that the North Vietnamese again be given the U.S. reformulation of North Vietnam's "Four Points" (a statement of their negotiating position, issued in April 1965),[44] and that they be told that the U.S.

[41] U.S. Department of State, Central File, Pol 27 Viet S, Saigon to Washington 3130, Aug. 10, 1966.

[42] Same location, Washington to Saigon 27973, Aug. 15, 1966.

[43] Library of Congress, Harriman Papers, Vietnam General, Memorandum for the President and the Secretary of State, Aug. 18, 1966. For the Committee's approval of the memorandum see U.S. Department of State, Lot File 70 D 207, Notes of Meeting of the Negotiations Committee, Aug. 18, 1966.

[44] Following are the texts of the North Vietnamese Four Points and the U.S. reformulation of those points. For the citation to the Four Points, see pt. III of this study, p. 218. The text of the U.S. reformulation is from Harriman's memorandum to the President cited in the next footnote below.

North Vietnam's Four Points	U.S. Reformulation
1. Recognition of the basic national right of the Vietnamese people—peace, independence, sovereignty, unity and territorial integrity. According to the Geneva agreements, the U.S. Government must withdraw from South Vietnam U.S. troops, military personnel, and weapons of all kinds, dismantle all U.S. military bases there, and cancel its "military alliance" with South Vietnam. It must end its policy of intervention and aggression in South Vietnam. According to the Geneva agreements, the U.S. Government must stop its acts of war against North Vietnam, completely cease all encroachments on the territory and sovereignty of the Democratic Republic of Vietnam.	Point I—The basic rights of the Vietnamese people to peace, independence, sovereignty, unity and territorial integrity are recognized as set forth in the Geneva Accords of 1954. Obtaining compliance with the essential principles in the Accords is an appropriate subject for immediate, international discussions or negotiations without preconditions. Such discussions or negotiations should consider, among other things, appropriate means including agreed states, for withdrawal of military and quasi-military personnel and weapons introduced into South Vietnam or North Vietnam from one area to the other or into either area from any other outside source; the dismantling of any military bases in either area, and the cancellation of any military alliances, that may contravene the Accords; and the regrouping and redeployment of indigenous forces.

was prepared to see the role of the NLF settled by the South Vietnamese themselves, and that the U.S. would be willing to stop bombing North Vietnam and cease military reinforcements in exchange for an "undertaking" by North Vietnam to stop infiltration.[45]

On September 15, however, Thieu was quoted as saying that negotiations with the North Vietnamese "are not possible now 'because Hanoi still believes that it will be victorious.'" South Vietnam, he said, "does not advocate invading the North but whenever the situation requires, we may send forces over the 17th parallel."[46]

In a meeting of the Negotiations Committee on August 25, 1966, there was further discussion of eliciting negotiations with North Vietnam. "Harriman said that we had to realize that reunification of Vietnam was the 'sacred aim' of Ho Chi Minh and his associates. It was clear that reunification on Hanoi's terms was unacceptable to us. Nevertheless we had to think realistically about the way in which we wanted to see relations between the North and the South develop." He asked "what bait we could offer Hanoi." "The group agreed that rice, favorable trade terms, and transport were fairly attractive items from Hanoi's point of view." U. Alexis Johnson added that admission of North Vietnam to the U.N. might also be "dangled in front of Hanoi."[47]

Harriman and the Negotiations Committee also continued to pursue the question of national reconciliation.[48] A draft of a speech for Ky to make announcing the program was sent to Lodge on Septem-

---

2. Pending the peaceful reunification of Vietnam, while Vietnam is temporarily divided into two zones, the military provisions of the 1954 Geneva agreements on Vietnam must be strictly respected—the two zones must refrain from joining any military alliance with foreign countries, there must be no foreign military bases, or military personnel in their respective territory.	Point II—Strict compliance with the military provisions of the Geneva Accords must be achieved in accordance with schedules and appropriate safeguards to be agreed upon in the said discussions or negotiations.
3. The internal affairs of South Vietnam must be settled by the South Vietnamese people themselves in accordance with the program of the South Vietnam National Front for Liberation, without any foreign interference.	Point III—The internal affairs of South and North Vietnam must be settled respectively by the South and North Vietnamese people themselves in conformity with the principles of self-determination. Neither shall interfere in the affairs of the other nor shall there be any interference from any outside source.
4. The peaceful reunification of Vietnam is to be settled by the Vietnamese people in both zones, without any foreign interference.	Point IV—The issue of reunification of Vietnam must be decided peacefully, on the basis of free determination by the peoples of South and North Vietnam without outside interference.

[45] U.S. Department of State, Lot File 70 D 207, Memorandum from Harriman for the Secretary, with attached draft memorandum for the President, "Establishing a Dialogue with Hanoi," Aug. 29, 1966. The memorandum for the President was based on a longer memorandum from Chester Cooper to Harriman, "A look at some key issues for possible use in establishing a dialogue with Hanoi," Aug. 26, 1966, same location.

[46] The Defense Department's public edition of the *Pentagon Papers* (Washington, D.C.: U.S. Govt. Print. Off., 1971) (hereafter cited as *PP*, DOD ed.), Book 12, VI. A., p. 32.

[47] U.S. Department of State, Lot File 70 D 207, Notes of Meeting of the Negotiations Committee, Aug. 25, 1966.

[48] See Cooper's Memorandum to Harriman," "The NLF and Where We Go from Here," Aug. 31, 1966, in the Department of State, Lot File 70 D 207, and the Negotiations Committee discussion of the memorandum in its meeting on September 15, notes of which are in the same location.

ber 22 with the suggestion that the proclamation be issued on November 1, 1966.[49]

In early October, Lodge held a long meeting with Ky, Thieu and Foreign Minister Tran Van Do to discuss national reconciliation and a peace settlement.[50] Lodge, who was concerned that if there were a cease-fire and withdrawal of U.S. and North Vietnamese forces without adequate provisions for preventing continued activity by the "200,000 Vietcong terrorists . . . [that] could not be coped with by the GVN alone in its beginning steps,"[51] was asked by Ky and Tran Van Do whether the U.S. would keep its forces in South Vietnam as a guarantee of the further security of the country. He replied (based on advice from Washington) that he was "authorized to state that the US will not withdraw our troops before security is assured or GVN is able to cope with terrorism, or while the VC infrastructure is intact; SVN would not be left without protection."[52] Tran Van Do asked about a possible multilateral commitment from the seven nation conference that was to be held in Manila at the end of the month. He said that the basis of the U.S. commitment was not clear. Lodge, saying that he would report this suggestion to Washington added that, as for the U.S. commitment, in addition to the SEATO treaty authority there was the Gulf of Tonkin Resolution, which was "a legal commitment as far as the U.S. alone was concerned."

Tran Van Do asked how, in practice, infiltration could be halted. Thieu and Ky said that this could be controlled by a system of border outposts, and Ky said that he preferred a multilateral guarantee together with border outposts. Although Ky insisted that the South Vietnamese "cannot sit down with the VC" in a conference, he thought that if there were adequate border control against infiltration from the North, "a secret agreement with the VC" would be the best option for ending the war.

Ky said that he preferred a "fade-away" solution with gradual cessation of hostilities by both sides, but he did not think the U.S. "would have time to accept a 'fade-away' solution. . . . He feared that prolonged war of this nature would find U.S. public opinion unprepared for the continued employment of U.S. troops in what would be a purely guerrilla-type, terroristic war even though casualties would be light."

The question of an amnesty as part of a program of national reconciliation was discussed, and Ky said he thought the timing of a proclamation on November 1 was premature and could adversely affect the morale of South Vietnamese troops "who would see their enemies being accepted back before they were defeated." Thieu, however, said he was planning a speech on November 1 which would contain a plea for national reconciliation.

---

[49] For the text of the proposed speech see, in the Department of State Central File, Pol 27 Viet S, Washington to Saigon 52727, Sept. 22, 1966. For related documents see Washington to Saigon 49407, September 17, and 52726, September 22. See also the discussion of the speech in the notes of the meeting of the Negotiations Committee on Sept. 23, 1966, Department of State, Lot File 70 D 207, and in the same location, the six-page memorandum, "Program of National Reconciliation," Sept. 29, 1966, probably drafted by Cooper.

[50] For Lodge's report on the meeting see his four-part cable in the Department of State Central File, Pol 27 Viet S, Saigon to Washington 7630, Oct. 4, 1966. For Lodge's earlier cable outlining and commenting on the agenda he intended to follow, see Saigon to Washington 7243, Sept. 29, 1966, same location.

[51] Saigon to Washington 7243, cited in preceding footnote.

[52] Saigon to Washington 7630, cited in second preceding footnote.

The aftermath of this effort by the United States to get the South Vietnamese Government to launch a program of national reconciliation with the hope that it would lead ultimately to an internal settlement of the war, was that although in the seven-nation meeting in Manila the Government of South Vietnam announced that it was preparing a national reconciliation program (and "declared its determination to open all doors to those Vietnamese who have been misled or coerced into casting their lot with the Viet Cong")[53] the statement scheduled for November 1 was postponed until December, and only on April 18, 1967 was a National Reconciliation Proclamation, considered by the Americans to be very inadequate, finally issued.[54]

It was obvious, as the discussion in the Negotiations Committee on November 10, 1966 emphasized, that there were differences in perspective between U.S. officials and the South Vietnamese military leaders about the content of "national reconciliation." The subject came up in connection with a comment by Harriman that he was "disturbed by indications that the new Vietnamese constitution [then being drafted by the Constituent Assembly elected in September 1966] would have a clause excluding 'Communists and neutralists.'" Harriman said that it was important for the constitution not to be inconsistent with the principle of national reconciliation. William Bundy's special assistant, Daniel Davidson, commented that even if the U.S. could get the South Vietnamese to launch a program of national reconciliation, it would be difficult to keep the provision on "neutralists and communists" out of the constitution. "We should realize," he said, "that when Ky and Thieu spoke of national reconciliation they were thinking in terms of defection from the NLF/VC [and] not of the NLF/VC itself playing a political role in South Vietnam."[55]

U.S. Diplomatic Moves, Fall 1966

Beginning in late September 1966, the Johnson administration, motivated in part by the need to counter criticism of the U.S. role in Vietnam and to offset the effects of increasing military activities, increased its efforts to seek a negotiated end to the war and to pacify public opinion. On September 22, Ambassador Goldberg made a major speech at the opening meeting of the U.N. General Assembly in which he explicitly accepted two of the three major conditions for peace talks that had been suggested by U.N. Secretary

---

[53] Manila Summit Conference Joint Communiqué, Oct. 25, 1966, in *Public Papers of the Presidents,* Lyndon B. Johnson, 1966, p. 1263.

[54] Saigon to Washington 23376, Apr. 18, 1967, cited in *PP,* Gravel ed., vol. II, p. 302. For the text of a concept paper on national reconciliation drafted by the U.S. Embassy in Saigon for use by the South Vietnamese Government, see in the Department of State Central File, Pol 27 Viet S, Saigon to Washington 11958, Nov. 29, 1966. For another paper prepared in the Embassy on "basic themes" for use by the South Vietnamese Government in the national reconciliation proclamation see, in the same location, Saigon to Washington 13123, Dec. 11, 1966. The "appeal to the Viet Cong to join in building the nation" would promise that they would be "welcomed as brothers," that each one "will have the chance, if he wishes, to serve the government and the nation in accordance with his talents and experience," or would be helped to find private employment, and that "Ralliers will enjoy full civil rights, including the right to engage in politics and to present themselves as candidates for elected office, on the sole condition that they renounce the use of arms against the nation."

[55] U.S. Department of State, Central File, Pol 27 Viet S, Notes of a Meeting of the Negotiations Committee, Nov. 10, 1966.

General U Thant[56]—cessation of bombing of North Vietnam and mutual reduction of military activity—and implied that the U.S. was also ready to accept a controversial third condition, the inclusion of the National Liberation Front in negotiations.[57] He also proposed that the U.S. would stop bombing North Vietnam "the moment we are assured privately or otherwise that this step will be answered promptly by a corresponding and appropriate de-escalation of the other side." Prior to that time, the U.S. had insisted that there should be an immediate and demonstrable reduction of infiltration of North Vietnamese men and matériel in return for a bombing halt.

This new proposal, the "Phase A-Phase B formula," became the cornerstone of the U.S. negotiating position in Operation MARIGOLD. In Phase A, U.S. bombing would cease after private North Vietnamese assurances that they would reciprocate. Because this would appear to be done by the U.S. unilaterally and unconditionally, the North Vietnamese could claim that the U.S. had acceded to their demand for an unconditional end to the bombing. In Phase B, which would follow in a week or two, and thus appear not to be associated with Phase A, both sides would deescalate, thereby meeting U.S. demands for mutual deescalation while also serving the presumed needs of the North Vietnamese for avoiding any connection between the stopping of bombing and subsequent deescalation.[58]

Goldberg's speech, denounced by the U.S.S.R., China and North Vietnam, was widely praised by American commentators, with Senators Mansfield and Fulbright, among others, expressing their support.[59] Senator Morse, however, said that the speech "represents sophistry and a concealment of the true motives of the U.S. Government." There was, he added, "no reason to believe that this administration intends to negotiate a peace in South Vietnam except upon the terms of this administration." He predicted further escalation of the war by the United States, and said, "Plans for doubling the American force of 300,000 are widely leaked in Washington."[60]

Senator Javits said that while the administration's peace initiative in the United Nations may have been a positive move, it was important to recognize that the U.N. "cannot be counted upon to deal with 'wars of national liberation,'" and that in order to extract from the Communists a reasonable agreement ending the war, the first step was "convincing them beyond doubt that we intend to

---

[56] U Thant had continued to press for a peace settlement, and in August 1966 he reported to the U.S. that he had a "recent contact with Hanoi's Ambassador in Moscow" that he thought was "an important new development," and that he was going to make further inquiries as to the interest of the North Vietnamese. After a meeting with Goldberg on August 17, the Negotiations Committee agreed on a proposal drafted by Cooper that U Thant could use in communicating with the North Vietnamese as well as through other channels, including contacts with Polish representatives by Lodge and by U.S. Ambassador John Gronowski in Warsaw. A memorandum for the President was then sent to Rusk by Harriman on August 29 on "Establishing a Dialogue with Hanoi." Its recommendations were approved by the President and U Thant was so informed and passed on the information to the North Vietnamese. They did not respond. Cooper, *The Lost Crusade*, p. 331.

[57] Goldberg's speech was reprinted in the *Department of State Bulletin*, Oct. 10, 1966. For background on the preparation of the speech see Cooper, *The Lost Crusade*, pp. 330–332. It will be recalled that Goldberg had been advocating U.S. acceptance of the inclusion of the NLF.

[58] On these developments, see Cooper, *The Lost Crusade*, pp. 332–334.

[59] *New York Times*, Sept. 23, 24, 1966.

[60] *CR*, vol. 112, p. 23851.

stay in Vietnam as long as necessary to back up our commitment and that the South Vietnamese Government can be legitimized and can make a go of it."[61]

In the weeks following Goldberg's speech, there was a flurry of activity as the U.S. sought to highlight the peace issue. On October 7, President Johnson talked with U Thant and "affirmed strongly to the SYG [Secretary General] that the U.S. would not be a barrier to efforts to achieve a peaceful settlement of the Vietnam problem."[62]

On November 10, 1966, Senator Mansfield proposed that all interested parties, including the North Vietnamese, the NLF and the Chinese, be invited by the U.N. Security Council to a meeting to discuss the war.[63] At President Johnson's request, Goldberg invited Mansfield to come to New York, where the two of them met privately with U Thant. Under Secretary of State Katzenbach was also present. According to Goldberg's report on the meeting, U Thant "very forthrightly said in his considered judgment no purpose would be served by having formal Security Council consideration of Vietnam conflict. He expressed vigorously his view to Mansfield that Security Council confrontation at this time would be highly undesirable and could only lead to increased tensions between Soviet Union and U.S. He further stated in his view only hope for peace in Vietnam would be through private diplomatic channels not excluding his own. He believed his channel was open as a result of his discussions in Moscow last summer with North Vietnamese ambassador."[64]

A memorandum on the meeting from Mansfield to the President also noted that, according to U Thant, "China is real key and cannot be contacted; it will continue to encourage Hanoi and thereby increase its dependance on China."[65]

Greater Priority for Pacification and Political Development

By August of 1966, as it became increasingly apparent that the bombing of POL had not significantly affected the war in the South, there was an even more perceptible shift against further military escalation on the part of McNamara and his associates. This was reflected in a cable to Westmoreland on August 3 from Chief of Staff of Pacific Command Lt. Gen. Paul S. Emrick at CINCPAC headquarters in Hawaii, in which Emrick warned that there was growing resistance in Washington to approving the increased troops for 1967 that had been requested by Westmoreland and CINCPAC—90 maneuver battalions, which would raise the level of U.S. forces to 542,588 by the end of 1967.[66] The CINCPAC/Westmoreland request was based on a new concept for Vietnam. "The four basic objectives remained as they had been set forth in CINCPAC's February concept. A new item in the June concept was that . . . conduct [of] sustained and coordinated operations with in-

---

[61] *Ibid.*, p. 24303.

[62] U.S. Department of State, Lot File 70 D 207, Memorandum to the Executive Secretary (Read) from Assistant Secretary Sisco, on Goldberg's report of the conversation to Sisco.

[63] *New York Times*, Nov. 11, 1966.

[64] U.S. Department of State, Lot File 70 D 48, USUN New York to Washington 2499, Nov. 20, 1966.

[65] There is a copy of the memorandum in the Johnson Library, NSF Files of Mike Mansfield.

[66] On June 18, 1966, CINCPAC had sent the request for 1967 to the JCS. *PP*, Gravel ed., vol. IV, p. 324.

creased effort in the Highlands and along the western border. This was in line with the generally increased emphasis given in the concept to restricting NVA/VC forces' access to the coastal and land borders through effective land, sea, and air interdiction operations."[67] The JCS, Emrick told Westmoreland, "are loathe to recommend approval of these requirements without additional rationale as to where we are now, why we will be needing additional forces, and what results can be achieved if and when additional forces are provided."[68] (On August 5, the JCS sent the CINCPAC/Westmoreland request to McNamara without making any specific recommendations.[69] McNamara replied that same day, saying, "I desire and expect a line by line analysis of these requirements to determine that each is truly essential to the carrying out of our war plan.")[70]

On August 7, Westmoreland cabled CINCPAC that he could not at that time justify a reduction in the force requirements for 1967. "The enemy," he said, "intends to continue a protracted war of attrition," and there could be increased infiltration from the North and an escalation of the war. If the North Vietnamese did not decide to escalate the war, the force request could be modified. To prepare for this possibility, he said, the MACV staff was studying various options, including that of a "balanced force that is designed to fight a long war of attrition and sustainable without national mobilization."[71]

While defending his request, Westmoreland was also taking steps to accommodate the pressure for greater emphasis on pacification. In a meeting of the U.S. Mission Council in Saigon on August 8, General Tillson, as noted earlier, gave a briefing on the PROVN Report in which he emphasized support for pacification and the need for South Vietnamese forces to be used primarily for that purpose, while U.S. forces, through operations against Communist main force units, provided the security "screen" behind which pacification could occur.[72]

On August 24, Westmoreland sought to clarify his position and strengthen his request for new forces with a message, "Concept of Military Operations in South Vietnam," in which he reviewed the military situation and explained his strategy for the coming year.[73]

---

[67] *Ibid.*, pp. 324–325.

[68] CMH, Westmoreland Papers, Message Files, Emrick to Westmoreland, 032207Z Aug. 1966.

[69] "JCS Policy Statements Concerning Operations in Southeast Asia," cited above, JCSM–506–66, Aug. 5, 1966.

[70] For the text of McNamara's reply see *PP*, Gravel ed., vol. IV, p. 326.

[71] CMH Westmoreland Papers, Message Files, Westmoreland to Sharp, MAC 6814, Aug. 7, 1966.

[72] In a cable to Washington on August 13, Lodge cited Sir Robert Thompson's statement that the North Vietnamese would desist only if the Communists were defeated in South Vietnam, and that U.S. strategy should be "to commit minimum forces against purely military forces enough to keep the Viet Cong off balance," while using remaining U.S. forces to provide "the punch and protection without which pacification, still left almost entirely in Vietnamese hands, would not gather momentum." (Saigon to Washington 4923, Aug. 13, 1966, as described by Lodge in his unpublished "Vietnam Memoirs," Pt. 4, I–13 Lodge Papers, Massachusetts Historical Society.)

In a cable to the President on August 31 (Saigon to Washington 4923, cited above) Lodge, referring again to Thompson's article, said that "We also have learnt, to use Thompson's words, that to lift helicopters into a jungle valley and win a battle, is certainly not the initiative required in counterinsurgency. American and South Vietnamese forces will not gain this [initiative] until they start to recover, by 'clear and hold' operations, the developed and populated areas of the countryside which are the 'popular bases' of the Viet Cong."

[73] Johnson Library, NSF Memos to the President—Walt Rostow, Westmoreland to Sharp, MACV 29797, Aug. 24, 1966.

During the period May 1-November 1, 1966, he said, MACV strategy had been to "contain the enemy through offensive tactical operations (referred to as 'spoiling attacks' because they catch the enemy in the preparation phases of his own offensives, force him to fight under conditions of our choosing, and deny him attainment of his own tactical objectives.)" "The threat of enemy main forces has been of such magnitude," however, "that fewer friendly troops could be devoted to general area security and support of revolutionary development than visualized at the time our plans were prepared for the period."

During the period beginning November 1, 1966, Westmoreland said, "Our strategy will be one of a general offensive with maximum practical support to area and population security in further support of revolutionary development." "The growing strength of US/Free World forces will provide the shield that will permit ARVN to shift its weight of effort to an extent not heretofore feasible to direct support of revolutionary development." In addition, he said that a "significant number" of "US/Free World" combat battalions would be committed to base security which would also have the effect of "spreading security radially from the bases to protect more of the population."

Rostow sent Westmoreland's cable on strategy to the President with a cover note stating: "It underlines the need to mount a maximum political campaign, overt and covert, designed to defect VC[74] and start Saigon VC negotiations as soon after the September 11 [South Vietnamese] election as possible." "That," he added, "is the political track required to match Westmoreland's military plan which is clearly in the right direction. . . ."[75] The President sent the memorandum back to Rostow with this handwritten note: "Let's get Komer to pick up and spark the inspirations."[76]

In a memorandum to the President on August 30, Maxwell Taylor said that Westmoreland's proposed strategy could advance pacification and speed up the end of the war, but he cautioned that it would increase the proportion of U.S. casualties as compared to those of South Vietnam, and that "Such a rise will reinforce the charges at home and abroad the U.S. has taken over the war and is accepting a disproportionate share of the losses."[77]

Taylor also noted that in Westmoreland's proposal "there are indications of emphasis which could carry very important implications for the future with respect to the size and the manner of employment of our ground forces in South Vietnam." "It is full of important implications and deserves close study and a considered reply." "It should not be accepted without a reply as this would convey tacit approval and would justify Westmoreland to feel that his concept had official approval."

Acceptance of Westmoreland's concept, Taylor warned, "would seem to create an open-ended requirement for U.S. forces. If our goal is to reestablish GVN authority over the entire territory, open and keep open the road and rail communications, and make good

---

[74] This is a reference to the effort to get South Vietnamese Communists to defect.

[75] Johnson Library, NSF Memos to the President—Walt Rostow, Memorandum from Rostow to the President, Aug. 29, 1966.

[76] Johnson Library, NSF Country File, Vietnam.

[77] Same location, Memorandum from Taylor to the President, Aug. 30, 1966.

the manpower deficiencies in the revolutionary development program, General Westmoreland will be justified in asking for almost any figure in terms of future reinforcements."

That same day (August 30), Rostow sent Taylor's memorandum to the President. Calling it a "thoughtful response," he agreed that there should be a careful analysis of Westmoreland's concept before it was approved. The dangers that Taylor foresaw, Rostow said, could be met by having the elite South Vietnamese units participate fully in U.S. ground combat operations, while "getting the ARVN [Army of the Republic of Vietnam] engaged effectively in pacification, which will require changes in attitude as well as in Vietnamese force missions."[78] In a handwritten note on Rostow's memorandum, the President replied that Rostow should talk to McNamara and should then request Defense, State and Komer to prepare an analysis of Westmoreland's concept and recommendations.

The next day Rostow reported to the President that he had talked to McNamara, who thought that rather than conducting a review in Washington of Westmoreland's message, a plan should be developed for reorganizing U.S. pacification resources in South Vietnam—a task he hoped to begin during a trip he would be making to Vietnam in October. Rostow said he agreed, and asked the President if the matter should be discussed at a Tuesday Lunch. The President approved, and told Rostow that Taylor should be present, and that meanwhile a message should be sent to Westmoreland ". . . so that he will not *assume* that we have approved." (emphasis in original)[79]

It is not known what the President's reaction was to Taylor's observation about the dilemma facing the U.S.—how to "win" the war when it was clear that this might require more men and resources than the American public could be expected to accept, and there is no record of a Tuesday Lunch discussion or of any other consideration of Taylor's memorandum.

In a cable to the President on August 31, Lodge declared that "The biggest recent American event affecting Vietnam was giving pacification the highest priority which it has ever had—making it, in effect, the main purpose of all our activities." This came about, he added, in several ways, one of which was Westmoreland's acceptance of the need for using both ARVN and U.S. forces to provide better security for pacification.[80]

---

[78] Same location, Rostow Memorandum to the President, Aug. 30, 1966.

[79] Johnson Library, Files of Walt W. Rostow, Memorandum from Rostow to the President, Aug. 31, 1966, with handwritten note from the President to Rostow.

[80] Saigon to Washington 4923, Aug. 31, 1966, cited above. Lodge also cited the cooperation of the U.S. Army and the ARVN, one example of which he described in a cable to the President on Aug. 24, 1966 (U.S. Department of State, Central File, Pol 27 Viet S, Saigon to Washington 4323):

"I visited the scene of a pacification operation taking place at a hamlet called Hoa Loi [in Binh Duong Province, just north of Saigon] with a population of some 2,500 people. US and ARVN troops had moved into position swiftly and without warning at 6:00 PM the previous evening and had completely surrounded the hamlet, using tanks—in effect sealing it off so that no one could enter or leave. All of the inhabitants were then moved out of their dwellings and into open fields where they were grouped under the shelter of a number of large tents. The atmosphere was festive. Both division bands were playing; a Vietnamese information service unit was showing movies; U.S. doctors of the 1st Division along with Vietnamese medical assistants were holding sick call for the villagers; a large field mess had been set up and big meals were being prepared for all the people. They were obviously enjoying everything that was being done for them.

In another report to the President in mid-August, Lodge said that he was optimistic about the situation: "The economic picture has brightened. . . . The number of civilian South Vietnamese officials killed or kidnapped by the Communists in July was the lowest in 18 months. . . . There is growing popular interest in the forthcoming election."[81]

"All adult members of the hamlet were being documented and given temporary identification cards. Most important, each individual (with the exception of very small children) was being 'interviewed' by intelligence representatives in order to elicit information on Viet Cong in the hamlet. I was glad to note that each villager was being interviewed alone—so that none of his neighbors knew what he was saying. While all of this was going on, ARVN search teams were carefully combing through the hamlet looking for Viet Cong hiding in holes in the ground, in hay stacks and wood-piles and for Viet cong weapons and supplies. The search was being aided by information produced by the so-called interviews of the hamlet residents. Everything involving fighting and contact with the Viet Cong was done by the ARVN. The Americans did the nice human things—the good hot lunch; the toothache cure; ointment for the baby's itch.

"Since each individual was not only questioned separately, but also for equal lengths of time, it would be subsequently impossible for the Viet Cong to learn who had given information and thus against whom to make reprisals. Earlier in the morning some 160 Vietnamese males, ranging in years from 15 to 45, had been segregated from the hamlet population and taken by helicopter to a nearby national police center for more thorough interrogation and identity checks. Forty of these personnel had no documentation to prove their identities. Some obviously were Viet Cong. This operation designed to ferret out the Viet Cong guerrillas and their infrastructure, was to take place throughout the day and at dark the ARVN and US forces would be removed as quickly and unexpectedly as they came. This particular village is simply too deep in Viet Cong territory for our forces to remain indefinitely to protect it, and we do not have enough forces to parcel out in this fashion.

"This operation, thus, did the following things:

"A. sealed off the village;

"B. combed out the Viet Cong;

"C. protected the villagers from murder, kidnapping and torture;

"D. and then fed, doctored, and amused them.

"Some of the results of this operation are:

"A. Valuable information was obtained about the Viet Cong.

"B. The removal of Viet Cong presence, if only temporarily, from the village demonstrated to the villagers and to the neighboring communities that the GVN and the US are able to go in and pull out the Viet Cong. Until now the people in this area had every right to think the Viet Cong was supreme and impregnable.

"C. This comb-out meant that when the GVN does come back, they will find friendly people who understand.

"D. It gives hope for the future—since it undoubtedly means that the men with gumption in the village will feel it worthwhile at least to make plans to resist—if indeed they do not do some actual resisting now that there has been tangible and dramatic proof that the GVN and the Americans are really not so far away.

"E. This was truly a precinct operation in the sense that at the end of the comb-out, every single human being was accounted for in one way or another. This looks to me like a solid way to go at it—particularly in a country which has suffered from sweeping programs which overlooked the vital factor of individual human psychology and treated people as a massive and faceless proletariat.

"F. It showed them and their neighbors a concrete example of the concept of government being nice to the people. The central government is traditionally looked upon as arbitrary, corrupt, and totally self-centered. There is a Vietnamese proverb that there are five evils that afflict mankind: fire, flood, famine, robbery, and central government. Now these villages have seen the government doing something nice for them and the ARVN have seen what it can mean to the ARVN to be nice to the people—if only in terms of getting information about the Viet Cong."

For a critique of the kind of operation described by Lodge, see Bergerud, *The Dynamics of Defeat*, pp. 152–153, 162.

Contrasted to Lodge's report was a report from Rufus Phillips, a member of Lansdale's team, that was sent to Lodge by Lansdale: "Last Thursday, 18 August, at 7:15 in the morning in broad daylight a reinforced VC company practically annihilated the Popular Forces and Combat Youth of An Phu ("Peace and Prosperity") Village, only three miles from the edge of Saigon—Cholon [a suburb of Saigon]. . . . Today, I visited An Phu with some Vietnamese friends. My conclusion is, that in this area so close to Saigon and in the middle of Hop Tac [the area designated by the U.S. as the first priority for pacification], we are losing the struggle that really counts—the political war for the people." U.S. Department of State, Lot File 70 D 207, Memorandum from Lansdale to Lodge, Aug. 23, 1966 enclosing memorandum to Lansdale from Phillips, Aug. 21, 1966.

[81] Johnson Library, NSF Memos to the President, Saigon to Washington 3129, Aug. 10, 1966.

Lodge concluded his August 10 report on yet another note of optimism. Chester Bowles, a prominent liberal Democratic politician and former Member of the House of Representatives, who, as Under Secretary of State under Kennedy and then Ambassador to India under President Kennedy and Johnson had been strongly opposed to U.S. military intervention in Vietnam,

Continued

Lodge described what he called "The Smell of Victory":

We are not losing; we cannot lose in the normal sense of the word; never have things been going so well. We are "on the track" with regard to almost every aspect of the war and we are winning in several.

All of this is a great tribute to the excellence of your policies and to the courage with which you have made your decisions. It is also a tribute to those who execute the policies, notably our magnificent military men.

But all of this is still not called "victory." Indeed, however much they disagree about many things, everyone—in Washington and Hanoi and in Saigon—seems to agree that what we have now is not "victory."

In truth, we do not need to define "victory" and then go ahead and achieve it 100 percent. If it becomes generally believed that we are sure to win (just as it is generally believed that we cannot lose) all else will be a mopping up. If there is the "smell of victory," we will be coasting.

What could be done to evoke a sense of victory?

There are a number of things which would psychologically mean "victory" to us, to Hanoi, to Saigon and to the world, as follows:

(A) First on the list would be some really smashing results as regards the "criminal" war: terrorism, subversion, village guerrilla. Figures indicate a diminution in assassinations of local officials, but we have as yet no good figures on the trend as regards civilian casualties in general.

(B) Important defections could mean a great deal.

(C) A successful advance towards constitutional democracy could bring a feeling of success.

(D) Really spectacular numbers of people coming into the Chieu Hoi [defector] camps would look like the end of the war.

(E) Of great significance psychologically would be a situation in which one could start at Camau and drive securely all the way to Quang Tri, since this would mean that the 50 percent of the population which is in Saigon and the Delta and the 35 percent of the population in the coastal strip from Hue to Qui Nhon had been effectively pacified. To be able to ride the whole length of the railroad would also mean much. (Several months ago I sent you a population map which illustrates this.)

(F) Other things which would have great meaning would be to be able to drive securely to Dalat or to Vung Tau.

Clearly, the type of "battle victories" which we have been winning, and the impressive 10 to 1 casualties we are inflicting, do not look like victory to many Vietnamese as much as

---

was visiting in Vietnam, and Lodge said that Bowles was "impressed with our entire operation." "Bowles believes this struggle is of both historical and world-wide importance and is the kind of thing that happens once in 100 years. If, he says, we succeed (and he is confident that we will) it will be the beginning of the end for world Communism. . . . He believes also that victory here will change America, in that so many young Americans have seen at first hand the importance of economic and social development, going hand in hand with security against violence." For Bowles' views during the 1961–64 period, see pt. II of this study.

> does the phenomenon of open roads. Driving the Viet Cong out of a certain place on the map seems to mean little in and of itself. In that sense this looks more like naval war in which one particular point in the ocean is much like another. The solid thing is the people and 85 percent of the people live in the area through which a traveller driving from Camau to Quang Tri would pass.

None of these things, Lodge said, was "just around the corner . . . it is obvious that we have quite a stretch of time ahead of us." "How much time?" he asked. And, because "time is not necessarily on the side of the U.S. or the Vietnamese," could the war be won more quickly, and, if so, how? His answer was as American as apple pie:

> In a war like this, in spite of everything, there is something tremendously effective about sheer mass. On the fifth floor of this building, I can see the port of Saigon, thick with shipping and in the green flat fields through which the Saigon River winds, I see more ships constantly making the sixty-mile trip to and from the open sea. When I flew over Vung Tau last week, I counted eighteen ships anchored there. There are undoubtedly more in the Philippines and elsewhere. This is American mass, which none can produce as we can.
>
> While I do not believe we can bring anything more into the city of Saigon (in fact, I think the American presence in this city must be reduced), I submit that if ports, piers and warehouses throughout Vietnam are ready and the military leaders can manage, and it can be done without political damage—three big "if's"—there is a strong case for "more" coming in "quicker."
>
> Such are the agonizing questions of history, since we never know what would have happened had the course which was not followed been followed. But common sense suggests that the more we bring in and the quicker we do it, the sooner there will be the "smell of victory," the sooner will the war be over and the fewer will be the casualties. Is this worth what it will cost in further dislocating the lives of Americans? Could they be made to understand that something is being asked of them now so as to avoid much great sufferings later?

Besides bringing in "more," and bringing it in faster, the U.S., Lodge reported, was preparing to take over responsibility for all major combat operations against the Communists. Westmoreland, he said, was completing a plan under which U.S. forces would conduct all search and destroy missions against Communist forces except for limited operations by some elite South Vietnamese Army units against Communist forces, leaving the South Vietnamese Army to support pacification by providing local security against guerrillas. This change in the role of the U.S. and South Vietnamese armies, Lodge added, would probably result in greater U.S. casualties.

At a briefing of the President's Cabinet on August 25 on the situation in Vietnam, McNamara used a chart which indicated that the strength of southern Communists was levelling off. Komer, who attended the briefing, sent McNamara a memorandum on September

2 in which he said that the chart, together with the conclusions of several recent CIA studies and reports, suggested that "the southern VC are becoming the 'weak sisters' in the enemy lineup, and thus perhaps especially vulnerable to stepped up efforts against them. . . . If VC infrastructure and local forces turn out to be weaker and more vulnerable than we currently think, pacification may not prove as slow and painful a task as many predict. There would also be a stronger case for stepping up several programs mounted from the civil side (e.g., Chieu Hoi, Refugees Resource Control/Economic Warfare, Police, RD Cadre) which, in conjunction with increased military efforts to provide local security might show substantial early results."[82]

Election of the Constituent Assembly—September 1966

On September 11, 1966, the election of a Constituent Assembly to draft a constitution was held in South Vietnam—the first major step toward re-establishing an elected government.

U.S. efforts to "develop" politics and government in South Vietnam, based on the implicit and explicit application of American concepts and values, had long been a primary goal of American policy.[83] A cornerstone of Eisenhower's Vietnam policy was what was then called the "essential premise"—that effective self-government was a prerequisite for U.S. assistance. Under Ngo Dinh Diem, who had been chosen in 1955 as Premier by the Americans and confirmed by a national plebiscite, there had been an elected Parliament, albeit with very limited powers. After Diem's assassination in 1963, the country had been ruled by a military junta which showed very little interest in moving toward a more democratic system.

In August 1965, at the time of the announcement of the decision to use U.S. forces to defend South Vietnam, there was considerable discussion of the need to develop the political life and institutions of South Vietnam. According to a paper prepared by Rostow's office in the State Department, unless there could be "some effective political expression of South Vietnamese anti-colonial nationalism," military and diplomatic successes could come to naught. Lodge was chosen as the new Ambassador in part because of his view of the central importance of political development.

As U.S. military operations gathered momentum during 1965–1966, there was continuing concern among the Americans as well as among many Vietnamese about the need for achieving more effective self-government. On January 1966, Premier Ky announced that a "Democracy Building Council" would be established to draft a new constitution preparatory to elections in 1967. At the Honolulu Conference in February 1966, Ky and Thieu repeated that promise, and a statement to that effect was incorporated in the Declaration of Honolulu. Final plans for the election of a Constituent Assembly, as it was called, were not announced, however, until, after pressure from the Buddhists as well as the Americans, the junta declared in May that the election would be held on September 11, 1966.

---

[82] Johnson Library, Warnke Papers, McNaughton Files.
[83] See pt. I of this study, p. 300.

During the months preceding the election, the U.S. engaged in a wide range of overt and covert activities, from advising government officials, especially Ky, to humoring the public. (As Lodge said in a cable to the President on August 10, "I am looking around for things to do which will put the people in a good humor as far as the Government is concerned during the first ten days of September. The General Supply Office is helping: through the sale of rice from the backs of trucks in low income areas, the transportation and sale of pork, and the importation of motorbikes.")[84]

Lansdale was put in charge of coordinating various efforts to get out the vote, and he and his team, augmented by several former members, launched a broad campaign to encourage voter participation.[85]

The U.S. also provided secret assistance to at least some of the candidates.[86]

In Washington, as noted, the State Department established a Political Development Working Group in late April 1966 to serve as the focal point for interagency discussion of the election, the drafting of the constitution, and related aspects of the political development of South Vietnam.[87] At its first meeting on April 26, the question of the role of the U.S. in the election was raised, and after some discussion the group agreed that "with the exception of some possible role for specific covert activity, the U.S. must make every effort to avoid appearing to be mixing in the elections, and that guidelines to this effect should be drafted for transmission to the Embassy."[88]

In subsequent meetings, the group considered a wide range of other questions as it continued to explore and to explicate the U.S. role in the election. Among other things, these included the terms of the law under which the election was to be held; whether there should be international observers; the desirability of releasing political prisoners before the election, especially Buddhist and former "Diemists"; whether Communists or neutralists should be allowed to stand for election; whether it would be advantageous, as a part of the electoral process, to seek to build a broad-based non-Communist political party.

---

[84] U.S. Department of State, Central File, Pol 27 Viet S, Saigon to Washington, 3129, Aug. 10, 1966.

[85] For example, a special effort was made to enlist the women, and a meeting of American women, chaired by Mrs. Lodge, was held at Lansdale's house on August 10 to develop plans for persuading Vietnamese women's groups to become active in the election. See Lansdale's memorandum to Lodge, "Women," on August 29, attached to which is a memorandum from Hank Miller to Lansdale on August 26 describing the results of these efforts. U.S. Department of State, Lot File, 70 D 207.

In a memorandum to Lodge on May 27, 1966, Lansdale said that his group had "one more service yet to perform," after which he planned to ask that the group be disbanded. This was "to help the Vietnamese gain their own popular political institutions" during the critical period from the election of the Constituent Assembly through the writing of the constitution, and ending with the election of a new government. He recommended that his group be responsible for "influencing the growth of coalitions of political groups . . . helping them grow strong enough to vie with the Communist political organization, and guiding them into moving towards an eventually more stable and meaningful political party structure in Vietnam." (U.S. Department of State, Central File, Pol 27 Viet S, Memorandum to Lodge from Lansdale, "The SLO Role," May 27, 1966, attached to letter to William Bundy from Lansdale, May 27.) There is no record of action by Lodge on this recommendation.

[86] As might be expected, there is very little available documentation on this aspect of the U.S. role, which was alluded to by Lodge in his unpublished memoir in the Lodge Papers at the Massachusetts Historical Society (pt. 4, II–8).

[87] See page 300 above.

[88] Same location, Summary Record of the Meeting on Apr. 26, 1966.

On the most pressing political question—how to handle the Buddhists—the Political Development Working Group agreed that it was important to keep Tri Quang and his followers "working within a 'pan-Buddhist' framework rather than driving them into a position of isolation from which they would be more inclined to go out on the streets."[89] Unger, expressing the consensus of the group, said that the Buddhists would probably dominate the election (they did not, as it turned out), and that the U.S. needed to maintain a position "from which we can work with the Buddhists and insure their continued desire for a U.S. presence in Vietnam at this time." "It follows," he added, "that we must not allow ourselves to slide into a position of opposition to the Buddhists, for example by supporting a Ky/military/other political groupings coalition which would be anti-Buddhist in orientation."[90]

In the election, 81 percent of those registered (approximately two-thirds of those eligible to vote were registered) voted for the 117 members (from 532 candidates) of the Constituent Assembly. Although the act of voting was a demonstration of political loyalty—in addition to checking identification cards, police checked to see if persons had cards showing they had voted—and there were restrictions on those who were eligible to stand for election or to vote,[91] the election was said to have been relatively honest and free of coercion[92] and those who voted seemed to have demonstrated that they were committed to some form of representative government, and that, given the chance, they would exercise their right to establish such a government.

President Johnson and a number of Members of Congress hailed the results of the election, as did major American newspapers.[93] Others, including Mansfield and Fulbright, questioned the significance of the election. In a private conversation with Harriman shortly before the election Fulbright, according to Harriman, "spoke disparagingly of the elections because the VC were not permitted to put up candidates."[94] Mansfield also was critical of the decision to exclude the "so-called neutralists and the Vietcong." "I would like to know," he said, "how anyone can tell the difference between a Vietcong and a citizen of South Vietnam loyal to the present government. They look alike, they talk alike, and they have

---

[89] Same location, Summary Record of the Meeting on May 2, 1966.

[90] Same location, Summary Record of Meeting of May 6, 1966.

During the period when the Political Development Working Group was formulating U.S. policy with respect to the election, there was a very active exchange between the Group and the U.S. Mission in Saigon, as indicated by State Department documents in the Central File, Pol 27 Viet S.

[91] See FitzGerald, *Fire in the Lake,* ch. 11, and Shaplen, *The Road from War.* According to FitzGerald, p. 435, "American fears to the contrary, there was very little evidence of direct NLF or government intimidation of the voters and no substantial case of election fraud." Shaplen said (p. 83) that it was "without doubt the fairest election ever held in South Vietnam."

[92] The South Vietnamese Government issued an electoral decree limiting candidates, which, as Bernard Fall observed was "designed to eliminate all neutralists, procommunists, or other possible opposition. . . ." He also notes that, in part because of these restrictions and other actions by the government to ensure that the election would be adequately controlled, out of the 117 members elected, 73 were originally from North Vietnam—a number considerably larger than the proportion of northerners to southerners in the total population. Bernard Fall, "Vietnam: The Quest for Stability," *Current History,* 52 (January 1967), pp. 8 ff. at pp. 10–11.

[93] See, for example, *CR,* vol. 112, for Sept. 12, 13, and 16, 1966, and the *New York Times* and the *Washington Post* for September 12. For Lodge's comments in a cable to President Johnson, see in the Johnson Library, NSF Memos to the President—Walt Rostow, Saigon to Washington 5970, Sept. 14, 1966.

[94] Library of Congress, Harriman Papers, Fulbright File, Memorandum of Conversation, Aug. 24, 1966.

the same traditions and customs. I think they should be allowed to vote to show how strong or weak they are; then we would have a better idea of what we are up against in Vietnam itself."[95]

After the election, U.S. officials worked closely with the South Vietnamese in drafting the constitution. In Washington, the Political Development Working Group considered in detail the various provisions and arrangements that the U.S. might want to propose,[96] and a Vietnam Drafting Group was created in the State Department to study and prepare papers on constitutional issues.[97] In Saigon, Lodge himself formulated a plan for the new constitutional government, patterned after the American system,[98] and U.S. personnel played an active role in assisting the Constituent Assembly in drafting the constitution. Two members of the Embassy's Political Section were assigned to attend all open sessions of the Assembly and to maintain daily contact with the members. In addition, Dr. Gisbert H. Flanz, an authority on constitutional law from New York University, who had provided similar assistance to the South Korean Government, was brought in to help with the drafting of the new South Vietnamese constitution.[99]

The Situation in Congress

During the late summer and early fall of 1966, as Members of the House of Representatives and one-third of the Members of the Senate prepared for November elections in which the war in Vietnam was considered to be an issue in several of the more prominent contests, Congress, despite the private doubts of many Members and the public opposition of a few, continued to provide strong support for U.S. policy. (On October 28, 1966, *Congressional Quarterly* reported that in its survey of 313 Senators and Representatives, 58.5 percent favored existing policy, 26.4 percent favored stronger military action, and 15.1 percent favored deescalation and negotiations.) After a long debate it also gave the President authority to callup the Reserves and the National Guard for use in Vietnam or elsewhere without declaring a national emergency.[100] (Under existing law, the President could call up the Reserves only after approval by Congress or by declaring a national emergency.) Under the terms of the amendment granting this authority, which was sponsored by Senator Russell—who had advocated greater equality between draftees and those who were able to avoid the draft and the war by enlisting in the Reserves as well as the need to make the Reserves available for use in the war—and cosponsored by Senator Saltonstall, Congress provided that the President could order to active duty any Reserve Unit or any member of the Ready Reserve who was not attached to a Ready Reserve Unit and who had not served on active duty (or "active duty for training") for 24 months, or members of units of the Ready Reserves who had

---

[95] *CR*, vol. 112, p. 21059.

[96] See summaries of meetings of the Working Group during October-December 1966, State Department Lot File 70 D 102.

[97] Relevant documents, including a "Constitutional Issues Paper" prepared by the Drafting Group, are in the same location.

[98] Massachusetts Historical Society, Lodge Papers, unpublished "Vietnam Memoir," pt. 4, II 10.

[99] U.S. Department of State, Lot File 70 D 102, memorandum for Rostow from Unger, "Mission Contacts with Vietnamese Constituent Assembly, Dec. 31, 1966.

[100] *Department of Defense Appropriations Act, Fiscal Year, 1967*, Public Law 89–687.

not received the required four months of training. These latter provisions would affect about 133,000 men who were said to have enlisted in the Reserves in order to avoid the draft.[101] This provision, which expired June 30, 1968, made available to the President an additional manpower pool of approximately 789,000 men.[102]

In addition, Congress approved all 1966 requests from the President for authority and funds to carry on the war with very little discussion of the war and without making any significant cuts. The Department of Defense Appropriations bill was passed by the House 392–1 (George Brown, the lone dissenter was a liberal Democrat from California) and by the Senate 86–0 (Morse and Gruening did not vote).[103] During the House proceedings, virtually nothing was said about the war and there were no amendments by opponents. In the Senate proceedings, very little was said about the war and there were no amendments by opponents except for proposals by Clark and McGovern to delete funds for several programs, unrelated to the war, that exceeded the amounts originally requested by the administration. Clark's amendment was defeated 14–73 and McGovern's by 18–69, both on August 18.[104] Those voting for the amendments included most of the more committed opponents of the war, and in that sense the amendments served as a referendum on the extent of Senate opposition to the war as of the summer of 1966.

Efforts in the Senate to pass provisions by which Congress would seek to enact statements of policy on the war or to legislate limitations or restrictions were unsuccessful except for an innocuous amendment to the foreign aid authorization bill providing that, "The furnishing of economic, military, or other assistance under this Act shall not be construed as creating a new commitment or as affecting any existing commitment to use armed forces of the United States for the defense of any foreign country."[105] Fulbright, who was concerned about what he saw as the connection between U.S. economic and military aid to Vietnam and the subsequent commitment of Armed Forces, had first introduced the amendment in March when the Foreign Relations Committee was acting on the supplemental foreign aid appropriations for Vietnam, but it was defeated in committee.

On April 19, 1966, during Senate testimony by Rusk on the foreign aid authorization bill for fiscal year 1967, Fulbright continued to express his concern about the foreign aid-military commitment connection. Referring to Rusk's testimony on that question in January, he told Rusk: "This frightened me more than any other single thing which happened recently and I don't propose to be a party to that."[106] "We no longer have a declaration of war in order to

---

[101] See the discussion in *CR*, vol. 112, pp. 26034–25035, and 26056–26064.

[102] For a good discussion of congressional action on the amendment, see the 1966 *Congressional Quarterly Almanac*, pp. 144 ff. President Johnson used the Russell amendment twice during the Vietnam war, once after the North Koreans had seized the U.S. intelligence ship, U.S.S. *Pueblo*, in February 1968, when he called up 14,000 reservists to strengthen the U.S. position in Korea, and again in May 1968, when about 22,000 reservists were called to active duty to provide troops for Vietnam and to rebuild U.S. Strategic Reserves drawn down by the use of active duty forces in Vietnam.

[103] See *CR*, vol. 112, pp. 16302, 19858.

[104] *Ibid.*, pp. 19834, 19853.

[105] *Ibid.*, pp. 16302, 19858.

[106] U.S. Congress, Senate, Committee on Foreign Relations, *Foreign Assistance, 1966*, Hearings on S. 2859 and S. 2861 (Washington, D.C.: U.S. Govt. Print. Off., 1966), p. 15.

wage a major war," he added, "and we ease into these situations. . . ."

Rusk testified again on May 9, and Pell raised the commitment question, expressing concern that "with the extension of aid goes a certain military responsibility." Rusk disagreed, saying that military commitments were made for "reasons vital to the security of the United States." [107]

In preparation for committee action on the bill, Church proposed adding a slightly modified version of the commitment amendment that Fulbright had offered in March. At the State Department, Rusk took the position, based on advice from Legal Adviser Meeker, that the amendment should be opposed. Meeker argued that it would create confusion at home and abroad with respect to congressional support of "the President's policies" in Vietnam. Rusk approved alternative language recommended by Meeker as a replacement for the language for the Church amendment in the event that the committee appeared to be intent on passing an amendment.[108]

Rusk asked President Johnson for his judgment, and the President responded with the handwritten note: "I would try to keep any amendment out—if not I'd try a modified [Meeker] amendment." [109]

Church offered his amendment in an executive session of the Foreign Relations Committee on May 24, 1966, and after some discussion the committee approved the amendment, as modified by the Meeker language provided by the State Department.[110]

In its report on the bill, the committee explained the amendment, saying in part, "The American people must be reassured that furnishing foreign aid does not constitute a back-door commitment of military forces to a potential series of brushfire wars in countries throughout the world. In addition, aid recipients need to be put on notice that regardless of the extent of aid, they should in no way interpret U.S. generosity as a promise to help with military forces in time of trouble." [111]

The foreign aid bill was considered by the Senate beginning on July 18, 1966.[112] Several days earlier, Bill Moyers held a dinner party at which Fulbright and Rostow had an extended conversation on U.S. policy in Asia. There are no records that would explain why the two men were brought together in this fashion, but, as noted earlier, Moyers was seeking to moderate the difference of opinion

---

[107] *Ibid.*, pp. 613–615.

[108] Church's amendment provided: "This Act, or the furnishing of economic, military, or other assistance under this Act, shall not be construed as a commitment to use armed forces of the United States for the defense of any foreign country." Meeker's language provided: "This Act, or the furnishing of economic, military, or other assistance under this Act, shall not be construed as enacting a new commitment or as affecting any existing commitment to use Armed Forces of the United States for the defense of any foreign country."

[109] Johnson Library, NSF Memos to President—Walt Rostow, Memorandum from Rostow to the President, May 13, enclosing memorandum from Read to the Secretary, May 13, to which was attached Meeker's memorandum to the Secretary. On May 16, Rusk sent a letter to Chairman Fulbright stating that the administration "strongly opposed" the Church amendment. U.S. Department of State, Central File, Pol 27 Viet S, Memorandum from Read to the Secretary, May 16, 1966, with letter attached.

[110] U.S. Congress, Senate, Committee on Foreign Relations, unpublished executive session transcript, May 24 and 26, 1966. As published in the committee's Historical Series, 1966, vol. XVIII, the minutes of meetings of the committee on May 24 and 26, 1966, while, referring to the "markup" of the Foreign Assistance Act, do not give any of the details which are provided by the unpublished transcript.

[111] S. Rept. 89–1359, p. 7.

[112] For Senate debate, see *CR*, vol. 112, pp. 16020–17073 passim.

between the President and Fulbright, and it is reasonable to assume that the dinner may have been arranged with that in mind. There are also no notes on the conversation, but, judging by a letter from Rostow to Fulbright on July 11, it ranged widely over U.S. policy, with Fulbright criticizing the creation of a "U.S. empire" of "client states" to prevent China from dominating Asia. Rostow said in his letter, "So far as China is concerned, I suspect you feel there is some natural historical force that decrees that its tradition, scale, and energy shall make it dominate Asia—or at least Southeast and South Asia."[113]

In his letter, which President Johnson, who was shown the draft, said was "excellent," Rostow argued that China would not be that important; rather, that unless there were a "series of wars like Europe," there would be in Asia "an equilibrium involving Japan-India China," and that the U.S. and the U.S.S.R. would "remain Asia powers." "The art of U.S. policy for the long pull," he said, "is for us not to pull out but to help Asia organize itself so as to maintain this equilibrium with a much diminished U.S. presence and effort." For the "foreseeable future," however, "the scale of the Chinese Communist armies and their emerging nuclear capability will require us to remain committed to non-Communist Asia if the military capabilities of the China mainland are to be persuasively deterred and the rest of Asia is to go forward in confidence." As for Fulbright's concern about "client states," Rostow argued that although there was a need for the U.S. to provide security for countries on the border of the "Communist world," this "irreducible interdependence" was "required for mutual security and progress."

In a speech on July 12 that seemed to embody Rostow's ideas, President Johnson emphasized the importance of Asia and of the need to defeat the Communists in Vietnam in order to bring stability and peace to the region. He spoke generally of U.S. "obligations in Asia as a Pacific power," and of the hope of building a "truly world civilization in the Pacific" that could lead to the "greatest of all human eras—the Pacific era." "As a Pacific power," he said, "we must help to achieve that outcome."[114]

According to William Bundy, in executive session testimony before the Senate Foreign Relations Committee on September 20, 1966, the President's speech was a deliberate effort to focus on the "broader sweep of the problem," and not just the war, in order "to get it [the war] into a wider framework."[115]

Fulbright, however, was concerned about the implications of Rostow's views and of the President's speech which, following the Vice President's comments after the Honolulu Conference the previous February and press reports of a "Johnson Doctrine" for Asia, seemed to suggest that the U.S. was assuming a broad role in Asia, and that commitments were being made without consultations with and approval by Congress. He expressed these concerns in a speech

---

[113] Johnson Library, Office of the President File, Memorandum from Rostow to the President, July 11, 1966, attaching a draft of his letter of that date which, with a minor addition suggested by the President, was sent that day to Fulbright.

[114] *Public Papers of the Presidents*, Lyndon B. Johnson, 1966, pp. 718–722.

[115] U.S. Congress, Senate Committee on Foreign Relations, *Executive Sessions of the Senate Foreign Relations Committee* (Historical Series), 1966, vol. XVIII (Washington, D.C.: U.S. Govt. Print. Off., 1993), p. 1011.

in the Senate on July 22, during debate on the foreign aid bill.[116] "Except for the Monroe Doctrine," he said, "the United States has traditionally rejected policies of unilateral responsibility for entire regions and continents." During the 20th Century, "events imposed" upon the United States certain commitments "far beyond our borders," but these had been "guided by two extremely important qualifying principles: First, that these responsibilities were limited to certain countries and certain purposes; second, that they would be discharged collectively either under the United Nations or in cooperation with our allies." "The emerging Asian doctrine," however, "represents a radical departure in American foreign policy in that it is virtually unlimited in what it purports to accomplish and unilateral in its execution. Without reference to the United Nations and with only perfunctory reference to the nonfunctioning SEATO treaty, the United States on its own has undertaken to win a victory for its proteges in the Vietnamese civil war and thereupon to build a 'great society' in Asia, whatever that might turn out to be." "Under the emerging Asian doctrine," he added, "the United States is taking on the role of policeman and provider for all of non-Communist Asia."

"All of this," Fulbright said, "must come as a big surprise to Senators who have not even been informed of these sweeping commitments, much less asked for their advice and consent. . . ."

Majority Leader Mansfield, while agreeing with Fulbright that Congress should be asked to approve a "doctrine" involving a broad U.S. commitment to Asia, argued that there was no "Johnson Doctrine" for Asia, and no commitment that needed to be brought before Congress.[117]

On July 27, Mansfield sent the President a letter in which he said that he had not understood why Fulbright had taken such strong exception to Johnson's speech on Asia. Having read the speech for a second time he said that the "misapprehension" may have stemmed from a confusion of the role of the U.S. as a "Pacific power" in contrast with that of an "Asian power." He urged that the distinction be made clear, inferring that it had not been. "As you know only too well," he said, "today's generalizations are, too often, tomorrow's sanction for the expansion of the permanent bureaucratic commitment in the conduct of American foreign policy."[118]

During his Senate speech, Fulbright also noted that he had discussed the subject of the U.S. role in Asia with Rostow, and that "my impression is that he believes it is the proper role for this country to become a major Asian power, to create a balance there as opposed to China and Russia." "I am not saying this policy is necessarily wrong," he added, but it "comes as a great shock to me to think that this concept of our role could be contemplated without consideration by the Senate."[119]

The day after Fulbright's speech, the *Washington Post,* in an article entitled "White House Resorts Sharply to Criticism," reported

---

[116] *CR,* vol. 112, pp. 16808–16814.

[117] *Ibid.*

[118] Mansfield's letter and a perfunctory reply by the President drafted by Rostow, are in the Johnson Library, NSF Memos to the President—Walt Rostow, transmittal memorandum to the President, Aug. 1, 1966, with Mansfield letter and draft reply attached.

[119] *CR,* vol. 112, p. 16813.

that Press Secretary Moyers had made a "lengthy rebuttal" in which he said, among other things, "I find it difficult to believe the Senator does not believe we should meet our obligations in Asia," and that, "I find it difficult and disappointing to believe that the Senator believes what he does about the President's policies." In reply to the charge that Congress was not being consulted about commitments, Moyers said, "I cannot nor can the President find any commitments in the President's speech which Senator Fulbright is not aware of." [120]

It was apparent that Fulbright was becoming more of a "problem" for the President and his policies, and that further steps needed to be taken to influence him as well as to counteract the effect of his growing opposition. Several days later, in the first meeting of Harriman's Negotiations Committee, Unger suggested the possibility of a congressional resolution on U.S. aims in Vietnam. "Amb. Unger said that he visualized such a resolution as a means of emphasizing the limited nature of our objectives and our readiness to engage in unconditional talks. If the right language could be worked out, such a resolution might be a way of getting Fulbright back on the track. Governor Harriman commented that it was hard to conceive of any resolution which would be acceptable to both Congressional hawks and doves—to Fulbright and Symington for example. The group agreed that there could be no more effective way of convincing Hanoi and the rest of the world of our unity and determination than to bring Fulbright around." [121]

Various emissaries were also sent during mid-August 1966 to see Fulbright, including, as noted earlier, William Sullivan and Averell Harriman, with little if any effect. On September 19, at the direction of the President, CIA Director Helms met with Fulbright, Mansfield and Russell to discuss the findings of a new CIA study, "The Will to Persist," which analyzed whether the Communists could persist in fighting the war. Helms reported to the President that "the three Senators talked largely among themselves, and it was clear that positions which each had previously held about the Vietnamese war failed to be influenced by the material in the study." [122]

> Senator Fulbright quite clearly remains convinced of two particular viewpoints: (a) He is persuaded that the Vietnamese war was initially a civil war, that it has always been a civil war, and that it has been internationalized by the United States in recent times; (b) He believes that Mendes-France, with whom he said he had talked, pulled the French Government out of Indo-China, not because the French people did not have the will to fight, but because it was the intelligent thing to do in light of economic resources of France which were being "wasted" in an unimportant country of the world. . . .
>
> At another point in the discussion, Senator Fulbright expressed his disagreement with the contention which he claims Secretary Rusk has made, i.e., that the United States military

---

[120] *Washington Post,* July 23, 1966.

[121] U.S. Department of State, Lot File 70 D 207, Notes of Meeting of Negotiations Committee, Aug. 2, 1966. Unger said that he would draft a resolution. Notes of subsequent meetings of the committee, however, do not mention the matter again.

[122] Johnson Library, NSF Agency File, CIA, Memorandum from Helms to Rostow, "Senatorial Briefing," Sept. 20, 1966.

presence in Vietnam is keeping the Chinese from expanding into Southeast Asia. The Senator commented that Communist China is in a bad mess politically and economically and that she is not going anywhere outside her borders for a long time to come. . . .

Senator Russell stated that he had been interested in the content of the briefing and that he would have by himself come to essentially the same conclusions, although perhaps not couched in such "fine phrases." Senator Mansfield, as he left the gathering, commented that he was particularly pleased to note that the Agency had presented to the President such an objective and thorough report.

"At one point," Helms reported, "Senator Fulbright asked me if the purpose of my briefing on the study finding was designed to stop Senator Mansfield and himself from criticizing the Administration's handling of the Vietnamese situation. I replied, 'I received no such instructions from the President or anyone else. I was simply asked to present to you gentlemen together the results of the study.'"

Helms concluded: "I truly believe the briefing was useful, but I am equally convinced that it did little to change the views of the three Senators present."

Toward the end of September 1966, as Congress prepared to adjourn prior to congressional elections in November, the Foreign Relations Committee held an executive session hearing on the situation in Thailand, especially what commitments the U.S. had and how they were entered into. The choice of U.S. commitments to Thailand as the subject of the hearing was prompted by reports of such commitments and of increasing U.S. military activity in relationship to Thailand, as well as by the concern of Fulbright and others on the committee with the role of Congress in the making of commitments that could involve the United States in military action. In a staff memorandum, Marcy, the chief of staff, explained what Fulbright hoped to accomplish:[123]

JWF want to use the occasion to get into the subject of how we get into these commitments without more formal action by the Congress. . . . He want to provoke a constitutional discussion of what is happening to Senate authority. . . . If the President can, in fact, commit the United States to irrevocable commitments, then shouldn't we make it clear now that Congress has no authority in the field? Thus, responsibility would attach to authority. We can't let the President say that all he is doing is carrying out the mandate of Congress as expressed in the Southeast Asia Resolution [Gulf of Tonkin Resolution].

What, in fact, do treaty commitments to 43 nations mean? What is the precise language? Why aren't the treaties reciprocal? Or are they? Do we interpret these as obligatory whilst the others treat them as simple agreements to consult?

What is meant by "in accordance with our constitutional process"? Is a Presidential statement a "constitutional process"?

[123] National Archives, RG 46, Papers of the Committee on Foreign Relations, Marcy Chron File, Memorandum from Marcy to Bill Bader, Aug. 29, 1966.

In the hearing, held on September 20, there was an extended discussion of the constitutional and legal basis of U.S. activities in Thailand and of why there was so much secrecy surrounding those activities. Senator Symington thought they should be explained to the American public. The witness, William Bundy, explained that the Thais were opposed to that kind of public disclosure.[124]

During September, there was also some discussion within the staff of the Foreign Relations Committee about plans for committee activities in the new Congress beginning in January 1967. In a memorandum to Marcy on September 12, Norvill Jones suggested that, based on comments from scholars and others, the committee should hold hearings on the role of the Senate and of the committee in foreign policy.[125] Such hearings, he said, "should create the proper atmosphere for what will probably be a crucial period for the Congress in foreign affairs. Public discussion of the Committee's role—and what can be done to make it more effective—should give the Committee a better sense of direction and serve notice on the Executive Branch that it will do whatever is necessary to bring an independent point of view to bear on foreign policy."

Jones explained the rationale of his proposal:

> Much of the Committee's concern this year has been over fundamental questions about how policy is made and what part Congress should have in the policy making process. Vietnam, Thailand, the "Johnson" doctrine—all illustrate either distortion of Congressional intent or the Executive Branch's taking a "Senate be damned" attitude. It seems to me that much of the tone of the Committee's work indicated a frustration or uncertainty over its proper role which went far deeper than doubts about who had the votes. There are strong indications that foreign policy will become more important in the future as a national political issue. And there is little doubt that the President (whoever he may be) will use the powers of his office to try to minimize the role of the Congress in formulation policy. The circumstances are appropriate for the Committee to make a thorough reassessment of its Constitutional role in the light of the changing world and the power structure of our Government with a view to updating its concept of its proper role in policy making.

Marcy responded on September 19:[126]

> My trouble with your suggestion that the Committee ought to seek expert advice on how to improve its effectiveness in the foreign policy making progress is that it reminds me of a monkey picking fleas while the forest fire gradually hems him in. I am afraid such an activity on the part of the Committee would be far too introspective if conducted on any formal basis—though I see no problems with a bull session or two on the subject. But if the Committee and staff spent much time

[124] U.S. Congress, Senate, Committee on Foreign Relations, *Executive Sessions of the Senate Foreign Relations Committee* (Historical Series), 1966, vol. XVIII (Washington, D.C.: U.S. Govt. Print. Off., 1993), p. 979.

[125] National Archives, RG 46, Papers of the Committee on Foreign Relations, Marcy Chron Files, Memorandum from Norvill Jones to Marcy, Sept. 12, 1966.

[126] Same location, Marcy Memorandum to Jones, Sept. 19, 1966.

on this project, I think we would see other Committees moving into the substantive field.

It seems to me that the Committee had been feeling its way this year into a new role which is becoming pretty effective. In brief, the Committee is doing the thinking which ought to be done downtown.

I wonder if the Committee might not wish to hold a series of hearings next January on the subject of "American Responsibilities as a World Power." This was suggested by Reinhold Niebuhr and would provide a framework for expert outside witnesses so hearings could be held on particular subjects such as "Responsibilities toward Maintenance of Free Nations"; "Responsibilities toward UnderDeveloped Countries"; etc.

Dissatisfaction with the conduct of the war was also being voiced by some Members of Congress who were strong supporters of U.S. policy but who advocated the deployment of larger forces and the use of greater military pressure. Among these was Senator Stennis, who declared in a speech in the Senate on October 13, 1966, the day McNamara returned from Saigon: "It is time that we take a good hard look at the realities." "I continue to be impressed and almost appalled," he said, "by the fact that a nation of this kind has been able to tie us down as it has, and that it apparently will continue to do so, even though it has very little industry and no semblance of a modern war machine in the sense with which we are familiar." Noting that the Communists did not seem interested in a peace settlement, Stennis said the time had come for the U.S. to "prepare for the long pull in Vietnam," including the deferral of some of the Great Society programs in order to make the necessary resources available for fighting the war, while avoiding adverse economic consequences from its costs. He was joined by Senator Symington, as well as by Senator Strom Thurmond (R/S.C.), who called for using the "full power" of the United States to fight the war. Arguing that there would continue to be a military stalemate unless the U.S. took the war to the enemy, Thurmond said: "When the time comes that the enemy feels the effects of this war, they will be glad to come to the peace table." [127]

In early December 1966, after Congress had adjourned for the year, Stennis, chairman of the Preparedness Subcommittee, the principal investigative arm of the Senate Armed Services Committee, made a speech in his home state of Mississippi, after a subcommittee trip to Vietnam, in which he said that the U.S. was not "significantly closer" to winning the war than it was a year earlier, and again took the position that a greater military effort was required to win the war. Present policies, he said, would not produce "victory," and would cost the U.S. $25 billion a year for the 10 years or more that would be needed to win. He recommended sending "enough troops now," supported by other actions, such as closing the port of Haiphong, to force the Communists to come to terms.[128]

In advance of the 1966 congressional elections, the Republicans, while strongly supporting the war, tried to make their best possible

[127] *CR*, vol. 112, pp. 16537–26541.
[128] *New York Times*, Dec. 9, 1966.

political case against it by chipping away at the President and at the Democrats with speeches about the "credibility gap," and charges that the President and congressional Democrats had attempted to protect domestic programs by manipulating budget requests for the war.[129] There was also renewed Republican criticism of the low budget estimates that they claimed had been made by the President in order to gain support for the war while protecting domestic programs.[130]

The Republicans also wanted to emphasize their interest in ending the war, and in August, under the leadership of Senator Morton of Kentucky, chairman of the Senate Republican Campaign Committee, Republican candidates for the Senate and the House were urged to endorse the idea of an "all-Asian peace conference" which, as noted above, had been proposed by Charles Percy, the Republican Senate nominee in Illinois, as a way of settling the conflict.

On September 20, 1966, the House Republican Conference issued an updated version of the report that it had first issued in 1965 on the record of the U.S. in the war in Vietnam.[131] This report concluded that the war was a stalemate; that no progress was being made in extending the control of the South Vietnamese Government; that enemy forces had increased, as had desertions of South Vietnamese forces; that terrorist activity was increasing and there had been little progress in economic development; and that a "satisfactory peace in Vietnam is not in sight." The report concluded:

> Administration policy has prevented Communist conquest of South Vietnam. However, peace or victory or stability there are still remote. Faced with a prospect of war for five to seven years, of the spread of conflict to Thailand and perhaps other parts of Southeast Asia, of Communist China equipped with nuclear weapons, the United States must give attention to basic questions about its future political and military strategy in Asia.
>
> A five-year war in Vietnam would, at the present rate, involve the frightful cost of 125,000 American casualties. This high cost is dwarfed by the catastrophic losses which South Vietnam would suffer in five more years of fighting. To the South Vietnamese and other threatened people of Asia, this type of limitless war may come to be an unattractive alternative to Communist domination.
>
> The urgent immediate question facing the nation is how to end this war more speedily and at small cost while safeguarding the independence and freedom of South Vietnam.
>
> Simultaneously, the nation must give sober thought to the means of preventing the spread of this war and the eruption of similar wars in other places in Asia.

This Republican "white paper" was attacked by Democratic leaders in the House, led by the whip, Hale Boggs, and the chairman of the Appropriations Committee, George Mahon, who criticized the Republicans for trying to make a partisan issue out of the war. Re-

[129] See, for example, *CR*, vol. 112, pp. 11732–11733, 16185 ff., and 16285 ff.
[130] See, for example, *ibid.*, pp. 16288–89.
[131] *Ibid.*, pp. 23309–23318.

publican leader Melvin Laird replied that the President had failed to clarify U.S. objectives. There was a "general mood of uneasiness," Laird said, with respect to the question, "What have we learned in Vietnam? What policy have we evolved from our years of involvement in Vietnam that will find us prepared to prevent this kind of war in Thailand, in Latin America, in Africa? What policy have we evolved that will enable us to cope with such 'wars of national liberation' in a fashion that will not lead to such a drain on our country's men and materiel?

"Is this drift and the drain on America's manpower and resources that has been the hallmark of our policy in Vietnam the prospect for future 'wars of national liberation'?

"Or have our leaders been attempting to fashion new policies that will work better both in preventing aggression and maintaining peace?

"These questions, these concerns, this uneasiness are in the minds of a great many Americans and they have not been satisfactorily answered for the American people."

Laird charged that the administration had withheld information about U.S. objectives and about the war from Congress and the public. He also asked whether there were plans for a peace settlement that would allow a coalition government in Vietnam, and said, "If we end up with a Southeast Asia Yalta Agreement, the objective is not worth fighting for."

House Republican Leader Gerald Ford argued that the administration was engaging in "deception and confusion" in relation to Vietnam as an issue in the 1966 political campaign, and that, "At the mid-term election, the voters will decide whether they want the Congress to exercise its responsibilities in the field of foreign policy more vigorously or want the Congress to be a docile instrument of the President—neither effectively questioning, nor investigating, nor checking and restraining the executive branch."[132]

Members of Congress generally seemed to pay little attention to these partisan tactics, however. Many of them supported the war out of belief or necessity, but, knowing that it was becoming unpopular, they avoided the issue whenever possible.

Adding to the increasing sense of uneasiness about U.S. involvement and to the political liabilities of the war there were new reports of the waste and corruption associated with U.S. economic aid to Vietnam. According to the Foreign Operations Subcommittee, chaired by Representative John Moss, of the House Government Operations Committee, large amounts of U.S. aid—as much as 40 percent of the annual $800-$900 million—were being lost to theft, bribery, the black market, and currency manipulation.[133] A former deputy director of the U.S. Foreign Aid Mission in Saigon testified

---

[132] These various comments appear in *ibid.*, pp. 23225–23228, and 23318.

[133] *Ibid.*, pp. 15443–15444, and H. Rept. 89–2257. For a discussion of similar reports by the subcommittee in the late 1950s, see pt. I of this study.

In 1967, the Moss subcommittee followed up its investigation of the aid program in Vietnam, including improvements made since its 1966 report. See H. Repts. 89–609, 89–610, 89–611.

During the years of active U.S. involvement in the war, in addition to audits by the General Accounting Office, there were numerous audits of U.S. programs by the Defense Department, State Department and the Agency for International Development. These, in turn, were regularly reviewed for Congress by the General Accounting Office. See, for example, the GAO's "Review of Audit and Inspection Programs Conducted by United States Agencies in Viet Nam During 1966," (GAO report B 159451, May 1967.)

before the subcommittee that "at least 60 percent of the aid is diverted from the purpose for which it is intended." [134]

"The system [commodity import] seemed to be rational on paper," one observer has explained, "but it went awry in practice." [135]

> Entrepreneurs with the right connections obtained licenses to import such merchandise as television sets, motor scooters, and refrigerators, which they sold principally to urban Vietnamese who were themselves reaping profits from the American presence and could afford luxuries. So the aid revolved in a narrow circle, with only a pittance reaching the peasants, whose allegiance was deemed crucial to the success of the war. And even the necessities that trickled down to the rural areas were frequently diverted into shady schemes. For example, speculators hoarded imported American fertilizer and created artificial shortages that sent prices skyrocketing. One of the most notorious speculators was the brother-in-law of General Nguyen Van Thieu. . . . But he was a piker compared to Thieu himself, who carried away millions of dollars in gold when he fled Vietnam in April 1975.

Such money-making schemes were said to be commonplace in the South Vietnamese Government: [136]

> Without an ideology or even a positive purpose to inspire loyalty, the Saigon leaders could only purchase fidelity—and they practiced a style of secular simony, trafficking in jobs that gave their subordinates the opportunity to make money. General Dang Van Quang, the Mekong delta commander, was therefore accorded the rice and opium franchise in his region; later, assigned to Saigon, he increased his considerable fortune by selling passports for upwards of twenty thousand dollars each. General Van Toan's infantry division, deployed among the cinnamon plantations near Dalat, devoted more of its time and energy to harvesting the precious spice than to fighting the enemy, while General Nguyen Huu Co, a defense minister, cashed in on lucrative real estate killings—and he even had the audacity to pocket the rent from the lease of government land to the U.S. army. Lesser South Vietnamese officials participated in the system as well, paying kickbacks to their superiors for a chance to share the plunder. The going rate for the post of district chief in 1967 was the equivalent of ten thousand dollars, payable to the corps commander. Officials in many regions also paid off local Vietcong chiefs, with whom they had arranged accommodations.

Budget and Fiscal Problems Continue to Multiply

Another important factor contributing to the growing uneasiness about the war was its impact on both the Government's budget and on tax policy. It will be recalled that in January 1966 the President had decided not to ask Congress for a tax increase, despite the advice of Gardner Ackley, Chairman of his Council of Economic Ad-

---

[134] *New York Times,* Oct. 13, 1966. AID replied that only $35–40 million would be lost in that fiscal year (1967). *Ibid.,* Nov. 18, 1966. For a report in January 1967 by AID on "Management of AID Commodity Programs, Vietnam, 1966," see *Department of State Bulletin,* Feb. 6, 1967.

[135] Stanley Karnow, *Vietnam: A History* (New York: Viking, 1983), p. 441.

[136] *Ibid.*

visers that there should be "a significant" tax increase "as soon as possible" in order to prevent "an intolerable degree of inflationary pressure." The other two members of the economic "Troika"—Budget Director Schultze and Treasury Secretary Fowler—also thought that a tax increase would be needed, but were uncertain about its timing. Representative Mills, chairman of the House Ways and Means Committee, however, advised against asking for a tax increase in 1966, saying that if one were requested the Republicans and some Democrats in Congress would "start tearing at the budget instead."

The President also decided to send to Congress in January 1966 a budget request that deliberately understated the cost of the Vietnam war for the 1967 fiscal year. This, too, was done on the advice of Mills and on the recommendation of Schultze that rather than providing for the estimated $16–18 billion increased expenditure for the cost of the war for FY 1967, the budget should provide for $10 billion. (This was accomplished, as explained earlier, by assuming that the war would end by June 30, 1967.) Based on this estimate, there would be a projected budget deficit of $1.8 billion.

By the summer of 1966, however, the economic situation had worsened, and it was apparent that action on taxes needed to be taken without delay. In the spring, as a result of the decision not to ask for new taxes, the Federal Reserve, as it had warned the President it would do, tightened monetary policy in an effort to slow inflation. As one analyst described the ensuing "credit crunch," "by summer the growth in the money stock had fallen to almost zero. Interest rates move to historic highs. Rates for prime commercial paper averaged 5.55 percent for the year, the highest by far in the postwar [World War II] years and nearly twice the 1961 level. Savings and loans became overextended, and mortgage money almost dried up. Rates on state and local bonds soared, and two leading bond houses, caught with large inventories of unsold bonds, almost failed." [137]

On July 18, the President discussed these problems with Democratic and Republican leaders of Congress and on July 19 with members of the House and Senate Appropriations Committees.[138] He said that there would need to be additional funding for the war—between 5 and 10 billion dollars (over the estimated cost of the war for FY 1967 of $10 billion)—and urged them not to increase appropriations for other programs beyond his budget requests. He was asked what the deficit would be in FY 1967, and he replied: "I don't think we should be guessing." He added—referring to McNamara's statement in January about the war ending by June 30, 1967, as a way of justifying and explaining the President's decision to ask for only a part of the money that it was estimated would be needed—"McNamara made a bad guess on bringing the troops home. I don't want to be caught like that."

On August 8, 1966, the President met with congressional leaders to discuss an income tax increase. According to Califano's notes of

---

[137] Kettl, "The Economic Education of Lyndon Johnson," *op. cit.*, p. 64.

[138] Notes of both meetings are in the Johnson Library, Tom Johnson's Notes of Meetings.

the meeting,[139] "House minority leader Gerald Ford reacted instantly, 'You'd have trouble getting more than fifteen votes.' Ford's Democratic counterpart, Carl Albert, trumped him, 'You wouldn't even get that many!' Senate Finance Committee Chairman Russell Long and House Ways and Means Committee Chairman Mills told Johnson they opposed any tax increase, but might go along with suspending the investment tax credit."

Toward the end of August, after the President's advisers again recommended action on a tax increase—Ackley and the Council of Economic Advisers advocated a tax surcharge and immediate suspension of the investment tax credit, Fowler favored a surcharge on business income, and key congressional leaders indicated that they would support suspension of the investment tax credit[140]—the stock market fell to its lowest point that year, and Ackley sent a memorandum to the President warning that this was sign of the seriousness of the financial situation and urging action on suspending the investment tax credit.[141]

On August 29, after a meeting of Ackley, Schultze, Fowler, and Califano, as well as McNamara, Katzenbach, Lawrence O'Brien, and David Ginsburg, to discuss the situation, Califano reported to the President "Ackley and Fowler urge very strongly that you announce an immediate program this week. They are very deeply concerned about the market, both in stocks and bonds, and believe that we could have a serious crisis if you do not act rapidly."[142] On September 2, at the request of the President, all of these advisers signed a joint memorandum to the President recommending suspension of the investment tax credit, a reduction in current government spending, and future tax measures sufficient to cover any new funds for the war.[143] The President agreed, and sent a special message to Congress on September 8 announcing an immediate reduction in spending of $1.5 billion and requesting the suspension of the investment tax credit.[144] The tax credit suspension was rapidly approved by Congress.

These actions eased the financial problem, but as Califano comments, "There was a gnawing sense that, however many fingers LBJ was able to put in the dike, without a tax increase he could not much longer prevent the waters from flowing over the top."[145]

The Protest Movement Becomes More Militant

By the fall of 1966, the antiwar movement, as Powers has pointed out, "was going through one of its periodic depressions, convinced that nothing could persuade Johnson of the folly of his

[139] Joseph A. Califano, *The Triumph and Tragedy of Lyndon Johnson: The White House Years* (New York: Simon and Schuster, 1991), p. 148 from Califano's personal diary. There apparently are no notes of the meeting in the files of the Johnson Library.

[140] See King, "The President and Fiscal Policy in 1966," *op. cit.*, pp. 698–699. See also Lawrence O'Brien's memorandum of August 30 on conversations with Mills and Russell Long, Johnson Library, Ex BE5.

[141] Califano, p. 148.

[142] King, p. 200.

[143] Califano, p. 148, King, p. 700, and Kettl, "The Economic Education of Lyndon Johnson," *op. cit.*, p. 64.

[144] Kettl, p. 65.

[145] Califano, p. 148.

course."[146] Politically frustrated, many antiwar activists were becoming more politically alienated.[147]

Among students, a similar trend was developing. The early phase of student protests in 1964–1965 "embodied concern, dissent, and protest about various social issues," but it "generally accepted the legitimacy of the American political community in general and especially of the university." In the second phase, "a considerable number of young people, particularly the activist core, experienced a progressive deterioration in their acceptance of national and university authority." This change was associated with the escalation of the Vietnam war, which made the draft more of a threat, as well as with what was perceived as misrepresentation by the President and others—the "credibility gap."[148]

In November 1966, after several months of discussions among the various antiwar groups, agreement was reached on establishing a new organization, the Spring Mobilization Committee to End the War in Vietnam (SMC), to conduct in the spring of 1967 a major demonstration against the war, the goal of which would be a cessation of U.S. bombing of North Vietnam, a U.S.-initiated cease-fire, negotiations among the parties to the war, and a phased withdrawal of U.S. forces. A. J. Muste was named as chairman.[149] Unlike the earlier committee, (the National Coordinating Committee to End the War in Vietnam) which had been organized and led by students, the SMC was organized and led by adults, many of whom were experienced protestors. Not only had the antiwar movement taken to the street, it was also becoming much more broadly based and inclusive, with stronger leadership.

A few weeks later, antiwar students from radical left groups organized a Student Mobilization Committee to End the War in Vietnam. Rather than sponsoring a student strike, which had been the original purpose of the meeting, the new student group—despite the announced opposition of the SDS—agreed to support the SMC's spring demonstration.[150]

The fall of 1966, Kirkpatrick Sale says, was also "the beginning of active student resistance."[151] Notable among the numerous protests occurring at colleges and universities throughout the country was one at Harvard University on November 6, 1966, organized by Students for a Democratic Society, in which Secretary of Defense McNamara's car, as he was leaving the campus, was stopped by an estimated 800 protestors. When they began rocking it back and forth, McNamara agreed to spend five minutes answering questions. This is a description of the exchange that followed:[152]

> McNamara told the crowd: "I spent four of the happiest years on the Berkeley campus doing some of the same things you're doing here. But there is one important difference: I was both tougher and more courteous." After laughter and shouts,

[146] Powers, *The War at Home,* p. 166.
[147] Vogelgesang, *The Long Dark Night of the Soul,* p. 115.
[148] *The Politics of Protest,* cited above, pp. 99–101.
[149] DeBenedetti and Chatfield, *An American Ordeal,* p. 163, Zaroulis and Sullivan, *Who Spoke Up?* pp. 93–97, Powers, *The War at Home,* pp. 166–167.
[150] DeBenedetti and Chatfield, p. 164, and Zaroulis and Sullivan, pp. 97–98.
[151] Sale, *SDS,* p. 299.
[152] This quotation from "New Left Notes" is taken from *ibid.,* pp. 303–304. See also the description in Shapley, *Promise and Power,* pp. 376–377.

> he shouted vehemently, "I was tougher then and I'm tougher now!"
>
> The audience loved it. Mac was blowing his cool—unable to handle himself, quite possibly scared. The first question was about the origins of the Vietnamese war. "It started in '54-'55 when a million North Vietnamese flooded into South Vietnam," McNamara said. "Goin home!" someone shouted. Mac countered "Why don't you guys get up here since you seem to know all the answers?" The next question asked for the number of civilian casualties in the South. "the number of casualties . . ." Mac began, but was drowned out by cries of *"Civilian! Civilian!* Napalm victims!" A few PL types [Progressive Labor] in front were jumping up and down screaming "Murderer! Fascist!" Mac tried to regain his composure and said "Look fellas, we had an agreement. . . ." A girl shrieked "What about your agreement to hold elections in 1956?"
>
> Things seemed to be breaking up. The police moved in and whisked McNamara into Leverett House; an SDS leader, fearing violence in the streets, took the microphone and ordered all SDS people to clear the area. The disciplined shock troops of the revolution turned and dispersed quickly, McNamara was hustled out through steam tunnels, and everyone went home to watch themselves on TV.

Following the incident, the university apologized to McNamara, and a large number of students signed a petition of apology. But as Thomas Powers so aptly says, "Passions over the war were rising like an inexorable tide. That brief confrontation had better expressed the true feelings of students than all of the speeches, debates, editorials, congressional hearings, and elections put together. When language fails, students were beginning to feel, only action is left."[153]

This was also a time in which, partly as a result of some of these trends noted above—especially the rejection of authority and the alienation from traditional forms and methods of political protest, and partly because of government efforts to suppress protests, there were increasing confrontations between civil authorities and some of the more radical protestors.[154] Hearings by the House Un-American Activities Committee in August 1966 were the scene of one such confrontation as the committee considered a bill to provide criminal penalties for: "(a) the solicitation, collection and delivery of any money, property, or thing to or for the use of any foreign power or organization involved in armed conflict with the United States, whether or not a formal state of war has been declared by

[153] Powers, *The War at Home,* pp. 136–137.

[154] One of the targets of FBI efforts to suppress protests was the Inter-University Committee for Debate on Foreign Policy, the umbrella group for the teach-ins being conducted in colleges and universities, which had begun at the University of Michigan in March of 1965. In October 1966, for example, an anonymous letter was sent by the Detroit office of the FBI to "influential" Michigan political figures, the media, the Board of Regents and the administration of the University of Michigan in an attempt "to discredit and neutralize" the "communist activities" of the committee. The letter decried the "undue publicity" given to antiwar protests which, it said "undoubtedly give 'aid and comfort' to the enemy," and encourage the Communists "in refusing to come to the bargaining table." It added: "I wonder if the strategy is to bleed the United States white by prolonging the war in Vietnam and pave the way for a takeover by Russia?" Final Report, Book II of the Senate Select Committee to Study Intelligence Activities, p. 214.

Congress, and (b) the obstruction of the movement of personnel or supplies of the Armed Forces of the United States."

The bill had been prompted by efforts, especially in Oakland, California, to obstruct trains carrying troops and supplies to a port of embarkation, and by efforts of various groups, especially some Quakers, to collect blood as well as money for medical supplies to be sent to North and South Vietnam.

The House hearings, which focused on the activities of several left and "new left" organizations, primarily student groups, resulted in what Senate Republican Leader Dirksen called a "spectacle [which] can do the Congress no good." According to one description, "Witnesses and spectators, many of them members of the so-called 'New Left,' shouted protests against the Vietnam war, the hearings, the bill and HUAC [House Un-American Activities Committee] itself; some witnesses wisecracked or refused to answer questions; police ejected and arrested boisterous spectators; and a lawyer, Arthur Kinoy, was carried bodily from the hearing room after he shouted his defense of a client. . . . The hearings closed in an uproar as witnesses and spectators were dragged from the hearing room. The last person ejected was a witness who had been subpoenaed but not called to testify. He was Jerry Clyde Rubin of Berkeley and he appeared wearing a Revolutionary War costume."[155]

The Johnson administration opposed the Un-American Activities Committee bill. Representatives of the Department of Defense and the Justice Department testified that it was unnecessary. Deputy Attorney General Ramsey Clark told the members of the committee that they were helping to publicize the activities of those in question—activities, he said, which "can hardly be considered a threat." He concluded:[156]

> Essentially, the Vietnam obstructionist movement has been a propaganda effort. What we do to exaggerate its dimension, which is miniscule, only aids it in the accomplishment of its purposes. That such a tiny handful of people could secure so much attention in so vast a Nation by what has largely been eccentric behavior, is in itself a cause for concern.

These views were brushed aside, and the bill was approved by the committee, which said in its report: "If we are not prepared to suppress hostile activities in their infancy, we shall be faced with

---

[155] *Congressional Quarterly Almanac,* 1966, pp. 623, 625. See also the *New York Times,* Aug. 18, 19, 1966. Rubin, a leader of the Berkeley Vietnam Day Committee who subsequently became a prominent leader of the antiwar movement said in an interview some years later that he wore the costume in order to do "something arresting, something shocking, something that would really make a statement." "It was the perfect message. It said, 'We're the revolutionaries. This country was founded on a revolution. You're violating your own ideals. You're violating your own traditions.' It was a visual statement . . . America is primarily a visual society. What could I possibly say that would be noticed as much as this image?"

"It worked perfectly," Rubin said. "They fell into my trap and decided not to let me testify. My purpose was not to testify but to be seen. But when they cancelled the hearings, I screamed, 'I came to testify! I want to testify!' And the chairman said, 'Sit down.' When I didn't sit down, they arrested me. And when the marshals dragged me out, it was like dragging Thomas Jefferson, Thomas Paine away from the House Un-American Activities Committee as they tried to testify . . . the whole thing was A-plus theater.

"So everything worked out perfectly. I thanked the federal marshals, I thanked the media. . . ." (Joan and Robert Morrison, *From Camelot to Kent State,* cited above, pp. 281–283.)

[156] U.S. Congress, House, Committee on Un-American Activities, *Hearings on H.R. 12047, H.R. 14925, H.R. 16175, H.R. 17140, and H.R. 17194—Bills to Make Punishable Assistance to Enemies of U.S. in Time of Undeclared War,* 89th Cong., 2d sess., 2 pts. (Washington, D.C.: U.S. Govt. Print. Off., 1966), pt. 2, p. 101.

greater problems as they mature. If we value our liberties, as we do, we shall not permit any impairment of our national security while powerful forces, avowedly hostile to our society, are preparing to make us their victim."[157]

When the bill was debated in the House on October 12, 1966, its opponents, seeking to dramatize their opposition, resorted to the parliamentary device of demanding that a quorum be present, and seven long and tedious quorum calls, each taking about 45 minutes, were held in the course of the debate. The bill was passed, however, 275–64, over the opposition of 56 antiwar Democratic liberals joined by 8 Republicans.[158] It was sent to the Senate, where it died in the Judiciary Committee.[159]

Public opinion, as measured by opinion surveys, generally continued to support the war by about a two to one margin, but by September-October 1966 the surge in support a few months earlier had waned and there was less support for escalation and more support for finding a way to end the fighting.

A Harris Survey in October 1966 reported the following decline in support for escalation:[160]

[In percent]

	Favor Escalation	*Favor De-escalation*
Mid-October 1966	44	56
September	52	48
July	60	40
May	47	53
March	53	47
January	48	52

In the same survey, respondents were asked for their opinion on U.N. Ambassador Goldberg's proposal to have both sides withdraw forces under U.N. supervision.

> *"Which would you consider the best thing that you would like to happen in Vietnam?"*

[In percent]

Both sides withdraw troops under U.N. Supervision	48
Win total military victory over Communists	38
Have U.S. move its troops out	8
Get neutralist government of South Vietnam	6

Judging by opinion surveys, the publics of other major western countries were opposed to the war and, by fairly decisive margins, wanted the U.S. to withdraw. In August and again in October 1966, a Gallup Poll in the U.S. and several other countries produced these results:[161]

> *"Just from what you have heard or read, which of these statements comes closest to the way you, yourself, feel about the war in Vietnam: A. The United States should begin to withdraw its troops. B. The United States should carry on*

[157] H. Rept. 89–1908.
[158] For the debate see *CR*, vol. 112, pp. 26213 ff. The vote is on pp. 26592–26593.
[159] The same bill that passed the House of Representatives was reintroduced in 1967. There were no hearings, but the bill was reported favorably to the House (H. Rept. 90–326), despite the continued opposition of the executive branch. It was never called up for debate, however.
[160] *Washington Post*, Oct. 25, 1966.
[161] Gallup, *The Gallup Poll*, vol. 3, pp. 2030 (Great Britain), 2035 (France and West Germany).

its present level of fighting. C. The United States should increase the strength of its attacks on North Vietnam?"

[In percent]

	U.S.	*Great Britain*	*France*	*West Germany*
Begin to withdraw troops	18	42	68	51
Carry on present level	18	17	8	19
Increase attacks	55	16	5	15
No opinion	9	25	19	15

In these other countries, as in the United States, leading intellectuals were in the forefront of antiwar sentiment and activity. One of the principal figures was the renowned English philosopher and mathematician, Bertrand Russell. In the early 1960s, after President Kennedy had approved the use of defoliants and had sent 16,000 American troops as advisers to the South Vietnamese (they began playing active combat roles as well as giving advice),[162] Lord Russell began collecting information on what he perceived to be the "crimes" being committed by the Americans.[163] In a letter to the *New York Times* in early 1963, he said that American conduct in Vietnam was "reminiscent of warfare as practiced by the Germans in Eastern Europe and the Japanese in South East Asia."[164] Beginning in 1964, he began sending observers to Indochina.

These activities were funded by the Bertrand Russell Peace Foundation, which in 1965 began to seek ways of revealing and dramatizing what Russell and his associates considered to be "crimes on a scale which it was difficult to imagine."[165] This led to the establishment by Russell in June 1966 of the Vietnam Solidarity Campaign which Russell said "brought together those groups which saw the Vietnam War as flagrant aggression by the world's mightiest nation against a small peasant people," and held that "the war must be ended quickly and that the only way to end it was to support the North Vietnamese and the Liberation Front unequivocally."[166]

At about the same time, Russell announced that he was inviting jurists, literary figures and eminent public figures from Africa, Asia, Latin America, Europe and the U.S. to form an International War Crimes Tribunal which would conduct investigations in Vietnam and hear evidence on the "crimes of the U.S. Government in Vietnam." Twenty-one accepted, including the French philosopher Jean Paul Sartre, who became the executive president of the Tribunal (Russell was honorary president), Simone de Beauvoir, a prominent French writer and philosopher, and Americans James Baldwin, an African-American novelist who lived in Paris, Stokely Carmichael, an African-American leader of SNCC (the Student Non-Violent Coordinating Committee), David Dellinger, a pacifist and

---

[162] See pt. II of this study.

[163] Bertrand Russell, *The Autobiography of Bertrand Russell, 1944–1969* (New York: Simon and Schuster, 1969), p. 242.

[164] *Ibid.*, p. 243.

[165] Ralph Schoenman, from p. 5 of his foreword to *Against the Crimes of Silence, Proceedings of the International War Crimes Tribunal*, John Duffett (ed.) (New York: Simon and Schuster, 1970). Schoenman, an assistant to Russell, was director of the American Foundation for Social Justice in New York, and in 1966 became Secretary-General of the Tribunal.

[166] Russell, *Autobiography*, p. 242.

editor of *Liberation* magazine, and Carl Oglesby, past president of the SDS.[167]

On June 18, 1966, Russell issued an "Appeal to the American Conscience," which called on Americans to consider what the U.S. was doing to the people of Vietnam, and to emancipate themselves from the "usurpers of American society" who had "traduced" America's revolutionary tradition and were waging a "barbaric . . . aggressive war of conquest" for the purpose of "continued control over the wealth of the region [Indochina and Southeast Asia] by American capitalists."[168]

In this statement, Russell also referred to the creation of the International Tribunal, declaring that "President Johnson, Dean Rusk, Robert McNamara, Henry Cabot Lodge, General Westmoreland and other fellow criminals will be brought before a wider justice than they recognize and a more profound condemnation than they are equipped to understand."

The Tribunal held an organizational meeting in November 1966 (its two public "trials," as will be seen, were held several months later). In his opening speech to the group, Russell said that the Tribunal had no "clear historical precedent," although the Nuremburg Trials had sought to judge and condemn Nazi war crimes. The Vietnam Tribunal, he said, would have the "same responsibility," even though it had no legal authority. "I feel certain," he said, "that this Tribunal will perform an historic role if its investigation is exhaustive. We must record the truth in Vietnam. We must pass judgment on what we find to be the truth. We must warn of the consequences of this truth."[169]

Prior to the organizational meeting, Russell had written to President Johnson on August 25, 1966, inviting him to testify before the

---

[167] For the complete list of members see *Against the Crimes of Silence,* p. 17.

[168] Bertrand Russell, *War Crimes in Vietnam* (London: Allen and Unwin, 1967), p. 124. The text of the Appeal is on pp. 116–124. This volume also includes other writings of Russell on the war.

[169] Russell, *Autobiography,* pp. 319–320. In an "Appeal for Support for the International War Crimes Tribunal" Russell said that the Tribunal had been created because the U.S. was waging a "war of atrocity" in Vietnam to protect the natural resources in its "empire" by destroying "popular resistance to American economic control." "It is because the Vietnamese revolution has challenged the aggression of the exploiting countries that the United States has moved its armed forces into Vietnam." *Against the Crimes of Silence,* pp. 37–39. For Sartre's opening statement, see pp. 40–45.

In a statement on "The Aims and Objectives of the Tribunal," prepared by Russell and issued by the Tribunal at the preliminary meeting (*Against the Crimes of Silence,* pp. 14–16), the members of the panel declared that they were undertaking the inquiry "in the firm belief that we express a deep anxiety and remorse felt by many of our fellow humans in many countries. We trust that our actions will help to arouse the conscience of the world." The inquiry, the statement said, would seek to answer the following questions.

"1. Has the United States Government (and the Governments of Australia, New Zealand, and South Korea) committed acts of aggression according to international law?

"2. Has the American Army made use of or experimented with new weapons or weapons forbidden by the laws of war (gas, special chemical products, napalm, etc.)?

"3. Has there been bombardment of targets of a purely civilian character, for example hospitals, schools, sanatoria, dams, etc., and on what scale has this occurred?

"4. Have Vietnamese prisoners been subjected to inhuman treatment forbidden by the laws of war and, in particular, to torture or to mutilation? Have there been unjustified reprisals against the civilian population, in particular, the execution of hostages?

"5. Have forced labour camps been created, has there been deportation of the population or other acts tending to the extermination of the population and which can be characterized judicially as acts of genocide?"

If the Tribunal found that crimes had been committed, it would then decide who bore the responsibility.

Tribunal.[170] The President did not reply to Russell's letter, but he and his associates did not treat the challenge lightly. Coming at a time when there was growing dissent at home and in other countries, and because it involved a number of prominent persons who were able to draw on the resources of the Russell Foundation for financial support, the Tribunal was viewed as a threat that had to be vigorously combatted. Accordingly, an interagency group was formed from the State Department, the CIA, USIA, and the Department of Defense, with Under Secretary of State Ball as chairman, to deal with the matter.[171] The 303 Committee, which was the committee of the National Security Council that handled covert operations, may also have been involved.

Beginning in July 1966, the U.S. Government organized an extensive program of intelligence and actions aimed at discrediting Russell and the Tribunal and its staff, preventing, if possible, the meeting of the Tribunal and dissuading persons from serving on the Tribunal or attending its meetings, as well as persuading others to withdraw from affiliation with and support of the Russell Foundation. Consideration also was given to possible legal remedies for the defamation of U.S. officials, but the State Department's Legal Adviser suggested that this should not be attempted.[172]

Although most of the documentary evidence remains classified, there is enough evidence available to indicate the seriousness with which the threat was viewed and the nature of U.S. responses. On August 5, for example, Ball talked to Adam Yarmolinsky, McNamara's assistant, who had been made available by McNamara to work on the problem. Yarmolinsky said "he did not think we could ignore the war crimes trial—it could hurt us a good deal in Europe and also Asia." He suggested having a private counsel file briefs with and/or appear before the Tribunal. Ball said he "did not want to dignify" it, and proposed instead that the U.S. promote a "competing trial" through the International Committee of Jurists at the Hague. He said he had spoken to McNamara as well as CIA Director Helms about the idea. Yarmolinsky agreed with Ball's proposal.[173] In a memorandum on August 25, 1966, assigning responsibility for various tasks, the CIA was directed to prepare dossiers on the principal persons involved in the Tribunal, including members and staff, and on the Russell Foundation. An official in the Public Affairs Bureau of the State Department agreed to approach

---

[170] For the text of the letter see *ibid.*, pp. 19–20. In the Johnson Library, Name File, there is also a folder of material on Bertrand Russell, including a copy of this letter, and in the NSF Country File, Vietnam, there is a folder of material on Russell and on the War Crimes Tribunal.

[171] U.S. Department of State, Lot File 74 D 164, Memorandum for the President from Ball, "Items for Evening Reading," Aug. 29, 1966. There is some documentation of the U.S. Government's effort to discredit Lord Russell and the Tribunal in the Department of State Central File, Pol 27-12.

[172] U.S. Department of State, Central File, Pol 27 Viet S, Memorandum for the Secretary from Richard L. Kearney of the Legal Adviser's Office, "Legal Remedies Available Against Persons Conducting a Mock 'Trial' of United States Officials for 'War Crimes' in Vietnam," July 15, 1966. This memorandum discussed the provisions for such actions in U.S., English and French law, concluding: "It would seem that we would want to avoid litigating in what would be essentially a private action the truth of allegations concerning issues of such great national significance as our policy and actions in Vietnam." Moreover, "the bringing of any suit against those involved in the mock trial would itself result in very unfavorable publicity for the United States both at home and abroad, as well as focus attention on Lord Russell's activities. He and his cohorts would undoubtedly find this most welcome."

[173] Johnson Library, Ball Telcons, telephone conversation between Ball and Yarmolinksy, Aug. 5, 1966.

on a "personal basis" an official of the *New York Times* to suggest a story on Ralph Schoenman's background and activities. USIA was to provide background and guidance for its posts. The State Department was to handle diplomatic contacts.[174]

In a memorandum to the President on August 29, Ball reported that the interagency group was "quietly exploring with the British and French available legal steps that could be taken to forestall this spectacle. We also plan to stimulate press articles criticizing the 'trials' and detailing the unsavory and leftwing background of the organizers and judges."[175]

In a memorandum to the President on September 16, 1966, Ball said that the State Department had directed U.S. Ambassadors in Ethiopia, India, Pakistan, Senegal, Tanzania and Zambia to talk to the heads of those countries (who were among the sponsors of the Russell Foundation.)[176] Ball said that each one would be informed as to "the manner in which his name is being misused to circulate pro-communist, anti-American propaganda. . . . We are pointing out that the 'Foundation' has been captured by a group of extreme left-wingers of the pro-Chicom [Chinese Communist] stripe, several of them American citizens, who are using the 94-year old Russell's name, perhaps without his full comprehension."

Ball added that he was going to discuss the matter with the British Home Secretary, and was also going to talk to Supreme Court Justice Fortas about asking cellist Pablo Casals, a friend of Fortas, to remove his name as one of the sponsors.

U.S. diplomatic efforts proved to be partially successful when the heads of State of Ethiopia, Senegal, Tanzania and Zambia withdrew as sponsors.[177]

On December 12, 1966, in a memorandum to Rostow from D. W. Ropa, a CIA officer on detail to the NSC staff who was the White House liaison with the agency, said that the CIA was "monitoring" preparations for the trials and recommended that the CIA be asked by Rostow to develop options for U.S. action, "possibly for consideration by the 303 Committee."[178]

During the fall of 1966, efforts also were underway to promote support for U.S. policy. Among these was a statement on November 29, 1966, instigated by Freedom House, an organization with close ties to the U.S. Government, that was signed by 145 leaders from business, labor, politics, religion, the arts, and colleges and universities, including former President Eisenhower, former Secretary of State Acheson, and Senator Javits (the only Member of Congress in the group). In the statement, which was also printed as an advertisement in the *New York Times,* entitled, "Leaders Warn that

---

[174] Same location. On Feb. 19, 1967, the *New York Times Magazine* carried what Under Secretary of State Katzenbach called "a long, highly critical" piece, "The Bertrand Russell 'War Crimes' Campaign," by British journalist Bernard Levin. In a memorandum to the President on February 17, with which he enclosed a copy of the article, Katzenbach said: "We provided background material for this article. . . ." Johnson Library, NSF Country File, Vietnam.

[175] U.S. Department of State, Lot File 74 D 164, Memorandum for the President from Ball, "Items for Evening Reading," Aug. 29, 1966.

[176] Same location, Memorandum for the President from Ball, "Bertrand Russell's 'War Crimes Trials,'" Sept. 16, 1966.

[177] Same location, State Department Activities Report sent to the White House on Nov. 14, 1966. As a result of other "careful approaches" by U.S. Embassies, India and Pakistan also disavowed the Russell Tribunal.

[178] This memorandum, heavily excised when it was declassified, is in the Johnson Library, NSF Country File, Vietnam.

Extremists Could Delay Vietnam Negotiations," the group said: "The American military presence in South Vietnam has demonstrated that the Communists cannot win their 'war of national liberation,' and has brought the struggle in Vietnam to the point where the possibility of negotiation may become an actuality." [179] They said they were not suggesting that critics of the war "end their opposition," but in order to avoid any misunderstanding by the Communists of U.S. determination to defend South Vietnam, and to ensure that negotiations result in a "just peace," they urged critics to "renounce such fantasies as":

—That this is "Lyndon Johnson's War" or "McNamara's war" or any other individual's war.

—That the American leaders are committing "war crimes" or indulging in "genocide."

—That military service in this country's armed forces is an option exercisable solely at the discretion of the individual.

—That this is a "race" war of white versus colored peoples.

—That this nation's leaders are obsessed with some compulsion to play "world policemen" or to conduct some "holy war" against the legitimate aspirations of underdeveloped people.

Several weeks later, a leading academic opponent of the war, Hans Morgenthau, a professor at the University of Chicago, replied in an article in which he said, among other things, "The Freedom House document is trying to establish a political orthodoxy with regard to our policies in Vietnam. It tells us that we are morally entitled to criticize the government, but not with regard to the fundamental issue it enumerates. That is to say, we are not morally entitled to criticize the government in any meaningful way." "The Freedom House document," Morgenthau added, "is a result of a misguided sense of patriotism. This patriotism deems it its duty to support the policies of the government in times of crisis, thus identifying the government with the nation, and in the process sacrifices the interests of the nation upon the alter of conformity." [180]

Former Presidential Assistant McGeorge Bundy also came to the defense of the administration in the lead article in the January 1967 issue of *Foreign Affairs*.[181] Citing Vietnam as an example of the complex and difficult problems faced by the United States, Bundy said he had supported the decisions to become involved, and felt that it was "right to persevere." It was, he said, "a test of Communist revolutionary doctrine, and what happens there will affect what happens elsewhere. . . ." But he added that a Communist victory would not necessarily mean "automatic communization of all Asia," and the defeat of the Communists would not necessarily bring an end to the threat of China. He thought that the war would continue for some time, but that the American public would support it. Furthermore, its financial costs were "quite manageable," and should not detract from domestic expenditures. Bombing of the North, he said, was only one military instrument. Moreover, it had not been done irresponsibly, and was still justified "by its value of hampering the work of infiltration and supply."

[179] *New York Times*, Nov. 30, 1966.
[180] *New Leader*, Jan. 2, 1967.
[181] McGeorge Bundy, "The End of Either/Or," *Foreign Affairs*, 45 (January 1967), pp. 189–201.

There was also strong support from executives of major U.S. companies, according to an article in the *New York Times* reporting on a meeting of the Business Council.[182] "Council members, without exception, continue to support the war in Vietnam, and most believe Mr. Johnson is following about the right policy there, although a few 'hawks' in the group would like to see an increased American commitment, with the aim of getting the war over faster."

[182] *New York Times,* Oct. 24, 1966. The Business Council is an organization of the heads of most of the major U.S. corporations.

CHAPTER 11

STALEMATE

By November 1966, the United States was deeply involved in helping the South Vietnamese to defeat the Communists, as well as in assisting with the operation and the "development" of the country's economy and political system. There were almost 400,000 U.S. troops engaged in trying to find and to destroy the enemy on the ground in the South and to bomb the enemy into submission in the North, while others trained local security forces and helped in locating and eliminating the Communist "infrastructure" in the villages. (In addition, there were 40,000 U.S. Navy personnel on ships off the coast of Vietnam, 35,000–40,000 U.S. military personnel in Thailand, and thousands of others playing supporting roles in Guam, Okinawa and the Philippines.) Altogether, it was a vast, expansive, and difficult undertaking which, because of its costs in men and money, was imposing heavy burdens on those Americans and South Vietnamese who were seeking to direct the effort while also defending its necessity and validity.

It had become increasingly evident, however, that, while the reasons originally stated as the rationale for the war might still be defensible—whether or not they were valid—the war was not being "won" through the application of military pressure on the Communists, and probably could not be won within the limitations on its conduct imposed by external factors or by the demands of the American political system. The problem, of course, as George Ball had predicted, was not being able to get off the tiger's back.

Negotiations, while more important than ever, seemed ever more futile given the perceived undesirability of meeting the enemy's terms. Yet, unilateral withdrawal was deemed impossible because of the effect on U.S. prestige, alliances and national "honor" of breaking what was considered and had often been referred to as a "commitment." This was based in part, of course, on U.S. political considerations, but it also flowed from a deeper wellspring of feelings of national pride and well-being. America, it was said, had never broken a treaty or lost a war, and this sense of allegiance, of invincibility, coupled with a strong strain of national mission, served to support the perpetuation of a policy even when it began to appear to be flawed. It was not and would not in the end be easy to admit that the cause was being lost.

To admit defeat would also have meant that Lyndon Johnson was prepared to face the political consequences of such an action in 1968, which he was not at that point, and that he was prepared to accept such a verdict psychologically, which he also was not prepared to do. This is Doris Kearns' explanation:[1]

> In the beginning, Johnson had feared his country would become obsessed with failure if Vietnam was lost. As the war went on, the obsession he feared for his country became his own. Indeed, as the Great Society disintegrated, the lower the President's popularity fell, the more Johnson had to see his decision to escalate as the only decision he could have made. He had committed everything he had to Vietnam. Regardless of all evidence, he simply had to be right. To think otherwise, to entertain even the slightest doubt, was to open himself to the pain of reliving old decisions, options, and possibilities long since discarded.

There was also enough time and enough support in the public and in Congress for the President and his associates to continue hoping for and trying to achieve the victory that was proving to be so elusive. But time was growing short, and unless it could be demonstrated that the war was being won it was clear that there would be increasing pressure for a change of policy in the months ahead.

Reports on the war in the fall of 1966 from two prominent American journalists illustrated the problems being encountered and the moral and practical dilemmas facing the U.S. Neil Sheehan, who had been in Vietnam with United Press International in 1962–1964, wrote an article for the October 9, 1966 *New York Times Magazine* after he returned from Vietnam from a year as a *New York Times* reporter. In the article, "Not a Dove, But no Longer a Hawk," Sheehan said that during his first tour he had believed in basic U.S. aims in Vietnam, but after his second tour he realized that he was "naive in believing the non-Communist Vietnamese could defeat the Communist insurgency and build a decent and progressive social structure."

> While there are some patriotic and decent individuals among them, most of the men who rule Saigon have, like the Bourbons, learned nothing and have forgotten nothing. They seek to retain what privileges they have and to regain those they have lost.
>
> In Vietnam, only the Communists represent revolution and social change, for better or worse according to a man's politics. The Communist party is the one truly national organization that permeates both North and South Vietnam. . . . The Communists, despite their brutality and deceit, remain the only Vietnamese capable of rallying millions of their countrymen to sacrifice and hardship in the name of the nation and the only group not dependent on foreign bayonets for survival. . . .
>
> For its own strategic and political ends, the United States is thus protecting a non-Communist Vietnamese social structure that cannot defend itself and that perhaps does not deserve to be defended. Our responsibility for prolonging what is essentially a civil conflict may be one of the major reasons for the considerable amount of confusion, guilt and soul-searching among Americans over the Vietnam war.

---

[1] Kearns, *Lyndon Johnson and the American Dream,* p. 310.

Sheehan thought that the U.S. had no choice but to continue prosecuting the war.

We can and should limit the violence and the suffering being inflicted on the civilians as much as possible, but, for whatever reasons, successive Administrations in Washington have carried the commitment in Vietnam to the point where it would be very difficult to prevent any precipitate retreat from degenerating into a rout. If the United States were to disengage from Vietnam under adverse conditions, I believe that the resulting political and psychological shockwaves might undermine our entire position in Southeast Asia. We shall, I am afraid, have to put up with our Vietnamese mandarin allies. We shall not be able to reform them and it is unlikely that we shall be able to find any other Vietnamese willing to cooperate with us. We shall have to continue to rely mainly on our military power, accept the odium attached to its use and hope that someday this power will bring us to a favorable settlement.

But I simply cannot help worrying that, in the process of waging this war, we are corrupting ourselves. I wonder, when I look at the bombed-out peasant hamlets, the orphans begging and stealing on the streets of Saigon and the women and children with napalm burns lying on the hospital cots, whether the United States or any nation has the right to inflict this suffering and degradation on another people for its own ends. And I hope we will not, in the name of some anti-Communist crusade, do this again.

Sheehan also thought that the war could be won.

I have the feeling that somehow we can muddle through this grim business. We may not win in Vietnam as we won in World War II, yet we may well prevail. Given our overwhelming military superiority, it is entirely possible that Washington, over a period of years, may be able to destroy the Vietcong and North Vietnamese main-force units in the South, and to transform what is currently a militarily sound but politically weak position into one of some, if doubtful, political strength. . . .

A similarly ambiguous and uncertain but determined mood prevailed among U.S. Government civilians and military in South Vietnam, as Max Frankel, White House correspondent for the *New York Times,* reported during a trip to Vietnam in November 1966:[2]

Almost every soldier, from private to colonel, counts the days until his year of duty here expires, and most civilians echo the doubts and confusions of Americans at home about the involvement here. Yet all believe there is no easy way out of the morass. They expect a long guerrilla war even after the bigger Communist units are hunted down and humbled. They expect that a longer time still will pass before Americans can safely leave the nation to the policing of the South Vietnamese. They simply cannot imagine any peace until the village-by-village organization of the Vietcong's political agents and paddy fighters is first uprooted and eventually replaced. And they cannot un-

[2] *New York Times,* Nov. 25, 1966.

derstand why Washington will not simply say so and rally American patriotism around that arduous yet challenging task.

Everywhere the men who sweat and fight here are begging the home folks for patience. Above all they are begging their own government to resign itself to the scope of the undertaking and to quit pressing for daily, weekly, monthly indicators of "success."

If Saigon, after enormous effort, sends 6,500 Vietnamese members of new pacification teams into the villages, Washington burns up the wires demanding a figure of 10,000.

If Saigon shoves and begs and maneuvers to clear the port here for faster deliveries, Washington fires off orders that the Vietnamese be told to do it yet another way.

"I thought the name of the game out here was to treat these people as sovereign and independent," says an army colonel.

"Sometimes you think they think of it as an occupied country," says a senior diplomat.

The Manila Conference, October 1966

In late September 1966, the White House announced that President Johnson would meet in Manila on October 23–25 with leaders of South Vietnam and those from the other Pacific nations with troops or other military units in Vietnam (South Korea, Thailand, the Philippines, Australia, and New Zealand).

At the NSC meeting on October 15 at which the trip was discussed, Moyers explained that the purpose of the Conference was to "show our friendship for Asian countries rather than accomplish substantive policy gains," and the President added: "The conference will probably accomplish little so we must consider now how to keep the initiative in the period ahead." [3]

When asked about his reaction to the announcement of the Manila meeting, Senator Fulbright questioned whether anything productive would come from a meeting of "such a cozy little group" of "our boys." [4] More good could come, he said, from a statement of

---

[3] Johnson Library, NSF NSC Meetings File.

In a memorandum to the President on Oct. 3, 1966, Rostow outlined the goals for the Manila meeting (Johnson Library, NSF Memos to the President—Walt Rostow):

"We want these results from the Philippines conference:

"1. A reaffirmation of the commitment among the fighting allies to see it through to an honorable peace.

"2. An agreed position among the fighting allies and Saigon on the terms on which peace will be sought.

"3. An approach by the Saigon government, backed by the fighting allies, to those now fighting with the VC, including perhaps an amnesty offer, which would go beyond the appeal made in the Honolulu declaration by the Vietnamese government.

"4. Increased emphasis by Saigon, backed by the fighting allies, on pacification, land reform, planning for long-term economic development (including future use of our bases), education, health, agriculture, etc.

"5. If possible, an agreed statement of support for Cambodian territorial integrity and independence.

"6. Support from all the governments for Asian regional economic development without creating or appearing to create a new Asian grouping made up of the fighting allies.

"In general, we want the government in Saigon to recommit itself to its allies and to the world to getting on with the Honolulu program, where much progress has been made, including the commitment to go forward in next steps towards constitutional government."

[4] *New York Times*, Sept. 29, 1966. Before leaving for Manila, the President talked to Fulbright about the Conference (Johnson Library, WHCF, Name File, Fulbright, Memorandum to the President from Marvin Watson, Oct. 15, 1966), but no notes of that meeting have been found. In addition, the State Department briefed Democratic and Republican congressional leaders and the chairmen and ranking members of the Senate Foreign Relations and House Foreign Affairs

willingness to withdraw U.S. forces and from unilateral suspension of bombing for a reasonable time as a way of testing North Vietnamese interest in negotiating. Most targets had already been hit, he added, and infiltration could be controlled by bombing supply routes. He repeated his suggestion that the National Liberation Front should be included in negotiations.

The items on the agenda for the Manila Conference were: a review of military and nonmilitary developments, a review of progress being made toward pacification and "revolutionary development," and a review of peace proposals and of "new measures for ending the war."[5]

During the Conference, the President held a meeting with Westmoreland, Rusk, Lodge and Rostow, who were joined later by Ky and Thieu, at which the military situation was discussed. The President asked Westmoreland to give Rostow a written statement of his views on bombing the North.[6] He also asked him whether he needed additional forces. Westmoreland replied that he "definitely needed" an increase, which he estimated to be about 35 percent above the level at the end of 1966. (At the end of 1966, the authorized U.S. troop level for Vietnam was approximately 395,000. Thus, Westmoreland was estimating that he needed approximately 138,000 more troops, for a total of 533,000.)

The item on a peaceful ending of the war was considered by the Americans to be particularly important. As will be seen, this was in keeping with the conclusions of McNamara after a trip to Vietnam in mid-October that there was no "reasonable way to bring the war to an end soon" and that, while strengthening the pacification program, the U.S. should stabilize its force structure and press ahead with seeking negotiations despite the apparent futility of doing so. Emphasis on negotiations was also being stimulated by Harriman and the other State Department officials on the Negotiations Committee who, along with Goldberg, were trying to develop a more effective and acceptable U.S. negotiating position and to explore new possibilities for a settlement.

The South Vietnamese, on the other hand, as well as Lodge and other American officials in the U.S. Mission, were very skeptical of negotiations, and tended to think that public discussion of peacemaking weakened efforts to defeat the Communists. It was decided to draft a set of conditions that would meet such objections and, once they were accepted by the South Vietnamese, "would give the South Vietnamese Government a badly-needed boost in world public opinion and, much more importantly, commit Saigon to a program that would advance the day of political settlement."[7]

Committees. U.S. Department of State, Lot File 74 D 164, Memorandum for the President—"Items for Evening Reading," Sept. 26, 1966.

[5] See CMH, Westmoreland Papers, History File, for a copy of the agenda as well as a "Talking Points" paper and various briefing papers.

[6] CMH, Westmoreland Papers, Message Files, Westmoreland to Wheeler and Sharp, MAC 9451, Oct. 27, 1966.

[7] Cooper, *The Lost Crusade*, p. 313. As stated in the communiqué issued at the end of the Conference, these were: "1) cessation of aggression, 2) preservation of the territorial integrity of South Vietnam, 3) reunification of Vietnam, 4) resolution of internal problem, 5) removal of allied military forces, and 6) effective guarantees." In the communiqué there was also a narrative statement about each of the six conditions.

For the text of the Manila Summit Conference Joint Communiqué Oct. 25, 1966, see *Public Papers of the Presidents*, Lyndon B. Johnson, 1966, p. 1263. For more details on the Conference

Continued

Emphasis on negotiations and on ending the war was also viewed in Washington as a way of responding to the increasing uncertainty of the American public and its impatience with the results of the war. Accordingly, a plan was conceived for having the South Vietnamese formally ask at Manila for the United States to withdraw its forces as soon as practicable, following which the U.S. would state its willingness to do so. Members of the U.S. staff attending the Manila Conference were put to work drafting such a plan, as well as both the Vietnamese and the American statements, and, after considerable debate between those who were concerned primarily about the substance of the proposal and those who wanted it largely for its publicity value, it was agreed to include in the final communiqué of the Conference a provision that U.S. forces would be withdrawn from South Vietnam "as the other side withdraws its forces to the North, ceases infiltration, and the level of violence thus subsides." Over the objection of at least some of those present from the State Department, (but not from McNaughton, the principal person present from the Defense Department), an American-sponsored provision was also included in the communiqué specifying that U.S. forces would be withdrawn "as soon as possible and not later than six months after the above conditions have been fulfilled."[8] As McNaughton (who said that he did not oppose the provision) reported to McNamara, the six-month provision was "negotiated personally by the President himself." ("I'll tell you the tale later," McNaughton said in his report.)

The President's decision to include the six-month provision in the Manila communiqué was based on earlier discussions between Rusk and Gromyko, the Foreign Minister of the U.S.S.R., in late September 1966, which had been initiated by the U.S.S.R.,[9] followed by a meeting between President Johnson and Gromyko on October 10 in which, according to Johnson in his memoirs, "Gromyko noted that our previous statements had been 'very general' on the matter of withdrawals, and he thought a more specific statement would be useful. . . . This was in mind when I suggested strongly to my colleagues at Manila that we make our stand on troop withdrawals as specific as possible."[10]

In a meeting of the newly established Negotiations Committee on September 15, 1966, to discuss the proposed Johnson-Gromyko meeting, Ambassador at Large Llewellyn Thompson, who, as noted,

---

and on the formulation of the final communiqué see Cooper, *The Lost Crusade*, pp. 310–318, and *PP*, Gravel ed., vol. II, pp. 607–608. See also the materials in the Johnson Library, President's Appointment File, Diary Backup, Box 48.

[8] For the debate within the U.S. staff see Cooper, *The Lost Crusade*. For McNaughton's support of and State's opposition to the provision, see his annotation on p. 10 of a copy of the Joint Communiqué on the Manila Conference which is attached to his report to McNamara on Oct. 26, 1966, Johnson Library, Warnke Papers, McNaughton Files.

[9] See the discussion on Sept. 1, 1966, in Harriman's Negotiations Committee, U.S. Department of State, Lot File 70 D 207, Memorandum of Meeting Sept. 1, 1966 in Governor Harriman's Office. The suggestion for talks was made by a senior member of the U.S.S.R.'s delegation to the U.N.

[10] Johnson, *The Vantage Point*, pp. 248–249. For an interpretation of the contemporary diplomatic context of U.S. relations with the U.S.S.R. as well as China, see Ralph B. Smith, *An International History of the Vietnam War*, vol. III, *The Making of Limited War, 1965–66* (New York: St. Martin's Press, 1991), pp. 400–401.

Apparently very few of the members of the American delegation to the Conference or in Washington or Saigon knew of President Johnson's reason for wanting to include the six-month provision, and the importance he attached to it. In a cable to Wheeler on October 27, Westmoreland said that he was "as surprised as most" to learn that the provision was in the Final Communiqué. CMH, Westmoreland Papers, Message Files, MAC 9451, Oct. 27, 1966.

was considered to be the leading State Department authority on the U.S.S.R., said that he was doubtful that the U.S.S.R. was prepared to "talk seriously" to the U.S. about Vietnam. But Ambassador at Large Averell Harriman, also a former Ambassador to the U.S.S.R., argued that the talks should not be prejudged.[11] He said that this was the first time that the U.S.S.R. had proposed private talks on Vietnam, and that the U.S. had a "valuable opportunity to urge the Soviets to meet their obligations and play a constructive role in bringing about a peaceful resolution of the Vietnam conflict." He saw the talks "as a glimmer of light at present, and believed we should not snuff it out by being excessively negative about the possibilities."[12]

The Negotiations Committee supported Harriman's position, and on October 3, 1966, Harriman sent a memorandum to the President and to Rusk in which he said he believed that the "only real chance now in sight to induce Hanoi to negotiate a settlement depends on the influence Moscow is willing and able to exert."[13] Noting that there were a number of signs that the U.S.S.R. "was seriously" considering how it could play a stronger role in ending the war, he suggested that the President emphasize the obligation of the U.S.S.R. to play a role, pursuant to the 1954 Geneva Agreement, in helping to resolve the dispute,[14] and the willingness of the U.S. to consider any proposals for talks.[15]

On October 6, the Negotiations Committee reviewed the draft of a Harriman memorandum of points for the President's meeting with Gromyko on October 10. Harriman told the group that Gromyko "would be negative or non-committal with the President. 'He would only listen with a long face.'" Harriman said that the principal point for the President to convey was the obligation of the U.S.S.R. in bringing about a peaceful settlement.[16]

In a related move, the U.S., without any announcement or explanation, ceased bombing in the eastern part of the demilitarized zone for several days prior to President Johnson's meeting with Gromyko, apparently to indicate to the U.S.S.R. the seriousness of U.S. interest in a settlement of the war. This would appear to have been prompted by a recommendation from Harriman and the Negotiations Committee after a meeting on September 1 when the Committee agreed that the U.S. should avoid further escalation of bombing during late September-early October before the Johnson-Gromyko meeting, as well as during the period immediately pre-

[11] Thompson also questioned whether the suggestion for the talks had been made on instructions from Moscow. See the memorandum of the meeting on Sept. 15, 1966 of the Negotiations Committee, Department of State, Lot File 70 D 207.

[12] *Ibid.* At the meeting of the Committee on Sept. 1, 1966 (memorandum cited above) Harriman commented on his trip to Moscow in July 1965 at the request of President Johnson, prior to Johnson's decision to deploy large-scale forces. (See pt. III of this study, p. 346.) He said that Premier Alexi Kosygin had told him that the North Vietnamese did not exclude a political settlement, "even one bypassing the Chinese," and that the U.S.S.R. envisaged a settlement on the basis of retaining the present division of Vietnam at the 17th parallel.

[13] Johnson Library, NSF Memos to the President—Walt Rostow, Harriman Memorandum, "Negotiations," to the President and the Secretary of State, Oct. 3, 1966.

[14] Under the terms of the Geneva Agreement of 1954, the U.S.S.R., as one of the nations that guaranteed the implementation of the Agreement, was considered responsible in a legal sense for maintaining peace in Vietnam.

[15] For Harriman's memorandum as well as one from Ambassador Thompson, see the Johnson Library, NSF Memos to the President—Walt Rostow, Rostow Memorandum to the President on Oct. 9, 1966, tabs A and B.

[16] Library of Congress, Harriman Papers, Vietnam Subject File, Memorandum of Meeting of Negotiations Committee, Oct. 6, 1966.

ceding the Manila Conference. Such escalation, Harriman said in a memorandum to the President and the Secretary of State on September 30, "could drown out talk of peaceful negotiation."[17]

The Manila Conference was generally considered by the Americans to have been a success. As McNaughton said in a memorandum to McNamara, "The Conference went well. I think we got what we wanted: Display of not-U.S.-aloneness, of resolve, of beginnings of an awakening responsible Asia, and of concern for the miseries of the Asian billions."[18]

Hope that the six-month provision would help to influence the Russians appears to have been misplaced. Several days before the Conference began, and a few days after the Johnson-Gromyko meeting, Brezhnev, responding to a speech by President Johnson on October 7 in which he had appealed for closer cooperation between the U.S. and the U.S.S.R., said that in order for there to be closer cooperation, "the piratical bombing attacks . . . must be halted and the aggression against the Vietnamese people stopped."[19] After the Conference, Llewellyn Thompson told Anatoly Dobrynin, U.S.S.R. Ambassador to the U.S., that the six-month provision was inserted in response to Gromyko's comment about the usefulness of a more specific statement on withdrawal. Dobrynin replied that he would so inform Gromyko.[20] The Soviet press agency, Tass, however, said that the countries participating in the meeting could not hide their real aim, which was to continue and broaden "the aggression" in Vietnam.[21] In his memoirs, Westmoreland speculates that the six-month offer "may well have been an effort by President Johnson to rid himself of the albatross of South Vietnam, whatever the long-range consequences." He adds that the North Vietnamese victory in 1975 "could have come much sooner" if they had accepted the offer. "For once the United States had pulled out under those circumstances and Giap had come back, what American President would have dared risk the political pitfalls involved in putting American troops back in?"[22]

After the Conference, Harriman was sent by the President to visit 11 countries (Malaysia, Indonesia, Ceylon, India, Pakistan, Iran, Italy, France, Germany, England and Morocco), to describe and explain the purported success of the Conference.[23] When he returned to Washington, Harriman submitted a secret report on the reaction of these countries to the Manila Conference. He said that all of them supported President Johnson's efforts to seek a peaceful solution, but that "in almost every conversation the subject of a suspension of the bombing was raised, particularly now that the military situation had improved. Almost all expressed the belief

[17] Memorandum on the Meeting of the Negotiations Committee, Sept. 1, 1966, cited above and Harriman's memorandum to the President and the Secretary of State of Sept. 30, 1966, Library of Congress, Harriman Papers, Vietnam General.

[18] McNaughton Memorandum to McNamara, Oct. 26, 1966, cited above.

[19] *New York Times*, Oct. 16, 1966.

[20] U.S. Department of State, Lot File 74 D 164, "State Department Activities Report," Oct. 28, 1966.

[21] *New York Times*, Oct. 26, 1966.

[22] Westmoreland, *A Soldiers Reports*, p. 406.

[23] Cooper accompanied Harriman on this trip. For his description see *The Lost Crusade*, pp. 320–324.

that talks could be gotten under way if we would stop the bombing. . . ."[24]

After President Johnson's return from Manila, he was scheduled to make a four-day trip to campaign for Democratic candidates in the congressional election on November 8, 1966. Many administration supporters in Congress, especially the 50-odd new Democratic representatives elected in the 1964 Democratic landslide, were faced with strong opposition and were fearful of the effects of the war on their reelection. There were also two Senate races in which the war was a central issue: in Illinois, between incumbent Senator Paul Douglas, a Democrat, and Republican challenger Charles Percy, and in Oregon between Representative Robert Duncan, a Democrat, and Governor Mark O. Hatfield, a Republican. The trip was cancelled at the last minute when it became apparent that in many of these races the President and the war were negative factors.[25]

In the election, Republican Percy won his race against Douglas as did Republican Hatfield against Duncan, and both new Senators became active participants in Senate opposition to the war. The Democrats, although retaining their majorities in the Senate and the House, lost forty seven House seats in the 1966 election, many of which had been won by Johnson supporters in 1964, as well as losing four in the Senate. Generally speaking, however, the election was not a referendum on the war. If anything, it confirmed the fact that the war, which, judging by opinion surveys, was considered to be the major problem facing the country, was not enough of a political issue, at least in a congressional election, to be a determining factor in voter choice.[26]

---

[24] Johnson Library, NSF Memos to the President—Walt Rostow, Harriman "Report of Post-Manila Trip," Nov. 22, 1966.

[25] Lawrence F. O'Brien, who had managed John F. Kennedy's campaign for the Presidency and was in charge of White House liaison with Congress for both Kennedy and Johnson, said that the trip was cancelled when it appeared that many of the Democratic candidates for whom the President would have campaigned were going to lose. See O'Brien, *No Final Victories: A Life in Politics—From John F. Kennedy to Watergate* (Garden City, N.Y.: Doubleday, 1974), p. 193. See also the account by Califano, *The Triumph and Tragedy of Lyndon Johnson*, pp. 151–152.

Eric Goldman, a Princeton University history professor who was a White House assistant at the time (he was succeeded by John Roche later that year), maintains that Johnson's preoccupation with the war was another factor in the cancellation of the campaign trip: "He [the President] cancelled the trip only in part because when the time came, he was convinced that he would be associated with a defeated cause. Also of importance was the fact that he found it difficult to get interested in anything not directly connected with the war. . . . By the Summer and Fall of 1966 the domestic reformer of the Great Society days had become a war chief, finding more and more congeniality with conservatives, even avoiding the phrase 'Great Society' in his speeches. The ebullient leader given to moments of testiness and rage was now, day after day, bitter, truculent, peevish—and suspicious of the fundamental good sense and integrity of anyone who did not endorse the Vietnam War." Eric Frederick Goldman, *The Tragedy of Lyndon Johnson* (New York: Knopf, 1969), pp. 498–499.

[26] In a Gallup poll on Sept. 11, 1966, 56 percent named Vietnam the most important problem facing the nation. (Others were "racial problems," 24 percent, and "inflation," 16 percent.) *The Gallup Poll*, vol. III, p. 2026.

Those New Left political activists who had organized the National Conference for New Politics (NCNP) in the spring of 1966 received very little encouragement from their efforts to start a new political movement to support "peace candidates" in the 1966 elections. Of the few candidates who ran under this banner and were supported by the NCNP, only one, Robert Scheer, who received 45 percent of the vote in the primary for the Democratic nomination for Congress from the Berkeley, California area, came close to winning. See Powers, *The War at Home*, pp. 123–128, and Zaroulis and Sullivan, *Who Spoke Up?* pp. 83–85.

At the conclusion of the Manila Conference, Senator Mansfield expressed his pleasure with it and suggested that it be followed by a peace conference.[27]

Among the dignitaries who greeted the President on his return from Manila was Senator Fulbright, who accompanied Vice President Humphrey to the airport. This led one observer to comment:[28]

> It is an index of the deepening crisis in foreign policy, and a tribute to the man [Fulbright], that he should have moved so far as he has into the uncongenial role of opportunist, but those who see him intimately note that he is depressed rather than exhilarated by it. He does not have the heretic's zeal for standing alone, and often succumbs to the temptation of returning to the fold. Those aware of this weakness did not miss its skillful exploitation by Vice President Humphrey when he brought Fulbright along to join in the welcome to the President on his return from Manila that wind-swept night at Dulles airport . . . nor the President's own masterly histrionics. First Johnson appeared coldly to ignore the prodigal's return, then rewarded him with a warm embrace. Next day the President gave Fulbright an hour's private briefing, and instructed Rusk to continue it over lunch. The result was a statement by Fulbright hailing the result of the Manila conference.

After meeting with Fulbright on November 3, the President sent him a letter saying, "Enjoyed our meeting. Let me have your suggestions from time to time."[29]

In a brief report on Rusk's luncheon with Fulbright on November 5, one of the President's aides told him that it had gone well and that Fulbright was "very relaxed on Vietnam and seemed to be moving closer to our position."[30]

Although Fulbright may have appeared to be moving toward the administration's position, he and other leading Senate Democratic critics of the war were, in fact, continuing to search for a way to end the war. Those in positions of leadership, particularly Mansfield and Fulbright, recognized, however, that they had a responsibility to a President of their own party, as well as to the party itself—especially so because of the pending congressional election—that required them to discuss and to try to settle their differences in private. Thus, staying in the fold—working within the system—was considered to be an integral part of their roles as political leaders.

In addition to these institutional and political factors, there was a very important factor which appears to have been influential in bringing the President and Senate leaders somewhat closer together in late 1966 and in encouraging Members of Congress to continue working within the system. This was the apparent failure of military means to bring an end to the war and the need to find a solution that would avoid even higher costs and casualties. In the

[27] *New York Times*, Oct. 26, 1966. Congress had adjourned for the year.

[28] I. F. Stone, *In a Time of Torment* (New York: Random House, 1967), pp. 346–347.

[29] Johnson Library, letter from the President to Senator Fulbright, Nov. 4, 1966, Ex FO 6–3. In the Johnson Library, President's Appointment File, Diary Backup for Nov. 3, 1966, there is also a memorandum to the President from Rostow suggesting points to make in talking to Fulbright. There apparently are no notes of the meeting.

[30] Johnson Library, WHCF, Name File, Fulbright, Memorandum to the President from Jake Jacobsen, Nov. 5, 1966.

words of the *Pentagon Papers,* "The illusion of quick victory 'on the cheap' had fled, and hard reality intervened. People in and out of government were beginning to seek alternatives to our policies in Vietnam with increased interest."[31]

On October 13, 1966, Senator Mansfield sent the President another private memorandum in which he again emphasized the need for a prompt settlement of the war. "The alternative of looking for a way out by continuing to raise the military ante," he said, "gets us in deeper all the time, with no terminus in sight." He recommended that the U.S. should be prepared to stop bombing North Vietnam and agree to an immediate "hold fire." This would be followed by a cease-fire and negotiations, with the National Liberation Front included as one of the parties. During the first week or so of negotiations, the U.S. should make a token, unilateral withdrawal of 30,000 troops. He suggested that U.N. Secretary General U Thant should act as a mediator in communicating these terms to North Vietnam.[32]

On November 1, 1966, Senator Church made a similar suggestion for a cease-fire in a private memorandum to U.N. Ambassador Goldberg. He said he recognized the "serious practical disadvantages" of a cease-fire, but that "the alternative of a stalemated war of attrition makes it imperative that an attempt be made." Church added: "The longer the war goes on the more world opinion will turn against the United States, and the greater the public pressure here will be for ending the war by more drastic methods."[33]

"Hanoi," Church added, "is hoping and expecting that the coming elections will show that the American people do not support the war, but the elections are not likely to give her any satisfaction. I doubt that the elections will prove anything one way or the other about overall public opinion. And because of this, the President will have much more room for maneuver. He will be in a position to take political risks in trying to end the war that he could not pursue before the election."

Norvill Jones, who, as noted earlier, was attending the U.N. General Assembly session that fall with Senator Church, and who apparently had drafted Church's memorandum, sent Marcy a copy of the memorandum with this handwritten note:[34]

> Carl—this probably won't do a bit of good but I think it's a logical step under the circumstances. There have been some indications around the U.N. that a cease-fire might be what is needed to break the deadlock. But here again Ky is the significant figure—he must be willing to negotiate and he isn't now. It's a frustrating picture. I'm not sure who is more dogmatic—Ky or Johnson!

On October 19, 1966, as the President was leaving for Manila, Senator Aiken gave a speech in the Senate that contained one of

---

[31] *PP,* Gravel ed., vol. IV, p. 385.

[32] For Mansfield's memo and Johnson's perfunctory reply, see Johnson Library, NSF Name File, Mansfield.

On Nov. 11, 1966, Mansfield also sent a private memo to U.N. Ambassador Goldberg (a copy of which he sent to the President on November 25) suggesting how the Vietnam question could be taken up by the U.N., and the importance of doing so in order to facilitate negotiations. Same location.

[33] National Archives, RG 46, Papers of the Senate Foreign Relations Committee.

[34] Same location, Jones memorandum to Marcy, no date, but probably early November 1966.

the most memorable suggestions offered during the war.[35] It was paraphrased and parodied, restated and misstated, but Aiken was perfectly serious, despite the seeming fatuousness of the idea. After briefly analyzing the development of U.S. policy since the deployment of ground forces in March 1965, he turned to the current situation. U.S. forces, he said, were not in any danger of being defeated, but the more forces there were, the greater casualties there would be, and the less the South Vietnamese Government could assert its own authority. "The size of the U.S. commitment," he said, already clearly is suffocating any serious possibility of self-determination in South Vietnam, for the simple reason that the whole defense of that country is now totally dependent on the U.S. armed presence."

Aiken then posed the alternatives and made his suggestion, which was to declare that the war had been won and to reduce the U.S. military commitment:

> Considering the fact that as every day goes by, the integrity and invincibility of the U.S. Armed Forces is further placed in question because there is no military objective, the United States faces only two choices: Either we can attempt to escape our predicament by escalating the war into a new dimension, where a new so-called aggressor is brought into play or we can deescalate the war on the ground that the clear and present danger of a military defeat no longer exists and therefore deescalation is necessary in order to avoid any danger of placing U.S. Armed Forces in a position of compromise.
>
> Faced with these alternatives, the United States could well declare unilaterally that this stage of the Vietnam war is over—that we have "won" in the sense that our Armed Forces are in control of most of the field and no potential enemy is in a position to establish its authority over South Vietnam.
>
> Such a declaration should be accompanied, not by announcement of a phased withdrawal, but by the gradual redeployment of U.S. military forces around strategic centers and the substitution of intensive reconnaissance for bombing.
>
> This unilateral declaration of military victory would herald the resumption of political warfare as the dominant theme in Vietnam.
>
> Until such a declaration is made, there is no real prospect for political negotiations.
>
> The credibility of such a unilateral declaration of military victory can only be successfully challenged by the Vietcong and the North Vietnamese themselves—assuming that the Chinese remain aloof.
>
> There is nobody in the United States or in Europe or in Russia that is at all likely to challenge a statement by the President of the United States that our military forces have discharged their duty in their usual competent manner and occupy the field as victors.
>
> Any charge against such an assertion directly challenges the ability of U.S. military power and makes the prospect of a wider war clear and present.

---

[35] *CR*, vol. 112, pp. 27523–27525.

> Right now in the eyes of most of the world, only the United States rejects that possibility.
>
> Once the burden of suggesting a wider war is shifted from us to others—others who question the integrity of U.S. military power—the United States is again in the position of leading from collective strength politically.
>
> This suggested strategy is not designed to solve the political problem of Vietnam.
>
> It is simply designed to remove the credibility of U.S. military power—or more loosely the question of "face"—as the factor which precludes a political solution.

Aiken said in an interview some years later that his speech had upset the President, and that this was "the only time he ever really got mad at me."[36]

In 1967, a year after Aiken's speech, and following the South Vietnamese national election, Leonard Marks, the Director of the U.S. Information Agency who had been a friend and supporter of the President for many years as well as one of his personal lawyers, was visiting with the President and brought up the Aiken speech. This is Marks' account in an interview several years later:[37]

> I was with the President in the morning in his bedroom. He would have these periods when he would sit there and he would read and hand you stuff, and there would be isolated conversations. He really wanted somebody around, and if you had any business you would try to work it in. So at an appropriate interval I said, "I want to talk to you, Mr. President, about the Vietnam situation. I know you don't approve of George Aiken's proposal, but I think we can adapt it. We can say, 'Now that the elections have been held in Vietnam, that they have elected a national and regional and a local government and in a democratic fashion, we have achieved our objectives. We can now withdraw our troop support and continue our military support: arms and money.'" After I had made that statement I waited, and he just glared at me. He had an ability just to look you down, stare you down so that you got impatient and you became nervous. Finally I said, "Well, what do you think?" He said, "Get out." Now, we had known each other since 1948, and I had never had a run-in with him, I had never had a cross word. We had differences of opinion, but our relationship I think was as admirable as any relationship I have ever enjoyed. So I picked up my papers and I left.
>
> For several weeks I knew that I was in the doghouse. I was not invited to National Security Council meetings, which I had always attended. I wasn't told about Cabinet meetings, which I had regularly attended. I wasn't invited over to the White House family quarters for little informal get-togethers. Finally one afternoon Lady Bird called and said that they were having a little surprise party for Lyndon and would my wife and I be available to go. So I did, and he was as warm and as effusive

[36] CRS Interview with George Aiken, Oct. 19, 1978.
[37] Johnson Library, Oral History Interview with Leonard H. Marks, Jan. 26, 1976.

as if nothing had ever happened. The incident was never discussed.

After he left the White House, I spent a weekend at the ranch. The two of us [were] together in the living room; there was nobody else around. And again he was sitting there reading and handing me papers and musing. I said, "I want to ask you something." I recalled this incident where he had gotten angry with me, and I said, "I don't understand why you got so mad." He looked at me and he said, "Because in my gut I knew that you and George Aiken were right, and I couldn't do anything about it."

McNamara Returns to Vietnam

Whatever hope the President and his associates may have gained from the election of the Constituent Assembly in September 1966, or from the forthcoming Manila Conference, was soon eclipsed by a grim report from McNamara after another visit to Vietnam on October 10–13. Also on the trip were Under Secretary of State Nicholas Katzenbach (who had succeeded Ball in September), JCS Chairman Wheeler, McNaughton, Komer, and others, including Henry Kissinger in his capacity as a State Department consultant.

In an editorial on October 11 commenting on McNamara's trip, the *New York Times* noted the "dreary sense of futility that has engulfed this most frustrating of all wars in which the United States has taken part," adding: "United States intervention has substituted Americans for Frenchmen . . . and brought more terror and destruction than France ever did. . . . If kept up long enough, the end will be the destruction of all of North Vietnam and most of South Vietnam."

A weekly casualty list issued at about the same time showed a total of 967 U.S. servicemen killed or wounded, the highest of the war.

McNamara was briefed in Vietnam by Lodge and Westmoreland and their staffs. He also talked with Thieu and Ky.[38] Lodge reported that the U.S. had been successful in the "military war," and that by the spring of 1967 he expected "a very different military situation indeed." (This was based on Westmoreland's conclusion, as stated in a brief set of notes that he prepared for Lodge on October 3, that the "cross-over point" would be reached by that time: "By April 1967 attrition on enemy should exceed input from local recruiting and infiltration.")[39] But the "heart of the matter," Lodge said, was the "criminal" or "terrorist" side of the war, where there had been little progress. Alluding to the goals set at the February 1966 Conference in Honolulu, he said: "The mileage of roads which are open to all categories of persons is just about what it has been; the percentage of the population living under secure conditions is only a little bit greater than it was; the percentage of the popu-

[38] For a report on the meeting with Thieu and Ky see U.S. Department of State, Central File, Pol 27 Viet S, Saigon to Washington 8161, Oct. 11, 1966.

[39] CMH, Westmoreland Papers, History File, "COMUSMACV Policy Points," Oct. 3, 1966, and Lodge's memorandum of Oct. 3, 1966, Massachusetts Historical Society, Lodge Papers, Vietnam Papers.

lation under Viet Cong domination is not substantially diminished. . . ."[40]

In a private conversation with McNamara on October 10, Lodge argued that Westmoreland's strategy of search-and-destroy was "wrong," and that U.S. forces should instead be trying to "split up and keep off balance" Communist forces. This was the text of the memorandum that Lodge had prepared on the subject and which he read to McNamara:[41]

> 1. We (Westy and I) agree that the heart of the matter in this war is the "criminal" or terrorist war and that operations are undertaken against main force units to give us the opportunity to destroy the terrorist organization. This is the real cancer. Success in counter-terrorism dries up Viet Cong manpower and thus, in the not so long run, has a devastating military effect on the enemy.
>
> 2. The operations against main force units are called "offensive operations," and I cannot determine whether this phrase means "seek out and destroy" or whether it means "split up and keep off balance" or whether it means that in order to "split up and keep off balance" you must first, at the very least, try to "seek out and destroy."
>
> 3. It seems to me that this is not an insignificant question and that a policy of "seek out and destroy" means many more casualties than does a policy of "split up and keep off balance."
>
> 4. "Seek out and destroy" should not be an end in itself, as it rightly was in World War II. This war will not be won by killing Viet Cong or soldiers of North Viet-Nam, but by destroying the terrorist organization in South Viet-Nam. We should kill enough Viet Cong and North Vietnamese soldiers so as to make it seem so dangerous to the young Viet Cong that he will stop fighting, or to the potential Viet Cong so that he will resist impressment.
>
> 5. In arguing, therefore, that "split up and keep off balance" is enough, I, of course, omit our clearly defensive reactions to such enemy operations as those coming from the Demilitarized Zone or Chu Phong. These are in a separate category and are a clearcut defensive response to enemy offensive operations.
>
> This proposal would, I believe, do the following things:
>
> > a. Make possible a reduction in the number of U.S. troops engaged in the "military" war.
> >
> > b. Reduce the number of U.S. casualties in the "military" war.
> >
> > c. Make possible the assignment of many more U.S. troops to the job of pacification—the "criminal" or "counter-terrorist" war.
> >
> > d. If U.S. troops, totalling in number ten percent of the number of men in the ARVN infantry divisions, were assigned on the "buddy" system to these divisions who, in turn, would be assigned to pacification, it would be the quickest way both to revamp the ARVN and also the

[40] Johnson Library, NSF Memos to the President—Walt Rostow, Saigon to Washington 8262, Oct. 12, 1966, which contains the text of Lodge's statement in the briefing.

[41] Massachusetts Historical Society, Lodge Papers, Vietnam Papers.

quickest way to get pacification going. It would be real "on the job training."

e. This would get to the heart of the matter in this war, which the "military" war does not.

f. As far as public opinion is concerned at home, the proposed stress on pacification would mean a war of a few years duration with a definite and satisfactory ending. But there would be few American casualties; time would be clearly on our side; and the light at the end of the tunnel would be steadily growing brighter.[42]

It is not known what McNamara may have said in response to Lodge's comments, but Lodge noted that in another conversation about two years later:[43]

> He [McNamara] recalled my conversation with him at my house in Saigon in the second half of 1966 when I expressed my conviction that our then strategy of "search and destroy" was wrong, and that it should instead be "split up and keep off balance." He recalled my precise phraseology, remarking that we had done far too much in the way of "destroying." He said he had tried to persuade the President of the correctness of this view but had not succeeded, and that the events which had followed were due to his failure to convince the President. He evidently meant that his resignation came about because of his difference of opinion on whether the U.S. military strategy should have been "split up and keep off balance," as I advocated, rather than "search and destroy."

As the briefings continued during the October 1966 trip, McNamara agreed with Lodge during a briefing on pacification that there had been little if any progress in that area. According to a summary of the meeting, he was "highly critical of the entire RD [Revolutionary Development] program. He stated that goals were unrealistic, planning was shallow and that we had failed miserably in this task for the past five years."[44]

With respect to progress on the military front, although Westmoreland was predicting that the cross-over point would be reached by the spring of 1967, a briefing for McNamara by Westmoreland's chief of intelligence (J–2), Maj. Gen. Joseph A. McChristian, did not seem to point to that conclusion.[45] According to McChristian, the Communists were gaining in strength, had not suffered any appar-

---

[42] Several weeks later, Lodge told Westmoreland that he thought the organization of the South Vietnamese Army as a conventional force had been a mistake. Westmoreland replied that Lodge had "misjudged the situation." In his notes on his activities that he kept for his own records, Westmoreland said, "I invited his [Lodge's] attention to the fact that it takes a conventionally organized military force to fight VC main forces as well as guerrillas. It is not a matter of organization but a matter of tactics which differ depending upon the mission or task. If a battalion is to fight guerrillas, it breaks down into small unit actions whereas if they are to fight main force units they should be under strong battalion control. In any case, men armed with individual and supporting weapons are essential." He added: "Ambassador Lodge does not have a deep feel of military tactics and strategy. He is inclined to over-simplify the military situation and to deal with it on a simple formula basis." CMH, Westmoreland Papers, History File, Notes for Dec. 2, 1966.

[43] Massachusetts Historical Society, Lodge Papers, unpublished "Vietnam Memoir," Pt. VI, Appendix dated July 1, 1968.

[44] U.S. Army Military History Institute, Carlisle Barracks, Pa., MACV records (microfilm), documents from Secretary of Defense Visit, Oct. 10–14, 1966, summary of the 13 briefings.

[45] For the transcript of McChristian's briefing see vol. I, tab 3 of *ibid.*

ent loss of will to fight,[46] and were using their forces to maximum advantage against the Americans. Infiltration, which had been averaging about 10,000 a month during the first months of 1966, had increased to over 13,000, and the North Vietnamese had the capability of sending over 15,000. Exclusive of guerrilla forces, the enemy was capable, he said, of increasing its combat and combat support forces in South Vietnam (local forces plus North Vietnamese) from the existing 131,000 to 202,000 by the end of 1967. Since the beginning of 1965, enemy combat battalions had increased from 47 to 149, and he predicted that by the middle of 1967 there would be 199.

It was also clear from McChristian's briefing, as well as that of Westmoreland, that the Communists were continuing to wage a protracted war of attrition at times and places of their own choosing, and that American forces, despite efforts to take the offensive through seek-and-destroy tactics ("spoiling attacks"), were unable to force the enemy to come out and fight (as General Wheeler had said in July 1965 that they would be forced to do.)[47]

The most conspicuous example of the way in which the enemy was controlling the choice of strategy and battleground, cited by both McChristian and Westmoreland, was the movement of a number of North Vietnamese forces into Quang Tri Province (I Corps) in what the American command assumed was a way of gaining a better advantage in that area preparatory to a drive to seize the entire northern part of South Vietnam. Both men also noted that another reason for this concentration of Communist forces, as Westmoreland told McNamara, appeared to be that of drawing U.S. and other forces to the northern and northwestern part of South Vietnam, thus weakening U.S. military operations in the remainder of the country—a move that Westmoreland said had been successful. (In response to the perceived threat, some U.S. forces had been redeployed to the North and Northwest.)

The proposed construction of an anti-infiltration barrier across the northern part of South Vietnam was also discussed at some length during the briefings for McNamara. For years, military strategists and planners had considered a possible cordon across the top of South Vietnam and continuing through Laos by which

---

[46] McChristian said that "interrogation of enemy captives and returnees indicate that inadequate rice, inadequate medicine, malaria, airstrikes, personal hardships and the prolonged conflict have definitely contributed to a general lowering of morale" but that, "In spite of lowering morale there has been no appreciable rise in military defections in the past six months, and we have not detected signs of imminent mass defection or any weakening of the will to fight among a significant number of enemy soldiers."

McChristian was referring to semi-annual studies of "Viet Cong Motivation and Morale" that were being made for the U.S. Government by Leon Gouré of the RAND Corporation, copies of which are in the Department of State Central File, Pol 27 Viet S.

McChristian's interpretation contrasts with Rostow's own interpretation in a memorandum to the President on Aug. 2, 1966, transmitting the latest Gouré study, in which Rostow said that the report showed a "progressive decline in the morale [of the VC]"—which it did, even though it did not claim that it was "progressive"—and in the "fighting capacity of the VC"—which it did not.

Rostow's memorandum is in the Johnson Library, NSF Memos to the President—Walt Rostow.

[47] See p. 401 of pt. III of this study.

During that same discussion in July 1965 Wheeler was asked by the President "What makes you think if we put in another 100,000 men Ho Chi Minh won't put in another 100,000?" Wheeler replied that there was only a 50–50 chance that this would happen, but that if it did there would be "greater bodies of men—which will allow us to cream them." According to McChristian the North Vietnamese had sent at least 100,000 men to the South since the July 1965 decision to deploy large-scale U.S. forces. Wheeler's prediction that this would greatly increase the ability of the U.S. to inflict casualties had proven to be highly inaccurate.

to block infiltration from the North. The idea had been rejected in part because of the manpower that would be required for essentially defensive positions, as well as the fact that there were multiple other points of entry, especially by sea.

In December 1965, McNamara met twice with Carl Kaysen, former Kennedy NSC staff member who had returned to Harvard University where he and others in the Cambridge, Massachusetts area had been discussing ways to control and resolve the war. Kaysen told McNamara (and McNaughton, who attended the second meeting) that one way to limit infiltration while reducing the bombing of the North would be to use U.S. technology to create an electronic barrier. McNamara, Kaysen said in an interview some years later, "loved the idea," and asked Kaysen to get him a proposal.[48] In late January 1966, McNaughton received the proposal in a memorandum from his friend Roger Fisher of the Harvard Law School, a former State Department Legal Adviser who was one of the Cambridge group, proposing the construction of an anti-infiltration barrier across South Vietnam and Laos near the demilitarized zone.[49] In March, McNaughton submitted the proposal to McNamara, who asked the JCS for its comment. As proposed by McNaughton, the plan would involve a line of mines and barbed wire, backed by troops, extending from the coast of South Vietnam along the DMZ and through Laos to the border of Thailand, a distance of approximately 160 miles.[50] CINCPAC studied the idea and reported on April 7, 1966 that it would take three and a half to four years to make it fully operational, that it would pose a logistical and construction problem, and that it would require seven or eight U.S. divisions whose mobile defense of the DMZ area would be reduced by having to monitor a stationary line of defense.[51] McNamara then asked the group of experts working on contract with the JASON Division of the Pentagon's Institute for Defense Analyses, in conjunction with the study they were making of the effectiveness of bombing North Vietnam, to explore the idea of a barrier as an alternative to bombing.

As proposed by the JASON group in its report in August 1966, the barrier would consist of two parts. One section across South Vietnam, running from the coast inland, would seek to block foot traffic across the DMZ.[52] It would be manned by ground forces located at strong points along the line. The other, which would stretch from the western part of South Vietnam across Laos, would seek to stop vehicular traffic along the Ho Chi Minh Trail through Laos. It would be patrolled by aircraft. Both barriers would involve the use of electronic acoustic sensors that could pick up signals from "button bomblets," small mines that make a loud noise when stepped on but do not cause injury. "Gravel mines," which cause injury to feet and legs, would also be used, and SADEYE cluster bombs, by which hundreds of small mine-like devices are scattered,

---

[48] Shapley, *Promise and Power*, pp. 362–363.

[49] Fisher's draft memorandum, Jan. 30, 1966, on a barrier strategy, is in the Johnson Library, Warnke Papers, McNaughton Files.

[50] *PP*, Gravel ed., vol. IV, pp. 113–114.

[51] *Ibid.*, from CINCPAC to JCS 071925Z, Apr. 7, 1966, p. 114.

[52] *PP*, Gravel ed., vol. IV, pp. 115–123, from Institute for Defense Analyses, JASON Division, Study S–255, Aug. 1966, "Air-Supported Anti-Infiltration Barrier."

would be dropped by air in areas where infiltration was detected. Ground teams could also be used to plant antitruck mines.

This system, the JASON report stated, could be built in about a year using available components, but more effective, newly-developed components would not be available for 18 months to two years.

The report also noted that the North Vietnamese would doubtless devise countermeasures, including the changing of infiltration routes, thus requiring constant improvements in the barrier (the report called this "a dynamic 'battle of the barrier'").

McNamara and McNaughton met twice with the JASON group, and on September 3, 1966, McNamara asked the JCS to comment on a proposed "Concept for Infiltration Interdiction System for Vietnam."[53] The JCS sent the proposal to CINCPAC, and on September 13 CINCPAC again responded adversely[54] as follows:

> The combat forces required before, during and after construction of the barrier; the initial and follow-on logistic support; the engineer construction effort and time required; and the existing logistic posture in Southeast Asia with respect to ports and land LOCs [lines of communication] make construction of such a barrier impracticable. . . .
>
> Military operations against North Vietnam and operations in South Vietnam are of transcendent importance. Operations elsewhere are complementary supporting undertakings. Priority and emphasis should be accorded in consideration of the forces and resources available to implement the strategy dictated by our objectives.

On September 15, 1966, without waiting for a formal response from the JCS, McNamara ordered the proposed project to be implemented. He appointed Lt. Gen. Alfred D. Starbird to be head of Joint Task Force 728, to develop the program, code-named Project PRACTICE NINE. (After this name was compromised by public disclosure, the troop-supported part of the project was code-named Project DYE MARKER, and the air-supported part was called Project MUSCLE SHOALS.) He told Starbird that the project was "a matter of highest priority," and directed that the system be made operational by September 15, 1967.[55] On September 17, the JCS sent to the Secretary of Defense their reply to his memorandum of September 3. Possibly in part because the project had already been approved, the JCS position was favorable: "The Joint Chiefs of Staff recognize the historic use of barriers and the potential inherent in this concept. The imaginative use of technology, and surprise can contribute considerably toward solving the infiltration problem."[56] Noting CINCPAC's position, the JCS told McNamara that they "appreciate and share the concern behind his [CINCPAC] reservations, but recognize that these issues could be

---

[53] For the text of the proposed concept, see CMH, Westmoreland Papers, Message Files, JCS 5586–66, Sept. 17, 1966.

[54] *PP*, Gravel ed., vol. IV, p. 123, from CINCPAC to JCS 130705Z September 1966.

[55] CMH, Westmoreland Papers, History File, Memorandum to Starbird from McNamara, Sept. 15, 1966.

[56] CMH, Westmoreland Papers, Message Files, JCSM–594–66, the text of which is in JCS 5586–66, cited above.

resolved by rigorous determination of feasibility that must precede execution or commitment of resources."

In their memorandum to McNamara, the Chiefs added that logistical support for the project should not divert critical munitions and strike forces from other operations. They also said that the date for making the system operational was "optimistic," but added that the concept "may have the potential of shortening the war and that proceeding in the manner directed will provide a quick determination of concept validity and accelerated development of associated hardware."

On October 5, 1966, Army Chief of Staff Johnson in a cable to Westmoreland commented on Starbird's initial report. He told Westmoreland that a review of the report "indicates direct competition for resources with those required by your command." Construction of the barrier, he said, would require 18,400 personnel, most of them Army support forces, and after completion there would be a need for an undetermined number of combat troops as well as munitions that were already in short supply. One result, General Johnson said, would be a delay of six months in providing the additional forces that Westmoreland had requested.[57] Westmoreland replied: "Although I had speculated the cost of this proposed project would be high, your analysis of the impact of forces requested by this command is far greater than my wildest assumptions."[58]

Faced with the fact that the barrier had been approved by McNamara, and that a Washington task force under Starbird was preparing plans for implementing the idea, Westmoreland presented his own plan for a barrier in the briefing in Saigon for McNamara on October 10. After Starbird had outlined the plan as reported by his task force on September 29, McNamara asked Westmoreland to comment, adding: "I do not know if this or any other barrier is practical. I am actually sure that we are never going to move into one unless we mobilize unusual forces behind it." Westmoreland responded by emphasizing that he had already instituted a very effective anti-infiltration program consisting of TIGER HOUND, by which the U.S. was bombing traffic on the Ho Chi Minh Trail in Laos, as well as deploying mobile defense units near the demilitarized zone. He went on to say that he also planned to erect a "physical barrier" ("strong point obstacle system") that would serve a "counter invasion" purpose in the South Vietnamese portion of the DMZ and a "counter infiltration" purpose in Laos.[59]

Following Westmoreland's description of what he proposed to do, McNamara said he thought that it was an "excellent plan," and he added: "I keep looking back for five years, and as far as I am concerned it is a failure. I keep asking where did we make a mistake?

---

[57] Same location, WDC 11776, Oct. 5, 1966.

[58] Same location, MAC 8710, Oct. 6, 1966. For Westmoreland's comments in his memoirs, see *A Soldier Reports*, pp. 199–200. For further details on the barrier plan, which became partly operational in the fall of 1967 but was never completed and was later abandoned, see p. 538 below, and Paul Dickson, *The Electronic Battlefield* (Bloomington: Indiana Univ. Press, 1976). The BDM Corporation's study, *Strategic Lessons Learned in Vietnam*, prepared in 1979–80 for the Strategic Studies Institute of the Army War College, concluded: "Thus died, silently and unmourned, another costly attempt to substitute money, technology, materiel and—most unfortunately—lives for a sound and coherent strategy." Vol. VI, bk. 1, pp. 3–70.

For a good description of how the barrier was intended to work, see Edgar C. Doleman, Jr. and the editors of Boston Publishing, *Tools of War* (Boston, Mass.: Boston Publishing, 1984), pp. 152 ff.

[59] Westmoreland, *A Soldier Reports*, pp. 199–200.

The first mistake was not putting in a barrier five years ago instead of talking about it today." Westmoreland replied, "We could have, five years ago," and McNamara responded: "Certainly, we could have. I keep thinking to myself that five years from now I might look back and say it was an error not doing it five years ago. So that is why I want to see this tremendous effort placed. I recognize all the problems; I know all the unknowns. I recognize that it might prove unwise once we get to the point, but for God's sake, let's get lined up so we can do it if we want it."

As the discussion ended, McNamara declared: "I will absolutely guarantee you that a year from today there is going to be a barrier up there. I guarantee that. It may not be all that we talked about today, but it will be 95% of what we talked about."[60]

During his visit McNamara discussed with Westmoreland his request for additional U.S. forces during 1967. (When the request was first submitted in June 1966, the proposed new level was 542,000. By October, the request had been raised to 570,000.) Westmoreland, who had, as noted, been advised by Wheeler and Army Chief of Staff Johnson that there was considerable resistance to an increase of that size, told McNamara that he was "now concerned about what size force could be sustained indefinitely without great degradation in quality,"[61] in light of the President's opposition to calling up the Reserves and in keeping, as will be seen, with McNamara's view that the U.S. should assume "a military posture that we credibly would maintain indefinitely—a posture that makes trying to 'wait us out' less attractive."[62] He added that, after studying the matter, his best estimate was that 480,000–500,000 troops would be needed by the end of 1967.

Westmoreland went on to explain why these new figures were lower than that in his earlier request:

> I made the point to the Secretary that I had been very sensitive to the President's position and had refrained from putting him in an awkward situation because of exorbitant demands by me. In this connection, I stated I was looking for a level-off strength that would support a well-balanced force which could be supported indefinitely by our manpower and industrial bases. I stated I was convinced it is to be a long war and we should gear ourselves for it. The alternate solution would be to continue to build forces which might be difficult to support indefinitely, which would involve degradation in quality [of U.S. troops], and which would put increasing strains on the piaster [South Vietnamese currency] economy. In my opinion, this course of action is not a wise one. . . .

By the time of the Manila Conference two weeks later, Westmoreland, as noted, had raised his estimate, however, and told the President that he would need about 138,000 more troops, for a total of approximately 530,000 by the end of 1967.

---

[60] These quotations are from the transcript of the meeting of October 10, MACV records, cited above.

[61] CMH, Westmoreland Papers, History File, History Notes, and Westmoreland's cable on September 5 to Army Chief of Staff General Johnson, MAC 7720, in the Westmoreland Papers, Message Files.

[62] See McNamara's Oct. 14, 1966 report to the President, cited below.

McNamara's Pessimistic Report, October 1966

In his top secret trip report to the President on October 14, 1966, McNamara began by recalling that after his last visit in November 1965 he had said the odds were about even that by early 1967, even after deploying additional forces, the U.S. would be faced with "a military stand-off at a much higher level of conflict and with still stalled pacification."[63] In the intervening period, he said, the military situation had improved somewhat more than he had expected, but, as he had predicted, there was still a military stalemate, and "pacification," which he called a "bad disappointment," "has if anything gone backward." "As compared with two, or four, years ago, enemy full-time regional forces and part-time guerrilla forces are larger; attacks, terrorism and sabotage have increased in scope and intensity; more railroads are closed and highways cut; the rice crop expected to come to market is smaller; we control little, if any, more of the population; the VC political infrastructure thrives in most of the country, continuing to give the enemy his enormous intelligence advantage; full security exists nowhere (not even behind the U.S. Marines' lines and in Saigon); in the countryside, the enemy almost completely controls the night."

> In essence, we find ourselves—from the point of view of the important war (for the complicity of the people)—no better, and if anything worse off. This important war must be fought and won by the Vietnamese themselves. We have known this from the beginning. But the discouraging truth is that, as was the case in 1961 and 1963 and 1965, we have not found the formula, the catalyst, for training and inspiring them into effective action.

McNamara was also pessimistic about the results of U.S. military operations:

> I see no reasonable way to bring the war to an end soon. Enemy morale has not broken—he apparently has adjusted to our stopping his drive for military victory and has adopted a strategy of keeping us busy and waiting us out (a strategy of attriting our national will). He knows that we have not been, and he believes we probably will not be, able to translate our military successes into the "end products"—broken enemy morale and political achievements by the GVN. . . .[64]

---

[63] The complete report of Oct. 14, 1966 declassified in 1982 and available at the Johnson Library, had already been printed in 1971 in the *Pentagon Papers.* See Gravel ed., vol. IV, pp. 348–355.

[64] In a draft memorandum for the President on November 17 (discussed below), McNamara explained the way in which the Communists, as predicted by Ball and others, had reacted to U.S. strategy by increasing their own buildup and by adapting their military strategy:

"[C]urrent enemy recruitment/infiltration rates and tactics have more than offset the increased friendly deployments, enabling the enemy to increase his forces in the past and in the foreseeable future. If we assume that the estimates of enemy strength are accurate, the ratio of total friendly to total enemy strength has only increased from 3.5 to 4.0 to 1 since the end of 1965. Under these circumstances, it does not appear that we have the favorable leverage required to achieve decisive attrition by introducing more forces. . . . Furthermore, the enemy is undertaking fewer large scale offensive operations in recent months and concentrating his small scale attacks, ambushes, and harassments against easier targets (troops in the field and isolated military posts). This indicates a possible regression to activities characteristic of earlier stages of guerrilla warfare, is inconsistent with large numbers of battalions and even divisions, and may reflect an increasing inability to conduct large scale operations without incurring unacceptably high casualties." *PP,* Gravel ed., vol. IV, pp. 371–373, from the text of the draft memorandum.

McNamara also concluded that ROLLING THUNDER had not "significantly affected infiltration or cracked the morale of Hanoi."[65]

"In such an unpromising state of affairs," McNamara said, "what should we do?" His answer was sobering if not startling: U.S. military operations should be stabilized and not expanded further, and primary emphasis should be given to pacification and the development of self-government in South Vietnam. The trend during 1967 in the pacification effort, he said, "will, I believe, be the main talisman of ultimate U.S. success or failure in Vietnam, [and] extraordinary imagination and effort should go into changing the stripes of that problem."

McNamara stressed the importance of demonstrating to the Communists that they could not win by "waiting us out." At the same time, the chances for bringing the war to a successful and timely conclusion through military or diplomatic efforts were not promising: "The prognosis is bad that the war can be brought to a satisfactory conclusion within the next two years [i.e., by the time of the 1968 U.S. Presidential election]. The large-unit operation will not do it; negotiations probably will not do it. *While we should continue to pursue both of these routes in trying for a solution in the short run, we should recognize that success from them is a mere possibility, not a probability.*" [emphasis in original] Thus, he concluded, "The solution lies in girding, openly, for a longer war and in taking actions immediately which will in 12 to 18 months give clear evidence that the continuing costs and risks to the American people are acceptably limited, that the formula for success has been found, and that the end of the war is merely a matter of time." This course of action, he said, was "a new ingredient forced on us by the facts."

The report recommended these specific steps, each of which was discussed in detail:

> (1) Stabilize US force levels in Vietnam . . . limit the increase in US forces in SVN in 1967 to 70,000 men . . . and level off at the total of 470,000, . . .[66] A stabilized US force level would . . . put us in a position where negotiations would be more likely to be productive, but if they were not we could pursue the all-important pacification task with proper atten-

[65] *Ibid.*, p. 136.

In his November 17 memorandum, he added that while interdiction by air was "clearly necessary and worthwhile," the scale of ROLLING THUNDER at that time "is yielding only small marginal returns, not worth the cost in pilot lives and aircraft." (Infiltration, for example, had gone up from an average weekly rate of 510 for 1965 to over 1100 in 1966.) This was his description (*ibid.*, p. 134):

"The increased damage to targets is not producing noticeable results. No serious shortage of POL in North Vietnam is evident, and stocks on hand, with recent imports, have been adequate to sustain necessary operations. No serious transport problem in the movement of supplies to or within North Vietnam is evident; most transportation routes appear to be open, and there has recently been a major logistical build-up in the area of the DMZ. The raids have disrupted the civil populace and caused isolated food shortages, but have not significantly weakened public morale. Air strikes continue to depress economic growth and have been responsible for abandonment of some plans for economic development, but essential economic activities continue. The increasing amounts of physical damage sustained by the North Vietnamese are in large measure compensated by aid received from other Communist countries. Thus, in spite of an interdiction campaign costing at least $250 million per month at current levels, no significant impact on the war in South Vietnam is evident."

[66] McNamara noted in a footnote in the report that Admiral Sharp (CINCPAC) had recommended a total of 570,000 by the end of 1967, but said, "I believe both he [Sharp] and General Westmoreland recognize that the danger of inflation [in South Vietnam] will probably force an end 1967 deployment limit of about 470,000."

tion and resources and without the spectre of apparently endless escalation of US deployments.

(2) Install a barrier . . . near the 17th parallel. . . .

(3) Stabilize the ROLLING THUNDER program against the North. Attack sorties in North Vietnam have risen from about 4,000 per month at the end of last year to 6,000 per month in the first quarter of this year and 12,000 per month at present. . . . I recommend, as a minimum, against increasing the level of bombing of North Vietnam and against increasing the intensity of operations by changing the areas or kinds of targets struck . . . as in the case of a stabilized level of US ground forces, the stabilization of ROLLING THUNDER would remove the prospect of ever-escalating bombing as a factor complicating our political posture and distracting from the main job of pacification in South Vietnam.

(4) Pursue a vigorous pacification program.

(5) Press for negotiations.

McNamara also recommended that in order to provide a better "security screen" for pacification programs, at least half of the Vietnamese Army, and perhaps some U.S. forces, should be assigned to clearing and holding operations. He added: "The US cannot do this pacification security job for the Vietnamese. All we can do is 'massage the heart.'" In order for pacification to succeed, however, various changes were needed, including better U.S. management. He suggested that all civilian activities be consolidated under one manager, and all security-related activities under a military officer in MACV who would work with the civilian manager. "From the political and public-relations viewpoint, this solution is preferable—if it works. But we cannot tolerate continued failure. If it fails after a fair trial, the only alternative in my view is to place the entire pacification program—civilian and military—under General Westmoreland."[67]

Under Secretary of State Katzenbach submitted to the President a separate report on the pacification program. The "military aspect" of pacification, he said, had been "spindly and weak," and the lack of a "military screen" had been a major factor in the shortcomings of pacification efforts. Preoccupied with the "main force military emergency," the U.S. had failed "effectively to press" the Vietnamese "to even start meeting their RD [Revolutionary Development] responsibilities." He noted, however: "I know of no one who believes that these should be met principally by American forces—unless we should wish the whole RD effort to collapse once we leave."

In addition to an "immediate and effective military screen," Katzenbach recommended steps to establish "authoritative and compelling administration of the efforts of civilian agencies." To accomplish these objectives he recommended, among other things, that Deputy Ambassador Porter should supervise all U.S. pacification activities and that one of the better generals of the Army be named

[67] In an earlier draft of his memorandum McNamara had proposed that Westmoreland take charge of pacification, rather than first trying the joint approach. Komer and the JCS agreed, but others, notably Lodge and the State Department, objected. *PP*, Gravel ed., vol. II, pp. 589–590.

as Porter's deputy to provide "the rank, and stature to insure optimum RD performance from MACV."[68]

This is the *Pentagon Papers'* assessment of the significance of McNamara's report:[69]

> In a sense, the memorandum was a clear "no" to the MACV, CINCPAC and JCS proposals for expanded bombing and major ground force increases, but it was a negative with a difference. It provided alternatives. From this time on, the judgment of the military as to how the war should be fought and what was needed would be subject to question. New estimates of what was needed in Vietnam would have to be calculated in light of new objectives and new criteria for success, as well as new assumptions about "winning." The warning had rung and unless dramatic outcomes measured in time and political advantage could be promised, additional force increases in the upward direction promised to be sticky indeed.

The reaction of the JCS to McNamara's recommendations was "predictably rapid—and violent."[70] The Chiefs agreed that the U.S. should prepare for a long war, but they thought that McNamara underestimated the improvements in the military situation. They disagreed with his assessment of the results of bombing, and advocated fewer bombing restraints. They also argued that bombing was one of two U.S. "trump cards" in negotiating an end to the war (the other was the presence of U.S. troops), and should be used accordingly. They recommended an expansion of ROLLING THUNDER and the authorization of new targets. They also urged a "sharp knock" against North Vietnam rather than gradual escalation: "Whatever the political merits of the latter course, we deprived ourselves of the military effect of early weight of effort and shock, and gave to the enemy time to adjust. . . ."

The Chiefs also recommended attacks by U.S. naval forces against North Vietnam and against coastal shipping.

With respect to pacification, the JCS agreed that the existing program was inadequate, and proposed that it be put under Westmoreland's control.[71]

In conclusion, the JCS said: "enemy strategy appears to be to wait it out; in other words, Communist leaders in both North and South Vietnam expect to win this war in Washington, just as they won the war with France in Paris," adding, "In this regard, the Joint Chiefs of Staff consider that there is reason for such expectations on the part of the communist leadership." Although U.S. offers to end the war had been "admirable," it would be a mistake to continue such overtures because of the uncertainty they created about U.S. resolve to fight the war to a successful conclusion. Rather, they recommended that the President reiterate U.S. determina-

---

[68] For Katzenbach's report of October 15, "Administration of Revolutionary Development," see U.S. Department of State, Central File, Pol 27 Viet S. There are excerpts in *PP*, Gravel ed., vol. II, pp. 591–594.

[69] *PP*, Gravel ed., vol. IV, p. 356.

[70] *Ibid.* For the full text of the JCS memorandum (JCSM–672–66) to McNamara on Oct. 14, 1966, see Johnson Library, NSF NSC Meetings File.

[71] In an article by journalist Hanson Baldwin a few weeks later, military authorities were reported to believe that 600,000–750,000 U.S. troops would be required to win the war, and that one of the reasons for needing additional manpower was the need to protect civilians in areas being pacified. They also reportedly took the position, however, that "unless pacification succeeds, military victories will have no durable effect." *New York Times*, Nov. 12, 1966.

tion to continue fighting, while also continuing peace explorations on a covert basis.

Rostow's assistant on the NSC staff, Col. Robert Ginsburgh, who was also the JCS liaison with the White House, sent Rostow his own analysis of McNamara's report with this cover memorandum:[72]

> Attached is my reaction to Secretary McNamara's memo on Vietnam—which seemed to me exceedingly and excessively pessimistic.
>
> I think this memo puts me farther out on a limb than anyone else has gone in writing.
>
> Nevertheless, some of my military colleagues with whom I have discussed this approach accuse me of being too conservative.

A memorandum by George Carver, Special Assistant for Vietnamese Affairs to the Director of the CIA, and a supporter of the war, which was prepared in response to a request from McNamara to Director Richard Helms (who had replaced Admiral Raborn in the summer of 1966), while agreeing with McNamara's assessment of the effects of bombing and with his recommendation for stabilizing the level of ROLLING THUNDER operations, disagreed with his implication that an expanded program of bombing would not be effective: "We continue to judge that a bombing program directed both against closing the port of Haiphong and continuously cutting the rail lines to China could have a significant impact."[73]

The Carver memorandum also disagreed with McNamara's criticism of pacification and concluded that pacification was beginning to work. With proper management, among other things, there were "at least fair prospects for substantial progress in pacification over the next two years."[74]

McNamara was scheduled to discuss his trip at a meeting of the National Security Council from 2:40 p.m. to 3:30 p.m. on October 15, 1966, attended by the President, the Vice President, Rusk, McNamara, Katzenbach, Vance, William Bundy, Rostow, Wheeler, Helms, McNaughton, Secretary of the Treasury Fowler, USIA Director Marks, Moyers, Komer, Kintner, Jorden, and Bromley Smith. As it turned out, most of the meeting was spent discussing the upcoming conference in Manila, and there was only a brief report by McNamara.

Before the NSC meeting began, the President met from 2:10 p.m. to 2:40 p.m. with McNamara and Wheeler, as well as the Vice President and Vance, to discuss the touchy question of whether to put the military in charge of pacification. According to a cable from Wheeler to Westmoreland, the President emphasized that pacification was "critical to the success of our effort in South Vietnam; that he is dissatisfied with the present direction and execution of the program; but that he is unwilling to override the strong objections of Secretary Rusk (in consonance with those of Ambassador Lodge) to transferring the control of the program from civilian to military

---

[72] Johnson Library, NSF Country File, Vietnam, Ginsburgh Memorandum to Rostow, Nov. 2, 1966.

[73] *PP*, Gravel ed., vol. IV, p. 129, from Carver's Memorandum for the Director, CIA, Subject: "Comments on Secretary McNamara's Trip Report," 15 Oct. 1966.

[74] *Ibid.*, vol. II, p. 598.

hands."[75] The President stated, however, that he expected results "soonest," and that further action would be taken if the situation had not improved in 90 days.

During the NSC meeting, there was also a brief discussion of the military situation, and the President, according to Wheeler's cable, said that he was opposed to reducing the sanctuary areas around Hanoi and Haiphong, but would be receptive to bombing new targets "despite advice he has had from some quarters to forego expanding the target system or increasing the weight of effort in the North."

McNamara, who seemed to be choosing his words carefully, said, according to the notes,[76] "The military situation in Vietnam is better than he expected it to be. Military preparations are progressing in an entirely satisfactory way." "Progress in pacification," he added, "is less than he had hoped. More emphasis needs to be placed on pacification programs. The pacification situation was worse than it had been when he was last in Vietnam." "We will be in Vietnam longer than we have thought," he said. "We should prepare now contingency plans looking toward the future so that if it turns out that we have to stay a long time, we should be prepared to do so."

General Wheeler described the fighting, and said, "There has been substantial improvement in the military situation. The morale of our troops is the best ever."

Under Secretary of State Katzenbach, who only a few weeks earlier had been serving as Attorney General and for whom Vietnam was virtually a new subject, briefly discussed pacification, saying that, "Efforts in the field of pacification are not as good as they should be."

The President Approves McNamara's Recommendations

On November 4 and 5, 1966, McNamara and JCS Chairman Wheeler met with the President to discuss the final troop request for 1967 (Program Four) that had just been made by the JCS following a military planning conference in Honolulu on October 20.[77] In a memorandum to McNamara on November 4, the JCS requested that the level of approximately 395,000 U.S. forces authorized for the end of 1966 be increased to 504,000 by the end of 1967, 522,000 by June of 1968, and 564,000 by the end of 1968. (These figures were exclusive of the additional forces that would be needed for the barrier along the DMZ.) The request of 504,000 for the end of 1967 represented, of course, a considerable reduction in the original estimate of 542,000 made in June 1966, the estimate of 570,000 made in October, or the 530,000 estimated by Westmoreland in Manila, but it was still higher than the 470,000 for the end of 1967 that McNamara had recommended in his report on October 14.

In their memorandum, the JCS endorsed an "updated and expanded" "new concept" of military operations in North and South Vietnam that had been prepared by Westmoreland and forwarded to Washington by CINCPAC on October 20. (No action had been

[75] CMH, Westmoreland Papers, Message Files, JCS 9339–66, Oct. 17, 1966.
[76] Johnson Library, NSF NSC Meetings File, Notes of the 565th NSC meeting, Oct. 15, 1966.
[77] JCSM–702–66, Nov. 4, 1966, is summarized in *PP*, Gravel ed., vol. IV, pp. 361–362. There are no known notes of the meetings of November 4 and 5.

taken by the JCS or by civilian authorities on Westmoreland's "Concept of Military Operations in South Vietnam" that he had submitted on August 24.) In describing this "expanded" concept, the JCS memorandum said, among other things:[78]

> As in past concepts, it goes beyond certain restraints that have been placed on US operating forces to date, such as those on the air campaign in North Vietnam, on cross border operations, on certain special operations, and on ground actions in the southern half of the demilitarized zone. Further, this concept should be carried out in its entirety, if achievement of US objectives is to be accomplished in the shortest time and at the least cost in men and materiel. The concept describes preparation for operations that have not as yet been authorized, such as mining ports, naval quarantine, spoiling attacks and raids against the enemy in Cambodia and Laos, and certain special operations. Such action will support intensified and accelerated revolutionary development and nation building programs. Since the force requirements are based on this concept in its entirety, continued restraints and the absence of authorization for recommended operations could generate significantly different requirements for forces and timing.

According to the *Pentagon Papers,* the "expanded" concept of military operations proposed by the JCS "In a sense embraced all of the right arguments . . . but unfortunately for all the wrong reasons. McNamara and Johnson were not politically and militarily enchanted with a costly major force increase at that time, nor with cross border and air operations which ran grave political risks."[79]

On November 11, 1966, there was another meeting of the President, McNamara, and Wheeler, and the President gave final approval to McNamara's recommendations that U.S. military operations in South Vietnam should be stabilized, that primary emphasis should be given to pacification and the development of effective self-government, and that the U.S. should press for negotiations.[80]

By approving McNamara's recommendations for stabilizing U.S. troop levels in Vietnam and for placing greater emphasis on pacification and negotiations, President Johnson also accepted the conclusion on which the recommendations were based: the war was not being won and could not be won militarily. Or did he? When he said later in his memoirs that "By early 1967 most of my advisers and I felt confident that the tide of war was moving strongly in favor of the South Vietnamese and their allies, and against the Communists,"[81] was he trying, in retrospect, to justify his policies, or did his statement reflect his belief that in early 1967 the South Vietnamese and the U.S. were, indeed, "winning"? And when he told Senators Mansfield and Dirksen on January 17, 1967, that the U.S. was "doing better now than we have ever done in Vietnam if we just don't blow it,"[82] was he engaging in a bit of hyperbole for

---

[78] *Ibid.,* pp. 361–362.
[79] *Ibid.,* p. 362.
[80] *Ibid.,* pp. 361–363. There are no known notes of that meeting.
[81] *The Vantage Point,* pp. 257–258.
[82] See below, p. 505.

the sake of getting their support, or was he convinced of what he was saying?

Despite McNamara's finding that the war was stalemated militarily and that pacification had "gone backward," the President may have believed—or, needing to believe, as Kearns suggests, had convinced himself—that progress was soon going to be made on both the military and civil fronts, and that, as Rostow and Komer were arguing, 1967 should be and would be the year in which, "at the minimum," it would be made "patently clear to all that the war is demonstrably being won."

In addition to stabilizing ground force deployment, McNamara recommended and the President approved the stabilization of U.S. bombing of North Vietnam.[83] In his October 14 report, McNamara said that, "as in the case of a stabilized level of U.S. ground forces, the stabilization of ROLLING THUNDER would remove the prospect of ever-escalating bombing as a factor complicating our political posture and distracting from the main job of pacification in South Vietnam."[84] The military disagreed, and in a memorandum to McNamara on November 8, 1966, the JCS recommended that in the next phase of U.S. bombing of the North authorization be given for reducing the restricted area around Hanoi and Haiphong and for bombing new targets: three surface-to-air missile installations, additional POL sites, elements of a steel plant and cement factory, two power plants, four waterway locks on water lines of communication, and selected areas of ports at Cam Pha and Haiphong.[85] The next day (November 9), Rostow sent the JCS memorandum to the President with a cover memorandum in which he said: "We must begin now to lean more heavily on the North. I have reviewed all the evidence and all the reports we have on the effect of bombing the North. It is clear that the attritional cost we are imposing is significant for the North Vietnamese in military and economic terms and increasingly significant for Moscow and the Eastern European countries which are being forced to expend military and economic aid sharply to compensate for our bombing; and they don't like it. That increased burden may add to their interest in a negotiated settlement."[86] Rostow did not state what "evidence" and "reports" he had reviewed[87] or the basis for his statements about the

[83] *The Vantage Point*, p. 133.

[84] McNamara memorandum to the President, Oct. 14, 1966, cited above.

[85] Johnson Library, NSF, Country File, Vietnam, CM–1906–66, Nov. 8, 1966.

[86] NSF Memos to the President—Walt Rostow, Memorandum from Rostow to the President, Nov. 9, 1966.

[87] In addition to a number of intelligence reports, the JASON report, and McNamara's own report of October 1966, the CIA sent a new Intelligence Memorandum to Rostow on Nov. 5, 1966, "The Effectiveness of the Rolling Thunder Program in North Vietnam, 1 January-30 September 1966," 62 pages, which was issued on Dec. 7, 1966, as SC No. 12898/66, and "The Effectiveness of the Air Campaign Against North Vietnam," 175 pages. Both are located in the Johnson Library, NSF Country File, Vietnam.

These reports concluded that despite increased bombing, the North Vietnamese were able not only to continue but to increase their war effort. Their transportation system had been improved; their infiltration of the South had increased, including an increase of more than three times the number of persons infiltrating the South in 1966 compared to 1965; their external aid from the U.S.S.R. and China had been five times the damage they had sustained from ROLLING THUNDER.

Nor had U.S. bombing adversely affected the support of the North Vietnamese for their Government or the determination of the regime to continue fighting.

The reports concluded that in order for ROLLING THUNDER to "maximize the costs to the enemy and reduce his capability to recuperate," it would have to concentrate on "high-yield

Continued

possible benefits of bombing for stimulating negotiations. His argument was, however, a departure from earlier arguments for bombing the North, none of which had proved to be valid.

Rostow said that in light of an impending visit of British Foreign Secretary George Brown to the U.S.S.R., during which Brown planned to discuss the possibility of Vietnam negotiations, the JCS program "goes too far at this time. There is no reason to be excessively hopeful about that visit; but we must give him a fair chance to probe." Rostow added that "It might help his mission if we signalled, between now and then, our intent to up the ante in the North; but it could destroy his mission if we did anything excessively dramatic or noisy." (Rostow did not suggest, nor was he apparently even considering, that the U.S. might consult the British as to what they thought of this idea.)

Rostow recommended, therefore, that the President approve at that time certain of the JCS proposals to "make clear to Hanoi and Moscow the seriousness of our future interest, without putting them under public challenge or ultimatum. For example, we might hit the SAM support sites, one or two thermo-power plants, one of the two unstruck POL storage facilities. . . ."

The President, however, apparently preferred McNamara's advice on the matter to that of Rostow, and approved McNamara's recommendation to stabilize U.S. military activities while increasing the emphasis on pacification and the search for a peaceful settlement. On November 11, McNamara sent a memorandum to the JCS stating that, in response to the JCS request of November 4 (JCSM–702–66), a new deployment program (Program Four) of

---

transport and logistics target systems" in the northern part of North Vietnam, such as rail and road lines from China.

Rostow also had received in early November a copy of a 92 page JCS study of bombing, "An Evaluation of the Air Campaign Against North Vietnam and Laos," Oct. 31, 1966, and an 11-page summary of the report. (The summary is in the Johnson Library, NSF Country File, Vietnam. The full report, in the same location, is still classified.) The summary of the report stated that the basic objective of the air war had been one of "general harassment" designed to accomplish five goals: "(a) Cut down his [the enemy's] over-all logistic capacity so that the North Vietnamese and the Chinese Communists would be less likely to unleash their ground forces in a major overt attack against SVN. (b) Make the transportation of men and supplies to the south more expensive, and destroy supplies en route to the south. (c) Contain localized attacks such as those across the DMZ. (d) Impose a cost on NVN for continuing the war as one element of influencing NVN to call off the war. (e) Impose a cost on the communist bloc countries for their continued support of the war." Success in achieving each of these goals was then discussed in the summary report.

According to the summary report, the air war was not designed to "(a) achieve victory through air power or (b) destroy North Vietnam or (c) destroy the civilian economy of North Vietnam or (d) destroy North Vietnamese military capabilities or (e) interdict the throughput of supplies from outside of North Vietnam." The summary report also noted that, "Up to the present, we have made the deliberate decision to deny ourselves the possibility of making a clear cut in the throughput of supplies by a variety of constraints in which we have chosen to avoid: mining the ports, attacking key NVN airfields, attacking his limited industrial capability, attacking a variety of major military facilities and headquarters in the Hanoi-Haiphong 'sanctuary areas,' and attacking of key bridges and locks."

Another report on bombing, which Rostow may or may not have seen, was made in October 1966 by the Chief of Naval Operations, and was sent by Secretary of the Navy Nitze to McNamara. Although the Navy's own commander in the Pacific (CINCPAC) was in charge of the air war against North Vietnam (ROLLING THUNDER) and was an advocate of the greater use of air power, and although the Navy's own Chief of Naval Operations was a member of the JCS and a party to the JCS recommendation for increased bombing, this report found that there was inadequate intelligence on the effects of bombing on the rate of infiltration and recommended that bombing be halted until better intelligence could be obtained. In a memorandum to McNamara, Nitze said that "the analysts were unable to develop a logical case either for or against the current air campaign or higher or lower levels of air effort." Paul Nitze and Steven L. Rearden, *From Hiroshima to Glasnost: At the Center of Decision: A Memoir* (New York: Grove Weidenfeld, 1989), p. 265. It will be recalled that the JASON report on bombing came to the same conclusion.

463,000 U.S. forces was approved for the end of 1967 (compared to the JCS request for 504,000), increasing to 469,300 by June 1968 (compared to the JCS request for 522,000),[88] but that the request for expanding the air war (with one small exception) was denied.[89]

In his memorandum to the JCS, McNamara, while disapproving the JCS force recommendations, did not respond to the proposal for a "new concept" and objectives for U.S. military operations. To some degree this was done, however, in a draft memorandum by McNamara for the President on November 17 on the subject of the forthcoming supplemental appropriations request for the war (to be submitted to Congress in January 1967).[90] In a section on "Military Strategy in Vietnam," McNamara said that there were two approaches to the "principal task" of U.S. forces to "eliminate the offensive capability of the regular units in order to allow the GVN to counter the guerrilla forces and to extend permanent control over areas from which regular units have been cleared." *"The first approach would be to continue in 1967 to increase friendly forces as rapidly as possible, and without limit, and employ them primarily in large-scale 'seek out and destroy' operations to destroy the main force VC/NVA units." "The second approach,"* which he recommended, *"is to follow a similarly aggressive strategy of 'seek out and destroy,' but to build friendly forces only to that level required to neutralize the large enemy units and prevent them from interfering with the pacification program."*[91] (emphasis in original) This was the preferred course, he said, for three reasons:

> (1) *If MACV estimates of enemy strength are correct* ["NC/NVA losses," he said, "increased by only 115 per week (less than 15%) during a period in which we increased friendly strength by 160,000"] *we have not been able to attrite the enemy forces fast enough to break their morale and more U.S. forces are unlikely to do so in the immediate future; (2) we cannot deploy more than about 470,000 personnel by the end of 1967 without a high probability of generating a self-defeating runaway inflation in SVN and (3) an endless escalation of U.S. deployments is not likely to be acceptable in the U.S. or to induce the enemy to believe that the U.S. is prepared to stay as long as is required to produce a secure non-communist SVN.* (emphasis in original)

"[T]he data suggest," McNamara added, "that we have no prospects of attriting the enemy force at a rate equal to or greater than his capability to infiltrate and recruit, and this will be true at either the 470,000 U.S. personnel level or 570,000. . . . It may be possible to reduce enemy strength substantially through improved tactics or other means such as an effective amnesty/defection program or effective pacification to dry up VC sources of recruitment,

---

[88] There is a copy of McNamara's November 11 memorandum to the JCS in the Johnson Library, Warkne Papers, McNaughton Files. See also *PP*, Gravel ed., vol. IV, pp. 364–365.

[89] On that same day (November 11), McNamara sent a letter to Rusk proposing an interdepartmental working group to analyze the problem of establishing effective international supervision of cessation of hostilities in Vietnam. In a letter of November 30, Rusk agreed. The 138-page report was completed in September 1967. McNamara's and Rusk's letters and the completed report are in the Department of State, Lot File 70 D207.

[90] A substantial part of McNamara's November 17 memorandum, "Recommended FY 67 Southeast Asia Supplemental Assistance," is in *PP*, Gravel ed., vol. IV, pp. 365–378. The memorandum cannot be found at the Johnson Library.

[91] *PP*, Gravel ed., vol. IV, p. 369.

but further large increases in U.S. forces do not appear to be the answer."[92]

In this statement of November 17, McNamara also discussed the air war, concluding that, "our bombing campaign may produce a beneficial effect on U.S. and SVN morale by making NVN pay a price for its aggression and by showing that we are doing what we can to interdict the enemy. But at the scale we are now operating, I believe our bombing is yielding very small marginal returns, not worth the cost in pilot lives and aircraft."[93]

According to the *Pentagon Papers,* the meaning of these decisions on Program Four requests was that "DOD and the President were beginning to question the concept of operations for Vietnam which had led to programs, now becoming increasingly costly and depressingly barren of tangible results. The illusion of quick victory 'on the cheap' had fled, and hard reality intervened. People in and out of government were beginning to seek alternatives to our policies in Vietnam with increased interest."[94]

"In November 1966," Chester Cooper said in his study, *The Lost Crusade,* "the Johnson Administration embarked on a sustained search for a way out."[95]

The Dispute Over Pacification

During the fall of 1966, as the U.S. Government continued to try to find more efficacious ways of conducting its military and nonmilitary operations in South Vietnam, the dispute over management of the pacification program became considerably more intense. The question was whether the program should be under the control of civilians or the military or both. Proponents of military control argued that the most important aspect of pacification was the providing of security, which, they said, was essentially a military function. Opponents argued that although security was critical, it could be provided by the military and by local forces while avoiding the adverse consequences for the development of civil functions that would result from military control of the entire pacification program.

In early 1966, as noted, Deputy Ambassador Porter was made coordinator of all U.S. civilian pacification activities while Westmoreland and his staff retained responsibility for the pacification work of the U.S. district and province military advisers, who constituted a large part of the U.S. personnel involved in pacification.[96]

By late summer 1966, with pacification assuming greater importance, there was renewed agitation for improved management. On August 7, Komer, who had been appointed in the spring to be Washington coordinator of U.S. civilian for pacification, drafted a proposal, "Giving a New Thrust to Pacification: Analysis, Concept, and Management," in which he examined the problem and possible management options. His own preference, based on the fact that the military had the necessary men and resources, was to assign

[92] *Ibid.*, pp. 370–371.
[93] *Ibid.*, p. 374.
[94] *Ibid.*, p. 385.
[95] Cooper, *The Lost Crusade*, p. 324.
[96] As of September 1966, according to a memorandum from Komer to McNamara on September 29, (U.S. Department of State, Central File, Pol 27 Viet S), there were 470 civilian advisers compared to 2540 military.

responsibility for pacification, including the military and most of the civilian aspects, to the U.S. military, with an integrated civil-military staff serving under a civilian deputy to Westmoreland.[97]

The reaction to Komer's memorandum was mixed. The State Department, including Lodge and Porter, as well as AID, the CIA, and USIA, were opposed, but there was a favorable response from McNamara and McNaughton. Working with McNaughton, Komer then "arranged for Secretary McNamara to make the official proposal," and a draft memorandum for the President was prepared on September 22, 1966. (McNaughton sent the memorandum to Ball with a cover memorandum stating that McNamara had been "asked" to prepare the draft.)[98]

In his memorandum, McNamara said that one major reason for the "lack of progress" in pacification was the split responsibility for pacification, and that, "For the sake of efficiency—in clarifying our concept, focusing our energies, and increasing the output we can generate on the part of the Vietnamese—this split responsibility on the U.S. side must be eliminated." He recommended, as had Komer, a deputy to Westmoreland for pacification.

There was strong opposition, especially from State and the CIA, to McNamara's recommendation, but strong support from Komer and the JCS.[99] Westmoreland was cautious, saying that he did not seek the task, but would, of course, undertake it.[100]

Several memoranda in opposition to McNamara's proposal were drafted in State, AID and the CIA.[101] The principal objections of the civilians were summed up by Robert Miller, head of the Vietnam desk in the State Department's Far East Division, who sent a memorandum to Unger in which he said he agreed with Unger's position:[102]

> In my view, an increased U.S. military takeover of the direction of the U.S. effort behind revolutionary development would mean inevitably an increased takeover of programs in the field and a commensurate displacement of the Vietnamese apparatus. It seems to me, that if this happens, this is a major step backward and represents in effect an admission of failure regarding revolutionary development. If revolutionary development has not made the progress we had hoped for, it is essen-

---

[97] There is a copy of Komer's memorandum in the Johnson Library, Office Files of Robert Komer. See also Scoville, *Reorganizing for Pacification Support,* cited above, *PP,* Gravel ed., vol. II, pp. 589 ff, and Komer's forthcoming memoirs.

[98] McNamara's draft and McNaughton's memorandum are in the Department of State, Lot File 70 D 48.

[99] A copy of Komer's memorandum to McNamara, Sept. 29, 1966, which he sent to Rusk, as well as a cover memorandum of September 29 to Rusk, is in the Department of State, Central File, Pol 27 Viet S. For the JCS, see JCSM–626–66, Wheeler to McNamara, Sept. 29, 1966, cited in Scoville, p. 36.

[100] Scoville, pp. 34, 38.

[101] In the Department of State, Lot File 71 D 88, see the memorandum from William Bundy to Ball (drafted by Unger), "Responsibility for Pacification/Revolutionary Development Program in Vietnam (McNamara Draft Proposal)," Sept. 27, 1966, and the attached "Notes on McNamara Draft Proposal," prepared by Rutherford M. Poats, assistant administrator for AID for the Far East, Sept. 26, 1966; Memorandum from U. Alexis Johnson to Rusk, "Secretary McNamara's Proposal for Placing Pacification Program in South Vietnam Under COMUSMACV: ACTION MEMORANDUM," Oct. 1, 1966 (also drafted by Unger); and an unsigned memorandum, "Comments on Mr. Komer's Views on Pacification Management," Oct. 3, 1966, which Scoville, *Reorganizing for Pacification Support* (p. 35), says was from someone in the CIA. It is not clear which of these memoranda were transmitted to designated recipients. On the U. Alexis Johnson memorandum, Unger made this handwritten notation: "Overtaken by events. Return to file."

[102] U.S. Department of State, Central File, Pol 27 Viet S, Memorandum from Miller to Unger, Sept. 26, 1966.

tially because of a lack of adequate motivation on the Vietnamese side, ineffective cadre training, ineffective police/intelligence efforts to weed out the VC infrastructure in the hamlets and villages, and as a consequence of all of these factors the absence of the villagers' interest in and commitment to the program. These major weaknesses in revolutionary development will not be alleviated by an increased U.S. military involvement in the program.

Miller added that, "revolutionary development in its later stages should be intimately tied in with the political development process. Increased military direction of the program is likely to interfere with this process at the local level in a major way and could even begin to smack of U.S. civil administration in rural areas."

Porter, according to a memorandum from Unger to Rusk, was also very opposed to McNamara's proposal, saying that it was "quite impractical and is opposed most strongly by those with most experience in Vietnam. He [Porter] considered that the military authorities who would be put in charge are markedly less competent than those presently responsible for the program and, despite their unquestioned abilities in the military field, they lack the kind of political understanding required to work effectively in this field. . . ."[103]

Lodge, who apparently had not been sent a copy of McNamara's memorandum but had heard of the recommendation, was strongly opposed, and drafted a statement on October 9, which he did not send, asking a series of rhetorical questions, including:[104]

> [I]s it not true that the military personnel is of a "wholesale" character needed for the business of combat, that they place a tremendous reliance on statistics which are seldom applicable to political situations, that they believe in telling and ordering and not in persuading, that they must always have a positive attitude toward the mission even though the facts indicate otherwise; that they tend to apply straight line change to situations which are not of that kind, that while they have merits they have serious liabilities? . . .
>
> Is it not true that military training and instruction do not train one to recognize political signs, which cannot be identified accurately like the fall of an artillery shell?
>
> Is it not true that a political organization must be based on interaction, walking on eggs, voluntarism, enthusiasm, hopes?
>
> Whereas a military organization rests on the authority of law, fear of punishment and certain knowledge of rewards for certain kinds of performance?

Lodge also noted the effects of the proposal on the Government of South Vietnam:

> Would it not tend to encourage military government in the GVN, slow up its move toward democracy?
>
> When you encourage the military to hold office, do you not thereby, however, unwittingly encourage instability and encourage coups?

---

[103] Johnson Library, NSF Memos to the President—Walt Rostow, Memorandum from Unger to Rusk, Oct. 2, 1966.

[104] Massachusetts Historical Society, Lodge Papers, draft of Oct. 9, 1966.

> Is it not true with men whose preoccupation is giving the people what they want, you have a greater stability than you have with people who are trained to give orders?
>
> Would not this proposal look like colonial authority? Would it not look like the same mistake the French made? . . .

In a personal letter to Lodge, Komer tried to appeal to his interest in pacification and political development: "Maybe the trick is to charge Westy with the Pacification chore, thus forcing him to produce the results you [Lodge] want. This would make a lot of soldiers unhappy, but you'd be in the driver's seat."[105]

Opposition to the proposal for giving the military control of pacification led McNamara to accept the alternative strongly preferred by the civilians, namely, a dual system of the kind that had been agreed upon in early 1966 but never fully implemented, and after his trip to Vietnam in mid-October he recommended consolidation of all civilian activities under one manager and all security-related activities under a MACV officer. Under Secretary of State Katzenbach, in his report, made the same recommendation. McNamara added that if, after a reasonable time, this system did not work satisfactorily, the entire program should be assigned to Westmoreland.

The JCS disagreed with McNamara's recommendation for a dual system, and reiterated their view that Westmoreland should assume control. If the President decided "for political reasons" to accept McNamara's recommendation, however, the JCS said they would not object.[106]

In a meeting on October 15 from 2:10 p.m. to 2:40 p.m. with the Vice President, McNamara, Vance and General Wheeler, the President, stating that he was dissatisfied with pacification but did not want at that point to override the objections to full military control, approved the dual system. He said he would give the new system 90–120 days to produce results.[107] After a meeting of the President, Rusk and McNamara on November 4, Lodge was informed of the new organizational arrangement.[108]

Lodge responded on November 6, saying that the crux of the problem was not organization but security, which civilian reorganization would not affect.[109] To provide better security, he said, the U.S. Army, in addition to getting the Vietnamese Army to take primary responsibility for local security, as agreed at Manila, should assign 10 percent of its forces to work on a "buddy system" with the Vietnamese on pacification. (He cited the examples of the U.S. Marines and the 1st and 25th U.S. Infantry Divisions.) While it would "take time" to change the habits of the Vietnamese Army from serving as regular forces to serving more as a counterguerrilla constabulary, "it would be clear to everyone at home that time was working for us and it might create a 'smell of victory.'"

---

[105] Same location, letter from Komer to Lodge, Sept. 30, 1966.

[106] *PP*, Gravel ed., vol. II, p. 599.

[107] There apparently are no notes of this meeting. The information used here is from JCS 6339–66, Wheeler to Sharp and Westmoreland, Oct. 17, 1966, cited by Scoville, *Reorganizing for Pacification Support*, p. 40.

[108] Johnson Library, NSF Memos to the President, Walt Rostow, Memorandum from Rostow to the President, Nov. 4, 1966, listing items on the agenda for the meeting that day, and Department of State, Central File, Pol 27 Viet S, Washington to Saigon 78865, Nov. 4, 1966.

[109] U.S. Department of State, Central File, Pol 27 Viet S, Saigon to Washington 10204, Nov. 6, 1966.

In his response on November 6 as well as in a letter to the President on November 7, Lodge urged, as he had when he talked to McNamara, that U.S. offensive military operations should be redefined. "Instead of defining it ["offensive operations"] as meaning 'seek out and destroy,' which I understand is now the case, it would be defined as 'split up the Viet Cong and keep him off balance.' This new definition . . . would mean fewer men for the purely 'military' war, fewer U.S. casualties and more pacification."[110]

The State Department, in a cable on November 12 cleared by the White House, thanked Lodge for his views on pacification, but directed him to proceed to implement the dual control plan.[111] With respect to his proposal for using U.S. forces in pacification, the cable stated that Westmoreland was planning to use a limited number under the buddy system "to guide and motivate" the pacification activities of the Vietnamese Army, but that, "we have serious doubts about any involvement U.S. troops beyond this in straight pacification operations. We fear this would tempt Vietnamese to leave this work more and more to us and we believe pacification, with its intimate contact with population, more appropriate for Vietnamese forces, who must after all, as arm of GVN, establish constructive relations with population. Hence we believe there should be no thought of U.S. taking on substantial share of pacification."

On November 15, after a meeting from 2:05 p.m. to 3:40 p.m. of the President with Rusk, McNamara, Rostow, Komer, Moyers and Justice Fortas, Lodge was told, in a cable drafted by William Bundy, that the new (dual control) plan had been "discussed today at highest levels, who wished to emphasize that this represents final and considered decision and who expressed hope that indicated measures could be put into effect just as rapidly as possible."[112]

On November 16, the President replied to Lodge in a letter drafted by Komer and approved by McNamara.[113] Avoiding Lodge's suggestions about redefining "offensive operations," the President said that there did not seem to be any "major differences" between Lodge's ideas and his own or those of his chief advisers as to how to make pacification "work." There was general agreement, he said, that "a limited number of U.S. combat forces must be detailed to be the catalysts for the Vietnamese." The problem was "that if the U.S. takes over too much of the [pacification] job, the ARVN will tend to sit back and let us fight that 'war' also."

The President added that he favored shifting responsibility for pacification to MACV, but was willing to try a compromise—the dual control plan.

"You have our full support and backing," he concluded. "In turn, we here depend on you not to let your people spend *too much time*

---

[110] There is a copy of Lodge's letter to the President on Nov. 7, 1966 in the Johnson Library, NSF Country File, Vietnam.

[111] U.S. Department of State, Central File, Pol 27 Viet S, Washington to Saigon 83699, Nov. 12, 1966.

[112] Same location, Washington to Saigon 85196, Nov. 15, 1966. There are very brief notes by Rostow on this meeting, Files of Walt W. Rostow, Meetings with the President, but they do not mention the new pacification plan. For follow-up action on the new plan, see Scoville, *Reorganizing for Pacification Support*, and *PP*, Gravel ed., vol. II, pp. 609 ff.

[113] Johnson Library, NSF Country File, Vietnam. Komer's draft of November 15 is in NSF Files of Robert W. Komer. The reply is identical to the draft.

in arguing details but to make them get on with the job." (emphasis added by hand by the President, who underlined the three words) In a handwritten note at the end of the letter, the President added: "When this reaches you it will be about a month since Manila and perhaps 500 of our boys are gone—Make them all follow your orders and lets get going."

Lodge replied on November 17 that he would comply with the decision and outlined the changes he planned to make. He added, however, that, in order for them to prove effective, "they need time to develop." [114]

Lodge also said he was gratified that Washington officials agreed with the need to revamp the South Vietnamese Army, but he added: "Doubt whether we can change over night habits and organization of ARVN acquired during the last ten years. Unless our success against main force daytime activity is equalled by success against guerrillas during the night, swift improvement cannot be expected to result simply by reorganization on the U.S.-civilian side." To the State Department's comments about his proposal for using 10 percent of U.S. forces in pacification, he replied that he had never advocated that U.S. forces should take on a "substantial" part of pacification, but he did believe "that an American presence in this field amounting to a very small percentage of the total manpower involved could induce ARVN to take the proper attitude by 'on the job' training and could give the necessary courage and confidence to the Vietnamese."

In a memorandum to the President that same day (November 17), Komer said that the new civilian arrangement for pacification "won't really be able to do the job, and that if we want solid results by end-1967 we'll have to give it to Westy. But at least we've already gone 25% of the way in the right direction. Your letter will set Lodge himself to thinking about whether to go the rest of the way. If he doesn't, *the time to take the next bite may be when Lodge leaves.* I'm sure he'd like to switch no later than next spring (he'd dearly love Rome and the Vatican as a reward), though I believe him when he says he'll stay as long as his Commander-in-Chief wants him. *However, I strongly believe that decisive results in 1967 demand an Ambassador who can take hold and manage that sprawling empire.* I'm sure McNamara would agree. (emphases in original) [115]

The decision to implement the dual control plan left the fate of Lansdale and his Senior Liaison Office (SLO) in even greater doubt, and on October 3, 1966, Lansdale sent Lodge a long memorandum on the question of "Future Plans." [116] He said that since his earlier suggestion that his office be closed at the end of 1966, he had, partly at the urging of other U.S. officials as well as Vietnamese, reconsidered the matter. Although he and his staff were "bone-weary," they were prepared to continue if there were a change in the U.S. approach coupled with a "clear-cut" assignment

[114] Lodge's reply, Saigon to Washington 11124 and 11125, Nov. 17, 1967, is in the Johnson Library, NSF Memos for the President—Walt Rostow.

[115] Johnson Library, NSF Files of Robert W. Komer.

[116] Massachusetts Historical Society, Lodge Papers, Vietnam, Memorandum from Lansdale to Lodge, "Future Plans," Oct. 3, 1966.

for SLO, backed by the support of Lodge, Westmoreland, and officials in Washington.

Lansdale was critical of the approach being used by the United States. "A fundamental requirement in Vietnam is to establish a political basis upon which all other actions can be mounted for success by our side." Yet, by "pouring in more and more thousands of Americans to do the job that we say belongs to the Vietnamese," the U.S. was "breaking prime rules for waging successful 'people's war.'" "[M]uch of our current policy and operations reflects a strong trend to a paternalism which belongs with Vietnam being a protectorate of the United States . . . with the Vietnamese assigned roles of 'dress extras' artistically arranged in groups to provide background as appropriate."

Another problem was the friction resulting from bureaucratic infighting, with each U.S. Government organization desirous of having a "clearly defined bailiwick in which success can be reported, while pointing to the laggardness of others as the reason why glorious victory is still far away." Noting that SLO had been criticized for encroaching on other domains, Lansdale, who had clashed frequently with Porter and with Habib, head of the Political Section, said that such reactions were understandable in view of the fact that SLO's role cut across organizational lines. But he added that in order for his operations to be effective he needed "freedom to operate as necessary for success, and with the only stipulations being that the work must assist your mission to Vietnam and that you be kept adequately informed of progress. In other words, the ball carrier must be given the ball and permitted to run with it." To alleviate the problem of coordination he suggested that Lodge reestablish the informal "political steering group" (Lodge, Porter, Habib and Lansdale).

If the U.S. approach were changed—and the memorandum did not discuss this point—and there were better understanding and support and greater freedom, as well as a clearer definition of its role, SLO could play a constructive part in "political development." Lansdale summarized this as "the sensing of the elements required to gain Vietnamese popular belief, and then citing these elements as the basis for practical advice to Vietnamese leaders." "In essence, it would be to do what Prime Minister Ky asked me to do in the Fall of 1965: to work with him, with other leaders, and with various political and religious groups, to promote more national unity, encourage political stability through understanding, and to guide political groups into more constructive roles for the national good." "[T]he war must be won by the Vietnamese themselves. We can only help."

Lansdale recommended that Lodge direct SLO to undertake the following actions:

a. To contact all key Vietnamese leaders, including military commanders, as required, to give them counsel on political development in accord with U.S. policy, to help create a bond of trust among these leaders, and to gain their true understanding of the value of the political principles we believe in.

b. To advise Vietnamese military commanders, with the support of MACV, on the critical political action role that the Vietnamese military must undertake in its relations with the Vietnamese people for success; concurrently, this probably would require MACV complementary action in guiding the issuance and enforcement of directives making Vietnamese troop behavior a command responsibility, including relief of commanders whose troops misbehave.

c. To encourage Vietnamese religious leaders to work together harmoniously in establishing a common acceptance of moral principles for the administration of government, for the military protection of the people in the war, for acts of forgiveness towards Qui Chanh in the Chieu Hoi program, political prisoners, and exiles, as well as for the defense of Vietnamese freedom.

d. To provide guidance to political groups for their growth across regional and religious boundaries into national groups with principled platforms; current needs for such help include Tran Quoc Buu with his farmer-labor movement and the Cao Dai Generals with their new political formation.

SLO's operations, Lansdale said, should be considered a "temporary expedient" which would "give a boost" to political development, after which the team would be withdrawn and the "regular" U.S. Government organizations would take over. A "rational breaking-off point," he said, would be after the election and establishment of the new Vietnamese Government under the constitution then being drafted.[117]

In late November 1966, after President Johnson had approved the new pacification organization, Porter, after talking with Lansdale, asked him to become the coordinator of U.S. civilian pacification operations in Region II, one of the four administrative subdivisions of South Vietnam. In response to this deliberate slight, Lansdale said, among other things,[118]

> As you pointed out in our talk on the 29th, I have not been as usefully employed in Viet Nam as I could have been. My true task in Viet Nam should be much the same as what I have done previously and successfully in Asia, including in Viet Nam. This task is to get the Vietnamese leaders, in and out of government, working together towards recognized goals that will cause the Vietnamese people to make a decisive choice for the precepts of the Free World and against the precepts of Communism. When this is done, we will be on our way to winning our cause here. Rather than finding a different assignment for me in Viet Nam, the real solution to my under-

[117] Of interest also is a paper by Lansdale, "The Battleground in 1967," Nov. 8, 1966, that he sent to Lodge as well as to several officials in Washington. Rostow sent it to the President with a cover memorandum saying, "This is Ed Lansdale at his best—worth reading." (Johnson Library, NSF Memos to the President—Walt Rostow, Memorandum from Rostow to the President, Nov. 17, 1966, to which Lansdale's memorandum of November 8 is attached.) In a cover memorandum to Lodge, Lansdale said "I believe it will help in your own thinking about the situation here. If you approve, I will distribute copies to the U.S. Mission Council members. A constructive result would be to stimulate some further thinking by them. Perhaps, for similar reasons, you would find it useful to pass copies discreetly to selected Vietnamese leaders." Lodge sent the paper to Porter for comment, and Porter replied in a personally typed note on November 8, saying, in part, "This paper is full of conventional wisdom. I don't understand why Ed should aim this stuff at you. It is the kind of thing that should be used to educate visitors. . . . All in all, the document appears to have been written for the record rather than to you." (Massachusetts Historical Society, Lodge Papers, Vietnam.)

[118] Massachusetts Historical Society, Lodge Papers, Lansdale Memorandum to Porter, "Assignment," Nov. 30, 1966.

employment is to let me do the task for which I came to Viet Nam.

You need this to help you gain success in the great undertaking you are now starting. The United States needs this. After an agonizing period, our government is beginning to understand some of the measures necessary to achieve victory in this kind of struggle. However, while we say that the Vietnamese themselves must finally do the winning, we have shown insufficient understanding of how better policies can be transmitted to the Vietnamese in a way which will generate effective action by the latter. Lacking this, we are tending towards a colonial paternalism over the Vietnamese that will prove fatal to our cause, to your work, and to our military effort. As a realist, I have tried hard to head off this tragedy in the making, even though I have been able to be effective only at times during the past 14 months, in the emergence of the RD program, in its unique progress during last Spring's "Struggle" crisis, in the conduct of last September's election, and indirectly through my memos and in my talks on policy matters with a wide range of Americans and Vietnamese. . . .

There is ample past evidence that every time I have been permitted to work intimately with Vietnamese leaders on programs of U.S. interest, those Vietnamese programs—civilian or military—started succeeding, and the U.S. officials responsible for American help to the programs succeeded equally. These results are actions that have spoken louder than words, whether my methods are understood or not. The vital nature of the 1967 campaign, with its need for results on the true battleground of a "people's war," underscores the fact that my best service to the U.S. in Viet Nam would be to work continually with all Vietnamese leaders concerned with gaining success on the 1967 battleground.

After meeting with Lodge on December 2, Lansdale sent him a memorandum on December 7 outlining ways in which SLO would seek to provide "further liaison." This would include:[119]

Leadership. As a means of supporting your own work with Chief of State Thieu and Prime Minister Ky, I will provide a more informal low-key relationship that permits sounding out their problems for you and gaining follow-up by them on matters you have discussed with them. In so doing, I hope also to be able to encourage closer teamwork between these two men at the top. . . .

Power Base. Chief of State Thieu and Prime Minister Ky have a relatively small "base" supporting them in power, which is not particularly cohesive, tending to divide into Ky and Thieu camps. It is primarily military, including the military members of the NLC and unit commanders. Our "senior liaison" efforts are being directed to encourage more unity of purpose among the military leaders of this "base," (with more awareness of national needs in political, social, and economic fields), as well as to gain expansion of this base through wider civilian support of the GVN leadership in the transitional pe-

[119] Same location, Memorandum from Lansdale to Lodge, "Senior Liaison," Dec. 7, 1966.

riod just ahead. Initial priority, in contacts with leaders, is being given to discussions of the role of the Vietnamese armed forces in support of RD. . . .

Political development. Longstanding friendships with Vietnamese leaders, many of whom are outside the GVN, open a number of doors to us. We are extending contacts, to promote more unity among politicians and political factions and between the latter and the GVN. This is, of course, vital in helping the Vietnamese make orderly progress toward Constitutional government. Further, particular emphasis will be placed on helping stimulate policies and actions endorsed by you which are designed to accomplish sound political development at the hamlet and village level. The forthcoming hamlet/village reorganization decree is only one of many actions needed, including meaningful follow-up steps after elections have been held in these communities.

Esprit. Special attention will be given to helping maintain and enhance healthy Vietnamese esprit and confidence. It would be disastrous if the massive American presence in Viet Nam should cause the Vietnamese to seek the sidelines and to "let the Americans do it," along with increased xenophobic attitudes. . . .

Later in December, Lansdale, on leave for the holidays, met in Washington with William Bundy, who then wrote to Porter on the question of Lansdale's role:[120]

In our lunch today, Ed's basic thesis was that the Constitution/election process must produce a setup that articulate Vietnamese would regard as new. He thinks that Thieu and Ky are probably working together with the aim of occupying the Presidency and the Prime Minister's job (order unspecified), and he further thinks that if this is the result, Vietnamese generally will regard it as an American-influenced continuation of the status quo offering very little hope for the future. He thinks the reaction would be such that there would be marked hostility and in all probability some kind of coup. This would be disastrous to the whole effort, however well we were then succeeding on the military and pacification fronts.

In the face of this prospect, as he sees it, Ed's recipe would be for a major "political development" effort of contacts with key political figures specifically including Thieu and Ky themselves but also of others who might emerge in positions of influence and leadership. The second prong of the effort should be, in his judgment, an effort to develop local institutions, on which he seems to be thinking of such things as agricultural cooperative organizations in the countryside and development of the labor union structure. . . .

What he wants, in effect, is a hunting license . . . to produce a national political grouping that would cut across military/civilian, north/south, and other divisions, and form a cohesive and progressive government in South Vietnam.

---

[120] U.S. Department of State, Lot File 85 D 240 (William Bundy Papers), Letter from Bundy to Porter, Dec. 29, 1966.

> And so say all of us. The question is whether Ed can serve effectively in helping toward this end. As I see him, and have always seen him, he has the unique gift of meeting with the Vietnamese, winning their confidence, and on many occasions getting opinions and feelings out of them that a regular line officer cannot hope to get. He himself thinks his credit with the Vietnamese is, if anything, better than ever, and frankly ascribes this in part to his own frictions and difficulties with the Embassy and others in the mission.
>
> The debits are equally obvious. My own hunch is that this relationship with Thang [head of Revolutionary Development—pacification] has been on balance helpful, but it can hardly improve the cohesion of the mission to have a man with no action responsibility constantly picking up the gripes that others then have to do something about. As to his operating in a field of "political development," the ultimate question will always remain whether he reports his activities fully and keeps them in line with the Ambassador's policy. I suppose he will always think that he can only really report to Cabot personally, and I can see the difficulty of this arrangement. I also know well the problem of his relations with Phil [Habib] and, I surmise, with you—and I have always been inclined to put the blame more on him, or rather on his initial team, than anywhere else.
>
> At any rate, what must now be clear to all of us, although he put it only gently to me, is that his job in Saigon will wind up in the near future unless he gets some fairly clear outlet.

Porter replied to Bundy in a letter on January 3, 1967, in which he said that Lansdale was "unable to move from the theoretical to the practical," and that "in the terrible world of Vietnam, sooner or later persons who have views should display a desire to put then into practice, not by having more conversations but through actions."[121] Noting that Lansdale wanted to work closely with principal political figures, Porter said "there can only be one Ambassador at a post, and given Ed's method of operating, we would soon be seeing in the press some speculation on this subject which could be embarrassing. Even more importantly, we might find that Ed would not necessarily pursue a policy line consistent with the Mission's but would follow his own desires. If past experience is any guide, he would neither consult with nor adequately inform the other elements of the Mission. His ideas are not that good, nor does he have the unique insight that he believes he has, to allow him largely to ignore the opinions of others." Porter added that it was "difficult to see how Ed and his group have advanced our work here," and he said that in his opinion SLO should be terminated.

In the weeks that followed, Porter's advice was not heeded, and Lansdale remained in Vietnam for the better part of 1967. In April 1967, Ellsworth Bunker replaced Lodge as Ambassador and asked Lansdale to stay. The U.S. program, however, rather than changing as Lansdale had hoped, became larger and more bureaucratic and paternalistic. Although he continued to perform some of the same functions, he never regained his earlier role.

---

[121] Same location, Porter letter to William Bundy, Jan. 3, 1967.

CHAPTER 12

SEARCHING

The awareness in November 1966 that the war was stalemated militarily and could not be won, within the imposed limits, by further escalation, as attested by the President's acceptance of McNamara's recommendations, was not followed, however, by the kind of general review and reconsideration of strategy that might have been deemed desirable under the circumstances. Rather, while stabilizing military programs, greater emphasis was placed on strengthening and expanding existing nonmilitary programs and on continuing to seek negotiations.

At the same time, some effort was made to develop new organizational mechanisms by which to improve the effectiveness of U.S. programs. In late September 1966, Komer proposed creation of a small "war cabinet" to provide better management of all aspects of the war, which he suggested should be chaired by Under Secretary of State Katzenbach, who had just replaced Ball. Komer sent a copy of his memorandum to Moyers, followed by a memorandum to Moyers on September 30 in which he elaborated on the idea. "The key problem," Komer said, "is how to organize at the level below the President or even Rusk and McNamara, who are also busy on so much else. Why not take advantage of a new wind at State, and make Nick Katzenbach chairman of a little kitchen cabinet—to meet at least biweekly and report direct to the President in writing (as well as Rusk and McNamara of course). Nick would be a good impartial chairman and has no hawk/dove image problem yet. Cy Vance and I should be members, and I presume Walt. But I would not add Gaud, Marks, Helms, or any others or we'd have a wobbly SIG[1] (a real non-starter in my view). Then the JCS would want in too."[2]

Later that same day, Komer sent Moyers a memorandum suggesting that an alternative way of organizing a "Vietnam kitchen cabinet" would be to set it up in the White House. "But only," he added, "if it could be run by you in lieu of those other duties we discussed the other day. Walt [Rostow] could *not* run it; besides he has the wrong image. For me to run it would create problems with Walt. Besides the whole virtue would be to give it to someone who has the President's constant ear." (emphasis in original)

[1] The SIG—Senior Interdepartmental Group—was a subcabinet level group, organized within the NSC and chaired by the Under Secretary of State, to assist with interdepartmental planning and coordination.

[2] Johnson Library, Files of Robert Komer, Memorandum to Moyers from Komer, Sept. 30, 1966.

"You and I plus Nick K. and Cy Vance, could do wonders. I'm prepared to tell the President that putting you 50% on Vietnam would be the smartest thing we could do between now and 1968."[3]

Moyers sent the President a memorandum on September 30 in which he repeated Komer's suggestions for a kitchen cabinet headed by Katzenbach.[4] Komer then sent a memorandum to the President on October 5 in which he suggested the need for *"an effective subcabinet level mechanism in Washington to monitor performance."* (emphasis in original) "We badly need," he said, "to organize more systematically to (1) keep you properly informed on key programs; (2) do the staff work necessary to present you with coordinated recommendations; and (3) follow through on your decisions."[5] (It is not clear whether this subcabinet mechanism to monitor performance was the same as, in addition to, or a substitute for the "war cabinet" which Komer also had proposed.)

On November 15, 1966, at a Tuesday Lunch meeting with his senior advisers, the President directed that a "group" be established, chaired by Katzenbach and consisting of Komer, Rostow, Vance and "a good military man," which should meet three times a week "on Vietnam and all its dimensions."[6]

Thus began the "Non-Group," as it was known within the very small circle of those who were aware of its existence.[7] Beginning in early 1967 and continuing until February 1968, it met almost every Thursday at 5:00 p.m., and occasionally on other days as well, in Katzenbach's office. In addition to Katzenbach, Vance, Komer (until he left for Vietnam in the spring of 1967), and Rostow, who were the principal members, other members were William Bundy (in 1967, his deputy, Philip Habib, sometimes attended with Bundy or in his place), Harriman, Helms, General Wheeler, and Benjamin Read. (When Vance resigned, Nitze took his place.) According to one source, McNamara also attended frequently, even though he was not considered a member, as did Rusk from time to time.[8] The atmosphere was congenial—drinks were served—and in-

[3] Same location, Memorandum to Moyers from Komer, Sept. 30, 1966.

[4] Johnson Library, NSF Files of Bill Moyers, Memorandum to the President from Moyers, Sept. 30, 1966.

[5] U.S. Department of State, Central File, Pol 27 Viet S, Komer Memorandum to the President, Oct. 5, 1966.

[6] Johnson Library, NSF Files of Walt W. Rostow, Meetings with the President, notes on the Tuesday Lunch meeting with the President, Nov. 15, 1966.

[7] The author appreciates the cooperation of William Bundy and Nicholas Katzenbach in providing some of the details about the Non-Group.

In his study, *The President's War* (Philadelphia, Pa.: Lippincott, 1971), Anthony Austin says that the Non-Group was, "at bottom, a bureaucratic plot to flush out doubts about the President's policy and induce him to alter his course," adding that Katzenbach, who, like Ball, did not favor escalation of the war, considered this a more promising approach than Ball's individual frontal criticism. The President's acceptance of the Non-Group idea, Austin says, "convinced Katzenbach that deep down the President had his own reservations as to whether he was getting anywhere."

Walter Isaacson and Evan Thomas in *The Wise Men: Six Friends and the World They Made: Acheson, Bohlen, Harriman, Kennan, Lovett, McCloy* (New York: Simon and Schuster, 1986), p. 684, state that the Non-Group consisted of officials "who were growing ever more doubtful about the war," and, faced with "a small, hawkish circle—principally Rusk and Rostow—began holding their own strategy sessions on Vietnam." Although there is some validity to these observations—some of the members of the Non-Group were opposed to further escalation, and there was considerable tension between State and Defense Department officials and Rostow—they do not take into account the fact that the Non-Group was established by the President and that Rostow and General Wheeler were members.

[8] U.S. Air Force Historical Research Center, Maxwell Air Force Base, Oral History Interview (#477) with Maj. Gen. Robert N. Ginsburgh, May 26, 1971, p. 67.

formal—although subjects for discussion were frequently known in advance, there was no formal agenda and no notes were kept.

Although the Non-Group met in great secrecy, it would appear that it played a very important role in the policymaking process. In a sense it was the counterpart to the Tuesday Lunch, and had been organized along similar lines—small, select, intimate, secretive—because, as in the case of the Tuesday Lunch, of the need to limit participation in the consideration and coordination of key decisions and the flow of information to a few officials from the State and Defense departments, the CIA and the White House. Originally, as Komer said in his memorandum of September 30, the military were not going to be included. General Ginsburgh, who was responsible for liaison between the NSC and the JCS, said in an interview several years later that he was specifically prohibited from telling the JCS of the existence of the Non-Group, a situation that he became increasingly concerned about, but which as noted, was corrected by the President's order on November 15 adding Wheeler to the group.[9]

Like the Tuesday Lunch the Non-Group concerned itself with the major issues and problems involved in the war.[10] It was particularly active during the spring of 1967 in the long and intense deliberations on U.S. policy and strategy resulting from a new request from Westmoreland for more troops and broader authority to intensify the war, and in planning in the fall of 1967 for priorities for 1968.[11] According to Rostow in a memorandum to Lyndon Johnson in 1970 on the decision in 1968 to halt the bombing of North Vietnam, the Non-Group also discussed "on many occasions" the idea

---

[9] *Ibid.*

[10] In a memorandum to Katzenbach on April 22, 1967, "Projects for the Group," (State Department, Central File, Pol 27 Viet S), William Bundy listed the following broad range of items:

"*A. DOD Projects*

"1. Alternative scenarios on troop increases. . . .

"2. Scenario on any plans involving invasion of the North, or extension of present ground rules for Laos and Cambodia. . . .

"3. Possible scenario for the barrier project. . . .

"4. At least the outline of McNamara's 'sharp and short' bombing program.

"5. An outline of present DOD thinking with respect to improving the military thinking within SVN. . . .

"*B. State Projects*

"1. An overall presentation of our present thinking on a final settlement. . . .

"2. A general analysis of political factors affecting extension of the war or the barrier to Laos. . . .

"3. A similar analysis for Cambodia. . . .

"*C. Intelligence Projects*

"*Immediate*

"1. An SNIE on Soviet intentions and capabilities. . . .

"2. A proper analysis of Hanoi's attitude in the light of the captured documents. . . .

"3. A new CIA evaluation of air operations in North Vietnam. . . .

"4. An independent evaluation of pacification programs. . . .

"5. A new review of the adequacy and margins of error in our estimates on infiltration, local recruitment, overall military status, and order of battle. . . .

"6. Evaluation of the Chinese situation and how Hanoi may look at it. . . .

"*Contingent*

"7. As we develop scenarios of possible military action, a small group should be designated to give us, under tightest security, estimates of Chinese and Soviet reactions to selected alternatives.

"*D. Other Projects*

"1. Proposals for improving U.S. public support and particularly strengthening the appearance of U.S. unity to Hanoi. . . ."

[11] For the former, see the Ginsburgh interview cited above, pp. 67–68; for the latter, see the Memorandum for the President from Katzenbach, "Highest Priority Areas in Vietnam," Nov. 13, 1967, in the State Department, Central File, Pol 27 Viet S.

of a peace initiative involving some kind of bombing halt or reduction.[12]

Efforts to Plan for 1967

Rostow (supported by Ginsburgh) and Komer, operating from their own perspectives and from the vantage point of the White House, apparently also thought that the development of a strategic plan and policy guidelines for 1967 would be in the President's interest as well as serving as a blueprint for more effective future programs. Development of such a plan was also seen as a way of engendering greater optimism and action on the part of both Defense and State, where, as reflected in McNamara's October report, a potentially serious combination of negativism and fatalism was perceived by Rostow and Komer to be setting in.

One of the reasons for generating a greater sense of urgency as well as better organization and more effective action was the timing of the next U.S. Presidential election. As Ginsburgh commented in a memorandum to Rostow on October 1, 1966, "The closer we get to the November 1968 elections, the greater will be the incentive for the VC/DRV to hold on at all costs in hopes of a political reversal of the US position in Vietnam."[13] Thus, Ginsburgh argued, "we must do our best to be clearly over the hump by then [the political conventions in the summer of 1968], and it would be extremely helpful to have started a phased troop withdrawal." He proposed the following action program:

1. Establish at top levels within the government the objective of winning—or at least passing the crest—by 1 June 1968. *Keep this goal out of the press.*

2. Allow the Communists one week to evaluate the political impact of the November [congressional] election.

3. After one week, get the word privately to the VC/DRV that the US is prepared to resume its program of increasing pressure—at a faster rate than before. Issue no public ultimatums.

4. If no satisfactory de-escalatory signals are received within 10 days to two weeks resume our program of increasing pressures:

a. Resume the POL campaign.

b. Over a 2–3 week period take out the remaining hydroelectric plants.

c. Destroy the steel plant.

d. Mine the ports.

e. Eliminate the NVN air forces.

f. Attack the air defense system.

g. As d and e are eliminated shift weight of effort back to interdiction campaign.

5. As soon as details are worked out announce reorganization of pacification activities and beginning of new phase of operations.

6. By 1 January announce intention and commence withdrawal of up to two divisions and appropriate air units from

[12] Johnson Library, Rostow Files, Memorandum to Lyndon Johnson from Rostow, "Decision to Halt the Bombing," Mar. 19, 1970.

[13] Johnson Library, NSF Memos to the President—Walt Rostow, Memorandum from Ginsburgh to Rostow, "Vietnam—the Next Phase," Oct. 1, 1966.

Europe for transfer to Vietnam, with redeployment determined on basis of logistic capability. Justify as a temporary move without committing US to necessarily redeploy to Europe after Vietnam war is over.

The policy review and strategic planning effort for 1967 began in September 1966 with a paper by Rostow and Komer, in consultation with William Bundy—"We are all in basic agreement," Rostow said—which Rostow sent to the President. In their paper, "A Strategy for the Next Phase in Vietnam," Rostow and Komer proposed a program to "force acceptance" by the Communists of negotiations.[14] "Present evidence," they said, "is that we have come to the point where Hanoi cannot win, but obviously we have not yet forced it to accept negotiations on our terms. Our problem is to present them with a situation where, whatever their will to hold on and sweat us out, they have no realistic option but to accept our terms." "Short of occupying North Vietnam," they added, there were two ways by which this could be done. First, to bomb the North so heavily that "the whole economic, social, and political infrastructure is endangered." They rejected this course, saying that it might bring in the Chinese, and that "the pressures at home and abroad we would have to bear would likely be excessive." The second way would be "to produce a palpable process of political and military disintegration of the Viet Cong." "Their morale is already declining more rapidly than that of the NVN infiltrators. Their strength has stopped increasing. Most of the rising number of defectors are VC. They are probably hardest hit by food and medicine shortages, and by the increasing success of the GVN in establishing itself." "By focusing on their vulnerabilities," the paper said, "we can accelerate their decline and possibly split them off from Hanoi, which could be a decisive step toward winning the war. At the same time, by continuing the cost to Hanoi, Hanoi might be more willing to accept such a splitting off."

Rostow and Komer proposed the following elements of a program to produce an "accelerated disintegration of the Viet Cong":

A. *A dramatic and sustained political and psychological appeal to the VC to join in the making of a new South Vietnamese nation*

(i) an amnesty offer.

(ii) enlarged and sustained efforts to defect VC leaders.

(iii) an expanded psywar effort to split the VC from Hanoi.

(iv) a radical expansion in Chieu Hoi efforts.

(v) Agreement on a Constitution followed by elections in accordance with the Constitution in which the VC who had accepted amnesty would be allowed to vote.

B. *Accelerated Pacification*

(i) new organizational arrangements providing more unified US/GVN civil/military management.

(ii) size of forces to be allocated.

(iii) converting appropriate ARVN forces to pacification functions.

[14] Johnson Library, C.F. ND 19/CO 312, Memorandum to the President from Rostow, Sept. 28, 1966, with attached memorandum dated Sept. 20, "A Strategy for the Next Phase in Vietnam."

(iv) 1967 targets to be set, including rapid pacification of certain key areas. . . .

(v) contributing programs to be expanded, e.g., RD [Revolutionary Development] cadres, agriculture, land reform, police.

C. *An accelerated, workable land reform scheme*

D. *Pressing forward rapidly and dramatically with formulation of post-war development program*

E. *Assuring good military-civil political relations in post-election period, including creation of a national political party embracing both elements*

F. *Avoiding another round of severe inflation*

G. *US/GVN military offenses* [sic] *against VC/NVA Main Force* maintaining the capacity to deal with present or enlarged North Vietnamese military formations introduced into the South, plus whatever we can do about infiltration.

H. *Bombing offensive in the North* continuing to impose a cost on the North for continuing the war.[15]

On October 5, 1966, Komer sent the President a memorandum making many of the same points.[16] *"We're doing much better than we think,"* Komer declared. "we have at the end of September 1966 achieved some real momentum in Vietnam." By "properly orchestrating and pushing on at least seven different major fronts in 1967," (he enumerated these, which were similar to those in the Rostow-Komer memorandum) "we can achieve sufficient cumulative impact either to force the enemy to negotiate or cripple his ability to sustain the war." The "real objective," he said, *"is achieving a satisfactory outcome by the end of 1967, or at the minimum achieving such momentum that it will be clear to all—including the US public—that it is only a matter of time."* Moreover, he believed that the U.S. could develop a "'win' strategy *without further major escalation against the North, or sizeable US deployments beyond what you've already approved."* (emphases in original)

Following McNamara's October 14 report, the Manila Conference, and the President's decision to accept McNamara's recommendations, Rostow again raised the question of formulating a strategy for 1967.[17] In a long paper for the President on November 30, which was sent also to Katzenbach and the members of the Non-Group, he outlined a plan "to maximize the chance that we force a decision by Hanoi in the course of the calendar year 1967 to end the war in Vietnam on terms compatible with our interests; that is, an end to hostilities in Laos as well as in Vietnam; the acceptance of the Geneva framework [from the 1954 Conference] for Southeast Asia; acceptance of an essentially independent South

---

[15] On November 18, Komer sent a copy of the Rostow-Komer Memorandum of September 20 to Vance and Katzenbach, saying that "As the evil promoter of our non-club, I feel obligated to propose a menu for our first non-session. I suggest we focus on two issues:

"A. Whether and how a little group like ours could usefully provide some greater focus and orchestration to our own Vietnam enterprises. I can brief you on the President's current thinking.

"B. Whether developing a 'strategic plan' for 1967 would be a useful device for systematizing and orchestrating our effort. I don't have in mind any tome but rather a set of brief, agreed guidelines at which the attached is a poor first stab."

[16] Johnson Library, NSF Files of Robert W. Komer, Memorandum for the President from Komer, Oct. 5, 1966.

[17] Johnson Library, NSF Memos to the President—Walt Rostow, Memorandum to the President from Rostow, Nov. 30, 1966, attaching a 26-page paper, "A Strategy for Vietnam, 1967."

Vietnam that can determine its future on a one-man, one-vote basis or a reasonable approximation thereof." After analyzing various factions, including the effect of bombing and the role of the U.S.S.R. and of China, Rostow concluded: "In short, while it has suffered a profound setback from its hopeful position in 1964 and early 1965, Hanoi has found, thus far, a rationale for continuing the conflict and a domestic and foreign policy strategy which permits it to continue." The object of U.S. policy, he said, "is to produce in 1967 a sense that all the factors judged relevant by Hanoi are moving unfavorably—or as many of them as we can move. . . ."

Rostow outlined an action program similar to that contained in the Rostow-Komer memorandum of September 20, and, as will be seen, similar to that in a draft NSAM on December 10. He stressed also the need for better organization of the war effort, and emphasized the importance of the Non-Group, which he said should "spot delays in implementing the agreed plan and end them; spot gaps in implementing the agreed plan and fill them; re-survey the evolving situation and make recommendations for changes in the plan."

Rostow also expressed concern about "certain fundamental, unsolved problems with domestic opinion," and urged greater action to "give our citizens a better sense of how to measure progress in a war of this kind." He also stressed the importance of strengthening bipartisan political support for the war: "By every device we can conceive, we should make the war a bipartisan venture in domestic political terms, reaching out to the Republicans for advice and engaging them with the fullest possible briefings."

If the war could not be ended in 1967, Rostow said, the groundwork would have to be laid in advance of the 1968 elections to permit the Johnson administration "to hold a position of: don't throw away a winning effort and defeat a position of: don't throw good men and money after bad."

In a cover memorandum to the President, Rostow said that the plan would require the following "three things to make it move":

—Westmoreland must allocate more of his own military resources to pacification as well as press the ARVN forward into this task; and he should work up a plan for the military side of pacification for 1967.

—We shall need in Saigon a vigorous Ambassador with great managerial skill, to drive forward hard this kind of program at that end.

—We need to tighten the backstopping of this whole program in Washington.

At about the same time, Komer drafted two papers in which he surveyed the situation and recommended a plan for 1967. The first, "Vietnam Prognosis for 1967–68," he sent to McNamara on November 29, 1966, with a cover note saying that his prognosis was "quite consistent with the proposals in your October memorandum to the President, even though it makes a rather more hopeful estimate."[18] He added that he favored drafting a program for 1967 for the

[18] Johnson Library, Warnke Papers, McNaughton Files, Komer letter to McNamara, Nov. 29, 1966 and attached "Vietnam Prognosis for 1967–68," Nov. 28, 1966.

President's approval, and suggested that the draft could be initiated by the Non-Group.

In his paper, Komer began with "Where we are today," saying that "Any prognosis for 1967 must start with one's premises about end-1966, which I daresay are quite 'optimistic'":

> A. Westy's spoiling strategy (accelerating search-and-destroy operations) has already succeeded in throwing Hanoi's phase III strategy [main forces warfare] way off balance. Thus we are well past the first turning point where we stopped losing the war.
>
> B. *My guess, though I can't prove it, is that we have also passed a second major turning point.* I suspect that we have reached the point where we are killing, defecting, or otherwise attriting more VC/NVA strength than the enemy can build up [the "cross-over point"]. . . .
>
> C. *We may also have passed a critical psychological turning point,* in that the bulk of SVN's population increasingly believe that we're winning the war. This to me was the chief significance of the 80% voter turnout on 11 September. Even if one regards it as an exercise in competitive coercion, the fact is that 80% of those who could vote (in daylight) listened to the GVN rather than the VC. The ever increasing weight of the US commitment now felt literally everywhere in SVN, contributes greatly to this growing attitude. (emphases in original)

Komer concluded: "In sum—slow, painful, and incredibly expensive though it may be—we're beginning to 'win' the war in Vietnam." "This is a far cry from saying, however, that we're going to win it—in any meaningful sense." The war would be won, Komer said, in the South, and it would be won by an "increasing erosion" of the strength of the southern Communists. The "key to success" was "an effective pacification program," together with encouraging more Communists to defect, and developing a "more dynamic, representative and thus more attractive" government. Effective orchestration and management of U.S. programs, and better utilization of the Vietnamese Armed Forces—"our most underutilized asset"—"can produce enough of a *bandwagon psychology*" in the South to lead to a "successful outcome" by the end of 1967 or during 1968. (emphasis in original) This would be subject, however, to "certain imponderables": whether the North Vietnamese would "materially increase" infiltration; whether the Communists would "revert to a guerrilla strategy" (he thought that such a "de-escalation would shatter VC morale"); whether the North Vietnamese would choose to negotiate; whether the South Vietnamese Government would remain intact or be subject to more crises; whether the new pacification program would be successful; and whether the U.S. could "settle down for a long pull if necessary."

In a prognosis of the course of events in 1967, Komer said that by the end of the year, if not before, there should be demonstrable progress in pacification, in the results of U.S. combat in the South as well as in bombing the North, and in the establishment of a representative government. This should produce a "bandwagon psychology" in South Vietnam as well as a willingness by the North Vietnamese to negotiate or to begin withdrawing.[19]

On November 29, Komer prepared another paper, "A Strategic Plan for 1967 in Vietnam,"[20] which he sent to Rostow on December 10 with a cover note asking him to "endorse it on to the President." Rostow did so, and sent Komer a note saying "I'd have some language changes of a minor kind to suggest—but it's a start."[21] Komer also sent a memorandum to the President in which he said that the paper for a Vietnam strategy for 1967 was intended "as a means of getting a clear focus on the all-out effort needed next year." He and Rostow, he added, suggested that the paper be issued as an NSAM in order to give it emphasis as well as to provide the basis for clear, assignment of responsibility. "I will confess to a case of the six-month frustration," Komer said, "having now been in the job long enough to realize both the immensity of the task and the sheer difficulty of getting things done. But I am equally

---

[19] In late December 1966, Johnson received a report on pacification from Ambassador William Leonhart, a Foreign Service Officer assigned to the White House as Komer's deputy, following a visit by Leonhart to Vietnam. Despite Komer's optimism, Leonhart found that there had been little if any progress on the civil side of the war:

"*The lack of progress in pacification remains the crux of the Vietnam problem,* largely determining duration and extent of the war, persistence or fade-away of the NVA/VC forces, and the likelihood of negotiations. We may get negotiations without an internal resolution of Vietnam's security situation. We are unlikely to have negotiations or withdrawal without some significant progress toward genuine pacification. Despite the substantial results our arms have achieved against the enemy's main force in 1966 and our civil successes, we have not yet found a way to assist the GVN to achieve continuous local security below the provincial level—or to impose its obverse: continuous local insecurity for the VC guerrillas. This is the gap in our line. Closing it is a major task for 1967."

Leonhart said that he found a deeper division of opinion between U.S. military and civilian personnel over the nature of the war and priorities for the United States than he had found on two previous trips in 1966:

"The military generally argue the unresolved and increasing main force threat and view the guerrillas and their political infrastructure as a supporting arm which can be readily dealt with once the main force war is won. . . . The civilians stress the VC guerrillas and their political apparatus as the decisive enemy. . . . In their view the shortest route to the enfeeblement or withdrawal of the NVA/VA main force is the destruction of the totalitarian revolutionary apparatus in the south and its replacement by a broad base of popular support for the GVN in the districts and villages and hamlets of Vietnam."

Urging that steps be taken to mitigate this division of opinion, Leonhart suggested that the U.S. should also take steps to correct the "inertia" of the Government of South Vietnam. *"The GVN, as matters stand now,"* he said, *"is likely to be an increasingly uncertain instrument in the first half of 1967."* (emphasis in original) He recommended a system of "graduated pressures" by which to goad the South Vietnamese into action. Johnson Library, NSF Country File, Vietnam, Leonhart report to the President, "Visit to Vietnam—1966, Report and Recommendations," Dec. 30, 1966.

Komer sent copies of Leonhart's report to various Presidential advisers. Ball's assistant, Jack Rosenthal, responded with this memorandum to Ball on Jan. 5, 1967 (Department of State, Central File, Pol 27 Viet S):

"Crudely, it doesn't seem to me that this tells us anything we didn't already know either about what's happening there or here.

"With respect to the former, it says ARVN deployment to RD/P is the key—hardly diverting in its novelty. With respect to the latter, it says Komer & Co. believe MACV should run the program—again not a bewilderingly fresh concept.

"The main failing of the paper, however, in my view, is in what it omits. It builds up to say that we should 'develop a system of graduated pressures' on the GVN to make ARVN do its RD job and that in the past, our threats and pressures have been too sporadic. Again in the last paragraph on page 8, the point is 'to increase ARVN effectiveness. . . .'

"To offer any meaningful comment on this paper thus would require some explanation of what is meant by such language, other than continued exhortation of the kind that appears to have accomplished little more than driving the Embassy to distraction. If Ambassador Leonhart and Bob Komer know of ways to apply effective pressure, then perhaps they might spell them out. But all this paper gives us of that is the 'personal' view that the only successful RD/P program is one run by MACV. (And that, among other things, leaves unanswered your question—if MACV can make ARVN move, why should it not be able to do so with civilian-run RD/P?)"

[20] Johnson Library, NSF Files of Robert W. Komer.

[21] Johnson Library, NSF Memos to the President—Walt Rostow.

convinced that if we can jack up the GVN a lot harder than we have, we'll be able to see daylight by the end of 1967."[22]

The President replied in a handwritten note: "Walt—I agree. It's good. Come in with Bob on Monday. L"[23]

Komer's paper, retitled "Strategic Guidelines for 1967 in Vietnam," was sent as a draft NSAM to Rusk and McNamara on December 12. In a cover memorandum, Rostow stated that the President wanted to issue such a set of guidelines.[24]

"Now that the extensive deployment and skillful use of U.S. forces has greatly improved our military position in Vietnam," the draft stated, "it is imperative that we mount and effectively orchestrate a concerted military, civil, and political effort to achieve a satisfactory outcome as soon as possible," based on the following strategic aims for 1967:

> A. Maximize the prospects for a satisfactory outcome in Vietnam by December 1967 or, if this is not possible, put us in the best position for the longer pull.
>
> B. Be equally suited to (a) forcing Hanoi to negotiate; (b) weakening the VC/NVA to the point where Hanoi will opt to fade away; or (c) at the minimum, making it patently clear to all that the war is demonstrably being won.
>
> C. Complement our anti-main force campaign and bombing offensive by greatly increased efforts to pacify the countryside and increase the attractive power of the GVN—all these to the end of accelerating the erosion of southern VC strength and creating a bandwagon psychology among the people of SVN. This strategy is also well-suited to exploiting any possibilities of a Hanoi/NLF split.

To achieve these strategic aims, "a maximum continuing effort" would be required in nine program areas:

> A. *Press a Major Pacification Effort,* employing the bulk of the RVNAF [Republic of Vietnam Armed Forces].
>
> > 1. Devise a concrete and detailed US/GVN pacification plan for 1967 which will: (a) set realistic goals by region and by province, with emphasis on areas or LOCs [lines of communication] where early results are possible; (b) provide for adequate force allocations and time-phasing; (c) properly dove-tail the military and civil programs.
> > 2. Retrain, re-motivate and deploy a steadily increasing proportion of ARVN in supporting the RF [Regional Forces] and PF [Popular Forces] in clear-and-hold operations as the key to pacification.
> > 3. Progressively open essential roads, railroad and canals on a planned schedule.
> > 4. Revitalize and accelerate the civil side of pacification.
> > 5. Devise improved techniques for measuring pacification progress and presenting them to the public.

[22] Johnson Library, NSF Files of Robert W. Komer, Memorandum from Komer to the President, Dec. 10, 1966.

[23] Same location.

[24] A copy of the cover memorandum from Rostow to Rusk and McNamara and of the draft NSAM are in the Johnson Library, Warnke Papers, McNaughton Files.

B. *Step up the Anti-Main Force Spoiling Offensive,* as made feasible by the increase in FW [Free World] maneuver battalions.

1. Introduce modest US forces into certain key Delta areas.
2. Stress offensive actions to clear VC base areas and LOCs around Saigon.
3. Lay on a major re-examination of our intelligence on VC/NVA strength.

C. *Make More Effective Programs to Limit Infiltration and Impose a Cost on Hanoi for the Aggression.*

1. Refine the bombing offensive with respect to both efficiency of route harassment and quality of targets.
2. Press forward with a barrier system [anti-infiltration barrier along the DMZ].
3. Examine other ways to apply military pressure on the North.

D. *Mount a Major, Continuing National Reconciliation Program,* designed to maximize the inducements aimed at eroding VC strength.

1. Expand and revitalize Chieu Hoi [amnesty] Program to handle 45,000 lower-level defectors a year.
2. Press a sustained middle and high-level defector program under appropriate auspices.
3. Ensure that new Constitution is consistent with reintegration of VC into the national life.
4. Develop a US contingency plan on how to handle VC/NLF in the next local and national elections, examining options of allowing VC to vote or perhaps even inviting NLF to run as a party in next national election.
5. Enlarge efforts to establish contacts with the VC/NLF.

E. *Press for the Emergence of a Popularly-Based GVN,* with adequate checks and balances between the civilians and the military, and between northerners and southerners.

1. Make clear well in advance to the Directory [ruling military junta] that the U.S. cannot accept a retrogression to military government, another coup, or blatant election rigging.
2. Press home to all—civilian and military—the importance of national unity and pulling together, as a minimum US condition for continued US support of SVN.
3. Use all our influence behind the scenes to bring about a smooth transition to a representative GVN, but one in which the still indispensable military role is not submerged.

F. *Press for Other Key Elements of the Manila Program which will enhance the GVN's attractiveness.*

1. Encourage better local government, including elected hamlet, village, and district/province officials.
2. Insist on a workable scheme of land reform, land tenure, and rent moratorium.
3. Vigorously attack corruption and misuses of US aid.

G. *Maintain the Civil Economy and Keep a Firm Lid on Inflation.*

1. Enforce a vigorous stabilization program.
2. Definitively lick the port bottleneck—both movement into the warehouses and movement out.
3. Maintain an adequate import level.
4. Generate more rice from the countryside.
5. Accelerate the creation of infrastructure for economic development.
6. Mount an imaginative postwar planning exercise.

H. *Devise a Pre-Negotiating and Negotiating Strategy Consistent with the Above.*

1. Take such initiatives as will credibly enhance our posture that we are always ready to talk and ever alert for new avenues to negotiation.
2. Vigorously pursue serious negotiating leads.

I. *Mount a Major Information Campaign* to inform both the US electorate and world opinion of the realities in Vietnam, finding ways credibly to measure progress.

The "mood that pervades the entire NSAM," the *Pentagon Papers* said, "is: victory is near." But State, Defense, the JCS, CINCPAC, and COMUSMACV took issue with the proposal, and the NSAM was never issued. According to the *Pentagon Papers,* "The evident division in DOD over the concept and objectives, coupled with State's lukewarm responses to producing any clear definition of aims/concepts convinced the White House that the best way to retain flexibility in South Vietnam and at home was to allow the ambiguity and uncertainty to continue."[25]

In his reply to the Rostow and Komer papers, Katzenbach made the point that there were two wars in South Vietnam—the "conventional" war in the highlands of the northern provinces and over North Vietnam, which was being fought by U.S. forces, and the "unconventional" war in the delta region of the southern provinces for which the South Vietnamese Army and Regional and Popular forces were responsible for local security.[26] The South Vietnamese Army, however, "had never escaped from its conventional warfare mold. Both in its military tactics and in its relations with the people, it has all too often acted counter to the basic principles of counterinsurgency rather than in support of them. The US military leadership in Vietnam has, on balance, done little to reorient ARVN toward counterinsurgency." "There was little doubt that most ARVN divisions and corps commanders continued to regard pacification operations as dull, less prestigious, and generally not in keeping with the basic mission, past tradition and organization of ARVN." Moreover, few South Vietnamese Government leaders understood or effectively supported the goals of pacification. "As a result," the Katzenbach memorandum said, "the GVN, despite increasing US assistance in men and materiel, has been relatively in-

---

[25] *PP,* Gravel ed., vol. IV, p. 400. This was the reaction of Deputy Ambassador Porter in Saigon (Lodge was in Washington). "I find the tone of the NSAM unnecessarily exhortative and many of the goals not possible of achievement. It does not provide guidelines, and it does not include priorities. Instead, it sets out a series of desirable objectives, all of which are already known and accepted. I therefore do not understand the need for this document." U.S. Department of State, Central File, Pol 27 Viet 14, Saigon to Washington 14767, Jan. 3, 1967.

[26] Excerpts from Katzenbach's memorandum, "Strategic Concept for Vietnam: An Analysis," Dec. 12, 1966, drafted by his assistant, Richard Holbrooke, are in *PP,* Gravel, ed. vol. IV, pp. 396–400.

effectual in meeting the Communist military and subversive threat at the rice-roots level. Pacification has thus far failed to give the peasant sufficient confidence in the GVN's ability to maintain security, the first prerequisite in pacification, or, in longer run, to redress basic economic, political, and social inequities."

Katzenbach's reply concluded that because of the slow progress in pacification, Americans would be inclined to take over the task from the South Vietnamese, and this, in turn, would increase U.S. manpower requirements.

There were also responses from William Bundy's office to the Rostow and Komer papers and the draft NSAM. In a paper on December 21, "1967 and Beyond in Vietnam," Bundy said that there were three factors that had not been fully considered in the Rostow-Komer papers:[27]

> A. The prospect of the 1968 US elections and their impact on our ability to maintain a prolonged struggle.
>
> B. The question of negotiations, including specifically the possibility of attempting a direct "package deal" negotiation with Hanoi—and above all the question any such deal would necessarily raise of just what risks we might be prepared to assume in connection with a VC/NLF role in South Vietnam.
>
> C. The vital importance of developing a reasonable and effective GVN, and whether this argues in some ways against certain types of US involvement and action that might, in the short-term sense, appear to make sense.

The prognosis for 1967, Bundy said, "was not comforting." "1967 will be slow going at best on the pacification front . . . [and] even if the GVN and we both do the best we possibly can, the odds are on the whole against a major strengthening of the GVN position or a true crack in NVA/VC/NLF morale during 1967 . . . its chances cannot be rated better than one in three for 1967."

In the 1968 U.S. elections, Bundy said, it was unlikely that any Republican candidate could offer a "clear and convincing" alternative to the policy being pursued, but a sharp and divisive debate could leave any administration in a weaker position.

This, he said, led to the question of seeking a negotiated settlement as soon as possible. He noted, however, that involving "major early risks of Communist takeover—whether or not this had come about before the 1968 elections—would in itself virtually doom the Administration to defeat and might well set off a wave of isolationist revulsion against all of our now-promising efforts in the rest of East Asia." "Yet, the need for seeking a negotiated settlement is acute," and there were recent indications that "the time was ripe." Two factors had to be taken into account. One was a possible Communist takeover. There was a 20% "irreducible minimum possibility that a Communist takeover could not be avoided in the best of circumstances. . . . The issue is whether we should be prepared to accept a settlement that increases the irreducible 20% to perhaps 30% or more." The other factor was bombing. "If we are to pursue a serious negotiating track . . . we simply must accept that we will not hit politically sensitive targets, and specifically the Hanoi and

[27] U.S. Department of State, Central File, Pol 27 Viet S, William P. Bundy draft memorandum, Dec. 21, 1966.

Haiphong areas, while we are pursuing such a track . . . they [the North Vietnamese] simply will not enter into serious discussions if we appear to be escalating, particularly during key periods of contact."[28]

In mid-January, Bundy's office responded to the draft NSAM in a memorandum to Katzenbach from Bundy drafted by Unger, which said that the draft NSAM was "generally satisfactory as an overall description of our continuing programs in Vietnam, although its language tends to be somewhat strident and in some places unrealistic in terms of what we are likely to accomplish during this year."[29] For one thing, Bundy said, "The draft NSAM assumes too readily that we can achieve results in internal programs which the Vietnamese are primarily responsible for carrying forward. . . ." In another instance, Bundy said, if the U.S. were able to "make good" on the statement in the draft about making clear to the military junta (Directory) that the U.S. could not accept a retrogression to military government, another coup, or blatant election rigging, "we will either have achieved the millennium or will be out of Vietnam before the year is out . . . to say that 'the U.S. cannot accept' such a failure is either naive in terms of its estimate of our influence on the international political situation or it assumes a U.S. withdrawal." "Certainly," he added, "we hope that national unity and pulling together will improve in 1967, but I doubt that we will pull out if it doesn't improve very much. If it's meant as a threat to the Vietnamese, it will undoubtedly be understood as an empty one."

Consistent with McNamara and McNaughton's growing doubts about the war, the Department of Defense reply to the draft NSAM, drafted by McNaughton's office, sought to prevent any broadening of the limited U.S. objectives in the war as well as any

---

[28] In the Department of State files, there is also a very interesting unsigned memorandum of Dec. 16, 1966, which probably came from State or the CIA, "Fifteen Brief and Purposely Contentious Points Outlining our Sole Practical Course in Vietnam in 1967 and 1968," (U.S. Department of State, Central File, Pol 27 Viet S.) that carried Bundy's argument to its logical extreme. The U.S., the memorandum said, did not have enough time before the 1968 elections in which to develop a workable, viable government in South Vietnam. "Such a government would take years to develop even if there were not a legacy of 20 years of war and even if there were not deep regional, ethnic and religious differences." Yet, "If we are not out of Vietnam by mid-1968—or, at a minimum, if we are not by then able to start withdrawing American troops—the consequences could be politically fatal." Moreover, continued increases in U.S. involvement would make it more difficult to withdraw and would make South Vietnam more vulnerable when the American "crutch" was removed.

"The inability to achieve a socially responsive government," the memorandum said, "leaves two alternatives. The first is for the United States simply to get out, on whatever basis we can continue (e.g., Senator Aiken's declaration of victory). This alternative is unacceptable. As a minimum reason, it would not be understood by the American public. . . . The second alternative—the only alternative—is to negotiate." There were two methods for persuading the North Vietnamese to negotiate: First, "to bomb Hanoi to the conference table." This had not worked, and a "major expansion" of bombing would not work and "would only increase Hanoi's tenacity." "The second method—the only method—of achieving negotiations is to take the initiative with Hanoi . . . to continue to stretch as far as we can, in every reasonable channel, to persuade Hanoi that our offer of negotiations is credible, indicating our willingness to talk and to indicate in advance and in detail the acceptability of terms which are politically realistic to NVN."

There were, the memorandum added, at least two factors on which the U.S. would have to insist: "a distinct, separate state in SVN, and a government which is not overtly Communist." There were at least two other factors that the U.S. could live with: "NLF participation in the new SVN government, and ultimate unification, if it results from some colorable *[sic]* expression of the will of the people."

[29] U.S. Department of State, Lot File 70 D 207, memorandum from Bundy to Katzenbach on the draft NSAM. Attached is a copy of the December 10 draft NSAM with suggested changes penciled in by Unger.

extension of the U.S. military mission.[30] Although the NSAM draft did not contain any reference to the U.S. commitment and objectives in the war, referring only to achieving a "satisfactory outcome," McNaughton and McNamara wanted to have it made clear that the U.S. was committed only to preventing external conquest of South Vietnam and not to suppressing the insurgency or dictating the form of government. Thus, the McNaughton memorandum proposed that the preamble to the NSAM should contain the following statement:

> The national commitment of the United States in South Vietnam (SVN), stated in Manila, is that the South Vietnamese people shall not be conquered by aggressive force and shall enjoy the inherent right to choose their own way of life and their own form of government. The United States is committed to continue our military and all other efforts, as firmly and as long as may be necessary, in close consultation with our allies until the aggression is ended.

McNaughton's paper also emphasized the responsibility of the South Vietnamese, with U.S. support, for pacification, and took the position that U.S. forces should not be used except in areas where there were North Vietnamese forces. On his copy of the draft NSAM, McNaughton penciled in a number of changes, and in item B. (1) of the draft, which provided for deploying "modest US forces into certain key Delta areas," McNaughton had penciled in this substitute: "Consistent with the limited U.S. objective in Vietnam, U.S. forces should not be deployed to the Delta unless there is added evidence that North Vietnamese forces are active there."

The JCS, in their reply to the draft NSAM, argued, on the other hand, that the "national objective" of the U.S. was a non-Communist South Vietnam ("free of Communist subversion"), which, they said, required an intensification of U.S. military and political programs. They also opposed any contact with the South Vietnamese Communists (items D. [4] and [5] in the draft.) "To encourage contact with the VC," they said, "would constitute a major shift in U.S. policy in Southeast Asia which would certainly appear to the communists as a sign of weakness and lack of firmness of purpose and undermine the resolve of the GVN."[31]

Comments from CINCPAC and Westmoreland, according to the *Pentagon Papers,* "had been less cautious, and their message unmistakable—we were militarily in South Vietnam to convincingly defeat the VC/NVA, that the war could be long and difficult, and the field commander should be granted the operational flexibility and resources he needed to do the job as he perceived it." They also made the point that many of the objectives listed in the draft NSAM could not be realized in 1967, and that currently approved resources and programs were inadequate for accomplishing in 1967 all of the programs planned for completion during the year.

---

[30] McNaughton's memorandum to McNamara, "Draft NSAM on Strategic Guidelines for 1967 in Vietnam," Jan. 20, 1967, was approved and sent to W. W. Rostow on January 28 by Deputy Secretary of Defense Vance. In the Johnson Library, Warnke Papers, McNaughton Files, there is a copy of the draft NSAM containing McNaughton's handwritten changes in its wording.

[31] *PP,* Gravel ed., vol. IV, p. 394–396. The JCS memorandum for McNamara, JCSM–792–66, "Draft NSAM," Dec. 27, 1966, was based on comments by CINCPAC to the JCS, 200805Z December 1966, and a cable from COMUSMACV to CINCPAC, 142018Z December 1966.

As a result of comments on the December 10, 1966, draft of the NSAM, a revised draft was distributed in the latter part of January 1967. One of the suggestions that it incorporated verbatim was the McNamara/McNaughton proposal that the preamble should contain a statement of U.S. objectives limiting the U.S. commitment to the prevention of the external conquest of South Vietnam.[32] In a memorandum to Katzenbach on February 9, Unger said, on behalf of Bundy's East Asia Bureau, that the revised draft was a "major improvement," and he recommended that, with some possible further modification, it be approved by the State Department.[33] The revised draft retained the statement in the original draft that the U.S. could not accept a "retrogression to military government" to which Bundy/Unger had objected in the earlier Far East Bureau's memorandum, but in his February 9 memorandum Unger said that he saw "no objection to saying 'cannot accept' for rhetorical purposes but I doubt the wisdom of our ever laying it on the line in just that form."

In another development, an interagency study of alternatives to the way the war was being waged was initiated in December 1966 by the Policy Planning Council of the State Department. The project originated in a meeting of the Council in which, after a military briefing by the Joint Staff (JCS), the question was raised as to whether the Joint Staff was studying the possibility of "radical military alternatives to the present scale and conduct of the war." The answer was that this was not being done, and that it would probably be useful to do such a study. The Policy Planning Council then put the same question to Rostow, McNaughton, Desmond Fitzgerald (CIA Deputy Director) and Unger, of whom all agreed that it should be done. As a result, with the Policy Planning Council as Chair, a group composed of persons from the White House, State, Defense, the JCS staff, and the CIA was assigned to make the study. It was to be "closely held," with knowledge restricted to the participants.[34]

The study was so closely held that when the four members of the group's Steering Committee[35] went to South Vietnam in January 1967 in connection with the study, they travelled separately, as Wheeler explained in a cable to Westmoreland, "in view of the sensitivity of the project."[36] The group, as will be seen, completed in June 1967 its 84-page Top Secret/Sensitive "Possible Alternatives to the Present Conduct of the War in Vietnam."

---

[32] For the revised draft of the NSAM, which is not dated but was distributed in the latter part of January, 1967, see the copy attached to a memorandum from Unger to Katzenbach, Feb. 9, 1967, in the Department of State, Lot File 70 D 207.

[33] Unger memorandum to Katzenbach, "NSAM—Strategic Guidelines for 1967 in Vietnam," Feb. 9, 1967, cited in foregoing footnote. On the attached copy of the draft NSAM Unger also penciled in suggested changes.

[34] U.S. Department of State, Central File, Pol 27 Viet S, Memorandum from Henry Owen, Chairman of the Policy Planning Council, to Katzenbach (serving as Acting Secretary of State in Rusk's absence), "New Planning Venture," Dec. 6, 1966.

[35] Gen. Theodore H. Andrews of the JCS staff, Joseph A. Yager, Policy Planning Council, Richard C. Steadman, Deputy Assistant Secretary, Office of International Security Affairs, Department of Defense, and George Carver of the CIA.

[36] CMH, Westmoreland Papers, Message Files, CJCS 0486, Wheeler to Sharp and Westmoreland, Jan. 18, 1967.

Controversy Over the Bombing of North Vietnam

Despite the secret efforts being made to arrange peace talks with the North Vietnamese (MARIGOLD), U.S. planes struck at new targets near Hanoi on December 2 and 4, 1966 (and again on December 13–14), in raids that had been scheduled for November 10 but were postponed because of weather. This was the first bombing of targets within five nautical miles of the center of Hanoi since the POL attacks in June, and the tonnage of bombs was twice that of June.

Prior to these attacks, leading State Department officials, concerned about the possible adverse effects of such attacks on MARIGOLD, had urged that steps be taken to cushion those effects. For a Tuesday Luncheon of the President, Rusk and McNamara, on November 15, Benjamin Read prepared a memorandum for Rusk on the issues that he might wish to discuss, and one of the items was that "EA [Bundy's East Asia bureau], U [Under Secretary Katzenbach], S/AH [Harriman] and S/AL [Thompson] urge that all strikes be spread out as much as possible."[37] According to the *Pentagon Papers*,[38]

> The intended targets of all of the December attacks were the Yen Vien Railroad Yard and the Van Dien Vehicle Depot, but apparently there was collateral damage in all areas. In particular, during the December 13–14 attacks, the Chinese and Rumanian Embassies seem to have been hit, along with some residential structures in central Hanoi. From the ground, then, there might appear to have been an increase in the intensity of attack, measured both in tons of ordnance expended and type of target, commencing December 2. . . .

After the raids, there were reports, denied by U.S. officials, of damage to residential areas and of increased civilian casualties.

The Polish Government said that the new raids on December 2 and 4 had jeopardized MARIGOLD.[39]

A U.S. official, described as a "senior official in the national security apparatus," is said to have reacted: "Oh my God. We lost control."[40]

On December 6, 1966, after the first two days of airstrikes, the President met in Texas for about an hour with McNamara, Vance, W. W. Rostow and the JCS to discuss the bombing operations, including their effect on possible negotiations.[41] On December 9 he again discussed this subject in a meeting from 4:35 p.m. to 5:02 p.m. with the Vice President, McNamara, Katzenbach (Rusk was in Asia), Vance, Wheeler, Rostow, Moyers and Kintner. Rostow's very brief note of the meeting states: "Broadly speaking, the decision was made to carry forward with what was necessary but at this particular moment not to expand our targeting."[42]

---

[37] U.S. Department of State, Lot File 74 D 164, Read Memorandum for the Secretary, Nov. 15, 1966. Apparently, there are no notes of the luncheon.

[38] Herring, *The Secret Diplomacy of the Vietnam War*, p. 232.

[39] For a discussion of the effects of the December bombing raids on MARIGOLD, see *The Secret Diplomacy of the Vietnam War;* Kraslow and Loory, *The Secret Search for Peace in Vietnam;* Thies, *When Governments Collide*, pp. 146 ff.; and Goodman, *The Lost Peace*, pp. 38 ff.

[40] Kraslow and Loory, p. 5.

[41] There are no known notes of that meeting.

[42] Johnson Library, NSF Memos to the President—Walt Rostow, Memorandum "For the President's Diary," Dec. 9, 1966.

On December 13–14, despite strong objections from McNamara, Katzenbach and Llewellyn Thompson, the U.S. again bombed near Hanoi, with twice the severity of the December 3–4 raids.[43] In public statements by the Department of Defense, the U.S. maintained that the attacks did not constitute an escalation of the air war, and that they were made against military targets. Government spokesmen added, however, that housing adjacent to military targets could have been damaged. Several days later they admitted that residential areas had been bombed by mistake, but they would not cite specific cases.[44]

On December 14, after the airstrikes on December 13–14, the Polish Government told the U.S. that the North Vietnamese had asked them to discontinue discussions with the Americans.[45] A principal official at the Russian Embassy in Washington told McNaughton that there had been a favorable atmosphere in Moscow about the prospects of negotiations, but that the bombing attacks on December 13 and 14 had "ruined it."[46] He said that there were forces in Hanoi who thought the war could not be won and would be interested in a compromise, but that they "cannot become active in an environment in which bombs . . . are falling in Hanoi."

Although Rostow favored increased pressure on the North Vietnamese, and apparently believed that the airstrikes were necessary and that they would not interfere with efforts to initiate negotiations, others were more cautious. As noted, McNamara, Katzenbach and Llewellyn Thompson were concerned about the effects of increased bombing of a sensitive area at the time talks were scheduled to begin, and McNamara subsequently stated that the bombing attacks on December 13 and 14 were responsible for the decision of the North Vietnamese not to begin negotiations.[47] Harriman was also known to be opposed, and the Negotiations Committee, it will be recalled, had urged restraint in bombing while efforts were being made to get talks started.

Goldberg also was opposed, and several weeks later told Rusk and the President that he did not want to continue as U.S. Ambassador to the U.N. In a memorandum to the President, Rusk said, "It is quite clear to me that he [Goldberg] is motivated by disagreement on Vietnam and feels that we have not done enough to probe for peace. He was especially critical of the two bombing strikes in the Hanoi area on December 13 and 14."[48]

---

[43] Cooper, *The Lost Crusade*, p. 339. Both Cooper and Thies should be consulted on the developments described here.

[44] See the *New York Times* for Dec. 14, 15, 16 and 27, 1966.

[45] Herring, *The Secret Diplomacy of the Vietnam War*, p. 233.

[46] Johnson Library, NSF Memos to the President—Walt Rostow, Memorandum of Conversation between McNaughton and Minister Alexander Zinchuk, Jan. 3, 1967.

[47] In a memorandum for the President on Mar. 9, 1967, McNamara stated that there were two factions in North Vietnam's leadership, one of which favored negotiations. "The group favoring negotiations," he said, "was in the ascendancy during the latter part of last year and was prepared to start negotiations in December but was deterred from doing so by our bombing attacks of December 13 and 14." (Johnson Library, NSF Files of Walt W. Rostow.) During his visit with Lodge on July 1, 1968, noted earlier, McNamara said he had "high hopes" for MARIGOLD, but that Rusk did not. McNamara said that it was the heavy bombing, especially on December 13, that caused the North Vietnamese to break off the contact. Massachusetts Historical Society, Lodge Papers, unpublished "Vietnam Memoirs," pt. VI, Appendix.

[48] Johnson Library, NSF Memos to the President—Walt Rostow, Rusk memorandum for the President, Mar. 8, 1967.

William Bundy, who was in Vietnam with Rusk at the time of the airstrikes, apparently was also concerned about the effects of the attacks, and in his memorandum on December 21, 1966, as noted, he declared that the U.S. "simply must accept that we will not hit politically sensitive targets" while pursuing serious negotiations based on a "package deal."[49]

There is no available documentary evidence with respect to Rusk's position, but he probably was affected by the opposition of all of his principal associates on Vietnam policy, who, prior to the airstrikes, as noted, had expressed their concern about the effect of bombing on MARIGOLD.

Growing concern about the bombing among some elements of the public was evidenced by the action on December 9, 1966, of the General Assembly of the National Council of Churches, which voted 750–20 to have the Vietnam issue raised at the United Nations and to have the U.S. Government consider a unilateral suspension of bombing even without advance assurance of reciprocity by the Communists.[50]

Congress was not in session at the time, but on December 13, after a White House announcement of a 48-hour cease-fire at Christmas and possibly others at New Year's and at the Vietnamese New Year (Tet) in early February, Senator Mansfield proposed a cease-fire and freeze on troop reinforcements from Christmas to Tet to test the interest of the North Vietnamese in negotiating. Senator Fulbright said he agreed with that suggestion.[51]

There does not appear to have been any discussion with Congress on MARIGOLD, knowledge of which among the President's advisers and their staffs was quite limited, but some information was provided to Fulbright, Dirksen and Hickenlooper (Mansfield was out of the city) at the end of November on the discussions in Moscow several days earlier of British Foreign Secretary George Brown with Gromyko and Premier Alexi Kosygin. Rusk, without revealing the U.S. position in detail, told them that Brown "had made no progress on Vietnam. While he had probed them [the Soviets] on what would happen if we stopped the bombing, they did not respond meaningfully."[52]

On December 23, President Johnson prohibited further attacks on military targets within 10 nautical miles of the center of Hanoi without his specific approval,[53] and, according to the *Pentagon Papers,* the U.S. informed the Communists that this was being done

[49] William Bundy memorandum, "1967 and Beyond in Vietnam," cited above.

[50] *New York Times,* Dec. 10, 1966.

[51] *Ibid.,* Dec. 14, 1966. On December 19, the U.S. asked U.N. Secretary U Thant to "take whatever steps you consider necessary" to bring about discussions that could lead to a cease-fire in Vietnam (*ibid.,* Dec. 20, 1966). On December 31 (*ibid.,* Jan. 1, 1967), U Thant repeated his position that the cessation of U.S. bombing of North Vietnam was a prerequisite for such discussions. Ambassador Goldberg replied that same day, saying to U Thant, in part: "I wish to assure you categorically that my Government is prepared to take the first step toward peace: specifically, we are ready to order a prior end to all bombing of North Vietnam the moment there is an assurance, private or otherwise, that there would be a reciprocal response toward peace from North Vietnam." (*Ibid.*) According to an article in the *New York Times* (December 20), the U.S. request to U Thant was not a new American peace initiative, but, rather, was a move to respond to U Thant's strong rebuke of the U.S. several days earlier in which he criticized U.S. bombing of Hanoi, as well as being intended as a way of drawing U Thant into U.S. efforts to bring about negotiations.

[52] U.S. Department of State, Lot File 74 D 164, "President's Evening Reading Items," State Department Activities Reports for Nov. 29, 1966 and Dec. 1, 1966.

[53] *PP,* Gravel ed., vol. IV, p. 135.

"as an act of goodwill in the hopes of reviving the Warsaw contact."[54]

Ironically, as the *Pentagon Papers* notes, this "good faith" effort may have caused the North Vietnamese to conclude "that propaganda repercussions, actual and prospective, had forced a change in the U.S. posture, causing Hanoi in turn to stiffen the conditions it imposed in exchange for talks. The Trinh formula of January 28, 1967, demanding an end to all bombing of the DRV, may have been based on this calculation."[55]

The reaction at CINCPAC to the prohibition on attacking within 10 nautical miles of the center of Hanoi was expressed in a very blunt back channel cable on December 24 from Admiral Sharp to General Wheeler, Chairman of the JCS:[56]

> We were just starting to put some real pressure on Hanoi. Our air strikes on the rail yard and the vehicle depot were hitting the enemy where it was beginning to hurt. Then, Hanoi complains that we have killed a few civilians, hoping that they would get a favorable reaction. And they did, more than they could have hoped for.
>
> Not only did we say we regretted it if any civilians were killed but we also stopped our pilots from striking within ten miles of Hanoi. Hanoi has been successful once again in getting the pressure removed. They will be encouraged to continue their aggression, hoping to outlast us.
>
> With nearly 400,000 U.S. fighting men in RVN it must be apparent to Hanoi that they can't take over the country by force. But they can fight a protracted guerrilla war, terrorize the countryside, make revolutionary development very difficult, and kill a lot of people, including Americans. This kind of war can go on for a long time if we let them get away with it.
>
> My limited sounding of public opinion, including the thoughts of quite a few Members of Congress, leads me to believe that we had better do what we can to bring this war to a successful conclusion as rapidly as possible. The American people can become aroused either for or against this war. At the moment, with no end in sight, they are more apt to become aroused against it. It's up to us to convince our people and Hanoi that there is an end in sight and that it is clearly defeat for Hanoi. However, our actions these last few days can only encourage the enemy to continue.
>
> When Hanoi complains about civilians being killed, is it not possible to say, "Perhaps some were killed, we try to avoid that, but this is a war and some civilians are bound to get killed. Hanoi can prevent it by calling off the aggression in SVN."
>
> If the enemy avoids major engagements in SVN and gets back to phase II of their plan, the guerrilla phase, then it becomes urgently important to step up the pressure in the North

---

[54] Herring, *Secret Diplomacy of the Vietnam War,* p. 233.

[55] *PP,* Gravel ed., vol. IV, p. 135. The Trinh formula (Nguyen Duy Trinh was Foreign Minister of North Vietnam), stated that talks could begin only after an unconditional end of bombing, whereas under MARIGOLD the Communists were believed to be willing to negotiate without a prior suspension of bombing. See Thies, *When Governments Collide,* p. 158.

[56] CMH, Westmoreland Papers, Message Files, Sharp to Wheeler, DTG 242142Z December 1966.

by hitting targets that hurt them. And if some civilians get killed in the course of these stepped up air attacks, we should recognize it as part of the increased pressure. This war is a dirty business, like all wars. We need to get hard-headed about it. That is the only kind of action that these tough Communists will respect. That is the way to get this war over soonest.

Let's roll up our sleeves and get on with this war. We have the power, I would like authority to use it. . . .

On December 26, 1966, the *New York Times* began a series of eight articles on the situation in North Vietnam by its assistant managing editor, Harrison E. Salisbury, who was on a trip to Hanoi from December 23 to January 7.[57] The Salisbury articles, which seemed to confirm reports that U.S. air raids had hit some civilian areas in North Vietnam, created quite a controversy.[58] President Johnson was so angry that his press secretary, Bill Moyers, told James Reston, Washington bureau chief for the *New York Times,* "'I can't even put it [a question on the bombing] to him.'"[59]

Phil G. Goulding, McNamara's press spokesman, said later that the effect of the Salisbury series on public support for the war and on public confidence in the veracity of the government was a "national disaster." Goulding was critical of Salisbury and the *New York Times* for creating doubts about the war, although he said later that Salisbury's articles "presented to the American people a reasonably accurate picture of the effect of our bombing in North Vietnam."[60] He added that the Pentagon had overemphasized the precision of U.S. bombing:[61]

What we should have done was to tell the people what we assumed they knew: despite our target selection and our care, of course we were killing North Vietnamese civilians—not in large numbers, not as civilians have been killed in other wars, but of course we were killing civilians.

We did not do so. And because we did not, when Harrison Salisbury wrote as he did in December, 1966, a great many

---

57 For Salisbury's account, see his books, *Behind the Lines—Hanoi, December 23, 1966-January 7, 1967* (New York: Harper and Row, 1967), which also reprints his dispatches to the *New York Times,* and *A Time of Change: A Reporter's Tale of Our Time* (New York: Harper and Row, 1988). There is also a very useful discussion of "The Salisbury Affair" in Hammond, *The Military and the Media,* pp. 274–279. For a good discussion of Salisbury's trip in relation to diplomatic moves then underway, see Thies, *When Governments Collide,* pp. 154–159.

58 For the State Department's cable to all of its diplomatic posts commenting on Salisbury's articles see U.S. Department of State, Central File, Pol 27 Viet S, Circular Telegram 111162, Dec. 31, 1966.

59 Salisbury, *A Time of Change,* p. 160.

60 Phil G. Goulding, *Confirm or Deny: Informing the People on National Security* (New York: Harper and Row, 1970), p. 54. For criticism of Salisbury by others, see Lewy, *America in Vietnam,* pp. 398–404, and Norman Podhoretz, *Why We Were in Vietnam* (New York: Simon and Schuster, 1982), pp. 117–120. For a defense of Salisbury, see James Aronson, *The Press and the Cold War* (Indianapolis: Bobbs-Merrill, 1970), pp. 254–260.

John Colvin, the British consul general in North Vietnam at the time, who met twice with Salisbury during his visit to Hanoi, has also been critical. The implication of Salisbury's articles, he says, "drawn chiefly from North Vietnamese falsehoods, that the United States was deliberately bombing civilian targets carried world wide conviction," and they "had a decisive effect throughout America in persuading Americans that their government was engaged in a brutal and inhumane campaign." Colvin, *Twice Around the World* (London: Leon Cooper, 1991), pp. 99–100. See also 101–102. But Colvin (pp. 117–120) is also very critical of the American "intellectuals," who, he says, were ashamed of America and "degraded" the "honor" of the U.S. by their failure to prosecute the war vigorously.

61 Goulding, p. 92.

Americans became more disillusioned with their government and more convinced that it was lying to them.

During his conversation with North Vietnamese Premier Pham Van Dong, Salisbury sensed that the Premier wanted him to convey a private message to President Johnson that North Vietnam would not insist on the cessation of all U.S. military activity before talks could begin. When he returned to the U.S. on January 11, he went immediately to Washington to convey this message personally to Rusk. When Salisbury arrived at the State Department on January 13 for the meeting, which he had viewed as strictly private, the State Department press officer was also there, and the first thing the State Department officials wanted to talk about, Salisbury said later in an interview, was the statement they were going to issue after the meeting, having assumed, apparently, that Salisbury was going to write a newspaper article about the meeting. Salisbury insisted that the meeting was private and that there should be no public statement. He then proceeded, after the press officer left, to tell Rusk and William Bundy, who also attended, about his talk with Pham Van Dong, but, according to Salisbury, "most of the input came from Rusk, who lectured me about the nature of the war. Whenever I tried to tell him something about what was actually going on, he was obviously not interested in anything I had to say."[62] Bundy, on the other hand, appeared very interested, and Salisbury thought he was able to communicate to him some of the information he had gained from the trip.[63] Generally, however, he gained the impression that information contrary to established policy was not acceptable to top U.S. officials:

> [T]here was plenty of information available if anybody wanted it. But these people, they just didn't want that information. That's a terrible thing. This isn't unusual, you understand. This is what happens to people who get involved in a cause . . . and by this time Johnson and Rusk—and Walt Rostow, as far as that was concerned—were so involved in this thing they weren't going to receive any information that might, in some fashion, destroy their image of what was going on out there.

Even if he had been able to convince Rusk that the North Vietnamese wanted to discuss the war, Salisbury added, the effect of this would probably have been to convince President Johnson that "this is the time to whack them. If they want to talk, that shows they're hurting." "This is the way that logic went," Salisbury added. "It's impervious; it's iron. What can you do?"[64]

---

[62] CRS interview with Harrison E. Salisbury, Jan. 9, 1979.

[63] Subsequently, however, Bundy wrote a personal letter to Salisbury criticizing his reporting. Both the letter and Salisbury's reply are in the State Department, Lot File 85 D 240 (William Bundy Papers).

[64] For a brief statement of Salisbury's views on the war, see his introduction to the report, which he edited, of a conference on Vietnam held in 1983: *Vietnam Reconsidered: Lessons from a War* (New York: Harper and Row, 1984).

Two other prominent Americans who went to Hanoi in January 1967, and, among other things, talked personally to Ho Chi Minh, reported that they met the same kind of resistance in Washington. See Harry S. Ashmore (former editor of the *Little Rock Gazette*) and William C. Baggs (editor of the *Miami News), Mission to Hanoi* (New York: Putnam's, 1968).

In the Johnson Library, NSF Memos to the President—Walt Rostow there is a memorandum to the President, Jan. 18, 1967, by Ashmore and Boggs on their conversation in Hanoi. The conclusion of the talks, they said, was that the North Vietnamese were prepared to negotiate but, as they had previously stated, would do so only after the U.S. stopped bombing the North.

Ashmore and Baggs testified in executive session before the Senate Foreign Relations Committee on Apr. 10, 1968. (This hearing has not been published.) They had been asked to testify

On February 2, 1967, Salisbury testified before a public session of the Senate Foreign Relations Committee.[65] He said that from his observations U.S. bombing was not achieving the objective either of reducing infiltration of men and supplies into the South or of encouraging the North Vietnamese to negotiate. On the contrary, the supply routes were continuing to function despite the bombing, and North Vietnamese public support for the war appeared to have been strengthened as a result of the cohesive effect of facing a "common peril."

According to Salisbury's testimony, the war was at a "turning-point—one which may lead either to a negotiated settlement or to a sharp and dangerous escalation," and he thought it would be advisable for the United States to seek to negotiate.

Most of the members of the Foreign Relations Committee were present for the hearing, and the questioning of Salisbury generally followed the division of opinion within the committee between Fulbright, Mansfield, Morse, Gore, Clark, Pell, and McCarthy, on the one hand (Church was not present), and those Democrats who defended the administration—chiefly Sparkman, Lausche and Symington—on the other (Dodd was not present), while the Republican members, who were also somewhat divided (Hickenlooper, Carlson, Williams, Mundt and Case tended to support the administration, while Aiken and Cooper were more critical), played a less prominent part. Lausche was very outspoken, while Symington, with his membership on the Armed Services Committee and his long and close association with the Air Force came well prepared with questions.

Further Efforts to Seek Negotiations

Although Rusk considered some of the information from Salisbury to be "mood music," he apparently thought that other information was valuable and that the North Vietnamese might be attempting to indicate that they wanted to talk. In a memorandum to the President in which he summarized his discussion with Salisbury, Rusk said that the comments made to Salisbury by Premier Pham Van Dong also pointed to the desirability of a "package deal" with the North Vietnamese reached through secret bilateral discussions with the U.S.[66]

On January 3, Rostow transmitted to the President a preliminary report on Salisbury's discussions with the North Vietnamese in which Salisbury said he believed that North Vietnam wanted to negotiate but did not know how to arrange for talks. In an accompanying memorandum, Rostow said he thought that it was "conceivable, if not probable, that they are trying to get out of the war

---

after they returned in January 1967, but at the request of Under Secretary of State Katzenbach they declined to do so in the expectation that the avoidance of public or even closed congressional appearances would enhance their chances of having better access to and influence with the administration. *Mission to Hanoi*, pp. 59 ff.

For a similar account, in which he describes his contacts with the White House in 1966 on possible peace feelers through representatives of the Polish Government, see Norman Cousins, "Vietnam: The Spurned Peace," *Saturday Review*, July 26, 1969.

[65] U.S. Congress, Senate, Committee on Foreign Relations, *Harrison E. Salisbury's Trip to North Vietnam* (Washington, D.C.: U.S. Govt. Print. Off., 1967).

[66] U.S. Department of State, Lot File 85 D 240 (William Bundy Papers), memorandum from Rusk to the President, "Highlights of Harrison Salisbury Private Report to Me," Jan. 14, 1967.

but don't know how."[67] By this, Rostow said he meant that the North Vietnamese "cannot openly negotiate with us. They must have a deal which saves them minimum face with the NLF and the Chinese to announce before negotiations are acknowledged. They lose their bargaining leverage if they are known to be negotiating, because the NLF might bug out."

If this was so, Rostow added, the U.S. should send a message to the North Vietnamese saying simply: "Your message to Salisbury has been received. You will be hearing from us soon." The U.S. would then send another direct communication indicating interest in a settlement and setting forth suggested terms. "Be clear," he told the President, "I don't give this very high odds. But I have had the nagging feeling that they could well be in a position of wanting to get out and not knowing how. . . . Therefore, I think it is worth a try."[68]

On January 3, the day Rostow sent his memorandum to the President reporting on Salisbury's discussion, the *New York Times* carried a dispatch from Salisbury quoting Premier Pham Van Dong as saying that the North Vietnamese "Four Points" were not conditions for negotiations, as the U.S. had been assuming, but were "a basis for settlement of the Vietnam problem." On January 4, a statement was issued by the State Department saying that it was not clear whether this represented a change, and, in effect, inviting the North Vietnamese to clarify their position on this point.[69]

On January 5, 1967, Rostow sent to Rusk the draft of a letter from the President to President Ho Chi Minh. Rusk apparently had reservations about Rostow's proposal, and, after talking with Rusk the next day, Rostow sent him the following memorandum:[70]

> My concern is this: we are, in diplomatic parlance, "following up" every lead we get back through the channel which generates or communicates the lead.
>
> The net effect in Hanoi must be to convey an image of confusion and uncertainty similar to the image of confusion and uncertainty that we have about their position.

---

[67] Johnson Library, NSF Memos to the President—Walt Rostow, and Salisbury, *A Time of Change*, p. 163.

Several days later, Rostow sent the President a memorandum of Rusk and Bundy's talk with Salisbury, and in an attached note he said that the "case against it [the memorandum of conversation] confirms: The possibility—if not probability—that they are looking for a way out; [and that] secret talks with us without an intermediary is the proper route." Johnson Library, NSF Country File, Vietnam, Note to the President from Rostow, Jan. 19, 1967 with Memorandum of Conversation of Rusk and Bundy with Salisbury, Jan. 13, 1967, attached.

[68] As noted earlier, Rostow had concluded, based in part on a conversation with Dobrynin, that secret bilateral talks between U.S. and North Vietnam, involving a "total deal," offered the best chance for negotiations. On November 17, he sent the President a memorandum describing this possibility (Johnson Library, Warnke Papers, McNaughton Files), and in an undated memorandum that he sent to the President on January 3 with the Salisbury report, he outlined a "scenario" by which such direct contact could be established and talks arranged. In a meeting of the Negotiations Committee on Dec. 21, 1966, at which agreement was reached on the negotiating package prepared by Chester Cooper, Harriman disagreed with Rostow's proposal for passing the package directly to North Vietnam. This would "smack too much of an ultimatum," he said, and it would be better to use an intermediary. (Library of Congress, Harriman Papers, Vietnam General, Memorandum of Meeting of the Negotiations Committee, Dec. 21, 1966.) Meanwhile, after its approval by the Negotiations Committee, Cooper's negotiating package had been sent to the White House. According to Cooper, it was sent back by Rostow "with the grumble that it was 'too soft' but with no specific criticism. It remained in Rusk's 'in box' for many weeks and then dropped from sight." Cooper, *The Lost Crusade*, p. 345.

[69] *New York Times*, Jan. 5, 1967.

[70] U.S. Department of State, Lot File 74 D 164, Rostow memorandum to Rusk, Jan. 5, 1967.

We have many indications from the Soviet Union and others that a direct bilateral clandestine approach is what is required.

Moreover, they must regard us—the greatest power in the world—as the critical factor in whether a deal livable for them can be brought off.

As I said this morning, in a curious way they are looking for some kind of guidance and leadership from us in this murky, delicately balanced situation. It is for that reason that I still recommend the letter, a draft of which I sent over yesterday. It offers the best opportunity I can perceive for crystallizing the decisions in Hanoi.[71]

As will be seen, the letter from President Johnson to President Ho Chi Minh was finally sent on February 8. Meanwhile, the U.S.

---

[71] Although diplomatic developments were being held very closely, the President appears to have communicated at least some information to a few key Members of Congress. As will be seen, he met with Senators Mansfield and Dirksen on January 17 in connection with the response of the North Vietnamese to a diplomatic probe on January 10. He also talked with Mansfield on January 6 in connection with the consideration being given to a U.S. response to the possible "signal" given to Salisbury. Mansfield replied in a memorandum that same day in which he said, based on the Salisbury and other reports, that he thought the North Vietnamese were trying to signal the U.S. "It would appear that Hanoi's 'signals' are intended to get across to us a message which goes something like this:

"1. Of course, we are hurting and we want the bombing stopped. But let us be leery about one thing: we are not going to say 'Uncle' to you no matter what you do in the way of bombardment.

"2. As of now, we are still masters in our own house in North Viet Nam. We can still talk settlement for ourselves with you or anyone and we don't have to ask the Chinese or the Russians for permission. We do not know how long that will go on, however, because our dependency on other Communist nations and, particularly China, is bound to grow as you pile on the pressure.

"3. Of course we will talk with the United States about a settlement but not unconditionally. We will not talk until it is clear that you, Americans, not only mean to withdraw your forces from Viet Nam, as you say you will, but also that there is no question that they will be withdrawn. That does not necessarily have to happen before a settlement but it has got to be assured in at least a reasonable period of time thereafter and your words on this point are not enough. After all, we thought we were finished with foreign troops on Vietnamese soil when we made the Geneva Agreements with France and look what happened. Furthermore, we will not talk with you, Americans, until your military operations make it crystal clear that you are not seeking through negotiations to stall the war into a more or less permanent division of Viet Nam, as in Korea, in which you and your Vietnamese allies in Saigon (who are mostly northerners, by the way) run the south, and we and our allies down there (who are mostly southerners, by the way) are excluded from the political leadership of South Viet Nam. To be frank, we want it the other way around and we think the people of Viet Nam see it our way and not yours.

"There is no point in talking to you Americans unconditionally at this time, because you do not even begin to see the situation as we see it. Well, we can wait because you have come a long way to fight this war and you are spending a lot of money and you are in a strange and inhospitable place here in Viet Nam and your allies in the south are not of much use. By contrast, we are defending our own land and our allies are mostly southerners who can live and fight very cheaply (even you experts figure the Viet Cong budget at less than $50 million a year) and, in any case, they have got no other place to go because they are already home. . . .

"In a paragraph," Mansfield continued, "I think Hanoi is trying to say:

"The basic question is not one of getting to negotiations with us. The basic problem is what do you Americans expect to result from negotiations and you ought to know that before you sit down. You know what we want; we have said it many times and always in the same language. Now, what do you expect to come, in the end, from your commitment and military activity in our country?"

Mansfield added, however, that in view of the high level of U.S. military activity, it was doubtful whether negotiations could be expected to take place.

The President replied to Mansfield on January 9, using a draft by W. W. Rostow which had been slightly amended by Rusk. "We don't rule out that there may be something serious here," he said, but there did not appear to have been a change in the position of the North Vietnamese. The "critical question for us, on the political side, is whether they are prepared to accept honest self-determination by the people of South Vietnam in an environment freed of aggression and terror." He referred to the U.S. "14 points" and said that the U.S. was prepared to see whether these and the "four points" of the North Vietnamese were compatible. "The immediate question is whether they [the North Vietnamese] are prepared to explore this possibility or whether they will continue to seek by means of force, harassment, and what they call 'protracted warfare' to achieve what they may not be able to achieve through honest self-determination." (Mansfield's memo and the draft reply are in the Johnson Library, NSF Name File, Mansfield, and a copy of the President's letter to Mansfield is in the White House Central File, Name File, Mansfield.

attempted to test whether the North Vietnamese were trying to signal their interest in talking. A message was sent on January 6 to the U.S. Embassy in Moscow to be delivered on January 10 to the North Vietnamese Embassy by John Guthrie, who, as Chargé, was the highest ranking American in Moscow. (Llewellyn Thompson, the new U.S. Ambassador, had not yet arrived.)[72] It read in part:

> The U.S. Government places the highest priority in finding a mutually agreeable, completely secure arrangement for exchanging communications with the government of the DRV about the possibilities of achieving a peaceful settlement of the Vietnamese dispute. If the DRV is willing to explore such possibilities with us we will attempt to meet any such suggestions they have to offer regarding the time and place of such discussions and we will be prepared to receive such information directly from the North Vietnamese through diplomatic contacts at any capital where we both maintain posts or otherwise.

W. W. Rostow said in an explanation accompanying the message that this approach could help to overcome the fear of the North Vietnamese that if they agreed to cease sending men and supplies to the South the Communists in the South would "collapse," thus depriving the North Vietnamese of their bargaining position and exposing them to the possibility that the U.S. and South Vietnam might then ignore their commitment to deescalate and break whatever promises they had made. To prevent this, Rostow said, the U.S. should make its position "credible" by "communicating" three things to the North Vietnamese: "(1) an end position which Hanoi and the Viet Cong could live with; (2) a way of making our guarantee of that position credible; (3) a way of getting there which would minimize the significance of Hanoi's and Viet Cong's weak bargaining leverage along the way."

Rostow said that there were "only two things" that the U.S. could offer the Communists in the South: "a guarantee against slaughter," and "a right to organize politically and to vote, but only after arms are laid down." "As for Hanoi, we can only offer them our withdrawal six months after they are out and violence subsides, plus a free Viet Cong run at peaceful politics plus the promise of an ultimate plebiscite or unity under peaceful conditions plus economic assistance in reconstruction as part of Southeast Asia if they want."

On January 17, the North Vietnamese told Guthrie that they wanted further information on two points: first, what did the U.S. mean by "completely secure arrangements"? and, second, what kind of a settlement did the U.S. have in mind?[73]

The State Department replied the same day with the text of a message, drafted by William Bundy, for Guthrie to give to the

---

[72] Washington to Moscow 112967, Jan. 5, 1967, in Herring (ed.), *The Secret Diplomacy of the Vietnam War,* pp. 412–413. Other sources which discuss this initiative, code-named SUNFLOWER, are Thies, *When Governments Collide;* Cooper, *The Lost Crusade;* Kraslow and Loory, *The Secret Search for Peace in Vietnam;* and Goodman, *The Lost Peace.*

[73] U.S. Department of State, Central File, Pol 27–14 Viet, Moscow to Washington 3066, Jan. 17, 1967, and also in *The Secret Diplomacy of the Vietnam War,* p. 415.

North Vietnamese, which included these possible items for talks between the two countries:[74]

(1) Arrangements for the reduction or the cessation of hostilities.

(2) Essential elements of the Geneva Accords of 1954 and 1962, including withdrawal of any forces coming from outside South Vietnam and now present there.

(3) Arrangements for a full determination by North Vietnam and South Vietnam on the issue of reunification.

(4) Recognition of the independence and territorial integrity of North and South Vietnam, or of all Vietnam if the people should choose reunification.

(5) The international posture of South Vietnam, including relationships with other nations.

(6) Appropriate provisions relating to the internal political structure of South Vietnam, including freedom from reprisals and free political participation.

(7) Appropriate objective means for insuring the integrity of all provisions agreed to.

At 7:30 p.m. on the day the U.S. received the North Vietnamese inquiry (January 17), the President met with Senators Mansfield and Dirksen (who were at the White House to attend a dinner later that evening).[75] Also present were Rostow, and White House Chief of Staff Marvin Watson. According to Watson's notes of the meeting, the President told the two Senate leaders, "This is the most important thing I have talked to you about since I became President. You must not divulge to anyone this meeting—this discussion. Is this agreeable?" Mansfield and Dirksen said it was. The President continued: "As you know, there have been many plays *[sic]*, many feelers—these have all been our initiative. Now we have a feeler back that seems reliable." He described the meetings of Guthrie with the North Vietnamese and the request which the North Vietnamese had made earlier that day, and he told Mansfield and Dirksen that the reason for meeting with them was to see if the Senate Foreign Relations Committee could delay further hearings on Vietnam. (On January 10, the committee had discussed the possibility of having new hearings.) "Just give me two or three—or a few weeks," the President said. "I want you to prayerfully consider what might be said to Senators Fulbright and Hickenlooper by morning—such as would they be willing to go on with consular treaty [a treaty between the U.S. and the U.S.S.R. which had been sent to the Senate for approval] and not have hearings on Vietnam now."

Dirksen asked the President if he had talked to Hickenlooper, and Mansfield asked him if he had talked to Fulbright. Dirksen suggested that the President should talk to both Hickenlooper and Fulbright.

As the discussion continued, the President commented that South Vietnamese morale was better than ever, and Rostow ex-

---

[74] U.S. Department of State, Central File, Pol 27–14 Viet, Washington to Moscow 120335, Jan. 17, 1967, also in *The Secret Diplomacy of the Vietnam War*, p. 417. For Guthrie's report on the meeting with the North Vietnamese Chargé on January 20 at which this message was delivered see U.S. Department of State, Central File, Pol 27–14, Moscow to Washington 3126, Jan. 20, 1967.

[75] Johnson Library, President's Appointment File, Diary Backup for Jan. 17, 1967.

plained why. The President said he "personally wished he had never heard of South Vietnam; wishes we were not there but we are there. . . ." But he added, without explanation, that he could not tell Fulbright about the contents of the cable from Guthrie.

"The President then read a proposed [congressional] resolution after stating that Senator Russell wanted a resolution last year. Senators Dirksen and Mansfield both said the worse *[sic]* thing you can do is send up a resolution. We have a resolution [Gulf of Tonkin]. It can be withdrawn by vote of House and Senate."

The President again emphasized the progress being made in Vietnam: "We are doing better now than we have ever done in Vietnam if we just don't blow it."

As the meeting ended, it was decided that Mansfield, Dirksen, Fulbright and Hickenlooper, along with Senators Russell and Margaret Chase Smith (R/Maine), the ranking Republican on the Senate Armed Services Committee, would meet with the President the next morning.

The meeting was held the next day (January 18) from 9:40 a.m. to 10:45 a.m. Smith was invited but could not attend. Senator Aiken also attended. Rostow was the only staff person present. It is not known what transpired, or whether Fulbright and Hickenlooper were persuaded that the Foreign Relations Committee should delay its hearings. On January 24, the Foreign Relations Committee met again and decided to hold its hearings, but by the time the first one was held on January 30, the North Vietnamese, through both a diplomatic message given to the U.S. Embassy in Moscow on January 27 and a public statement by the Foreign Minister on January 28, had denounced the U.S. and repeated their demand that bombing "and all other acts of war" against North Vietnam had to be stopped before talks could begin.[76]

In their reply on January 27 to the U.S. message of January 17, the North Vietnamese, as noted earlier, seemed to be stiffening their terms by calling for an "unconditional" end to U.S. bombing of the North, whereas during MARIGOLD it appeared that they might be willing to talk without prior suspension of U.S. bombing. The following is the text of the reply:[77]

> A. The United States is intensifying the war in South Vietnam and escalating the bombing of North Vietnam. President Johnson has made clear his scheme to go on intensifying the war of aggression against Vietnam. But the Vietnamese people are determined to fight for their fundamental national rights and the United States is doomed to dismal defeat.
>
> B. The United States talks peace but makes war. The conditions which the United States demands the Vietnamese people to accept are absurd and arrogant. "Conditional suspension of bombing," "Conditional withdrawal of troops" are in fact schemes to cling to South Vietnam, to turn South Vietnam into a new-type colony and a military base of the United States, to prolong indefinitely the partition of Vietnam.

---

[76] For these developments see Herring, *The Secret Diplomacy of the Vietnam War*, pp. 383–385, 416–427.

[77] U.S. Department of State, Central File, Pol 27–14 Viet, Moscow to Washington 3218, Jan. 17, 1967.

C. The four-point stand of the government of the Democratic Republic of Vietnam embodies the fundamental principles and the main provisions of the 1954 Geneva Agreements on Vietnam. It is the basis for the most correct political solution to the Vietnam Problem. The government of the Democratic Republic of Vietnam has declared that if the United States really wants peace and seeks a political solution, it must recognize the four-point stand of the government of the Democratic Republic of Vietnam and the five-point statement of South Vietnam National Front for Liberation, the only genuine representative of the South Vietnamese people.

D. The Democratic Republic of Vietnam is an independent and sovereign country. The U.S. bombing of the Democratic Republic of Vietnam is a blatant act of aggression. The United States must end immediately and unconditionally the bombing and all other acts of war against the Democratic Republic of Vietnam, that is the urgent demand on the people of all countries, of all men of common sense throughout the world. The unconditional cessation of bombing and all other acts of war against the Democratic Republic of Vietnam being materialized, the Democratic Republic of Vietnam could then exchange views with the United States concerning the place or date for contact between the two parties as the Government of the United States proposed in its message handed over on January 10, 1967.

Washington officials did not comment publicly on the North Vietnamese statements, but privately they were concerned that the North Vietnamese were using the issue of talks as a political weapon. A cable drafted by William Bundy to the U.S. Embassies in Moscow and Saigon on January 31 called the statements "all-out efforts to build up public pressures on us to stop bombing in return for talks." [78]

After receiving the diplomatic message from the North Vietnamese on January 27, the State Department later that day asked Ambassador Thompson, who by then had arrived in Moscow, to comment on the North Vietnam position, including whether it represented the "start of a dialogue with the other side staking out an opening extreme position." [79]

---

[78] Washington to Moscow and Saigon 128175, Jan. 31, 1967, in Herring, *The Secret Diplomacy of the Vietnam War,* p. 424. A circular cable to U.S. diplomatic missions in Asia several days later, drafted by Bundy, concluded: "[O]ur reading remains that Hanoi is clearly embarked on a major campaign to get us to stop bombing in return for a mere willingness to talk, but that it is conceivable that some deeper change is in progress." U.S. Department of State, Central File, Pol 27 Viet S, Washington 137148, circular cable to diplomatic posts in Asia, Feb. 14, 1967.

[79] Washington to Moscow 127220, Jan. 27, 1967, in Herring, p. 421. On January 27, the State Department also approved an expanded version of the Fourteen Points for Peace in Southeast Asia, which had first been issued on Jan. 17, 1966. Released on Feb. 9, 1967, (*Department of State Bulletin,* Feb. 13, 1967) it was as follows:

"1. The Geneva Agreements of 1954 and 1962 are an adequate basis for peace in Southeast Asia.

"2. We would welcome a conference on Southeast Asia or any part thereof:

"—We are ready to negotiate a settlement based on a strict observance of the 1954 and 1962 Geneva Agreements, which observance was called for in the declaration on Viet-Nam of the meeting of the Warsaw Pact countries in Bucharest on July 6, 1966. And we will support a reconvening of the Geneva Conference, or an Asian conference, or any other generally acceptable forum.

"3. We would welcome 'negotiations without preconditions' as called for by 17 nonalined nations in an appeal delivered to Secretary Rusk on April 1, 1965.

Continued

Thompson replied: "DRV message strikes me as first round in oriental rug trading." He suggested several options. First, the U.S. could stop bombing and press for negotiations, "or alternatively state we are doing so on assumption there will be prompt meeting and mutual de-escalation." Second, the U.S. could "state that as evidence of good faith we will confine bombing to infiltration routes in southern part of DRV and press for prompt meeting." If neither of these was acceptable to Washington policymakers, he suggested that the U.S. should either compose a message which would have maximum publicity value "if publication forced by them [the North Vietnamese]," or that the U.S. should ask the North Vietnamese for further comments on certain parts of their message.[80]

"4. We would welcome 'unconditional discussions' as called for by President Johnson on April 7, 1965:

"—If the other side will not come to a conference, we are prepared to engage in direct discussions or discussions through an intermediary.

"5. A cessation of hostilities could be the first order of business at a conference or could be the subject of preliminary discussions:

"—We have attempted, many times, to engage the other side in a discussion of a mutual deescalation of the level of violence, and we remain prepared to engage in such a mutual deescalation.

"—We stand ready to cooperate fully in getting discussions which could lead to a cessation of hostilities started promptly and brought to a successful completion.

"6. Hanoi's four points could be discussed along with other points which others may wish to propose:

"—We would be prepared to accept preliminary discussions to reach agreement on a set of points as a basis for negotiations.

"7. We want no U.S. bases in Southeast Asia:

"—We are prepared to assist in the conversion of these bases for peaceful uses that will benefit the peoples of the entire area.

"8. We do not desire to retain U.S. troops in South Viet-Nam after peace is assured:

"—We seek no permanent military bases, no permanent establishment of troops, no permanent alliances, no permanent American 'presence' of any kind in South Viet-Nam.

"—We have pledged in the Manila Communique that 'Allied forces are in the Republic of Vietnam because that country is the object of aggression and its government requested support in the resistance of its people to aggression. They shall be withdrawn, after close consultation, as the other side withdraws its forces to the North, ceases infiltration, and the level of violence thus subsides. Those forces will be withdrawn as soon as possible and not later than six months after the above conditions have been fulfilled.'

"9. We support free elections in South Viet-Nam to give the South Vietnamese a government of their own choice.

"—We support the development of broadly based democratic institutions in South Viet-Nam.

"—We do not seek to exclude any segment of the South Vietnamese people from peaceful participation in their country's future.

"10. The question of reunification of Viet-Nam should be determined by the Vietnamese through their own free decision:

"—It should not be decided by the use of force.

"—We are fully prepared to support the decision of the Vietnamese people.

"11. The countries of Southeast Asia can be nonalined or neutral if that be their option:

"—We do not seek to impose a policy of alinement on South Viet-Nam.

"—We support the neutrality policy of the Royal Government of Laos, and we support the neutrality and territorial integrity of Cambodia.

"12. We would much prefer to use our resources for the economic reconstruction of Southeast Asia than in war. If there is peace, North Viet-Nam could participate in a regional effort to which we would be prepared to contribute at least one billion dollars:

"—We support the growing efforts by the nations of the area to cooperate in the achievement of their economic and social goals.

"13. The President has said 'The Viet Cong would have no difficulty in being represented and having their views presented if Hanoi for a moment decides she wants to cease aggression. And I would not think that would be an insurmountable problem at all.'

"14. We have said publicly and privately that we could stop the bombing of North Viet-Nam as a step toward peace although there has not been the slightest hint or suggestion from the other side as to what they would do if the bombing stopped:

"—We are prepared to order a cessation of all bombing of North VietNam, the moment we are assured—privately or otherwise—that this step will be answered promptly by a corresponding and appropriate deescalation of the other side.

"—We do not seek the unconditional surrender of North Viet-Nam; what we do seek is to assure for the people of South Viet-Nam the right to decide their own political destiny, free of force."

[80] Moscow to Washington 3231, Jan. 28, 1967, in Herring, *The Secret Diplomacy of the Vietnam War*, pp. 421–422.

On January 31, the State Department replied to Thompson in a cable drafted by William Bundy. Guthrie was told to deliver another message to the North Vietnamese reiterating the desire of the U.S. for talks with the North Vietnamese "covering any elements that either side believes should be considered in reaching a peaceful solution to the Vietnamese problem." Noting the concern of North Vietnamese about increased bombing of the North, the message pointed out that by establishing the 10-mile limit in bombing Hanoi the U.S. had already taken one step to deescalate the air war, and was prepared to take additional steps, including the cessation of bombing, "to create conditions conducive to the success of talks with the DRV." Bombing could be stopped "as a prior and ostensibly unilateral action," but before doing so the U.S. wanted a "private understanding" with the North Vietnamese that they would respond with "similar acts of restraint" which, together with U.S. action, would "amount in the aggregate to an equitable and reciprocal reduction of hostile actions."[81]

Guthrie gave the January 31 message to the North Vietnamese Chargé on February 2, who raised further questions but did not reply to the substance of the message.[82] In a press conference on February 2, President Johnson said that there had not been any indication of "seriousness" about negotiations on the part of the North Vietnamese. He was asked what kinds of steps the North Vietnamese should take to demonstrate their interest, and he replied: "Just almost any step." But when he was asked directly whether it would be enough for them to say they were willing to talk in return for a cessation of bombing or whether some military move on their part would be required, he avoided answering, repeating that he had not seen any indication of seriousness, and was waiting for whatever offer "they might care to make."[83]

McNamara and McNaughton appear to have strongly supported the effort to open talks with the North Vietnamese and to avoid an escalation of the war. McNamara agreed with a proposed "scenario" sent to him on or about February 3, 1967 by McNaughton, by which the U.S. would unilaterally extend the February 8–12 bombing pause at Tet (but not other military activities) whether or not the North Vietnamese reduced their activities or promised to do so.[84] If talks did not start and the U.S. resumed the air war, bombing should begin in the southern part of North Vietnam, and, if necessary, proceed northward. This was McNaughton's proposal:

SCENARIO

1. President tell DRV before Tet, "We are stopping bombing at start of Tet and at the end of Tet we will not resume."

---

[81] *Ibid.*, pp. 425–427.

[82] U.S. Department of State, Central File, Pol 27–14 Viet, Moscow to Washington 3321, Feb. 2, 1967, also in *The Secret Diplomacy of the Vietnam War*, p. 428.

[83] *Public Papers of the Presidents*, Lyndon B. Johnson, 1967, pp. 128–133. According to Kraslow and Loory (pp. 180–185), the President's press statement was "carefully prepared" and did not represent a relaxation of the U.S. position.

[84] For the text of McNaughton's scenario see *PP*, Gravel ed., vol. IV, p. 142. In the margin of his copy of this proposal McNaughton made the following note after talking to McNamara: "SecDef [McNamara] (2/3/67): 'Agreed we will do this if answer to note is unproductive' (?) Something like this even if productive. JTM [John T. McNaughton]." *Ibid.*, p. 143. It is not known what McNaughton meant by "note," but in all probability he was referring to the letter from President Johnson to President Ho Chi Minh which had been in preparation since late January.

2. During Tet and in days thereafter:
   a. Observe DRV/VC conduct for "signs."
   b. Try to get talks started.

3. Meantime, avoid changes in "noise level" in other areas of conduct—e.g., no large U.S. troop deployments for couple weeks, no dramatic changes in rules of engagement in South, etc.

4. As for public handling:
   a. At end of 4 days of Tet merely extend to 7 days.
   b. At end of 7 days just keep pausing, making no explanation.
   c. Later say "We are seeing what happens."
   d. Even later, say (if time) infiltration down, etc.

5. If we must resume RT [ROLLING THUNDER], have justifications and start in Route Packages 2 and 3 [southern part of North Vietnam], working North as excuses appear (and excuses will appear).

6. If talks start and DRV demands ceasefire in South or cessation of U.S. troop additions consider exact deal then.

7. Accelerate readiness of Project 728 [anti-infiltration barrier].

8. Avoid allowing our terms to harden just because things appear to be going better. . . .

On February 8, the bombing of North Vietnam and the status of U.S. peace probes were among the subjects considered at a brief meeting of the National Security Council from 10:32 a.m. to 11:08 a.m.[85] Rostow opened the meeting with a summary of the history of U.S. bombing of North Vietnam. Wheeler then read a statement of the military objectives of bombing and the results of the air war, in which he concluded: "our air campaign against North Vietnam is damaging their capability to move men and supplies into South Vietnam and is making them pay a substantial price for their aggression against South Vietnam."[86] "It is my judgment," he added, "that our air campaign is an integral and indispensable component of our over-all operations in Southeast Asia . . . [and] that bombing operations in North Vietnam should not be stopped unless a substantial reciprocal action is undertaken by North Vietnam. In my view a promise to talk does not meet the criteria for a substantial reciprocal action."

McNamara responded that "Bombing of North Vietnam could be stopped if we got in return a symmetrical de-escalation."

Rusk reviewed U.S. "peace probes," and concluded by saying: "All our efforts have encountered silence. We have had no serious response, public or private. We have come to feel that the North Vietnamese may think we are paniking *[sic]*. This risk we took." The President added: "We have our people all over the world who are ready to listen. We have pursued every hint that the North Vietnamese were willing to give up something if we give up some-

---

[85] In attendance at the 568th NSC meeting were the President, the Vice President, Rusk, McNamara, Rostow, Katzenbach, Vance, McNaughton, Goldberg, Helms, General Wheeler, Fowler, Marks, Komer, George Christian and several other administration officials and White House staff. Notes of the NSC meeting are in the Johnson Library, NSF NSC Meetings File. After the NSC meeting, the President continued meeting (until 11:40 a.m.) with Rusk, McNamara and Rostow, but there apparently are no notes of that meeting.

[86] A copy of Wheeler's statement is attached to the notes of the meeting.

thing." "Hanoi," he said, "is trying to force us to give up the bombing of North Vietnam. We will keep on until we get something from the North Vietnamese."

Project SUNFLOWER

As the Tet bombing pause (February 8–12, 1967) approached, Soviet Premier Kosygin arrived in London for talks with the British. There were strong indications that he was interested in resuming the discussion of the war which he and British Foreign Secretary George Brown had begun in Moscow in November 1966.[87]

After a session on February 7 between Kosygin and Prime Minister Wilson, Chester Cooper, Harriman's assistant, who was in London to help the British with the discussions with Kosygin, cabled a report to the State Department on the meeting.[88] He said that Wilson had told Kosygin about the Phase A–Phase B formula, but he noted that the version proposed by Wilson had been changed from the version that Cooper had sent to Washington earlier that day in a cable asking for clarification of the U.S. position.[89] Cooper said that Kosygin "evidently had not understood it [Phase A–Phase B] when Brown presented it to him last November," but showed "considerable interest" in the proposal as presented by Wilson, and the British thought that Kosygin would send it to the North Vietnamese. (He apparently did so.) Cooper was asked by the British whether the U.S. also planned to send a message to the North Vietnamese containing the Phase A–Phase B proposal. Cooper replied that he believed this was going to be done. If so, Cooper said, the British requested that if there were differences in the British formulation and that presented by the U.S., that the North Vietnamese be told that the British text was authoritative in substance even though the two might be different in style.

Later that same day (February 7), President Johnson sent a cable to Prime Minister Wilson, drafted by W. W. Rostow, commenting on the question "as to whether the U.S. would stop the bombing of North Vietnam in exchange for an indication that Hanoi would enter into talks without any military acts of deescalation on their side."[90] The U.S., Johnson told Wilson, had agreed in early December to hold talks with the North Vietnamese, and after the North Vietnamese had complained about U.S. bombing near Hanoi on December 13–14 the order had been given to refrain from bombing within 10 nautical miles of the center of Hanoi to demonstrate U.S. interest in negotiating. Since that time, there had been "neither a corresponding military step on their side nor a use of existing channels to get on with discussions." The U.S. remained ready to talk, Johnson said, but before it could take any additional deescalatory military actions it had to know what the North Vietnamese would do in return. He added: "We have noted that a sus-

---

[87] For Project SUNFLOWER, see Herring, *The Secret Diplomacy of the Vietnam War,* pp. 431 ff. See also *The Vantage Point,* pp. 253–255; Harold Wilson, *The Labour Government;* Cooper, *The Lost Crusade;* and Thies, *When Governments Collide.*

[88] Johnson Library, NSF Memos to the President—Walt Rostow, London to Washington 6360, Feb. 7, 1967.

[89] *Ibid.* The text of the Wilson version of Phase A–Phase B, which Cooper included in London 6360, was excised entirely when the cable was declassified in 1991.

[90] Washington to London 132481, Feb. 7, 1967, in *The Secret Diplomacy of the Vietnam War,* p. 436.

pension of the bombing has been termed by the other side as unacceptable and that we must accept an unconditional and permanent cessation of bombing. That makes it all the more necessary to know what military action Hanoi would take if we in fact stopped the bombing." Specifically," Johnson said, "we are prepared to and plan, through established channels, to inform Hanoi that if they will agree to an assured stoppage of infiltration into South Vietnam, we will stop the bombing of North Vietnam and stop further augmentation of U.S. forces in South Vietnam." "What we cannot accept," the cable concluded, is the exchange of guarantee of a safe haven for North Vietnam merely for discussions which thus far have no form or content, during which they could continue to expand their military operations without limit."

Meanwhile, the President had decided to send the personal letter to President Ho Chi Minh that was drafted by Rostow on January 5, and on February 8 this was delivered by Guthrie to the North Vietnamese Embassy in Moscow.[91] The text of the letter does not appear, however, to have been sent also to the U.S. Ambassador to Great Britain, David K. E. Bruce, Cooper and the British for their information in dealing with Kosygin. Cooper had told Wilson about the plan to send the letter, but the draft which Cooper had seen before he left Washington contained a version of the Phase A-Phase B formula by which the U.S. would agree to stop bombing after private assurances from the North Vietnamese that they would reciprocate after several days, whereas the final version of the letter stipulated that the U.S. would stop bombing only after the U.S. was assured that the North Vietnamese had stopped infiltrating men and supplies to the South.

This was the text of Johnson's letter to Ho Chi Minh:[92]

February 8, 1967.

Dear Mr. President:

I am writing to you in the hope that the conflict in Vietnam can be brought to an end. That conflict has already taken a heavy toll—in lives lost, in wounds inflicted, in property destroyed, and in simple human misery. If we fail to find a just and peaceful solution, history will judge us harshly.

Therefore, I believe that we both have a heavy obligation to seek earnestly the path to peace. It is in response to that obligation that I am writing directly to you.

We have tried over the past several years, in a variety of ways and through a number of channels, to convey to you and your colleagues our desire to achieve a peaceful settlement. For whatever reasons, these efforts have not achieved any results.

It may be that our thoughts and yours, our attitudes and yours, have been distorted or misinterpreted as they passed

---

[91] See Schoenbaum, *Waging Peace and War,* p. 456. Rostow's draft of Jan. 6, 1967 is in the Department of State Central File, Pol 27 Viet S.

[92] *Public Papers of the Presidents,* Lyndon B. Johnson, 1966, pp. 390–391. On February 9, 1967, Secretary of State Rusk held a news conference in which, without mentioning the letter, he made the point which had been made in the letter with respect to the need for reciprocity. Before agreeing to a "permanent cessation" of bombing, he said, the U.S. had to know the military consequences. A bombing halt without reciprocity would be "closing off one-half of the war while the rest of it goes on full force." (*Department of State Bulletin,* Feb. 27, 1967.) Also on February 9, the State Department released the revised text of the "Fourteen Points," listing the terms and conditions proposed by the U.S. for a settlement of the conflict.

through these various channels. Certainly that is always a danger in indirect communication.

There is one good way to overcome this problem and to move forward in the search for a peaceful settlement. That is for us to arrange for direct talks between trusted representatives in a secure setting and away from the glare of publicity. Such talks should not be used as a propaganda exercise but should be a serious effort to find a workable and mutually acceptable solution.

In the past two weeks, I have noted public statements by representatives of your government suggesting that you would be prepared to enter into direct bilateral talks with representatives of the U.S. Government, provided that we ceased "unconditionally" and permanently our bombing operations against your country and all military actions against it. In the last day, serious and responsible parties have assured us indirectly that this is in fact your proposal.

Let me frankly state that I see two great difficulties with this proposal. In view of your public position, such action on our part would inevitably produce worldwide speculation that discussions were under way and would impair the privacy and secrecy of those discussions. Secondly, there would inevitably be grave concern on our part whether your Government would make use of such action by us to improve its military position.

With these problems in mind, I am prepared to move even further towards an ending of hostilities than your Government has proposed in either public statements or through private diplomatic channels. I am prepared to order a cessation of bombing against your country and the stopping of further augmentation of U.S. forces in South Viet-Nam as soon as I am assured that infiltration into South Viet-Nam by land and by sea has stopped. These acts of restraint on both sides would, I believe, make it possible for us to conduct serious and private discussions leading toward an early peace.

I make this proposal to you now with a specific sense of urgency arising from the imminent New Year holidays in Viet-Nam. If you are able to accept this proposal I see no reason why it could not take effect at the end of the New Year, or Tet, holidays. The proposal I have made would be greatly strengthened if your military authorities and those of the Government of South Viet-Nam could promptly negotiate an extension of the Tet truce.

As to the site of the bilateral discussions I propose, there are several possibilities. We could, for example, have our representatives meet in Moscow where contacts have already occurred. They could meet in some other country such as Burma. You may have other arrangements or sites in mind, and I would try to meet your suggestions.

The important thing is to end a conflict that has brought burdens to both our peoples, and above all to the people of South Viet-Nam. If you have any thoughts about the actions I propose, it would be most important that I receive them as soon as possible.

Sincerely,

LYNDON B. JOHNSON

On February 10, unaware that the President's letter to Ho Chi Minh had changed Phase A/Phase B to provide that U.S. bombing would stop only after the U.S. had been assured that North Vietnamese infiltration had stopped, Cooper sent Washington a new draft of Phase A/Phase B which the British wanted to give to Kosygin at his request.[93] The new draft provided that the U.S. would stop bombing "as soon as they are assured that infiltration from North Vietnam to South Vietnam will stop."

After Cooper's cable of February 10 was received in Washington, the President met with Rusk, McNamara, and W. W. Rostow. Cooper was summoned from the theater in London by a phone call from Rostow, who said that the draft that Cooper had sent to Washington did not represent the American position that bombing would be stopped only after infiltration "has stopped," rather than "will stop."

A cable was sent immediately to Cooper with the approved text of Phase A/Phase B, as follows:[94]

(A) the United States will order a cessation of bombing of North Vietnam as soon as they are assured that infiltration from North Vietnam to South Vietnam has stopped. This assurance can be communicated in secret if North Vietnam so wishes.

(B) Within a few days (with a period to be agreed with the two sides before the bombing stops) the United States will stop further augmenting their force in South Vietnam. The cessation of bombing of North Vietnam is an action which will be immediately apparent. This requires that the stoppage of infiltration becomes public very quickly thereafter. If Hanoi is unwilling to announce the stoppage of infiltration, the United States must itself do so and, in that case, Hanoi must not deny it.

(C) Any assurances from Hanoi can reach the United States direct, or through Soviet channels, or through the Soviet and British Governments. This is for North Vietnam to decide.

COMMENTS FOR WILSON:

You should be clear that the stoppage of augumentation by us would still permit the rotation of United States forces and their continued supply. Augumentation means no net increase. Stoppage of infiltration, however, means that men and arms cannot come from North Vietnam into South Vietnam.

The phraseology of paragraph A above is to prevent the sudden movement of two or three divisions across the 17th parallel during the "few days" referred to in paragraph B.

---

[93] U.S. Department of State, Central File, Pol 27–14 Viet, London to Washington 6456, Feb. 10, 1967.

[94] U.S. Department of State, Central File, Pol 27–14 Viet. Typed text, Feb. 10, 1967, of message from Washington to Bruce and Cooper, with "Attention Burke Trent [Secretary of the British Cabinet] from Walt Rostow" written in hand by Rostow.

Rusk's biographer, Thomas Schoenbaum, says that Rusk was "disappointed" with the President's decision, at Rostow's urging, to insist on this formulation of Phase A/Phase B. Schoenbaum, *Waging Peace and War*, p. 457.

> It is very important that this arrangement in Vietnam not be translated into a communist seizure of Laos. The two Co-chairmen should agree between themselves that both will make a maximum effort in support of the 1954 and 1962 accords.
>
> Assurance about infiltration ought to lead to prompt measures by the ICC, either as a Commission or as governments, to provide assurances to all concerned that these arrangements are being carried out. This should mean ICC observed in the DMZ and in whatever places in Laos may be required to keep the Ho Chi Minh trail under surveillance.

The cable said that the reason for using "has stopped" in Paragraph A was to "to prevent the sudden movement of two or three divisions" across the 17th parallel during the "few days" referred to in Paragraph B.

Hastily, the new, "has stopped" version of Phase A/Phase B received from Rostow was typed and given to Kosygin as he was leaving on the night train for Scotland. The British, Cooper said in a telephone call to Benjamin Read, noted that the new American version directly conflicted with the position stated by Rusk in a press conference on February 9 in which Rusk referred to Point 14 of the modified "Fourteen Points for Peace in Southeast Asia," which read, "We are prepared to order a cessation of all bombing of North Vietnam, the moment we are assured—privately or otherwise—that this step *will* be answered promptly by a corresponding and appropriate deescalation on the other side."[95] (emphasis in original)

Wilson cabled Johnson that the "change of tense" had created a "hell of a situation" for his last day of talks with Kosygin.[96] The reply from the State Department on February 11, drafted by William Bundy, explained that the change of tense resulted from the fact that "we face immediate specific problem of three [North Vietnamese] divisions poised just north of DMZ. We must be in position to insist that these cannot be moved into SVN just before their [North Vietnamese] undertaking [to stop infiltration] takes effect." Moreover, the new U.S. proposal called for two U.S. commitments—cessation of troop augmentation as well as of bombing, whereas the original Phase A/Phase B formula applied only to bombing cessation. Finally, the State Department cable said, the British and the American team in London should understand that the Russians already knew of the change in the American position through the North Vietnamese, and therefore it came as no surprise to them and could not have impaired British credibility.[97]

This explanation did not assuage the British or American negotiators,[98] and there was another exchange of messages between London and Washington. President Johnson told Wilson in a cable on February 12, drafted by W. W. Rostow, that the change of tense was not significant. The North Vietnamese and the Russians had known about the Phase A/Phase B offer since November 1966, Johnson said, but had not shown any interest in it. Meanwhile, the

---

[95] U.S. Department of State, Central File, Pol 27–14 Viet, Memorandum of Cooper-Read Telephone Conversation, Feb. 11, 1967.

[96] Wilson, *The Labour Government*, p. 359.

[97] Washington to London 135662, Feb. 11, 1967, in Herring, *The Secret Diplomacy of the Vietnam War*, p. 459.

[98] See the discussion in *ibid.*, pp. 460–461.

North Vietnamese had continued their buildup, and had used the three truces for increased infiltration. "Everyone seems to wish to negotiate except Hanoi," Johnson added. "I wish someone would produce a real live North Vietnamese prepared to talk."

Johnson denied that there was any inconsistency between his message to Wilson on February 7, in which he had said that the U.S. would stop bombing if the North Vietnamese would agree to "an assured stoppage of infiltration into South Vietnam," and his letter to Ho Chi Minh on February 8. Wilson's February 10 version of Phase A/Phase B, he said, "transmuted" the U.S. position that there must be an "assured stoppage" of infiltration into "an assurance that infiltration 'will stop,'" which was "quite a different matter." "From an operational point of view," Johnson told Wilson, "we cannot stop the bombing while three (possibly four) divisions dash south from the DMZ before their promise is to take effect."[99]

On February 11, Ambassador Bruce, having learned that a decision had been made on February 10 to resume bombing North Vietnam on the night of February 11, sent an urgent message to Washington asking that resumption be delayed until the end of the Kosygin visit on February 13. Rusk sent a memorandum to the President (drafted by William Bundy) recommending that this be done, and the President agreed.[100]

On Sunday, February 12, Wilson, Cooper and Bruce made a final attempt to reach an agreement with the North Vietnamese through Kosygin. They proposed, and asked Washington to approve, that North Vietnamese forces remain in place north of the 17th parallel in return for U.S. extension of the Tet bombing pause. During the evening at Chequers, the Prime Minister's country home, the British kept stalling for time while Cooper sat in an attic room with a direct telephone connection to Washington. This is Cooper's description of what transpired as he sat waiting for the phone to ring:[101]

> The hours sped by. Two or three needling calls produced only assurances that the proposition was under consideration and that I would be informed when the President had made a decision.[102] Dinner was over downstairs—and still no word from Washington. I made yet another call. This time I was told an answer would be coming very shortly; the Prime Minister should try to detain Kosygin. All the business had been done, the joint communique had been approved, coffee, brandy, and cigars had been consumed. Kosygin was becoming increasingly impatient to return to London, and Wilson was practically hanging on to his guest's coattails. I heard the police rev up their motorcycles in the courtyard below. In utter desperation I called Rostow and dangled the telephone as far out of the window as I could get it so that he could hear the sound of the

---

[99] Washington to London 135718, Feb. 12, 1967, in *ibid.*, pp. 462–463. See also *The Vantage Point*, p. 253.

[100] For Bruce's cable see the Department of State, Central File Pol 27–14 Viet, London to Washington 6493, Feb. 11, 1967. In the same location are brief notes on two telephone conversations between Rusk and Bruce on February 11. For Rusk's memorandum to the President, "Resumption of Operations Against North Vietnam Over the Next Two Days," Feb. 11, 1967, see Department of State, Central File, Pol 27 Viet S.

[101] Cooper, *The Lost Crusade*, p. 365.

[102] In the Department of State Central File, Pol 27–14 Viet, there is a transcript of one of these telephone calls from Cooper to Benjamin Read at 1:52 p.m. on Feb. 12, 1967.

roaring motors. That did it. By about midnight, Walt thought, the Washington version of the new proposition would be ready. Wilson was to ask Kosygin to stand by for an important message after he returned to Claridges. Ambassador Bruce should be contacted, and both of us should join Wilson at Downing Street.

The reason for the delay, according to Schoenbaum, was that a "bitter argument" was raging in Washington between Rostow and the military, who opposed extending the pause, and Rusk and McNamara who favored an extension.[103]

The answer from Washington arrived as the group gathered at the Prime Minister's residence at 10 Downing Street. Washington agreed to Wilson's proposal, but set a deadline of 10 a.m. (London time) on Monday, February 13, for the North Vietnamese to accept.[104] By the time Wilson got to Kosygin's hotel it was 1 a.m., on Sunday night. Wilson thought the proposed time-table was "utterly unrealistic," as did Bruce and Cooper and Kosygin. After talking with Kosygin, Wilson cabled President Johnson to ask for an extension, and Johnson responded by extending the deadline to 4 p.m. Monday (London time). According to Cooper's account, Bruce then attempted to get a further extension: "Bruce called Secretary Rusk and came directly to the point: the deadline was ridiculous, several days were needed. He urged Rusk to see the President and argue for more time. I didn't hear Rusk's reply. I didn't have to. I could read it in the Ambassador's face. The conversation ended with a brusque 'good night.' Rusk had told Bruce the British had been given all they were going to get, and Bruce was not to call him again on that subject."[105] According to Schoenbaum, "Rusk's brusque attitude reflected his own disappointment."[106]

On Monday, February 13, President Johnson met from 8:29 a.m. to 10:45 a.m. with the Vice President, McNamara, Katzenbach, Vance, Rostow, William Bundy, Foy Kohler, Maxwell Taylor, and General Wheeler. Rusk was not present. The question was whether to extend the deadline another seven hours (beyond the deadline of 4 p.m. that afternoon), apparently as requested by Bruce. Vice President Humphrey was in favor of doing so, and the President said that he would agree "if military people are satisfied."[107] General Wheeler said he favored the postponement; that it was a "po-

---

[103] Schoenbaum, *Waging Peace and War,* p. 457. According to Schoenbaum's account (p. 458), "Vietnam was becoming Rusk's personal agony. He increasingly felt caught between the President, who was under the influence of the hawkish Rostow and the military . . . and the doves . . . who wanted to pull out. . . . The only way to win the war was to negotiate, but negotiations on terms the President was willing to accept seemed to be out of reach, and withdrawal was unthinkable. Rusk also worried that, with the rising tide of American dissent against the war, Hanoi would lose any incentive for negotiations."

[104] This was the "U.S. Formula" that Washington accepted (Johnson Library, NSF Memos to the President—Walt Rostow):

"If you can get a North Vietnamese assurance—communicated either direct to the U.S. or through you—before 10:00 a.m. British time tomorrow that all movement of troops and supplies into South Viet Nam will stop at that time, I will get an assurance from the U.S. that they will not resume bombing of North Viet Nam from that time. Of course the U.S. buildup would also then stop within a matter of days.

"This would then give you and me the opportunity to try to consolidate and build on what has been achieved by bringing the parties together and promoting further balanced measures of deescalation."

[105] Cooper, *The Lost Crusade,* pp. 366–367.

[106] *Ibid.,* p. 458.

[107] Johnson Library, Tom Johnson's Notes of Meetings, Notes of meeting of Feb. 13, 1967. These and other notes of meetings taken by W. Thomas Johnson are quoted with his permission.

litical decision [and] not going to make that much difference militarily." Rostow also approved the extension. McNamara was the only adviser who expressed opposition. "We gave them 6 hours more than expected," he said. The U.S. proposal "cannot be accepted by Hanoi," and if the North Vietnamese should reply with a "moderated no [i.e., a qualified response rather than outright rejection] and we haven't bombed, we're in a hell of a fix." Vice President Humphrey disagreed, arguing that even a few hours could make a difference and that it was a risk worth taking. The President, who had noted that he did not want to approve another extension "if not doing any good," apparently was persuaded that it would do little if any harm, and approved another extension of 3 hours.[108]

As he left London on February 13, Kosygin was told about the extension of the deadline for resuming bombing, but there was no response from Hanoi, and U.S. bombing of North Vietnam resumed at 7 p.m. Washington time on February 13, 1967.

In a memorandum to the President that afternoon, Rostow said he had talked by telephone to Cooper and Philip M. Kaiser (Deputy Chief of Mission) at the U.S. Embassy in London who reported that Prime Minister Wilson had thought the problem lay in the unwillingness of the North Vietnamese to respond to the U.S. offer, and that he had "'put the monkey on their back.'" "Kaiser went on to say," Rostow told the President, "that he found no hostility or ill-feeling about our role in the week with Wilson," and that Wilson "seemed quite at peace" with the decision to resume bombing.[109]

In his memoirs, Wilson presented quite a different interpretation: "A historic opportunity had been missed. The Washington decision on the Friday [to require that infiltration should end before bombing was halted] was decisive and disastrous. Some two years later I had the opportunity of discussing these events with a senior U.S. statesman who had been involved in the Washington policy reversal at the operative time. I expressed the view that, in terms of influence on his master, the more I saw of certain of the White House advisers the more I thought that Rasputin was a much-maligned man. There was no dissent."[110]

Referring to Johnson's subsequent decision not to seek re-election, coupled with his unilateral, unconditional termination of the bombing of North Vietnam in March 1968, Wilson commented: "As one who was so close to him in these years, and in these moments of decision, I have never been able to get away from an impression of a classical Greek tragedy. February 1967 was the re-enactment, in our time, of the Sibylline books."[111]

On February 14, the State Department, in a cable drafted by William Bundy and sent to U.S. Embassies in New Zealand, Australia, the Philippines, Korea and Thailand, explained the negotiating situation. Although it was assumed that the North Vietnamese

---

[108] It will be noted that, contrary to Schoenman's statement quoted above, during this meeting, at least—and there are apparently no notes from the meeting on February 12, where the positions of those involved may have been different—Rostow and the military were in favor of the extension and McNamara was opposed.

[109] Johnson Library, NSF Memos to the President—Walt Rostow, Memorandum to the President from Rostow, Feb. 13, 1967.

[110] Harold Wilson, *The Labour Government,* p. 365.

[111] *Ibid.,* p. 366.

were attempting to get the U.S. to stop bombing in return for "a mere willingness to talk," it was "conceivable that some deeper change is in process." "We are impressed," the cable said, "by forceful reassurance in Hong Kong 5584 [a cable from the U.S. consul general] that Hanoi fears further disruption in China, may be deeply concerned about growing rupture in Sino-Soviet relations and its effect on Soviet shipments, and also fears possible Chinese dictating," and that "we do not regard an early Hanoi move [toward negotiations] as out of the question." Thus, the cable stated, while "we continue to believe that odds are substantially against any serious move by Hanoi in near future . . . we do see over-all factors that make this significantly more of a possibility than it has been for a very long time, if ever."[112]

On February 15, 1967, a representative of the North Vietnamese Embassy in Moscow, saying that he could no longer meet with U.S. representatives, handed Guthrie the following reply from Ho Chi Minh to Lyndon Johnson's letter of February 8:[113]

February 15, 1967.

To His Excellency Mr. Lyndon B. Johnson,
President,
United States of America,

Your Excellency:

On February 10, 1967, I received your message. This is my reply.

Vietnam is thousands of miles away from the United States. The Vietnamese people have never done any harm to the United States. But contrary to the pledges made by its representative at the 1954 Geneva conference, the U.S. Government has ceaselessly intervened in Vietnam, it has unleashed and intensified the war of aggression in South Vietnam with a view to prolonging the partition of Vietnam and turning South Vietnam into a neocolony and a military base of the United States. For over two years now, the U.S. Government has, with its air and naval forces, carried the war to the Democratic Republic of Vietnam, an independent and sovereign country.

The U.S. Government has committed war crimes, crimes against peace and against mankind. In South Vietnam, half a million U.S. and satellite troops have resorted to the most inhuman weapons and the most barbarous methods of warfare, such as napalm, toxic chemicals and gasses, to massacre our compatriots, destroy crops, and raze villages to the ground. In

[112] U.S. Department of State, Central File, Pol 27 Viet S, Washington 137148 to Canberra, Wellington, Manila, Seoul and Bangkok, Feb. 14, 1967.

[113] Herring, *The Secret Diplomacy of the Vietnam War,* pp. 476–477. When he presented the letter, the North Vietnamese representative said, according to a cable from the U.S. Embassy in Moscow (Department of State, Central File, Pol 27–14, Moscow to Washington 3503, Feb. 15, 1967):

"A. Position and attitude of DRV Govt are very correct and serious, and enjoy strong support of world public opinion, including American people. US, however, always obstinate and perfidious, and it continues advance conditions for cessation of bombings.

"B. US had made use of DRV representative's receiving US representative in Moscow to deceive public opinion that secret negotiations going on while bombings continue.

"C. Lately, US extended so-called suspension of bombings during Tet. Less than two days later, bombings were resumed on pretext that there had been no response from Hanoi. This constitutes insolent ultimatum to compel Vietnamese people to accept unacceptable conditions.

"D. In such circumstances, DRV representative does not consider it possible receive US representative in Moscow on US proposal. Responsibility for this rests completely with US."

North Vietnam, thousands of U.S. aircraft have dropped hundreds of thousands of tons of bombs, destroying towns, villages, factories, schools. In your message, you apparently deplore the sufferings and destruction in Vietnam. May I ask you: Who has perpetrated these monstrous crimes? It is the United States and satellite troops. The U.S. Government is entirely responsible for the extremely serious situation in Vietnam.

The U.S. war of aggression against the Vietnamese people constitutes a challenge to the countries of the socialist camp, a threat to the national independence movement, and a serious danger to peace in Asia and the world.

The Vietnamese people deeply love independence, freedom and peace. But in the face of the U.S. aggression, they have risen up, united as one man, fearless of sacrifices and hardships. They are determined to carry on their resistance until they have won genuine independence and freedom and true peace. Our just cause enjoys strong sympathy and support from the peoples of the whole world, including broad sections of the American people.

The U.S. Government has unleashed the war of aggression in Vietnam. It must cease this aggression. That is the only way to the restoration of peace. The U.S. Government must stop definitively and unconditionally its bombing raids and all other acts of war against the Democratic Republic of Vietnam, withdraw from South Vietnam all U.S. and satellite troops, recognize the South Vietnam National Front for Liberation, and let the Vietnamese people settle themselves their own affairs. Such is the basic content of the five-point stand of the government of the Democratic Republic of Vietnam, which embodies the essential principles and provisions of the 1954 Geneva agreements on Vietnam, it is the basis of a correct political solution to the Vietnam problem.

In your message, you suggested direct talks between the Democratic Republic of Vietnam and the United States. If the U.S. Government really wants these talks, it must first of all stop unconditionally its bombing raids and all other acts of war against the Democratic Republic of Vietnam. It is only after the unconditional cessation of the U.S. bombing raids and all other acts of war against the Democratic Republic of Vietnam that the Democratic Republic of Vietnam and the United States could enter into talks and discuss questions concerning the two sides.

The Vietnamese people will never submit to force, they will never accept talks under the threat of bombs.

Our cause is absolutely just. It is to be hoped that the U.S. Government will act in accordance with reason.

Sincerely,

HO CHI MINH

On March 21, 1967, North Vietnam released to the press the texts of Lyndon Johnson's letter and Ho Chi Minh's reply.[114]

---

[114] *New York Times,* Mar. 22, 1967. For congressional reaction, including a statement by House Speaker McCormack condemning Ho Chi Minh's position that was greeted by a standing ovation in the House, see *CR,* vol. 112, pp. 7647–7649 and 7982–7983.

On April 6, President Johnson sent another letter to President Ho Chi Minh:[115]

April 6, 1967.

Dear Mr. President:

I was, of course, disappointed that you did not feel able to respond positively to my letter to you of February 8.

But I would recall to you the words Abraham Lincoln addressed to his fellow Americans in 1861:

> "Suppose you go to war, you cannot fight always; and when, after much loss on both sides, and no gain on either, you cease fighting, the identical old question as to terms of intercourse are again upon you."

In that spirit I wish to reaffirm the offers I made in my earlier letter. We remain prepared to talk quietly with your representatives to establish the terms of a peaceful settlement and then bring the fighting to a stop; or we are prepared to undertake steps of mutual de-escalation which might make it easier for discussions of a peaceful settlement to take place. Talks to either of these ends could take place in Moscow, Rangoon, or elsewhere.

Despite public discussion of our previous exchange of views, our responsibilities to our own peoples and to the world remain; and those responsibilities include bringing the war in Southeast Asia to an end at the earliest possible date.

It is surely clear that one day we must agree to reestablish and make effective the Geneva Accords of 1954 and 1962; let the people of South Vietnam determine in peace the kind of government they want, let the peoples of North and South Vietnam determine peacefully whether and how they should unite; and permit the peoples of Southeast Asia to turn all their energies to their economic and social development.

You and I will be judged in history by whether we worked to bring about this result sooner rather than later.

I venture to address you directly again in the hope that we can find the way to rise above all other considerations and fulfill that common duty. I would be glad to receive your views on these matters.

Sincerely,

LYNDON B. JOHNSON

This letter was delivered by Guthrie to the North Vietnamese Embassy in Moscow, but it was returned to the U.S. Embassy, which sent Washington this cable:[116]

> President's message returned by DRV Embassy. Original envelope which had been opened, found in embassy mail box at 1745 and bore following in French: "Non conforme! Retour a l'expediteur." (Unacceptable! Return to sender.)

Discussions between the U.S. and North Vietnam on ending the war finally began only after President Johnson announced on March 31, 1968, that the U.S. would stop bombing North Vietnam. During 1965–68, despite strong differences of opinion in the U.S.

---

[115] The text is reprinted in *The Vantage Point,* p. 596.

[116] U.S. Department of State, Central File, Pol 27–14. Moscow to Washington 4294, Apr. 6, 1967, in Herring, *The Secret Diplomacy of the Vietnam War,* p. 504.

Government and possibly in North Vietnam as well, neither side seemed to feel the need or was willing to make the necessary concessions for a compromise to be reached. Indeed, the reverse seems to have been true: Both sides appear to have believed in the rightness of their cause and to have been convinced that they were prevailing or would prevail, and this, in turn, seems to have resulted in a mutual hardening of attitudes which lessened the chance for talks. This was especially true in early 1967 when, as the *Pentagon Papers* said, neither side "was prepared to make further military concessions at this point . . . neither side *expected* to enter talks at this time."[117] (emphasis in original)

In fact, as Allan E. Goodman has pointed out, the war was probably prolonged by the strategies of the two sides:[118]

> Hanoi's strategy of negotiating in order to protract the fighting and Washington's counter-strategy of gradual escalation in order to raise the cost to Hanoi of fighting rather than negotiating contributed to both prolonging the war and vitiating efforts to end it with a negotiated settlement.
>
> In particular, the U.S. strategy of escalation, more than Hanoi's strategy of protracted struggle, prolonged the war. Hanoi had little choice with respect to strategy. Its resources and political military capabilities in the south required a protracted war. Escalation (one of a number of ways the United States could have chosen to fight the war) provided Hanoi with a symbol (the bombing) with which to rally support for holding out. Escalation also gave Hanoi time to adjust to each new increment of force and—in terms of the public antipathy that each step up the escalation ladder generated in the United States from 1966 onward—a ready index of America's waning will to continue the war.

[117] *Ibid.*, p. 385.
[118] Goodman, *The Lost Peace*, pp. 3–4.

Goodman has also concluded, however, that the "real obstacle" to a negotiated settlement was the determination of the Communists to force the U.S. to leave Vietnam. "As a result, Hanoi repeatedly told Washington, there was basically nothing to negotiate about."[119]

---

[119] *Ibid.*, p. 6. In his foreword to Goodman's book, pp. xiv-xv, William Sullivan takes a similar position:

"[T]he Lao Dong [Vietnamese Communist Party], in contrast to the sophisticated, nuanced, 'think-tank' effort that went into the American negotiating posture, had a primitive simplistic system that was directed without diversion or equivocation toward the single goal of achieving political dominance in Indochina.

"In retrospect, therefore, we can see that all the elaborate negotiating signals . . . were wasted on Hanoi. In most instances, it is probable that the signals were never even noticed, and many that were noticed were probably misinterpreted while those that were interpreted correctly were doubtless resented. They were resented because they were based on the presumption that the Lao Dong lacked conviction, or fortitude, or confidence in its goals. At the same time, because these signals were so ambiguous and reflected such ambiguous objectives, they could only generate contempt and the conclusion that they reflected an attitude of weakness."

Thies, (*When Governments Collide*, p. 5) argues that during the 1965–68 period there were three times when the North Vietnamese seemed to be willing to talk without a prior cessation of bombing: the XYZ contacts in August 1965-February 1966, the PINTA initiative in December 1965 (during the U.S. bombing pause) between the U.S. Ambassador to Burma and the North Vietnamese Consul General in Rangoon, and Project MARIGOLD. He analyzes in detail the reasons for the apparent willingness of the North Vietnamese to talk at those times.

Thies (p. 418) also argues that the U.S. did not have an adequate understanding of the difficulties of using coercive diplomacy techniques to force the North Vietnamese to modify their behavior, and concludes: "It is one of the great tragedies of the Johnson Administration that the information contained in the Study Group's report [Vietnam Coordinating Committee Report of March 1965], and in the results of the Sigma Games [war games in 1965], should have been either suppressed or ignored by high-level officials." He is referring to the Vietnam Committee's conclusion that U.S. pressure against North Vietnam would not cause the North to cease aiding the struggle in the South, and to a similar conclusion in the war games.

CHAPTER 13

1967: A YEAR OF RECKONING

If 1967 were to go according to plan, by July, and certainly by the end of the year, remaining Communist forces and base areas would be destroyed or incapacitated, all of South Vietnam would be pacified, and the war would be ended. The "plan," of course, was the one prepared by Westmoreland's command in the summer of 1965 and presented to the President by McNamara in July 1965 as the basis for U.S. military operations after the deployment of large-scale forces.

In reality, as McNamara said in his report to the President in October 1966, the war was stalemated militarily and there had been few if any gains in pacification. One indication of the lack of progress was the situation in the critical area around Saigon where, according to General Westmoreland's command history, "At the beginning of the year [1967] the enemy still enjoyed relative security in the huge War Zones in the III Corps, and our use of roads was generally restricted to Saigon and the immediate vicinity. Even our vital water lines on the Long Tau and Dong Ngai shipping channels connecting the Saigon area with the sea were never totally secure. With the exception of operation ATTLEBORO in late 1966, we had not yet entered these enemy areas on large-scale offensive operations, so that many of them were still largely untouched."[1]

---

[1] Admiral Sharp and General Westmoreland, *Report on the War in South Vietnam: January 1964-June 1968,* Section II (Washington, D.C.: U.S. Govt Print. Off.), pp. 132–133. See also the report of John Paul Vann, U.S. pacification chief in III Corps, cited in Dale Adrade, *Ashes to Ashes: The Phoenix Program and the Vietnam War* (Lexington, Mass.: Lexington Books, 1990), p. 48.

A case could be and to some extent was being made that the war was not being fought effectively and that it could be "won" if the plan proposed by the military in 1965, based on which they had given assurances that the U.S. could "win," were executed according to its assumptions and design. As stated in the JCS (Goodpaster) Report prepared in July 1965 in response to the question: Could the U.S. win "if we do everything we can" (see pt. III of this study, pp. 359 ff.), the war could be "won" if the U.S. acted "within the bounds of reasonable assumptions," provided there was the "will" to win and that will was manifested in strategy and tactical operations. (As has been noted, this report was never approved, nor were the plans for U.S. strategy and tactics that were submitted by the JCS in August and November 1965.) One of the assumptions was that except for three restrictions—no invasion of North Vietnam, no use of nuclear or chemical weapons, and no mass bombing of centers of population—U.S. military operations would not be subjected to "restriction, delay, or planning uncertainties" in implementing the proposed military concept (described in the Goodpaster Report as "progressively destroying the war-supporting power of North Vietnam, and pressing the fight against VC/DRV main force units in SVN to run them to ground and destroy them"). This assumption, which would have given the military considerable discretion, was not acceptable to the President and his chief advisers, who wanted to keep the war limited in order to avoid adversely affecting other U.S. foreign policy interests and the "Great Society." They were also attempting to wage, through the use of "graduated pressure," what McGeorge Bundy referred to as "a military campaign with an essentially political purpose," (see p. 54 above) and this led them to become involved in the making of decisions with respect to military plans and operations that the military traditionally regarded as being their responsibility.

An article in the *New York Times* described how a hamlet located only 18 miles from Saigon had been "pacified" in the spring of 1967 for the fifth time in ten years.[2]

The CIA also continued to report a lack of progress. In a memorandum, "The War in Vietnam," January 7, 1967, the Office of National Estimates concluded that although the "chances that the Communists would win South Vietnam by military victory have vanished," in other respects the "course of the struggle" was "inconclusive:"[3]

> In Saigon the political health of the South Vietnamese Government is still precarious, though much better than it was a year ago. The program for pacification of the countryside has made some progress, but results continue to be spotty. The fighting capabilities of the South Vietnamese army remain generally poor, and its eventual usefulness in pacification remains uncertain.[4]

The struggle, "if it is aimed at the creation of a peaceful South Vietnamese state which can stand on its own feet," would be long and costly. "There is no evident diminution of the Communist capability to continue the struggle. In any case, there is no evidence of a diminution of Communist will to continue the war."

"The matter of will is crucial," the memorandum said. "Hanoi's determination probably is strengthened by hopes that the US will lose heart if the struggle is prolonged and by its belief that South Vietnam cannot create a viable political structure capable of winning mass support."

Commenting more specifically on the military aspect of the war, the memorandum noted that despite increasingly effective U.S. military operations, Communist main forces (South Vietnamese Communist main forces plus North Vietnamese main force units fighting in the South) had increased in 1966 from 83,000 to 106,000, (although the memorandum noted that no new North Vietnamese units had been identified in the South since July 1, 1966), and that "There is no reason to doubt that the present force level can be sustained if Hanoi chooses." Furthermore, "capabilities for transporting supplies [from the north] to the main force units have been more than adequate and well above requirements."

In the face of increasing U.S. and allied military effectiveness against their main forces, the Communists, the memorandum said, appeared to be relying more on guerrilla warfare in order to maintain a lower attrition rate and thereby support a longer war. This development, it said, would pose a "serious challenge" for the U.S. and South Vietnam, especially in view of the fact that the strength of the Communist "irregulars [guerrillas] may have been underestimated in the past." "For some years it has been estimated that there were about 100,000–120,000 irregulars, but there is now documentary evidence which strongly suggests that at the beginning of 1965, irregular strength was about 200,000 and that the goal for

---

[2] *New York Times*, Apr. 12, 1967.

[3] Johnson Library, NSF Country File, Vietnam, "The War in Vietnam," Memorandum for the Director of Central Intelligence from Sherman Kent, chairman of the Board of National Estimates, Jan. 9, 1967.

[4] According to the memorandum, "The ARVN today is not in good shape. In general, its morale is poor, and its training has improved little. Only 4 of its 11 divisions are capable of reasonable performance in combat."

the end of 1965 was 250,000–300,000. More recent documentary evidence suggests that this goal was probably reached, at least during 1966."[5]

Morale was also more of a problem for the Communists than in the past, partly because Communist main force units "no longer have the capability of gaining the kind of major tactical successes which would sustain their morale." But none of these problems appeared critical, the memorandum concluded. "Thus, from the purely military standpoint there are good reasons to believe that the Communists will persevere."

On the question of U.S. bombing of North Vietnam, the memorandum concluded, as previous CIA studies had, that the air war was not achieving anticipated results:

> It is not demonstrable that the bombing of North Vietnam has thus far weakened Hanoi's will to continue the war. There appears to be confidence that North Vietnam can live with the present types and scale of attack and can also increase the attackers' losses. The principal economic cost to Hanoi has been the diversion of manpower, although we estimate that the diversion reached its peak in late 1965, and may now be declining. Losses to the economy are almost certainly viewed by Hanoi's leaders as tolerable given what is at stake in the war. The bombing of infiltration routes has not resulted in shortages of materiel for the forces in South Vietnam, or significantly reduced Hanoi's ability to maintain logistic support of these forces. It seems clear now that the air campaign by itself cannot persuade Hanoi to abandon the war. Other factors would weigh much more heavily in the North Vietnamese leaders' appraisal of the prospects of victory and therefore in influencing their will to persist.[6]

---

[5] The memorandum also touched on Communist manpower and morale problems. It noted that total losses in the South for 1966 were about 120,000, including 65,000–75,000 from main forces, 30,000–35,000 of which were North Vietnamese. North Vietnam was capable, however, of sustaining an infiltration rate of about 75,000, and in 1966 it had been better able to provide the necessary manpower than it had in 1965. During 1967, the Communists in the South would have to provide 10,000 a month for main force units, which was close to their maximum capability. The growth in irregulars by recruitment in the South would compensate, however, for any shortfall in main force manpower.

According to a 1968 study by the Defense Department's Office of Systems Analysis, the Communists were capable of replacing losses of 200,000 troops a year over many years. Alain C. Enthoven (Assistant Secretary of Defense for Systems Analysis) and K. Wayne Smith (Enthoven's special assistant), *How Much is Enough? Shaping the Defense Program, 1961–1969* (New York: Harper and Row, 1971), p. 296.

[6] A report from the CIA in January 1967 again concluded that bombing of the North had not significantly affected infiltration of men and supplies into the South or the morale or will of the North Vietnamese and their determination to continue the struggle. (*PP*, Gravel ed., vol. IV, pp. 136–140, from CIA SC No. 04442/67, "The Rolling Thunder Program—Present and Potential Target Systems," January 1967.) According to the report, although bombing had "disrupted normal military practices, caused the abandonment of many facilities, and forced the widespread dispersal of equipment . . . overall military capabilities had continued at a high level." "[T]he attacks had not eliminated any important sector of the NVN economy or the military establishment. They had not succeeded in cutting route capacities south of Hanoi to the point where the flow of supplies required in SVN was significantly impeded. The POL attacks had eliminated 76% of JCS-targeted storage capacity, but not until after NVN had implemented a system of dispersed storage, and the POL flow had been maintained at adequate levels. 32% of NVN's power-generating capacity had been put out of action, but the remaining capacity was adequate to supply most industrial consumers. Hundreds of bridges were knocked down, but virtually all of them had been quickly repaired, replaced, or bypassed, and traffic continued. Several thousand freight cars, trucks, barges, and other vehicles were also destroyed or damaged, but inventories were maintained through imports and there was no evidence of a serious transport problem due to equipment shortages. The railroad and highway networks were considerably expanded and improved during the year."

Continued

Moreover, North Vietnam had been able to take political advantage of U.S. bombing. "Together with its allies and supporters it has used the bombing to discredit the whole US effort in Vietnam."

The CIA memorandum also concluded that there was "no persuasive evidence at this time that a halt to the bombing would produce a Communist move for a truce and negotiations." Unless the Communists decided that a continuation of the war was not in their interest, the memorandum said, they would not negotiate. "Though they probably recognize that a decisive victory is not now in sight, they probably still hope that persistence in a protracted war will bring the U.S. to withdraw or consent to a settlement clearly advantageous to Hanoi."

Commenting more specifically on the "political struggle," the memorandum stated:

> The Communists lost ground in 1966 in terms of what they can offer the people. They are likely to lose even more ground in 1967. The development of a degree of stability in Saigon, the holding of elections, and the process of building national institutions began to provide the first credible political alternative since Diem. At the level of more particular and immediate concern to the villagers there was no decisive shift, but the strains on the VC apparatus and the pressure of US/ARVN military, pacification, civic action, and economic and construction programs were beginning to tell in particular areas, if not generally throughout South Vietnam. The VC have been driven increasingly to treat the population more harshly. Increased taxation, forced recruitment, and less selective acts of terrorism have hurt their image as defenders of the people. And association with the VC seems increasingly the wrong path to what the villagers want most of all—peace and security.
>
> The VC ability to defend villages against US/ARVN attacks has declined, and it has become increasingly likely that the presence of VC forces in a village will bring down a rain of bombs and gunfire. In contrast, in government-controlled areas schools are being built, medical assistance is available, economic activity is possible, there is a degree of immunity from bombings and battles, and the sheer weight of the resources available—trucks, earthmovers, airplanes—suggests that this may be the winning side. There are, of course, many shortcomings on the government side, including the pervasive threat of terrorism against those who go over or take active roles. Nevertheless, whole villages have moved to government areas, others have been "pacified," and recruits have been found among the people to take an active role in all the various phases of revolutionary development and pacification.

Despite these gains, the memorandum concluded, "the outlook for the political phase of the war is quite mixed. Progress in pacifica-

---

The only potentially effective bombing program, the report concluded, would be unlimited and "highly successful" attacks on transportation, including mining the harbors and waterways, and attacks on remaining targets. "If an unlimited interdiction program were highly successful, the regime would encounter increasing difficulty and cost in maintaining the flow of some of their most essential military and economic goods. In the long term the uncertainties and difficulties resulting from the cumulative effect of the air campaigns would probably cause Hanoi to undertake a basic reassessment of the probable course of the war and the extent of the regime's commitment to it."

tion and winning over the population is likely to come slowly and painfully. The Communists are going to wage the political battle as vigorously as the military contest. They will almost certainly allow one and probably two years to determine the success of their strategy in the next phase. But if the pacification program moves forward steadily, even if slowly, and Saigon continues to gain in stability, then the impact on Hanoi is likely to be far greater than any statistical measures of progress might suggest."

The CIA memorandum concluded with this statement:

> We conclude not only that the Communists are capable of fighting on for at least another year, but that they are probably determined to do so. In our view, however, they face important problems, and we believe that the Communist position, both militarily and politically in South Vietnam, will deteriorate further over the next year. Yet, Hanoi has a strong political incentive to keep the war going, especially until it has some clearer notion about the stability of the GVN, the US Presidential elections, and the possible impact of both on US policy.

On the military side, General Wheeler, after a trip to Vietnam, met with the President, Rusk, McNamara, Katzenbach, Vance, and Rostow from 2:42 p.m. to 4:25 p.m. on January 13, 1967, and assured the President that the Communists could "no longer hope to win militarily."[7]

After a five-day visit to South Vietnam in January 1967, General Taylor also praised the progress made by U.S. forces and recommended continued military pressure. He warned, however, as he had earlier, that the increased role for U.S. forces in pacification proposed by Westmoreland "could generate requirements for large increases in U.S. forces and, hence, needs to be carefully monitored. . . . RD [Revolutionary Development] is essentially a Vietnamese job and we will make a great mistake if we try to take it over."[8]

Each Side Assesses the Other's Strategy

In early January 1967, Westmoreland's staff prepared an assessment of the military situation and of enemy strategy which con-

---

[7] There are no known notes of the January 13 meeting, and Wheeler apparently did not make a written report. However, in a subsequent cable to Sharp and Westmoreland he reported that he had made that comment in the meeting. CMH, Westmoreland Papers, Message Files, Wheeler to Sharp and Westmoreland, JCS 1284–67, Feb. 17, 1967. In an NSC meeting on February 8, 1967, as noted above, Wheeler made similar comments.

By "winning," Wheeler explained in his cable that he meant "we could create a situation such that the North Vietnamese would be unable effectively to support the war in the South. At that point, the war would be essentially won, although much would remain to be accomplished in the revolutionary development field."

[8] Johnson Library, NSF, Files of Robert W. Komer, Taylor Memorandum for the Record "Vietnam Visit, January 20-25, 1967" attached to a letter from Taylor to the President, Jan. 30, 1967. See also Maxwell D. Taylor, *Swords and Plowshares* (New York: W. W. Norton, 1972), p. 375, and Taylor's "Comments on Vietnam, January 1, 1967," attached to a letter to the President on January 3 in which he again recommended that there should be a "searching analysis" of the added troop requirement that would result from Westmoreland's proposal to use U.S. forces in pacification. If no limits were set on the U.S. role, Taylor said, "Washington will continue to receive from Westmoreland repeated requests for troops which it may be hard to decline. If he is not given policy guidance, Westmoreland will be justified in assuming that his concepts for the employment of our troops are consistent with Washington policy." (A copy of this paper, which is in the Taylor Papers, National Defense University, was kindly provided by Gen. Douglas Kinnard.)

On January 31, Taylor attended a Tuesday Luncheon meeting from 2:20 p.m. to 3:20 p.m. with the President, Rusk, McNamara, Rostow, Komer and Press Secretary George Christian, at which his report of January 30 was discussed, but there are no known notes of that meeting.

cluded that, based on the principles of insurgency warfare and guided by the doctrine of "strategic mobility," the Communists would continue in 1967 to seek to attrit U.S. and South Vietnamese forces and to protract the war, by

(1) developing strong, multi-division forces in dispersed regions accessible to supplies and security;

(2) enticing US/FWMA [Free World Military Assistance—forces provided by other countries, primarily Korea, Australia and New Zealand] forces into prepared positions where dug-in communist forces may inflict heavy casualties upon them;

(3) conducting concurrent, intensified guerrilla and harassment pressure country-wide to tie down our forces, destroy small units, attack morale, and extend his control.[9]

The enemy, the assessment said, was capable of both main force and guerrilla operations, but because of U.S. offensive operations "he is avoiding major contact, fighting defensively when forced to do so, and attempting to rebuild and reinforce for winter-spring campaign operations." The assessment added, however, that there was no indication that the Communists were intending to "fragment" their main forces and "revert exclusively to guerrilla-type operations." Moreover, the capability to infiltrate from the North at a rate of about 8,400 men a month and to recruit about 3,500 men a month in the South, by which 42,000 new forces had been added in 1966—a buildup proportionate to that of U.S. and other allied forces—would enable the enemy to continue to inflict casualties, maintain and expand the insurgency base, and prolong the war.

The enemy, Westmoreland concluded, "is waging against us a conflict of strategic political attrition in which, according to his equation, victory equals time plus pressure. His main forces present a credible threat only as long as they exist, and he is not disposed to risk them prematurely, as he did against the French in 1951. Rather, he intends to wait until he thinks the time has come when their commitment will prove decisive."[10] "That point would be reached," Westmoreland said, in a comment that presaged what actually happened after the cease-fire in 1973, "if his war of political attrition forced U.S. withdrawal. The NLF infrastructure, supported by forces in country or conveniently located to launch counter-offensive (Phase III) operations against a dispirited RVNAF [Armed Forces of the Republic of Vietnam], then could emerge to take over the country."[11]

---

[9] CMH, Westmoreland Papers, Message Files, Westmoreland to Sharp and Wheeler, "Year-End Assessment of Enemy Situation and Enemy Strategy," MAC 00160, Jan. 2, 1967. There is also a copy of this cable in the Johnson Library, NSF Country File, Vietnam, and a summary in *PP*, Gravel ed., vol. IV, pp. 403–406. On Feb. 23, 1967, Westmoreland sent to Wheeler and Sharp another and similar "Assessment of the Enemy Situation," a copy of which is in the National Archives in the Westmoreland-CBS Papers, which concluded: "The enemy's strategy is a practical and clever one designed to continue a protracted war, inflict unacceptable casualties on our forces, establish a favorable political posture, minimize risks to main forces, and maintain the option of going on the military offensive or negotiating from a position of strength by virtue of his covert troop deployment." On March 20, an interagency (agencies in the U.S. Mission) "Assessment of the Enemy Situation," dated March 18, was presented to the Mission Council in Saigon. (National Archives, Westmoreland-CBS Papers.) The analysis and conclusions were quite similar to the February 23 assessment by MACV.

[10] CMH, Westmoreland Papers, Message Files, backchannel message from Westmoreland to Wheeler and Sharp, MAC 0030, Jan. 2, 1967.

[11] The Political Section of the U.S. Embassy in Saigon made a somewhat similar assessment of Communist strategy in January 1967, concluding that, "we believe the direction of Viet Cong military action, along with the necessary political adjustments, will be toward increasing reli-

Westmoreland pointed out that during 1966, the North Vietnamese had changed their strategy by sending major units into the demilitarized zone and into the area along the Cambodian border in the central highlands. One of the principal reasons for this move, he said, was "diverting Vietnamese and allied troops from the more populated areas. . . ."[12] And, indeed, as noted earlier, it had that effect. Beginning in the summer of 1966, a number of U.S. forces were shifted to the north and the border areas, and the U.S. Marines were ordered by Westmoreland to take up a defensive position at Khe Sanh, a remote outpost in Quang Tri province, at the northwestern tip of the country near the Laotian border.[13]

The Communists were also assessing U.S. strategy. During Operation CEDAR FALLS in January 1967, the U.S. Army recovered a number of Communist documents, including a long letter written in the spring of 1966 analyzing the political-military situation, assessing the strategy of the Americans, and providing guidance for Communist party cadre and military forces in the South.[14] "Our aim," the letter stated, "is to defeat the enemy at all costs." Communist forces "should not underestimate the mobility ability of U.S. troops as well as the superiority of their weapons, but should clearly realize that U.S. troops are not only strategically but also technically and tactically deadlocked because they are forced to fight the tactics of our people's war, and because under the present circumstances the southern people's armed forces have taken the initiative in their strategy. Accordingly, U.S. troops must passively cope with our attack and cannot fight in their own way." "[T]hose [Communist] forces can stand firm on the important strongholds which they have secured, relying on political strength, manpower, and resources of the locality to fight the enemy at any time, and

---

ance upon a highly developed guerrilla war of attrition, involving the relegation of main force units to a backseat position for the time being, and including more terrorism." U.S. Department of State, Central File, Pol 27 Viet S, Airgram from Saigon to Washington, A–367, Jan. 12, 1967.

[12] CMH, Westmoreland Papers, History File, "Highlights of 1966," Jan. 10, 1967.

[13] For the objections of the Marines to committing forces to Khe Sanh, which they did not think had any strategic significance, see General Krulak, *First to Fight,* cited above, pp. 207 ff. In *A Bright Shining Lie,* Sheehan (p. 641) discusses Krulak's dispute with Westmoreland, and quotes from a Krulak to Westmoreland cable in September 1966: "Our current actions in Quang Tri are probably agreeable to the North Vietnamese. I believe they are glad we have a battalion invested in the defense of Khe Sanh, and that we have five other [Marine] battalions operating in the inhospitable jungle which might otherwise be engaged in Revolutionary Development Support. . . ." According to Krulak (*First to Fight,* p. 208), "Westmoreland saw it all quite differently. To him, holding Khe Sanh was critical to monitoring enemy north-south movements, an effective block to enemy use in Route 9, a source of good intelligence, a western anchor to U.S. defense of the Demilitarized Zone, and a strategic jumping-off place should his dream of an expedition into Laos to cut the Ho Chi Minh Trail ever be realized. And he said that he saw Khe Sanh as offering an excellent opportunity to tie down and destroy thousands of enemy soldiers. Of all these reasons, I was sure that the last was the dominant one in Westmoreland's mind, representing his own conception of how to defeat the large North Vietnamese forces. As he saw it, firepower was the classic answer. . . ."

In *A Soldier Reports* (pp. 193 ff), Westmoreland explains why he shifted forces to the North and sent the Marines to Khe Sanh. For one thing he was concerned that prior to U.S. congressional elections in the fall of 1966, the Communists might attempt to gain a victory comparable to Dien Bien Phu in 1954, and thus "achieve a battlefield spectacular that might be used as a bargaining point at a future negotiating table and a psychological shock to the American people."

[14] There is an English translation of the letter in the Department of State, Central File, Pol 27 Viet S, Airgram 488, Mar. 7, 1967.

According to a CIA report in the spring of 1967, the letter was written by Le Duan, Secretary General of the Lao Dong (Communist) Party. (Johnson Library, NSF Memos to the President—Walt Rostow, Memorandum for the President from Rostow, Apr. 19, 1967, with undated text of a CIA Report "Viet Cong Status and Prospects—1966–67." As noted earlier, Le Duan was an advocate of an aggressive policy in the South.

can fight forever with enemy troops who outnumber them five or ten times, thereby putting the enemy on the constant defensive."

The gradual escalation of the war by the "U.S. imperialists," the letter said, "testifies to both their stubborn and bellicose nature and their weak, isolated and defensive position." "Escalating the war in such a disadvantageous position, the enemy cannot succeed in expanding the war on any scale at any time." If the U.S. should try to expand the war by using ground forces against the North and "to convert the present war into an ideological conflict," this would lengthen the period of time required to defeat the Americans, but Vietnamese Communist resources, supported by the "socialist bloc" and the Chinese, were inexhaustible. "At length, in war, whoever has the resources will win."

The letter stressed the importance of "restricting" the war to the South, where U.S. forces were "deadlocked" and unable to take the offensive because of the Communists "people's war" tactics, and where they could be kept on the defensive and defeated more easily and quickly.

Although forced to fight a protracted war because of the "superior strength" of the Americans, Communist forces should make "tremendous efforts . . . to obtain decisive victory within a relatively short period of time."

"Heavy emphasis," the letter concluded, "is to be placed on the political struggle which includes the diplomatic struggle, which is of prime importance."

Also captured during CEDAR FALLS were tapes of a long speech on "The 1966–1967 Winter-Spring Task."[15] According to the speaker, the Communists had begun to defeat the "limited war" being waged by the U.S. and the South Vietnamese. "Previously, only twenty three thousand advisors were bogged down, but now an entire army has been caught in the quicksand." These victories, the speaker said, had created a military and political dilemma for the Americans, who wanted to end the war quickly but were being deadlocked. If they did not increase their forces, they would be defeated. If they increased their forces, the Communists would do the same. "[W]e can defeat the Americans under whatever circumstances. . . . If the Americans bring in here as many as six hundred or seven hundred and fifty thousand men, they will encounter a region of conflicting conditions and problems. . . . We will mobilize thirty one million people from both South Vietnam and North Vietnam. Our armed forces in North Vietnam will grow stronger, our artillery will be more powerful. If the enemy invades North Vietnam, we will continue to concentrate forces in South Vietnam to fight him there. If our guerrilla warfare in the coming period can achieve what has been set forth by COSVN, the enemy will have to use five hundred of the seven hundred and fifty thousand men just to face our guerrillas. . . . Other countries are prepared to send us volunteers. . . . If China sends her volunteers . . . we may have five hundred thousand or one million men easily."

Deadlocked in South Vietnam, the U.S., the speaker said, was increasing its attacks on North Vietnam, but had escalated "almost

[15] CMH, Westmoreland Papers, MACJ 261, English translation of the speech, May 7, 1967.

to the top rung of the ladder. Now there is nothing but escalating to strike dikes, dams, and the cities of Hanoi and Haiphong."

"At home, the enemy's political situation is unstable whereas ours grows stronger from day to day. Internationally, the enemy is also politically on the defensive." "[I]t is a very arduous task for the Americans to fight a protracted war although they are well-to-do people. We can endure the hardships of a lengthy war but they are unable to endure the hardships of such a war because they are well-to-do people."

"[T]he Americans publicly say that they are determined to go on fighting. . . . They may be able to go on for a short period of time with their stubborn nature. If they intend to continue for five or ten years, they will learn that we are a terribly difficult lot to deal with."

"The Americans are falling into an unsolvable, self-contradictory position. They want to fight fast to avoid a protracted war but they have continuously sunk more and more deeply into a muddy marsh and thus have to endure protraction. That is why, even Johnson and Westmoreland dare not now speak of victory, especially quick victory. They dare not say the problem will be solved in the near future. Instead, they insist on the American people having to endure a prolonged war. But in reality they are afraid of protraction and only want to go fast. And the faster they try to go, the more deeply they sink. The more men they throw in, the more deeply they sink."

In a report on Communist plans for 1967, the CIA concluded that the party leadership made a "major strategic error" in early 1966, after the initial experience in fighting U.S. forces in the fall of 1965, in building up main force units and seeking to defeat Allied forces militarily.[16] "The military results envisaged by the build up of the Main Force units simply were not achieved. . . . The Party leadership now finds itself in a dilemma. Continuation of the present policy will lead to increasingly serious military defeats [with] disastrous political and morale effect upon the local Party structure throughout South Vietnam. On the other hand, a sharp change in strategy to either negotiations or a reversion to pure guerrilla warfare would be a tacit admission of failure by the Party leadership, and the local Party apparatus in South Vietnam may not be able to survive such a blow to its already-shaky morale." The Party would be forced, therefore, to place greater reliance on political action and guerrilla warfare in 1967, rather than on main forces, "in an effort to wear down and harass Allied units and counter Government of Vietnam pacification and political development."

Military Planning for 1967

Westmoreland's proposed plan of military operations for 1967 and his request for troops to carry it out, first submitted to the JCS by CINCPAC in June of 1966, provided for a "new concept" for Vietnam based on "containing" Communist forces in their "sanctuaries" in Laos, Cambodia and north of the demilitarized zone,

---

[16] CIA report on "Viet Cong Status and Prospects—1966–67," cited above.

thus preventing major assaults on U.S. forces in adjacent areas of South Vietnam and diversionary attacks further south.[17]

On November 4, 1966, the JCS submitted the final troop request for Vietnam for 1967 together with estimates for subsequent years. (For the end of 1967, the JCS requested 504,000, compared to the original JCS estimate of 542,000 in July, Westmoreland's 530,000 at the Manila Conference, and McNamara's recommendation of 470,000 in his report on his trip in October.) In their memorandum, the JCS endorsed the "new concept" of operations proposed by Westmoreland. When the President decided on November 11 to approve only 470,000 troops for 1967, Sharp, in a cable to Westmoreland on December 16 commenting on the need to find ways of dealing more effectively with infiltration "which are reasonably attainable," advised Westmoreland that, "The indications are that we must accomplish our present objectives within programmed force levels. . . ." Referring to possible deployment of U.S. forces in Laos or in North Vietnam, he added, "It appears unlikely that we can hope for any change in political policy to permit maneuvers of ground troops in the NVN or Laos."[18] Accordingly, in early January 1967, Westmoreland proposed a revised plan of operations for 1967 that provided for increased U.S. operations against Communist main force units and bases in South Vietnam, on the one hand, and guerrilla forces on the other (in conjunction with the South Vietnamese Army, which would be primarily responsible for counterguerrilla operations and local security), but did not provide for expanded operations against the sanctuaries.[19]

On January 3, 1967, citing "the cost of the effort required to establish credibility, and in light of stated national policy," Westmoreland told Sharp that two "cover and deception concepts" on which he had briefed Sharp in early December were not "practical at this time." One, FIRE BREAK, was an airborne operation against the Communists in the Panhandle of Laos, and the other, BLUE PAGE, was an amphibious landing threat ("feint") against the southern part of the coast of North Vietnam.[20]

On January 28, however, Westmoreland, possibly sensing that a shift in "political policy" was about to occur, resumed planning for operations in Laos and directed his staff to develop a "scenario" for additional U.S. military action to block infiltration. In the notes he

---

[17] *PP*, Gravel ed., vol. IV, p. 324. CMH, Westmoreland Papers, Message Files, MAC 41191, Sept. 13, 1966, MAC 41676, Sept. 16, and MAC 8212, Sept. 20, 1966.

Westmoreland proposed increased surveillance and interdiction of infiltration routes, including intensive operations in key target areas to be known as "slams," ("seek, locate, annihilate, and monitor.") "Once an area [of Laos] was designated as a slam it would be hit with B–52 and Tactical Air Strikes to neutralize it. This action would be followed by visual and air photo reconnaissance and/or ground reconnaissance patrols and, if appropriate, exploitation forces [Special Forces teams]. Upon their withdrawal they would leave mines and booby traps, and the Air Force would follow with air delivered land mines." In some instances, reconnaissance parties would remain at the scene. (MAC 41676.)

Another program being developed, Project POPEYE, which was tested in the fall of 1966, involved cloud seeding to increase rainfall in selected areas for the purpose of impeding truck traffic. (U.S. Department of State, Central File, Pol 27 Viet S, Washington to Vientiane 41012, Sept. 2, 1966, Vientiane to Washington 1318, Sept. 4, 1966, and 3623, Dec. 16, 1966.)

[18] CMH, Westmoreland Papers, Message Files, Sharp to Westmoreland 160150Z Dec. 1966.

[19] CMH, Westmoreland Papers, History File, Memorandum from Westmoreland to Sharp, "Strategy and Concept of Operations for 1967," no date, but a notation that it was sent in January 1967. Westmoreland said in this brief memorandum that the document on which his plans for 1967 were based, and from which the memorandum was derived, was the "Combined Campaign Plan, 1967" signed by the U.S. and South Vietnam on Nov. 7, 1966. See *PP*, Gravel ed., vol. IV, p. 379.

[20] CMH, Westmoreland Papers, Message Files, MAC 0050, Jan. 3, 1967.

kept in his history file he stated: "Having studied the situation in South Vietnam for some months, I am convinced that the Panhandle in Laos [the area in the vicinity of Tchepone, near the 17th parallel] must be cleared of enemy elements and secured before we can expect any stability in Southeast Asia. Little thought has been given to this solution by the State Department so I have decided to develop a scenario which could be presented and hopefully accepted."[21] The resulting plan, Operation DRAG HUNT, provided for deploying U.S. forces in the Laotian Panhandle by late 1968-early 1969. According to Col. Charles F. Brower's interpretation, "in 1967 ground operations in the Laotian Panhandle (that part of Laos south of the 18th Parallel, forming a corridor between Thailand and the narrow waist of Vietnam), to interdict infiltration down the Ho Chi Minh Trail and isolate the battlefield in South Vietnam increasingly seemed the strategic key to Westmoreland." Although the idea of using U.S. forces for interdiction in Laos had been considered for some time, it was in early 1967, "as Westmoreland's misgivings about the attrition in Laos strategy grew," and as public opposition to the war rose and McNamara and his associates became increasingly critical of attrition, that such operations "assumed greater strategic significance."[22]

Westmoreland, Brower says, began in January 1967 "to stimulate a [strategic] reassessment" and to formulate an "alternate strategy." Rather than a strategy of attrition, the objective of which was to destroy Communist forces in South Vietnam, the alternate strategy would be based on "convincing Hanoi, through the isolation of the battlefield by ground operations in Laos and North Vietnam [through an "amphibious hook" into the southern part of North Vietnam], that it could not win." "Throughout much of 1967," Brower says, "Westmoreland's consistently grim assessments about the pace of North Vietnamese infiltration and the length of the war, his development of logistics and fire support bases in South Vietnam opposite the Laotian panhandle, his pressure on Saigon both to mobilize its manpower more expeditiously and to seek approval for South Vietnamese ground operations into Laos, and his own request for a substantial increase in American troops, all evidenced a systematic effort on his part to stimulate such a recommendation and to secure the adoption of his alternate strategy."

Gen. Bruce Palmer says that "Westmoreland from the beginning had considered operations in the Laotian Panhandle and against enemy bases along the Cambodian border. What prevented any serious consideration of such a course of action, however, was the unalterable opposition of Averell Harriman, who negotiated the Geneva Accords of 1962 designed to neutralize Laos, but would never admit that the Accords were essentially a fraud. Although the United States respected the agreement, Hanoi did not, refusing to withdraw its North Vietnamese forces from Laos as agreed; instead escalating its political and military actions against the Laotian Government. As a result, the 'secret war' in Laos continued. Harriman, however, succeeded in preserving the figment of neutrality

---

[21] CMH, Westmoreland Papers, History File.

[22] Col. Charles F. Brower, IV, "Strategic Reassessment in Vietnam: The Westmoreland 'Alternate Strategy' of 1967–1968," *Naval War College Review*, 44 (Spring 1991), pp. 20–51.

with respect to Laos and blocked any proposals to operate openly in Laos with U.S. and allied forces. This was, in my view a tragic mistake."[23]

Palmer adds that by 1967, it was too late for a Laotian Panhandle strategy. "The feasible time was in 1966 while the US troop and logistic buildup was underway and before US and allied troop stationing and base construction were set in concrete."[24]

The military also continued efforts to get the State Department to relax restrictions on and to augment covert cross-border operations into Laos, particularly to extend the zone of operations of SHINING BRASS—reconnaissance teams operating across the South Vietnamese border into Laos—from the existing 5 kilometers to 20 or 30 kilometers, as well as relaxing other restrictions on ground and air operations. The State Department, while opposed to the extension of the zone for SHINING BRASS, said it was willing to consider relaxing several other restrictions.[25]

With respect to Cambodia, which the Communists were using as a route for infiltrated supplies and for bases and as a refuge for troops, it had been agreed at a meeting in November 1966 of U.S. Ambassadors and military officials from Southeast Asia—SEACOORD—that further steps should be taken to control the increasing use by the Communists of Cambodian territory.[26] A few days later, Deputy Secretary of Defense Vance wrote to Under Secretary of State Katzenbach suggesting the establishment of a State-Defense-CIA group, chaired by State, to study the Cambodian problem, which Vance said was of "deep concern" to the JCS.[27]

In a message to the JCS on January 25, 1967, Admiral Sharp reemphasized the need to block infiltration from Cambodia: "The importance of Cambodia as sanctuary and as a source of supplies, particularly rice, cannot be overemphasized." If nonmilitary pressures on the Cambodian Government did not produce the desired results, Sharp said, "then we must be prepared in all respects to use the necessary degree of force to attain our objectives."[28] The JCS agreed, but a Special National Intelligence Estimate, "Signifi-

---

[23] Letter to the author from Gen. Bruce B. Palmer, Jr., Dec. 6, 1993. See also Palmer, *The 25-Year War*, pp. 11–12.

[24] Letter to the author, Dec. 6, 1993. For further comments on Westmoreland's Laotian Panhandle strategy and on Brower's analysis, see pt. V of this study, forthcoming.

[25] See CMH, Westmoreland Papers, Message Files, Westmoreland to Sharp, MAC 11222, Dec. 25, 1966, and MACV 1567, Feb. 14, 1967, and State Department Central File, Pol 27 Viet S, Washington to Vientiane 131711, Feb. 4, 1967.

[26] See Saigon to Washington 10958, November 1966. In response, the State Department said, in part, "our desire to avoid an expansion of the war in Vietnam remains a basic consideration in our policy in SEA [Southeast Asia]. Actions which threaten to bring such an expansion into Cambodia or elsewhere would raise misunderstanding as to our intentions and weaken base of national and international support for our effort in SEA.

"We recognize the problems created by VC use of Cambodian territory and the need to protect the safety of our forces fighting in South Vietnam. Problem remains to be certain that remedial action does not involve us in greater problems and dangers than those which it is intended to correct. We continue [to] believe that best means of achieving our objectives in Cambodia, including a reduction in VC/NVA use of Cambodian territory, is through political and diplomatic efforts . . . actions which push Sihanouk into a close collaboration with the Communists would make it far easier than at present for VC/NVN forces to use the extensive and well-adapted Cambodian territory for base areas, for refuge, for training and for infiltration of men and supplies into South Vietnam. Resulting demands on U.S. and allied military forces to cope with the situation would thus be correspondingly greater." State Department, Central File, Pol 27 Viet S, Washington to Saigon 89498, Nov. 22, 1966.

[27] U.S. Department of State, Central File, Pol 27 Viet S, Letter from Vance to Katzenbach, no date, but apparently sent in early December 1966, and reply from Foy Kohler to Vance, Dec. 13, 1966.

[28] *PP*, Gravel ed., vol. IV, p. 417, from CINCPAC to the JCS 252126Z Jan. 1967.

cance of Cambodia to Vietnamese Communist War Effort," concluded that while it would be more difficult for the Communists to function without a sanctuary in Cambodia, "it would not constitute a decisive element in their ability to conduct military operations in South Vietnam."[29]

In March 1967, the State-Defense-CIA Cambodia study group chaired by Unger completed an initial report on the proposals advanced by the JCS.[30] "[O]ur efforts to deal with this problem," the report said, "should continue to be primarily in the political sphere and should be on a priority basis. Provocative actions which would seriously prejudice the success of such efforts and threaten to expand the conflict into Cambodia should be avoided. However, those actions which are clearly required in terms of self-defense of our forces in South Vietnam "should continue to be authorized as necessary."

Although it was difficult to measure the benefits to the Communists of being able to use Cambodian territory for sanctuary and supplies, there was general agreement that such usage provided a "considerable advantage." Some steps had been taken by Cambodia to address the problem but, according to the report, Sihanouk was more concerned about keeping the war from spreading into Cambodia; thus, the need for preserving the country's neutrality and defending its interests against the Vietnamese and Thais:

> Over the past few years Sihanouk, while continuing to assert his country's neutral status, has led Cambodia into a progressively closer relationship with Communist China and given vigorous public support to the Communist position in Vietnam. The basic and continuing motivation behind Sihanouk's foreign policy has been to secure reassurance for Cambodia's future, which he believed to be endangered more by the historical threat of Thai and Vietnamese territorial encroachments than by Communist ambitions.

Noting that in May 1965 Cambodia had broken diplomatic relations with the U.S., the report explained that this stemmed from U.S. relations with the traditional enemies—Vietnam and Thailand, incidents on the Cambodian border involving U.S. and South Vietnamese forces, and Sihanouk's irritation with the U.S. over other factors. The U.S. had sought to repair the break, but while there were some signs of a possible reconciliation, the impasse continued.

In 1966, in response to requests from Westmoreland, U.S. forces had been authorized to undertake limited covert operations in Cambodia, including some pursuit of Communist forces across the border, aerial reconnaissance and photography, and clandestine intelligence operations on the ground. In its report, the Cambodia study group, while taking the position that "the best course available to us is to intensify efforts to bring about an improvement in relations with Cambodia and get its cooperation in reducing VC/NVA ability to use Cambodia," and approving new efforts to open discussions with Cambodia, also approved an expansion of the ex-

[29] *Ibid.*, p. 414, from SNIE 57–67, Jan. 26, 1967.

[30] U.S. Department of State, Central File, Pol 27 Viet S, "Initial Report of Joint State DOD/CIA Study Group on Cambodia," no authorship or date, but "3/67" was written by hand on the cover page.

isting covert programs for aerial photography and psychological operations, but denied the request to expand the authorization for immediate pursuit of Communist forces across the border, and approved only a very limited operation involving intelligence gathering by small teams (each consisting of 3 U.S. Special Forces and 8 South Vietnamese), code-named DANIEL BOONE.[31]

While continuing to press for more troops and operating authority for the ground war in the South, the military also advocated an intensification of the air war against the North. On January 14 and 18, 1967, CINCPAC submitted to the JCS a proposal for striking new targets, the goal of which would be to destroy the military and industrial base around Hanoi and Haiphong, including most of the power plants in the area.[32] On February 1, CINCPAC proposed mining North Vietnamese ports. On February 2, the JCS proposed instead the mining of certain rivers and coastal areas of North Vietnam.[33]

Westmoreland, supported by Sharp and generally by the JCS, also continued to resist McNamara's "barrier" plan for controlling infiltration. In order to forestall McNamara's plan, Westmoreland began developing a plan of his own by which only a small part of a barrier, in the east near the coast, would be constructed (this was also the area where the U.S. Marines had major military responsibility, and by assigning the project primarily to the Marines it was possible to minimize the commitment of Army units).[34] In the western portion, along the DMZ in the area of Khe Sanh and extending across the Laotian Panhandle, Westmoreland proposed "selective interdiction" by bombing—rather than ground troops—using the program already established (TIGER HOUND).

In a memorandum to McNamara on December 1, 1966, the JCS again recommended that the barrier not be constructed.[35] The forces required for the barrier, the JCS said, could not be allocated from those forces already authorized for Vietnam "without jeopardizing on-going programs and revising fundamental strategy for SE Asia," and if other U.S. forces from Europe or the continental United States were brought in it would not be possible to meet McNamara's deadline of September 1967 for making the barrier operational. Moreover, there was not enough time to test the technical and operational feasibility of the plan.

McNamara did not respond to the JCS recommendations except to indicate, as he had in the meeting in Saigon in November, that

---

[31] In his letter on May 9 to Vance transmitting the initial report of the Cambodian study group (same location), Katzenbach stated that he had approved the initial report. He also urged the Department of Defense to approve the limited DANIEL BOONE operation, saying "I understand that the initiation of these operations is being pressed by MACV and CINCPAC as a matter of military urgency."

[32] *PP*, Gravel ed., vol. IV, p. 139, from CINCPAC to the JCS 142140Z and 182210Z, January 1967. On January 25, in 252126Z, CINCPAC again urged attacks on Haiphong and an intensification of ROLLING THUNDER.

By 1967, the "94-target" list of 1965 had increased to 244 active and 265 contingency targets. Gen. William W. Momyer (U.S. Air Force, Ret.), *Air Power in Three Wars* (Washington, D.C.: U.S. Govt. Print. Off., for the Dept. of the Air Force, 1978), p. 15.

[33] *PP*, Gravel ed., vol. IV, pp. 144–145, 415, from CINCPAC to the JCS 012005Z, January 1967, and JCS 59–67, Feb. 2, 1967.

[34] The Marines objected vigorously to the barrier and the strong point obstacle system and to being assigned the principal role in the construction and operation of either system. See Maj. Gary L. Telfer, Lt. Col. Lane Rogers, and V. Keith Fleming, Jr., *U.S. Marines in Vietnam, Fighting the North Vietnamese, 1967,* Marine Corps Vietnamese Operational Histories Series (Washington, D.C.: History and Museums Division, Headquarters, U.S. Marine Corps, 1984), p. 87.

[35] CMH, Westmoreland Papers, Message Files, JCSM 740–66, Dec. 1, 1966.

he would be amenable to a modification of the original concept of the barrier. Accordingly, on January 26, 1967, Westmoreland submitted his plan for establishing a strong point obstacle system along 30 kilometers of the eastern end, followed by the extension of the system to the western end if there were adequate forces to do so at a later date.[36] In mid-March, McNamara approved Westmoreland's proposal.[37]

While seeking authorization to expand U.S. military operations in the border areas of South Vietnam, Westmoreland had become increasingly concerned about the situation in IV Corps, the delta south of Saigon, where three South Vietnamese divisions with the help of U.S. military advisers had been responsible for security in a region long dominated by the Communists. Conditions had not improved, and Westmoreland and his associates concluded in 1966 that U.S. forces were needed. The State Department resisted, but finally agreed to a limited deployment to determine if U.S. forces could be used effectively. In a combined operation (Operation DECKHOUSE V), two battalions of South Vietnamese Marines, reinforced by one U.S. Marine battalion landing team (about 1,350 men) and supported by U.S. helicopters, landed on January 7, 1967, on the coast of one of the delta provinces.[38] They spent a week vainly trying to find the Communists who had been reported to be there before the invasion occurred, but who apparently had received advance warning and avoided contact, resorting instead to sniping and harassment.[39]

Despite the results of DECKHOUSE V, the plan to use U.S. forces continued to be implemented, and the 9th Infantry Division was sent into the delta early in 1967.

These moves produced a "storm of criticism," according to the *Pentagon Papers,* from those who were concerned that the U.S. was assuming too much responsibility for the war, especially in areas like the delta where the war was primarily one of small-scale guerrilla activity, and where South Vietnamese forces had primary responsibility.[40] In a hearing before a joint meeting of the Senate Armed Services Committee and the Defense Subcommittee of the Senate Appropriations Committee during the last week in January 1967, several members of the committee who had been stalwart supporters of the war pointed out that administration spokesmen had previously stated that the delta could be adequately protected by the South Vietnamese, and questioned why it was necessary to

[36] MACV, "PRACTICE NINE Requirements Plan," transmitted to McNamara by JCSM–97–67, Feb. 22, 1967. Wheeler, while agreeing with Westmoreland's modified plan, said that it would be advantageous to proceed with building the barrier. See his argument in *PP,* Gravel ed., vol. IV, p. 414, from CM–2134–67, Feb. 22, 1967.

[37] U.S. Department of State, Central File, Pol 27 Viet S, Washington to Saigon 156207, Mar. 16, 1967. See also General Starbird's Fact Sheet "Practice Nine," Mar. 15, 1967, prepared for McNamara. (same location) In a briefing paper prepared for the Guam Conference, "Optimum U.S. Force Level in SVN," Mar. 16, 1967, the Defense Department's Systems Analysis Office estimated that the first phase of PRACTICE NINE (the eastern end) would require 7,700 additional U.S. troops, and that if the system were fully implemented a total of 40,000 would be required. (This memorandum is also in Pol 27 Viet S.)

[38] For a joint Embassy/COMUSMACV message to Washington discussing the proposed use of U.S. forces in the delta, see Department of State, Central File, Pol 27 Viet S, Saigon to Washington 6696, Sept. 23, 1966. For Lodge's own views see 6837, Sept. 24 and 11978, Nov. 29. For Westmoreland's reply to Lodge, see 14308, Dec. 27. See also Westmoreland, *A Soldier Reports,* pp. 207–209.

[39] See Telfer, et. al., *U.S. Marines in Vietnam, 1967,* p. 151.

[40] *PP,* Gravel ed., vol. IV, p. 384.

use U.S. forces. The response from Army Chief of Staff Gen. Harold Johnson was that the area was too large for the South Vietnamese to handle alone. He agreed, however, that there were serious problems connected with using U.S. forces and firepower in an area containing 70 percent of the total population of South Vietnam, where the Communists were so strong that it was very difficult to distinguish friend from foe or to avoid civilian casualties. Although control of the population in the delta could be expanded by using U.S. forces, he said, "maintaining that control results in the type of thing that occurred a couple of nights ago when civilian fleeing the Vietcong occupation of their villages were taken under fire by our forces. We are dealing with a very simple people who have never been very far away from their homes, and they just don't understand a lot of this."[41]

"I don't think you can pacify the villages with white people," Senator Symington said.

Symington again criticized the cost of the war: "We need billions more dollars, tens of thousands more men, but don't know precisely where we are going or what we are getting. . . . The people of Missouri are getting restless about the costs, as against the accomplishments, of this war."[42]

January-February 1967: Operations CEDAR FALLS and JUNCTION CITY

While recognizing that the strategy of the Communists was to attrit U.S. and South Vietnamese forces and to prolong the war, the U.S. continued to rely primarily on a strategy of attrition based on large search-and-destroy missions, combined with the use of airpower (Navy and Air Force) against North Vietnam. Despite the growing evidence that large unit operations were not accomplishing their intended goal (and arguments from within the Army—the PROVN report—and from the Marines that in important respects they were counterproductive), and evidence that the air war, as it was being conducted, was unsuccessful, the U.S. launched a series of large-scale search and destroy missions in 1967 and greatly in-

---

[41] U.S. Congress, Senate, Committee on Armed Services, *Military Procurement Authorizations for Fiscal Year 1968* (Washington, D.C.: U.S. Govt. Print. Off., 1967), p. 579.

[42] *Ibid.*, p. 597. In the same hearing, Senator Russell, who was chairman of both the Armed Services Committee and the Defense Appropriations Subcommittee, again expressed his concern about authorizing the means by which the U.S. could more easily and effectively intervene militarily in other countries. *Ibid.*, pp. 360–361. The issue was a proposal for five more Fast Deployment Logistics Ships (FDLs)—two had been authorized and funded by Congress in 1966—by which the U.S. could "preposition" heavy equipment as well as supplies in areas where U.S. forces might be deployed, thus, along with rapid airlift of troops by C–5A aircraft, facilitating a more rapid and effective response. Russell said: "I was enthusiastic about this concept when the plan was first laid before the committee, but I have seen some things recently that cause me to have grave misgivings about it. It seems to me this will increase the dependence of all of our allies all over the world on the United States to straighten out anything that goes wrong anywhere, and also to enforce all of the views of the United Nations.

"I have supported prepositioning. I can see where it would be very helpful in a conflict between the United States and another power. But when I read an article in a reputable British newspaper, after the gallant efforts to declare Rhodesia a threat to world peace and to vote sanctions against her, that the United States would have to enforce any sanction on South Africa and Rhodesia, it chilled my enthusiasm for these ships. If we build anything like this, we are just going to be handed more and more of this business of fighting everybody's wars everywhere."

Russell added that he was fearful the U.S. would end up sending three or four divisions to Rhodesia which could result in having "another pretty goodsized Vietnam on our hands." "[T]he building of these ships is a very decided step in that direction in my opinion."

General Wheeler replied that "the dependence of many of our allies for American military action in contingencies will continue whether we have the means to respond or not."

creased the bombing of North Vietnam. "[A]s the Communists moved away from big-unit operations," Krepinevich observes, "the Americans emphasized them all the more. . . . MACV failed to adopt a strategy to exploit the potential weaknesses of the People's War strategy, and instead adopted a strategy congruent with its emphasis on conventional military operations. In so doing, MACV accelerated the dissipation of US public support for the war effort, and failed to defeat either the internal or the external threats to South Vietnam."[43]

Lodge, who had privately told McNamara and the President in the summer of 1965 and again in the fall of 1966 of his doubts about search-and-destroy missions, was so strongly opposed to attrition strategy that he contemplated resigning in the spring of 1967 and making a public statement of his opposition.[44]

Again it should be noted, however, that according to Westmoreland and other military officials they had no choice; that because of political decisions which had placed limits and restrictions on military operations, they were left with having to resort to a strategy of attrition.

On January 9, 1967, U.S. forces launched the largest search-and-destroy mission of the war, Operation CEDAR FALLS, against a Communist stronghold about 20 miles north of Saigon in the so-called "Iron Triangle." The results of CEDAR FALLS were hailed by American military and political leaders. Major General DePuy, then the commander of the "Big Red One," the U.S. First Infantry Division, who had previously served as Westmoreland's chief operations officer (J–3) and strategist, said in a personal "Dear Joe" letter to columnist Joseph Alsop on January 24, 1967: "We have just concluded an operation [CEDAR FALLS] which I believe represents THE turning point in the war."[45] (emphasis in original) In his official report on the operation, DePuy, whose division was the principal military unit involved, called it "a blow from which the VC in this area may never recover."[46]

President Johnson said in his memoirs that after Operation CEDAR FALLS, "This once 'safe' area would never be safe again for the Viet Cong."[47]

The objectives of CEDAR FALLS were to "destroy enemy forces, infrastructure, installation, and Military Region IV headquarters" (the Communist headquarters in the region, from which activities in the area, including Saigon, were said to be directed); to evacuate the populace, and, by removing the people, to turn the Iron Triangle into a "free-fire zone," then called "specified strike zone" or

---

[43] Krepinevich, "Vietnam: Evaluating the Ground War, 1965–1968," cited above.

[44] Massachusetts Historical Society, Lodge Papers, Draft of "Vietnam Memoir," pt. I, p. 4.

[45] DePuy papers, Military History Institute, quoted in *The Strategic Lessons Learned in Vietnam,* a study prepared in 1979–80 for the Strategic Studies Institute of the U.S. Army by the BDM Corporation, vol. VI, book 1, pp. 3–37. According to Gen. Douglas Kinnard, "DePuy was convinced in the early days of United States troop involvement in Vietnam that the answer was the massive deployment of United States troops. If Westmoreland needed any convincing, DePuy was there to provide it. Inclined toward introspection, he told me after the war had ended that he had not been perspicacious enough in those days. We should, he said, have thought through the military problem better." Kinnard, *The War Managers,* pp. 40–41. See also DePuy's comments in pt. III of this study, p. 455.

[46] See Bernard William Rogers, *Cedar Falls—Junction City: A Turning Point,* Department of the Army Vietnam Studies (Washington, D.C.: U.S. Govt. Print. Off., 1974), p. 78. See also the discussion in Sharp and Westmoreland's *Report on the War in Vietnam,* pp. 133–134, 137–138.

[47] Johnson, *The Vantage Point,* p. 258.

SSZ, where U.S. commanders could order unrestricted bombing and indiscriminate, unobserved artillery fire—so-called "harassment and interdiction fire" (H and I). The destruction of the headquarters, according to an official history of the operation, was the principal objective.[48]

Although elaborate precautions were taken to achieve complete surprise, there was only light resistance. The Communists had learned of the attack and had moved their main force units from the area.[49]

The populace was evacuated, and 5,987 refugees (582 men, 1,651 women, and 3,754 children) were taken to a relocation center just outside the Iron Triangle. Most of these came from Ben Suc, the principal town in the area, and reportedly the site of the Communist's Military Region IV Headquarters. The following description of the evacuation of Ben Suc and nearby villages is from a history of the operation written by Gen. Bernard W. Rogers, then the assistant commander of the First Infantry Division:[50]

> It was to be expected that uprooting the natives of these villages would evoke resentment, and it did. They had lived under and with the Viet Cong and had supported them for the past three years [since South Vietnamese forces had abandoned the area]; nor was it easy for the natives to give up their homes and the land they had been working. The villagers were permitted to take with them anything they could carry, pull, or herd, to include their water buffalo. What they could not take was retrieved by the U.S. and South Vietnamese troops and returned to the natives at the relocation center. . . .
>
> As the villagers and their belongings moved out, bulldozers, tankdozers, and demolition teams moved in. . . . The bulldozers moved through the former Viet Cong stronghold and razed the structures to the ground, crushing ruins, collapsing tunnels, and obliterating bunkers and underground storage rooms. . . . A large cavity was scooped out near the center of the area . . . filled with ten thousand pounds of explosives . . . covered, tamped, and then set off by a chemical fuze. . . . The hope was that the blast might crush any undiscovered tunnels in the village.
>
> One of the major objectives of Operation CEDAR FALLS had been achieved: the village of Ben Suc no longer existed.[51]

---

[48] Rogers, *Cedar Falls—Junction City,* p. 19. On Jan. 24, 1967, General Wheeler, Chairman of the JCS, told the Senate Armed Services Committee that the objective of CEDAR FALLS was "to ferret out all of the caves, all of the tunnels, all of the underground supply installations . . . the intent is to destroy the [Communist facilities in the Iron Triangle] once and for all." U.S. Congress, Senate, Committee on Armed Services and the Subcommittee on Department of Defense of the Committee on Appropriations, *Supplemental Military Procurement and Construction Authorization, Fiscal Year 1967,* Hearings on S. 665, 90th Cong., 1st sess. (Washington, D.C.: U.S. Govt. Print. Off., 1967), pp. 169–170.

[49] Tom Mangold and John Penycate, *The Tunnels of Cu Chi* (New York: Random House, 1985), p. 166. There were 750 confirmed enemy dead, compared to 72 Americans, and an estimated 540 Communists surrendered to join the Chieu Hoi amnesty program. Rogers, *Cedar Falls—Junction City, p. 74.*

[50] Rogers, *Cedar Falls—Junction City,* pp. 39, 40–41.

[51] For an account of the Ben Suc operation, see Jonathan Schell, *The Village of Ben Suc* (New York: Knopf, 1967). Also of interest is Schell's account of a similar operation late in 1967: *The Military Half: An Account of Destruction in Quang Ngai and Quang Tin* (New York: Knopf, 1968). In late 1967, the U.S. Mission in Saigon submitted to Washington a detailed report on Schell's allegations about the effects on civilians of military operations. U.S. Department of State, Central File, Pol 27 Viet S, Saigon 715, Dec. 30, 1967.

In addition to destroying Ben Suc and other villages, U.S. Army Engineers completely cleared a large area in the Iron Triangle in order to make it easier to detect Communist military activity and to conduct bombing and shelling.

CEDAR FALLS was followed in late February 1967 by Operation JUNCTION CITY, an even larger search-and-destroy mission in an area northwest of Saigon extending from the Iron Triangle to the Cambodian border, where the Communists were also well-entrenched, and where it was thought they had their main headquarters in South Vietnam, the Central Office of South Vietnam, or COSVN. The principal objectives of JUNCTION CITY were to "eradicate" COSVN as well as other supporting facilities, to engage enemy main forces, and to construct airfields and other facilities that U.S. forces could use in the future. When JUNCTION CITY ended in mid-May 1967, its results, like those of CEDAR FALLS, were acclaimed by U.S. military authorities. According to General Rogers:[52]

> Disruption of the headquarters of the Central Office of South Vietnam caused its forces to withdraw to Cambodia and affected its control over Viet Cong activity. Coupled with the loss of large quantities of important documents and the destruction of many important installations and communication networks, this disruption led to a reversal in planning and control during this period and for some time to come. But probably one of the most far-reaching effects of all upon the enemy was the realization that his bases, even in the outer reaches of War Zone C [the area involved in JUNCTION CITY] were no longer havens.

Once again, however, as in the case of CEDAR FALLS, "All objectives were accomplished in considerable degree with the exception of the destruction of COSVN forces."[53] Communist troops again evaded U.S. forces, while continuously harassing them with guerrilla type actions. According to General Rogers, "It was a sheer physical impossibility to keep him [the enemy soldier] from slipping away whenever he wished if he were in terrain with which he was familiar—generally the case. The jungle is usually just too thick and too widespread to hope ever to keep him from getting away; thus the option to fight was usually his." "We also found it very difficult," General Rogers added, "to prevent him from mining the roads at night. The routes were just too extensive for the number of troops available. We could not expect our men to outpost the roads all night and beat the jungle on search and destroy all day."[54]

Soon after U.S. forces completed their CEDAR FALLS and JUNCTION CITY missions and withdrew, the Communists re-

---

[52] Rogers, *Cedar Falls—Junction City,* p. 151. Official figures showed 1,776 enemy dead, compared to 282 U.S. A number of facilities were destroyed and a quantity of supplies was captured.

[53] *Ibid.,* p. 152. According to Krepinevich, *The Army and Vietnam,* p. 191, "the operation [JUNCTION CITY] was anything but a success. The target, the 9th VC Division, was not rendered ineffective, and with one exception, the only significant engagements were those initiated by the VC."

[54] Rogers, *Cedar Falls—Junction City,* p. 157.

turned, and in his history of the two missions General Rogers said:[55]

> One of the most discouraging features of both CEDAR FALLS and JUNCTION CITY was the fact that we had insufficient forces, either U.S. or South Vietnamese, to permit us to continue to operate in the Iron Triangle and War Zone C and thereby prevent the Viet Cong from returning. In neither instance were we able to stay around, and it was not long before there was evidence of the enemy's return. Only two days after the termination of CEDAR FALLS, I was checking out the Iron Triangle by helicopter and saw many persons who appeared to be Viet Cong riding bicycles or wandering around on foot. . . . During the cease-fire for Tet, 8–12 February [1967], the Iron Triangle was again literally crawling with what appeared to be Viet Cong.

Some villagers returned home despite the danger of doing so. According to Westmoreland's official report on the war, "As in the earlier Strategic Hamlet Program under the Diem government, the separation of a rural people from their ancestral lands caused fear and resentment. Their usual reaction is to attempt to slip back as soon as the opportunity arises. Notwithstanding the efforts of the government to care for these unfortunate victims of the prolonged war, this pattern was repeated at Ben Suc. . . ."[56]

Within a short time, the jungle undergrowth had also returned, even in areas where the U.S. Army Engineers had used huge "Rome Plows" to dig up the terrain. General Rogers commented: "the discouraging aspect of such operations is that it takes but a short time for the jungle to grow again. . . . Once the jungle has been cut, some system must be devised to keep it from growing back; otherwise it must be cut again and again."[57]

Some years later, Gen. Bruce Palmer, who commanded the Field Force II which carried out JUNCTION CITY, appraised this and other large search and destroy missions. Referring specifically to JUNCTION CITY and to a smaller operation, MANHATTEN, he said that they had "mixed results." On the one hand they disrupted enemy bases and demonstrated that no base area was secure from U.S. troops. On the other hand, Palmer said, "these large operations were of questionable utility, for they involved large numbers of troops, only a few of whom were actually engaged in combat, and they consumed large amounts of U.S. resources." Moreover, "Vast, heavily vegetated areas were involved, and it was simply not feasible to seal them off, search them completely, and police them permanently. . . . It was also very apparent that the war was a small unit affair, mostly of rifle companies and battalions."[58]

As a result of bombing and H and I artillery fire, together with operations like CEDAR FALLS and JUNCTION CITY, the number of South Vietnamese refugees more than doubled during 1967.[59]

---

[55] *Ibid.*, p. 158. See also the discussion by military analyst Dave Richard Palmer, *Summons of the Trumpet*, ch. 16, and Mangold and Penycate, *The Tunnels of Cu Chi*, ch. 14.

[56] Admiral Sharp and General Westmoreland, *Report on the War in Vietnam*, p. 149, cited above.

[57] Rogers, *Cedar Falls—Junction City*, p. 155.

[58] Palmer, *The 25-Year War*, cited above, p. 60.

[59] There was considerable criticism within the Army of the practice of H and I fire. It will be recalled that the Army's PROVN Report in the spring of 1966 emphasized "as a cardinal

Even though some refugees ignored the authorities and returned to their villages, the estimated total of half a million refugees climbed to over one million, and may have reached two million, by the end of the year.[60]

On January 20, 1967, just after the conclusion of CEDAR FALLS, Senator Edward Kennedy, chairman of the Subcommittee to Investigate Problems Connected with Refugees and Escapees of the Senate Judiciary Committee, met with Richard Holbrooke, then on the NSC staff, to discuss the effects of the operation. Holbrooke assured him that "harsh as Cedar Falls might appear in the United States, it was the only way to deal with the problem." He also told Kennedy that, despite the slow improvement in pacification, "we have made real progress in the last 18 months."[61]

U.S. military authorities generally took the position that the displacement of population was an asset to military operations, first, in depriving the enemy of recruits and assistance, and, second, by

---

principle" the need to engage in "selective warfare . . . to avoid elimination of the population through universe application of military force," and proposed a set of rules that included "no unobserved [H and I] artillery fire in populated areas. . . ." Army Chief of Staff Harold Johnson, who had initiated the PROVN study, said in a later interview that in late 1965 and 1966, "far too much of our own artillery fire in Vietnam was unobserved fire." "[W]e got into a firepower war over there, where firepower was not really effective. Ammunition costs were simply astronomical, and when we first began to examine where our artillery ammunition went, we found something in the neighborhood of 85% of it was unobserved fire, which was a rather staggering volume. I don't know what good it was doing." Noting that controls on unobserved H and I were subsequently ordered, he said that this "indiscriminate application of firepower . . . was not compatible . . . with respect to being people-oriented. . . . If we were really oriented after people we should have been discriminating against those people that we were after and not against all people. I think we sort of devastated the countryside." "The alternative," Johnson added, "is that you control closely all of your supporting fires, direct and indirect, and that your indirect fire particularly, would be used very sparingly." Interview with General Johnson, 1973, Senior Officer Oral History Program, U.S. Army Military History Institute, Carlisle Barracks, Pa. See also the Military History Institute's interview with Lt. Gen. Arthur S. Collins, Jr., who was assistant deputy chief of staff for Military Operations (under General Palmer) in 1964–1965, and later served in Vietnam as commander of the 4th Infantry Division and then of the 1st Field Force, for his description of his own experience in reducing H and I fire. "[W]e don't defeat the enemy tactically," he said. "We tend to overpower them. In Vietnam we carried this to an extreme."

A study in 1967 by the Systems Analysis Office in the Defense Department of unobserved air and artillery strikes concluded that "In 1966, some 65 percent of the total tonnage of bombs and artillery rounds used in Vietnam was expended against places where the enemy *might* be, but without reliable information that he was there." [emphasis in original] "In 1966, such unobserved strikes probably killed fewer than 100 VC/NVA; the 27,000 tons of dud bombs and shells from such attacks provided the enemy with more than enough material for mines and booby traps . . . the effects of such strikes on civilians in VC and friendly areas were often undesirable, probably creating more VC than they eliminated; the more than $2 billion a year the United States was spending for such strikes could probably be spent with greater effectiveness elsewhere. . . ." Enthoven and Smith, *How Much Is Enough?* pp. 305–306.

Douglas Kinnard, who on one of his two tours of duty in Vietnam was commanding general of an artillery unit, says in his survey of U.S. general officers who had commanded in Vietnam that it is "surprising . . . that a substantial minority [30 percent] of the generals themselves felt that there was too much firepower. . . . In particular, comments were very critical of H and I fires; one respondent said that such fires were 'madness.'" Kinnard, *The War Managers,* p. 47.

On the adverse effects of H and I fire and search-and-destroy missions, and "the futility of attempting to fight a guerrilla enemy with the wrong techniques," see Blaufarb, *op. cit.,* pp. 252–256.

[60] A number of humanitarian groups volunteered to help the refugees in cooperation with the U.S. foreign aid program (the Agency for International Development of the Department of State), which was responsible for U.S. Government assistance. One of the groups directly involved was International Voluntary Services (IVS), a humanitarian organization founded in 1953, under which Americans assisted other countries with agriculture, education and community development. IVS, which had begun working in South Vietnam in 1957, had about 80 persons working in the countryside, and its volunteers often experienced first-hand the effects of U.S. and Communist military activity. For a description by two IVS leaders of the effects of U.S. harassment and interdiction fire and search-and-destroy missions, see Don Luce and John Sommer, *Viet Nam—The Unheard Voices,* pp. 169–176.

[61] Johnson Library, ND 19/CO 312, Memorandum from Richard Holbrooke to Robert W. Komer, Jan. 20, 1967.

the clearing of areas which could then be used as free-fire zones. In a report in late 1967 to the JCS, General DePuy, then the JCS Special Assistant for Counterinsurgency and Special Activities, stated: "Although the policy to create refugees for military purposes does not, in so many words, appear in any MACV document, the necessity is openly recognized as a realistic requirement." DePuy recommended that the number of refugees be doubled in 1968.[62]

U.S. civilian officials also considered refugees an asset. The argument continued to be made, as it had been made in 1954, that they were "voting with their feet" by fleeing the Communists, and that, according to a memorandum from the U.S. refugee chief in Saigon, they constituted a source of labor as well as "a singular and readily exploitable opportunity to increase popular support of the GVN within Vietnam and abroad."[63] As a State Department cable to Saigon in September 1966 stated: "This [the flow of refugees] helps deny recruits, food producers, porters [persons carrying supplies] etc. to VC, and clears the battlefield of innocent civilians. Indeed in some cases we might suggest military operations specifically designed to generate refugees—very temporary or longer term depending on local weighing of our interests and capacity to handle them well. Measures to encourage refugee flow might be targeted where they will hurt the VC most and embitter people toward US/GVN forces least."[64]

Besides uprooting people from their homes and destroying their villages, military operations by allied and Communist forces resulted in an increasing number of civilian casualties, primarily women and children. By the summer of 1967, the number of those who required hospitalization for more than 24 hours was at least 50,000 (and perhaps as high as 100,000) a year.[65] In addition, an undetermined number of civilians were being killed. U.S. officials said they did not know how many were killed, and that in order to compile the statistics they would have to assign a number of people to the task who could be better used elsewhere in the war. It was estimated however, based on U.S. military ratios of five or six wounded to one killed, that 10,000 South Vietnamese civilians a year were being killed in the war as of the summer of 1967.[66]

---

[62] Cited by Lewy, *America in Vietnam*, p. 65, from military history files.

[63] For the text of the memorandum, see the 1967 hearings of Senator Edward Kennedy's Subcommittee to Investigate Problems Connected with Refugees and Escapees of the Senate Judiciary Committee, *Civilian Casualty, Social Welfare, and Refugee Problems in South Vietnam* (Washington, D.C.: U.S. Govt. Print. Off., 1968), pp. 183–184. For the 1954 parallel, see pt. I of this study, pp. 265–266.

[64] Cited in Lewy, *America in Vietnam*, p. 111, from a copy of the cable in military history files. Similar suggestions for deliberately increasing the flow of refugees in order to deprive the Communists of a recruitment base were made in the spring of 1967 by, among others, Komer, the newly-appointed chief of U.S. pacification programs, and Under Secretary of State Katzenbach. See *PP*, Gravel ed., vol. IV, pp. 441, 508.

[65] The estimate of 50,000 was based on reported figures of 4,000 a month treated at government hospitals, and does not include those treated at other hospitals or not receiving treatment.

[66] These statistics are from testimony before Kennedy's subcommittee by medical teams sent by the U.S. Government to survey the situation in mid-1967. Kennedy himself estimated the number of wounded at 150,000–180,000 a year. See the hearings, *Civilian Casualty, Social Welfare, and Refugee Problems in South Vietnam*, pp. 217, 222, 239, 325. See also Lewy's discussion, *America in Vietnam*, pp. 446–449.

Subsequent estimates were that 75,000–100,000 civilians a year were wounded, but estimates for civilian deaths are considerably higher than the 10,000 a year figure used in 1967. The Kennedy subcommittee's estimate of war-related deaths between 1965 and 1974 was 430,000. *Humanitarian Problems in South Vietnam and Cambodia: Two Years After the Cease-Fire, A Study Mission Report*, January 27, 1975, 94th Cong., 1st sess. (Washington, D.C.: U.S. Govt. Print. Off., 1975), p. 7.

According to the Defense Department's Chief of Statistics on the war, there were more than one million South Vietnamese civilian casualties during 1965–1972, of which 200,000 were killed and 500,000 seriously wounded.[67] These estimates were based primarily on hospital admissions, however, and, among other things, did not include civilians killed outright.

Congressional and Public Concerns Deepen

In Washington on January 10, 1967, the day after Operation CEDAR FALLS was launched, President Johnson took a determined stand in his State of the Union Address to Congress. It was, he said, a "time of testing for our Nation. At home, the question is whether we will continue working for better opportunities for all Americans, when most American are already living better than any people in history. Abroad, the question is whether we have the staying power to fight a very costly war, when the objective is limited and the danger to us is seemingly remote."[68] "We have chosen to fight a limited war," he said, "in an attempt to prevent a larger war—a war almost certain to follow, I believe, if the Communists succeed in overrunning and taking over South Vietnam by aggression and by force. . . ." "I wish I could report to you that the conflict is almost over. This I cannot do. We face more cost, more loss, and more agony." But the U.S., he concluded, "will stand firm in Vietnam."

On the evening before his speech, the President met with 23 Democratic Senators, including all of the Senate committee chairmen except for one as well as all of the members of the Senate Democratic Policy Committee. Vice President Humphrey also attended.[69] The meeting had been suggested by Majority Leader Mansfield, who told White House aide Mike Manatos that he thought it would be helpful. Manatos reported this in a memorandum to the President, attached to which was a cover note asking:

There were no estimates as to the number of active Communists among those civilians who were killed or wounded, nor was there any agreement on the percentage of casualties which resulted from U.S. action, Communist action (including mines and booby traps), or fighting between U.S. and Communist forces. One U.S. official said that 50 percent of the civilian casualties was caused by allied military action and the rest by the Communists. Other U.S. officials said that most of the casualties resulted from allied action. *New York Times*, May 8, 1967.

In view of the prominence given during the war to civilian casualties resulting from the use of napalm, it should be noted that a team of six American doctors, selected by the U.S. Government, which also paid their expenses, reported after a survey of civilian war casualties during a three-week trip to South Vietnam in September 1967 that burns from all causes were "relatively limited in number in relation to other injuries and illnesses, and we saw no justification for the undue emphasis which had been placed by the press upon civilian burns caused by napalm. A greater number of burns appeared to be caused by the careless use of gasoline in stoves which were not intended for gasoline. Probably most burns occurred from this source." *Civilian Casualty, Social Welfare, and Refugee Problems in South Vietnam*, p. 306.

[67] Thomas C. Thayer, *War Without Fronts: The American Experience in Vietnam* (Boulder, Colo.: Westview Press, 1985), p. 125.

[68] *Public Papers of the Presidents*, Lyndon B. Johnson, 1967, p. 2.

[69] There are two sets of White House notes on this meeting on file in the Johnson Library. One set, the author of which is not known, is in the President's Appointment File for Jan. 9, 1967. The other, by Mike Manatos, a White House assistant responsible for liaison with the Senate, is in Ex FG 400. Both have been used in the present discussion and in the quotations. In addition, Vice President Humphrey made a few brief notes which are in his papers at the Minnesota Historical Society, VP Notes: White House Meetings 1967, Memorandum for the Files, Jan. 10, 1967.

Present were: Clinton Anderson, Alan Bible, Daniel Brewster, James Eastland, Allen Ellender, William Fulbright, Philip Hart, Carl Hayden, Lister Hill, Daniel Inouye, Everett Jordan, Russell Long, John McClellan, Warren Magnuson, Mike Mansfield, A. S. Mike Monroney, Edmund Muskie, John Pastore, Jennings Randolph, Richard Russell, George Smathers, John Sparkman, and Stuart Symington.

"Do you want such a meeting? Yes————No————." The President checked "yes" and sent the memorandum back, but he changed "Do you want such a meeting?" to "I would attend such a meeting." Rather than for the invitation to come from the White House, as Manatos had proposed, the President wrote on the Manatos memo, "Let Mansfield do it."[70]

The meeting was opened by Mansfield, who stressed the need for cooperation and teamwork. He said there had recently been an "unusual amount of criticism of the President personally and that everyone was blaming the President for all of their troubles." "This has gone pretty far," he said, and he hoped the meeting would provide the opportunity for an expression of views. The President responded that he would make every effort to work harmoniously with the Senate. He then invited comments from those in attendance, and, judging by the White House notes of the meeting, most of those present were concerned primarily about Vietnam, both the war itself and its effects on U.S. domestic interests and on American politics. Except for Mansfield, who played his role as loyal lieutenant of the President and did not speak on the issues (as noted, he had also just communicated privately with the President), the only other opponent of the war among those present was Fulbright, who "laid great emphasis on the need to find a way to 'get out' of Vietnam which he believes was the strongest undercurrent in last year's elections," to which Warren Magnuson, chairman of the Interior Committee, replied, "we should quit 'nit-picking' on Vietnam, 'with all due respect to my colleague from Arkansas [Fulbright], . .'" and "get on with it. People want action."[71]

Fulbright said he regretted his differences with the President on the conduct of the war, which was the only substantive issue, he added, on which he differed from the President.

In response to Fulbright, the President reviewed his efforts to negotiate a settlement. Fulbright thanked him, and said he believed "every word" that the President had said, but that Rusk's position that "Hanoi must surrender before the war can end" was not consistent with the President's statements. The President replied that this was not Rusk's position, and told Fulbright that if he would give him a statement showing the differences between himself (Johnson) and Rusk that he would ask Rusk about it and then talk to Fulbright. (There is no indication that Fulbright followed through on this suggestion.)

Others, including several of the most prominent Senate Democratic moderates and liberals, repeated their support for the President. Senator Muskie said that "both withdrawal and escalation are unacceptable," and that most people favored the President's middle-of-the-road position. But he said that the war was "difficult for people to understand" and there was a "need to clarify who is for what."[72] Senator John Pastore said he supported the President "even when it hurts," adding, "and I will continue to do so." He said he was concerned, however, about intensified bombing, and he favored a pause and mediation by U.N. Secretary General U Thant.

---

[70] Johnson Library, President's Appointment File, Jan. 9, 1967.

[71] The quotation beginning "and get on with it" is from Vice President Humphrey's notes cited above.

[72] The quotation beginning "difficult for people" is from *ibid.*

If that did not work, "the President should then use his 'Sunday punch.'"

Senators Russell Long of Louisiana, Jennings Randolph of West Virginia, and Daniel B. Brewster of Maryland said they supported the President.

George Smathers of Florida, one of the President's closest allies among the younger Democrats in the Senate, said that he had one son who had just returned from Vietnam and another who was going, and that the former had told him that Senate dissent was a "serious damper" on the morale of U.S. forces. Smathers "urged upon his colleagues a more careful and thoughtful attitude which would not give comfort to the enemy."

Among those who favored increased military action, Russell, chairman of the Armed Services Committee, supported by Lister Hill of Alabama, chairman of the Senate Education and Labor Committee, said, "We should 'go in and win, or get out.'" Referring to the unstable domestic situation in China, and the tension between China and the U.S.S.R., Russell added that it would be "'better now than later'" to end the war "'before we get in trouble.'"

Senator Symington, agreeing with Russell, advocated greater use of airpower with fewer restrictions.

Symington also said, however, that he was "'not as optimistic'" about Vietnam, and that it was "costing too much." Others who had also supported the war expressed similar concerns. B. Everett Jordan, a conservative from North Carolina, called U.S. involvement in the war "'bad.'" Alan Bible of Nevada "urged some way be found to resolve Vietnam which he felt was most important factor in Nevada elections." Others expressed concern about the cost of the war and its effect on the budget.

It was apparent that, despite continued public support from most Senate Democrats for the President's Vietnam policy and for the war, there was a rising tide of private doubt, even among those rank and file moderates and conservatives from the smaller states who were the backbone of Senate support for the war.

Lawrence O'Brien, who attended the meeting, said in his memoirs that the meeting showed two things: "The first is that, clearly, in early 1967, the President was not hearing outspoken criticism of the war from the Democratic leaders in the Senate," and that, second, "this meeting, however mild its criticisms, was nonetheless the strongest face-to-face criticism of the war the President had heard. In previous meetings, the war had hardly been discussed at all."[73]

In mid-January, 1967, possibly in response to this softening of support, the President, apparently on his own initiative, raised with his advisers the question of whether Congress should be asked to approve a new resolution on Vietnam that would reaffirm U.S. policy and provide a new statement of legislative consensus on which future actions could be based. Rusk and McNamara were requested to give their views at a Tuesday Luncheon to be held on January 17.

In a memorandum to Rusk on January 17 listing the issues to be discussed at the Luncheon, his assistant, Benjamin Read (Exec-

---

[73] Lawrence F. O'Brien, *No Final Victories*, pp. 213–214.

utive Secretary of the State Department), stated that the question of a congressional resolution was on the agenda, but that "No drafting [of a resolution] has been done. Consensus here—Katzenbach, Bundy—and at White House staff levels—McPherson—is opposed to submission of such resolution for following reasons: (1) Vote at best would show considerable fall off from 1964 resolution 502–2 vote; (2) There has been sufficient continuing Congressional support for Vietnam evidenced by appropriation bill votes, failure to press censure resolution, etc.; (3) Seeking such a resolution in 1967 casts doubt on legality of our actions during 1965 and 1966."[74]

There are no known notes of the Tuesday Luncheon meeting of the President with Rusk, McNamara, Rostow and Tom Johnson, held from 1:15 p.m. to 3:10 p.m. on January 17, but the President decided not to pursue further the question of a resolution. On his copy of the agenda for the meeting, Rostow noted next to the item on "Congressional Resolution on Vietnam," apparently in reference to the position of the President and his advisers: "No, put off. Skeptical. No decision."[75]

During the first several weeks of the new Congress the differences of opinion expressed in the January 9 meeting of Senators with the President continued to be voiced in speeches in the Senate. Supporters of the war urged increased military pressure. On January 20, Senator Stennis, the ranking Democratic member on the Armed Services Committee, who had given a pessimistic report after a trip to Vietnam in November 1966, said that 500,000 U.S. troops would be needed by the end of 1967—at the time there were about 400,000—and he called for striking new targets in North Vietnam, not just those that had been defined as "military" targets, but industrial targets such as steel mills, concrete plants, and power plants.[76]

Senator John Tower, a Texas Republican on the Armed Services Committee and its chairman some years later, reported after a trip to Vietnam that the U.S. was winning, but could win much more rapidly by intensifying its military operations. "We must continue," he said, "to apply *unrelenting* pressure." (emphasis in original) He disagreed with those who argued that bombing had not been effective, and said that the U.S. should bomb every "military target," including steel mills, powers plants, and airfields, and should also close the harbor at Haiphong.[77]

On the other hand, Senator Jacob Javits, a liberal Republican from New York who had supported the war, announced that he opposed further military escalation and favored an unconditional cessation of bombing and further efforts to negotiate. Asked why he had changed his position, he said: "Our situation in Vietnam is a national dilemma. I just thought it was about time someone gave the Republican party a stance on the issue."[78]

---

[74] U.S. Department of State, Lot File 74 D 164, memorandum to the Secretary from Read, "Your Luncheon Meeting with the President," Jan. 17, 1967.

[75] Johnson Library, NSF Files of Walt W. Rostow, Agenda for Lunch with the President, Jan. 17, 1967.

[76] *New York Times*, Jan. 21, 1967. On March 27, Stennis' Preparedness Subcommittee issued a staff report criticizing restrictions on the conduct of the air war. See the *New York Times*, Mar. 28, 1967.

[77] *CR*, vol. 113, p. 3815.

[78] *New York Times*, Feb. 13, 1967. See also Jacob K. Javits and Raphael Steinberg, *The Autobiography of a Public Man* (Boston: Houghton Mifflin, 1981), pp. 398–399.

In a speech reporting on his recent trip to Vietnam, Senator Symington said, as he stated in the meeting at the White House on January 9, that the U.S. was not attacking enough important military targets in the North, and that U.S. pilots were being subjected to unreasonable restrictions. He added, however, that there had been "no outstanding success" in reducing infiltration by bombing, and that "The number of troops coming down from the North today is considerably greater than we were told last year would be coming down at this time." Nevertheless, he favored bombing of more military targets in the North as a way of reducing infiltration, even though he recognized that there might be adverse reactions from other countries, especially the Chinese, to the bombing of some targets, and that this could prove detrimental to the U.S. In general, Symington said he was less optimistic than he had been a year earlier, and that "the monetary situation and other problems have increased my desire for a political settlement more so than before, if it can be arranged on a proper basis." [79]

On February 5, *Newsweek* reported that Senator Robert Kennedy had returned from a tour to Europe with a Vietnam "peace feeler" from the North Vietnamese via the French. While in Paris, Kennedy had met with President de Gaulle and with Etienne Manac'h, Director of Asian Affairs in the French Foreign Office. According to *Newsweek,* Manac'h passed along a message purportedly from Mai Van Bo, the North Vietnamese representative in Paris, to the effect that peace talks could begin once the U.S. stopped bombing the North. Information on the Kennedy-Manac'h meeting was reported to Washington by John Gunther Dean, a member of the U.S. Embassy staff who accompanied Kennedy to the session, and apparently *Newsweek* heard about the meeting through someone in the State Department who had seen Dean's cable. When the President saw the story in *Newsweek* he was reported to have been furious, and he told Katzenbach to investigate the source of the *Newsweek* story and to discuss the trip with Kennedy. When contacted on February 6, Kennedy denied to Katzenbach that he was the source of the story.[80] Meanwhile, Kennedy had proposed a meeting with

---

[79] *CR,* vol. 113, p. 548. See also Symington's comments on pp. 1191–1192 and 1707–1710. Symington gave a report on his trip to the Armed Services Committee, which, after security deletions, was made public on March 26. See the *New York Times*, Mar. 27, 1967.

Before making the trip, Symington had talked to Rostow, who sent a memorandum to the President on the conversation (Johnson Library, C.F. ND 19/CO 312, memorandum from Rostow to the President, Nov. 28, 1966):

"Stu Symington called me. He said: 'You and I have been hawks on Viet Nam since 1961. I am thinking of getting off the train soon. If I do, the first one to know will be the President; but we are old friends and I wanted to give you this warning.

"'It looks to me that with the restraints on the use of airpower, we can't win. We are getting in deeper and deeper with no end in sight.

"'In 1968 Nixon will murder us. He will become the biggest dove of all times. There never has been a man in American public life that could turn so fast on a dime.

"'I am going out now to Asia and will stop in Viet Nam. I'll be in touch with you when I get back. But I wanted you to know that this is how I feel right now.'"

The President replied: "Dear Walt: Thanks for your note about Symington and his evaluation of Nixon. I know at least one more fellow who can turn faster on a dime than Nixon. Guess who!" (Same location, handwritten note from President Johnson to Rostow, Nov. 30, 1966.)

[80] This description of the origins of the incident is from David Wise, *The Politics of Lying: Government Deception, Secrecy and Power* (New York: Random House, 1973), pp. 78–80. For Katzenbach's memorandum to the President reporting on his investigation of the source of the *Newsweek* story—he said he thought it came from someone in the State Department—see Johnson Library, NSF Files of Walt W. Rostow, Katzenbach memorandum to the President, Feb. 14, 1967. For the transcript of the Kennedy-Manac'h talk, see Department of State, Central File, Pol 27 Viet S, Paris to Washington 11650, Feb. 2, 1967.

the President to clarify the situation, and later that day, he met from 4:34 p.m. to 5:52 p.m. with the President, Katzenbach, and Rostow. This is Arthur Schlesinger's description of what happened:[81]

> "The President started right in by getting mad at me for leaking the story," Kennedy told [Frank] Mankiewicz [his press secretary]. Kennedy replied that he had not leaked the story; he was not aware there had been a peace feeler and still was not sure there had been one. "I think," Kennedy said, "the leak came from someone in your State Department." "It's not my State Department, God damn it," Johnson said angrily. "It's your State Department." The president went on about the irrelevance of negotiations. "Those guys are out of their minds," Kennedy told Mankiewicz. "They think they're going to win a military victory in Vietnam by summer. They really believe it." Johnson told him that the war would be over by June or July. "I'll destroy you and every one of your dove friends [he specified Fulbright, Church and a couple of other unfortunates] in six months. You'll be dead politically in six months."
>
> After a time Kennedy asked whether Johnson would like to know what Kennedy thought he should do. Johnson said yes, go ahead. "Say that you'll stop the bombing if they'll come to the negotiating table," Kennedy said, "and then you should be prepared to negotiate." He outlined a series of possibilities—a cease-fire in stages, an expanded International Control Commission to deter further escalation, an international presence gradually replacing American forces, a political settlement allowing all major elements in South Vietnam to participate in the choice of a government. "There just isn't a chance in hell that I will do that," Johnson said, "not the slightest chance." Kennedy and his friends, he said, were responsible for prolonging the war and for killing Americans in Vietnam. Blood was on their hands. Kennedy said, "Look, I don't have to take that from you," and started to leave.
>
> Katzenbach and Rostow tried to compose the situation. They asked Kennedy to tell the waiting press that there had been no peace feelers. Kennedy refused, saying he did not know whether there had been peace feelers or not. "I didn't know what the hell had been said to me." He finally agreed to say that he had not brought home any feelers—true enough, since the message had been transmitted to Washington by [John Gunther] Dean. "Well, that wasn't a very pleasant meeting," Kennedy told his aides when he was safely back on the Hill. "He was very abusive. . . . He was shouting and seemed very unstable. I kept thinking that if he exploded like that with me, how could he ever negotiate with Hanoi."

During the first several weeks of the new (90th) Congress, which convened in January 1967, and which contained 47 new Members

---

[81] *Robert Kennedy and His Times*, pp. 768–769. Bracketed material was added by Schlesinger. A similar account appears in Kraslow and Loory, *The Secret Search for Peace in Vietnam*, pp. 200–204. On Mar. 13, 1967, *Time* magazine carried a story on the meeting which characterized the argument as being considerably harsher than the Schlesinger account. This version was called inaccurate by both Kennedy and a spokesman for the White House. See the *New York Times*, Mar. 15, 1967. President Johnson does not mention the meeting with Kennedy in his memoirs, and there are no notes of the meeting in the Johnson Library.

of the House of Representatives and 4 new Senators, the President invited the entire Congress to attend "briefings" at the White House, primarily on foreign policy, especially Vietnam.[82] At each of eight meetings attended by Members of the Senate or House the President, Rusk and McNamara spoke and there were questions from the group. Budget Director Schultze and Gardner Ackley, Chairman of the Council of Economic Advisers, also participated. Other officials and staff, including the Vice President, Katzenbach, Rostow and a number of other members of the White House staff also attended.[83] The purpose of the briefings was to exhort new and old Members to support the President's program, and Fulbright, who attended on January 19, reportedly reacted by saying to Senator Clark (D/Pa.), a fellow member of the Foreign Relations Committee: "Joe, I'm tired of listening to these prejudices and propaganda . . . let's get out of here," whereupon they left.[84]

In one briefing, Under Secretary of State Katzenbach, substituting for Rusk, was quite firm in his support for U.S. policy in Vietnam. Saying that the significance of Vietnam was "whether or not the word of the United States . . . is any good at all," he asserted that the war was "going to come out all right." He did not have any doubt that U.S. goals were going to be accomplished. "[W]e're not going to give up. We don't give up. We're not quitters. . . . We are going to stay in there until the reasons that we are in there have been vindicated and they are accomplished."[85]

Congressional concern about the war reflected growing public concern. Harrison Salisbury's articles on the bombing of North Vietnam had given greater impetus to the antiwar movement. On January 15, 1967, 462 members of the Yale University faculty and administration, including five deans and 15 department chairmen, sent President Johnson a letter citing Salisbury's articles and recommending an unconditional halt to the bombing of North Vietnam.[86] Similar letters were sent by 100 members of the faculty and administration at Dartmouth College and by 239 faculty at Cornell University on January 30.[87] On January 21, 1967, a group of faculty members calling themselves the Ad Hoc Faculty Committee on Vietnam, chaired by Hilary Putnam, a professor of philosophy at Harvard University, announced that it had 6,000 signatures from faculty at 200 institutions in 37 states opposed to further bombing of North Vietnam.[88]

---

[82] Briefings were held on Jan. 19 and 23, Feb. 6, 15, 18, 21, 23 and Mar. 2, 1967. Transcripts of the portions of each meeting dealing with Vietnam are in the Johnson Library, Congressional Briefing Notes.

[83] The format was for the Members of Congress to gather for the briefing, while their spouses met separately with Mrs. Johnson and were entertained with various programs, after which all of the guests were served a buffet dinner. On at least two occasions, the briefings on February 6 and 8, the President asked Postmaster General Lawrence O'Brien (who was still performing his earlier role as head of congressional liaison) for a report on the meeting from the White House staff members who attended. Johnson Library, President's Appointment File, Diary Backup for Feb. 6, 1967, Memorandum to the President from Lawrence O'Brien, "Congressional Briefing on February 6, 1967," Feb. 7, 1967, with attached reports, and, in the same location, O'Brien's memorandum on the meeting on February 8 with attached reports.

[84] Johnson Library, Ex ND 19/CO 312, note to the President on Jan. 19, 1967 from John Gonella, a State Department staff member, reporting that he overheard the remark.

[85] Johnson Library, Congressional Briefing Notes, Transcript of the briefing of Feb. 15, 1967.

[86] *New York Times*, Jan. 16, 1967.

[87] *CR*, vol. 113, pp. 4021–4022, and the *New York Times*, Jan. 31, 1967.

[88] *New York Times*, Jan. 22, 1967.

On January 31, a group of about 2,000 from Clergy and Laymen Concerned About Vietnam, which, it will be recalled, had been organized in January 1966, demonstrated at the White House as part of a three-day-mobilization against the war.[89] On February 1, seven of the leading clergymen in the group met at the White House with W. W. Rostow, who was reported to have expressed confidence that negotiations would eventually take place, and told the group that the administration "was under terrific pressure from people who want to go militarily further."[90]

Following the mobilization in Washington, there was a three-day Fast for Peace in Vietnam on February 8-10 called by Clergy and Laymen Concerned About Vietnam, involving an estimated one million people in hundreds of churches throughout the country.[91]

A significant development occurred in early February 1967 when some members of the business community began to oppose further escalation of the war. In a letter to the President on February 7, 174 corporate executives, including 89 presidents or board chairmen, declared: "This war is against our national interest and world interest." They urged the President to stop bombing the North, deescalate fighting in the South and negotiate with the Communists, including the National Liberation Front.[92] Several months later, as will be seen, members of this group established Business Executives Move for Peace (BEM), headed by Henry E. Niles, a Quaker, who was Chairman of the Board of the Baltimore Life Insurance Company. As was noted earlier, however, the executives of most major corporations, as represented by the Business Council, strongly supported U.S. policy in Vietnam.

On February 13, 1967, the White House announced that the U.S. was resuming the bombing of North Vietnam after a pause during the Vietnamese New Year (Tet). On February 15, an estimated 2,500 people from Women Strike for Peace, mostly from Philadelphia and New York City, marched on the Pentagon. They demanded to see McNamara, who sent an assistant to meet with them.[91] The next day, Senator Stennis condemned the demonstration.[92] Calling it "unruly," he said: "the best that can be said for them [the demonstrators] is that they are badly misguided and uninformed. Otherwise they would not have mounted such a demonstration, which inevitably plays into the hands of and provides tremendous propaganda ammunition for our enemies." Stennis said that he, too, wanted to end the war, but the Communists had re-

[89] *Ibid*, Feb. 1, 1967. For the text of a position paper, "Vietnam: The Clergyman's Dilemma," prepared for the mobilization by Clergy and Layman Concerned About Vietnam, see *CR*, vol. 113, pp. 2947–2949.

[90] *New York Times*, Feb. 2, 1967.

[91] For a description see *ibid.*, Feb. 12, 1967. There was also a campaign to organize letters protesting the war, led by activist Allard Lowenstein, who attended a meeting of Clergy and Laymen Concerned about Vietnam on January 31, where he recruited a number of students from Union Theological Seminary in New York City. Together, they arranged for a letter to the President from 200 college and university student body presidents, "a petition to allow draftees to choose an alternative service signed by ten thousand students on nine campuses, and a letter to McNamara signed by one thousand young seminarians." Powers, *The War at Home*, p. 178. But also see David Harris, *Dreams Die Hard* (New York: St. Martin's/Marek, 1982), for comments on how Lowenstein manufactured some of this opposition.

[92] *Washington Post*, Feb. 8, 1967. For the text of the letter and a list of those who signed, see *CR*, vol. 113, pp. 4892–4894.

[91] *New York Times*, Feb. 16, 1967. See also Zaroulis and Sullivan, *Who Spoke Up?* p. 103.

[92] *CR*, vol. 113, p. 3665.

fused to "conclude a peace on honorable terms," and therefore the U.S. had to "fight this war to win."

On February 20, Vice President Humphrey received a mixed reception at Stanford University in California. After an all night teach-in on the war, about 100 of an estimated crowd of 1700 students walked out of a speech by Humphrey, and as he left after delivering the speech, about 300 students, "Screaming 'Shame, Shame' . . . rushed at Humphrey as he went to his limousine. . . . They banged on the windows and doors with their fists. Some shouted 'Burn, baby, burn.' Agents ran ahead of the vehicle, shoving demonstrators out of the way . . . Humphrey, visibly shaken at first, smiled as the car moved past the demonstrators enroute to San Francisco."[93]

On February 21-23, there were similar demonstrations by SDS students at the University of Wisconsin, and the chancellor, blockaded in his office, announced that he would call in police if necessary to control further disorder. He was supported by the faculty and by a large number of other students.[94]

The general public, however, seemed to support the war and the bombing of North Vietnam by a slightly better margin than it had since a poll in May 1966, and, following the brief increase in support for deescalation in the fall of 1966, there was increased support for intensifying military pressure on the Communists. In a Gallup Poll taken on February 16-21, 1967, and announced on February 26 after the United States had resumed the bombing of North Vietnam on February 13, the response to the "mistake" question was (with earlier responses given for comparison):[95]

[In percent]

	February 1967	*May 1966*	*August 1965*
Not a mistake	52	49	61
Mistake	32	36	24
No opinion	16	15	15

In the same poll, a high percentage of respondents—67 percent—said that they approved continued bombing of North Vietnam; 24 percent disapproved, and 9 percent had no opinion. The principal reason cited by those who favored bombing was that it was the only way to end the war; and by those opposed, that too many civilians were being killed.

An analysis by Louis Harris in February also concluded that there was strong public support for intensified military pressure as "the best and perhaps the only method to achieve an honorable liquidation of the war."[96] According to Harris,

> The dominant middle-ground opinion [70 percent of the public] is now convinced that intensified military activity, including bombing of North Vietnam, represents the best chance to bring the Communists to the negotiating table. Nationwide,

[93] *Washington Post*, Feb. 21, 1967.

[94] *New York Times*, Feb. 24 and *Washington Post*, Feb. 26, 1967.

[95] *The Gallup Poll*, p. 2052. The "mistake" question was: "In view of the developments since we entered the fighting in Vietnam, do you think the United States made a mistake in sending troops to fight in Vietnam?" For a breakdown of both polls by sex, race, education, etc., see *Vietnam War, A Compilation: 1964–1990*, vol. 2.

[96] Louis Harris, "How the U.S. Public Now Feels About Vietnam," *Newsweek*, Feb. 27, 1967, pp. 24–25.

> the number who want to keep up present military pressures in Vietnam has risen from 43 to 55 per cent. Continued bombing of North Vietnam is supported by 67 per cent. What is more, 71 per cent of the public sees the struggle as a long war, not one that will be settled in the near future. So the grit and determination and will to see this war through has now become an integral part of the majority view.

Another Harris survey in February found that 43 percent of respondents favored "total military victory," compared to 31 percent in November 1966, while 44 percent favored withdrawal of forces of both sides under U.N. supervision, compared to 57 percent who favored withdrawal in the November poll.[97]

Harris also pointed out, however, that when President Johnson "overplayed his hand by raising hopes for a settlement, he has been met with disillusionment among the people." "The real dilemma of Lyndon Johnson," Harris said, "rests squarely with his own behavior in handling the war. If he slips, if he raises false hopes, he will be in irreparable trouble."

[97] *Washington Post,* May 16, 1967.

CHAPTER 14

THE PRESIDENT DECIDES TO USE GREATER FORCE

In mid-January 1967, after the failure of MARIGOLD and the adverse publicity resulting from Harrison Salisbury's articles, the President asked Rostow to explore with Clark Clifford the creation of a committee to examine the effects of the bombing of North Vietnam. Rostow met with Clifford on January 18, and reported the next day that Clifford had doubts about the idea. Clifford, he said, recommended instead that if the President wanted more information and a wider spectrum of views he should ask a very small group to study the question and, without filing a report, to meet very privately with the President to present its views. Rostow said he agreed with Clifford that an "informal non-committee" would be the preferable way of helping the President to form his own opinions and to decide on a course of action.[1]

"The problem," Rostow said, "is this: If we do not get a diplomatic breakthrough in the next three weeks or so, it probably means that they [the Communists] plan to sweat us out down to the election of 1968. As you know, I share your view that we would then have to think hard about how to apply our military power against the North with maximum effect and minimum risk of enlarging the war as a whole." To prepare for such a "fresh appraisal of all the courses open and the pros and cons," Rostow said that he had "stimulated" Vance and the Non-Group to examine the three broad strategic alternatives:

—Cut off supplies coming from outside North Vietnam (mining, etc.);

—Bomb so as to disrupt the whole North Vietnamese economy, without interdicting external supplies;

—Apply our military power with great concentration in the southern part of North Vietnam—at the bottom of the funnel—in effect, to separate North and South Vietnam.

Although there is no evidence that the Non-Group acted at the time on the proposed review, within several weeks, as will be seen, such a review was conducted after Westmoreland made a new request for troops. It is important to note, however, that while the immediate impetus for the review was Westmoreland's request, the President and his advisers had anticipated the need for a review of options before deciding how U.S. power could be used with maximum effect if there were no diplomatic breakthrough.

Although he had accepted McNamara's recommendation to stabilize U.S. military operations, and had resisted the pleading of the military for more flexible authority and for the stronger use of force, by mid-February 1967 the President apparently concluded

[1] Johnson Library, Memos to the President—Walt Rostow, Jan. 19, 1967.

that something more had to be done, and done urgently, to increase the pressure on North Vietnam as well as on the battlefield in South Vietnam and in nonmilitary programs.

The "diplomatic breakthrough" had not occurred, and hope for negotiations appeared to be fading. Several days after the President told Senators Mansfield and Dirksen that the U.S. had received a "feeler" from North Vietnam "that seems reliable," the North Vietnamese appeared to be taking a harder line, and at an NSC meeting on February 8, Rusk said that there had not been a "serious response" to any U.S. peace probe. He and the President both noted that the Communists believed that the U.S. was "panicking" and were trying to use negotiations as a way of getting the U.S. to stop bombing the north. A few days later, the British initiative with Kosygin ended inconclusively. Two days after that (February 15), Ho Chi Minh said in a reply to the letter he had received from President Johnson that North Vietnam would negotiate only if bombing stopped unconditionally.

The President's decision to use greater force may also have been a response to increasing public support for stronger military action and to the need to achieve greater progress before the 1968 Presidential and congressional campaign. Growing public opposition to the war may have played a role as well, at least in making the President and his associates more aware of the potential unrest that could result from a long, costly and inconclusive conflict.

Congress was also becoming more restive, and it was clear that, from the administration's standpoint, steps to demonstrate greater effort—and, hopefully, greater progress—needed to be taken to maintain congressional support while seeking to protect other parts of the President's program from serious congressional challenges.

In addition, U.S. military officials were expressing optimism and urging greater action. On January 13, as noted earlier, JCS Chairman Wheeler reported after his trip to Vietnam that, "The adverse military tide has been reversed, and General Westmoreland now has the initiative. . . . We can win the war if we apply pressure upon the enemy relentlessly in the north and in the south."

On February 17, General Wheeler talked to McNamara, and in a backchannel cable to Sharp and Westmoreland later that day he reported that "highest authority" [the President] appeared to have become more receptive to increased U.S. military pressure, having been "swayed by" three recent events: [2]

> A. The dramatic logistic buildup undertaken by the North Vietnamese during the Tet standdown and in the extension period prior to our resumption of offensive actions against the north;
>
> B. The hardnosed reply which Ho Chi Minh gave to the Pope's plea for peace, [3] and
>
> C. The possibility that the current chaotic situation in mainland China offers opportunities which may be exploitable by U.S. to the end of getting ahead with the war.

[2] CMH, Westmoreland Papers, Message Files, Wheeler to Sharp and Westmoreland, JCS 1284–67, Feb. 17, 1967.

[3] See Lyndon Johnson, *The Vantage Point*, pp. 253, 255.

Wheeler added that McNamara and he were going to meet with the President to discuss "certain courses of action, among them a broadening of the target system in North Vietnam." "Additionally," he said, "we will probably discuss what measures we can take to accelerate the pace of the war in South Vietnam and thereby increase directly the pressures upon VC/NVA forces, and, indirectly, upon the Hanoi leadership.

Wheeler said that McNamara asked him whether Westmoreland was "engaging the enemy as speedily and with as much force as is prudent." Wheeler replied that, in his opinion, this was being done. "I surmised," he added, "that, if COMUSMACV were asked could he accelerate the pace and scope of operations in South Vietnam, the reply would be additional forces would be necessary." McNamara responded to this comment by Wheeler by asking him to talk to Army Chief of Staff Harold Johnson about accelerating the deployment of Army units already approved as a part of Program IV. In his cable to Westmoreland, Wheeler said that he had done so, and that General Johnson said that the units remaining to be deployed under Program IV would not increase substantially the offensive capabilities of U.S. troops. Wheeler said he asked Johnson to examine the possibility of providing Westmoreland some additional combat battalions beyond those that had been authorized.

Sharp and Westmoreland replied to Wheeler the same day (February 17). Sharp said that Wheeler's report was "most encouraging," and that the war "may have reached a stage where a good hard offensive push might start the ball rolling down hill." He mentioned recent messages he had sent to Washington on increasing ROLLING THUNDER, and added that it might also be a "good time to try for more freedom to operate in Laos."[4]

Westmoreland replied that the ground war in South Vietnam could not be "significantly" accelerated. "The limitations on the pace of the war," he said, "are established in general by intelligence, troop availability, and helicopter support. . . . The situation will improve during the year," he added, "but my requirements will not be met until approximately a year from now. . . . Yes, I need additional maneuver battalions, but I also need helicopters, artillery, engineers, and supply and maintenance elements to support them."

In response to Wheeler's comment about additional troops, Westmoreland said that he had asked for considerably more troops than had been approved for Program IV—550,000 for calendar year 1967, compared to the 470,000 that had been authorized—and he thought that the estimate of 550,000 was still valid. But he added, "if Pandora's Box is to be opened and the ceiling set by Program IV is to be voided, I would want to restudy the situation and resubmit new requirements [above the 550,000 level] in line with my current estimate of the enemy and our experiences during the last several months."[5]

The following day (February 18), Wheeler cabled Sharp and Westmoreland that there had been further developments. In a

---

[4] CMH, Westmoreland Papers, Message Files, Sharp to Wheeler, CINCPAC 170820Z, Feb. 17, 1967.

[5] Same location, Westmoreland to Sharp and Wheeler, MAC 1658, Feb. 17, 1967.

meeting from 12:25 p.m. to 2:04 p.m. on February 17 with McNamara, Wheeler, Rostow and Taylor, the purpose of which was to consider Wheeler's recommendation for destroying the entire North Vietnamese electric power system (no one attended from the State Department), the President said that on February 22 he wanted to consider alternative courses of action for applying greater pressure on the Communists.[6] "I am not optimistic," Wheeler said, "that many of the items which will be contained in Program C, [the strongest of three alternatives being developed by the JCS staff] will receive early or even late approval. However, it is quite evident that there is a new sense of urgency in the atmosphere; therefore, while I cannot forecast now early approval of more drastic actions than a slight broadening of the target base for ROLLING THUNDER, I believe that certain actions to bring increased pressure on the enemy will be approved in the near future."[7]

In response to the President's expressed desire to consider alternative courses of action against the North, Rostow sent him a memorandum on February 17 (which he prepared in advance of the meeting that afternoon) describing the three strategies from which the U.S. could choose.[8] The first was to interdict supplies originating outside North Vietnam by mining the harbors and bombing the rail line between Hanoi and the Chinese border. (He termed this *"Strategy A. Interdicting or Narrowing the Top of the Funnel,"* using "funnel" to describe the supply line from the points of ingress of supplies down to the border with South Vietnam where supplies entered the South.) This, he said, would be "the most effective military course of action and it might force an early negotiated end to the war by creating a crisis so severe for everyone on the other end that they would have to decide either to end the war or to undertake extremely risky or undesirable courses of action." The risk would be that there might be a major reaction from the U.S.S.R. and/or China. "It is not clear that the Soviet Union could do anything very effective in North Vietnam itself. It might react elsewhere in the world, notably in East-West matters." "On the other hand—and we simply do not know—closing access to the sea routes might lead the Soviet Union to press Hanoi harder for a settlement." There was "relatively little" China could do in North or South Vietnam, Rostow added. "They might use the occasion to put forces into Laos, Thailand, or even Burma, thus enlarging the war at points where it is extremely difficult for us to get at them. But thus far, they have shown a marked tendency to avoid putting themselves in a position where we might justifiably attack the Chinese mainland.

"The problem here is simple ignorance on our side as to what the reaction might be."[9]

---

[6] There apparently are no notes of the meeting on Feb. 17, 1967.

[7] CMH, Westmoreland Papers, Message Files, Wheeler to Sharp and Westmoreland, JCS 1337–67, Feb. 18, 1967.

[8] Johnson Library, NSF, Memos to the President—Walt Rostow.

[9] In contrast to Rostow's estimation of the reactions of the U.S.S.R. and China to U.S. mining of the harbors, Llewellyn Thompson, in a memorandum to Katzenbach on Dec. 12, 1966, said that "While this [mining the harbors] would not greatly increase the possibility of direct Chicom intervention, it would bring about a direct confrontation with the Soviet Union. After the Soviet backdown in the Cuban crisis, a further Soviet humiliation would be very difficult for them to take and they would probably respond with some drastic action, the nature of which is difficult to predict. In addition, the mining of Haiphong would make North Vietnam entirely dependent upon Communist China. It appears clear that Communist China desires the war to continue

The second strategy, Rostow said, was "Hammering the middle of the Funnel," by which he meant increasing attacks on targets in the Hanoi-Haiphong area, including attacks on 8 power plants (which he said provided 82 percent of North Vietnam's remaining power capacity), the cement plant, the steel plant, perhaps certain port installations, and more intense attacks on lines of communication and military supplies and barracks. The advantage, he said, would be that this would "place an awkward further burden directly on Hanoi, making the operation of their economic life substantially more difficult, interfering marginally with the war effort in the South." The cost would be "increased noises from the British left wing, our own opposition to Vietnam policy, U Thant, etc."

The third strategy was "Narrowing the broad Bottom of the Funnel," by which Rostow meant operations to choke off the supply line at its bottom. These would include mining the mouths of two rivers in the southern part of North Vietnam which were important transhipment points, naval to shore gun fire, and an expansion of SHINING BRASS, the intelligence gathering and harassment teams operating into Laos from South Vietnam. These, he said, would risk few costs.

Rostow concluded his recommendations to the President by saying that he did not believe the U.S. should move into a "maximum campaign against the North, convulsively, right now," but he thought the first option should not be ruled out, and he recommended that "a few sober and objective minds" should clarify the possible gains and costs involved in that option.

As for the next move, he recommended attacking electric power plants, and doing so "thoroughly" but at a "deliberate pace."

Three days later (February 20), Rostow sent another memorandum to the President in which he explained that he was not going to be able to attend the meeting scheduled for February 22, and that he wanted to give the President his conclusions on what the

---

and their influence in Hanoi would be strengthened by Hanoi's dependence upon them for supplies." U.S. Department of State, Central File, Pol 27 Viet S, Memorandum for the Under Secretary from Llewellyn E. Thompson, "Soviet and Communist Chinese involvement in Vietnam," Dec. 12, 1966.

In a memorandum on Apr. 12, 1967, on "Communist Policy and the Next Phase in Vietnam," (Johnson Library, NSF Country File, Vietnam), the CIA's Office of National Estimates came to conclusions similar to those of Thompson. If the U.S. mined North Vietnamese harbors, the memorandum said, the U.S.S.R. probably would not risk major confrontation with the U.S. in Southeast Asia by attempting to reopen shipping routes. They "might consider," however, responding elsewhere. "Greatly heightened tensions in Korea is a possibility, though a dangerous one. Turkey and Iran could be candidates, or the Middle East in general." But the most likely place would be Berlin, where, without risking a major crisis which would "threaten the gains Moscow is seeking at U.S. expense in Europe by pursuing the line of detente," they might put "minor pressure on access routes, to create the impression of impending crisis and to lead European opinion to blame the U.S. rather than Soviet policy for causing the trouble."

"Of one thing only can we be fairly certain: the U.S.S.R. would respond to the mining with across the board hostility toward the U.S. They would demonstrate this by interrupting any ongoing conversations, such as the discussion of ABMs, non-proliferation and a freeze on strategic weapons. In addition they might interfere with various [cultural] exchanges, and delay ratification or implementation of the consular treaty and air agreements. They might go so far as to abrogate existing agreements, the test ban and other space agreements, though this seems much less likely. . . ."

The Office of National Estimates agreed with Rostow that mining might stimulate diplomatic activity. "There would be a good chance," the memorandum said, "that the Soviets would at this juncture begin to exert greater efforts to bring about peace."

With respect to the reaction of the Chinese, the memorandum added that, "It is possible that the mining of the harbors and the anticipated effects on North Vietnam would cause the Chinese to intervene in the war with combat troops and air power."

U.S. should do.[10] In order of priority these were: (all emphases in original)

1. *Keep pouring it on in the South.* . . .

2. *Pacification and opening of roads.* . . .

3. *Bombing the North.* . . . I am for applying more weight . . . but I believe it should be applied step-by-step, not convulsively. . . .

4. *The Russians.* We should keep in steady frank conversations with them. . . . We should tell them politely that since they can't deliver Hanoi on a sensible deal, we'll have to do it. . . .

5. *Negotiations.* We should stop projecting an atmosphere of great anxiety about negotiations to Hanoi—a kind of "you call me" posture is about right.

6. *Politics in South Vietnam.* This is the sleeper for 1967 if it comes out right. The critical issue is increasingly this: Westy and Lodge should take Thieu up on a mountain and let him see what a grand role he could play if he took over the Vietnamese military and modernized them for the long pull while keeping unity and backing the constitutional process. Ky looks to me the more likely politician for the next phase; but it may matter that Thieu knows he will have all kinds of U.S. support if he undertakes the critical backstop military job. . . .

When the Ky-Thieu matter is settled—and the sooner the better—we can really go to work to encourage them to organize solidly a military-civil coalition; a national program; a consolidation of political parties into a great big national party; an election with maximum turn-out; a forthcoming amnesty position; and all the rest.

Because it doesn't involve hardware and much money, this is the dimension we tend to neglect; but doing it will make all the difference to whether we get a settlement this year.

On February 22, the President met from 1:15 p.m. to 3:25 p.m. with Rusk, McNamara, Wheeler and Taylor. Bromley Smith and George Christian also attended. The major subject on the agenda was "Vietnam: A. Accelerating operations in the South, B. Operations in the North, C. Next steps in negotiations, if any."[11]

The following outline of possible additional military actions in North Vietnam and Laos and in South Vietnam was distributed by McNamara to the President and others present for the meeting:[12]

---

[10] Same location.

[11] Johnson Library, NSF Files of Walt W. Rostow, "Agenda" for lunch with the President Feb. 22, 1967. At the bottom of the agenda Rostow added: "Mr. President: You should know that Sects. Rusk and McNamara plan to meet at 8:00 a.m. tomorrow morning [the day of the lunch] to see if they can come up with an agreed package [on Vietnam] for lunch. Brom Smith will be there and report to you before lunch."

Except for a few cursory notations that Rostow made on his copy of the agenda, there are no known notes of either the meeting of Rusk and McNamara or the meeting with the President.

[12] This outline along with a 19-page narrative analysis which was also distributed at the meeting, was prepared by McNaughton's office based on material prepared by the JCS. The outline and narrative statements, undated and unsigned, are in the Johnson Library, NSF Files of Walt W. Rostow, attached to the agenda for the meeting.

In the *Pentagon Papers*, Gravel ed., vol. IV, pp. 421–423, there is the text of the alternative programs prepared by the JCS at the request of Vance, entitled, "Military Action Programs for Southeast Asia" (for the few words missing in the Gravel ed. see the DOD ed., Book 5, IV C.6.(b), pp. 50–51), which is footnoted as having been sent to Katzenbach by Vance on February 21 as an attachment to a note from Vance to Katzenbach asking for State to "check the political judgments." It is also noted (p. 420) that a statement of alternatives was prepared on that date

JCS PROGRAM			
A	B	C	OUTLINE
			I. Military actions against North Vietnam and in Laos
			A. Present Program
			B. Options for increased military programs
			1. Destroy modern industry
X	X	X	—Thermal power
X	X	X	—Steel and cement
	X	X	—Machine tool plant
			—Other
		X	2. Destroy dikes and levees
			3. Mine ports and water entrances
	X	X	—Mine Haiphong, Cam Pha and Hong Gai, and estuaries south of 20°
		X	—Mine major port approaches
			4. Unrestricted LOC attacks
X	X	X	—Eliminate 10-mile Hanoi prohibited area
	X	X	—Reduce Haiphong restricted area to 4 miles
		X	—Eliminate prohibited/restricted areas
	X	X	—Elements of 3 ports
		X	—4 ports
	X	X	—Selected rail facilities
	X	X	—Mine inland waterways south of 20°
		X	—Mine all inland waterways
	X	X	—7 locks
			5. Expand naval surface operations
X	X	X	—Fire at shore targets south of 19°
	X	X	—Expand to 20°
		X	—Expand to Chicom buffer zone
			6. Destroy MiG airfields
	X	X	—Kep and Hoa Lac
		X	—4 other
			7. SHINING BRASS ground operations in Laos
	X	X	—Expand operational limits to 20 km into Laos, increase helo [helicopter] operations, authorize larger forces, increase frequency of operation
		X	—Battalion-size exploitation forces; start guerrilla warfare
X	X	X	8. Cause interdicting rains in Laos and North Vietnam [Operation POPEYE]
			9. Miscellaneous
X	X	X	—Base part of B–52 operations at U-Tapao, Thailand
	X	X	—Fire artillery from positions in South Vietnam against targets in Laos
		X	—Air defense HQ and Ministry of Defense HQ
	X	X	—Ammunition dump
			II. Actions in South Vietnam
			A. Expand U.S. forces and/or their role
X	X	X	—Continue present force build-up
	X	X	—Accelerate build-up; and deploy 2 additional battalions and 2 air squadrons
		X	—Deploy up to 4 divisions and 9 air squadrons
			B. Improve pacification

The *Pentagon Papers,* Gravel ed., vol. IV, p. 423, summarizes the three alternative courses of action proposed by the JCS:

> *Program A* included ROLLING THUNDER, naval surface operations, SHINING BRASS, Laos operations, land artillery firing across the DMZ and ground force deployments. The deployment recommended under Program A consisted of merely accelerating Program 4 deployments and possibly adding three Army maneuver battalions. The reminder of Program A rep-

---

for the President's night reading by McNaughton's office and the JCS "with an assist from Department of State."

resented no more than minor expansions in operations, recommendations for which the JCS had been on record since last fall [1966].

Program B featured expanded ROLLING THUNDER operations to include attacking the North Vietnamese ports, mining the inland waterways and estuaries south of 20° North, attacking the MiG airfields previously excepted, expansion of SHINING BRASS operations into Laos and . . . the deployment of the 9th Marine Amphibious Brigade from Okinawa/Japan to the I Corps Tactical Zone [the area near the DMZ where U.S. Marines were already positioned] in March 1967.

Program C subsumed all of the recommendations of the two preceding Programs A and B, but added an expansion of the mining quantitatively, to include all approaches and inland waterways north of 20°, authorized battalion-sized expeditions in the SHINING BRASS area [Laos] and recommended deployments of up to four U.S. divisions (3 Army, 1 USMC) and up to nine tactical fighter squadrons (5 Air Force, 4 USMC).

An analysis prepared by McNaughton's office and distributed by McNamara to those attending the meeting on February 22 contained a number of comments that indicated the McNamara/McNaughton position on the JCS proposals. "The present bombing program," the paper said," has increased the cost of the war to Hanoi and has perhaps put a ceiling on the level of infiltration. It has not, however, succeeded in denying the VC/NVN the less than 120 tons per day of logistic support necessary to continue operations [in South Vietnam] at present levels. . . . [It] has hurt North Vietnam but has not resulted in a material weakening of the will of the Hanoi regime. Hanoi is expected to be able and willing to persevere indefinitely in the face of the present bombing program."

The first option in the JCS proposal, the paper said—to "destroy modern industry" in North Vietnam—although putting greater pressure on North Vietnam, would not affect infiltration or the "will" to continue the war. "The North Vietnamese economy is essentially agrarian; and the people have been prepared for such bombing." Such actions would result, however, in increased imports from the U.S.S.R. and China, and would lead to considerable criticism from other countries as well as within the United States. "There is a serious risk that this action would lose us British support for the war and push certain marginal Senators and Congressmen into opposition."

The second option, "destroy dikes and levees," also would not affect infiltration and would probably increase the will to resist. There would, however, be a "massive loss of support both internationally and domestically" from such attacks on a "population" target system.

The third option, "mine ports and water entrances," even if it achieved maximum effectiveness (estimated at 80 percent, reducing imports from 3,000 to 600 tons a day), would have such a small effect compared with North Vietnam's total import potential that it would not affect infiltration to the South. "All normal traffic could be handled by resorting to rail, road and inland water routes." Although it would "cause serious pain and concern to Hanoi . . .

their resolve to fight on would remain." China, among other things, would probably add to its troops in North Vietnam. The U.S.S.R., "severely embarrassed by their inability to prevent or counter the U.S. mines . . . would at least send a token number of volunteers to North Vietnam if Hanoi asked for them, and would provide Hanoi with new forces of military assistance, e.g., floating mines and cruise missiles . . . which could appear as a direct response to the U.S. mining and which would endanger our ships in the area." "It is an open question whether they [the U.S.S.R.] would be willing to take the risks involved in committing their own ships and aircraft to an effort to reopen the ports." "The situation could of course become explosive if the mining operations resulted in serious damage to a Soviet ship." International reaction, the paper added, "would be one of fright, because of the possibility of U.S.-U.S.S.R. confrontation, and of disapproval."

The fourth option, "unrestricted attacks on roads, railroads and waterways," would result in high civilian casualties, perhaps 1,000 a month. By itself, this option would not affect infiltration and would be "unlikely to have a significant effect on Hanoi's will to keep fighting." If combined with options 1–3, the effect could be "increasing cost in maintaining the 'minimum' flow of some of their most essential military and economic goods," but infiltration would continue, and, unless the war in the South was "going badly for them," the North Vietnamese would have the "will" to continue the war "despite their concern over the increasing destruction of their country, the effect of this on their people, and their increasing apprehension that the U.S. would invade the North." As to the reaction of other countries, only if the combination of options 1–4 were so successful that the collapse of the North Vietnamese Government seemed certain would the Chinese intervene. The U.S.S.R. would probably be urging the North to seek peace, and might be applying pressure on the U.S. in Berlin as well as conducting a vigorous propaganda campaign. "All marginal international and domestic support for U.S. policy in Vietnam would be lost."

The fifth option, "extend naval surface operations," and the sixth, "destroy MiG airfields," would not affect infiltration or the will to fight, but would have some serious international ramifications.

With respect to options 7 and 8 dealing with Laos, the McNamara/McNaughton paper said that option 7, "enlarge SHINING BRASS ground operations in Laos," would increase intelligence and make infiltration more difficult, but "only together with other actions could it have effect on the will of North Vietnam." Option 8, "cause interdicting rains in Laos and North Vietnam," could make infiltration of matériel very difficult," and, if so, could affect the war in the South and thereby the will of the North Vietnamese to continue supporting the war. International and domestic reactions, however, "might be great" if this were viewed as "a new form of warfare akin to biological and nuclear warfare."

With respect to the JCS proposal for increasing actions in the South, the McNamara/McNaughton paper said the deployment of U.S. forces could be accelerated, reaching the 1967 level of 462,000 by September rather than December, and their mission could be expanded "to include more spoiling offensives against enemy base areas, more activity in the Delta, and a larger role in small-unit activities required to provide security to populated areas." The paper did not comment on the JCS proposal, as part of Program C, to add 4 divisions and 9 air squadrons.

Finally, the paper commented on pacification: "The most important factor in convincing Hanoi to accept a political settlement of the war is the way that war is going in the South. And the way that war is going is determined by the extent to which Saigon is gaining control and support of the people." "[A]s of this moment, the Saigon Government has made no discernible progress in the 'real war'—the war for support and control especially of the rural population." "Efforts to revamp the South Vietnamese army into a pacification force have not yet borne fruit—the army still misbehaves and fails to take steps to provide security for the population. Attempts to improve government at the village and hamlet level are very slow in producing results. There is no hard evidence that our neutralization and frustration of enemy main-force units has started a collapse of enemy strength at the grass-roots level. . . ."

Thus, it can be seen that the Secretary of Defense found very little merit in any of the JCS options for applying greater pressure on North Vietnam.

There are no notes of the meeting of February 22 at which the JCS proposals were considered except for several notations made by Rostow on his copy of the summary of the three alternative programs, but from these and a cable from Wheeler to Sharp and Westmoreland the next day it is possible to ascertain the decisions made by the President.[13] These decisions confirm Wheeler's comment that there was "a new sense of urgency in the atmosphere," but also, as Wheeler had indicated, that the President was not prepared to approve the full range of measures in Program C.

The President approved almost all of the actions in Program A, and several in Program B. (All of these, of course were also in Program C.) However, of the actions in Program C which went beyond Programs A and B he gave conditional approval to only two—first, he approved A.7. (SHINING BRASS ground operations in Laos), "if McNamara and Wheeler agree," using battalion-sized forces ("exploitation forces," as contracted with the small reconnaissance units used in SHINING BRASS), by which to start guerrilla warfare in Laos against North Vietnamese forces in the area of the Ho Chi Minh Trail; and, second, he approved B.9. (Miscellaneous), air attacks on the North Vietnamese Air Defense Headquarters and Ministry of Defense Headquarters in Hanoi if the Communists again attacked the U.S. military command headquarters in Saigon.

He also approved (B.9.) attacks on a major North Vietnamese ammunition dump in Haiphong, "depending on civil casualties estimate." He agreed to eliminate the 10-mile prohibited area at Hanoi, but said "not now" to reducing the Haiphong area to 4 miles.

[13] Rostow's notations are on his copy of the agenda for the meeting, NSF Files of Walt W. Rostow, and Wheeler's cable is in CMH, Westmoreland Papers, Message Files, JCS 1422–67, Feb. 23, 1967.

In approving increased ROLLING THUNDER operations, the President said, as Rostow had recommended, that new targets should be struck "one-by-one: gradual buildup." [14]

In the case of actions in the South, the President approved—"if Westy desires"—the acceleration of deployment of Program IV forces already authorized, but, as McNamara had in his memorandum, he ignored or disregarded the JCS provision in Program C (II.A. on the above outline) for increasing U.S. forces by "up to 4 divisions and 9 air squadrons."

With respect to pacification, the President agreed with the recommendation that improvements were needed, and said, according to Rostow's notes, "especially campaign against hard-core cadres" (later called the PHOENIX Program).

Wheeler's cable to Westmoreland summarized the President's decisions as follows: [15]

> A. ROLLING THUNDER 54 will be comprised of ROLLING THUNDER 53 targets not yet struck plus the Thai Nguyen steel plant, Thai Nguyen thermal power plant, Viet Tri thermal power plant, Bac Giang thermal power plant and Hon Gai thermal power plant.
>
> B. Selective mining of inland waterways and estuaries of North Vietnam south of 20 degrees north latitude.
>
> C. Naval gunfire against coastal shipping in North Vietnamese waters up to 20 degrees north latitude.
>
> D. Naval gunfire against military shore targets in North Vietnam up to 20 degrees north latitude.
>
> E. Artillery fire from positions in South Vietnam against valid military targets in Laos, the DMZ and North Vietnam north of the DMZ to the effective range of the artillery employed.
>
> 2. SHINING BRASS operations will be modified as follows:
>
> A. Width of the northern sector will be expanded from 5 kilometers to 20 kilometers.
>
> B. Helicopters may be used for infiltration to the full depth of the zone of operations.
>
> C. Exploitation forces may be used to the full depth of the zone of operations.
>
> D. Exploitation forces up to 3 platoons in size may be deployed. (Operational authority will be delegated to CINCPAC and American Ambassador, Vientiane.)
>
> 3. POPEYE [cloud seeding along the Ho Chi Minh Trail in Laos to produce heavy rainfall] has been approved; however, in order to maintain utmost security separate instructions will be forthcoming in a couple of days.[16]
>
> 4. It was agreed to pursue with the Thais the basing of about 15 B–52s at U TAPAO.

---

[14] Several days later, the CIA sent to Rostow a CIA "intelligence memorandum," entitled "An Evaluation of the Effects of Bombing on Infiltration Into South Vietnam," Mar. 9, 1967, which, Helms said in a cover memorandum, had been prepared for the President at Rostow's request. Johnson Library, NSF Country File, Vietnam.

[15] JCS 1422–67, cited above.

[16] Project COPATRIOT (the new name for POPEYE) began in late March, and in early May the JCS reported that it was successful and requested that it be expanded. U.S. Department of State Central File, Pol 27 Viet S, Memorandum to McNamara from Wheeler CM–2306–67, May 3, 1967.

The President's decision of February 22, 1967, to use greater force was made quickly with very little advance preparation or consultation. The State Department received the alternative proposals paper from the Defense Department on the day before the meeting was to be held with the President, and in his note to Katzenbach, Vance said, "The President wants the paper for his night reading tonight."[17] William Bundy drafted a few comments, but further consideration seems to have been precluded by lack of time and the apparent desire of the President for prompt action.[18]

The President also sought to downplay the significance of the decision in order to avoid having it become an issue domestically or internationally. It was, of course, made in secret and there were no announcements of the fact that the U.S. was increasing military pressure. Within several days, however, there were news reports from Saigon that military operations had increased and that new kinds of action were being initiated, and at a press conference on February 27, the President was asked whether this represented "a step-up in U.S. activities . . . [a] change in the level of the war."[19] In a very evasive reply he said that these actions were "more far-reaching than previous U.S. operations," but that "step-up may connote something that I wouldn't want to embrace. . . ."

After the decision was made, U.S. planes began to bomb some of the newly approved targets in North Vietnam, but bad weather delayed a number of strikes for several weeks. During March, there were attacks on a major steel mill near Hanoi (Thai Nguyen) and on power plants. On April 8, the President approved additional targets, including MiG airbases, the Haiphong cement plant and ammunition dump, and the Haiphong thermal power plant.[20] On May 16, he approved bombing the principal Hanoi power plant, one mile from the center of the city. On May 26, the CIA reported that the bombing of electric power facilities had produced extensive physical damage.[21]

One of the actions approved by the President on February 22, as listed in Wheeler's cable to Westmoreland on February 23, was long range artillery attacks by U.S. artillery located just south of the DMZ against North Vietnamese troops and supplies north of the DMZ. Firing began immediately after the President's approval, and, in a memorandum on March 14, the Defense Intelligence Agency reported that these attacks were "hurting the North Vietnamese . . . because of the 'hue and cry' that went up from Hanoi when they began, and the immediate and continuing attacks that

---

[17] Johnson Library, Warnke Papers, McNaughton Files.

[18] In his memorandum to Rusk, Bundy generally agreed with the paper from Defense, but argued against bombing the dikes and levees, and recommended that waterways be mined but that the mining of ports be deferred. *PP*, Gravel ed., vol. IV, "Comment on DoD Analysis—Courses of Action," Feb. 21, 1967, pp. 147–148.

[19] *Public Papers of the Presidents*, Lyndon B. Johnson, 1967, p. 219.

[20] This decision, a sensitive one, apparently was made without the involvement or knowledge of the State Department. In a memorandum to Rusk on April 15, the Department's executive secretary, Benjamin Read, who apparently had been asked by Rusk to check the matter, reported that the message approving the bombing of the power plant was sent following a discussion on April 14 between McNamara and the President's plane. U.S. Department of State, Lot File 70 D 207, Read memorandum to the Secretary, Apr. 15, 1967, with JCS cable from Wheeler to Sharp and Westmoreland, JCS 2766–67, Apr. 15, 1967, attached.

[21] *PP*, Gravel ed., vol. IV, p. 153.

have been launched by NVA/VC forces against these artillery positions."[22]

The decision to apply greater pressure on the Communists, coming on the heels of inconclusive negotiating efforts in late 1966-early 1967, had the effect of giving greater credence and force to the arguments of Westmoreland, Sharp and the JCS for stronger military actions, as well as to the arguments of Walt Rostow (and Ginsburgh) and Komer that the U.S. needed to develop a "win" strategy for 1967, and that through both military actions against the North and a variety of military and nonmilitary actions in the South the Communists could and should be "forced" to accept negotiations.

The President's decision to increase the use of force apparently encouraged the military to think that they could get even broader authority and larger numbers of forces. In a cable to Sharp on February 27, Westmoreland, following up on his earlier comment to Wheeler, said that to attain U.S. strategic objectives the troop level of 470,000 established in November 1966 should be expanded by the equivalent of two and one-third division forces (which would raise the total of U.S. forces up to or above the 550,000 level requested in 1966).[23] On March 6, Wheeler stated in a backchannel cable to Sharp and Westmoreland: "My assessment of the sentiment at highest level persuades me that even broader authority to exert additional military pressure on North Vietnam can be obtained in the near future if we and our people exercise good judgment." This "sentiment," he explained, had resulted from several factors:[24]

> First, our forces have demonstrably inflicted heavy losses on the enemy in the field. Second, the frantic efforts of the North Vietnamese to move supplies into Laos and into the southern areas of North Vietnam during Tet underscored the fact that our attacks against the lines of communications have been effective. Third, the massive propaganda effort on the part of North Vietnam and Communist countries worldwide, supported by domestic dissident groups, to force us to cease unconditionally our air attacks on North Vietnam convinced the highest level that we are hurting them badly. Fourth, criticism of administration policy and actions and fuzzy proposals for ending the war emanating from opposition political elements have instigated a sense of urgency to get on with the war militarily, i.e., to apply further pressure on the enemy in order to capitalize on our successes in that respect to date. Fifth, I believe that highest authority recognizes that the advice he has received from the military to date has been fundamentally sound and is, in fact, the basis of the successes we have achieved in the war; therefore, he is inclined to discount more readily and more heavily contrary advice which has not achieved similar success.

---

[22] Johnson Library, Warnke Papers, McNaughton Files, "Usefulness and Effect of Actions Outside SVN," prepared by the Southeast Asia Branch of the Defense Intelligence Agency, Mar. 14, 1967, as a briefing paper for the upcoming conference at Guam, discussed below.

[23] CMH, Westmoreland Papers, Message Files, Westmoreland to Sharp, MAC 01928, Feb. 27, 1967.

[24] Same location, Wheeler to Sharp and Westmoreland, JCS 1691–67, Mar. 6, 1967.

The one obstacle to obtaining broader Presidential approval, Wheeler said, would be if there were reports of complaints by the military about civilian restrictions, such as the method for selecting bombing targets, and he urged upon Sharp and Westmoreland "the absolute necessity for every military man to keep his mouth shut and get on with the war."

The President's decision to approve the increased use of military force also had the effect of inhibiting efforts to secure a political settlement of the war. The President, who, from the beginning, seems to have been doubtful about negotiating prospects, apparently continued to be skeptical.[25] At a Tuesday Luncheon from 12:45 p.m. to 2:30 p.m. on March 7 with Rusk, McNamara, Katzenbach, Rostow and Christian, he asked for "an orderly public account" of efforts to negotiate made during the bombing pause of May 1965 and December-January 1966–1967 as well as during "Kosygin week" (the meetings of Prime Minister Wilson and Kosygin in London in February 1967), and said he was "sick and tired of being afraid to blow a [diplomatic] contact."[26]

He added that he wanted to put "more pressure—every possible item of pressure in Vietnam. . . ."

After a meeting at the White House, congressional leaders said that the President "had little hope for peace feelers soon," and Senate Republican Leader Dirksen predicted increased bombing, saying, "When you are at war and the enemy refuses to talk except on terms that would mean you surrender, you turn the screws on him . . . you do everything necessary to bring him down."[27]

On March 9, McNamara sent the President a memorandum in which he proposed attacks during the following two weeks on all

[25] Although there is very little evidence on the subject, it may be that President Johnson, who gave very little indication that he was thinking along such a line, was inclined to believe that the war would end as a result of actions by the "great powers," rather than by negotiations with the North Vietnamese. In a meeting with Washington columnist Drew Pearson, the President, according to Pearson's unpublished notes, "seemed very optimistic" about the prospects for peace, saying: "When I talked to Gromyko, he promised to throw his weight on our side for peace, and I am sure he did his best. But he just didn't have the same weight that apparently the Chinese have. When the Chinese get a little weaker and the Russians stronger, we're going to have a peace." Johnson Library, Drew Pearson Papers, Notes of a meeting of Pearson with the President, Mar. 11, 1967, cited above.

[26] Johnson Library, NSF Files of Walt W. Rostow, Notes on the Luncheon Meeting with the President, March 7, 1967, no attribution but probably written by Rostow.

White House Counsel, Harry McPherson, who, while loyal and supportive, was becoming concerned that there was not more of a public display of the efforts being made to negotiate a settlement, said in a memorandum to the President: "Unless we give some additional outward manifestations of searching for peace we can very easily find ourselves identified, along with Ky and the generals, as 'war-lovers.' The Russians, the British, the French, the Pope, the intellectual community, the students, Bobby Kennedy—will be the 'peace-lovers.' Even Ho Chi Minh will look like a seeker after peace—'if they will just stop bombing I will talk about peace.'

"If our only response is 1) we've tried everything before, 2) all we can do is increase the bombing (though McNamara says it is not slowing the infiltration rate anyway) and 3) we are really looking for a peaceful settlement (through secret channels, but can't tell the public anything about that) we may be isolated by world opinion and ultimately forced to yield to it—through a bad bargain that gets us out of the war at any price. The only alternative to that is to ignore world opinion altogether, and escalate massively in a way that threatens to widen the conflict.

"I think we may be needlessly creating problems for ourselves by not making more of a public, visible effort to bring about peace. The real warlovers like [L.] Mendel Rivers [D/S.C., chairman of the House Armed Services Committee] don't even like what you are doing covertly, in search of peace; you run no great additional risks with the hawks by making a more open effort."

The President coolly replied to McPherson in a letter drafted by Rostow, saying that he had asked Rostow to talk to McPherson about his suggestion, "and to inform you of some of the intense planning that is going forward on negotiations." Johnson Library, ND 19/CO 312, letter from the President to McPherson, Mar. 13, 1967, with attached memorandum to the President from McPherson, Mar. 11, 1967. There is no available documentation on whatever followup may have occurred, if any.

[27] *New York Times*, Mar. 24, 1967.

eight power plants in North Vietnam, after which, as an inducement for negotiations, attacks would be restricted temporarily to the area south of the 20th parallel and the U.S.S.R. would be asked to facilitate secret talks by the North Vietnamese with a U.S. representative—Llewellyn Thompson.[28] On March 10, Rostow sent a very revealing "literally eyes only" memorandum to the President in which he attempted to explain McNamara's position.[29] "First and foremost, he [McNamara] is deeply troubled about the possibility that the war will run on into next year; and then political pressures will rise, in one form or another, that would force us into an unsatisfactory settlement unworthy of what the nation has put into the struggle. Therefore, he is in a great hurry—as are we all. He is now even willing to contemplate the possibility of forcing a major crisis with the Soviet Union and Communist China by mining the Haiphong harbor and otherwise interdicting supplies from outside North Vietnam. . . . Like all of us, he hesitates to recommend this because of the risk of enlarging the war. . . ."

McNamara's "main thrust," Rostow said, "is to seek a quick end to the war by action which does not run the risks involved in mining Haiphong. He has some hopes that the present high casualty rates being inflicted on the VC plus high levels of defection will force some kind of crack in the organizational and political structure of the NLF. . . He is frustrated but does not know what he can do from here about the slow pace of pacification."

"Against this background—of one course of action which may be too dangerous and another which may be too slow—he is passionately interested in finding a way to negotiate an end to the war. . . ."

Rostow said he did not think McNamara could be described as a "dove." "He wants the Vietnam operation to succeed because of the nation's stake in it; your stake in it; and—perhaps—his stake in it. He is afraid it is endangered by the passage of time. He is thrashing about for a short cut."

Rostow added that his main difference with McNamara was whether the North Vietnamese would "seriously try to get out of the war" if the U.S. stopped bombing in the North. "Moreover," he said, "I do believe that if we are systematic about electric power we can do something significant about their war effort."

In closing, Rostow told the President, "My advice would be to support Bob in his efforts to ensure that every possible negotiating track is explored; unleash his full energies . . . at trying to accelerate pacification; but exercise great caution in surrendering prematurely or without adequate compensation our bombing in the North. In addition, you may wish to look hard and afresh at a po-

---

[28] This is the description of McNamara's memorandum of Mar. 9, 1967 in Rostow's memorandum to the President on March 10 in which he discussed McNamara's memorandum. (See following footnote.) The Johnson Library staff reports that McNamara's memorandum cannot be found.

The Office of National Estimates of the CIA concluded in a memorandum on Apr. 12, 1967, "Communist Policy and the Next Phase in Vietnam," cited above, that, contrary to McNamara's hopes, "All signs continue to indicate that their [U.S.S.R.] influence in Hanoi is limited, and that they are unwilling to risk applying real pressure in an attempt to move Hanoi toward negotiations. For the present, new appeals to the Soviets to be helpful in getting talks started would probably bring only stone-walling responses that the bombing must stop first."

[29] Johnson Library, NSF Files of Walt W. Rostow.

litical-military diplomatic plan for forcing a major crisis some time late in the spring."

New Peace Moves

It was apparent that unless the Communists yielded to additional U.S. military pressure, negotiations would be necessary if the United States was going to avoid a larger and much more costly war with no assurance, even then, that it would be possible to end the war by military means (and with the possibility that escalation might lead to a war with China and possibly the U.S.S.R.). Conceivably, there was the alternative of substituting counterinsurgency for search-and-destroy, but such a major change of strategy would have been extremely difficult to achieve and impossible to implement effectively before the 1968 election. Moreover, it, too, might not have succeeded.

Thus, while military pressure might help in promoting negotiations, the circumstances under which the war was being fought made it essential for the United States to continue to seek a political settlement rather than a military victory. As Chester Cooper concluded in a memorandum on March 11, "The Negotiations Track—Another Look," there was "one practical and compelling" argument: "We have no choice but to continue to press for a political settlement."[30]

In his memorandum, Cooper recommended that the U.S. should seek to open direct communication with the North Vietnamese,[31] and should press for early negotiations to try to keep the North Vietnamese from postponing negotiations until after the 1968 U.S. election.

Cooper also proposed changes in the U.S. position, including a reformulated version of Phase A-Phase B under which the U.S., rather than insisting that infiltration must stop before bombing ceased, would agree to stop bombing if the North Vietnamese gave private assurances that they would stop infiltration at an agreed time. In addition, Cooper suggested an approach to "mutual deescalation" by which troops from both sides would pull back from the DMZ, the

---

[30] U.S. Department of State, Central File, Pol 27-14 Viet. Cooper's memorandum is attached to a cover memorandum to the Secretary from Harriman, Mar. 11, 1967, which states that it had been considered by the Negotiations Committee.

[31] The possibility of direct negotiations by the South Vietnamese with the NLF/VC was also being considered within the State Department. On the evening of Mar. 12, 1967, a small group met at Chester Cooper's house to discuss the question. Present were Cooper, and, from the East Asia Bureau, Daniel Davidson, Heyward Isham, William A. K. Lake, and Robert Miller, as well as William R. Smyser from the Office of Intelligence and Research, and Monteagle Sterns, who, like Cooper, was working with Harriman. Cooper explained to the group that Ball thought it would be "worthwhile to explore on a theoretical basis the problems and possibilities of encouraging GVN negotiations with the NLF/VC. Was it conceivable that the NLF/VC could develop a negotiating position independent from that of Hanoi? Were there significant non-Communist elements in the NLF/VC leadership which might eventually agree to negotiate even if the hard core refused?" The response of the group was that the NLF/VC "was in no position to act independently of Hanoi. . . . An over-all settlement required a conscious decision on the part of the Front's Communist leadership to negotiate a compromise. At present, there was no sign that Hanoi or the southern leaders of the Front were willing to cooperate."

The group discussed the attitude of the South Vietnamese Government toward negotiating with the NLF/VC. It was agreed that there was little hope for such negotiations, unless the U.S. were "to use muscle on the GVN," which would have serious consequences. "It was clear that if the United States decided to use its influence to bring about a compromise settlement with the NLF/VC after elections, or to encourage formation of a neutralist party before elections, our relations with the present military leaders in Saigon would be badly strained and we might have to use our military presence in Vietnam to prevent the situation from deteriorating into chaos." (Library of Congress, Harriman Papers, Subject File, Memorandum, for the Record, Mar. 24, 1967, by Monteagle Sterns, "Subject: Negotiations with NLF/VC.")

U.S. would end the bombing of North Vietnam, and there would then be secret talks between the two sides. Under this plan, the North Vietnamese would not be asked to stop infiltrating and U.S. bombing of infiltration routes in Laos would continue.

On April 11, the Canadian Government publicly proposed a similar plan, and on April 19 the U.S. proposed that both sides move their forces back 10 miles from the DMZ, following which the U.S. would be prepared to begin peace talks. Subsequently, the zone of withdrawal could continue to expand. Harriman explained the concept to the Russians and the British. The Canadians, who were a member of the International Control Commission (ICC, an inspection group provided for by the 1954 Geneva Agreement), were asked to suggest to the two other members of the Commission, India and Poland, that they explore the possibility of an ICC peacekeeping role in the expanded DMZ (as contrasted with its prescribed monitoring functions). The Defense Department was asked to study the requirements for such a peacekeeping force.[32]

Cooper says that an hour or so after the U.S. announcement on April 19 of the proposed mutual deescalation he learned that an attack was scheduled later that day on major new targets in Haiphong. Rusk was not in Washington, and "no one else in the State Department hierarchy was ready to face up to the admittedly distasteful chore of confronting the President on the touchy bombing issue. I made a few distraught pleading phone calls to the Pentagon and to the West Basement [Rostow's office] of the White House—but with no success. The sorties had been scheduled and the President was determined that they would proceed on schedule." Soon afterwards, the diplomat from the U.S.S.R. who had been briefed on the deescalation proposal met with Harriman again and asked how the U.S. could expect, after the bombing, that the U.S.S.R. could assure the North Vietnamese that the Americans were seriously interested in a deescalation of the war. The next day, Cooper said, the North Vietnamese rejected the pull-back proposal.[33] According to Cooper,[34] the bombing attack:

> did not stem from a conscious high-level decision to sabotage the efforts of the peacemakers. Nor was it a "carrot/stick" attempt to signal Hanoi that, even though we were making a new diplomatic initiative, the pressure was still on. Either of these would at least have had the merit of reflecting some thinking on the subject at high levels of the government. But there was none at this point in time, instead, there was inertia, lethargy, and a reluctance "to upset the President." There was just no interest or effort expended in orchestrating military and diplomatic moves; every one was doing his own thing. . . .

"Even the most determined optimist," Cooper adds, "was forced to conclude after this miserable performance that there were those at the top-level who had no interest in any new ideas, approaches,

---

[32] Cooper, *The Lost Crusade*, p. 373.
[33] *Ibid.*, pp. 373–374.
[34] *Ibid.*, p. 374.

or initiatives with respect to negotiations. The current operative concept was 'Hit 'em again, but harder.'"[35]

As the U.S. military pressure intensified, there were new efforts by U.N. Secretary General U Thant to find a way to end the war. On March 6, Ambassador Goldberg met with U Thant, who had just returned from Burma where he had been visited by officials from the North Vietnamese Foreign Office. After the North Vietnamese had discussed their terms for negotiations (stop the bombing, withdraw U.S. forces, accept the North Vietnamese Four Points), U Thant told them that these terms would not be acceptable to the Americans and therefore could not serve as the basis for a settlement. He added that he thought one avenue to settlement might be a "stand down" (cessation) of all military activities by both sides. The North Vietnamese said they had no authority to discuss that idea, but that they would report it to their government and would respond at a later date. Rostow sent Goldberg's report of the conversation to the President, saying "It poses the question of a total ceasefire; although we don't have to move with U Thant until he hears from Hanoi."[36]

The next day (March 7), at the meeting noted earlier of the President, from 12:45 p.m. to 2:30 p.m. with Rusk, McNamara, Katzenbach, Rostow and Christian, after some discussion of U Thant's proposal, the President said that U Thant should be asked to put it in writing and that the U.S. would then reply.[37]

---

[35]The Canadian proposal was discussed again in June (see William Bundy's memorandum of June 16, 1967, "Linking Demilitarization of the DMZ and Some Form of Stopping the Bomb," in the Department of State, Central File, Pol 27 Viet S), but no action was taken on it.

During April, May and June 1967, Harriman's office and the East Asia Bureau continued to prepare papers on negotiations. On April 4, saying that "the President and the Secretary have expressed a desire that we develop our thinking about the problem of a cease-fire on an urgent basis," Unger circulated a paper, "Problems of a Cease-Fire," drafted by Ralph N. Clough of State's Policy Planning Council. (U.S. Department of State, Lot File 70 D 207.) On April 11, Unger sent the same recipients another paper by the same title, drafted by Robert Miller, head of the Vietnam Task Force, which discussed additional aspects of the subject.

In May, an undated, unsigned paper was prepared, probably in the East Asia Bureau, on "Summary of Positions on Negotiations, and Key Issues." (Same location) Later in May, Chester Cooper and others prepared, at Ball's request, a 60-page, single-spaced paper, "A Settlement in Vietnam," which was sent to Ball on May 25 with a cover memorandum from Cooper describing the paper as follows: "It reviews where we stand in our efforts to end the hostilities; assesses the forces and influences that must be taken into account, presents a settlement model and scenario that meet our basic objectives without prejudicing serious consideration by Hanoi and the NLF; examines alternatives to a negotiated settlement; and projects a picture of South Vietnam several years after hostilities have been concluded." (Same location.)

[36]The Goldberg report of Mar. 7, 1967 and Rostow's memorandum of the same date are in the Johnson Library, NSF, Memos to the President—Walt Rostow.

That same day, Ginsburgh prepared for Rostow a paper, "Mutual Stand Down," examining the idea. (U.S. Department of State, Central File, Pol 27 Viet S, Memorandum for Rostow from Ginsburgh, Mar. 7, 1967.) He said that U Thant's proposal "offers interesting possibilities for satisfactorily concluding the war in Vietnam. At the same time, it has its perils." By accepting the proposal, the North Vietnamese could "attempt to win by diplomacy what they have been unable to achieve by force of arms." Once a stand down was agreed upon, they could consolidate their control over large parts of South Vietnam during a period of extended negotiations, thus creating a situation where the settlement would require a "Laos-type solution" which the Government of South Vietnam could not survive.

Ginsburgh said that it was possible, however, that the North Vietnamese might want a cease-fire, and the U.S. therefore needed to respond in good faith to the proposal while deciding "as quickly as possible" what terms would be acceptable. After suggesting possible U.S. terms, he discussed the implementation of a stand down, which would involve, among other things, the movement of all Communist forces in South Vietnam into "sanctuary areas," where they would remain during negotiations.

[37]Johnson Library, NSF Files of Walt W. Rostow, Notes of the Luncheon Meeting with the President, Mar. 7, 1967.

On March 14, U Thant gave Goldberg an Aide Memoire describing the proposal.[38] The next day, Rostow sent a memorandum to the President in which he pointed out some of the problems with a stand down, but said he thought the U.S. should agree to talk about a total cease-fire.[39] On March 18, the State Department told Goldberg to support the idea of a stand down.[40]

On March 22, as will be seen, the Senate Foreign Relations Committee traveled to New York City to meet with U Thant for a discussion of possible United Nations action to settle the Vietnam conflict. Goldberg, acting on a suggestion from Katzenbach, told Senators Fulbright and Carlson (the ranking Republican on the trip), about U Thant's proposal and the U.S. response, but they agreed that this information should not be given to the other members of the committee, and U Thant said he would not raise the matter at his meeting with the committee.[41]

On March 29, the U.S. was notified that the North Vietnamese had rejected U Thant's proposal, among other things, according to a report from Goldberg to the President, because a standstill truce "equated the aggressor and the victim of aggression" and was "advantageous" to the United States. U Thant, Goldberg added, was under the impression that the North Vietnamese did not want him to continue with the initiative; the UN, the North Vietnamese said, had "nothing to do with Vietnam."[42]

Should Westmoreland be Appointed Ambassador?

In early March 1967, after deciding to increase U.S. military pressure, the President made another decision, in the course of which he may have considered taking certain actions that could have had significant effects on the U.S. role in the war. For several months, there had been increasing support for replacing Lodge with someone who could better manage U.S. programs, especially pacification, and who would be more effective in dealing with the South Vietnamese.[43] On January 11, 1967, the President and

---

[38] For the text see U.S. Department of State, Lot File 70 D 48, Washington circular telegram 155315, Mar. 15, 1967, to Saigon and several other U.S. Embassies.

[39] Johnson Library, NSF, Memos to the President—Walt Rostow, Memorandum for the President from Rostow, Mar. 15, 1967.

[40] For the text of the U.S. response see U.S. Department of State, Central File, Pol 27 Viet S, circular telegram 158177, Mar. 18, 1967, to Saigon and other U.S. Embassies. In a memorandum to the President earlier that day, Rostow set forth the points that he said Rusk wanted Goldberg to make orally to U Thant. (See Johnson Library, NSF Memos to the President—Walt Rostow, Mar. 18, 1967, 10:35 a.m.) At 2:15 p.m., Rostow sent another memorandum to the President (same location), in which he said he had talked with General Taylor, and that he and Taylor would prefer not to make a "substantive reply because we have not in fact thought through the problems of a general cessation of hostilities and because some of the language in this message could rise up to haunt us; for example 'standstill truce.'" He explained, saying, in part, that "'Standstill truce' has overtones of freezing the sovereignty and limiting the police powers in Saigon which 'cessation of hostilities' avoids. . . ." On the other hand, Rostow said, Rusk's argument for a prompt response "is quite strong."

The President approved the reply, leaving the words "standstill truce."

That evening (March 18), Goldberg met with U Thant and presented the U.S. reply. For a memorandum on the meeting see U.S. State Department, Central File, Pol 27 Viet S, USUN New York to Washington 4479, Mar. 18, 1967.

[41] Same location, USUN to Washington 4526, Mar. 22, 1967.

[42] Johnson Library, NSF, Memos to the President—Walt Rostow, USUN to Washington 4640, Mar. 30, 1967.

[43] One of the principal advocates of replacing Lodge was Komer. After visiting Vietnam in February 1967, he reported to the President that better management of U.S. programs was "the key to earlier success," and that *"the sooner you replace Lodge with a top manager the better."*

Continued

Lodge discussed the question,[44] and the President apparently mentioned the possibility of replacing him with McGeorge Bundy or McNamara. On January 21, Lodge sent a handwritten note to the President saying that the nominations of either man "could not be faulted," and that Clark Clifford would also be an excellent choice.[45]

The subject was then discussed at a Tuesday Luncheon from 2:20 p.m. to 3:20 p.m. on January 31, attended by the President, Rusk, McNamara, Taylor, Rostow, Komer and George Christian, at which there was some discussion of appointing Westmoreland as Ambassador. There are no notes of the meeting, but it seems likely that McNamara suggested Westmoreland's appointment.[46]

On February 6, Taylor sent a letter to the President responding to the latter's request at the January 31 luncheon for suggestions as to alternative ways this could be done.[47] Taylor said that, "in the absence of a very outstanding civilian candidate for Ambassador, I feel that in the selection of Westmoreland, the pros outweigh the cons by a substantial margin." Although there might be charges of undue military control, there would be the advantages of Westmoreland's experience and prestige and the "improved leverage" which he could exert on the South Vietnamese military in connection with the 1967 elections. His appointment would also consolidate all U.S. programs under "the effective direction of a single official."

If Westmoreland were appointed, Taylor added, he should be made Ambassador and Commander in Chief of all U.S. forces in South Vietnam, with a senior military assistant to command U.S. forces, a civilian assistant for nonmilitary operations, and a third assistant for management of the U.S. Mission.

Replying for the State Department, Katzenbach said in a memorandum to the President on February 11 that it would be "unwise" to appoint Westmoreland as Ambassador for these reasons:[48]

> (a) The Ambassador's function would, in effect, be placed under MACV, and we would lose the Ambassador's freedom of action to monitor our operations from a political point of view.
>
> (b) The appointment would present to the world, and particularly to the Vietnamese, an image of a U.S. move towards greater military control, with overtones of a "Governor General" appointment. It even suggests military occupation, like Germany after World War II.
>
> (c) It could have a most unfortunate effect on the thinking of the Vietnamese at a time when we are trying to promote

(emphasis in original) U.S. Department of State, Central File, Pol 27 Viet S, Memorandum from Komer to the President, Mar. 2, 1967.

[44] See in the Johnson Library, NSF Country File, Rostow's memorandum to the President, Jan. 4, 1967, on Lodge's "wishes," and in NSF, Memos for the President—Walt Rostow, Rostow's memorandum of January 10 on "talking points" for the President for his meeting with Lodge the next day.

[45] Johnson Library, NSF Memos to the President—Walt Rostow, handwritten note from Lodge to the President, Jan. 21, 1967.

[46] For Westmoreland's account of being considered for appointment as Ambassador see, *A Soldier Reports*, pp. 212–217.

[47] Johnson Library, NSF Files of Robert W. Komer, letter from Taylor to the President, Feb. 6, 1967. Taylor, had left his earlier post as Presidential consultant to become president of the Institute for Defense Analyses, a research organization affiliated with the Defense Department.

[48] Johnson Library, NSF Files of Walt W. Rostow, Memorandum to the President from Katzenbach, Feb. 11, 1967.

greater participation in the government by Vietnamese civilians rather than generals.

(d) Westmoreland's dual position would make it difficult for the Departments of State and Defense to instruct him effectively in their respective areas of concern.

Katzenbach stressed the importance of appointing an outstanding civilian with "extraordinary political sensitivity in order to operate effectively during the coming period of intense Vietnamese political activity and factionalism"—someone, he said, like Ellsworth Bunker, who had been U.S. Ambassador to the Dominican Republic during a difficult period in 1965–1966. If there were no outstanding civilians available, Katzenbach said that he "would have no serious objection" to Westmoreland, provided he first resigned from the Army, but thought he would be more valuable in his role as military commander.

McNamara and Wheeler favored Westmoreland's appointment. On February 14, Wheeler sent a backchannel message to Westmoreland saying that McNamara had raised the matter with the President, and that "there is interest."[49] McNamara's position, Wheeler said, was the same as when he and Wheeler first discussed the matter with Westmoreland (which he noted had been in November 1966), namely, that the management of the war required "a MacArthur-type operation" in which Westmoreland, as Ambassador and Commander in Chief, would plan and coordinate military strategy. Wheeler added that, "As we see it, the military effort is going extremely well; the problem area today lies in the non-military areas, and it is to these areas that you must be able to devote the same time and effort that has made the military effort a success."

On February 27, McGeorge Bundy wrote a "personal" memorandum to the President on the question of Lodge's replacement, saying that McNamara had pressed him for ideas.[50] Bundy recommended Bunker, who, he said, "has the precise combination of strength and sensitivity that Saigon now needs. . . . The spotlight on Saigon politics will be very intense in the next twelve months, and Bunker would be the ideal man to play the U.S. hand. There is no good in saying that we don't have a hand in these matters, and we have lost many tricks in the past because of the insensitivity of very brave and decent men like [Frederick E.] Nolting [Jr., former Ambassador to Vietnam] Taylor and even Lodge." At the conclusion of the memorandum Bundy added this comment: "The last time you have had this problem, I have tried to persuade you to let me do the job. I greatly regret that I cannot mount the same campaign this time—it would be a break of faith with my Trustees [the Ford Foundation, of which Bundy was then President] for me to get myself another job so soon."

On March 3, after the President's decision on February 22 to increase the use of force, Wheeler cabled Westmoreland that there had been further discussions between the President, Rusk and

[49] CMH, Westmoreland Papers, Message Files, Wheeler to Westmoreland, JCS 1190–67, Feb. 14, 1967.

[50] Johnson Library, NSF Files of Walt W. Rostow, Memorandum for the President from Bundy, Feb. 27, 1967.

McNamara of appointing Westmoreland as Ambassador.[51] Rusk said he "has no objection to you as an individual assuming the role; however, he does have concern at the prospect of a complete 'militarization' of our senior structure in South Vietnam, particularly at a time when the GVN is moving toward elections which undoubtedly will result in either Thieu or Ky being installed as President." McNamara said that, based on Westmoreland's preference not to resign from the Army,[52] he had advised the President against appointing him to the post in a civilian status. McNamara, Wheeler said, asked whether Westmoreland and he agreed that rather than for Westmoreland to be appointed Ambassador in a civilian status with someone else commanding U.S. forces, it would be preferable to leave Westmoreland in his present post. Wheeler said he felt that way and was sure that Westmoreland did also.

On March 10, Wheeler cabled Westmoreland that the idea of appointing him as Ambassador was being dropped.[53] He regretted that decision, he said, because he thought that the appointment of one man to be in charge of all U.S. military and nonmilitary programs would have greatly aided pacification.

Within a few days, as will be seen, the President announced the appointment of Ellsworth Bunker to succeed Lodge.

A few days after Wheeler's cable saying that the idea was being dropped, the President met with Washington columnist Drew Pearson, who, in notes he made of the conversation, said that the President reported that the war "was going very well," but that "Lodge has got to go," and "probably Westmoreland will go," and that he was thinking about replacing him with Gen. Bruce Palmer. (Palmer had been in charge of U.S. forces sent to the Dominican Republic in 1965–1966, where he had worked closely with Bunker. He was sent to Vietnam in early March 1967 where Westmoreland assigned him as Commander of the II Field Force, consisting of three divisions and four brigades in III Corps.)[54]

This report of the President's comment about replacing Westmoreland raises the interesting question of what the President had in mind when he first considered and then decided against appointing Westmoreland as Ambassador. Further interest is aroused by Palmer's report that when the President talked to Bunker about taking the post as Ambassador he said, with no one else present, that he wanted him, as Bunker later told Palmer, to "wind up the war for American troops as quickly as possible."[55] According to Palmer, Bunker's report of what the President said, "threw quite a different light on the period and came as a distinct surprise. In early 1967 it seemed clear enough that the President was unwilling to widen the war, that his objectives were limited, that he realized that the prospect of a protracted war was not going down well with the American people, and that he was deeply troubled about growing dissent. Nevertheless, I was under the impression in early 1967 that the President's determination to prosecute the war was strong

---

[51] CMH, Westmoreland Papers, Message Files, Wheeler to Westmoreland JCS 1637–67, Mar. 3, 1967.

[52] In the same location, see CJCS 1527–67, Feb. 28, 1967.

[53] Same location, Wheeler to Westmoreland, JCS 1815–67, Mar. 10, 1967.

[54] Johnson Library, Papers of Drew Pearson. I am grateful to Mary Knill and David Humphrey of the Johnson Library for bringing this document to my attention.

[55] Palmer, *The 25-Year War*, cited above, pp. 47–48.

and that he did not look for a lesser way out until much later in 1967."[56]

There is the additional element of Palmer's own doubts about the war. In his book, *The 25-Year War,* he indicates that he did not think that the war, as it was being fought, could be won. He says that after Bunker became Ambassador in April 1967, he talked with him privately about the situation. "I stressed my private reservations about the feasibility of our pacifying South Vietnam, given the depth of the insurgency and our passive defense strategy that could not prevent the infiltration of large forces from North Vietnam into the south. I voiced the thought that a clear-cut decision over the insurgents might not be possible and that eventually an accommodation between the two sides might have to be negotiated unless U.S. strategy was fundamentally changed."[57]

Palmer also confided his doubts to Westmoreland, "who really didn't want to talk about it," and to Abrams, then Vice Chief of Staff of the Army (who shortly thereafter became Westmoreland's deputy), who was on a visit to Vietnam. "Abrams listened but was pretty non-committal." "Later," Palmer says, "it became clear to me that both Westmoreland and Abrams realized that President Johnson would not change the way the war was being prosecuted, and that their job was to concentrate on improving South Vietnamese performance so that U.S. forces could disengage." He adds: "This was *before* Tet 1968. . . ." (emphasis in original)[58]

In considering replacing Westmoreland or making him the Ambassador, was the President trying to find a way of removing him from active military command in the hope of making some changes in the way the war was being fought? One way to do this would have been to make him Ambassador, but in that role, even as a civilian, he could still have considerable influence on the conduct of military operations. Another possibility would be to appoint a new Ambassador and to charge him with quickly ending U.S. troop involvement while at the same time replacing Westmoreland with someone who would redirect U.S. strategy and operations.

This interpretation is not necessarily inconsistent with the President's action in ordering the use of greater force. The purpose of that action was not to win the war by overcoming the enemy, but to try to compel the Communists to accept a negotiated settlement in order to help abate growing public and congressional pressure for "winning or getting out" and to meet some of the demands of the military. Moreover, while the President may have encouraged the military to think that his sentiment toward the greater use of force was changing, in fact, he approved, with several exceptions, the weakest of the three programs proposed by the JCS.

New Hearings by the Foreign Relations Committee

As the 90th Congress began in January 1967, those on the Senate Foreign Relations Committee who opposed the war—Fulbright, Mansfield, Morse, Gore, Church, Clark, Pell, and McCarthy, and,

---

[56] *Ibid.*, pp. 40–49.

[57] *Ibid.*, p. 65. Palmer says that in April 1967 he also expressed these reservations to Westmoreland and General Creighton Abrams, then Deputy Chief of Staff of the Army, who shortly afterwards became Westmoreland's deputy. See *ibid.*, p. 63.

[58] Johnson Library, Transcript of Vietnam Round Table, March 9–10, 1991, Appendix IV, Comments by General Palmer in a letter to Harry Middleton, director of the Johnson Library.

on the Republican side, Aiken—were still outnumbered 10–8 by the five Democrats and five Republicans who supported existing policy—Democrats Sparkman, Lausche, Symington, Dodd, and McGee, and Republicans Hickenlooper, Carlson, Williams of Delaware, Mundt, and Case of New Jersey, and in the full Senate by an even larger margin. Moreover, support for the administration was so strong in the House of Representatives that even if the Senate were to act, the House would continue to block action by Congress. Another factor was that, unlike the previous year, the administration's request for additional funds for Vietnam for 1967–1968 did not include economic aid funds, and the Senate Foreign Relations Committee was precluded from using hearings on economic aid, as it had in 1966, as a way of raising questions about and dramatizing opposition to the war.

On January 11, 1967, the Foreign Relations Committee held its first organizational meeting of the new Congress, and Fulbright suggested that the committee conduct hearings on the general subject, "The Responsibilities of the U.S. as a World Power." This focus, he said, would avoid some of the rancor and animosity in and out of the committee that had been generated by the 1966 hearings on Vietnam. He said he "wanted to guard against an accusation that he was starting another vendetta against the administration."[59] Pell commented that, in holding the hearings, the committee could "do it with a little modesty and criticism and self-criticism by suggesting we are doing now [in the case of Thailand] what we should have done [for Vietnam] 5 years ago. . . ." (He was referring to the concern of some members of the committee about possible commitments to Thailand that might result in an expansion of the war.) Fulbright replied that he did not realize what the U.S. was getting into in Vietnam when he supported the Gulf of Tonkin Resolution in 1964. "I am quite willing to say I was shortsighted. I had no idea that we were going to go this way." "This would be a good opening," Pell commented, and Fulbright continued, "I thought he [President Johnson] was just as determined as I was to keep out of major war out there."

Preparations for new hearings had begun several months earlier. On November 28, 1966, Chief of Staff Carl Marcy sent Fulbright a memorandum suggesting possible subjects for hearings, including "American Responsibilities as a World Power," which Marcy apparently favored. He said that he preferred holding hearings that could have an "immediate and, hopefully, a decisive impact" on U.S. policy. The 1966 hearings of the committee on Vietnam and China, he added, had "moved in that direction, although they were not as decisive as we might have wished." "My inclination," Marcy said, "is to opt for hearings on a subject with enough sex appeal to attract the attention of the press and the Committee, and with the potentiality of changing (reversing) policy within the next year or two. The Foreign Relations Committee is the only instrumentality within the Government which has that potentiality—with all its dangers." "Finally, I believe a majority of the Committee will go along with hearings in the bolder format in the hope that such

[59] U.S. Congress, Senate, Committee on Foreign Relations, unpublished executive session transcript, Jan. 11, 1967.

hearings might have a restraining influence on the President."[60] On December 12, Marcy drafted a memorandum outlining the possible content of hearings on the U.S. as a world power. The aim of such hearings, he said, would be "educational"—to "focus public attention on aspects of American foreign policy that Americans should be thinking about . . . which will help citizens deal rationally with issues which are too often dealt with on the basis of pure emotion."[61]

On January 24, the committee met again in executive session and, after some disagreement about possible witnesses, agreed to hold the hearings and, as in 1966, to make Fulbright and Hickenlooper, the ranking Republican, responsible for selecting the witnesses.[62]

On January 30, 1967, the Foreign Relations Committee held the first of its new set of hearings on "The Responsibilities of the U.S. as a World Power." The subject was "The Communist World in 1967." (In the weeks that followed, hearings were held on "Asia, the Pacific, and the United States," "Changing American Attitudes Toward Foreign Policy," and "Conflict Between United States Capabilities and Foreign Commitments.") The witness was George Kennan, renowned specialist on the Soviet Union, who talked generally about opportunities for improving U.S.-U.S.S.R relations.[63]

On January 31, Edwin Reischauer, a professor of Far Eastern history at Harvard University and former U.S. Ambassador to Japan under Presidents Kennedy and Johnson, testified that the U.S. should not have become involved in Vietnam, but that once the commitment was made it should be supported. Although he favored a "prudent deescalation" of U.S. military activities and emphasized the need for "clear and hold" and pacification rather than search and destroy, he did not think the U.S. should withdraw

---

[60] National Archives, RG 46, Papers of the Senate Foreign Relations Committee, Marcy Chron File, Memorandum from Marcy to Fulbright, Nov. 28, 1966.

[61] Same location.

[62] Unpublished executive session transcript, Jan. 24, 1967. Meanwhile there had been two other executive sessions involving members of the Foreign Relations Committee at which Vietnam was discussed. The first was an executive session on January 9 of the CIA joint subcommittee of the Armed Services and Appropriations Committees, the small group of trusted Senators which met periodically to receive briefings from the CIA, to which Russell had invited Fulbright, Mansfield and Hickenlooper for a general briefing by CIA Director Helms. The meeting was completely off-the-record, but Helms sent a summary of it to the President. Although the briefing was primarily on other subjects on which Russell had asked Helms to speak, several Senators raised specific questions on Vietnam—civilian casualties, progress of pacification, and the work of the Constituent Assembly. Fulbright asked about the effectiveness of bombing North Vietnam, and Mansfield expressed surprise at Helms' view that recent North Vietnamese statements were not less rigid than earlier statements. "The tone of the discussion," Helms memorandum concluded, "was thoughtful, businesslike, and cordial." Johnson Library, NSF Agency File, CIA.

The second was an executive session of the Foreign Relations Committee on January 16 at which Rusk spoke generally about the world situation. Most of his presentation was on Vietnam, but there was very little discussion of significance. Fulbright continued to dwell on the question of the legal basis for the U.S. role in Vietnam. After Rusk commented about congressional support for the U.S. role, Fulbright challenged him on the applicability of the SEATO Treaty. Fulbright also said that his actions on behalf of the Gulf of Tonkin Resolution were prompted by his support for the President in the 1964 election and the hope of preventing a war, and that he did not think Congress had voted for the kind of war being waged in 1967. In 1964, he said "The circumstances were very, very different." U.S. Congress, Senate, Committee on Foreign Relations, unpublished executive session transcript, Jan. 16, 1967. For Rusk's memorandum for the President summarizing the January 16 meeting, see Department of State, Lot file 74 D 164, Rusk Memorandum for the President, "Items for Evening Reading," Jan. 16, 1967, to which Rusk's summary is attached.

[63] U.S. Congress, Senate, Committee on Foreign Relations, *The Communist World in 1967*, Hearing, January 30, 1967, 90th Cong., 1st sess. (Washington, D.C.: U.S. Govt. Print. Off., 1967).

from Vietnam. "I am myself," he said, "a supporter of the administration's objective in Vietnam, which, as I understand it, is to bring the war to as speedy an end as possible, without resorting to either of the dangerous alternatives of withdrawal or major escalation."[64]

Reischauer suggested that U.S. relations with Asia should be based on the following propositions:[65]

1. We should seek to minimize our military involvement and military commitments in Asia, because our vital interests are not likely to be threatened in most of Asia, because our type of military strength is not very effective in meeting subversion and guerrilla warfare, which are the chief threats to the stability of most Asian countries, and because our military presence is likely to stir up anti-American reactions and have other influences adverse to our long-range interests.

2. We should not try to induce most Asian countries to align themselves formally with us, since such alignments do not add to our security and are not likely to be as effective in giving them security as their own unfettered nationalism and, possibly, regional groupings of like-minded countries. Far more useful, both to the security of most Asian nations and to our own, are multilateral involvements of these states with one another and with all the developed nations.

3. We should not sponsor political, social, or economic change in Asian countries, though we should be responsive to requests from them for aid in carrying out such changes whenever we judge that these changes would help in the healthy development of these countries and that our aid could usefully contribute to this end. We run serious and unwarranted dangers when we take the initiative in sponsoring important internal changes in Asian lands or when our influence becomes so preponderant that we assume responsibility for the existence or nature of a regime. Such situations are all too likely to produce serious friction between our well-meaning efforts and their nationalism.

4. We should not seek to play the role of leader in Asia, rallying allies to our policies, but should attempt to withdraw to the role of a friendly outside supporter of individual or collective Asian initiatives. In such a role, we are more likely to be able to give effective aid to Asian countries than when we assume the leadership ourselves.

On February 20, Henry Steele Commager, a prominent historian, testified that U.S. involvement in the Vietnam war was a mistake, and that fighting should be ended.[66] He sketched for the committee some of the ideas underlying the U.S. role in world affairs, especially the concept of "mission" that had influenced American territorial expansion. He also stressed the experience of the United States as the first "new nation" and Americans as believers in

[64] U.S. Congress, Senate, Committee on Foreign Relations, *Asia, the Pacific, and the United States,* Hearing, January 31, 1967, 90th Cong., 1st sess. (Washington, D.C.: U.S. Govt. Print. Off., 1967), pp. 4, 14.

[65] *Ibid.,* pp. 8–9. Several months later, Reischauer expounded on these and related points in *Beyond Vietnam: The United States and Asia* (New York: Knopf, 1967).

[66] U.S. Congress, Senate, Committee on Foreign Relations, *Changing American Attitudes Toward Foreign Policy,* Hearing, February 20, 1967, 90th Cong., 1st sess. (Washington, D.C.: U.S. Govt. Print. Off., 1967), pp. 3–14.

change, which he said should make the U.S. more sympathetic to those in other countries struggling for change and independence.

Commager argued that the U.S. role in the Vietnam war was not supported by either the SEATO Treaty or the Gulf of Tonkin Resolution. U.S. action, he said, was also in conflict with the United Nations Charter, and he recommended that, in keeping with the Charter, the U.S. should turn the matter over to the U.N.[67]

Commager was asked about the attitude of intellectuals toward the war, and he replied:[68]

> I think the effort of some to pretend that there is a great deal of support among the intellectuals for our foreign policy is a mistaken one. . . . I do not know any war in our history where the hostility was so deep or so widespread among intellectuals—in the academic world, the religious world, the journalistic world as it is here and now. . . . There is a feeling not only are we launched upon dangerous courses, but that it is impossible to reach those in positions of high authority or to bring home to them the causes for our discontent and our disillusionment. There is a deep feeling that we have lost our moral leadership in much of the Western World, that we are now not so much naked to our enemies in Vietnam, but naked before our friends. . . .

On February 21, the Foreign Relations Committee held the last of these "educational" hearings, with retired General Gavin, who had testified in the 1966 hearings, appearing again as a witness.[69] "What is now needed," Gavin said, "is a political solution." "Undoubtedly, the terms that we will be confronted with will seem to us to be rather a stiff price to pay for peace, but the alternative is a protracted conflict for many years that will ultimately assume an Orwellian character; a war that will go on for years and will take many lives, Vietnamese and American, and a war in which ultimately the basic issues on which it began will, no doubt, have become forgotten by the participants."[70]

He also opposed continuation of the war because of its effects on the United States. "I am afraid that our society is going to be torn apart," he said, adding that he was more concerned about the effects of the war at home than he was about what was happening in Vietnam.[71]

Gavin opposed the bombing of North Vietnam, which he said "has caused considerable civilian casualties, has not stopped the flow of supplies to the south, and has aroused the ill will of people throughout the world." He also took the position that the U.S. should negotiate with Ho Chi Minh and the National Liberation Front for the establishment of an independent, neutral, non-Communist status for Vietnam comparable to that for Laos provided by

---

[67] *Ibid.*, p. 18.

[68] *Ibid.*, pp. 47–48.

[69] U.S. Congress, Senate, Committee on Foreign Relations, *Conflicts Between United States Capabilities and Foreign Commitments,* Hearing on February 21, 1967, 90th Cong., 1st sess. (Washington, D.C.: U.S. Govt. Print. Off., 1967). Gavin, who had been involved in 1954 in planning for the possible intervention of U.S. forces in Indochina, had testified before the committee in February 1966 that he had never favored major U.S. military involvement in Vietnam, and in his testimony he proposed an "enclave" strategy by which U.S. forces would establish strategic strong points rather than seeking to take and control territory throughout Vietnam.

[70] *Ibid.*, p. 4.

[71] *Ibid.*, pp. 25–26.

the 1962 Geneva Accords.[72] He was asked whether the neutrality of Vietnam would threaten U.S. vital interests, and he replied that it would be the "best thing that could happen to us. Not only would it not be a threat to our vital interests but it would enable us to redeploy our vast resources in that area to deal with the more pressing serious problems we have at home and in other parts abroad."[73]

Three days after the Gavin hearings, Chief of Staff Marcy sent Chairman Fulbright a memorandum saying, "If the Committee is to keep the initiative of influence in foreign policy it must begin to plan now for the next few moves."[74] He suggested three possible moves. First, noting that "the local press is putting the [educational] hearings back with the brassiere adds," he said that to "rejuvenate" the hearings, and to meet the criticism "that witnesses thus far have been handpicked to please the Chairman," Fulbright should consider inviting witnesses who probably disagreed with him. "Specifically, could the staff have your O.K. to draft letters to [John] McCone [former Director of the CIA], [McGeorge] Bundy, and possibly [retired Air Force Commander] Curtis LeMay. We would also like to invite General [David] Shoup [former Commandant of the Marines]—letting the chips fall where they may. He might support your position, or be against it."[75]

Marcy's second suggestion was that the Foreign Relations Committee should make a two-week trip to Tokyo, Hong Kong, Saigon and Bangkok to talk with U.S. officials and national leaders. (The committee had made a trip of this nature to Europe in 1951, he said, but there had been none since that time.) "Johnson went to Honolulu and to Manila last year," Marcy said. "Rusk roams the world. This Committee sits in Washington and offers advice."

"I know of personal knowledge," he added, "that Senators Pell and Case are looking for an excuse to go to Vietnam and Senator Carlson also wants to go. Members who will be up for election next year ought to go—and this includes Senator Hickenlooper and you, as well as Senators Church, Clark, Morse, and Lausche."

Marcy said that the committee could find time for such a trip if it did not hold public hearings on the foreign aid authorization bill for fiscal year 1968, which he said was a rewrite of previous aid bills.

Third, Marcy suggested that the committee should issue a declaration of its views on the "minimum terms of a settlement in Vietnam." "I would hope we can get a draft that would appeal to a majority of the members and thus, perhaps, get a dialogue going with Hanoi and the NLF that would compel the Administration to articulate the acceptable conditions for a settlement of the war—perhaps through hearings."[76]

---

[72] *Ibid.*, pp. 3, 26.

[73] *Ibid.*, p. 27. General Gavin's proposal for negotiating a neutral status for Vietnam, while criticized at the time by military spokesmen for the Johnson administration, was quite similar to that suggested in retrospect by General William Rosson. (See pt. III of this study, pp. 456–457.)

[74] National Archives, RG 46, Papers of the Committee on Foreign Relations, Marcy Chron File, Memorandum from Marcy to Fulbright, Feb. 24, 1967.

[75] For Shoup's opposition to the war, as well as that of Gavin and other military leaders, see Bob Buzzanco, "The American Military's Rationale Against the Vietnam War," *Political Science Quarterly*, 101 (Nov. 4, 1986), pp. 559–577.

[76] Marcy attached to his memorandum to Fulbright the draft of such a declaration, the operative part of which was as follows:

"After all," he added, "this Committee has a duty to advise. I would guess that at least five members of the Committee have spent more time thinking about Vietnam than has the President—at least, they think about the broad policy rather than picking the targets. [This was a reference to the President's involvement in decisions about which targets to bomb in North Vietnam.] Moreover, neither the President nor his advisers have a monopoly on judgment, which is what we need more than these mixed up facts about infiltration, etc."

None of these suggestions by Marcy was carried out (in part because the Senate meanwhile had begun to debate the request for supplemental funds for Vietnam). The educational hearings were not continued, the committee held public hearings on the foreign aid bill and did not consider a trip to the Far East, and the declaration was not issued. There was, however, a series of four informal coffees for interested Senators held at the committee's offices at which guest speakers discussed various aspects of the war. According to Fulbright, 10–15 Senators were involved, and it was out of that nucleus that the various Senate amendments to control the war developed subsequently.[77]

Congress Approves a Policy Statement; Rejects Limitations on Presidential Action

While the Foreign Relations Committee was skirting the issue of the war with "educational" hearings, and the House Foreign Affairs Committee was generally avoiding the subject,[78] congressional interest in and debate on the war once again centered around the need for funds. This process began on January 24, 1967, when President Johnson in his Budget Message for Fiscal Year 1968 asked Congress for two appropriations for the war: a $12.3 billion supplemental request for the remainder of the fiscal year then in progress (fiscal year 1967, ending June 30, 1967) and $21.9 billion

---

"We believe the national interests of the United States would not be jeopardized and the cause of international peace would be promoted if the following principles were accepted by all parties to the conflict as the basis for a cessation of hostilities:

"1. The existing line of demarcation between North and South Vietnam (17th parallel) established by the Geneva Conference of 1954 should be accepted by all parties and honored as a de facto boundary until a final settlement can be reached.

"2. The people of North and South Vietnam should be free without outside interference to determine their own form of Government. For its part, the United States would not interfere with the establishment of a national Government in Saigon. It would hope to see all significant groups in South Vietnam participate in the political process and would support efforts to provide temporary international supervision of the process should that prove necessary and feasible.

"3. The Governments of North Vietnam and South Vietnam should undertake reciprocally not to interfere directly or indirectly in the political, economic or military posture of each other; the policing of such an undertaking to be vested in such multinational surveillance as may be mutually acceptable to the parties directly concerned.

"4. Efforts should be made to find a means of giving Vietnam representation in the United Nations.

"5. All foreign forces stationed in either North or South Vietnam (including such North Vietnamese forces as may be in South Vietnam, and vice versa) should be withdrawn in a time-phased, orderly manner, so that in due course no foreign troops or bases shall remain in either North or South Vietnam.

"6. A settlement should look toward a neutralized Vietnam and the United States should support steps toward that end.

"7. As a concrete step toward promoting a settlement the United States should cease its bombing of the North and thereby evidence this nation's desire to terminate hostilities in Vietnam."

[77] CRS Interview with J. William Fulbright, Feb. 18, 1983.

[78] During February-May, the Asian and Pacific Affairs Subcommittee of the House Foreign Affairs Committee held three weeks of hearings on rural development in Asia, including Vietnam. See U.S. Congress, House, Committee on Foreign Affairs, *Rural Development in Asia*, Hearings, 90th Cong., 1st sess. (Washington, D.C.: U.S. Govt. Print. Off., 1967), published in two parts.

in regular appropriations for the following fiscal year (FY 1968, ending June 30, 1968).[79]

In the Budget Message the President also notified Congress that in order to meet both domestic needs and the costs of the war, he would, depending upon economic conditions at the time, ask Congress later in the year for a temporary 6 percent tax surcharge on personal and corporate income, to be effective July 1, 1967.[80] Congressional reactions to the proposed 6 percent surcharge were quite unfavorable. According to one source, "The request was met with almost no enthusiasm. Constituent mail against the proposal was said to be extraordinarily heavy."[81] A Harris Survey in February indicated that the proposed surcharge was opposed by 65 percent of the public and approved by 24 percent, compared to 49 percent opposed and 44 percent in favor a year earlier. Spending cuts were preferred over increased taxes by 75 percent of respondents.[82]

The first round in Congress' action on the request for $12.3 billion in supplemental funds for the remainder of fiscal year 1967 occurred on January 23–25, 1967, in joint meetings of the Senate Armed Services Committee and the Department of Defense Subcommittee of the Senate Appropriations Committee. (Senator Russell was chairman of both the Armed Services Committee and the

---

[79] For the text of the President's Annual Budget Message to the Congress, Fiscal Year 1968, see *Public Papers of the Presidents,* Lyndon B. Johnson, 1967, pp. 39–61. For his request for a $12.3 billion supplemental for Vietnam, see pp. 61–62.

It will be recalled that in making his fiscal year 1967 request to Congress in January of 1966 for $10 billion, the President and his associates had taken the position that, for planning purposes, the budget for the war was based on the assumption that the war would be over by the end of fiscal year 1967 (June 30, 1967). This tactic had been strongly criticized in Congress, where it was predicted that the administration would have to return in early 1967, half-way through the fiscal year, for as much or more in additional funds to finance the war for the remainder of the year. As a result of this congressional criticism, as well as the fact that by 1967 the cost of the war had leveled out at about $25 billion per year, thus enabling the administration to project costs more accurately, the fiscal year 1968 request was not based on a projected date by which the war would end.

For a discussion of these budgetary questions and the general questions of the effects of the war on the economy, see U.S. Congress, Joint Economic Committee, *Economic Effects of Vietnam Spending,* especially the testimony of Senator Stennis, pp. 70 ff. of vol. I. Several economists also testified, including Murray L. Weidenbaum of Washington University, whose study, "Impact of the Vietnam War on American Economy," published in April 1967 by the Center of Strategic Studies of Georgetown University, is reprinted on pp. 193–236 of vol. I. The title of the hearings is misleading, however. They dealt primarily with the economic effects of the ending of the Vietnam war and the problems of economic adjustments after the war.

On July 9, 1967, the Joint Economic Committee issued a report on the hearings (S. Rept. 90–394) in which it charged that underestimates in 1966 of the cost of the war had caused "havoc" in the economy, and that "the same dreary cycle of events threaten again in calendar 1967." For a summary of the report see *Congressional Quarterly Almanac,* 1967, pp. 930–931.

[80] *Annual Budget Message to the Congress,* Fiscal Year 1968, cited above, pp. 40–41.

After the President decided in early 1966 not to request a tax increase, the Federal Reserve had tightened monetary policy to slow inflation and by the summer of 1966 interest rates had risen, rates on municipal bonds had increased, and mortgage money had become scarce. In September 1966, the President, on the advice of his economic advisers, asked Congress to approve a limited tax increase by suspending the investment tax credit. This request was approved in October.

By the end of 1966, the President was advised that although inflation and the increased budget deficit were serious problems, because of the declining rate of economic growth he should not ask Congress for a tax increase until later in 1967. See King, "The President and Fiscal Policy in 1966," p. 702, Kettl, "The Economic Education of Lyndon Johnson," pp. 56–67, and Califano, *The Triumph and Tragedy of Lyndon Johnson,* pp. 181–182.

For a useful paper on economic trends during 1966, see "1966—Year of Excessive Demands and Their Control," *Federal Reserve Bank of St. Louis Review,* December 1966, reprinted in vol. II, pp. 556–596 of *Economic Effect of Vietnam Spending.* See also *Economic Report of the President,* January 1967, together with the *Annual Report of the Council of Economic Advisers* (Washington, D.C.: U.S. Govt. Print. Off., 1967).

[81] *Congressional Quarterly Almanac,* 1967, p. 643. See also Califano, p. 184 and King, p. 705.

[82] Kettl, p. 66.

Defense Subcommittee of the Appropriations Committee.)[83] These hearings proved to be somewhat eventful when Secretary of Defense McNamara testified that the bombing of North Vietnam had not "significantly reduced, nor any bombing that I could contemplate in the future would significantly reduce, the actual flow of men and materiel to the South," and JCS Chairman Wheeler, disagreed, saying that he thought bombing had reduced the flow of men and materiel from North Vietnam "to an extent which limits the number of people that they can deploy into South Vietnam."

In response to McNamara, Senator Howard W. Cannon (D/Nev.) commented, "Why do we keep sending the tremendous sorties up there, risking our men, our equipment and material, losing a lot of American lives and expending a lot of effort, if we are not significantly reducing the flow?" McNamara replied that the number of lives lost was small in comparison to those lost in the main battle in the South, adding that, from the beginning, bombing of the North had been conceived as a "penalty" against the North Vietnamese to help induce them to cease their operations against the South rather than as a way of preventing infiltration or as a substitute for military operations against Communist forces in the South.[84] This statement ran somewhat counter, however, to his previous testimony to congressional committees about the value of ROLLING THUNDER in reducing infiltration.

Although few if any Members of Congress knew that in his October 1966 report McNamara had recommended stabilizing military activities and placing greater emphasis on pacification, he strongly hinted at it in his testimony when, in addition to questioning the value of bombing, he said that while U.S. search and destroy operations had been an "unqualified success," there had not been satisfactory progress in the securing of local areas against the Communists and in pacification, which was the key to ultimate success in the war.[85]

Senate debate on the authorization bill for the Vietnam supplemental request for fiscal year 1966, which had been reported without change from the Armed Services Committee, began on February 23, 1967, the day after the President approved (but did not announce publicly) an expanded program of U.S. military actions. Almost immediately after the bill was taken up, Senator Joseph Clark, Democrat of Pennsylvania, a member of the Foreign Relations Committee and a critic of the war, introduced an amendment, which Morse, also a member of the committee, joined in sponsoring, entitled a "Statement of Congressional Policy," as follows:[86]

> It is hereby declared to be the sense of the Congress—
>
> (1) that none of the funds authorized by this Act or any other Act shall be used to carry out military operations in

[83] A small part of the $12.3 billion request for military funds had to be authorized before being appropriated, which is the reason why the Armed Services Committees were involved. As was mentioned earlier, the fiscal year 1967 supplemental request was entirely military, however, and did not include any foreign aid funds. Thus, the Foreign Relations and Foreign Affairs Committees were not involved in its consideration.

[84] *Supplemental Military Procurement and Construction Authorizations for Fiscal Year 1967,* cited above, pp. 69–70. See also p. 57 for McNamara's more specific explanation of the accomplishments of bombing the North.

[85] *Ibid.*, p. 13.

[86] *CR,* vol. 113, p. 4295. For Clark's statement of his position on the war see pp. 4607–4620 and 4764–4766.

> or over North Vietnam or to increase the number of United States military personnel in South Vietnam above 500,000, unless there shall have been a declaration of war against North Vietnam by the Congress in accordance with article I, section 8, of the Constitution of the United States; and
>
> (2) that the Congress supports those efforts being made by men of good will throughout the world to prevent an expansion of the war in Vietnam and to bring that conflict to an end through a negotiated settlement which will preserve the honor of the United States, protect the vital interests of this country, and allow the people of South Vietnam to determine the affairs of that nation in their own way.

Knowing that the chances for passage of the amendment were slim, even though it was only a "sense of Congress" amendment which would not be binding on the Executive, Clark then introduced a second and more limited amendment:[87]

> The Congress hereby declares—
>
> (1) its firm intentions to provide all necessary support for members of the Armed Forces of the United States fighting in Vietnam;
>
> (2) [same language as (2) from the first amendment]
>
> (3) its support of the Geneva Conference Agreement of 1954 and the Final Declaration of that Conference as a basis for settlement of the Vietnam War, and to that end urges that the Conference be reconvened as soon as practicable for the purpose of formulating plans to effectively implement that agreement.

Senator Russell, who, as chairman of the Armed Services Committee, was the floor manager of the bill, opposed the Clark amendment. He said that nothing would be gained by a declaration of war, and that it could result in an escalation of the war because of possible secret treaties of mutual assistance between North Vietnam and the U.S.S.R. and China that might be triggered by such a U.S. declaration.[88] If Congress wanted to assert its authority, Russell, said, it should repeal the Gulf of Tonkin Resolution. Fulbright replied: "I think it would be impractical to do that." He asked Russell whether he thought that in adopting the Gulf of Tonkin Resolution the Senate had intended to give advance approval "for the President to involve the Nation in a conflict of this magnitude," to which Russell replied, "Personally, at that time I did not contemplate anything of this magnitude."[89]

Continuing his comments on Clark's proposal, Russell said he was opposed to any amendment that proposed reducing U.S. military operations. Airstrikes on North Vietnam, he said, "hurt them as badly as anything does," and the only way to end the war would be, as in Korea, "by keeping the pressure on North Vietnam until Ho Chi Minh concludes that he cannot possibly win. . . ."[90] He added, however, a very significant statement—significant because

---

[87] *Ibid.*, pp. 4295–4296.
[88] *Ibid.*, p. 4717.
[89] *Ibid.*, p. 4723.
[90] *Ibid.*, pp. 4717, 4723.

of his close relationship with the President, his standing in Congress, and his power and reputation in the military community. He said he was "strongly opposed to any invasion of North Vietnam."

Symington agreed with Russell's opposition to the amendment. If the President decided to get out of Vietnam, Symington said that he too was "ready to get out," but while the war was being waged he objected to the restrictions on the Air Force.[91]

The Clark amendment was also opposed by another highly respected Senator, Cooper, a Republican from Kentucky, who took the position that under the Constitution Congress could not limit the President's authority as Commander in Chief, and that Congress could not and should not attempt to direct the war.[92]

Others were also opposed, including both Thurmond and Ernest F. Hollings (Democrat) from South Carolina. Thurmond said it was not a time to discuss policy. He recommended bombing all of the strategic and military targets in North Vietnam and closing all of the North Vietnamese ports. The enemy had to be convinced, he said, that the U.S. would use its power, and only through punishment could the enemy be brought to terms. Hollings said that the U.S. was "winning politically and militarily in Vietnam today," and that it was essential to let the North Vietnamese know that Americans were united in their determination to win.[93]

On February 28, Majority Leader Mansfield offered a substitute to Clark's amendment in the form of a slightly revised version of Clark's second amendment. This was the text of Mansfield's amendment:[94]

> The Congress hereby declares—
>
> (1) its firm intentions to provide all necessary support for members of the Armed Forces of the United States fighting in Vietnam;
>
> (2) its support of efforts being made by the President of the United States and other men of good will throughout the world to prevent an expansion of the war in Vietnam and to bring that conflict to an end through a negotiated settlement which will preserve the honor of the United States, protect the vital interests of this country, and allow the people of South Vietnam to determine the affairs of that nation in their own way; and
>
> (3) its support of the Geneva accords of 1954 and 1962 and urges the convening of that Conference or any other meeting of nations similarly involved and interested as soon as possible for the purpose of formulating plans for bringing the conflict to an honorable conclusion in accordance with the principles of those accords.

In response to a question from Russell as to whether the substitute amendment was intended to bring about any "modification or change or limitation" in the Gulf of Tonkin Resolution, Mansfield said that he had introduced the substitute amendment because of his concern that if the original Clark amendment were defeated, that vote could be interpreted as a rejection of the limita-

---

[91] *Ibid.*, p. 4724.
[92] *Ibid.*, p. 4727.
[93] *Ibid.*, pp. 4728, 4763.
[94] *Ibid.*, p. 4766, as amended by Mansfield on p. 4938.

tions of the Clark amendment, and thus as approval of an open-ended authorization. He added that in offering the amendment he hoped "to bring out a valid consensus of Senate sentiment."[95]

Mansfield said that he had not discussed the substitute amendment with the administration or with any other Members of the Senate, although he had told Clark that he was going to offer it. Credit for the amendment, he said, should go to Clark, who had originally offered it.[96]

For its part, the administration welcomed the Mansfield amendment, whatever its role in devising it may have been.[97]

The Mansfield-Clark amendment was crafted in such a way as to satisfy the political and policy needs of most Members of Congress and to express general Senate and congressional attitudes on the war. Members of Congress who wanted to voice their desire for ending the war, but with honor, could do so, while reaffirming their support for America's fighting men. Supporters of the war could reaffirm their goals. Antiwar activists, especially those on the Foreign Relations Committee, could take some encouragement from the fact that Congress was finally taking a policy stand on the need to end the war. The administration and its supporters could be heartened by the fact that Congress was not challenging the President's authority or his expressed intentions to prosecute the war militarily while seeking a negotiated settlement. Those who thought the United States was playing a legitimate and necessary role in Vietnam could be reassured; while those who thought that the South Vietnamese should assume more responsibility for their own destiny could gain new confidence that this was the congressionally approved goal of U.S. policy.

Because it served all of these purposes, the second Clark amendment as revised by Mansfield passed the Senate on February 28 by a vote of 72–19, with nine conservative Southern Democrats, including Russell and Stennis, and ten conservative Republicans opposed.[98] Those who voted against it argued that it was not needed, that it should be voted on separately rather than in connection with the defense authorization bill, and that it would mislead and encourage the enemy. Those who voted for it, and they included some of the stalwart supporters of the administration's Vietnam policy such as Dirksen, Dodd, Hickenlooper, Lausche, McGee, Smathers, and Symington, based their support on the fact that, as Mansfield emphasized, the major purpose of the amendment was to declare that the U.S. objective in Vietnam was an honorable peace, and that this was consistent with administration policy. There seemed to be general agreement with Mansfield's statement: "We do not intend to withdraw. We will not withdraw. The question of how we got in is moot. The immediate question is: 'How do we get out and how do we get out under honorable circumstances?'"[99]

Despite disclaimers that the Mansfield-Clark amendment was only a restatement of U.S. policy and did not add to or change existing policy, and denials that it would interfere with the conduct

---

[95] *Ibid.*, p. 4946.
[96] *Ibid.*, p. 4938.
[97] See statements by McNamara and General Wheeler below, p. 597.
[98] *CR*, vol. 113, p. 4948.
[99] *Ibid.*, p. 4945.

of the war or encourage the enemy to think that the United States was becoming disillusioned with the war and would not continue to prosecute it as vigorously, the North Vietnamese may have interpreted the amendment as signifying, as indeed it did signify, that the U.S. wanted to end the war. It may have reinforced their strategy of encouraging Americans to think that there was a military stalemate, and that the war could not be won and was not worth winning in terms of its human and financial cost and the problems of developing an honest, effective, popularly supported Government in South Vietnam.

Apart from its possible effect on the enemy, however, this and subsequent amendments to limit and end the war served a basic purpose in the American political system. Although there had not been any major breaks in the ranks of administration loyalists—these came later in 1967—Members of Congress were aware of the increasing dissatisfaction of the public, and this, together with the lack of progress in the war, caused them to be receptive to a move that would help them politically as well as represent their own concerns about the lack of progress and the need to find an honorable way out of Vietnam.

The President and his associates were more sensitive to the lack of progress in the war than might have been assumed by those who did not know about McNamara's doubts that the war could be "won," and the President's acceptance of McNamara's recommendation to put a cap on troop deployment and to give primary emphasis to pacification. While appearing to be confident, and while endeavoring to shore up public and congressional support for the war, the President, as was mentioned earlier, may well have believed that success was eluding him and his country, and that it was only a matter of time before the public would tire of the war and force the Government to end it. While the President probably did not relish the idea of Congress' passing the Mansfield-Clark amendment because of its infringement on his own role, he understood the political pressures which he and Members of Congress were facing together, and the need, therefore, for an expression of sentiment that would help Members of Congress to respond to public discontent without undermining him politically or interfering with U.S. policy.

From the standpoint of the significance of the Mansfield-Clark amendment in the policy process, it is important to understand that although the amendment may have been a restatement of existing U.S. policy and of the President's own position, this action had a significance for the future direction of U.S. policy that may not have been fully appreciated at the time. It was the first statement by Congress about limiting the war and seeking a negotiated settlement. It also put Congress on record, for the first time, in support of the Geneva Accords.

Moreover, both Congress and the President (by approving the bill in which the amendment appeared) went on record as favoring complete freedom for the South Vietnamese to "determine the affairs of that nation in their own way," which left open the question of a coalition government with the Communists, unification with the North, or neutrality. As long as the "honor of the United States" was preserved—which, it should be noted, was the first objective stated in the resolution—and the settlement protected the "vital interests" of the United States, there was no explicit recognition in the amendment of any continuing obligation on the part of the United States to defend South Vietnam, or even to assist it in defending itself.

Thus, a year before the "Tet offensive" and six years before the 1973 Paris Agreement, the Mansfield-Clark amendment established the policy framework for the termination of the war and the withdrawal of American forces. In this sense, the amendment occupies an important place in the sequence of events that led to eventual U.S. disengagement from Vietnam, as well as being important from the standpoint of the role of Congress and legislative-executive collaboration in the making of U.S. policy during the war.

Congress Approves New Funds

Senate debate on the authorization bill for the supplemental appropriations request ended on March 1, and the bill passed 89–2, with Morse and Nelson opposed. Gruening, who was absent, announced that he would have voted no.

As debate ended, Senator Javits again made the point that the Gulf of Tonkin Resolution was out of date and should be replaced by another resolution. He said he would support the supplemental request, but he thought the U.S. should attempt to be more conciliatory in its terms for peace talks, and, as a step in this direction, that it should cease bombing the North. He added that the first priority for the U.S., and the best way of ending the war, was to "legitimize the Saigon government at its roots" by helping to bring about the adoption of the constitution then being prepared and the elections which were to follow.[100]

Senator Aiken alluded to his speech of October 1966 in which he had called for the U.S. to declare that it had won and to discontinue offensive military operations, and asked, "What is it that we have not won which we still seek to win?" The problem in Vietnam, he said, was "social re-engineering," which only the Vietnamese could accomplish:[101]

> What makes the Vietnam war so incredible to so many here and abroad is the spectacle of the United States, largely through deployment of its matchless military power, attempting to reengineer the society of Vietnam.
>
> Of course, sweeping changes in Vietnamese society are needed if the Vietnamese people are to defend themselves against the depredations of the Vietcong's Murder, Inc., policy.
>
> But how can we believe that this is a task which can be accomplished largely by Americans, and by American Armed Forces at that?

Aiken said that the U.S. could not and should not withdraw from Vietnam, and that U.S. forces would have to remain in Vietnam and in Southeast Asia for many years. Both the idea of withdrawal and the idea of victory through airpower were rooted in the illusion that withdrawal would be possible in the foreseeable future, he said. Neither total victory nor withdrawal was possible, "Yet we

---

[100] *Ibid.*, p. 4938. On Mar. 3, 1967, the administration replied to Javits in a speech by Smathers. See *ibid.*, pp. 5327–5328.

[101] *Ibid.*, p. 4870.

can say that we have won militarily all that is necessary and no power on earth will rise to challenge our word. What would such a declaration mean? It would mean a radical change in strategy—a change from a strategy of trying to re-engineer Vietnamese society to one of mounting a strong watch over that society, a watch maintained at strong points on the coast and at sea."

"We would be saying to our friends in Saigon that social change must be their job and that it is time they got down to it. If this means they will turn to negotiations with the Vietcong, so be it; it is their country."

"[W]e are in a very real sense our own worst enemy in that country," Aiken concluded. "We have chosen a strategy that ill befits our vast military power; we have persevered with that strategy to the point where we are encouraging even our own people to believe that we face either an unthinkable retreat or a hideous escape into a wider and more terrible war. This is a strategy that denies options; it is a strategy that has failed."

On March 2, 1967, Senator Robert Kennedy, who, according to Arthur Schlesinger, had become convinced of the need to speak out more forcefully on the war as a result of his meeting with the President on February 6, gave a major speech on Vietnam.[102] Asserting that "Nearly all Americans share with us the determination and intention to remain in Vietnam until we have fulfilled our commitments," Kennedy said: "Three Presidents have taken action in Vietnam. As one who was involved in many of those decisions, I can testify that if fault is to be found or responsibility assessed, there is enough to go around for all—including myself." The issue, he said, was how best to support President Johnson's "middle road between withdrawal and ever-widening war." He proposed a three-point program:

> (1) The United States would halt the bombing of North Vietnam and state that it would be ready to start negotiations within a week.
>
> (2) If negotiations began, the United States should seek agreement that neither side would "substantially increase" the scale of the war in the South by "infiltration or reinforcement," and should attempt to secure international supervision of this provision.
>
> (3) With an "international presence gradually replacing American troops," a final settlement should allow all major political factions in South Vietnam, including the National Liberation Front, to participate in elections to select a national leadership.

Kennedy's speech was hailed by Democrats Mansfield, Fulbright, Clark, McGovern, Gore, and Hartke, among others, as well as by Republicans Cooper and Percy, the latter having previously made a similar suggestion. Senate Republican leader Dirksen said he stood by the President, and various Democrats, including McGee,

---

[102] *Ibid.*, pp. 5279 ff. In preparing the speech, Kennedy had consulted McNamara, Taylor and Harriman.

For a summary and analysis of the speech by NSC staff member William Jorden, see Johnson Library, NSF Files of Walt W. Rostow, Memorandum to the President from Rostow, Mar. 3, 1967, with attached memorandum to Rostow from Jorden, March 3. See Schlesinger, *Robert F. Kennedy and His Times*, pp. 770–775 for background on Kennedy's decision to give the speech, the process of drafting, and reaction to the speech.

Lausche, Jackson, and Robert C. Byrd of West Virginia indicated their skepticism or disagreement with Kennedy's proposal in a series of questions to him during a brief discussion after his speech.

The President, who had learned in advance that the speech was going to be made, directed Rusk to respond, and asked Westmoreland to hold a news conference on the progress of the war, especially the value of the bombing of North Vietnam. Rusk responded with a statement that Kennedy's proposal had already been tried, and that the Communists had not given any "signal" of their interest in negotiating.[103] In a cable to Lodge approved personally by Rusk, the State Department took the position that the South Vietnamese Government should be told that Kennedy's proposal had already been tried, in order "to steer GVN away from any sharp denunciations of peaceful initiatives of sort Kennedy sketched out." [104]

Wheeler cabled Westmoreland on March 1 that, "We are being subjected to a new flood of propaganda, domestic and foreign, charging that our air campaign against North Vietnam is ineffective, and, therefore, we could discontinue it with no detriment to our war effort in Southeast Asia." "Substantial rumor has it," he said "that a major speech [Kennedy's] will soon be made by a leading Democratic politician echoing the foregoing thesis," and "Highest authority" wants Westmoreland to hold a press conference as soon as possible and to state the results of air operations in "positive terms." [105]

The President asked Rusk, McNamara, Taylor and Rostow for their recommendations on Kennedy's proposals.[106] Rusk replied that the North Vietnamese had "made it clear that they would strongly oppose every essential point in them. The Senator's problem, therefore, is not with us but with Hanoi." He added that he believed the U.S. should continue to probe possible interest in negotiations, and "should be prepared to consider a suspension of the bombing if in fact a serious prospect of peace opens up. But a suspension is quite different from a permanent cessation; for the latter, we must have some corresponding action by Hanoi or we will find ourselves in a struggle that could last for years." [107]

In his memorandum to the President, Rostow said that Kennedy's proposal was similar in substance to the proposals that had been made by the administration, but that he was suggesting a "conditional halt to bombing"—which the U.S. had already proposed and which had been rejected—whereas the North Vietnamese wanted an unconditional halt.[108]

---

[103] *New York Times*, Mar. 4, 1967. Kennedy disagreed with Rusk. *Ibid.*, Mar. 5, 1967.

[104] U.S. Department of State, Central File, Pol 27 Viet S, Washington to Manila 147883, Mar. 2, 1967. The cable was sent to William Bundy, who was enroute to a meeting with South Vietnamese leaders.

[105] CMH, Westmoreland Papers, Message Files, CJCS 1594–67 and 1613–67, Mar. 1 and 2, 1967. Wheeler cautioned Westmoreland against mentioning the bombing of Laos, as well as in referring to the effects of bombing on infiltration, "since it is most difficult to prove or disprove the effect of bombing on the movement of personnel."

[106] For Taylor's reply of Mar. 9, 1967 see Johnson Library, NSF Memos to the President—Walt Rostow. There apparently was no reply from McNamara, but in a memorandum to the President on March 10, Rostow summarized what he called "Sec. McNamara's thoughts." Johnson Library, NSF Files of Walt W. Rostow.

[107] Johnson Library, NSF Files of Walt W. Rostow, Memorandum to the President from Rusk, Mar. 10, 1967.

[108] Same location, Memorandum to the President from Rostow, Mar. 9, 1967.

Three weeks after Kennedy's speech, the President expressed considerable pleasure at a report from Senator Edward W. Brooke of Massachusetts, who had been elected in 1966 to succeed Senator Leverett Saltonstall. During the 1966 campaign, Brooke, a liberal Republican and the first African-American to be elected to the Senate since Reconstruction, said he was troubled about the war and hoped there would be an early disengagement. In March 1967, Brooke made a tour of the Far East, and upon his return he said in a Senate speech on March 23 that although he had been critical of U.S. policy in Vietnam, he had become convinced that the Communists were not going to negotiate "in a meaningful way" at that time and that the U.S. must persevere in its military efforts to win the war. He was opposed to escalating or widening the war, but he said it was essential for the Communists to understand that the U.S. was committed to support the South Vietnamese "as long as is necessary." Moreover, he said, the Communists were waiting for a "collapse of the American will to persist," and, "It is quite possible that the North Vietnamese base their calculations on the expectation of a growing division in the American body politic on the question of our basic commitment in Vietnam"—the implication, of course, being that dissent in the U.S. was prolonging the war.

Brooke concluded that the American public was "beginning to accept, reluctantly but definitely, that this struggle could conceivably last another decade," although it was also possible, he said, that continued military pressure might end the war much sooner.[109]

Meanwhile, the House was also acting on the President's supplemental request, and, like the Senate, even the most determined supporters of the war were concerned about the state of affairs. In the hearings of the House Armed Services Committee during the first two weeks in February 1967, for example, Chairman Mendel Rivers, one of the strongest congressional proponents of the war, and Representative Charles A. Halleck (Indiana), formerly the House Republican leader (he had been defeated for the post in January 1967 by Representative Gerald Ford), who also supported the war, told McNamara that the public was becoming frustrated. Rivers said he was worried that people, "many respectable people . . . good folks," were "getting tired . . . getting weary of the fight." Representative Halleck added that "a lot of real good people are disturbed," and that there was "a growing lack of enthusiasm in respect to this effort in Vietnam." People were beginning to wonder when and how the U.S. was going to be able to "get through with this business." McNamara, replied that he agreed with their appraisal of the public's reaction, "and I think it is our job to try to meet it." The U.S., he said, was not running out of the resources necessary to fight the war; "we are just running out of patience and

[109] For Brooke's speech and comments by other Senators, see *CR*, vol. 113, pp. 7968–7979. For an appreciative statement by President Johnson, see the *New York Times*, Mar. 27, 1967. According to Alton Frye, Brooke's legislative aide at the time, Brooke was "unhappy, intellectually, and emotionally discontented that he had reached a policy judgment on the evidence different from his preferences." CRS Interview with Alton Frye, Feb. 7, 1979.

On March 27, the State Department sent a copy of Brooke's speech to all of its diplomatic missions, saying that it had "received considerable attention," and had been "widely praised as thoughtful and constructive." U.S. Department of State, Central File, Pol 27 Viet S, Airgram CA–7351, Mar. 27, 1967.

will."[110] The committee continued its practice of supporting the war, however, and voted unanimously to report the full authorization for the supplemental appropriation.[111]

Similar concerns were expressed during hearings in the last week of February before the House Appropriations Committee on the bill to provide the appropriation for the supplemental request for Vietnam, which was moving through Congress on the heels of the authorization bill. Several of the senior members of the committee voiced doubts about progress in the war, and said that the public was becoming frustrated and would not support a long, inconclusive war. Representative William E. Minshall, a conservative Republican from Ohio, said that antiwar feeling (he called it "'we are the aggressors' sentiment") was growing rapidly. "The war was just a ripple 2 or 3 years ago. Now it is becoming a big swell. Before long you are going to have a tidal wave." Many people, he added, were sincere, "but many others are being duped and misled by this Communist line of propaganda."[112] Representative George Andrews, a conservative Alabama Democrat, said that the people who were complaining to him "are complaining because we are not winning the war, bringing it to an end." "They are the ones," he added, "who are going to have a ground swell next year."[113] Andrews said that he had "started off as a 'Hawk,' a convinced one," but because of the restraints placed on fighting the war, and the failure to take the necessary military action to win it, he was "fast getting to be a 'Dove.'"

McNamara, the witness, told Minshall and Andrews that there were two minority groups, "one wanting us to get out and one wanting us to try to win more rapidly than we are." "In each case," he said, "they suffer from lack of patience." He disagreed with Minshall that more people were opposing the war or that protests were having more of an effect, although, he said, they were having the effect of encouraging North Vietnam to think that opposition in the U.S. was growing, and thus causing them to doubt the U.S. "will to continue." He urged greater education of the public by executive branch officials and Members of Congress: "I think as we meet with these dissident groups we can dampen down their criticism and seek to explain to them the basis on which we are in Southeast Asia, the objectives we have and the restraint with which we are applying our military power to achieve these objectives in the sense of trying to minimize the cost to our Nation in terms of human lives. If we continue to do that, I think it will continue to be a small minority of citizens who object to the program."[114]

In the same hearing on February 20, 1967, leading Republicans on the House Appropriations Committee also challenged McNamara on two issues that Republicans in Congress were using politi-

---

[110] U.S. Congress, House, Committee on Armed Services, *Fiscal Year 1967 Supplemental Authorization for Southeast Asia,* Hearings, 90th Cong., 1st sess. (Washington, D.C.: U.S. Govt. Print. Off., 1967), pp. 142, 153, 157.

[111] *Ibid.,* p. 291.

[112] U.S. Congress, House, Committee on Appropriations, *Supplemental Defense Appropriations for 1967,* Hearings before the Subcommittee on Department of Defense and the Subcommittee on Military Construction, 90th Cong., 1st sess. (Washington, D.C.: U.S. Govt. Print. Off., 1967), pp. 113–114.

[113] *Ibid.,* p. 61.

[114] *Ibid.,* pp. 60–62, 113–114.

cally against the Democrats and the Johnson administration, both of which were also important substantive issues. The first was the question of Congress' control over the Defense budget, and Representative Glenard P. Lipscomb (R/Calif.), the ranking Republican on the Defense Appropriations Subcommittee, raised with McNamara a series of questions as to why Congress had not been given better information on the budget situation in 1966.[115]

The second issue was the question of U.S. objectives, which was raised by Representative Laird. Referring to a letter he had written to President on February 9, 1967,[116] Laird said that he was particularly concerned about the U.S. offer of mutual withdrawal from South Vietnam by the U.S. and the North Vietnamese, and about the problem that the South Vietnamese would have in withstanding Communist pressure even if North Vietnamese forces were to leave the South and there were no further supplies from the North. McNamara replied that if troops from the North were withdrawn and supplies stopped, the "Vietcong" forces in the South "can't continue for long." Laird said that the southern Communists could function militarily without supplies from the North, and "this idea that they would not be able to operate effectively against the South Vietnamese Government just amazes me." McNamara replied that Laird underestimated the South Vietnamese Government and military, and that he (McNamara) had "faith in the ability of the people of South Vietnam to develop a government and govern themselves." Laird said he hoped "never [to be] proved to be correct on this [South Vietnam's inability to withstand Communist pressure after the withdrawal of U.S. forces] because if this does take place, then everything we have done in Vietnam has been in vain."[117]

On March 2, the House took up the authorization bill for the supplemental appropriations. (That morning, the House Armed Services Committee held a hearing on the regular Defense Department authorization for military procurement appropriations for FY 1968, with McNamara as the witness. The subject of the Mansfield-Clark amendment came up, and McNamara, as well as JCS Chairman Wheeler, said that the administration supported the amendment. It was obvious from the discussion that there was also little or no dissent concerning the amendment among members of the committee.)[118] Opponents of the war made several unsuccessful attempts to amend the bill. Representative Henry Reuss, a liberal Democrat from Wisconsin, offered the Mansfield-Clark amendment,[119] but it was ruled out of order because the subject of it was considered to fall under the jurisdiction of the Foreign Affairs Committee rather than the Armed Service Committee. Representative Sidney R. Yates, a liberal Democrat from Illinois, then offered the first two

---

[115] For the exchange, see *ibid.*, pp. 67 ff.

[116] For the text of Laird's letter, see *ibid.*, pp. 46–48.

[117] *Ibid.*, pp. 40–44.

[118] Hearings on Military Posture and H.R. 9250, House Committee on Armed Services, *op. cit.*, pp. 419, 421.

[119] *CR*, vol. 113, p. 5139. Under House rules, which are more stringent than those of the Senate, the amendment in the form in which it was passed by the Senate could have been declared to be nongermane to the bill and therefore out of order. To prevent this, Reuss substituted introductory language intended to make the amendment conform to House rules. In place of the statement, "The Congress hereby declares," he used the following language as a way of establishing the amendment as one involving a limitation on the use of authorized funds, which would be germane, rather than as a statement of policy: "None of the funds authorized by this Act shall be used except in accordance with the following declaration by Congress. . . ."

parts of the Mansfield-Clark amendment, omitting the third section about an international conference, but this was also ruled out of order for the same reason.[120]

Representative George Brown, Jr., a liberal Democrat from California, who had been one of the earliest and strongest House opponents of the war, then offered the following amendment:[121]

> It is hereby declared to be the sense of the Congress that none of the funds authorized by this Act shall be used to carry out military operations in or over North Vietnam.

The Brown amendment was not a prohibition on the use of funds, as it would have been if the wording of it had begun at the point where the word "none" appears and the words about the sense of Congress had been omitted. Rather, it was an expression of the sense of Congress that none of the funds should be so used, reflecting Brown's perception that there would be stronger support in the House for a sense of Congress amendment than for a prohibition.

Rivers said that Brown's amendment was policy, and made a point of order that it was not germane. The chair ruled, however, that it was germane because it involved a restriction on funds, a point that Brown had in mind when he offered the amendment in that form. As Brown said when he offered it, "This amendment is the only way I know of to get to the heart of the policy involved in this war in Vietnam."

Explaining his amendment, Brown said that there was "no such thing" as a military victory because U.S. "political goals" were "unattainable." As the U.S. increased its military forces and role, the Communists did the same, and this produced a continuing escalation of an "open-ended war" which could lead to "a tragedy the likes of which we have never seen." The war could only be ended through negotiations, Brown said, and negotiations could begin only if the U.S. stopped bombing the North.

Brown's amendment was opposed by several of the leading Democrats and Republicans on the Armed Services Committee, including Chairman Rivers and William Bates of Massachusetts, the ranking Republican, as well as by Samuel Stratton, Otis G. Pike (D/N.Y.), and Halleck, all of whom argued that it would, in Rivers' words, be "declaring open season on every GI in southeast Asia." The U.S., they argued, had tried to encourage negotiations by ceasing bombing the North, but the enemy had responded by increasing infiltration.

Halleck said he wanted to "get out" of the war, but "with honor." The amendment would "pull the rug out from under the boys taking it on the chin over there." He said he did not know the best way to get out, but that the war could not be run from the floor of the House.

There was some support for the amendment from liberal Democrats, but it failed on a voice vote, 15–128, and on a roll-call, 18–372. The bill then was passed by a voice vote.[122]

---

[120] *Ibid.*, p. 5141.

[121] *Ibid.*, p. 5143. The debate on the amendment, from which the quotes here were taken, is on pp. 5143–5151.

[122] *Ibid.*, pp. 5150, 5156. All of the 18 voting for the Brown amendment were liberal Democrats (11 were from California and New York): Jonathan B. Bingham (N.Y.), Brown (Calif.), Phillip

During the debate on the bill, it was apparent that there was considerable support in the House for accepting the Mansfield-Clark amendment. Several Members, including Pike, said that they would have voted for the Mansfield-Clark amendment if it had been ruled germane.

Given this feeling, and the support of the administration, it was not surprising, therefore, that the House members of the House-Senate conference committee agreed to accept the Mansfield-Clark amendment, after which the House approved the conference report containing the amendment by a vote of 364–13 on March 8, 1967.[123] Rivers himself defended the amendment, saying that even though he was considered "the granddaddy of all hawks," he wanted to end the war, "if it can be brought to an end in an honorable and positive fashion," adding, "I would not want to associate myself in any way with the idea of wanting to continue this kind of meatgrinder of a ground war in Asia." Bates, the ranking Republican on Armed Services, called the amendment "almost innocuous."[124]

Thus, for the first time since the Gulf of Tonkin Resolution, Congress approved a statement of U.S. policy which, while it may have been considered innocuous by some, was an important step in the effort to prevent expansion of the war and to seek an honorable negotiated settlement. At the same time, the very heavy vote against the Brown amendment restricting the use of U.S. forces was a sign of the reluctance of the House, and of Congress, to interfere with the President or to move toward the stronger use of Congress' power over appropriations as a way of exercising greater control over the war. It was also further evidence of the continuing broad

---

Burton (Calif.), John Conyers, Jr. (Mich.), Charles C. Diggs, Jr. (Mich.), Don Edwards (Calif.), Leonard Farbstein (N.Y.), Donald Fraser (Minn.), Edith Green (Oreg.), Henry Helstoski (N.J.), Robert W. Kastenmeier (Wisc.), Patsy T. Mink (Hawaii), Thomas M. Rees (Calif.), Benjamin Rosenthal (N.Y.), Edward R. Roybal (Calif.), William Ryan (N.Y.), James H. Scheuer (N.Y.), and Sidney Yates (Ill.).

Eleven liberal Democrats, including ten of the eighteen who voted for the Brown amendment—Brown, Burton, Conyers, Edwards, Fraser, Helstoski, Kastenmeier, Rees, Rosenthal, Ryan, along with John Dow, who voted against the Brown amendment, issued at the beginning of the debate on the bill a statement saying that the war was escalating and opportunities for negotiations were not being fully exploited, and proposing these four U.S. initiatives (*ibid.*, p. 5103):

"(1) The U.S. should cease bombing North Vietnam immediately and without preconditions.

"(2) The U.S. must support truly free elections in South Vietnam. We must be prepared to accept whatever role for the National Liberation Front results from such elections.

"(3) The U.S. should propose to the North Vietnamese government, the South Vietnamese government, and the National Liberation Front, four-party negotiations to secure a cease-fire in Vietnam.

"(4) The U.S. should seek appropriate sponsorship of an international conference to guarantee agreements reached by the belligerents."

Ten other liberal Democrats, mostly from New York—Joseph P. Addabbo (N.Y.), Jonathan Bingham (N.Y.), Frank J. Brasco (N.Y.), Jeffrey Cohelan (Calif.), Leonard Farbstein (N.Y.), Jacob Gilbert (N.Y.), Richard L. Ottinger (N.Y.), James Scheuer (N.Y.), Herbert Tenzer (N.Y.), Sidney Yates (Ill.)—issued a statement saying that they had previously suggested similar initiatives, and that in general they agreed with the statement of the 11 other Members. *Ibid.*, p. 5075. Of these ten, only four—Bingham, Farbstein, Scheuer, and Yates—voted for the Brown amendment.

In addition to 10 of the 11 who issued the original statement, and 4 of the 10 who signed the supporting statement, the 4 others who voted for the Brown amendment were: Diggs, Green, Mink, and Roybal.

[123] Of the 13 who voted against the bill, 9 were liberal Democrats—Brown (Calif.), Burton (Calif.), Edwards (Calif.), Rees (Calif.), Dow of New York (the only one of the 9 who had voted against the Brown amendment), Rosenthal, Ryan, Fraser, and Kastenmeier—and 4 were conservative Republicans—William Bray (Ind.), William L. Dickenson (Ala.), H. R. Gross (Iowa), and Charles A. Mosher (Ohio), who opposed it because of the Mansfield-Clark amendment.

[124] *Ibid.*, pp. 5768–5772. Senate action on the conference report is on p. 5930.

base of congressional and public support for U.S. policy in Vietnam. Even though there was growing opposition to the war, both from those who opposed it and those who wanted to "win or get out," most Members of Congress, like the general public, thought that the United States should be helping to defend South Vietnam and should not withdraw before reaching an honorable settlement. This was exemplified by the positions taken by two leading liberal Democrats, both members of the Foreign Affairs Committee, who, while supporting Brown's amendment, were still persuaded that the U.S. role in Vietnam was important. One was Fraser of Minnesota, who favored increased efforts to negotiate a settlement, including stopping the bombing and talking directly with the National Liberation Front, but who also advocated increasing military pressure on the Communists in the South, including possible increases in U.S. forces for that purpose. The other was Bingham of New York, who said that both a military victory and unilateral withdrawal were impossible. He said that the war might be won by programs to win popular support in the South, combined with providing better security, but that this would take 4–10 years, and with growing public pressure for a quick end to the war, the U.S. should seek to negotiate a settlement.[125]

On March 16, 1967, about a week after final congressional passage of the authorization bill for the Vietnam supplemental appropriation request, the House took up the Vietnam supplemental appropriations request itself. Faced with increasing pressure from both opponents of the war and proponents of stronger military action, the President and his supporters waged an intensive campaign to bolster House support for the bill as well as congressional and public support for the administration's Vietnam policy.

Although the President continued to stress his willingness to negotiate with the North Vietnamese,[126] he was becoming more militant. On March 15, 1967, he gave a speech to the Tennessee legislature that represented, according to James Reston of the *New York Times,* "another, harder turn of the screw."[127] "President Johnson," Reston wrote, "looks more and more like a man who has decided to go for a military victory in Vietnam, and thinks he can make it."

In the House, a similar mood prevailed among the President's supporters, especially on the Armed Services Committee, and prior to the beginning of the debate on March 16 they arranged a classified presentation to the committee by the Defense Intelligence Agency which was intended to show how the North Vietnamese had taken advantage of the recent suspension of bombing to resupply forces in the South, and had again rejected an effort by the U.S. to show its willingness to negotiate. This briefing was repeated twice for others in the House, the second time being the morning of the day when House debate began.[128] Meanwhile, key House supporters of the administration were emphasizing in brief speech-

---

[125] For the comments by Fraser and Bingham, see *ibid.*, pp. 5131 and 5132.

[126] See his remarks in a press conference on Mar. 9, 1967, *Public Papers of the Presidents,* Lyndon B. Johnson, 1967, pp. 303 ff.

[127] *New York Times,* Mar. 16, 1967. For the text of the speech see *Public Papers of the Presidents,* Lyndon B. Johnson, 1967, pp. 348–354.

[128] *CR,* vol. 113, pp. 5755, 6007, 6673.

es the President's continuing commitment to a peaceful settlement.[129]

On March 16, after a brief general debate on the supplemental appropriations bill, Representative Brown again offered an amendment, as follows:[130]

> None of the funds appropriated in this Act shall be available for the implementation of any plan to invade North Vietnam with ground forces of the United States, except in time of war.

Unlike Brown's earlier amendment, which was a sense of Congress amendment, this new version was a limitation on the use of funds, and had it passed the Executive would have been prohibited from using funds from that appropriations act "for the implementation of any plan to invade North Vietnam with ground forces of the United States, except in time of war." Unlike the earlier version, however, it covered only ground forces and did not apply to bombing or shelling. The language "in time of war," Brown said, meant that there had to be a declaration of war by Congress before such funds could be so allocated. However, the wording did not specifically require a declaration of war. Moreover, the amendment applied only to funds from the supplemental appropriations act and not to any other act, thus leaving the Executive free to use other funds. (In later years, congressional amendments to control and end the war used the wording: "funds from this or any other act.") The wording "for the implementation of any plan" was also vague. Did it mean that no funds from that act could be used for invading North Vietnam with U.S. forces?

In arguing for the amendment, Brown, who cited Senator Russell's statement opposing any U.S. invasion of North Vietnam, said that passage of the amendment was a way to begin to exercise congressional control over the war.

The amendment was opposed by leading Democrats and Republicans. George Mahon from Texas, chairman of the Appropriations Committee and of the Defense Appropriations Subcommittee, said that it would interfere with the conduct of the war by the President and the military, and "would tend to give a sanctuary to the enemy . . . would tip the hand of this country in advance . . . would give aid and comfort to those in Hanoi who are holding out against settlement of the controversy. . . ." The ranking Republican on the Defense Subcommittee, Lipscomb of California, opposed it for similar reasons. Republican H. R. Gross of Iowa, who frequently nettled the Democrats, asked whether the U.S. had not already invaded North Vietnam.[131] Brown replied that although the U.S. was bombing and shelling the North, the amendment was limited to the use of ground forces.

Despite the fact that the amendment was designed to be politically palatable, the House, which was in no mood to begin trying to control the conduct of the war, and did not seem to feel that there was a serious threat of U.S. invasion of the North, emphati-

---

[129] See, for example, *ibid.*, pp. 6277 and 6328. See also pp. 5810–5819 for a series of speeches by 14 members of the Texas congressional delegation, joined by several other members, praising the President for his handling of Vietnam, and pp. 7296–7303, for supporting speeches by eight freshmen Members of Congress, all from the South.

[130] *Ibid.*, p. 6886.

[131] Gross favored stronger military action. See *ibid.*, p. 5819.

cally defeated Brown's proposal on a division (nonrollcall) vote, 2–123. The supplemental appropriations bill was then passed on May 16 by a vote of 385–11.[132]

On March 20, the Senate passed the bill 77–3 after a brief and perfunctory debate.[133] Voting "no" were Gruening, Morse, and Nelson. All of the other opponents of the war, including Church, Clark, Cooper, Fulbright, Hartke, Hatfield, both Kennedys, Mansfield, McCarthy, McGovern, and Young of Ohio, supported the bill.

Nelson said he voted against the bill "with great reluctance:"[134]

> From a purely political point of view it would be easier to vote for the appropriations and pretend that no other issues are at stake here. But to do so would not be honest with myself or with my constituents.
>
> I wish to make it abundantly clear that I believe, as do all Americans, that our soldiers must be supplied, equipped, and supported to the very limit of our capacity as a nation. If there were any question about the adequacy of supplies or equipment for our troops, I would vote whatever appropriations were necessary to remedy it.
>
> My vote against the appropriation is simply and purely to express my dissent to the past escalation without congressional consent or debate; to future escalation without congressional consent or debate; and to express my concern over administration failure to explore the possibility of negotiations by a temporary cessation of bombing the north.
>
> This war is going to end at the negotiating table, as we have repeatedly and solemnly assured the world. The sooner we start negotiating, the fewer lives will be lost, and the sooner peace will be achieved.

After the Senate vote, Majority Leader Mansfield, commenting on a statement by Senator Russell, who was in charge of the bill, said that Russell "voiced the opinion of the great majority of us in the Senate when he stated that as long as American men are in southeast Asia, they will be given our unstinting support."[135]

Several weeks later, other bills affecting the war were also passed. One was a bill to authorize Defense procurement and research and development which contained substantial funds for the Vietnam war, which passed the House by a vote of 401–3 (the three were liberal Democrats Brown and Edwards of California and Fraser of Minnesota) and passed the Senate by a vote of 86–2 (Morse and Gruening).[136]

The other was a bill to amend and extend the Selective Service Act (the draft), which passed the House by a vote of 362–9 and the Senate by a vote of 70–2.[137] During House debate, Representative Paul Findley (R/Ill.) offered an amendment to provide that induct-

---

[132] *Ibid.*, p. 6889. Ten of the eleven were liberal Democrats: Brown, Burton (Calif.), Conyers, Dow, Edwards (Calif.), Fraser, Kastenmeier, Reuss, Rosenthal, Ryan. They were joined by one conservative Republican, Mosher of Ohio.

[133] For Senate proceedings, see *ibid.*, pp. 7188–7212. As approved by Congress, the FY 1967 Vietnam supplemental appropriations bill contained all but $79,350,000 of the $12,196,520,000 requested by the President.

[134] *Ibid.*, p. 7212.

[135] *Ibid.*, p. 7524.

[136] *Ibid.*, pp. 12015–12016.

[137] *Ibid.*, pp. 12504, 14154.

ees "can be dispatched to a foreign country as a part of combat personnel units of the United States Army or United States Marine Corps only if authorized by specific act of Congress except in military operations required pursuant to a treaty to which the United States is a party." No other Member of the House spoke on behalf of the amendment, however, and it was defeated by a voice vote.[138] In the Senate, Gruening introduced an amendment to provide that no inductee should be sent to Southeast Asia unless he volunteered for such an assignment. This was rejected 2–75, with Gruening and Morse voting aye.[139]

The White House Plans a Counterattack as Protests Increase

In early February 1967, White House aides began discussing the need for a stronger public relations program to support U.S. policy and to strengthen the President's position prior to the 1968 election. Two proposals emerged: first, the establishment of a group in the White House staff to provide more effective and better coordinated information to those seeking to defend U.S. policy, and, second, creation of a citizens' organization to campaign for the administration's position.

The proposal for a White House information group (the "Vietnam Information Group"), appears to have been made by John Roche. On February 6, following a discussion a few days earlier with Postmaster General Lawrence O'Brien, Roche sent O'Brien a memorandum (with a copy to W. W. Rostow) suggesting the creation of the information group:[140]

> It seems to me that we must start with the presumption that the worst alternative may occur—in this instance that the war in Vietnam will *not* be settled before the 1968 election.
>
> Assuming that the war will not *in itself* be an issue (except for a few peace types), but that it will provide a psychological background for the campaign, we can anticipate what I have called the "Korean whipsaw": On Mondays, Wednesdays and Fridays, we will be the war party; on Tuesdays, Thursdays and Saturdays, the party of appeasement. (emphases in original)

To avoid being whipsawed in this manner by the Republicans, Roche said, the administration needed to provide better information on Vietnam to its friends, especially in Congress. The State Department, he added, "is simply incompetent to do the kind of job we need. They have all kinds of material, and plenty of talent, but for reasons which defy rational explanation, the two can never coincide." Therefore, he concluded, "we must do the job ourselves." He proposed creating a small office in the White House headed by Harold Kaplan from the public affairs staff of the State Department, who had previously been on the U.S. Embassy's public affairs staff in Saigon.

The origins of the idea for a citizens' committee are somewhat obscure. In early March 1967, Walt Rostow discussed it with Abbott Washburn of the Washington public relations firm of Washburn, Stringer Associates, Inc. In a letter to Rostow on March

---

[138] *Ibid.*, pp. 14142–14143.
[139] *Ibid.*, p. 12480.
[140] Johnson Library, NSF Name File, Roche Memos.

15, Washburn, an official of the U.S. Information Agency during the Eisenhower administration and a self-styled "Eisenhower Republican," said that the issue of mobilizing public opinion in support of U.S. policy on Vietnam was one that "transcends party." In a memorandum with the letter Washburn suggested three steps: first, the President should "go to the people" in weekly 10-minute TV "fireside chats" from the White House in which he would report on developments in the war and explain the reasons for and goals of U.S. involvement in the war, emphasizing the "historical imperatives" for action by the United States to block Communist aggression in other parts of the world. Using as much "first-hand evidence" such as captured films, exhibits of captured equipment, filmed interviews with defectors, and personal reports from U.S. servicemen, as well as civilian officials, the President "would invest those few minutes with a high factor of immediacy, a you-are-in-on-it-from-where-I-sit quality. Faithfully and honestly he would assess: *how it's going in Vietnam right now, what your sons and brothers and husbands are accomplishing, what the hopeful signs are, what the negative ones."*[141] (emphasis in original) If the President were unable to appear, the Vice President or Rusk or McNamara would substitute in making the weekly report.

Washburn's second suggestion was that the President should hold meetings with "opinion leaders" in different parts of the country for an "exchange of views" on Vietnam, using a format similar to the weekly TV programs. Such sessions with bipartisan groups of 75–100 leaders would also be televised, and the President would also hold dinners or luncheons with local returned Vietnam veterans and visit the families of those servicemen who had been killed in the war.

One advantage of meeting with "responsible leaders," Washburn said, was that "there would be no discourtesy" to the President or other officials by persons opposed to the war.

His third suggestion was for a bipartisan national citizens' committee, to be backed by local committees and by public affairs experts around the country. "Like myself," Washburn said, "many of the . . . [public affairs experts] are disturbed and angry at the negative attitude of elements in their communities toward the sacrifices of our men in Vietnam."

Rostow sent Washburn's letter and memorandum to the President, who replied: "Walt: I like this. Bring this up on the way out [a reference to the pending trip to Guam]—it's very important. I quite agree with it. LBJ"[142]

After his letter of March 15, Washburn met with several others with experience in government and public affairs—including Kermit ("Kim") Roosevelt, the grandson of Theodore, and an experienced CIA operative who headed the firm of Roosevelt and Associates—and on March 22 he sent another memorandum to Rostow outlining the proposed national citizens' committee.[143] The rationale for the group, the memorandum stated, was:

[141] Johnson Library, Ex ND 19/CO 312, Memorandum to the President from Rostow, Mar. 17, 1967, with Washburn's letter and memorandum attached.

[142] *Ibid.* The President's reply of March 17 has been photocopied onto the file copy of Rostow's memorandum of that day.

[143] Same location.

a.) To support our fellow Americans in Vietnam, civilians as well as servicemen; one of the saddest aspects of this conflict is that those who are out there don't feel the solid backing of the people at home.

b.) The Communist aggressors are counting heavily on the divisiveness within the U.S. to work in their favor—particularly going into a Presidential election year; we mean to deny them that advantage, to the greatest extent possible. (We have no interest of trying to check the amount of criticism, but rather to give a banner and voice to those who support U.S. policy.)[144]

Washburn also sent Rostow a list of possible members of the national committee, and suggested that the emphasis should be on younger leaders, avoiding the "same old names."[145]

Rostow, Katzenbach, and McNaughton seem to have been given responsibility for exploring the possibility of a citizens' committee,[146] but others on the White House staff were more actively involved, particularly McPherson, who apparently was put in charge, and Roche, who took charge several weeks later. In early April, McPherson organized a lunch, attended by Roche as well as by James Rowe, a former assistant to President Roosevelt and an experienced Washington lawyer and politician who was a close personal friend and adviser to President Johnson, and Louis Martin, deputy director of the Democratic National Committee, at which the idea of a committee was discussed.[147] As will be seen, however, action on the idea was slow in coming.

On April 20, Secretary of Health, Education and Welfare John Gardner brought a businessman from California to see McPherson who, according to a memorandum later that day from McPherson to the President, "was concerned about the noisiness of the anti-Vietnam Left, and the relative inertness of the majority that sup-

---

[144] In addition to the usual kinds of publicity, the memorandum suggested this "symbol:"

"As a symbol of the defense of individual dignity and the right of free choice, a huge Bell or Gong of Freedom would be cast in Philadelphia and presented by the American people—through the efforts of the Committee—to the men and women of South Vietnam and their allies. Bells and gongs hold unusual significance in the cultures of the East. Such a gift would have particular meaning throughout the Far East. The symbol would tour the United States and be seen (and contributed to) by millions of Americans prior to its departure. The dedication ceremonies in South Vietnam would offer opportunities to stress unity and support. The bell's daily sound would be a constant reminder. It might well, also, be regularly used on radio programs beamed to the North."

[145] The list contained 59 names from the "important categories: Labor, Business, Education, Women, Veterans, Church, Hyphenated-American Groups, Medicine, Science, Negro, et al," of which 10 were on the roster of the 109 members of the committee when its formation was announced in October 1967. There were 38 more names written by hand by McNaughton on his copy of the list, of which two were on the final roster. Many of those listed by Washburn were Republican business leaders who had been active during the Eisenhower administration, whereas the final roster contained more Democrats, fewer "same old names," and more academicians.

[146] On March 27, Rostow, Katzenbach and McNaughton met to discuss the Washburn proposal, and in a memorandum to the President on March 29, Rostow indicated that the group was skeptical of the idea. (Johnson Library, NSF Memos to the President—Walt Rostow) "While we probably could generate a broadly based, effective continuing group, it would be done only at a sacrifice of some of your freedom of action—e.g., implied assurance by you that you will not sharply escalate the war against the North. A continuing group would not be worth the candle if, at some stage, we had a batch of noisy resignations." They proposed the organization by private citizens "at some distance from the Government" of a committee which would be broadened beyond Washburn's list to include educators, labor, and minorities, the principal function of which would be to issue a statement of support of U.S. policy, couched in moderate terms for broad appeal.

[147] Johnson Library, Office Files of Harry McPherson.

ports our efforts there."[148] The businessman proposed that a brief telegram should be composed that could be sent to the Pentagon by citizens, pledging support "to our brave men in Vietnam." A national committee, perhaps chaired by former Presidents Eisenhower and Truman, would be organized for the purpose of conducting this campaign.

McPherson's memorandum continued:

> *There should be no overt White House involvement in this.* The committee would ask a public relations specialist, perhaps someone from the networks, to serve as its director. He would contact the Advertising Council, publishers, and the networks, to provide free time and space for this request from Eisenhower and Truman. He and other volunteers would ask business and labor leaders to bring the campaign to the attention of their employees and members. He would background the press that he hopes for at least as many signatories as marched last Saturday—175,000 or whatever it was. (With an aggressive campaign he should be able to hit half a million or more.) The call would be simple: here is a way for you to express *your* feelings about the fight Americans are making tonight in Vietnam.
>
> The whole thing would be done within 10 days, if possible—so as to be completed by Loyalty Day, May 1. The message and its signatures would be transmitted to Vietnam thereafter, with publicity. (emphases in original)

McPherson added that Katzenbach, Valenti and Roche all supported the idea. But the President, when he was given three choices at the end of McPherson's memo: "——— yes, ——— no, ——— see me," checked "see me," and although there is no record of what he told McPherson, the idea was not implemented. One of the reasons could have been that General Westmoreland was about to return to Washington for a series of appearances, and the President doubtless viewed these as having a greater impact on the public than a telegram campaign.

[148] Same location.

CHAPTER 15

WESTMORELAND REQUESTS MORE TROOPS

By mid-March 1967, the U.S. was increasing its military operations against North Vietnam and the President was emphasizing the need to stand fast to win the war. In a speech to the Tennessee legislature on March 15, probably the most definitive and strident defense of U.S. policy in Vietnam of his entire Presidency, he declared: "This generation of Americans is making its imprint on history. It is making it in the fierce hills and the sweltering jungles of Vietnam."[1] Referring to the decision to enter the war, he said, "if we were prepared to stay the course in Vietnam, we could help to lay the cornerstone for a diverse and independent Asia, full of promise and resolute in the course of peaceful economic development for her long-suffering peoples. But if we faltered, the forces of chaos would scent victory and decades of strife and aggression would stretch endlessly before us. The choice was clear. We would stay the course. And we will stay the course. . . . We must not—we shall not—we will not—fail."[2]

Although with McNamara's growing opposition there was no longer as strong a consensus about the war among his principal advisers, the President continued to receive support and encouragement from Rusk and Rostow. For Rusk, the issue was one of loyalty and responsibility, as well as policy, as David Halberstam explained: "If by 1966, and increasingly in 1967, McNamara was beginning to move away from the policy, then Rusk was, if anything, more steadfast than ever. He not only believed in the policy, he had a sense of profound constitutional consequences if the President, already at loggerheads with one of his chief advisers, was separated from the other. If Rusk too dissented, if that gossipy town even thought he was a critic, then in Rusk's opinion the country would be in a constitutional crisis."[3]

Rostow was actively optimistic. In a memorandum to the President on March 18, prior to a meeting of the President with Vietnamese leaders a few days later, he said that the "two key ideas in Vietnamese/U.S. relations are: confidence in the future and confidence in one another. We have come through a great deal in the last six years and especially in the last two years. If victory is not in sight, it is on the way. We must set our sights high; work hard

[1] The text of the speech is in *Public Papers of the Presidents*, Lyndon B. Johnson, 1967, pp. 348–354.

[2] In the speech the President described objectives of U.S. policy, the military and political progress being made, the efforts to negotiate, and the U.S. position on negotiations.

[3] Halberstam, *The Best and the Brightest*, p. 634.

for a breakthrough, whether on the battlefield or in diplomacy; and look to the future of a democratic, modern South Vietnam."[4]

Komer was also a strong supporter. After a trip to Vietnam February 13–23, 1967, he reported to the President:[5] "I return more optimistic than ever before. Indeed, I'll affirm even more vigorously my prognosis of last November (which few shared then) that growing momentum would be achieved in 1967 on almost every front in Vietnam." "Wastefully, expensively, but nonetheless indisputably, we are winning the war in the South. Few of our programs—civil or military—are very efficient, but we are grinding down the enemy by sheer weight and mass." Pacification, he added, "lags the most, yet even it is moving forward."

By the end of 1967 if not before, Komer concluded, it "would be clear to all that we were 'winning' the war in the South. . . . It now seems quite conceivable that gathering momentum in the South, plus the turmoil in China and our continued pressure on the North, could lead to negotiation or Hanoi fadeaway in 1967. . . . Even if the VC/NVA manage to sustain a protracted war, it seems likely that we can inflict such damage on them in the next 12-18 months—and achieve sufficient pacification, political and economic progress in the south—to reduce the enemy threat to proportions permitting redeployment of some U.S. forces."

Komer sent copies of his report to the President's principal advisers, and on the copy he sent to Katzenbach he noted: "Nick, we're doing even better than I thought!"[6]

And from the CIA, where throughout the war analysts generally had reported little progress, George Carver, the Director's special assistant for Vietnam, returned from a trip to Vietnam in early March 1967 with a confident report. His "net assessment" was one of "progress, achievement and promise"—although he rated pacification "last in terms of progress."[7] Moreover, "there is a better than even chance that within eighteen months the total situation in Vietnam will have improved to the point where nearly everyone will have to recognize that the Communist insurgency is failing, that the South Vietnamese are well on the way to building an independent nation, that our basic assessment of the situation in Viet-

---

[4] Johnson Library, NSF Memos to the President—Walt Rostow. This same theme was being repeated in other Rostow memoranda. See, for example, in the Johnson Library, NSF Country File, Vietnam, Rostow's memoranda to the President on February 21, (advice on an interview with journalists), March 8 (the benefits of bombing), March 11 (progress against Communist guerrilla apparatus), April 6 (progress in program to encourage defections).

This is Halberstam's description (*The Best and the Brightest,* pp. 637–638): "With the White House under siege, with increasing evidence that the American military commitment to Vietnam had been stalemated, Rostow fought back; in the White House basement aides culled through the reams of information coming in from Saigon and picked the items which they knew Rostow was following, particularly the good ones. They would send this up to Rostow, and he would package it and pass it on to the President, usually with covering notes which said things such as—this would give confirmation to the statement which the President had wisely made to the congressional leadership the day before. The notes were similar—there were little touches of flattery: The record of your success indicates. . . . Your place in history will bring you. . . . The theme was the greatness of the course and the immortality of Lyndon Johnson." See also Kearns, *Lyndon Johnson and the American Dream,* p. 320.

[5] Johnson Library, NSF Files of Robert W. Komer, Memorandum for the President from Komer, "Change for the Better—Latest Impressions from Vietnam," Feb. 28, 1967.

[6] U.S. Department of State, Central File, Pol 27 Viet S. On February 27, the President held a press conference at which Komer reported on his trip. For a summary of Komer's remarks see *Public Papers of the Presidents*, Lyndon B. Johnson, 1967, p. 241.

[7] Johnson Library, Office Files of George Christian, Memorandum for the President from Christian, Mar. 8, 1967. Although Christian's memorandum stated that the Carver report was attached, it is not attached and has not been found in the Johnson Library.

nam was correct, and that, with U.S. support, free men in underdeveloped areas can successfully cope with Communist wars of national liberation."

It is doubtful whether the President was significantly influenced by these optimistic forecasts. Although there is not sufficient evidence to support a categorical judgment, it would appear that he knew the war was not going well and that it could be "won" only by a political settlement. At this stage, after almost two years of effort, and faced with what his Secretary of Defense called a military stalemate, little or no progress in pacification, mounting costs and casualties, and growing public and congressional dissent, he seemed to be more intent on ending than on winning the war. It had become the albatross he had feared from the beginning.

Yet, with the 1968 U.S. elections looming nearer, negotiations, in part because of the elections, seemed more elusive and unattainable than ever. And the hopes being expressed in many of the deliberations and the communications in and between Washington and Saigon during those months in the spring of 1967 that a new, elected government in South Vietnam would want to seek negotiations with the North, were parried by the stubborn fact that military control would probably continue, as indeed it did, and that the South Vietnamese Government would try to block rather than facilitate a negotiated agreement—as it did.

The Communists' assessment of the U.S. strategic dilemma was quite perceptive—U.S. forces were deadlocked, and the war of attrition being waged against them was succeeding in frustrating this large and powerful military force, while causing discontent and doubt at home. Moreover, it was clear that stronger U.S. action would produce a corresponding reaction.

The Guam Conference, March 1967

On March 20-21, 1967, President Johnson met on the island of Guam with U.S. officials from Washington and Saigon and with Chief of State Thieu and Prime Minister Ky. The stated purpose of the conference was to review nonmilitary programs, especially the adoption of a constitution and election of a government, and to announce and bring together with Thieu and Ky the new American team of Ellsworth Bunker as Ambassador, replacing Lodge, Eugene M. Locke, a Texan and friend of the President, as Deputy Ambassador replacing Porter, and Robert Komer as the new head of the pacification program (CORDS—Civil Operations and Revolutionary Development Support), which was to be transferred from civilian control through the Embassy, where Porter had been in charge, to the military, with Komer, who was given the rank of Ambassador, serving as a deputy to Westmoreland.[8] The more important and unstated purpose of the conference was to demonstrate to Congress and the public, as well as to audiences in South Vietnam and other countries, that progress was being made toward accomplishing U.S. goals.

Lodge, supported by his principal associates, argued strenuously against including Ky and Thieu in the conference, not only because

---

[8] This new pacification arrangement was promulgated by NSAM 362, May 9, 1967, "Responsibility for U.S. Role in Pacification." Johnson Library, NSF Memos to the President—Walt Rostow.

it would appear to be an American "show," but because both were running for President in the 1967 election and the U.S. would thus be in the position of conveying to the South Vietnamese the impression that it supported a military candidate.[9] Although Lodge thought that the election of a military leader might be preferable, he was also concerned about weakening the civilian element in South Vietnam's political structure. On the other hand, he said he recognized "the absolutely vital [U.S.] political base," and the reasons why the President would feel the need to invite Ky and Thieu.[10]

Rostow, however, thought that the presence of Ky and Thieu would be beneficial. In a memorandum and a proposed agenda for the conference which he sent to the President on February 27, Rostow said that "One of the greatest virtues of the meeting is that it will force Ky and Thieu to stay together. If they have not settled, by late March, which will run, you may have to settle it by taking Thieu up on a mountain and letting him see that leading the military, with our full backing, is his destiny [i.e., the U.S. did not want Thieu to run for President] for the next five years. I think I know how you could do this and what you could offer him." [11]

The conference was planned to coincide with the completion of the new South Vietnamese constitution by a Constituent Assembly elected in September 1966 for that purpose. Delegates to the Assembly had worked through the night before the conference opened in order to finish the document in time for its presentation to the Americans by Premier Ky on the first day of the meeting (March 20).[12] President Johnson and his associates were lavish with their praise. "'I looked at it,' Mr. Johnson said later, 'just as proudly as I looked at Lynda, my first baby.'" [13]

The following day (March 21) the President met with U.S. officials. According to the *Pentagon Papers,* Westmoreland expressed "basically optimistic" views: "that the enemy was weakening, that ROLLING THUNDER did help, and that the enemy's losses would

[9] U.S. Department of State, Central File, Pol 27 Viet S, Saigon to Washington 20198, Mar. 13, 1967.

[10] See also Rusk's statement of the objectives of the meeting in which he said, among other things: "Continued GVN unity and broadly based government are critical to the maintenance of the U.S. political base." *PP*, Gravel ed., vol. 4, p. 424.

[11] Johnson Library, NSF Memos to the President—Walt Rostow.

[12] Ky's speech to the conference was drafted by a member of the U.S. staff in Saigon. See U.S. Department of State, Central File, Pol 27 Viet S, Saigon to Washington 20692, Mar. 18, 1967.

[13] *Newsweek,* Apr. 3, 1967. For a copy of the constitution, which had been drafted with U.S. assistance, and which was modeled in part after that of the United States, see *CR*, vol. 113, pp. 14758–14762. For comment on the constitution by the U.S. Embassy in Saigon see U.S. Department of State, Central File, Pol 27 Viet S, Saigon to Washington 20396, Mar. 15, 1967. For President Johnson's various statements in connection with the Guam Conference see *Public Papers of the Presidents*, Lyndon B. Johnson, 1967, pp. 375–387, and *The Vantage Point,* pp. 259–260. Background papers for the Guam Conference are in the Johnson Library, NSF International Meetings and Travel File, as well as in the McNaughton Files in the Warnke Papers. Notes of the meetings by George Carver are in the International Meetings and Travel File.

Some U.S. officials in Saigon were reported to feel that the kind of political development ("democracy building") represented by the completion of the constitution and the forthcoming election was a better method of "pacification" than "revolutionary development." (*New York Times*, Mar. 25, 1967.) For one thing, Revolutionary Development depended upon the maintenance of local security by 59-person Revolutionary Development teams backed by the Vietnamese Army, and in the year prior to the Guam Conference, during which there had been a twelvefold increase in Communist armed attacks on the teams, there had been little observable progress in providing such security. Moreover, there were only 416 such teams in being, and at the rate of 30 new teams a month it was estimated that it might take 5–10 years to create the kind of secure environment in which revolutionary development could become an effective method of pacification.

soon exceed his gains [the 'crossover point']." "Recent American successes," the *Pentagon Papers* added, "reinforced the belief that we had hit upon the key to winning—despite continued large scale infiltration."[14] In his memoirs, however, Westmoreland paints a somewhat different picture of the reaction to his presentation:[15]

> If the Viet Cong organization failed to disintegrate, which I saw as unlikely, and we were unable to find a way to halt North Vietnamese infiltration, the war could go on indefinitely. As I sat down, my audience was painfully silent. On the faces of many of the Washington officials, who had obviously been hoping for some optimistic assessment, were looks of shock. John McNaughton, in particular, wore an air of disbelief.

Although Westmoreland's comment about the possibility that the war could "go on indefinitely" may have been somewhat unsettling, it should not have come as a surprise that he would be speaking in such a cautionary manner, or that he should continue trying to straddle the line between reporting progress and recommending a stronger response.

What apparently did come as a surprise was Westmoreland's request for substantial additional troops, the specifics of which, although he had submitted the request several days before the conference, were not presented at the conference.[16] In this request, sent to CINCPAC on March 18, Westmoreland asked for 100,000-200,000 more troops and for authority to take further action against infiltration routes in Laos and Cambodia as well as to increase bombing and to mine harbors in North Vietnam. Communist forces, he said, had been strengthened, and the 470,000 U.S. troops then authorized would not "permit sustained operations of the scope and intensity required to avoid an unreasonably protracted war." Another 100,000 in fiscal year 1968 (a total of about 570,000) would provide a "minimum essential force," but with yet another 100,000 in fiscal year 1969 (a total of 670,000, or 750,000 counting other U.S. forces in the area that were involved in the war), he would have the "optimum force" needed to win the war.[17]

As frequently happened in such a changing environment, these estimates of 100,000 and 200,000 were increased by late May to 125,000 and 250,000 (with the 250,000 there would be a total of 670,000, or 800,000 counting other U.S. forces in the area), as a result, according to the JCS, of "additional requirements" estimated by CINCPAC.[18]

In a long cable on March 28, Westmoreland gave a detailed explanation of and justification for the request.[19] "The enemy," he

[14] *PP*, Gravel ed., vol. IV, p. 425.

[15] Westmoreland, *A Soldier Reports*, p. 214.

[16] See *PP*, Gravel ed., vol. IV, p. 425.

[17] Johnson Library, Warnke Papers, McNaughton Files, COMUSMACV 09101 to CINCPAC, "Force Requirements," Mar. 18, 1967. The 470,000 had been authorized by Program Four in November 1966, a reduction of 85,000 from the original request for 555,000.

As Krepinevich points out, the four and two-thirds divisions represented by the 200,000 would raise the total of U.S. maneuver battalions to 130, almost four times the number (34) requested by Westmoreland in June, 1965. Krepinevich, "Vietnam: Evaluating the Ground War, 1965–68," p. 32.

[18] Johnson Library, Warnke Papers, McNaughton Files, Memorandum for the Secretary of Defense from JCS Chairman Wheeler, CM 2381–67, May 29, 1967, citing CM 2377–67, May 24, 1967.

[19] CMH, Westmoreland Papers, Message Files, COMUSMACV 10311, Mar. 28, 1967.

said, "has altered neither his objectives nor his intention of continuing the protracted war of attrition. He continues to augment his forces. . . ." U.S. forces, whose operations during 1966 "were primarily holding actions characterized by border surveillance, reconnaissance to locate enemy forces, and spoiling attacks to disrupt the enemy offensive," had planned and initiated a general offensive and, having gained the tactical advantage, were "conducting continuous small and occasional large-scale offensive operations to decimate the enemy forces; to destroy enemy base areas and disrupt his infrastructure; to interdict his land and water LOCs [lines of communication] and to convince him, through the vigor of our offensive and accompanying psychological operations, that he faces inevitable defeat."

In 1967–1968, Westmoreland said, "With requisite forces, we shall be able to complete more quickly the destruction or neutralization of the enemy main forces and bases and, by continued presence, deny to him those areas in RVN [Republic of Vietnam] long considered safe havens. As the enemy main forces are destroyed or broken up, increasingly greater efforts can be devoted to rooting out and destroying the VC guerrilla and Communist infrastructure. Moreover, increased assistance can be provided the RVNAF [Republic of Vietnam Armed Forces] in support of its effort to provide the required level of security for the expanding areas undergoing revolutionary development."

According to the *Pentagon Papers,* "It is quite clear that the 'minimum essential forces' [100,000] which COMUSMACV requested was intended to be employed against VC/NVA main force units in a containment role in the border areas and a destruction-disruption mode in I CTZ [the northern part of South Vietnam] as well as the base areas within the country itself," while the additional 100,000 [the "optimum force" of 200,000] were to be used "to take up the slack in the RD [Revolutionary Development] 'shield' role."[20]

CINCPAC and the JCS supported Westmoreland's request, but although the JCS recommended the 100,000 increase they did not recommend the 200,000 increase. In their memorandum to the Secretary of Defense on April 20, 1967,[21] the Chiefs reaffirmed the basic objectives and strategic concepts that had been stated in their November 1966 memorandum. Among other things, the Chiefs said that to meet Westmoreland's need for troops there should be a Reserve callup for a minimum of 24 months and an extension of terms of service for 12 months.

Once again, the Secretary of Defense, who had not approved or commented on the strategic concepts propounded by the Chiefs in November 1966, did not approve or comment on this latest JCS memorandum.

Westmoreland's request for more troops which, as noted, appears to have been encouraged if not invited by the President's decision on February 22 to use greater force, came at an awkward time from the standpoint of U.S. public support for the war. This was reflected in comments by Rusk in a private meeting on April 24 with West German Foreign Minister Willy Brandt, when he was

[20] *PP*, Gravel ed., vol. IV, p. 435.

[21] There are excerpts from the JCS memorandum, JCSM–218–67, Apr. 20, 1967, in *PP*, Gravel ed., vol. IV, pp. 436–438.

asked whether the U.S. was "now stronger in Vietnam." "The Secretary said 'yes' on the military side. There has been some improvement. But there are no signs of peace from Hanoi. . . . It looks as if the war will go on." He added: "The domestic problem is not with the 'doves,' but with the growing impatience of Americans. This has been aggravated by the fact that we have suffered 2,500 killed since January. Something must give, and give shortly."[22]

In an effort to shore up U.S. public and congressional opinion as well as for consultation on the troop request, the President asked Westmoreland to return to Washington. On April 25, he arrived, and on April 27 he, Rusk, McNamara, Katzenbach, Vance, McNaughton, Rostow, Wheeler, Komer, and Christian met with the President from 10:35 a.m. to 11:50 a.m. and again from 4:45 p.m. to 6:30 p.m.[23]

At the meeting, according to McNaughton's notes, Westmoreland and Wheeler stressed the need for the additional 100,000-200,000 troops requested by Westmoreland to avoid "losing the momentum" and lengthening the war.[24] With the existing force level of 470,000, Westmoreland said, "'we will not be in danger of being defeated but it will be nip and tuck to oppose the reinforcements the enemy is capable of providing.'" "'In the final analysis,'" he said, "'we are fighting a war of attrition in Southeast Asia . . . [and] unless the will of the enemy is broken or unless there was an unraveling of the VC infrastructure, the war could go on for 5 years.'" With 100,000 more troops, he said, it could go on for three years, and with 200,000, for two years.

Westmoreland said in his memoirs that he made these predictions after McNamara had "wrung" the estimates from him during the meeting, but that, looking back, he was "struck by the accuracy" of his prediction that with approximately 550,000 men it would be five years before U.S. forces could be withdrawn.[25]

On the subject of the air war against North Vietnam, Westmoreland said, "I am frankly dismayed at even the thought of stopping the bombing program." Wheeler added that "The bombing campaign is reaching the point where we will have struck all worthwhile fixed targets except the ports. At this time we will have to address the requirement to deny to the DRV the use of the ports."

The President appeared to be skeptical of the troop increase, asking several times what the effect on infiltration would be and whether the Communists would try to match the U.S. Westmore-

---

[22] U.S. Department of State, Central File, Pol 27 Viet S, Memorandum of Conversation between Rusk and Brandt, Apr. 24, 1967.

[23] Prior to each of the two parts of the meeting, which will be treated here as a single meeting, Rostow sent a memorandum to the President suggesting issues to be raised and questions to be asked. (Johnson Library, NSF Memos to the President—Walt Rostow). In his memorandum for the afternoon session he said that it would be difficult to call up the Reserves "if we were to do just a bit more of the same. We would be creating a major political crisis in the U.S. without being able to promise an early or decisive result." Prior to a decision on a callup, he suggested considering possible additional military actions, including the mining of Haiphong and other harbors, the landing of U.S. forces in North Vietnam to "clean out" the North Vietnamese divisions that were diverting and harassing U.S. forces at the DMZ, sending U.S. forces into Laos to interdict infiltration routes just south of the DMZ. At the meeting, as will be seen, Rostow raised the possibility of sending U.S. forces into North Vietnam.

[24] Johnson Library, Warnke Papers, McNaughton Files, McNaughton Notes on discussions with the President, Apr. 27, 1967. In *PP*, Gravel ed., vol. IV, pp. 442–443, the analyst used McNaughton's notes as the basis for his description of what transpired at the meeting.

Rostow also made extensive hand-written notes of the meeting which are located in his files in the Johnson Library. Except where indicated, the notes quoted here are McNaughton's.

[25] Westmoreland, *A Soldier Reports*, pp. 227–228.

land replied that the war was one of action and reaction, and that when the U.S. added troops the Communists did also. "If so," the President asked, "where does it all end?" Westmoreland replied that the Communists, who had eight divisions in South Vietnam, could deploy twelve, but would have difficulty supporting them. The President: "At what point does the enemy ask for volunteers?" General Westmoreland: "That is a good question."[26]

After comments by General Wheeler endorsing Westmoreland's remarks and suggesting that the U.S. should consider moving against Communist troops in Laos and Cambodia, as well as a possible invasion of North Vietnam, Westmoreland explained Operation HIGH PORT, a plan for moving a division of South Vietnamese forces into Laos, in the area around Tchepone, followed by the construction of military facilities that could be used for larger operations. He said that Laos "would become more and more the battlefield and this would take the pressure off the South."

There is no indication in the notes of the meeting that there were any questions or discussion of Wheeler and Westmoreland's remarks about moving against Communist troops in Laos. On May 1, William Sullivan, U.S. Ambassador to Laos, in a memorandum requested by William Bundy, discussed Westmoreland's several proposals for extending military special operations actions in Laos.[27] He noted that the request of the military for extending the zone for PRAIRIE FIRE operations had been approved, and these cross-border teams were authorized to penetrate from 20-35 kilometers along the Laotian border with South Vietnam. Other rules had also been relaxed, permitting larger teams and allowing them to conduct harassment and ambush actions. But he said that the targets in the current PRAIRIE FIRE zone exceeded the forces available, and that until the military could "handle everything it already has on its platter" (PRAIRIE FIRE, together with SLAMS—similar operations against base areas) further extensions of the operational zone should not even be contemplated.

Partly because of over-extension of PRAIRIE FIRE and SLAM forces, Sullivan said, Westmoreland proposed using an airborne battalion to undertake such operations. "There are two problems with this proposal," Sullivan said. "The first is that it would probably destroy completely the element of clandestinity which is an essential factor of PRAIRIE FIRE. The second is that the airborne battalion would by definition not be trained in those special skills which make the PRAIRIE FIRE teams capable of operating in hostile territory. In other words, the airborne battalions would very likely be decimated on its first operation."

In addition, Sullivan said, "jumping from clandestine teams to conspicuous airborne operations would cross the threshold of Souvanna's tolerance. He has made it clear that he cannot provide positive acceptance to an overt ground force operating in Laos."

---

[26] Westmoreland recalled (*ibid.*, p. 227), referring to the meeting: "In prolonged discussion of the two proposals [A and B], I discerned that the President was leaning toward a call-up of Reserves but that Secretary McNamara was reluctant. . . ." There is nothing in the notes of the meeting to support this statement about the President's inclination. But Westmoreland only says that he discerned this to be the President's inclination, and does not state that the President actually said so.

[27] Johnson Library, Warnke Papers, McNaughton Files, Memorandum from William Sullivan to William Bundy, "Limitations on Military Actions in Laos," May 1, 1967.

Sullivan said that Operation HIGH PORT was an extension of the airborne battalion concept and that the objections to the airborne battalion "would be present in spades for the ARVN division." "Moreover," he added, "given the consequences of taking and holding territory, rather than just raiding into it, I feel that this one goes well beyond the limitations of anything which really requires serious consideration."

Sullivan concluded that if the U.S. ignored Souvanna Phouma's objections to some of the proposals being advanced for extending U.S. military operations into Laos, there would be "serious consequences." "At the very least, these consequences would involve the withdrawal of Souvanna's collaboration on many other matters of importance to us, including ground actions within Laos which are designed to protect the Mekong Valley area. At the very worst, he could chuck in his job, retire to France and let the country degenerate into a Pathet Lao occupied, Communist controlled fief. If he retired, the Soviets would predictably support the Pathet Lao. The North Vietnamese would directly attack toward the Mekong and we would lose all the territorial gains we have made in the past three years. Therefore, for limited operational advantages on the Ho Chi Minh Trail (none of which I am convinced would succeed) we would probably lose the entire Mekong Valley. To quote President Kennedy, this would be really trading an apple for an orchard."

At the meeting with the President on April 27 during which these proposals for extending military operations in Laos were discussed, there was also a discussion of a U.S. invasion of the southern part of North Vietnam. Rostow proposed landing U.S. troops in the vicinity of the city of Vinh, "in order to block infiltration routes and to hold the area hostage against North Vietnamese withdrawal from Laos and Cambodia as well as from South Vietnam." In his memoirs, Rostow explained his position:[28]

> On balance, I thought this a more effective way to proceed than going into the difficult terrain of Laos during the dry season, which, in any case, lay a half-year or more in the future. I did not believe Communist China would march the length of Vietnam, risking long supply lines, vulnerable to air and sea harassment, if American forces moved in south of Vinh. Intelligence evaluations supported this assessment. Not only would Hanoi not be anxious to have massive Chinese units on its soil, but every bit of evidence we had in 1967 suggested that the internal struggle over the Cultural Revolution and Peking's anxiety about both the growing Soviet force on its frontiers and its emerging, but vulnerable, nuclear capability would be paramount considerations.
>
> So far as American opinion was concerned, I argued that it would be difficult to justify further large increases on a more-of-the-same basis. An effort to force a conclusion to the war was desirable.

It will be recalled that a similar proposal by William Sullivan was strongly criticized by Russian and Chinese specialists in the State Department. State was not asked to evaluate Rostow's pro-

[28] Rostow, *The Diffusion of Power*, p. 513.

posal, but there probably would have been strong opposition from the same quarters. In a memorandum to Katzenbach, Llewellyn Thompson (then posted in Washington) said that, "The direct invasion of North Vietnam by U.S. forces would in my view make probable direct Chinese Communist intervention in the war. The Chinese are publicly committed to this and the only thing that would let them off the hook would be for the North Vietnamese to refuse their aid. In the circumstances described, I should think that the North Vietnamese would be desperate not to refuse it. If the Chinese Communists would intervene directly, their action would probably not be confined to Vietnam. . . . Faced with such a situation the Chinese would probably attempt to secure Soviet involvement. Although the Soviets might not officially enter the conflict, I believe they would send volunteers in large numbers and perhaps unofficially furnish air support or take other similar actions."[29]

The CIA also estimated that China would enter the war if North Vietnam were invaded.[30]

In the meeting, Westmoreland respond to Rostow's suggestion by saying that studies of an amphibious landing in North Vietnam indicated that it "was militarily feasible and could produce significant military results, if the political results were considered acceptable." He pointed out, however, that because of the weather factor the invasion would need to occur in the spring or summer. The next few months would be a good time, but there were not enough troops available, and it would be a year therefore, before the operation could be mounted. "No one around the table," Westmoreland said in his "History Notes," written several days later, "to include *[sic]* the President, expressed any great enthusiasm for the [amphibious] operation, and the discussion died with only Rostow and me participating."[31]

Rusk, who said very little, wondered, "Have hands been tied by gradualism?" "If asked," he queried, "would the war be fought the same way?" Westmoreland replied that if it were to be done again, U.S. forces, if possible, should move into Laos, the pattern of deployments should change, and there should be a gradual buildup.[32]

The meeting appeared to end inconclusively, without any decisions, and with very little indication on the President's part of his reaction to Westmoreland's request or to the various suggestions made during the meeting. Rostow, however, believes that the decision on the troop request which was finally made three months later was, in fact, made that day: "My impression," he says, "is that the decision was almost made on the spot once and for all, after that presentation in April 1967."[33]

Talk of a possible invasion of North Vietnam stirred up considerable opposition in Congress, including some of the administration's key supporters. During the last week in February 1967, an amendment had been offered to disapprove of U.S. military operations "in

---

[29] U.S. Department of State, Central File, Pol 27 Viet S, Memorandum for the Under Secretary from Thompson, "Soviet and Chinese Communist involvement in Vietnam," Dec. 12, 1966.

[30] See, for example, the memorandum from the CIA Office of National Estimates, "Communist Policy and the Next Phase in Vietnam," Apr. 12, 1967, p. 23, Johnson Library, NSF Country File, Vietnam.

[31] CMH, Westmoreland Papers, History File, History Notes, entry for Apr. 27, 1967.

[32] Material in this paragraph is from Rostow's notes of the meeting.

[33] Johnson Library, transcript of Vietnam Round Table, Mar. 9–10, 1991.

or over" North Vietnam. Senator Russell, chairman of the Armed Services Committee, opposed it, but said also that he was "strongly opposed" to any invasion of North Vietnam. Toward the end of May the subject came up again and several Republican Senators, led by Cooper and Morton of Kentucky, expressed opposition. Morton said, "I do not know of any member of this body who wants an invasion of North Vietnam by our forces or by the South Vietnamese." Senator Symington said that an invasion of North Vietnam could require many more U.S. troops, lead to greatly increased casualties, and probably result in a clash with Chinese combat forces. "The results of such action on our part, therefore, are incalculable."[34] On May 21, General Wheeler declared that the U.S. had no intention of invading North Vietnam. (This statement was made in the context of operations against North Vietnamese forces which had moved into the demilitarized zone.)[35]

While in the U.S., Westmoreland also spoke at the annual meeting of the Associated Press, at a private meeting of the Council on Foreign Relations in New York, and on April 28 to a joint session of Congress followed by a White House luncheon to which all of the Nation's governors and selected Members of Congress were invited. In his memoirs, Westmoreland said he was reluctant to make public appearances while the fighting continued, but that he "appreciated the President's desire to keep the American people informed, particularly in view of manifold misinformation disseminated by antiwar activists. By providing a sober, authoritative explanation of the American role in Vietnam, I reasoned, I might contribute to thwarting North Vietnamese efforts to weaken American resolve."[36]

In his speech to the Associated Press, Westmoreland emphasized that the war was not a civil war, but a "massive campaign of external aggression from Communist North Vietnam."[37] The Communists in the South, he said, were controlled by the Government of North Vietnam, and did not constitute a "legitimate nationalist movement."

Westmoreland said that the military picture was "favorable," but that the enemy "needs a victory for political, psychological and morale purposes, and he will continue to strive for one."

The major point of his speech to the Associated Press—that dissent against the war was encouraging the Communists—came in his concluding remarks:

> [T]he military war in South Vietnam is, from the enemy's point of view, only part of a protracted and carefully coordinated attack, waged in the international arena. Regrettably, I see signs of enemy success in the world arena which he cannot match on the battlefield. He does not understand that American democracy is founded on debate, and he sees every protest as evidence of crumbling morale and diminishing resolve. Thus, discouraged by repeated military defeats but encouraged by what he believes to be popular opposition to our effort in Vietnam, he is determined to continue his aggression from the

[34] *CR*, vol. 113, p. 12113.
[35] *New York Times*, May 22, 1967.
[36] Westmoreland, *A Soldier Reports*, p. 224.
[37] For the text, see *CR*, vol. 113, pp. 10699–10700.

north. This, inevitably will cost lives—American, Vietnamese, and those of our brave allies.

The reaction of several leading Senate critics of the war, as well as among some critics in the press, was that the President was using Westmoreland as part of a campaign to stifle opposition to the war.[38] Senator McGovern declared on April 25 that, "Frustrated by the failure of the escalation policy to produce anything other than a bloodier war . . . the administration is now trying to blame their failure on those who have warned them all along that they were playing with fire."[39] Senator Fulbright agreed, and said he felt that Westmoreland's visit was part of a "final drive for a vastly enlarged manpower commitment and a great drive for a military victory." "There is a legitimate difference of opinion as to our best course of action as a nation," he added. "It is clear, however, that there is a growing implication that dissent will lead to charges of disloyalty and muddleheadedness and then finally to implications of treason. This, I fear, is one of the last times that anybody will have courage to say anything else about the war."[40]

Senator Spessard Holland, a conservative Democrat from Florida who supported the war, suggested to Fulbright that Westmoreland be invited to meet with the Foreign Relations Committee, and that he should also be invited to meet with the Armed Services Committee.[41] On April 27, Fulbright reported that invitations had been extended by the Foreign Relations Committee, but that Westmoreland's schedule was said to be too full to meet with either group.[42] In fact, his schedule had been arranged to keep him from having to appear before congressional committees, especially the Senate Foreign Relations Committee. In a backchannel cable on March 24, Wheeler told Westmoreland:[43]

> Of greatest concern to me is the fact that, as soon as it becomes known you will be visiting CONUS [continental U.S.], the Congress will start immediately to get into the act. I have discussed briefly with Secretary McNamara the desirability of protecting you from demands by various committees to have you appear before them. The Armed Services committees should not be too difficult; however, I would expect Senator Fulbright to attempt to get you before his committee, possibly in an open hearing complete with TV and Radio, to question

[38] For journalistic criticism see, for example, Walter Lippmann in the *Washington Post*, Apr. 27, 1967; James Wechsler in the *New York Post*, Apr. 26, 1967, and Mary McGrory in the *Washington Evening Star*, Apr. 27, 1967. In the *New York Times* on April 27, James Reston quoted McNamara as saying, when asked about Westmoreland's comment, that he "would not like to see any action taken to any way restrict" free speech. Reston concluded: "Secretary McNamara has his critics, but nobody should mistake him on this point, and he is certainly not alone in Washington in feeling this way. The question, therefore, is why other leaders of the Administration have allowed themselves to get in the position of seeming to want to shame their critics into silence, and the answer is that the pressures of war are doing what the pressures of war usually do. They are distorting and corrupting the priorities of many men and leading them to say things under emotion that they do not really believe and probably would not act on even if they could."

[39] *CR*, vol. 113, p. 10611. In the May 1967 *Progressive* magazine, McGovern, in an article, "The Lessons of Vietnam," called the war "the most tragic diplomatic and moral failure in our national experience," and developed his argument for ending the war and for avoiding a similar problem in the future.

[40] *CR*, vol. 113, pp. 10618, 10622.

[41] *Ibid.*, p. 10621.

[42] *Ibid.*, p. 11042.

[43] CMH, Westmoreland Papers, Message Files, Wheeler to Westmoreland, JCS 2218–67, Mar. 24, 1967.

you about the implementation of US policy in Southeast Asia. Therefore, the problem is to keep you away from all congressional committees.

The tactic of not allowing Westmoreland to meet with the committees provoked comments by two important Senators who had been strong supporters of the war, but who were beginning to waver: Democrat Symington and Republican Thruston Morton of Kentucky, chairman of the Senate Republican Campaign Committee. Symington said, "there is nobody who has greater respect than I for General Westmoreland as a man and as a soldier. But it is unfortunate, if he has the time to come over here and deliver talks in Washington and New York and other places that upon the request of the Armed Services Committee he is not available to answer questions with respect to the conduct of the war. . . ."[44] Morton took a similar position, asking whether Westmoreland had been brought back to report on the conduct of the war, "Or is he, indeed, here merely to put a sort of a sack, if you will, over discussion, and try to muffle dissension?"[45]

On April 28, Westmoreland spoke before a joint session of Congress in much the same vein as in his speech to the Associated Press,[46] but with a more oblique reference to dissent:

> [I]t is evident to me that he [the enemy] believes our Achilles' heel is our resolve. Your continued strong support is necessary to our mission. . . . Backed at home by resolve, confidence, patience, determination, and continued support, we will prevail in Vietnam over the Communist aggressor.

Congressional reaction to the speech was muted. Several supporters of the war praised it; several opponents criticized it, including Senator Morse who said, "Wrapping a bad policy in the American flag does not improve its chances for success one iota." He said that he had great respect for Westmoreland, but that he should not be asked to perform a political function while in uniform. Mansfield made this same point:[47] "no field commander has ever had to look over his shoulder to find out if he is 'supported,' because constitutionally, the duty of the military is to carry out policies made by their civilian superiors."

After the speech, the President held a luncheon for members of the House and Senate foreign policy, armed services, and appropriations committees, as well as all of the Nation's governors. After brief comments by the President, Westmoreland spoke, followed by Rusk.[48]

After the luncheon, Westmoreland and Wheeler went to Capitol Hill for individual visits with Russell, Stennis, Fulbright, and George Mahon, chairman of the House Appropriations Committee.

---

[44] *CR*, vol. 113, p. 11049.

[45] *Ibid.*, pp. 11051. See also the speech by Senator Mark Hatfield on Apr. 26, 1967, before the Yale Political Union, in which he criticized the handling of the war, and accused the administration of "using political blackmail to eliminate the painful but democratic necessity of giving all views a fair hearing." *Ibid.*, pp. 11049–11051.

[46] *Ibid.*, pp. 11153–11155.

[47] For Morse's statement, see *ibid.*, pp. 11186–11187; for Mansfield, see 11194. For other congressional comments on Westmoreland's speeches see pp. 10613–10623, 10995–10996, 11155, 11162–11163, 11189–11190.

[48] For the text of the statements see *Public Papers of the Presidents*, Lyndon B. Johnson, 1967, pp. 469–477.

In his notes, Westmoreland said, "Discussions were all cordial and addressed the future course of the war and additional troop requirements." [49]

New Request Leads to a General Review

Following Westmoreland's request for more troops, U.S. officials conducted what the *Pentagon Papers* called "a searching reappraisal of the course of U.S. strategy in the war." [50] Lasting two months, it was the most thorough and intense review conducted during the entire course of the war; and, accordingly, it will be treated here at some length.

On April 24, after a meeting of the Non-Group on April 21, Katzenbach sent a memorandum to Vance, Walt Rostow, William Bundy, McNaughton, Helms and Komer asking that papers be prepared within three weeks on the following three aspects of Westmoreland's request: [51]

> (1) the current situation in Vietnam and the various political and military actions which could be taken to bring the [the war] to a successful conclusion;
>
> (2) the possibilities for negotiation, including an assessment of the ultimate U.S. position in relationship to the DRV [Democratic Republic of (North) Vietnam] and NLF [National Liberation Front]; and
>
> (3) the military and political effects of intensification of the war in South Vietnam and North Vietnam.

With his memorandum of April 24 or shortly thereafter Katzenbach sent a draft description of each of four papers (pacification had been added as a fourth paper).[52] The State Department was assigned the paper on negotiations, the White House (Leonhart, Komer's deputy, who had succeeded him) was assigned the paper on pacification, the CIA was assigned the paper on the political and economic situation as well as the effects of future military actions, and the Department of Defense was assigned the paper on military aspects of the war. As will be seen, although all of these subjects were addressed during the course of the review, these original assignments did not hold firm and the papers that were produced did not follow the original division of subject matter or the descriptions of who should be responsible for what.

In addition to negotiations, State was asked to analyze the political factors involved in extending the war in Laos and Cambodia. It was also asked to analyze "domestic support" in the U.S., and "the connection, if any, with race problems, youth rebellion, disregard for law and order, isolation, polarization of hawks and doves, etc." and to propose actions "to unify domestic support. . . ." including the creation of citizens' committees, "'recantations' by well-known dissidents," and better explanation of

---

[49] CMH, Westmoreland Papers, History File, History Notes, entry for Apr. 27, 1967.

[50] *PP*, Gravel ed., vol. IV, p. 154.

[51] U.S. Department of State, Central File, Pol 27 Viet S.

[52] Same location. This memorandum was based on the discussion of the meeting on April 21 and on two draft descriptions, one prepared by William Bundy on April 22 and another which has no date or author but may have been prepared by McNaughton. Both are in the same location. This was followed by descriptions of each paper as approved by the group at its next meeting, probably held on April 24. These are in the same location.

the war. It was also asked to make a "head count" of congressional opinion on Vietnam, and to consider a congressional resolution.

State was also asked to consider ways of "strengthening the appearance of U.S. unity to Hanoi." Omitted from the final version of the outline, however, was the succeeding sentence in the original draft of the papers, which provided that such consideration "might also include more systematic thinking about using U.S. and other 'doves'—as we have already done to some extent—to get the idea across to Hanoi that the U.S. is really united in basic support of the President's policy, and if anything, tougher."

Defense was asked to analyze in detail the two alternatives proposed by Westmoreland: "Course A," which would add 200,000 troops, with greatly intensified military activity outside South Vietnam, including the possible invasion by U.S. and South Vietnamese forces of North Vietnam, Laos, and Cambodia; and "Course B," which would add only those troops that could be sent without calling up the Reserves—about 10,000 during the following year, and a total of about 35,000. On April 26, Vance asked the JCS to analyze the two options.[53]

Defense was also asked to study possible measures for strengthening South Vietnamese forces as a substitute for U.S. troops, an alternative known as "Vietnamization," which later became the primary emphasis of the Nixon administration as it began to withdraw U.S. forces. In addition, studies were to be made of the more efficient use of U.S. forces in ground combat, of bombing strategy, and of the effect of Courses A and B on Congress and the U.S. public as well as on other countries.

On April 24, Komer, who was about to leave the White House staff for his new post as pacification chief, sent a memorandum to the President questioning the need for additional troops, saying that there was "light at the end of the tunnel," and that the U.S. should concentrate on the war in the South and on defeating the "VC." This, he said, "might at the optimum force Hanoi to fade away, or at the minimum achieve such success as to make clear to all that the war was being won. Such a course would also reinforce the pressures for negotiations. But if we can't get a settlement in 12-18 months, at the least we should shoot for such concrete results in South Vietnam that it might permit us to start bringing a few troops home rather than sending even more out." He suggested the following as "Crucial Variables Which Will Determine Success in Vietnam:"[54]

> a. *It is Unlikely that Hanoi will Negotiate.* We can't count on a negotiated compromise. Perhaps the NLF would prove more flexible, but it seems increasingly under the thumb of Hanoi.
>
> b. *More Bombing or Mining Would Raise the Pain Level but Probably Wouldn't Force Hanoi to Cry Uncle.* I'm no expert on this, but can't see it as decisive. Could it prevent Hanoi from maintaining substantial infiltration if it chose? Moreover, some facets of it contain dangerous risks.
>
> c. *Thus the Critical Variable is in the South!* The greatest opportunity for decisive gains in the next 12-18 months lies in ac-

---

[53] *PP*, Gravel ed., vol. IV, p. 492. For the JCS analysis see p. 640 below.

[54] Johnson Library, Warnke Papers, McNaughton Files, Memorandum to the President from Komer, "Thoughts on Future Strategy in Vietnam," Apr. 24, 1967.

celerating the erosion of the VC in South Vietnam, and in building a viable alternative with attractive power. Let's assume that the NVA could replace its losses. *I doubt that the VC could.* They are now the "weak sisters" of the enemy team. The evidence is not conclusive, but certainly points in this direction. Indeed, the NVA strategy in I Corps seems designed to take pressure off the VC in the South. [emphases in original]

Instead of more U.S. troops, Komer argued that the U.S. should seek to stimulate a greater effort by the South Vietnamese Armed Forces. He recommended a number of specific measures, including more U.S. advisers, higher pay and other incentives, and better weapons. The U.S. should also exert greater pressure for competent military leadership: "Insist on dismissal of incompetent commanders. Find U.S. means for rewarding competent ones, such as withholding MAP [Military Assistance Program funds] from ineffective units." He also proposed a joint command, with Westmoreland in charge of all South Vietnamese as well as U.S. forces.

Civilian pacification programs, Komer added, should be strengthened along similar lines.

On May 1, 1967, William Bundy explained his position in a memorandum to Katzenbach.[55] He, too, opposed large troop increases. It was essential, he said, to withstand Communist pressure in the northern part of South Vietnam, but he said that Nitze had told him that an additional 50,000 U.S. troops would be sufficient to handle that problem. Moreover, Bundy said, he was skeptical of using U.S. forces in the delta.

Bundy thought the key factor was a combination of the situation in South Vietnam and the situation in China, which was then undergoing considerable domestic unrest. "If we go on as we are doing, if the political process in the South comes off well, and if the Chinese do not settle down, I myself would reckon that by the end of 1967 there is at least a 50-50 chance that a favorable tide will be running really strongly in the South, and that Hanoi will be very discouraged. Whether they will move to negotiate is of course a slightly different question, but we could be visibly and strongly on the way." "If China should go into a real convulsion," he said, "it [is] clearly more likely that Hanoi would choose a negotiating path to the conclusion [of the Vietnam war]."

Bundy also opposed any increase in U.S. troops that would require calling up the Reserves and thus precipitate a debate in Congress. "Under present circumstances," he said, "I believe such a debate could only encourage Hanoi, and might also lead to pressures to go beyond what is wise in the North, specifically mining Haiphong. Unless there are over-riding military reasons—which I do not myself see—we should not get into such a debate this summer."

Bundy opposed increased bombing of the North—he said he would agree to bombing the Hanoi power station "but then let it go at that"—and the mining of Haiphong, "unless the Soviets categorically use it to send in combat weapons." The mining of Hai-

[55] U.S. Department of State, Central File, Pol 27 Viet S, Memorandum from William Bundy to the Under Secretary, "Thoughts on Strategy in Vietnam," May 1, 1967. There is also a copy in the Johnson Library, Warnke Papers, McNaughton Files, and there are excerpts in *PP*, Gravel ed., vol. IV, pp. 115–156 and 444–447.

phong, he said, "is bound to risk a confrontation with the Soviets and to throw Hanoi into greater dependence on Communist China. These in themselves would be very dangerous and adverse to the whole notion of getting Hanoi to change its attitude. Moreover, I think they would somehow manage to get the stuff in through China no matter what we did to Haiphong." The possibility of a renewed convulsion in China, which might lead the North Vietnamese to be more amenable to a settlement of the Vietnam war, was added reason, he believed, for the U.S. not to increase military action against the North.

Bundy was also "totally against" an invasion of the North, "for the single reason that I believe the chances are 75–25 that it would bring the Chinese truly into the war and, almost equally important, stabilize the internal Chinese situation at least temporarily."

As for U.S. ground action in Laos, Bundy said he agreed with William Sullivan that Souvanna Phouma would "object violently and feel that his whole position had been seriously compromised." Bundy also agreed with Sullivan that small unit over-the-border operations against the Ho Chi Minh Trail in Laos were acceptable, even though both he and Sullivan doubted whether these would do more than make the use of the trail "somewhat more difficult."

Bundy said that Cambodia was becoming more important in the war, but he questioned whether military action against Communist supply routes in Cambodia would be effective or "worth the broad political damage of appearing to attack Cambodia." Moreover, he thought that Sihanouk was "slowly moving to a more truly neutral position and is doing about all he can to ease the problem."

Finally, William Bundy recommended that the U.S. should maintain a "steady and considered program of action for the next nine months" in order to convince the North Vietnamese of American determination to prosecute the war. Since December of 1966, he said, the U.S. had "given a very jerky and impatient impression to Hanoi . . . related more to the timing and suddenness of our bombing and negotiating actions than to the substance of what we have done." This, he said, may have encouraged the North Vietnamese to think that the U.S. wanted to end the war before the 1968 American elections, believing, as they did, that the elections could lead to a change in the U.S. position.

McGeorge Bundy, who had left the White House earlier in 1966 to become president of the Ford Foundation, was still very much involved in discussions of U.S. policy toward Vietnam, and he, too, sent the President a letter (May 3) and a memorandum of his views on the troop request.[56] He said that large increases in U.S. forces or escalation of the war—recommendations that were "inevitable, in the framework of strictly military analysis"—would be a mistake. They would not bring an end to the war, and would further inflame the U.S. public, which was "increasingly uneasy about Vietnam because there appears to be no defined limits to the levels of force and danger that may lie ahead."

Moreover, escalation of the war would not bring a victory over the North Vietnamese before the 1968 American elections because

[56] Johnson Library, NSF Files of Walt W. Rostow, letter and memorandum to the President from McGeorge Bundy, May 3, 1967. There are excerpts in *PP*, Gravel ed., vol. IV, pp. 157–160.

the North would hold out until then in anticipation that, like the French in 1954, the U.S. would change its course after the election if the war appeared to be unwinnable. The Johnson administration should plan, therefore, to justify its Vietnam policy in the 1968 election, not by a victory over Hanoi, but by the "growing success—and self-reliance—in the South."

With respect to the request for an extension of the air war against North Vietnam, McGeorge Bundy said he preferred a "middle course" that would limit bombing in the North, "but you know me too well to mistake this for a sudden switch to appeasement. I have been for bombing from the beginning and I am sure it has been and still is indispensable, but I just don't believe the people who think that a lot more of it brings us nearer to solution today." "Ho Chi Minh and his colleagues," he said, "simply are not going to change their policy on the basis of losses from the air in North Vietnam." He added, however, that he was opposed to stopping the bombing at that time. To do so "would be to give the Communists something for nothing, and in a very short time all the doves in this country and around the world would be asking for some further unilateral concessions."

Tactical bombing of communications and troop concentrations "and of airfields as necessary" was still justifiable as a way of attempting to control infiltration, but he argued that strategic bombing of such targets as power plants was "nonproductive and unwise." "We are attacking them [the power plants], I fear, mainly because we have 'run out' of other targets. Is it a very good reason? Can anyone demonstrate that such targets have been very rewarding? Remembering the claims for attacks on oil supplies, should we not be very skeptical of new promises?"

Strategic bombing, McGeorge Bundy added, had little effect on the "military capability of a primitive country," and tended "to divide the U.S., to distract us all from the real struggle in the South, and to accentuate the unease and distemper which surround the war in Vietnam, both at home and abroad." "There is certainly a point," he said, "at which such bombing does increase the risk of conflict with China or the Soviet Union. . . ."

The case against the request for 100,000–200,000 additional troops, Bundy said, was "more complicated and I advance it with less conviction." Although U.S. forces had been "decisive in preventing defeat and in opening a hope of real success, in the absence of major Communist escalation, we are reaching the point of diminishing returns from U.S. troop buildups." Moreover, the war would not end "as long as it merely pits foreign troops against Communists." "In the end, it is safety in the villages that is the object of the war," he added, and a "clearly defined limit on the American forces in South Vietnam would serve to focus the attention of all on this centrally *Vietnamese* task and on the continuing responsibility of the South Vietnamese themselves." (emphasis in original) The "requirement for 1965 was for proof of the American effort," but the requirement for 1967 was for "re-emphasis upon the role of the Vietnamese themselves, always with our advice and support."

Restrictions on bombing and troops were even more justified, Bundy said, "by their value in stabilizing American opinion." "The best observers agree that the only hope in Hanoi today is for American disunity and war weariness," and that argument "underlines the critical importance of holding the country together and giving it a solid basis for confident determination in its persistence."

McGeorge Bundy said that the President's Johns Hopkins speech in May 1965 had provided a good "platform" for the "balanced program of military firmness and readiness for unconditional negotiations." "Now we need a fresh and clear statement which will limit the fears of our own people and at the same time underline our national determination to stay the course." Such a "policy of announced restraint" would be criticized by "some civil and military hawks," but that criticism could be countered by a "powerful assembly of technical and expert opinion:"

> I am confident, on the basis of a recent conversation, that General Laurie Norstad would be willing to accept the task of rounding up senior Air Force heroes like Spaatz and Twining—and he thinks perhaps even LeMay—to support a policy of bombing restraint. (Norstad himself would actually stop the bombing in the North—at least for a while—but I think he would gladly fall in with the present proposal to restrict ourselves to the "tactical.") I suspect that a similar effort could be launched through General Bradley in favor of a policy of troop limitation. (Obviously, the position will be greatly reinforced as and when we are able to refer to a new and stronger military/technological barricade against infiltration.)
>
> More generally, I think there is no one on earth who could win an argument that an active deployment of some 500,000 men, firmly supported by tactical bombing in both South and North Vietnam, represented an undercommitment at this time. I would not want to be the politician or the general, who whined about such a limitation.

Finally, McGeorge Bundy commented on the question of diplomatic negotiations. He recommended postponing any further "public campaigns for negotiations . . . while maintaining every possible private diplomatic contact." "I think we got a clear No in February and should wait a while before we go back to the well. I also think we ought to wait until after the South Vietnamese election."

> The present issue is not "negotiation." It is "escalation." What is undermining national unity now is the prospect of one more unrewarding debate between the advocates and the opponents of escalation, each shouting at the other against a backdrop of worldwide fear of a third war. The most valuable single step for all of us now would be a clear public demonstration, by a publicly proclaimed decision, of what the top of the government knows so well—that the President himself is a man of peace *and* determination, restraint *and* perseverance, who knows what the war is really about, and how to keep it in bounds while pressing it towards success. Above all we need a renewed demonstration that the President is in charge of the war, and not the other way around. (emphases in original)

McGeorge Bundy concluded by stressing the need not to obscure the gains already made by "seeming to act as if we have to do much more lest we fail." The "great and central achievement of these last two years," he said, was "the defeat we have prevented. The fact that South Vietnam has not been lost and is not going to be lost is a fact of truly massive importance in the history of Asia, the Pacific, and the U.S. An articulate minority of 'Eastern intellectuals' (like Bill Fulbright) may not believe in what they call the domino theory, but most Americans (along with nearly all Asians) know better."

The President asked McNamara to get the JCS's reaction to McGeorge Bundy's memorandum, but to do so without revealing its source. Chairman Wheeler replied the next day (May 5) in a memorandum to the President listing the advantages of bombing the power plants, and arguing that "Unless and until we find some means of obstructing and reducing the flow of war supporting material through Haiphong, the North Vietnamese will continue to be able to support their war effort both in North Vietnam and South Vietnam."[57]

Doubts about increasing U.S. troop strength were also expressed by one of McNamara's chief lieutenants, Alain Enthoven, Assistant Secretary of Defense for Systems Analysis. In a briefing paper on March 16 for the Guam Conference, Enthoven's office stated that the forces already approved, together with South Vietnamese and other allied forces, "should provide adequate forces to neutralize the large enemy units and prevent them from interfering with the pacification program as well as to conduct a large scale interdiction campaign against NVN efforts to supply Communist forces in the South."[58] Additional U.S. troops, the paper argued, would provide a "marginal return." "The VC/NVA have the capability to recruit and infiltrate at an adequate rate to replace their current or expected losses, offsetting our buildup. Moreover, VC/NVA losses per 1,000 additional U.S. troops deployed appear to be dropping off." "The best alternatives," the paper said, "are to increase the effectiveness of the force already deployed. This may be done through improved tactics and intelligence as well as through greater firepower and mobility."

The Systems Analysis paper, noting that deployments "must fit the capacity of the Vietnamese economy to bear them without undue inflation," also stated that "Any sizeable increase in forces over those now planned would almost certainly result in a sharp increase in inflation . . . [which] might well destroy our hopes of establishing a relatively stable and effective government in SVN."

Finally, the paper considered some of the factors that might lead to "significant changes" in the approved program of U.S. deployments. Significant implementation of the barrier plan (PRACTICE NINE) could require an additional force of 40,000. But, depending on the success of military operations, there could also be reductions in U.S. forces. In addition to a possible reduction of 10-15,000 in construction and support personnel beginning mid-1968, "if the war against the hard-core VC/NVA units should drop off sharply next year, it may be possible to withdraw a major slice of U.S. combat and support units—perhaps as many as 100,000." In a comment

[57] Johnson Library, NSF Memos to the President—Walt Rostow, Memorandum from Rostow to the President, May 6, 1967, transmitting CM-3218-67, May 5, 1967.

[58] Johnson Library, Warnke Papers, McNaughton Files, "Optimum Force Levels in SVN," Office of the Assistant Secretary of Defense for Systems Analysis, Mar. 16, 1967.

reminiscent of a similar plan in the fall of 1963[59] the paper added that "Such a step would reduce the overall cost of the war to the U.S. and hopefully stimulate the GVN to play a more responsible role. It would also lessen the economic dislocations caused by the massive U.S. presence, and ease the burden in the U.S. of supporting the effort in SEA."

In response to Westmoreland's request for additional troops, Enthoven sent McNamara on May 1, 1967, what the *Pentagon Papers* called "the most cogent critique of MACV's strategy. . . . Here a concentrated attack was launched on the two most vulnerable aspects of COMUSMACV's operations: the feasibility of the 'war of attrition' strategy pursued in the face of the uncertainty about NVN infiltration, and 'search and destroy tactics to support it.'"[60]

Enthoven said that the U.S. was "up against an enemy who just may have found a dangerously clever strategy for licking the United States." "They believe that public opinion will eventually force our retirement. And they could be right." "If, as I believe, their strategy is to wait us out, they will control their losses to a level low enough to be sustained indefinitely, but high enough to tempt us to increase our forces to the point of U.S. public rejection of the war."

Enthoven saw the war "as a race between, on the one hand, the development of a viable South Vietnam and, on the other, a gradual loss in public support, or even tolerance, for the war. Hanoi is betting that we'll lose public support in the United States before we build a nation in South Vietnam. We must do what we can to make sure that doesn't happen. We must work on both problems together, slow the loss in public support; and speed the development of South Vietnam. Our horse must cross the finish first." He concluded: "I feel that adding more U.S. combat forces would be a step in the wrong direction. They are not needed for military security, and they could not force higher losses on the North Vietnamese. But they might play right into the hands of Hanoi by burdening the United States and increasing internal opposition to the war, while delaying the birth of the strong nation in the South which is our only hope of real stability."

With respect to military objectives which assertedly would be served by additional forces, Enthoven argued as follows:

> 1) To deter a Communist Chinese invasion, I see no sign of a change in Communist Chinese intentions. Were they to invade, they would face a formidable force already in place, and more available if needed, particularly with mobilization. Furthermore, I feel that the very nationalism which drives the North Vietnamese also inhibits them from calling in the same Chinese who have subjugated them in the past.
>
> 2) To prevent a military defeat in South Vietnam. I do not think there is danger of any significant military defeat, given the forces we have in place now. . . .

---

[59] See pt. 2 of this study, p. 185.

[60] Enthoven's memorandum for McNamara, "Increase of Southeast Asia Forces," May 1, 1967, is in the Johnson Library, Warnke Papers, McNaughton Files, as well as in *PP*, Gravel ed., vol. IV, pp. 463–466. Enthoven later published a book on the application of systems analysis to the defense program in which he discussed efforts to analyze aspects of the Vietnam war and the lack of adequate analysis of the war. See Enthoven and Smith, *How Much is Enough?*

3) To prevent terrorism. Though there is terrorism in South Vietnam now, I doubt that additional U.S. combat forces would significantly reduce it. This is a job for police-type forces, not maneuver battalions.

4) To raise VC/NVA losses to a level they cannot sustain. Presumably, this would be something above the weekly loss rate of 3,265 which the DIA/USIB [Defense Intelligence Agency/U.S. Intelligence Board] estimate they can swallow indefinitely.

On the most optimistic basis, 200,000 more Americans would raise their weekly losses to about 3,700, or about 400 a week more than they could stand. In theory, we'd then wipe them out in 10 years. But to bank on that, you have to assume that (1) enemy losses are just proportional to friendly strength, and (2) that the unusually favorable kill ratio of the first quarter of 1967 will continue. However, if the kill ratio should be no better than the 1966 average, their losses would be about 2,100—less than 2/3 of their sustaining capability.

But even that figure is misleading. Losses just aren't directly related to the size of our force. Between the first and fourth quarters of 1966, our forces increased 23%, but their losses increased only 13%—little more than half as much.

Finally, the most important factor of all is that the enemy can control his losses within wide limits. The VC/NVA started the shooting in over 90% of the company-sized fire fights; over 80% began with a well-organized enemy attack. Since their losses rise (as in the first quarter of 1967) and fall (as they have done since) with their choice of whether or not to fight, they can probably hold their losses to about 2,000 a week regardless of our force levels.

Enthoven joined Komer and William Bundy in arguing that additional U.S. forces would hurt rather than help the pacification program. "[M]ore United States forces aren't going to solve the pacification problem," he said. "The pacification program depends . . . on better support for Vietnamese forces and a more energetic national Government. This program requires not only time and patience, but political and economic progress rather than military victories. . . . Furthermore, if we continue to add forces and to Americanize the war, we will only erode whatever incentives the South Vietnamese people may now have to help themselves in this fight. Similarly, it would be a further sign to the South Vietnamese leaders that we will carry any load, regardless of their actions. That will not help us build a strong nation." Enthoven added that "There is no indication MACV has the same sense of urgency about increasing ARVN effectiveness as it has about increasing the number of U.S. forces."[61]

According to Enthoven's analysis, there was an excess of U.S. forces in Vietnam. Assuming that the existing threat from the Communists remained constant, the "minimum essential force" was 28 battalions smaller than the 470,000 already authorized in Program 4. This was his analysis:[62]

---

[61] *PP*, Gravel ed., vol. IV, p. 467.

[62] From the appendix to Enthoven's memorandum, *ibid.*, pp. 467–468.

Before U.S. intervention, the VC decimated and demoralized the ARVN reaction and reserve force by successful ambushes and attacks. The 17 US/FW [Free World] battalions deployed by July 1965 ended the deteriorating trend. In both I CTZ [Corps Tactical Zone I] and II CTZ, VC control over the population peaked by July 1965, and it declined even earlier in III and IV CTZ.

Since then, the enemy increased from 99 to 151 infantry-type battalions at the end of December 1966. As of 31 December 1966 we had 98 infantry-type battalions, more than enough to counter the enemy force considering the intelligence available. Of the 98 battalions 34 were engaged in TAOR [tactical area of responsibility] patrol; 46 were engaged in operations that were initiated by hard intelligence; and the 18 others were predictably unproductive. The 46 battalions were obviously sufficient to counter the 151 VC/NVA infantry-type battalions, witness the total lack of enemy success. This suggests that we need 1 battalion for each 3 enemy infantry-type battalions, in addition to those needed for static defense. The 18 battalions ineffectively employed plus the 10 additional infantry-type battalions in Program 4 that close after January 1, 1967 are enough to counter 84 additional enemy battalions. Thus we need deploy no more forces until the enemy goes above 235 battalions, which does not seem to be his present intent. (The enemy peak was 155 infantry-type battalions in July 1966, and was 144 at 31 March 1967).

US/FW FORCE REQUIREMENT

Enemy Force	*Required Mobile US/FW Force*	*US/FW Force for TAOR Patrols*	*Total Required U.S. Force*
151	46	34	80
235	74	34	108

The 3 to 1 ratio is supported by results in battle. Our forces routinely defeat enemy forces outnumbering them two or three to one. In no instance has a dug-in U.S. company been overrun, regardless of the size of the attacking enemy force, and nothing larger than a company has come close to annihilation when caught moving. Seven battalions of Marines defeated two NVA divisions in HASTINGS, and single battalions of 1st Air Cavalry defeated regimental-sized forces in pitched battles in the Ia Drang Valley in the Fall of 1965.

These factors need confirmation, in actual practice, by how well the forces are doing in the field and by progress in RD [Rural Development]. VC/NVA military victories and large areas succumbing to VC require a reaction regardless of calculated force requirements. But there is no sign of anything like that in the foreseeable future. Moreover, a sharp improvement in our effectiveness should result from improvements in the flow of intelligence and in the tactical employment of our forces. Achieving such improvements should be the main objective at this time.

Preparation of Memoranda for the President on Troops and Bombing

In late April 1967, McNaughton's office began preparing the draft of a Presidential memorandum (DPM) on the new troop request. McNaughton felt strongly that more U.S. troops were not needed and would be detrimental both in Vietnam and at home. In the U.S., he said, in commenting on an early draft of the DPM on troops, "A feeling is widely and strongly held that 'the Establishment' is out of its mind. The feeling is that we are trying to impose some U.S. image on distant peoples we cannot understand (anymore than we can the younger generation here at home), and that we are carrying the thing to absurd lengths." "Related to this," he added, "is the increased polarization that is taking place in the United States with seeds of the worst split in our people in more than a century."[63] "In this connection," he added, "I fear that 'natural selection' in this environment will lead the Administration itself to become more and more homogenized—Mac Bundy, George Ball, Bill Moyers are gone. Who next?"

McNaughton argued that "to avoid another diplomatic default and military misuse of the forces," it was essential to thrash out more general questions of policy and strategy:

> I am afraid there is the fatal flaw in the strategy in the draft. It is that the strategy falls into the trap that has ensnared us for the past three years. It actually *gives* the troops while only *praying* for their proper use and for constructive diplomatic action. Limiting the present decision to an 80,000 add-on [the number provided in the May 1 DPM] does the very important business of postponing the issue of a Reserve call-up (and all of its horrible baggage), but postpone it is all that it does—probably to a worse time, 1968. Providing the 80,000 troops is tantamount to acceding to the whole Westmoreland-Sharp request. This being the case, they will "accept" the 80,000. But six months from now, in will come messages like the "470,000–570,000" messages, saying that the requirement remains at 201,000 (or more). Since no pressure will have been put on anyone, the military war will have gone on as before and no diplomatic progress will have been made. It follows that the "philosophy" of the war should be fought out now so everyone will not be proceeding on their own major premises, and getting us in deeper and deeper; at the very least, the President should give General Westmoreland his limit (as President Truman did to General MacArthur). That is, if General Westmoreland is to get 550,000 men, he should be told "that will be all, and we mean it." (emphasis in original)

By early May 1967, the President and his associates began considering ways of applying additional military pressure on the Communists without substantially increasing the number of U.S. forces. Major consideration was given to troop contributions by other countries—a "troop community chest operation" as Walt Rostow called it.[64] Another possibility was to expand the air war against the

[63] Johnson Library, Warnke Papers, McNaughton Files, McNaughton memorandum to McNamara, "My Comments on the 5 May 'First Rough Draft,'" May 6, 1967.
[64] *PP*, Gravel ed., vol. IV, pp. 469–470.

North. Because of the relevance of the air war to the proposal for more troops, as well as because of the greater sensitivity of the troop question, the two issues tended to become separated to some extent during the policy review in May and June, with priority given to deciding about the air war before acting on the troop request.

On Tuesday, May 2, the President held a luncheon meeting from 1:27 p.m. to 2:50 p.m. with Rusk, McNamara and Rostow. George Christian also attended. According to the agenda, the group considered a proposal by McNamara that the U.S. should complete the bombing of major targets, especially the major power plants in Hanoi and Haiphong, and that after airstrikes had eliminated the major power systems for North Vietnam the U.S. should shift its bombing to the area south of the 20th parallel while holding open the possibility of returning to the Hanoi/Haiphong area. The Russians would be "quietly notified" of this shift in the hope of encouraging them to play more of a peacemaking role.[65] (It will be recalled that McNamara made a similar proposal in early March.)

At another luncheon meeting two days later (May 4) from 1:32 p.m. to 3:00 p.m. attended by the President, Rusk, McNamara, Rostow, McPherson and Christian, the question of whether to attack the power plants in Hanoi and Haiphong was again discussed, as well as the plan to reduce the bombing program after those targets were struck. It was decided to postpone the attacks.[66]

Meanwhile, on May 3 the troop request was made public in an article in the *New York Times* reporting that Westmoreland had asked for a large number of additional troops.[67] In response, the President denied that a buildup in Vietnam was "imminent."[68]

On May 5, concurrently with the preparation of the DPM on the new troop request, McNaughton's office prepared a separate DPM on bombing, based on McNamara's proposal at the meeting with the President on May 2.[69] This DPM, which was distributed under Vance's name, took the position that there were few important targets left in North Vietnam, and that ROLLING THUNDER had strengthened rather than broken the will of the North Vietnamese. Moreover, the U.S. loss rate for bombing the Hanoi-Haiphong area was more than six times the rate for the area of North Vietnam below the 20th parallel (50–75 miles to the south of Hanoi/Haiphong.) Accordingly, the memorandum recommended that future U.S. operations should be in the North Vietnamese "panhandle" area below the 20th parallel, the "funnel" through which men and

---

[65] There apparently are no notes of the meeting. The agenda for the meeting is in the Johnson Library, NSF Files of Walt W. Rostow.

Prior to the meeting, William Bundy sent a memorandum to Rusk in which he urged that in the case of such additional bombing the U.S. should not bomb the Doumer bridge or the Phuc Yen airport. The former was in a civilian area and there could be major casualties. Bombing the airport, the principal base for North Vietnamese MiGs, might drive the North Vietnamese to seek Chinese help in basing the planes in China, and that could have "most dangerous" consequences in terms of future incidents and the possible further involvement of the Chinese in the war. U.S. Department of State, Central File, Pol 27 Viet S, Memorandum to the Secretary from William Bundy, May 2, 1967.

[66] There apparently are no notes of the meeting. The agenda is in the Johnson Library, NSF Files of Walt W. Rostow. On his copy of the agenda Rostow noted "put off" next to the items on whether to bomb the sensitive targets.

[67] *New York Times*, May 3, 1967.

[68] *Ibid.*, May 4, 1967.

[69] Johnson Library, Warnke Papers, McNaughton Files, Draft Memorandum for the President, May 6, 1967, "Proposed Bombing Program Against North Vietnam."

supplies flowed south, but with occasional strikes against the area north of that "as necessary to keep the enemy's investment in defense and in repair crews high throughout the country."

The Vance/McNaughton memo also opposed closing the ports by bombing and mining, primarily because of the risk of a confrontation with the Soviet Union.

The next day (May 6), Walt Rostow stated his position in a memorandum, "U.S. Strategy in Vietnam," which he sent to the President as well as to Rusk, Vance, Katzenbach, McNaughton, William Bundy and Helms.[70] Bombing in the Hanoi-Haiphong area, he said, had forced the North Vietnamese to divert manpower and resources to repair work and related tasks. It had also imposed other "economic, political and psychological difficulties." But, it had not hardened their will to resist.[71] Nor was there any "direct, immediate connection" between the bombing of the Hanoi-Haiphong area and the capability of the Communists to carry on the fighting in the South. Moreover, with the bombing of the Hanoi power plant, which constituted 80 percent of the north's remaining electrical generating capacity, and which Rostow agreed should be attacked, most of the targets "whose destruction imposes serious military-civil costs on the North" would have been hit.

Again describing the North Vietnamese supply line as a funnel, as he had in a memorandum to the President on February 17, noted earlier, Rostow said he opposed "closing the top of the funnel" by mining and bombing of ports and bombing of rail lines between Hanoi and China as proposed by the military. He doubted that the Soviet Union would go to war over Vietnam, with the possible exception of an effort by the U.S. to occupy North Vietnam. China, he said, would enter the war if the U.S. invaded the northern part of North Vietnam. However, even though Russian or Chinese intervention was unlikely, efforts to close the top of the funnel would increase tension between the U.S. and the Soviet Union and China, and benefits would not be commensurate with risks.

Rather than either trying to close the top of the funnel or continuing to bomb in the Hanoi-Haiphong area, as he had recommended in his February memorandum, Rostow agreed with McNamara, Vance, McNaughton and both Bundys that it would be

---

[70] Johnson Library, NSF Country File, Vietnam. See also Rostow's comments in *The Diffusion of Power*, pp. 510–513.

In his transmittal memorandum, Rostow noted that his memorandum of May 6 was "for discussion on Monday, May 8, 1967." Presumably, this was to be (and was) a meeting of the Non-Group principals to whom the transmitted memorandum was addressed, of which there are no notes.

[71] According to Rostow, *The Diffusion of Power*, p. 511, "As of March 1967, the best estimate in the government was that the air and naval bombardment of North Vietnam had tied up from 600,000 to 700,000 North Vietnamese who were diverted from other tasks to repair, reconstruction, dispersal, and transport programs, and to civil defense activities. The figures also includes about 83,000 military personnel, or 20 percent of North Vietnam's military strength, who were directly engaged in air defense activities, and an additional 25,500 personnel who were indirectly involved. These diversions of manpower limited North Vietnam's capability for sustained large-scale conventional military operations against South Vietnam. Additionally, air attacks destroyed or inactivated significant percentages of direct military or war-supporting targets, like military bases, ammunition depots, petroleum storage, electric power, radar sites, explosives manufacturing, and communications facilities. And there was ample evidence that the bombing slowed transit to the south and inflicted attrition on men and supplies in transit of up to 20 percent."

preferable to shift bombing to the area below the 20th parallel, with occasional strikes as needed in the Hanoi-Haiphong area.[72]

On May 9, 1967, William Bundy prepared a memorandum on "Bombing Strategy Options for the Rest of 1967" (which he said represented his views as well as those of Katzenbach and Helms), which came to conclusions similar to those of Rostow.[73] It argued that besides saving American lives, this alternative would be at least as effective militarily as the existing bombing program, and would also be the option most likely to induce the North to change its behavior. Existing or heavier levels of bombing, on the other hand, would harden the will of the North. Heavier bombing, especially of sensitive targets, would also induce the Russians and Chinese to increase their aid to North Vietnam, whereas more restricted bombing would reduce the dependence of the North Vietnamese on Chinese and Russian supplies, which in turn would lessen Russian and Chinese influence in North Vietnam. Moreover, heavy bombing of the North could also affect China's internal situation, and this, the memorandum explained, could have a very important bearing on the willingness of the North Vietnamese to negotiate an end to the war:

> [O]ur China experts have recently pointed to a danger that a continued high level of bombing against North Vietnam may tend either to calm down the Chinese internal situation or to assist Mao to gain control. The argument is that a state of high tension might have these effects, even though Peking remained well short of any decision to intervene in a major military way.
>
> Some of us believe we must take this argument very seriously. As things now stand, the odds look better than 50–50 that the Chinese internal struggle will get worse. If so, this could be a major favorable factor at some point in changing Hanoi's attitude, both by tending to reduce Chinese leverage and by causing Hanoi to worry as to whether disorder alone may not affect the Chinese supply routes. . . .[74]

---

[72] In his memoirs, Rostow says that the President rejected his argument "on the ground that an ending of bombing attacks in the Hanoi-Haiphong area would weaken his political support at home and deny him a possible negotiating asset." (*Ibid.*, p. 512.) At the end of this sentence he cites a statement to this effect in the President's own memoirs, *The Vantage Point*, p. 368.

[73] Johnson Library, NSF Country File, Vietnam. There are excerpts in *PP*, Gravel ed., vol. IV, pp. 165–168.

[74] This was a reference to a cable to William Bundy from Rice, the State Department's chief China analyst in Hong Kong, (U.S. Department of State, Central File, Pol 27 Viet S, Hong Kong to Washington 7581, May 1, 1967), responding to a query from Bundy (same location, Washington to Hong Kong 184833, Apr. 28, 1967). On May 8, the Director of Intelligence for the State Department (INR), Thomas Hughes, sent to Secretary Rusk a memorandum (same location) on the Hong Kong cable, saying that its conclusions were quite similar to those of an INR paper, "Probable North Vietnamese and Chinese Reactions to Augmented Military Pressure Against North Vietnam," among them:

"—Augmentation of US military pressure on NVN would—added to other considerations—suggest to Peking that the US intended ultimately to attack China;

"—Despite present Chinese defensive policy and desire not to become involved in a war with the US, developing circumstances, including situations involving combative Chinese elements, could result in a US-Chinese confrontation;

"—Bombing NVN will not achieve our objectives if only because China and NVN's other supporters can funnel in all the aid necessary to replace what we destroy and maintain the Communist military effort in North and South;

"—If the Hanoi regime felt itself nearing collapse, China would be on balance willing and able to intervene;

"—As long as NVN has not lost its struggle in the South, it will not be disposed to compromise, whatever foreseeable military pressure is exerted upon the North."

With respect to domestic factors, the Bundy/Katzenbach/Helms memorandum stated that there would be a "really serious outcry" from the "doves" against heavier bombing of all targets, which was described as Option A, and that Option B, the existing program, "would cause substantial continuing concern and criticism." Option C, bombing below the 20th parallel, "would not satisfy the 'doves' but would probably mean criticism within more controllable limits from this quarter." Missing from this analysis, however, was any comment on the reaction of the "hawks" to the three options.

Finally, as to targets to be struck before shifting to more restricted bombing, the memorandum took the position that most of the President's civilian advisers had been taking, namely, that of the three remaining targets of military value in the Hanoi-Haiphong area, the Doumer bridge over the Red River and the Phuc Yen airport were located too close to residential areas and should not be bombed. The Hanoi power plant, the only major remaining power source, could be hit, but it, too, was located near residences and "the choice could go either way."

On May 9, the McNaughton Draft Presidential Memorandum on bombing, signed by both McNamara and Vance, was sent to the President.[75] It took virtually the same position that Rostow and William Bundy (joined by Katzenbach and Helms) had taken, that bombing should be concentrated on the "funnel" area south of 20 degrees. "The military gain from destruction of additional military targets north of 20 will be slight," the memorandum said. "If we believed that air attacks in that area would change Hanoi's will, they might be worth the added loss of American life and the risks of expansion of the war. However, there is no evidence that this will be the case, while there is considerable evidence that such bombing will strengthen Hanoi's will." (Rostow disagreed that bombing would strengthen Hanoi's will.)

Although this change of policy would not be undertaken for the purpose of "getting Hanoi to change its ways or to negotiate," McNamara and Vance suggested that "to optimize the chances of a favorable Hanoi reaction" the U.S.S.R. should be told of the decision. The U.S.S.R. could be expected to tell the North Vietnamese who, "not having been asked a question by us and having no ultimatum-like time limit, might be in a better posture to react favorably than has been the case in the past." The U.S., however, should not expect a favorable reply from the North.

In a memorandum to the President that same day (May 9), Rostow, noting that there had been a meeting of the Non-Group on the previous afternoon, summarized the common elements of the Vance, Bundy, Rostow papers.[76] He also described what happened to cause this reexamination of U.S. bombing strategy:

> I believe what has happened is something like this:
>
> —We expanded our targets list in the Hanoi/Haiphong areas. CINCPAC, feeling a general go-ahead, began to propose targets which had two characteristics: they were either increasingly

---

[75] Johnson Library, NSF Country File, Vietnam, "Proposed Bombing Program Against North Vietnam," May 9, 1967. That day Rostow sent the McNamara-Vance memorandum, Bundy's memorandum of May 9, and his own memorandum of May 6 to the President, but he did not comment on them in his transmittal memorandum (same location).

[76] Johnson Library, NSF Memos to the President—Walt Rostow.

unimportant in relation to the losses sustained, or they began to foreshadow the mining of the ports and the cutting of supplies from China.

—Sect. Rusk began to worry about the Soviet and Chinese Communist reaction to what was happening and, especially, to what was projected;

—Sect. McNamara, who does not feel bombing in Hanoi/Haiphong relates directly to the war in the South, became increasingly uneasy and felt that rational control over targeting was getting out of his hands.

On May 12, there was another meeting from 1:24 p.m. to 2:45 p.m. of the President with Rusk, McNamara, Rostow and Christian. According to the agenda, the principal Vietnam item to be considered was U.S. bombing policy.[77] Judging by the few notations Rostow made on his copy of the agenda, there may also have been some discussion of a "plan to win [the] war," and of the drawing up of such a plan (another notation was "draw up plan").

In a memorandum to the President on May 10 before the meeting on bombing policy, Rostow summarized the Vance-Bundy-Rostow consensus as follows: The North Vietnamese import system would not be attacked, but a study would be made of doing so; a plan for attacking the Hanoi power plant would be submitted to the President with a statement on the risks of civilian casualties and damage; there would be an assessment of bombing and on estimates of the costs and benefits of bombing new targets, and meanwhile, requested attacks on airfields would be held in abeyance.[78]

On May 15, prior to a Tuesday Luncheon the next day, Rostow sent the President a memorandum "on the issue that will be before you tomorrow at lunch"—the bombing of the Hanoi power plant.[79] McNamara, he said, wanted to launch the attack as soon as possible. "As you know, he is quite prepared for a cutback in our targeting pattern; but he feels that it will be very difficult unless the Hanoi TPP [thermal power plant] is out, and he can claim with the JCS that all of the truly significant targets in the Hanoi/Haiphong area have been hit." "I do not know what position Sec. Rusk will take, but I do know they have been trying in the State Department to work up a way of using our cutback in targets to put some kind of direct or indirect pressure on the Russians to move us towards a settlement of the war. Such an effort does not necessarily imply that we should hold attack on the Hanoi TPP; but there could be argument that we will hold that target as 'hostage.'"

Rostow added that, "The central problem in talking with the Russians is that if we tell them that we've run out of good targets and are going to stand down, generally speaking, to the 20th parallel, they may simply heave a sigh of relief that some of the pressure is off them and go on about their business. They will also tell Hanoi—which is having a quite rough time—and they will also relax. What the Russians are afraid of is a confrontation that might arise from mining Haiphong or other operations in the North

[77] Johnson Library, NSF Files of Walt W. Rostow, "Agenda for Lunch with the President, Friday, May 12, 1967." There are no known notes of the meeting. For related comments made to Senator Russell by the President at an informal dinner that night see p. 685 below.

[78] Johnson Library, NSF Memos to the President—Walt Rostow.

[79] Same location.

that would increase the pressure on them from Hanoi and from the demonstration of their relative importance to defend a Communist country."

On May 16, the President held another Tuesday Luncheon from 1:10 p.m. to 3:05 p.m. with the Vice President, Rusk, McNamara, Rostow, Helms, Wheeler and Christian to discuss, according to the agenda, the bombing of the Hanoi power plant.[80]

In a memorandum on May 16, Deputy Under Secretary of State Foy Kohler, who had preceded Llewellyn Thompson as U.S. Ambassador to the U.S.S.R., said that bombing the Hanoi power plant would be inconsistent with U.S. efforts to seek assistance from the Russians in negotiating an end to the war, and he recommended that it be dropped permanently from consideration.[81]

From Moscow, Llewellyn Thompson was giving similar advice. In cables to Washington toward the end of April he expressed concern about the possible consequences for U.S.-U.S.S.R. relations of U.S. escalation of the air war. Apparently, warnings were being received in both Moscow and Washington to the effect that the U.S.S.R. was threatening to become more involved in the war. On April 18, for example, Walt Rostow reported that at a meeting the previous evening Georgi A. ("Yuri") Zhukov, a correspondent for *Pravda* and vice president of the Institute of Soviet-American Relations, stated, as Rostow said Zhukov had told Ambassador Thompson in Moscow before coming to the U.S., that the U.S.S.R. was going to increase its aid to North Vietnam, and that the summer of 1967 would be "a long, hot summer."[82] Rostow said it was *his* judgment that Zhukov's purpose was to "increase the pressure on the U.S. for negotiation on Hanoi's terms." (Zhukov also urged that the U.S. "unconditionally" stop bombing the North, saying that if it did the North Vietnamese would negotiate.)

On May 1, Eugene Rostow, Deputy Under Secretary of State for Political Affairs, sent a letter to Thompson, in which he said that he had been trying "to arrange a reconsideration of the approach to the Soviets about Vietnam we [he and Thompson] have discussed at intervals since I came to the Department last fall" but had been delayed by several trips.[82] "Meanwhile, the process of hostilities in Vietnam asserts a dynamic force which continues to cause both of us great concern. We—we, the civilians, that is—have failed to produce a political solution for the war. It is almost reflexive action to allow more leeway for the soldiers, and especially to the Air Force. In turn, the pressure on China and the Soviet Union mounts."

"I believe as you do," Rostow said, referring to several of Thompson's recent cables, "that we are on a tricky and dangerous course, and that relative success in South Vietnam is increasing the risk

---

[80] Johnson Library, Files of Walt W. Rostow, Agenda for Lunch with the President, Tuesday, May 16, 1967. There are no known notes of the meeting.

[81] U.S. Department of State, Central File, Pol 27 Viet S, May 16, 1967. Kohler's memorandum was in response to one by Bundy that same day (May 16) discussing the bombing of the power station and communications with the Russians. (Same location.) See also Bundy's memorandum on May 19 to Secretary Rusk, "Bombing Policy and Possible Communication with the Soviets," same location.

[82] Johnson Library, Warnke Papers, McNaughton Files, W. W. Rostow Memorandum of Conversation with Yuri Zhukov, Apr. 18, 1967.

[83] U.S. Department of State, Central File, Pol 27 Viet S, letter to Llewellyn Thompson from Eugene Rostow, May 1, 1967. Copies of the letter were sent to Rusk, Katzenbach, Foy Kohler, Harriman, William Bundy and Walt Rostow.

of a confrontation with the U.S.S.R. . . . at some point, over some issue. . . ." "[T]he risk would be less," he added, "if bombing could be confined to the infiltration routes."

"As you know," Rostow continued, "I have felt for some time that unless the war were settled, it would enter a more dangerous phase—a phase of danger for the Soviet Union as well as for other people—and that sooner or later we should have to follow the procedure which, with some variations, led to the end of all the post-war crises, that is, a secret low-keyed warning to the U.S.S.R., followed by a joint or parallel U.S.-Soviet action to put out the fire. . . . My thought, as you know, is to convey both a warning and an offer to the U.S.S.R.: a warning that the present course of action could get out of hand, with results no one wants; an offer, in the spirit of our 'special relationship' to join with them in procedures that could bring this affair to an end," including a proposal by the U.S. for a joint guarantee with the U.S.S.R. of whatever settlement might be reached by which the war would be ended. "The essence of that approach," Rostow said, "(at least the second part there was no visible warning) was put to Dobrynin by the Secretary [Rusk] in January, and recently followed up by Harriman and me. There are different ways to formulate the idea. It rests in the end on the assumption that we have a common interest in ending the war on the basis of the status quo ante, since further hostilities carry risks we both wish to avoid."

"I'm sure that some people in the Soviet Union would like to see us continue to flounder in Vietnam, and to have the President punished politically in 1968. Such a result would paralyze American foreign policy for the foreseeable future, and open the door to a renewal (or should I say intensification?) of Soviet adventurism in the many soft under-bellies of the world."

"Even though there are risks . . . that efforts to involve the Soviets may be understood or rebuffed, I remain convinced that the time has come to try. The alternatives are all worse."

Thompson replied by letter from Moscow on May 8, 1967.[84] With respect to Rostow's proposal for an "offer" to the U.S.S.R., he said, "God knows we have made it clear to the Soviets that we are prepared to negotiate, and the only new factor which you suggest is an expression of our willingness to jointly guarantee a settlement. In the first place, I think the present situation is such that the Soviets would not believe us and, in the second place, I can see great difficulties both for the Soviets and ourselves. For them this means openly joining with us in a move largely directed against Communist China. While they would have no regard for how the Chinese might receive this, it would cause problems for them with the rest of the Communist world. Moreover, the Soviet objective is surely a Communist North and South Vietnam not dominated by China and, to the extent that the settlement left South Vietnam free, the guarantee would work against Soviet interests." "So far as we are concerned, if we ever succeed in disengaging ourselves militarily, I would hate to see us committed to come back if the settlement were violated. For both of us there would be the problem of establishing when a violation had occurred. If it did occur, it would

[84] Same location, Letter to Eugene Rostow from Llewellyn Thompson, May 8, 1967.

undoubtedly be by North Vietnamese support for Viet Cong elements in the South, and this would be very hard to establish.

"This brings me to the subject of the settlement itself. Perhaps there have been some decisions in Washington of which I am not aware, but if the North Vietnamese did agree to negotiations, I cringe to think of what our position would be on the role of the NLF. Unless they were brought into the Government in some way, I think we would be even worse off in world opinion than we are now, and Ky's position seems to me tenable only in the event that we have achieved a military victory. It seems to me that you are suggesting that we agree to guarantee a settlement, the nature of which we do not know, and in short my view is that any settlement we could achieve now would be one which I would hate to see us have to guarantee. Despite the foregoing objections, I can see that at some stage we might sound the Soviets out on this, but I think surely it would have to be a guarantee in which others, and probably the UN, were involved."

"I feel much more strongly about the warning," Thompson said. "In the first place, the Soviets are well aware of the risks involved in the continuation of the present situation. You suggest it would not be difficult to work out a formula for a warning, but I can myself think of none that would be effective which would not be taken by them as a threat, and if there is one thing I have learned about this place it is that they react badly to threats. They should never be made unless we mean them and, because of their great inferiority complex, threats tend to make them dig in all the deeper. . . ."

"My own view," Thompson concluded, "is that neither the Soviets nor the North Vietnamese hold the key to this situation. The Soviets do not want to take the blame for any settlement that would be acceptable to us, as this would greatly enhance the standing of the Chinese Communists in the whole area at their expense. Similarly, the North Vietnamese will not want to pull the rug out from under the Viet Cong. They have made enormous sacrifices in this affair, and if they move before the Viet Cong are willing to settle, they will have jeopardized their own position in South Vietnam. It seems to me therefore that the NLF and the Viet Cong constitute the key factor and I am afraid that the only satisfactory solution is for us to continue and step up our efforts in the South, although this involves heavy sacrifices on our part. I certainly do not think that the Soviets would be willing to cut off supplies in order to bring pressure on North Vietnam for fear that this would mean handing over North Vietnam to the Chinese. As long as our main effort is confined to the South, I think there is little risk of Soviet intervention and I only wish that we could have levelled off our bombing in the North some time ago, and even better to have confined it to the southern part of North Vietnam, although I realize the pressures on the President from the military and others. . . ."

During this period in mid-May 1967, there were CIA reports that generally supported the consensus among civilian policymakers against increased bombing of the North.[85] On May 12, 1967, the

[85] On April 12, the Office of National Estimates of the CIA, responding to a request (probably from the Defense Department), issued a memorandum, "Communist Policy and the Next Phase in Vietnam," cited above, which discussed the Communists' view of the current situation and

CIA concluded that although bombing had "significantly eroded the capabilities of North Vietnam's limited industrial and military base," this had not "meaningfully degraded North Vietnam's material ability to continue the war in South Vietnam."[86] A related CIA study of "The Effect of Bombing on North Vietnamese Thinking," concluded:[87]

> Twenty-seven months of US bombing of North Vietnam have had remarkably little effect on Hanoi's over-all strategy in prosecuting the war, on its confident view of long-term Communist prospects, and on its political tactics regarding negotiations. The growing pressure of US air operations has not shaken the North Vietnamese leaders' conviction that they can withstand the bombing and outlast the US and South Vietnam in a protracted war of attrition. Nor has it caused them to waver in their belief that the outcome of this test of will and endurance will be determined primarily by the course of the conflict on the ground in the South, not by the air war in the North.

Another CIA study on May 23 concluded that even though an optimum interdiction of all land and water transportation of supplies into North Vietnam would cut import capacity by about 70 percent, this would not prevent essential supplies from getting through:[88]

> A mining program [of ports] coupled with intensified armed reconnaissance against the railroads and roads in the northern part of North Vietnam would have serious economic consequences, but it would not be likely to weaken the military establishment seriously or to prevent Hanoi from continuing its aggression in the south.
>
> The disruption caused by mining would depend upon the type and extent of the program. A substantial portion of imports could be maintained by sea and coastal water movements despite a conventional mining program designed to prevent the discharge of deep-draft oceangoing ships in harbors. However, almost complete denial of water access to North Vietnam could result from a mining program which also used a newly developed mine effective against shallowdraft shipping.
>
> An optimum program against all means of land and water transportation probably could interdict at most 70 percent of North Vietnam's transport *capacity* to import, reducing it from about 14,000 tons a day at present to about 3,900 a day. Interdiction to this extent would reduce the present level of goods *actually imported* by about 25 percent.*
>
> North Vietnam could, however, reduce the flow of supplies from outside the country to manageable levels by eliminating nonessential imports. The military supplies and essential eco-

---

estimated their likely reaction to three possible U.S. courses of action. The substance of this memorandum also appears in subsequent CIA memoranda issued during May.

[86] Johnson Library, NSF Country File, Vietnam, CIA Intelligence Memorandum 0643/67, "Bomb Damage Inflicted on North Vietnam Through April 1967," May 12, 1967.

[87] *PP*, Gravel ed., vol. IV, p. 168. Another CIA study on May 12, "The Current State of Morale in North Vietnam," Intelligence Memorandum 0642/67, also concluded that bombing had had little effect on morale. See *ibid.*, p. 168.

[88] CIA Intelligence Memorandum 0649/67, May 23, 1967, Johnson Library, NSF Country File, Vietnam.

*At that time, only about a third of imports capacity was being used; thus, reducing imports to 3,900 would be a reduction of about one-fourth.

nomic goods needed by Hanoi to continue with the war would not exceed an estimated 3,000 tons a day. This amount of traffic could be handled even if the capacity of North Vietnam's transport system were reduced by 70 percent.

Imports at this level would not be sufficient to continue operations of modern industrial plants or to restore operation of those which have received extensive bomb damage. The economy would be reduced to its essential subsistence character, but those modern sectors such as transportation, construction, communications and other elements essential to support the military establishment in North Vietnam and in the South could be sustained. (emphases in original)

Recommendations of the Draft Presidential Memorandum on Troops

On May 19, 1967, McNamara sent the President the Draft Presidential Memorandum on Westmoreland's request for more troops. It began as follows:[89]

This memorandum is written at a time when there appears to be no attractive course of action. The probabilities are that

[89] Johnson Library, NSF Country File, Vietnam, Draft Presidential Memorandum, "Future Action in Vietnam," May 19, 1967. Excerpts are in *PP*, Gravel ed., vol. IV, pp. 478–489. The JCS sent McNamara a memorandum on May 29, CM 2381–67 (Johnson Library, Warnke Papers, McNaughton Files), containing corrections and annotations to the DPM, on his copy of which McNaughton made marginal notes indicating whether he agreed. This was followed on May 31 by JCSM–307–67 in which the JCS said that the DPM "does not support current U.S. national policy and objectives in Vietnam and should not be considered further." (Apparently unaware that the President had already seen it, they recommended that the DPM should not be sent to him.) "The DPM would, in effect," the Chiefs argued, "limit U.S. objectives to merely guaranteeing the South Vietnamese the right to determine their own future on the one hand and offsetting the effect of North Vietnam's application of force on the other," and this would mean that the U.S. would remain committed to these two objectives and to remaining in Vietnam only so long as the South Vietnamese continued to help themselves. Such a position, they said, was not consistent with existing U.S. policy and goals as enunciated originally by NSAM 288 of March 17, 1964, which, they pointed out, was still the governing policy document for U.S. participation in the war.

The JCS rejected the two alternatives suggested by the DPM. They said that Course B would prevent the achievement of U.S. goals: "The strategy embodied in this alternative—largely designed to 'make do' with military resources currently approved for Southeast Asia—would not permit early termination of hostilities on terms acceptable to the United States, supporting Free World nations, and the Government of Vietnam. The force structure envisaged provides little capability for initiative action and insufficient resources to maintain momentum required for expeditious prosecution of the war. Further, this approach would result in a significant downgrading of the Revolutionary Development Program considered so essential to the realization of our goals in Vietnam. It would also result in the abandonment of the important delta region on the basis of its being primarily a problem for the Republic of Vietnam to solve without additional external assistance."

The Chiefs argued that the formulation in the DPM of Course A, on the other hand, did not reflect their views or recommendations, especially with respect to the statement of U.S. objectives. (In the Johnson Library, Warnke Papers, McNaughton Files, there is a memorandum, "Response to JCS Statement that 'Course A' does not Accurately Reflect JCS Position," June 8, 1967, by a member of McNaughton's staff.) U.S. policy in NSAM 288 should be maintained, they said, and the military objectives and strategy which they had proposed in their original memorandum of April 20 supporting Westmoreland's request should be approved.

The Chiefs also disagreed with the prediction of an adverse public reaction to a Reserve callup, saying: "The Joint Chiefs of Staff firmly believe that the American people, when well informed about the issues at stake, expect their Government to uphold its commitments. History illustrates that they will, in turn, support their Government in its necessary actions. The Joint Chiefs of Staff believe that there is no significant sentiment for peace at any price. They believe also that despite some predictable debate a Reserve callup would be willingly accepted, and there would be no 'irresistible' drive from any quarter for unnecessary escalation of the conflict."

In another paper the Chiefs also argued that while in the short-run there would be greater public opposition to Course A than to Course B, in the long-run there would be greater support for Course A because of the "new determination and resolve to terminate the war on acceptable terms, particularly if diplomatic efforts for negotiated settlement continue." With Course B, on the other hand, "lack of marked results in long term could result in further disenchantment with the war in Southeast Asia and increased pressure for the U.S. to withdraw under less than acceptable terms." "Alternative Courses of Action for Southeast Asia," cited above.

Hanoi has decided not to negotiate until the American electorate has been heard in November 1968. Continuation of our present moderate policy, while avoiding a larger war, will not change Hanoi's mind, so it is not enough to satisfy the American people; increased force levels and actions against the North are likewise unlikely to change Hanoi's mind, and are likely to get us in even deeper in Southeast Asia and into a serious confrontation, if not war, with China and Russia; and we are not willing to yield. So we must choose among imperfect alternatives.

The DPM recommended that Westmoreland's request for the 200,000 additional troops (which, as noted, had been changed to 250,000), for bombing additional targets in the Hanoi-Haiphong area, for mining the harbors, and for attacking the "sanctuaries" in Laos and Cambodia and possibly invading North Vietnam and Laos, all of which were called "Course A" in accordance with Katzenbach's memo of April 24, be rejected in favor of Course B, under which 30,000 additional troops would be deployed, bombing would be concentrated below the 20th parallel, and efforts would be increased to "settle the war." [90]

According to the DPM, the "big war" in the South between U.S. and North Vietnamese forces was "going well," and "there is consensus that we are no longer in danger of losing this war militarily." It added, however, that "The enemy retains the ability to initiate both large and small-scale attacks," and noted that "Small-scale attacks in the first quarter of 1967 are running at double the 1966 average; larger-scale attacks are again on the increase after falling off substantially in 1966."

(In a meeting that same week with his military commanders, Westmoreland painted a somewhat different picture.[90] "The main

---

[90] On May 11, McGeorge Bundy, who received from McNamara a draft of the memorandum being prepared for the President, sent McNamara a memorandum supporting the position in favor of Course B, which he said should be the "fixed and final maximum unless they escalate again, and a lot." (Johnson Library, Warnke Papers, McNaughton Files.) Concerning the reasons for the United States to continue fighting the war Bundy said, "I think the basic reason for staying in there until we get a satisfactory (non-Communist) result is that anything less will be (a) not what the South Vietnamese would freely choose and (b) for this reason with others, a terrible failure for the U.S. after a very great investment. I do not find this minimum view sufficiently presented in the paper. . . ." (In another comment he also said, however, that "holding some sort of line" around China "remains very important.")

McGeorge Bundy also objected to a paragraph dealing with admitting the NLF into the Government of South Vietnam: "There is a vast difference between generous treatment of individual VC leaders and a place in the national government for the NLF. The latter is not justified—as far as I can see—on any ground. This paragraph, along with one or two others, seems to me to stretch out toward disaster; nor do I see its usefulness in present arguments. [Here McNaughton commented in the margin: "To get deal!"] I wholly agree with the general notion that we should encourage the Saigon Government to keep moving out toward political settlement. But I foresee no endurable settlement with the NLF as a party sharing power, and I think it is deceptive to urge this as a practical possibility. The evidence doesn't support it."

McNamara gave a copy of McGeorge Bundy's memorandum to McNaughton, who said in a marginal note on his copy of Bundy's memorandum: "I told SecDef this was a big disappointment to me. 1600 5/13/67." (Johnson Library, Warnke Papers, McNaughton Files.) In other marginal notes on his copy, McNaughton also said that McGeorge Bundy:

"1. *Finesses 'fundamentals'*—e.g., what our interests are in the East, views as to who's right—except as to point that we must not 'fail.' (Does say that 'holding some sort of a line around [China] remains very important.')

"2. [Almost] equates 'success' with 'free choice' by SVNese and states conviction that 'free choice' would be non-Communist; ergo Communist choice = U.S. failure.

"3. NLF in govt = disaster." (emphasis in original)

[90] CMH, Westmoreland Papers, History File, Memorandum for the Record, "MACV Commanders' Conference, May 13, 1967," May 21, 1967.

force war," he said, "is accelerating at a rapid, almost alarming, rate. . . . The NVA [North Vietnamese Army] is taking over the main force war in I, II, and III Corps [IV Corps, the delta, was still a Communist-guerrilla stronghold]. . . . Infiltration continues and at a greater rate than in the past. Individuals and units are better equipped and have some of the best weapons from the U.S.S.R. . . ." "The challenge for the next several months is formidable in both the main force war and RD [Revolutionary Development—pacification].)[91]

McNamara said in the DPM that even though the U.S. was no longer in danger of losing the war militarily, neither was it winning; the war was still "stalemated." "The enemy," he said, "has the capability to tailor his actions to his supplies and manpower and, by hit-and-run terror, to make government and pacification very difficult in large parts of the country almost without regard to the size of U.S. forces there; and . . . the enemy can and almost certainly will maintain the military 'stalemate' by matching our added deployments as necessary."

By contrast to the military situation, "Regrettably, the 'other war' against the VC is still not going well. Corruption is widespread. Real government control is confined to enclaves . . . and there is little evidence that the revolutionary development program is gaining any momentum."[92]

In the U.S. itself, the DPM said, the "state of mind" produced by the war "generates impatience in the political structure of the United States:"

> The Vietnam war is unpopular in this country. It is becoming increasingly unpopular as it escalates—causing more American casualties, more fear of its growing into a wider war, more privation of the domestic sector, and more distress at the amount of suffering being visited on the non-combatants in Vietnam, South and North. Most Americans do not know how we got where we are, and most, without knowing why, but tak-

---

[91] See also Westmoreland's cable to Sharp and Wheeler on the increased pace of the war, CMH, Westmoreland Papers, Message Files, MAC 5310, June 4, 1967.

[92] Long An Province, adjacent to and south of Saigon, was a good example of the difficulty in bringing under government control those areas where the Communists had traditionally been strong. At a conference in Saigon on May 13, 1967, of U.S. military commanders in South Vietnam, Col. Samuel V. Wilson, one of the most experienced of U.S. politico-military experts, who had been sent in the fall of 1966 to Long An Province as the Senior U.S. Representative, explained that "After some 25 years of enemy influence, resistance to the GVN [Government of South Vietnam] by the people has become a way of life. . . ." In November 1966, when he arrived in the province, 4 percent of the area was considered secure during the day and 1 percent at night. The government had "fairly firm control" over 20 percent of the population. "Now," Wilson reported, "six months later, 10 percent of the area is secure during the day and 3 percent at night and 30 percent of the population is under GVN control." This improvement, he added, "was not overwhelming but does indicate success."

Wilson also said that he was "appalled at the rampant corruption of the VN officials," but he had been able to get a number of officials relieved and "the problem had lessened."

The reason for the success in achieving increased security, Wilson said, was the presence of U.S. forces, three battalions of which had been deployed to Long An to test whether U.S. forces could operate effectively in the delta and whether their presence would make a difference.

Wilson estimated, however, that it would take 10 years to bring the province under government control, or 5 years if current operations produced the intended "snowball effect." If operations were changed from the existing "oilspot" system of expanding secure areas to a system of going into areas where Communist control was "soft," he estimated that 2 1/2 years would be required, but he cautioned that there would be problems in such operations in "soft" areas.

Wilson's very interesting presentation is in the memorandum of the MACV Commanders' conference, May 13, 1967, cited above. See Wilson's detailed report to Lodge, "Critique of Long An Experiment," Apr. 15, 1967, in Massachusetts Historical Society, Lodge Papers, Vietnam. See also the study by Jeffrey Race, *War Comes to Long An: Revolutionary Conflict in a Vietnamese Province* (Berkeley, Calif.: Univ. of California Press, 1972).

> ing advantage of hindsight, are convinced that somehow we should not have gotten this deeply in. All want the war ended and expect their President to end it. Successfully. Or else.

The DPM analyzed Course A (200,000 more troops) and Course B (30,000 more troops). It said that because of American impatience with the war, Course A, which would require a $12 billion increase in the budget, a Reserve callup, and an "eventual increase" of about 600,000 in total U.S. military troop strength (from 3,600,000 to 4,200,000), "would involve accepting the risk—the virtual certainty—that these actions, especially the Reserve callup, would stimulate irresistible pressures in the United States for further escalation against North Vietnam, and for ground actions against 'sanctuaries' in Cambodia and Laos." Furthermore, the Reserve callup would "almost certainly set off bitter congressional debate and irresistible domestic pressures for stronger action outside South Vietnam."

> Cries would go up—much louder than they already have—to "take the wraps off the men in the field." The actions would include more intense bombing—not only around-the-clock bombing of targets already authorized, but also bombing of strategic targets such as locks and dikes, and mining of the harbors against Soviet and other ships. Associated actions impelled by the situation would be major ground actions in Laos, in Cambodia, and probably in North Vietnam—first as a pincer operation north of the DMZ and then at a point such as Vinh. The use of tactical nuclear and area-denial radiological-bacteriological-chemical weapons would probably be suggested at some point if the Chinese entered the war in Vietnam or Korea or if U.S. losses were running high while conventional efforts were not producing desired results.

The DPM did not forecast as much of a potential problem from those who opposed the war. Unless pressure from the proponents of stronger military action led to the wider war just described, the memorandum concluded that even though there would be a "divisive debate" in Congress over a Reserve callup, "increased forces will not lead to massive civil disobedience."

With respect to bombing, the draft DPM on troops took the position that the application of greater pressure on North Vietnam, as proposed by Course A, have not the effect of compelling the North to modify its behavior or the effect of choking off the war by denying enemy forces in the South the arms and men necessary to fight. The "will" of the North Vietnamese to continue fighting "can and will hold out at least so long as a prospect of winning the 'war of attrition' in the South exists." Moreover, interdiction of men and supplies could be accomplished as well by bombing in the southern third of North Vietnam below the 20th parallel, where supplies were funneled down the Ho Chi Minh Trail, as by bombing in the Hanoi/Haiphong area. This would also save U.S. pilots, who were being lost at the rate of one pilot for every 40 sorties. (This high loss rate was for sorties in the Hanoi/Haiphong area, where many of the sorties over North Vietnam were being directed.) More limited bombing in less-populated areas would also help the image of the United States: "The picture of the world's greatest superpower killing or seriously injuring 1000 noncombatants a week, while trying to pound a tiny backward nation into submission on an issue whose merits are hotly disputed, is not a pretty one."

No amount of limited bombing, whatever the location, would prevent the North Vietnamese from effectively aiding the Communists in the South: "[I]t now appears that no combination of attacks against the North short of destruction of the regime or occupation of North Vietnamese territory will physically reduce the flow of men and materiel below the relatively small amount needed by enemy forces to continue the war in the South."

Even though, according to the DPM, bombing was not seriously affecting the North's will to fight or its infiltration of men and supplies, the DPM concluded that under Course A increased bombing of the targets which had already been bombed would not produce much of a counterreaction from China or Russia. This would not be true, however, if the U.S. were to mine North Vietnamese harbors:

> *Mining the harbors* would be much more serious. It would place *Moscow* in a particularly galling dilemma as to how to preserve the Soviet position and prestige in such a disadvantageous place. The Soviets might, but probably would not, force a confrontation in Southeast Asia—where even with minesweepers they would be at as great a military disadvantage as we were when they blocked the corridor to Berlin in 1961, but where their vital interest, unlike ours in Berlin (and in Cuba), is not so clearly at stake. Moscow in this case should be expected to send volunteers, including pilots, to North Vietnam; to provide some new and better weapons and equipment; to consider some action in Korea, Turkey, Iran, the Middle East or, most likely, Berlin, where the Soviets can control the degree of crisis better; and to show across-the-board hostility toward the US. . . . *China* could be expected to seize upon the harbor-mining as the opportunity to reduce Soviet political influence in Hanoi and to discredit the USSR if the Soviets took no military action to open the ports. Peking might read the harbor-mining as indicating that the US was going to apply military pressure until North Vietnam capitulated, and that this meant an eventual invasion. If so, China might decide to intervene in the war with combat troops and air power, to which we would eventually have to respond by bombing Chinese airfields and perhaps other targets as well. *Hanoi* would tighten belts, refuse to talk, and persevere—as it could without too much difficulty. North Vietnam would of course be fully dependent for supplies on China's will, and Soviet influence in Hanoi would therefore be reduced. (emphases in original)

With respect to possible invasions of North Vietnam and Laos, "To U.S. ground actions in North Vietnam, we would expect China to respond by entering the war with both ground and air forces," and the Soviet Union could be expected to respond, among other things, by "a serious confrontation with the United States at one or more places of her own choosing." If the U.S. attacked across the border into Laos (Cambodia was not discussed), "We would simply have a wider war, with Souvanna back in Paris, world opinion against us, and no solution either to the wider war or to the one we already have in Vietnam."

"COURSE B," the DPM stated, "implies a conviction that neither military defeat nor military victory is in the cards, with or without the large added deployments, and that the price of the large added deployments and the strategy of COURSE A will be to expand the war dangerously. COURSE B is designed to improve the negotiating environment within a limited deployment of U.S. forces by combining continuous attacks against VC/NVA main force units with slow improvements in pacification (which may follow the new constitution, the national reconciliation proclamation, our added efforts and the Vietnamese elections this fall) and a restrained program of actions against the North."

> The strategy of proponents of COURSE B is based on their belief that we are in a military situation that cannot be changed materially by expanding our military effort, that the politico-pacification situation in South Vietnam will improve but not fast, and that (in view of all this) Hanoi will not capitulate soon. An aspect of the strategy is a "cool" drive to settle the war—a deliberate process on three fronts: Large unit, politico-pacification, and diplomatic. Its approach on the large unit front is to maintain the initiative that "Program 4-plus" forces will permit, to move on with pacification efforts and with the national election in September, and to lay the groundwork by periodic peace probes, perhaps suggesting secret talks associated with limitation of bombing and with a view to *finding a compromise involving, inter alia, a role in the South for members of the VC.* (emphasis in original)

In accordance with the general design of Course B, the DPM questioned whether U.S. forces should be used in pacification, and whether they should be sent into the delta, where guerrillas were especially active. "Are these not matters for the Vietnamese?" it asked. "If our 'success' objective is solely to check or offset North Vietnam's forceful intervention in the South we are in that position already in the Delta! Must we go further and do the job for the South Vietnamese?"

After analyzing Courses A and B, the DPM turned to the broader question of U.S. interests in Asia.[93] There was a difference of opinion, it said, as to the potential threat of China to the interests of the U.S., but "most US Asian experts believe that China's history, current troubles, interests and capabilities do not make her a significant military threat outside certain fairly limited geographical areas." Moreover, the "trends in Asia today are running mostly for, not against, our interests (witness Indonesia and the Chinese confusion)," and in the future the U.S. could establish alliances, especially with Japan and India, to contain the Chinese.

The memorandum then drew an important conclusion: "To the extent that our original intervention and our existing actions in Vietnam were motivated by the perceived need to draw the line against Chinese expansionism in Asia, our objective has already

[93] For unexplained reasons, this key section of the DPM is not quoted or discussed in the *Pentagon Papers*, although the proposed strategy on which it was based, which was quoted (see below), referred to "U.S. policy as described herein."

been attained. . . ." "COURSE B," it added, "will suffice to consolidate it [drawing the line against Chinese expansionism]."

In terms of American interests in Asia, therefore, the major reason for U.S. involvement in Vietnam no longer existed once the containment of China, which had been the principal regional factor in the constellation of reasons for U.S. involvement, had been achieved. Other reasons, especially those of maintaining U.S. international credibility and prestige, and deterring the use by the Communists of the technique of a "war of national liberation," were not discussed in the DPM. Judging by the recommendations made in the concluding portion of the memorandum, however, these, too, no longer justified U.S. involvement. The only remaining reason for U.S. involvement appeared to be the "objective" or "commitment" of the United States to help the South Vietnamese "to determine their own future," an objective to which McNaughton attributed very little importance in comparison with other objectives or reasons for involvement. Even this was not an absolute commitment, however: "This commitment ceases if the country ceases to help itself."

> It follows that no matter how much we might *hope* for some things, our *commitment* is not:
>
> —to expel from South Vietnam regroupees [southerners who went north in 1954 or later, and returned to fight on the Communist side in the South], who are South Vietnamese (though we do not like them),
>
> —to ensure that a particular person or group remains in power, nor that that power runs to every corner of the land (though we prefer certain types and we hope their writ will run throughout South Vietnam),
>
> —to guarantee that the self-chosen government is non-Communist (though we believe and strongly hope it will be), and
>
> —to insist that the independent South Vietnam remain separate from North Vietnam (though in the short-run, we would prefer it that way).
>
> (Nor do we have an obligation to pour in effort out of proportion to the effort contributed by the people of South Vietnam or in the face of coups, corruption, apathy or other indications of Saigon failure to cooperate effectively with us.) (emphases in original)

The DPM took the position that the United States had already fulfilled its commitment, as defined in these terms, and, reminiscent of Senator Aiken's suggestion, it proposed that after the September election the U.S. Government should declare that it had achieved success.

Based on this concept of the U.S. commitment, the DPM suggested the following strategy: (all emphases in original)

> (1) *Now:* Not to panic because of a belief that Hanoi must be made to capitulate before the 1968 elections. No one's proposal achieves that end.
>
> (2) *Now:* Press on energetically with the military, pacification and political programs in the South, including groundwork

for successful elections in September. Drive hard to increase the productivity of Vietnamese military forces.

(3) *Now:* Issue a NSAM nailing down US policy as described herein. Thereafter, publicly, (a) emphasize consistently that the sole US objective in Vietnam has been and is to permit the people of South Vietnam to determine their own future, and (b) declare that we have already either denied or offset the North Vietnamese intervention and that after the September elections in Vietnam we will have achieved success. The necessary steps having been taken to deny the North the ability to take over South Vietnam and an elected government sitting in Saigon, *the South will be in position, albeit imperfect, to start the business of producing a full-spectrum government in South Vietnam.*

(4) *End-May:* Concentrate the bombing of North Vietnam on physical interdiction of men and materiel. This would mean terminating, except where the interdiction objective clearly dictates otherwise, all bombing north of 20° and improving interdiction as much as possible in the infiltration "funnel" south of 20° by concentration of sorties and by an all-out effort to improve detection devices, denial weapons, and interdiction tactics. . . .

(5) *July:* Avoid the explosive Congressional debate and US Reserve call-up implicit in the Westmoreland troop request. Decide that, unless the military situation worsens dramatically, US deployments will be limited to Program 4-plus (which, according to General Westmoreland, will not put us in danger of being defeated, but will mean slow progress in the South). Associated with this decision are decisions not to use large numbers of US troops in the Delta and not to use large number of them in grassroots pacification work.

(6) *September:* Move (force, if necessary)[94] the newly elected Saigon government well beyond its National Reconciliation program to a political settlement with non-Communist members of the NLF—to try to arrange a ceasefire and to reach an accommodation with the large numbers of South Vietnamese who are under the VC banner; to accept the non-Communist members of the NLF as members of an opposition political party, and, if necessary, to accept their individual participation in the national government—in sum, a settlement to transform the members of the VC from military opponents to political opponents.

(7) *September:* Explain the situation to the Canadians, Indians, British, UN and others, as well as nations now contributing forces, requesting them to contribute border forces to help make the inside-South Vietnam accommodation possible, and—consistent with our desire neither to occupy nor to have bases in Vietnam—offering to remove later an equivalent number of US forces. (This initiative is worth taking despite its slim chance of success.)

---

[94] This parenthetical phrase was dropped from the *Pentagon Papers'* quotation of this paragraph from the DPM. There are discrepancies also in several other words. See *PP*, Gravel ed., vol. IV, p. 489.

The U.S. would have to be prepared to deal with contingencies that might arise from this new strategy:

1. *Hanoi will continue efforts to take over South Vietnam by force.* This is to be expected. Indeed, even if we have a negotiated arrangement with Hanoi, we should expect them to struggle on, as Communists are wont to do.

2. *The Saigon government might collapse under the strain.* We would then have to decide whether to snip a piece of stem, plant it, nurture it, and start over again with the VC excluded, or to follow the example of the Dominican Republic and, to the extent that we could, to force a compromise under our own auspices. The situation would be messy, but, in the eyes of the world, our course would have been honorable and our commitment upheld. We have certainly done enough in fulfilling our commitment to give us the right to knock a few heads together! (We need a contingency plan covering the case of the GVN and perhaps the ARVN falling apart.)

3. *No progress might be made toward the accommodation government.* This would put us in no worse, and probably in a better, position than we now are. If the scenario is faithfully carried out, the "rules of the game" will have been changed by then; *the definition of "success" will have been changed.* Attention will more and more be focused on Saigon's attempt to produce a working consensus of South Vietnamese people, with the US (and hopefully other countries) role more and more that of fending off or canceling out interference from outside, letting the chips inside fall where they may.

4. *An accommodation government might be formed, but it might choose to go neutral or otherwise to ask us to leave.* We should leave, maintaining the guarantee if the government wished it.[95] This might mean we had a "Finland" or a "Cambodia" in South Vietnam.

5. *The accommodation government might go Communist. This could happen but would almost certainly take some time—perhaps 3 to 5 years.* This is a bad outcome because it is unlikely the result would be a "Yugoslavia." "Yugoslavians" are created by countervailing force, e.g., NATO, of which there is "none" in Southeast Asia. Instead, a *Communist-dominated SVN would probably join with North Vietnam to carry on subversive attacks on Laos, Thailand and Cambodia.* (There is less likelihood that North Vietnam would be a puppet of China under this scenario than under one in which we try to press North Vietnam to capitulation. For Hanoi has made clear that, while it dislikes the Chinese, it prefers a Chinese invasion to an American invasion.) *How much this case would appear to be a "defeat" for the US in, say, 1970 would depend on many factors not now foreseeable.*

These were the conclusions of the DPM:

The war in Vietnam is acquiring a momentum of its own that must be stopped. Dramatic increases in US troop deployments, in attacks on the North, or in ground actions in Laos

[95] It is not clear what the DPM meant by "the guarantee." Presumably this referred to permitting the people of South Vietnam to determine their own future.

or Cambodia are not necessary and are not the answer. The enemy can absorb them or counter them, bogging us down further and risking even more serious escalation of the war.

COURSE A could lead to a major national disaster; it would not win the Vietnam war, but only submerge it in a larger one. COURSE B likewise will not win the Vietnam war in a military sense in a short time; it does avoid the larger war, however, and it is part of a sound military-political/pacification-diplomatic package that gets things moving toward a successful outcome in a few years. More than that cannot be expected. No plan can be fashioned that will give a better chance of success by 1968 or later. Attempts to do so not only produce dangerous plans but also are counterproductive in that they make us look overeager to Hanoi.

We recommend COURSE B because it has the combined advantages of being a lever toward negotiations and towards ending the war on satisfactory terms, of helping our general position with the Soviets, of improving our image in the eyes of international opinion, of reducing the danger of confrontation with China and with the Soviet Union, and of reducing US losses.

The importance of the May 19, 1967 DPM, other than its recommendation with respect to Westmoreland's request for new troops and authority to expand the war, was its redefinition of the U.S. commitment and objectives in Vietnam and thereby what was meant by "success" in achieving those objectives or "winning" the war. Unlike the Truman and Eisenhower administrations, especially Eisenhower's, in which there had been carefully formulated and detailed statements of national policy on the U.S. role in Vietnam, the Kennedy and Johnson administrations, reflecting the operating style of those two Presidents, tended to avoid such policy formulations. One result of this less structured, less formal approach was the lack of comprehensive statements of U.S. policy toward Vietnam. During the entire eight years between 1961 and 1969 there were only two formal NSC statements of U.S. policy and objectives in Vietnam, the first under Kennedy in May 1961, NSAM 52, and the second under Johnson in March 1964, NSAM 288.[96] Both documents were prepared in conjunction with proposed augmentation of U.S. programs in Vietnam rather than as statements of general policy and were more operational than conceptual in character. One of them in fact—NSAM 288—was simply the text of a report by McNamara.

It is also likely that neither the Kennedy nor the Johnson administration felt the need to discuss or define the U.S. commitment and the objectives being sought in Vietnam. Previous administrations had already done so and further elaboration was probably considered unnecessary. Politically, the Kennedy and Johnson administrations doubtless preferred to base the legitimacy and necessity of their actions on the commitments and programs of previous

[96] For discussion of these, see pp. 40, 238–240 in pt. II of this study. For comparison with the Eisenhower administration, see the NSC policy papers discussed in pt. I. In December 1966, it will be recalled, Walt Rostow had distributed for comment a new draft NSAM, "Strategic Guidelines for 1967 in Vietnam," but after disagreement from State, Defense, and the JCS, the proposal was dropped.

administrations, especially the preceding Republican administration.

In the case of Kennedy and particularly of Johnson it was assumed that there would also be greater Presidential flexibility and control if policy remained somewhat informal, unstated, and contingent. In dealing with the military and the other large government bureaucracies involved in the war, it may have been considered an advantage not to have established criteria and guidelines which they could use in arguing their own positions, as, indeed, the military did in invoking NSAM 288 against the policy position recommended in the May 19, 1967 DPM. Those who wanted to prevent further escalation of the war were, of course, using the DPM for that purpose, and it is ironic that one of the most definitive statements of U.S. policy and objectives during the whole of the Johnson administration should have been prepared as a justification for not continuing to escalate the war rather than to justify U.S. involvement and participation in the war.

Action on the Draft Presidential Memorandum on Bombing

On May 19, 1967, the President met from 5:38 p.m. to 6:59 p.m. with Rusk, McNamara, Rostow and Christian. According to the agenda for the meeting, the major Vietnam subjects to be considered were: "Bombing Policy"—whether to attack the Hanoi power station and whether to shift toward bombing south of the 20th parallel, and "Diplomacy"—"What, if anything, to tell the Russians or to negotiate about."[97] Earlier that day there had been a meeting of Katzenbach, Vance, William Bundy, General Wheeler, Helms, Eugene Rostow, and, for part of the time, Walt Rostow, at which Vance presented the proposal of the McNamara/Vance memorandum of May 9, which had also been recommended by William Bundy, Katzenbach and Helms and with which Walt Rostow also agreed, to bomb primarily below the 20th parallel rather than in the Hanoi-Haiphong area. During the discussions that followed, Wheeler raised a series of objections and various members of the group expressed their views.[98] After the meeting and before the meeting with the President, Walt Rostow, based on comments at the earlier meeting, sent the President a very sensitive memorandum, so sensitive that it was marked "Top Secret—Literally Eyes Only," in which he proposed a "scenario" for handling the bombing issue. That issue, he said, had aroused "dangerously strong feelings in your official family which tend to overwhelm the strictly military factors." He described these as follows:[99]

> Sect. Rusk feels the diplomatic cost of bombing Hanoi-Haiphong overwhelms whatever the military advantage might be; but has not devised—nor can he guarantee—a diplomatic payoff for moving the bombing pattern to the south.
>
> Sect. McNamara feels the domestic and diplomatic cost is enormous; and believes Hanoi-Haiphong bombing is not cost-effective, if effectiveness is measured against Communist oper-

---

[97] Johnson Library, NSF Files of Walt W. Rostow, "Agenda for Meeting with the President, May 19, 1967."

[98] U.S. Department of State, Central File, Pol 27 Viet S, Memorandum to the Secretary from Eugene Rostow, May 19, 1967.

[99] Johnson Library, NSF Country File, Vietnam, Memorandum to the President from Walt Rostow, May 19, 1967.

ations in the South. And that is how he thinks it should be measured.

General Wheeler feels a withdrawal from Hanoi-Haiphong bombing would stir deep resentment at home, among our troops, and be regarded by the Communists as an aerial Dien Bien Phu. He argues there is net military advantage in hitting Hanoi-Haiphong targets; but finds it hard to make a firm, lucid case because none of us really knows what the cumulative and indirect effects of the bombing are around Hanoi-Haiphong, except that they are making one hell of a military and political effort to try to make us stop. General Wheeler wants to keep the pressure up via armed recce [reconnaissance] in the North plus attacks on airfields.

"The question," Rostow said, "is what kind of a scenario can hold our family together in ways that look after the nation's interests and make military sense." He proposed that after bombing the Hanoi power plant the U.S. should "radically" cut back on bombing in the Hanoi-Haiphong area for several weeks while telling the Russians that they had those two or three weeks to "deliver something by way of negotiations." Meanwhile, the U.S. would continue to consider bombing options. By the end of that period, he said, McNamara and Wheeler would have returned from a trip to Vietnam planned for July 1967 and the decision on bombing could then be made as part of the overall decision on Westmoreland's requests. Rostow concluded:

This scenario would give:

—Sect. Rusk and Sect. McNamara a break in what they feel is a dangerous pattern of progressive bombing escalation;

—Sect. Rusk and the State Department a chance to prove if they can buy anything important to us through diplomacy at this time;

—General Wheeler would get a temporary rather than a permanent change of bombing pattern, with the opportunity to refine his case and make it to you in, say, a month's time.

At the meeting with his advisers on May 19, the President apparently accepted Rostow's proposed scenario.[100] Later that day, the Hanoi power plant was bombed,[101] but on May 22 bombing was

---

[100] The only known notes of the meeting, apparently taken by Rostow, are very abbreviated and do not refer to the discussion or to the decision to bomb the power plant. Johnson Library, NSF Files of Walt W. Rostow, "Meeting with the President, Friday, May 19, 1967."

[101] This is Chester Cooper's account (p. 375 of *The Lost Crusade)*: "Hopes were high for the President's approval, and a telegram was drafted informing Saigon of the new bombing policy. On the night of the White House meeting [of May 19], I waited at the State Department with the draft telegram for the go ahead signal. In due course I was told to put the draft away. The Joint Chiefs wanted the President first to approve a raid on the one juicy target left in Hanoi. Only then would they be prepared, though with many reservations, to limit all bombing to the area south of the 20th parallel. The President agreed to postpone his decision to limit bombing until the Chiefs had been given their opportunity to 'take out' Hanoi's thermal power plant. It would be a simple matter that could be executed with 'surgical precision'; one strike would do the job. . . .

"The power plant was bombed. But the target was not destroyed with 'one strike.' Nor was the raid characterized by the precision that had been advertised. Many more attacks over many months were necessary before it was put out of operation; in the process the surrounding area took a beating. The power plant was located in downtown Hanoi and was bounded on two sides by residential areas. 'Subsidiary damage' was significant, and it was another case of 'sorry about

Continued

cutback, in part in an effort to persuade the U.S.S.R. to get the North Vietnamese to agree to negotiate. Meanwhile, on May 19 the President wrote to Kosygin to make that suggestion.[102]

The President's decision to bomb only the power plant and then to restrict bombing again was viewed by the military as a sign of diminishing support for the program of increased military pressures on North Vietnam that had been approved on February 22, and General Wheeler cabled Sharp and Westmoreland to "batten down for rough weather ahead."[103] In a top secret backchannel cable to Sharp and Westmoreland several days later, Wheeler gave his explanation as to why bombing was being cut back:[104]

> A. The feeling in high circles that our recent strikes in the Hanoi area have raised the temperature of the war in a manner which could elicit additional Soviet assistance to the North Vietnamese;
>
> B. The feeling at the same levels that the losses sustained by our forces are not commensurate with the results attained;
>
> C. A desire to "let the dust settle" for a bit while we watch Soviet/Chicom reactions, and
>
> D. Expressed doubts that our air strikes in the northern portion of North Vietnam do indeed obstruct and reduce the flow of men and materials to the South.

Wheeler said he shared the feeling of Sharp and Westmoreland that airstrikes were hurting the North Vietnamese, and he added that the JCS had made a strong recommendation with respect to the need for attacking ports, airfields, and rail lines between China and North Vietnam.

After the meeting on May 19, 1967, "the Washington papermill," the *Pentagon Papers* said, must have broken all previous production records. The JCS in particular literally bombarded the Secretary [McNamara] with memoranda. . . ."[105]

On May 20, the JCS sent McNamara an urgent memorandum stressing the need to cut off supplies by bombing and mining the ports of Haiphong and bombing roads and rail lines into China. In addition, the Chiefs recommended attacks on MiG fighters at eight North Vietnamese airfields.[106] The Chiefs asked that the memoran-

---

that.' Hanoi claimed that the premises of the Rumanian and North Korean Embassies were hit. In time, of course, the lights went out in Hanoi, but the people there used kerosene lamps and candles, and the regime neither softened its stand on negotiations nor relaxed its efforts in the South. The President had been given two pieces of bum advice—by those who claimed the bombers could drop their cargo down the smokestacks of the power plant, and by those who equated the simple and resilient economy of Hanoi with the power-dependent cities of the United States."

[102] The May 19 letter is still classified.

[103] CMH, Westmoreland Papers, Message Files, Wheeler to Sharp and Westmoreland, JCS 3891, May 26, 1967.

[104] CMH, Westmoreland Papers, Message Files, Wheeler to Sharp and Westmoreland, JCS 3903, May 27, 1967.

[105] *PP*, Gravel ed., vol. IV, p. 177. Memoranda from the JCS and its Chairman included: JCSM-286-67, "Operations Against North Vietnam," May 20, 1967 (Johnson Library, NSF Country File, Vietnam); JCSM-288-67, "U.S. Worldwide Military Posture," May 20, 1967 (same location); CM-2377-67, "Alternative Courses of Action," May 24, 1967 with attached 120-page JCS study, "Alternative Courses of Action for Southeast Asia" (Johnson Library, Warnke Papers, McNaughton Files); CM-2381-67, "Future Actions In Vietnam," May 29, 1967 (same location); JCSM-307-67, "Draft Memorandum for the President on Future Actions in Vietnam," May 31, 1967; JCSM-312-67, "Air Operations Against NVN," June 2, 1967, (Johnson Library, Warnke Papers, McNaughton Files). For summaries of their contents see *PP*, Gravel ed., vol. IV, pp. 177-181, 489-501.

[106] JCSM-286-67, "Operations Against North Vietnam," May 20, 1967, cited above. See *PP*, Gravel ed., vol IV, pp. 489-490 for a good statement of the contents of this memorandum.

dum be given to the President, and McNamara did so with a cover memorandum in which, without commenting on the substance of the JCS memorandum, he said he would analyze it and give the President his comments.[107]

McNamara responded to the JCS that same day in a memorandum to the JCS, the Secretaries of the Navy and the Air Force, and the Director of the CIA.[108] Noting that "considerable controversy surrounds our current program of bombing North Vietnam," he asked for comments on the two "most promising" alternatives that had been suggested (in essence, Courses B and A respectively):

> I. Concentrate the bombing of North Vietnam on the lines of communication in the Panhandle Area (Route Sectors I, II, and III) and terminate bombing in the remainder of North Vietnam unless there occurs reconstruction of important fixed targets which have been destroyed by prior raids or unless new military activities appear.
>
> II. Terminate the bombing of fixed targets not directly associated with LOCs in Route Sectors VIa and VIb and simultaneously expand the armed reconnaissance operations in those Sectors by authorizing strikes on all LOCs, excepting only those in an eight-mile circle around the center of Hanoi and an eight-mile circle around the center of Haiphong. This program would undoubtedly require continuous strikes against MiG aircraft on all airfields. Further, the program should be examined under two alternative assumptions in one of which strikes against ports and port facilities are precluded and in the other of which every effort is made to deny importation from the sea. (This latter program is essentially that recommended in JCSM- 286–67 dated May 20.)

McNamara's memorandum stated that replies to this request, which did not need to be limited to these alternatives, "should examine the extent to which the proposed bombing pattern will reduce the flow of men and materiel to the South, affect the losses of U.S. pilot and aircraft, and affect the risk of increased military or political pressure from the Soviet Union and/or Red China."

In its reply on June 1 to McNamara's request of May 20, the CIA repeated many of the points made in its earlier assessments and evaluations, concluding: "In general, we do not believe that any of the programs presented in your memorandum is capable of reducing the flow of military and other essential goods sufficiently to affect the war in the South or to decrease Hanoi's determination to

---

[107] Johnson Library, NSF Country File, Vietnam, Memorandum to the President from McNamara, May 20, 1967. The President wrote on the face of McNamara's cover memorandum (attached to which was the JCS memorandum), "Put on my desk." Also on the face of the document is the capital letter L (in cursive) with a small letter s, indicating that the President (L) had seen the memorandum. This notation was used by the White House staff to indicate that the President had seen and possibly perused a document but had not necessarily read it.

McNamara did not send the President his comments on the JCS memorandum. Instead, on July 26, after the issue of the request for new troops had finally been settled, Vance sent a memorandum to Wheeler saying that a final decision on the JCS bombing proposal of May 20 would be made in connection with the overall decision on the troop request and on the future U.S. course of action in Vietnam. *PP*, Gravel ed., vol. IV, p. 490.

[108] Johnson Library, Warnke Papers, McNaughton Files, Memorandum from McNamara to JCS, CIA, Navy, Air Force, "Bombing Options in NVN," May 20, 1967.

persist in the war."[109] Either Alternative I or Alternative II would reduce, at least temporarily, loss of U.S. aircraft and pilots, but such losses would probably increase again as the North Vietnamese, relieved of bombing in the Hanoi/Haiphong area, shifted air defenses to the panhandle area.

Alternative I would also "reduce the chances of increased military or political pressure on the U.S." from China and the Soviet Union, but the Chinese would assume that the changes in U.S. bombing demonstrated "a lack of will in the face of rising domestic and international criticism and to a general frustration in the US over its inability to bring the war to a successful conclusion . . . [and] would almost certainly advise Hanoi that, having scored an important gain, the North Vietnamese had even greater incentive to persist in their current strategy of protracted war."

The U.S.S.R. would be "relieved that the US had broken the cycle of escalation." They, too, would assume that the change signified a lack of will, but they might also conclude that it was made for valid military reasons, and that the effect might be to put the U.S. in a better position to carry on the ground war in the South.

As for its effect, however, on North Vietnamese infiltration of men and supplies, the CIA said that Alternative I, although increasing North Vietnamese costs in manpower and materiel, would not reduce infiltration below existing levels. Moreover, these additional costs "could be met easily." There were an estimated 200,000 full-time and 100,000–200,000 part-time workers engaged in "repair, reconstruction, dispersal and transport programs," and a number of these could be shifted to the panhandle if necessary. Moreover, from its 12,000–13,000 trucks, the North Vietnamese could replace losses to intensified U.S. bombing of infiltration routes, even if twice the number of trucks were destroyed. Imports of trucks could also be increased, although that probably would not be necessary. During the previous 16 months it was estimated that 4,400 trucks were imported while only 3,400 were destroyed, leaving a net gain of 1,000 trucks for the period.

As for roads, it was estimated by the CIA that in bombing the roads in North Vietnam ROLLING THUNDER had reduced infiltration by a maximum of 25 percent, but that even if this rate of interdiction were doubled, the remaining capacity of two major roads along the infiltration routes into Laos would still be five times greater than required to move supplies at the rate they were being moved in the 1966–67 dry season. "The ability of North Vietnam to maintain and improve its logistical network is impressive," the report said. "During 1966, for example, more than 400 miles of new road were constructed in Laos, more than doubling the road network."

"In summary," the CIA report stated, "the excess capacity on the road networks in Route Packages I, II, and III [the major infiltration routes through the panhandle] provides such a deep cushion that it is almost certain that no interdiction program can neutralize the logistics target system to the extent necessary to reduce the

---

[109] Letter from Helms to McNamara, June 1, 1967, transmitting CIA memorandum 196752/67 of June 1, "Alternative Programs for Bombing North Vietnam," Johnson Library, Warnke Papers, McNaughton Files.

flow of men and supplies to South Vietnam below their present levels."

With respect to Alternative II, which would provide for concentrated bombing of lines of communication in North Vietnam in the area near Hanoi-Haiphong (but outside an eight-mile radius from the center of each city), as well as continuous strikes against North Vietnamese fighters on all airfields, and either no strikes against ports or the opposite ("every effort to deny importation from sea"), the CIA report took the position that none of these proposals "could obstruct or reduce North Vietnam's supply of military or war-supporting materials sufficiently to degrade its ability to carry on the war." This would also be true if the plan involved airstrikes on lines of communication in the northern part of North Vietnam near the Chinese border, a provision which had not been included in the statement of Alternative II in McNamara's memorandum. (The CIA memorandum also pointed out that McNamara's Alternative II, although permitting attacks on all lines of communication, would not permit attacks on military and industrial "fixed targets" other than airfields.)

Citing statistics similar to those in its earlier memoranda, the CIA said that even an "optimum program against all means of land and water transportation" would not prevent essential supplies from getting through. Although the North Vietnamese economy might thereby be reduced to its "essential subsistence character," those elements of the economy needed to carry on the war in the North and the South "could be sustained."

Under Alternative II, U.S. losses of planes and pilots, which had been increasing during the spring of 1967, would continue to be costly, particularly if ports were attacked.

As for the effect of Alternative II on the Chinese and the Russians, the CIA report said that if ports were not attacked it was doubtful whether their responses would be very different. If ports were attacked, the Russians would probably increase their aid to North Vietnam through China, while increasing political pressure on the U.S. by mobilizing world opinion against the U.S. for blocking free passage for shipping. Chinese assistance probably would also increase, and, "If requested, the Chinese might introduce some combat troops in North Vietnam." Moreover, since the remaining supply lines would be those through China, this would increase China's influence, which "would be directed toward persuading Hanoi to continue the fight." The Russians might make a greater effort toward negotiations, but even so they probably would not be willing to condition continued support for North Vietnam on the willingness of the North to negotiate.

In the Navy's reply on June 2 to McNamara's request for comments, Secretary Nitze agreed with McNamara that bombing south of the 20th parallel would be preferable to the existing program, and that while closing the port of Haiphong and increased bombing of the North might cause more of an interruption in supplies, the North Vietnamese would develop substitute supply routes. He concluded: "Reducing imports below NVN's minimum requirements was probably beyond the current capability of the bombing campaign."[110]

Secretary of the Air Force Harold Brown argued, however, that if bombing were limited to the area south of the 20th parallel it would be possible for the North to increase the volume of men and supplies flowing into the top of the funnel, thus increasing the flow into South Vietnam.[111] Moreover, while U.S. losses would be reduced, they would increase when the North Vietnamese responded by moving their antiaircraft defenses further south. The North would also view the shift in bombing as a sign of U.S. weakness, thus increasing its resistance.

Brown also continued to maintain that heavier attacks on roads and railroads in North Vietnam, combined with closing the port of Haiphong, would reduce infiltration into South Vietnam. Closure of Haiphong, however, could increase the risks of a wider war. For this reason, he advocated a continuation of the existing program plus new efforts to cut off Hanoi along with Haiphong from the rest of the transportation system and attacks on airfields "as necessary to minimize overall losses in the air campaign." This program, he said, "will keep our losses no higher than they are at present, and will impose additional difficulties on the North Vietnamese in trying to maintain their support of the war in SVN at its present level."[112]

In its reply to McNamara on June 2, the JCS, agreeing generally with the Air Force position, reiterated their support for heavier bombing of the North and for closing the port of Haiphong.[113] The alternative of bombing below the 20th parallel, the Chiefs argued, would not be as effective in interdicting infiltration, would not significantly reduce loss of planes and pilots, and could signify a decline in U.S. will and determination. Contrary to the position of Air Force Secretary Brown, however, the JCS contended that bombing of North Vietnam would be much more effective if combined with closing the port of Haiphong.

The Chiefs suggested a third alternative which they said would be more effective than either of the two alternatives suggested by McNamara. They proposed, in addition to attacking all lines of communication and North Vietnamese fighter planes on all airfields, that bombing of fixed targets should be continued and expanded, and that "every effort will continue to be made to deny importations from the sea except that strikes will not be made in the immediate vicinity of the Haiphong commercial wharf . . . and mines will not be laid in the deep water approaches to the maritime ports north of 20° N [fifty or more miles to the south of Haiphong] or in waters contiguous to commercial wharves."

In their memorandum, the Chiefs criticized Alternative I, saying that it would not "appreciably reduce" infiltration, and would "decrease the burden that NVN must bear for support of the war in

[110] Johnson Library, Warnke Papers, McNaughton Files, Nitze Memorandum to McNamara, "Bombing Options," June 2, 1967.

[111] Brown's memorandum to McNamara, "Possible Courses of Action in Southeast Asia," June 3, 1967, is in the same location, as are supplementary memoranda from Brown on June 5 and 9 and July 3.

[112] Quoted from a one-page untitled memorandum from Brown to McNaughton, June 5, 1967, in the same location.

[113] JCSM-312-67, cited above.

the South." Although it might initially reduce combat losses, it might eventually increase them over current levels as the North Vietnamese imported more weapons and strengthened air defenses in the panhandle. In addition, Alternative I would probably be interpreted as a weakening of U.S. resolve, and would "serve the Communists' interest" by encouraging the North Vietnamese to continue the war and to press for greater concessions.

Alternative II (Ports Open), the JCS said, would not provide for attacking "all elements of the import system," and would not provide for strikes against fixed targets.

Alternative II (Ports Closed), while permitting attacks on all modes of transportation and reducing imports, "fails to provide for exerting simultaneous military pressures on NVN internal resources through attacks on important fixed targets and new military targets."

After reading the JCS memorandum, John McNaughton sent it to one of his aides with the notation, "See if JCS *agree* with us on any key points—eg. unlikelihood of meaningful interdiction." (emphasis in original)

Discussion of the DPM on Troops Continues

On May 20, Rostow sent the President a "Top Secret-Sensitive" memorandum in which he explained his own views on McNamara's proposals in the May 19 Draft Presidential Memorandum on troops.[114] McNamara's proposals, he said, were "a reaction against the JCS position as he [McNamara] understands it and projects it—a reaction that goes a bit too far." It is a strategy further towards the other end of the scale than the one I would recommend." He said he agreed with McNamara that the U.S. should not, at that stage, invade Cambodian or Laos or the southern part of North Vietnam, although cutting infiltration routes by an invasion of North Vietnam might become necessary in 1968 if the North Vietnamese sent additional forces into the South. He also agreed with McNamara that U.S. plans should not be based on blockading North Vietnamese ports or interdicting rail and road lines to China.

Rostow said he disagreed with McNamara on two points. First, "Like him, I do not wish to see progressive and mindless escalation of the bombing in the Hanoi-Haiphong area; but I am anxious that we not take the heat off that area without an adequate return and would, therefore, like to see continuance of a selective attack based on an examination of what we have achieved thus far and a reexamination of targets." Second, Rostow disagreed with McNamara (and with Enthoven) on the question of additional troops. He thought more troops were needed, in part to assist South Vietnamese forces in areas which were not considered "war zones" where they were primarily responsible for providing security. Although the South Vietnamese should continue to provide security in the hamlets and villages, U.S. forces, besides being used against main force units in the areas which were considered to be war zones and

[114] Johnson Library, NSF Country File, Vietnam, Rostow memorandum for the President, May 20, 1967. On May 22, Rostow sent the same memorandum to Vance, Helms and William Bundy. See the copy of the May 22 memorandum in NSF Country File, Vietnam.

along the border, should help the South Vietnamese to fight Communist "provincial forces." He quoted a report by General DePuy:

> It is perfectly clear that progress in Revolutionary Development in large measure can be equated directly to the scope and pace of US/Free World Forces Operations against provincial VC forces contiguous to those areas in which Revolutionary Development activities are in progress. . . .
>
> In those provinces in which Vietnamese forces have had the responsibility for both the security of RD cadre and for sustained offensive operations against VC provincial forces, progress has been very modest or non-existent. In those provinces where US/Free World forces have diminished or discontinued offensive operations against VC provincial forces because of participation in long-term offensive operations against the VC/NVA main forces in the war zones and along the borders, there has been a marked adverse impact on Revolutionary Development.

In addition, Rostow said, increased U.S. forces in the I Corps area south of the demilitarized zone could help to prevent infiltration and harassment by North Vietnamese forces, as well as a possible invasion across the DMZ, and to make the new electronic anti-infiltration barrier "stick." Another 100,000 U.S. troops in I Corps, Rostow also said, would bring the ratio of allied forces to Communist forces into line with that of II and III Corps.[115]

Contrary to McNamara's advice, Rostow also favored a Reserve callup to provide the additional manpower needed for these purposes as well as for a possible "shallow" invasion of North Vietnam in 1968. A callup would also help to convince North Vietnamese that the U.S. was serious, and that it was in a position to fight an even larger war. "Nothing you could do would more seriously impress Hanoi that the jig was up." Because of this beneficial effect of a callup, as well as because of the time needed to bring Reserves into active duty, he recommended to the President that he order a callup in the summer of 1967, "if you judge it politically possible." For this purpose, Rostow outlined a speech which the President could give to a joint session of Congress or to the nation to explain this action. He proposed, first, a discussion of the enemy's strategy, which he described as follows:

> —harass SVN pacification efforts and the drive to Constitutional government;
>
> —use the DMZ illegally to maintain pressure on us and to limit the forces available for pacification;
>
> —buy time until the will and capacity of the United States are broken.

This would be followed by a discussion of the enemy's view of the United States: "Having failed to achieve military victory, they are testing the will and capacity of the U.S. They do not believe we can sustain this kind of grueling war. They are still looking for a French outcome."

---

[115] The existing ratios were: I Corps 3:3, II Corps 5:3, III Corps 4:6, IV Corps 2:2. (IV Corps was the delta, where there were no North Vietnamese forces and only 12,000 U.S. forces.) According to Rostow, "it is, essentially, a VC–GVN stand-off which might best be resolved politically when we block infiltration better, control the DMZ, and drive forward pacification in III, II, and I Corps."

Then the speech would discuss why the enemy refuses to negotiate: "It is because they still believe in military victory; and they think in the end we will cave."

Finally, the proposed speech would discuss U.S. strategy:

> *Our strategy.*
>
> We shall:
>
> —reduce to the maximum their illegal infiltration and impose a price for aggression in the North;
>
> —protect the 17th Parallel from invasion;
>
> —support the South Vietnamese pacification effort;
>
> —encourage the movement to Constitutional government;
>
> —encourage the process of reconciliation in the South;
>
> —seek a negotiated end to the war at the earliest date on the principles of the 1954 and 1962 Accords and of South Vietnamese determination.

Rostow concluded by re-emphasizing that in order to carry out this strategy the U.S. needed more troops in Vietnam or ready for assignment there. Although he did not state how many were needed, saying only that it would be less than the 200,000 recommended by Westmoreland as a maximum and that the number should be determined after further consideration, it was clear that he generally supported the troop request even though he did not support an expanded air war. "[T]he provision of this manpower," he said, "is a test of the proposition on which the men in Hanoi are basing their calculations; whether the U.S. has the potential and the spirit to see this through. Not only Hanoi but the emerging New Asia is watching our decision—hundreds of millions of people whose future hopes and commitments are rooted in the proposition that we shall see it through."

On June 2, 1967, William Bundy commented on the May 19 DPM on troops in a memorandum to the other members of the Non-Group—Katzenbach, Walt Rostow, Vance, Helms and McNaughton. The U.S., he said, was playing an essential and successful role in the war: "Our effort in Viet-Nam in the past two years has not only prevented the catastrophe that would otherwise have unfolded but has laid a foundation for a progress that now appears to be truly possible and of the greatest historical significance." Bundy was deeply concerned, however, about the possible effect on the South Vietnamese of sending additional U.S. forces and taking more aggressive military action:[116]

> The gut point can almost be summed up in a pair of sentences. If we can get a reasonably solid GVN political structure and GVN performance at all levels, favorable trends could become really marked over the next 18 months, the war will be won for practical purposes at some point, and the resulting peace will be secured. On the other hand, if we do not get these results from the GVN and the South Vietnamese people, *no amount* of US effort will achieve our basic objective in South Viet-Nam—a return to the essential provisions of the

[116] William Bundy, "Comments on DOD First Rough Draft of 19 May," May 30, 1967, with a cover memorandum of June 2, Johnson Library, Warnke Papers, McNaughton Files.

> Geneva Accords of 1954 and a reasonably stable peace for many years based on these Accords. [emphasis in original]
>
> It follows that perhaps the most critical of all factors in assessing our whole strategy—bombing, major force increases, and all the rest—lies in the effect they have on the South Vietnamese. On the one hand, it is obvious that there must be a strong enough US role to maintain and increase GVN and popular confidence and physical security; although the point is not covered in the CIA papers, it surely is the fact that in early 1965 virtually all South Vietnamese believed they were headed for defeat, whereas the general assumption today is strongly in the opposite direction, that with massive US help the country has a present chance to learn to run itself and a future expulsion of the North Vietnamese will take place although not perhaps for a long time. We have got to maintain and fortify this underlying confidence and sense that it is worthwhile to get ahead and run the country properly.
>
> On the other hand, many observers are already reporting, and South Vietnamese performance appears to confirm, that the massive US intervention has in fact had a significant adverse effect in that South Vietnamese tend to think that Uncle Sam will do their job for them.

Applying this logic to the request for troop increases, William Bundy said that another 200,000 troops would not make the "difference between victory and defeat," and would at most, by Westmoreland's calculations, bring victory in three years rather than five. The effect on the South Vietnamese of adding that many more Americans was, however, a "much more serious factor."

> [I]n facing decisions whether to make a further major increase in the US performance and whether to maintain at a high level that portion of the war that is wholly US—bombing—we must at least ask ourselves whether we are not . . . putting in an undue proportion of US effort in relation to the essential fact that in the last analysis the South Vietnamese have got to do the job themselves. By "do the job themselves" we mean concretely a much more effective South Vietnamese role in security, pacification, and solid government while the war is going on. But we also mean the progressive development of a South Viet-Nam that can stand on its own feet whenever North Viet-Nam calls it off, and can nail down at that point what could otherwise be a temporary and illusory "victory" which, if it unraveled, would make our whole effort look ridiculous, undermine the gains in confidence that have been achieved in southeast Asia and elsewhere, and have the most disastrous effects on our own American resolve to bear burdens in Asia and indeed throughout the world.

While he, too, supported Course B, Bundy agreed to some extent with Walt Rostow and the JCS and took exception to certain aspects of the DPM's statement about U.S. commitments and objectives. "In Asian eyes," he said, "the struggle is a test case, and indeed much more black and white than even we ourselves see it. The Asian view bears little resemblance to the breastbeating in Europe or at home. Asians would quite literally be appalled—and this includes India—if we were to pull out from Viet-Nam or if we were to settle for an illusory peace that produced Hanoi control over all Viet-Nam in short order."

Moreover, with respect to the statement in the DPM that the objective of containing Chinese expansionism had "already been obtained," Bundy said that it was "absurd" to say that this had been accomplished "and that we can in any sense rest on our oars. The fact is that we are nearer to having an Asia, and even a Southeast Asia, that can stand on its feet than would have appeared conceivable 2, 5, or 10 years ago. But we could throw away and reverse all these gains if we do not achieve an ending of the Vietnamese conflict that preserves what all Asians would recognize as a clear and firm opportunity for the South Vietnamese to run their own show."

The DPM, according to Bundy, "conveys the flavor, particularly in the commitment section, that we can define our commitment in limited terms and not have to worry unduly about the impact in Asia if a minimum commitment fails to achieve its goals." He disagreed, arguing that "the achieving and nailing down of a South Viet-Nam running its own affairs remains vital at least for the next decade in Asia."

"How, then, should our commitment and objective in Viet-Nam be defined?" he asked. "The minimum statement is certainly 'to see that the people of South Viet-Nam are permitted to determine their own future.' But it seems much too pat to say that [as the DPM stated] 'this commitment ceases if the country ceases to help itself,' or that there are not further elements in our commitment that relate not only to getting North Vietnamese forces off the backs of the South Vietnamese but to making sure that the political board in South Viet-Nam is not tilted to the advantage of the NLF."

The U.S. commitment, Bundy said, was two-fold:

> To prevent any imposed political role for the NLF in South Vietnamese political life, and specifically the coalition demanded by point 3 of Hanoi's Four Points, or indeed any NLF part in government or political life that is not safe and acceptable voluntarily to the South Vietnamese Government and people.
>
> To insist in our negotiating position that "regroupees," that is, people who went North in 1954 and returned from 1959 onward, should be expelled as a matter of principle in the settlement. Alternatively, such people could remain in South Viet-Nam if, but only if, the South Vietnamese Government itself was prepared to receive them back under a reconciliation concept, which would provide in essence that they must be prepared to accept peaceful political activity under the Constitution . . . the South Vietnamese are not obliged to accept as citizens people whose total pattern of conduct shows that they seek to overthrow the structure of government by force and violence.

"In sum," Bundy said, "we could define our commitment as being to see that the people of South Viet-Nam are permitted to determine their own future, and to see that the political board is level and not tilted in favor of elements that believe in force. And we should at least hold open the possibility that a future South Vietnamese Government will need continuing military and security assistance, and should be entitled to get it."

He concluded that the May 17 draft memorandum was not faithful to this conception of the U.S. commitment:

> In terms of our course of action, the major implication—as compared with the DOD draft—is that we will not take our forces out until the political board is level. The implication of the DOD draft is that we could afford to go home the moment the North Vietnamese *regulars* went home. This is not what we said at Manila, and the argument here is that we should not in any way modify the Manila position. Nor should we be any more hospitable than the South Vietnamese to coalitions with the NLF, and we should stoutly resist the imposition of such coalitions. (emphasis in original)

Finally, William Bundy asked what would happen "if South Viet-Nam performs so badly that it simply is not going to be able to govern itself or to resist the slightest internal pressure." Although the U.S. could "do nothing to prevent this," the "real underlying question is to what extent we tolerate imperfection, even gross imperfection, by the South Vietnamese while they are still under the present grinding pressure from Hanoi and the NLF. . . . Are we to walk away from the South Vietnamese, at least as a matter of principle, simply because they failed in what was always conceded to be a courageous and extremely difficult effort to become a true democracy during a guerrilla war?" He cautioned against looking at such a contingency "in quite the negative way that the DOD draft suggests. For the effects in Asia may not be significantly reduced if we walk away from Viet-Nam even under what we ourselves and many others saw as a gross failure by the South Vietnamese to use the opportunity that we had given them."

Under Secretary of State Katzenbach took a similar position. In a memorandum to McNamara on June 8, he said that the U.S. should withdraw from Vietnam only after three goals had been accomplished: "(1) that we would be behind a stable democratic government (democratic by Asian standards); (2) that we would confront the prospect of a reasonably stable peace in Southeast Asia for several years; and (3) that we will have demonstrated that we met our commitments to the government of Vietnam."[117] "To do these," he added, "we had to persuade the North Vietnamese to give up their aggression and we had to neutralize the internal Viet Cong threat while in the process being careful not to create an American satellite nor to generate widespread anti-American sentiment nor destroy the social fabric of South Vietnam, nor incur disproportionate losses in our relations with other countries or bring in so called 'enemy' countries." He was not optimistic that these goals could be accomplished in the next 12-18 months (i.e., before the 1968 U.S. Presidential election), although he was more optimistic about the prospects two or three years thence.

Katzenbach did not favor expanded military action against North Vietnam, believing that the battle of attrition in the South was "the key." He said he found it difficult, however, to appraise the re-

[117] See *PP*, Gravel ed., vol. IV, pp. 505–508 for excerpts from Katzenbach's memorandum "Preliminary Comments on the DOD Draft of May 19," June 8, 1967.

sults of military action in the South given such apparently inconclusive evidence as the fact that enemy losses were up 70 percent in the first quarter of 1967 but U.S. losses were up 90 percent. It was also clear to him that pacification was not going well. "[I]t appeared that GVN and ARVN were going to continue moving slowly, corruption was becoming more widespread and the population was increasingly apathetic."

After examining the pros and cons of sending 200,000 more troops, Katzenbach recommended a "middle" strategy patterned after Course B of the May 19 DPM. In the South, he proposed the following:

> a. Add 30,000 more troops, in small increments, over the next 18 months. This would show Hanoi and our own forces that we are not levelling off, and yet we would not appear impatient or run into the risks and dangers which attend force increases. Continue to try to get as many more third country forces as possible.
>
> b. Make a major effort to get the South Vietnamese more fully involved and effective. . . . Tell the GVN early in 1968 that we plan to start withdrawing troops at the end of 1968, or earlier if possible, in view of progress in the "big war." Pacification will be up to them.
>
> c. Use the great bulk of US forces for search and destroy rather than pacification—thus playing for a break in morale. Emphasize combat units rather than engineers. Leave all but the upper Delta to the Vietnamese.
>
> d. Use a small number of US troops with South Vietnamese forces in pacification, targeted primarily on enemy provincial main force units. Recognize that pacification is not the ultimate answer—we have neither the time nor the manpower. In any event, only the Vietnamese can make meaningful pacification progress. The GVN should therefore hold what it has and expand where possible. Any progress will (1) discourage the enemy and (2) deprive him of manpower.
>
> e. We should stimulate a greater refugee flow through psychological inducements to further decrease the enemy's manpower base. Improve our ability to handle the flow and win the refugees' loyalty.
>
> f. Devote more attention to attacking the enemy infrastructure [Communist cadres in the south]. Consider giving MACV primary responsibility for US efforts in this regard.
>
> g. Use all the political pressure we have to keep the GVN clean in its running of the elections. Press for some form of international observation. Play down the elections until they are held, then exploit them and their winner (probably Ky) in the international and domestic press.
>
> h. After the elections, but prior to the Christmas-Tet period, press hard for the GVN to open negotiations with the NLF and for a meaningful National Reconciliation program.

This was his recommendation for U.S. policy toward the North:

> In the North—the object is to cut the North off from the South as much as possible, and to shake Hanoi from its obdurate position. Concentrate on shaking enemy morale in both

the South and North by limiting Hanoi's ability to support the forces in South Viet-Nam.

a. A barrier [the "McNamara Line" across the DMZ], if it will work . . . or

b. Concentrate bombing on lines of communication throughout NVN, thus specifically concentrating on infiltration but not running into the problems we have had and will have with bombing oriented towards "strategic" targets in the Hanoi/Haiphong area. By continuing to bomb throughout NVN in this manner we would indicate neither a lessening of will nor undue impatience.

On June 8, 1967, there was a meeting of the Non-Group on the subject of redrafting the May 19 DPM. There apparently are no notes of the meeting, but the *Pentagon Papers* contain the full text of an outline by either McNaughton or Katzenbach describing major differences among and between the participants.[118] There were several major differences between Deputy Secretary of Defense Vance and the CIA. Vance took the position that an invasion of North Vietnam or mining of the ports would result in Chinese intervention in the war. The CIA disagreed on both points, maintaining that in the event of an invasion the Chinese might not intervene if the invasion did not seem to threaten the survival of the Hanoi regime. There was also a difference of opinion between the CIA and Vance as to how well the war was going, and whether the U.S. had reached the "crossover point" where Communist casualties exceeded replacements, with Vance taking a more pessimistic position. William Bundy, however, quoted one CIA paper as contradicting another on the subject of the enemy's strength and strategic position.

There were also differences between the CIA and the Intelligence and Research Office (INR) of the State Department, with INR arguing that bombing was more effective than the CIA believed, and that the North Vietnamese were seeking positive victories in the South, contrary to the CIA's conclusion that they were determined to engage in a more passive form of protracted warfare.

There was also disagreement between Vance and the JCS about the effectiveness of bombing only below the 20th parallel.

Revision of the DPM on Bombing

On June 12, 1967, McNamara sent the President a new DPM on bombing, drafted in McNaughton's office, which generally took the same position and contained some of the same language as those parts of the May 19 DPM which dealt with the air war.

The June 12 DPM on bombing stated that there were three alternatives for the air war against North Vietnam:[119]

ALTERNATIVE A. *Intensified attack on the Hanoi-Haiphong logistical base.* Under this alternative, we would continue at-

---

[118] See *ibid.*, p. 188. On pp. 505–506, of *ibid.*, this outline is attributed to Katzenbach, but it may have been McNaughton's. The original copy of the outline is in the Johnson Library, Warnke Papers, McNaughton Files.

When the outline was made available at the Johnson Library in 1985, it was sanitized in part by the State Department, despite the fact that the full text had been printed in the *Pentagon Papers* 10 years earlier.

[119] Johnson Library, NSF Country File, Vietnam, "Alternative Military Actions Against North Vietnam," June 12, 1967.

tacks on enemy installations and industry and would conduct an intensified, concurrent and sustained effort against all elements of land, sea and air lines of communication in North Vietnam—especially those entering and departing the Hanoi-Haiphong areas. Foreign shipping would be "shouldered out" of Haiphong by a series of air attacks that close in on the center of the port complex. The harbor and approaches would be mined, forcing foreign shipping out into the nearby estuaries for offloading by lighterage [small boats]. Intensive and systematic armed reconnaissance would be carried out against the roads and railroads from China (especially the northeast railroad), against coastal shipping and coastal transshipment locations, and against all other land lines of communications. The eight major operational airfields would be systematically attacked, and the deep-water ports of Cam Pha and Hon Gai would be struck or mined as required. ALTERNATIVE A could be pursued full-force between now and September (thereafter the onset of unfavorable weather conditions would seriously impair operations).

ALTERNATIVE B. *Emphasis on the infiltration routes south of the 20th Parallel.* Under this alternative, the dominant emphasis would be, not on preventing material from flowing into North Vietnam (and thus not on "economic pressure" on the regime), but on preventing military men and materiel from flowing *out* [emphasis in original] of the North into the South. We would terminate bombing in the Red River basin [the Hanoi-Haiphong area] except for occasional sorties (perhaps 3%)—those necessary to keep enemy air defenses and damage-repair crews positioned there and to keep important fixed targets knocked out. The same total number of sorties envisioned under ALTERNATIVE A—together with naval gunfire at targets ashore and afloat and mining of inland waterways, estuaries and coastal waters—would be concentrated in the neck of North Vietnam, between 17° and 20°, through which all land infiltration must pass and in which the "extended battle zone" north of the DMZ lies. The effort would be intensive and sustained, designed especially to saturate choke points and to complement similar new intensive interdiction efforts in adjacent areas in Laos and near the 17th Parallel inside South Vietnam.

ALTERNATIVE C. *Extension of the current program.* This alternative would be essentially a refinement of the currently approved program and therefore a compromise between ALTERNATIVE A and ALTERNATIVE B. Under it, while avoiding attacks within the 10-mile prohibited zone around Hanoi and strikes at or mining of the ports, we could conduct a heavy effort against all other land, sea, and air lines of communication. Important fixed targets would be kept knocked out; intensive, sustained and systematic armed reconnaissance would be carried out against the roads and railroads and coastal shipping throughout the country; and the eight major airfields would be systematically attacked. The total number of sorties would be the same as under the other two alternatives.

The division of opinion in DOD with respect to these alternatives, McNamara said, was as follows:

> *Mr. Vance and I recommend* ALTERNATIVE B.
>
> *The Joint Chiefs of Staff* recommend ALTERNATIVE A.
>
> *The Secretary of the Navy* recommends ALTERNATIVE B.
>
> *The Secretary of the Air Force* recommends ALTERNATIVE C modified to add some targets (especially LOC [lines of communications] targets) to the present list and to eliminate others.
>
> *The Director of the CIA* does not make a recommendation. The CIA judgment is that none of the alternatives is capable of decreasing Hanoi's determination to persist in the war or of reducing the flow of goods sufficiently to affect the war in the South.

As for using bombing to force North Vietnam to agree to withdraw from the war, McNamara repeated the statement in the May 19 DPM that "nothing short of toppling the Hanoi regime will pressure North Vietnam to settle so long as they believe they have a chance to win the 'war of attrition' in the South. . . ." The use of the force necessary to topple the regime, he said, would lead to a war with the Soviet Union and China.

Ambassador Bunker generally supported the position on bombing taken in Course B of the June 12 DPM, arguing that while strategic bombing was important, it had not "interdicted infiltration nor broken the will of the NVN and it is doubtful that it can accomplish either."[120] He endorsed McNamara's proposal for an anti-infiltration barrier.

Although the JCS recommended Course A, it was clear, as Wheeler had warned in his cable on May 26 and as Admiral Sharp said in a backchannel cable to Westmoreland on June 13, that this was not going to be approved.[121] Sharp said that both Course B and Course C were "unacceptable," but that the forces for Course A "are simply not going to be provided. The country is not going to call up the reserves and we had best accept that." "On the other hand," he added, "the actions outlined for Course B are a blueprint for defeat. Our job then is to develop a logical and feasible course which lies somewhere between A and B. . . ."

"If we are going to be forced to fight this war with less than we would like," Sharp said, "we need to take a hard look at how best to do it. I think Washington intends to give us the forces listed for Course B. What we need is a well thought out concept which takes the forces of Course B and employs them not in the manner they suggest in Course B but rather so that we make best possible

---

[120] *PP*, Gravel ed., vol. IV, p. 192, from Saigon to Washington (Bunker to Rusk) 28293, June 17, 1967.

In a cable to the JCS, CINCPAC objected to reduced bombing, arguing that in the spring of 1967 "air power began for the first time to realize the sort of effectiveness of which it is capable . . . We are at an important point in this conflict. . . . In our judgment the enemy is now hurting and the operations to which we attribute this impact should be continued with widest latitude in planning and execution. . . ." *Ibid.*, p. 193 from CINCPAC to JCS 210430Z, June 21, 1967.

During June, Air Force Secretary Harold Brown continued to make the case for increased bombing of targets north of the 20th parallel as well as infiltration routes in the area below the 20th. *Ibid.*, pp. 193–195.

[121] CMH, Westmoreland Papers, Message Files, Sharp to Westmoreland, 130013Z, June 13, 1967.

progress toward accomplishing our objectives." He cautioned Westmoreland against "too gloomy an appraisal of this Course of Action [B] for it is probably the one we are going to pursue." Westmoreland replied that he agreed with Sharp, but he, in turn, cautioned Sharp "against too gloomy an appraisal" with respect to what could be accomplished by Course B."[122]

On June 13, the President met from 1:10 p.m. to 2:35 p.m. with McNamara, Katzenbach, Rostow and Christian, who were joined by McGeorge Bundy and Llewellyn Thompson, for a discussion of the three bombing options—the JCS proposal to expand bombing to include mining of ports and attacks on roads and bridges closer to Hanoi and Haiphong, the McNamara/Vance/Nitze proposal to continue the present program of attacks but restrict it generally to the area below the 20th parallel, and the option, supported by Air Force Secretary Brown, of continuing and refining the existing program. It was tentatively decided to continue at existing levels until McNamara returned from his trip to Vietnam.[123]

In a memorandum to Rusk summarizing actions taken at the Tuesday Lunch, Benjamin Read also reported that "DCI [Director of Central Intelligence] Helms estimates that none of the alternatives 'is capable of reducing the flow of military and other essential goods sufficiently to affect the war in the south or to decrease Hanoi's determination to persist in the war.'"[124]

On June 15, the President met again with Rusk, McNamara, Walt Rostow, Eugene Rostow, Wheeler, Helms, and Christian. Also attending was McGeorge Bundy, who was in Washington, at the President's request, to assist with discussions of the situation in the Middle East from 11:55 a.m. to 1:06 p.m. to discuss bombing options. There are no known notes of the meeting. According to the agenda prepared that morning by Rostow, the questions to be considered were:[125]

> 1. Do we give the USSR an interval of several weeks to produce a negotiation, while cutting down around Hanoi-Haiphong?[126]

---

[122] Same location, Westmoreland to Sharp, MAC 5601, June 13, 1967.

On June 12, 1967, the President met with General Walt, Commander of U.S. Marine forces in Vietnam. The meeting had been arranged by General Greene, Commandant of the Marine Corps, who had suggested that the President see General Walt and get a "complete briefing on what is going on in I Corps." (I Corps, in the northern part of South Vietnam, was the area for which the Marines had major responsibility, and where they had been involved in major battles with the Communists during May-June 1967.)

Walt met with the President at 1:24 p.m., apparently expecting to be able to give him a complete briefing. There is no indication that anyone else attended the meeting, for which there apparently are no notes.) At 1:28 p.m., the meeting ended and Walt held a prearranged meeting with the press. (Johnson Library, President's Daily Diary for June 12, 1967)

There is no documentary explanation for the brevity of this session, but given the fact that the President's other appointments that afternoon do not seem to have been such as to preclude a longer meeting with Walt, it would appear that it was the President's choice to meet for only four minutes.

The treatment of Walt may have been indicative of the President's growing disillusionment with the use of military means. It probably was also the result of the effect on Johnson of Westmoreland's complaints that the Marines were not fully engaging the enemy.

[123] There are no known notes of this meeting. Information cited here is from a June 15, 1967 memorandum to Rusk from his assistant, Benjamin Read, State Department, Lot File 74 D 164.

[124] *Ibid.*

[125] Johnson Library, NSF Rostow Memos to the President.

[126] On May 19, as noted above, President Johnson wrote to Premier Kosygin to suggest that he try to get the North Vietnamese to enter negotiations. Same location, Rostow note to the President, June 9, 1967, with attached draft of letter to Kosygin. On May 22, also as noted above, the U.S. had reduced bombing apparently in part as a way of indicating to the U.S.S.R.

Continued

2. If that effort fails (or is not attempted), should we go for:

a. *Intensified attack versus Hanoi-Haiphong logistical base, including mining of ports.*

b. *Concentration south of the 20th parallel.*

c. *Extension of current programs, short of mining the ports.*

3. Relation of bombing decisions to troop decision. (emphasis in original)

Prior to the meeting, Rostow also sent the President a memorandum of his own views on bombing policy: [127]

Mr. President:

Here are my views on bombing policy.

1. Bob McNamara believes that we may have to live with the war through 1968 and beyond. He holds that we can best do this if we adopt a relatively low-key strategy. This means two things:

—We should not go for a big troop increase but work patiently and gradually to improve the performance of the Vietnamese; and

—Limit our bombing to the region south of the 20th parallel.

He believes this is the setting in which the U.S. public will best accommodate itself to seeing the war through; and he holds that in this setting the forces of moderation in Hanoi are most likely to move towards a gradual decline in the level of hostilities and, perhaps, negotiations.

2. Pending the results of the investigation of manpower requirements [a reference to McNamara's impending trip to Vietnam] by Bob, Bus [Wheeler] and Nick [Katzenbach], I am inclined to think that we need:

—more troops to work with the Vietnamese in getting at the provincial main force units and thus lay the base for pacification;

—a decision for some limited call-ups would impress Moscow and Hanoi more than anything else that we have the capacity to see the war through, which is the critical issue of judgment in Hanoi; and

—that if we do this, we need a strong bombing policy in the northern part of Viet Nam, but short of direct attack on shipping. (Current evidence is that the port is bottlenecking for one reason or another and, therefore, it is internal transport and concentrations of supply rather than ships which are the appropriate attritional targets.)

3. Therefore, I would propose:

---

and the North Vietnamese its bona fide interest in negotiations. There had been no response, and on June 9, Rostow proposed that the President write again to Kosygin to suggest that the U.S.S.R. seek to persuade the North Vietnamese to end the war by letting a settlement be worked out "by a negotiation between South Vietnamese, designed to transfer the present bloody conflict from the battlefield to the ballot box," after which international negotiations could "reestablish and insure the effectiveness" of the Geneva Accords. According to Rostow's draft of the proposed letter, the President would also tell Kosygin that, for its part, the U.S. was prepared to deescalate the air war, and would stop bombing in the previously prohibited areas around Hanoi and Haiphong. It is not known whether this proposed letter was sent.

[127] Johnson Library, NSF Memos to the President—Walt Rostow.

—that you give the Russians an interval of several weeks, perhaps via the Kosygin trip, to get Hanoi into serious negotiations, while holding bombing in the north well away from Hanoi and Haiphong;

—and then make your decision on manpower and bombing policy together, as a package, after Bob returns.

CHAPTER 16

CONGRESS IN A QUANDARY

As the financial and human cost of the war increased, and "victory" became more elusive, Congress, like the President, was faced with the problem of continuing to expend men and money in a struggle that seemed to have no end, while at the same time maintaining adequate defenses in other parts of the world, providing funds for the Great Society programs that had been established, keeping inflation and budgetary deficits under control without increasing taxes, and avoiding adverse political repercussions in the 1968 election.

There was still strong bipartisan support for the war, but storm flags were beginning to fly as leading Republican liberals and moderates began criticizing the President's policy. In the Senate these included two newly-elected Members, Percy and Hatfield, as well as Javits, Aiken, Cooper, Morton and Case, and in the House of Representatives a growing number of Republicans including Findley (Ill.), Morse (Mass.), Dellenback (Ore.), Esch (Mich.), Horton (N.Y.), Mathias (Md.), Mosher (Ohio), Schweiker (Pa.), and Stafford (Vt.).[1]

[1] Percy proposed "full participation of the Vietcong in peace negotiations in Vietnam so that they might become 'a legal political party competing peacefully at the polls and shunning violence.'" *(New York Times,* Apr. 23, 1967.) He was also critical of the Johnson administration for insisting, as a condition for negotiations, that North Vietnam cease infiltration. "To ask Hanoi to end the resupply and reinforcements of its forces in the South was unrealistic," he said. And to those who advocated "total victory," he said, "We must answer whether we are prepared to allow our men to die at the rate of 150 to 250 a month, for an interminable number of years, in search of a total victory which cannot, in my judgment, really be achieved."

Hatfield called for a cessation of bombing and a deescalation of the war, as well as a reconvening of the 1954 Geneva Conference and U.S. action to get the U.N. involved in initiating negotiations. He also advocated, as Percy had proposed in 1966, an all-Asian conference of America's allies which could consider replacing U.S. troops in Vietnam with Asian troops, as well as helping bring about negotiations to end the war. *(CR,* vol. 113, pp. 7527–7530.)

See below for the views of Javits, Aiken, Cooper, and Morton.

In May 1967, Case went on a three-week study mission to Vietnam and other parts of Southeast Asia, and returned with the somber forecast that the war was not being won, that there appeared to be little likelihood of a negotiated peace, and that the U.S. "was in for a long pull—measured in years—if we are to see the job through." He said he was opposed to escalation and thought that bombing of the North should be limited to targets directly related to infiltration. *(CR,* vol. 113, June 5, 1967, p. 14685.) The war, he said, "may be unwinnable." *(Ibid.,* July 26, 1967, p. 10897.)

Findley, a member of the House Foreign Affairs Committee, introduced a congressional resolution to provide for referring the Vietnam dispute to the International Court of Justice (World Court) for adjudication. *(Ibid.,* May 18, 1967, pp. 13159–13160.) Among the list of questions to be raised was whether, if the North Vietnamese violated the 1954 Geneva Accords, the use of U.S. forces was "consistent with the principles of international law." All parties to the dispute would be asked to accept the judgment of the court as binding. If parties refused to accept the use of the court, the U.S. could then take the matter to the U.N. and request the General Assembly to seek an advisory opinion from the court which the U.S. could ask the Security Council to enforce. If action by the Security Council were vetoed, the U.S. could ask the General Assembly to order the members of SEATO to enforce the decision or to enforce it through a U.N. military force.

Many Democrats who had supported the war were becoming uneasy and were beginning to speak out. This was Presidential Counsel Harry McPherson's description:[2]

> Like an acid, it [the war] was eating into everything. It threatened to wipe out public awareness of Johnson's great achievements; it had already corroded his relationships with members of Congress.
>
> Joe Tydings [D/Md.] asked me to come up and talk about it. In the Senate, he had been a pretty firm supporter of the war. But it had become such a political albatross in Maryland that "any reasonably good Republican could clobber me if the election were held today." He did not hold the President personally responsible for his troubles; but "every political advisor I have says I can save myself only by attacking him. I won't do that, but I'm going to have to speak out against the war. It's dragging the country down, and Democrats along with it." He said that other senators friendly to the Administration—[Birch] Bayh [Ind.], [Fred R.] Harris [Okla.], Muskie [Maine], and Hart [Mich.]—had reported the same bitterness in their states. Senator Russell said, "For the first time in my life, I don't have any idea what to recommend."[3]

Through their congressional political party structure, Republicans continued to blame the Democrats for getting the U.S. involved in Vietnam in the first place, and then, after Eisenhower's careful avoidance of overcommitment, getting the U.S. more committed under Kennedy and fully involved under Johnson. This was the essence of a "White Paper" published in August of 1965 and reissued in September of 1966 by the Republican organization in the House, and the same position was reiterated in a white paper released on May 1, 1967, by Senator Hickenlooper, chairman of the Senate Republican Policy Committee:[4]

> As of April 1967, the war to contain Communist aggression in Vietnam has assumed for the United States these unusual dimensions:
>
> It means a conflict that has escalated from a small force of 600 American technicians to over a half-million fighting men.
>
> It means over 8,000 men killed.
>
> It means over 50,000 wounded.
>
> It means greatly increased American conscription at a time when the rest of the Western world has done away with its draft.
>
> It means our longest war since the American Revolution—six years—a weary nightmare and yet the men who fight are fighting with extraordinary bravery and skill.
>
> It means not knowing at any given moment precisely who the enemy is.
>
> It means a war which is not simply fought over this tiny land of Vietnam; for this war, unlike all others in American

[2] Harry McPherson, *A Political Education* (New York: Boston, Little, Brown, 1972), p. 420. McPherson's memorandum to the President on Aug. 25, 1967, reporting on his talk with Senator Joe Tydings on August 24, is in the Johnson Library, Office Files of Harry McPherson.

[3] Another Democratic loyalist, Senator Harrison Williams of New Jersey, urged that the war be deescalated. *New York Times*, Apr. 24, 1967.

[4] For the text of the May 1, 1967 report, "The War in Vietnam," see *CR*, vol. 113, pp. 12030–12041.

history, is more and more justified as much on geopolitical grounds as on the defense of one small government.

It means our relative isolation as the world's policeman, for here we have no Grand Alliance as in World War II, no United Nations Combined Forces as in Korea. In addition to South Vietnamese troops, four Pacific nations have provided some fighting help—with our financial assistance.

It means fighting a people who claim this is a civil war, and who in turn are spurred on by two giant powers quarreling openly with each other.

It means that while we have committed 550,000 men to battle communism, neither the Soviet Union nor Red China—the great Communist powers—has found it necessary to commit troops.

It means the most frustrating sort of war, with no front lines, which breaks out here and there, even across national borders in Laos and Cambodia, neither of which is involved.

It means spending over $300,000 to kill each enemy soldier.

It means spending $24 billion a year, with another increase in taxes threatened, a further drain on an already inadequate gold supply, and an escalation of inflation.

It means enormous discretionary powers assumed by the President, with Congress asked to approve his actions after the fact.

It means the Nation which started the war—France—and lost it, now has become our most outspoken critic while profiting heavily from the war.

It means a war where, in the eyes of many Asiatics, we are fighting against indigenous Asiatic nationalism, much as France did in the past.

It means the first war in our history fought not only on the battlefield but brought into the American livingroom, every day, through the raw emotionalism of today's mass communications.

It means a war in which religious controversy between Catholic minority and Buddhist majority has come dangerously close to causing collapse of the successive governments of South Vietnam.

The Senate Republican white paper concluded that Republicans should be wary of supporting the policy of the Johnson administration:

Republicans—for two decades—have believed the United States must not become involved in a land war on the Asian continent. We are so involved today.

Republicans have believed that no American military intervention should be unilateral. Our commitment today in Vietnam is primarily unilateral.

Republicans, in 1954, made a limited commitment to the South Vietnam Government. Under the Democrats, our commitment has become open-ended.

Before making any further decisions to support or differ with the President, Republicans might agree to seek hard, realistic answers to two basic questions:

1. What precisely is our national interest in Thailand, Cambodia, Vietnam, and Laos?

2. To what further lengths are we prepared to go in support of this interest?

The white paper had been prepared after a meeting of the Senate Republican Policy Committee in late March 1967 in which Senator Javits had suggested that Senate Republicans should reach a consensus on Vietnam.[5] When news accounts of the study portrayed it as a partisan document, however, Senate Republican Leader Dirksen objected to that interpretation as well as any implication that the Republicans were seeking to separate themselves from the Democrats prior to the 1968 election.[6] "We reaffirm our position standing four-square behind him [President Johnson] and our field, air and sea commanders in Southeast Asia . . . ," Dirksen said. Asked if the report represented an effort by the Republicans to dissociate themselves from Johnson administration policy, he said: "Not for a minute."[7] Dirksen was supported by Senate Republican Whip Kuchel and by House Republican Leader Ford, who said that the "overwhelming" number of House Republicans supported the fight against Communist aggression in Vietnam.[8]

Among the Democrats, Fulbright welcomed the Senate Republican statement, saying that it was "the most fruitful and promising movement on the part of the minority party that I can remember." He said he preferred the report to the "Madison Avenue gimcrackery of the Administration." "This is the only break in the clouds that I have seen in a long time," he said, adding: "If my committee staff had put it out, all hell would have broken loose."[9]

Senator Sparkman, the ranking Democrat on the Foreign Relations Committee, said, however, that the report would be "a powerful weapon in the hands of Ho Chi Minh, for it would provide him with his most important policy objective: to divide the American people and bring about the complete collapse of American foreign policy."[10]

Senator Stennis, who was the acting chairman of the Armed Services Committee during Russell's illness, declared that the war "should not be made a political football" and warned against giving the impression that the United States was divided: "We simply cannot afford to stop in the midst of a shooting war and take time out to debate whether we have been wise or unwise and whether our past actions were sound or unsound. At this critical time, we need unity and a sense of national purpose, not disunity and divisiveness." Javits replied that "Unity does not mean blindness," and that the Republicans had an obligation to develop the facts and present alternatives. This, he said, would strengthen the Nation in

---

[5] *New York Times,* May 2, 1967.

[6] The *New York Times* headline for its May 2 article was "Senate G. O. P. Study Calls U.S. War Role Error by Democrats," and the article said that the white paper "could lay the groundwork for the Republican party to dissociate itself next year from the Johnson Administration's policy in Vietnam."

[7] *Ibid.,* May 3, 1967. For the full text of Dirksen's statement see *CR,* vol. 113, p. 11528. See also his comments reprinted in the *New York Times,* May 10, 1967.

[8] *New York Times,* May 4, 1967. For Kuchel's statement, see *CR,* vol. 113, p. 12115.

[9] *CR,* vol. 113, p. 11528, and *New York Times,* May 3 and 5, 1967.

[10] *New York Times,* May 2, 1967.

its efforts to find a way to bring the war to an "honorable conclusion."[11]

Aiken, second-ranking Republican on the Foreign Relations Committee and the senior Republican in the Senate, said that he had been coming "more and more to believe that the present administration cannot achieve an honorable peace in Vietnam." It was "too bound by its own vague criteria, its own predictions, its own predilections, its own conceptions and emotional commitments to see the interest of the Nation except in terms of its own survival as the government in power." Public confidence in U.S. policy had been shaken, he said, and the Republican Party should "promise a new look at U.S. policy in Asia," a "fresh appraisal which can come only from a Republican administration."[12]

Congressional concern about the war was becoming so intense that a new consular treaty with the U.S.S.R., which was intended to be a central feature of efforts by the Johnson administration to improve relations with the Soviet Union, passed the Senate on March 25 by only three votes more than the required two-thirds, partly because of a feeling by many conservatives that the U.S. should not enter into a commercial treaty which would provide economic benefits to the U.S.S.R. while it was supplying North Vietnam with war matériel.[13]

---

[11] *CR*, vol. 113, pp. 11526–11529.

[12] *Ibid.*, pp. 11436–11437. The administration did not respond to the Senate Republican white paper of May 1, but memoranda were prepared for use in possible responses. See U.S. Department of State, Central File, Pol 27 Viet S, Memorandum from Harold Kaplan in Public Affairs to Unger in East Asia, "Credibility and the Senate Republican Policy Committee's 'The War in Vietnam,'" May 8, 1967, and in Lot File 71 D 88, a joint memorandum from William Bundy and McNaughton to Rusk and McNamara, May 10, 1967.

[13] Senator Karl Mundt (R/S.D.) offered an amendment ("executive reservation") to the treaty to provide that it should not take effect until the President reported to Congress that it was no longer necessary for U.S. forces to fight in Vietnam, or the removal of U.S. forces was "not being prevented or delayed because of military assistance furnished North Vietnam by the Soviet Union." This was defeated 25–67, and the treaty was then approved 66–28. See *CR*, vol. 113, p. 6834.

Even seemingly unrelated matters were being affected by the war. A case in point was the request for additional funds to support development of Fast Deployment Logistics Ships (FDL) by which the heavy supplies for U.S. ground forces could be stored in specially equipped ships and the ships could be prepositioned in areas where U.S. forces might have to be deployed. It was estimated that four ships could be required to supply one U.S. infantry division, or eight ships for an armored division, and the plan at that time called for building 30 ships. In 1965, Congress was asked to approve the idea, which it did, and to authorize money for four ships. It authorized two. In 1966, additional funds were approved. In the spring of 1967, however, a request for five more ships ran afoul Senator Russell's opposition, based on his experience with Vietnam, and prompted also by reports that the U.S. might become involved in enforcing U.N. sanctions against Rhodesia.

In its report (S. Rept. 90–76), which recommended against the request the Senate Armed Services Committee gave this explanation: "The committee is concerned about the possible creation of an impression that the United States has assumed the function of policing the world and that it can be thought to be at least considering intervention in any kind of strife or commotion occurring in any of the nations of the world. Moreover, if our involvement in foreign conflicts can be made quicker and easier, there is the temptation to intervene in many situations."

The Senate agreed with the recommendations of its committee, and the House yielded to the Senate and no funds were authorized in FY 1968 for the Fast Deployment Logistics Ships. A year later, in 1968, the Senate Armed Services Committee approved the administration's request for more funds, and the Senate agreed, but there was concern in the House about the effect on commercial shipping and shipbuilding of a government program to build transport vessels for its own use, and the House refused to approve the request. In 1969, both the House and the Senate rejected a request for more funds. In 1970, the Nixon administration announced that it was considering alternatives and would not make a new request. There the matter rested until 1980, when the Carter administration, prompted by events in the Middle East and Southwest Asia, decided to create a Rapid Deployment Force (RDF), and again requested funds for prepositioning supply ships. The name was changed to Maritime Prepositioning Vessel (MPV). This time the request was readily approved, partly because some of the fears of intervention

Continued

During March-June 1967, as the tempo of the war increased and it became apparent that the President was considering sending more troops, those Members of Congress who were opposed to expanded military action continued to seek ways of preventing further U.S. involvement and, instead, of moving toward a negotiated settlement. Having passed the Mansfield-Clark amendment, they began to explore other possibilities. One, as Morse had long argued, and as Mansfield had also begun to advocate,[14] was to take the problem to the United Nations, an approach that the President and most of his advisers, as well as many Members of Congress, thought was unworkable and unwise. In their view, the United Nations was not capable of resolving a dispute of this kind; thus, any effort to do so would be viewed as insincere, while also signifying U.S. weakness. The argument was also made that the North Vietnamese and the Soviet Union did not want the U.N. involved.

In an effort to explore the possibility of U.N. action, the Senate Foreign Relations Committee arranged to meet with U.N. Secretary General U Thant for a private discussion of the war, and on March 22, 1967, Democrats Fulbright, Sparkman, Gore, Church, Symington, Clark, Pell, and McCarthy, and Republicans Carlson, Mundt, Case, and Cooper flew to New York City, where they met with Ambassador Goldberg and members of the U.S. Mission to the U.N. Without any executive branch officials taking part, they talked to U Thant for three hours. According to the notes of that meeting, which were released five years later, U Thant said that the North Vietnamese would never surrender; that they were convinced of the justice of their cause.[15] Nor would they negotiate until bombing ceased. If bombing were stopped, negotiations could begin in a matter of weeks.

U Thant reviewed for the members of the committee his three-point proposal of January 1966: "(1) Stop bombing the North; (2) mutual deescalation, and (3) participation in talks by all parties involved in the fighting." He added, however, that the North Vietnamese did not believe that the U.S. wanted to withdraw. "Hanoi believes the United States wants to make a South Korea out of South Vietnam and legalize the government of General Ky." The U.S., he said, "'must dispel this suspicion.'" Fulbright commented that, "it may not be a suspicion but that, in fact, some elements in the United States may want to keep U.S. forces in South Vietnam."

Senator Clark raised the question of a cease-fire, and U Thant's associate, Dr. Ralph J. Bunche, an American who was U.N. Under Secretary for Special Political Affairs, said he doubted whether this would be possible, "inasmuch as the American position seemed to be to talk and shoot at the same time."

By pre-arrangement, as noted earlier, U Thant did not discuss with the committee his latest plan for a truce, followed by talks,

---

had dissipated, and because the new plan had been developed in consultation with U.S. maritime interests.

The author wishes to thank his former colleague in CRS, Alva Bowen (Capt., U.S. Navy, Ret.), for information and assistance on this subject.

[14] For Mansfield's position, which he discussed on Nov. 10, 1966, in a speech at Johns Hopkins University, Mansfield, see *CR*, vol. 113, pp. 12594 ff.

[15] U.S. Congress, Senate, Committee on Foreign Relations, *A Conversation With U Thant, Secretary General of the United Nations*, Committee Print, 92d Cong., 2d sess. (Washington, D.C.: U.S. Govt. Print. Off., 1972).

and Fulbright and Carlson, who had been told about the plan by Goldberg, agreed not to raise it during the committee's meeting with U Thant.

After the private meeting of the Foreign Relations Committee with U Thant, Fulbright said in a press conference that the talk had been productive, but when asked for details he said they were "for the administration and not the press." He emphasized, however, his own feeling that bombing should be stopped "'not for a day or two or a weekend,' but for good."[16]

Although neither Mansfield nor Morse attended the meeting with U Thant, a few weeks later Mansfield proposed a new approach through the U.N. which he and Morse then discussed with the President. In a memorandum to the President on April 29, 1967, Mansfield suggested that the U.S. should invite the North Vietnamese, the NLF, and China, as well as the South Vietnamese, to present to the U.N. Security Council their views on the war and on possible solutions, while at the same time the U.S. should seek an advisory opinion from the International Court of Justice (World Court) on the applicability of the Geneva Accords of 1954 to the situation in Vietnam.[17]

In his memorandum, Mansfield also said that "our bombings will continue to make Hanoi ever more heavily dependent on China," and that "the road to settlement with Hanoi, now, very likely runs by way of Peking rather than Moscow." He renewed a suggestion he said he had made earlier of a "quiet and clearly conciliatory approach to China," which he said he could undertake to make with the President's approval, to explore the Chinese view of a possible settlement of the war as well as the "restoration of more normal relations throughout the Western Pacific."

After Mansfield's memorandum reached the White House, Rostow met with Katzenbach and Goldberg to discuss it and reported on April 30 to the President: "They agree it's a gimmick. Nick leans against; Arthur for."[18]

Rusk also talked to Goldberg and Katzenbach, and, according to another memorandum on April 30 from Rostow to the President, Rusk said he was prepared to take Mansfield's proposal to the Security Council but that Mansfield "should be clear that this proposal will be opposed by the Secretary General and a number of other members of the Security Council who will not wish to press this proposal because Hanoi has made it clear that it does not wish

---

[16] *New York Times*, March 23, 1967. On Apr. 1, 1967, Senator Clark proposed that on April 15 the U.S. should declare a unilateral cease-fire, both in bombing the North and in military operations in the South, in the hope that U Thant could arrange for the North Vietnamese to reciprocate, and that negotiations could then begin. U Thant endorsed Clark's proposal, saying that the impasse in Vietnam could be broken "only if one side or the other shows the wisdom and the courage and the compassion for humanity to take the initiative on the first step. . . . The United States, with power and wealth unprecedented in human history, is in a position to take this initiative." Goldberg replied that the United States had already accepted U Thant's three-point plan of January 1966, except that the U.S. wanted talks on details of the truce to precede the cease-fire, whereas, as U Thant had said many times, the North Vietnamese would not talk until bombing had stopped. *Washington Post*, Apr. 2, 1967. On April 3, Senator Byrd of West Virginia criticized U Thant's statement. See *CR*, vol. 113, pp. 8023–8024.

[17] Johnson Library, NSF Name File, Mansfield, Memorandum from Mansfield to the President, "Vietnam," Apr. 29, 1967.

[18] Same location.

the United Nations to get in a peace-making role in southeast Asia."[19]

Concerning the World Court proposal, Rusk said that the court did not have jurisdiction and that few members of the court would support a move to accept jurisdiction.

Rusk disagreed with Mansfield's contention that the road to peace was through Peking, and said he was "strongly opposed" to Mansfield's suggestion that he (Mansfield) should undertake a mission to China. According to Rostow's memo, Rusk said that it would be "a major intervention in a troubled situation. The Soviet Union would be upset and suspicious. Above all, Senator Mansfield should remember that he is 'an officer of the United States Government,' as a member of the legislative branch. Therefore there would be great confusion among our friends in free Asia, including the fear that we were about to sell them out." Rusk said the proper way to proceed would be to elevate to the foreign ministers' level the informal talks then going on in Warsaw between the U.S. Ambassador and a representative of the Chinese Government, but he said he had wanted to wait "until the situation within Communist China has somewhat settled down."[20]

In his memorandum to the President, Rostow said that he generally agreed with Rusk.

The next day (May 1), the President, joined by Rusk, Rostow, Katzenbach, Goldberg and Califano, had a breakfast meeting from 8:30 a.m. to 10:03 a.m. with Mansfield and Morse to discuss the matter. There is no record of their conversation.

On May 2 the President held a luncheon meeting from 1:27 p.m. to 2:50 p.m. with Rusk, McNamara, Walt Rostow and Press Secretary George Christian for another discussion.[21] There are no

---

[19] Same location.

[20] The Warsaw talks between the U.S. and China (the Ambassadors to Poland of the two countries), had begun in 1958 and by 1967 there had been about 135 meetings. There is very little available information on the nature and content of the talks, but they would appear to have been an important diplomatic channel between the U.S. and China during the period when the U.S. had not recognized the Chinese Communist Government and did not have diplomatic representatives in China. In the mid-1960s, after the U.S. became heavily involved in Vietnam, this was the private channel through which the U.S. sent and received messages on U.S. and Chinese actions and policy in the war. See Smith, *An International History of the Vietnam War*, vol. III.

[21] In a memorandum to Rusk that morning in which he commented on some of the issues which were scheduled to be discussed at the meeting, William Bundy had advised against going to the U.N., saying that he had read a paper by Joseph Sisco (Assistant Secretary of State for International Organization Affairs) on the pros and cons of taking the matter to the Security Council and that he "came out overwhelmingly negative." (Sisco's paper, "Possible Recourse to United Nations on Vietnam, May 2, 1967, which was prepared for the May 2 White House meeting and apparently was discussed at the meeting, is in U.S. Department of State, Central File, Pol 27 Viet S, appended to a memorandum to Rusk from Sisco, "Possible Security Council Consideration of the Vietnam Problem," May 12, 1967.)

Some of Sisco's major "pro" arguments were that such a move would help to demonstrate U.S. determination to seek a settlement, and that Mansfield and Morse's endorsement of the proposal could help it to obtain broad public support. Moreover, if the Security Council voted to consider the proposal, the ensuing debate "might possibly open some new diplomatic avenue towards a peaceful settlement. At the very least, direct contact with Hanoi, the Viet Cong, Peking, the Co-Chairmen of the Geneva Conference [the U.S.S.R. and Britain], and the members of the International Control Commission, if it could be achieved, might put into train some new dialogue." If the Communists refused to participate in the U.N. debate, they would "bear a substantial part of the onus for the collapse of the initiative."

"In the past," Sisco added, "we have sought to avoid putting the Soviets on the spot unduly in hopes they would press Hanoi towards a peaceful solution. Since the Soviets are not being helpful to this end and at this time, we need not hesitate in putting them in the docket."

Among the principal "con" arguments was that it was unlikely the U.S. could get the nine votes required for the issue to be put on the agenda of the Security Council. In the earlier effort in February 1966, it had been put on the agenda with only nine affirmative votes, only, Sisco

known notes of the meeting, but a memorandum several days later stated that the President had decided to defer the question of Security Council actions at least until June, and that he had "expressed particular concern that any resort to the Security Council not interfere with our military operations in Vietnam."[22] In a memorandum to the President later that day, Rostow said, "As you gathered at today's lunch, Sec. Rusk thinks, on balance, we can go ahead, but play it low key and try to make it appear credible."[23]

There was a second breakfast meeting on May 3 from 8:30 a.m. to 9:55 a.m. of the President with Mansfield, Morse, Rusk, Rostow, Katzenbach and Goldberg to continue the discussion of May 1, but, again, there are no known notes of the meeting.

After the breakfast on May 3, Mansfield sent the President a memorandum in which he said:[24]

> Mr. Katzenbach put his finger on a key problem with his reference to the possibility of an international interpretation of the proposal as a "phony." If we give the slightest pretext for such an interpretation, it would almost guarantee the failure of the proposal.
>
> Certainly I would want no part of any "phony" proposal and I cannot imagine anyone in position of responsibility in this government proceeding on that basis. The danger, as I see it, is not that we would take a "phony" initiative. The danger is that a bonafide initiative in the U.N. might be subject to such an interpretation because of some unwitting action or ineptitude in its pursuit. That might be the case, for example, in any of the following circumstances.
>
> 1. if the tone of the initiative is such as to suggest that we are advancing the proposal to prove that only we want peace and that Hanoi has not the slightest interest in negotiations;
>
> 2. if the initiative is accompanied, coincidentally, by some announcement of a new military enterprise on our part in Viet Nam or a significant intensification of military activity;

---

said, "by applying maximum pressure on Jordan." But he said that the present composition of the Security Council was not as favorable. The likely vote would be: *For:* Argentina, Brazil, Canada, [Nationalist] China, Japan, U.K., U.S.; *Against:* Bulgaria, France, India, Mali, U.S.S.R.; *Abstain:* Denmark, Ethiopia, Nigeria. "Maximum pressure," he added, "would have to be applied on Denmark, Ethiopia, and Nigeria."

Failure to get the nine votes, Sisco said, would be construed as a defeat for the U.S. and lack of support for U.S. policy. Moreover, in connection with U.N. Security Council consideration of the issue, the U.S. would be pressed to make concessions, especially suspension of bombing of North Vietnam.

In addition, because the proposal came during a period of increased U.S. military action "and in the context of well known Communist opposition to U.N. involvement, the U.S.S.R., many non-aligned countries, and even U.S. allies, would interpret the move as a "cynical ploy," and the proposal would not be taken as credible.

Further, if the U.N. decided to hear the U.S. proposal and to take up the case, there would be pressure on the U.S. to refrain from intensifying military operations.

The reaction of the North Vietnamese would probably be that the U.S. action indicated weakness and irresolution, and U.S. allies would tend to interpret it "as a nervous reaction motivated primarily by domestic considerations." "I really think," Bundy said, "the whole exercise . . . would give the wrong signal to Hanoi and tend to put our good faith in jeopardy in whatever quarters were consulted or heard of it. It simply has no serious chance of making a substantive contribution at present, and it would be regarded, in my honest judgment, as a rather cheap piece of theater that was really totally cynical in view of our bombing actions of these weeks." (Same location, Memorandum to Rusk from William Bundy, "Bombing Program and UN Approach—Information Memorandum for Today's Lunch," May 2, 1967.

[22] Sisco memorandum to Rusk, May 12, 1967, cited above.

[23] Johnson Library, NSF Files of Mike Mansfield, Memorandum for the President from Rostow, May 2, 1967.

[24] Same location.

3. if "anonymous officials" leak to the press non-attributed explanations of the purposes of the initiative as anything other than a straightforward desire to proceed at once through the U.N. to try to find a path to peace and if these leaks are not promptly disavowed by the appropriate information officers of the White House, the Departments of State and Defense, the Embassy in Saigon, the U.S. Mission at the U.N., and other appropriate officers.

If, in the pursuit of a U.N. initiative, the above pitfalls cannot be avoided by the Executive Branch, then it would seem to me preferable not to pursue the proposal at all.

In speeches in the Senate on May 15, 18, and 24, Mansfield continued to urge that the U.S. should seek a peace conference through the U.N. On May 18, Rusk told reporters that the administration was considering the possibility. He said the U.S. had been in favor of such a move, but that the North Vietnamese and the Soviet Union were opposed.[25]

At a news conference on May 18, the President was also asked to comment, and his reply was that he would "welcome any constructive action" the UN might take, but, in answer to another question he said that his objectives in the war had not changed and that his determination to persevere was "just as strong as it has ever been."[26]

Proposals for Congressional Action

During this period in the spring of 1967, as U.S. military and nonmilitary programs intensified and an increasing number of Senators and Representatives, while voting for appropriations for the war, were becoming more concerned about the situation, Fulbright and others on the Foreign Relations Committee and on its staff continued to consider what the committee could and should do. The committee had not held a public session with Rusk since February 1966, but efforts to arrange for a public hearing had been rebuffed. On April 27, Fulbright again inquired whether Rusk would testify in a public session on U.S. foreign policy, and Rusk replied that he would be pleased to do so but that the meeting should be in executive session rather than in public.[27] (The hearing was held—in executive session—on May 23, but the situation in the Middle East [the Israeli-Arab "Six Day" war] was about to erupt and it dominated the session.)

On May 4, perhaps prompted in part by Fulbright's effort to get Rusk to testify publicly on Vietnam, the President commented to a White House assistant that Press Secretary George Christian "should someday get a carefully prepared statement saying the President is not going to argue with Fulbright. He will depend on the basic fairness of the American people. This man is doing everything he can to create problems for the President who is doing ev-

[25] For Mansfield's statements see *CR,* vol. 113, pp. 12593–12594, 13213–13214, 13728. For Rusk's, see the *New York Times,* May 19, 1967.

[26] *Public Papers of the Presidents,* Lyndon B. Johnson, 1967, pp. 543, 547.

[27] U.S. Department of State, Lot File 74 D 164, letter from Rusk to Fulbright, May 2, 1967, with Fulbright's letter of April 27 attached.

erything he can to make the best of a difficult situation. Less caustic carping and more constructive criticism would be welcome."[28]

Two ideas were being considered within the Foreign Relations Committee staff. One was to hold public hearings with primarily academic witnesses on the role of the Senate in the making of foreign policy and in decisions to go to war. This was suggested in a memorandum to Fulbright from Seth Tillman, a member of the committee staff, on May 8.[29]

The other idea was to hold further hearings on Vietnam with public witnesses, academic and nonacademic. In a memorandum to Fulbright on May 16, Chief of Staff Marcy noted that the committee had been discussing a number of other subjects "while public protest takes such forms as marches on Washington, draft-card burnings, and sleeping on the Pentagon steps." "This Committee," he said, "has a duty—a constitutional duty—to advise. We also have a duty to listen to petitioners. . . ." "Hopefully," he said, such hearings "will be instructive to the Committee and, hopefully, will let off some of the steam now being generated by frustrated citizens who cannot get a hearing except by engaging in acts of violence or public protest."[30]

Marcy suggested four days of hearings during June, the first on the role of Congress in foreign policy, as suggested by Tillman, the second on "U.S. interests in Vietnam," the third on domestic impact of U.S. policy in Vietnam, and the fourth on foreign impact.

Meanwhile, Fulbright apparently had decided to talk to Russell, chairman of the Armed Services Committee, about the possibility of working together on the problem of Vietnam, and on May 18, Marcy sent Fulbright a memorandum suggesting points that he might want to raise with Russell.[31] Constitutionally, Marcy said, it was the responsibility of the Foreign Relations and Armed Services Committees to advise the President on the U.S. national interest. "There is growing evidence that the U.S. may be 'hellbent' to stay in Asia 'till the end of the century' in the words of General Wheeler or, as Secretary Rusk predicts, 'It's going to be useful for some time to come for American power to be able to control every move of the Pacific, if necessary.' If these aims are in the 'national interest,' then the Armed Services and Foreign Relations Committees have a duty to begin now to build up U.S. forces and rally national support. If these aims are *not* in the national interest, it is *only* these Committees that can call a halt." (emphases in original)

Marcy posed three possible collaborative efforts for Fulbright to suggest to Russell: first, a joint subcommittee of five members from each of their committees to hold public hearings on Vietnam and the national interest; second, support of a resolution "expressing the sense of the Senate that the U.S. national interest is so directly involved in Vietnam the U.S. should commit such resources as may be necessary to confirm U.S. domination of the area; and, third, whether Russell would join Fulbright in a private discussion with

[28] Johnson Library, Ex FG 1 ND 19/CO 312, unsigned note, May 4, 1967, with notation "J. [James R.] Jones passed this to George on 5–4–67, 10 pm."

[29] National Archives, RG 46, Papers of the Senate Foreign Relations Committee, Memorandum to Fulbright from Tillman, "Hearings on the Role of the Senate in the Making of Foreign Policy, May 8, 1967. In the memorandum, Tillman listed the names of possible witnesses.

[30] Same location, Marcy Chron File, Memorandum to Fulbright from Marcy, May 16, 1967.

[31] Same location, Memorandum to Fulbright from Marcy, May 18, 1967.

the President on "the growing concern of the Senate," in which they could also indicate the possibility of joint hearings on U.S. interests and submit to the President a proposal for disengagement.[32]

Fulbright and Russell had lunch on May 18, and the next day Fulbright sent him a note with which he enclosed a memorandum prepared by Marcy on how joint hearings—which Russell apparently thought had some merit—could be handled.[33]

On the note Fulbright added this handwritten comment: "I really believe such hearings would make them [the Executive] examine their premises with more care and in greater depth, and I think they would help the atmosphere here on the Hill, which gets pretty ugly at times."

As submitted to Russell, Fulbright's proposal was that a joint subcommittee of five members from each of the two committees hold hearings with the following focus:

> 1. What precisely is the nature and extent of the United States national interest in Southeast Asia, Vietnam in particular?

---

[32] A copy of a draft of this proposal was attached to his memorandum to Fulbright on May 18, cited above. Marcy had been developing the idea for some months, and had sent in a slightly different version to Senator Aiken on May 8, with the comment that he or Percy or Hatfield "might grab it." Same location, Memorandum to Senator Aiken from Carl Marcy, May 8, 1967, with attached "Proposal for Honorable Disengagement in Vietnam," May 8, 1967.)

Marcy's proposal began with the following statement: "*The fundamental national interest of the United States in Southeast Asia is to maintain such base facilities there as will protect the sea and air routes of the area from domination by hostile forces, and to do so without involving American manpower in combat with the manpower of Asia.*" (emphasis in original) "Subsidiary national interests might include 'stopping aggression' wherever it occurs, protecting General Ky and his supporters, promoting 'Democracy' or individual freedom in Vietnam, and stopping the expansion of China."

The memorandum continued:

"In order to protect the fundamental national interest the following proposal is submitted:

"The President should state a Johnson doctrine for Asia somewhat as follows:

"Three Presidents have conceived that the interests of world peace and the defense of free people in Southeast Asia required the U.S. military defense of South Vietnam.

"Despite numerous appeals and the sacrifice of many American lives to these ends, neither the peoples, the Governments of the states directly concerned, nor the majority of the members of the United Nations, have been willing to support the U.S. and its few allies in this judgment.

"Therefore, it is the intention of this Administration to re-fashion its policies in Southeast Asia so as to support the fundamental national interests of the United States as distinct from its heretofore more ephemeral efforts to extend unilaterally its power in such a way as to promote its conception of 'world peace' generally or the defense of 'free people.'

"To give effect to this statement, the United States will, in the months ahead, with care and discrimination take the following steps:

"1. The United States will by January, 1969 withdraw all American forces to a base area in South Vietnam which will be about 1500 square miles in area (Cam Ranh Bay), establishing there a *permanent* base which will be maintained for the purpose of protecting international sea and air routes, responding to such acts of international aggression as the United Nations determines exist, and for the purpose of providing protection for political refugees in the area. [emphasis in original]

"2. The United States will withdraw from this base area at such time as the foregoing purposes can be achieved by the United Nations or by states within the area.

"3. The United States will reconsider this decision only provided that not less than six months prior to January 1969 a majority of the states of the United Nations by resolution request the United States to continue its military action in South Vietnam as in the interest of international peace and security or, provided a majority of the Asian governments directly concerned ask the United States to remain in Vietnam and are willing to support the continued American presence there with substantial contributions of manpower and materiel."

Marcy also wanted the State Department to be apprised of his proposal. At a luncheon which he arranged on May 17 with George C. Denney, Jr., deputy director of Intelligence and Research in the Department, who had previously been on the staff of the Foreign Relations Committee, he discussed the plan, and Denney then summarized the conversation in a memorandum which was sent to several officials in the department. A copy of Denney's memorandum is in the National Archives, RG 46, Papers of the Senate Foreign Relations Committee.

[33] Same location, Letter to Russell from Fulbright, May 19, 1967, with attached draft of proposed joint hearings, May 19, 1967.

2. To what lengths in terms of manpower and materiel should the United States go to support this interest?

3. What evidence is there leading to the conclusion that China, and eventually the Russians, will not eventually become directly involved in the war, and does the national interest require a military victory in that case?

4. Should China become involved, what nations may be expected to ally themselves with the United States?

IN SUMMARY: the fundamental question to be examined is whether the United States may have gradually re-defined its "national interest" to mean that the United States must do in Southeast Asia what neither the United Nations nor the states directly in the area are either willing or capable of doing, i.e. "stopping aggression" or promoting "peace and security."

If the fundamental national interest of the United States were defined more narrowly as the maintenance in Southeast Asia of such base facilities there as will protect the sea and air routes of the area from domination by hostile forces (Admiral Mahan), and to do so without involving American manpower in combat with the manpower of Asia (General Ridgway, General Bradley, and others), is our present military involvement in Vietnam still justified?

Fulbright suggested as government witnesses Rusk, McNamara, Walt Rostow, General Taylor and General Wheeler. Public witnesses could include General Omar Bradley, historian Henry Steele Commager, and China specialist John Fairbank.

There are no known notes of the Fulbright-Russell conversation nor is there further available information on its outcome. No joint hearings were held, no resolution was introduced, and there was no discussion between the two men and the President. Several weeks later, however, as will be seen, Fulbright and Russell agreed on a resolution that led to hearings and Senate action to assert the role of Congress in the making of "national commitments."

On May 15, 1967, amid reports that the President was considering sending more troops to Vietnam and speculation that the U.S. was considering an invasion of North Vietnam—to which the Chinese responded that if this happened they would send their own forces to help the North Vietnamese—Senator John Sherman Cooper warned in a speech that increased U.S. military activity might foreclose the possibility of negotiations and bring China and the Soviet Union into the war.[34] There was even the "dread possibility," Cooper said, "that the matching of power by power will lead relentlessly to a third world war."

To prevent further escalation, Cooper urged that the U.S. limit bombing to the southern Panhandle of North Vietnam (the same proposal as that being made in the executive branch by most of the President's associates), and, if the North Vietnamese responded by indicating an interest in negotiating, the U.S. should then suspend all bombing of the North in the interest of achieving a negotiated settlement.

[34] Cooper's speech and comments by other Senators are in *CR*, vol. 113, pp. 12578–12610. See also the *New York Times*, May 16, 1967.

The depth of concern in the Senate about the possible consequences of escalating the war, and the need to take restraining action that would encourage negotiations, was indicated by the comments on Cooper's statement by Senator Milton Young of North Dakota, a conservative Republican who had supported the war. Young did not have a national reputation and was not an active participant in foreign policy matters, but he was well-regarded in the Senate, and when he rose to commend Cooper for his speech, saying that he found "much merit" to Cooper's proposal, those who understood the Senate knew that Young's remarks were a further sign that the consensus on the war was crumbling. Young did not criticize the administration or oppose the war. In fact, he continued to support the war and to oppose amendments limiting U.S. action. But he was troubled by the cost and lack of success of the war, and he was worried, as were many congressional supporters of the war, that the U.S. was mired in Vietnam and would stay mired unless a way could be found to end the conflict. "This war," he said, "has been going on for some time and it could go on for years and years to come. I am fearful that even after we win—and we shall win one day—it will be necessary for us to keep several hundreds of thousands of troops there for years to come."

Cooper's colleague, from Kentucky, Senator Thruston Morton, who was chairman of the Senate Republican Campaign Committee, and formerly Assistant Secretary of State for Congressional Relations in the Eisenhower administration, was also beginning to question the war, and he praised Cooper's proposal for limiting bombing. Morton had supported the war, although never enthusiastically, but he wanted to keep it limited, both because of the nature of the war and of U.S. goals and because of his concern that the public was becoming more militant and that this, in turn, could make it more difficult for the U.S. to achieve a negotiated settlement. In a Senate speech on May 11, 1967, Morton noted that U.S. pacification activities had just been put under direct military command (the appointment of Komer to serve under Westmoreland), and he wondered whether this would lead to the assignment of U.S. forces to carry out pacification.[35] Noting that American forces had recently been sent to the delta to help with pacification in that area, he warned that the U.S. should not attempt to take the place of Vietnamese forces in pacification, "an operation that, while difficult for the Vietnamese, is probably impossible for Americans, as it was for the French before us." The use of U.S. forces for pacification, he said, "could very well become another step in the Americanization of the entire conflict." He added:

> [T]he course of the war in Vietnam, and the spiraling American participation in it, has been an almost unbroken series of promising programs followed by disappointing results followed by increased U.S. involvement followed by promising programs.

The question of using U.S. forces in pacification should be carefully examined, Morton said. "I have no doubts that if we had asked searching questions about the prospects in Vietnam 5 years ago rather than allowing ourselves to be soothed by administration

[35] *CR*, vol. 113, p. 12494.

reassurances, we would not find ourselves sinking further into an Asian quagmire today."

Senator Eugene McCarthy, a Democrat from Minnesota and a member of the Foreign Relations Committee, took a position similar to Morton. "It appears," he said, "that we are on the threshold of a period in which demands for some kind of all-out and total war may be made. Once that demand is made, the disposition is for the country to make a kind of total response, and what should be a shared objective . . . made on a rational basis becomes overburdened with demands for attacks on China and total war." McCarthy, who within several months would decide to run for President, partly out of concern for the way in which he felt the President was ignoring the constitutional role of Congress in the making of foreign policy and war, added that Senators had a constitutional responsibility to speak out on the war in order to attempt to influence the making of policy. Those who drafted the Constitution, he said, if they had known how important foreign policy would become, would have provided a "different procedure whereby our suggestions could be brought to bear," but, lacking that, it was incumbent for Senators to express their views on the Senate floor.[36]

Other Senators joined in praising Cooper's proposals, including Mansfield, Church, Aiken, Fulbright, Pell, Carlson, and Morse.[37]

Three days earlier (May 12), the President got opposite advice from Senator Russell at a private, informal White House dinner of the President, Russell, Mrs. Johnson, and Presidential counsel, Harry McPherson, following a meeting of the President and his senior advisers earlier that day to discuss the bombing of North Vietnam:[38]

> At dinner, the President told Senator Russell that what he needed to talk to him about was Vietnam (it was obvious that the two had discussed the same matter earlier in the evening). The President outlined three choices open to him:
>
> "1. I can move further in the North—but they tell me that moving further in the north with the bombing will result in only killing civilians and will not accomplish anything that we've not already accomplished.
>
> "2. I can concentrate completely on the DMZ.
>
> "3. I can concentrate on the areas between the seventeenth and twentieth parallels and make my planes make that a desert. Just destroy anything that moves."
>
> Senator Russell feels that dragging this out each day leans more toward getting us in a big war. "We've just got to finish it soon," said the Senator, "because time is working against you both here and there." The Senator suggested that his feel-

---

[36] *Ibid.*, pp. 12582–12583.

[37] Commenting on the Senate speeches, James Reston said in his column in the *New York Times* on May 17, 1967 that the debate "had a different tone. Last winter's loud and strenuous argument between hawks and doves has given way to a kind of distracted anxiety. The President's critics are no longer shouting at him to turn back, but imploring him to be careful. It is not that they are resigned to the steadily rising violence, but merely that they feel helpless to do anything about it. . . . The issue here is no longer whether the United States can crush the enemy, but what the consequences of doing so will be." There was a "new mood of apprehension in Washington," Reston added. "It is not merely that Senators feel helpless to change the present course of the war, but the fear that the President himself has set in motion a train of action that he cannot wholly control."

[38] Johnson Library, notes typed on the President's Daily Diary for May 12, 1967, by a White House secretary who was present at the dinner.

ing was that the only way to end the war was to blockade the ports and stop their lines of supply. . . . The President expressed sincere belief that this would get us into war sooner than anything. He also felt that number (1) above would get us into war. "The only thing left to take out up there," said the President, "is a power plant which is located ½ mile from Ho's headquarters." "Suppose we missed," said the President.

On May 17, under the leadership of Church, a group of 16 Senators issued a statement that had been coordinated with the State Department in which they sought to make clear that while they disagreed with U.S. policy in Vietnam and wanted a negotiated settlement, they were opposed to unilateral U.S. withdrawal. Intended for the benefit of the North Vietnamese, the statement, "A Plea for Realism," said: "The conflict now appears to have reached an acute phase. At this critical juncture, it would be tragic indeed if there were any misconceptions in Hanoi about the realities of the political situation in the United States. . . . The signers of this declaration . . . share the conviction that the tragic war in Vietnam should be ended by negotiations of a mutually acceptable settlement. However, in the absence of such a settlement, we remain steadfastly opposed to any unilateral withdrawal of American troops from South Vietnam."[39]

After a Harris Survey on May 17, 1967, showed substantial public support for "total military victory,"[40] Senator Morton warned in a speech in the Senate on May 23 that the Johnson administration had not adequately explained the nature of the war and of U.S. goals, and that the public was being led to believe that "military victory" was possible.[41] What, he asked, did "total military victory" mean?

> It means successfully carrying out a pacification program in South Vietnam with American troops. It means locating and identifying those dissident Vietnamese who now control 75 percent of that nation's 12,000 hamlets. It means persuading them of the righteousness of the Saigon junta's cause, or putting them in concentration camps, or killing them.
>
> Total military victory in South Vietnam means destroying or driving out the main force units from the north, and preventing their re-entry. According to a high Defense Department official, it means, "anywhere from half-a-million to 2 million U.S. troops" to win the war in as little as 5 years.
>
> But let us not forget North Vietnam. In order to prevent that country from continuing its policy of aggression and subversion against South Vietnam, we would have to demolish her military installations and much of her population centers from the

---

[39] The statement was signed by Democrats Church, McGovern, Fulbright, Moss, Bartlett, Metcalf, Hartke, Nelson, Burdick, Clark, Young, Robert Kennedy, Morse, and Pell, and Republicans Cooper and Hatfield. See the text and comments by Church and others in *CR*, vol. 113, pp. 13011–13013. See also the *New York Times* for May 17 and 18, 1967.

The statement was supported by 18 liberal House Democrats: George Brown, Phillip Burton, Jeffrey Cohelan, Don Edwards, Augustus F. Hawkins, Thomas M. Rees, and Edward Roybal, all from California, and by Jonathan Bingham, Leonard Farbstein, Benjamin S. Rosenthal, James H. Scheuer from New York, John Conyers, Jr. of Michigan, Donald Fraser of Minnesota, Edith Green of Oregon, Henry Helstoski of New Jersey, Robert W. Kastenmeier of Wisconsin, Patsy T. Mink of Hawaii, and Sidney R. Yates of Illinois.

[40] For the results of the May 17 Harris Survey, see p. 692 below.

[41] *CR*, vol. 113, pp. 13534–13535.

air. And to do a really thorough job, we would have to mount a massive land invasion, defeat her armies in the field, and be prepared to occupy the ground taken for the foreseeable future.

And what about Laos and Cambodia? Could these countries be effectively neutralized from without, or would the United States have to go in with military might and set up a military government?

And then there is China. Seventeen years ago, the vision of an American army chasing the North Koreans toward the Yalu brought us into bloody battle with a million Chinese "volunteers." At what stage of the course toward total military victory can we expect to run into the Chinese army, supported by modern nuclear weaponry? And what of the Soviet Union. How long will it be in her national interest to limit assistance to Hanoi, or would it by then be China, to technical and logistical support?

"These are harsh and perhaps exaggerated questions, Morton added. "But I believe the administration is committing a tragic oversight if it permits the dangerous illusion to persist across our country that total military victory in Vietnam is in the cards. I believe an unhealthy and unproductive war fever is mounting in the United States, and that only the most careful and calculated program initiated from the White House will be able to lower the temperature."

"War fever," Morton said, could make it difficult for the U.S. to achieve its "stated policy of reaching a negotiated settlement with limited objectives." "If the polls are right, if nearly half of the American people believe that a total military victory in Vietnam is possible and vital to our national interest, then there is going to be hell to pay if we settle for anything less."

Pell's Diplomatic Initiative

That same day (May 23, 1967), Senator Claiborne Pell, Democrat of Rhode Island and a member and future chairman of the Foreign Relations Committee, made a major Senate speech on the importance of keeping the war from escalating and on the need for a Government in South Vietnam that would, as he put it, "reflect all the diverse political forces of the area" and lead to a settlement of the war and to military neutralization of all of Indochina.[42]

Pell generally agreed with Mansfield's position on the need to settle the war, but he also took the position, as did Mansfield, that the U.S. should not withdraw unilaterally. To do so, as he had said in a speech in 1965, would leave a "vacuum" in that part of Asia.[43] "I believe we must continue to hold on, seeking to arrive at a point when we can honorably negotiate a reasonable, solid, and forceful agreement that meets the interests of the Geneva powers, of ourselves, and, most important, of the Vietnamese people."

Pell began his speech by expressing concern about what he sensed was the "growing impatience and frustration regarding the

---

[42] *Ibid.*, pp. 13498–13502. Mansfield, Morse and Gore praised it as a thoughtful, well-balanced speech. Morse, referring to Pell's earlier experience as a Foreign Service Officer, said it was "one of the most constructive contributions that has been made to the historic debate on Vietnam that has been going on in this Chamber for 3½ years."

[43] See pt. III of this study, p. 82.

Vietnam war" that led people to favor escalation "without recognizing that achieving a military victory through constant escalation will probably lead, at best and only after many more deaths, to a permanent commitment of hundreds of thousands of our young men and billions of dollars annually for many years to come." "More important, such a so-called victory will, I believe, contain the seeds of far greater future bitterness and disaster. . . . [T]he most probable end result of continued escalation . . . will be a vacuum of power in North Vietnam which would, of necessity, be filled by China, with consequences hurtful to our national interest." If the Chinese come into North Vietnam, we will obviously be drawn into the conflict far more than is even now the case. Popular opinion at home may well demand we erase China's nuclear potential." If the Chinese used troops, there would be "domestic clamor for us to use nuclear weapons. . . ." If this happened, he said, the U.S.S.R. might join the war, and "all of us know the result of such an eventuality."

The "main reason" for U.S. involvement in the Vietnam war, Pell added, was that otherwise a stand would have to be taken against Communist expansion in other countries. "But have we not by our valiant, lengthy stand, already made this point and underlined it in scarlet?"

"To my mind," Pell said, "America's national interest, Vietnam's national interest, and the world's self-interest are all the same when it comes to the common aim of achieving a sane resolution to the conflict in Vietnam. To cool it down, to slow down, would appear to me the correct, commonsense, immediate course to follow." This could also lead to a settlement: "If, by following this course, we can demonstrate in South Vietnam that we are willing to face a low-key, minimum-casualty, long drawn out struggle in preference to a high-key, high-casualty war that has a good chance of escalating into world war III, then it would obviously be to the advantage of the North Vietnamese and the National Liberation Front to negotiate with us since they would have no other way to get us out of their area."

As a first step toward cooling and slowing down the war, Pell proposed that the U.S. should cease bombing the North and refrain from increasing its troop strength in the South. Search-and-destroy missions should be curtailed, and U.S. forces should be used to secure and assist the more economically viable and populous areas. "We would, of course, not assume a 'sitting duck' position but would continue to engage in active patrolling around these areas, searching out and eliminating any offensive Vietcong efforts to attack us."

While ceasing bombing and holding the existing level of troops, the U.S. should seek "either North Vietnamese assurance or some responsible third party guarantee that the North Vietnamese will not increase their level of men in the south and will negotiate and agree upon a cease-fire and an end to the violence." This, Pell said, should be followed by these steps:

> First, verified free election, with candidacies for office and right to vote open to every citizen of South Vietnam;
>
> Second, in accordance with principles of self-determination, internal affairs of South Vietnam, including constitutional is-

sues, to be settled by the South Vietnam Government resulting from the [1967] election;

Third, agreement in principle to eventual complete American withdrawal of troops, and withdrawal in fact based on completion of arrangements leading to election, replacement by Asian troops, and the withdrawal of North Vietnamese forces;

Fourth, immediate release of all political prisoners, amnesty for any political actions in the past, and right of asylum for any South Vietnamese wishing it.

"In the civilian sector," Pell added, "we would press harder for more education, public health, improved agricultural methods, and the start of industry. More particularly, we should return the American responsibility for pacification from our Army to civilian leadership and encourage increasing Vietnamese direction. . . ."

The U.S., Pell added, should seek to work through the United Nations "to the maximum extent possible," and "should particularly seek more participation by other Asian nations to dispel the notion that this is a white man's war or that the regime which follows it will be an extension of white colonialism. And we should strive to achieve a military neutralization of the whole of Southeast Asia, guaranteed either by the Geneva Convention powers together with the United States, or by the United Nations."

In negotiations, Pell said, the U.S. and North Vietnam "must return to the Geneva Convention [of 1954] and follow it; on our part, accepting the fact that we must negotiate with the Vietcong and accepting the possibility that a nationalist Communist regime may eventually emerge."

If, in the pending election, Ky or Thieu were elected President, Pell said, that government "would remain in power just as long as we would continue to shore it up with a quarter-million-man occupation force and several billions of dollars a year . . . there simply will be no broad political base for that government. The presently scheduled election will not permit the large numbers of people in the National Liberation Front areas to vote, and even those in the Ky government areas who believe in a neutral solution will be denied a choice, because no candidate offering this view will be allowed."

After his speech, Pell stopped in Paris en route to a meeting in Geneva, where he talked to John Gunther Dean in the American Embassy about seeing Mai Van Bo, the senior North Vietnamese diplomat in Paris. (In 1965, prior to major U.S. troop deployment, Pell suggested to the State Department that it might be useful for him to have a private conversation with Bo, but the Department discouraged it.)[44] He told Dean that he would like to discuss Vietnam and would like to get some reaction from the North Vietnamese to his May 23 speech. However, if the State Department felt that such a contact would be adverse to U.S. interests he said he would not proceed. Dean replied, in the words of a cable from U.S. Ambassador Charles Bohlen sent that day to Washington, "that it appeared to him that Mai Van Bo might interpret and publicize Senator's initiative as evidence [of] increasing lack of support in US for administration's policy and that therefore Senator's initiative

[44] See pt. III of this study, pp. 257–279.

might harden DRV position and make North Vietnamese persist in their present inflexible policy rather than move Hanoi closer to accepting compromise solution."[45] Alternatively, Dean suggested, Pell might send a copy of his speech to Mai Van Bo through his old friend from his Foreign Service days,[46] Etienne Manac'h, Director of Asian Affairs in the French Foreign Office, who could then report to Pell on Bo's reactions.

Pell also saw Bohlen, who, as he had said in his cable he would do, sought to discourage Pell from seeing Bo. (The Department of State replied that Dean's response to Pell was "entirely right," and agreed that Bohlen should reinforce Dean's reply. Before leaving for Paris, the cable added, Pell had talked to Harriman about the idea of seeing Bo, and Harriman also discouraged the idea.)

According to Pell, the French Embassy in Washington had sent a copy of the May 23 speech to Paris, where the Foreign Office, presumably Manac'h, sent it to Hanoi. While in Paris, Pell told Manac'h that he was available to talk to Bo.[47]

On his return from Geneva, Pell stopped in Paris, but missed a call from Manac'h saying that Bo would like to talk to him.[48] After receiving a letter from Manac'h on about June 17 saying that Bo was not only willing but "desirous" of seeing him, Pell went back to Paris on June 19, saw Bo for one and a half hours, and returned to Washington the same day. Pell said in an interview several years later, "I took a flight over, and I was worried about the Logan Act, worried about finding Marines at the other end blocking me from getting off the American plane, so I took an Air France plane."[49]

In a memorandum on his conversation with Bo (who, the memorandum states, "was expressly authorized by his government to talk with me"), Pell reported that Bo kept repeating that North Vietnam would negotiate if and when bombing of the North ended "'without condition.'" Pell asked whether an agreement not to increase the level of forces in South Vietnam or a "mutual deescalation of violence" might be included in a diplomatic package on ending the bombing. Bo replied that he "'took note of this thought.'" He added that the other proposals made by Pell in his speech could be discussed during negotiations.

Pell "emphasized that the mood of the American people was to escalate the war and that our Administration is subject to far more pressure to escalate, rather than to deescalate." Bo did not deny this, but said, according to Pell's memorandum of the conversation,

---

[45] U.S. Department of State, Central File, Pol 27 Viet S, Paris to Washington 19123, May 25, 1967.

[46] Pell had been in the Foreign Service before his election to the Senate.

[47] These and following details are from Senator Pell's "Memorandum of Conversation Between Mai Van Bo, Delegate of North Vietnam in Paris, and Claiborne Pell, 19 June 1967," June 20, 1967, in Senator Pell's personal papers, and a memorandum of a conversation between Pell and William Bundy, June 29, 1965, Johnson Library, NSF Country File, Vietnam.

[48] While in Geneva, Pell talked about his speech with South Vietnamese Foreign Minister Tran Van Do, who said that his government agreed with the idea of implementing the Geneva Agreements. Pell's other proposals were also acceptable in principle, he said, except that he did not like the idea of unilateral cessation of bombing without some sort of understanding as to what would follow, and he felt that U.S. troops should not be withdrawn until after the withdrawal of North Vietnamese troops.

[49] CRS Interview with Senator Pell, Jan. 24, 1979. The Logan Act, a 1799 law that has never been enforced, prohibits an American citizen without authority from interfering in foreign relations between the United States and a foreign government. For more details, see fn. 52, p. 95 above.

"that his government had to make use of propaganda just as did any other." (In other words, Bo was arguing that U.S. emphasis on the public's demand for escalation was propaganda.)

After returning from Paris, Pell met with Rostow on June 20, gave him a copy for the President of the memorandum of his conversation with Bo, and asked to see the President. Rostow sent the President a memorandum on his conversation with Pell.[50] He said that Pell was "disappointed" with his talk with Bo, but he did not elaborate as to why Pell was disappointed. He said he explained to Pell how difficult it would be to stop bombing if the North Vietnamese continued "to violate the DMZ and put pressure on our men in I Corp." Pell replied that this was the reason he emphasized "mutual deescalation."

Pell, who finally saw the President on July 13 from 11:25 a.m. to 11:55 a.m., said that Johnson "was very nice and very courteous and didn't say to me, 'Claiborne, you're upsetting our foreign policy,' or 'You're going outside the Logan Act.' He could not have been more courteous and listened to me more attentively."[51]

On June 29, William Bundy also met with Pell to discuss the meeting with Mai Van Bo, and Bundy prepared a memorandum of that conversation which he sent to Rusk and to the White House relating essentially the same information provided by Pell's own memorandum.[52] At the conclusion of Bundy's memorandum he added a section of comments on Pell's meeting with Bo. Bo's motives in seeking the meeting, he said, "seem obscure . . . but the most likely explanation would be that he wished to convey to a respected 'semi-dove' the most forthcoming possible picture of North Vietnamese willingness to talk seriously if we stopped the bombing." After noting that several of Bo's reactions to various points raised by Pell were "noteworthy" for what he did or did not say, compared to previous North Vietnamese statements, Bundy added that Pell's "obvious suggestion of preliminary conversations" between the U.S. and North Vietnam before the beginning of more formal talks, "may well have had an impact on Bo."

Bundy attached the memorandum of his conversation with Pell to a memorandum on June 30 to Rusk on "Possible Developments in Hanoi, and Their Implications for the Negotiating Situation."[53] There were two pieces of evidence, Bundy said, "that Hanoi *may* be taking really serious stock of its negotiating situation." (emphasis in original) The first was the recall to Hanoi of key North Vietnamese overseas representatives, including Mai Van Bo. Secondly, "the 'nibble board' has been lighting up in the past month in several ways that are quite at variance with the totally negative readings of February through April. . . ." One of these was the greater accessibility of Mai Van Bo to Americans, and the lengths to which he went to see Pell. My "over-all feel," Bundy said, "is that something is at work. It may just be an attempt to make the bombing/

---

[50] Johnson Library, Memos to the President—Walt Rostow, Memorandum to the President from Rostow, June 20, 1967.

[51] CRS Interview with Pell, cited above. There are no White House notes on the meeting.

[52] Bundy's two-part memorandum of conversation with Pell (part I covers the Bo-Pell meeting; part II covers Bundy's comments to Pell on his May 23 speech), June 29, 1967, is in the Johnson Library, Warnke Papers, McNaughton Files.

[53] U.S. Department of State, Lot File 85 D 240 (William Bundy Papers).

talks gambit seem more appealing. It may be just tactics. But it just might be an indication of some serious re-thinking."[54]

Although, as noted, the U.S. Embassy in Paris had taken the position that discussions between Pell and Mai Van Bo would probably "harden" the North Vietnamese position on negotiations, Rostow concluded in a memorandum to the President on July 22 that the discussion might have had the opposite effect by indicating that "certain dovish Senators are not prepared to accept Hanoi's terms. . . ."[55]

In early August 1967, Pell went to Paris again, hoping to see Mai Van Bo, but he was out of the country. At the end of August, Bo sent a message to Pell in Washington saying, in effect, that there was nothing to talk about as long as the U.S. continued bombing the North.[56]

Public Opinion Hardens; Protests Increase

According to a Harris Survey in mid-May 1967, the public was becoming more dissatisfied with the war and more inclined to be belligerent. The poll reported that there was stronger support for increased military pressure and less support for withdrawal: 45 percent of respondents favored "total military victory," up from 43 percent in February, while 41 percent favored withdrawal of U.S. and Communist forces under U.N. supervision, down from 44 percent in February.[57] In the same poll, 81 percent of respondents said that they believed the war would be a long one—a sharp increase of 10 percent from a similar poll in February. Public support for President Johnson's handling of the war was stronger, with 70 percent in favor, an increase of two points since February. Only 55 percent thought that bombing of North Vietnam was helping to win the war, however, compared to 61 percent in February.

A Gallup Poll released on May 14, showed, however, that support for U.S. involvement was also declining. In response to the "mistake question" *("In view of the developments since we entered the fighting in Vietnam, do you think the United States made a mistake sending troops to fight in Vietnam?"),* 37 percent thought the U.S. had made a mistake, an increase of 7 points over the 30 percent recorded in February.[58]

On June 18, 1967, another Gallup Poll provided further details on the public's perception of the war. Only 48 percent had a "clear idea of what the Vietnam war is all about—that is, what we are

---

[54] "All of this suggests," Bundy said, "that the present might be an excellent time for us to push some buttons or to have a third nation push it." Because the U.S. "apparently cannot make direct contact" with the North Vietnamese, Bundy suggested a possible approach through the Canadians, using a proposal made by the Canadians several months earlier of a halt in U.S. bombing of the North in return for North Vietnamese agreement to ban military activity by both sides in the demilitarized zone, presumably including North Vietnamese infiltration through the DMZ to South Vietnam, with supervision by a force organized by the International Control Commission, of which Canada was a member.

[55] Johnson Library, NSF Memos to the President—Walt Rostow, Memorandum from Rostow to the President, July 23, 1967.

[56] U.S. Department of State, Lot File 85 D 240 (William Bundy Papers), "Note for the President's Evening Reading," Sept. 15, 1967, enclosing a letter from Pell to William Bundy, September 14.

[57] *New York Times,* May 17, 1967.

[58] *The Gallup Poll,* 1967, *op. cit.,* p. 2063. For a breakdown of both of these polls by sex, race, education, etc., see *Vietnam War, A Compilation: 1964–1990,* vol. 2. In the same poll respondents were asked: *"Some people say we should go all-out to win a military victory in Vietnam, using atom bombs and weapons. Do you agree or disagree with this view?"* The responses were: 26 percent agreed; 64 percent disagreed; 10 percent had no opinion.

fighting for," while 48 did not; 55 percent thought the war would end in a compromise, while 15 percent thought it would end in "all-out victory," and 5 in defeat (25 percent had no opinion). In answer to the question, "If the United States and North Vietnam come to peace terms and United States troops are withdrawn from Vietnam, do you think a strong enough government can be developed in South Vietnam to withstand Communist pressures?" 25 percent of respondents answered yes and 52 percent answered no; (23 percent were undecided).[59]

Meanwhile, the antiwar movement continued to gain momentum. On April 4, 1967, Rev. Martin Luther King, Jr. took a strong stand against the war in a speech to an overflow crowd at the Riverside Church in New York City at a meeting sponsored by Clergy and Laymen Concerned About Vietnam.[60] Dr. King called on African-Americans and "all white people of goodwill" to become conscientious objectors. Declaring that the U.S. Government was "the greatest purveyor of violence in the world today," King said that the use by the U.S. of new weapons on the Vietnamese peasants was like the testing by the Germans "of new medicine and new tortures in the concentration camps of Europe." He spoke of Vietnamese peasants

> who watch as we poison their water, as we kill a million acres of their crops.
>
> They must weep as the bulldozers roar through their areas preparing to destroy the precious trees.
>
> They wander into the hospitals with at least 20 casualties from American firepower for one Vietcong-inflicted injury.
>
> So far, we may have killed a million of them—mostly children.

The Vietnamese, King added, "wander into the towns and see thousands of the children, homeless, without clothes, running in packs on the streets like animals. They see the children degraded by our soldiers as they beg for food. They see the children selling their sisters to our soldiers, soliciting for their mothers."

Sharing the platform with King was historian Henry Steele Commager, who described the war as the "product of a body of political and historical miscalculations and of moral and psychological obsessions."

King offered a five point program for "extricating ourselves from this nightmarish conflict: (1) the end of all bombing of North and South Vietnam; (2) a unilateral ceasefire; (3) curtailment of the military buildup in Thailand and of interference in Laos; (4) inclusion of the National Liberation Front in negotiations and in a future government, (5) announcement of a date for the removal of all foreign troops from Vietnam."[61]

---

[59] *The Gallup Poll,* 1967, *op. cit.,* p. 2068. For a breakdown of this poll by sex, race, education, etc., see *Vietnam War, A Compilation: 1964–1990.*

[60] Clergy and Laymen Concerned About Vietnam, with a membership of about 5,000, was formed in January 1966.

[61] *New York Times,* Apr. 5, 1967. For the text of King's speech see *CR,* vol. 113, pp. 13223–13225. See also Zaroulis and Sullivan, *Who Spoke Up?* pp. 108–110.

King's position was criticized by several prominent African-American leaders, including Roy Wilkins and Carl Rowan, who supported Lyndon Johnson and who did not want King's activities to interfere with the administration's strong commitment to civil rights. Following a statement by Whitney Young, Jr., director of the National Urban League, that the peace and civil rights

Continued

Six days later, the FBI sent to the White House, Secretary of State, Secretary of Defense, Attorney General, and the Director of Secret Service an updated version of a statement it had prepared on King's alleged subversive activities which contained allegations about Communist influence on King, as well as personally derogatory allegations.[62]

On April 15, 1967—following "Vietnam Week," April 8–15, during which students organized a variety of protests on a number of campuses—"Spring Mobilization," the largest demonstration ever held against the Vietnam war, took place in New York City. The crowd was estimated at 100,000–125,000 by the police, but the organizers estimated that there were 400,000–500,000.[63] Another demonstration, which police estimated was attended by 50,000, took place in San Francisco. Both events were organized by the Spring Mobilization to End the War in Vietnam, the antiwar coordinating group formed in September 1966.[64] Other groups had joined as sponsors, including Women Strike for Peace and the American Friends Service Committee, as well as an assortment of Trotskyites, anarchists, Communists and Maoists. SANE had declined to become a sponsor, once again because of the involvement

---

movements had different goals, and that it would not be appropriate to merge them, the board of the National Association for the Advancement of Colored People voted unanimously against King's suggestion that African-Americans should work against the war by becoming conscientious objectors. The N.A.A.C.P. said that it was not "a peace organization nor a foreign policy association," but was committed to civil rights, and that "civil rights battles will have to be fought and won on their own merits, irrespective of the state of war or peace in the world." *New York Times,* Apr. 11, 1967.

King was also criticized by a liberal Democrat in the House of Representatives, Jonathan Bingham of New York, who later became an opponent of the war, who said, among other things, that King's position "can only be interpreted by Hanoi as approval of its intransigent stand," *(CR,* vol. 113, p. 8497), and by Freedom House, an organization which had long supported U.S. policy in Vietnam. See the *New York Times,* May 21, 1967.

[62] Final Report, Book III of the Senate Select Committee to Study Intelligence Activities, p. 173, cited in full above.

On April 5, John Roche sent the President the following memorandum (Johnson Library, Confidential File, Name File "KI:):

"Yesterday's speech by Nobel Laureate Martin Luther King was quite an item. To me it indicates that King—in desperate search of a constituency—has thrown in with the commies.

"As you know, the civil rights movement is shot—disorganized and broke. King, who is inordinately ambitious and quite stupid (a bad combination), is thus looking back to a promising future.

"The Communist-oriented 'peace' types have played him (and his driving wife) like trout. They have—in effect—guaranteed him ideological valet service. There will always be a crowd to applaud, money to keep up his standard of living, etc.

"In my judgment, however, his recruitment to 'peace' will cut two ways: He will become the folk-hero of the alienated whites, but lose his Negro support *both* among 'black nationalists' (who see him as a threat to their operations) and among the great bulk of the Negro community (who are solid, sensible supporters of the Administration).

"In short, King is destroying his reputation as a 'Negro leader' for a mess of 'Charlies'' pottage. He is painting himself into a corner with a bunch of losers.

"For your *private* information, a group of non-Comnmunist peace advocates including Norman Thomas, Bayard Rustin, and several Quakers, spent hours trying to convince King *not* to make this speech or commitment."

He rejected their counsel. I am presently finding out who wrote the speech." (emphases in original)

[63] *New York Times,* Apr. 16, 1967. See also Zaroulis and Sullivan, *Who Spoke Up?* pp. 110 ff.

[64] Leaders of Spring Mobilization were A. J. Muste, the veteran 82-year old pacifist, as chairman (Muste died in February 1967), and as vice chairmen: David Dellinger, editor of *Liberation* magazine; Edward M. Keating, publisher of *Ramparts* magazine; Sidney M. Peck, a professor of sociology at Case Western Reserve University in Cleveland; Robert Greenblatt, an assistant professor of mathematics at Cornell University (both Peck and Greenblatt were leaders of the Inter-University Committee which sponsored the Vietnam war teach-ins); and Cleveland Robinson, vice president of District 65 of the Retail, Wholesale and Department Store Workers Union in New York City. The director of Spring Mobilization was Rev. James Bevel, a member of the staff of King's Southern Christian Leadership Conference. For more details, see Powers, *The War at Home,* pp. 166–169, and the *New York Times,* Feb. 26, 1967.

of far-left groups, but said that its members were free to participate.[65]

The major speech at the New York demonstration was made by Dr. King. Other speakers included Floyd McKissick, the national chairman of the Congress of Racial Equality (CORE); Stokely Carmichael, head of SNCC; Dr. Benjamin Spock (who was co-chairman of SANE). Among the participants were singers Harry Belafonte, Pete Seeger, and the group Peter, Paul and Mary, as well as actor Tony Randall, playwright Harold Pinter, and Nobel Prize winner Dr. Linus Pauling.

Prior to the demonstrations, the House Un-American Activities Committee issued a report claiming that the Vietnam Week and Spring Moblization were "completely Communist in origin," and that the organizing group was dominated and controlled by the Communists.[66] "There are, of course, many non-Communists who are sponsors of the Spring Mobilization Committee," the report said. "Not one of the top officers of the committee is known to be a Communist. With this excellent cover, there is little doubt but that the many Communists who are giving their all-out support to the group's activities will succeed in hoodwinking many persons who are sincere pacifists, liberals, and critics of U.S. policy in Vietnam into supporting the April 15 demonstrations—which the Communists look upon primarily as a means of undermining the United States and promoting Communist interests not only in Vietnam, but in all parts of the world."[67]

The objective of Spring Mobilization, according to the Un-American Activities Committee report, was to "reverse the U.S. policy of resisting communism in Vietnam":

> The constant professions of a desire for "peace" which have appeared in the literature and publicity related to Vietnam Week are completely insincere; the real, ultimate aim of the dominant Communist element in this movement is not peace, but the undermining of the United States, the destruction of any possibility of establishing a stable democratic government in Vietnam, the promotion of a Communist takeover in Vietnam, and the general advance of world communism.

The committee report added that while genuine pacifist groups were also involved, it was clear that they were playing a "minor role." "Every major, large-scale demonstration against the war in Vietnam which has taken place in this country has had all-out Communist support. They have, in fact, achieved the status of 'large-scale' and 'major' mainly because of the effort put into them by Communist elements." The April 15 demonstrations, the report concluded, would "give aid and comfort to Communists everywhere, particularly Vietnam;" would tend to create "the false impression"

---

[65] *New York Times*, Apr. 16, 1967.

[66] H. Doc. 90–186, p. 53. Several Members of Congress took a similar position. See *CR*, vol. 113, pp. 8173–1895, 9186–9188, 9702, 9720–9721, 9804–9806, 9830–9831, 9915, 10006–10007.

Freedom House declared that although the "majority of the marchers may have been motivated by their devotion to the cause of peace, the Communists were clearly in evidence among parade managers." It added, however, that "It would be absurd to describe the demonstration as 'Communist' or even 'Communist-controlled.' It would also be foolish and dangerous to ignore the Communists' participation or their rising hopes for exploiting King and other non-Communists for their own ends in the future." *New York Times*, May 21, 1967.

[67] H. Doc. 90–186, p. 35.

that a large segment of the country opposed the war; and would make it harder for U.S. leaders to persuade other countries to support U.S. policy.

On the day of the march, President Johnson "let it be known that the Federal Bureau of Investigation was keeping an eye on 'antiwar activity.'"[68] As a later investigation revealed, after a meeting of J. Edgar Hoover with President Johnson in April 1965, the FBI was not only "keeping an eye" on antiwar activity, but was engaged in a campaign to weaken and discredit antiwar activists and programs. In the case of Spring Mobilization, for example, the FBI, among other things, furnished information to the news media on the participation of the Socialist Workers Party in order to promote the idea that Spring Mobilization was being influenced by the far left.[69]

Although most of the participants in the demonstrations were college students, there were also a number of older persons, including at least several prominent Washingtonians who flew to New York in the private plane of Cyrus Eaton, a wealthy industrialist known for his support of peace causes. Mrs. Eaton, active in Women Strike for Peace, organized the trip, and among those on the plane were Supreme Court Justice William 0. Douglas and his wife; Mrs. Drew Pearson, wife of the columnist; and Mrs. Henry Reuss, wife of the congressman. Mrs. Fulbright, wife of the Senator, reportedly was to have gone, but was ill. Scottie Lanahan, a writer and political activist, daughter of novelist F. Scott Fitzgerald, was also a member of the party, and on April 17, 1967, the *Washington Post* published her diary-style account of the day's events and her description of the kinds of people who were taking part: "Look for Communists, Trotsky Revisionists, Black Muslims and so on . . . only see masses of Greenwich-village young people wearing blue jeans and daffodils, apparently new rage imported from London."[70]

One of the features of the New York demonstration was the burning of draft cards by about 200 protestors led by Tom Bell and other students from Cornell University. This move, which had been planned in advance, was intended as a way not only to protest but to resist the war.[71]

---

[68] *New York Times,* Apr. 16, 1967.

[69] Final Report, Book II of the Senate Select Committee to Study Intelligence Activities, cited above, p. 247.

[70] On the way back to Washington, the Eaton party expressed pleasure at the turnout but some voiced concern over the possible impact on the antiwar movement of the merging of the civil rights and the antiwar causes, just as some African-American leaders had expressed their concern that African-American involvement in the antiwar movement would adversely affect the civil rights campaign. According to Lanahan, Anne Eaton commented, "We need as many people under the umbrella of the fight for peace as we can get. Maybe they're not all our best friends, and maybe we don't approve of everything they said, but as long as we have a common end, we're getting somewhere." The group agreed, Lanahan said, "that in a subtle way, deep in the national consciousness, the fight for racial equality and national self-determination are related. Marchers were not 'just a bunch of beatniks,' we agree. Do not feel entirely comfortable, however, with the sudden shift, much as we're all for civil rights."

[71] See *New York Times,* Apr. 16, 1967, and Zaroulis and Sullivan, *Who Spoke Up?* pp. 112–114. The first draft card-burning had occurred in the spring of 1965, after which Congress passed a new law with harsh penalties. In October 1965, David Miller, a young pacifist and member of the Catholic Worker Movement, publicly defied the new law by burning his card at the time of the first major demonstration against the war. He was arrested, tried, and given a suspended sentence. In March 1967, after an appeals court had reversed the sentence for burning his card, he was convicted of not having his card in his possession and sentenced to two and a half years, again suspended. He was told to get a new card. Continuing to resist, he was carried from the courtroom. On Apr. 1, 1967, he obstructed the entrance to the Selective

At about the same time, a new resistance organization, "The Resistance," was formed, and David Harris, who had recently been the student body president at Stanford University (and who later married singer Joan Baez, another opponent of the war), called for students nationwide to turn in their draft cards on October 16, 1967, as a way of protesting and resisting the war.[72]

During this period in the spring of 1967, Congress, as noted earlier, was considering a bill to extend the selective service law, and some antiwar activists in Congress, as well as some elements of the antiwar movement, took the opportunity to protest the Vietnam war as well as the inequities of the draft. At that time, there were two million male students deferred from the draft, with the result that males who were not in college made up a disproportionately large part of the 45 percent of Army personnel in Vietnam in the spring of 1967 who had been inducted into service.

Within the antiwar movement, a group called the Vietnam Draft Hearings Committee was organized to conduct a demonstration at the May 8 hearing of the House Armed Services Committee on the new draft bill which sponsors said would be a "direct confrontation" rather than a "march down an otherwise empty street."[73] Hopes for a confrontation were dashed, however, when the House committee, preferring not to give the group any publicity, cancelled the hearing. A committee aide offered to meet a delegation from the group of about 50 demonstrators, but they insisted on attending as a group. This was refused. When one of them started making a speech against the war, they were ejected from the House office building for violating the law against demonstrations on the Capitol grounds.[74]

Prior to the aborted demonstration on May 8, about 70 members of the draft opposition group, primarily college students from the New York and Boston areas, met in Washington at St. Mark's Episcopal Church on Capitol Hill on May 6 for a discussion and strategy session. One of the speakers was Rev. James Bevel, a member of Rev. Martin Luther King's staff who was director of Spring Mobilization. The pastor of St. Mark's Church, Rev. James R. Adams, also attended. These and other facts about the meeting were reported to President Johnson on May 12 in a memorandum from Thomas L. Johns of the U.S. Secret Service, based on information from Secret Service agents who, Johns said, attended the meeting "under suitable guise."[75] According to Johns' memorandum, Rev. Adams seemed "very sympathetic to this group."

Johns said he was sending the information to the President because of his possible attendance at St. Mark's.

Johns also discussed the information with White House Counsel Harry McPherson, a member of the St. Mark's congregation and a friend of the pastor. In a memorandum to the President on May 15,

---

Service headquarters in New York City by sitting in the doorway, thereby hoping to get arrested. Authorities did not press charges. Powers, *The War at Home,* pp. 85, 189, and *New York Times,* Apr. 1, 1967.

[72] See Harris, *Dreams Die Hard.*

[73] For a copy of the group's announcement, see *CR,* vol. 113, p. 10423.

[74] *New York Times,* May 9, 1967.

[75] A copy of the Johns memorandum is in the Johnson Library, Office Files of Harry McPherson, Vietnam, 1967.

McPherson said that while the church was used by many groups, "politically it made no sense to let this crowd in the door."[76]

After the April 15 demonstration in New York and San Francisco, plans for a "Vietnam Summer," an idea developed among antiwar activists at Harvard University, was announced on April 23 as a follow-up to the demonstration. Headed by Rev. King, Dr. Spock, and Robert Scheer, publisher of *Ramparts* magazine, and staffed by faculty and students at Harvard, this was to be aimed at recruiting 10,000 volunteers to organize local antiwar efforts throughout the country.[77]

The following day, in a speech in New York, General Westmoreland said that antiwar protests were costing American lives and encouraging the enemy.

Former Vice President Richard Nixon also criticized U.S. dissenters. On April 17, while visiting Vietnam, he was reported to have said that American political leaders who criticized the war were giving aid and comfort to the enemy. Singling out Mansfield and Robert Kennedy, Nixon said they were "prolonging the war" by opposing U.S. policy. Urging unity, he recommended increased military pressure to end the war, adding, "It can be said now that the defeat of the Communist forces in South Vietnam is inevitable. The only question is, how soon?"

Nixon also said "there was no question," that the Communists were promoting the peace movement, and he called Reverend King's position on the relationship between civil rights and the war "very unfortunate."[78]

On April 24, Reverend King joined with Joseph L. Rauh, Jr., vice chairman of the Americans for Democratic Action, to announce the formation of "Negotiations Now!"—a group which planned to get one million signatures on a petition to President Johnson, as well as to hold a lobbying campaign to demand the end of the bombing of North Vietnam and the negotiation of a truce.[79]

---

[76] Same location. McPherson said he was "set to tackle Jim [Adams] about this yesterday [May 14] when he preached on it. This is the essence of what he said:

"Last Sunday the Bishop came here to preach, and it was a disaster. Small congregation, rainy day, lifeless spirit—particularly the Bishop's. Nothing happened.

"Last Wednesday a group of demonstrators asked permission to use the church. I said O.K. The first one to arrive—a young fellow about 25—asked, 'Where are the factories in Washington?' I asked him why he wanted to know. He said, 'Because we have to take the word to the exploited workers.'

"It was as if we were back in the thirties. It was absolutely kooky.

"Not all the group was Marxist. Some were very angry about ghettos, some about Negroes, all about Vietnam. The Marxists seized the occasion to hand around literature about workers' wars and bosses' profits to anyone who would take it.

"As kooky as these people were, though, there was a spirit going among them. They actually thought the world could be changed; they thought it was possible for people to love one another; to work with one another. Maybe they are going about it wrong; certainly they are naive; certainly they don't take enough account of their own capacity to hate. But last Wednesday they were alive, and trying to be responsible and caring. That is more than you could say about this congregation last Sunday."

[77] *New York Times* and *Washington Post*, Apr. 24, 1967. For comments on the problems encountered in carrying out the idea, and the lack of public response, see DeBenedetti and Chatfield, *An American Ordeal*, pp. 182–183.

[78] *New York Times*, Apr. 18, 1967.

[79] *Ibid.*, Apr. 25, 1967. See also Zaroulis and Sullivan, *Who Spoke Up?* pp. 117–118. Others involved were Rabbi Maurice Eisendrath, president of the Union of American Hebrew Congregations; Gerhard Elston, director of Vietnam Affairs for the National Council of Churches; Philip Baum, executive director of the American Jewish Congress, and William J. Butler, general counsel for SANE. In late June 1967, the group held a meeting in Washington at which John Kenneth Galbraith proposed a plan for reducing U.S. involvement in South Vietnam. See the *Washington Post*, June 29, 1967.

Beginning May 17, 1967, a delegation representing the Spring Mobilization Committee led by Dr. Spock, and including Mrs. Martin Luther King and Reverend James Bevel, who had been the national coordinator for the April 15 demonstrations, went to the front gate of the White House asking to see the President. They were told by a White House aide that he was not available. Dr. Spock read a petition from the group urging that the war be ended, and the aide said he would transmit it. On May 18, the group appeared again with a letter from Bevel asking the President to speak to a conference against the war which they were holding in Washington that weekend. White House Aide Richard Moose (subsequently a member of the Senate Foreign Relations Committee staff, where he was involved in investigating the war) was sent to receive the letter, which was then sent to the President by Rostow and Marvin Watson. In his cover note, Watson said: "Mr. President. Obviously we will regret but wanted you to know what was received today." On the face of Rostow's transmittal memo the President wrote: "Walt. Have Moose reply—L [Lyndon]" On May 19, Moose told Bevel that the President could not accept the invitation. In a memorandum to Rostow, Moose related what happened after he spoke to Bevel:

> A member of the group, who introduced himself as a professor, then read yesterday's letter and presented a well-balanced slate of 3-minute speakers, leading off with a representative of the Women's Strike for Peace, followed by a long-haired blonde, an American Indian (who invoked the Indian treaty rights), a draft-age youth "representing half-a-million students," a female journalist, who has visited North Vietnam, a Negro-Vietnam veteran, a labor representative ("Local 65"), an aged Negro farm worker from Mississippi (carrying a bundle of cotton and a rambling complaint about cotton allegedly taken from him), another potential draft evader, and a goateed Washington Negro interested in D.C. home rule.
>
> At mid-point in the Chatequa *[sic]* session, I suggested their messages be put on paper; but they said they had been told their statements would be taped for the President. I decided it was better to hear them out (there were very few cameras compared to yesterday), rather than agitate them by refusing.
>
> I did not comment on their statements (most of which were fairly restrained), except at one point to remind them that the President was not able to see everyone who wanted to see him or everyone whom he would like to see. At the end, I assured them that their views would be made known to the president and, in response to a specific question, that the farm worker's grievance would be considered by the "appropriate officials." Little did he know that the Agricultural Stabilization Committee people had been inside!
>
> It was an orderly group. Hopefully, the absence of press coverage will discourage them—or maybe it will snow again.[80]

On May 20–21, there was a meeting in Washington to plan future events, and it was agreed to carry out a mass protest in Wash-

[80] This and other documents on this incident are in the Johnson Library, NSF Country File, Vietnam.

ington on October 21.[81] The *ad hoc* Spring Mobilization Committee became the National Mobilization to End the War in Vietnam (MOBE).

There were also numerous protests at colleges and universities. On May 10, a "National Day of Inquiry," a "teach-in" organized by a group led by a student leader at Harvard University was held on more than 80 campuses.[82]

On May 11, 321 faculty members at Columbia University signed a letter to President Johnson and to the Senate—to date, the largest concerted pronouncement from a single university—calling for stopping the bombing and ending the "detestable" war. The group included two winners of the Nobel Prize, a two-times winner of the Pulitzer Prize, 11 members of the National Academy of Science, and 21 department chairmen.[83]

President Johnson held a White House luncheon on May 22 "to find out," according to a report by *New York Times* correspondent Max Frankel, "why he was having trouble communicating with the country's luminous intellectuals." All of the 16 "intellectuals" who attended were then serving in the Johnson administration.[84]

There was, Frankel reported, a "spirited one hour discussion of what he [President Johnson] might do about the intellectuals and what they would have him do about the war." The President was said to have "described himself as puzzled by the alienation and protests of thoughtful men." What would they have him do? "Perhaps, the President is said to have remarked, intellectuals really wanted him to do something he did not think a President could do and something that most other citizens would not want him to do; to agonize about his problems in public."

The extent of disaffection among intellectuals was described by some members of the group as "not much greater than that of a noisy minority of the general population." It was agreed that there was a communications problem, but while some said the President should do more to explain Vietnam policy, others doubted that this would help.

On May 10, the 16-member International Tribunal on War Crimes Trials sponsored by Bertrand Russell and presided over by Jean Paul Sartre, which met from May 1–10 in Stockholm, Sweden, after the Government of France barred it from meeting in

---

[81] DeBenedetti and Chatfield, *An American Ordeal,* p. 180, and Zaroulis and Sullivan, *Who Spoke Up?* p. 117.

[82] *New York Times,* May 11, 1967.

[83] *Ibid.,* May 12, 1967.

[84] *Ibid.,* May 22, 1967. Participants were:
Gardner Ackley, Chairman of the Council of Economic Advisers
Francis M. Bator, a member of the NSC staff
Harold Brown, Secretary of the Air Force
Zbigniew Brzezinski, a member of the State Department's Policy Planning Council
Douglass Cater, a special assistant to the President
James S. Duesenberry, a member of the Council of Economic Advisers
Alain Enthoven, an Assistant Secretary of Defense
John W. Gardner, Secretary of the Department of Health, Education and Welfare
William Gorham, an Assistant Secretary of Health, Education and Welfare
Charles M. Haar, an Assistant Secretary of Housing and Urban Development
Harry C. McPherson, Jr., White House Counsel
Arthur M. Okun, a member of the Council of Economic Advisers
John P. Roche, a special assistant to the President
John A. Schnittker, Under Secretary of the Department of Agriculture
Charles L. Schultze, Director of the Bureau of the Budget
Robert C. Wood, Under Secretary of the Department of Housing and Urban Development

Paris, announced its finding that the U.S. was guilty of "crimes against peace and crimes against humanity," consisting of aggression and the bombing of civilian targets in Vietnam. Australia, New Zealand and Korea were named as accomplices. The U.S. was also found guilty of violating the neutrality of territorial integrity of Cambodia.[85] The group based its findings on reports from five international teams, on studies produced by medical, scientific and legal commissions which had been established to conduct such inquiries, and on testimony from various witnesses.[86] As noted earlier, several Americans sat on the Tribunal while others participated in the studies.[87]

The U.S. Government, having taken a number of steps to block and to discredit the Russell Tribunal, deliberately ignored the proceedings in Stockholm. The Swedish Government, for its part, apparently was concerned about the effects on its relations with the U.S. On April 25, at a luncheon following the funeral for Chancellor Konrad Adenauer in Germany which President Johnson attended, the Prime Minister of Sweden, according to a note in the President's Daily Diary dictated by Rostow, "was desperately anxious to explain to him [President Johnson]" why the Swedes, "due to their complex laws," had allowed the Tribunal to meet. As the Prime Minister tried to speak to Johnson, there were a number of interruptions, and afterwards Johnson "dispatched Rostow in the middle of the night to find the PM of Sweden to tell him how concerned the President was and to listen to his story."[88]

During the spring of 1967, preparations also continued for establishment of a National Committee For Peace With Freedom in Vietnam which, as noted, was being organized by the White House. Toward the end of April, John Roche, the White House staff member who was handling the project, met with Vice President Humphrey and Max Kampelman, a Washington lawyer who had once been an assistant to Vice President Humphrey. After their discussion of the project, Roche received from Kampelman a list of names of possible sponsors. This was followed by another meeting on May 24 with the Vice President.[89]

On May 17, James Rowe, a close political adviser, gave the President a memorandum proposing the organization of the committee. He said that, "at Louis Martin's instigation," he, McPherson and Roche had been discussing the idea of establishing such a "'Third Force'. . . led by independents, preferably members of the Republican Party along with some university intellectuals" to provide a

---

[85] *Ibid.*, May 11, 1967. A second and final meeting of the Tribunal was held in Copenhagen, Denmark, in November 1967.

[86] *Ibid.*

[87] Gabriel Kolko, a member of the history faculty at the University of Pennsylvania and Samuel Rosenheim, an American lawyer, presented long briefs on the international legal aspects of U.S. involvement in Vietnam.

For an interview with Carol Brightman, an antiwar activist who published *Viet Report,* on her trip to North Vietnam in January 1967 as part of one of the teams, see Harry Maurer, *Strange Ground: Americans in Vietnam, 1945–1975, An Oral History* (New York: Henry Holt, 1989), pp. 428–436.

[88] Johnson Library, President's Daily Diary for Apr. 25, 1967. For a discussion of the Russell Tribunal issue and of U.S.-Swedish relations during the war, see Frederik Logevall, "The Swedish-American Conflict Over Vietnam," *Diplomatic History,* 17 (Summer 1993), pp. 421–445.

[89] Johnson Library, C.F. ND 19/CO 312, Memorandum from Kampelman to Roche, Apr. 30, 1967. This memorandum mentions the May 24 meeting; there are no known notes of either meeting.

"rally ground" for those who supported the war. This was Rowe's description of the state of public opinion:[90]

> It is elementary that this is an unpopular war. Even though the bulk of the country presently supports the President's policies it is clear there is restlessness on the subject of the Vietnam struggle. This is particularly true among the "intellectuals"—the universities, the columnists and the large city "intellectuals." Not only is it fashionable among them to be against the war, it is unfashionable to be for it.
>
> The common people, in the form of the American Legion, the labor unions, the boiler makers and the bartenders, may parade down Fifth Avenue to "support the boys" in Vietnam. Yet the "opinion makers" in the press, on the magazines and in the universities are more and more attacking the Vietnam policy. Eventually these "opinion makers" may convert the people, particularly if unopposed. Inevitably, their widely publicized, noisy and loud point of view will have the effect of a war of attrition against those who would support the Vietnam policy.
>
> Here and there, on the campuses, in the editorial offices, among the "opinion makers" are a number of people who think the policy is correct. But more and more these people feel they are outnumbered, that they have no allies, there is no place to turn and their own doubts are beginning to creep in. If everyone is against them, they may feel perhaps they themselves are wrong.

Plans to improve the government's own public relations effort on behalf of U.S. policy in South Vietnam were still being discussed, based on Roche's suggestion in February, mentioned above, of creating an information staff in the White House headed by Harold Kaplan, then on the public affairs staff of the State Department. Apparently, very little progress had been made in implementing the idea, judging by a memorandum on May 29 to Kaplan, who was still in the State Department, from Robert Miller, head of State's Vietnam Working Group, proposing ways of increasing the number of qualified officers from the Department to speak before academic audiences, as well as ways of providing more and better printed material to faculty and students.[91] This was Miller's apt description of the problem:

> Among the most characteristic attitudes encountered in academic communities are: (1) deep moral and ethical concern voiced by many students over the Administration's course in what they see as an area not vital to United States security, (2) a disposition to accept the most cynical interpretations placed on the Government's actions and statements; (3) skepticism about the Administration's rationality in combatting Communism which has elsewhere been forced to liberalize as

[90] Same location, Memorandum from Rowe to the President, "Vietnam and a 'Third Force,'" May 17, 1967, with cover transmittal note from Rowe to Califano, May 17, 1967.

Rowe sent a copy of the memorandum to Presidential Assistant Califano, who, apparently not knowing about activities underway, sent it to McPherson with the note: "This looks like a great idea to me. Are we doing something about it?" Califano's note has been photocopied onto the Rowe transmittal memoranda.

[91] U.S. Department of State, Lot File 72 D 207, Memorandum to Kaplan from Miller, "Need for an Intensified Vietnam Information Effort Directed at Academic Communities," May 29, 1967.

the price of survival and which in any event is weakened by the Sino-Soviet split; and finally, (4) a widespread belief that the war is essentially a civil war rather than aggression from Hanoi, and hence none of our business. The collapse of various peace initiatives in the early winter, the intensification of fighting around the DMZ, the threat of greater Soviet or Chinese intervention, evidence of rivalry among the generals in Saigon on the eve of the presidential campaign, the tenor of recent senatorial comments on escalation—all these have accentuated the unease within the academic world and the sense of being cut adrift from the Administration's thinking.

This set of opinions is sharpened by a general feeling that there is no wish in Washington to talk to the undergraduates honestly. As thoughtful persons who hope one day to assume leading positions in this country, they feel the Administration has deliberately appealed to the broad majority of Americans who are less well-equipped than they to analyze and to criticize. They feel they deserve more candid, sophisticated and detailed presentations than they have received.

CHAPTER 17

THE DEEPENING DILEMMA

It was the summer of 1967, two years after U.S. forces had entered the Vietnam war, and scarcely more than a year away from the next Presidential and congressional elections in which the war seemed destined to play a crucial role. Yet, at the very point when, according to the original plan, the war should have been largely over, the U.S. was still searching for a winning strategy, and the President, after receiving another first-hand report from McNamara in July, is quoted as asking him, "'Are we going to be able to win this goddamned war?'"[1]

Publicly, the President and his associates seemed confident that the war could be won. Privately, there was deepening doubt that this was possible. A paper prepared for McNaughton in early June concluded: "If we are winning, we are not winning quickly. It has become a question of the will to persist on either side rather than of the attainment of an overwhelming military victory."[2] This mood was described by General Wheeler in a top-secret backchannel cable to Sharp and Westmoreland on June 6 in which he summed up the "assertions" on which he said the Draft Presidential Memorandum on Westmoreland's troop request was "generally based:"[3]

> A. Short of population bombing or closure of an international port (neither of which would be politically acceptable) the bombing campaign in the North has not and cannot succeed in coercing the North Vietnamese into a settlement or reduce the flow of men and materiel to the south to the extent that victory is possible.
>
> B. The main-force war in the South is stalemated and even with significant added deployment will continue to fail to achieve an attrition level above that which the North Vietnamese can tolerate.
>
> C. Pacification efforts have failed to achieve significant results and there is no evidence that pacification will ever succeed in view of the widespread rot and corruption in the government, the pervasive economic and social ills, and the tired, passive and accommodation prone attitude of the armed forces of South Vietnam.

---

[1] Harry Middleton, *LBJ: The White House Years* (New York: Harry N. Abrams, 1990), p. 178. Middleton, now director of the Lyndon Johnson Library, was a member of the White House staff at the time.

[2] Johnson Library, Warnke Papers, McNaughton Files, untitled, unattributed paper discussing U.S. goals, the current situation, and U.S. strategy, apparently drafted in connection with the preparation of the Draft Presidential Memorandum. In the upper right hand corner of the first page there is this notation in McNaughton's handwriting: "6/8/67 This paper to be seen by McNaughton only."

[3] CMH, Westmoreland Papers, Message Files, Wheeler to Sharp and Westmoreland, JCS 4200, June 6, 1967.

D. Because of the low attrition rate in the South and the relative effectiveness of the bombing in the North, any reasonable reinforcement of our effort in the South will be matched by reinforcement from the North, resulting only in a new stalemate at a higher level in cost.

Whatever the President may have hoped to accomplish by the decision in February 1967 to increase the use of force against North Vietnam—which had been followed by five weeks of heavy bombardment beginning in late April during which, according to Admiral Sharp, "the level of stress against the Hanoi government was greater than during the entire previous Rolling Thunder program"[4]—the reaction of the North Vietnamese was to increase the evacuation of citizens from populated areas, to intensify air defenses, and to claim that they were winning.[5]

General Nguyen Chi Thanh, head of Communist forces in the South, declared on May 31: "All the strategic objectives set forth and all methods used by the U.S. aggressors have been frustrated. The U.S. expeditionary troops are on the decline. The puppet troops are even worse. The U.S. ruling clique is facing difficult, insoluble problems. When and how can the Viet Cong main force be destroyed? When and how can the so-called pacification task be fulfilled? To what extent must the war of destruction against the North be escalated to become effective? What is to be done to win a turning point on the battlefield? Johnson himself had to say, 'The Americans are in a deadlocked and bloody situation in South Vietnam.'"[6]

In Paris on June 15, Vo Van Sung, deputy to North Vietnamese diplomat Mai Van Bo, claimed in a press briefing that recent Communist objectives had been achieved:[7] From these successful military operations, he said, five lessons could be learned: "(1) know your enemy and break his strategic will; (2) maintain a continuous offensive; (3) intensify the coordination of military, political and economic action; (4) increase the operational and strategic capacity of a people's war; and (5) develop the quality of forces rather than the quantity because quality is decisive." Communist guerrilla tactics, Vo Van Sung explained, were to "prevent the enemy from encircling us so that guerrillas can encircle the enemy. By not forming a continuous battle line and by forcing the adversary to be constantly on the move, we wish to force Americans to eat their soup with chop sticks."

In the search for a winning U.S. strategy, the military continued to propose plans for operations in Laos. One such plan, developed

[4] U.S. Department of State, Lot File 70 D 48, text of Sharp's briefing for McNamara during the latter's visit to Vietnam, July 7–12, 1967.

[5] In a memorandum for the President in late August, 1967, Helms commented on the effects of intensified bombing of the North, which had caused almost as much damage between March and July as in the whole of 1966. "Hanoi," he said, "continues to meet the needs of the Communists in South Vietnam and essential military and economic traffic continues to flow." Johnson Library, NSF Country File, Vietnam, Helms memorandum to the President, "Effects of the Intensified Air War Against North Vietnam," Aug. 29, 1967.

[6] McGarvey, *Visions of Victory*, p. 116.

[7] "(1) to defeat the million men fighting with the U.S. and to break the counter offensive during the dry season; (2) to increase the factors leading to a U.S. defeat; (3) to gain control over new strategic positions." U.S. Department of State, Central File, Pol 27 Viet S, Paris to Washington, Airgram A–2006, June 20, 1967.

at CINCPAC in mid-summer, brought this pointed reaction from Ambassador Sullivan.[8]

> If the CINCPAC staff officer who wrote reftel [referenced telegram] will kindly raise his right hand, he can have my job tomorrow. However, when he comes (and if he persuades higher authority to accept his plans) he had better bring out the 200,000 U.S. troops with him to "pacify" the area he wants to occupy in Laos and to defend it against North Vietnamese forces operating against it on short DMZ-type logistics lines.

"I am disappointed," Sullivan added, "that messages of this type are permitted to move in official channels and receive wide dissemination. It is the sort of thing which is giving marijuana a good name."

In mid-June 1967, the highly secret study of "radical military alternatives to the present scale and conduct of the war" that had been initiated the previous December by the Policy Planning Council of the State Department in cooperation with the Defense Department, the JCS and the CIA,[9] was completed and distributed to a limited number of senior officials.[10] These were the major findings and conclusions of the study:

"*Checking Infiltration Within South Vietnam.* A continuous physical barrier along South Vietnam's land frontiers would have definite value, but it does not appear to be presently feasible within the limits of available resources. Extension into Laos of the strong point obstacle system now under construction south of the DMZ appears to be a more promising alternative.

"Further study should be given to the artificial stimulation of rainfall and the laying down of a belt of radioactive material as anti-infiltration measures."[11]

"Defeating or Neutralizing Enemy Forces and Consolidating Secure Areas in South Vietnam." Should the "war of attrition" against main-force units be downgraded in favor of more direct support for Revolutionary Development? "The answer to this problem is neither simple nor clear. Large-scale military operations do produce sizeable gains in terms of VC/NVA disruption and losses. Also, tak-

---

[8] U.S. Department of State, Central File, Pol 27 Viet S, Vientiane to CINCPAC 433, July 24, 1967.

[9] See p. 494 above.

[10] U.S. Department of State, Lot File 72 D 139, memorandum to the Secretary from Henry Owen, (chairman of the Policy Planning Council), June 20, 1967, with attached 84-page report from the Policy Planning Council, "Possible Alternatives to the Present Conduct of the War in Vietnam," June 15, 1967. The study examined "major alternatives to the present conduct of the war in Vietnam" under the following categories, each of which was divided into "Present Approaches," "Other Possible Approaches," and "Conclusions:"

"I. Checking Infiltration Within South Vietnam
"II. Defeating or Neutralizing Enemy Forces and Consolidating Secure Areas in South Vietnam.
"III. Actions Against the Enemy in Cambodia and Laos
"IV. Actions Against North Vietnam
"V. Dealing with the Displeased Population in GVN Areas
"VI. Seeking Optimum U.S. Role in War
"VII. Imposing GVN Ability to Prosecute the War
"VIII. Diplomatic Actions."

These were followed by a final section on "De-Escalation."

The study specifically did not include the question of whether additional U.S. forces were needed.

[11] At another point in the report there is this further statement: "The technical feasibility of this method [radioactive belt] has not been examined in this study. It would appear to warrant further examination, despite the clear political costs of using radioactive material for military purposes."

ing the pressure off main force units might greatly compound our security problems. On the other hand, large-scale operations are sometimes possible only at the expense of temporarily relaxing US/ARVN control over previously secured areas. . . ."

The report concluded that large-scale operations were fully justified "only where such operations relieve pressures against heavily populated areas," and that "over all, a shift in emphasis away from the war of attrition and toward Revolutionary Development may be wise, at least on an experimental basis."

"Actions Against the Enemy in Laos and Cambodia. A large-scale ground and air operation in the panhandle of Laos would appear to be ruled out because of adverse international repercussions, the large-scale of the effort, and the possibility of Chinese/NVA actions in northern Laos. Serious consideration should, however, be given to the installation of a belt of sensors intersecting enemy infiltration routes in Laos.

"Except in the case of self-defense, military actions against enemy forces in Cambodia, because of serious political disadvantages which we would incur, should be limited essentially to intelligence efforts. Primary reliance must be placed on diplomatic efforts to reduce enemy use of Cambodian territory. . . .

"Actions Against North Vietnam. Serious consideration might be given to a graduated approach involving phased application of some or all of the following measures:

"a. An interdiction campaign against the road, rail and waterway lines of communication leading to and from the Hanoi-Haiphong logistics base within the limits imposed by the present China buffer zone. . . .

"b. Offensive naval surface ship operations against targets in North Vietnamese coastal waters along the entire North Vietnamese coast, less the Chinese buffer zone.

"c. Aerial mining of the principal ports (Haiphong, Hon Gai, and Cam Pha) as well as smaller ports, river estuaries and coastal waters north of 20° N.

"d. A naval blockade.

"e. Air attacks against ports with the objective of achieving a level of damage that would render them inoperable.

"Since these actions would run progressively greater risk of Soviet or Chinese intervention on a larger scale than at present, each successive step should be withheld until a determination of the effectiveness of prior steps could be made and attitudes of the Communist governments re-assessed.

"Ground invasions of North Vietnam would be very costly in terms of U.S. divisions required and potential reactions by the Chinese and Soviets; they should not be attempted. However, raids into southern North Vietnam—or perhaps better, merely the threat of such raids—might promote some maldeployment of the North Vietnamese army and should be considered.

"Special operations in North Vietnam designed to promote a resistance movement in that country offer some advantages, although these advantages might be slow in coming. The possibility of early initiation of such actions should be examined further. The U.S. should avoid commitment to the objective of overthrowing the Hanoi regime.

"Introducing counterfeit currency and ration cards into North Vietnam and replacing present currency in south Vietnam would be marginally useful as a way of harassing the enemy. The latter proposal would meet resistance with the GVN and neither scheme deserves a very high priority.

"*Diplomatic Actions.* If we assume that the USSR is more interested in seeing the war in Vietnam ended than is the CPR [Chinese Peoples Republic], the object of US policy should be to try for a split between Hanoi and Peking while making clear to Moscow that a continuation of the war poses various risks for Soviet interests. Somewhat paradoxically, it can be argued that moves which threaten to make Hanoi more dependent on Peking might have this effect. The DRV leadership evidently disagrees with Peking on the proper conduct of the war and presumably wishes to avoid becoming a satellite of China. If faced with a choice of becoming more heavily dependent on China or of phasing down the war, it is possible that Hanoi might opt for the latter. This might also be the choice of Moscow. The most obvious way in which diplomacy might succeed in presenting this choice clearly to Hanoi and to Moscow is to build on some combination of threats, such as a threat not only to intensify the bombing but also to mine Haiphong and other harbors in North Vietnam if the DRV's support for the VC was not terminated. . . .

"Assuming that our object is to keep open the possibility of Moscow's eventually taking an active hand in diplomacy to end the war, it would seem desirable to combine elements of several approaches:

"—Maintaining or enhancing somewhat the element of threat. Demonstrable US willingness to escalate the war as needs dictate would pose fresh uncertainties for Moscow both as to potential involvement and as to possible effects upon their relations with the US in other fields.

"—At the same time, and not without an element of contradiction, keeping open channels and keeping alive other issues in which the Soviets have intrinsic interests in order to maintain a hostage in US-Soviet relations which can be threatened.

"—Turning aside any Soviet efforts to create artificial trade-offs designed to divert us from our objectives in Vietnam.

"—Occasionally rattling the skeleton of a settlement which excluded Moscow.

"This would not be predicated on the premise that Moscow would soon be moved. In fact, there are no diplomatic or propaganda moves which seem to have reliably predictable effects in terms of moving the conflict to a favorable resolution. Rather, the calculation would be that the Soviets would—whenever the military situation in Vietnam or the stresses in intracommunist relations create a new circumstance—have incentive to move.

"With respect to diplomatic actions towards the NLF, it would appear that no basically new approach is tenable at this time. However, it would be desirable to place added emphasis on the Chieu Hoi and the National Reconciliation programs as a means of internally splitting the Viet Cong/NLF.

"*De-Escalation.* Limiting the geographical scope of operations by either U.S. or all friendly forces in South Vietnam is not a promising means of de-escalation and should be accepted or rejected on other grounds. . . . Similarly, there are no grounds at present for believing that unilateral suspension of bombing in part or all of NVN would lead to reciprocal de-escalation by Hanoi.

"The reciprocal withdrawal of part of the US and NVN troops in SVN would, up to a point, work to our advantage if an agreement to this effect included a DRV commitment to stop infiltration—and if such a commitment were in fact honored. If NVN troop withdrawals from Laos were included, the deal would be even more attractive, but even in this case care would have to be taken not to withdraw so many US troops as to expose the ARVN unduly to the superior VC forces. A total US withdrawal should therefore be contingent upon achievement of a satisfactory settlement, including adequate peacekeeping arrangements. . . .

"Trading bomb-free zones in NVN for freedom of comparable zones in SVN from enemy military or terrorist actions is theoretically very attractive. There is no reason to believe that the enemy could be interested in such a trade at this time, but the concept merits further study for possible future application."

The most notable feature of the Policy Planning Council report, which began as a study of "radical" military alternatives, was its conventionality and its conformity to existing policy and programs. It is little wonder, therefore, that the report does not appear to have had any impact on policymaking or operations, and, indeed, may never even have been discussed or considered further after it was issued. In itself, this was indicative of the problems faced by the U.S. at this stage in the war. "Radical" alternatives either were not acceptable or were unworkable or both and, thus, as the study made clear, the only hope for improvement in the conduct of the war was to seek to improve and develop existing programs.

On July 1, 1967, a Defense Department official, Richard Steadman, Deputy Assistant Secretary for the Far East in the Office of International Security Affairs, drafted a brief memorandum, "A Plan for the Termination of Hostilities in Vietnam," which, in contrast to the Policy Planning Council study, could have been considered a "radical" alternative to existing policy. Steadman proposed that after the South Vietnamese Presidential elections in September 1967, the U.S. should negotiate with the North Vietnamese and then with the South Vietnamese a settlement of the war based on the following terms: [12]

A. US ceases bombing of NVN

B. NVN agrees to cease or slow down infiltration or to withdraw their regular forces in SVN.

C. Depending upon B, US agrees to cease or slow down troop levels or to withdraw troops. . . .

D. US agrees to force (i.e., to withdraw forces and support unless) an election in SVN on 1 January, 1969 (or perhaps during their TET holiday in February) with two choices on the ballot—to stick with the recently elected government or to join now the present regime in NVN.

[12] Johnson Library, Warnke Papers, McNaughton Files, "A Plan for the Termination of Hostilities in Vietnam," undated and unsigned, but McNaughton had noted by hand on the first page of the memorandum that it had been drafted by Steadman on 7/1/67.

E. US agrees that this election will be supervised by ICC [International Control Commission] or some other group which will provide controls at least not hostile to communists.

F. US agrees to withdraw all troops after 1969 election, regardless of outcome.

G. US agrees that all support will be withdrawn from GVN if after 1969 election it conducts bloodbath or purge of NLF.

H. NVN and NLF agree to live with results of election and thereafter to cease armed attempt to take over government of South Vietnam. U.S. reserves right to re-introduce force if NLF resorts to armed conflict after 1969 election.

I. NVN/NLF agree to permit all who so desire to leave SVN if SVN elects to join the NVN regime in 1969 election. SVN makes similar agreement. US/Japan/Korea/Taiwan/Thailand agree to accept refugees.

J. NVN/NLF agree to withdraw from Laos and Cambodia and to keep hands off after 1969 election.

K. Russians agree to withdraw support for NVN if it violates terms of the above deal. . . .

Steadman said that the proposal "was designed to accomplish the following objectives:"

1. Fulfill our commitment of permitting people of SVN to determine own destiny.

2. Grant the new SVN government a fair opportunity to win confidence of people.

3. Give ARVN incentive for strong action in 1968.

4. Give US forces strong incentive to help GVN and ARVN win territory to win people to win votes.

5. Give the NLF assurance of survival in any event and of possible political victory.

6. Give NVN a clear shot at immediate reunification and assurance that its assets in SVN would survive in any case, and thus a chance at later (if not now) unification.

7. Save NVN face with a bombing cessation while war continues.

8. Provide the US public with an honorable solution to an involvement in Vietnam. And the final results of this solution would be unknown in November 1968.

There is no indication that there was any consideration of Steadman's proposal or that it was even circulated outside of McNaughton's office. It is of interest here because it is suggestive of the urgency felt by U.S. officials to end the war, as well as being indicative of what at least one high official in the Defense Department's ISA staff considered to be a possible approach to a settlement.

"Takeoff"?

Reports from South Vietnam in May-June 1967 tended to confirm the pessimistic view about pacification which Wheeler said in his cable to Westmoreland on June 6 was one of the assertions on which the Draft Presidential Memorandum was "generally based," namely, that pacification had failed to achieve "significant results" and might never succeed.[13] In a trip report to Leonhart on May 18, Richard H. Moorsteen, who had worked in Southeast Asia with the RAND Corporation for several years and for Komer and Leonhart at the White House for about a year, said that while "more of the country belongs to us, and VC recruiting is impaired . . . the VC apparatus still functions effectively in every province. Cadres are not defecting or lying down on the job." [14] "[T]he VC/NVA are hurting and unpopular but are still tough—with no good indication they will soon give up or disintegrate."

There was "not enough security to support present RD plans," Moorsteen said, and U.S. effort to improve the armed forces of South Vietnam had "not been very successful." Moreover, "The better RD teams generate good will and local intelligence, but the GVN is seldom able to exploit these openings by introducing effective leadership . . . at the village level."

Moorsteen concluded:

> It seems unlikely that simply attriting the enemy will make him quit or that passing US commodities into the Vietnamese country side will separate him from the peasantry. For the US to get out of Vietnam, therefore, it is not only necessary to cut the communists down to size, RVNAF [the armed forces of the Republic of Vietnam] has to learn more about fighting guerrillas and the GVN about governing villages. On present showing, it will take a long time for any such improvement to occur—if it happens at all. For the US, this means digging in for the long haul:
>
> —Chasing after victory through attrition is a will-o'-the wisp that costs us too much in dollars, draft calls and casualties, makes it too hard to stay the course. Putting additional US forces into Vietnam may even be counterproductive, in that the enemy expects our endurance to shorten as our costs go up. If our forces were employed more prudently at present levels, they could defend themselves and keep the enemy sufficiently off balance to give the GVN and RVNAF time for improvements.
>
> —Civilian casualties should be reduced. They occur in part out of sheer sloppiness and in part from our efforts to speed attrition of the enemy by massive use of firepower. They are a rapidly growing political liability, both here and in Vietnam, one that can make it both difficult and costly to sustain the war.
>
> —Like it or not, our stake in improving the GVN and RVNAF is so great that we should accept the risks of a more active policy. "Stability" and "good working relations" are inadequate objectives. We are unlikely to get either victory or a viable negotiated settlement unless the GVN and RVNAF improve.

A similar report was made to Leonhart on June 6 by Richard Holbrooke, a Foreign Service Officer with experience in Vietnam who was assigned to the Komer/Leonhart office, and had just re-

---

[13] Cited above, p. 705.

[14] U.S. Department of State, Central File, Pol 27 Viet S, Memorandum to Leonhart from Moorsteen, May 18, 1967, attached to cover memorandum from Leonhart to Katzenbach, Rostow and Vance, May 18.

turned from a trip to Vietnam.[15] "The 1967 pacification program is in deep trouble almost everywhere in Vietnam," Holbrooke said. Describing the situation in each of the four corps areas, he said that "In the difficult and critical area around Saigon, despite major US efforts to clear the area, we have succeeded only in reducing the level of violence and rebuilding a few roads and bridges. We have not done anything significant to eliminate the VC shadow government, which still exists throughout the area."

"Pacification," Holbrook declared, "is simply not going to change the face of the war in the foreseeable future, and is currently overemphasized. This is automatically putting GVN/US troops on defensive missions and easing the pressure on the VC. As presently conceived, pacification is nothing more than 'bringing security to the people' and then, behind this security, building a few schools and dispensaries. All this is commendable, but to win at Vietnam by this route—which neither destroys the Viet Cong nor builds any permanent governmental structure—would require nothing less than the full scale occupation of Vietnam by some mix of American, Vietnamese, and Korean troops. Our present forces, although already over 1.3 million strong, are wholly inadequate for this task. If we are to follow this route seriously—and this would be most inadvisable—then we must send enormous numbers of additional troops there."

The fallacy, Holbrooke said, was to assume that because "the people want security" that it should be provided when the people themselves were "invariably unwilling to assume any portion of the burden. . . ." "[T]hey are unwilling, for example, to tell allied troops where the VC political cadre are; they are unwilling to form volunteer hamlet militias, or serve in local self-defensive units." "They are unwilling to do these things," Holbrooke said, because they still have no feeling that either side in the war is on their side—and because they are scared." Thus, he concluded:

> a. The most valuable use of troops in support of pacification is effective anti-main force action in VC areas near the area to be pacified;
>
> b. We should not undertake the pacification of a new area if the effort will increase the static defensive commitments of GVN/US/and Free World forces;
>
> c. We should not begin the attempt to pacify an area until we have penetrated it with agents, have measured its receptivity to the GVN, and know that it is ready for pacification (in sharp distinction to the present approach of always taking on the next area on the map, no matter how hard it is to pacify);
>
> d. We should not try to begin the *build phase* of pacification prematurely: it should follow a successful destroy phase in which all efforts support the anti-infrastructure campaign. . . . (emphasis in original)

Holbrook stressed the need for a more effective "anti-infrastructure" effort—i.e., the program (later called "Phoenix") to eliminate the personnel and structure of the Communist insurgency organi-

[15] U.S. Department of State, Lot File 70 D 48, Memorandum for Leonhart from Holbrooke, "Some Observations about the Success and Importance of Pacification in Vietnam," June 5, 1967.

zation. "Until we mount a successful *effort to destroy,* the VC at the lower levels, we will be pouring fresh troops into never-ending mine fields and ambushes. . . ." (emphasis in original)

Efforts to help the South Vietnamese to develop "something to take the place of the VC" also needed to be improved, Holbrooke said. The U.S. aid program "has shown no ability to do what might have been its most important job—build up local government." And the CIA had "substituted 'made in America' programs like the RD Cadre for a genuine effort to build up basic government institutions such as village/hamlet government, RF [Regional Forces] and PF [Popular Forces]."

During the trip to Vietnam in May on which he based his report to Leonhart on June 5, Holbrook, together with a U.S. provincial representative, Richard Bumham, also prepared a comprehensive report for Komer, at his request, on the Binh Chanh District in Gia Dinh Province.[16]

In 1964, Binh Chanh, located south of Saigon, was designated as the highest priority area for pacification under the Hop Tac program (a plan to pacify seven provinces around Saigon, based on the "oil spot" concept of expanding security outward in concentric circles from a secure center—Saigon—as areas were cleared, secured and then pacified).[17] When Lodge returned as Ambassador in August 1965, he stressed the importance of Hop Tac. In their report to Komer, Bumham and Holbrooke noted that "When the Americans began their first 'top priority' effort in the area surrounding Saigon in the late summer of 1964 a high-ranking member of the U.S. Mission visited us at the Hop Tac headquarters and, pointing to Binh Chanh District just south of Saigon, he said, 'This is where we start. If we can't win here, we can't win.'" Yet, despite an enormous effort, including a large search-and-destroy operation in late 1966, Operation FAIRFAX, and the continuing presence in Binh Chanh of one U.S. Army battalion and another part-time, Bunham and Holbrooke reported that as of May 1967, the situation in Binh Chanh was "unusually bad." "The pacification program is virtually non-existent. . . . One of the three [RD] cadre teams is virtually non-existent; the other two are not going to accomplish much." "The VC, despite the improvement in security that has accompanied Operation FAIRFAX, have not been badly hurt." "[They] are as well entrenched in Binh Chanh as they were when it became our highest priority area in 1964."[18]

Bumham and Holbrooke pointed out that the date for withdrawing Operation FAIRFAX forces had been postponed twice, and that the operation would continue at least until after the election in September 1967. "The commitment in Binh Chanh (and as a matter of fact in all of Gia Dinh) may thus turn out to be far greater and longer than anyone originally intended. But as long as the VC infrastructure remains virtually intact the US troops will have to stay, not as pacifiers, not as genuine search-and-destroy troops, but primarily as defensive troops guarding the GVN strongpoints in the

---

[16] Same location, Memorandum for Komer from Bumham and Holbrooke, "Binh Chanh," May 24, 1967.

[17] See p. 58 above.

[18] U.S. Department of State, Lot File 70 D 48, Memorandum for Leonhart from Holbrooke, "Binh Chanh and the Misuse of Force," June 12, 1967.

district." "As long as US troops remain," the report said, "the VC will probably have to stay submerged, waiting for the day when we leave. . . . Meanwhile they continue to collect taxes, recruit, observe the US troops, and inflict a shockingly high casualty rate on the Americans with mines and booby traps."

Bumham and Holbrooke concluded that "the answer to the VC in Binh Chanh is not more US troops . . . it is an intensive campaign against the shadow VC government (infrastructure) that is still in Binh Chanh." Yet, the only force in Binh Chanh assigned to eliminate the infrastructure was a "poor and ineffective" 21-man South Vietnamese PRU group (Provincial Reconnaissance Unit—the anti-infrastructure teams). According to one report, however, there were only seven members of the PRU in Binh Chanh, and in late May they were jailed after a drunken attack on an RD team.

Moreover, although there were a number of South Vietnamese and U.S. intelligence "nets" operating in Binh Chanh, there was very little coordination and "almost no information of exploitable value is yet being collected there." "The blacklists [lists of persons purportedly in the infrastructure] have proved inadequate, both being outdated, and unable to bridge the gap between name or alias, and physical identification."

Finally, the report was very critical of the South Vietnamese for failing to follow-up Operation FAIRFAX, not only their failure to pursue the opportunity thus afforded to move against the infrastructure, but their failure to build a strong local government in areas that had been under the control of the Communists. "In the six months since Fairfax began," Bunham and Holbrooke said, "there has been no significant effort to build a more responsible and responsive government—the prime *positive* ingredient of a pacification program." "This failure," they added, "seems to extend through every aspect of the GVN's presence in Binh Chang." [19] (emphasis in originial)

In the State Department, William A.K. Lake, special assistant to Katzenbach, had obtained through "underground channels" a copy of two reports, one of which was on the situation in Binh Chanh, and he sent them to Katzenbach saying, "They show our inability to make progress without the GVN's local officials taking the lead (and receiving support from the GVN at higher levels). Indeed, it is criminal to waste American lives in situations like that in Binh Chanh." [20]

In mid-June, Komer submitted to Bunker a general plan of action to give the pacification program "a new thrust"—"Project TAKEOFF." As described by Bunker in a cable to the President, "the plan would concentrate on these eight programs:" [21]

---

[19] In the State Department, Pol 27 Viet S, there is another useful report on the problems of pacification as seen through experience in a single province. It was sent on June 14, 1967, as a letter to Holbrooke from David W. P. Elliott, a RAND Corporation employee attached to a U.S. advisory team in Dinh Tuong Province in the delta, south of Saigon, which was also among the provinces included in Hop Tac.

[20] U.S. Department of State, Central File, Pol 27 Viet S, Memorandum for the Under Secretary from Tony Lake, June 17, 1967.

[21] *The Bunker Papers*, Douglas Pike (ed.) *Reports to the President from Vietnam, 1967–1973*, three volumes (Berkeley: Univ. of California Institute of East Asia Studies, 1990), vol. I, p. 52, Bunker telegram to the President, June 21, 1967. See also Blaufarb, *The Counterinsurgency Era*, pp. 243 ff. For the text of the plan, "Project TAKEOFF—Action Program," no date, see U.S. Department of State, Central File, Pol 27 Viet S.

A. Improve 1968 Pacification planning.

B. Accelerate the Chieu Hoi program.

C. Mount an intensified attack on the Viet Cong infrastructure.

D. Expand and improve support by the Vietnamese armed forces . . . add as soon as possible 50,000 RF/PF [Regional Force/Popular Force] troops and another 50,000 in 1968, the bulk of which will be assigned to pacification.

E. Expand and supplement RD team effort. . . .

F. Increase capability to handle refugees.

G. Improve and expand the national police and the police field forces. . . .

H. We plan to increase the [U.S.] advisory structure and increase the number of ARVN battalions in direct support of RD programs from 53 to 60 or more. We also plan to put greater emphasis on night patrolling, active defense instead of digging in, and rapid employment of mobile reaction forces.

"As is often the case," Bunker added, "GVN performance remains the crucial factor."

The problem of the performance of the South Vietnamese Government was addressed in a section of the plan entitled "U.S. Influence—The Necessity, Feasibility and Desirability of Asserting Greater Leverage."[22] "Present U.S. influence on Vietnamese performance," it stated, "is dependent upon our ability to persuade, cajole, suggest or plead. Political and practical considerations usually have argued against developing any systematic use of the various levers of power at our disposal. . . . However, the factors of corruption, antique administrative financial procedures and regulations, and widespread lack of leadership probably can be overcome in the short run only if the U.S. increases its influence on Vietnamese performance."

In late August, the U.S. Mission in Saigon completed a long paper, *Blueprint for Vietnam,* which, after a general assessment of the situation, discussed the several areas of U.S. programs—political, military and economic—and made recommendations for the future. A chapter on pacification was based on the Project TAKEOFF action plan.[23]

The *Blueprint,* the *Pentagon Papers* observes, "struck a consistently optimistic note,"[24] as the assessment chapter suggested:[25] "Progress in the war has been steady on all fronts. We can defeat the enemy by patient, continued, and concerted effort." However, the paper also recognized that there was "no magic way to insure quick victory short of an unacceptable degree of risk of war with Communist China or the Soviet Union," and concluded: "We still have a long way to go. Much of the country is still in VC hands, the enemy can still shell our bases and commit acts of terrorism

---

[22] See *PP,* Gravel ed., vol. II, pp. 502–503.

[23] There is a copy of the paper in the Johnson Library, NSF Country File, Vietnam, as well as in the Department of State, Lot File 70 D 48. Accompanying the State Department copy there is a brief transmittal memorandum from Bunker to Rusk on Aug. 26, 1967. A volume of backup papers is also in Lot File 70 D 48.

For Bunker's specific recommendations for U.S. action to implement the blueprint, see Saigon to Washington 4958, Sept. 5, 1967, in *PP,* Gravel ed., vol. II, pp. 403–404.

[24] *PP,* Gravel ed., vol. II, p. 402.

[25] *"Blueprint,"* ch. I, p. 1.

in the securest areas, VC can still mount large scale attacks, most of the populace has not actively committed itself to the Government, and a VC infrastructure still exists throughout the country."

"Now that the initiative is ours and the enemy is beginning to hurt," the paper said, "maximum pressure must be maintained on him by (a) intensifying military activity in the South; (b) developing new methods of interdicting infiltration; (c) bombing all targets in the North connected with the enemy's war effort that do not result in unacceptable risk of uncontrolled escalation; (d) accelerating the program of pacification (including better security, more effective attacks on the infrastructure, stepped up National Reconciliation and Chieu Hoi programs, a greater involvement of the people in solving their own problems at the village and hamlet level); (e) encouraging reforms in the government structure and continued improvement in the armed forces; (f) attacking the problem of corruption; (g) using influence to effect a strong, freely elected government with political stability; and (h) taking actions necessary to the continued growth and stability of the economy."[26]

The chapter on military operations gave a brief presentation of U.S. strategy for the following year, noting that "Our overall strategy can be interpreted as one of applying such pressure on the enemy as necessary to destroy his will to continue his aggression. He must be convinced that victory is impossible, and that time is not on his side."[27]

The *Blueprint* also supported, as had Bunker in the July meeting with McNamara, Westmoreland's proposed use of South Vietnamese troops in Laos. Infiltration, it said, was continuing at a high rate, perhaps higher than in 1966, and it was "essential that every acceptable action be taken to stem the flow of men and supplies into SVN, including operations in Laos and Cambodia."

In the case of Cambodia, "It is becoming increasingly important that we prepare to take the necessary steps to stop, or at least to impede, increased infiltration through Cambodia." In addition to intensive study of how this could be done, "the Embassy recommends that we begin now to disseminate through both diplomatic and public channels evidence of the VC/NVA use of Cambodian territory as a means of exerting pressure on Sihanouk and preparing the ground for action we may decide later to take."[28]

Deputy Ambassador Locke went to Washington to discuss the *Blueprint* with the President on September 11. This was followed by a discussion of it at a meeting of the Luncheon Group the next day.[29] Although some of the proposals in the *Blueprint* exceeded existing policy and authority, such as those dealing with Laos and Cambodia, it is not clear what, specifically, the Mission was asking for approval to do or needed to have approval to do. The reaction in Washington, including the President, seems to have been that the *Blueprint* was useful as a broad, comprehensive statement, but

---

[26] *Ibid.*, ch. I, p. 5.

[27] *Ibid.*, ch. II, p. 5.

[28] *Ibid.*, p. 12.

[29] See Leonhart's memorandum to Rostow, September 11, commenting on the *Blueprint*, Johnson Library, NSF Komer-Leonhart File, and Locke's memorandum for the President, September 12, giving his recommendations for steps the U.S. should take, U.S. Department of State, Central File, Pol 27 Viet S.

For the meeting of the Luncheon Group on September 12, see Johnson Library, Meeting Notes File, Notes of James Jones of Weekly Luncheon, Sept. 12, 1967.

needed to be reviewed in order to establish priorities, "time-phasing," and costs.[30] The President appears to have accepted the *Blueprint*, but was not asked to and did not make any decisions on the plan.

The Glassboro Summit Conference, June 1967

A basic premise of American strategy was that the Communists eventually would yield to the application of pressure and would take steps to wind down or end the war. A corollary premise was that greater use of force against North Vietnam could have the effect of encouraging the U.S.S.R., because of its own interests in its relations with North Vietnam and the U.S., to play a more active role in helping to negotiate an end to the war.

In order to use force effectively to achieve these political results, it was essential to be able, through "fine tuning"—turning pressure up or down, on or off—to communicate one's intentions to the other side and to provide opportunity and time for a possible response. Thus, U.S. policymakers agreed in early May to reduce the pressure on North Vietnam later in the month in order to test whether the North Vietnamese would then be willing to consider negotiations and, more likely, whether the U.S.S.R. would show more interest in facilitating a settlement. (Another consideration, as noted, was the preference of most of the President's civilian advisers for reducing bombing in the northeastern part of North Vietnam and shifting the emphasis to the southern infiltration routes. There was also concern that the increased bombing program, rather than encouraging cooperation with the U.S., might result in greater pressure on the U.S.S.R. to assist the North Vietnamese.) On May 22, as noted, bombing was eased somewhat and the 10-mile limit on bombing Hanoi was reimposed. Although there was no obvious response from either the North Vietnamese or the U.S.S.R., officials at the State Department saw some hopeful signs during early June that the North Vietnamese might be softening their position. William Bundy, as noted, concluded that "something's at work . . . [that] might be an indication of some serious re-thinking." Thomas Hughes, head of State's intelligence office (INR), sent Rusk a memorandum on June 15 on prospects for negotiations which concluded in part that "The past three weeks have seen several highly tentative signs that Hanoi may again be interested in testing the atmosphere for opening talks which could lead to a negotiated political solution of the Vietnam problem."[31]

On June 5, 1967, the Israeli-Arab "Six Day War" began. One of the results was increased U.S.-U.S.S.R. diplomatic contact and cooperation which, in turn, spurred hope that there could be cooperation on other international issues, including Vietnam. In the Senate, Mansfield, Fulbright and Morton urged greater U.S.-U.S.S.R. cooperation on Vietnam. Fulbright advocated "quiet diplomacy looking toward the possibility of a [U.S.-U.S.S.R.] conference." Morton said that greater cooperation might be encouraged if the U.S.

---

[30] See Leonhart's comments in his memorandum of Sept. 11 cited above.

[31] U.S. Department of State, Central File, Pol 27 Viet S, Memorandum for Rusk from Thomas Hughes, "Prospects for Vietnam Negotiations in Next Three Months," June 15, 1967.

eased bombing and shifted to targets south of Hanoi and Haiphong.[32]

Several days later, the U.S. was informed that Kosygin was coming to the United Nations for a meeting on the Middle East crisis and "would welcome" a meeting with President Johnson.[33]

On the evening of June 13, the President "sought out" Fulbright, as Fulbright characterized it, at a White House reception.[34] The next day, Llewellyn Thompson, U.S. Ambassador to the U.S.S.R., paid a visit to Fulbright. In his report on their conversation[35] Thompson said that Fulbright "began by saying he assumed I had been sent to see him." Thompson replied that the President and Katzenbach thought that the visit would be useful. He told Fulbright that Premier Kosygin might be coming to the U.S., and that this could offer an opportunity "to start the process of moving toward an understanding with the Soviets." Fulbright said he was quite pleased that the President had sought him out the previous evening, "and seemed to attach significance to this as an indication that the President might be reconsidering our Vietnam policy." Fulbright stressed the need to reduce bombing, "as he feared Chinese and/or Soviet involvement." He also repeatedly referred to the impact of the war on U.S. internal affairs.

In a letter to the President on June 17, Fulbright urged him to meet with Kosygin to discuss the Middle East and Vietnam as well as attitudes of the U.S. and the U.S.S.R. toward each other. "I believe," he said, "we have reached the time when further progress can be made toward encouraging more positive attitudes on both sides, attitudes which might give rise to a general expectation on the part of each of the two great powers that cooperation with the other is not only desirable but possible."[36]

Fulbright's letter was received in the White House at 3:25 p.m. At 3:45 p.m., Marvin Watson read it to the President, who immediately sent a copy to Rusk and telephoned Fulbright that night.[37]

On June 19, Fulbright sent Johnson another letter urging him to meet with Kosygin. The President responded by letter, which he personally dictated, thanking Fulbright, and repeating the comments he had made in their telephone conversation: "We are ready to meet with him if there is any indication that he wishes and is willing to discuss with us substantive problems of common interest. . . ."[38]

On June 21, Walt Rostow sent the President a memorandum in which he argued "the case for seeing Kosygin."[39] There was a "20% chance," he said, that the meeting would have a "net favorable effect in U.S.-Soviet policy," and "well under 10%" that it could have an adverse effect. As for the substance of the meeting, Rostow said

---

[32] *New York Times*, June 10, 1967.

[33] Johnson, *The Vantage Point*, p. 481.

[34] U.S. Department of State, Lot File 74 D 164, Thompson memorandum, June 14, 1967, of meeting with Fulbright June 14.

[35] *Ibid.*

[36] Johnson Library, WHCF, Ex ND 19/CO 1–6.

[37] There is no record of the telephone conversation.

[38] Fulbright's letter and the President's reply are in the Johnson Library, WHCF, Ex FO/Kosygin.

[39] Johnson Library, NSF Country File, U.S.S.R., Memorandum for the President from Rostow, June 21, 1967.

that "the serious case for talking with Kosygin is Vietnam." He apparently agreed that there might be some interest in negotiating:

> Frankly, I am a little impressed by the fact that the North Vietnamese have initiated contacts with us at several points. I am impressed by the fact that Kosygin dropped "permanent" from his bombing formula. It may be that our polls, which show popular support for a harder policy, have led them to believe that they will not be saved by the election of 1968; they may believe that we are about to make important decisions to increase our forces and perhaps apply more pressure against the North; that the bombing we have been doing is too unpleasant to be accepted over a period of either a clear-cut Hanoi defeat or a U.S./Soviet confrontation which they do not want; and that Hanoi is coming to believe that time is no longer its friend.
>
> If there is anything at all in this line of thought then, of course, a meeting with Kosygin could be most important. And certainly the most important thing on which you must make up your mind is what you say to Kosygin—after hearing him out—on Viet Nam.

He continued:

> My own thoughts are not final, but here they are. You might say that he knows our commitment and our views; and that the formula of the Foreign Minister in Hanoi is not satisfactory to us. We cannot accept a stoppage of bombing simply for the possibility of talk. What are his views? If it emerges that he does not repeat the permanent formula and goes on to say he is sure talks could take place if we stop bombing unconditionally, you could then explain that as long as the DMZ is being violated you cannot make a commitment to stop bombing. You might ask him if they would respect the DMZ if we stopped bombing the North. He is most unlikely to be able to give you a definite answer on this; but he might agree to find out.
>
> You could then indicate that there is a certain urgency in this matter. Your forces are under great pressure. They are taking heavy casualties every week. Secretary McNamara is going out to review the situation and to make recommendations. You might then add this: every mature American remembers that we lost more casualties during the Panmunjom negotiating period than we did during the Korean War. The critical question that must be answered by Hanoi is whether they are or are not willing to make peace on the basis of the 1954 and 1962 agreements and leave the South Vietnamese to settle their own political affairs on the basis of politics and not violence. We are looking for peace in Southeast Asia at the earliest possible time; but not on the basis of turning South Vietnam over to North Vietnam.

The President decided to meet with Premier Kosygin, and on June 23 and 25, 1967, the two leaders conferred at Glassboro State College, Glassboro, New Jersey. Others in the delegation were Rusk, McNamara, Harriman, Llewellyn Thompson, Rostow, Marvin Watson and McGeorge Bundy (who had been called back to the White House temporarily to assist with the Middle East crisis.) At the first meeting on the morning of June 23, where the only other persons present were the two interpreters, the principal subjects discussed were the situation in the Middle East and the "arms race" between the U.S. and the U.S.S.R. Toward the end of the meeting, President Johnson raised the question of Vietnam.[40] He said he wanted Premier Kosygin "to understand the following: North Vietnamese soldiers were being sent through the DMZ to attack South Vietnam. Some of our military people advocated our replying in kind [sending U.S. ground forces from South Vietnam into North Vietnam]. We did not however want to conquer North Vietnam, we merely wanted to prevent the North Vietnamese from completing their aggression against South Vietnam. It was for this reason that we sent planes to North Vietnam to bomb instead of men to fight." If the North would stay north of the DMZ, Johnson said, U.S. troops would stay south of it and would cease bombing the North. "In that case," he added, "the co-chairmen of the [1954] Geneva Accords [the U.S.S.R. and Great Britain] would have a chance to supervise free elections in South Vietnam and the people of South Vietnam would be given a chance to express their view as to what government they wanted to have." Kosygin, who, judging by the record of the meeting, did not comment on these remarks, returned to the subject of the Middle East.

At the afternoon meeting, according to the memorandum of conversation, "Mr. Kosygin informed the President in strictest confidence as follows: In anticipation of a meeting with President Johnson he had two days ago contacted Hanoi in the person of Pham Van Dong [the Prime Minister of North Vietnam] as to what he could do during his meeting with the President to help bring this war to an end. Just now, while he was having lunch with the President, a reply from Hanoi had been received. In substance, it amounted to the following: Stop the bombing and they would immediately go to the conference table. Mr. Kosygin did not know what the President's views of this proposal would be, but he wanted to express his own opinion very strongly, to the effect that he thought the President should follow-up this proposal. It provided for the first time the opportunity of talking directly with Hanoi at no risk for the United States. He asked the President to recall the experience of President de Gaulle of France who had fought in Algiers for seven years and still wound up at the conference table. He was sure of the North Vietnamese will to continue to fight for many years if necessary. And what would the President accomplish? He would carry on a war for ten years or more, killing off the best of the young people of his nation. . . . In his view, it was now time to end the war and to sit down at the conference table

[40] Johnson Library, NSF Country File, Addendum, U.S.S.R. [Glassboro Memcons], Memorandum of Conversation, meeting of President Johnson and Premier Kosygin, June 23, 1967, 11:15 a.m. to 1:30 p.m., prepared by the U.S. interpreter, William D. Krimer. According to Mr. Krimer, who made notes as Johnson spoke and then translated, the memcon is "as nearly verbatim as possible." Author's telephone conversation with Mr. Krimer, Jan. 11, 1993. Contrary to the times stated in the memorandum of conversation, Mr. Krimer recalls that the meeting took place at 9:00 a.m. and ended at 12 noon. Author's telephone conversation with Mr. Krimer, Jan. 23, 1994.

Except for the account of the Glassboro Conference in President Johnson's memoirs (*The Vantage Point*, pp. 256–287, 481–485), very little has been written about the Conference. This was confirmed by a bibliographical search by Allen Fisher, archivist at the Johnson Library, who says that perhaps "the paucity of original source material has contributed to the lack of treatment the conference has received." (Letter to the author from Fisher, Sept. 3, 1992.)

and then the President could see what would develop. This could be the very greatest problem which the two of them could resolve here together today: to end this obnoxious war and to let the rest of the world breathe easier because the danger of it spilling over into a bigger war had been removed."[41] "Sooner or later," Kosygin added, "American forces would have to be withdrawn from Vietnam and it was better sooner than later."

It should be noted that three days before the North Vietnamese submitted to President Johnson through Prime Minister Kosygin their proposal to hold talks immediately upon cessation of bombing, Mai Van Bo made the same proposal in his conversation with Senator Pell, when he said that if the U.S. stopped bombing there could be talks "without condition." This, and the fact that, as will be seen, the North Vietnamese took a similar position in the Paris talks in the summer of 1967, adds weight to William Bundy's observation in June 1967, after Pell's report, that the North Vietnamese might be taking "serious stock" of their negotiating position.

In his reply, President Johnson asked whether, if the U.S. agreed to a conference and stopped bombing, fighting would continue as it had during the Korean peace talks. He said that the North Vietnamese had five divisions immediately north of the DMZ which, if bombing ceased, would enter South Vietnam and engage U.S. Marines, resulting in a "great many casualties among our boys." "Surely Mr. Kosygin realized," the President continued, "that should this happen following the President's decision to stop the bombing, he would be crucified in this country for having taken the decision."[42]

According to the memorandum of conversation, "Chairman Kosygin thought that from a practical point of view the question could be put as follows: If the bombing stopped today, representatives of the United States and North Viet-Nam would meet tomorrow, wherever the President wished—Hanoi or New York or Moscow or Paris or Geneva or any other place. From that point on, it would be up to the negotiators to work out what was to follow. In establishing such direct contact with Hanoi, the President could present all questions between the United States and North Viet-Nam and the other side could do the same. Certainly, this could save hundreds of thousands of lives which would otherwise perish in vain. The President could set the condition that if the bombing were stopped, representatives of the two countries should meet at any place designated in, say, two days. Without such direct contact, no solution was possible. The President did not know what they wanted and indeed North Viet-Nam did not know what the President wanted. Mr. Kosygin urged the President to try this step, which in addition carried no risk to the position of the United States."

The President asked Kosygin whether he "would and could provide assistance at the conference table, if such a meeting took place, in obtaining self-determination for the people of South Viet-

[41] Memorandum of Conversation, Meeting of President Johnson and Premier Kosygin, June 23, 1967, 3:15 p.m. to 4:30 p.m., prepared by William Krimer. Mr. Krimer recalls that the meeting lasted from 2 p.m. to 5 p.m.

[42] According to Chester Cooper, who was closely involved in negotiations activities in his role as deputy to Ambassador Harriman, "The bombing cutback proposal was revived in the State Department" prior to the President's meeting with Kosygin, "but the White House gave it a cool reception. In the end, the idea was dropped." Cooper, *The Lost Crusade*, p. 376.

nam" and thus enable the U.S. to withdraw its forces. Premier Kosygin replied that he could not answer without consulting the North Vietnamese, and urged the President to put the question in writing for him to present to them.

The two leaders agreed to meet again two days later (June 25) and as the meeting ended Kosygin, according to the memorandum of conversation, "stressed again that all problems between the two nations could be solved if it were not for the grave problem in Viet-Nam and the new problems which have arisen in the Middle East. He felt very strongly that Viet-Nam had destroyed much that had developed between the United States and the USSR and had given China a chance to raise its head with consequent great danger for the peace of the entire world. Viet-Nam also led the United States into something unknown and had finally resulted in a military budget today which was greater than that of 1943. He asked if this could be considered to be a sober and reasonable policy. If it came to a question of prestige, he wanted to remind the President of the example of de Gaulle who had fought in Algiers for 7 years and then had withdrawn; in consequence, his prestige had not decreased at all, on the contrary it had risen throughout the world."

After the meeting on June 23, the President, according to his memoirs, "studied Hanoi's message carefully . . . [and] discussed it at length with Secretaries Rusk and McNamara,"[43] and on June 24 Rusk prepared a message for the President to give to Kosygin for transmittal to the North Vietnamese stating that the U.S. was prepared to stop bombing on the assumption that talks would then begin immediately. In addition, U.S. and other forces in the South would not advance to the north, and the U.S. would expect North Vietnamese forces not to advance to the south.[44]

This was the text of the U.S. statement:[45]

> The United States anticipates that it could stop the bombing of the Democratic Republic of Viet-Nam. The United States further anticipates that, following the cessation of bombing, there could be immediate discussions between representatives of the United States and of the Democratic Republic of Viet-Nam. These discussions could be held in Geneva, Moscow, Vientiane, or any other suitable location. The United States further anticipates that its own and allied forces in the northern provinces of South Viet-Nam would not advance to the north and that elements of the armed forces of the Democratic Republic of Viet-Nam in the northern part of south VietNam and in the southern portions of North Viet-Nam would not advance to the south. The United States anticipates that, if discussions are held between its representatives and those of the Democratic Republic of Viet-Nam, all questions which either side might wish to raise could be raised. The United States would hope, on the basis of the anticipations expressed above, that the results of such talks could be the stabilization of peace

---

[43] Johnson, *The Vantage Point*, p. 257. According to the President's Daily Diary, the President talked with Rusk and McNamara from 4:50 p.m. to 5:14 p.m. that day (Friday, June 23), after which he flew to California for a speech that night, flew on Saturday morning to his ranch in Texas, and returned to Washington and then to Glassboro, where on Sunday morning, June 25, he met with the U.S. delegation from 12:53 p.m. to 1:29 p.m. before meeting again with Kosygin.

[44] This "no military advantage" formula was used subsequently in the 1968 Paris talks.

[45] Johnson Library, NSF country File, Addendum, U.S.S.R. [Glassboro Memcons].

in Southeast Asia. The United States would be glad to know of the reactions of the Democratic Republic of Viet-Nam to the thoughts expressed above.

It is important to note that this formulation represented a substantial change in the U.S. position, which previously had stipulated, in one form or another, that the U.S. would cease bombing only on the condition that the North Vietnamese had stopped infiltration. As will be seen, the Glassboro formula became the basis for the U.S. position in the subsequent discussions in Paris in the summer of 1967 and the President's proposal in his San Antonio speech in September.

Rusk also prepared on June 24 a brief statement for the President for his meeting with Kosygin on June 25, as follows:[46]

> Mr. Chairman, you and I have a very special responsibility on matters involving peace. It is of the greatest importance that you and I not misunderstand each other and that no problems of good faith arise between us. Therefore, I want you personally to know that we are prepared to stop the bombing as a step toward peace. We are not prepared to stop the bombing merely to remove one-half of the war while the other half of the war proceeds without limit. I am accepting very large risks in giving you the message for transmittal to Hanoi which I have just given you. I want you to know that if talks do not lead to peace or if protracted talks are used to achieve one-sided military advantage against us, we shall have to resume full freedom of action. I say this to you and not to Hanoi because I think it is of great importance that you and I fully understand each other. I do not ask you to agree; I am merely asking you to understand what is in my mind.

Johnson and Kosygin met again with interpreters on June 25. Johnson read aloud the message from the U.S. to the North Vietnamese. Kosygin's response was that "although it contained certain qualifications, it looked alright *[sic]* to him on the whole."[47] "Stressing the need for complete confidence between the Chairman and himself," the President then read the statement that Rusk had prepared for him to use in talking to Kosygin. In reply, Kosygin said he would keep the matter "strictly confidential," and would transmit promptly the U.S. message to the North Vietnamese, "and if and when a reaction was received, the United States would be immediately informed."

"No response to our proposal ever came back," Johnson said in his memoirs, "either directly or through Moscow. Despite many subsequent exchanges with the Soviets on Vietnam, they never gave us an answer. Nor did anything ever come from Hanoi. The door to peace was still tightly barred."[48]

Based on what he called "our recent conversations," as well as conversations with Rusk about the Glassboro meeting, Fulbright wrote to the President on June 30 about the situation in Vietnam.

---

[46] Johnson Library, NSF Country File, Addendum, U.S.S.R. [Glassboro Memcons], Memorandum for the President from Rusk, June 24, 1967.

[47] Same location, Memorandum of Conversation, Meeting of President Johnson and Premier Kosygin, June 25, 1967, 2:45 p.m. to 6:30 p.m., drafted by the U.S. interpreter for the meeting, Alexander Akalovsky.

[48] Johnson, *The Vantage Point*, p. 257.

Noting the President and Rusk held contrary views, he suggested a halt in the bombing of North Vietnam for "an indefinite period just to see what would happen." "I am not suggesting," he said, "a public announcement of an 'unconditional' and definitive cessation, and I am certainly not suggesting a promise never to bomb again, no matter what. I am suggesting simply that the bombing be quietly and progressively reduced over a period of, say, a week or two and then terminated. I do believe that this might encourage Mr. Kosygin over the summer to take some new initiative."[49]

"[R]egardless of what is done about the bombing," Fulbright added, "I most strongly urge you to proceed with great caution in any significant increase in the number of American troops in Vietnam," both because it would be prejudicial to the "fragile beginning" at Glassboro, and because it would be a "grievous mistake to increase our involvement in Vietnam before we have a clearer idea of how political events in that country are going to unfold in connection with the September elections. . . . We may have to face a very unsatisfactory political situation there prior to and following the elections—possibly so unsatisfactory that we would want to make a major reassessment of our position. In such a situation, we would have a little more room for maneuver if we were not in the process of major augmentation of our forces."

Rostow replied for the President: "The President has read with interest your thoughtful letter of June 30 on Vietnam. As always, I am sure he will take your views into account in the decisions which lie ahead."

Apparently the President's handling of the Middle East situation and his meeting with Kosygin were well-received by Members of the Senate. In a memorandum to the President on July 5, 1967, in which he suggested capitalizing on it for the remainder of the 1967 congressional session and in 1968, Mike Manatos, White House liaison with the Senate, said that the President's actions had created goodwill among Democratic and Republican Senate leaders, "from Mansfield and Dirksen on down." "Particularly is this change telling on Senator Fulbright," he said, "who likes to think his views on the advisability of the Kosygin meeting had some measure of influence on the end decision."[50]

McNamara and Westmoreland Agree on a Compromise

In early July 1967, the President sent McNamara to Vietnam, accompanied by Katzenbach, McNaughton and Wheeler, to work out an agreement with Westmoreland on the request he had made in March for more troops and broader bombing authority. Others on the trip included White House Counsel McPherson and William Leonhart, a Foreign Service Officer assigned to the White House (Special Assistant for Vietnam Civil Affairs) to assist Komer with pacification.[51]

---

[49] Johnson Library, WHCF, Ex ND 19/CO 312, letter from Fulbright to the President, June 30, 1967, with reply by Rostow, July 7, 1967.

[50] Johnson Library, WHCF, Ex ND 19/CO 1–6, memorandum for the President from Mike Manatos, July 5, 1967.

[51] Several weeks earlier, McPherson and William Jorden had visited South Vietnam for two weeks, and on June 13 McPherson gave the President a report on his "impressions." (Johnson Library, Office Files of Harry McPherson.) He spoke highly of the quality of the Americans in-

Continued

Westmoreland viewed the meeting as the "last chance" to get additional forces, and "enormous energy was used in making the briefings for McNamara as persuasive as possible."[52]

During his meeting with McNamara on July 7, Westmoreland again expressed optimism about the war. "The situation is not a stalemate," he said. "We are winning slowly but steadily and this pace can accelerate if we reinforce our successes."[53] Westmoreland and his top staff officers also criticized Course of Action B in the May 19 DPM, under which only 30,000 troops would be added and bombing would be shifted to the area below the 20th parallel. The J–3 (operations) officer commented:[54]

> In summary, the reduced forces under course of action B; the limitation of air operations north of 20° latitude; and the restriction of ground action to South Vietnam could reinforce Hanoi's determination to prolong the conflict. In particular, the restriction of out-of-country air and ground operations would increase the enemy's capability to concentrate his defense, maintain his LOCs and require us to divert additional ground forces to the containment role. Under these circumstances, we present the enemy increased options to prolonging the war. Course of action B does not provide us with reasonable assurance that, given the present objectives, there would be any

---

volved in the war but noted that the military "tend to defend the status quo, that is, whatever is being done at the moment," and that "the embassy people tend to be absorbed in specific political questions—who is down and who is up in Saigon." Neither group, he said, "seems to be looking for a new kind of politics, a politics of programs instead of personalities."

Most of the military, McPherson said, had "'accepted' revolutionary development as an assignment, but only in their heads; their hearts are committed to the shooting war against the VC main forces." The OCO [Office of Civilian Operations] people—Komer excluded—seems to be hesitant about occupying the driver's seat and calling for more effort in the unglamorous pacification campaign." "It will require constant pressure from here [the White House] to keep the pacification effort at the fore-front."

"Most of our chips in the pacification field," McPherson said, "are riding on the revolutionary development program." He said he had visited the RD training center and had been impressed with the director, Major Nguyen Be, but that it was "hard to say" how well the RD teams were doing in the hamlets. And he quoted Americans "whose instincts seemed right to me," who said: "'Nothing can really work unless there is *political change*. RD had been tried before, under Diem; almost everything has been tried. But until there is a government in Saigon that can gain the people's trust, and make its will felt in the provinces, all of these schemes will break apart on the same old rocks: suspicion of the government, corrupt officials, lack of response by those in a position to help.'" (emphasis in original)

McPherson noted the "constant dilemma" faced by Americans in Vietnam of "how much to run the show, and run it well, as we can; how much to hang back and try to bring the government along, frustrating as that is."

On military operations, he praised U.S. forces and said that American firepower was "unbelievable." But he added that the Communists, though "in trouble in most areas," "can still operate in many villages throughout the country," and that "some well-spring of idealism and romanticism is being reached by the Viet Cong, and that it will continue being reached until the government finds a way to top it for itself."

He touched briefly on the problem of the conduct of the war. Air Force intelligence officers, he said, "seemed to me deeply imbedded in ideology, to wit, give us two or three months and less restricted targets and we'll bring this thing to a . . . to a what? Well, to the point where Ho has to decide whether he can go on with it. Maybe I had just heard one too many briefings—this was my last day there—but it seemed thin soup to me."

"I came back neither optimistic nor pessimistic," McPherson concluded, "neither hawk nor dove. We are simply there, and we should be. . . . Every aspect of our national life and our role in the world is involved in Vietnam. I feel that I am only another of those many men who have a part of their soul at stake there."

[52] Gen. Douglas Kinnard, telephone conversation with the author, June 8, 1993. Kinnard says he had been put in charge of making the preparation for the presentation of the case for more troops.

[53] For more details on Westmoreland's briefing see *PP*, Gravel ed., vol. IV, pp. 517–518. The text of Westmoreland's statement, together with those of several officers from the staff who participated in the briefing, is contained in a compilation, "Vietnam Sec Def Briefings, 7–8 July 1967—COMUSMACV Assessment," a copy of which is in the Department of State, Lot File 70 D 48.

[54] *PP*, Gravel ed., vol. IV, p. 522.

> prospects of an early settlement of the conflict. This is not to imply we might not eventually win the war of attrition but it would be a long drawn out process and would postpone the time when US forces could redeploy from South Vietnam.

The J–2 (intelligence) officer emphasized also the increasing use being made by the Communists of "sanctuaries" in Laos and Cambodia.[55]

Ambassador Bunker told McNamara that he, too, thought the war was being won, but he agreed with Westmoreland that steps to control infiltration, including attacks across the Laotian border, were of the "highest priority."[56] Military operations into Laos, Bunker contended, were legally justified because North Vietnam, a signatory to the 1962 Geneva Accords, had its troops in Laos and was using Laos to infiltrate South Vietnam. "Is it not logical and reasonable, therefore," he asked, "that South Vietnamese troops should oppose and combat North Vietnamese offensive action by whatever method can be devised in order to prevent the invasion of their country?"

After stressing also the importance of nonmilitary programs, especially pacification and the upcoming national elections in September 1967, Bunker concluded that the next several months might be viewed by the North Vietnamese as a "critical time of testing of wills." "Hanoi," he said, "may be set to hold on in the expectation that we cannot significantly curb infiltration or destroy the VC's military and political capability in the South."

"In the end," Bunker said, "they [the South Vietnamese] must win it themselves." This would require better leadership, however, both civilian and military, especially in the pacification program. A "serious deficiency" in improving government programs, he added, was the "lack of adequate means of finding out what the Vietnamese people are really thinking and what their aspirations are." But, from "soundings throughout the country," he said, "security and social justice, especially getting rid of corruption, seem to be highest on the list. There is obviously great deficiency in both."

Bunker concluded:

> The Vietnamese are intelligent, hardworking and if properly guided, encouraged and well led can perform effectively. We have had a good measure of success and I believe that we are gradually achieving our aims in Viet-Nam. If we stick with it long enough—and this is not a short-term proposition—I am confident that we shall have reasonable success in achieving our objectives.

Rostow sent President Johnson a copy of Bunker's statement with the comment, "Herewith Amb. Bunker's briefing—with all the scope, balance, lucidity about priorities and tasks we would expect."[57]

---

[55] See *ibid.*, pp. 518–520.

[56] Johnson Library, NSF Country File, Vietnam. See also Bunker's weekly report to the President, July 12, 1967, Douglas Pike (ed.) *The Bunker Papers*, vol. 1, pp. 78 ff. In a cable to Rusk several weeks earlier, Bunker had advocated, as a way of controlling infiltration, the extension across Laos of the physical barrier being constructed in Vietnam south of the DMZ. See Johnson Library, NSF Memos to the President—Walt Rostow, Saigon to Washington 28293, June 17, 1967.

[57] Johnson Library, NSF Country File, Vietnam.

McNamara also heard from Admiral Sharp (CINCPAC) as well as Air Force and Navy commanders on the need to increase the air war. "If we eliminate the only offensive element of our strategy," Sharp said, "I do not see how we can expect to win." Bunker did not agree that bombing should be increased, however, and again expressed the hope that the anti-infiltration barrier, combined with attacks on supply lines and bases in Laos and Cambodia, would help to control infiltration.[58]

During the meeting, there were briefings on a number of aspects of the war, including preparations for the barrier along the DMZ. At one point McNamara declared: "I think we are candid with ourselves—I doubt very much if this [the barrier] will stop it [infiltration], but we are putting a tremendous amount of effort in on this. We have already incorporated about $800,000,000 for the whole system, but the cost is really quite small if we get some benefit out of it." "I, myself," he added, "have been very dissatisfied, and I know most of you have been as well, with our inability through application and with tremendous amounts of air power to interdict these lines of communications. What we are trying to do here is to get a tremendous step forward in air effectiveness."[59]

There was considerable discussion of ways of increasing troop strength other than by adding more Americans. McNamara strongly emphasized the need for South Vietnam, where the draft age was 20 (compared to 18 for the U.S.), to lower the age and extend the length of service. General McGovern responded, "we feel that we could get the GVN [Government of Vietnam] this year, without too much difficulty, to lower the draft age to 19 and also extend the terms of service for one year. Psychologically, we hope they will accept this. . . ." McNamara interrupted him:

> Let me just say this, General, psychologically, I cannot accept it. I am sick and tired of having problems in what the GVN accept when the American society is under the strain it is under today. And, you men out here are under a strain. There is no damn reason in the world why we should worry about whether the GVN will accept it psychologically. We can't break their society, they are under a strain, I realize that, but there are certain things that they are just going to have to face forcefully. And, one of them is that our Government is not going to send additional tens of thousands of U.S. personnel over here until they [GVN] get fully mobilized. That's all there is to it. It just is not going to be done. It is politically impossible. The people won't stand for it. So, they are going to have to get this done out here. . . .

On the night of July 8, McNamara met with Westmoreland and a compromise was reached on Westmoreland's original request for 100,000–200,000 more troops. Based on new studies by Enthoven's Systems Analysis Office on ways by which 45,000–50,000, and up to 86,000 if need be, could be sent from existing forces rather than by increasing the draft or calling up the Reserves, it was agreed that Westmoreland would get 45,000 more men—only 15,000 more

---

[58] *PP*, Gravel ed., vol. IV, p. 196. There is a copy of Sharp's statement in the State Department, Lot File 70 D 48.

[59] National Archives, Westmoreland-CBS Papers, partial transcript of questions and answers during briefings for McNamara, July 7–8, 1967.

than the May 19 DPM had recommended. This would bring the total authorized strength to 525,000 for Program 5 (which was the level originally requested by the military for the previous year's Program 4). Although the available records are not clear on this point, it would appear that McNamara and Westmoreland also agreed to continue the air war at its existing level and scope rather than increasing it or limiting it to the area below the 20th parallel. In a cable to the President on July 12 in which he summarized the results of the discussions, Bunker said it was agreed that the U.S. should "maintain our bombing of North Vietnam through the remaining months of good weather. We can then decide whether to cut back to the 20th parallel and whether we then think a pause to test out Hanoi's intentions would be advisable."[60]

Apparently Komer had been asked by the President for his personal assessments of the Vietnam situation and his recommendations for action, and the new Deputy Ambassador, Eugene Locke, had also been asked by the President for his personal recommendations. Komer responded in an "eyes only" backchannel cable to the President on July 9.[61] "No matter how many call me a rosy optimist," he said, "I feel more confident than ever that at long last we are slowly but surely winning war of attrition in South. After fifteen months full-time on VN, including two months out here, I will stick to my guns despite more skeptical views SecDef [Secretary of Defense] and others who are not as intimately familiar with myriad day-to-day details which add up to what really happening in VN." "Westy clearly thinks we are winning military war. His real pitch is that the more you give him the faster he can reinforce success."

Bombing of the North, Komer said, was helping to limit infiltration, and should continue. Moreover, Bunker, Westmoreland and he believed that there should be stronger cross-border raids against supply lines in Laos. "Combination of continued bombing, the new barrier, and raids into Laos offers," he said, "real hope of limiting NVA infiltration, thus complementing our growing attrition of southern VC."

In pacification, Komer said, "we are doing much better than last year," adding, "Though McNamara still skeptical on pacification, I feel in much better position than he to see that we are finally making some progress. . . ."

Komer said that the "biggest worry" was that the September 1967 election in South Vietnam, "will go sour. Thieu/Ky are running scared . . . which increases risk they'll rig elections. We can't live with a sham election, partly because resulting regime would simply be so lacking in popular support that it would be under constant pressure. Hence we must weigh in heavily (and publicly as means of pressuring Ky/Thieu) for reasonably fair election."

"Provided we can make sure elections not a show," Komer concluded, "and can sustain present military pressure, enemy summer/fall offensive will prove even more of a fizzle than last year. This could lead Hanoi to rethink whether it can really afford to wait us out through 1968 elections. Even if it decides to outwait us, I am

---

[60] *The Bunker Papers,* cited above, cable of July 12, 1967.

[61] Johnson Library, C.F. ND 19/CO 312, Komer 164 from Saigon to the President, July 9, 1967, sent immediately to the LBJ Ranch by Rostow, CAP 67721, July 9.

convinced that by mid-1968 we will be so visibly winning that even press here won't be able to deny it."

Therefore, Komer said, he recommended:

A. Keep bombing North through remaining months of good weather. Hold off pause or cutback to 20 degrees until fall, when onset monsoon will force some diminution anyway. I fear military would scream publicly if we cut back just when they claim they're finally getting results.

B. Allow up to brigade size ARVN raids into Laos as added means of getting at infiltration routes.

C. Whatever added US forces you decide to give Westy, put positive public face on it. Also get him to say it's enough for now by promising to let him reargue case later if necessary.

D. Keep heat on to revamp ARVN. Westy has made real progress, but a lot more is possible and will reduce US troop needs.

E. Tell us in spades we'd better make sure elections clean.

Deputy Ambassador Locke's recommendations were summarized for the President by Rostow in a memorandum on July 12:[62]

A. Military

1. Prevent infiltration of enemy forces through Laos

a. use South Vietnamese battalions in Laos and build strong points or other feasible barriers;

b. intensify and expand bombing in Laos

c. intensify and expand bombing of selected targets in North Vietnam.

d. maximize use of new weapons (bombs, mines and detection devices)

e. expedite search for technical aids to night fighting.

f. experiment with chemical techniques to destroy permanently roads and pathways.

2. Avoid mining Haiphong harbor but consider bombing warehouses at the port and blocking the harbor by sinking a ship in the channel.

3. Encourage reorganization of South Vietnam security forces to increase their effectiveness in providing the security necessary for the new pacification program.

4. Much greater use of U.S. military leadership in Vietnamese regional and Popular Force units including integration of some U.S. and Vietnamese units.

5. Use South Vietnamese regular troops in combat missions with U.S. troops as much as possible.

6. Provide adequate U.S. supporting personnel and equipment to an enlarged Vietnamese Navy which would expand its river operations in the Delta.

B. Pacification

1. Encourage and support new programs to identify and destroy the Viet Cong organization in South Vietnam.

2. Regain U.S. control of the use by the South Vietnamese Government of counterpart funds to reduce corruption

---

[62] Johnson Library, NSF Memos to the President—Walt Rostow, memorandum to the President, July 12, 1967.

and give U.S. leverage to accomplish changes in existing Vietnamese village and province programs.

C. Political-Economic

1. Encourage Thieu and Ky to reach an understanding which will keep them together before and after the elections, if they win.

2. Make clear that free elections are essential to present and future political stability.

3. Find a way for General Westmoreland to relieve some of his present logistic soldiers for combat duty so that he can obtain combat soldiers he needs with minimum new U.S. troops.

4. Ensure that South Vietnamese do their part in mobilizing their manpower.

5. Increase meetings between ranking U.S. and South Vietnamese leaders.

6. After the South Vietnamese election, encourage the new leaders to initiate political discussions with members of the National Liberation Front.

McNamara returned to Washington on July 11, and, after talking by telephone to the President four times during the morning of July 12, he reported orally (there was no written report) to him at a meeting from 1:05 p.m. to 2:38 p.m. that day, attended also by Rusk, Katzenbach, Rostow, Wheeler, Taylor, Helms, Komer, Clark Clifford, William Leonhart, McPherson, Tom Johnson and George Christian.[63] McNamara said that military operations were proceeding well and "There is reason to expect significant military losses by the Viet Cong in coming months." "There is not," he added, "a military stalemate."

On the question of sending additional U.S. troops, McNamara said that "we can get by with less" than the 100,000 Westmoreland wanted by putting civilians into military jobs, asking the Koreans for more troops, and getting the South Vietnamese to reduce the draft age and extend tours of service. Australia, New Zealand, Thailand and the Philippines should also be asked to send more combat troops.

McNamara said he thought that the South Vietnamese Army should be authorized to expand ground operations into Laos, adding that he considered Cambodia to be "growing as a Viet Cong base."

With regard to bombing of North Vietnam, he reported that U.S. commanders wanted to expand the target system and to mine and attack the ports, a move he said he did not support. Noting that

---

[63] Notes of the meeting at 1:05 p.m. on July 12 were prepared by Tom Johnson and are in his Notes of Meetings at the Johnson Library. In addition, the President made some notes, which are located in the Handwriting File. The President's notes follow the general lines of the presentations made at the meeting and do not add anything to Tom Johnson's notes, nor do they suggest any special interest of the President in what was being said.

With respect to the accuracy and authority of his notes of meetings Tom Johnson says that after each day's notes were typed he sent them to the President, who reviewed them and sent them back the next day. According to Johnson, the President, to his knowledge, never amended them. Johnson Library, Transcript of the Vietnam Round Table, Mar. 9–10, 1991, p. 212.

In addition to Tom Johnson's notes, there is a "Memorandum for Record" on the meeting by Taylor, located in the Taylor Papers at the National Defense University, a copy of which was kindly provided by Gen. Douglas Kinnard.

Quotations used here are from both Tom Johnson's notes and Taylor's memorandum.

considerable progress had been made toward crippling the rail line between Hanoi and the border of China, he said he did not agree with military commanders that there had been progress in the air war since his last trip. "We have destroyed more but what we have destroyed has less effect on the war effort in the South."

Wheeler reported that there had been "steady progress," and that "there are no great military problems in sight." He disagreed with McNamara on the effects of bombing, and "argued strongly" in favor of an increased program. He recommended reducing the prohibited areas around Hanoi and Haiphong to 10 miles and 4 miles, and urged strikes on all targets except population centers.

Wheeler also said that the Navy's efforts to mine inland waterways had not been effective and that new methods were being sought. "The President directed that the Navy be energized to the maximum extent to improve performance in closing inland waterways."

In reporting on his findings, Under Secretary of State Katzenbach told the President that "U.S. and allied forces can win depending on the performance, if we get it, of the government of Vietnam." He said he agreed that military pressure must continue to be applied.

Komer, reporting on pacification, said that he was "more encouraged than when he left" about pacification in general.

Komer also "advanced the thought that it was time to get the [Vietnamese] generals out of politics. He would send them back to the battlefield and hope that a civilian government would be at least as efficient and probably less corrupt. He expressed confidence that our large military presence could prevent a coup or military disunity."

There was broad agreement among Katzenbach, McNamara and Komer that the political situation was, as McNamara said, "the greatest danger facing us." With only two months remaining before the South Vietnamese election, Ky and Thieu were feuding for power, and, as Katzenbach said, "the government could fall apart if Ky, who was 'bitter,' should refuse to cooperate in accommodating the interests of both men and maintaining the unity of the armed forces in the election." There were only two or three weeks left, he said, for the U.S. "to work on the political situation" and to work out an agreement between the two men with the U.S. as the "guarantor."

Rusk commented, "We are going to come through this thing, [and] we must get the American people to realize that the U.S. forces are going to come through this."

The President responded that there was "an attitude in this country today that we are not doing all we should to get the war over as quickly as it should be." "[T]he U.S. people," he added, "do think, perhaps, that this war cannot be won." He said he was "more frightened by this than by the Thieu-Ky difficulties." Ky, he said, had been "number one" and Thieu had been "number two" for several years, "and perhaps some accommodation can be reached with a division of responsibility." Katzenbach replied that "if the American people give us a chance here at home, that he had every reason to believe that we could win the war in the field."

Clark Clifford, referring to public feeling that the war could not be won, asked McNamara whether this was true. McNamara replied that U.S. units were destroying "a significant capacity" of the Communists' main force units, and that there was a limit to the troops that would be supplied from the North. "Hanoi," he added, "is testing the unity and patience of the American people."

According to Tom Johnson's notes, which President Johnson later quoted in his memoirs, McNamara said in response to Clifford's question, "for the first time [since U.S. forces were sent in 1965] . . . he felt that if we follow the same program we will win the war and end the fighting."[64]

In summing up the meeting, the President "expressed his fear that U.S. patience would progressively decline and with it the will to continue the war in Vietnam. He feels that energetic, affirmative action is necessary to countrovert the impression that we are not doing everything possible to gain a speedy success. He concedes that some troop reinforcement will be necessary but wants the Westmoreland requirement squeezed down to the absolute minimum acceptable."

Although the notes of this meeting do not contain any references to the subject, it would appear that, as a memorandum from Cooper to Harriman on July 17 stated, McNamara and Katzenbach "returned from Vietnam each convinced we must exert a maximum effort to stimulate negotiations," and were "now thinking of a concentrated, 'all-out' attack on the problem."[65]

The meeting on the morning of July 12 was followed by a brief meeting from 2:50 p.m. to 3:40 p.m. of the Tuesday Luncheon group—the President, Rusk, McNamara, Rostow, Christian and Tom Johnson—at which the President asked McNamara to brief the press after the luncheon and to make these points:[66]

—Announcement that some more troops would be required.

—That the troops currently there should be used better.

—That we would be talking with other governments about more troops (this is a matter for the 7 nations and not just me).

—There would be no call up of reserves to meet current manpower requirements.

—There is no military stalemate.

That night (July 12), Westmoreland, who had returned to the United States for his mother's funeral, arrived in Washington, where he was an overnight guest at the White House. He had dinner with the President, following which the two men talked for an hour and a half. Westmoreland apparently was upset about press

[64] Johnson Library, Tom Johnson's Notes of Meetings, Notes of meeting July 12, 1967. See also Lyndon Johnson, *The Vantage Point*, p. 262. In his Memorandum for the Record, cited above, Taylor says that McNamara "volunteered that for the first time he was feeling that the war could be won if the home-front could be kept stable and the will to carry on could be maintained."

[65] Library of Congress, Harriman Papers, Cooper File, Memorandum from Cooper to Harriman, "Organizing for Negotiations," July 17, 1967.

[66] Johnson Library, Tom Johnson's Notes of Meetings, Notes of Meeting July 12, 1967, 2:50 p.m. with Rusk, McNamara, Rostow, Christian and Tom Johnson. In his press briefing, McNamara, according to the President's wishes, "cited the judgment of several hundred officers in Vietnam—all senior Americans and Vietnamese officials and many allied and many American junior officers—that reports of a stalemate were, in their words, 'the most ridiculous statements they ever heard.'" *New York Times*, July 13, 1967.

reports of McNamara's briefing which indicated that McNamara had questioned Westmoreland's management of the war. The next day (July 13) the President met from 12:40 p.m. to 1:02 p.m. with McNamara, Westmoreland, Wheeler and Christian. He said that, in response to Westmoreland's concern, he had told him that:[67]

—He would carefully review everything.

—Secretary McNamara, General Westmoreland, and the President feel that General Westmoreland's team in Vietnam is the best we have ever seen.

—The President said he had never heard anybody who has ever been critical of General Westmoreland in any way.

—The President said that Westmoreland has been assured that he will have the troops he needs. The President referred back to many earlier statements he has made which said that the General's suggestions would be reviewed in light of existing situations and the General would be given whatever he needed. The President said there is an acceptable area on the number of troops and that we will be announcing these numbers in a few weeks. This agreement is fully shared by General Westmoreland, Secretary McNamara, and General Wheeler of the Joint Chiefs of Staff.

That same afternoon (July 13), the President met from 1:25 p.m. to 2:45 p.m. with McNamara, Westmoreland, Wheeler and Christian (Rusk and Rostow did not attend) to discuss the final agreement on sending new U.S. troops to Vietnam.[68] McNamara, who had met with Westmoreland that morning, reported that there was "'complete accord'" on sending 45,000 additional U.S. troops. (As noted, this would raise the total to 525,000, which was the level Westmoreland had requested a year earlier.) Wheeler agreed, and said "this meets the need for Vietnam." Westmoreland said that he was "delighted with the outcome," and that "with the additional men 'we will have a formidable force' . . . [and] that progress can be accelerated once the troops are deployed and placed." He added that he had not asked for a specific number of troops," and that his recommendations "have been honored."[69]

There was also some discussion of getting more troops from other countries. Wheeler said that the Australians might be able to provide one more battalion and that Korea might be asked for another combat brigade. He and McNamara agreed that "'we should put the bite' on Thailand for a larger troop commitment."

---

[67] Johnson Library, Tom Johnson's Notes of Meetings, Notes of meeting July 13, 1967, 12:40 p.m. of the President with McNamara, Westmoreland, Wheeler and Christian.

[68] Same location, Notes of the President's Meeting on July 13, 1967, at 1:25 p.m. with McNamara, Westmoreland, Wheeler and Christian.

[69] In his memoirs, however, Westmoreland said that he was "extremely disappointed for I knew that failure to provide major troop augmentation would extend the time required to do the job." *A Soldier Reports*, p. 230.

The decision on troop strength was based in part on avoiding mobilization, as the *Pentagon Papers* explained (*PP*, Gravel ed., vol. IV, pp. 527–528): "The program which emerged . . . was essentially the result of the circular path traced far back to the optimum request of Program 4. Its origins and its limits can be traced to one primary factor—that of mobilization. When the President and the Secretary of Defense, as well as other Congressional leaders and politically attuned decision makers in the government began to search for the illusive point at which the costs of Vietnam would become inordinate, they always settled upon the mobilization line, the point at which Reserves and large units would have to be called up to support a war which was becoming increasingly distasteful and intolerable to the American public. Domestic resource constraints with all of their political and social repercussions, not strategic or tactical military considerations in Vietnam, were to dictate American war policy from that time on."

The possibility of press censorship was also discussed. (In reporting on their trip McNamara and Katzenbach had lamented the criticism of U.S. policy by American reporters in Vietnam.) McNamara, Westmoreland, Wheeler and Christian agreed, however, "that while they are for censorship at times, that we would pay a terrible price for it." Christian (White House press secretary) said that censorship would be "a morass," and that "'we cannot do it.'" According to Tom Johnson's notes of the meeting, "It was agreed that no censorship would be taken."

As the meeting ended, the President asked the group whether South Vietnam would "go Communist" after the election if the U.S. stopped bombing North Vietnam. McNamara, the only one to reply according to the meeting notes, said that, "from what he had learned in the field, definitely no—the country would not go Communist."

After the meeting, the President, together with McNamara, Wheeler and Westmoreland held a press conference in which he said, "we are generally pleased with the progress we have made militarily. We are very sure that we are on the right track."[70] "[A]dditional troops are going to be needed and are going to be supplied," he said, but he refrained from stating that he had approved sending 45,000. The President then called on Wheeler and Westmoreland. Wheeler said "we are in accord." Westmoreland said that he had not asked for a specific number of troops. "I have recommended a deployment to Vietnam for a certain number of combat units that would comprise a part of a balanced force. I am being provided the forces, as I have recommended." In response to a question as to whether the increased forces would "fully meet" Westmoreland's request, the President replied:

> The answer is: Yes, we have reached a meeting of the minds. The troops that General Westmoreland needs and requests, as we feel it necessary will be supplied. General Westmoreland feels that is acceptable, General Wheeler thinks that is acceptable, and Secretary McNamara thinks that is acceptable. It is acceptable to me and we hope it is acceptable to you.
>
> Is that not true, General Westmoreland?
>
> General Westmoreland. I agree, Mr. President.
>
> The President. General Wheeler?
>
> General Wheeler. That is correct, Mr. President.
>
> The President. Secretary McNamara?
>
> Secretary McNamara. Yes, sir.

During the press conference, the President called upon Westmoreland to comment on the progress being made, and to "touch on this 'stalemate' creature." Westmoreland replied in part: "The statement that we are in a stalemate is complete fiction. . . . During the past year tremendous progress has been made."

The question of additional bombing authority was taken up at a meeting on July 18 of the President with the Tuesday luncheon group—Rusk, McNamara, Rostow, Christian and Tom Johnson—

---

[70] *Public Papers of the Presidents,* Lyndon B. Johnson, 1967, pp. 690–696 at 690.

from 6:06 p.m. to 7:30 p.m.[71] "The President read a letter to the group from a man in Arizona and quoted such in saying that U.S. people do not think the U.S. is sincere in its desire to end the war. The letter said, 'People believe that civilian heads have ignored the advice of the military.' The President said he read the letter only because he believes it is symptomatic of what we will be facing on the Hill and around the country in coming months."

McNamara then reviewed the targets that had been recommended by CINCPAC for the next phase of bombing. These, he said, were "largely unimportant." Some were in the 25-mile buffer zone near the Chinese border, a number were within the ten-mile radius of Hanoi, and 23 were within the four-mile circle of Haiphong. Among the targets recommended by the JCS was the Phuc Yen airbase, which had never been bombed. McNamara added that there was a "very strong potential" for civilian casualties if those in Hanoi and Haiphong were bombed, and that the targets near the center of Hanoi "are not worth the loss of a single U.S. plane or pilot." U.S. military commanders, he commented, "are interested in 'free bombing.'"

McNamara concluded by saying that he would recommend at least 17 targets outside the Hanoi-Haiphong prohibited zones (it is not clear whether these were included in the JCS recommendations), but would not recommend striking the North Vietnamese air base at Phuc Yen, "because the air base is heavily defended and the MIGs are of no threat to us at this point." But he told the President, "'Mr. President, your responsibility is to the people of this country. Whatever you feel we must do let's do it.'"

The notes of the meeting do not indicate what was decided at the meeting, but, based on a JCS cable to CINCPAC later that day, it would appear that some new targets were approved.[72] The message reported that the next phase of ROLLING THUNDER (RT57), "will be only a limited extension of previous targets. No cutback is planned."

The Clifford-Taylor Recommendations

In July 1967, shortly after deciding to send Westmoreland only 45,000 of the troops he had requested, the President sent Clark Clifford and Maxwell Taylor on a trip to South Vietnam and to the countries in the Pacific area that were assisting with the war ef-

---

[71] Johnson Library, Tom Johnson's Notes of Meetings, Meeting of the President with Rusk, et al., July 18, 1967, at 6:06 p.m.

Within the State Department, both the East Asia Bureau and the Bureau of Intelligence and Research (INR) were advising that, while it appeared that the North Vietnamese were suffering from the bombing and that they were conducting an evaluation of the situation and might be preparing to make some kind of a negotiating move, they were probably waiting for the results of the 1968 U.S. elections and any move they might make prior to that time would likely be a "tactical maneuver." The response of the U.S., William Bundy argued in a memorandum to Rusk on July 18, should be to avoid any "drastic" military actions, and "to create the impression of steady firmness, without a major shift in direction." (Bundy made these same points in a longer memorandum to McNamara on July 3, "Thoughts on Vietnam," following a telephone conversation between the two men.) Thomas Hughes, Director of INR, responded to Bundy on the same day (July 18), and agreed with his analysis and his conclusion. "Accordingly," Hughes said, "the logic of the situation would argue very strongly for no drastic shifts in our present pattern of operations against the North which might prejudice moves by Hanoi toward a less militant stance. The present pattern could probably be continued without such an effect, however. Operations which could lead to a greater degree of Chinese involvement should in any case be avoided." Hughes' memorandum is in U.S. Department of State, Central File, Pol 27 Viet S. Bundy's memoranda to Rusk and McNamara are in Lot File 85 D 240 (William Bundy Papers).

[72] *PP*, Gravel ed., vol. IV, p. 13, from JCS to CINCPAC 1859, July 18, 1967.

fort—Australia, New Zealand, Korea, Thailand and the Philippines to consult about the situation and to urge those countries to send more combat troops.[73]

The requests for troops, Clifford said, "fell on deaf ears."[74] The South Vietnamese said that they would add 65,000 troops, lower the draft age to 18 and increase the terms of service, but this decision had already been made and communicated to the U.S. None of the other governments offered to send more troops, but said they would consider the request. (When it became known that the issue of troops was going to be raised, the Filipinos, who had sent a hospital corps and an engineer battalion but no combat troops, cancelled Clifford and Taylor's visit.)

Clifford subsequently maintained that he returned from the trip "puzzled and troubled, dismayed by our failure to get more support from our allies. I could only hint at the level of my concern in our joint report to the President, since Taylor did not share it. Privately, though, I told President Johnson I was shocked at the failure of the countries whose security we believed we were defending to do more for themselves."[75]

In a report to the President on August 5, as well as in their meeting with the President, Rusk, Ball, Rostow, Nitze (sitting in for McNamara), McPherson, Christian and Tom Johnson, on August 5 from 1:49 p.m. to 4:08 p.m., Clifford and Taylor said that all the countries they had visited supported the war and rejected the "stalemate theory." "The movement is not dramatic, and all felt we should increase our pressure to get movement." All also endorsed "the essentiality of the bombing campaign against the north."[76] The Asian nations, Clifford and Taylor said, "were inclined to press it [the bombing] harder and with less regard for civilian casualties," whereas the Commonwealth countries (Australia and New Zealand) "are more inclined to continue it about as at present." Likewise, in discussions of closing the harbor at Haiphong by bombing or mining, there was less concern among the Asian nations about the possible consequences of bombing a Russian ship.

Clifford and Taylor also reported that none of the governments consulted was "interested in extending the war as a matter of policy," but that some of their suggestions, if followed, would have that effect. . . ."[77] "Almost everyone," they said, "would like to use troops to cut the infiltration routes in Laos and the concept of an Inchon-type landing [behind the lines, as at Inchon in the Korean war] behind the North Vietnamese forces at the 17th parallel had appeal for some. However, our reminder of the need for increased

[73] For a cable to U.S. Ambassadors in each of these countries announcing the trip, which included the text of the letter that President Johnson sent to each leader, see Department of State, Central File, Pol 27 Viet S, Washington 9005, July 19, 1967, to Bangkok, Canberra, Manila, Saigon, Seoul, and Wellington. The trip was discussed at a brief meeting of the President with McNamara, Katzenbach, Wheeler, Clifford, Rostow and Tom Johnson from 12:51 p.m. to 1:15 p.m. on July 14, 1967, notes of which are in the Johnson Library, Tom Johnson's Notes of Meetings.

[74] Clark M. Clifford, "A Viet Nam Reappraisal," *Foreign Affairs,* 47 (July 1969), pp. 601–622 at 606, and Clifford, *Counsel to the President,* p. 449.

[75] Clifford, *Counsel to the President,* p. 451. See also Clifford, "A Viet Nam Reappraisal," p. 607, and the Johnson Library's oral history interview with Clifford, Tape 3, July 14, 1969.

[76] The Clifford-Taylor report is in the Johnson Library, NSF Country File, Vietnam, and the notes of the meeting of August 5 are in Tom Johnson's Notes of Meetings. Quotations used here are from these two documents.

[77] At this point in the report there is a one-line excision.

ground forces to carry out these operations served to dampen their enthusiasm."

While in South Vietnam, Clifford and Taylor met privately with Ky and Thieu separately, and, joined by Bunker, Westmoreland and others from the U.S. Mission, they met with Ky, Thieu and other South Vietnamese officials.[78] During their meeting with the President on August 5, Clifford commented on these discussions. He said that there was a "truce" between Ky and Thieu, but he did not know how long it would last.[79]

The Clifford-Taylor mission, in addition to serving the purposes indicated above, had a concealed purpose. Although there is very little documentation, and existing evidence is scanty, it is clear from available information that the President, deeply worried about not "winning" or settling the war, privately asked Clifford (or Clifford and Taylor) to advise him on ways of increasing the pressure on the North Vietnamese.[80] The advice that the President had been getting from the Defense and State Departments, as represented by the DPM, was that the level of U.S. ground forces should be stabilized and that the air war should be concentrated on infiltration routes (lines of communications) rather than attacking strategic targets in the Hanoi-Haiphong area or near the Chinese border. There was also a general feeling among all of the principal civilian officials, except for Rostow, that the war could only be "won" by the success of the South Vietnamese in promoting internal strength and security. As expressed by William Bundy in his memorandum of June 2, "If we can get a reasonably solid GVN political structure and GVN performance at all levels, favorable trends could become really marked over the next 18 months, the war will be won for practical purposes at some point, and the resulting peace will be secured. On the other hand, if we do not get those results from the GVN and the South Vietnamese people, no amount of US effort will achieve our basic objective in South Vietnam. . . . It follows that perhaps the most critical of all factors in assessing our whole strategy—bombing, major force increases, and all the rest—lies in the effect they have on the South Vietnamese."[81]

Rostow, supported by Ginsburgh, while agreeing that South Vietnamese effort was essential, was more committed to the use of

---

[78] For the meetings of Clifford and Taylor with South Vietnamese leaders see, in addition to their report, the summary sent to Washington by Bunker, U.S. Department of State, Lot File 72 D 207, Saigon to Washington 1871, July 25, 1967.

[79] Notes of the meeting of August 5, cited above.

[80] In notes he made in connection with the trip (which are not dated), Clifford summarized what he was told were or perceived to be the President's views at that time (Johnson Library, Clifford Papers, Handwritten Notes):

"1. Chinese now occupied—time to strike decisive blows.

"2. More and more American public views war as not Vietnamese—but Southeast Asian war.

"3. President's feeling that Hanoi is hurting now—much more than before.

"a) Presume increasing on ground in S. Vietnam and in air in N. Vietnam.

"b) Viet Cong not as strong as before.

"c) Political progress is serious blow to Viet Cong. . . .

"4. American public support for war has strengthened.

[*Note:* a line was drawn through all of #4, apparently, judging by the width of the pen that was used, after the notes had first been completed.]

"5. President Johnson feels the time has come to exert maximum pressure on the enemy. . . .

"6. President feels only one solution to war——

"1. Keep up pressure.

"2. Increase pressure.

"3. Present forceful image of solidarity among allies."

[81] Bundy memorandum of June 2, 1967, cited above.

force. He favored a callup of the Reserves and the deployment of 100,000 more U.S. troops, and, while agreeing that bombing should concentrate on infiltration routes, he believed that pressure should be increased in North Vietnam and that there should be selective attacks on strategic targets in the northeast. In a memorandum to the President on July 22, he said that although the North Vietnamese might decide to negotiate, this was unlikely, and that "the only way to maximize the chance of an early end of the war is to proceed on the assumption that the war will last a long time."[82] Rostow said that he "spent some time reading literally hundreds of particular intelligence reports on the situation in the various provinces of South Vietnam. They show, in different degrees, strain on Viet Cong morale and manpower; a weakening of military effectiveness; increased concentration on finding food and recruits rather than actual military operations; but no definitive break in the resilient Viet Cong structure." Moreover, "the bombing of North Vietnam is hurting them, but not to the point of necessitating an early decision."

Rostow concluded the memorandum by arguing that the U.S., while needing to be prepared for a North Vietnamese peace overture "soon rather than late," "should make every effort to increase the pressure on them in the South and in the North."

The President, faced with the growing disaffection of his principal civilian advisers and increasing pressure from Congress and the military for stronger action, especially in the air war, and apparently feeling that bombing should be increased, decided to enlist Clifford and Taylor's help as a way of confirming and bolstering his position and justifying decisions that ran counter to the advice he was receiving not to increase bombing. Clifford and Taylor, who approached this concealed assignment with great discretion, discussed the military situation with Westmoreland, who then sent the following cable to Admiral Sharp:[83]

> During my discussions yesterday with Mr. Clifford and General Taylor, great interest was expressed in targets that had not been struck in North Vietnam. I discussed the matter in generalities but recommended that they withhold further discussion on this subject until they met with you in Honolulu. This they agreed to do.
>
> It was suggested by General Taylor that I alert you to this matter. Furthermore, Mr. Clifford has requested that you have prepared for discussion and submission a list of targets that are considered important but have not been struck because of restriction and that an explanation be given as to why we consider the targets important and our best estimate of the risks involved in attacking these targets.
>
> As you know, this subject is outside of the Mission assigned to them by the President and it is desired that their interest in this subject be closely held.

After the trip, but separate from their report, Clifford and Taylor submitted to the President a private memorandum on their mili-

---

[82] Johnson Library, NSF Memos to the President—Walt Rostow.

[83] CMH, Westmoreland Papers, Message Files, Westmoreland to Sharp, MAC 6978, July 25, 1967.

tary recommendations which was described as follows in a State Department document:[84]

> After the above presentation [the trip report], Mr. Clifford and General Taylor will give the President privately a memorandum embodying their recommendations on the bombing of North Viet-Nam. They will present their view that the bombing must be stepped up considerably to bring as much pressure as possible against Hanoi and as the least dangerous and expensive means to shorten the war. They will recommend the bombing of all major targets presently not approved short of strictly civilian targets. They will recommend reductions in the size of the prohibited circles around Hanoi and Haiphong and will propose exceptions for specific targets within the 30 and 25 mile buffer zones along the Chinese border. They will also recommend careful re-examination of the closing of Haiphong Harbor, citing the military need to do so to cut off the influx of supplies. They have already asked CINCPAC to study carefully the possibility of blocking the Harbor by means other than mines, such as perhaps sinking a ship in the narrow channel. Both Mr. Clifford and General Taylor, but especially the former, believe that additional means must be found to bring pressure against Hanoi and keep the war from dragging on with continuing high casualties.

Although the lack of evidence makes it difficult to appraise the full significance of the effects of the Clifford-Taylor recommendations on bombing on subsequent events, they probably played an important role in the President's growing determination to apply greater force on the Communists through heavier bombing of North Vietnam.

During the meeting of the President with Clifford and Taylor on August 5, the private memorandum was not mentioned, but there was some discussion of the military situation and of the need for greater pressure. Clifford said that the South Vietnamese wanted to reduce the prohibited zones around Hanoi and Haiphong as well as the 30-mile buffer zone between North Vietnam and China. The President replied that he did not mind reducing the buffer zone, but that he was "afraid of the fliers going over the Chinese border." He asked Rostow "to look into the matter of [bombing] sanctuaries."

According to the notes of the meeting, Rusk reacted sharply to the proposals for bombing closer to the cities and to the Chinese border, saying, "the Russians have every reason to blockade Berlin now, that it probably would do that right away and attribute it to Vietnam."

As the meeting ended, Clifford said, in summary,

> [I]f we continue at the same level of ground effort and bombing that he is unable to see that this will bring us to the point we want to be. He said he believes that a year from now we

[84] U.S. Department of State, Lot File 72 D 207, "Secret-Sensitive" Memorandum for the Secretary from Philip Habib (who had replaced Unger as Bundy's deputy in the East Asia Bureau), Aug. 5, 1967, "Subject: Report to the President by the Clifford/Taylor Mission." The memorandum, drafted by H. Freeman Matthews who had been on the Clifford-Taylor trip, summarized the trip report. The author has not been able to locate a copy of the private Clifford-Taylor memorandum on bombing.

again will be taking stock. We may be no closer a year from now than we are now.

As long as the supplies continue to reach the troops in the South coming in from Laos, over the Northeast Railroad, through Haiphong Harbor, and down from Cambodia we can't get the war over. As long as the faucets are on, we cannot reach our objective.

We have to give increased attention to stopping this flow. The attitude of the allies is that we must increase this pressure. As long as Hanoi continues, there seems to be no diminishing of Hanoi's will to continue the war. We must focus on the supply. There was no concern anywhere in the countries visited about Red China entering the war. There was the same reaction to the Soviets entering the war.

Clifford suggested that the margins be moved closer to Red China and that additional targets be approved. He said the rewards justified the risks.

General Taylor added that the "graduated application of force was working, but there is a very great need to keep the pressure on."

In the weeks that followed the Clifford-Taylor report, the President, as will be seen, overrode the objections of McNamara and Rusk and their subordinates and the bombing recommendations of the DPM, and authorized much heavier bombing of strategic targets in the northeastern part of North Vietnam as proposed by the JCS and supported by Clifford and Taylor as well as by Rostow.

In a Tuesday Luncheon meeting on August 8, 1967, from 1:25 p.m. to 2:50 p.m. of the President, McNamara, Katzenbach (sitting in for Rusk), Rostow and Christian (Califano was also present), McNamara reported that the JCS recommended additional bombing, to include re-strikes of the Hanoi thermal power plant (which had been attacked in May but was operating again at 75 percent capacity), the Paul Doumer Bridge in Hanoi and 10 targets in the buffer zone between North Vietnam and China.[85] In addition, the JCS requested that the restrictions around Hanoi and Haiphong be lifted. McNamara said he had talked to Rusk, who was opposed to all of the recommendations except for the power plant.[86] McNamara took the same position. He said that he was fearful of an invasion of Chinese air space if the buffer zone targets were bombed. The President responded that he was going to emphasize to Wheeler the dangers and the need for extreme caution.

McNamara said he was opposed to additional bombing around Hanoi and Haiphong "for fear of civilian casualties, additional difficulties this may create for negotiations, and the domestic controversy it would create on possible escalation." The President responded that "it doesn't look as though we have escalated enough to win." McNamara replied that "hitting the targets would not necessarily mean that we would win."

---

[85] Johnson Library, Tom Johnson's Notes of Meeting, notes of Tuesday Luncheon, Aug. 8, 1967.

[86] In a memorandum to Katzenbach prior to the luncheon, William Bundy said that changes in the prohibition against bombing within 25–30 miles of the Chinese border could have serious effects, and urged a State-Defense review before taking further action. U.S. Department of State, Lot File, 85 D 240 (William Bundy Papers), Memorandum from Bundy to the Acting Secretary, Aug. 8, 1967.

The question of the Hanoi bridge was discussed. McNamara reported that the JCS said the chance of civilian casualties was almost zero, but he said that the JCS was incorrect. "They would be more on the order of 100–500, possibly more."

"It was decided" that the bridge would be bombed if, after reviewing the maps, Katzenbach, on behalf of the State Department, agreed.

On the question of buffer zone targets, Katzenbach said he was not sure of their importance. McNamara replied that they were not "terribly important targets, but that they were more important than some of the targets we are hitting."

Katzenbach also said that he would approve of eliminating the restricted zones if specific targets were approved, rather than having blanket authority to bomb any target.

The President said that, with the exception of lifting the restricted zones around Hanoi and Haiphong, he would approve all targets, including those in the buffer zone "if General Wheeler can do it without going into China." He said he would also approve bombing the bridge in Hanoi "if it is essential to transportation." "We have got to do something to win," he added. "We aren't doing much now." The President added that McNamara "should worry about the heat he has to take on the Hill about bombing limitations." (The Stennis hearings, as will be seen, were to open the next day.) McNamara replied that he was "not worried about the heat as long as he knew what we were doing is right. 'Does this help get it [the war] over?'" he asked. Katzenbach added that bombing alone "'isn't going to be the magic.' He said that total pressure, a combination of strong ground action in the South and good bombing in the North, was the combination for progress."

Later in the meeting, the President asked Rostow for his opinion on bombing. Rostow replied that he favored a re-strike on the thermal power plant, the bridge transportation links inside the restricted areas, and the proposed targets in the buffer zone. The President responded that "propaganda about a stalemate has us wobbling now. . . ."[87] He said he "no longer was worried about the stop the bombing pitch."

Finally, there was a discussion of the effects of bombing on infiltration. "Rostow said some reports showed that as much as 50% of the infiltration was impeded by bombing. Secretary McNamara disputed this. Some reports, he said, showed only 1% of the infiltration was stopped by bombing."

If the President believed that by intensified bombing he was "doing something to win," he could have received little comfort from a CIA memorandum in late September 1967 on the effects of bombing. In the memorandum, which he may or may not have seen, the

---

[87] The previous day (August 7) there had been a long article in the *New York Times* by R. W. Apple, Jr. from Saigon, "Vietnam, the Signs of Stalemate," in which Apple said that "in the opinion of most disinterested observers, the war is not going well. Victory is not close at hand. It may be beyond reach. It is clearly unlikely in the next year or even the next two years, and American officers talk somberly about fighting here for decades." "Stalemate," he said, "is a fighting word in Washington . . . but it is the word used by almost all Americans here, except the top officials, to characterize what is happening." Westmoreland's reaction was that Apple "is pessimistic and suspicious. . . . I have watched Apple become more critical and more argumentative during recent months. . . . He is probably bucking for a Pulitzer Prize." Berman, *Lyndon Johnson's War,* p. 59 from Westmoreland cable to Wheeler, Aug. 12, 1967.

For an "Outline Response to Stalemate Thesis," prepared by Walt Rostow on August 7, see Johnson Library, Files of Walt W. Rostow.

CIA once again concluded that bombing was not appreciably affecting the course of the war. Although it found that, as a result of the increased bombing of lines of communication in the North, "Transport operations have been seriously disrupted, losses of transportation equipment have increased sharply, and the costs and difficulties of maintaining traffic movements have multiplied," it said that, "as a result of countermeasures, the use of alternate routes, and foreign assistance, North Vietnam's logistic capabilities have not been reduced, and there is convincing evidence that the military and economic goods needed to support the war have continued to move."[88] "The North Vietnamese transport system has emerged from more than 30 months of bombing with greater capacity and flexibility than it had when the Rolling Thunder program was started." "Even a more intense interdiction campaign in the North," the memorandum concluded, "would fail to reduce the flow of supplies sufficiently to restrict military operations."

The Stennis Hearings on the Air War, August 1967

Beginning on August 9, 1967, the Preparedness Investigating Subcommittee, chaired by Senator Stennis, of the Senate Armed Services Committee, held seven days of executive session hearings on the conduct of the air war against North Vietnam.[89]

Stennis set the tone for the hearings in his brief opening statement when he commented that "the question was growing in Congress as to whether it is wise to send more men if we are going to just leave them at the mercy of the guerrilla war without trying to cut off the enemy's supplies more effectively." "My own personal opinion," he said, "is that it would be a tragic and perhaps fatal mistake for us to suspend or restrict the bombing. I am gratified by the step up in the air operations which has occurred since this hearing was announced. It has brought increased pressure on the enemy. I hope this pressure will be further increased and expanded and that it will hasten the end of this unhappy war.

"By slowing, reducing, and restricting the flow of supplies to the south the bombing of North Vietnam has saved the lives of many brave Americans. . . .

"In my opinion this is no time to reduce or diminish the pressure or to throw away any military advantage. . . .

"The real question is whether we are doing what we can and should do in the opinion of our military experts to hit the enemy when and where and in a manner that will end the war soonest and thus save American lives."[90]

Several days later, Stennis said in the course of Senate debate on the Foreign Assistance Act of 1967, "Unfortunately, things do not look good. There is no bright light at the end of any tunnel. It is highly uncertain how much further we will have to go or how much longer we will have to fight. I did not say how much longer

---

[88] Johnson Library, NSF Country File, Vietnam, Memorandum from the Directorate of Intelligence, "Rolling Thunder: The 1967 Campaign Against LOC's," September 1967.

[89] U.S. Congress, Senate, Preparedness Investigating Subcommittee of the Armed Services Committee, *Air War Against North Vietnam,* 5 pts., 90th Cong., 1st sess. (Washington, D.C.: U.S. Govt. Print. Off., 1967). In this published version of the hearings there are numerous security deletions.

[90] *Ibid.*, pt. I, pp. 2–3.

we will have to stay there. I think it is clear we will have to stay there a long, long time after the fighting has stopped."[91]

Witnesses before the Stennis subcommittee included the Secretary of Defense and all of the principal military officials concerned with the war with the exception of Westmoreland:

August 9 and 10—Adm. Ulysses S. G. Sharp, Jr., Commander in Chief of U.S. Forces in the Pacific (CINCPAC), accompanied by Gen. John Ryan, Commanding General of the Pacific Air Force (CINCPACAF) and Adm. Roy Johnson, Commander in Chief of the Pacific Fleet (CINCPACFLT)

August 16—Gen. Earle G. Wheeler, U.S. Army, Chairman, Joint Chiefs of Staff, and Lt. Gen. William W. Momyer, U.S. Air Force, Commander 7th Air Force

August 22–23—Gen. John P. McConnell, Chief of Staff, U.S. Air Force, and Adm. Thomas H. Moorer, Chief of Naval Operations

August 25—Secretary of Defense Robert S. McNamara

August—28 Gen. Harold K. Johnson, Chief of Staff, U.S. Army, and Gen. Wallace M. Greene, Commandant, U.S. Marine Corps

August 29—Maj. Gen. Gilbert L. Myers (U.S. Air Force, Ret.), Former Deputy Commander of the 7th Air Force.

This is the *Pentagon Papers'* summary of the testimony of U.S. military leaders (excluding McNamara):[92]

The subcommittee . . . was told that the air war in the North was an important and indispensable part of the U.S. strategy for fighting the war in the South. It was told that the bombing had inflicted extensive destruction and disruption on NVN, holding down the infiltration of men and supplies, restricting the level of forces that could be sustained in the South and reducing the ability of those forces to mount major sustained combat operations, thus resulting in fewer U.S. casualties. It was told that without the bombing, NVN could have doubled its forces in the South, requiring as many as 800,000 additional U.S. troops at a cost of $75 billion more just to hold our own. It was told that without the bombing NVN could have freed 500,000 people who were at work maintaining and repairing the LOCs in the North for additional support of the insurgency in the South. It was told that a cessation of the bombing now would be "a disaster," resulting in increased U.S. losses and an indefinite extension of the war.

The subcommittee was also told that the bombing had been much less effective than it might have been—and could still be—if civilian leaders heeded military advice and lifted the overly restrictive controls which had been imposed on the campaign. The slow tempo of the bombing; its concentration for so long well south of the vital Hanoi/Haiphong areas, leaving the important targets untouched; the existence of sanctuaries; the failure to close or neutralize the port of Haiphong—these and other limitations prevented the bombing from achieving great-

[91] *CR,* vol. 113, p. 22566.
[92] *PP*, Gravel ed., vol. IV., p. 199.

er results. The "doctrine of gradualism" and the long delays in approving targets of real significance, moreover, gave NVN time to build up formidable air defenses, contributing to U.S. aircraft and pilot losses, and enabled NVN to prepare for the anticipated destruction of its facilities (such as POL) by building up reserve stocks and dispersing them.

Several weeks after the hearings were held, the President, in a meeting with the Tuesday Luncheon group (which Wheeler had joined as a regular member), told Wheeler, "Buz, your generals almost destroyed us with their testimony before the Stennis Committee. We were murdered on the Hearings."[93]

The President and his associates, aware of the potential damage from the hearings, took some steps to try to limit their adverse effect. In a memorandum to the President on August 8, Rostow proposed a "roundup session" prior to Wheeler's testimony to review the targets available for attack and to develop justification for explaining specifically why others were not considered available. Rostow said he had been told that Wheeler felt his hand would be strengthened in the hearings "if he could state flatly that he has been fully and personally consulted in all of the major decision made . . . to head off the argument that bombing decisions have been made by civilians without the benefit of JCS recommendations and discussions." Rostow said he was convinced that Wheeler "wishes to defend our bombing policy. . . ." Apparently, no action was taken on the suggestion of a roundup session, but on August 11, McNamara sent a memorandum to the President summarizing information on the targets that had been attacked and listing those being proposed by the JCS, along with his own recommendations. The JCS recommended attacks on 70 targets. McNamara recommended that six of these be approved at that time. Four were minor targets near Hanoi (three of which were re-strikes). The other two were air fields—Phuc Yen, the North Vietnamese MiG base which the military had long recommended as a target, but which McNamara had previously opposed, and Cat Bi, a "MiG-capable" base near Haiphong which could be used as a substitute base. He did not explain his change of position on Phuc Yen except to say that operations from the base had recently increased.[94]

On August 16, 1967, the day of Wheeler's testimony before the Stennis subcommittee, the President met from 2:10 p.m. to 4:00 p.m. with Rusk, McNamara, Rostow, Helms and Christian.[95] Rusk opened the discussion of bombing by saying, "We need to clarify our strategy on bombing policy."

The President: Our strategy, as I see it, is that we destroy all we can without involving China and Russia between now and September 1. I do not believe China and Russia will come in. The [American] people will not stay with us if we do not get destroyed all we can. The targets we have authorized are in the Hanoi, Haiphong, and buffer zone areas. It's better to

---

[93] Johnson Library, Tom Johnson's Notes of Meetings, Notes of the meeting of Oct. 17, 1967.

[94] Johnson Library, NSF Country File, Vietnam, Memorandum to the President from McNamara, "Recommendations on Additional Fixed Targets in North Vietnam," Aug. 11, 1967. A memorandum from Ginsburgh to Rostow on August 16, commenting on McNamara's recommendations, is in the same location.

[95] Johnson Library, Tom Johnson's Notes of Meetings, Notes of meeting Aug. 16, 1967.

hit those targets authorized now rather than waiting six months.

Secretary Rusk: In the buffer zone there is a question as to whether these are specifically authorized strikes or repeaters. The larger the number of sorties in there, the higher the chances are of mistakes.

Secretary McNamara: I must point out that we could invade Chinese air space. Secretary McNamara said he proposed nothing new until next Tuesday. I would like to have a week go by to check the accuracy of what we are doing.

Secretary Rusk: There appears to be no ascertainable connection between some of these targets and winning the war. We are trying to wage the war without enlarging it and without causing the Soviets or the Chinese to give us problems in Berlin or Korea. I have no reservations except on these targets.

The President: Let us find the least dangerous and the most productive targets. I would like to be able to say that we have hit six out of every seven targets requested. We have some weather now that is my type of weather. I think we should get every target as quickly as we can. There are three areas that we are not going to hit. We are not going to hit Haiphong Harbor because we are not going to hit any ships. We are not going to bomb Hanoi because we are not going to hit civilians. And we must be careful about the buffer zone because of the danger in going over the border. But we have got to put more pressure on.

The notes of the meeting are not clear as to what decisions were made except that it was agreed that targets "more than eight to ten miles away from the buffer zone could be hit without danger." (This probably should read: targets in the buffer zone but more than eight-ten miles from the Chinese border.) In all, seven new targets were approved.[96]

In a meeting of the President, Rusk, McNamara and Rostow on August 18, from 8:35 p.m. to 9:55 p.m. which Wheeler also at-

[96]On August 14, William Bundy sent a memorandum to Rusk cautioning against bombing near the Chinese border in which he argued that it "could become highly dangerous to continue the attacks." (There had been three days of airstrikes against targets in the buffer zone since the August 8 White House meeting referred to above and Bundy said that "the odds of major Chinese intervention in the war could be significantly increased by continuing our attacks for more days.") "It has for some months—and increasingly—been the firm conclusion of all experts that the irrational element in Chinese Communist behavior has grown markedly . . . they could well see systematic attacks as an attempt by us to take advantage of their internal weaknesses and confusion, and this is the very thing that could drive them to action however irrational." Secondly, Bundy said, systematic (rather that periodic) attacks in the buffer zone might cause the Chinese Army and the Maoists, who were then at odds, to unite, and, by reducing the internal confusion existing in China, this could vitiate the benefits that might be derived from that state of affairs: "that confusion [in China]—and how it affects Hanoi—may quite well be the *only* hole card we have that could bring about peace between now and our 1968 elections." (emphasis in original) U.S. Department of State, Lot File 85 D 240 (William Bundy Papers), Memorandum to the Secretary from William Bundy, Aug. 14, 1967.

That same day the *New York Times* said in an editorial that "United States policy in the Vietnam war has now been reduced to brinkmanship. The idea seems to be to see how far the United States can go without pulling Communist China and/or the Soviet Union into the conflict. At the same time, of course, it is hoped that escalated bombing will so punish North Vietnam that she will sue for peace. On both counts the new policy is likely to prove as futile as it is dangerous." "The most tragic feature of the latest escalation," the editorial concluded, "is that it drives the possibility of a negotiated peace—the only kind of peace that is ultimately going to be possible—still further into the distant future."

tended, McNamara said that Wheeler "'did a helluva good job,'" in his testimony before the Stennis subcommittee.[97]

During the meeting, there was further discussion of bombing targets. In addition to the seven targets already approved, two more were approved by the President.

The President asked Wheeler about the "stalemate issue." "Wheeler responded there is no stalemate. The President said that's not a good enough answer. He said McNamara gets ridiculed when he says it. The President said he answered it today by saying it was pure Communist propaganda."[98] "[W]e should have some colorful general like MacArthur with his shirt neck open to go in there and say this is pure propaganda and cite them Gen. [Stanley R. "Swede"] Larsen's figures [on the progress in II Corps] . . . get a colorful general to go to Saigon and argue with the press." "We've got to do something dramatic."[99]

At this point in the meeting the President sent an aide to get summaries of the Larsen report which he gave to those present, saying that he had been using the information in "backgrounder" meetings with reporters, and "they all practically surrender." Some of these reports, he said "are so optimistic that he believes Komer must be writing them."[100] But "today we have no songs, no parades, no bond drives, etc. and . . . we can't win the war otherwise."

Meanwhile, Army Chief of Staff General Johnson had returned on August 10 from an 11-day visit to South Vietnam. On August 11, Rostow sent the President a memorandum saying that General Johnson had returned and that "he comes back with the most optimistic reports." Rostow recommended that the President meet with General Johnson and that, "After meeting with him, you might

---

[97] Johnson Library, Meetings Notes File, Notes of meeting Aug. 18, 1967.

[98] This refers to the President's press conference on Aug. 18, 1967, the transcript of which is in *Public Papers of the Presidents,* Lyndon B. Johnson, 1964, pp. 788–795.

[99] Larsen, who had just completed two years as commanding general of U.S. forces in II Corps, submitted a memorandum to the Under Secretary of Defense on August 11 giving a statistical summary of the progress being made in II Corps, in which he said: "there is an air of refreshing optimism." On August 16, Bromley Smith sent a memorandum to the President on the highlights of Larsen's report. Both documents are in the Johnson Library, NSF Memos to the President—Walt Rostow.

Wheeler, Sharp and Westmoreland had also become concerned about some of the adverse publicity, especially the "stalemate" issue, and were taking steps to generate more favorable reporting. See CMH, Westmoreland Papers, Message Files, Wheeler to Westmoreland, JCS 6105, Aug. 2, 1967. Among other things, reports on progress were going to be prepared for all four corps areas. (For the first of these see CMH, Westmoreland Papers, History File MAC8073, Aug. 25, 1967, in which Westmoreland concluded, "From the summaries provided above, it is readily apparent that we have made considerable, although not always dramatic, progress and that the stage is being set for even greater progress. It is also just as apparent that there is no stalemate.") Other steps included a background news conference by Westmoreland and by U.S. commanders in each corps area, together with talking with more newsmen and taking more of them on trips to the field.

In a cable to Wheeler reporting on what was being done, Westmoreland's description of the military situation seemed to confirm the lack of progress in U.S. ground force operations resulting from the Communist guerrilla tactics: "If the enemy was exercising even modest initiative the more than 30 large operations under way and more than 5,000 small unit actions undertaken each day would have more success in finding him. . . . Enemy strategy is smart and economical, but basically defensive. He accepts major combat occasionally along the DMZ or in the highlands where he has both sanctuary and short lines of communication. Elsewhere he reacts against revolutionary development and growing civilian commerce by attacking RD operations and sabotaging LOCs. His only real initiative is expressed in long-range attacks against our base areas."

[100] Several days later, Komer was in Washington, and Rostow reported to the President that Komer's "sense of confidence is increasing daily; and it is shared by Westy and Ambassador Bunker." Johnson Library, NSF Memos to the President—Walt Rostow, Memorandum to the President from Rostow, Aug. 22, 1967.

want to unleash him on the White House Press Corps."[101] The President returned Rostow's memorandum with a handwritten note: "Bring him in Saturday if George [Christian] agrees."[102] On Saturday, August 12, the President met from 11:47 a.m. to 12:10 p.m. with General Johnson, who then held a press conference at the President's suggestion[103] at which he challenged reports that the war was a stalemate. "We're winning the war," he declared. By the end of 1967 he said he expected to see "very real evidence of progress and forward movement," especially on the economic and social fronts. When asked whether the additional 45,000 U.S. troops approved in July would be the last increase that would be needed, he replied that if the war continued to be waged at its current level, with no reduction of the bombing of the North, and if no other Communist countries entered the war, the troop increase "should be adequate to provide a degree of momentum that will see us through to a solution in South Vietnam."

On August 20, there were 209 U.S. bombing sorties over North Vietnam, the highest of the war. Meanwhile on August 19, CINCPAC had been ordered—without explanation—to cease bombing inside the Hanoi 10-mile zone between August 24 and September 4. (On September 7, this was extended indefinitely.)[104] This action was taken, as will be seen, in connection with a highly secret effort to initiate discussions with the North Vietnamese.

On August 22, the President met from 1:20 p.m. to 3:10 p.m. with Rusk, McNamara, Rostow, Wheeler, Helms and Christian.[105] According to a report on the meeting that Wheeler sent to Westmoreland, Rusk, "who from time to time had raised the thought that at a selected time, all our forces in South Vietnam should go on the offensive in an all-out effort to defeat the enemy on the broadest possible front and in as many areas as possible," made the proposal again. Labeling it a "peace offensive," Rusk, Wheeler said, suggested that four to six weeks after the South Vietnamese Presidential elections in early September, all U.S. forces should undertake such an all-out attack. Wheeler said he started to respond "by pointing out that you [Westmoreland] endeavor as a matter of policy to get the maximum combat return from your forces at all times, not merely at selected times," but the President, he said, told him not to respond but to think it over and talk to him the following week.

In his cable Wheeler added: "As you will recognize, Secretary Rusk is thinking in terms of the big offensive of past and more conventional types of war. Nevertheless I need your views and whatever facts and figures you can supply me in order to respond adequately next week."

Westmoreland replied on August 26:[106]

---

[101] Same location, memorandum to the President from Rostow, Aug. 11, 1967.

[102] Johnson Library, President's Appointment File, Diary Backup for Aug. 12, 1967. Christian was White House press secretary.

[103] There are no known notes of the meeting. The text of the press conference is in the Johnson Library, Diary Backup for Aug. 12, 1967.

[104] *PP*, Gravel ed., vol. IV, p. 13.

[105] Wheeler's report to Westmoreland, (CMH, Westmoreland Papers, Message Files, JCS 6878, Aug. 23, 1967), is the only known source of information on what was discussed at the meeting. There are no White House notes.

[106] Same location, MAC8095, Aug. 26, 1967.

> It appears to me also that Secretary Rusk is thinking in terms of the more conventional type warfare where our forces could launch such an all-out offensive from a reasonably secure area of departure, leaving behind a pacified rear area, and against identified enemy formations disposed along a recognizable front. Such is not the case in SVN. We have three major tasks that must be accomplished simultaneously and which compete for available resources. Forces are required to oppose the enemy in his sanctuaries in the DMZ area, Laos, and Cambodia; to conduct major offensives against enemy units, base areas, and lines of communication in country; and to expand and improve the security conditions in and around the populated and resource rich areas of the country in support of pacification programs.

"We are," he added, "maintaining relentless pressure on all levels of the enemy force spectrum—from infrastructure to North Vietnamese main force units. . . . As additional assets become available, our operations will be stepped up."

"If more drastic evidence of our determination to win this war at the earliest date is required," Westmoreland said in conclusion, "I suggest that consideration be given to carrying the ground attack to the known areas of enemy concentration north of the DMZ and along the border sanctuaries. These moves would not be without their pitfalls, but I am confident that they could be undertaken successfully."

In a meeting with the President on August 29, as will be seen, Rusk's proposal was discussed again.

On August 24 the President met from 5:33 p.m. to 6:25 p.m. with Rusk, McNamara, General Harold Johnson, Acting Chairman of the JCS in the absence of General Wheeler, General McConnell, Air Force Chief of Staff (who had testified before the Stennis committee two days before), and Deputy Secretary of Defense Nitze (who had replaced Vance).[107] The issue was whether to authorize the bombing of the Phuc Yen airfield as requested by the JCS and recommended by McNamara in his memorandum of August 13. General Johnson reported that Admiral Sharp (CINCPAC), who was directly in command of ROLLING THUNDER, was strongly opposed to bombing Phuc Yen, but wanted to bomb Gia Lam, a nearby airfield. General Johnson said that he and General Wheeler favored bombing both airfields. The President asked how many MiGs there were at Phuc Yen. General McConnell said there were approximately 11. (There were 9 at Gia Lam.) "Why is it so important to get 11 airplanes?" the President asked. General McConnell replied that eliminating even one MiG would help American pilots who "have a growing frustration against our not knocking this MiG base out." The President asked McNamara if he was in favor of the strike. Reversing the position he took on August 12, McNamara replied, "No, Mr. President, I am not. It will cost more pilots than it will save. It puts more pressure on the Chinese and the Soviets to react. . . . They will move their planes to Gia Lam, and we won't have accomplished anything." The President, saying he was "inclined to hit it," asked Rusk's opinion. Rusk replied that he "had

[107] Johnson Library, Tom Johnson's Notes of Meetings, Notes of meeting Aug. 24, 1967.

some problems with this." There could be a serious problem, he said, if the MiGs were moved to China and operated out of Chinese airfields. General McConnell said he would "rather face them from China," where they would have only "half the time over target because of fuel." Rusk responded: "This would be considered Chinese intervention. We have braced ourselves for a major reaction from the Soviets and the Chinese. We've got to brace ourselves on this one. This doesn't mean that we should cut and run. But we should know what the margins are. The losses would not be made up with what we gain."

> The President: Well, that's two for and two against. As I see it, by some estimates, we could lose 11 planes for the 11 planes we knock out. We could have many civilian casualties because of the location. We may have to hit it every three days or so to effectively knock it out. There are possible problems with China and Russia. It could be handled by other means.
>
> For those reasons, I am not going to authorize it today. Personally, I am inclined to hit it. I know that it is a constant danger and a constant threat. I think we have to get in now and knock out everything we can get. We have got to prevent our being hobbled out there. We also have problems here at home. It is better to hit these targets now than wait. So much of the people believe this pure propaganda which is coming out about the war.
>
> We can't take it much longer. . . .

On August 25, 1967, McNamara testified before the Stennis subcommittee.[108] Bombing of North Vietnam had been successful, he said, but it had "always been considered a supplement to and not a substitute for an effective counterinsurgency land and air campaign in South Vietnam." Proponents of greater bombing wanted to use it to break the will of the North Vietnamese and to achieve more complete interdiction of men and supplies, but neither goal, he said, was realistic, adding:[109]

> A selective, carefully targeted bombing campaign, such as we are presently conducting, can be directed toward reasonable and realizable goals. This discriminating use of air power can and does render the infiltration of men and supplies more difficult and more costly. At the same time, it demonstrates to both South and North Vietnam our resolve to see that aggression does not succeed. A less discriminating bombing campaign against North Vietnam would, in my opinion, do no more. We have no reason to believe that it would break the will of the North Vietnamese people or sway the purpose of their leaders. If it does not lead to such a change of mind, bombing the North at any level of intensity would not meet our objective. We would still have to prove by ground operations in the South that Hanoi's aggression could not succeed. Nor would a decision to close [the ports], by whatever means, prevent the movement in and through North Vietnam of the essentials to continue their present level of military activity in South Vietnam.

---

[108] *Air War Against North Vietnam*, pt. 4, pp. 273–373. There is also a good description of McNamara's testimony in Goulding, *Confirm or Deny*, ch. 6.

[109] See *Air War Against North Vietnam*, pt. 4, pp. 275, 281–282.

> On the other side of the equation, our resort to a less selective campaign of air attack against the North would involve risks which at present I regard as too high to accept for this dubious prospect of successful results.

During the course of the six-hour hearing, the members and the chief counsel of the subcommittee asked McNamara such questions as why the U.S. had not bombed key targets earlier in the war, why targets recommended by the military had not been bombed—Phuc Yen and the port of Haiphong were emphasized, whether bombing could succeed in reducing infiltration below the level that was essential to sustain the war in the South, and the effect of bombing on the "will" of the North to continue supporting the war. He answered these skillfully, forcefully and in considerable detail, and urged members of the subcommittee to examine for themselves the targets that had been recommended but not yet approved and to reach their own conclusions as to whether they should be.

According to his former deputy, Roswell Gilpatric, when McNamara testified before the Stennis subcommittee, he was "tremendously troubled. It was one of those great moments of anguish for him when he had to come out with testimony that he knew would infuriate Johnson. It was just a question of how large the explosion would be and what the denouement would be."[110]

After the hearing, McNamara started to return to the Pentagon, but was summoned to the White House by a telephone call to his car. There, he spent about three hours being "upbraided and roared at . . . getting the LBJ treatment. . . ."[111]

Wheeler and the members of the JCS are said to have been "stunned" by McNamara's testimony.[112] According to Mark Perry's study of the JCS, "The highest-ranking officers now believed that they had been betrayed by their civilian leaders, that the war could not continue without an irrational loss of American lives, and that, given McNamara's bad-faith defense of a clearly discredited strategy, there was little reason to hope for an eventual American victory."[113] Late on the afternoon of August 25 after the hearing ended, Wheeler is said to have convened a meeting of the JCS in his office. This is Perry's description of what happened:[114]

> The meeting was unprecedented. Not only did it not take place in the tank [the JCS meeting room], Wheeler barred all JCS aides and did not allow anyone to take notes. His instructions to his staff . . . were exact: the JCS would accept calls from the President but from no one else. His next step was even more unusual. When the chiefs convened in his office, he asked each of them to pledge that what they were about to discuss would be kept strictly secret as long as any of them remained alive; they agreed. Facing his colleagues from a chair pulled in front of his desk, Wheeler said that he believed they should resign "en masse" during a press conference to be held the next morning. . . . There was no vote. The chiefs dis-

---

[110] CRS Interview with Roswell Gilpatric, Jan. 9, 1979.

[111] *Ibid.* At present, there is very little information, other than this account by Gilpatric, of the President's reaction to McNamara's testimony. Hopefully McNamara will provide additional details in his forthcoming autobiography.

[112] Perry, *Four Stars,* p. 162.

[113] *Ibid.*, p. 163.

[114] *Ibid.*, pp. 163–164.

> cussed McNamara's testimony matter-of-factly. Moorer [Chief of Naval Operations] said he hadn't been surprised, only disappointed that the administration had not changed its position on JCS targeting. McConnell [Air Force Chief of Staff] . . . said he would agree to whatever anyone else wanted. They were a team, he said, and he would do anything to help his flyers. Johnson [Army Chief of Staff] was the most outspoken proponent of resignation, saying that the military was being blamed for a conflict over which it had little control. The discussion went on for three hours before agreement was reached. Wheeler said they would call for a press conference early the next day. . . .

Overnight, Wheeler is said to have changed his mind, and in another meeting of the JCS in his office early the next morning (August 26) he announced, according to Perry's account: "'We can't do it. It's mutiny . . .' Johnson stood fast, arguing that the chiefs should resign because it was apparent to him that 'no one was really paying any attention' to their recommendations. 'If we're going to go to war, then we'd better be honest with the American people,' he added. . . . 'This is mutiny,' he [Wheeler] said again. 'If we resign they'll just get someone else. And we'll be forgotten. Twenty-four hours from now there will be new guys sitting in our places and they'll do what they're told.' Wheeler added that as military men they had dedicated their lives to their country, to carry out the orders of their civilian leaders. 'All our lives we've been told to obey orders, we've been schooled in it. We've been told to give our lives for our country. Now, we're going to throw all of that away.' Johnson responded by raising other arguments. The war was being lost, he said, and the military would 'take the fall.' Wheeler pleaded with him. 'Give it some time,' he said. 'You never know, maybe we can pull it out.'"

In the aftermath of this remarkable episode, Wheeler is said to have insisted on being included in the Tuesday Luncheon Group, and in October 1967 he began attending regularly.[115]

On August 31, 1967, the Stennis subcommittee submitted its report to the full committee. In the words of the *Pentagon Papers,* the report "castigated the Administration's conduct of the bombing campaign, deferred to the authority of the professional military judgments it had heard, accepted virtually all of the military criticisms of the program, and advocated a switch-over to escalating 'pressure' concepts."[116]

According to the report, lack of success in the air war resulted from "the fragmentation of our air might by overly restrictive controls, limitations, and the doctrine of 'gradualism.' . . . [W]e have employed military aviation in a carefully controlled, restricted, and graduated buildup of bombing pressure which discounted the professional judgment of our best military experts and substituted civilian judgment in the details of target selection and the timing of

[115] *Ibid.*, p. 169.

[116] *PP*, Gravel ed., vol. IV, p. 203. The report of the Preparedness Investigating Subcommittee, *Air War Against North Vietnam,* was issued on Aug. 31, 1967 as a committee print (i.e., for the use of the committee and without being numbered as a committee report) and is contained in the compilation of committee prints of the Senate Armed Services Committee issued during 1967, cited above.

strikes. We shackled the true potential of airpower and permitted the buildup of what has become the world's most formidable aircraft defenses." Noting that more than 660 U.S. planes had been shot down, the report declared that, "The long delay in approving targets in North Vietnam has almost certainly contributed to our aircraft and pilot losses since it gave the North Vietnamese the time to build up formidable air defenses. Moreover, the long delay enabled the enemy to prepare for a response to the anticipated loss of installations, such as petroleum storage, by dispersal of facilities and building reserve stocks."

The report also noted that, while the air war "has been crucial and vital in saving many American and allied lives," the "overwhelming weight" of the testimony by military witnesses was that the limitations and restrictions on the air war had resulted in increased U.S. casualties in the ground war in the South.

U.S. policy in the air war against North Vietnam, the report said, "has not done the job. . . . What is needed now is the hard decision to do whatever is necessary! take the risks that have to be taken, and apply the force that is required to see the job through. . . . The subcommittee is of the opinion that we cannot, in good conscience, ask our ground forces to continue their fight in South Vietnam unless we are prepared to press the air war in the north in the most effective way possible. This requires closing the port of Haiphong, isolating it from the rest of the country, striking all meaningful targets with a military significance, and increasing the interdiction of the lines of communication from Red China." "Obviously," the report added, "the question of closing or neutralizing Haiphong has important policy and political considerations over and above the pure military requirements, including the reaction, if any, of the U.S.S.R. or Red China." Moreover, "we emphasize that nothing in this report is meant to suggest the indiscriminate bombing of civilians or civilian population centers. . . ," but "within this limitation" there were still many targets that could be attacked.[117]

The Stennis subcommittee hearings and report appear to have had several effects. First, as the *Pentagon Papers* comments,[118] "The subcommittee's summary report, which sided with the military and sharply criticized McNamara's reasoning, forced the Administration into an awkward position. Ultimately, the President felt compelled to overrule McNamara's logic in his own version of

[117] Several days after the report was issued, McGeorge Bundy responded in a long letter to the *Washington Post* in which he said that the subcommittee's recommendation of an expanded air war had four "decisive weaknesses" (*Washington Post*, Sept. 11, 1967):

"First, the Senators appeal not to evidence but to authority . . . their position is that the generals and admirals are right simply because they are professionals. . . .

"Second, the Subcommittee report pushes aside all political and diplomatic considerations—and all risks of wider conflict. . . .

"Third, while the Subcommittee gives lip-service to the principle of civilian control, its main line of argument tends to deny that principle. . . . But civilian control means civilian control, and in a complex contest the exercise of that control will inevitably place limits upon both strategy and tactics.

"Fourth, the Subcommittee report moves into dangerous ground when it suggests that the course chosen by the Administration has increased the cost of the war in American lives."

Bundy said his own position was that "both the advocates and the opponents of the bombing continue to exaggerate its importance. . . ." "To me it is the struggle in and for the South that will be decisive—bombing or no bombing. . . . I believe with McNamara that limited bombing helps in the Southern struggle, but neither in expanded bombing nor in any unconditional suspension do I see a likely substitute for the very hard work ahead in the South. . . ."

[118] *PP*, Gravel ed., vol. IV, p. 199.

the matter. Once again the President was caught unhappily in the middle satisfying neither his critics of the right nor the left." Second, the end of McNamara's long tenure as Secretary of Defense, while probably imminent in any event, may have been hastened by his testimony. Third, the hearings and report probably increased public and congressional dissatisfaction with the conduct and progress of the war, while tending also to polarize opinion even further. Fourth, the hearings increased the concern of military leaders about the conduct of the war, and led Wheeler and the JCS to press even harder for authority to use greater force and for more of a voice in decisionmaking.

Phil Goulding, Assistant Secretary of Defense for Public Affairs at the time, argues persuasively that while bombing increased after the hearings, against McNamara's recommendations, that his testimony, together with the position he took inside the government, had the effect of preventing an expanded air war which could have had "chilling ramifications."[119]

The Tax Surcharge

During the late summer and early fall of 1967, as the war escalated and its costs rose, congressional opposition increased. Part of the reason was the President's request to Congress on August 3, 1967, for a 10 percent tax surcharge to help to meet the ballooning national deficit.[120] As Rusk commented in a meeting of the Luncheon Group, "the tax bill made many doves."[121]

It will be recalled that in 1966, after warnings by his economic advisers of an inflationary trend, the President had asked for a small tax increase, which Congress approved, and in January 1967

---

[119] Goulding, *Confirm or Deny*, p. 201.

Goulding also says the hearings gave McNamara the public forum he needed in order to make his case. In the summer of 1967, following his efforts for more than a year to restrict and limit the bombing of North Vietnam, McNamara began searching, Goulding says, for new ways of convincing the President and the public that the escalation of bombing would be a mistake. The announcement of Stennis' hearings, which came at a time when Pentagon officials were considering what might be the best type of forum, was "fortuitous" (*Ibid.*, p. 181):

"No platform could have been more ideal for a detailed analysis of what McNamara was trying to accomplish with the bombing and what tactical bombing could never achieve. He could support the President's basic bombing policy, state his own honest view that the objectives he and the President sought were conceived soundly and yet puncture arguments for an expanded campaign. Committee members, nearly all of whom were Hawkish, would interrogate him at length—which also was desirable for producing a worthwhile public record. Since the confrontation would be in the closed session of a Congressional committee, the press would be writing first from our prepared statement and later at leisure from a transcript of the proceedings instead of dashing in and out of an open committee room during the testimony to report each 'hot exchange.'"

Another "fortuitous" event occurred on August 8 when House Republican Leader Gerald Ford attacked the administration for "handcuffing" the military in the conduct of the air war. Ford's speech, Goulding says, "afforded us an outstanding opportunity to lay the groundwork for the lengthy statement which McNamara would be reading to the committee. In a short response to him, we could counter in advance some of the Hawkish military testimony which the committee and the public would be receiving prior to McNamara's appearance and, of immeasurable importance to help compensate for the antibombing tone of the Secretary's testimony, could simultaneously defend President Johnson against a rough political attack by one of the nation's top Republicans." *Ibid.*, pp. 182–183. For Ford's speech see p. 800 below. For McNamara's reply to Ford, see *PP*, Gravel ed., vol. IV, p. 184 and *Air War Against North Vietnam*, pt. 4, pp. 358–361.

[120] For the text of the President's message to Congress see *Public Papers of the Presidents*, Lyndon B. Johnson, 1967, pp. 733–740. For secondary sources on the tax surcharge see Johnson, *The Vantage Point*, ch. 19, Califano, *The Triumph and Tragedy of Lyndon Johnson*, ch. 15, and Kettl, "The Economic Education of Lyndon Johnson: Guns, Butter, and Taxes," in Devine (ed.), *The Johnson Years*, vol. 2, pp. 67 ff; Lawrence C. Pierce, *The Politics of Fiscal Policy Formation*, pp. 146 ff.

[121] Johnson Library, Tom Johnson's Notes of Meetings, Notes of meeting Oct. 3, 1967.

he had notified Congress that later in the year, depending on economic conditions, he would request a six percent tax surcharge. On June 7, at a meeting with his economic advisers—Secretary of the Treasury Fowler, Secretary of Commerce Alexander B. Trowbridge, Jr., Secretary of Labor Wirtz, Chairman of the Council of Economic Advisers Ackley, Director of the Bureau of the Budget Schultze—the President was urged to proceed with the request for the surcharge. Fowler said that the deficit for the fiscal year ending June 30, 1967, would be $23 to $28 billion without the surcharge—twice that which had been predicted six months earlier. The President replied that he would "'refuse to run a deficit for the magnitude projected'"; that he would "'slash the hell out of domestic programs if necessary. . . . I've gone as far as I can without increased support for these programs. The country and Democratic Congressmen in particular will have to choose between the domestic programs and a tax increase. . . . The Cabinet and the Congress have to muster more support for these programs or they'll have to be cut back.'"[122]

Presidential Assistant Joe Califano says in his memoirs, "I had never heard Johnson talk that way. I thought he was trying to impress Fowler with his fiscal responsibility and encourage the rest of us to fight harder for the program and the taxes to preserve them. I sensed he was also expressing his frustration about the uncertainty, the divisions among his advisers, and the lonely fight he was facing with congress."[123]

On July 14, Califano sent a memorandum to the President in which he stated, "It is abundantly clear that [Wilbur] Mills [chairman of the House Ways and Means Committee] is anxious to be called down to the White House by you and to be consulted on your economic proposals." The President, according to Califano, refused to meet with Mills.[124]

On July 26, however, the President met from 5:10 p.m. to 7:33 p.m. with Mills, and with Treasury Secretary Fowler (Ackley, Califano, and Califano's assistant Larry Levinson, and McPherson joined the meeting at 5:48 p.m.) to go over a draft of the proposed tax message, following a unanimous recommendation on July 22 by the President's economic advisers that a 10 percent surcharge should be requested. According to Califano's account of the meeting, "Mills helped draft the message, but made it clear he was distancing himself until the President delivered more spending cuts."[125]

On August 16, after the Ways and Means Committee completed two days of hearings on the tax bill on August 14–15, the President, as he told the Luncheon Group at its meeting on that day,

---

[122] Califano, *The Triumph and Tragedy of Lyndon Johnson,* p. 243 and Johnson Library, Office Files of White House Aides, Califano Memorandum for the Files, June 9, 1967, on the meeting of June 7.

[123] Califano, *The Triumph and Tragedy of Lyndon Johnson,* p. 243.

[124] *Ibid.*

[125] *Ibid.*, p. 244. Notes on this and other meetings on the tax bill for which Califano's book is cited as the source are in Califano's papers at the Johnson Library, but the papers have not yet been processed.

"had Mills down here this morning to see what *[sic]* the bodies are."[126]

In his tax message to Congress on August 3, the President said that the country faced a serious budget deficit that posed a "clear and present danger to America's security and economic health," and that unless Congress increased taxes and reduced spending such a deficit would have extremely serious inflationary consequences. Referring to Vietnam he said, "there are times in a Nation's life when its armies must be equipped and fielded and the Nation's business must still go on. For America, that time is now."

Prior to his request for the 10 percent surcharge the President met with Members of Congress to discuss the situation and to promote the proposed tax. On July 25, from 6:10 p.m. to 8:00 p.m., he met with Majority Leader Mansfield and 15 other Senate Democrats, all chairmen of committees.[127] The President told the group, "The Budget is in bad shape." In order to avoid a large deficit it would be necessary to raise taxes and reduce expenditures, especially in Defense.

Fulbright responded, "'Mr. President, what you really need to do is to stop the war. That will solve all your problems.'" "'I think there is a change in attitude on the war,'" he added. "'The Vietnam war is a hopeless venture. Nobody likes it . . . [It] is ruining our domestic and our foreign policy. I will not support it any longer.'" Because of his opposition to the war, he said that for the first time in 20 years he might vote against the foreign aid bill, "'and may try to bottle the whole bill up in the [Foreign Relations] Committee.'"

The President replied, "if the Congress wants to tell the rest of the world to go to hell, that's their prerogative. . . . I believe foreign assistance is vital, but I can understand the depression and distress of all of you on this matter." He added that he did not want "to get into defense of his position because, 'I understand all of you feel like you are under the gun when you are down here, at least according to Bill Fulbright.'"

Fulbright responded: "'Well, my position is that Vietnam is central to the whole problem. We need a new look. The effects of Vietnam are hurting the budget and foreign relations generally.'"

The President retorted, "'Bill, everybody doesn't have a blind spot like you do. You say don't bomb North Vietnam on just about everything. I don't have the simple solution you have. We haven't delivered Ho yet. Everything which has been proposed to Ho has been rejected. As far as stopping the bombing in North Vietnam, I am not going to tell our men in the field to put their right hands behind their backs and fight only with their left.'" "'If you want to get out of Vietnam,'" he said, "'then you have the prerogative of taking the resolution under which we are out there now. You can repeal it tomorrow. You can tell the troops to come home. You can tell General Westmoreland that he doesn't know what he is doing.'"

---

[126] Johnson Library, Tom Johnson's Notes of Meetings, Notes of meeting Aug. 16, 1967. There apparently are no notes of the meeting of the President and Mills.

[127] Johnson Library, Tom Johnson's Notes of Meetings, Notes of meeting July 25, 1967. The following Senators attended the meeting: Anderson, Bible, Eastland, Ellender, Fulbright, Hayden, Hill, Jackson, Jordan, Long (Louisiana), John L. McClellan (D/Ark.), Magnuson, Mansfield, Monroney, Pastore, and Randolph.

At this point, Mansfield diverted the discussion to other subjects.

On July 31, the President met from 5:46 p.m. to 6:35 p.m. with Democratic congressional leaders from the House and Senate to discuss the tax bill. Attending were Senators Mansfield, Long (La.) and Byrd (Va.), and Speaker McCormack, Majority Leader Albert and Democratic Whip Boggs. Califano, Christian, Manatos, and Harold Barefoot Sanders, the head of White House congressional liaison, also attended.[128] The group indicated its support of the tax increase. Boggs commented that in every war Congress had raised taxes. Mansfield said he would support the proposal, and that the President "should tell the Congress that it must face up to the situation. He said the President would then have done his duty." McCormack said, "'You do your duty and we'll do ours. If the Congress doesn't want the responsibility, it's up to them.'"

The President held 13 other meetings with Members of Congress in an effort to promote the tax bill, including a meeting on August 3 from 9:00 a.m. to 10:30 a.m. with the House leadership and chairmen and members of the Ways and Means and Appropriations Committees, followed by meetings later in the day with the Democratic members of the Joint Economic Committee from 5:15 p.m. to 6:45 p.m. and with 13 freshmen House Democrats from 6:45 p.m. to 9:55 p.m. There was also a meeting on August 9 from 9:02 a.m. to 10:25 a.m. with 58 Democratic Members of the House, and on August 17 from 6:20 p.m. to 7:44 p.m. with freshmen Republican Representatives.[129]

At a meeting with the Luncheon Group on August 18, Rusk said that Senator Hugh Scott suggested having a group of Republican "moderates" to the White House for a "pep talk." The President replied, "you can't trust them. He said he met with 48 House Republicans Freshmen and took all their questions on Vietnam . . . [and] tonight they are all out telling what he said."[130]

The President also met with 14 prominent business leaders in an effort to rally business support for the tax bill.[131] He explained that to cover the projected deficit of $29–30 billion he was proposing that 25 percent of the total would be met by the tax increase, another 25 percent by reductions in existing programs, and the remaining 50 percent by borrowing. The reaction was one of reluctant support. Frederick R. Kappel, chairman of the board of the Amer-

---

[128] Johnson Library, Tom Johnson's Notes of Meetings, Notes of meeting July 31, 1967.

[129] There are apparently no notes of the meetings on August 3 and August 9. Notes of the meeting on August 17 are in the Johnson Library, Tom Johnson's Notes of Meetings.

[130] Johnson Library, Meetings Notes File, Notes of meeting Aug. 18, 1967.

[131] Johnson Library, Meetings Notes File, George Christian Notes of meeting of Aug. 10, 1967, dated Aug. 15, 1967. The business leaders who attended were:

C. Douglas Dillon, banker and former Secretary of the Treasury
Henry Ford II, president, Ford Motor Company
Thomas S. Gates, Jr., chairman of the board, Morgan Guaranty Trust Co. (former Secretary of Defense)
Werner P. Gullander, president, National Association of Manufacturers
Frederick R. Kappel, chairman of the board, American Telephone and Telegraph Co. (AT&T)
William B. Murphy, president, Campbell Soup Co.
Albert L. Nickerson, chairman, Mobil Oil Corp.
Rudolph A. Peterson, president, Bank of America
David Rockefeller
Stuart T. Saunders, chairman of the board, Pennsylvania Railroad
J. Harris Ward, chairman, Commonwealth Edison (Chicago)
Sidney J. Weinberg, Goldman-Sachs Co.
Frazar B. Wilde, chairman, Connecticut General Life Insurance Co.
Walter B. Wriston, president, First City National Bank

ican Telephone and Telegraph Company (AT & T), probably expressed the group's concerns when he commented "I have the feeling you are in a position where you can't do anything else." Thomas S. Gates, Jr., chairman of the board of the Morgan Guaranty Trust Company, said "the people will buy this as a war tax. Couple this tax with some cuts and it will help psychologically." Stuart T. Saunders, chairman of the board of the Pennsylvania Railroad agreed: "The people need to know you will cut these things. Then they will be willing to support the tax bill."

Following a statement by Secretary of the Treasury Fowler on the importance of business support for the tax, the President suggested that the group should organize to promote the proposal. On a show of hands, "all of those present supported the President's position in general," and the group discussed forming the organization. Subsequently, 13 of those who met with the President formed the organization, which by the middle of September had been subscribed to by 455 leaders.[132]

In his tax message to Congress, the President revealed for the first time that he had approved deployment of another 45,000 U.S. troops. There were also signs that U.S. bombing of North Vietnam was going to be stepped up. These developments prompted Senate Majority Leader Mansfield on August 7, 1967, to object to further escalation by the U.S., "in which the enemy can match and outmatch us," and to urge instead that the U.S. should stop bombing North Vietnam and should concentrate on bombing supply lines on the 17th parallel as Senator Cooper had proposed, should complete the defensive barrier at the southern end of demilitarized zone, and should "resurrect" the U.S. resolution of January 1966 in the U.N. Security Council.[133]

Other Members of Congress questioned the President's decision to send 45,000 more troops. Republican Senators Clifford Case and Cooper emphasized the need for the South Vietnamese to make more of an effort, and Case asked, "is the Johnson administration blind to the signs of growing public unrest about Vietnam? Is it deaf to the continuing advice of Members of Congress?"[134]

Senator Jacob Javits, Republican of New York, whose support for the war had been waning for several months, said on August 11 that there was "an imperative need to reassess our commitment in Vietnam."[135] The President's decision to send more troops, reports of military stalemates and lack of progress in pacification, and the budgetary impact of the war, combined, he said, "to project Vietnam as the prime issue before the country." "Notwithstanding stalemate, the momentum of the past decade in Vietnam is threatening to push us into a new and disastrous commitment. . . . There is a great danger that piecemeal decisions will be taken in the near future, in response to the present impasse brought on by the inability of the South Vietnamese to help themselves, which

---

[132] See p. 673 of the House hearings on the bill, cited below.

[133] *CR*, vol. 113, pp. 21636–21637. Senator Cooper supported Mansfield's recommendations. See *ibid.*, pp. 21637–21638.

For suggested responses to Mansfield's speech which were prepared for the President (at his request) by McNamara and Rostow, see McNamara's memorandum for the President, Aug. 7, 1967, in the Johnson Library, WHCF, ND 19/CO 312, and Rostow's memorandum of August 7 in NSF Memos to the President—Walt Rostow.

[134] *CR*, vol. 113, Aug. 11, 1967, pp. 22362–22364.

[135] *Ibid.*, pp. 22348 ff.

will plunge us irrevocably—though over a period of time—into a full-blown colonial venture, where we will be fighting both North Vietnamese and the guerrillas."

Javits said that the South Vietnamese "must stand now and be counted." The September elections, he said, should mark the beginning of the end of the U.S. commitment and the point at which the South Vietnamese would assume "crucial political responsibility to reform the Armed Forces and establish social and political reform, including land reform. . . ." The U.S. should also begin the process of ending its commitment. Bombing of the North should be either ended or limited to the infiltration routes near the DMZ, and plans should be made for phasing out U.S. forces.

At the conclusion of the speech, which Javits said he made after "an enormous amount of deep soul searching," Senator Clark congratulated him and said he welcomed him "to the ranks of the 'nervous nellies' and the 'doves.'"

Tax Increases Deferred; New Funds Approved for the War

Hearings on the President's tax request were held on August 14–15, 21–28 and September 12–14, 1967, by the House Ways and Means Committee.[136] Mills continued to express his reservations, questioning whether the tax would be "temporary," as it was intended to be, "in the light of all the demands that are being made by people for additional Federal service—problems within our cities, this drive presently underway for Federal sharing of reserve, and things of that kind. . . ." He also urged again that new taxes be accompanied by spending cuts: "It just seems to me," he said, "like we are going to have to find some way to bring about reductions on the spending side to coincide and go along with increases in revenues if we are going to get any acceptance by the American people of a tax increase."[135]

In a memorandum to the President on September 13, Barefoot Sanders reported that in a conversation with the Treasury Department's liaison officer Mills had said "that the Administration has simply got to make a choice between 'guns and butter'; that you should go on national TV and explain that the choice must be made and that the choice is 'guns'; that because of Vietnam we must cut domestic spending *and* pass the Tax increase; that if you take this position you can count on him to go with you all the way."[138] (emphasis in original) Mills also said he wanted some commitments from the executive branch on major reductions in domestic spending.

Sanders suggested that the President should consider seeing Mills. "My own view," he added, "is that it would be a mistake to make a public choice between 'guns and butter.' While choosing 'guns' might be popular with the more conservative Democrats, I believe it would leave you wide open to attack from the liberal side." "We have just got to have it both ways and Mills has to be convinced of this."

---

[136] U.S. Congress, House, Committee on Ways and Means, *President's 1967 Tax Proposal,* Hearings, 2 pts., 90th Cong., 1st sess. (Washington, D.C.: U.S. Govt. Print. Off., 1967). For a good summary of the testimony see *Congressional Quarterly Almanac,* 1967, pp. 643 ff.

[137] House Hearings on Tax Proposals, pp. 76, 95.

[138] Johnson Library, Memorandum to the President from Barefoot Sanders, Sept. 13, 1967, Ex FG 1.

At the Luncheon Group meeting on September 15, following three days of testimony before the Ways and Means Committee by private witnesses (economists and business leaders) at which Mills and others on the committee continued to state their reservations about the tax increase, the President said, "'I have given serious thought that if I cannot get the tax bill that I will send a message to the Congress saying that I just cannot have a $30 billion deficit and I will ask the Congress to review all appropriations and cut them by 10 percent.'" McNamara responded: "'I'd stick it to Mills, and not let him get away with what he's done in the last three or four days.'"[139]

Budget Director Schultze also urged the President to take a strong stand. "I do *not* think we should be pushed into making much larger civilian cuts than the $2 billion."[140] (emphasis in original) A deeper cut, he said would "wreck our domestic programs." He also recommended telling Mills and the committee that there was increasing evidence of the need for the tax increase and of the support of business and economists for the increase. "Under these conditions do they [the committee] *really* want to take the risk of being the ones to be blamed for inflation, high interest rates, and a sadly depressed housing market!" (emphasis in originial)

"I think," Schultze concluded, "Mills and the Committee are playing 'chicken,' in an 'eyeball-to-eyeball' confrontation. I can't be positive—and obviously I'm not the world's greatest expert on what moves the Congress—but I think that if we are willing to take a strong and unyielding stand, they will blink first. They won't blink right away until they test our resolve. More economic signals will be necessary. But blink they will."

On September 19, the President met from 8:36 a.m. to 9:35 a.m. with congressional Democratic leaders for his weekly breakfast meeting to discuss the legislative situation. The Vice President also attended. The President said that "his biggest problem now is with Mills and the Ways and Means Committee and the budget." House Democratic Whip Boggs declared, "With Mills you can get it [the tax bill] out of Committee, and without Mills you can't.'"[141]

On October 3, the Ways and Means Committee voted 20–5 to postpone consideration of the tax request until the President and Congress could "reach an understanding on a means of implementing more effective expenditure reductions and controls."[142] In a statement on October 6, Mills defended this decision, saying that it was "an expression of the anxiety which many Members of Con-

[139] Johnson Library, Meetings Notes File, Jim Jones' notes of meeting of the President with Rusk, McNamara and Rostow, Sept. 15, 1967.

[140] Johnson Library, WHCF Ex LE/FI 11–3, Memorandum for the President from Schultze, "Wilbur Mills and the Tax Bill," Sept. 16, 1967.

The administration told the committee that it would cut $2 billion in civilian programs, but the committee apparently wanted a cut of $3 billion. See *ibid.*, and the memorandum to a senior member of the committee of a conversation with Representative Al Ullman (D/Ore.), attached to a memorandum for the President from Fowler, "Ways and Means Committee and the Tax Bill," Sept. 20, 1967, same location.

The administration also told the committee that it would cut Defense Department expenditures in order to offset increases in military expenditures for the war, but it not state an amount. The committee apparently proposed a $2 billion cut in defense expenditures. See both documents cited immediately above.

[141] Same location, Jones' notes of congressional leadership meeting Sept. 19, 1967.

[142] *Congressional Quarterly Almanac,* 1967, p. 653.

gress feel . . . about the recent sharp rise in Federal outlays and the proliferation of Federal Government activity." He told reporters "that the surcharge proposal was 'dead' unless the president made some basic long-range changes in federal spending policies. Even if this were done, he said, he did not know if the bill could be 'resurrected.'"[143]

Despite predictions of serious consequences in the absence of either spending cuts and/or new taxes, Congress approved the President's full request for appropriations for the war of about $22 billion as part of the Defense Department appropriation bill for the next fiscal year (FY 1968). No amendments to the provisions for funding the war were approved in either the House or the Senate. In both houses, however, amendments were offered to reduce overall defense appropriations as indirect, symbolic gestures against the war. In the House, Democrat George Brown, a long-time opponent of the war, offered an amendment to limit defense expenditures to 95 percent of the total defense expenditures as estimated in the President's budget. This was defeated by a voice vote.

George Mahon, chairman of the House Appropriations Committee, interpreted approval of the bill as an affirmation of support for the war: "The passage of this bill today," he said, "will unequivocally establish the fact, in my judgment, that the House of Representatives is in support of the war effort in Southeast Asia, because if we vote for this bill we will vote for approximately $20 billion to carry on the war. . . . I would estimate that probably 99 percent of the members of the House will vote for the bill. The world should interpret this . . . as evidence that the elected Representatives of the people in the House of Representatives are in support of the prosecution of the war for freedom in Southeast Asia. . . . It is not that we are entirely happy with the progress of the war, or all of the tactics being followed but we are in support of the overall objectives of the nation."[144]

In the Senate, Morse offered an amendment to reduce the bill by 10 percent and to let the Secretary of Defense decide which items to cut. (Thus, he could choose to exempt Vietnam funds). This was defeated 5–85. Supporting the amendment were Morse, Gruening, Fulbright, Young of Ohio and Clark. Clark then offered an amendment to reduce the funds by 5 percent and this was defeated 6–83, with Philip Hart joining the other five.

During a hearing the following day (August 23, 1967) by the Senate Foreign Relations Committee on a proposed resolution to assert the role of Congress in the making of "national commitments," Clark asked Representative Paul Findley, who was testifying in favor of the resolution, about use of the "power of the purse":

> Senator Clark. . . . the one thing that Congress has which we have been completely unwilling to exercise in connection with the Vietnamese situation in both Houses is the power of the purse. If we really get far enough into a clash with the Executive, I think that is the power we ought to utilize.
>
> Yesterday, I tried to indicate it in a very mild way, and to my glee, the Chairman joined me, but there were only six of

[143] *Ibid.*
[144] *CR*, vol. 113, pp. 15541–15542.

us. It does not look very good when you get licked 83 to 6 on a question of whether you are going to continue to give the Pentagon and the President all the money they want to wage any kind of warfare anywhere in the world under the Tonkin Bay resolution or under the powers of the commander in chief.

I would like to get your reaction as to whether you think it is perfectly futile to rely on the power of the purse—because everybody is too scared of the American Legion and the Veterans of Foreign Wars—or whether you think that is not really the ultimate weapon which we have. Until we are ready to use it maybe we ought to shut up.

Mr. Findley. I do not think it arises entirely from fear of the Legion and the VFW because I do not have such a fear. But I do feel——

Senator Clark. You are a brave man. [laughter] I voted for the appropriations yesterday when the chips were down.[145]

During Senate debate on August 22 on the Morse and Clark amendments, there was considerable criticism of U.S. policy in Vietnam. Among the critics was Case, who, following his earlier critique of the conduct of the war,[146] was concerned about the failure of the South Vietnamese to take the social, political and military steps necessary to "make victory possible." He also criticized the President for the decision to send 45,000 more troops without offering any justification to Congress or the public and "in the face of evidence that this has already become too much of an American war." He was also critical of increasing bombing "in apparent disregard of concerns expressed by many Americans"—an action which was "feeding the unfortunate illusion that victory is to be found in the north rather than in the south." "The missing ingredient in Vietnam," Case argued, "is not manpower or airpower, but willpower—the will of the present rulers of South Vietnam to mobilize and focus all their resources on the task of nation building." Unrest about Vietnam within the United States, Case said, reflected "a growing anxiety and deepening resentment at the admin-

---

[145] Hearings before the Committee on Foreign Relations on "National Commitments," cited in full below, p. 811. Findley had also voted for the same Defense appropriations bill.

[146] In a Senate speech on July 10 after returning from a trip to South Vietnam, Senator Case said that the common goals of the U.S. and the South Vietnamese could not be achieved unless the South Vietnamese Government and military could provide greater security and stability and gain the confidence and support of the people. (*CR*, vol. 113, pp. 18097 ff.) He said he did not think the U.S. could withdraw, and he quoted Edwin Reischauer, a professor of Asian history at Harvard University who had recently been U.S. Ambassador to Japan, as saying that withdrawal "would seriously shake confidence in our word and would be interpreted as a great triumph for the Communist program of immediate world revolution. This in turn would encourage further warfare and instability throughout Asia," and that the "least unsatisfactory course would seem to be our present one of limited warfare to pacify South Vietnam, and economic and political development to build up a government and society more resistant to internal subversion." Case, who said he opposed further U.S. troop deployments, argued that the escalation of the war would be a mistake, and that the greater the U.S. effort, the less the South Vietnamese would do for themselves.

Only by using "all our influence to get the South Vietnamese to do the things we are convinced must be done," Case added, could the U.S. avoid "catastrophic failure" in South Vietnam. "I think we must, once and for all, make up our minds that we must exercise the full weight of our influence on every important issue, whether it be to restrain the personal ambitions of military leaders, to force reforms both in the civilian and military establishments, to reduce the corruption and get rid of the corruptors, to limit censorship to a minimum instead of permitting its use without restraint as a campaign tool and for other improper purposes, to restore vigor, discipline, and morale to the Vietnamese armed forces and get them doing their job." "All this and more," Case said, "must be accomplished if we are not to see the whole Vietnamese effort bog down in complete chaos and eventual failure with effects which will last for decades and will be felt far beyond that remote and relatively tiny area of the world."

istration's continuing claims of progress when the American people are increasingly persuaded that . . . there has been no progress." Case said he thought that, having been "oversold by the administration as a replica of the American political process," the forthcoming South Vietnamese elections had "taken on the appearance of travesty in Western eyes. . . ." That was highly unfortunate, he said, because the question was not whether the elections met "ideal" Western standards, but whether they could, by bringing about reforms, give people confidence in their government and increase their will to win the war.

Stennis, the floor manager of the bill in Russell's absence, argued that the U.S. was sending more troops because South Vietnamese forces "cannot get the job done," but he thought that it was not reasonable to expect rapid social and political change. "It takes time to bring about new political institutions, new political thought, and new political practices. I am afraid that we do not realize that fact. That is one of the main troubles there." "I am about convinced," Stennis added, "that due to the differences in outlook, religion, culture, background, and history, those people are not going to learn very much about self-government from Americans."[147]

Gale McGee, who supported the war and was one of the principal spokesmen for the administration, said that Case's concerns were of secondary importance to the question of what effect the war was having in Southeast Asia. "Heaven knows, it is going to take a long time for any kind of elections with great meaning to take place, for any kind of self-participation on a local level in Vietnam." But the "big question is really not what happens to Vietnam at all, but what happens to that part of the world." What has happened as a result of U.S. involvement, he said, "is that the gloom, the despair, and the despondency that once dominated that part of the world have shifted . . . to the very firm conviction that they are winning a chance." "[I]f we vacillate now in Vietnam, . . if we begin to worry about what Mr. Ky, if we begin to worry about what Mr. Thieu, if we begin to worry about what the men in Hanoi are going to do, we will lose sight of the central question . . . which is the imperative requirement that someone successfully hold the line against erosions of the chance for a less violent procedure and a more orderly change in that part of the world." Case replied that he did not disagree. He said he did not want to withdraw U.S. forces or to lose the war. "We cannot win in the big picture unless we win in South Vietnam. We have chosen to make this the battleground, wisely or not." But "success means stabilization in South Vietnam, and that depends upon getting the South Vietnamese Government into such shape that the people will support it."

In the end, once again, Congress passed the bill providing funds to fight the war by nearly unanimous votes—407–1 in the House, with only George Brown dissenting, and 87–3 in the Senate (Morse and Gruening, and Young of Ohio who opposed the war but voted no on the bill for a specific reason not involving Vietnam).[148]

---

[147] For Case and Stennis' comments, see *ibid.*, pp. 23454–23455.

[148] *Ibid.*, pp. 11587, 23498.

CHAPTER 18

SOUTH VIETNAMESE ELECTIONS AND A NEW DIPLOMATIC INITIATIVE

On September 3, 1967, the South Vietnamese chose a new government, the first elected since the overthrow of Ngo Dinh Diem by the military junta in 1963. U.S. policymakers had spent months preparing for the event which, in their eyes, was an essential step toward creating a government based on popular support that could rally the public and defeat the Communists.[1] They also considered it to be an important aspect of the effort to promote U.S. support for the war by demonstrating that the Vietnamese, even in the middle of a war, could conduct a political campaign and an election that would be considered fair and honest, and that could lead to the establishment of a system of self-government.

As the U.S. began in early 1967 to lay plans for the election, the salient consideration was the need to find a way of making the transition from a military government to an elected government without losing the support of the military, and to do so while continuing to prosecute the war. In a message to Ambassador Lodge on January 12, 1967, the State Department said that it was essential to have a government "strong and unified enough to continue to prosecute the war (or to negotiate a peaceful settlement) and at the same time broadly enough based to attract increasing local and national political strength away from the V.C." "Constitutional regime most likely to fulfill both criteria would seem to us," the message said, "to be a genuine alliance or partnership between progressive civilian political and military elements and including Southern representation."[2] "For such a government to be viable over longer term, Vietnamese military leadership would have to forego their traditional practice of dictating political solutions through exercise of military power; similarly, civilian political elements would have to recognize reality of military power and cooperate with it."[3]

"What continues to concern us," the message continued, "is whether Vietnamese military leadership . . . is prepared to accept a genuine alliance with responsible civilian elements, or whether Vietnamese military will instinctively think in terms of their domination of government with some democratic window dressing." The

[1] "There is general agreement that, aside from military successes, advent of a popularly-based GVN could be our most important Vietnam success in 1967. Conversely, the most visible cloud now on the 1967 horizon is a major political crisis (or series of them) between military/civilian or Northerners/Southerners which could evolve into a major setback." Memorandum from Komer to Katzenbach, Vance, Rostow (the Non-Group), "Action Program to Promote a Favorable Political Evolution in Saigon," Jan. 13, 1967, Johnson Library, NSF Files of Robert W. Komer.

[2] After the division of Vietnam in 1954, the Government of South Vietnam had been dominated by Northerners.

[3] Johnson Library, NSF Country File, Vietnam, Washington to Saigon 117709, Jan. 12, 1967. This message was drafted by Robert Miller and approved by Unger and William Bundy. See also Washington to Saigon 128939, Jan. 31, 1967, to Lodge from Rusk.

U.S. Mission in Saigon replied that "a genuine sharing of power between the military and the civilian political leaders is required . . . [but] the military is in many respects the most experienced, cohesive and reliable of the nation building forces in this country." Rather than thinking of "controlling" the military, the U.S. should understand their role in providing unity, stability and political strength. "In the early years of the civilian-military partnership it may be best if the military is the senior partner." "Surely nothing could be more imprudent than to leave them out in the cold with no duties. An overthrow of the government would soon result." [4]

In its message, the State Department went on to argue that the U.S. should be "prepared to take risk of reducing to some degree governmental effectiveness which continued military leadership might provide . . . and of supporting emergence of a regime which has better prospects . . . for attracting and exploiting local political strength to the disadvantage of the VC." Accordingly, "we are inclined to prefer prominent civilian political figure as President, with military man as Prime Minister or Vice President." In its reply, the Mission agreed that "a new, more broadly-based government requires the infusion of some civilian elements into the executive branch and an elected legislature should at least have some degree of influence on the executive," but, that "does not necessarily mean a government dominated by civilians."

The State Department message also noted that "When we come down to personalities, we are inclined to agree with Ky that Thieu lacks sufficient support (except possibly within the military establishment) and inspires too much mistrust to gain key elected leadership position in honest campaign. While Ky does not share some of Thieu's disadvantages (associations with past regimes, Catholic religion, and relationships with northern Dai Viets [a political party]), Ky's northern birth is probably a disadvantage. Moreover, we see little sign that Ky has garnered any significant degree of popular support during his tenure as Prime Minister, and therefore seriously doubt his claim to such support." "Moreover," the State Department message added, "we would be concerned that either one or really any military man as president of constitutional government would be widely considered as 'more of the same' both in South Vietnam and abroad."

The Mission replied that at that time the leading candidates for President were Generals Ky and Thieu and former Premier Tran Van Huong, a civilian. Thieu was "acceptable to a wide range of Vietnamese opinions . . . but generates little enthusiasm," whereas "people are generally either positively for or against Ky." The most likely "winning ticket" would be Thieu or Ky supported by prominent civilians as Vice President and Prime Minister.

In a meeting of the Mission Council on February 27, 1967, Lodge cautioned officials not to "get in bed" with the Thieu-Ky government. "Our aim," he said, "is to be cool and correct—no more, no less." "If we do anything," he added, "we must not get caught." [5]

In a report to the President on February 28 after returning from a trip to Vietnam, Komer said that Lodge, Westmoreland, Porter,

[4] Same location, Saigon to Washington 17704, Feb. 9, 1967.

[5] Massachusetts Historical Society, Lodge Papers, Vietnam Papers, statement by Lodge to Mission Council meeting, Feb. 27, 1967.

and all senior officials in the Mission "believe that Ky would be at least marginally better than Thieu." They also believed, he said, that the winner would come from the military, and that "of our top people, only Porter and Lansdale strongly favor a civilian government; Porter because he thinks it would look better from our viewpoint and because a civilian regime would be more willing to negotiate. He says the generals, 'have it too good to want the war to end.' Habib [the Embassy political officer] disagrees; he sees a civilian regime as afraid to negotiate lest it trigger a military coup. He also sees Ky as evolving toward willingness to negotiate, and better able to do so because the military could least be accused of weakness in such case."[6]

Komer added that if the U.S. preferred a civilian Government "it will take early forceful exertion of our influence to get one." "This," he added, "would seem to call for a civilian Prime Minister and Vice President, which Ky or Thieu would probably be willing to accept if the U.S. discreetly made known its views—but might not otherwise."

There was general agreement among U.S. officials in Washington and Saigon that, as Lodge said in a message to Washington on February 18, "unity of the military is essential to governmental stability in Vietnam." And it was this factor he said, which "makes a political contest between Ky and Thieu highly dangerous. It could be a disaster which would jeopardize much that we have labored to build."[7] "I believe," he added, "we should continue to stress the importance of: keeping the military together; keeping the military and non-Communist civilians together; nominating a ticket in which the military and civilian elements are joined; and having a clean election, the results of which will be accepted as binding by all concerned."

On the other hand, there was also general agreement among U.S. officials that Thieu and Ky should not run together on the same political ticket. This, Komer said, "would be a disaster. Even if they could win legitimately, which most experts doubt, few in Vietnam or elsewhere would believe that it was not a rigged affair." Thieu, Komer said, should be encouraged "to 'return to the Army' to make pacification work."[8]

By June 1967, both Ky and Thieu had announced that they would run for President.[9] After meeting separately with the two men, Bunker cabled the President on June 15, "We do not see how dual military candidacies or Thieu's ultimate joining with a civilian ticket can fail to have some divisive effect on the military, especially on regional grounds."[10] Ky, he said, was "determined to run

---

[6] Johnson Library, NSF Files of Robert W. Komer, Memorandum for the President from Komer, Feb. 28, 1967.

[7] Johnson Library, NSF Memos to the President—Walt Rostow, Saigon to Washington 18354, Feb. 18, 1967.

[8] Johnson Library, NSF Files of Robert W. Komer, Memorandum to Katzenbach, Vance, Rostow from Komer, Jan. 13, 1967.

[9] For developments during the spring see CMH, Westmoreland Papers, History File, History Notes, notes of meeting May 7, 1967 of Westmoreland and Thieu; Johnson Library, NSF Memos to the President—Walt Rostow, Saigon to Washington 25083 and 25233, May 10, 1967, reporting on Bunker talks with Thieu and Ky; Saigon to Washington 26779 and 26790, May 26, reporting on meetings of Bunker and Bui Diem and Bunker and Thieu; and Saigon to Washington, (number not known), May 30, reporting on Bunker meeting with Ky.

[10] Johnson Library, NSF Country File, Vietnam, Saigon to Washington 28218, June 15, 1967.

and to win, and, as of now, he appears prepared to use whatever means are needed for this purpose unless we bring our influence to bear directly and forcefully on him regarding some of the pressure moves he has already initiated to assure his election." On the other hand, direct pressure on Thieu to withdraw, Bunker said, would run "the unacceptable risk of failing and of giving Thieu a major weapon to use against us and against Ky, who would then be the 'American candidate.'"

Ky's actions, Bunker said, were destroying the possibility of a fair election. "All political elements are fully aware of what is going on and have concluded that Ky is getting away with it because the Americans support him and condone his methods. Even if we think Ky is the most efficient and energetic leader on the scene, and this is not entirely certain, his election as a result of clearly repressive measures would in the long run destroy his effectiveness and sow the seeds of disunion and dissidence."

"To demonstrate that we stand for a fair election ahead of support for any one individual," Bunker said, "I am convinced that we must force Ky to take certain measures to counteract the damage that has already been done. . . . [T]here might then be a basis for seeing how we could encourage the leading candidates to prepare the ground for working together in a government of national union whatever the election outcome may be."[11] One possibility, Bunker said, would be "prompt exportation of General Loan, perhaps an invitation to an extended training visit and program in the U.S." (Nguyen Ngoc Loan, the director of the National Police and head of the Military Security Service, who was a close associate of Ky, was known for his strong-arm tactics.)[12]

On July 19, Bunker sent a very secret cable to Rusk through the communications facilities of the CIA in which he said: "If Ky were not virtually certain to win, whether by proper or improper means, and if he were not on balance the best available candidate, though not exactly a prize package, the problem could be viewed from a different perspective. However, since we shall almost certainly have to contend with him as the President and dominant political force for some time to come, it is my judgment urgent that we can take steps to restore faith in the fairness of his administration and of the honesty of the forthcoming elections."

Bunker repeated his judgment that one of the steps required to restore faith in Ky was to persuade him to remove Loan. Another was to try to persuade Thieu to withdraw as a candidate. "The core of the problem which we face, however," Bunker added, "remains the fact that Ky does not have enough experience or political wisdom of his own at this point to conduct his campaign without sounder advice than he can command from his compatriots. It is

---

[11] For the State Department response to this cable (Saigon 28218), see, in the same location, Washington to Saigon 212155, June 16, 1967.

[12] On June 14, 1967, Bunker reported that Loan "has begun systematically summoning police and military security officers from throughout the country in order to instruct them on how to assure that Ky is elected . . . each officer is being instructed to submit weekly reports on the political situation in his province, including information on activities of presidential and legislative candidacies. Candidates who are not supporters of Ky are to be persuaded to switch their loyalties to Ky, by means of bribes if necessary. . . . It is further stated that there will be a number of changes in police and military security personnel in the pre-election period determined by the willingness of the incumbent's loyalty to Loan and Ky and their willingness to engage in manipulation of the elections." Pike (ed.), *The Bunker Papers*, vol. I, p. 48.

therefore incumbent upon us to establish a special relationship with Ky in order to exert on him the kind of continuous influence which is impossible through formal official contacts."[13]

Bunker proposals were transmitted to Rostow's office, and the next day (June 20) William Jorden sent Rostow a memorandum taking exception.[14] "I don't think they will work," he said. "I think they would do more harm than good." He said he did not agree with the Mission's appraisal, which he said was "shared to a great extent by [the] State [Department]," "that Ky is the only choice and that any other would be a disaster. As you know, I think highly of Ky and he might be an effective president. But I have come to believe that the healthiest thing that could happen in Vietnam right now would be the election of a civilian. The best government I can think of would be: Huong as President, [Duong Van] Big Minh as Vice President, Ky as Prime Minister, and Thieu as Chief of the Army."

Jorden said that the kind of direct U.S. involvement proposed by Bunker "would be a great mistake. It would be known. It would put us right in the middle of internal contention." Instead of backing one man, Jorden said, "we should be working clearly with *all* candidates." (emphasis in original) "I would pick four good men to work with Ky, Thieu, Huong and Suu [Phan Khac Suu, who was briefly Chief of State in early 1964] on a full-time basis. . . . They could provide advice, suggestions, and ideas, and help to keep their man on the track. They would make clear that the U.S. interest was in real democracy and the development of a solidly-based political process. They would also, by their actions, make clear on strict neutrality in the electoral process."

A "power play against Thieu would backfire badly," Jorden said, and the removal of Loan "would not in itself solve the problem of chicanery and manipulation." Moreover, financial assistance for Ky (which Bunker had apparently proposed) was a "bad idea." "This, too, will become known."

"I would put real heat on Ky," Jorden said, "to rein in his followers. . . . There are three principal items that need correcting: the use of the police and security apparatus in support of Ky; inept use of censorship on political matters; Ky's use of his position and the machinery of government for political purposes." Jorden recommended that Rostow call in the South Vietnamese Ambassador and "lay down the law" and urge him to return to Saigon immediately with the message that a "dishonest election would undercut our President's position and endanger continued American support. . . ."

In a cable to Westmoreland on June 24, JCS Chairman Wheeler reported that there was "much high-level concern here" about the consequences of the split between Ky and Thieu, and that at meetings of a "fairly prestigious committee of which I am a member [probably the Non-Group] we are at a loss as to what, if anything, we can and should do. Our basic concern, of course, revolves about

---

[13] Johnson Library, NSF Memos to the President—Walt Rostow, Saigon to Washington 8185, June 19, 1967, sent to Rusk via the CIA. After the final sentence quoted above, the remainder of the cable, about 1½ pages, was deleted when it was released in 1993. The cable is not included in *The Bunker Papers*.

[14] Johnson Library, NSF Memos to the President—Walt Rostow, Memorandum to Rostow from William Jorden, "Ambassador Bunker's Proposals," June 20, 1967.

the grave possibility that the candidacies of both men, coupled with a growing antipathy between the two, will split the armed forces and create once again a situation where senior officers devote their time to politicking rather than defeating the common enemy."[15]

On June 27, as a result of U.S. pressure, Loan was removed as chief of the Military Security Service (but remained as director of the National Police).

On June 28–30, an extraordinary meeting was held in Saigon of the general officers in the Armed Forces Council (the junta that governed the country). This is Robert Shaplen's account of what happened:[16]

> The meeting began with the forty-eight generals berating each other for corruption. Some of them suggested that Thieu and Ky both withdraw and let a civilian be elected President. Others said that the civilians would ruin the country and that the junta should just tear up the new constitution and go on ruling without one. General Thieu then spoke, in a humble vein. He said that he realized that some of those in the room resented him and were embarrassed by his actions, and as he said this, according to reports by those present, tears rolled down his cheeks. At that point, Ky offered to withdraw, whereupon, just as he had surmised, a sufficient number of generals rallied behind him to persuade him that he couldn't.
>
> During the second day's sessions, while the customary rumors of a coup by the forces of one man or the other swept the city, Thieu had apparently reached a private decision to quit the race, but overnight, at the urging of his advisers, and especially of his wife (wives have always played prominent behind-the-scenes political roles in Vietnam), he changed his mind, and in the morning he returned to the meeting loaded for bear. He attacked Ky at Ky's most vulnerable point—the Premier's failure to fulfill his promise to eradicate corruption—and listed, one by one, various corrupt activities in the ranks of the police in Saigon and among officials at the district and province level throughout the country. By implication, Thieu was thus attacking Ky's closest ally, General Nguyen Ngoc Loan, a swashbuckling, pistol-packing, erratic officer who was the head of both the police and the Military Security Service. At this moment, histrionics took over completely. Three of the country's four corps commanders are said to have torn off their stars and refused to go back to their commands until the Thieu-Ky deadlock was broken. Thieu is said to have wept again and thanked his fellow-officers for their loyalty. Ky is said to have wept, too, and to have offered once more to quit, and it is said that this time, worn out by the whole performance, the other generals accepted his withdrawal. But they subsequently prevailed upon him to accept the Vice-Presidential nomination, and the American Embassy had no choice but to indicate that it thought this a fine idea.

---

[15] CMH, Westmoreland Papers, Messages Files, Wheeler to Westmoreland, JCS 4736, June 24, 1967.

[16] Robert Shaplen, article from Saigon October 7, 1967, printed in the *New Yorker* on that date and reprinted in Shaplen, *The Road from War,* pp. 151–169. Quotation used here is from pp. 156–157.

According to a cable from Bunker to the President on June 30, 1967, Ky, in agreeing to become the Vice Presidential candidate, "laid down the conditions that he would have the right to name the cabinet and to control the armed forces," and these conditions were accepted by the Armed Forces Council.[17]

In his subsequent account, Ky explained that the generals, in order to make sure that after the election "Thieu would have to obey the military, and I would have a share of power, not normally allowed under the constitution," formed a "secret organization, with a non-constitutional framework, called the Military Council," which included all of the high ranking military officers as well as the President, Vice President and Minister of Defense, who, of course were part of the military as well." "The Military Council," Ky stated, "had the right to set up national policies, promote military and civil officials in the government," and any member of the Council who was elected President would be required to "observe directives outlined by the chairman of the Military Council." "In other words, the Military Council was organized beyond the boundaries and scope of the law." [18]

Toward the end of June, General Duong Van ("Big") Minh, former head of the junta that assassinated Ngo Dinh Diem and took power in 1963, announced that he was going to run for President. Big Minh, who was very popular with many South Vietnamese, had been exiled to Thailand in 1964.[19] Minh's candidacy for President was filed by proxy on June 30, shortly after the Government announced that, for reasons of "national security," Minh and others in exile would not be permitted to return. Faced with the threat that Minh would disrupt the unity of the armed forces in the election, and that in a divided contest he or a civilian might be elected, the junta (Directorate) moved quickly to prevent him from running. Defense Minister Cao Van Vien, the highest ranking military officer in South Vietnam, met with Minh in Thailand and told him that if he returned he would be arrested when he stepped off the plane. Minh replied that he was going to return. Several days later, the Provincial National Assembly, which, under the election law, had to approve candidates, approved Minh's candidacy by a substantial vote.[20]

The U.S. Government, while officially neutral, was very opposed to Minh's candidacy. In a cable to the President on July 12, Bunker said that it could "pose a serious threat to military unity . . . [and] might also divide the country in other ways. The Catholics are strongly opposed to his candidacy and would probably react vigorously if he continued to be a candidate. He had some Buddhist support, and while this strength is difficult to gauge, it could turn out to be enough to threaten a revival of religious tension and even

---

[17] Johnson Library, NSF Memos to the President—Walt Rostow, Saigon to Washington 29258, June 30, 1967.

[18] Nguyen Cao Ky, *Twenty Years and Twenty Days*, pp. 156–157. Ky added that over the years Thieu "cunningly grabbed more power for himself and sidestepped the Military Council." Thieu's "blatant corruption," Ky said "finally led South Vietnam to defeat. . . . I should never have ceded power to someone so unworthy." *Ibid.*, p. 157.

[19] In May 1965, when a change of Government in South Vietnam became imminent, Minh attempted to return in response to pressure for him to replace the current Premier, but the Government, fearing his popularity, ordered air force planes to turn back the commercial plane on which he was flying. See p. 274 of pt. III of this study.

[20] CIA Files, Intelligence Report, "The Situation in South Vietnam (Weekly)," July 3, 1967, No. 0357/67.

open religious conflict such as that which erupted between Catholics and Buddhists in 1964. Thus, the Minh candidacy appears to me to pose a clear threat to the essential degree of political stability without which we cannot get further progress toward democratic government in this country."[21]

The junta, supported by the U.S., successfully blocked Minh's candidacy, and in the middle of July the Assembly voted not to allow Minh to run. It also refused to allow the candidacy of Au Truong Thanh, a former Minister of Economy under Ky, who had been well regarded by the Americans but who favored a cease-fire and was running as a "peace" candidate. (The action against Thanh was taken under the provision of the electoral law barring persons who "have directly or indirectly worked for communist or pro-communist neutralization or worked in the interests of communism.")[22]

During the campaign, which began August 3, there were numerous charges of unfairness and election rigging by the civilian candidates who had been permitted to run.[23] This resulted in considerable publicity in the U.S., and led to a number of complaints from Members of Congress. Fifty seven liberal Democrats in the House of Representatives, led by Sidney Yates and Jonathan Bingham, sent a letter to the President on August 10 urging him "to make the strongest representations that steps be taken to prevent a further eroding of confidence in the elections." Moreover, "If the governmental authorities of South Vietnam continue to refuse to assure free and fair elections, they should be informed that the United States may very well undertake a serious reappraisal of its policies in Vietnam."[24]

On August 11, Senators Javits and Robert Kennedy, joined by Case, Pastore, Clark, Fulbright, Young of Ohio, Symington, McGovern, Church, Cooper, and Morse, argued forcefully in speeches in the Senate that the elections should be free and that restrictions on civilian candidates should be removed.[25]

On August 23, the White House announced that the President had asked a group of distinguished Americans to observe the elections. In a meeting with his advisers on August 18 at which this was discussed, the President suggested that, in addition to others, the chairmen of the House and Senate Armed Services Committee and House Foreign Affairs and Senate Foreign Relations Committees should be included. He said that Fulbright "won't go any further than Hawaii," and Rusk responded, "it's not safe for Fulbright to go farther than Hawaii because nobody in Asia wants to see Fulbright."[26]

The observers consisted of 22 men, including three Senators (but no Members of the House of Representatives or chairmen of the four committees):[27]

---

[21] *The Bunker Papers*, vol. I, p. 82, Bunker to the President, July 12, 1967.

[22] *Ibid.*, pp. 82–83, Bunker to the President, July 12, 1967, and p. 89, Bunker to the President, July 19, 1967.

[23] See Bunker's weekly reports to the President for August 9, 16 and 23, in *ibid.*, pp. 111–138. See also Bunker's cable, on Aug. 17, 1967, summarizing the criticisms and the answers suggested by the U.S. Mission. U.S. Department of State, Central File, Pol 27 Viet S, Saigon to Washington 2972.

[24] *CR*, vol. 113, pp. 22262–22263.

[25] *Ibid.*, pp. 22348 ff. and *New York Times*, Aug. 12, 1967.

[26] Johnson Library, Meetings Notes File, Jim Jones' notes of meeting of the President with Rusk, McNamara, Rostow and Wheeler, Aug. 18, 1967.

[27] Johnson, *The Vantage Point*, p. 264.

	Senators	
1.	Bourke B. Hickenlooper (R/Iowa)	Ranking Republican Member of the Foreign Relations Committee
2.	Edmund S. Muskie (D/Maine)	Chairman, Senate Democratic Campaign Committee
3.	George L. Murphy (R/Calif.)	Chairman, Senate Republican Campaign Committee
	Governors	
4.	William L. Guy	Democrat of North Dakota
5.	Thomas L. McCall	Republican of Oregon
6.	Richard J. Hughes	Democrat of New Jersey
	Mayors	
7.	Joseph M. Barr	Democrat of Pittsburgh
8.	Theodore R. McKeldin	Republican of Baltimore
	Veterans	
9.	Joseph Scerra	Incoming Commander, Veterans of Foreign Wars
10.	Eldon James	Former National Commander, American Legion
	Labor	
11.	David Sullivan	President, Building Services Employees Union (Vice President, AFL–CIO)
	Business	
12.	James B. Antell	President, Junior Chamber of Commerce
13.	Werner P. Gullander	President, National Association of Manufacturers
	Churches	
14.	Archbishop Robert E. Lucey	Archbishop of the Diocese of San Antonio
15.	Rabbi Jacob P. Rudin	President, Synagogue Council of America
16.	Dr. Edward L. R. Elson	Pastor, National Presbyterian Church, Washington, D.C.
	News Media	
17.	John S. Knight	President, Knight Newspapers
18.	Stanford Smith	General Manager, American Newspapers Publishers Association
19.	Eugene C. Patterson	Editor, *Atlanta Constitution*
20.	Donald H. McGannon	President, Westinghouse Broadcasting Company
	Others	
21.	Whitney M. Young, Jr.	President, Urban League
22.	Ed Munro	President, National Association of Counties

After the group returned to Washington from its visit to South Vietnam on August 30-September 4, there was a White House meeting with the President on September 6 at which members of the group were called upon to comment about the election. According to the President's memoirs, they were "enormously enthusiastic."[28] Eugene Patterson, editor of the *Atlantic Constitution,* said in a later interview that the way the President set the scene, "It was

[28] *Ibid.*, p. 265.

a performance and not a report."[29] When Patterson was called upon, he said "he suggested that the glowing praise of democracy amidst battle had neglected to place the elections within their context, including the fact that the current South Vietnamese government had barred several popular candidates from even entering the race." The President, Patterson said,

> had been taking notes with a pencil and he looked up at each person as he spoke, . . . and looked steadily at him and nodded and listened to the encouraging talk. But when I put the sour note into it, he looked quickly from his pad and glared at me with obvious anger as if I were doing an unfair thing. Then he put his head back down, and wrote studiedly with his pencil without looking at me again.[30]

As the election approached, Bunker, who said that Thieu and Ky would win with 35–45 percent of the vote, and that Huong would be second with 25–30 percent,[31] cabled Washington on August 26 that Thieu and Ky estimated they would receive as little as 35 percent of the vote, and that if they were willing to settle for this small a mandate they would not need to "rig" the election. If a major civilian candidate were to withdraw, however, the race would be very uncertain and Thieu and Ky might end up rigging the election. If a civilian were to win, there could be a coup, in which case, Bunker said, "we must be prepared for the possibility of firmer and more intervention than has been required at any time in recent past."[32]

In the election, Thieu and Ky were the winners, receiving 35 percent of the vote. Huong came in fourth with only 10 percent. In second place, to the great surprise of the South Vietnamese and the Americans, was a lawyer and peace candidate, Truong Dinh Dzu, who received 17.2 percent of the vote. According to a cable from Bunker to the President on September 6, "Dzu's strong showing, which surprised everyone, was due in part to the fact that he was the most articulate and vociferous critic of the government. . . . His simplistic and insistent exploitation of the peace theme undoubtedly also had a strong appeal."[33]

---

[29] Kathleen J. Turner, *Lyndon Johnson's Dual War: Vietnam and the Press* (Chicago: Univ. of Chicago Press, 1985), p. 189.

[30] In the Johnson Library, Meetings Notes File, there is a memorandum on the meeting of September 6 which contains comments made by the observers, including Patterson, but the notes do not include any of Patterson's less favorable comments.

[31] Pike (ed.), *The Bunker Papers,* vol. I, Weekly report to the President, Aug. 23, 1967, p. 135.

[32] U.S. Department of State, Central File, Pol 14 Viet S, Saigon to Washington 4105, Aug. 26, 1967.

[33] *The Bunker Papers,* vol. I, p. 148. Bunker said (p. 152) that Dzu's peace plan "involves proposing to the U.S. an unconditional halt to the bombing of North Vietnam; talks between the GVN and Hanoi aimed at halting the infiltration of men and equipment from North to South and the withdrawal of North Vietnamese troops from the South; talks with the U.S. and other allied governments to reach agreements on troop levels, the period during which Allied troops would be stationed in Vietnam, and timing of ultimate withdrawal, talks with the Liberation Front 'to find out the aspirations of the Liberation Front' and 'to exchange rational proposals with the Liberation Front'; and negotiations of an international guarantee through a reconvened Geneva Conference to support the arrangements reached directly between the parties concerned."

For an analysis of the election and an explanation of Dzu's strong showing, see Allan E. Goodman, *Politics in War: The Bases of Political Community in South Vietnam* (Cambridge, Mass.: Harvard Univ. Press, 1973), ch. 3.

For a description of Dzu and of his political campaign, see Bernard Weinraub, "South Vietnam's No. 1 Dove," *New York Times Magazine,* Oct. 8, 1967.

In an informal talk to a U.S. subcabinet group on September 12, William Bundy called Dzu "well heeled, articulate. We think he may have got some dough from the French . . . but he has dough from somewhere, and he is a smarty." "But he is not," Bundy added, "a significant figure. He will not be able to put together a significant opposition coalition."[34]

President Johnson sent Thieu a letter congratulating him in which he said, "The election was a milestone along the path toward the goal you have set for yourselves—a free, secure, and peaceful Vietnam."[35] Others were not as sanguine. Robert Shaplen said in an article on October 7, "The assumption—primarily an American one—that the Vietnamese elections have had, or are likely to have, any salutary effect on the war or on the internal political situation here [Saigon] is regarded by most Vietnamese as unwarranted and unrealistic. This reaction can be attributed partly to national cynicism but much more to an enduring conviction that the whole elective process is strongly an American-directed performance with a Vietnamese cast."[36]

Ambassador Averell Harriman, who at the end of his service with the Johnson administration (having been in Paris during 1968 as head of the U.S. delegation to the peace talks), wrote an "absolutely personal" memorandum for his files on December 14, 1968, sharply criticized the 1967 election. "Thieu/Ky," he said, "were elected by 34% of the people living in the part of the country secure enough to participate in the election. Komer figures this at 67%. Two-thirds of 34 is less than 23% of the people. For us to try to maintain that these officials are the free choice of the South Vietnamese people cannot be maintained. A new election must be held under appropriate conditions."[37]

Immediately after the election, at a meeting on September 5 with the Luncheon Group (Rusk, McNamara, Rostow, Helms, General Johnson sitting in for Wheeler, and Christian), President Johnson strongly emphasized the need for the new government to go into action.[38] "The President said we should get a speech worked up for Thieu and let him make it as quickly as possible." He said that Thieu "should be grabbing the headlines from Dzu by proposing several programs." "'Instead of Dzu taking the headlines,'" he said, "'Thieu and Ky should fill the news with Operation Takeoff.'"

The President said to get a cable out to Bunker along these lines. "'Get out the programs they can try to get proposed. Have Westmoreland talk to them about reforming the Army. Have them (Thieu and Ky) give backgrounders. First tell them how to broaden the government and make it as much civilian as possible. Clean up the government. Give out their programs on reconciliation in the Chieu Hoi program; land reform; peace initiatives. I'd have the *New York Times* believe that they will get what they want from this government."

"The President said to let Ky talk about the things he wants done, especially those things that would appeal to the opposition in

---

[34] U.S. Department of State, Lot File 85 D 240 (William Bundy Papers), notes of Bundy speech to subcabinet, Sept. 12, 1967.

[35] *New York Times*, Sept. 10, 1967.

[36] Shaplen, *The Road from War*, p. 151.

[37] Johnson Library, Papers of Francis M. Bator, Harriman memorandum, Dec. 14, 1968.

[38] Johnson Library, Meetings Notes File, Jim Jones' notes of meeting Sept. 5, 1967.

the U.S. . . . we've got to minimize our opposition. The major threat we have is from the doves."

After the meeting, Rostow called Benjamin Read, Rusk's assistant, to urge the State Department to act. According to Read's notes, Rostow said, "Get the notion to Thieu and Ky. They have to grasp the initiative from Dzu." "Don't sit back," he told Read. "Have initiative . . . go, go, go!"[39]

Toward the end of September, the State Department gave Thieu the text of a draft platform for an action program together with the text of a suggested inaugural address.[40]

Meanwhile, Dzu and other civilian candidates protested election irregularities and sought to invalidate the election. This was blocked by Thieu/Ky supporters with active assistance from the Americans. As Westmoreland said in notes he made after a U.S. Mission Council meeting on October 2, "members of the Mission made it clear to various [South Vietnamese] contacts that to invalidate the elections would be a major blow to American public support of the war."[41] Later that day, the Assembly voted 58–43 to validate the results of the election. (Bunker had predicted that the chances for validation were only 50–50).[42]

The next day (October 3), in a meeting with the Luncheon Group (Rusk, McNamara, Rostow, Helms and Christian), the President said that "with validation behind us, we should get Thieu to get the most progressive civilians in government . . . there is a need to 'get with it' out there. We need programs for health and education and land reform. They have got to show that they know what they are doing. We need to get General Westmoreland to get the South Vietnamese Army in line. They have got to get in where the fighting is."[43]

The "M–A/K Channel"—A New Attempt to Open Talks

During July-October 1967, the U.S. again sought to open direct communications with the North Vietnamese in the hope of finding a way of ending the war. At the same time, South Vietnamese leaders were being encouraged to work toward reconciliation and direct talks with the National Liberation Front after the September election.

The reaction of the North Vietnamese, as will be seen, was that the U.S. was "talking while fighting" as a tactical move prior to heavier fighting, which, of course, was the attitude of the U.S. toward similar efforts by the Communists.

Since the beginning of active U.S. military involvement in the war, the President had been doubtful that the Communists would negotiate unless they were sufficiently punished. He remained

---

[39] Johnson Library, NSF Files of Benjamin Read, "Telephone Conversation between Walt Rostow and Read, September 5, 1967.

[40] See the text in U.S. Department of State, Lot File 70 D 207, memorandum to Katzenbach from Phillip Habib, Sept. 28, 1967.

[41] CMH, Westmoreland Papers, History File, History Notes, Oct. 2, 1967.

[42] See his cable, Saigon to Katmandu, Nepal 7407, Oct. 2, 1967, in the Department of State, Lot File 74 D 417.

According to a CIA situation report on October 1, a factor in the support for validation was Thieu's appeal to the "patriotism and common sense of recalcitrant deputies and to their openly expressed desire for some financial quid-pro-quo." Johnson Library, NSF Country File, Vietnam, Rostow to the President, CAP 67853, Oct. 1, 1967.

[43] Johnson Library, Tom Johnson's Notes of Meetings, Notes of meeting Oct. 3, 1967.

hopeful that the Communists could be compelled to come to terms—that there was a "breaking point." Yet as desirous as he may have been to force his opponent to capitulate, and as confident as he was of the ability of the U.S. to achieve that goal, from the beginning he had also understood the logic of fighting a limited war for limited objectives—a war which, by definition, would end in some form of limited victory, either a negotiated settlement or a simple withdrawal, partial or complete, on the part of the enemy.

The nub of the problem, of course, was that the Communists apparently did not desire or see the necessity to negotiate, at least until the U.S. ceased bombing the North, while the U.S., seeking to fashion a formula by which to preserve its principal "blue chip" (bombing) and to prevent the Communists from "taking advantage" of a cessation of bombing, took the position that bombing would be suspended (or would end) when there was proof that infiltration from North Vietnam had stopped. (As noted, this was later modified somewhat from the original formulation, and was changed substantially by the U.S. proposal at the Glassboro Summit Conference in June 1967.)

During 1966 and early 1967, various efforts had been made to initiate negotiations, but following the failure of the British initiative in February 1967, there appears to have been less diplomatic activity as fighting escalated. In the summer of 1967, however, there was a potentially promising development. On June 5, the day the Israeli-Arab war began, Herbert Marcovich, a French biologist and member of the International Continuing Committee of the Pugwash Conference (a group of leading intellectuals concerned about world problems) asked the conference's secretary general to convene a small meeting to discuss the Middle East situation. The conference's executive committee agreed, but the Russian representative asked that the meeting also consider Vietnam. Two weeks later (and several days before the Glassboro Summit) the meeting was held in Paris. Those present included Marcovich, a participant from the U.S.S.R., and Henry Kissinger, a member of Pugwash and a friend of Marcovich.[44] (It will be recalled that Kissinger was actively involved in Vietnam matters as a consultant to the State Department.) At the session, it was agreed that Marcovich and another Frenchman, Raymond Aubrac, a friend of Marcovich and Kissinger who was an old friend of Ho Chi Minh, should visit Hanoi and attempt to discuss negotiations with Ho.[45]

The extent of U.S. Government involvement in proposing this initiative is not known, but Kissinger was acting, in effect, as a government agent, and continued to do so as the matter developed.

At a meeting of Harriman's Negotiations Committee on July 7, 1967, Cooper discussed the trip. Marcovich and Aubrac, he re-

---

[44] David Landau, *Kissinger: The Uses of Power* (Boston: Houghton Mifflin, 1972), p. 164.

[45] The basic published source of information on "Pennsylvania," the codename for this initiative, is *The Negotiating Volumes of the Pentagon Papers*, edited by Herring, *The Secret Diplomacy of the Vietnam War.* See also Lyndon Johnson, *The Vantage Point*, pp. 266–268, Cooper, *The Lost Crusade*, pp. 377–381, Walter Isaacson, *Kissinger: A Biography* (New York: Simon and Schuster, 1992), pp. 121–123, Kraslow and Loory, *The Secret Search for Peace in Vietnam*, Thies, *When Governments Collide*, pp. 180–194.

ported, had received de Gaulle's permission to go to Hanoi, but not as an official French Mission.[46]

Marcovich and Aubrac went to Hanoi on July 21–26, where Aubrac met with Ho Chi Minh and Aubrac and Marcovich met with Premier Pham Van Dong. They told Pham Van Dong that they would report to Kissinger, who would report to the U.S. Government. As advised by Kissinger, they discussed the Phase A-Phase B formula whereby the U.S. would suspend or end bombing based on a commitment by the North to take reciprocal action. Pham Van Dong replied, "We want an unconditional end of bombing and if that happens, there will be no further obstacles to negotiations."[47] Pham Van Dong added that the situation on the battlefield in South Vietnam was "improving all the time. . . . We fight only when we choose; we economize on our resources, we fight only for political purposes. . . . We have been fighting for our independence for four thousand years. We have defeated the Mongols three times. The United States Army, strong as it is, is not as terrifying as Genghis Khan."

In closing, Pham Van Dong told Marcovich and Aubrac that they could communicate with him through Mai Van Bo, the North Vietnamese diplomat in Paris.

Kissinger met Marcovich and Aubrac one hour after they returned to Paris, and sent a report to Washington on the results of the Hanoi trip.

On August 8, the report of the Hanoi trip was discussed at a meeting of the President with McNamara, Katzenbach (sitting in for Rusk), Rostow and Christian. Califano was also present.[48] After a brief statement about the discussions which had occurred in Hanoi (which was excised when the notes of the meeting were declassified), McNamara said it was "the most interesting message on the matter of negotiations which we have ever had." The President "questioned about the reliability of the two men," and McNamara replied that to his knowledge they were "completely reliable," and that Kissinger was "a tough, shrewd negotiator."

The President responded that "he saw no need until the facts became clearer to slow up the bombing. He said the moment they are willing, we certainly are ready to sit down. We will discontinue all bombing north of the 17th parallel [the demarcation line] if we know they will not take advantage of it."

On August 11, the President approved the following statement:[49]

> The United States is willing to stop the aerial and naval bombardment of North Vietnam if this will lead promptly to productive discussions between representatives of the U.S. and the DRV looking toward a resolution of the issues between them. We would assume that, while discussions proceed either with public knowledge or secretly, the DRV would not take advantage of the bombing cessation or limitation. Any such move on their part would obviously be inconsistent with the move-

---

[46] Library of Congress, Harriman Papers, Subject File, Memorandum of Meeting of the Negotiations Committee, July 7, 1967.

[47] "Conversations with Pham Van Dong and Ho," prepared by Kissinger from reports by Marcovich and Aubrac, attached to memorandum from Cooper to members of the Negotiations Committee, Aug. 2, 1967, Herring, *The Secret Diplomacy of the Vietnam War,* p. 717.

[48] Johnson Library, Tom Johnson's Notes of Meetings, Notes of meeting Aug. 8, 1967.

[49] Herring, *The Secret Diplomacy of the Vietnam War,* p. 726.

ment toward resolution of the issues between the U.S. and the DRV which the negotiations are intended to achieve.

Kissinger returned to Paris on August 17 where, joined by Chester Cooper, he held a series of meetings with Marcovich and Aubrac, who meanwhile had applied for visas for another trip to Hanoi. According to Cooper, M and A (as they were referred to in the cables) "repeatedly pressed us as to how they could convince the North Vietnamese that the United States was seriously interested in negotiations when our bombing had reached record levels of intensity." They asked whether, during their next trip to Hanoi, the U.S. could reduce bombing "as a signal to Hanoi that their mission was seriously regarded by the United States." Kissinger (referred to as K in the cables) and Cooper said they would raise the issue with Washington.[50]

On August 19, at a meeting from 8:35 p.m. to 9:55 p.m. of the President, Rusk, McNamara, Rostow, and General Wheeler, it was agreed that the Hanoi 10-mile limit would be reimposed for ten days. Rusk said, "these fellows [M and A] will get there on the 25th and it's not good to hit them when they get there.'" He added that "a few days ago he felt there was one chance in 100—but today he feels there is one chance in 50 that out of this may come secret contact." McNamara replied that he thought the chances were one in ten.[51]

Later that day, Kissinger told M and A that beginning August 21, the U.S. would modify its bombing in the Hanoi area "to guarantee their personal safety and as a token of our good will." Kissinger said that this would last for 10 days. "When M and A asked whether this was an ultimatum, Kissinger replied that we would hardly talk of an ultimatum when we had offered to end bombing altogether."[52]

On August 21–23, U.S. bombing of Hanoi outside the 10-mile limit was the heaviest of the war. On August 21, the North Vietnamese rejected M and A's application for a visa, an action, according to Mai Van Bo, that was taken because it would have been too dangerous to visit Hanoi because of the bombing, and to have let them come at that time "would have discredited us and ultimately you."[53]

On, August 25, M and A gave Bo the text of President Johnson's statement of August 11.

On September 3, M and A told Bo that the Americans were extending the suspension of bombing in the area of Hanoi for three days beyond the original 10 days. (This was subsequently amended by a decision to extend it indefinitely.)

On September 8, M and A told Bo that Kissinger would be coming to Paris for about 10 days beginning September 9, and Bo commented that if there were no bombing of Hanoi "something could well happen" during that period.[54]

There was no bombing of Hanoi, but there was no further response from the North Vietnamese.

---

[50] Cooper, *The Lost Crusade*, p. 379.
[51] Johnson Library, Meetings Notes File, Jim Jones' Notes of Meeting of Aug. 19, 1967.
[52] Herring, *The Secret Diplomacy of the Vietnam War*, p. 729.
[53] *Ibid.*, pp. 730, 745.
[54] *Ibid.*, p. 736.

Bombing continued in other areas, including a heavy raid in and around Haiphong on September 11. On that day, North Vietnam rejected President Johnson's proposal in a statement which said in part:[55] "The American message has been communicated after an escalation of the attacks against Hanoi and under the threat of continuation of the attacks against Hanoi. It is clear that this constitutes an ultimatum to the Vietnamese people. . . . It is only after the unconditional stopping by the United States of the bombing and all other acts of war against the Democratic Republic of Vietnam, that it would be possible to engage in conversation." At the same time, Bo told M and A that "because of the continued threat of bombing Hanoi which has the character of an ultimatum, a direct meeting with Kissinger cannot take place."[56]

The U.S., Kissinger said in a cable to Washington later that day, had two choices: "(a) to take the message at face value and end the A–M channel; (b) to treat the message as a first step in a complicated bargaining process." "[O]n balance," he said, "I would favor going along a little further. . . ."[57]

The next day (September 12) from 1:25 p.m. to 3:10 p.m. the President met with the Luncheon Group—Rusk, McNamara, Rostow and Christian. General Harold Johnson attended in place of General Wheeler. James R. Jones, a Presidential assistant, also attended. Among other things the group discussed the report from Paris.[58] The President asked Rusk "if he had confidence in Kissinger's trustworthiness and character. . . ." "Is he a dove and critic of our policy?" Rusk replied that he had confidence in Kissinger, who, he said, "is for us." Rostow observed that Kissinger "is a good analyst and his only weakness is, that he may go a little soft when you get down to the crunch." The President asked "Who is M?" Rusk replied: "Marcovich, and he is not a Communist. . . . A is a Communist."

The President wondered, "why shouldn't we quit explaining so much and just say we will stop bombing, if a conference is arranged and if it will lead to fruitful discussions." Rusk replied that he felt it was important "to keep this message [to the North Vietnamese via the A–M/K channel] the same as what we said before. Otherwise we would be charged with bad faith." The President repeated his statement, adding that bombing could be resumed if necessary. McNamara said he agreed. Rusk said: "'It really turns on what our policy is. Are we prepared to go through with a series of talks that may not be productive. Then if the talks are not productive, you are faced with the decision of resuming the bombing.'" He said, however, "'I'll go along if you want to change our policy.'" The President continued his line of argument, pointing out that "'we did not have reciprocity when we had the bombing pause. The conditions [in the U.S. proposal transmitted through Bo on August 25] are prompt and productive discussions. . . . That has more conditions than the pause.'" Rusk said he did not object to dropping that provision, but that "he knows that if we are not prepared

[55] *Ibid.*, pp. 737–738.
[56] *Ibid.*, p. 739.
[57] Johnson Library, NSF Files of Walt W. Rostow, Paris to Washington 3143, Sept. 11, 1967. This cable is not in the negotiating volume of the *Pentagon Papers*.
[58] Johnson Library, Meetings Notes File, Jim Jones' Notes of Weekly Luncheon, Sept. 12, 1967.

to follow through, then we have a public record and they may make us eat our words." "'My guess,'" Rusk continued, "'is that we won't get very much from talks. We will be faced with the position of resuming the bombing because the other side has bad faith.'"

It was agreed that the words in question would be dropped, and the President approved the proposal to continue using the A–M/K channel.

On the following day (September 13), after the U.S. again bombed around Hanoi and Haiphong, Kissinger cabled from Paris that he had given Marcovich the text of the message to Bo that had been agreed upon at the White House meeting the previous day, and M said "that every time I brought a message we bombed the center of a North Vietnamese city. If this happened one more time he was no longer prepared to serve as channel."[59]

In a meeting on September 26 from 1:15 p.m. to 2:35 p.m. with McNamara, Katzenbach, Helms, Rostow and Christian, the President asked about the situation in Paris.[60] Katzenbach replied that the channel was still open, but the question was whether the North Vietnamese would talk to Kissinger while bombing continued. "The odds are against talks at this time," Katzenbach said, but "The chances of getting Vietnam resolved before November, 1968, depends on our ability to get talks going." "We should try even if there is little hope for success." "Even if you were to get them started and nothing happened it would be good. We would step down some if secret talks began. I do not see a better channel at the moment."

McNamara brought up the subject of new bombing targets recommended by the JCS, who wanted to eliminate the 10-mile restriction and resume bombing of Hanoi as well as to bomb the Phuc Yen airbase. He said that intensification of the bombing would be harmful to the Paris negotiating effort. Rostow responded that he did not see any connection between bombing and negotiations, to which Katzenbach replied: "I do not think we are going to get negotiations by bombing."

"I do not see holding off again," the President said. "What have we gotten out of this so far?" Katzenbach replied that communications had been established for the first time since February, and that the "tone of the communications was less strident than before." "Bo has been careful not to slam the door." "It is important," he added, "to try to get them to talk . . . even at the price of our hitting within the Hanoi circle."

Katzenbach said he did not think the U.S. should stop bombing North Vietnam unless peace talks could begin. A pause, he added, could help in promoting such talks, and he favored one during the period prior to February 1968.

The President, interestingly enough (in view of his long-standing skepticism on the subject), said that he, too, favored a pause. "We get nothing, in return for giving all we have got. But I guess a pause won't hurt because the weather is bad any way." "But we are too quick to pick up what any professor may get going. I think we should get those targets now [25 targets had been authorized but

---

[59] Johnson Library, NSF Files of Walt W. Rostow, Paris to Washington 3242, Sept. 13, 1967.
[60] Johnson Library, Tom Johnson's Notes of Meetings, Notes of meeting Sept. 26, 1967.

not struck]. A pause won't change the political situation. It will give them an answer though that we are prepared to go the last mile. But I do want to get all those targets before a pause." "History may make us look silly on this whole thing," he added, commenting that bombing of Hanoi was stopped for five weeks in conjunction with the second visit of M and A to Hanoi. "We are losing support in this country. The people just do not understand the war. But nobody can justify holding off for five weeks."

He continued:

> I think they are playing us for suckers. They have no more intention of talking than we have of surrendering.
>
> In my judgment everything you hit is important. It makes them hurt more. Relatively few men are holding down a lot of men. I think we should get them down and hold them down. We will give them an opportunity to speak and talk if they will.
>
> If we believe that we should bomb, then we should hit their bridges, their power plants, and other strategic targets outside the ones which we ruled off-limits. . . . If they do not talk we will have to take more drastic steps.

The President asked: "How do you wrap up the channel if it is getting us nowhere?" McNamara replied that the President could authorize the bombing of Phuc Yen airbase, and then watch all of the replies through the A–M/K channel and cancel the talks "if nothing comes of it." The President responded: "I am ready to do that. Wait a week. If they give any indication I am ready to do it." He asked Katzenbach for a memorandum "on what hopes you and State see in this thing. I just do not see them. But I want a paper on this. You have already given them five weeks." "But it did not cost us anything," Katzenbach said. The President replied: "You built a big umbrella which gives them a chance to rebuild. I would deny them that. . . ."

CIA Director Helms, who had begun to attend the Tuesday Luncheon Group on a fairly regular basis, commented, "I do not think it will pay to continue holding off hitting Hanoi." "Let's get the public relations aspect out," he said. "Let Bob [McNamara] go ahead and tell his people that we destroy every military target in North Vietnam with the exception of Hanoi and China restricted areas. We have offered a scenario related to bombing. This was unconditional. This could lead to talks. They said no. We regard this as their answer for the time being. We must design a scenario that would lead to a pause."

A few minutes later the President repeated his request to Katzenbach for a memorandum on why the U.S. should continue using the M–A/K channel and a "scenario for wrapping it up, because we have been met twice with a firm no. We owe it to our men to do everything we can. We're not."

> Katzenbach: We are talking about a very small area [Hanoi] in exchange for what we are doing.
>
> President: But all of this adds up. It is a question of which one of us can last the longest.

Later that same day (September 26), Katzenbach sent the President the memorandum he had requested on why the U.S. should continue to work through the Paris channel. It represented his own views, he said, and he did not know whether Rusk would agree.[61] "The significance of the Paris-Kissinger exercise," Katzenbach stated, "lies in the fact that it is the closest thing we have yet had to establishing a dialogue with North Vietnam." He noted the objections of the North Vietnamese to bombing by the U.S. while at the same time seeking to open talks. "It is entirely possible—I think probable—that these actions were seized upon as excuses by Hanoi. But it is not possible to prove that point and there is sufficient plausibility in their position to cast doubt in the minds of other governments and a substantial segment of American public opinion as to the sincerity of our efforts." He said he would "like to eliminate all possible doubt" by continuing to refrain from bombing in Hanoi at least until Bo refused to see Kissinger. "I do not believe that Hanoi is presently likely to enter into serious discussions. But I think that it is important in terms of both circumstances and public relations that we test that possibility to the hilt. I do not think we pay a heavy price in delaying hitting again a very small percentage of the targets in North Vietnam. We know that destruction of those targets this week or next week can have absolutely no significance in terms of the conduct of the war. There is an outside chance that it could have some impact on the search for peace. And I would play along with that chance—which I acknowledge to be very small indeed—because the consequences are so great."

On September 29, the President gave a speech in San Antonio, Texas, in which he publicly stated the same proposal which had been secretly offered at Glassboro and in the Paris talks:[62] "The United States is willing to stop all aerial and naval bombardments of North Vietnam when this will lend promptly to productive discussions. We, of course, assume that while discussions proceeded, North Vietnam would not take advantage of the bombing cessation or limitations." In his memoirs, the President explained that this "San Antonio Formula," as it came to be called, "relaxed somewhat the proposal we had made to Ho Chi Minh in February. We were not asking him to restrict his military actions before a bombing halt, and once the bombing ended we were not insisting that he immediately end his military effort, only that he not increase it. Since the leaders in Hanoi seemed to be having difficulty with the idea of making any military commitments prior to a bombing halt, we made it clear that we were prepared to assume they would not take advantage of the cessation. All we asked was that a cessation of bombing would lead promptly to peace talks and that those talks would be productive."[63]

The North Vietnamese immediately rejected the offer. Mai Van Bo called the speech "insulting," and a North Vietnamese news-

[61] There is a copy of Katzenbach's memorandum of Sept. 26, 1967, "Negotiation with North Vietnam," in the Johnson Library, NSF Files of Walt W. Rostow.

[62] The text of the speech is in *Public Papers of the Presidents*, Lyndon B. Johnson, 1967, pp. 876–881. For the origins and preparation of the speech and reaction to it, see Turner, *Lyndon Johnson's Dual War*, pp. 193–198.

[63] Johnson, *The Vantage Point*, p. 267.

paper said that it was a "faked desire for peace" and "sheer deception."[64]

Several days after the speech, Marvin Watson, the White House Chief of Staff, sent word to Rostow that the President wanted to see the telegram responses to his speech. Watson also suggested that the telegrams opposing the speech be sent to the FBI "to run a check on" the persons who sent them. Rostow's office complied with both requests.[65]

The Paris Initiative Collapses

On October 3, the President met from 6:10 p.m. to 9:32 p.m. with Rusk, McNamara, Rostow, Helms, Christian and Tom Johnson.[66] He asked Rusk for a report on his discussions at the United Nations. Rusk said that, among other things, there had been some discussion of Vietnam, and that "Many said there was a need for us to stop the bombing of the North. I told them that we have not been able to find anybody who can tell us what will happen if we were to stop the bombing." The President asked Rusk whether he had talked to Russian Foreign Minister Gromyko about the bombing. Rusk replied: "I told him nobody would tell us what would happen if the bombing stopped." "The Russians," he said, "have given up any attempt to try to influence Hanoi."

The President then asked about the Paris talks. "We will know in two days," Rusk replied. "Kissinger told them that we are against waiting any longer, that we are getting impatient."[67]

The question of stopping the bombing came up, and the President said he would not do so unless the North Vietnamese agreed "1. To meet promptly; 2. To push for a settlement." McNamara said it was important to know the facts about the bombing, but most of his brief explanation of this statement was excised when the notes of the meeting were released.

Rusk then asked why, if the bombing was not having much effect, the North Vietnamese wanted so much to have it stopped. Rostow, responding that bombing was making it "very unpleasant and very costly for them," summed up the effects of bombing:

—Industrial and agricultural production has been cut.

—500,000 men have been diverted full and some part time as a result of the bombing.

"It is a heavy cost," he added, "but they have the kind of tactics that can still sustain them at this cost if they choose to. If we stop the bombing, it will bring their economy back up and permit them to increase their commitment in the South. No bombing means less strain and less cost." McNamara replied: "I do not agree with that," whereupon the President asked both Rostow and McNamara for papers on their respective positions on additional bombing.[68]

---

[64] For Mai Van Bo's reactions, see the letter from Marcovich to Kissinger, Oct. 2, 1967, based on his meeting that day with Bo, Johnson Library, NSF Files of Walt W. Rostow, attachment to Read Memorandum for the Record, Oct. 6, 1967. The newspaper comments appear in *PP*, Gravel ed., vol. IV, p. 206.

[65] Johnson Library, NSF Country File, Vietnam, Note from LN, a member of Rostow's staff, to Rostow, Oct. 4, 1967.

[66] Johnson Library, Tom Johnson's Notes of Meetings, Notes of meeting Oct. 3, 1967.

[67] See Herring, *The Secret Negotiations of the Vietnam War,* p. 756.

[68] It is not known whether Rostow and McNamara prepared papers on their positions on bombing.

The following day (October 4), the President met from 7:02 p.m. to 7:55 p.m. with Rusk, McNamara, Rostow and Christian.[69] Rusk reported that two messages had been received from Paris.[70] "We ought not to hurry," he said. "We need our scenario. It's best to do it on a steady basis. We should keep the dialogue going and not let the matter come to a head quickly."

Rusk reported that in the second message a "crucial phrase"—"solemn engagement to talk"—was withdrawn. "They are still weaseling on us," he said.

The President responded: "In view of that, why don't we leave the circle around Hanoi but clear up everything short of Hanoi. We need to get our target list down to the lowest level possible. I know this bombing must be hurting them. Despite any reports to the contrary, I can feel it in my bones. We need to pour the steel on. Let's hit them every day and go every place except Hanoi. I want you to get me in shape to make a decision when I can."

McNamara said that there were 24 remaining targets that had not been struck (out of 412 "important fixed targets" on the JCS list), 9 in Haiphong and 15 in Hanoi. Why had these not been hit? the President asked. McNamara replied: "The basic argument in Hanoi is that the strikes would result in a very high civilian casualities. The basic argument in Haiphong is the fear of hitting Soviet ships." A few minutes later, the President returned to the subject and told McNamara to "Hit all you can" of the 24 remaining targets.

Discussion of the Kissinger-Bo communications continued, with the President expressing the need "to get all of this straight. What are they saying exactly? Is this it: We would stop the bombing if prompt and productive discussions began, assuming they would not take military advantage of it?" After McNamara reviewed what Bo had said, the President asked, "Well, where does that leave us now?" "I'm not as encouraged by all of this as you all are." Again he asked who M and A were. "They aren't our people, are they?" Rusk replied, "No, A is a scientist; M is a Communist." [*sic*—This is incorrect. A was the Communist, as Rusk says on page 780.] McNamara commented that Kissinger "has been a shrewd negotiator. He is the best I've seen in my seven years."

---

[69] Johnson Library, Tom Johnson's Notes of Meetings, Notes of meeting Oct. 4, 1967.

[70] The first message was a note to Kissinger from Marcovich reporting on his meeting with Bo on October 2 at which Bo said that the statement made by Foreign Minister Trinh early in 1967 constituted a "solemn engagement" to talk after the unconditional end of bombing, and that a public statement by the United States of a cessation of bombing would be considered to be "a reply having the same character of commitment."

The second message reported on a followup meeting of Marcovich with Bo on October 4 to show Bo the text of M's October 2 note to Kissinger in order to seek confirmation of one point. During the conversation, Bo denied that he had used the words "solemn engagement." "M took strong exception with Bo, saying that M's own notes and clear recollection of their conversation on this point were very clear. M said to Bo that if he (M) was capable of such misunderstanding M's usefulness was at an end. Bo energetically denied that M's utility was an end and expressed the view that the channel was of definite continuing utility. Bo and M discussed what phrase should be used in place of 'solemn engagement' without reaching a firm conclusion." Later that day, after Washington objected to removing the words "solemn engagement," M met with Bo to review the statement. Bo would not discuss further the use of the words. M drafted a new statement, which Bo accepted, and this was telephoned to Washington from Kissinger in Paris at 8:30 p.m. on Oct. 4, as follows: "[I]f the U.S. really wants to talk it is necessary first to stop without conditions the bombing and all other acts of war against the DVN . . . the scenario would be as follows: The Government of the United States would send a first message through our channel announcing unequivocally the unconditional cessation of bombing. Once this has been effectively realized, a second message still through our channel might suggest the opening of the dialogue at a date and site proposed by you." Herring, *The Secret Diplomacy of the Vietnam War,* pp. 756–759.

The next day (October 5), the President met from 6:55 p.m. to 8:25 p.m. with Rusk, McNamara and Rostow.[71] Rusk presented the draft of a new message to Bo containing a reformulation of the U.S. position. The President noted that it did not include the provision of the August 25 proposals that "the United States would assume that the Democratic Republic of Vietnam would not take advantage of the bombing cessation," and he asked what would happen if the Communists attacked during the talks. McNamara replied, "We would open fire, of course," to which the President responded: "Wouldn't that be acting in bad faith if we do not state it in plain terms in this message that we assume they will not take advantage of the bombing cessation?" "I think it is important we know what we are saying, and they know what we are saying."

The draft also contained a new phrase—"without expression of condition"—that was intended to meet objections from the North Vietnamese to alleged "conditions" in the August 25 proposal. This caused the President some concern, and he proposed deleting the phrase. "What I want them to know is that I will stop the bombing and enter negotiations which are prompt and productive. We have always assumed that they would not take advantage of the bombing. Let's not let them say we have retracted our assumption." "This proposal may lead them to a meeting," he added, "but it may lead me into a trap."

The President's advisers apparently did not fully share his concern. McNamara said, "They have not contracted not to take advantage of the pause. In other words talks could go on while the level of current fighting continues—just so long as they do not increase it." Rusk commented, "They can come back after this message and debate anything they want to." And Rostow added, "None of us believe that the private assumption is forgotten," adding, however, that he preferred to have it expressly stated in the proposal.

The President persisted: "I know I will be charged with bad faith if they enter talks [and] then begin firing at us. I must respond. I don't think this message gives me room to respond. . . . I want talks which I can depend on." Rusk suggested adding the words "in accordance with its proposal of August 25." This, he said, would incorporate the "no-advantage" assumption. McNamara said he agreed, but he wanted to retain the phrase "limited expression of conditions." Rusk said that he did too, and the President acquiesced in keeping the phrase, saying, "I guess that is because it makes it a little more appealing to them."

The President asked McNamara about Wheeler's position. McNamara said he had not talked to him (Wheeler was hospitalized), but he believed that Wheeler would support it if no military advantage were taken. The President asked McNamara to talk to Wheeler. "I want to get Wheeler aboard. On the last pause, he did not favor it but he was willing to defend the decision." He added: "Otherwise I am a man without a country."

Rostow raised the question as to when Mansfield and Dirksen should be told about the Paris track. "Not until we have something," the President replied.

---

[71] Johnson Library, Tom Johnson's Notes of Meeting, Notes of meeting Oct. 5, 1967.

On October 6, the following revision of the U.S. proposal was dispatched to Kissinger for delivery to Bo by M and A:[72]

> The United States Government understands the position of the Democratic Republic of Vietnam to be as follows: That upon the cessation by the United States of all forms of bombardment of the Democratic Republic of Vietnam, without expression of condition, the Democratic Republic of Vietnam would enter promptly into productive discussions with the United States. The purpose of these discussions would be to resolve the issues between the United States and the Democratic Republic of Vietnam.
>
> Assuming the correctness of this understanding of the position of the Democratic Republic of Vietnam, the United States Government is prepared, in accordance with its proposal of August 25, to transmit in advance to the Democratic Republic of Vietnam the precise date upon which bombardment of the Democratic Republic of Vietnam would cease and to suggest a date and a place for the commencement of discussions.[73]

On October 8, Kissinger, through M and A, presented the new version of the U.S. proposal to Bo, who read the note and commented that he thought all of the language after the words "without expression of conditions," constituted conditions, in particular the words "prompt," "productive," and "in accordance with the proposal of August 25."[74]

On October 11, the President met from 12:55 p.m. to 1:03 p.m. with Rusk, McNamara, General McConnell (Chief of the Air Force), who was Acting Chairman of the JCS, Rostow and Christian to hear the recommendations of the JCS and of General McConnell on bombing the Phuc Yen airfield.[75] General McConnell explained that although the need was no greater than it had been, North Vietnamese MiGs were becoming more active and the U.S. was losing more planes in aerial combat. The President asked what would be accomplished by the strikes and whether there was any urgency "in the next week or so . . ." (i.e., while the U.S. was waiting to hear if talks could begin). General McConnell replied that the longer the wait, the more U.S. losses there would be.

McNamara said that the Phuc Yen base was "militarily marginal," and that it would have to be bombed more than once. Rusk agreed, and suggested that no attack be made for several days. The President said he would wait before deciding.

---

[72] The text is in Herring, *The Secret Diplomacy of the Vietnam War,* p. 761.

[73] That same day (October 6), Rostow sent the President a memorandum in which he gave a brief explanation of each of the terms used in the revision of the U.S. proposal that had been agreed to at the meeting that day, as well as suggesting "How we might use to best advantage militarily the period when North Vietnam is not being bombed." He also proposed that the President should make a speech on Vietnam to "give our people a fresh view of the war; one that we can live with over the whole next year, if necessary. . . ," the conclusion of which would be that "We have clearly turned the corner in this struggle for Vietnam and the future of Southeast Asia. We hope that through negotiations we are very nearly *[sic]* the end. But, if negotiations do not succeed, we can be confident that we are already well on the road to success and to peace." Johnson Library, NSF Files of Walt W. Rostow, Memorandum to the President from Rostow, Oct. 6, 1967.

[74] Herring, *The Secret Diplomacy of the Vietnam War,* pp. 763.

[75] Johnson Library, Meetings Notes File, Notes of Meeting of Oct. 11, 1967.

The President told the group that he wanted "strategy for the next 12 months on Vietnam—military, political, negotiating." He said there was "too much vague talk."[76]

On October 16, the President met with Rusk, McNamara, Rostow, Helms and Christian.[77] The President told Rusk he wanted to know "all you know and think" about the Paris talks. Rusk replied: "We haven't seen any serious response from Hanoi. They are not in the business of telling about negotiations at this stage. It has been a one way conversation." He added that Bo wanted the talks to continue, and not just because of the advantage gained by the continuation of the 10-mile limit on bombing in and around Hanoi. McNamara agreed, and said that the question was what the U.S. did in the next three to four months. He did not expect anything in the next two weeks. He added that if the President wanted a pause it should be done through the M–A channel.

The President asked about Wheeler's response to the question of a bombing pause or halt. McNamara replied that Wheeler would not be concerned provided that the North Vietnamese did not take military advantage of a bombing halt. Wheeler did not think a pause would bring about negotiations, but he was "tolerant of our views given the domestic situation we have."

The President asked McNamara what damage would be suffered from a pause, and McNamara replied that there was a possibility that the U.S. would not suffer any damage. "We could develop our own talk and fight strategy." He added that he would recommend a pause "because of the domestic plus it would be." Rusk asked how long a pause he would recommend. McNamara responded, "You will never have a long enough pause to satisfy Fulbright and others. A pause of at least a month would be necessary."

Rusk remarked, as he said the others present already knew, that in the next issue of *Life* magazine (which had strongly supported U.S. policy), there would be an editorial advocating a bombing pause.

Helms said that he did not think anything would come out of the Paris talks, and Rusk responded that the U.S. proposal "was almost too reasonable."

At this point, the President made a comment that doubtless summed up his feeling of frustration and futility, as well as his obvious disagreement with those who were saying that the war was being won, when he said to the group: "How are we ever going to win?"

McNamara's answer was, "We are making progress. But it is slow. I have no idea how we can win it in the next 12 months. We have to do something to increase the support for the war in this country. I know of no better way to do it except by a pause." The President replied, "We may lose if we have a pause. I do not think it would change any of these folks."

Helms said that a short pause would not help, and it would be difficult to begin bombing again. "If we have a pause, it must be a very long, deep breath." The President replied, "I do not see how we can get into a long one."

---

[76] Johnson Library, NSF Files of Walt W. Rostow, brief typed notes prepared by Rostow on decisions made at the meeting of the Luncheon Group on Oct. 11, 1967.

[77] Johnson Library, Tom Johnson's Notes of Meetings, Notes of meeting Oct. 16, 1967.

The next day (October 17), the President met from 1:40 pm. to 2:50 p.m. with Rusk, McNamara, Wheeler, Helms, Rostow and Christian.[78] "It looks as though the news is all bad," the President said, reading aloud a memorandum about a large protest in Oakland, California, the number of U.S. casualties the day before, and the downing of more American planes. On the Paris talks, Rusk reported that there had been no word from the North Vietnamese. McNamara suggested that the Paris initiative should be made public. The President agreed, saying, "I think we should let our folks know. We quit bombing August 22 inside the 10-mile perimeter of Hanoi. It has been two months." McNamara added that if there was not going to be a pause, "let's make as much of this as we can."

An account of the Paris talks could be released, the President said, by having Rusk "disclose it under strong questioning" at a closed session of a congressional committee. "It will take about two days to leak." "I would not identify the individuals. I would say that we had outside, fresh professional minds at work on this." "We have to have something to carry us in this country. Every hawk and every dove and every general seems to be against us." "Bob," he added, "I want you to spend as much time as you can with Senator Russell. Dean, you need to get your people to pull their gloves off in their public speeches and press conferences. Too many signs are bad now. There has been nothing good since the [Stennis] hearings. We need to be a little more outspoken."

The President told the group that he would wait until Friday, October 20, and if the North Vietnamese had not responded by then he would approve the resumption of bombing in the Hanoi area.

On October 17, Bo gave Marcovich the following message:[79]

> Actually the U.S. has been following a policy of escalation of an extremely serious nature. In these conditions the U.S. proposals of peace are double-faced. At a time when the U.S. is pursuing a policy of escalation we cannot receive Kissinger, nor comment on the American proposals transmitted through this channel.
>
> The position of the Government of the DRV is perfectly clear: it is only when the U.S. has ended without condition the bombardment that discussions *can* take place. (emphasis in original)

That same day (October 17), McGeorge Bundy, who had been asked by the President to advise him on the direction of U.S. policy in Vietnam, sent the President a memorandum in which, among other things, he commented on the question of the Paris talks and on having a pause in bombing:[80] "There is one and only one condition on which I would order an extended pause—it is that there should be a recorded and acknowledged diplomatic position like the one which we have been stating to Hanoi through the Harvard pro-

---

[78] *Ibid.*, Notes of meeting Oct. 17, 1967.

[79] Herring, *The Secret Diplomacy of the Vietnam War*, p. 766, from a Kissinger/Read telecon, Oct. 17, 1967.

[80] Johnson Library, NSF Country File, Vietnam, memorandum for the President from McGeorge Bundy, "Vietnam—October 1967," Oct. 17, 1967. See below for further discussion of the memorandum.

fessor. A quick review of this exchange persuades me that it has been extremely well handled and that it is to our advantage to keep it going. If it leads to a nibble, and we should get grounds for a bombing suspension, we would have a clear predicate on which to base any necessary resumption if the truce were not productive or if there were heavy reinforcements from the North. If, on the other hand, we get no response, we have certainly established a record which will show plainly that we were ready to stop the bombing on a still more forthcoming basis than any we have yet started—even in the Texas speech."

On the morning of the following day (October 18), Rostow sent the President a memorandum, "Strategy on Negotiations and a Pause,"[81] in which he said that there were three alternatives:

> 1. To take the latest Paris message as a flat negative and move into a posture of you-call-me, resuming our full bombing program in the north, including Hanoi.
>
> 2. Close out the Paris channel, resume bombing, including Hanoi, for an interval; and then find a fit occasion for a pause.
>
> 3. Build a scenario on the Paris channel which would lead us into a pause at or very close to the time of Thieu's inaugural, October 31.

Without stating that he preferred it, Rostow said that his memorandum would consider the third alternative. He listed one disadvantage—that it would put off the resumption of bombing of Hanoi for several weeks—and three advantages: first, that "it would avoid a big debate on whether we had correctly interpreted the Paris exchanges and lost the opportunity for a serious negotiation;" second, it would allow for the possibility, "small as it may be," that the North Vietnamese were moving toward negotiating; and, third, "It would permit us to orchestrate three elements [the Paris channel, diplomatic approaches to those who had urged a bombing cessation "to put up or shut up in getting Hanoi to perform, and efforts to unite the American public during and after the pause] into quite a dramatic scenario which might, if well handled, leave us both with a clean record for Life magazine, the more moderate doves like Senator Brooke, etc.; and leave us with a more united political and international base for the conduct of the war over the next year." (Rostow went on to develop in the memorandum the "full scenario" for this third alternative.)

Later that day (October 18), the President met from 7:30 p.m. to 9:30 p.m. with Rusk, McNamara, Katzenbach and Rostow. Kissinger also attended.[82] In addition, the President invited his two close friends and advisers, Clark Clifford and Supreme Court Justice Abe Fortas to attend, as well as General Maxwell Taylor.[83] Rusk reviewed the status of the Paris talks, and concluded by saying "we have had nothing constructive from this exchange," and although the "mood" of the North Vietnamese seemed "more definite," there

---

[81] Johnson Library, NSF Memos to the President—Walt Rostow, memorandum for the President from Rostow, "Strategy on Negotiations and a Pause," Oct. 18, 1967.

[82] According to Isaacson, *Kissinger,* p. 122, Kissinger received a telephone call from the President, who said he had grave doubts about the outcome of the Paris talks. Kissinger urged him to try a reformulated version of the earlier proposal. "Johnson reluctantly agreed. 'I'm going to give it one more try,' he growled to Kissinger, 'and if it doesn't work, I'm going to come up to Cambridge and cut off your balls.'"

[83] Johnson Library, Tom Johnson's notes of Meetings, Notes of meeting Oct. 18, 1967.

was no assurance that talks would start. Kissinger responded, "I have seen some indication of Bo's eagerness to keep the channel open. . . . When one looks at the whole record it shows that Bo is eager to keep this going. There has been a slight movement in their position."

The President asked Kissinger for his recommendations, and he replied:

> If there is an intention to have a bombing pause it would be desirable to do this through the existing channel. I would recommend in this case that we interpret their last message under conditions of de-escalation and ask that they receive me or somebody else in conjunction with the cessation of bombing. I would notify them of the time and date of the beginning of significant de-escalation.
>
> If there is no pause it becomes a question of how to wind up this channel diplomatically and publicly. Confronted with a termination they may yield. We could indicate that we can only construe their last message as a refusal. If it is not a refusal I would give them a chance to say why it isn't a refusal. I would give them ten days, the normal time required for turn around; if there is no response then I would resume full-scale activities.

Rusk said he saw no need to close out the Paris channel, and he would make it clear that the U.S. offer remained open.

The President said he thought the North Vietnamese were keeping the Paris channel open because the U.S. was not bombing Hanoi. "The net of it is that he [the enemy] has a sanctuary in Hanoi in return for having his Consul talk with two scientists who talked with an American citizen." Katzenbach replied: "I disagree with that very much." The President asked him which alternative he preferred, and Katzenbach responded that the pause "does make more sense. It would bring together the ranks in this country and abroad. I would favor a pause in mid-November or early December." "Just pause, period?" the President asked, and Katzenbach replied, "Yes, I would say very loud and clear that we are ready. I would make clear through private channels that the assumption that they would not take advantage of the bombing still holds. If they attacked us along the DMZ I would respond immediately. If they were to begin a major resupply we should deal with that immediately."

The President asked McNamara how effectively the U.S. could deal with the resupply problem in the event of a pause. McNamara replied, "I believe I can show beyond a shadow of a doubt that bombing in Hanoi and Haiphong will not affect resupply in the South one bit. If they take military advantage we should counter with military reciprocal action. If they unleash artillery across the DMZ, we should pound it. If they begin a step up in infiltration we should hit their lines of communication in North Vietnam and South Vietnam and in the panhandle."

Rusk said that "to convince anybody" a pause would have to be longer than 37 days (which was the length of the pause in December 1966-February 1967). Katzenbach recommended 30–40 days. "As I see it," the President said, "you would wait 40 days and resume only on a tit for tat basis."

General Taylor, who said he thought that this was "one of the few times we have had an authentic link," recommended that the reply of the North Vietnamese to the U.S. proposal be accepted as a rejection, but that the channel be kept open. He also urged that a pause be based on the "principle of reciprocity," and that it be requested by Thieu to avoid the appearance of weakness if it came from Washington.

Clark Clifford said that the Paris channel had not produced anything new, and that the U.S. should tell the North Vietnamese it would be terminated, but that if they had a different view the U.S. would consider it. He did not think that the channel would be used by the Communists if they were serious about talking. He preferred more formal contacts, and suggested using the North Vietnamese diplomatic mission in Moscow.

On bombing, Clifford said that the Hanoi 10-mile limit "might lead to some development later on" and should be continued. He said he saw no basis for suspending or ceasing bombing, which he thought would indicate a weakening of resolve that could be misinterpreted by the North Vietnamese and used by them to rebuild their industries, their transportation lines, their food supplies and their communications. "In my opinion," he said, "a bombing pause makes the possibility of peace much more remote." The attitude of the Asians with whom he and Taylor talked on their trip, he said, was that "without the bombing . . . there is no inducement for the North Vietnamese to seek peace. This thing could go on for twenty years." It was also the "wrong time" for a pause, the "right time" for which would be after the election of the South Vietnamese assembly, and after the Government of South Vietnam had become a "functioning unit." He also thought that Thieu should propose the pause.

Fortas said he believed the Paris channel was closed, and that "We need to summon all our courage and strength from the Lord and maintain our position here." Bombing pauses, he added, had intensified criticism in the U.S., and "the next time you suspend bombing you have quit bombing."

McNamara disagreed with Fortas and said he believed that a pause would increase domestic support. He also thought that the Paris channel represented "an important dramatic change in attitude" on the part of the North Vietnamese and should not be cut off. Moreover, he thought that if bombing were halted, talks will begin quickly and could lead to a settlement. He did not think public support for the war could be maintained for 12 months and that "We need to move toward settlement in the next 12 months."

Rusk recommended that Kissinger return to Paris the following day as planned and tell M "that 'my people back home don't think I've got anything.' I would scare him. I would tell him that if he has anything he had better put it in right away."

Rostow recommended that the U.S. should keep the channel open "and adopt the posture of waiting for a signal" from the North Vietnamese. He argued that the military position of the North in the South was weak, but that "The major field of battle is no longer in the South or even I Corps but in American politics. . . ." "Domestic politics is the active front now," he added, and the question was: "would a pause," which he called "no more than an exercise of domestic politics and international politics," "destroy our strength with the hawks and the doves?" "I would put in all of the creative imagination of this government," he asserted, "in order that we not lose the hawks and come out in support of the doves."

The President concluded the meeting, saying that he saw no necessity to break off the talks and that Kissinger should inform the North Vietnamese of the U.S. reaction. "After we see what happens, then we can go to another phase and discuss the possibilities of a pause."[84]

On October 20, Bo refused to see M and A, telling them, "There is nothing new to say. The situation is worsening. There is no reason to talk again."[85]

On October 21, as will be seen, there was a large antiwar demonstration in Washington, D.C. and at the Pentagon.

On October 23, the President met from 1:05 p.m. to 3:40 p.m. with Rusk, McNamara, Rostow, Wheeler and Christian. Helms discussed a CIA analysis of the Paris talks, which, he said, "showed no new movement on the part of the Hanoi government toward peace negotiations. . . . In short, Mr. President, you ended up where you began." The President responded by asking, "Isn't there a lot we could gain by exposing this channel?" Rusk replied. "The doves will make trouble if we publicize the message. In addition, we may want to talk some serious business through this channel at a later time."

The President then asked the group, "Are we now ready to take the wraps off the bombing?" McNamara responded: "It depends on what you want to do for the rest of the year." General Wheeler recommended against a pause and urged bombing the Phuc Yen airfield and lifting the 10-mile limitation. Rusk responded that he did not object to lifting the 10-mile restriction, but believed the attacks should be "spread out." He said he had no strong objections to bombing Phuc Yen, but that it would have to be bombed repeatedly and could result in the loss of more U.S. planes than North Vietnamese planes destroyed on the ground.

"The attack on Phuc Yen will require two or three hundred aircraft, won't it?" Rusk asked, and Wheeler replied: "All totaled, it will require a couple of hundred. There will be four different waves of attack aircraft." Rusk said he wondered what the rationale was when there were only 12 aircraft on the Phuc Yen field. Wheeler replied: "To destroy the support facilities as well as the aircraft. . . . Their air effectiveness will be further reduced by hitting Phuc Yen."

---

[84] For the State Department's instructions to Kissinger after the meeting, see Herring, *The Secret Diplomacy of the Vietnam War*, pp. 767–768. On the next day (October 19), the President met from 11:05 a.m. to 11:15 a.m. with Rusk, McNamara and Rostow. The Daily Diary states that the meeting was "Off the Record." There are no known notes.

[85] Herring, p. 769. On October 20, an article by the Australian journalist Wilfred Burchett, who frequently reported on the North Vietnamese position, reaffirmed the stand that the Communists had continued to take. According to Burchett, based on interviews with Premier Pham Van Dong, Foreign Minister and Deputy Premier Nguyen Duy Trinh and other high-ranking officials, talks could not begin unless and until bombing was halted. "The mood of Hanoi," Burchett stated, "is one of toughness and confidence. Although leaders expect Hanoi and Haiphong will probably be destroyed and that the war may last many more years, they feel the worst is behind them. . . . It is repeated at every level that total independence, with complete American withdrawal from South Vietnam, is the unalterable aim of the Hanoi government and of the National Liberation Front, the political arm of the Viet Cong. They are prepared to fight 10 or 20 years to achieve this, and life is being reorganized at this basis." Dispatch to the Associated Press from Burchett, Oct. 20, 1967, *New York Times*, Oct. 21, 1967.

At this point, the President, according to the notes of the meeting, reminded those present that Phuc Yen had been authorized previously, subject only to winding up the Kissinger talks. "Now we have gotten rid of the excuses," he declared. "Let's go with it."

McNamara announced the consensus: "Then we are agreed that Phuc Yen is authorized; the two bridges are authorized, and the power plant is authorized."

The President asked Rusk, "Dean, are you ready to go on Phuc Yen?" Rusk replied: "Yes, if you can spread out the number of strikes." The President: "Bob, are you ready to go on Phuc Yen?" McNamara: "Yes."

The President then returned to the question of publicizing the Paris talks and again expressed his feeling of frustration and futility:

> My political instinct is to make public this exchange in Paris but say we are unable to make a proposal which we can stand on publicly. It doesn't seem we can win the war militarily. I asked the JCS for suggestions on how to shorten the war but all of their proposals related to suggestions outside South Vietnam.[86]
>
> We can't win diplomatically either. We ought to make the proposals so clear and get such clear answers back that we can tell a farmer what has taken place and be able to have him understand it.
>
> Now we are back to where we started.
>
> We've tried all your suggestions. We've almost lost the war in the last two months in the court of public opinion. These demonstrators and others are trying to show that we need somebody else to take over this country.
>
> People who want us to stop the bombing should know all we have gone through in this exchange. There are men at this table who do not know what all has taken place. We have not seen one change in their position. They are filling the air waves with this propaganda. Your two departments must provide answers to these charges. Senator Russell won't even talk about it. The hawks are throwing in the towel. Everybody is hitting you. San Antonio did not get through. I cannot mount a better explanation.
>
> If we cannot get negotiations, why don't we hit all the military targets short of provoking Russia and China. It astounds me that our boys in Vietnam have such good morale with all of this going on.
>
> We've got to do something about public opinion. . . .
>
> We must show the American people we have tried and failed after going the very last mile.

And then, as if casting about for some way of winning the war he knew he was losing, the President asked as the meeting ended: "What about the reserves?" "We do not need them in Vietnam now," McNamara replied, and Wheeler added, "We certainly do not need them at the current level of operations."

For the President to raise the issue of the Reserves, which, as has been seen, had never been considered a feasible option, re-

[86] See p. 925 below.

vealed his sense of frustration and futility that the war could ever be won. The measure of his desperation was his willingness to consider breaking the barrier (the "Plimsoll Line") he himself had erected in 1965 in order to keep the war limited and, by controlling its cost, to protect his domestic programs. It must have surprised and saddened Wheeler, who had recommended, as had McNamara, that the Reserves be called up in July 1965, and had renewed the recommendation on several occasions since that time. And the further irony is that only six days earlier, the JCS had sent a report to the President, prepared at his request, describing measures by which military pressure on North Vietnam could be increased, including measures that would require additional U.S. forces, and that the President, as noted, had rejected these proposals.

Later that afternoon (October 23), the President met with congressional leaders McCormack, Albert, Mansfield, Long and Byrd (West Virginia) to discuss legislative business. Also attending were Representative John Moss, as well as O'Brien, Sanders, Califano and Manatos. This was followed by a meeting from 5:36 p.m. to 7:04 p.m. at which the President told the group about the Paris negotiating effort and the decision to resume bombing. Joining the group for this meeting were Rusk, McNamara and Helms as well as Senate Republican Leader Dirksen and the following chairmen and senior Republicans on key congressional committees:[87] Bates (ranking Republican on the House Armed Services Committee), Hickenlooper (ranking Republican on the Senate Foreign Relations Committee), Smith, (ranking Republican on the Senate Armed Services Committee), Hayden (chairman of the Senate Appropriations Committee), Sparkman (a senior Democrat of the Senate Foreign Relations Committee), and Mahon, (chairman of the House Appropriations Committee).

After reviewing briefly the history of earlier negotiating efforts, the President told the group in general terms about the Paris channel. He said there was no evidence that the North Vietnamese were "seriously interested in meaningful peace negotiations at this time," and that "The best judgment and advice I have is that the current policies are best to bring us to an honorable peace."

Some of the Members of Congress then expressed their opinions:

> *Senator Hickenlooper:* If we stop bombing, we will surrender in effect. I do not know what other objections the President has, but I think perhaps we should do more damage than we are doing. I would support a continuation in the bombing.
>
> *Senator Dirksen:* I am still in your corner. Do not lose this leverage of bombing. Remember how many casualties resulted from the talks during the Korean war.
>
> *Congressman Bates:* Senator Dirksen expressed my view. . . .

---

[87] Johnson Library, Tom Johnson's Notes of Meetings, Notes of meeting Oct. 23, 1967, drafted on Oct. 25, 1967. The notes do not include the earlier part of the meeting, for which there apparently are no notes.

There is no explanation for Moss' attendance. He was chairman of the House subcommittee that had been actively investigating the handling of U.S. foreign aid in South Vietnam, but he was not a member of the elected leadership of the House.

Fulbright did not attend the meeting, and it is not known whether he was not invited or was unavailable.

Congressman Mahon: You should keep the pressure on. Continue the bombing.

Senator Long: Don't stop the bombing. If anything, step it up. Anytime you want to lose a war you can. If we lose Vietnam we lose influence in this entire area of the world. We must make a stand here.

Senator Smith: I don't see any good coming out of our other pauses. Stand firm is my position. I don't know the President's alternatives but I don't think you should stop the bombing. I have a great admiration for the firm stand you have taken.

Senator Byrd [W. Va.]: You can't do more than you've done. If anything, you have been overly eager. I am not surprised these people feel the way they do.

These people have every reason to believe they should hold out until the next election. I hope you continue to be firm. I hope you try to work through the U.N. If you feel what you are doing is right I hope you continue to do it. You may lose next year's election because of it, but I believe that history will vindicate you.

Senator Sparkman: You have done all you could. I think you should stand firm.

Senator Mansfield: I am not in accord on the matter of the effectiveness of the bombing. We could bomb North Vietnam into the stone age if we wanted to. I do not believe we have reached the objective which was stopping the flow of men and material into the South. We have lost many planes and we are flying within 24 seconds of China. I think there is much to what Senator Cooper said. We should think of contact between the NLF and Saigon to try to cut them out from North Vietnam.

After several other questions and comments, the President ended the meeting by saying that the U.S. had pursued the Paris channel "religiously," adding, "We are trying all we can. We will try again," to which House Majority Leader Albert responded: "I would tell them to jump in the lake. We must continue to do what we have to do."

With the end of the Paris channel, the U.S. resumed the bombing of Hanoi and on October 25, 1967, the Phuc Yen airfield, which Admiral Sharp and the JCS had been seeking permission to bomb for three years, was bombed for the first time. In following weeks, U.S. bombing continued to increase.

In the aftermath of the Paris talks, Charles Bohlen, U.S. Ambassador to France, one of the most knowledgeable and respected senior members of the Foreign Service, sent a message to Washington commenting on certain psychological aspects of the Paris experience:[88]

> [W]e would have a much better chance of success if we avoided any attempt to qualify the nature or content of the talks. For example to the Communist mind for US to insist that talks must be "productive" means that we would already have determined how the talks should come out and would amount to the

[88] U.S. Department of State, Central File, Pol 27–14 Viet, Paris to Washington 5578, Oct. 23, 1967.

acceptance of an American solution to the talks before they have even begun. Since no one can possibly tell whether the talks would be productive, I would recommend that this and any other qualification be dropped. A simple statement to the effect that as soon as a date and place have been agreed upon for a meeting we would cease all aerial and naval bombardment of North Vietnam should be sufficient.

I would make no reference whatsoever to any conditions or time limit or character of bombing. I would assume that if the talks went on for a certain period and proved to be completely non-productive and we had clear evidence that Hanoi was continuing to supply the troops south of the DMZ, we could then resume bombardment on both of these grounds.

It will be recalled that the President had taken a similar position with respect to the statement of the nature and content of the U.S. position. In the Tuesday Lunch meeting on September 12 he commented to Rusk, "why shouldn't we quit explaining so much and just say 'we will stop bombing, if a conference is arranged and if it will lead to fruitful discussions.'"

After the Paris talks ended, the U.S. continued to explore ways of initiating negotiations. One, as noted, was for the new South Vietnamese Government to raise the question with the North Vietnamese. On October 24, Bunker discussed this with Thieu and later that day with Ky, and the U.S. agreed with Thieu's proposal that after his inaugural address he would send a message to Ho Chi Minh expressing a desire for a peaceful settlement and for direct discussions. If Ho responded favorably, Thieu would then ask the U.S. to halt bombing.[89]

Another possibility emerged when a Rumanian channel opened in November 1967, and for a time, according to Herring, it "seems to have raised American hopes as high as at any time since the onset of the war."[90] It, too, led to a suspension of U.S. bombing around Hanoi and Haiphong during January 1968, but nothing materialized, and the effort was abandoned in mid-February. Meanwhile, the Tet offensive had begun.

---

[89] U.S. Department of State, Central File, Pol 27–14 Viet, Saigon to Washington 9433, Oct. 24, 1967.

On December 19, 1967, the President urged the National Liberation Front to negotiate with the South Vietnamese Government, and on December 21, Presidents Johnson and Thieu issued a statement in which Thieu agreed that he would seek talks with the NLF. See Johnson, *The Vantage Point*, p. 589.

[90] Herring, *The Secret Diplomacy of the Vietnam War*, p. 523. See also Johnson, *The Vantage Point*, p. 268 and Thies, *When Governments Collide*, pp. 196–200.

CHAPTER 19

THE CRUMBLING CONSENSUS

During the summer of 1967, as the U.S. applied greater pressure on North Vietnam and the President approved the deployment of more troops while continuing to probe for a negotiated settlement, there was a rapid increase in congressional advice and dissent: advice on how the war should be conducted and how negotiations could be initiated; dissent, ranging from those who wanted stronger action to those who wanted to stop the bombing and find a way out.

In the two years since the U.S. decided to deploy large scale forces, there had been general support from Democrats and Republicans for the President's policy and for the funds necessary to fight the war, and, except for the Mansfield/Clark policy amendment in the spring of 1967, no action had been taken by Congress to control or limit the war. However, when the war escalated and costs and casualties increased, while the military stalemate continued and there was little progress in pacification, the public and Congress became more restive and there were a number of challenges and proposals for change from Members of Congress.

As congressional opposition to the war had increased, the President and his associates had made a number of tactical political moves to ward off or blunt such attacks, to put critics on the defensive, and to promote administration policy. One of the principal moves was to give increased attention to the House of Representatives, where, because of the size of the membership, frequency of election, and the nature of the rules and organization, among other factors, it was more difficult for any one individual or small group to gain publicity and public attention than in the Senate. In addition, the leadership hierarchy could exercise more direction of legislative proceedings, debate was more constrained, and the initiation of legislative action was more cumbersome and more highly controlled. Another important element was the circumstantial factor that, unlike the Senate, where the majority leader and the chairman of the Foreign Relations Committee were both opposed to the war, in the House, the Speaker, majority leader and majority whip, together with the chairman of the House Foreign Affairs Committee, happened to be strong supporters of the war.

The President also sought to appeal to the minority party to give bipartisan support to the war, and as part of this effort he maintained close and continuing consultation with former President Eisenhower and with leading Republicans who were members of the Wise Men.

Another important tactical political move was the President's effort to curry favor with Senate Republican Leader Dirksen as a way of curbing Republican opposition in the Senate and as a way of splitting congressional Republicans through Dirksen's disagreements with some of his fellow Republican Senators as well as with the positions taken by House Republican leaders.

These political tactics and efforts to maintain bipartisan support and to split the opposition appear to have been at least partially successful, but this is difficult to determine, in part because the war, which had not been a political issue, was rapidly becoming an issue in the 1968 election. Previously, with the exception of Aiken and Cooper, there had been little Republican opposition except for those who thought that the war should be waged more vigorously. This began to change in 1967 as several leading Republican Senators, particularly Morton, Case and Javits and the newly elected Percy and Hatfield, voiced opposition to the war, the House Republican leadership of Ford and Laird became more actively opposed, and various House Republicans began to express their growing concern.

Advice and Dissent from Congress

On August 8, 1967, House Minority Leader Ford made a speech in the House challenging the President's conduct of the war.[1] He said he had "grave misgivings . . . about the way the war in Vietnam is going." Referring to the President's decision to send 45,000 more troops and to ask for a tax surcharge, he said that a larger force was not the answer. The answer was to allow the military to implement their plans for bombing and shelling (by sea) the North, and for blocking shipping into Haiphong (a "sea quarantine"). In a news conference before the speech, Ford said he considered the speech "a break with Administration policy."[2]

At a White House briefing on the tax bill the next day for a group of House Democrats, the President, responding to a question about Ford's speech, said: "I am not going to do what Ford says, because we would be in a war with China tonight if we did. Much as we want it, there is no easy way out."[3]

Several days later, Presidential Assistant Douglass Cater reported that he had talked to columnist Rowland Evans, who, he said, "professed to be deeply disturbed about new developments in the Vietnam debate which he believes mark a major turning point. He says Ford and Laird have embarked on a deliberate policy of setting conditions which you cannot possibly meet. They will then use your failure to meet these conditions as rationale for embracing a 'Get Out of Vietnam' policy."[4]

Although Ford may have expressed the feelings of many if not most House Republicans, a growing number of Republicans were actively searching for ways to end the war. One conservative Republican, Tim Lee Carter, from a rural area of Kentucky, denounced the war and urged U.S. withdrawal in a speech in the House on August 28, 1967, in which he declared: "Let us now,

---

[1] *CR*, vol. 113, pp. 21897 ff.

[2] *New York Times*, Aug. 9, 1967.

[3] Johnson Library, Tom Johnson's Notes of Meeting, Notes of meeting Aug. 9, 1967.

[4] Johnson Library, Office Files of Douglass Cater, Memos to the President, Memorandum for the President from Cater, Aug. 12, 1967.

while we are yet strong, bring our men home, every man jack of them."[5]

"The Vietcong," Carter said, "fight fiercely and tenaciously, because it is their land and we are foreigners and intervening in their civil war." "If we must fight, let us fight in defense of our homeland and our own hemisphere."

On July 10, 1967, a group of House Republicans led by Representative F. Bradford Morse of Massachusetts and joined by Representatives Mathias of Maryland, John R. Dellenback of Oregon, Marvin L. Esch of Michigan, Charles A. Mosher of Ohio, Richard S. Schweiker of Pennsylvania, Robert T. Stafford of Vermont, and Frank Horton of New York, proposed a "Grid Plan" for "staged deescalation" of the war.[6] The plan provided that the U.S. would stop bombing above the 21st parallel for 60 days. If the North Vietnamese undertook a corresponding "similarly limited, similarly visible, similarly measurable" deescalatory step, the U.S. would then stop bombing for 60 days above the next (20th) parallel to the south, and so on until all bombing ceased. If at any time the North Vietnamese failed to reciprocate, the U.S. would resume bombing.[7]

Representative Morse was critical of those who favored military escalation as well as those who favored total withdrawal or complete cessation of bombing. Both sets of critics, he said, did not understood the nature of a limited war which imposed "special requirements not only on our military planning but on our diplomatic efforts as well." He argued, among other things, that "the end of a limited war requires that the combatants that meet at the peace table appear to be equals. If one side were to appear to 'lose face' by negotiating, negotiations in a limited war context would not occur. . . ." In addition, "negotiations to end a limited war must appear to be at the initiative of both sides, must appear to some degree to be the result of a military stalemate in which both sides can claim success, and must result in an agreement which each side can convincingly claim as a major achievement in pursuit of its objectives."

Morse was critical of the Johnson administration for being "unyielding and inflexible—rigidly insisting that the first concrete step toward deescalation be taken by North Vietnam—dogmatically demanding that North Vietnam demonstrate its genuine sincerity for negotiations before the United States does." "It is an attitude," Morse said, "which may reflect a misunderstanding of the nature of limited war, for it asks the enemy to risk losing face. The administration insists on publicly putting the Government of North Viet-

---

[5] *CR*, vol. 113, p. 24279, and CRS Interview with Tim Lee Carter, Mar. 19, 1979. It will be recalled that a year earlier, Carter, after a congressional trip to Vietnam, had told President Johnson that the U.S. was not winning the war.

[6] *CR*, vol. 113, pp. 18233 ff., speeches by Bradford Morse and others on July 10, 1967. Quotations used here are from this source unless otherwise indicated. The author of the plan was Dr. Douglas Bailey, who was employed by the Wednesday Group, an organization of Republicans that had been initiated by Bradford Morse.

The Grid Plan, which had been developed over the course of a year, had been discussed by Morse with Harriman, who had a very favorable reaction and encouraged Morse to present it publicly. CRS Interview with Bradford Morse, Oct. 16, 1978.

[7] Deescalatory steps could include "the cessation of shipments to and from specific military supply depots in the southern portion of North Vietnam; the erection of barriers on and the nonuse of specific supply routes in North Vietnam and Laos along the Ho Chi Minh trail; the withdrawal of all MiG fighters to distant bases in North Vietnam; the cessation of all terrorist bombing in specific areas of South Vietnam; the release of U.S. prisoners of war; et cetera."

nam on the spot by insisting that she back down first. It is a position which comes dangerously close to changing the atmosphere of restraint to an atmosphere of power—and a limited war cannot stay limited or be ended in an atmosphere of power."

In a memorandum to Rostow drafted by William Bundy, the State Department took the position that even though Representative Morse was in error in stating that the U.S. had insisted that the North Vietnamese should take the first step, the Grid Plan was "thoughtful and constructive," and "a not unreasonable specific suggestion along the lines of mutual deescalation."[8] It was also consistent with the administration's willingness to engage in mutual deescalation. The weakness of the plan was that "we would necessarily accept the military advantages, even for a 60-day period, that Hanoi would get from immunity to bombing in the exempt areas. These areas contain major routes into North Vietnam as well as major production facilities directly related to the war. The area proposed for exemption by Morse is substantially greater and more strategically significant than the immediate area around Hanoi, which we exempted for four months earlier in the year without response. Their immunity for even 60 days would confer significant advantage on Hanoi, at a time when we have no indication that Hanoi would in fact respond favorably."

The memorandum to Rostow also suggested that the Department of State should contact Representative Morse and explain its position, "which we think will satisfy him that we have carefully considered his proposal."

As far as "public treatment" was concerned, the memorandum recommended that "If the proposal excites public attention, it might be sufficient simply to go on saying that it is a responsible one and that we are always studying such serious suggestions. To the degree necessary, we might then go on to say that we have frequently stated that steps in the direction of mutual deescalation could be one of the possible avenues to peace. This specific proposal involves certain military disadvantages, and these would have to be weighed in in the light of the absence of any present indication that Hanoi wishes peace or would take responsive action."[9]

The reaction in the House of Representatives to the Grid Plan suggests that the President and his legislative leaders wanted to discredit the proposal. In a speech that probably was written by the State Department, Democratic Majority Leader Carl Albert strongly attacked the plan, saying that it "implies that the key to peace in Vietnam lies not in Hanoi, but in Washington." Reciting the peace proposals that he said had been made and had been accepted by the U.S. but rejected by the North Vietnamese, Albert declared that "there can no longer be the slightest doubt who wants peace and who wants the war to continue."[10]

Representative Rivers, chairman of the Armed Services Committee, commended Morse and his colleagues for making the effort to

---

[8] U.S. Department of State, Central File, Pol 27 Viet S, Memorandum to W. W. Rostow from Benjamin Read, "Comments on Republican Proposal for Staged De-Escalation in Vietnam," July 10, 1967.

[9] According to a note by Read on July 11 on his copy of the memorandum, Rostow approved the proposed public treatment, but apparently did not approve having a Department representative meet with Morse.

[10] *CR*, vol. 113, pp. 18193–18194.

develop a plan, but said that, based on experience, he did not think it would work. His position was that the U.S. had not "punished them [the North Vietnamese] enough."[11]

No action was taken on the Grid Plan. According to Morse, "nobody paid much attention to it . . . until March 31, 1968, when Lyndon Johnson proposed rolling the bombing back to the 20th parallel."[12]

Another proposal from the Republicans was made by Representative Paul Findley, a member of the House Foreign Affairs Committee, who introduced in mid-August 1967 a resolution (House Resolution 869 of the 90th Congress), cosponsored by 24 other Republicans, calling for the Foreign Affairs Committee "to review the implementation of the Gulf of Tonkin Resolution and to consider whether it empowers the President to carry forward military operations of the current scope and magnitude in Southeast Asia, whether it requires modification in light of "changing political and military conditions, and whether alternative legislative action is necessary."[13] Subsequently, Findley decided to modify his proposal. Rather than raising the issue of Presidential authority under the Gulf of Tonkin Resolution and limiting the inquiry to the House, he introduced a resolution (House Concurrent Resolution 509 of the 90th Congress) on September 25 providing "that . . . the appropriate committees of each House of Congress shall immediately consider and report to their respective bodies their determination as to whether further Congressional action is desirable in respect to policies in Southeast Asia." The resolution was cosponsored by Bradford Morse and by 47 other Republicans and four Democrats.[14]

In a speech in the House on August 14,[15] in testimony before the Senate Foreign Relations Committee on August 23, and in a speech on September 25 when he introduced the modified resolution, Fin-

---

[11] *Ibid.*, p. 18227.

[12] CRS Interview with Bradford Morse, Oct. 16, 1978.

[13] *CR*, vol. 113, pp. 22281–22282. These were the 24 Republicans who cosponsored Findley's resolution: Mark Andrews (N. Dak.), J. Herbert Burke (Fla.), Don H. Clausen (Calif.), Harold R. Collier (Ill.), Bob Dole (Kans.), John J. Duncan (Tenn.), John N. Erlenborn (Ill.), Paul A. Fino (N.Y.), Charles S. Gubser (Calif.), Edward Gurney, Seymour Halpern (N.Y.), Theodore R. Kupferman (N.Y.), Robert McClory (Ill.), Thomas J. Meskill (Conn.), Rogers C. B. Morton (Md.), Albert H. Quie (Minn.), Howard W. Robison (N.Y.), Herman T. Schneebeli (Penn.), Joe Skubitz (Kan.), Sam Steiger (Ariz.), Vernon W. Thomson (Wisc.), Lawrence G. Williams (Penn.), Larry Winn (Kan.), and John M. Zwach (Minn.).

[14] *CR*, vol. 113, pp. 26598 ff. In addition to Bradford Morse, cosponsors of H. Con. Res. 509 or sponsors of identical resolutions included Republicans Mark Andrews (N. Dak.), Edward G. Biester, Jr. (Penn.), Laurence J. Burton (Utah), Daniel E. Button (N.Y.), Tim Lee Carter (Ky.), Don H. Clausen (Calif.), James C. Cleveland (N. H.), Harold R. Collier (Ill.), Barber B. Conable, Jr. (N.Y.), William C. Cramer (Fla.), Thomas B. Curtis (Mo.), John J. Duncan (Tenn.), Florence P. Dwyer (N.J.), John N. Erlenborn (Ill.), Edwin D. Eshleman (Penn.), George A. Gooding (Penn.), Gilbert Gude (Md.), Edward J. Gurney (Fla.), Seymour Halpern (N.Y.), Frank J. Horton (N.Y.), Hastings Keith (Mass.), Theodore R. Kupferman (N.Y.), Sherman P. Lloyd (Utah), Robert McClory (Ill.), Clark MacGregor (Minn.), William S. Mailliard (Calif.), Charles McC. Mathias (Md.), Thomas J. Meskill (Conn.), Chester L. Mize (Kan.), Rogers C. B. Morton (Md.), Charles A. Mosher (Ohio), Thomas M. Pelly (Wash.), Albert H. Quie (Minn.), Howard W. Robison, (N.Y.), Donald Rumsfeld (Ill.), Herman T. Schneebeli (Penn.), William L. Scott, (Va.), Robert T. Stafford (Vt.), William A. Steiger (Wisc.), Vernon W. Thomson (Wisc.), Charles W. Whalen, Jr. (Ohio), Lawrence G. Williams (Penn.), Larry Winn, Jr. (Kan.), John M. Zwach (Minn.) and Democrats Joseph P. Addabbo (N.Y.), William L. Hungate (Mo.), Robert W. Kastenmeier (Wisc.), Richard L. Ottinger (N.Y.).

By October 30, when there was another discussion in the House, led by Findley, of the need for Congress to reconsider U.S. policy in Vietnam (*ibid.*, pp. 30465 ff.), the number of sponsors of Findley's proposal had reached 56.

[15] *Ibid.*, pp. 22505–22506.

dley explained the purpose of the proposal.[16] The most important reason for Congress to consider whether further congressional action on U.S. Vietnam policy was desirable was that the war was "so far-reaching and touches so intimately the lives of the American people." The "lack of compliance with constitutional procedures had the effect of denying our Nation a powerful, unifying influence," and congressional action on a new resolution could "forge a policy acceptable to the American people, one which will answer the grave fundamental questions that are now being asked." Moreover, Congress had "never debated in any degree the question of military policy in Vietnam," and such a resolution would provide a means for doing so at a time when the U.S. appeared to be stepping up the war.[17] In a colloquy in the House on September 25, Bradford Morse agreed, saying that it was "a new war." "Are we," he asked, "in the conduct of what has become a major war, to rely forever on one resolution passed in a different time and under totally different circumstances?"[18]

The State Department responded in a memorandum to the President from Katzenbach on September 26, 1967: "We see this [the revised Findley resolution] as a matter of considerable delicacy, and for dealing with the press we have developed an informal, low-key response to the effect that the Administration will continue to operate under certain authorities granted by the Congress and will continue to keep the Congress informed as we have done in the past of developments in Vietnam."[19]

The "Friendly Five" Survey of Congressional Attitudes

In early August 1967, after riots in several major American cities and with rapidly increasing opposition in Congress to the Vietnam war, the President, whose popularity was falling sharply in public opinion polls, decided to take a secret poll of his own. Apparently feeling the need to find out the current state of opinion among Democrats in Congress, he asked each of the directors of congressional liaison in the departments and agencies of the government to talk privately with five Members of Congress they knew best (the "Friendly Five") and to report back to him.[20] Arrangements for

---

[16] For Findley's testimony, see U.S. Congress, Senate, Committee on Foreign Relations, *U.S. Commitments to Foreign Powers,* Hearings, 90th Cong., 1st sess. (Washington, D.C.: U.S. Govt. Print. Off., 1976). For Findley's speech on September 25, see *CR*, vol. 113, pp. 26598–26603.

In another statement of his views, Findley suggested that Congress should clarify and strengthen its constitutional "power of the sword," by a statutory definition of its right to commit troops "so that the legislative history of this statutory definition hopefully can be used in accomplishing a strict construction of the exercise of these powers." Moreover, in cases where the President exercised his own power to repel attacks to protect the lives and property of U.S. citizens, or to fulfill treaty obligations, he should be required by law to present to Congress "after such a commitment a documentation of his reasons for believing it was required." See Findley's statement in U.S. Congress, Senate, Committee on the Judiciary, Subcommittee on Separation of Powers, *Separation of Powers,* pp. 179–184.

[17] These comments by Findley are from his September 25 speech and his testimony before the Foreign Relations Committee on August 23.

[18] *CR*, vol. 113, p. 26599.

[19] U.S. Department of State, Lot File 70 D 207, Memorandum for the President from Katzenbach, Sept. 26, 1967, "Subject: Congressional Criticism and Action, September 25." On September 27, according to "Congressional Criticism and Action September 26," (same location), the State Department sent the President a classified memorandum on its "thinking" about the revised Findley-Morse resolution, but the Johnson Library apparently does not have the memorandum in its files, and the author has not found it in State Department files.

[20] On August 4, 1967, each congressional liaison officer was asked to submit to the White House congressional liaison staff a brief list of those Members of Congress he knew best. Assign-

the talks were to be made as casually as possible to avoid the appearance of preplanning, and neither the purpose of the talks nor the fact that they were being conducted for the President was to be revealed to Members of Congress being surveyed. Information about the entire operation was to remain highly confidential.[21]

Further, the talks were to be informal, unstructured and open-ended in order to encourage frankness and communication in depth by the Members of Congress being surveyed. Members themselves were to be seen, not staff (although in a few cases this instruction was not followed). Reports on all talks were to contain all pertinent information no matter how critical the Member of Congress might be of the President or administration policy.

In all, 169 interviews were conducted during August and September (137 Representatives and 32 Senators).[22]

Jean P. Lewis, in a careful study of the reports on the interviews, concludes that of the 169 interviews, "104 were negative [with respect to the war, and its domestic political effects], 22 were positive, 18 contained both good and bad news, and 25 were noncommittal or irrelevant."[23] Lewis adds that this high rate of disapproval occurred despite the fact that the President had "lavished attention" on congressional Democrats (and Republicans as well):[24]

> Every Democratic Congressman [House and Senate], each one of the 59 Freshmen Republicans in the House, all Chairmen and ranking Republican members of House and Senate Committees and the Democratic and Republican Leadership of House and Senate had been invited to the White House for briefings, for supper parties, for question-and-answer sessions. They had been congratulated on their birthdays, commiserated with when they were ill, consoled when there was a death in the family. Their constituents had received congratulations on special birthdays and anniversaries. Their children and grandchildren from first grade through high school had been entertained at an old-fashioned country fair on the White House lawn even as the dismaying reports were coming to the President's desk.

Except for the surtax legislation, Lewis says, the legislative program was moving well at the time the survey was made. "The President had long been aware of the opposition of the Fulbright-led group in the Senate; yet he had been able to count on the support of most of his old Democratic friends and such Republicans as Dirksen and Saltonstall. Now he had in cold print reports of the disaffection of many of the Democrats. He was leading the country—and the Democratic Party—toward disaster. . . . Johnson, the consummate politician, the master of persuasion and compromise, the seeker after consensus, had failed for three years to find a mid-

---

ments were made by the White House. Some liaison officers had more and some less than five. The President met with all of the liaison officers on Aug. 21, 1967 to discuss the survey.

[21] Even though information about talks was closely held, Rowland Evans and Robert Novak learned about it and described it in their column in the *Washington Post* on Sept. 6, 1967, "Johnson Secretly Uses Top Aides as His Personal Political Scouts."

[22] These reports are in the Johnson Library, Papers of Harold Barefoot Sanders. Of the 169 interviews, there are copies of only 137 reports in the file, and there is no explanation of the absence of others.

[23] Jean P. Lewis, "President Johnson Surveys the Congress," a paper prepared for the Senior Seminar in History, Georgetown Univ., May 1990, p. 80.

[24] *Ibid.*, p. 81.

dle ground that would satisfy the Fulbrights and the Stennises—and the American people."[25]

Typical of the responses of the Friendly Five survey were Senator John Pastore, Democrat of Rhode Island, and Representative Julia Butler Hansen, Democrat from Washington, both influential and respected Members who supported the administration on the war. Pastore commented that "our problem is Vietnam—boxes coming back, casualties going up—back home not a good word from anyone for us and this attitude is reflected in the Senate. We're losing Democrats in droves—a paradox, [an] affluent society that fears riots but fears Vietnam more. Attitude now is any Republican can do a better job." Mrs. Hansen was reported as saying that the "present course of action in Vietnam will defeat not just the President but the Democratic Party"; that the public "wants the war over quickly, not because it wants to win but because it wants out. People would rather pull out without victory if this would avoid new taxes. They think Vietnam is not worth a tax increase."[26]

The report on Pastore was prepared by Postmaster General O'Brien, a very experienced and trusted political adviser to Presidents Kennedy and Johnson, who says that during 1967, "while I remained uncertain as to whether the war was right militarily or diplomatically, I became increasingly aware that it was a disaster politically." Referring to his report on Pastore, O'Brien says: "It didn't much impress Johnson to learn that, say, Senator McGovern was talking against the war, because he'd been against it for a long time. But when someone like Pastore questioned the war, someone who'd been a staunch supporter of ours, the President had to be impressed with the seriousness of the situation."[27]

The President, Lewis says, "sought consolation in the polls." In a Luncheon Group meeting on September 15, as the last of the Friendly Five reports were being sent to the White House, he spoke of "what we have to be thankful for and pointed out the recent August and September polls showing the President's performance in relation to the four leading Republican Presidential candidates. He noted that he led [Richard M.] Nixon 49–41 in a September poll; led [George] Romney 52–48 in August and 45–41 in September; led [Nelson A.] Rockefeller 59–41; and led [Ronald] Reagan 55–45." "There are three groups hitting us," he said, "1) Bobby [Kennedy] and his crowd, 2) all of the Republicans; the ADA [Americans for Democratic Action] and other liberal groups. What will they do if Nixon or Reagan or Romney runs against me. If I get a hawk running against me, then I'll get all the doves votes. If I get a dove, then I'll get the hawks vote. So, these things are just relative."[28]

What the President apparently feared most, however, was not the Republicans but a challenge from Robert Kennedy, even though a Harris Survey taken in July 1967 indicated that among the Democrats Johnson led Kennedy 45 to 39 percent. A Harris survey taken in October, however, gave Kennedy the lead, 51 percent to

---

[25] *Ibid.*

[26] Another critic, House Majority Leader Carl Albert, was interviewed (CRS Interview with Carl Albert, Oct. 31, 1978), but although the report of the interview was submitted to the White House, it is not in Sanders' file.

[27] O'Brien, *No Final Victories*, p. 214.

[28] *Ibid.*, p. 83, and Johnson Library, Meetings Notes File, Jim Jones notes of meeting Sept. 15, 1967.

Johnson's 39 percent.[29] Moreover, in the October Harris Survey Johnson trailed all of the Republicans he had led several weeks earlier. He trailed Nixon 48–41, Romney 46–37, Rockefeller 52–35, and Reagan 46–41. "Most shocking of all, however, was the additional news that LBJ was behind two young and relatively unknown Republicans: By 40–39 he was edged out by Major John Lindsay [of New York City] and by 41–40 he ran behind Senator Charles Percy."[30]

In a meeting of the Luncheon Group (Rusk, McNamara, Rostow, Christian and Tom Johnson) from 6:10 p.m. to about 9:30 p.m. on October 3, 1967, the President read from some of the Friendly Five reports about what Members of Congress were saying about Vietnam. According to the notes of the meeting, "The President said that 95% of the people [this probably referred to those Members of Congress who were interviewed] believe there has been a change of attitude on Vietnam. They all think that we will lose the [1968] election if we do not do something about Vietnam quick. They are all worried about expenses."[31]

The discussion during the meeting ranged over a number of subjects—the lack of progress at the Paris talks; Rusk's report on his conversation with Gromyko—"The Russians have given up any attempt to influence Hanoi"; the large demonstration against the war planned for late October in Washington—the President said he had asked McNamara to plan for protecting the White House, the Pentagon and the Capitol, but he asserted "they are not going to run me out of town"; the lack of action by the new South Vietnamese Government, and the problem of getting the Vietnamese Army to "get in where the fighting is"; increasing resistance to the draft; opposition to the war from an influential and formerly staunch supporter, Representative Thomas P. "Tip" O'Neill (D/Mass.);[32] the state of public opinion—"The President said that he believed we had lost people away from us in the last two weeks. . ."; opposition in Congress to the tax surcharge request, where the Ways and Means Committee had just announced that day (October 3) that it was shelving the request.

As the meeting drew to a close, the President, saying that "he did not want any of the information he was about to discuss to go outside of the room," asked the group what the effect on the war would be if he announced that he was not going to run for another term. "He said if it were set either way today, the decision would be that he would not run." "Our people will not hold out four more years," he said, adding: "I just don't know if I want four more years of this. . . . We [referring to himself] are very divisive. We don't have the press, the newspapers or the polls with us. . . ." Rusk responded firmly: "You must not go down. You are the Commander-in-Chief, and we are in a war. This would have a very serious effect on the country."

The President observed that if he ran and were re-elected he would be the first President to have served a part of a term and

---

[29] *Washington Post*, Aug. 28 and Nov. 13, 1967.

[30] Louis Harris, *The Anguish of Change* (New York: Norton, 1973), p. 61. See also Gallup's similar findings, *The Gallup Poll, op. cit.*, vol. II, pp. 2086–2087.

[31] Johnson Library, Tom Johnson's Notes of Meetings, Notes of meeting Oct. 3, 1967.

[32] See p. 835 below.

to have been elected for two full terms. "I don't think you should appear too cute on this," McNamara replied.

"What I'm asking," the President repeated, "is what would this do to the war." Rusk replied: "Hanoi would think they have got it made." McNamara said that he thought there would still be support for money and men to fight the war, but he did not know about the effect on the public, the morale of U.S. troops or the North Vietnamese, but that after such an announcement the North Vietnamese would not negotiate and would wait for the results of the 1968 U.S. election.

This was one of several similar episodes that occurred during the fall of 1967 as the President expressed to a few associates and friends, including General Westmoreland, his inclination not to run for re-election.[33] Lewis concludes that "the August 1967 survey of the Congress and the defections of his old friends in the Senate on whom he had felt he could depend must have profoundly shaken his confidence in his ability to govern." "[D]espite astounding domestic accomplishments, support had eroded to such an extent that President Johnson, on reading the comments of the Democrats in Congress—months before the Tet offensive and the political challenges of Senator McCarthy and Senator Kennedy—may have made a firm, irrevocable decision that he would not run for reelection."[34]

Foreign Relations Committee Hearings on "National Commitments," August 1967

In August 1967, the Senate Foreign Relations Committee began hearings on a resolution stating the "sense of the Senate" that a "national commitment" by the United States to another country results from action by both the legislative and the executive branches of the government.

Since the President's decision in 1965 to send large-scale U.S. forces to fight the war, some Members of Congress, Fulbright in particular, had become concerned—and their concern increased as the war escalated—that in approving the Gulf of Tonkin Resolution Congress was not acting in accordance with its constitutional role in the making of decisions to go to war. Apart from questions as to whether the Executive had misrepresented the facts in asking for Congress' approval, there were issues with respect to the procedures used in passing the resolution quickly and with almost no debate, the use of a resolution rather than a declaration of war, and the terms of the resolution, in particular the President's subsequent expansion of the war far beyond Congress' original intent.

Since early 1966, the question of what Congress might do about the matter had been the subject of discussion among those, especially in the Senate, who believed that some kind of action was desirable. The most extreme remedy—repeal of the Gulf of Tonkin Resolution—was ruled out as unnecessary and undesirable. Moreover, it would doubtless be defeated, as the Senate vote in March of 1966 on Morse's repeal amendment had demonstrated. The more

[33] In his memoirs, Johnson states that, beginning in 1965, he told a number of people that he was not going to run again in 1968. See *The Vantage Point*, pp. 427–429. See also the analysis in Lewis, "President Johnson Surveys the Congress."

[34] Lewis, pp. 12, 98.

practicable alternative, and the one which was generally preferred by those who believed that some action should be taken, would be to pass a resolution stating more precisely the terms on which Congress agreed to the U.S. involvement in the war. This was the impetus behind the Mansfield-Clark amendment, which, although it fell far short of the desires of those who wanted to pass a revised or new resolution, constituted the first step by Congress toward a better definition of its view of U.S. policy and goals.

In April-May, 1967, when it began to appear that the President and his associates were preparing to escalate and possibly to expand the war, and to do so without seeking congressional approval, the question of such approval became more acute. This led to consideration of what should and could be done, and to recommendations from the staff of the Foreign Relations Committee that the committee should hold hearings on the war and/or on the role of Congress in foreign policy. Fulbright considered talking to Russell, who had opposed U.S. involvement in South Vietnam in 1953 and was known to be concerned about Congress' war power, about possible joint hearings on the war by a special subcommittee of the Armed Services Committee and the Foreign Relations Committee.

In early July 1967 an incident occurred which brought Fulbright and Russell together in support of a resolution seeking to assert Congress' role in the making of "national commitments." The incident involved action taken by President Johnson in response to an internal disturbance in the Congo. Apparently without any consultation with Congress,[35] he sent three U.S. transport planes and a small number of U.S. military personnel to assist in suppressing the revolt. There was a sharp reaction in Congress from Democrats and Republicans, liberals and conservatives alike. These included Democrats Russell, Stennis, Fulbright, Mansfield, Morse, McCarthy and Republicans Case (N.J), James B. Pearson (Kans.), Strom Thurmond (S.C.), and Milton Young, as well as House Minority Leader Ford. In a Senate speech on July 10, Russell deplored intervention in a country "where we have no commitment or any vital interest whatever." U.S. involvement in Vietnam, he said, began with a limited commitment, and the commitment in the Congo could become a major intervention if U.S. planes were lost or there were military casualties.[36]

---

[35] After the decision had been made, Rusk telephoned Fulbright and Russell to inform them of the action that was being taken. Russell is said to have told Rusk that he saw no reason for U.S. intervention in the Congo's internal crisis, and that if U.S. military personnel were to become endangered, or there were casualties, there would be increasing pressure to send more troops. Don Oberdorfer, "Nonintervention, 1967 Style," *New York Times Magazine* (Sept. 17, 1967). In this article, Oberdorfer, after interviews with Russell, Stennis, Milton Young, Mansfield and Morton, described the growing feeling in the Senate that the U.S. was overcommitted around the world. "The growing frustration of Vietnam," he said, "is the root of the new noninterventionism. . . . Vietnam has impressed them as never before with the staggering price tag which may accompany intervention, while trouble at home has raised new questions about the nation's ability or willingness to pay."

[36] *CR*, vol. 113, pp. 18093 ff.

Six months later, after U.S. planes and personnel had been withdrawn from the Congo, the President informed Russell that the mission had been successfully completed without casualties. Russell replied in a letter on Dec. 21, 1967 (University of Georgia Libraries, Richard B. Russell Memorial Library, Richard B. Russell Papers):

"While I am happy over the safe return of our men and planes from this mission, I must regretfully advise that I still do not believe in the United States moving into situations of this kind unilaterally. I note from your letter that the lives and property of fifty thousand European nationals were involved, along with seventeen hundred Americans. I am quite sure that most,

Continued

Several days later, Russell and Fulbright talked at lunch about the Congo, and agreed that they should do what they could to "dissuade the administration from intervening physically in the Congo civil war."[37] According to Fulbright, Russell said to him "'Why don't you prepare a resolution to see if we can express our right to be consulted [on such decisions].'"[38] Fulbright responded that Russell should introduce it, and that he would co-sponsor it "and do the work." Russell said that it would be more appropriate for Fulbright to introduce it, but that he would support it.[39]

A day or two later, Fulbright sent Russell the draft of a resolution, as follows:[40]

> *Whereas* accurate definition of the term, national commitment, in recent years had become obscured: Therefore be it
>
> *Resolved,* That it is the sense of the Senate that a national commitment by the United States to a foreign power necessarily and exclusively results from affirmative action taken by the executive and legislative branches of the U.S. Government through means of a treaty, convention, or other legislative instrumentality specifically intended to give effect to such a commitment.

In an accompanying letter, Fulbright repeated his hope that Russell would introduce the resolution, and in a handwritten note he added: "If you sponsor such a resolution, I am confident that it would inspire a very healthy and beneficial discussion of this subject and probably bring about much better relations between the Senate and the President than we presently enjoy.

"It is timely, in view of the Congo—and it is of fundamental importance."

Russell sent word that he preferred not to introduce the resolution "BUT WILL jump to his feet to support JWF," Marcy said, in a memorandum to the member of the Foreign Relations Committee staff who was drafting Fulbright's introduction speech.[41] Marcy added: "This could be a pretty important statement—the break between JWF and LBJ openeth again. JWF told LBJ last night that he doubted he could support the foreign aid bill this year in light of our mixed up national priorities—priorities which have been determined by national commitments."

---

if not all, of these people are citizens of countries that are likewise members of the United Nations. If any of them contributed in any degree to averting the great dangers which you say the utilization of these aircraft, their crews and guards prevented, I did not hear of it. It would seem that some one of those countries would likewise have been willing to make some contribution to such a vital mission.

"I cannot subscribe to any policy predicated upon the assumption that the United States alone has an obligation to avoid domestic strife in Africa or elsewhere. Despite any great advancement that may have been made in Africa in recent years, from what I have been able to learn, tribal loyalties are still superior to any feeling of nationalism and we are likely to have tribal rebellions and wars for some time to come. A number of other countries that have aircraft and armed forces have a much greater stake in Africa than the United States and I shall continue to protest our country rushing in unilaterally to aid the side that we may temporarily favor in any African country confronted with domestic disorders and conflicts."

[37] Russell Papers, Oral History Interview with J. William Fulbright, Apr. 19, 1971.

[38] U.S. Congress, Senate, Committee on Foreign Relations, unpublished executive session transcript, Nov. 1, 1967, p. 69, and Russell Papers, Fulbright Oral History.

[39] Russell Papers, Fulbright Oral History.

[40] University of Arkansas, Fulbright Papers, letter to Russell from Fulbright, July 14, 1967, with draft resolution attached.

[41] National Archives, RG 46, Papers of the Committee on Foreign Relations, Marcy Chron File, Memorandum from Marcy to Don (Donald) Henderson July 27, 1967.

On July 31, 1967, Fulbright introduced the resolution in the form that it had been sent to Russell.[42] In a brief statement, he said that it "represents a conservative position which seeks to recover in some degree the constitutional role of the Senate in the making of foreign policy—a role which the Senate itself has permitted to be obscured and diminished over the years."[43]

A number of Senators, Republicans as well as Democrats, beginning with Russell, supported Fulbright's action in introducing the resolution.[44]

Later that afternoon, Rostow sent a copy of Fulbright's statement and the resolution to the President with a note saying "I am getting State's legal people to have an urgent look at it; and we shall be studying it."[45]

Beginning August 16, 1967, the Foreign Relations Committee held five days of open public hearings on the national commitments resolution.[46] The principal government witness was Under Secretary of State Katzenbach.[47]

Prior to the hearings, the Foreign Relations Committee asked the State Department for a statement of its views on the resolution, as well as "a full list of all nations which upon the basis of past official statements, communiques, or other public or private understandings, as well as formal treaties, reasonably assume that they have a United States commitment under some set of circumstances involving either an economic or military threat to their existence, to receive either economic or military assistance from the United States."[48]

In its reply on August 15, the Department of State avoided commenting on the resolution, saying that the views of the Department "can best be presented" in Katzenbach's testimony. In response to the question on commitments, the Department provided a long list of provisions of "formal treaties and agreements, and official declarations by the Congress, the President, the Vice President, and the Secretary of State concerning actions the United States would

---

[42] Senate Resolution 151 of the 90th Congress, *CR*, vol. 113, pp. 20702 ff.

[43] Fulbright inserted in the *Congressional Record* the text of a statement on "Congress and Foreign Policy" which he made on July 20, 1967 in a hearing by the Subcommittee on Separation of Powers of the Senate Judiciary Committee, *Separation of Powers,* Hearings, Pt. 1, July 19 and 20, August 2, and September 13 and 15, 1967, 90th Cong., 1st sess. (Washington, D.C., U.S. Govt. Print. Off., 1967), pp. 41–53. Senator Morse also testified before the subcommittee on constitutional aspects of the Congress' war power and its role in foreign policy. See pp. 55 ff.

[44] *CR*, vol. 113, pp. 20706–20719.

[45] Johnson Library, NSF Files of J. William Fulbright.

[46] U.S. Congress, Senate, Committee on Foreign Relations, *U.S. Commitments to Foreign Powers,* Hearings, 90th Cong., 1st sess. (Washington, D.C.: U.S. Govt. Print. Off., 1967).

[47] Three Members of Congress, Senator Sam J. Ervin, Jr., (D/N.C.) chairman of the Separation of Powers Subcommittee of the Judiciary Committee, Senator Charles Percy (R/Ill.), and Representative Paul G. Findley (R/Ill.) also testified. In addition, there were two academic authorities, Professor W. Stull Holt of the University of Wisconsin and Ruhl J. Bartlett of the Fletcher School of Law and Diplomacy at Tufts University, and testimony by or statements from several other private witnesses.

[48] Letter from Fulbright to Rusk, Aug. 1, 1967, quoted in *U.S. Commitments to Foreign Powers,* p. 51. The request for information or commitments set in motion in the Department of State, the Department of Defense and the Agency for International Development a search for the facts for a reply. Decisions also had to be made as to what information should and should not be provided. In the latter category—information that was considered "internal" and was not to be provided—were the highly secret actions taken and commitments made by the so-called "NSC 1550" commitments (a reference to NSC directive 1550) under the presumed authority of the President to take such actions and make such commitments.

take if another country were the victim of aggression."[49] No information was provided on secret commitments.

On August 17, Under Secretary of State Katzenbach testified before a large audience that included most of the members of the Foreign Relations Committee, a number of members of the press, other government officials and staff, and private citizens. Outside the committee room there was a long line of people waiting for seats. Even though the hearing was not on Vietnam directly, and was not being televised, it created considerable interest because the underlying issue was Vietnam, and, as Marcy said, Fulbright and the committee were again challenging the President.

In his prepared statement, Katzenbach reviewed the constitutional arrangements for the making and conduct of foreign policy as well as describing the main lines of U.S. foreign policy since World War II. The Constitution, he said, "recognized that the voice of the United States in foreign affairs was that of the President," who has "a preeminent responsibility in this field." The President, however, "acts most effectively when he acts with the support and authority of the Congress. . . . The Congress is and must be a participant in formulating the broad outlines of our foreign policy, in supporting those fundamental and enduring commitments on which the conduct of day-to-day diplomacy depend."[50]

Asked by Fulbright to state more precisely the position of the Department of State on the resolution, Katzenbach replied:[51]

> I could not support the resolution, Mr. Chairman, because it seems to me that . . . it tries to do precisely what the Founding Fathers of this country declined to do in writing the Constitution in that it purports to take a position, through a Senate Resolution, on matters that it seems to me have worked out successfully, in terms of distribution of functions between the Executive branch and the Congress. And it seems to me that it could be interpreted to seek to join the Congress with the President on those matters which I think the President, in his capacity of conducting foreign relations of the United States has the constitutional authority to do. So, in short, I see no need for it. I find it confusing, and I doubt that even in our almost 200 years we have achieved the wisdom to resolve these problems which our forefathers, in drafting the Constitution, decided that they would leave to the Congress and the President in their wisdom, in their political experience . . . to work out for themselves.

Fulbright asked about the constitutional power of Congress to declare war. Katzenbach answered that "The function of the Congress is one to declare. It is not one to wage, not one to conduct, but simply one to declare." Fulbright said, "To declare the war and to authorize the war, I guess." Katzenbach replied: "To declare it." Fulbright continued: "I think the Constitution contemplated that the Congress should make the decision of whether or not we should engage in war. Don't you agree with that?" Katzenbach replied: "Yes, Mr. Chairman, I agree that the Congress should, except in the case

[49] *Ibid.*, pp. 51–71.
[50] *Ibid.*, pp. 76–77.
[51] *Ibid.*, pp. 77–78.

of emergencies, participate in major decisions of that kind." He went on to say that the phrase "to declare war" was outmoded; that it "came from a context that recognized 'war' to be an instrument of implementing the acceptable policy, but which is not acceptable in the climate today, which rejects the idea of aggression, which rejects the idea of conquest."[52]

With respect to Vietnam, Katzenbach said that a declaration of war would not "correctly reflect the very limited objectives of the United States," but that there "is an obligation on the part of the Executive to give Congress the opportunity, which that language was meant to reflect in the Constitution of the United States, to express its views with respect to this." In the case of Vietnam, Senate approval of the Southeast Asian Treaty (SEATO) and congressional approval of the Gulf of Tonkin Resolution "fully fulfill the obligation of the Executive in a situation of this kind to participate with the Congress to give the Congress a full and effective voice, the *functional equivalent* of the constitutional obligation expressed in the provision of the Constitution with respect to declaring war." (emphasis added)

It was this expression—functional equivalent—that, after Katzenbach's testimony, became fixed in the minds of many Members of Congress and others who were concerned about maintaining constitutionality in the conduct of foreign policy. For them, it epitomized the attitude that because a declaration of war was anachronistic and outmoded, Congress' constitutional war power was obsolete and superfluous and whatever constitutional power or obligation, if any, remained for Congress to exercise, could and should be carried out through some mechanism by which Congress could "participate" in decisions involving the use of the Armed Forces, thus leaving the Executive with the power to determine what the role of Congress should and would be.[53]

Fulbright replied, "You haven't requested and you don't intend to request a declaration of war, as I understand it." Katzenbach responded ("angrily" according to a *New York Times* reporter)[54] "that is correct, Mr. Chairman, but didn't that resolution authorize the President to use the armed forces of the United States in whatever way was necessary? Didn't it? What could a declaration of war have done that would have given the President more authority and a clear voice of the Congress of the United States than that did?"

[52] *Ibid.*, pp. 79–81.

[53] Although the expression functional equivalent of a declaration of war originated with Katzenbach (these, as noted above, were not his exact words), in 1954, when describing to Congress the request that the President would make if he were to ask Congress to approve the use of the Armed Forces in Indochina, Secretary of State John Foster Dulles used the term "the equivalent of war authority." (See pt. I of this study, p. 232.)

In a letter to the author, Dec. 7, 1993, Katzenbach said "perhaps the way in which I used the term 'functional equivalent' might suggest that I did not then and do not now believe that the Tonkin Gulf resolution and a Declaration of War were in fact functional equivalents. They are—as I think most international and constitutional law scholars agree.

"The point of functional equivalency is essentially a simple one. The process within the Congress for a Declaration of War and the process by which the resolution with respect to the Tonkin gulf were passed are identical. Under a normal declaration of war the President is delegated extremely broad powers to use force. These can be implied or expressed. Under the Tonkin Gulf resolution the President was delegated extremely broad powers to use force in exactly the same way that would have been inferred from a Declaration of War. Since the Constitutional process is identical it seems to me that one resolution is the functional equivalent of the other. And which ever way it was done the Congress would have been performing the Constitutional role in precisely the same way."

[54] *New York Times*, Aug. 18, 1967, article by E. W. Kenworthy.

Fulbright replied that he did not think the Gulf of Tonkin Resolution was a proper substitute for a declaration of war, "especially having been made under conditions of great emergency. It wasn't a deliberate decision by the Congress to wage war in that full-fledged sense against a foreign government." The resolution, he added, was drafted by the Executive and sent to Congress. "We didn't draft it, but we did, under the impulse of the emergency, accept it . . . largely without any consideration." Katzenbach responded: "Mr. Chairman, how much debate was there on that resolution as compared with a declaration of war when President Roosevelt sent that up? How quickly did the Congress respond? If you say there was pressure, there was the urgency. Maybe people regret afterward a declaration of war or a vote for it, but that situation inherently is one of urgency, it is one of commitment."[55]

Senator Gore's reaction to Katzenbach's testimony was that his interpretation of the Gulf of Tonkin Resolution as granting broad authority to the Executive to conduct the war made the hearing more important than he previously thought it would be. "I did not," Gore said, "vote for the resolution with any understanding that it was tantamount to a declaration of war." Katzenbach replied: "I do not wish to be understood as saying, for reasons that I have indicated, that the Tonkin resolution was tantamount to a direct declaration of war. . . . What I attempted to say was . . . that the Tonkin Gulf resolution gave Congress a voice in this, and that they expressed their will and their voice."[56]

Gore added that in voting for the Gulf of Tonkin Resolution he did not intend, nor did he think Congress intended, to authorize the use of U.S. ground combat troops in Vietnam. Katzenbach replied that Congress authorized the use of the Armed Forces, and that under the Constitution Congress could not "proceed to tell the President what he shall bomb, what he shall not bomb, where he shall dispose his troops, where he shall not."

Gore asked if the Gulf of Tonkin Resolution would authorize U.S. bombing of China. Katzenbach replied that the resolution provided for taking "all necessary steps to repel any armed attack against the forces of the United States and to prevent further aggression against South Vietnam," and that, depending on the circumstances, bombing of China could be considered to be authorized by the resolution if it were necessary to repel aggression against South Vietnam. He added, however, that if China were to invade South Vietnam, "that would present a very different factual situation than exists today. I think the limitation on it, Senator, is a limitation on what is necessary and proper in carrying out the authorization as was made today."[57]

In a press conference the next day (August 18), the President, in a long response to what may have been a pre-arranged question about the Gulf of Tonkin Resolution, said, among other things, "We stated then [at the time the resolution was passed], and we repeat now, we did not think the resolution was necessary to do what we

---

[55] *U.S. Commitments to Foreign Powers*, pp. 81–83.
[56] *Ibid.*, p. 88.
[57] *Ibid.*, pp. 89–91.

did and what we are doing."[58] He added that under the provision in the resolution for its repeal by a majority vote of Congress "the machinery is there any time the Congress decides to withdraw its views on the matter." (Note that he carefully avoided any reference to "authority" or "authorization.") He also said, without explanation, "'The remedy is there if we have acted unwisely or improperly.'"

As will be seen, these comments by the President were considered by some Members of the Senate and the Foreign Relations Committee to have been a dare or taunt, and to have strengthened the desire of Senators to assert Congress' war power and to repeal or replace the Gulf of Tonkin Resolution. On August 19, 1967, the Associated Press reported that in a survey of the Senate, out of 84 Senators willing to express an opinion, 40 (26 Democrats and 19 Republicans) said they disapproved of what the President was doing in Vietnam, but this group included those who wanted to escalate the war. (Among the 44 who supported the President, there were 27 Democrats and 17 Republicans.) According to the report, "The substance of the comments of individual Senators indicates there is such widespread dissatisfaction with the way the war is going that it would be risky for the President to seek any formal endorsement of his position, as he did in the Gulf of Tonkin Resolution in August, 1964."[59]

Among those interviewed in the survey, three members of the Foreign Relations Committee—McCarthy, Aiken and Cooper—said that Congress had not envisioned a major war when it approved the resolution, but they "saw no point" in rescinding it. Aiken's comment was that the President "'knows perfectly well it's impossible to rescind. . . . We're in a war now.'"

On August 20, in an interview on the American Broadcasting Company's television program, "Issues and Answers," Fulbright said he thought that in making his comment in the press conference the President might have been denying the validity of Congress' constitutional authority to declare war. He added that he saw "no likelihood" of a repeal of the Resolution. "Politically, this would be a direct slap at a leader in time of war. It will not be done that way. The disillusionment, the dissent, that will be expressed in other ways." Moreover, it would be useless to repeal the Resolution because of the argument of Katzenbach that the President had a right to fight the war without congressional approval, and because Congress would not cut off funds for the war. The only "real" sanction, Fulbright added, would be impeachment, but that would be "politically impractical."[60]

---

[58] *Public Papers of the Presidents,* Lyndon B. Johnson, 1967, p. 794. On August 17, the day before the press conference, NSC Aide Bromley Smith sent the President, at his request, all of the pertinent documents on the development of and passage by Congress of the Gulf of Tonkin Resolution. Johnson Library, NSF NSC History, Gulf of Tonkin.

[59] *Washington Post,* Aug. 20, 1967.

[60] *New York Times* and *Washington Post,* Aug. 21, 1967. At about that same time, Morse, who, it will be recalled, had introduced an amendment in the spring of 1966 to repeal the Gulf of Tonkin Resolution, apparently considered introducing a new resolution to provide for disengagement. He talked about it with Marcy, who seemed to share his feelings, and Marcy drafted a resolution for Morse's use, as follows: "That the Congress hereby affirms the desire of the American people honorably to disengage their armed forces from Southeast Asia at the earliest possible time when that area is secure from external attack and, to that end, the Congress urges the President of the United States on an urgent basis to take appropriate steps to encourage

Continued

On August 21, as he resumed his testimony before the Foreign Relations Committee, Katzenbach answered a question that Fulbright had sent to him after the first day of testimony. This was the question:[61]

> What would be the situation today regarding American involvement in Vietnam if the Tonkin Resolution had not been passed? Would the President then be with, or without, constitutional authority to send U.S. soldiers to South Vietnam in the numbers that are there today; would he have had authority to bomb in the north? In short, did the Gulf of Tonkin Resolution give the President authority which otherwise he constitutionally would not have had, and, if so, what?

Katzenbach replied that he thought the President had the authority both to send troops and to bomb the North, but that it would be "extremely difficult, in a situation of that kind, for a President to exercise that authority on his own. . . ." "He [the President] knew as a constitutional matter that he would have to depend upon the Congress if he were to exercise the policy in that way, and he wanted in a sense an indication that the Congress would support the exercise of that authority. He also wanted to avoid the constitutional questions that had come up at the time of Korea."[62]

If Congress were to repeal the Resolution, Katzenbach said, this "would by itself" not prevent the President from continuing the war. But it would put the President and the country in "an extremely difficult position, because I would assume . . . they would then continue with other powers which they have to not support the President in his decisions. They would not raise armies, they would not support them and maintain them for this purpose. They would exercise a variety of other constitutional rights." "So I think," Katzenbach said, "we would then be in a situation which every President and Congress over the years have responsibly sought to avoid in the conduct of international matters, the situation where they do not act together."[63]

In response to a question from Senator Hickenlooper, the senior Republican on the committee, Katzenbach said that although he did not believe that, under the Constitution, Congress could order U.S. troops out of Vietnam (this, he said, would be interfering with the President's power as Commander in Chief), he thought there was "a much closer question" with respect to support of such troops. "On that I think as a practical matter it is perfectly obvious Congress can do this." Senator Hickenlooper: "'Do what?'" Mr. Katzenbach: "'Can get the troops out of Vietnam if it chooses to do

---

negotiation of a cease-fire as between the forces supporting the Government of Vietnam and those forces opposed to that Government." (National Archives, RG 46, Papers of the Committee on Foreign Relations, Marcy Chron File, Marcy Memorandum to Senator Morse, Aug. 25, 1967.) In the memorandum to Morse, Marcy said that the resolution "has the advantage of giving members something they can vote for. Aside from you and Senator Gruening, a good many Members find themselves in this dilemma—they voted for the Tonkin resolution, which they wish they hadn't, but don't feel they can vote against appropriations. Thus, there has not been a vehicle by which Congress is able to express itself." Morse decided not to introduce a new resolution. Instead, he introduced in September, 1967 a resolution to urge the President to seek U.N. Security Council action on Vietnam.

[61] *U.S. Commitments to Foreign Powers,* p. 129.
[62] *Ibid.,* p. 141.
[63] *Ibid.,* p. 147.

it.'" Hickenlooper said that he could not accept the doctrine that, except by use of its appropriations power, Congress could not control the use or withholding of troops.[64]

Katzenbach's testimony produced a sharp reaction among most of the members of the Foreign Relations Committee and many others in the Senate. One member of the committee, Senator Eugene McCarthy, Democrat of Minnesota, said that Katzenbach's statement was a prescription "for a kind of four-year dictatorship in foreign policy."[65] As he left the hearing room, he told a reporter, "'This is the wildest testimony I ever heard. There is no limit to what he says the President could do. There is only one thing to do—take it to the country.'"[66] And that, as will be seen, is what McCarthy did on November 30, 1967, when he announced that he was going to run for President in 1968.[67]

Senator Case said that "for the President to come to the Congress with a resolution which turns over the whole matter to him for an indefinite time seems to me was taking advantage of a situation in which Congress has no choice, and had to go along with the form of words which later is thrown back into its teeth as a complete abdication of authority . . . if we are going to have cooperation and accommodation and make this system work with its ambiguous line between the authority of the President and the authority of Congress, we cannot have this kind of thing. We can't have it."[68]

Katzenbach's testimony was also the subject of considerable comment in Senate debate on the Defense Appropriations Bill on August 22, the day after he finished testifying. Morse, referring to Katzenbach's statement that the constitutional provision for a declaration of war was outmoded, declared: "We have an Under Secretary of State, a former Attorney General of the United States, who, in public testimony tells us that a key section of the Constitution of the United States is outmoded . . . did you ever think you would live so long as to hear that?" "I say to Mr. Katzenbach, what else in that Constitution do you regard as 'outmoded'?"

Morse called Katzenbach's testimony "naught but a testimony to rationalize a government by executive supremacy." "I say to the American people you have an administration that even tells you that if the Tonkin Gulf resolution were rescinded, the President could continue to do what he wants in Vietnam and elsewhere in the field of foreign policy." "If the President is to be taken at his word—if it is true that there are no limits to his discretion—if it is true Congress cannot change the course of the war by repealing the Tonkin Gulf resolution because he will pursue his policy with or without such a resolution—then the conclusion that must be drawn by the American people is that their only means of changing an unsound policy is to vote the President out of office."[69]

---

[64] *Ibid.*, pp. 170–171.

[65] *Ibid.*, p. 133.

[66] *New York Times*, Aug. 18, 1967. According to one knowledgeable journalist, McCarthy had said "essentially the same thing" at a private dinner party in March 1967. Richard T. Stout, *People* (New York: Harper & Row, 1970), p. 70.

[67] See Eugene McCarthy, *The Year of the People*, p. 257.

[68] *U.S. Commitments to Foreign Powers*, p. 163.

[69] *CR*, vol. 113, pp. 23463–23464, 23498.

For his part, Katzenbach said in an interview some years later that he had not wanted to testify about Vietnam. On the evening before the August 17 hearing, he went to Capitol Hill to talk to Fulbright, who, he says, promised him that he would not ask him any questions about Vietnam. At the hearing, Katzenbach said, it was the first question Fulbright asked, and "I felt taken."[70]

Katzenbach said in the interview that when he used the expression "functional equivalent" "it just came out. I hadn't thought about it much . . . because Bill Fulbright had promised me he wasn't going to ask any questions about Vietnam."

Katzenbach added that he was surprised at the adverse reaction, "because I thought it was a very pro-Congress thing. I was saying, Congress should be involved in this . . . Congress had the authority to do this . . . and they gave him [the President] that authority." Katzenbach was asked how he accounted for the adverse reaction and he replied: "Because Congress didn't like being told they had given the President the authority they had very clearly given him."

In the interview, Katzenbach was asked the same question that he had been asked by Fulbright in the hearing: would the President have had the authority to fight the war in the absence of the Gulf of Tonkin Resolution? This was his reply, in which he gives a further explanation of his views:

> I think at the time I was there I would have said "yes," mainly because it seems to me if you are in the executive branch you didn't want to indicate any doubts as to what the executive authority is. There is so much precedent that goes one way or the other on this subject that it is rather hard to tell. The only thing that at least was clear to me then, and is clear to me now, is that the whole constitutional structure is such that Congress has enormous powers and the President really has very little. If Congress wants to exercise those powers, I have no doubt it can tell the President what time he has to get up in the morning. In the area of foreign affairs, they have very rarely exercised those powers, and normally, and perhaps wisely, they have followed executive leadership. I think Presidents have rarely done things in foreign affairs that were not popular and for which they could not get congressional support if they needed it. Sometimes they have chosen to get it, and sometimes they have chosen to do it on their own. So I would guess that the President probably did not need authority up to some point that would be difficult to say. Before then he had.

He continued:

> When I testified for Fulbright he asked me whether without the Gulf of Tonkin Resolution the President would have had the authority to do this sort of thing. I tried to avoid the question about four times, and he was insisting on an answer, so finally I said, "yes." I had, I guess, some reservations as to whether that answer was right. I wasn't about to say "No." I think you could defend either position. It seems to me that when you get the country as involved as we were in Vietnam,

[70] CRS Interview with Nicholas Katzenbach, Nov. 7, 1978.

by constitutional standards you really ought to have some congressional authority for it; probably constitutional and certainly political.

Katzenbach was also asked whether there should have been further action by Congress, after the Gulf of Tonkin Resolution, with respect to approving the war. He replied that the President "was very unhappy about the Gulf of Tonkin Resolution . . . he thought it gave him more authority than he wanted. He wanted Congress with him. He was constantly saying, 'Let me go back. I want Congress to affirm this. I want Congress to redo this'. . . . He was pleased when he got it, because he never intended to use it. Then when he started to use it, he was very concerned about having that much authority and very concerned about the fact that Congress was dumping the whole problem in his lap." Katzenbach said that he advised the President not to seek further action by Congress. "If they [Congress] wanted to take it [the resolution] back, they could take it back . . . they could have repealed it. . . . I don't have any question of the authority of Congress to tell the President to get out of there [Vietnam] day before yesterday." "I would suppose that if they had simply rescinded the resolution that that would have been all that would have been required."

Katzenbach was asked what authority the President would have if the resolution were rescinded. Would it be "simply authority to withdraw?" "Yes, I suppose so," he replied.

Finally, Katzenbach was asked whether he still believed that the Gulf of Tonkin Resolution was the functional equivalent of a declaration of war. He replied:

> Absolutely, absolutely. I guess people have never understood what I was trying to say. I thought I said very clearly that under the Constitution, if you are really going to get that heavily involved with . . . a war, that it is not something the President ought to do on his own. He ought to have the authority of Congress to do it. . . . The form, "declaration of war," doesn't seem to me to be particularly important as a form. What is important is that both houses of Congress authorize the President to do this; that they participate in that very important basic decision. That is what the Constitution requires. . . . The Constitution . . . says that on decisions this important both houses of Congress should act, and they did. That is why I said it was the functional equivalent of war. I still believe it.[71]

After completing its national commitments hearings in mid-September 1967, the Foreign Relations Committee met several times in executive session to discuss and revise the resolution. Toward

---

[71] In testimony before Congress in 1970 on proposed war powers resolutions, Katzenbach commented at some length on the constitutional aspects of the Vietnam war and the Gulf of Tonkin Resolution. Among other things, he said that "Congress does have the clear constitutional right to participate in decisions to use force in a major and prolonged war and, absent congressional authorization, the President has no authority to do so on his own." Without the authority of the Gulf of Tonkin Resolution, he said, "the President could not, in my judgment, have constitutionally deployed combat troops to Vietnam. . . ." He also reiterated his opinion that the Gulf of Tonkin Resolution was the "functional equivalent to that participation of Congress contemplated by the Constitution in giving Congress power to declare war." U.S. Congress, House, Committee on Foreign Affairs, Hearings before the Subcommittee on National Security Policy and Scientific Developments, *Congress, The President, and the War Powers*, 91st Cong., 2d sess. (Washington, D.C.: U.S. Govt. Print. Off., 1970), pp. 299–324 at p. 302.

the end of October, in an effort to respond to criticisms of the original resolution, the committee staff drafted two alternative revisions which were placed before the members at an executive session on November 1. One provided for the addition of language that "commitment" was the promise to another country of using U.S. forces and/or "other resources" "either immediately or upon the happening of certain events."

In a lengthy discussion at the November 1 meeting, Fulbright took the position that the committee should complete action on the resolution and make its report, but that he did not expect to call up the resolution for debate in the Senate until the next session of Congress in 1968. "This, after all," he said, "is not a legislative act, it is an educational gesture for the benefit of the Senate and the Executive. . . . This business of these people going around and making fine speeches and then coming and saying it is a commitment, I just want to get it out of their minds that it is a commitment."[72] "When you have officials going out and saying we have a new doctrine at Honolulu or something on the Asian Doctrine which the Vice President, and others, made the statement that we are committed to bringing the Great Society to Southeast Asia and everyone asked what does this mean, this is the type of thing we are getting at."

Fulbright was challenged by Lausche, who argued that in the midst of the war was not an appropriate time to be challenging the legality or constitutionality of the President's use of troops in Vietnam. He said he would support a resolution provided it contained a provision stating specifically that the Gulf of Tonkin Resolution gave the President that authority.

Fulbright, replying to Lausche's comment about the timing of the resolution, said that "if you don't do these things when the matter is critical and on the public's mind then you don't do it at all. If you don't do it now it will be absolutely forgotten."

Hickenlooper, the senior Republican on the committee, said that he was "unhappy" about the resolution. He favored the idea, but was concerned about finding better language.

Aiken, another senior Republican, was concerned that the resolution would be defeated in the Senate. "[I]f it goes to the floor and comes up for action next spring it is going to be put on the basis of are you for the boys who are fighting and dying in Vietnam or are you for Hanoi, and it will be defeated by a four to one vote and that would undo much of the good which the resolution itself had done." "I have seen so many times," he added, "when a resolution or a bill has done much more good than its passage would do, and I am not sure but what we have got one of those here." Aiken said that the President had "grossly abused" his power, but that "I don't know how I can stop him. He is President, [and] you can't stop him until next November. . . ."

Republicans Cooper and Case also had reservations about the resolution. Cooper was concerned about finding better language, and thought that the resolution as originally introduced would unduly restrict the President. In addition, he thought it should re-

[72] U.S. Congress, Senate, Committee on Foreign Relations, unpublished executive session transcript, Nov. 1, 1967. Quotations used here are from this transcript.

quire congressional approval not just to use troops in combat but to deploy them in a foreign country where, as in Vietnam, they could become progressively involved in belligerent activities.

Case favored the idea of a resolution but believed that the committee had not adequately considered the issues involved, especially the effect of a resolution on the conduct of foreign policy. The "real issue," he said, was the President's asserted authority, whether or not there is a "commitment," to deploy and use the Armed Forces as he chooses. Because the resolution provided only for national commitments and not for the deployment of forces, it did not address that central problem. For these reasons, Case proposed that the committee should not act on the resolution until after additional hearings, adding that he did not think that the hearings had built "in the public mind enough of a base for effective action."

Morse strongly disagreed with Case, saying "I think you are just as wrong as you can be. The public is crying for this committee to stand up to its responsibility."

Fulbright responded to Case and Cooper by saying that the "practical situation" was that he did not know how much longer Congress would stay in session in 1967. But if the committee did not wish to approve the resolution, "and if the Committee doesn't wish to play a part in the formulation of policy, of course, that is its right. We can leave it all up to the President if we want to." That, he added, would be the result of not challenging Katzenbach's interpretation that the "participation of Congress is obsolete" and that the President "can do as he pleases." "It seems to me his testimony alone compels us to take some action or to accept this interpretation which means this Senate has no part to play."

Other members of the committee who favored the resolution, including Symington and Pell, wanted to improve the language and to develop more of a consensus. Pell also thought that the resolution should be applied only to commitments to use the Armed Forces, and that the reference to "other resources" in the new draft should be dropped. He also questioned the meaning of the term "affirmative action" by Congress, and asked whether it meant "affirmative action afterward." Fulbright said he would not object to dropping "other resources." "Broadly speaking," he said, "no one will take [all of] the language. All I am saying is I don't think the United States ought to become involved in a major undertaking in the foreign field without participation of Congress, and this is a challenge which I think has arisen from the statement of Katzenbach and of the President himself. I don't think we ought to abdicate a part in it . . . the whole basis of our system is that the Congress has something to contribute, that we do not believe that an authoritarian government is the right kind of government, that the Executive should have a sole responsibility."

Sparkman, a senior Democrat on the committee who had supported the war, said that unless the resolution clearly did not apply to Vietnam it would be taken as critical of the war and of U.S. policy. "Everything that goes out of here [the committee] is going to be construed by the press as being critical of what we are doing there, and I think we ought to support them [U.S. forces] just as strongly as we can as long as we are in there and get out the best way we can as soon as we can."

On November 6, Chief of Staff Marcy sent a memorandum to the members of the committee along with a new draft resolution prepared by the staff that incorporated changes suggested at the meeting on November 1, a draft by Hickenlooper that was quite similar, and a draft by Cooper that was limited to congressional approval of the assignment of troops overseas. In the memorandum, Marcy said that the staff had drafted language for possible use in the committee report that would make it clear that the resolution applied only to future military commitments and would not affect existing commitments.[73]

The revised resolution as drafted by the staff and the Hickenlooper draft were quite similar, and the resolution that was finally passed by the committee was a combination of the two.[74]

On November 16, the committee met to consider the three alternative drafts. Most members preferred the staff draft or Hickenlooper's. Fulbright and others were opposed to Cooper's because it was limited to the providing of military assistance and assignment of forces overseas rather than the use of forces in a war. According to Fulbright, "the main thing we are after . . . is the responsibility of Congress in participating in a major decision of war."[75] Case, who supported Cooper, commented: "I think we have to decide whether we are going to deal with the question of whether the President is right or not to move troops in any number or massive numbers."

Lausche argued that the resolution was "the product of our involvement in South Vietnam," and offered an amendment to state specifically that it did not apply to the Vietnam war. Mansfield opposed the amendment, saying "I think we would be creating a hornet's nest where none is intended." Hickenlooper agreed, saying that the substance of the amendment could be included in the committee report. (No one supported the amendment, which was withdrawn by Lausche.)

---

[73] The copy of Marcy' memorandum that was consulted for this study was clipped inside the committee's copy of the unpublished transcript of the executive session of the Foreign Relations Committee on Nov. 11, 1967.

[74] In response to comments by Pell and others, the staff draft omitted reference to "other resources," thus limiting commitments to the use of the Armed Forces, whereas Hickenlooper's draft retained "other resources." The staff draft referred to committing the Armed Forces "to hostilities on foreign territory," whereas Hickenlooper's referred to committing forces "to foreign territory." Both drafts, as well as Cooper's, referred to future commitments, thus excluding existing commitments, but Hickenlooper also added the words, "pertaining to situations in which the United States is not already involved."

Both the staff draft and Hickenlooper's provided that there would have to be affirmative action by Congress "specifically intended to give rise to such commitment," thus clarifying Pell's question as to whether "affirmative action" referred to action before or after the fact.

The staff version also stated that a decision to commit forces would be made "in accordance with constitutional processes," which would require legislative as well as executive action. This was intended to cover treaties which provided that the U.S. would respond in accordance with its constitutional processes but did not define the term, thus giving the Executive the option of defining it as it saw fit.

In his draft, Cooper provided only for congressional approval by treaty, statute, or concurrent resolution, of the assignment of the Armed Forces outside of the U.S. for the purpose of giving military assistance or helping to defend any country. For his explanation of his draft, see his statement on pp. 28–29 of the committee report on the resolution, S. Rept. 90–797, *National Commitments*, Nov. 20, 1967.

[75] U.S. Congress, Senate, Committee on Foreign Relations, unpublished executive session transcript, Nov. 16, 1967.

The final vote on a combination of the staff draft and Hickenlooper's [76] was 16–0 (after a poll of absentees it was 19–0), and the committee reported the National Commitments Resolution to the Senate on November 20, 1967.[77]

This is the text of the National Commitments Resolution (Senate Resolution 187, 90th Congress) as approved by the Committee:

> Whereas the executive and legislative branches of the United States Government have joint responsibility and authority to formulate the foreign policy of the United States; and
>
> Whereas the authority to initiate war is vested in Congress by the Constitution: Now, therefore, be it
>
> *Resolved,* That a commitment for purposes of this resolution means the use of, or promise to a foreign state or people to use, the armed forces of the United States either immediately or upon the happening of certain events, and
>
> That it is the sense of the Senate that, under any circumstances which may arise in the future pertaining to situations in which the United States is not already involved, the commitment of the armed forces of the United States to hostilities on foreign territory for any purpose other than to repel an attack on the United States or to protect United States citizens or property properly will result from a decision made in accordance with constitutional processes, which, in addition to appropriate executive actions, require affirmative action by Congress specifically intended to give rise to such commitment.

In its report, the Foreign Relations Committee stated that "The purpose of the resolution is . . . an assertion of Congressional responsibility in any decision to initiate war as that responsibility is spelled out in Article I, Section 8, of the Constitution [the provision for Congress to declare war]." "Our country has come far toward the concentration in its national executive of the unchecked power over foreign relations, particularly over the disposition and use of the armed forces. . . . The prevailing view in the executive branch seems to be that the President has the authority to commit the country to war but that the consent of Congress is desirable and convenient." "The concentration in the hands of the President of virtually unlimited authority over matters of war and peace," the report concluded, "has all but removed the limits to executive power in the most important single area of our national life. Until they are restored the American people will be threatened with tyranny or disaster."

The report, observing that the Gulf of Tonkin Resolution "represents the extreme point in the process of constitutional erosion that began in the first years of this century," described the expansion of executive power and the steps that led to congressional acquiescence. In the case of the Gulf of Tonkin Resolution, it said, "there was a discrepancy between the language of the resolution and the intent of Congress. Although the language of the resolution lends itself to the interpretation that Congress was consenting in advance to a full-scale war in Asia should the President think it

[76] The major change was to drop Hickenlooper's reference to "other resources"; otherwise the language of the final resolution closely followed Hickenlooper's.

[77] Senate Rept. 90–797, *National Commitments,* Nov. 20, 1967.

necessary, that was not the expectation of Congress at the time. In adopting the resolution Congress was closer to believing that it was helping to prevent a large-scale war by taking a firm stand than it was to laying the legal basis for the conduct of such a war. . . . In adopting a resolution with such sweeping language, however, Congress committed the error of making a *personal* judgment as to how President Johnson would implement the resolution when it had a responsibility to make an *institutional* judgment, first as to what any President would do with so great an acknowledgment of power, and, second, as to whether, under the Constitution, Congress had the right to grant or concede the authority in question." (emphases in original)

In conclusion, the committee report recommended that in considering future resolutions involving the use of the Armed Forces, Congress should take the following steps:

(1) debate the proposed resolution at sufficient length to establish a legislative record stating the intent of Congress;

(2) use the words *authorize* or *empower* or such other language as will leave no doubt that Congress alone has the right to authorize the initiation of war and that, in granting the President authority to use the armed forces, Congress is granting him power that he would not otherwise have; (emphasis in original)

(3) state in the resolution as explicitly as possible under the circumstances the kind of military action that is being authorized and the place and purpose of its use; and

(4) put a time limit on the resolution, thereby assuring Congress the opportunity to review its decisions and extend or terminate the President's authority to use military force.

On the same day (November 16, 1967) that it approved the National Commitments Resolution, the Foreign Relations Committee, as will be seen, approved, by the same unanimous vote, a resolution sponsored by Mansfield and co-sponsored by about half of the Senate, urging the Johnson administration to take the Vietnam dispute to the United Nations.

In a statement in the Senate that same day, Fulbright said that he did not intend at that time to press for action on the National Commitments Resolution, but that it was of "fundamental importance to every Senator who takes seriously his duties in the field of foreign relations"[78] to study the resolution and the committee report.

Congressional Criticism Intensifies

Beginning in late September 1967, there was a barrage of other congressional criticism and proposals to control and end the war and to assert Congress' war power. So much was happening, in fact, that the State Department instituted a daily report to the White House on "Congressional Criticism and Action."[79]

Case, Morton and Cooper pressed their opposition. On September 26, Case repeated his earlier charge that the President's handling

[78] *CR*, vol. 113, p. 33139.

[79] These reports, located in the Department of State, Lot File 70 D 207, began on Sept. 20, 1967 and continued until Jan. 25, 1968.

of the war had produced a "crisis of confidence" springing from a "growing conviction" in Congress and the public that the administration was not telling the truth—"that the administration's continuing assurances of progress in Vietnam simply do not square with the cold fact that toward our basic objective—that of creating an independent self-governing society supported by its citizens—there has been no significant progress at all." "Recently," Case added, this "clash between administration words and deeds" had also involved bombing policy, and he cited the fact that testimony by McNamara that air attacks on North Vietnamese ports would not be an effective means of stopping infiltration had been followed by airstrikes against targets in two of the three major ports.[80]

Case also sharply criticized the President for his "perversion" of the Gulf of Tonkin Resolution. He said that the resolution had been presented to Congress "in an atmosphere of emergency," and that Members of Congress had been "given specific assurance" that the resolution "was not intended to grant the unlimited sanction which, stretched to their ultimate, the words could be taken to convey." Yet, the President had used the resolution to justify sending half a million U.S. forces to Vietnam, bombing the North, and turning the war "into a largely American war with no end in sight." "[T]he President," Case said, "has done more than to squander his credibility; he has dealt a grievous blow at the process by which we have arrived at the expression of national unity in the face of international crises since the Second World War. The 'sense of Congress' resolution has served an invaluable purpose in this respect under President Truman, President Eisenhower, and President Kennedy. But President Johnson's perversion of the Tonkin Gulf resolution has so undermined the mutual confidence and trust upon which this technique was built that its future utility may have been irreparably compromised."

Case, a member of the Foreign Relations Committee, who was known as a well-informed, responsible Republican, had voted for the Gulf of Tonkin Resolution and had supported the war until 1967, and his criticism of the President and of the war produced a strong reaction. In the two-hour Senate debate following his speech, he was attacked, by prearrangement with the White House, by Mansfield and Dirksen, as well as by Long, Lausche, and McGee.[81] Mansfield said that he was "surprised at the vehemence" of Case's attacks on the President and at placing all of the blame on the President for something that Congress had also been responsible for. Moreover, he said that although he was "not happy" about the Gulf of Tonkin Resolution or U.S. involvement in Vietnam, he thought that rather than argue about the past, the impor-

---

[80] *CR*, vol. 113, pp. 26699 ff.

[81] At the Tuesday Lunch that day (September 26), the President asked Rostow, "Walt, did you get the information to Senator Dirksen and Senator Mansfield? They are battling with Senator Case today." Rostow replied that he had. The President also asked Katzenbach whether he had collected information on the Gulf of Tonkin Resolution. "I want the opinions and procedures on this." Johnson Library, Tom Johnson's Notes on Meetings, Notes of the meeting of the President with McNamara, Katzenbach, Helms, Rostow and Christian, Sept. 26, 1967. For Katzenbach's response to Case's arguments, see his 25-page paper, "A Response to Senator Case's Attack on the Administration's Handling of Vietnam," no date, Johnson Library, NSF NSC History, which was transmitted to the President by Rostow on Oct. 10, 1967.

tant question was: "How do we get out and how do we get out under honorable circumstances?"

Dirksen, too, argued that Congress knew what it was approving when it passed the resolution, and that Members "ought not to complain afterwards if the language rises up and hits them in the face."

Stennis asserted that it was a "grievous error" to continue to debate the Gulf of Tonkin Resolution. This, he said, "unintentionally gives comfort, encouragement and hope to the enemy. While I did not say 'aid,' in a sense it amounts to that. . . ."[82] Rather, "we should support a policy that will bring this war to an end upon honorable terms just as quickly as possible."

Case agreed with Stennis that rather than talking about how the U.S. got into the war, the Senate should consider what to do about it. But, he added, "This discussion of the Tonkin Gulf resolution was not as to whether its words were understood at that time, or whether it should have been adopted at that time. . . . It was a protest against the misuse of the language, currently, by the President and by the administration, to shut off debate, and to say to Congress, 'You gave me complete authority, and you have no right to question what is going on now.'"

Long of Louisiana, the Senate Democratic whip, and Lausche, a Democrat from Ohio, who was a member of the Foreign Relations Committee, also attacked Case for giving "comfort" to the enemy.

Case, the *New York Times* reported, "paced back and forth across the center aisle, pounding on desks as he responded to the criticism."[83]

Case's views were also attacked by Wayne Morse and Gruening, the only two Senators who voted against the Gulf of Tonkin Resolution. Morse argued that "there never was anything obscure or misleading about the language of the Tonkin Gulf resolution," and that it was "unfair to criticize the sincerity, the dedication, and the motivation of the President of the United States in offering the Tonkin Gulf resolution." "Every Senator who voted for this resolution," he said, "is just as responsible for what has been done under it as the President. . . ."

Gaylord Nelson, a liberal Democrat from Wisconsin who had been very concerned about the apparently unlimited approval of the use of Presidential use of force provided by the Gulf of Tonkin Resolution, and had questioned Fulbright about it during Senate debate on the resolution in 1964,[84] agreed with Case about the

---

[82] To give "aid and comfort to the enemy" is language that is generally considered to define "treason."

[83] *New York Times*, Sept. 27, 1967.

[84] See pt. II of this study, pp. 323–324, 327–328. During the 1964 debate on the resolution, Fulbright said in reply to Nelson that although he thought it would be "very unwise under any circumstances to put a large land army on the Asian continent," he did not know what the limits were of the action that could be taken under the terms of the resolution. He added that he thought the resolution would help to deter the Communists. Moreover, he did not believe that the resolution "would substantially alter the President's power to use whatever means seems appropriate under the circumstances." In a private conversation, Fulbright told Nelson, according to an account by Senator McGovern, who was present, that the resolution was "'harmless'"—"that we had to help Johnson against Goldwater. We were just backing the President on his Tonkin response, not giving him a blank check for war." Nelson proposed an amendment to declare that Congress supported the efforts of the President to take the Vietnam problem to the U.N. and approved the President's statement that the U.S. did not want to expand the war and would "respond to provocation in a manner that is 'limited and fitting,'" and that it was the "sense of Congress that, except when provoked to a greater response, we should continue

misuse of the resolution. "It is rather ironic now," he said, "to see how many otherwise responsible and thoughtful people have been 'taken in' by the line that Congress did in fact by its Tonkin vote authorize this whole vast involvement in Vietnam. The fact is neither Congress nor the Administration thought that was the meaning of Tonkin. . . ."

Javits joined the debate, arguing, as he had for some time, that the Gulf of Tonkin Resolution was obsolete and that Congress should pass a new resolution to "give Members of Congress an opportunity to assert the way they believe this matter should be handled now." He predicted that the President "would get about as big a majority on a new resolution as he got on the old one. But he would get a much more unified country."

Several days later, Javits returned to this subject.[85] The question, he said, was whether the U.S. commitment to South Vietnam should continue to be unlimited. He said he thought the U.S. had interests in Vietnam "that are worth fighting for," but its commitment should be limited by the extent to which South Vietnam can help itself." If the South Vietnamese were not willing to help themselves, "then we have got to consider disengaging. . . ."

The Gulf of Tonkin Resolution, Javits said, was "no longer germane to the situation we face today," and Congress should enact a new resolution defining U.S. objectives and placing both scale and time limits on the U.S. commitment in Vietnam "conditioned on self-help." In a colloquy with Fulbright, he said he was working on drafting such a resolution. Fulbright said that Javits' new resolution "would be most helpful" if it did nothing more than to clarify U.S. objectives. "I can assure the Senator that the committee is very much interested in anything he or any other Senator has to propose in this connection. I think it is high time we think about it." (Javits did not introduce a new resolution.)

Republican Thruston Morton also announced his opposition to the war. In a speech before the National Committee of Business Executives for Peace in Vietnam on September 27, 1967, he told the group, "The last three years have witnessed a disastrous decline in the effectiveness of American foreign policy. The root cause of the trouble is the bankruptcy of our position in Vietnam." But, he added, "If the President has been mistaken, so have I. In early 1965 when the President began to escalate the war, I supported the increased American military involvement. I was wrong!" "I have grave doubts today that any military action, then or now, would have decisively influenced the conflict."[86]

"The Americanization of the conflict in Vietnam," Morton said, "has created a kind of myopia that prevents the administration from effectively coping with major problems elsewhere. The number one priority of United States foreign policy must be to reach an accord with the Soviet Union . . . that will prevent holocaust, and

---

to attempt to avoid a direct military involvement in the Southeast Asia conflict." Fulbright said that the amendment would frustrate the President's purpose and that he could not accept it. Nelson agreed to withdraw the amendment after offering it, in return for a colloquy on the Senate floor during which Fulbright would say that he did not object to the amendment, which he thought was an "accurate reflection . . . of the President's policy," but that he could not accept it.

[85] *CR*, vol. 113, pp. 28852–28854.

[86] The text of the speech is in *ibid.*, p. 27131.

permit peaceful progress, however bitterly competitive. Vietnam stands in the way!"

"In Europe a revolution of independence challenges American initiative, but Vietnam stands in the way. In Latin America a revolution of rising population and rising expectations threatens the future of our own continent. More imagination and energy must be devoted to these areas—*vital to our national interest*—but Vietnam stands in the way. [emphasis in original]

"On our domestic front, apprehension and misunderstanding of our involvement in Southeast Asia are contributing to a dangerous political polarization. Extremists of the left and right are poised to destroy our basic social fabric, while men of reason are reduced to answering 'after Vietnam.'"

The "basic mistake" in U.S. policy, Morton said, was "failure to give proper emphasis to the political nature of the war," but a "political victory may well be out of reach."

"I am convinced," he concluded, "that unless we gradually and, if necessary, unilaterally reduce the scope of our military involvement we may well destroy the very society we sought to save. The President has said the war 'is worth the price.' There is absolutely no indication that the Vietnamese agree.

"We must decide without delay on a course of political and diplomatic action that offers some hope of settlement. We must make it crystal clear to the American people that there is no military solution in Vietnam. We must put an immediate ceiling on further U.S. military action and open up every possible avenue toward negotiations."

Morton suggested the following six steps:

(1) An immediate cessation of all bombing of North Vietnam.

(2) An end to all search and destroy missions in South Vietnam.

(3) A gradual concentration of efforts to secure the coastal and population centers of South Vietnam.

(4) Increased pressure upon the Saigon Government to negotiate and institute widespread reform.

(5) An internal and regional settlement through an all-Asia peace conference.

(6) The issuance of a statement to Hanoi and the world that the United States seeks an appropriate response to its unilateral disengagement.

Later that day, in the daily State Department memorandum to the President on congressional criticism and actions, Katzenbach said that he was "having prepared talking points to answer Morton's speech, which I will get to Ev Dirksen tonight for his possible use tomorrow."[87]

After Morton's speech, the President called him down to the White House where, according to Morton, "he really twisted my arm." "He gave me a long lecture on how wrong I was and how vital it was for our country and its position of leadership in the world that we see this thing through in Vietnam."[88] During the

[87] U.S. Department of State, Lot File 70 D 207, Memorandum for the President from Katzenbach, "Congressional Criticism and Action, September 27, 1967."

[88] CRS Interview with Thruston Morton, Jan. 29, 1979.

conversation, Morton, who said that he and Johnson had become "quite good friends" over the years, told Johnson that he was not sure he was going to run for re-election in 1968. Johnson, he said, replied: "I'm not sure I'm going to run again."

In an interview some years later, Morton said that, despite his break with administration policy on Vietnam, Johnson asked him, "Who have you got on your staff that you've got to take care of?" Morton named one person he would like to help, and Johnson replied that he knew him, and that he had a Republican vacancy "on the Federal Power Commission and would appoint him."[89]

In an article on "The 'Wobble' on Capitol Hill," *Washington Post* Reporter Don Oberdorfer said that because of Morton's "reputation as a political weathervane and the forthrightness of his confession of error," his reversal was "an instant sensation," but that it was not unique. It reflected the fact that during the summer and fall of 1967 "millions of American voters—along with many religious leaders, editorial writers and elected officials—appeared to be changing their views about the war."[90]

On October 2, Morton's colleague, John Sherman Cooper, again advocated the unconditional cessation of bombing and said he favored action by the U.N. to reconvene the Geneva Conference and begin negotiations. If a bombing halt did not lead to negotiations, Cooper said, it should be continued nevertheless, and U.S. military action should be confined to South Vietnam in order to "reverse the present dangerous expansion of the war" and bring about eventual negotiations.[91] Cooper's speech was followed by comments from Mansfield, Fulbright, Pell, Morton, Javits and Percy supporting his position, and comments in opposition by some of his fellow Republicans, including Kuchel of California, who was the minority whip, Miller of Iowa, Thurmond of South Carolina, George Murphy of California and Peter H. Dominick of Colorado, as well as by Gale McGee of Wyoming, one of the most articulate and active proponents of the President's Vietnam policy on the Democratic side.

Percy said that the war was dividing Americans and causing them to lose confidence in the President. In his attacks on his critics the President "failed to understand that widespread dissent indicates something may be wrong with this policy, rather than with his critics." In addition to this failure (the seventh on a list of seven), the President had failed in six other ways:

> First is his failure to persuade the South Vietnamese Government to institute truly democratic reforms which could win the support of the people of their own country.
>
> Second is his failure to persuade the South Vietnamese Army to carry its rightful share of the combat, so that our American men will not have to bear the heaviest burden of the fighting by themselves.
>
> Third is his failure to persuade our other Asian allies to participate substantially in the military, economic, psychological, and diplomatic tasks confronting us in Vietnam. Further, he has been unable to persuade a single country in Western Europe to provide any meaningful help or support.

---

[89] *Ibid.*
[90] Don Oberdorfer, "The 'Wobble' on Capitol Hill," *New York Times Magazine,* Dec. 17, 1967.
[91] *CR*, vol. 113, pp. 27441 ff.

> Fourth is his failure to pursue every possibility for negotiations leading to a settlement of the war.
>
> Fifth is his failure to learn from experience that every U.S. escalation is matched by the enemy and only brings more casualties.
>
> Sixth is his failure to recognize that bombing so near China has already caused the Chinese and the Soviets to massively increase their military role in support of Hanoi. . . .

At the end of Percy's speech, McGee, who questioned him at length about each of these seven statements, argued that "the real issue at stake" was protecting eastern Asia from the Chinese. "The Vietnam question," he said, "is incidental. It happened to happen. It could have happened in half a dozen other places."

"The fact we come down to," McGee concluded, "is that as we assess the picture in Southeast Asia, as we weigh the alternatives that confront us, there is very little wiggling room where rational men have to go. We may disagree . . . on carrying out a particular aspect, but the basis is there, the direction is there, the concept of limiting this conflict is there, and the wish to end it and to somehow bring it to a close pervades everywhere. The disagreements are in the methods.

"I suspect we are living in a time where wars can never be won but can be lost. . . . The old cliches about victory and defeat no longer have meaning and no longer apply because you have to keep your priorities and objectives on what the main goals are. Our main goal is a more peaceful world.

"I believe what we seek to help to do in Southeast Asia is achieve the chance that we will move a little closer to that kind of opportunity. Mr. Lee Kuan Yew [the Prime Minister of Singapore, who supported U.S. policy], stated it better when he said: 'If you Americans succeed in standing firm in Vietnam, Southeast Asia will be closer to stability than at anytime during this century.'"[92]

Following his speech in the Senate on October 2, Percy introduced a resolution (Senate Resolution 173 of the 90th Congress) on October 5 calling for a greater Asian contribution to the war.[93] The resolution was cosponsored by a bipartisan group of 16 Republicans and 5 Democrats, including 5 critics of the war (Democrats Clark and Ribicoff, and, in addition to Percy, Republicans Hatfield, Javits, and Morton).[94]

---

[92] On Oct. 18, 1967, Prime Minister Lee Kuan Yew of Singapore, visiting the U.S. for the first time since he led Singapore's successful drive for independence in 1965, said in talks in Washington with officials of the Executive and Members of Congress that the North Vietnamese would move toward a negotiated settlement only when convinced of U.S. determination, but would probably wait in any event until after the 1968 U.S. elections. *New York Times*, Oct. 19, 1967.

[93] *CR*, vol. 113, p. 28038. The resolution provided:

"(a) The Armed Forces of the United States should not continue to bear an ever-increasing proportion of the fighting in Vietnam; and

"(b) The non-Communist nations of Asia, including South Vietnam, should contribute substantially more manpower and resources to share the military, diplomatic, economic and psychological tasks in Vietnam; and

"(c) The President of the United States should move with greater determination to obtain commitments of such manpower and resources in support of the effort in Vietnam."

[94] Other sponsors were: Wallace F. Bennett (R/Utah), J. Caleb Boggs, (R/Del.), Daniel B. Brewster (D/Md.), Harry F. Byrd, Jr. (D/Va.), Frank Carlson (R/Kan.), Norris Cotton (R/N. Hamp.), Paul J. Fannin (R/Ariz.), Clifford P. Hansen (R/Wyom.), Roman L. Hruska (R/Nebr.), Len B. Jordan, (R/Idaho), James B. Pearson (R/Kan.), Winston L. Prouty (R/Vt.), Jennings Randolph (D/W. Va.), Hugh Scott (R/Penn.), Abraham A. Ribicoff (D/Conn.), Herman E. Talmadge (D/Ga.), Strom Thurmond (R/S.C.) and Milton R. Young (R/N. Dak.).

The war, Percy said, "has become our war . . . American men and money are being sucked into the quicksand of Vietnam in extravagant numbers, and the end is nowhere in sight."

Senate Republican Leader Dirksen commented that Percy's resolution was "full of mischief."[95]

Both Deputy Secretary of Defense Nitze, acting at McNamara's direction, and Assistant Secretary of State William Bundy, told Percy that the resolution "might have a significant adverse effect on the internal political situations of these [Asian] countries, since it could well be interpreted as U.S. pressure." Percy said that he did not intend to press for hearings or a vote, and would consult further with the Executive if and when he did.[96]

At a White House Tuesday Luncheon on October 4, the President asked Rusk, McNamara and Rostow whether any of them had talked to Percy about his resolution. McNamara and Rostow "said they had discussed his resolution, pointing out the flaws in it." McNamara added: "Percy has a nasty resolution, but he says he wants to help us. He is saying that the Johnson Administration will not listen to him." The President replied: "Tell Percy we will listen to him at any time and any place. There certainly is no doubt about our willingness to have him heard."[97]

On October 3, Senator Symington proposed that the U.S. should cease all military operations in North and South Vietnam and all reinforcements as a way of testing the interest of the Communists in a negotiated settlement.[98] If fighting continued, the U.S. would resume military operations. In addition, the Government of South Vietnam should announce its willingness to negotiate a settlement and to provide amnesty.

Symington wanted restrictions removed on U.S. bombing of the North, and believed that unless the military could be given greater freedom of action, the U.S. should find a way to withdraw its forces.[99]

The administration, as could be expected, reacted very unfavorably to Symington's proposal. Various officials from the State and Defense Departments met with him to try to persuade him of the error of his ways, and papers opposing the proposal were sent to

---

[95] *New York Times*, Oct. 6, 1967.

[96] Johnson Library, NSF Country File, Vietnam, William Bundy, "Late Note for the President's Evening Reading," Oct. 4, 1967, attached to transmittal memorandum from Rostow to the President, Oct. 4, 1967.

[97] Johnson Library, Tom Johnson's Notes of Meetings, Notes of meeting of the President with Rusk, McNamara, Rostow and Christian, Oct. 4, 1967.

[98] *CR*, vol. 113, pp. 28090–28091.

[99] In a private conversation with former Presidential Assistant Jack Valenti several weeks after his speech, Symington said he thought the U.S. had made three major mistakes in Vietnam: first, "underestimating the durability of the Viet Cong," second, the "theory of gradualism [which] has consistently underestimated the Viet Cong in Hanoi," and, third, "overestimating the concept of nationhood of [South] Vietnam. They couldn't last 24 hours without us and it is a matter of common knowledge that most of the top leaders are crooks." Johnson Library, Office Files of Marvin Watson, Note to Watson from Valenti, Dec. 14, 1967, enclosing summary of his discussion with Symington on December 13.

In the Fulbright Papers in the University of Arkansas Library, Series 48, Box 44, there is also a statement by Symington on his position on Vietnam 1965–1967 which he prepared after a trip to Asia in September 1967. This is attached to a letter from Symington to Fulbright, Oct. 26, 1967, asking for his comments on the statement.

the President by the State Department (Katzenbach) and the JCS.[100]

In his memorandum to the President, Katzenbach called Symington's proposal "a clumsily formulated hawk-dove position that we will see more of as frustration with the prolonged and limited effort makes allies of all those whose primary interest is a quick end to the war." "The odds," he said, "are overwhelmingly against DRV [North Vietnam] acceptance of negotiations as a result of such a public offer, with its implied ultimatum and time limits." "The only purpose of formulating cessation of military actions in this way would be to justify major escalation."

On October 3, 1967, after being supplied information by the executive branch at the direction of the President, Senate Majority Leader Dirksen delivered an impassioned speech in defense of U.S. policy.[101] Earlier in the day, Kuchel, the Republican whip, who had recently returned from Vietnam, argued that progress was being made and that dissension in the U.S. was hurting the U.S. war effort.[102] After Kuchel's speech, Rusk called to congratulate him for his "fine work."[103]

Without referring to specific individuals, Dirksen took issue with proposals for a bombing halt and the end of search-and-destroy tactics, and argued that Congress should not attempt to interfere with the President's conduct of the war. Demeaning criticism of the President, he said, would "demean the prestige of this Republic."

Dirksen also defended the role of the U.S. in the war as being necessary for American security. "There is no holding line between Saigon and Singapore," he asserted, "and when you are at one of the clogged water courses that I am confident the Soviets are going to try to control . . . control Panama, control Singapore, the two ends of the Gulf of Aden and Suez, and, you have just about command of the world."

Pounding on his desk "until his curly grey hair shook in all directions,"[104] Dirksen declared that Vietnam represented "our outside security line." "Let freedom slip and it begins to slip everywhere. We remember that Churchill said he was not made the King's first minister to preside over the liquidation of the British Empire. Let me say that I was not made a Senator to preside over the liquidation of the holy fabric of freedom."

At the conclusion of Dirksen's speech, Case, one of the targets of his own party leader's remarks, rose to say that "Just as it was proper for the Senator from Illinois to call to the attention of all of us our responsibility not to weaken the cause of our Nation, the cause of freedom in the world, so I think it is equally important for all of us to meet our responsibility, when we disagree with the conduct of affairs by our Government, to state that disagreement

---

[100] See U.S. Department of State, Lot File 70 D 207, Memorandum to the President from Katzenbach, "Congressional Criticism and Action, October 3," Oct. 4, 1967. Katzenbach's memorandum to the President on Oct. 19, 1967, "Responses to Senator Symington's Proposal of October 2," is in the State Department Central File, Pol 27 Viet S. The JCS paper is in the Johnson Library, NSF Country File, Vietnam, attached to a transmittal memorandum to the President from Rostow, Oct. 19, 1967.

[101] *CR*, vol. 113, pp. 27576–27584.

[102] *Ibid.*, pp. 27442 ff.

[103] U.S. Department of State, Lot File 70 D 207, Memorandum for the President from Katzenbach, "Congressional Criticism and Action, October 3," Oct. 4, 1967.

[104] *New York Times*, Oct. 14, 1967.

as clearly and distinctly as possible, whether in time of peace or in time of war."

Fulbright also challenged Dirksen's statement, saying that "the pursuit of this war under the conditions that exist is more likely designed to liquidate the holy fabric of freedom because of what could well be a war of indefinite tenure, indefinite existence, and possibly involving China." Vietnam, he said, was not essential to U.S. security, and was not worth the cost in money and lives. He added that he did not know what the answer was, but that there needed to be a resolution of the problem. He pressed Dirksen to describe and to justify the object of the war, and after a brief exchange Dirksen sought to turn the question. "You have been quarreling for the last year about the conduct of the war," he told Fulbright. "What does the Senator want to do?" Fulbright replied that he would like to have the Geneva Conference reconvened and to have the U.S. abide by the results. And so it went for nearly two hours, as "the principal defender and the principal critic of Administration policy in Vietnam, standing only three desks apart, clashed in a sometimes bristling argument over whether American security was at stake in Vietnam."[105]

According to accounts of Dirksen's speech, it was directed primarily at dissenting Republicans, and there was "historic irony" in the spectacle of the opposition leader defending the President from members of the opposition party.[106] More particularly, the speech was a reply to Morton "who is emerging as the most outspoken Republican critic of the Administration policy, as well as a personal rival for leadership of the Republican forces in the Senate,"[107] and "a tactical skirmish" by Dirksen "in a larger strategy to defend himself within the Republican Party and to maintain his own influence on the party's decisions."[108]

In a meeting of the Luncheon Group on October 4, 1967, the day after Dirksen's speech, the President said he told Dirksen, "we do not want to supplant South Vietnam but do want to support it. I told him that I want him to go out there and look at it from stem to stern."[109]

On October 9, 1967, Senator Hugh Scott, a moderate Republican of Pennsylvania and a former chairman of the Republican National Committee, who later succeeded Dirksen as the Republican leader of the Senate, gave a speech in the Senate in which he reiterated his support for U.S. policy in Vietnam and for the President as Commander in Chief.[110] "I believe it is imperative," he said, "that we not undermine the stature of the President as Commander in Chief and as the Nation's chief diplomat." The war, he added, "is

---

[105] *Ibid.* In a Senate speech on October 11, Fulbright made some additional comments on Dirksen's speech of October 3. See *CR*, vol. 113, pp. 28590 ff.

[106] *New York Times*, Oct. 4, 1967, and MacNeil, *Dirksen*, *op. cit.*, p. 301.

[107] *New York Times*, Oct. 4, 1967. In an interview some years later, Morton said that Dirksen was worried that he was going to run against him for the leadership post, but he never thought of doing so. CRS Interview with Thruston Morton, Jan. 29, 1979.

[108] MacNeil, *Dirksen*, p. 301. "What troubled the Republican moderates most was Dirksen's friendship with Lyndon Johnson, presumably the 1968 Democratic nominee for President, and his support of Johnson's Vietnam policies. One Republican Senator went so far as to say that if the Republican Party ever died, 'Ev Dirksen will have killed it.'" *Ibid.*, p. 303.

[109] Johnson Library, Tom Johnson's Notes of Meeting, Notes of the meeting of the President with Rusk, McNamara, Rostow and Christian, Oct. 4, 1967.

[110] *CR*, vol. 113, pp. 28203 ff.

not, and must not become a political issue, either between or within political parties."

Scott said that his views had not changed—a none-too-subtle reference to those, especially Republicans, and particularly Morton, whose positions had shifted. He still supported the nine-point statement of principles on Vietnam that he, Javits and Percy had developed in May 1967. But although he was opposed to a widening of the war, and supported "any honorable means to bring the aggressor to the conference table," he said that he thought the President was "pursuing the only course open to us," and that "disapproval of present action" was not "valid justification for attacks upon the President, especially in the light of the absence of alternative courses of action based on anything more substantial than a desire to get it over with and the hope that the other side will behave like good fellows."

Kuchel and John G. Tower (R/Tex.) praised Scott's speech. Case and Percy, who may have considered his remarks directed at them among others, engaged him in a brief colloquy but did not criticize him nor he them. Percy pointed out Scott's participation in the May 1967 statement of principles. Case inserted in the *Congressional Record* a statement by the Ripon Society, a private national Republican research and policy organization, based in Cambridge, Massachusetts, and composed of centrist/moderate young businessmen, professionals and academics, proposing an alternative Republican plan for ending the war.[111]

During this period—September and October of 1967—a number of other Members of Congress who had supported the war announced their support for steps to limit and end the war.[112] These included Democrats Al Ullman of Oregon, who had been the only Representative from Oregon who had consistently approved the President's position, Democrat Jerome Waldie of California, Democrat Claude Pepper of Florida, Democrat Morris Udall of Arizona.

Udall, a respected liberal who had supported the war even after it came under strong attack from the liberals, announced that he had been wrong, and that the U.S. should "start bringing American boys home and start turning this war back to the Vietnamese."[113] He proposed a cessation of bombing, enclaves for U.S. forces, and a negotiated settlement. "I refuse any longer," he said, "to accept a tortured logic which allows little mistakes to be admitted, but requires big ones to be pursued to the bitter end, regardless of their

---

[111] *Ibid.*, pp. 27916–27933. According to the proposal, which was published on Oct. 3, 1967 in the *Ripon Forum*, U.S. policy was misdirected. "Vietnam is largely a counterinsurgency war" which would take two million allied troops to fight successfully. Bombing of the North was a failure, and bombing of the Chinese railway into North Vietnam "will ultimately bring the Chinese into the war." Heavy bombing of Haiphong would lead to a confrontation with the Russians.

The alternative was to reduce bombing in the North, use U.S. forces to defend areas loyal to Saigon, and to reduce gradually the U.S. commitment by a three-phased "confederal strategy" by which, in contrast to the existing emphasis on centralized government in South Vietnam, local autonomy would be given, first to non-Communist groups who were able to maintain order in their areas of the country, second, to villages where there was both Communist and non-Communist leadership—thus splitting off local Communist groups from the hierarchy—and, third, extending recognition of local control "hard-core Viet Cong areas" as part of a program of national reconciliation.

[112] A survey of 205 Members of the House of Representatives conducted in late September by the Christian Science Monitor found that 43 of the 205 had changed from being wholehearted supporters to, "'more emphasis on finding a way out.'" Oberdorfer, "The 'Wobble' on Capitol Hill," cited above.

[113] *Ibid.*

cost in lives and in money. As a nation, let's not adopt the senseless psychology of the compulsive gambler at the race track. If he's lost a whole week's wages on some unfortunate nag, he ought to quit and go home, sadder but wiser. But no, he'll go to the bank, draw out his savings, mortgage his house and wipe out his children's chances for a college education, all in the vain hope he can recoup his losses. I think this is the direction we're headed in Vietnam."

On October 18, Udall sent the following letter to the President:[114]

> Dear Mr. President:
>
> I am a loyal Democrat who greatly admires your exceptional leadership and is deeply grateful for the many historic things you have accomplished for our country. Thus, this is, for me, a letter which is painful to write, containing a message I am sorry to have to send.
>
> After many months of careful and responsible deliberation, I have reluctantly but firmly concluded that our Vietnam policies are unwise and should be substantially modified. . . .
>
> Because the expression of my views may in some small measure add to the heavy burdens you already bear, I want you to know that I have acted in sorrow and in friendship. . . .
>
> Respectfully,
> Morris K. Udall

After talking to Udall at the President's request, Katzenbach reported that Udall had raised "some of the difficulties we foresaw in the speech he was planning, pointing out that it would get wide publicity. He said his speech was essentially the same as the proposals put forward by Senator Mansfield. Besides, it had been printed and 20,000 copies had been mailed to his constituents. I told him I still thought it was wrong, but it did appear, under the circumstances, that little could be done."[115]

The President also asked Rostow to analyze the speech. In a memorandum to the President on October 21, Rostow said that it was "the most politically effective statement I have yet seen for a policy of unilateral deescalation plus enclave, because he makes it personal and apparently—perhaps truly—sincere." Rostow added, however, that the speech was "based on factually false assumptions and arguments" (which he enumerated).[116]

Of all of the congressional changes of position on the war, perhaps the most significant politically was that of Representative (later Speaker) Thomas ("Tip") O'Neill, Democrat of Massachusetts. O'Neill, who held the seat previously held by John F. Kennedy, was a moderate-liberal, very close to Speaker McCormack, and, as a member of the House Rules Committee, he was considered to be a member of the inner circle in the House. He had supported the President and the war even though in his district in Boston and

[114] For location, see second footnote below.

[115] U.S. Department of State, Lot File 70 D 207, Memorandum to the President from Katzenbach, "Congressional Criticism and Action," Oct. 20, 1967.

[116] Johnson Library, NSF Country File, Vietnam, Rostow Memorandum to the President, Oct. 21, 1967, with attached copy of Udall's letter to the President, October 18.

Cambridge there were, in addition to strongly prowar elements, a number of active antiwar "academians," as he called them.

O'Neill's new position was stated without any fanfare in a newsletter mailed to his constituents in early September 1967. As he tells the story, "I sent about 150,000 copies to my district. The *Boston Globe* nor the *Boston Herald* never picked the story up. And so, one day in about September a reporter from the *Washington Star* is walking down through the room where newsletters are being printed to see if he can get some kind of story. And he picked an old one up off of the floor that gave my viewpoint. And he said, 'Gee, has this ever been used?' And that afternoon in the *Star* there was a front-page story, and it said, 'Member of the Establishment Splits with Leadership—Closest Friend to Speaker McCormack Leaves the Administration.'"

In the newsletter, O'Neill said he had come to these conclusions:[117]

> First, because peace is so crucial and the war so severe, we must avoid further escalation and attempt to bring the peacekeeping mechanisms of the United Nations into the conflict. . . .
>
> Second, in order to promote meaningful negotiations, we must stop the bombing of the North, and rely on explanations, not explosions, to bring our adversaries to the conference table.
>
> Third, in order to promote an Asian solution to what is essentially an Asian problem, we should deploy our troops in strategic enclaves throughout the South and encourage an expansion of democratic institutions within the government.

Like many other Members of Congress who were revising their views in the summer and fall of 1967, O'Neill had been troubled about the war for some time and had discussed the situation with a wide variety of people, including a daughter who was in college and some of her friends, and various civilian and military officials or former officials in the government. One was General Gavin, then president of a corporation in Boston, whose proposals for limiting the war he apparently found persuasive.[118]

According to O'Neill, several months before he sent the newsletter he talked with Senator Edward Kennedy, who urged him to re-examine his position on the war. He then arranged a series of private meetings with executive branch personnel, ranging in viewpoint from those who favored negotiations and ending the war to those who favored escalation.[119]

This is O'Neill's description:[120]

> I started making inquiries, assistant secretaries of State, General Shoup with the Marines—I used to play poker with

---

[117] Johnson Library, C.F. ND 19/CO 312, copy of O'Neill's "Report from Washington," Sept. 1967, attached to a memorandum to the President from Postmaster General Lawrence F. O'Brien, Sept. 29, 1967.

[118] Johnson Library, NSF Country File, Vietnam, Memorandum to Benjamin Read from John P. White, "Congressional Consultation with Congressman Thomas P. O'Neill," Oct. 20, 1967, reporting on a conversation of September 14, attached to a transmittal memorandum to the President from Rostow, Oct. 24, 1967.

[119] Johnson, Library, C.F. ND 19/C0 312, Memorandum to Postmaster General O'Brien from Claude Desautels (White House Congressional Liaison staff), Sept. 27, 1967, reporting on his conversation with O'Neill.

[120] CRS Interview with Speaker Thomas P. O'Neill, Jr., May 7, 1979. See also O'Neill's memoirs, *Man of the House* (New York: Random House, 1987).

him on occasion—and I said to him one night at the Army Engineers Club, "General, you know, the war's got me bitterly upset. I wonder if I've been on the right side of the thing." And he said, "I have just resigned. I've written a book and I'm coming out with why we shouldn't be in the Vietnam war." And then we sat down a couple of nights later and had supper before a poker game, and he told me his viewpoints of the war. . . .

I got a telephone call one night. It's a fellow from the CIA. And he says, "I'd like to have you come in and meet with a group of my friends." He says, "They're bitterly opposed to the war. Would you come to my house for supper?" So I went to his house for supper. . . . He had about 7 or 8 fellows there. And I said, "What did you send for me for?" "Well," he said, "we understand that you're making a study as to the war; that you're thinking of changing your viewpoint." I said, "Well, that's interesting. How did you know that?" And they said, "Well we have methods of knowing it." "Well, why do you want to see me?" "Well, we want you to know that we take the messages of the President of the United States and the administration's viewpoint and we deliver them to all of the CIA agencies around the world, and we get reports back—who's opposed to it, how they're opposed to it. Our messages never get to the desk of the President." I said, "I can't believe it, but what are you telling me for? I'm just a member of Congress." And they said, "Well, you're the closest person in the Congress to John W. McCormack. . . ." And I said, "I'm as close to John McCormack as to anybody. We understand each other. Our districts abut each other. But if I were to tell John McCormack about opposing the war, it would be like hitting my head against the wall. It's ridiculous. John McCormack wouldn't even accept a message like that." Well, anyway, to make a long story short, I probably told McCormack, I don't recall. But I knew I'd be wasting my time. But anyway, it was the combination of those things that turned me against the war. . . .

In June of 1967, O'Neill and his wife were visiting a daughter who was in the Foreign Service and was stationed in Malta.

Millie and I were in a restaurant, and there must have been 50 American Marines [from the Naval base] in the cocktail bar, and this fellow came in and he said, "I understand you're a Congressman from Massachusetts. I live down in Woods Hole down at the Cape." And I said, "Oh, is that so?" and he said, "Yes." I asked him a million questions about the war, and these kids are coming back from the war and they are totally disgusted. What the hell kind of war, are you fighting. You can't shoot until you're shot at. I've been there 19 months and I've been there 20 months. This was their feeling. They didn't know what they were fighting for. What are we over there for? What are we fighting for? In those days Malta was a Commonwealth island, and the British had a governor there and he had a big cocktail party. And I went to about four parties in a row. And the head of the [U.S. Mediterranean] fleet was there, the admiral of the fleet. . . . [H]e kicked the living hell out of the war—"We shouldn't be in the son of a bitch. We're not trying to win it." The only way that we can win this war, he says, is by an invasion, by knocking out the power plants in Hanoi and by mining the coast. "You've got to shut off the Chinese railroad. The supply lines. This is crazy. You're never going to win the war. We ought to get out of there." [121]

In an interview some years later O'Neill recounted what happened on the night the article about his change of position appeared in the *Washington Star* (an afternoon newspaper).[122]

[T]hat night I went out to play poker, which I did most of my adult life down here. It kept me out of trouble. . . . Well, I came in about 1 o'clock in the morning, put my car in the garage. I came upstairs and Eddie Boland, [a Democratic Representative from Massachusetts with whom O'Neill shared, a house] said, "Where the hell have you been? I've called all over town." I said, "For what?" He says, "The White House must have called 25 times. There's a Secret Service man sitting downstairs in the front office. How did you come in?" I said, "I came in through the garage." He said, "The Secret Service are waiting. You're supposed to call the White House no matter what time you get in." I said, "About what?" He said, "You didn't see the *Star*? Boy, the President is wild!" So anyway, I called the White House, and they said, "The President would like to see you at 9 o'clock in the morning."

I went over at 9 o'clock in the morning and I saw the President. And he said, "I've known you from the first day that you arrived here. You've been John McCormack's friend and Sam Rayburn's friend. You were in the "Board of Education," [informal afternoon gatherings of selected Members of Congress hosted by Speaker Rayburn] Mr. McCormack would bring you there. I don't mind the Ryans [William Fitts Ryan, D/N.Y., who opposed the war] and a few of those, but when a guy is as close as you leaves me like this, I am bitterly disappointed." And I said, "Hey, Mr. President. I made a complete study about this and I just think you're wrong. I feel as though I have to change." "You mean to tell me that you know more about this war, than I do? I'm briefed six times a day. You think that I didn't roll and toss all night and every night about the lives of those kids over there. I certainly do." And I said, "Hey, Mr. President, look it, I've gone all over this. I've talked to different people. I've talked to people who advise you and they go along with your policy but they tell me that you are wrong. . . ." And he said, "You believe in your heart that I'm wrong?" And I said, "I believe in my heart that you are wrong." "Well," he said, "I'm glad of that because I thought you did it for political reasons because the academians in your area had politically scared you." I said, "Hey, Mr. President, you've got the wrong guy. The academians have never been with me. I get elected in the back street. The academians aren't with Tip O'Neill. I just, in my heart and in my mind, feel we're fighting a war we can't win, not trying to win and why are we over there and nobody's giving us any help, and there's loss of life," and I went

---

[121] *Ibid.*
[122] *Ibid.*

> along the whole route. Well, I want you to know he said, "the first thing I'm going to look at every day is the CIA report from now on. I'm happy that you did it. One thing, I want you to do me a favor." I said, "What is it?" He said, "Tip, make no statements to the press. You know, I think I'm right, you think you're right." I said, "Hey, Mr. President, you know, I had to do what I did." He said, "Well, I'm afraid you may have started a snowball on me. I don't want the thing to gather momentum. A Tip O'Neill, he's part of the establishment; when he leaves, they're all going to start to leave. And you're wrong." I said, "Gee, Mr. President, I'm only speaking for myself. I'm not speaking for others. Let the others do what I did."

In a memorandum on September 27, reporting on a conversation with O'Neill, an experienced member of the White House Congressional Liaison staff stated: "there is no question in my mind that the various government spokesmen with whom he met privately convinced him that what he now advocates is the right position—stop the bombing, the use of the Security Council, etc." [123]

The memorandum added that O'Neill "went to great lengths to demonstrate that had he realized the importance that would be attached to it [the announcement in the newsletter], he, as a Democrat, would never have released such a letter. 'As you well know, I am a Democrat and I love the President as a brother.'"

At a Tuesday Luncheon on October 3, the President, referring to O'Neill's meetings with executive branch officials, said he was "astounded to find that there were several groups of people who were working to get Congressmen who are in agreement with our position to make a reassessment." According to reports, the President added, "it was the President's own people that were responsible for the change." [124]

On October 12, a group of 30 Representatives—27 Democrats (all liberals primarily from New York and California) and 3 Republicans—led by Representative William Fitts Ryan sent the President a letter urging him to stop bombing North Vietnam.[125] On October 31, Rusk met with the group, and in a report to the President the next day Katzenbach said: "All were opposed to our present Vietnam policy, but it became clear from the discussion that there was no unanimity as to why our policy was wrong or as to what type of policy should be substituted for the present one. While no doves were converted, they may well have come away from the

---

[123] Memorandum from Claude Desautels, cited above, attached to a memorandum to the President from Postmaster General Lawrence F. O'Brien, Sept. 29, 1967.

[124] Johnson Library, Tom Johnson's Notes of Meetings, Notes of meeting of the President with Rusk, McNamara, Rostow, Helms, and Christian, Oct. 3, 1967.

[125] Johnson Library, WHCF, Name File, "Ryan, William F." The three Republicans were: Daniel Button, Seymour Halpern and Theodore Kupferman, all of New York, and the 26 Democrats (in addition to Ryan) were: Jonathan B. Bingham (N.Y.), Frank J. Brasco (N.Y.), George E. Brown, Jr. (Calif.), Phillip Burton (Calif.), Jeffrey Cohelan (Calif.), John Conyers, Jr. (Mich.), Charles C. Diggs, Jr. (Mich.), John G. Dow (N.Y.), Don Edwards (Calif.), Leonard Farbstein (N.Y.), Donald M. Fraser (Minn.), Samuel N. Friedel (Md.), Jacob H. Gilbert (N.Y.), Edith Green (Ore.), Augustus F. Hawkins (Calif.), Joseph E. Karth (Minn.), Robert W. Kastenmeier (Wisc.), Robert L. Leggett (Calif.), Patsy T. Mink (Hawaii), Thomas M. Rees (Calif.), Henry S. Reuss (Wisc.), Benjamin S. Rosenthal (N.Y.), Edward R. Roybal (Calif.), James H. Scheuer (N.Y.), and Lester L. Wolff (N.Y.).

On that same day, *Life* magazine, which had strongly supported the war, proposed in an editorial that there should be a pause in the bombing of North Vietnam. The most important reason for a pause, the editorial said, "is to recapture support for the U.S. presence and commitment in Vietnam."

meeting with an increased realization of the fundamental determination of the U.S. Government to see the situation through in South Vietnam." [126]

That same day, Senator Brooke, a Republican of Massachusetts, who, it will be recalled, had gained considerable attention in the spring of 1967 when, after a trip to South Vietnam, he announced his support for the President's policies, proposed a reassessment of bombing, [127] said he hoped there could be a bombing halt, adding, "If the President has any valid reasons as to why there should not be a cessation of bombing, I think he should make those reasons crystal clear to the American people." Brooke also declared that no additional U.S. forces should be deployed "until South Vietnam has made a total commitment" to winning the war.

On October 11, 1967, the *New York Times* published a report on an article in the North Vietnamese Armed Forces newspaper by General Giap. The U.S., Giap said, had sought to capitalize on larger numbers of troops, mobility, and superior firepower, but had failed to do so and the war was stalemated. The U.S. had two choices, he said: to invade North Vietnam or to continue to escalate the war in the South with limited reinforcements. "As of now," Giap added, "they [the U.S.] have not finished making preparations for a new world war," but if the U.S. should invade North Vietnam, it would "meet with incalculable serious consequences." Additional U.S. reinforcements of 50,000 or 100,000 would not break the stalemate. Moreover, "The more the war is Americanized, the more disintegrated the puppet Saigon army and Administration becomes."

Giap also said that although the decisive factor was the strategy of wearing down the Americans through a protracted war, opposition to the war in the United States was a "valuable mark of sympathy."

The following day (October 12), the Speaker of the House of Representatives, Democrat John McCormack of Massachusetts, delivered what a reporter called "an emotional table-pounding speech . . . [that] drew a standing ovation from some 100 Representatives on the House floor." [128] Quoting Giap's comment in the *New York Times* about the "valuable mark of sympathy" represented by U.S. dissent, McCormack, "rolling the newspaper in his hand and pounding it on a table for emphasis," declared: "If I were one of those [dissenters], my conscience would be such that it would disturb me the rest of my life." U.S. opponents of the war, he said, were giving comfort to the enemy.

Efforts to Bolster Support for the War

By the end of September 1967, public and congressional support for the war was falling rapidly, and the President and those of his associates who remained committed to his policy, together with supporters in Congress and the public, were faced with the urgent need to prevent further disaffection and to bolster confidence and support.

---

[126] U.S. Department of State, Lot File 70 D 207, Memorandum for the President from Katzenbach, "Congressional Criticism and Action," Nov. 1, 1967.

[127] *New York Times*, Oct. 13, 1967.

[128] *Ibid.*, Oct. 12, 1967. For McCormack's speech, see *CR*, vol. 113, p. 28611.

Opinion surveys indicated that the trend toward disapproval of the conduct of the war and toward a polarization of attitudes was becoming even stronger. A *New York Times* survey of Governors and Members of Congress, reported on October 7, found that there was "increased sentiment for less military action and more negotiations." In addition, "A significant number of those interviewed reported a discernible polarization of Vietnam sentiment," with the "large middle group that formerly accepted the war tending to split into two vocal critical factions, one advocating every possible peace effort and the other an all-out offensive for victory."[129] More than two-thirds of those interviewed reported "rising criticism of the war as it is now being prosecuted, some of it from people who favor further intensification but the preponderance from those who want a more limited commitment or an end to the conflict."

According to the report, "many of the replies reflected discouragement that the investment of men and money did not seem to be achieving visible progress rather than any basic quarrel with the aims of the investment," but the "single specific factor most often cited as a basis for the shift of opinion against the war was the growing casualty list."

The *New York Times* report concluded that Vietnam posed a "serious problem" for the President and the Democrats in the 1968 election: "Unless the public sentiment shown by the survey changes materially in 1968, Mr. Johnson will clearly be running in the face of criticism from two directions: those who think his policy is too belligerent and those who do not think it is belligerent enough. Dwindling support can be expected between these two extremes."

On the day after the report on the *New York Times* survey, Gallup released his most recent poll on the question, *"Do you approve or disapprove of the way President Johnson is handling the situation in Vietnam?"*[130] which indicated a sharp drop in support since August:

[In percent]

	Approve	*Disapprove*	*No opinion*
August 1967	33	52	15
October 1967	28	57	15

[129] *New York Times*, Oct. 8, 1967.

[130] *Washington Post*, Oct. 8, 1967. Although these data are useful in indicating the level of public satisfaction/dissatisfaction with the President's handling of the war, they do not provide an accurate picture of the division between those who wanted to maintain or increase the existing level of U.S. action versus those who wanted to decrease U.S. action. This can be ascertained, however, in the case of this particular poll by examining the results of a followup question that was asked of the 57 percent who said they disapproved of the way the war was being handled. (In other Gallup polls on the same approval/disapproval question, there had not been such a followup question.) The followup question was whether the U.S. should scale down the fighting and get out or step up the fighting. Of the 57 percent who had said they disapproved of Johnson's handling of the war, 37 percent replied that the fighting should be increased and 48 percent thought it should be scaled down. Thus, the total of those who said that they approved of the way the President was handling the war and those who disapproved but wanted the war stepped up, was 49 percent. (The figure of 49 percent is the sum of the 28 percent approval and the percentage of the 57 percent disapproval which wanted the war increased—21 percent, or 37 percent of 57.) Conversely, the true figure for those who were unfavorable and who wanted the war scaled down was 27 percent. The results of the poll can therefore be recalculated as follows:

[In percent]

in favor of existing action or of stepping up the war	49
in favor of withdrawing or scaling down the war	27
no opinion	15

In response to reports of lack of progress in the war and a rapid decline in public support, and on orders of the President through Rostow and Leonhart, a group of 12 of the Government's Vietnam experts was sent to a CIA facility near Washington to develop a "Dow Jones" formula for measuring progress in the war. According to one of the participants, Volney Warner (a colonel in the Army, then on Leonhart's staff, who, it will be recalled, had assisted with the PROVN Report), the group was put "in isolation" and was told not to come back until they had developed the formula.[131]

The group, which met at Vint Hill Farms near Warrenton, Virginia in early October 1967, consisted of representatives from the White House, the CIA and DIA, the military and the Department of Defense, and USIA. It met for several days, but in the end was unable to agree on a formula. According to Warner in an interview, "We sat there for two-and-a-half weeks or longer, I can't even remember. And we argued and we fought and we screamed and we wrote on blackboards and finally we prayed, and then asked permission to please come back to our homes and regular jobs."[132]

This is Warner's description of the effort to find a formula:[133]

> We argued for 1 or 2 days about the accuracy of the data, then decided to assume that it was all accurate and merely instead to identify what factors should be considered in the equation. We looked at maps of pacified and unpacified areas. We considered body counts, weapons captured, number of small unit operations, number of large unit operations, Chieu Hois, dollars spent in the Corn/Pig Program, quantities of Bulgar Wheat issued, cement block produced, Revolutionary Development cadre trained. The thought was that if we could aggregate and statistically weigh some of these factors then combine them into a formula equated to programs, we could then determine a "K factor" to take care of the balance of the variance in the model. The result would be our Dow Jones Index on Vietnam. Thereafter we would merely plug numbers into the formula and quantify progress or lack of it.

"It didn't work," Warner says. "We could not even agree on the equation—much less guarantee the validity of the input data."

In his interview, Warner explained that at the root of this lack of agreement was a perceptual difference with respect to the nature of the war. "If you view that war as essentially starting as a civil war, political in its beginnings, and essentially one where the people have rejected the government, then all of the programs, all of the force structure, all of the chains of command, all of the reporting procedures, everything you do looks infinitely different than if you have the mystic view that I think Rostow and the President did and Westmoreland did. They were seeing Vietnam as tied to an umbilical that goes from Moscow to Peking to Hanoi, and we're fighting communism. And, unfortunately, I think the field advisors began to realize early on that simply wasn't true. . . ."[134]

---

[131] Johnson Library, Volney Warner Oral History, May 3, 1984, and letter to the author from General Warner (U.S. Army, Ret.), Dec. 6, 1993.

[132] Interview cited above.

[133] Letter to author cited above.

[134] Interview cited above.

During this same period—mid-October 1967—President Johnson also asked McGeorge Bundy to review the progress being made and to recommend what else could be done to improve the situation. After meeting with his brother William and with McNamara, Helms, and "a knowledgeable junior interdepartmental staff team," McGeorge Bundy reported to the President on October 17: "Basically, I think your policy is as right as ever and that the weight of the evidence from the field is encouraging. I also believe that we are in a long, slow business in which we cannot expect decisive results soon. And while I think that there are several things which we can usefully do to strengthen our position, my most important preliminary conclusions are negative [with respect to other things that could be done]." [135]

Rather than changing course, the President and his associates and his allies in Congress and in the public decided to wage a more vigorous campaign to persuade Congress and the public that the war was being won. This was carried out in a number of ways, including private meetings at the White House with Members of Congress, reassuring public speeches, a meeting of the Wise Men, and public appearances in the U.S. by Westmoreland and Bunker. In addition, after several months of preparation, action finally was taken on establishing a White House Vietnam Information Group [136] and a national public support group—the Citizens Committee for Peace with Freedom in Vietnam.

The role of the White House Vietnam Information Group was to gather information and to act as a "quick reaction team" to prepare material for the President and speech and background material for use on Capitol Hill; to "provide background material to leak to correspondents regularly, with the President's approval"; and to work with information officers at the State and Defense Departments to coordinate and improve the flow of information.[137] Rostow and Christian advised that the "main themes" should be U.S. objectives, reasons for bombing the North, results of the war (new confidence in Asia), consequences of a U.S. pull-out or "resort to static enclaves." There should be emphasis on the evidence that there was no stalemate, and on the strategy of the Communists in seeking to influence U.S. public opinion—"The war could be lost—but only in the United States," Rostow said.[138]

On October 25, 1967, the establishment of a new Citizens Committee for Peace with Freedom in Vietnam, which had been conceived and organized by the White House, was announced by former Senator Paul Douglas, the organizing chairman.[139] Mem-

[135] Johnson Library, NSF, Country File, Vietnam, Memorandum to the President from McGeorge Bundy, "Vietnam—October 1967," Oct. 17, 1967.

[136] For the establishment of the White House Vietnam Information Group, headed for a short time by Harold Kaplan, who had been Deputy Assistant Secretary of State for Public Affairs, see Turner, *Lyndon Johnson's Dual War*, and the following documents from the Johnson Library: Kaplan Memorandum to George Christian, Aug. 8, 1967 (from Office Files of George Christian); memorandum to Christian from Tom Johnson, Aug. 15, 1967 (from C.F. PR 18 ND 19/CO 312); memorandum for the President from Christian, Aug. 22, 1967 (from Office Files of Fred Panzer); memorandum from Kaplan to Rostow, Oct. 9, 1967 (from NSF, Country File, Vietnam); and from the State Department, Lot File 70 D 207, a memorandum for the Secretary from Ernest K. Lindley, "White House Meeting on Public Relations Activities," Aug. 30, 1967.

[137] Christian Memorandum for the President, Aug. 22, 1967, cited in previous footnote.

[138] Lindley memorandum for the Secretary of State, Aug. 30, 1967, cited above.

[139] *Washington Post* and *New York Times*, Oct. 26, 1967. John Roche was the principal White House staff member involved in the enterprise, which had been started in the spring of 1967.

Continued

bers were former Presidents Truman and Eisenhower and over 100 other notables.[140] The press release announcing the new committee was drafted by the White House staff.[141]

Concurrently with this effort in Washington to generate greater and more favorable publicity for the war, U.S. officials in South Vietnam were emphasizing the need to answer the charge of a "stalemate" and to gain more favorable publicity. On September 2, Westmoreland talked to General Momyer about a trip the latter had just made to Washington. According to Westmoreland's notes,[142] "He [Momyer] has the opinion that our public relations programs are of major magnitude with the Doves becoming more Dovish and the Hawks beginning to conclude that if we cannot escalate we should pull out. His impressions give cause for concern."

In a MACV Commanders' Conference on September 24, General Winant Sidle, Chief of Information for Westmoreland's command, discussed the need for reducing the "credibility gap" and maintaining U.S. support for the war.[143] He said, among other things, "Much of the credibility gap stems from an inaccurate and often misleading picture of the U.S. war effort as painted by the various news media. Some would lay the blame for this on prejudiced reporters with preconceived ideas. This is not completely true. Many newsmen, it is granted, have their prejudices. Most, however, are basically objective in their reporting and will listen to us if we can prove our point.

"There are a number of causes for the growing doubt in the public mind. Neither MACV nor Washington are completely blameless in this respect. It is a common American characteristic to oversell. Virtually all U.S. headquarters in the past have been guilty of over-optimism and have passed their enthusiasm on to the press. . . .

For pertinent documents on the role of the White House, see Roche's Memoranda to the President, Sept. 5, Oct. 7, and Oct. 19, 1967, in which he kept the President informed about progress being made in launching the organization, including recruitment of members, raising of funds, and obtaining an Internal Revenue Service tax-exempt ruling.

Even though the President had been kept fully informed by Roche, and had been asked for his assistance on several occasions, Roche suggested to George Christian on October 24 that, when asked about the White House role he should state to the press that "The President had nothing to do with the formation of the group . . . [and] everything the President knows about the committee he has read in the newspapers." (Notes for Christian from Roche, Oct. 24, 1967, same location.)

It will be recalled that two years earlier, a similar group, the Committee for an Effective and Durable Peace in Asia, had been created at the instigation of the White House.

[140] These included former Secretary of State Dean Acheson; General Omar Bradley; former Governor Edmund G. Brown of California; former Secretary of State James F. Byrnes; General Lucius Clay; Dr. James Conant, former president of Harvard University; Thomas Gates, former Secretary of Defense; Professors Oscar Handlin and Arthur Smithies of Harvard University; Professor Louis M. Hacker of Columbia University; Professor Myrnes McDougal of Yale University; George Meany, president of the AFL–CIO; Allan Nevins, retired professor, Columbia University; James Rowe, lawyer and former assistant to President Roosevelt; Professor Milton Sacks, dean at Brandeis College; Professors Robert A. Scalapino and Paul Seabury, University of California; Dr. Frederick Seltz, president of the National Academy of Sciences; Dr. George N. Schuster, former president of Hunter College; news commentator Howard Smith; Professor Ithiel de Sola Pool of the Massachusetts Institute of Technology; Professor Roger Swearingen, University of Southern California; Professor Harold C. Urey, University of California; John Hay Whitney, former U.S. Ambassador to Great Britain; Professor Eugene P. Wigner, Princeton University; Joseph C. Wilson, chairman of the Board of the Xerox Corporation. For the complete list see the *Washington Post*, Oct. 25, 1967.

[141] See Johnson Library, NSF Country File, Vietnam, Box 99 ("Vietnam Public Relations Activities," 7E(1) a 9/67–10/67.

[142] CMH, Westmoreland Papers, History File.

[143] Same location, "Briefing Summary" of General Sidle's remarks.

"We must change our approach. A good public information program emphasizes getting credit for a job well-done. We are doing a good job but progress varies in many areas. The military effort is proceeding well; the pacification effort is not progressing with equal success. We must not be over optimistic in fields where progress is slower."

The President also was urging U.S. officials in Saigon to step up publicity, and on September 27, 1967 Rostow sent the following "eyes only" cable to Bunker:[144]

> The President requests you, Westy, Bob Komer to search urgently [the word urgently was added by hand by the President] for occasions to present sound evidence of progress in Vietnam.
>
> Press and TV here are dominated by DMZ [heavy fighting between U.S. Marines and North Vietnamese forces], Thieu-Ky split, alleged election irregularities, newspaper closings, debates on bombing, etc. We must somehow get hard evidence out of Saigon on steady if slow progress in population control, pacification, VC manpower problems, economic progress in the countryside, ARVN improvement, etc. All are happening. Little comes through despite what we know to be most serious efforts out your way.
>
> President's judgment is that this is at present stage a critically important dimension of fighting the war.

Bunker replied in a long cable on October 7 which Rostow sent to the President with this note: "As you will see, we have at last gotten Saigon moving in the right direction on public relations. We shall be following up hard here."[145]

As part of the public relations campaign, Rusk held a press conference on October 12, 1967, in which he sought to answer critics and promote support for U.S. policy.[146] He began with a statement re-emphasizing the need to maintain the U.S. commitment to South Vietnam, based on the SEATO treaty and on the Gulf of Tonkin Resolution. "If any who would be our adversary should sup-

---

[144] Johnson Library, NSF Country File, Vietnam, Rostow cable to Bunker, Sept. 27, 1967.

[145] Johnson Library, NSF Country File, Vietnam, Saigon to Washington 7867, Oct. 7, 1967, Rostow note to the President of the same date.

[146] Rusk chose a press conference in preference to a speech in order to get better press coverage. In his remarks at his staff conference on October 5, cited above, he had commented on the difficulties of getting national press coverage for his speeches.

Some indication of the importance attached to Rusk's statement on U.S. policy in his press conference, and of the significance of the statement as a major step in the campaign for support for the war, was evident in the memorandum to Rusk from Dixon Donnelley (State Department Office of Public Affairs) on Oct. 13, 1967, "Follow-up on your Press Conference." (U.S. Department of State, Central File, Pol 27 Viet S.) These were some of the follow-up steps that were taken:

"1. Yesterday afternoon, we sent tapes of the entire conference to 310 radio stations throughout the 50 states.

"2. We prepared 6 short speeches summarizing your major points for H [the designation, derived from the letter H in Capitol Hill, for the State Department's Congressional Liaison staff] to place with members of the Congress. H also sent copies of the transcript to all members of the Congress.

"3. The transcript was sent to all Cabinet members and other senior Government officials.

"4. This afternoon at 3:30, we arranged for State and AID employees to hear a complete recording."

"5. A tape of the conference, plus a transcript, were pouched to all of our overseas posts today.

"6. The State Department Bulletin of October 30 will carry an edited version of the transcript. Meanwhile, 20,000 copies of this version will be sent to our special mailing lists on October 20. . . ."

pose that our treaties are a bluff, or will be abandoned if the going gets tough, the result could be catastrophe for all mankind."[147]

In response to criticism in the Senate with respect to the Gulf of Tonkin Resolution, Rusk said he did not understand how the peace and security of Southeast Asia could have been deemed in the Resolution to have been a vital national interest, "and then 2 years later, some of the [Senators] seem to brush that aside as having no validity." "If people change their minds," he added, "then it is fair to ask the question, On which occasion were they right?" "[T]hese are not matters that change with the wind. These have to do with the possibility of organizing a peace on a planet on which human beings can destroy each other. . . . And I believe that those who think you can have peace by letting one small country after the other be overrun have got a tremendous burden of proof in the light of the history of the past four decades; and they have not sustained that burden of proof."

The "overriding object" of U.S. policy, Rusk said, "is . . . the establishment of a reliable peace." The President had emphasized his interest in a "prompt and peaceful settlement," most recently in his speech in San Antonio, but the North Vietnamese had rejected the offer. This rejection meant that the U.S. faced some "sober conclusions. It would mean that Hanoi has not abandoned its effort to seize South Vietnam by force. It would give reality and credibility to captured documents which describe a 'fight and negotiate' strategy by Vietcong and the North Vietnamese forces. It would reflect a view in Hanoi that they can gamble upon the character of [i.e., expect dissent from] the American people and on our allies in the Pacific."

In response to questions, Rusk went on to say that there was no stalemate in Vietnam, that this was a word "invented" by some reporter in Saigon. Moreover, the South Vietnamese election represented "almost a miracle in politics." He said there was "no reason to be gloomy simply because it [the war] is not over yet." "The situation is moving."

Rusk was asked whether U.S. national security was "really at stake in Vietnam and whether Vietnam represents an integral part of our defense perimeter in the Pacific." He replied that "Within the next decade or two, there will be a billion Chinese on the mainland, armed with nuclear weapons, with no certainty about what their attitudes toward the rest of Asia will be." The U.S. hoped that Chinese leaders would emerge who "would think seriously about 'peaceful coexistence.'" "From a strategic point of view," he added, "it is not very attractive to think of the world cut in two by Asian communism reaching out through Southeast Asia and Indonesia" and that "these hundreds of millions of people in the free nations of Asia should be under the deadly and constant pressure of the authorities in Peking. . . ."[148]

During the press conference, Rusk was also asked whether the U.S. "was informed by the Soviet Government, on the authorization

---

[147] For the transcript of Rusk's press conference of Oct. 12, 1967, see the *Department of State Bulletin*, Oct. 30, 1967.

[148] After the press conference, there was some criticism of Rusk for invoking the specter of a "yellow peril" of millions of Chinese armed with nuclear weapons. See, for example, the statement on Oct. 16, 1967 by Senator Eugene McCarthy, *CR*, vol. 113, pp. 28929–28931.

of Hanoi, that if the bombing was stopped there would be a conference between the United States and North Vietnam within 3 or 4 weeks." He replied, "No, we were not informed of that. There was a public statement by Mr. Kosygin in London [February 1967]. But Hanoi has not said that to our knowledge. . . . There is no one in the world who has been able to tell us what Hanoi would do if we stopped the bombing."

This statement by Rusk is inconsistent with the record of the Glassboro Summit Conference, where the U.S. was informed by Kosygin that he had received a message from the North Vietnamese saying that talks would be held if the U.S. stopped bombing, as well as inconsistent with similar statements from Mai Van Bo.

In appealing to Congress to support U.S. policy, the President, besides continuing to press for increased efforts by the State and Defense Departments to maintain very close relationships with Members and committees—answering mail, providing information, getting speeches made and having material inserted in the *Congressional Record,* initiating discussions with those who criticized or raised questions—invited a number of Members of the House and Senate to the White House for "stag" dinners beginning in September and continuing into November 1967. In all, there were eight such sessions.[149] Unlike previous meetings of this kind, however, in which the presentation was usually made by Rusk and McNamara with the President acting more as director of production, in these meetings in the fall of 1967 Rusk and McNamara were not present and the President did the talking. (One exception was a meeting in November in which Westmoreland was the speaker.)

It is not clear what prompted the use of this politician-to-politician format—which had been recommended to the President from time to time as a way of establishing more of a direct connection and exchange of ideas, unencumbered by the presence and the role of Presidential advisers. The most likely explanation is that, as the President perceived it, the situation called for less of an emphasis on policy and operations as such and more direct, personal, political efforts to explain, justify, and urge support of the course being followed and to urge Democrats to be less divisive.

The choice of this format also made it possible for there to be more give-and-take, more opportunity for questions and discussion, more "consultation" between the President and his fellow elected officials. But that was not Lyndon Johnson's style. Moreover, he apparently felt the need to explain and defend his policies, especially with members of his own party. The result was that he spoke at great length at these meetings, leaving almost no opportunity for questions or discussion. This was the pattern even at some of the smaller meetings, such as a stag dinner on September 21, 1967, of the President, Vice President, and Democratic Senators Mansfield, Long, Hayden, Nelson, Clark, Church, Magnuson, Monroney,

149 White House records at the Johnson Library, (WHCF, Social Entertainment), indicate that there were the following meetings: Sept. 12, 21, and 26, 1967 with Democratic Senators, October 4 with Senators of both parties, October 24 with Members of the House (both parties), October 25 with Democratic Senators, November 2 with Members of the House (both parties), and November 16 with House Democrats. All of these sessions were off-the-record and there are no White House notes of what was said. For lists of those who attended, see the President's Daily Diary.

Morse and McGovern. In a memorandum the next day for his personal file, McGovern observed: "The President is a tortured and confused man—literally tortured by the mess he has gotten into in Vietnam. He is restless, almost like a caged lion, as if some great force has overtaken him. He seemed to be almost begging for political advice; yet, when we would try to interject, he would immediately break in. I think one time—I didn't time him—but he went on for 45 minutes without interruption. You almost want to put your hand on his shoulder and say, 'Now, Lyndon, calm down, back away a little and take a cooler look.'"[150]

At a dinner party and reception for Members of the House on October 24, the President spoke the entire time, with no questions or comments from others.[151] He began his informal, impromptu talk by noting the fact that the 1968 election would be "tough" for Democratic candidates for Congress and the Democratic candidate for President. "I think we are all professionals, or should be," he said, "and I understand that a Congressman at times must establish a very visible public distance between himself and the policies of even the President of his own party. . . . But as a professional, I know something else about dissent within a party, and I hope you know it too. In November of next year we are all going to be on the same line of the ballot . . . all I ask of you tonight—and I think you have the same right to ask it of me—is that we disagree with each other when necessary, but that we do it in a spirit of appreciation for the other fellow's position. . . ."

"[A]ll of you have a handicap. You have to carry a Democratic President . . . in the middle of a war when there is a great deal of frustration and dissatisfaction. . . ." "They [the public] are unhappy about the war. And they are unhappy about taxes. And they are unhappy about farm income dropping from 80 percent of parity to 73. And they're just plain unhappy with me. And I don't know how they could be any other way, when you read the columns in the magazines and the commentators—every single day putting it to them."

After touching on several other topics: similar problems that Presidents had experienced in other wars; recent meetings with Asian leaders Prime Ministers Lee and Souvanna Phouma,[152] who,

---

[150] Princeton University, Seely Mudd Library, McGovern Papers, McGovern Memorandum to Personal File "Re: Informal Stag Dinner Meeting at the White House, 9/21/67," Sept. 22, 1967. The author appreciates the kindness of Gen. Douglas Kinnard in providing a copy of this document, as well as a copy of a memorandum on Vietnam (same location) from McGovern to the President on Oct. 12, 1967. In the latter document, McGovern recommended that the U.S. should cease bombing North Vietnam. Most of the military targets had been destroyed, he said, and the costs of continued bombing would not be offset by its benefits. The U.S. should urge the U.S.S.R. to "secure a pullback" of North Vietnamese divisions. Search-and-destroy operations should be replaced by clear and hold. Finally, the U.S. should get the South Vietnamese to assume more of the burden of fighting the war and should encourage them to explore negotiations with the NLF.

[151] Johnson Library, Notes of Congressional Meetings, Notes of a meeting of the President with House Members, Oct. 24, 1967.

[152] On Oct. 20, 1967, Prince Souvanna Phouma, Prime Minister of Laos, in a meeting with President Johnson at the White House, emphasized the impact of the war on Laos, which had 100,000 men in its Armed Forces and spent half of its national budget for defense. He said he would be "very happy if the U.S. Government would help in some circuitous way . . . to relieve those financial pressures." It would need to be circuitous because "the neutrality of Laos had to be maintained." (U.S. Department of State, Central File, Pol 27 Viet S, Memorandum of Conversation of meeting of the President and Prince Souvanna Phouma, Oct. 20, 1967.)

Souvanna Phouma said that he had read the President's San Antonio speech, but that there had been no change in the attitude of the North Vietnamese and he wondered what the U.S. would do. The President replied that the U.S. would continue applying pressure. Souvanna

he said, emphasized the need for the U.S. to persevere; an American Federation of Labor poll that showed strong support for the war; the numerous suggestions being made to him and his response to the proposal to stop bombing (if there could be a "prompt meeting and a productive discussion . . . I'll stop the bombing"), the President returned to the central theme of his remarks, the need for Democrats to stand firm and stand together. He said he knew that a tax bill was "not the way to win friends and influence people and get elected." "And I know that to keep on fighting and putting [in] more men and having more casualties—that's not going to make you popular with the mothers of the country, or the wives of the country. But, we just can't look at our own popularity. At least I can't. I'll excuse all of you when it's absolutely necessary to look after yourself. . . ." "I don't ask for your sympathy, and I don't criticize anything you have done. I just want you to know that what I'm doing may be wrong. But from the best information I have, and the best advice I can get, and the people that you have surrounded me with to give me counsel, I at least think it's right.

"[W]hat we are going to do is pray for peace, and work for peace, and try every plan we can in every capital we can with anything that offers any hope because there is no human being would sleep better tonight than I would if we didn't have Vietnam. But we're going to do it honorably, and we're not going to surrender, and we're not going to run out, and we're not going to stop bombing and sit there while they bomb our people."

The President ended as he began, by appealing for unity and less public criticism. "So, let us Democrats, let's don't let them stampede us. Let's don't let them steam-roller us. Let's don't be worried because we get a few . . . Gallup Polls." (On the previous day, as noted, Gallup had reported that in a Presidential "trial heat" for the 1968 election, all of the leading Republican candidates outpolled Johnson.) I looked at the [*Congressional*] *Record* last week and I had 21 attacks made upon me in the Senate. . . . [In] the House of Representatives, during that period, I had three or four. . . . So, I am very grateful to the House and very hopeful that we can reestablish . . . as much unity as we can . . . our job is to perpetuate what we have and preserve what we have and protect what we have, and we can't do it chewing on each other."

In addition to meeting with Members of Congress to appeal for support for his policies, the President also met with a group of senior faculty members from Harvard University who had written to him on August 3 asking if there was "anything we can do, now or

---

Phouma "stressed the vital interest of his country in this subject because the majority of the North Vietnamese equipment that infiltrated to the south went through Laos. If the U.S. Government hardened its stand, the Lao would be happy if all passes from North Vietnam into Laos are very heavily bombed." He said that the Lao feared that during the next dry season, North Vietnam, having failed to achieve victory in the South or at the demilitarized zone, might launch an offensive against Laos. The President replied that the U.S. would "do all we could to prevent such an event."

The President asked Souvanna Phouma how he thought the war could be ended. "The Prime Minister replied that he thought pressure could be brought upon the Soviet Union to exert its influence on Hanoi toward that end. The President pointed out that the Soviet Union had already tried this but the Chinese Communists were opposed."

The President asked Souvanna Phouma if he felt peace was nearer at hand. He replied that this might be true although it was "a difficult question." "His own feeling was that during November and December we should try to subject North Vietnam to extremely heavy bombings including all of the access roads into Laos. Then there would remain no strategic targets in the north."

in the future, which will make it easier for you to forward the cause of peace in Vietnam."[153] In their letter, they said that they had not signed any of the various public statements on the war, but that recent events had caused them to "intensify our mutual discussions of the situation with the result that we have chosen to address this private letter to you." They said they understood the "extreme pressures" on the President to escalate the war, and said they appreciated the fact that he had not done so. "We realize that you want peace," they said "[and] you will have our support for any moves toward deescalation of the conflict and we will stand ready to express that support in any way that will aid you in accomplishing this objective." "[A]s we see it, the cost of the war (in all senses) now exceeds any foreseeable gains and no increase in commitment is likely to improve the situation."

John Roche, a college professor and political activist who had joined the White House staff in 1966 as a Special Consultant, was given responsibility for handling this request, and, after getting the President's approval for a meeting, he drafted a reply for the President to send to the group, in response to their letter, which said that the issues the group had raised were complicated and that it would be preferable to discuss them in person.[154] Roche then set up meetings for the group with William Bundy, McNamara, and the President.[155]

On September 26, the President met with the Harvard University group from 5:46 p.m. to 7:10 p.m.[156] He began the meeting by saying that he welcomed the chance to hear from the group, and that he had "the same feeling you have on the problems we face." The group's spokesman (who is not identified in the notes), said,

---

[153] Johnson Library, President's Appointment File, Diary Backup, Sept. 26, 1967, letter of Aug. 3, 1967, to the President from Franklin L. Ford, professor of history, dean of the faculty of arts and sciences; Roger Revelle, professor of population policy, director of the Center for Population Studies; Mary I. Bunting, lecturer on biology, president of Radcliffe College; Edward M. Purcell, university professor; Merle Fainsod, university professor, director of the university library; Robert G. McCloskey, professor of government; Abram Bergson, professor of economics, director of the Russian Research Center; E. Bright Wilson, Jr., professor of chemistry; Paul Doty, professor of chemistry; Simon S. Kuznets, professor of economics; R. B. Woodward, professor of science; Talcott Parsons, professor of sociology; J. H. Van Vleck, professor of mathematics and natural philosophy; R. V. Pound, professor of physics; Howard W. Emmons, professor of mechanical engineering; and Paul D. Bartlett, professor of chemistry. Another member of the Harvard University faculty, Wassily Leontief, professor of political economy, sent the President a separate letter on August 3 supporting the group's appeal. (Same location.)

[154] Same location, letter from the President to Prof. Robert G. McCloskey, Harvard University, Sept. 5, 1967.

[155] Same location, Memorandum from Roche to McNamara and Bundy, Sept. 13, 1967. In the memorandum, Roche commented on some of the members of the group:

"Franklin Ford is Mac Bundy's successor as Dean of the Faculty of Arts and Sciences at Harvard, and is an extremely able European historian.

"Mary Bunting is President of Radcliffe College.

"Merle Fainsod, the distinguished historian of Soviet politics, is also President-elect of the American Political Science Association.

"Bob McCloskey is one of the outstanding figures in American constitutional history and law.

"Bergson, Leontief and Kuznets are probably three of the most distinguished economists in the country.

"Talcott Parsons has achieved an enormous reputation in Sociology by writing books which even other Sociologists can't understand."

[156] Johnson Library, Tom Johnson's Notes of Meetings, "Notes of the President's meeting with Educators from Cambridge, Massachusetts Colleges and Universities," Sept. 26, 1967.

In a memorandum to the President before the meeting, Roche commented about the group: "They are not worshippers at the Shrine of John Kennedy. . . . These are good people who need reassurance. They have been living inside the snare drum in Cambridge. . . . I suggest you simply let them lead and play it low key. As you can see from their letter, they are serious and essentially want proof that this Administration is run with sanity, commitment and intelligence." Same location, Memorandum to the President from Roche, Sept. 25, 1967.

"Our principal question is how can we open the way to a stable, acceptable solution of the Vietnam problem. The doors must be open for the national aspirations of North Vietnam. . . . By intensifying the air war we may be closing doors which would otherwise open. . . . There is a common slogan of get it over with. But we do not believe there is a military way to get it over. Our belief is that we must contract this war in the north by measured steps coordinated with diplomatic steps. Some restriction or halt in the bombing is needed. . . . What we want to know is this: is there any way we can help in thinking through a rational route to a peaceful settlement?" The President replied at some length. "There is much that you can do. There has been no time when you could do more. I am greatly disturbed by the division in this country. . . . The President and the country have to have support.

"I have stopped the bombing six times. I did not get any indication of action on their part. We are in touch with Ho Chi Minh today. The problem is not one of conviction. The problem is that Ho wants South Vietnam. He isn't going to give it up. He doesn't want to talk about it." "Ho has been told by me, very recently, that we would stop all naval and air bombardment if he would agree to enter negotiations." (This was a reference to the proposal made through the Paris channel.)

"We do not want to invade North Vietnam. We never thought it would bring us military victory." "The bombing does have a deterring effect," he said. "It might motivate them to talk or at least make them inclined to talk."

"I think there are two significant handicaps. The first is my overzealousness to do anything for peace. The second is the enemy listening to our Senators. This dissent encourages the enemy to think that we will bring our own government to its knees. . . . The problem is not here with your government. Every time we talk about the morality of our position and the faults with our government, it makes Hanoi think they will win in Washington what they won in Paris [in 1954, when the French agreed to withdraw from Vietnam]. I believe we are misleading Ho."

"Frankly, I do not know how much longer North Vietnam can hold out. Their losses have been very heavy. . . . The question is where do we go from here? We are providing the maximum deterrent. We believe the time will come when their power to make war will no longer be there. The price will be enough to make them talk."

The spokesman for the group said that they shared the President's concern about the effects of dissent. "We worry about whether this country will hold on."

Mary Bunting, the president of Radcliffe College and a lecturer at Harvard University, commented that after listening to the President and to McNamara, "the alternatives seem even more difficult than they did before. And the solutions seem even less promising." "We do want to know," she added, "what we can do to help." The President responded: "If all of you can put the throttle on extremism in this country, it would help." "I am in deep trouble," he said. "What you can try to do is to 'cool it.' Many people are being used in this country and are hurting the country perhaps without even knowing it."

As the meeting ended, the President asked the group some questions which are included in the notes of the meeting along with the replies:

> [President] Would you do the following:
>
> (1) Would you pull out of Vietnam? Let me see the hands of those who think you would. There was a comment, "Not this group. We believe it is in our interest to be there and not to pull out. We are 100% on this. None of us would pull out."
>
> (2) Who would bomb Haiphong harbor or Hanoi? None would. There was 100% agreement.
>
> (3) Which of you would stop the bombing along the DMZ, in line of the position of our men? None said they would. One spokesman said there was an alternative to this, moving the men back out of range of the weapons and then bombing only certain segments of the north.

In a memorandum to the President the next day (September 27), Roche said: "You did an extraordinary job yesterday with the Harvard contingent. I practically had to carry them out—Talcott Parsons, the distinguished sociologist, grabbed me by the shoulders and said, 'This has been the greatest experience of my life.' And I must say you really shot the gun right out of Mary Bunting's hand. . . ."[157]

---

[157] Johnson Library, President's Appointment File, Diary Backup for Sept. 26, 1967, Memorandum for the President from Roche, Sept. 27, 1967.

CHAPTER 20

CRUCIBLE

While trying to develop stronger public support for U.S. policy, the Government was also taking steps to counteract the increasing militancy of the antiwar movement and the greater use of violence in certain quarters of the civil rights movement. For some months, the FBI, the Army (the military service designated as the one responsible for the role of the military), and, to an increasing extent, the CIA, had been strengthening their capabilities for intelligence and counterintelligence and for action in matters relating to domestic disturbances.[1] The FBI had continued to expand its program of gathering information on the "subversive activity" of individuals and groups (COMINFIL—Communist Infiltration) and its program for disrupting such activities (COINTELPRO—Counterintelligence Program), both of which had been developed in response to perceived external threats to the United States in the 1930s and 1940s.[2] These programs had been directed primarily at the Communist Party, but in 1960 the emphasis began shifting "from targeting Communist Party members, to those allegedly under Communist 'influence,' to persons taking positions supported by the Communists."[3] As the dissent associated with the Vietnam war came to be viewed by many in the FBI and elsewhere in the Government as a threat to internal security, both COMINFIL and COINTELPRO were increasingly used for investigation of antiwar and "New Left" individuals and groups, as well as for disrupting their activities.[4]

---

[1] For background on the development during the years prior to 1967 of U.S. Government programs for gathering information on domestic dissent and related activities and for taking steps to prevent and control internal "disorders," see especially the Final Report, Book II of the Senate Select Committee to Study Intelligence Activities. Also useful are Theoharis, *Spying on Americans,* and Joan M. Jensen, *Army Surveillance in America 1775–1980* (New Haven, Conn.: Yale Univ. Press, 1991).

[2] Final Report, Book II of the Senate Select Committee to Study Intelligence Activities, pp. 65–66. For a thorough treatment of COINTELPRO, see the staff study "COINTELPRO: The FBI's Covert Action Programs Against American Citizens," in Final Report, Book III of the Senate Select Committee to Study Intelligence Activities.

[3] Final Report, Book II of the Senate Select Committee to Study Intelligence Activities, p. 67.

[4] In January 1968, FBI offices were directed to designate as "Key Activists" leaders in the SDS and in the antiwar movement and to conduct intensive investigations of each one, including "technical and physical surveillance." *Ibid.,* p. 90. In May of 1968, the FBI initiated a broad program of COINTELPRO activities to "expose, disrupt and otherwise neutralize" the activities of the New Left. *(Ibid.,* pp. 88–89.) Field offices were directed to:

"(1) prepare leaflets using 'the most obnoxious pictures' of New Left leaders at various universities;

"(2) instigate 'personal conflicts or animosities' between New Left leaders;

"(3) create the impression that leaders are 'informants for the Bureau or other law enforcement agencies' (the 'snitch jacket' technique);

"(4) send articles from student or 'underground' newspapers which show 'depravity' ('use of narcotics and free sex') of New Left leaders to university officials, donors, legislators, and parents;

"(5) have members arrested on marijuana charges;

Continued

The role of the Army in relation to domestic disturbances had also been expanded. Beginning in 1965 with the establishment within the newly-created U.S. Army Intelligence Command (USAINTC) of a unit for coordinating domestic intelligence and counterintelligence which became known as CONUS Intel (Continental U.S. Intelligence), the Army increased its surveillance, photographing and reporting of antiwar activities and its infiltration of civilian groups and organizations.[5]

In addition to the Intelligence Command's CONUS Intel, there was another Army domestic intelligence and counterintelligence system operated by CONARC—the Continental Army Command, the Army's command center for its six districts in the U.S. (one for each of the five U.S. Armies stationed in the U.S. plus the Military District of Washington). CONARC's intelligence and counterintelligence program paralleled and in many respects appears to have duplicated CONUS Intel.[6]

CONARC's operations were carried out through Military Intelligence units in all of the Army commands across the country, and information was computerized centrally at CONARC headquarters in Fort Monroe, Virginia. Files were also maintained in virtually every subordinate command and field office across the country.[7]

Both CONARC and CONUS Intel also drew on files collected by other branches of the military as well as the files of the FBI, and, in turn, Army intelligence was made available to the FBI.

"(6) send anonymous letters about a student's activities to parents, neighbors, and the parents' employers;

"(7) send anonymous letters about New Left faculty members (signed 'A Concerned Alumni' or 'A Concerned Taxpayer') to university officials, legislators, Board of Regents, and the press;

"(8) use 'cooperative press contacts';

"(9) exploit the 'hostility' between New Left and Old Left groups;

"(10) disrupt New Left coffee houses near military bases which are attempting to 'influence members of the Armed forces';

"(11) use cartoons, photographs, and anonymous letters to 'ridicule' the New Left;

"(12) use 'misinformation' to 'confuse and disrupt' New Left activities, such as by notifying members that events have been cancelled."

[5] Jensen, *Army Surveillance in America*, pp. 240–241. A communications network, "Operation IV," was established at Fort Holabird, Maryland, served by a nationwide teletype system reporting information gathered by over 1,500 plainclothes Army agents operating out of 300 military intelligence (MI) posts across the country. (*Ibid.*, p. 246.)

Very extensive studies were conducted by the Senate of the military's—especially the Army's—role and operations in U.S. domestic intelligence and counterintelligence relating to antiwar activities. For the (Church) Select Committee to Study Governmental Operations with Respect to Intelligence Activities, see vol. II of the Committee's final report, cited above, and, in Final Report, Book III of the Senate Select Committee to Study Intelligence Activities, also cited above, see the staff report, "Improper Surveillance of Private Citizens by the Military," pp. 785–834.

The principal Senate study of the role and operations of the military was the series of hearings, studies and reports in 1971–1974 by the Subcommittee on Constitutional Rights, chaired by Senator Sam Ervin, of the Senate Judiciary Committee. See especially the Ervin subcommittee's 1971 hearings, *Federal Data Banks, Computers and the Bill of Rights*, 2 pts. (Washington, D.C.: U.S. Govt. Print. Off., 1971); the staff study, *Army Surveillance of Civilians: A Documentary Analysis* (Washington, D.C.: U.S. Govt. Print. Off., 1972); the 1973 subcommittee report, *Military Surveillance of Civilian Politics* (Washington, D.C.: U.S. Govt. Print. Off., 1973); and the 1974 hearings, *Military Surveillance* (Washington, D.C.: U.S. Govt. Print. Off., 1974).

These hearings by the Ervin subcommittee were prompted in part by an article by Christopher H. Pyle, "CONUS Intelligence: The Army Watches Civilian Politics," *Washington Monthly* (January 1970), pp. 4–16. Pyle, a lawyer who was a captain in Army Military Intelligence and served on the CONUS staff, subsequently testified before the Ervin subcommittee. His Ph.D. dissertation, *Military Surveillance of Civilian Politics, 1967–1970,* was published in 1986 by Garland Press in New York.

Pyle also wrote a second article for the *Washington Monthly* (July 1970), pp. 49–58, "CONUS Revisited: The Army Covers Up."

[6] For a further explanation of the organization and operations of CONUS Intel and CONARC, see the Ervin subcommittee report on *Military Surveillance of Civilian Politics.*

[7] *Ibid.*, p. 6.

In all, the Army had over 350 separate records centers across the country which contained "substantial files on civilian political activity" (there were a number of similar intelligence and counterintelligence programs operated by the other military services). It is estimated that there were Army files on at least 100,000 citizens.[8]

After the July 1967 riots in Newark, Detroit and other cities (during which Army units were sent to Detroit) and following the antiwar demonstration in Washington in October 1967, plans were approved in December 1967 for expanding the Army's domestic intelligence and counterintelligence role and operations with respect to civil disturbances. Immediately after the October demonstration, McNamara asked the Under Secretary of the Army to review the role of the Army in civil disturbances. After meetings of representatives from the Defense Department, the Justice Department, the FBI and the White House, the Army created a task force which produced a Civil Disturbance Plan that was approved in December 1967. According to the plan, "continuous counterintelligence investigations are required to obtain factual information on the participation of subversive personalities, groups or organizations" in civil rights or antiwar activities that could result in civil disturbances.[9] Dissident groups, the plan explained, were susceptible to control by "subversives," and there was "very strong support to the antiwar movement" from the Communist Party and Communist front organizations. It concluded that "Although it cannot be substantiated that the antiwar and antidraft movements are acting in response to foreign direction, it must be pointed out that by their activities they are supporting the stated objectives of foreign elements which are detrimental to the United States." [10]

In the spring of 1968, the Defense Department created a Directorate for Civil Disturbance Planning and Operations (later called the Directorate of Military Support), which established a "domestic war room," a suite of offices in the Pentagon manned by 150 people, with "watch teams" on duty 24 hours a day which were capable of directing 25 1,000-man civil disturbance task forces simultaneously.[11]

Under the broad mandate of the Civil Disturbance Plan, the Army was called on "to monitor virtually every aspect of civilian protest politics." "No individual, organization, or activity which expressed 'dissident views' was immune from such surveillance and, once identified, no information was too irrelevant to place on the Army computer . . . no demonstration was too small or too peaceful to merit direct or indirect monitoring. No church meeting was too sacred and no political gathering too sensitive to be declared off limits." [12]

From the massive data collection produced by CONUS Intel and CONARC surveillance, not to mention the many other military

---

[8] *Ibid.*, p. 96.

[9] Final Report, Book III of the Senate Select Committee to Study Intelligence Activities, p. 707.

[10] "Improper Surveillance of Private Citizens by the Military," in *ibid.*, pp. 797–798; the Ervin subcommittee report, *Military Surveillance of Civilian Politics*, pp. 34–35.

[11] "The war room's equipment includes extensive teletype networks to Military Intelligence emergency operation centers throughout the country, situation maps, closed circuit television, hot lines, an illuminated switchboard, and a computerized data processing center." *Military Surveillance of Civilian Politics*, p. 30.

[12] *Ibid.*, pp. 36, 3, 10.

units that were engaged in surveillance of dissidents, there was a veritable flood of information in the form of printouts of raw data, reports and summaries of various kinds issued daily, weekly and monthly, predictions of trouble spots, "incident reports," "personality reports," trend reports.[13]

From its data bank, CONUS Intel, beginning in the fall of 1967, compiled, printed and distributed to users of such information in the military and other parts of the Government two collections of information on dissidents (civil rights and antiwar). One was a two-volume set called "The Compendium," with the formal title "Civil Disturbances and Dissidence" (volume 1 concerned "Cities and Organizations of Interest," and volume 2 covered "Personalities of Interest"). The purported purpose of the Compendium was to provide information for use in cases of civil disturbances. The other collection of information was a six-volume compilation of information on "Individuals Active in Civil Disturbances," commonly called "the mug book" or "the blacklist," containing a picture and information on each of 1,000 persons in the antiwar and civil rights movements.[14]

A variety of methods were used by Army and other military personnel to obtain the information used in civil disturbance operations, including covert means such as infiltrating organizations and meetings; passing as press photographers and newsmen, sometimes with bogus credentials; posing as students.

There is very little information on the extent to which the military engaged not only in collection of data but in efforts to disrupt antiwar or other dissident activity. Based on its very extensive investigation of military surveillance, the Senate Subcommittee on Constitutional Rights stated in its report:[15]

> The subcommittee has sought without success to determine whether Army intelligence has used offensive or aggressive counterintelligence operations against civilian groups within the United States in order to neutralize their capacity to promote civil disturbances. So far the evidence establishes (1) frequent petty harassment of protest groups by agents acting on their own to steal bus tickets, handbills and petitions; (2) infiltrations of such groups as the Southern Christian Leadership Conference, the National Mobilization Committee . . . (3) the existence of several secret coded source operations by the name of Rook Castle, Rook Tower, and Royal Queen, the nature of which remains unknown despite subcommittee inquiries.

In some instances, Army and other military personnel who infiltrated dissident groups joined the members of those groups in conducting various dissident activities. A sampling of this by the Senate subcommittee included a demonstration at a university where rocks were thrown by the demonstrators, some of whom, including Army agents, were arrested. During another demonstration in Washington, D.C., covert Army agents supplied the demonstrators with marijuana and alcohol, the procurement of which had been authorized by the government.[16]

---

[13] See *ibid.*, p. 48.

[14] For further information on the Compendium and the blacklist, see *ibid.*, pp. 50 ff.

[15] *Ibid.*, p. 37.

[16] *Ibid.*, p. 45.

The CIA, although prohibited by law from exercising "internal security functions," was also increasingly drawn into collecting intelligence about antiwar groups. In 1967, two such programs, MERRIMAC and RESISTANCE, were established by the CIA's Office of Security based on the alleged need to protect CIA facilities in the United States. MERRIMAC involved CIA infiltration of antiwar/peace groups in the Washington, D.C. area in order to gather, in advance of demonstrations, information on the organizations, their members, sources of funds and plans. This included covertly photographing persons attending meetings, or license plates, and following people to their homes in order to identify them. If necessary to establish their credibility, agents (or "assets"—persons who were not regular CIA employees who were used for intelligence or counterintelligence activities) were directed to participate at a low-level in the activities of such organizations. Surveillance of particular activities or leaders was also conducted as a part of MERRIMAC.

RESISTANCE was a nationwide CIA program to gather information on radical groups, especially students.[17]

In August 1967, in response to "Presidential requests made in the face of growing domestic disorder,"[18] the CIA created within its counterintelligence staff a new and highly secret group—the Special Operations Group—to collect, coordinate, evaluate and report on foreign influence on domestic dissidence. This program, which came to be known as Operation CHAOS, remained in existence for six years, during which it engaged in widespread surveillance of antiwar individuals and groups in the United States.[19] In addition to the information it developed within its own staff, CHAOS also obtained information from "proprietaries"—businesses created, funded and directed by the CIA which operated or appeared to operate as private firms but were, in fact, CIA "cover" operations. CHAOS also received a steady stream of information from MERRIMAC and RESISTANCE, from the FBI, from the communications intercept activity of the CIA and the National Security Agency, and, beginning in 1969, from the CIA's Directorate of Operations (the component of the CIA which was responsible for the collection of intelligence information and for covert operations in foreign countries, and which, in support of those roles, maintained extensive relationships with and collected intelligence from individuals and groups in the United States including, as noted,

[17] See *ibid.*, p. 103, and the *Report to the President by the Commission on CIA Activities Within the United States*, June 1975 (Washington, D.C.: U.S. Govt. Print. Off., 1975), published also by Manor Books in New York in 1975. This commission was chaired by Vice President Nelson Rockefeller, and the report was known as the Rockefeller Report, the term which will be used here when it is cited.

[18] Rockefeller Report, p. 23 and Final Report, Book II of the Senate Select Committee to Study Intelligence Activities, p. 100.

[19] For Operation CHAOS, see generally the Rockefeller Report; Final Report, Book II of the Senate Select Committee to Study Intelligence Activities; and the Senate staff study, "CIA Intelligence Collection About Americans: CHAOS and the Office of Security," in Final Report, Book III of the Senate Select Committee to Study Intelligence Activities, pp. 679–732. Theoharis, *Spying on Americans*, is also useful, as is David Wise, *The American Police State* (New York: Vintage Books, 1978), pp. 193–196. The study by Rhodri Jeffreys-Jones, *The CIA and American Democracy* (New Haven, Conn.: Yale Univ. Press, 1989), while useful as an appraisal of the role and operations of the CIA, contains very little information on CHAOS and related CIA activities.

MERRIMAC and RESISTANCE).[20] Some of the informants for CHAOS were recruited from the antiwar movement.

During its seven years of operation, Operation CHAOS compiled 13,000 different files, including files on 107 private American organizations and 7,500 U.S. citizens, containing information on 300,000 persons. This information, maintained in a computerized system appropriately named HYDRA, served as the basis for memoranda for the White House and a special series of high-level memoranda—"M" memoranda on particularly sensitive items—as well as numerous studies and thousands of reports.[21]

In order to carry out their roles, CHAOS agents, like those in MERRIMAC, were directed in certain cases to join in protest activities.[22]

In addition to the counterintelligence programs of the FBI, the Army, and the CIA, the Justice Department established in December 1967 an Interdivision Information Unit (IDIU) responsible for gathering, evaluating and issuing reports on information "relating to organizations and individuals throughout the country who may play a role, whether purposefully or not, either in instigating or spreading civil disorders or in preventing or checking them."[23] IDIU, which obtained most of its information from the FBI (an agency within the Justice Department), eventually developed a listing of 10–12,000 dissidents which also described their activities.

Another important source of information for government counterintelligence programs was the communications intercept activity of the National Security Agency (NSA), the FBI and the CIA. NSA conducted two such operations. The first, which had been started in 1945 under a secret arrangement with three U.S. telegraph (cable) companies, involved the screening of every telegram or cable sent from or to the United States, including coded (enciphered) telegrams. Over the years, this included millions of telegrams, and in the latter years of the program, which was said to have ended in 1975, NSA analysts examined approximately 150,000 telegrams a month.[24]

The second NSA interception program consisted of monitoring telephone and radio communications between the U.S. and other countries using a "watch list" of words and phrases as well as the names of individuals and organizations, based in part on requests of other government agencies for such information, predominately the CIA (including CHAOS), the FBI, and the Army but also including the other military services, the Secret Service, and the Defense Intelligence Agency. Between 1967 and 1973, 1,200 names of Americans appeared on the watch lists, as well as hundreds of names of non-Americans and names of organizations.

---

[20] See the Rockefeller Report, p. 210, which states that at that time—1975—the CIA Operations Directorate had a master list of 150,000 names and 50,000 active files, many of which "reflect relationships with prominent Americans who have voluntarily assisted the Agency, including past and present Members of Congress."

[21] Final Report, Book III of the Senate Select Committee to Study Intelligence Activities, p. 698, and Rockefeller Report, p. 24.

[22] Final Report, Book II of the Senate Select Committee to Study Intelligence Activities, p. 101.

[23] Rockefeller Report, p. 118. Several months later the IDIU was placed under the framework of a Civil Disturbance Group created by the Justice Department to coordinate such counterintelligence activities within the Department. *Ibid.*, p. 121.

[24] Final Report, Book III of the Senate Select Committee to Study Intelligence Activities, "National Security Agency Surveillance Affecting Americans," pp. 733–784.

In addition to its communications intercept activity, NSA also maintained files derived from those intercepts on approximately 75,000 U.S. citizens, including many prominent persons from business, the arts, and politics. NSA itself did not use this information directly, but it was used extensively by the CIA, and it is likely that some of it was used by Operation CHAOS.[25]

Another communications interception program used against the antiwar movement involved the opening of mail by the CIA and the FBI. The CIA conducted mail opening programs in four different U.S. cities between 1953 and 1973. The major program, which lasted the full 20 years, was in New York, where a total of 28,322,796 letters, mostly to or from American citizens, were screened by the CIA through arrangements with the U.S. Postal Service. Of these, the envelopes of 2,705,706 were photographed and 215,820 were opened, read, and, where useful, the contents were photographed before the envelopes were resealed. The busiest year was 1967, when 23,617 letters were opened, read and an unknown number were photographed.[26] CIA mail opening was done both randomly and selectively. Selective opening was based on a "watch list" of names of individuals and organizations. "Numerous domestic dissidents, including peace and civil rights groups, were specifically targeted. . . ."[27] CHAOS supplied 41 names for the list.[28]

The FBI's mail cover (photographing of the envelopes) and mail opening program was conducted in eight cities between 1940 and 1966. The largest, which ran the entire 26 years, was conducted in Washington and New York. Although the FBI program was intended to be a counterespionage operation aimed at detecting and identifying foreign agents, it also generated counterintelligence information about individuals and groups involved in antiwar activities. It was not as large and inclusive as the CIA program, nor was it based on a target list, but the volume of mail that was screened was substantial—more than 425,000 letters a week between the U.S. and Western Europe (of which 1,011 in the period 1959–1966 were opened and photographed), with at least 130,000 first-class letters opened and photographed during the course of the program.[29]

The FBI mail opening program was terminated in 1966, but beginning in 1969 the FBI received such information from names it submitted to the CIA mail opening watch list.[30]

The October 1967 Demonstration in Washington

During the summer of 1967 the antiwar movement had continued to gain strength,[31] but it was becoming more fragmented and polarized, with the younger, more radical elements moving toward resistance while the older, liberal elements remained committed to

[25] *Ibid.*, p. 778.

[26] Final Report, Book III of the Senate Select Committee to Study Intelligence Activities, "Domestic CIA and FBI Mail Opening," pp. 559–678 at 571.

[27] *Ibid.*, p. 565.

[28] *Ibid.*, p. 705.

[29] *Ibid.*, pp. 638 ff; and the Final Report, Book II of the Senate Select Committee to Study Intelligence Activities, p. 6.

[30] Final Report, Book II of the Senate Select Committee to Study Intelligence Activities, p. 107.

[31] See DeBenedetti and Chatfield, *An American Ordeal*, pp. 185 ff.

traditional methods of dissent.[32] This, as has been seen, paralleled a similar trend toward more sharply polarized public and congressional attitudes. In both cases, the root causes were perceptions of the war: protracted, stalemated, seemingly winless and endless and increasingly costly in lives and money, and, in the eyes of many, unjust and inhumane if not immoral—a war of debatable necessity and uncertain purposes, whose goals seemed to have been attained or to be unattainable. In the case of the antiwar movement, there was also a growing feeling among the more radical elements that the war could not be controlled and ended through the normal functioning of the political system, and that such action could only be obtained through resistance, ranging from civil disobedience to the deliberate breaking of the law by such methods as refusal to register for the draft and burning of draft cards. (Under the law, those acts were considered felonies.)[33]

At a planning meeting after the antiwar march in New York City in April 1967, it was decided to hold a large demonstration in Washington in October that would include acts of civil disobedience. Leadership of the march, under the auspices of the National Mobilization Committee to End the War in Vietnam—Mobe, which replaced the Spring Mobilization Committee, was to be provided by the older pacifist element. As Charles DeBenedetti and Charles Chatfield explain: "At the outset its guiding spirits, Dave Dellinger, Jim Peck and Robert Greenblatt,[34] had intended to include direct action in order to escalate the movement into a 'stage of structured confrontation.' They intended to radicalize the demonstrators and to confront the administration. . . . And yet they also intended to mass a broadly inclusive demonstration. The only way these goals could be reconciled was by including alternatives—from verbal protest to direct action."[35] Several organizations, including SANE, the SDS, and the Women's International League for Peace and Freedom, disliked the concept and refused to participate, although the Women's League did so in the end.[36]

By August 1967, plans for the October march were mired in controversy, and Dellinger turned to the younger, more radical element for leadership. Jerry Rubin became the director. He recruited Abbie Hoffman, and "Together, and to the dismay of their radical

---

[32] "By 1967 the weight and initiative in the antiwar movement had shifted to the left. It was attracted there by the social turbulence that now swirled around the war issue, and it was driven there by the apparent inflexibility of national policy." *Ibid.*, p. 391. This quotation is from the final chapter in the book, which was written by Chatfield, assisting author, who completed the book after DeBenedetti's death.

[33] Developments in the antiwar movement were affected by a number of factors other than the war itself. See Kenneth Keniston, *Young Radicals: Notes on Committed Youth* (New York: Harcourt, Brace, and World, 1968) and *Youth and Dissent: The Rise of a New Opposition* (New York: Harcourt Brace Jovanovich, 1971).

[34] Dellinger was editor of *Liberation*, Peck was a professor at Western Reserve University, and Greenblatt was a professor at Cornell University. All three had been vice chairmen of the Spring Mobilization.

In the Johnson Library, NSF Country File, Vietnam, "U.S. Peace Group Ties with Hanoi," box 143, there is a memorandum from Rostow to the President on October 23 which states "Mr. President: This evidence on Dellinger's direct ties with Hanoi will interest you, if you haven't seen it." The attachment containing the "evidence" is still classified. When the author requested that it be declassified the response from the archivist was that it was too soon since the last request, which had been made in 1993. Four previous requests for declassification, beginning in 1978, were also denied.

[35] DeBenedetti and Chatfield, *An American Ordeal*, p. 188.

[36] For further information, see the references to studies of SANE and SDS cited above, p. 93.

colleagues in the Mobe, they began to give the mobilization vitality with a counterculture twist."[37]

Leaders of Mobe announced in August 1967 that the October demonstration would "obstruct the war machine."

Hoffman attempted to put out publicity that would help to mobilize the counterculture, but Mobe leaders took the position that some of Hoffman's ideas would alienate more moderate elements and announced that the theme of the demonstration would be: "from dissent to resistance."[38]

Although the President and his associates deliberately took no official notice of the planned demonstration, there was considerable concern and preparation. On September 21, the President met with McNamara, Katzenbach, Attorney General Ramsey Clark, Secretary of the Interior Stewart Udall and the administrator of the General Services Administration to discuss preparations for the march.[39] McNamara said that there would be enough troops to handle the situation. The question, he said, was whether a possible injunction or legislation should be considered, and whether someone should be named to supervise the various government preparations. Attorney General Clark recommended an overall command post in either the Defense Department or the Justice Department. Under Secretary of State Katzenbach agreed that there should be a central command post, "and possibly preliminary steps taken to discourage attendance." "In any event," he said, "steps must be taken to make certain all essential and central roads are kept open and an effort made to learn the plans of this group."

Clark said that the group had attempted to get 1,000 buses in New York, "but the indication is that they will be only able to secure about 150 buses." McNamara "pointed out that as of now no buses have been contracted for." (The information about buses probably came from the FBI, which, as will be seen, was covertly working with bus companies to deny protesters the use of buses.)

The President asked the Justice Department to supervise government preparations.

Clark, McNamara, and Katzenbach suggested that the President might consider being out of Washington during the demonstration. At a meeting of the Luncheon Group several days later, however, the President declared that he would be in Washington during the demonstration. "They are not going to run me out of town."[40]

On October 3, the President sent a memorandum to Attorney General Clark asking for a report to be submitted that day on preparations "together with new FBI information," and later that day Clark responded.[41]

At a meeting of the President with his Cabinet on October 4, Clark reported on preparations, including efforts "to create other

---

[37] DeBenedetti and Chatfield, *An American Ordeal*, p. 188. For a description of Hoffman's role see Marty Jezer, *Abbie Hoffman: American Rebel* (New Brunswick, N.J.: Rutgers Univ. Press, 1992), ch. 5.

[38] Zaroulis and Sullivan, *Who Spoke Up?* p. 126.

[39] Johnson Library, Meetings Notes File, Memorandum (unsigned) of notes on meeting of Sept. 20, 1967.

[40] Johnson Library, Tom Johnson's Notes of Meetings, Notes of meeting Oct. 3, 1967.

[41] Both memoranda are in the Johnson Library, President's Appointment File, Daily Backup for Oct. 3, 1967.

diversionary events on day and night of March" in order to reduce the attendance.[42]

There was this exchange:

The President: "Who are the sponsoring groups? Pacifist? Communists?"

Attorney General Clark: They are a combination of both. There is a heavy representation of "extreme Left-wing groups with long lines of Communist affiliations. . . . They are doing all they can to encourage the March."

The President: "Is that a secret?"

Attorney General Clark: "No."

Secretary Rusk: "Wouldn't it help to leak that?"

Secretary Gardner [John Gardner was Secretary of the Department of Health, Education and Welfare]: "The people have got to know that . . . they must know that!"

(Strong vocal agreement from Cabinet.)

Attorney General Clark: The fact of Communist involvement and encouragement has been given to some columnists.

The President: "Let's see it some more."

"It is time," the President declared, "that this Administration stopped setting back and taking it from the Vietnam critics. We have the evidence to refute the charges and we must begin answering back. Every day, Senators attack us and return to the attack encouraged by our silence. We should head them off . . . call them over . . . show them the evidence . . . ask them and tell them not to spoil our initiatives with their charges."

On October 16, Califano reported to the President that preparations were proceeding as planned, and that leaks to the press about Communist influence "should discourage many less extreme antiwar sympathizers from attending."[43]

The demonstration in Washington on October 21–22, 1967, was preceded by draft resistance in the form of a national "Stop the Draft Week," during which there were numerous activities around the country, including protests at induction centers, and October 16 was designated as the day for protestors to burn or to turn in their draft cards to resistance leaders.[44] In addition to this effort, which was student-led, there was a corresponding effort among adults—RESIST—to support draft resistance. Arthur Waskow and Marcus Raskin prepared "A Call to Resist Illegitimate Authority," which was circulated for signature in the summer of 1967, and was released on October 2.[45]

On October 16, 1967, more than 1,000 draft cards were turned in at meetings in 18 cities.[46] The largest, attended by 4,000 people,

---

[42] Johnson Library, Cabinet Papers, Notes of Cabinet meeting, Oct. 4, 1967. For a further report by Clark to a Cabinet meeting on October 18, see the notes of the meeting for that date, same location.

[43] Johnson Library, WHCF, HU 4 Freedoms, Memorandum to the President from Califano, Oct. 16, 1967.

[44] This facet of antiwar action, initiated by David Harris in the spring of 1967, became known as The Resistance. See Harris, *Dreams Die Hard.* See also DeBenedetti and Chatfield, *An American Ordeal,* p. 184, Michael Ferber and Staughton Lynd, *The Resistance* (Boston: Beacon Press, 1971), and Michael Useem, *Conscription, Protest, and Social Conflict: The Life and Death of a Draft Resistance Movement* (New York: Wiley, 1973).

[45] For the text of the statement and a partial list of signers, see *New York Review of Books,* Oct. 12, 1967.

[46] See the *New York Times,* Oct. 17, 1967.

was in Boston, where draft cards were handed in to the Reverend William Sloan Coffin, chaplain of Yale University and a leader in civil rights and antiwar activities, and there were speeches by Coffin, George Williams (a professor at the Harvard Divinity School), and Michael Ferber (a Harvard graduate student).[47]

It was decided that the cards that had been turned in would be taken to the Justice Department on October 20, the day before the demonstration was to begin, by Coffin, Dr. Spock, Waskow, novelist Norman Mailer, writer Mitchell Goodman, Professor R.W.B. Lewis of Yale University and Professor Seymour Melman of Columbia University. At the last minute, Marcus Raskin replaced Goodman. Poet Robert Lowell joined the group, as did Professor William Davidon of Haverford College.

At the Justice Department on October 20, Coffin made a statement of support for the draft resisters, saying, among other things,[48]

> We cannot shield them. We can only expose ourselves as they have done. The law of the land is clear. Section 12 of the National Selective Service Act declares that any one "who knowingly counsels, aids, or abets another to refuse or evade registration or service in the armed forces . . . shall be liable to imprisonment for not more than five years or a fine of ten thousand dollars or both."
>
> We hereby counsel these young men to continue in their refusal to serve in the armed forces as long as the war in Vietnam continues, and we pledge ourselves to aid and abet them in all the ways we can. This means that if they are now arrested for failing to comply with a law that violates their consciences, we too must be arrested, for in the sight of the law we are now as guilty as they.

A Justice Department representative refused to accept the cards, so Coffin simply left them.[49]

At the White House on the night of October 20, after the draft cards had been left earlier that day at the Justice Department, the President told Califano, "I want a memo to the Attorney General tonight. I want the FBI investigating." Later that evening, Califano

---

[47] See Coffin, *Once to Every Man,* pp. 241–243. For Ferber's role, see his study cited above. His speech, "A Time to Say No," is reprinted in Teodori, *The New Left, op. cit.,* pp. 300–303.

[48] Coffin, *Once to Every Man,* p. 247.

[49] See Coffin's description of the incident, *ibid.,* pp. 245–251, and Coffin's statement in Morrison and Morrison, *From Camelot to Kent State, op. cit.*

On Jan. 5, 1968, Coffin, Spock, Goodman, Raskin and Ferber—the "Boston Five"—were indicted by a Federal grand jury for conspiring to counsel, aid and abet draft resistance. After the trial in May, at which all except Raskin were found guilty, four were sentenced to two years in prison and a $5,000 fine (Ferber was fined $1,000). On appeal, Spock and Ferber were acquitted and Coffin and Goodman were ordered to be tried again. Eventually, however, the Government decided not to continue prosecuting the case. See Coffin, *Once to Every Man,* pp. 260–285, Jessica Mitford, *The Trial of Dr. Spock, the Reverend William Sloane Coffin, Jr., Michael Ferber, Mitchell Goodman and Marcus Raskin* (New York: Knopf, 1969), and Noam Chomsky, Paul Lauter and Florence Howe, "Reflections on a Political Trial," *New York Review of Books,* Aug. 22, 1968.

Some years later, Coffin said, "When I found out who the other five were in the conspiracy trial, I realized that Ramsey Clark had clearly decided to arrest five older people who would take care of themselves, rather than hundreds of students. . . . I asked him about that later—we are very good friends now—and he said, 'Yes, that was my decision. You were pushing the law pretty hard, and with civil disobedience the law has to hold at some point. I was as set against the war as you were, but either I had to resign or have you arrested, as I saw it, and I preferred to stay in, because I had a lot of unfinished civil rights business to do.'" Coffin's comments are on p. 104 of Morrison and Morrison, *From Camelot to Kent State,* cited above.

relates, "as we sat in the living quarters before dinner, the President called General [Lewis] Hershey [head of the Selective Service System] and delivered a monologue about the need to punish draft protestors. At times he was infuriated; at others he seemed genuinely struggling to understand what could drive a young American to burn his draft card. He wanted to know who 'the dumb sonofabitch was who would let somebody leave a bunch of draft cards in front of the Justice Department and then let them just walk away.' If Ramsey [Clark] wouldn't act, the President wanted Hershey to do something about draft-card burners and people disrupting the Selective Service System."[50]

Late that night (October 20), the President signed a bill that Congress had passed that day quickly (and almost unanimously) in preparation for the demonstration, which updated and strengthened existing law regarding security measures to protect Congress.[51] The new law covered a variety of disorderly and disruptive acts, including picketing, demonstrating or using loud, threatening or abusive language, as well as carrying weapons or explosives onto the Capitol grounds or entering with force and violence either the House or Senate chamber.

During dinner, according to Califano, the President also talked about the demonstration which was to take place on the following two days, and said he was "worried that 'Communist elements' would take advantage of the situation to 'make sure that there will be big trouble in the Negro ghetto.' He wondered whether to deploy Army troops around the White House and how much of the 82nd Airborne should be alerted to deal with the demonstration." The President, Califano says, "decided to prepare for the worst. He had troops, including regular Army soldiers, Marines, and police, deployed or on the alert to protect the Pentagon, Capitol, and the White House. Army troops were even secretly stationed in the basement of the Commerce Department [which is about three blocks from the White House], so they could rapidly assume positions surrounding the White House if such action became necessary."[52]

The Army was also preparing to use its intelligence and counterintelligence capabilities to impede and control the demonstration. "The Army Intelligence Command [which operated CONUS Intel] went all out . . . Agents from every MI [Military Intelligence] group in the country rode the buses and trains to Washington. Others joined FBI agents to question the managers of charter bus companies, interrogations which in some cases led companies to break their contracts with antiwar groups. Still others counted demonstrators and buses at armories in New York and from the over-

---

[50] Califano, *The Triumph and Tragedy of Lyndon Johnson*, pp. 198–199. The Johnson Memorandum of October 20 for Clark, Hershey and FBI Director Hoover is in the Johnson Library, WHCF, Ex ND 9–4. For the actions taken by the Government in response to the President's orders to Hershey, see Califano, pp. 200–203. The President had Califano prepare a list of all of the criminal statutes on sabotage, espionage and interference with the government, which he then sent to the Attorney General with directions to instruct U.S. attorneys that, consistent with the right of freedom of speech and assembly, it was the Government's "firm policy that persons who violate the law—for example, by disrupting peaceful meetings, preventing public officials from carrying on their work, impeding the operations of the Armed Forces and the Selective Service System—will be prosecuted to the full extent of the law." *Ibid.*, p. 201.

[51] *New York Times*, Oct. 22, 1967.

[52] Califano., p. 199. The 1st Brigade of the 82d Airborne Division was moved to Washington for the occasion. In all, there were approximately 3,000 troops on standby and 15,000 in reserve.

passes on the Baltimore-Washington Expressway. Phony draft cards were issued to agents from the 108th MI group in New York to immunize them from prosecution should they be arrested in Washington."[53] Other Army intelligence agents "were used to penetrate the groups in Washington who were planning the March; and still other were used to penetrate and report on the line of march. Army agents, moreover, took still and motion pictures of the crowds, and secretly used amateur radio bands to learn of the demonstrators' plans."[54]

The Army Assistant Chief of Staff for Intelligence requested for the demonstration (as well as on a continuing basis) information from the National Security Agency on efforts by foreign governments or individuals or groups acting as their agents to influence or control activities of U.S. "peace" or "Black Power" groups; the nature of such instruction or advice; identification of U.S. individuals or groups in contact with foreign agents.[55]

As part of its role in preparing for and responding to the October 1967 demonstration, the Army also broke with tradition, and with established regulations banning such practices in the U.S., and authorized units of its Security Agency (ASA—Army Security Agency, which intercepted international communications for the Army as well as engaging in "jamming" and "deceptive transmitting") to support Army units which would be used to control the demonstration, including jamming and deceptive transmitting if necessary. During the weekend of the demonstrations, ASA units monitored citizen band, police band, taxi band and amateur radio bands from 36 listening posts in the Pentagon and around the Washington, D.C. area.[56]

The FBI was also heavily involved in COINTELPRO efforts to weaken and impede the demonstration.[57]

The antiwar demonstration began on Saturday, October 21, 1967, with a large, peaceful gathering at the Lincoln Memorial, where there were speeches and music. The crowd was estimated to be at least 50,000, and probably closer to 100,000.[58] In the afternoon, at

---

[53] Testimony by Christopher Pyle before the Ervin subcommittee, p. 190 of the subcommittee's 1971 hearings cited above.

[54] Final Report, Book III of the Senate Select Committee to Study Intelligence Activities, p. 796.

The Army established a unit to coordinate its role in the October demonstration—"Task Force Washington." *Ibid.*, p. 808.

[55] *Ibid.*, and Final Report, Book II of the Senate Select Committee to Study Intelligence Activities, p. 108.

[56] Final Report, Book III of the Senate Select Committee to Study Intelligence Activities, pp. 808–809.

[57] There is very little available information on specific action taken by the FBI in connection with the demonstration. As noted above, the FBI was involved in trying to block transportation. In another incident, a New York newspaper declared that its contribution to the demonstration would be the symbolic act of dropping flowers on the crowd from an airplane. It ran an add seeking a pilot. The FBI responded under an assumed name of a pilot, and kept up the pretense to the point where the publisher of the newspaper showed up with the flowers to put them on the nonexistent plane. U.S. Congress, Senate, Select Committee to Study Governmental Operations with Respect to Intelligence Activities, Hearings on the Federal Bureau of Investigation, vol. 6, Nov. 18, 19 and Dec. 2, 3, 9, 10 and 11, 1975, 94th Cong., 1st sess. (Washington, D.C.: U.S. Govt. Print. Off., 1976), p. 28.

[58] For the most complete account of the demonstration by a participant, see Norman Mailer, *The Armies of the Night* (New York: New American Library, 1968). Also useful are Paul Goodman, "A Causerie at the Military-Industrial," *New York Review of Books*, Nov. 23, 1967; Noam Chomsky, "On Resistance," *New York Review of Books*, Dec. 7, 1967; Small, *Johnson, Nixon and the Doves*, pp. 110 ff; Zaroulis and Sullivan, *Who Spoke Up?* pp. 138–152; Bruce Jackson, "The Battle of the Pentagon," *Atlantic* (January 1968); Matusow, *The Unraveling of America*, pp. 328–

Continued

least half of the demonstrators marched to the Pentagon, where another gathering was held with speeches and music. At that point the situation became confusing as the various groups began to engage in their own actions. One group of more radical students reached the Pentagon and briefly gained entry before being subdued by security forces.

Plans called for some of the "notables," including Spock, Mailer, poet Robert Lowell, and literary critic Dwight Macdonald to get themselves arrested, but only Mailer managed to do so, as he recounts in his *The Armies of the Night.*[59] Mailer was jailed and released on bond late the next day. Other leaders who were arrested, detained briefly and released included Noam Chomsky, Dagmar Wilson (head of Women Strike for Peace) and Dellinger.

By nightfall, most of the demonstrators had left, but several thousand, mostly students, camped overnight on the plaza in front of the main entrance to the Pentagon where they burned draft cards and tried to talk to, taunt or harass the lines of soldiers and National Guard drawn up around the building—they called it a "teach-in." Some of the women, in a gesture that provided one of the most graphic images of the war, put flowers in the upturned barrels of soldiers' rifles. Around midnight on Saturday, after most of the media had departed, the troops, backed by Federal marshals, closed in on the remaining demonstrators and began beating them and making arrests.

The demonstration ended at midnight on Sunday, October 22. Several hundred refused to leave and were arrested. In all, estimates of those arrested ranged from 647 to 693. Scores of others were beaten, and 47 were hospitalized.[60] Of those who were arrested, charges were pressed against 600, but there were no felony charges for assault and of 12 charged with assault only two were tried. Both were acquitted.[61]

During the demonstration, the President, who had refused to leave the city, made a point of carrying on business as usual. On Saturday morning he and McNamara and Rusk met with Laotian Prince Souvanna Phouma to discuss the war. On Sunday morning he went to church and then drove around the scene of the demonstration. "He wanted to see what the remaining hippies looked like—their dress, sex, and ages, their flags, bed rolls, blankets, flight bags, and flowers."[62]

---

330. Newspaper accounts should also be consulted, although participants, such as Mailer, generally denounced them as incomplete and inaccurate and as overly influenced by the Government's rendition of the facts.

[59] It will be recalled that in June 1965 Lowell had refused, because of his opposition to the war, to participate in a White House Festival of the Arts. See pt. III of this study, p. 269. For Lowell's poem on the October demonstration, see "The March (for Dwight Macdonald)," *New York Review of Books,* Nov. 23, 1967.

[60] DeBenedetti and Chatfield, pp. 198, 443 n. 21.

[61] Mailer, *The Armies of the Night,* p. 285. Mailer states, however (pp. 286–287) that a number of those who were arrested remained for some days in the jail in Washington, D.C., where they "refused in many ways to cooperate, obstructed prison work, went on strikes. Some were put in solitary. A group from the Quaker Farm in Voluntown, Connecticut, practiced non-cooperation in prison . . . some of them refused to eat or drink and were fed intravenously. Several men . . . would not wear prison clothing. Stripped of their own, naked, they were thrown in the Hole. There they lived in cells so small that not all could lie down at once to sleep. For a day they lay naked on the floor, for many days naked with blankets and mattress on the floor. For many days they did not eat nor drink water. Dehydration brought them near to madness."

[62] Califano, *The Triumph and Tragedy of Lyndon Johnson,* pp. 199–200.

White House Press Secretary George Christian later recalled, however, that during the week-end there was "a tense White House, the feeling of siege," and Assistant Press Secretary Tom Johnson said that the demonstration was "'troubling' to the President," who, he said, "monitored television news all weekend and was impressed with the number of people participating."[63]

Except for attending the meeting with Souvanna Phouma, McNamara spent most of his time during the demonstration in his office in the Pentagon or in a command center in the building where he was joined by his deputy, Cyrus Vance, General Wheeler, Attorney General Clark, and Deputy Attorney General Warren Christopher. In an interview some years later by *Washington Post* feature writer Paul Hendrickson, McNamara said that the sight of the mass of demonstrators was "terrifying . . . I was scared. You had to be scared. A mob is an uncontrollable force." He added that the demonstrators "did it all wrong. The way to have done it would to have been Gandhilike. Had they retained their discipline, they could have achieved their ends. My God, if 50,000 people had been disciplined and I had been the leader, I absolutely guarantee you I could have shut down the whole goddam place. You see, they didn't set up proper procedure for maximizing the forces of the day."[64]

There were, as could be expected, a number of reactions within the antiwar movement, but generally, at least among the more radical elements, the feeling was that the demonstration represented the successful transition from protest to resistance, and that there was now the potential, as one of the principal movement leaders said, of creating "a movement of resistance people on a mass basis who would refuse to be complicit, who would refuse to pay taxes, to do the research, to accept the draft, who would refuse to fight, to produce the transport, the weaponry. . . ."[65]

After the demonstration, antiwar protests increased and became more confrontational. An SDS leader proposed a new strategy on the campuses of "institutional resistance" which called for "the disruption, dislocation and destruction of the military's access to the manpower, intelligence or resources of our universities" for the purpose of "1) the weakening of the resisted dominant institution and 2) developing a consciousness of power among those resisting the dominant institution."[66]

Public and congressional reaction to the October demonstration and other forms of antiwar protest was generally negative, however. These were the conclusions of a Harris Survey published on December 18, 1967:[67]

> A rising reaction against anti-Vietnam demonstrations is developing among the American people. The peace march to the Pentagon, the picketing of Administration officials, campus uprisings and clashes between draft protestors and police ap-

---

[63] Small, *Johnson, Nixon and the Doves*, p. 117. Christian sees the demonstration "as a major turning point" in the war, noting that in following weeks, White House staffers began looking for new jobs after 1968.

[64] *Washington Post*, May 10, 1984, feature article by Paul Hendrickson, "McNamara: Specters of Vietnam."

[65] Zaroulis and Sullivan, *Who Spoke Up?* p. 142. See also Powers, *The War At Home*, pp. 243, 249–251, and Sale, *SDS*, pp. 386–287.

[66] Article by Carl Davidson, Nov. 13, 1967, quoted by Sale, *SDS*, p. 387.

[67] *Washington Post*, Dec. 18, 1967.

pear to have had an effect opposite to that intended by the organizers.

The public response to these events has been a firming up of support for President Johnson and the military effort in Vietnam.

These were some of the results of the survey:

- 76 percent of the American people felt that recent anti-Vietnam demonstrations "encourage Communists to fight all the harder."
- 70 percent estimate that the marches and demonstrations have hurt the cause of opposing the war.
- 68 percent believe that such demonstrations are "acts of disloyalty against the boys in Vietnam."

Harris also reported that "By 59 percent the public estimates that 'sentiment against the war is rising and people have a right to feel that way.' And 58 percent are prepared to accept demonstrators 'as long as they are peaceful.' However, seven in 10 Americans object to the way the protest has been conducted. They cite a 'lack of dignity,' 'lack of respect for law and order' and exhibitionist behavior as marks of the demonstrations."

In the same survey, Harris also found a "rising trend against recognizing the right to demonstrate peacefully," as indicated by responses to the following question:

"Do you feel that people who are against the war in Vietnam have the right to undertake peaceful demonstrations against the war?"

[In percent]

	December 1967	*July 1967*
Have right	54	61
Don't have right	40	[1] 30
Not sure	6	9

[1] In the *Washington Post,* this figure was given as 40 rather than 30. In the article, however, there is this statement: "The number who doubt the right of peaceful protest against the war has risen to 40 percent, up ten points from July." Based on this, and the fact that the total would be 110 rather than 100 if the figure of 40 were used, it is clear that there was a misprint.

On Monday, October 23, the President met from 1:05 p.m. to 3:40 p.m. with Rusk, McNamara, Rostow, General Wheeler and George Christian for a discussion of several matters, including—in view of the final collapse of the Paris channel cables the previous week—the resumption of bombing of North Vietnam.[68] During the meeting the President brought up the subject of the demonstrations and the march on the Pentagon. The President said, "As long as I am President we are going to make sure that justice is given to all but that the laws are enforced and applied. I think we handled the Pentagon problem very well." "I am concerned," he added, "as to how we handle the draft card burners who are handing in their draft cards at various federal centers." Rusk responded: "I would enforce the law." "Not to enforce the law," General Wheeler said, "is going to create unrest among Americans who do support the law."

[68] Johnson Library, Tom Johnson's Notes of Meetings, Notes of meeting Oct. 23, 1967.

Later in the meeting, the President, who had asked in a meeting a week earlier "How are we ever going to win?"[69] again registered his frustration and concern: "It doesn't seem we can win the war militarily. We can't win diplomatically either. . . . We've [referring to himself] tried all your suggestions. We've almost lost the war in the last two months in the court of public opinion. These demonstrators and others are trying to show that we need somebody else to take over the country. People who want us to stop the bombing should know all we have gone through in this exchange [negotiations through the Paris channel]. The hawks are throwing in the towel. Everybody is hitting you. San Antonio did not get through. I cannot mount a better explanation. . . . We've got to do something about public opinion. We must show the American people we have tried and failed after going the very last mile."

In a meeting with Democratic congressional leaders on October 31, the President noted that "Of the 256 who allegedly burned their draft cards, a substantial number were crazy people who had previous history in mental institutions according to the FBI reports.[70] Also, most of the cards supposedly burned were xeroxes or photostats or facsimiles of the draft card and therefore no prosecution is possible. The President noted that he did not want to be like a McCarthyite, but his country is in a little more danger than we think and someone has to uncover this information."

In a meeting with the Luncheon Group on Saturday, November 4, from 2:30 p.m. to 3:55 p.m., the President, referring to antiwar opposition, said "'I'm not going to let the Communists take this government and they're doing it right now.'"[71] "'I told the Attorney General that I'm not going to let 200,000 of these people ruin everything for the 200 million Americans. I've got my belly full of seeing these people put on a Communist plane and shipped all over this country.'" "'I want someone to carefully look at who leaves this country, where they go, why they are going, and if they're going to Hanoi, how are we going to keep them from getting back into this country.'" CIA Director Helms responded that "under the laws today you cannot prosecute anybody for anything."

The President apparently had become convinced, as had Rusk,[72] that the U.S. antiwar peace movement was being promoted from abroad as well as receiving some of its funding from foreign sources. A few days after the demonstration, the President directed the CIA to conduct a study of the connections of antiwar groups to sources outside the United States.[73] On November 15, having quickly canvassed its overseas posts, the CIA made its report, "International Connections of U.S. Peace Groups,"[74] which was

---

[69] Notes of Tuesday Lunch Group on Oct. 16, 1967, cited above.

[70] Notes of Meeting of October 31, cited above. It is not clear what card burning episode the President was referring to. The notes of the meeting say in the preceding sentence that he "talked about some of the protestors from the peace march of October 21."

[71] Johnson Library, Meetings Notes File, Jim Jones notes of luncheon meeting Nov. 4, 1967.

[72] "On the eve of the march on the Pentagon, Secretary of State Rusk announced that the White House had secret evidence that the antiwar movement was communist-controlled." DeBenedetti and Chatfield, *An American Ordeal*, p. 204.

[73] Final Report, Book III of the Senate Select Committee to Study Intelligence Activities, p. 691. There is no mention of this request in Johnson's memoirs.

[74] The 27-page report, with 15 pages of appendices, and with a cover memorandum from Helms to the President dated Nov. 15, 1967, is in the Johnson Library, NSF Intelligence File.

Continued

sent to the White House with the following cover memorandum from Helms to the President:

> Preparation of this study, "International Connections of the U.S. Peace Movement" involved extensive research and examination of the Agency's own files as well as access to data in the hands of the Federal Bureau of Investigation and the National Security Agency [as well as the intelligence agencies of the Army, Navy and Air Force]. From this intimate review of the bulk of the material on hand in Washington, we conclude that there are significant holes in the story. We lack information on certain aspects of the movement which could only be met by levying requirements on the FBI, which we have not done.
>
> First, we found little or no information on the financing of the principal peace movement groups. Specifically, we were unable to uncover any source of funds for the costly travel schedules of prominent peace movement coordinators, many of whom are on the wing almost constantly.
>
> Second, we could find no evidence of any contact between the most prominent peace movement leaders and foreign embassies, either in the U.S. or abroad. Of course, there may not be any such contact, but on the other hand we are woefully short of information on the day-to-day activities and itineraries of these men.
>
> Finally, there is little information available about radical peace movement groups on U.S. college campuses. These groups are, of course, highly mobile and sometimes even difficult to identify, but their more prominent leaders are certainly visible and active enough for monitoring.

"The American peace 'movement,'" the CIA report said, "is not one but many movements; and the groups involved are as varied as they are numerous. The most striking single characteristic of the peace front is its diversity. "Under the peace umbrella one finds pacifists and fighters, idealists and materialists, internationalists and isolationists, democrats and totalitarians, conservatives and revolutionaries, capitalists and socialists, patriots and subversives, lawyers and anarchists, Stalinists and Trotskyites, Muscovites and Pekingese, racists and universalists, zealots and nonbelievers, puritans and hippies, do-gooders and evildoers, nonviolent and very violent.

"One thing brings them all together: their opposition to U.S. action in Vietnam. . . ."

This diversity, the report said, "makes it impossible to attach specific political or ideological labels to any significant section of

---

The report was prepared by the CIA's Office of Current Intelligence with the assistance of the Clandestine Services.

There were two appendices to the report. The first, "U.S. 'Peace' Groups with Significant International Communist Contacts," gave a brief description of and commentary on each of the following groups: National Mobilization Committee to End the War in Vietnam, Students for a Democratic Society, Radical Education Project (the "intellectual arm" of SDS), Tri-Continental Information Center (created to maintain contact with world peace organizations—according to the report, it "appears to be almost completely under the domination of the Communist party, U.S.A."), Student Non-Violent Coordinating Committee, Women Strike for Peace, the War Resisters League (a long-standing pacifist organization), and the Bertrand Russell Peace Foundation. The second appendix, "American Organizations Participating in Anti-Vietnam War Activities," listed 127 such organizations, many of them minor and small.

the movement. Diversity means that there is no single form. . . . Joint action on an international scale is possible only because coordination is handled by a small group of dedicated men, most of them radically oriented, who have volunteered themselves for active leadership in the key organizations." Many of these, the report said, "have close Communist associations but they do not appear to be under Communist direction. . . . In terms of the political spectrum . . . the activists generally range from somewhere left of center to the farthest limits of the left. Many are Marxist-oriented, but the Marxists come in all colors. Take the Communists: the 'orthodox' Moscow-oriented Communists, the Peking-influenced 'Marxist-Leninists,' and the self-oriented Trotskyites are all energetically active in the Vietnam protest activity. It would be surprising if they were not since the objectives of the movement are consistent with the national interests of the USSR and Communist China."

"The peace movement," the CIA report concluded, "can be described in ideological terms only if one political element is dominant or exerts a controlling influence. A careful review of the evidence does not substantiate either conclusion in the case of any of the groups." "This is not to say," the report continued, "that the Communist role is not substantial. Both the individual peace groups and the coordinating organizations are well infiltrated with Communists of one stripe or another. . . . As a result of their infiltration of the leadership of key peace groups, the Communists manage to exert disproportionate influence over the groups' policies and actions. It remains doubtful, however, that this influence is controlling. Most of the Vietnam protest activity would be there with or without the Communist element."

The CIA report also described and analyzed the record of foreign contacts by American peace groups. It found that contact with the North Vietnamese "has developed to the point where it is almost continuous." Apart from this, however, U.S. peace groups had few contacts with foreign governments. "Their relations are with foreign, private institutions such as the Bertrand Russell Peace Foundation. . . ." "Moscow exploits and may indeed influence the U.S. delegates to these bodies, through its front organizations, but the indications—at least at this stage—of covert or overt connections between these U.S. activities and foreign governments are limited."

The President, failing to get the evidence he had hoped for and expected, refused to release the CIA report or even to allow a public statement about its findings, "although pressed to do so by House minority leader Gerald Ford who, as a result of the president's private briefing, had claimed publicly that the October march was 'cranked up in Hanoi.' Instead, the administration continued to denigrate the antiwar movement as communist inspired."[75]

---

[75] DeBenedetti and Chatfield, *An American Ordeal*, p. 205.

On Dec. 21, 1967, the CIA sent the President a follow-up memorandum, "The Peace Movement: A Review of Developments Since 15 November," and on Jan. 5, 1968, a memorandum on "Student Dissent and Its Techniques in the U.S." Both studies reaffirmed the findings of the November 15 study with respect to Communist influence and the international connections of the U.S. peace movement, as did a study for President Johnson in early September 1968, "Restless Youth," which was updated in February 1969 for President Nixon.

Advice from the Wise Men, November 1967

By the end of October 1967, two major questions were begging to be answered: what changes, if any, should the U.S. make in waging the war? and what should be done to shore up congressional and public opinion? For help with both questions, the President again called on his "senior advisory group"—the Wise Men—for advice. The Wise Men, a group of about 16 prominent Americans who were considered to be influential in shaping foreign and defense policy, were first convened in September 1964 as a way of giving greater stature and strength to Johnson's campaign for President. They had met again in July 1965 as the President prepared to send large-scale forces to South Vietnam, a decision which they endorsed.[76] Although they were asked for and gave advice, their principal function in 1965 and again in November 1967 was to lend support and credibility to the President's program.

Before convening the Wise Men on November 1–2, the President, as noted earlier, asked McGeorge Bundy, who would also be meeting with the group, to evaluate U.S. policy options. On October 17, Bundy, after a day of discussions in Washington with his brother William, McNamara, Helms, and others (he said he would be seeing the Vice President, Clark Clifford and Walt Rostow later in the day), reported to the President in a memorandum, "Basically, I think your policy is as right as ever and that the weight of the evidence from the field is encouraging."[77] "I also believe," he said, "that we are in a long, slow business in which we cannot expect decisive results soon."

Bundy said he was opposed to an unconditional bombing pause. The U.S. would probably have to resume, and to do so after making an unconditional promise would be "very damaging" at home and abroad. By an unconditional pause, he added, "we impale ourselves on a terrible dilemma: a. to accept continuing and visible reinforcement from the North without reply; b. to resume on our own say-so, thus 'destroying the hope of peace' by unilateral action." He recommended that a "considered and careful exposition" of the argument against an unconditional pause be made, preferably under Katzenbach's direction. Once this was done and the decision was made not to have an unconditional pause, "we will end some of the chatter [by those advocating such a pause] and we will lay a base for looking at other less categorical alternatives."

Bundy said he was also opposed to having an extended pause "for the sake of appearances." "[N]othing which pretends to be a pause and has conditions attached to it," he said, "is likely to have any useful effect whatever upon people like the *New York Times.* They will simply say once more that we have done it wrong, that we were insincere, and that we have proved again that we cannot be trusted by Hanoi. Since in fact Hanoi will not accept any such conditional or limited pause, we can only get the worst of both worlds by offering it."

The only condition for an extended pause would be if there were a "recorded and acknowledged diplomatic position" like that which

---

[76] The single exception to this was Arthur Larson's dissent in 1965. See pt. III of this study, p. 348.

[77] Johnson Library, NSF Country File, Vietnam, Memorandum for the President from McGeorge Bundy, Oct. 17, 1967, "Vietnam—October 1967."

the U.S. had taken through Kissinger and the Paris channel. "A quick review of this exchange," he said, "persuades me that it has been extremely well handled and that it is to our advantage to keep it going. If it leads to a nibble, and we should get grounds for a bombing suspension, we would have a clear predicate on which to base any necessary resumption if the truce were not productive or if there was heavy reinforcement from the North. If, on the other hand, we get no response, we have certainly established a record which will plainly show that we were ready to stop the bombing on a still more forthcoming basis than any we have yet stated. . . ."

Bundy was also opposed to any "headline-making intensification of the bombing," and especially to any further bombing in Hanoi. "[T]he bombing of the North is quite intense enough as it stands," he said. "While I strongly support bombing of communications lines and supply depots—*tactical* bombing—I see no evidence whatever that North Vietnam is a good object for a major *strategic* campaign. Dick Helms told me solemnly today that every single member of his intelligence staff agrees with the view that bombing in the Hanoi-Haiphong area has no significant effect whatever on the level of supplies that reaches the Southern battlefield. Nor does any intelligence officer of standing believe that strategic bombing will break the will of Hanoi in the foreseeable future." "We have everything to gain politically and almost nothing to lose militarily," he added, "if we will firmly hold our bombing to demonstrably useful target areas." (emphases in original)

Bundy said he was aware that, in the past, the President had not felt he could break with the military and their supporters on the issue of bombing, but the balance of opinion, he said, was shifting rapidly, "and it is more and more to our advantage to put a distance between ourselves and people like Symington, Rivers . . . and even Russell. They are overwhelmingly wrong, on all the evidence, and the belief that you are gradually giving in to them is the most serious single fear of reasonable men in all parts of the country."

Bundy said he favored a careful study of "the possibilities for continuous bombing in the North which avoids startling targets and has the public effect of deescalation without seriously lightening the burden on the North Vietnamese." He said that after his conversations with the President's advisers, he was persuaded "that we can have both the essence of the present real military advantages of bombing and much of the advantage of seeming to exercise a new Presidential restraint."

On other aspects of the situation, Bundy advised against further large-scale troop increases and recommended that efforts to increase participation by the South Vietnamese be continued.

On October 18, McGeorge Bundy sent another memorandum to the President. He reported that he had seen the Vice President and Clifford.[78] The Vice President, he said, had made a "number of searching and interesting comments," which Bundy said he agreed with in the main. He also agreed with Clifford except for bombing

[78] Johnson Library, C.F. ND 19/CO 312, FG 440, Memorandum for the President from McGeorge Bundy, Oct. 18, 1967, attached to a letter from the President to Bundy, Oct. 23, 1967.

policy. Clifford, he said, "is in favor of a gradually increasing squeeze [on the North] because he simply doesn't think much of the argument against it. He shares the view which he has heard from the Far Eastern leaders he has visited:[79] the people in Hanoi need to know that they will be hurt for what they are doing."

In the memorandum, Bundy thanked the President for his hospitality (Bundy and his wife had spent the night at the White House), and, referring to the previous evening, he said, "I was deeply struck last evening by the contrast between the President I was talking *with* and the President a lot of commentators are talking *about*. The courage and confidence and good cheer which filled your house last night are very different from the talk of 'hunkered-up defensiveness' which I see in the papers."[80] (emphases in original) He added that there was one other thing he should have said during the evening's conversation: "while there are many interesting variations in detail in your Administration, there is among the people I talked with a steadfast and energetic commitment to the cause in Vietnam, and to its leader, who reflects great credit to all concerned. You are surrounded by people you can trust."

It will be recalled that on October 18 the President met with the Luncheon Group to consider a response to the rejection by Mai Van Bo of U.S. terms for negotiations. At that meeting, the group also discussed what action to take if, as it appeared, efforts to stimulate negotiations through the Paris channel had failed. McNamara and Katzenbach favored a bombing pause, both to encourage negotiations and to seek to respond to the mounting criticism of bombing in Congress and the public. Clark Clifford and Abe Fortas, who had been invited to attend by the President, were strongly opposed to a pause. Rusk did not comment directly on the question.

As a result of the October 18 meeting, the President, who seems to have been very unsure about, if not opposed to, a pause, met on October 19 with Clifford and Rostow to discuss how to handle the mounting pressure for a pause.[81] It was decided that the issue should be put to the Wise Men, and on October 20, Rostow sent the President a joint Clifford-Rostow memorandum recommending a meeting of 10 Wise Men "to explore the problem of a pause. . . ."[82] On October 23, however, after Mai Van Bo had told the U.S. that there was "no reason to talk again," the President in a meeting with the Luncheon Group declared, "If we cannot get negotiations, why don't we hit all the military targets short of provoking Russia and China." The question of a pause came up again, and General Wheeler recommended against it and agreed with the President on the desirability of heavier bombing, including the Phuc Yen airfield. As noted earlier, the President, after specifically asking Rusk and McNamara if they agreed, then ordered the intensification of bombing, including Phuc Yen and other targets in the Hanoi area that had not been bombed during the latter stages of the Paris channel talks.

[79] This is a reference to the Clifford-Taylor trip in July 1967.

[80] On the evening of October 17, Bundy and his wife were among the guests at a dinner party given by the President for the Prime Minister of Singapore.

[81] Clifford, *Counsel to the President*, p. 454.

[82] Johnson Library, President's Appointment File, Diary Backup for Oct. 20, 1967.

As a result of this decision to resume and increase bombing, which settled for the moment the question of a pause, the agenda for the meeting of the Wise Men was modified. In a memorandum to the President on October 25, Rostow, for himself and Clifford, proposed a plan for the meeting.[83] After an evening briefing at the State Department, the group would meet with the President the next morning for a general discussion of U.S. policy and of the war. "Since there is no single issue like a pause to deal with," the memorandum stated, the group should be asked for advice on U.S. policy in Vietnam, including bombing of the North, the issue of an unconditional bombing pause, peace initiatives, conduct of the war in the South, and efforts to improve U.S. public support for the war.

The meeting of the Wise Men was scheduled for November 1–2, 1967. A list of 10 participants was submitted to the President by Rostow and Clifford. The President struck the names of Acheson and Fortas, putting a question mark after each one, and he added the names of Maxwell Taylor and Henry Cabot Lodge. Subsequently, Acheson and Fortas were included. The final list of the 11 who were invited to and did attend the meeting was as follows:

Dean Acheson
George Ball
Omar Bradley
McGeorge Bundy
Clark Clifford
Arthur H. Dean
Douglas Dillon
Justice Abe Fortas
Henry Cabot Lodge
Robert Murphy
Maxwell Taylor[84]

John J. McCloy, who had been a key member of the group, apparently was not invited to attend, and Lovett, although invited, did not attend. According to Isaacson and Thomas, "By the autumn of 1967, McCloy and Lovett had decided to have nothing further to do with Vietnam. . . . [They] apparently decided that since they could no longer support the war, they would absent themselves from Johnson's war councils."[85]

At the briefing session on November 1, the Wise Men heard from General Wheeler and George Carver, Helms' assistant for Vietnamese affairs, and then from Rusk and McNamara.[86] The next day, the President met with the group at the White House from 10:42 a.m. to 2:15 p.m. Also attending were Rusk, McNamara, Rostow,

[83] Johnson Library, NSF Country File, Vietnam.

[84] See the President's handwritten notes on the Rostow-Clifford Memorandum of October 20, cited above. According to that memorandum, Taylor's name had not been included on the list because it was assumed his advice was available to the President "independently." Taylor was still serving part-time as a White House consultant on Vietnam.

The President also agreed with the suggestions of Clifford and Rostow not to invite to the meeting the following Wise Men who had been in the 1964–1965 group: Eugene Black, John Cowles, Roswell Gilpatrick, Paul Hoffman, George Kistiakowsky, Arthur Larson, Morris Leibman, Teodoro Moscoso, James Perkins, James Wadsworth.

Of the 12 who were invited to the meeting on November 1–2, eight had been added to the group since 1965: Ball, Bundy, Clifford, Dillon, Fortas, Lodge, Murphy and Taylor.

[85] Isaacson and Thomas, *The Wise Men*, pp. 677–678.

Several days after the meeting, William Bundy talked to Lovett, who said that although the effects of bombing the north were exaggerated, there were some benefits and the U.S. "*cannot* give it up." (emphasis in original) Bombing of Haiphong or the dikes should be avoided, however. The U.S. could not withdraw, but should not keep saying that it would not. William Bundy notes, in his possession, on conversation with Lovett, 2–3 days after the meeting of November 2.

[86] For a brief summary, see Rostow's memorandum for the President, Nov. 2, 1967 (sent at 8:15 a.m.), Johnson Library, Meetings Notes File.

Katzenbach, William Bundy, Helms, and Christian. Harriman also joined the meeting. The President began by saying that he was "deeply concerned about the deterioration of public support and the lack of editorial support for our policies." [87] He said he wanted the group's advice on five questions: "1) What could we do that we are not doing in South Vietnam? 2) Concerning the North, should we continue what we are doing, or should we mine the ports and take out the dikes, or should we eliminate the bombing of the North? 3) On negotiations, should we adopt a passive policy of willingness to negotiate, or should we be more aggressive, or should we bow out? 4) Should we get out of Vietnam? 5) What positive steps should the Administration take to unite the people and to communicate with the nation better?"

In response to the first question on action in South Vietnam, there was general agreement that progress was being made and that the existing program should be continued. Henry Cabot Lodge raised several issues, including his concern about the adverse effects on pacification of "search-and-destroy" tactics, and suggested, as he had in earlier conversations with McNamara and Westmoreland, greater emphasis on "split up and keep off balance" operations by smaller military units. Murphy and Fortas agreed with Lodge.[88]

On the second question, bombing the North, there was broad agreement that bombing should be continued but should be restricted to military targets (which would exclude bombing the dikes). Ball, arguing that bombing in the North was not effective and would "make it almost impossible for them [the North Vietnamese] to stop the war," suggested shifting from the area around Hanoi and Haiphong to interdiction bombing in the area around the DMZ. Clifford and Fortas strongly favored a continuation of U.S. bombing of the North. Fortas rejected Ball's proposal and said that the bombing "is not the way to end the war but a way to make cessation of the hostilities on a basis acceptable to us a possibility." Clifford argued that "Any cutback in the South or the North will be interpreted as a sign of weakness of the American people. If we keep the pressure on them, gradually the will of the Viet Cong and the North Vietnamese will wear down." [89]

Acheson, Bundy, Murphy and Lodge argued that there was too much emphasis on the importance of bombing. Bundy argued that "the South is the focus." The President, referring to the Stennis hearings, responded that the Senate "won't let us play down the bombing issue." "I am," he said, "like the steering wheel of a car without any control." Acheson responded: "The cross you have to

---

[87] Johnson Library, Meetings Notes File, notes by Jim Jones of the meeting of the President with foreign policy advisers, Nov. 2, 1967. Jones also sent the President a summary of the views expressed during the meeting, which is in the same location.

William Bundy also made some notes of the meeting, which are in his personal possession, but they do not add anything significant to the notes by Jones.

[88] The source of this and following summaries of comments made and positions taken at the November 2 meeting is Jones' notes (which report what each individual said), Jones' summary, and a summary (with comment) by McGeorge Bundy, which he prepared at the President's request and submitted on Nov. 10, 1967. (For Bundy's memorandum, see Johnson Library, President's Appointments File, Nov. 2, 1967.) Jones' and Bundy's summaries are organized by the questions that were asked.

The President does not mention this meeting of the Wise Men in his memoirs.

[89] In Clifford's papers in the Johnson Library, Handwritten Notes, there are several pages of handwritten notes on the meeting of November 2.

bear is a lousy Senate Foreign Relations Committee. You have a dilettante Fool at the head of the Committee." (Later in the meeting, Harriman said he wished that Acheson would make that statement publicly.)

On the third question—negotiations—there was general agreement that there was little hope for progress until after the 1968 U.S. election. Acheson argued that the Communists would not negotiate, but would simply quit when they found they could not win. Fortas contended that the U.S. public was not interested in negotiations. "That is why the people don't understand you when you say you're willing to negotiate, because the American people really don't believe in negotiations." He and several others emphasized the need to talk less about negotiating. "To continue to talk about negotiations," Fortas said, "only signals to the Communists that they are succeeding in winning over American public opinion."

In response to the fourth question, withdrawal from South Vietnam, there was, McGeorge Bundy said in his summary of the meeting, "a strong and unanimous negative. No one present would quit without a satisfactory settlement."[90]

The Wise Men made a number of suggestions in response to the President's fifth question on how to communicate better with the public and how to unite the Nation. According to Bundy's summary, "the advice . . . was very mixed. Some seemed to feel that the best course was to march straight ahead without fretting over criticism. While others shared the view that the Administration should not seem to be worried about its critics, they did not seem to feel that nothing ought to be done." As Bundy noted, there was a variety of proposals: "to develop friendly television programs, to organize committees of speech-makers, to bring in the responsible top educators, to reach past the Congress to the people, to promote visits by Bunker or Thieu, and to publicize such favorable assessments as George Carver's (which he gave to the Wise Men at the November 1 meeting). . . ." "My own view of all this," Bundy told the President, "is that the advice to keep calm is excellent and that most of the rest is of marginal value. . . ." (Bundy's own comment during the meeting had been that the communications people in New York "cannot be won over, but they should not be allowed to set the tone of the debate." What is eroding public support, he added, "are the battles and deaths and dangers . . . with no picture of a result in sight. If we can permeate to the public that we are seeing the results and the end of the road, this will be helpful.")

As the meeting ended, the President said that the consensus of the group was that there was general agreement with the present course in the South and with not extending bombing in the North, and some sentiment for reducing bombing. He then called on McGeorge Bundy to summarize the feelings of the group. Bundy re-

[90] In his summary of the meeting, Jim Jones gave this description of answers to the withdrawal question:

"'Absolutely not,' said Acheson.

"'As impossible as it is undesirable,' said Bundy.

"'Definitely not,' said Dillon.

"'Unthinkable,' said Lodge, 'we are trying to divert a change in the balance of power.'

"'No one in the group thinks we should get out,' said George Ball, 'and no one gives propriety to the Gavin or Galbraith enclave theory.'

"'The public would be outraged if we got out,' said Fortas."

sponded that there was "a sense of clarity and calmness among the group with a heavy majority agreed about what we should or should not do." There was agreement, he said, that bombing was important but overemphasized. He noted that the group had not discussed the question of a pause, which, judging by the lack of comment, did not appear to be a critical issue.

Harriman, "eyes heavy, jaws slack . . . had sat quietly through the Wise Men meeting."[91] The next day, he sent a memorandum to the President urging that, despite some of the comments made at the meeting, the President's efforts to seek negotiations should be continued.[92] With respect to comments that such efforts only encouraged the Communists to refrain from negotiating because of perceived U.S. weakness, he said that there was "no evidence whatever supporting this contention." He said he agreed with other comments that the Communists would probably wait until after the 1968 U.S. election to begin talks, but he argued that talks could begin earlier and that U.S. actions could increase the likelihood of that happening.

In early December, Acheson was quoted as saying that there was "no possibility of negotiating our way out of Vietnam."[93] Harriman, who had known him since he was his rowing coach at Yale University, walked to Acheson's nearby residence and spent several hours trying to persuade him that it was important to continue pursuing negotiations. He also urged Acheson to talk to the President, "to level with him about his doubts about the war. . . . Acheson made no promises, but he seemed interested in trying to help."[94]

McNamara Proposes an Alternative Plan

In his summary of and commentary on the meeting of the Wise Men, McGeorge Bundy said that in his estimation the Wise Men would support a course of action which he said the President had outlined at the end of the meeting (but which is not in the meeting notes), "namely that when the currently approved targets have been struck, you should clearly rule out any proposal for major widening of the bombing of the North, and should ask the Chiefs to plan a redeployment of air power against targets which would *not* constitute 'escalation'—with due allowance for necessary restrikes."[95] (emphasis in original) "If you should decide to move in this direction," Bundy said, "I believe it would be highly desirable for you and the two Secretaries [McNamara and Rusk] and the Joint Chiefs to come to a solid internal understanding on this whole question which would apply to the next fifteen months." The "pulling and hauling" between McNamara and the Chiefs, he said, had "created some confusion," but a "command decision" by the President along the lines of the course of action he had proposed at the end of the meeting, which "clearly defines the future of bombing in the North," could put an end to the pulling and haul-

---

[91] Isaacson and Thomas, *The Wise Men,* p. 681.

[92] Library of Congress, Harriman Papers, Memorandum for the President from Harriman, Nov. 3, 1967.

[93] *New York Times,* Dec. 4, 1967.

[94] Isaacson and Thomas, *The Wise Men,* p. 682. Douglas Brinkley, *Dean Acheson: The Cold War Years, 1953–71* (New Haven, Conn.: Yale Univ. Press, 1992), p. 255, says that "To his pleasant surprise, Harriman found Acheson much less rigid than he had supposed." "Indeed," he adds, "by late December Acheson was beginning to sour on Vietnam."

[95] Bundy's memorandum of November 10, cited above.

ing. In addition, Bundy said, "such a clear delimitation would be of real political value with moderates at home and with worried friends abroad. It would help to stop the foolish and false talk about a collision course with China, and it would help to meet the need for a real focusing of the attention of all toward the South, which remains the real battlefield."

Bundy went on to suggest that, based on comments during the meeting about U.S. military tactics in South Vietnam, there should be a high-level review of the conduct of the war. "For extremely good reasons the top men in Washington have kept their hands off the tactical conduct of the war, and most discussions have been directed rather to questions of force levels in the South and bombing limits in the North. . . . But now that the principal battleground is in domestic opinion, I believe the Commander-in-Chief has both the right and the duty to go further. I don't think anyone can predict the results of such an inquiry, but neither do I see how you can be asked to deal with the home front until you are satisfied that the plan of action in Vietnam—North *and* South—is the one you want." (emphasis in original) "What I am recommending is simply that the Commander-in-Chief should visibly take command of a contest that is more political in its character than any in our history except the Civil War (where Lincoln interfered much more than you have). I think the visible exercise of his authority is not only best for the war but also best for public opinion—and also best for the internal confidence of the Government."

Bundy said that he thought that through such a review there was "a really good chance of reaching an agreed program, among civilians and military men alike, which would have these general characteristics:

"(1) It could be *less* expensive in lives by involving fewer exposures to ambush and also by adopting the best tactics of the most successful local commanders.[96]

"(2) It could be *much less* expensive in money. (There just has to be an end of the cost of build-up at some point, and we ought not to let anyone believe that the dollar in Vietnam doesn't matter. It matters like Hell in our ability to stay the course.)

"(3) It could be *more* effective politically in South Vietnam: all evidence of care and control and patient endurance will help on this front.

"(4) It could *enlarge* the real and visible role of the South Vietnamese. There is a good deal of reason for driving home our insistence on their help even by just not doing things they won't join in.

"(5) It could still keep plenty of pressure on the Communists.

"(6) It could make it plain that we are over the hump. . . .

"(7) It could establish a pattern of gradually decreasing cost that would be endurable for the *five or ten years* that I think are predicted by most of the wisest officials in Vietnam. If one thing is more clear than another, it is that we simply are not going to go on at the present rate for that length of time, and since I think the Communists have proved more stubborn than we expected at every stage, I think that sooner or later we are going to have to find a way of doing this job that is endurable in cost for a long pull."

---

[96] All of the emphases in this list of seven characteristics are in the original.

Bundy said he still held to the views he had stated in his memorandum on October 17 about not pausing, not negotiating, and not escalating, but "I now go on to say that I think some visible de-escalation, based on success and not failure, is the most promising path I can see. I can't prove the path exists, but I think we should search for it."

In his deft and artful way, Bundy, who may have heard about the proposal, was propounding an alternative to existing U.S. policy that was quite similar to that which McNamara had proposed several days earlier—a similarity that the President doubtless noted.[97] The President may also have reflected on the irony that it had been McGeorge Bundy and McNamara who had joined in a memorandum to him on January 27, 1965, arguing that it was urgent for the President to make a firm decision with respect to U.S. policy in Vietnam, and recommending that he use U.S. military power to defend South Vietnam and to "force a change of Communist policy."

McNamara's proposal for an alternative course of action was set forth in a memorandum to the President on November 1, 1967, following a meeting of the Luncheon Group on October 31 at which he took the position that the "present course of action in Southeast Asia would be dangerous, costly in lives, and unsatisfactory to the American people."[98] The memorandum began with a discussion of "Outlook If Present Course of Action is Continued." Gradual expansion of U.S. forces in the months ahead from the existing level of 465,000 to 525,000 would not, McNamara said, "produce any significant change in the nature of our military operations," but would be "likely to lead to a proportionate increase in encounters with the enemy, and some increase in the number of casualties inflicted on both sides." "But neither the additional troops now scheduled nor augmentation of our forces by a much greater amount hold great promise of bringing the North Vietnamese and Viet Cong forces visibly closer to collapse during the next 15 months." "Nonetheless," he added, "we will be faced with requests for additional ground forces requiring an increased draft and/or a call-up of reserves."

U.S. ground operations in the South would continue along the same lines, McNamara said, but casualties would probably increase to between 700 and 1,000 killed in action each month. There would be renewed requests for ground operations against the "sanctuaries" in Laos and Cambodia.

There would be slow progress in the nonmilitary aspects of the war in the South, including pacification and political evolution, but while the development of representative government was encourag-

---

[97] The President, for unstated reasons, had asked Rostow to compare the positions of McNamara and Bundy, prior to Bundy's memorandum of November 10. See Rostow's response in his "literally eyes only" memorandum to the President on Nov. 4, 1967, Johnson Library, NSF Country File, Vietnam.

[98] This quotation is from McNamara's cover memorandum of Nov. 1, 1967 to his memorandum to the President of that date entitled "A Fifteen Month Program for Military Operations in Southeast Asia." Both memoranda are in the Johnson Library, NSF Country File, Vietnam.

The Luncheon Group met on October 31 from 1:57 p.m. to 4:10 p.m. In attendance were the President, Rusk, McNamara, Rostow, General Wheeler, Helms, Christian and Tom Johnson. For unknown reasons, there are no notes of the meeting, despite the presence of Tom Johnson.

McNamara stated that his memorandum represented his personal views and because these "may be incompatible with your own," he told the President that he had not shown the paper to Rusk, Rostow or General Wheeler. Cover memorandum of Nov. 1, 1967.

ing, "it is not at all clear that the image or performances of this government over the next 15 months will make it appear to the U.S. public to be a government worthy of continued U.S. support in blood and treasure."

In the air war against the North, "the continuing destruction of previously authorized targets will lead inexorably to requests for authority to attack more and more sensitive targets in the centers of Hanoi and Haiphong." There would also be increased pressure for mining the harbors and bombing the dikes. However, the bombing of additional targets, improvement in tactics and munitions, or a shift toward bombing farther south would be unlikely to reduce significantly the infiltration of troops and supplies. Nor would bombing of the North combined with greater success in the South break the will of the Communists to continue fighting. "Nothing can be expected to break this will other than the conviction that they cannot succeed. This conviction will not be created unless and until they come to the conclusion that the U.S. is prepared to remain in Vietnam for whatever period of time is necessary to assure the independent choice of the South Vietnamese people." But this could depend upon the American public, "And the American public, frustrated by the slow rate of progress, fearing continued escalation, and doubting that all approaches to peace have been sincerely probed, does not give the appearance of having the will to persist."

"As the months go by," McNamara said, "there will be both increasing pressure for widening the war and continued lack of support for American participation in the struggle. There will be increasing calls for American withdrawal. There is, in my opinion a very real question whether under these circumstances it will be possible to maintain our efforts in South Vietnam for the time necessary to accomplish our objective there."

The next section of McNamara's memorandum to the President dealt with two alternative courses of action. The first would be to intensify and expand U.S. military operations to include increased bombing of the North, expansion of the war into Laos and Cambodia, and an invasion of North Vietnam in the area above the demilitarized zone, or a combination of these options. He rejected this course of action. Bombing, he said, could not prevent the infiltration necessary to maintain the existing level of military effort in the South, and supplies would move on other routes if the ports were closed. Bombing of dikes would create greater public hardships but would not have significant military effects, and, like the bombing of cities, would be severely criticized as direct attacks on the civilian population.

Expansion of the war into North Vietnam, Laos and Cambodia would also provide few military benefits and would involve serious diplomatic consequences. An invasion of the North could lead to various counteractions by the Chinese and the Russians, including the use of Chinese troops. And although an invasion could relieve some of the pressure on U.S. forces from North Vietnamese shelling and rocket fire, this would be temporary unless the invaded territory were secured and held. If U.S. forces continued to occupy such territory, however, they would be subjected to attacks by North Vietnamese forces. "Our repeated response to this renewal of pressure would lead to our inching the area of conflict further into North Vietnam. The net result would be a broader battlefield, part of which would be contested by opponents fighting for their own homeland and an even higher American casualty list. If Chinese forces enter the fray, or more sophisticated Russian weapons are introduced, our losses would continue to climb."[99]

The other alternative, McNamara said, would be to stabilize U.S. military operations, both ground operations in the South and bombing in the North. The objectives of such a policy could be "to attract greater support by allaying apprehensions that the conflict would be expanded by our actions into North Vietnam . . . [and] to increase pressure on Hanoi to enter into negotiations and/or to reduce their military efforts in the South."

Such a stabilization policy would include the following:

1. No increase is to be made in US forces above the current approved level.
2. There will be no call up of reserves.
3. No expansion of ground action will be undertaken in North Vietnam, Laos or Cambodia.
4. No attempt will be made to deny sea imports into North Vietnam.
5. No effort will be made to break the will of the North by an air campaign on the dikes, locks or populated targets—efforts will be made to hold down civilian casualties in the North.
6. We will engage in continued efforts to restrict the war.
7. We will endeavor to maintain our current rates of progress but with lesser US casualties and lesser destruction in South Vietnam.
8. We will be willing to accept slow but steady progress for whatever period is required to move the North Vietnamese to abandon their attempt to gain political control in South Vietnam by military means.
9. In light of the political progress of the GVN, we will gradually transfer the major burden of the fighting to the South Vietnamese forces.

In addition, McNamara proposed a "complete cessation" in bombing of the North in order to induce the North Vietnamese to negotiate or at least to reduce their offensive military action, or, if they did not so respond, to demonstrate that it was North Vietnam and not the United States that was blocking a peaceful settlement.[100]

---

[99] These quotes are from the report's appendix 1 "Expanded Ground and Air Operations Against North Vietnam, Laos and Cambodia," in which McNamara discussed these options in greater detail.

[100] White House Counsel Harry McPherson also urged the President to stop the bombing. In a memorandum on Oct. 27, 1967 (Johnson Library, NSF Country File, Vietnam), McPherson, who began by saying he knew little about the bombing, suggested that the U.S. should refrain from bombing around Hanoi and Haiphong and should shift bombing to the southern part of North Vietnam. By this move, the President could "recapture a good deal of the moderate support we are now losing, without any appreciable loss in military effectiveness."

In arguing his case, McPherson made this point among others: "It appears to some people that you are escalating the air war, and running a kind of numbers game on remaining targets, solely in order to quit or escape criticism from right-wing Senators and Congressmen and your own military leaders. But you are the Commander in Chief. If you think a policy is wrong, you should not follow it just to quiet the generals and admirals. Generals and admirals like to bomb. People trust their judgment when it is a question of this or that *military* tactic; but when it is a question of this or that *policy*, they mistrust the military. It appears to some people that

A bombing cessation, McNamara said in his memorandum, would have the following consequences:

1. It is probable that Hanoi would move to "talks," perhaps within a few weeks after the bombing stopped.

2. There is a strong possibility that, whether or not talks ensued, a halt would be accompanied by a cessation of enemy military activities across the DMZ.

3. Hanoi, at least initially, would be likely to use the talks for propaganda purposes rather than as a forum for serious negotiation.

4. As the talks, continue, however, the internal dynamics of the situation would create pressures and opportunities for both parties that might well result in productive discussions moving toward a settlement short of the total elimination of North Vietnam's intervention in the South but consistent with our objective of permitting the South Vietnamese to shape their own future.

5. If large scale shelling and infiltration across the DMZ does not stop, or if Hanoi prolongs fruitless discussions while taking military advantage, resumption of the bombing could be made acceptable to the majority of the American people.

6. At a minimum, we would have made clear that our bombing is not preventing peaceful political settlement.

The President took issue with numbers 1 and 2 on this list, and on the memorandum he circled the word "probable" in number 1, and added by hand, "How do we get this conclusion?" In number 2, he circled the words "strong possibility" and added by hand, "Chapter and verse—why believe this?"

In the case of number 3, he added by hand at the end of the sentence, "I agree." [101]

The third section of McNamara's memorandum consisted of recommendations, as follows:

1. Decide on, and announce, the policy of stabilization outlined above. . . .

2. Plan a halt in the bombing for some time before the end of the year. . . .

3. Review intensively the conduct of military operations in the South and consider programs which involve (a) reduced U.S. casualties, (b) procedures for the progressive turn-over to the GVN of greater responsibility for security in the South, and (c) lesser destruction of the people and wealth of South Vietnam.

After McNamara gave his memorandum to the President, Rostow sent the President a memorandum the next day (November 2) in which he commented on McNamara's analysis and recommendations.[102] He said he agreed with points 1–5 and 9 in the nine-point list of elements of the stabilization program, but generally he thought McNamara's advice was wrong, and that "both a unilateral bombing cessation and an announced policy of 'stabilization' would

---

the military are blackmailing you into following their policy toward North Vietnam." (emphasis in original)

[101] These were the only notations by the President on the memorandum.

[102] Johnson Library, NSF Country File, Vietnam.

be judged in Hanoi a mark of weakness rather than evidence of increased U.S. capacity to sweat out the war." "Although I certainly will not predict for you an early end of the war, I believe that, with a little luck and reasonable performance by the South Vietnamese under the new government, the evidence of solid progress will become increasingly clear to one and all." Moreover, Rostow said, McNamara's proposed strategy could "take you away from your present middle position; that is, using rationally all the power available, but avoiding actions likely to engage the Soviet Union and Communist China. If we shift unilaterally towards deescalation, the Republicans will move in and crystallize a majority around a stronger policy."

With respect to the possibility of a diplomatic settlement, Rostow said that intelligence information suggested the occurrence of "a shift of the following kind":

—an increase in Soviet influence in Hanoi, partially caused by our bombing and a consequent requirement for very large increases in Soviet aid;

—a shift in Hanoi to the view that they cannot directly take over the South now and, therefore, they have to accept the 17th parallel for a considerable time period;

—within this framework, a probing for what the status of the Communists would be within South Vietnam in a time of peace.

Rostow suggested that, as a result of this shift, the military operations of the Communists "are designed not to produce victory but to improve their position in a negotiation which is, in a sense, already under way." "If and when we come into contact and begin to exchange views, it may well turn out that their minimum price for National Liberation Front status is higher than we and the government of South Vietnam are prepared to pay. In that case, we shall have to prove that their bargaining power diminishes with the passage of time—not increases. That, in turn, means high costs in the North; maximum pressure in the South on their manpower base. I believe Bob's strategy would ease their problem and permit them rationally to protract the negotiation—unless Bob is correct on domestic politics and I am wrong. That is, if the country settled down for the long pull comfortably with Bob's program, he could be right. If his policy opened up a debate between united Republicans claiming we had gone soft and a Democratic Administration, with the JCS in disagreement if not open revolt, then my view is correct."

At the President's request, Rusk, Katzenbach, Taylor, Fortas and Clifford also commented on McNamara's paper, as well as Westmoreland and Bunker through reports by Rostow.[103]

Rusk generally agreed with McNamara's recommendations for stabilizing U.S. military operations in South Vietnam, but while agreeing that the bombing of the North should be more limited, he did not approve a bombing halt or a pause. "Purely from a political point of view *in relation to Hanoi,*" he said, "we have two major cards to play: (1) growing success in the South and (2) the bombing

[103] All of these memoranda are in the Johnson Library, NSF Country File, Vietnam. In chronological order their dates are as follows: Taylor, November 3; Fortas, November 5; Clifford November, 7; Katzenbach, November 16; Rusk, November 20; and Rostow's memorandum on Westmoreland, November 20; and on Bunker, November 21.

of the North." (emphasis in original) Any cessation of bombing "should be related to what will happen next. The Kissinger exercise did not even produce a discussion as to what your San Antonio formula means. They have never said that cessation will lead to talks. . . . I do not believe that we should cease the bombing before further probing on what the result would be."

As for a pause in the bombing, Rusk said he was skeptical "because I don't know who would be persuaded. Hanoi would call any pause (i.e., not permanent) an ultimatum. . . . For those in the outside world pressing for a halt in the bombing, no pause would be long enough."

Rusk said that he strongly supported bombing of infiltration routes in North Vietnam and Laos and areas around the demilitarized zone, but he rejected the argument that continuous escalation of bombing would break the will of the North Vietnamese, and favored limiting bombing in the Hanoi-Haiphong area to major military targets. He proposed the following guidelines:

> (a) we should bomb sufficiently to hold in place the AA [antiaircraft] defenses of the area;
>
> (b) we should bomb sufficiently to require substantial diversions of manpower to repairs and to maintaining communications;
>
> (c) we should not permit a complete sanctuary in the northern part of North Vietnam and thereby eliminate this incentive for peace.

"I believe," Rusk added, "we must resist pressure to take direct action against foreign shipping entering Haiphong or to bomb irrigation dikes."

In the South, where Rusk said that he and Bunker were "somewhat more optimistic" than McNamara about political developments, he said he generally agreed with the concept of stabilization, "on the assumption that actual results in the South would continue to accelerate," but that to announce it would help the Communists to plan and use their resources. He said he was strongly opposed to conducting U.S. ground operations against Laos and Cambodia, except that he favored "increased operations against infiltration routes through Laos, but not with U.S. combat units of significant size." He was also opposed to a U.S. invasion of North Vietnam. "If we cannot deal satisfactorily with forces now in South Vietnam, I do not see how we could improve the position by taking on more than 300,000 additional forces in North Vietnam." Moreover, there was a "very high risk" that ground action against North Vietnam "would cross the flash point" at which China and the U.S.S.R. might become more involved militarily in aiding North Vietnam.

The comments of Bunker and Westmoreland on McNamara's memorandum were made orally to Rostow, who then sent a memorandum to the President summarizing their views. Bunker's response, according to Rostow's summary, was that there was "no reason to believe that a bombing stand-down now would lead to serious negotiations, but he favored anti-infiltration operations (specifically the barrier and small unit ground operation in Laos against supply lines) that could put the U.S. in a better position to propose a pause at a later date. He was opposed to mining Haiphong harbor and to bombing dikes.

Bunker favored stabilization of U.S. forces and military operations in the South and the effort to transfer functions to the South Vietnamese military, but said it was important to avoid giving the South Vietnamese the impression that the U.S. was preparing to withdraw or relaxing in its efforts to win the war.

Bunker, Rostow said, "would make no statement committing us against ground operations in North Vietnam, Laos and Cambodia." His advice was to "keep them guessing."

Westmoreland, Rostow said, was opposed to a bombing halt or pause or to further limits on bombing in the Hanoi-Haiphong area. He believed, however, that U.S. efforts to harass and isolate Haiphong were effective, and he did not recommend mining Haiphong harbor. He also did not favor bombing the dikes.

As for stabilization in the South, Westmoreland said that it would be "foolish" to announce a 525,000 limit on U.S. forces, but he hoped it would prove to be the maximum requirement. He favored transferring functions to the South Vietnamese military and said that, over the next two years, this was his "central purpose," adding that while such a plan had been studied, "a mature operational program to transfer functions does not yet exist." He resisted, however, McNamara's proposal for a review of the conduct of U.S. military operations in which consideration would be given to programs that involved "reduced U.S. casualties" and "lesser destruction of the people and wealth of South Vietnam." (McNamara's third recommendation.) He said that every operation was based on respecting these considerations, but that he could not permit his tactical operations to be controlled by those criteria.

On the question of ground operations against North Vietnam, Laos and Cambodia, Westmoreland said that he wanted to have the capability, should the U.S. position in the area of the demilitarized zone require it at the time, of raiding North Vietnam "in force" above the DMZ in May or June of 1968—the earliest this would be "technically possible." He also was thinking, and had discussed with McNamara, of using South Vietnamese forces to conduct raids into Laos in the spring of 1968 against base areas being used by the Communists to support operations against U.S. forces in the highlands of South Vietnam. In Cambodia, where there were "'dozens, even hundreds,'" of Communist bases, he was sensitive to the political problem, but did not want to rule out the possibility of some kind of military action.

In his reply to the President's request for comment on McNamara's paper, Taylor commented as follows:

> While this course of action might tend to allay the fears of those who are concerned over an expansion of the conflict, it would provide fresh ammunition for the numerically larger number of critics who say that we are embarked on an endless and hopeless struggle or that we are really not trying to win. The decrease in our efforts implicit in this proposal would tend to nullify by a form of self-stagnation the progress which we properly contend that we are now making and would give renewed stimulus to our impatient fellow citizens who are even now crying for a quick solution or get out. . . .

> The curtailment of the bombing under this proposal has all the liabilities which we have noted in previous discussions of this issue. The South Vietnamese would be deeply discouraged by this lifting of the penalty which the bombing imposes on the North. I would suspect that our other allies contributing troops would object strongly to this course of action—they are convinced of the essentiality of the bombing. Our own forces would regard this action as a deliberate decrease in the protection which, they feel, is afforded them by the bombing. The large majority of our citizens who believe in the bombing but who thus far have been silent could be expected to raise violent objections on the home front, probably surpassing in volume the present criticism of the anti-bombers.
>
> Probably the most serious objection of all to this Pull-back Alternative would be the effect upon the enemy. Any such retreat will be interpreted as weakness and will add to the difficulty of getting any kind of eventual solution compatible with our overall objective of an independent South Vietnam free from the threat of subversive aggression.
>
> I would recommend strongly against adopting any such course of action.

In his reply, Justice Fortas said that he was strongly opposed to McNamara's proposal. "I can think of nothing worse than the suggested program. . . . This is an invitation to slaughter. *It will, indeed, produce demands in this country to withdraw* . . . it means *not* domestic appeasement, but domestic repudiation (which it would deserve); a powerful tonic to Chinese communist effectiveness in the world; and a powerful retreat to the Asian dominoes." (emphases in original) He added, "I must frankly state again that I am not convinced that our military program in South Vietnam is as flexible or ingenious as it could be. I know that new proposals have been sought from our military. But perhaps a new and fresh look, including new people—civilian as well as military—might be warranted."

Clifford said in his reply that McNamara's proposal would "retard the possibility of concluding the conflict rather than accelerating it." "Hanoi will never seek a cessation of the conflict if they think our determination is lessening. On the other hand, if our pressure is unremitting and their losses continue to grow, and hope fades for any sign of weakening on our part, then some day they will conclude that the game is not worth the candle."

With respect to the bombing halt, Clifford said:

> Would the unconditional suspension of the bombing, without any effort to extract a quid pro quo persuade Hanoi that we were firm and unyielding in our conviction to force them to desist from their aggressive designs?
>
> The answer is a loud and resounding "no."
>
> It would be interpreted by Hanoi as (a) evidence of our discouragement and frustration, and (b) an admission of the wrongness and immorality of our bombing of the North, and (c) the first step in our ultimate total disengagement from the conflict.
>
> It would give an enormous lift to the spirits and morale of the North, and an equally grave setback to the will and deter-

mination of the South Vietnamese and our other allies fighting with us.

It would dramatically confirm the conviction of the North that Premier Pham Van Dong was correct when he said, "Americans do not like long, inconclusive wars; thus we are sure to win in the end."

Concerning the proposal to announce a policy of stabilization, Clifford said:

Can there be any doubt as to the North Vietnamese reaction to such an announcement? The chortles of unholy glee issuing from Hanoi would be audible in every capital of the world.

Is this evidence of our zeal and courage to stay the course? Of course not! It would be interpreted to be exactly what it is. A resigned and discouraged effort to find a way out of a conflict for which we had lost our will and dedication.

And what of our bargaining position? It would have been utterly destroyed. Hanoi would be secure in the comforting thought that we had informed the world that we would refrain from practically all activities that would be damaging to North Vietnam.

It would be tantamount to turning over our hole card and showing Hanoi that it was a deuce.

For his part, Katzenbach sent the President on November 16, 1967, a long memorandum that included comments on the issues raised by McNamara but was more in the nature of a statement of Katzenbach's own views than his reaction to McNamara's proposal. In the paper, Katzenbach stated the premises of U.S. strategy, analyzed the two options which he said the President had in deciding future strategy, and discussed the steps necessary for carrying out the preferred option. This was his argument: "Until we can build the Government of Vietnam as a government and as a fighting force to the point where it can, with moderate levels of outside assistance, both sustain itself and deal adequately with DRV-supported [Democratic Republic of Vietnam—North Vietnam] insurrection and terror, we must base our strategy on six fundamental premises:

1. *The war is being actively fought on two fronts: One, in Viet-Nam* with our military and civilian efforts; the other, in the United States with our efforts to maintain whatever level of popular and Congressional support is necessary to continue our efforts.

2. *Hanoi's strategy is based on winning the war in the United States, not in Viet-Nam* where our military might obviously forecloses that possibility.

The DRV strategy should not be analyzed in terms of phase 1, phase 2 warfare. Hanoi uses time the way the Russians used terrain before Napoleon's advance on Moscow, always retreating, losing every battle, but eventually creating conditions in which the enemy can no longer function. For Napoleon it was his long supply lines and the cold Russian winter; Hanoi hopes that for us it will be the mounting dissension, impatience, and frustration caused by a protracted war without fronts or other visible signs of success; a growing need to choose between guns and butter; and an increasing American repugnance at finding, for the first time, their own country cast as "the heavy" with massive fire power brought to bear against a "small Asian nation."

3. *The war can be lost in the United States.* There is considerable justification for Hanoi's belief that public and Congressional opinion will not permit the United States to keep meeting immense costs in men, money, and—above all—severe internal divisions for many more months without an end visibly in sight.

4. *The military requirements of Hanoi's strategy are minimal and well within the DRV's capabilities.* Even if it never wins a battle, the DRV can create the conditions of growing dissension in the United States merely by denying us crucial victories, inflicting (as well as taking) sizeable casualties and requiring us to maintain a large and expensive force in Viet-Nam. Unless we undertake a full-scale and unlimited war on the North—and almost certainly, even then—this will continue to be well within the DRV's capacities for years to come.

5. *Hanoi will continue to fight, so long as it continues to believe it will win the South; and it will continue to believe it will win the South so long as dissension flourishes and grows in the United States.* The additional costs we can still impose on North Viet-Nam without invading the DRV weigh far less in Hanoi's scales than the value of continuing a fight which they believe we will be prepared to abandon relatively soon. Unless and until they are persuaded that we are not going to abandon Viet-Nam, they thus have little incentive for negotiation.

6. *While the position of the DRV/VC in the field may be weakened by increasing our commitment of men and money to the war and/or reducing our self-imposed restrictions as to how and where we fight, this result is by no means certain. What is certain is that these actions at the same time increase the level of dissent at home and thus bolster the sole basis for Hanoi's hopes.* (emphases in original)

Katzenbach said that the President had two broad strategic options:

1. *You can increase the commitment of men and money and reduce the restrictions on how and where we fight in an effort to score a quick "knock-out" of enemy forces in Viet-Nam before dissent at home—which will be greatly increased by these actions—becomes overwhelming.*

2. *You can concentrate on adjusting the United States to a longer pull by gradually attacking the sources of at least much of the growing opposition to the war.* (emphases in original)

The U.S., Katzenbach said, should follow the first strategic option "only if we believe that we can destroy the enemy's military forces, eliminate its infrastructure and destroy its will to persist well before American public opinion decides to wash its hands of the whole Vietnam problem." "[I]f we believe we do have this capability, then it would be logical to grant General Westmoreland a virtual carte blanche, authorizing an extension of the war into North Vietnam, Laos and Cambodia, remove all target restrictions in the North, make an all-out effort to increase other free world commitments in Vietnam, send U.S. troops into the Mekong Delta in a major campaign, etc. . . . In effect, most of this General Westmoreland wants to do. He has been given an extremely difficult mission, and naturally seeks every possible military means with which to carry it out. If I were in his shoes I would do the same thing." "The rub is that we can't in this way destroy the continuing capacity of the DRV/VC to inflict heavy casualties and to tie down large numbers of American troops so long as there is a sanctuary in North Vietnam, a reserve of 400,000 troops, and a willingness of Communist allies to provide material support. And if we cannot destroy the DRV's capacity to continue fighting, it will be our democratic will to fight on—not Hanoi's dictatorial will—that will suffer the harder blow. . . . Only from Hanoi's point of view is there much to recommend a strategy that promises greatly to increase dissension, impatience, and frustration within the United States without greatly reducing the capacity of the DRV to stop fighting."

The alternative, Katzenbach said, "is to pursue a strategy whose principal purpose is to restore the center position here in the United States," and by reducing domestic dissent, "eliminate the basis for Hanoi's hope that we will abandon Vietnam before the GVN is able to withstand Communist pressures on its own."

This alternative strategy, which Katzenbach discussed at some length in his paper, was quite similar to McNamara's proposal: a bombing halt or at least the cessation of bombing in the Hanoi-Haiphong area, stabilization of U.S. military forces and operations, no significant extension of ground operations into North Vietnam, Laos or Cambodia, greater emphasis on South Vietnamese responsibility for military and political functions, and less destructive ground war operations in the South.

Katzenbach concluded by recommending steps to re-build public confidence, including major statements by the President and other civilian and military leaders, statements by Thieu and Ky emphasizing their hope for peace and for assuming responsibility for the security and government of the country, and clarification of U.S. objectives, both within the government and for the public, to make it clear that the main objective was *"to provide the military cover and non-military assistance needed to enable the Government of Vietnam to grow in capacity and popular support to the point where it can survive and, over a period of years, deal with what will remain a continuing and serious Communist problem."* (emphasis in original) This, Katzenbach said, would be a "far more limited, far more attainable objective than an alternative formulation we sometimes suggest: to administer all significant bases of Communist antigovernment power in South Vietnam and to convince North Vietnam to allow the South to follow an independent course without outside interference." Such a change in objective, he said, "should mean that MACV would deploy its forces so as to minimize their involvement with the population, and to reduce substantially American involvement in those measures which should be the GVN's responsibility. It would probably mean:

—a vigorous review of free bombing zones,

—a policy on refugees which would sharply reduce our vulnerabilities at home and around the world on this festering sore point,

—dramatic new efforts to reduce civilian casualties,

—and an end to the continual military requests for incremental expansion of the war into Laos, Cambodia and North Vietnam.

What was the President's reaction to McNamara's paper and the responses of other senior associates? There are no notes on the Luncheon Group meeting of October 31, at which McNamara explained his position, and there was apparently no group discussion of the memorandum subsequently. Based on a few comments by the President in other meetings of the Luncheon Group in following weeks, however, it would appear that he was reflecting on some of the ideas expressed in the memorandum from McNamara and other senior advisers, especially with respect to the bombing of North Vietnam. Although additional targets in the Hanoi-Haiphong area were attacked during November—on November 16–17 one of the major Haiphong shipyards and Bac Mai airfield near the center of Hanoi were bombed for the first time—the President apparently was becoming more concerned about the trade-off between the military benefits and the losses of planes and crews as well as the unfavorable publicity. At a meeting of the Luncheon Group on November 4, he "wondered whether the bombing of the small tire factories, steel mills and airfields are 'worth all the hell we are catching here.'" At the same meeting he asked about "how we are going to do a better job of winning the war in the South." "'We've been on dead center for the last year,'" he said.[104]

At another meeting of the group on November 9, the President rejected a request from General Wheeler on October 27 to allow more bombing in the Hanoi-Haiphong area by reducing the size of the prohibited area.[105]

At a meeting of the group on November 15 attended by Rusk, McNamara, Rostow, Wheeler, Helms, Christian and Tom Johnson, and by Ambassador Bunker who, as will be seen, was in the country for consultation and public appearances, the President told the group that he wanted them to "get the number of [North Vietnamese] targets down to the absolute minimum."[106]

At a breakfast meeting on November 21 with those who attended the meeting on the 16th, joined by the Vice President and by General Westmoreland, who was also in the U.S. for consultation and public appearances, the President "asked about the increase in the number of planes lost. 'I am beginning,'" he said, "'to agree with Bob McNamara that it does not appear the targets are worth the loss in planes.'"[107]

"The President emphasized 'the clock is ticking.' [This was a reference to U.S. public opinion.] Get the targets you have to hit. The bombing arouses so much opposition in the country."

---

[104] Jim Jones' Notes of the meeting on November 4, cited above.
[105] *PP*, Gravel ed., vol. IV, p. 14. There are no notes of this meeting.
[106] Johnson Library, Tom Johnson's Notes of Meetings, Notes of meeting Nov. 16, 1967.
[107] Same location, Notes of meeting November 21.

On November 28, the President announced that McNamara would become President of the World Bank and would be replaced by Clark Clifford.[108]

On December 18, 1967, President Johnson, having studied McNamara's proposed course of action "with the utmost care," wrote a "memorandum for the file" stating his conclusions:[109]

> The memorandum of Secretary McNamara dated November 1, 1967 . . . raises fundamental questions of policy with reference to the conduct of the war in Vietnam.
>
> I have read it, and studied it, with the utmost care. In addition, I have asked certain advisers to give their written reactions to the memo. These reactions are attached.
>
> I have consulted at length with Ambassador Bunker and General Westmoreland on their recent trip to Washington.
>
> At my suggestion, a group of senior advisers [the Wise Men] attended a lengthy briefing at the State Department and then met for a full discussion with me.
>
> I have carefully considered the questions presented and the individual views expressed, and I have reached the following conclusions:
>
> With respect to bombing North Vietnam, I would wish for us to
>
> > —authorize and strike those remaining targets which, after study, we judge to have significant military content but which would not involve excessive civilian casualties; excessive U.S. losses; or substantial increased risk of engaging the USSR or Communist China in the war;
> >
> > —maintain on a routine basis a restrike program for major targets through North Vietnam;
> >
> > —strive to remove the drama and public attention given to our North Vietnamese bombing operations.
>
> I have concluded that, under the present circumstances, a unilateral and unrequited bombing stand-down would be read in both Hanoi and the United States as a sign of weakening will. It would encourage the extreme doves; increase the pressure for withdrawal from those who argue "bomb and get out"; decrease support from our most steady friends; and pick up support from only a small group of moderate doves.
>
> I would not, of course, rule out playing our bombing card under circumstances where there is reason for confidence that it would move us toward peace. But with the failure of the Paris track and the opening of Buttercup [contacts in late 1967 between U.S. Embassy officials in Saigon and agents purport-

---

[108] For information and commentary on this event see Shapley, *Promise and Power,* pp. 427, 437–440, Johnson, *The Vantage Point,* p. 20, and Kearns, *Lyndon Johnson and the American Dream,* pp. 320–321.

Washington Post reporter Chalmers M. Roberts provides this vignette in his memoirs, *First Rough Draft: A Journalist's Journal of Our Times* (New York, Praeger, 1973), p. 264: "In the end, McNamara turned dove on the war. . . . He deeply felt a sense of responsibility for the lost lives. And he was close to a physical breakdown. LBJ had denied that he fired McNamara, contending that he simply was fulfilling a McNamara request by shifting him to the top job at the World Bank. The day that shift was announced, Benjamin Bradlee, by now the *Post's* managing editor, and I went to see LBJ to talk about the shift. While we were in his office, the phone rang. It was McNamara. . . . We could hear only Johnson's end of the conversation. His pregnant sentence: 'Yes, Bob, I'm sitting here with tears in my eyes, too.' LBJ was as dry-eyed as any human being could be."

[109] Johnson, *The Vantage Point,* pp. 600–601.

edly representing the NLF]—at a time when the North is being bombed—I do not believe we should move from our present policy unless hard evidence suggests such a change would be profitable.

With respect to operations on the ground, I do not believe we should announce a so-called policy of stabilization. An announced change would have, in my judgment, some of the political effects in Hanoi and in the United States of a unilateral bombing stand-down.

On the other hand, at the moment I see no basis for increasing U.S. forces above the current approved level.

As for the movement of U.S. forces across the frontiers of South Vietnam, I am inclined to be extremely reserved unless a powerful case can be made. There are two reasons: the political risks involved, and the diversion of forces from pressure on the VC and from all the other dimensions of pacification. But I believe it unwise to announce a policy that would deny us these options.

The third recommendation of Secretary McNamara has merit. I agree that we should review the conduct of military operations in South Vietnam with a view to reducing U.S. casualties, accelerating the turnover of responsibility to the GVN, and working toward less destruction and fewer casualties in South Vietnam.

As can be seen by reviewing the responses of senior advisors to McNamara's memorandum, the President's own position was very similar to that of Rusk and Katzenbach as well as the general position of McGeorge Bundy. Indeed, except for differences on the bombing halt—which were critical, of course, given the fact that a bombing halt appeared to be the prerequisite for negotiations—and the *announcement* of stabilization, the President generally agreed with McNamara. While believing that U.S. national interest required the war to be continued until the Communists could be defeated or forced to negotiate, he had become disillusioned about the possibility of winning a military victory and about the ability of air power to break the will of the North Vietnamese or to prevent necessary supplies and troops from infiltrating the South. On the other hand, he did not believe that a bombing halt would lead to negotiations. (Therein lay the rub, for without a bombing halt there could be no negotiations.) Yet, he was also aware, as Harriman continued to argue, that under the circumstances, a negotiated settlement was necessary and inevitable. Generally, he agreed with his advisers that the war had to be won in the South and by the South Vietamese. While recognizing that some progress appeared to have been made, he was not optimistic about whether effective self-government could be achieved, or whether it could be achieved in a timely manner before the loss of U.S. public support for the war would necessitate a change of policy.[110]

[110] In early December 1967, a group of 24 prominent Americans took a position quite similar to that of McNamara and Katzenbach. After a meeting in Bermuda on December 1–3 sponsored by the Carnegie Endowment for International Peace, they issued a statement warning that "There now appears to be a serious danger that the momentum of the Vietnam conflict may carry hostilities to disproportionate and even perilous levels . . . if we were to pursue present

Continued

Vice President Humphrey's Trip to Vietnam and General Westmoreland's Trip to Washington, November 1967

On October 31, 1967, Thieu and Ky took office as President and Vice President in a ceremony in Saigon in which Vice President Humphrey represented the United States. In cables to President Johnson on October 30 and November 1, Humphrey reported that good progress was being made.[111] "I am encouraged," he said in his October 30 cable, "not only by the evident progress I have seen over February, 1966, when I was last here, but by the expressed

---

objectives by widening the war as by ground probes into Laos and Cambodia, our commitments would escalate along with our risks, and the next step would be an invasion of North Vietnam. Such developments would entail unacceptable risks and threaten world peace."

The text of the "Bermuda paper" is in the *New York Times,* Jan. 17, 1968. Those attending the meeting included Hedley Donovan, editor of *Time* magazine, Gen. Matthew Ridgway, and three former members of the Wise Men—John Cowles, publisher of the *Minneapolis Star and Tribune,* attorney Roswell Gilpatrick, former Deputy Secretary of Defense, and George Kistiakowsky, a professor at Harvard University who had been a Presidential science adviser.

The group recommended that U.S. policy "should aim at moderating the level of hostilities regardless of whether formal negotiations for an ultimate settlement are now possible. . . . American posture should be one that can be sustained for an indefinite period with reduced risks and increased political benefits until such time as the conflict can be resolved in an honorable and peaceful fashion." Specifically, "The emphasis should not be on the military destruction of Communist forces in the South but on the protection of the people of South Vietnam and the stabilization of the situation at a politically tolerable level. Tactically, this would involve a shift in emphasis from 'search-and-destroy' to 'clear-and-hold' operations." The U.S. should also stop the bombing of North Vietnam. The South Vietnamese Government "should be steadily pressed to assume greater and greater responsibility, both political and military, for the defense and pacification of the country." In addition the U.S. needed to recognize the National Liberation Front "as an organized factor in the political life of South Vietnam."

On December 19, three representatives of the Bermuda group presented their case to William Leonhart, the NSC staff member who worked with Komer on pacification, and to Marshall Wright, who worked with Leonhart. See Wright's memorandum to Rostow, December 19, Johnson Library, NSF Country File, Vietnam. A list of the 24 participants in the Bermuda meeting is attached to this memorandum.

At about the same time as the Bermuda Conference, a group of Asian scholars held a three-day conference on the U.S. and Eastern Asia, sponsored by Freedom House, an organization, as noted earlier, which for many years had worked closely with the U.S. Government. The conference had been initiated by John Roche, White House Consultant, working with Professor Robert Scalapino of the University of California, a supporter of U.S. policy in Vietnam.

Among other faculty and experts who attended the conference were William W. Lockwood of Princeton University, Lucian Pye of the Massachusetts Institute of Technology and Edwin Reischauer of Harvard University. See the report of the meeting, which includes a list of conferees, "The United States and Eastern Asia," issued on Dec. 20, 1967 by Freedom House.

In their report on the conference, the Asian scholars took the position that "To avoid a major war in the Asia-Pacific region, it is essential that the United States continue to deter, restrain, and counterbalance Chinese power."

"The stakes in Vietnam," the report said, "now go far beyond that nation. . . . To accept a Communist victory in Vietnam would serve as a major encouragement to those forces in the world opposing peaceful coexistence, to those elements committed to the thesis that violence is the best means of affecting change. It would gravely jeopardize the possibilities of a political equilibrium in Asia, seriously damage our credibility, deeply affect the morale—and the policies—of our Asia allies and the neutrals."

But although these Asian scholars supported U.S. policy, they also took a position quite similar to that of McNamara and Katzenbach as well as to the position of the group that issued the Bermuda statement. For one thing, they warned against the danger of escalating the war into a regional or global conflict, and argued that "Nothing would do more to strengthen American support for our basic position than to show a capacity for innovation of a deescalatory nature. . . ." They also took the position that, "An increasing emphasis must be placed upon 'seize and hold,' rather than 'search and destroy' operations with the peasants being given the protection against extortion and pillage from all sides. . . ." Moreover, they said, "Corruption must be rigorously attacked. Social reforms, especially those that would enhance rural support, must be strongly supported."

In a memorandum for Marvin Watson on December 14, with an attached copy of the Asian scholars' report, Roche said "At the risk of sounding boastful, another of my enterprises has reached fruition. I got Scalapino and [Leo] Cherne [who was associated with Freedom House] going on this last spring." "We are trying," he added, "to get maximum publicity for it. Walt [Rostow] sent a copy to Hedley Donovan of *Time-Life,* and tomorrow a delegation of the signers is visiting [Turner] Catledge of the *New York Times.* (Johnson Library, Office Files of Harry McPherson, Memorandum for Marvin Watson from John Roche, Dec. 14, 1967.

[111] U.S. Department of State, Pol 7 US/Humphrey, Saigon to Washington 9985, Oct. 30, 1967, and Kuala Lumpur to Washington 1709, Nov. 1, 1967.

determination of both Thieu and Ky to move strongly not only militarily but in building a responsive, representative government." "There is solid reason," he said in his November 1 cable, "for satisfaction and optimism if the true picture can be shown and the public can be made to understand it. I am certain that our country can steadily be mobilized in support of our efforts here. We are winning—steady progress is everywhere evident. . . . More than ever, I am convinced that what we are doing here is right and that we have no choice but to persevere and see it through to success."

To his close friend Edgar Berman, who accompanied him on the trip, Humphrey reportedly said the opposite: "From what I know and see here now," he told Berman in Saigon, "I think we're in real trouble. America is throwing lives and money down a corrupt rat hole."[112]

On the return trip to Washington, Berman asked Humphrey what he was going to say to President Johnson. "He answered obliquely: 'I hope they know what they're doing. As of right now I'm damn sure we're not doing the Vietnamese or ourselves any good. We're murdering civilians by the thousands and our boys are dying in rotten jungles—for what? A corrupt, selfish government that has no feeling—no morality. I'm going to tell Johnson exactly what I think, and I just hope and pray he'll take it like I give it." [113]

Upon his return to Washington, the Vice President met on November 8 from 9:42 a.m. to 10:03 a.m. with the President and Rostow, to make his report. The President responded by suggesting to him which aspects he should emphasize in discussing it at the larger meeting which followed and in public appearances.[114]

From 10:03 a.m. to 10:55 a.m. there was a meeting of the National Security Council attended by the President, the Vice President, Rusk, McNamara, Rostow, Wheeler, Cabinet Secretaries and other government officials and White House staff. In addition, several Members of Congress had been invited to attend: Senators Mansfield, Russell, Smith, Fulbright, Hayden, Speaker McCormack, and Representatives Bates and Mahon. Humphrey reported on his trip, stressing, as the President had suggested, that pacification was "beginning to move," action was being taken to eliminate corruption, the spirit and morale of U.S. forces was high, South Vietnamese forces were greatly improved, the election had produced a "very good affect."[115] "On my last trip to Vietnam," Humphrey

---

[112] Edgar Berman, *Hubert*, p. 115.

[113] *Ibid.*, p. 116. In his autobiography, Humphrey said, "If my first trip to Vietnam, almost two years before, had made me certain that what we were doing there was right, my second trip brought back many uncertainties. . . . Americanization of the war was virtually total. We had taken over the economy, we had taken over the fighting, we had taken over South Vietnam. . . . Even Thieu's inaugural address had been largely written by our embassy. I knew then the American people would not stand for this kind of involvement much longer." Hubert H. Humphrey, *The Education of a Public Man: My Life in Politics* (Garden City, N.Y.: Doubleday, 1976), pp. 348–349.

[114] Johnson Library, Tom Johnson's Notes of Meetings, Notes of meeting Nov. 8, 1967 in the President's office. It is not known whether Humphrey made a written report to the President. According to archivist John Wilson at the LBJ Library, no report can be found. To date, the search for a copy in the Humphrey Papers at the Minnesota Historical Society has also been unsuccessful.

[115] In the Johnson Library there are two sets of notes on the NSC meeting of November 8. The first, by Tom Johnson, is in Tom Johnson's Notes of Meetings. The second, by Bromley Smith, is in the NSF NSC Meetings File.

told the group, "I came back 'impressed.' Today, I returned 'encouraged.'"

The President asked for questions from the Members of Congress who were present. Senator Fulbright asked the Vice President, "What is our objective out there?" Humphrey replied that the objective had not changed. "Before you can build a country, you have to put down the insurgency. Many of the Asian leaders told me that their number one enemy is Asian militant communism with headquarters in Peking."

"Senator Fulbright said he was confused as to what the Vice President thinks our objective is. 'Is the enemy the North Vietnamese or the Chinese? I think it makes a big difference.'"

"The Vice President said that the South Vietnamese know who the enemy is. Those boys out there who are being shot and maimed don't have any difficulty recognizing who the enemy is."

Senator Mansfield said that the Vice President's report was "mildly encouraging." He asked about the rate of infiltration and the Communists' troop strength in South Vietnam compared to the previous year. Humphrey replied that he had not inquired about infiltration. The troop strength was about the same as a year earlier.

Senator Russell praised Humphrey for his report. He noted that the enemy buildup along the DMZ led him to conclude that bombing had not been effective in closing infiltration routes and supply lines, and he wondered about the possible closing of the port of Haiphong. Humphrey replied that this was discussed, but that it was a "policy decision."

After the meeting concluded, the President met from 1:00 p.m. to 2:15 p.m. with the Luncheon Group—Rusk, McNamara, Rostow and Christian, but there are apparently no notes on the meeting.

A week later (November 15), General Westmoreland and Ambassador Bunker, accompanied by Komer, arrived in Washington for a visit which, like Humphrey's trip to Vietnam, was intended to serve primarily as a way of promoting U.S. public and congressional support for the war. As Westmoreland said in his memoirs, the trip was "ostensibly for further consultations, but in reality for public relations purposes."[116]

While in Washington, in addition to meeting with the President, Westmoreland met with McNamara and then with the JCS and with the House and Senate Armed Services Committees in executive session. He also made speeches to the National Press Club and to a dinner meeting at the White House for Democratic Members of the House of Representatives. Westmoreland and Bunker also appeared on the National Broadcasting Company's television program, "Meet the Press," and Bunker met with the Senate Foreign Relations Committee in executive session.[117]

When he arrived in Washington, Westmoreland told the press, "I have never been more encouraged in my four years in Vietnam."[118] In his speech to the Press Club on November 19, he said that the war was going well, and had reached the point "when the end be-

[116] Westmoreland, *A Soldier Reports*, p. 231.

[117] For news stories on these various meetings and speeches see the *New York Times*, Nov. 15–22, 1967.

[118] *Ibid.*, Nov. 16, 1967.

gins to come into view."[119] Although he said he was reluctant to estimate how long it would be before U.S. troops could start withdrawing, he was quoted as saying in congressional testimony that the U.S. could begin to phase down its commitment in two years or less—a statement that he confirmed on "Meet the Press." He made the same statement in meetings with the President, McNamara and the JCS, and at the White House dinner.[120]

In a cable on November 26 to his deputy, General Abrams, Westmoreland said he took this position "on my own initiative . . . after considerable thought based on the following considerations:[121]

> I believe the concept and objective plan for our forces, as well as those of the Vietnamese [is feasible] and as such it should serve as an incentive. The concept is compatible with the evolution of the war since our initial commitment and portrays to the American people "some light at the end of the tunnel." The concept justifies the augmentation of troops I've asked for based on the principle of reinforcing success and also supports an increase in the strength of the Vietnamese forces and their modernization. The concept straddles the Presidential election of November 1968, implying that the election is not a bench mark from a military point of view. Finally, it puts emphasis on the essential role of the Vietnamese in carrying a major burden of their war against the Communists but also suggests that we must be prepared for a protracted commitment.

He told Abrams to have the MACV staff begin to study "the specific areas and time frames in which responsibility might be transferred from the U.S. to the Vietnamese. Based on these studies, I visualize a program that would initiate and manage the multiple actions necessary to put the Vietnamese in a posture to make possible some transfer of responsibility at the earliest practical time."[122]

For his part, Bunker also emphasized the progress that was being made. In his closed meeting with the Senate Foreign Relations Committee on November 16 he said, among other things, "the military situation has greatly improved," "pacification has gained momentum." "It is my opinion," he told the committee, "that we have had a good measure of success, that we are making steady, not spectacular but steady progress, and that we are gradually achieving our aims in Vietnam. . . . We are also at the point

---

[119] *Ibid.*, Nov. 20, 1967.

[120] For Westmoreland's notes for these meetings see National Archives, Westmoreland-CBS Papers, "Notes for Talk With the President (Also used in Briefing Sec Def, JCS, Senate and House Armed Services Committees), November 1967." See also "Substance of General Westmoreland's Opening Remarks to the JCS, Friday, 17 November 1967," Johnson Library, NSF Country File, Vietnam. For notes on the White House dinner for Democratic Members of Congress see in the Johnson Library, Congressional Briefings, the transcript (from tape) of the meeting of Nov. 16, 1967.

[121] CMH, Westmoreland Papers, Message Files, Westmoreland to Abrams, HWA 3445, Nov. 26, 1967.

[122] In an interview some years later, Westmoreland gave this further explanation: "Now, I did not visualize how long that process would take. My thought was it might take ten years, and our rate of withdrawal would depend to a great degree on the conduct of the enemy, and what we were able to, say, negotiate with the enemy. And a very important element of that strategy was the increase in bombing in order to weaken the enemy in the North, weaken him by accentuating the pressure, and in strengthening our friends by modernizing their equipment and by leaving our troops there as long as necessary. . . ." Michael Charlton and Anthony Moncrieff, *Many Reasons Why: The American Involvement in Vietnam* (New York: Hill and Wang, 1978), p. 145.

where the steady progress I have referred to can be accelerated in all of these fields. . . ."[123]

Members of the committee asked Bunker how and when the war would end. He replied that he could not predict when it would end, but that "we are going to win." As to how it would end, he said he thought, as Lodge had suggested, that it might end when the Communists simply faded away.

There was considerable discussion about the variance between press reports on the war and the statements of U.S. officials. Senator Case said, "I have never seen a situation in which there was almost a unanimous impression on the part of the newspaper reporters in the face of what has been more or less continuous, general optimistic reports by our agencies of government, and this is something that people cannot understand and is the main cause of our difficulty." Bunker said he agreed that this was a problem. Many of the reporters, he said, were young and inexperienced, and had preconceived ideas. But he added, "I don't know any more than you do, Senator [Case], how we get what we do. . . . But certainly as far as my objective view, as far as I can be objective, and I try to be, I just think the general impression that is created about the Vietnamese Armed Forces, about pacification, gives a very distorted view."

On November 21, the President met from 8:30 a.m. to 10:30 a.m. with Westmoreland, Bunker, the Vice President, Rusk, McNamara, Rostow, Wheeler, Helms, Komer, Christian and Tom Johnson. Justice Fortas also attended.[124] The President asked if the State and Defense Departments had "done all they could" to get the additional troops from other allied countries as well as those promised by the South Vietnamese. "'The clock is ticking,'" he said. "We need to get all the additional troops as fast as we can."[125] He said his "main concern was that General Westmoreland get what he wants as soon as possible." Westmoreland replied that "from a practical standpoint he had all he needed at this stage . . . 525,000 men [the total of U.S. forces approved for Program V] will be a well-balanced, hard-hitting force."

"The President stressed the need to bring the South Vietnamese Government to the center of the stage stressing tax needs, anti-corruption measures and a need for a reform image."

The President also asked, "if there is anything else that the United States government should be doing to bring about peace." Bunker replied, "we have tried everything. The more efforts we make now, the more Ho believes we want to get out."

The President asked Rostow to gather information on four or five U.S. peace initiatives. "'I don't expect to do any more talking,'" he said, "'until I hear from them [the North Vietnamese]. There has been enough talk on this.'"

---

[123] U.S. Congress, Senate, Committee on Foreign Relations, unpublished executive session transcript, Nov. 16, 1967.

[124] Fortas' name is not on the President's Daily Diary list of those who attended, but on the copy of his "Memorandum for the Record," Nov. 22, 1967, in which he listed the names and summarized the major points covered at the meeting, Westmoreland notes, after the list of names: "plus Justice Fortas." CMH, Westmoreland Papers, History File.

[125] Johnson Library, Tom Johnson's Notes of Meetings, notes of meeting Nov. 21, 1967, Nov. 24, 1967.

The President "asked why we are so silent about the Cambodian situation, particularly in light of recent press reports about base camps along the Cambodian border." "Why not raise hell," he asked.[126] He said he was "tired of Sihanouk's actions." McNamara suggested that the U.S. should "surface more information about Cambodia." The President suggested getting Ambassador Goldberg to make some speeches on the subject.

The President asked for recommendations for operations in Laos. Westmoreland said he wanted to initiate action in a border area of Laos, using two South Vietnamese battalions for a raid of three to four days (Operation SOUTHPAW). Bunker said he agreed. "'80% of their supplies come through Laos. To give them a free hand is suicidal.'"

Wheeler said that the JCS agreed that Westmoreland should be authorized to initiate the raid within the next 60–90 days.

On the air war, the President asked about increased losses of U.S. planes, saying, as was noted earlier, "'I am beginning to agree with Bob McNamara that it does not appear the targets are worth the loss in planes.'" He added, "I want to pull out of Hanoi-Haiphong some time."[127] Emphasizing again that "the clock is ticking," he said, "Get the targets you have to hit. The bombing arouses so much opposition in this country."

In a cable to Abrams after the meeting, Westmoreland listed the "guidance" which the President had given at the meeting:[128]

> A. We should encourage the GVN to pursue their anticorruption campaign and to publicize it.
>
> B. We should do all possible to make credible to the press body count reports on enemy KIA [killed in action] (there is a strong school of thought at senior level that we should discontinue reporting enemy casualties).
>
> C. We should differentiate between hospitalized WIA's [wounded in action] and those not hospitalized.
>
> D. We should advertise the association of the people with the government.
>
> E. We should do all possible to reduce civilian casualties and to publicize our concern for these casualties and the extraordinary steps taken to minimize them. We should stress that fewer civilians are getting killed and wounded in this war than in other wars of this century.
>
> F. We should cooperate with the press in identifying areas in Cambodia used by the enemy.
>
> G. We should plan on more visitors from the US and take steps to give them the picture. These will primarily involved preachers, educators, and Congressmen.
>
> H. Ambassador Bunker and I should plan on periodically making a report to the folks back home.
>
> I. As a matter of priority, we must put ARVN in the center of the stage, with the objective of improving their image and

---

[126] Johnson Library, Papers of Walt W. Rostow, handwritten notes by Rostow on the meeting of November 21.

[127] The remark about pulling out appears in Rostow's handwritten notes cited above.

[128] CMH, Westmoreland Papers, Message Files, Westmoreland to Abrams, HWA 3424, Nov. 23, 1967.

convincing the American people that they want to fight and are fighting.

Although Westmoreland, in response to the President's request for recommendations concerning Laos, had said he wanted to initiate raids under Operation SOUTHPAW, and Bunker and Wheeler had agreed, the President apparently did not comment on the proposal and did not approve the recommendation.

On the night of November 20, before the meeting the following morning, Westmoreland and his wife, who were staying at the White House, had dinner with the President and Mrs. Johnson and Senator Russell. In a private conversation with Westmoreland later in the evening, the President, Westmoreland said in his notes, "let his hair down." He told Westmoreland that McNamara was leaving and would be replaced by Clifford. He also said that his health was not good, that he and Lady Bird were tired, and he did not plan to be a candidate in 1968. He wondered what the reaction of the troops would be. As noted earlier, Westmoreland replied that if the troops were told why he had made the decision, "they would understand and it would not adversely affect their morale." [129]

Polls Indicate Greater Public Confidence and Support for Military Action

Toward the end of 1967, public confidence in President Johnson's handling of the war rebounded from the lowest rating of his Presidency in late October, rising 11 points between then and late November according to a Harris Survey: [130]

"How would you rate the job President Johnson has been doing in handling the war in Vietnam?"

[In percent]

	Positive	*Negative*
Late November, 1967	34	66
Late October	23	77
September	31	69
August	33	67
June	46	54

The Gallup Poll reported a similar increase: [131]

"Do you approve or disapprove of the way Johnson is handling the situation in Vietnam?"

[In percent]

	Approve	*Disapprove*	*No Opinion*
November	35	52	13
December	40	48	12

Attitudes toward the war also changed substantially toward the end of the year. On December 23, 1967, Harris reported that "The prevailing mood in America today toward the Vietnam conflict is to intensify military pressure without limits and see the war through. . . . Public opinion has now crystallized, at least tempo-

---

[129] CMH, Westmoreland Papers, History Notes for November 20, 1967, and *A Soldier Reports*, p. 233.
[130] Harris Survey, *Washington Post*, Dec. 4, 1967.
[131] *Vietnam War, A Compilation: 1964–1990*, vol. 2.

rarily, on the side of those who have been saying that a 'war of attrition' may eventually bring about a political settlement. . . . In the absence of any other acceptable alternatives the American people have turned to the view that an intensification of military pressure might be the surest and speediest way out of Vietnam." [132]

"In general," Harris said, "escalation is favoured over deescalation by 63 to 37 per cent. This is a high-water mark for feelings that the military effort should be intensified. The previous high was 59 percent last May. However, last July a majority of people wanted to see the war de-escalated."

"By 58 to 24 percent the public feels that the road to a negotiated peace is 'to convince the Communists they will lose the war if they continue the fighting.' In July, the division on the same proposition was a slim 45 to 42 percent."

"By 63 to 24 per cent, people reject the suggestion that the United States halt bombings of North Vietnam 'to see if the Communists will come to the negotiating table.' In October, sentiment against a halt in the bombing stood at 53 to 29 percent, and in September it was only 48 to 37 percent. Clearly the trend is toward no let-up in the air strike pressure on the North Vietnamese."

Likewise, when respondents were asked whether, as a step toward trying to get a negotiated peace, the U.S. should "de-escalate fighting to show the Communists we have peaceful intentions," they rejected the idea by 62 to 22 percent (15 percent were undecided).

Harris also asked about specific military steps, including whether the U.S. should mine Haiphong harbor "even at the risk of sinking Russian ships"—42 percent were in favor and 33 percent opposed (25 percent were undecided).

In response to a question as to whether the U.S. should invade North Vietnam, 49 percent were in favor and 29 percent opposed (22 percent were undecided), which Harris said was a slight increase over the response to the same question in July 1967. A similar question asked at about the same time by Gallup, however, produced a somewhat different response: [133]

> *"We are now bombing North Vietnam, but we have not yet sent troops into North Vietnam. Would you favor or oppose extending the ground war into North Vietnam?"*

[In percent]

Favor	39	Oppose	44	No opinion	17

While favoring stronger military action, the public also favored 66 percent to 15 percent (with 19 percent undecided), the policy of stabilizing U.S. forces and of building up the South Vietnamese Army to take over the fighting.

Harris' explanation for this hardening of public opinion was that "A combination of three circumstances have coincided and may be fairly assured to have contributed to the change: [134]

---

[132] *Washington Post*, Dec. 23, 1967.
[133] *Vietnam War, A Compilation: 1964–1990*, vol. 2.
[134] *Washington Post*, Dec. 23, 1967.

"1. The reassurances of General Westmoreland and Ambassador Bunker that the war is now going better and will go better in the future with the implication that future U.S. troop demands in Vietnam may level off.

"2. The deeply negative reaction of the public to the tactics of the anti-Vietnam war demonstrations, especially the violence which has occurred.

"3. The difficulty for opponents of the war to outline any convincing alternative to the course the Johnson Administration has followed."

Buoyed by the resurgence in public support for the President's handling of the war, a White House staff assistant who was responsible for such matters sent a memorandum to the President on December 28, 1967, a month before the Tet offensive, expressing confidence in the situation: "All in all it looks like the public has greater understanding of what the Administration is trying to do in Vietnam—and accepts it."[135] "Thus, Vietnam is well in hand. The time has now come, I believe, to shift gears to the domestic side."

---

[135] Johnson Library, C.F. PR 16, Memorandum to the President from Fred Panzer, Dec. 28, 1967.

CONCLUSION

THE END OF STRATEGY

Autumn turned to winter, but there was little change in the situation in Vietnam. Among U.S. officials, even the military, there seemed to be a mood of resignation, as if, after years of effort and almost three years of active U.S. military and political intervention, the U.S. had reached the limit of its effectiveness, its sacrifice and its endurance. When the Joint Chiefs were asked to recommend new programs that might shorten the war, they repeated earlier requests, all of which involved action outside South Vietnam and had already been denied by the President. And when the Non-Group was asked to recommend the "highest priority areas" for U.S. programs in South Vietnam for 1968, it listed the same areas that were already considered to have priority, most of which had experienced little if any improvement during 1967.[1]

This mood was reflected in a report from Saigon by correspondent Robert Shaplen. There was "increasing sentiment," he said, in favor of "pushing ahead as best we can with Revolutionary Development and pacification, meanwhile depending on American military and economic might to eventually 'smother the Communists,' as several top-level officials keep saying. The mere fact that at this point in the history of the American involvement in South Vietnam those in charge of prosecuting policy here can speak of smothering the Vietcong and the North Vietnamese amounts to an admission that politics and ideology have failed." "Obviously," Shaplen added, "in what has always been a political war, there can never be a purely military solution, even if General William C. Westmoreland is given a million troops and North Vietnam is obliterated by bombing. The fact that a growing number of ultrahawks, here and

---

[1] In response to a request from the President, Katzenbach, on behalf of the Non-Group (then consisting of Katzenbach, William Bundy, Nitze, Rostow, Wheeler, Helms, Harriman, Warnke and Habib), prepared a memorandum on Nov. 13, 1967 listing what the group considered the "highest priority areas in Vietnam for U.S. action during the following year"—a list, they said, which was quite similar to the priorities of the U.S. Mission in Saigon. (U.S. Department of State, Central File, Pol 27 Viet S, memorandum for the President from Katzenbach, Nov. 13, 1967.) This was the list:

"1. *Anti-corruption effort*—There was unanimous agreement that a visible and credible anti-corruption effort would help a great deal in improving the [Johnson] Administration's position, and in building a more effective GVN [Government of Vietnam]. . . .

"2. *ARVN performance*—Everything that can be done must be done to make the Vietnamese Army assume a greater portion of the war burden—visibly. . . .

"3. *Anti-infrastructure efforts*—This is probably the quickest payoff item around; while the CIA is going all out now on this effort, I think we can and should demand more from the GVN.

"4. *Building political institutions*—We all agree that this is important, but, unlike Walt Rostow, I tend to doubt that we can anticipate a really dramatic breakthrough on this one in the next year. . . .

"5. *Economic stability*—We are anticipating a probable inflation of about 40%. At the very best we could reduce it to about 25%, but if things get out of hand there could be as much as a 75% increase.

"6. *Efforts to get the GVN into contact with the VC*—We can't push the GVN too hard, or they will think we are asking them to commit suicide. But we can definitely push them harder than they have been pushed in the past. . . ."

in the United States . . . are now saying that if we can't 'bomb the hell' out of North Vietnam and 'force it to buckle under' we ought to get out indicates the current mood and emphasizes our political bankruptcy."[2]

David Halberstam, who had covered the war for the *New York Times* from 1962 to 1964, returned to South Vietnam at the end of 1967 to observe what had happened since he left. In his report he said, "I do not think we are winning, . . . nor do I see any signs we are about to win." "I have a sense that we are once again coming to a dead end in Indochina." "The society is rotten, tired and numb. It no longer cares. . . . The government of Vietnam is largely meaningless to its citizens . . . most province and district chiefs are corrupt and incompetent . . . the army is still poorly led and barely motivated. . . . At very best there is creeping pacification." "The other war, the nation building, helping the Vietnamese to help themselves, has not changed."[3]

In protest against the effects of the war, the chief of International Voluntary Services (IVS) in South Vietnam, Don Luce, and three other key staff members, resigned in late September 1967, and 45 of the 170 volunteers sent a letter to President Johnson calling the war "an overwhelming atrocity" and urging the President to stop bombing in both North and South Vietnam, to recognize the National Liberation Front as one step toward negotiations, and to "turn the [peace] question over to an international peace commission and be prepared to accept its recommendations."[4]

After returning to Washington, Luce, who had been in South Vietnam with IVS for nine years, said in a meeting at the State Department with Robert Miller, director of the Vietnam Working Group, that the "increasing militarization" of the U.S. effort and the destructiveness of the war were alienating the South Vietnamese. According to Miller's memorandum on the conversation, Luce said that "rapidly growing numbers of Vietnamese, both inside and outside the government, were becoming increasingly anti-American. In Luce's view, this was going to lead to the ultimate defeat of the United States in Vietnam, even if we were militarily successful in staying there indefinitely." In response to a question from Miller, Luce said that Revolutionary Development/pacification "was making no progress and in fact in real terms [was] slipping behind." Regarding the elections, Luce said that "almost all the Vietnamese he knew believed that the elections were rigged and that the United States assisted in their rigging."[5]

---

[2] Robert Shaplen, "Saigon, October 7, 1967," published in the *New Yorker* magazine of that date and reprinted in Shaplen's *Road from War, op. cit.*, pp. 165–166.

[3] David Halberstam, "Return to Vietnam," *Harper's* (December 1967), pp. 47–58.

[4] *New York Times*, Sept. 20, 1967. See the text of the letter in Luce and Sommer, *Vietnam: The Unheard Voices, op. cit., pp.* 315–321. IVS, as noted earlier, was a private, nonprofit organization, the prototype of the Peace Corps, which, beginning in 1956, contracted with the U.S. Government to render technical advice and assistance in agriculture and education, especially in rural areas. As the war increased, IVS volunteers became more involved in working with refugees. According to a State Department briefing sheet for Secretary Rusk to use in congressional testimony, "Throughout these activities IVS volunteers have displayed exemplary courage while moving about in a hostile countryside. Often they have been the only contact with distant villages." U.S. Department of State, Lot File 71 D 88, briefing paper for Secretary Rusk, Nov. 7, 1967.

[5] U.S. Department of State, Lot File 71 D 88, Robert Miller memorandum of conversation with Don Luce, Oct. 9, 1967.

A report from Bien Hoa Province, where, as noted, the U.S. and the South Vietnamese had been making a major effort in Revolutionary Development/Pacification, gave a frank appraisal of the situation:[6]

> The GVN in Bien Hoa Province has not met with any measure of success in furthering the pacification effort during 1967 . . . at all levels [the GVN] has grown weaker, become more corrupt and, today, displays even less vitality and will than it did one year ago. . . .
>
> The primary interest of GVN officials in Bien Hoa Province is money. The lucrative U.S. presence with all the various service trades that cater to the soldier, have created a virtual gold mine of wealth which is directly or indirectly syphoned off and pocketed by the officials. Thus, revolutionary development with all the ultimate implications of broadening the governing base of this society, is viewed as some sort of necessary device that needs to be propped up and nominally catered to by the GVN in order to keep U.S. and Free World's interest and faith intact. However, any serious or meaningful gesture in support of a program which ultimately is designed to displace the powers-to-be (or at least force them to become accountable or share in the power) is not forthcoming. Infrastructure [Communist

---

Frances FitzGerald said that Luce and his colleagues "acted upon their convictions," and that "in this the young men were unique, for no other American official in Vietnam resigned publicly for reasons of conscience." (FitzGerald, *Fire in the Lake,* p. 361.) She added: "For the rest of American officials nothing seemed to have changed. In the air-conditioned offices of Saigon, the mission 'regulars' pored over plans for dredging of a long canal through NLF territory—a project that would employ the labors of some eight or nine thousand people for months in order to bring the Delta rice two days closer to Saigon. . . . The confidence of the Americans was something quite extraordinary—indeed it was probably incredible to those who had not spent time in Vietnam. After thirteen years of failed programs and fallen governments, the officials were still planning new approaches not only to winning the war, but to building a prosperous, independent nation out of the shreds of non-Communist Vietnam. 'Democratic elections . . . rooting out corruption . . . rooting in the government . . . land reform . . . rural electrification . . . revolutionary development' [ellipses in original]—the phrases had become so familiar that it was difficult now to grasp the magnitude of the changes they implied, or to sort out the intellectual confusion. In Da Nang one might find (as one writer did) a Marine colonel distributing carpentry sets paid for by Marine Reserve officers in the United States and saying, 'Of course we try to make what we do seem as though it comes from the government, not us. We want the villagers to think their own people are looking after them and not Uncle Sam. We're trying to get some other kind of training for people. Maybe in ten or fifteen years there'll be some ground to build democracy on here.'

"Confusion of goals and motives extended not only to the soldiers and the junior AID officials. By 1967 Vietnam was inundated with social scientists working under contract to the Defense Department. Herman Kahn and his colleagues at the Hudson Institute briefed colonels on increasing 'security' by means of substituting German shepherd dogs for Vietnamese soldiers on night patrols and building a moat all the way around Saigon. . . . Professor Ithiel de Sola Pool of MIT and the Simulmatics Corporation spoke about the great success of the Vietnamese elections and the drive against corruption, proposing that the United States 'build a bridge' between the new legislature and the elected village councils so as to reduce and finally eliminate the autonomy of the Vietnamese military bureaucracy. Dr. Pool, in other words, proposed that the U.S. mission destroy the whole infrastructure of the war and deliver power to a group of unarmed legislators, whom the Vietnamese generals tolerated as creatures of an American whim.

"In this third year of a major war that had made the Vietnamese civilians into survivors and refugees, the mission had an air of freshness and newness about it. Young men from RAND and Simulmatics bounded about the countryside in Land Rovers studying 'upward mobility among village elites' or 'the interrelationship of land reform with peasant political motivation.' 'Of course,' they would say with a slight swagger as they emptied the clips from their Swedish K submachine guns, 'if the GVN realized the RF–PF potential, the lower-level Viet Cong village hierarchies would disappear in a matter of weeks.' The old-timers would scoff at their naivete. In the embassy weary State Department officials would look up from their desks to describe the disasters that had occurred to the RF–PF in Quang Ngai, Quang Tin, and Quang Nam provinces. 'So the program isn't working,' a journalist might conclude. 'Not working?' They would look up startled. 'Why, just look at An Giang province. The GVN is really pulling itself together this year. . . .'"

[6] *PP*, Gravel ed., vol. II, pp. 406–407, from MACCORDS report for the period ending Dec. 31, 1967.

> cadre] is not attacked even though the target is known, budgets are not spent although the funds are available; GVN officials steadfastly refuse to visit their districts or villages or hamlets although it is there that most immediate problems exist. . . .
>
> [I]t is the considered opinion of CORDS Bien Hoa that unless major revisions are brought about . . . there is only [going] to be a continuation of the same ordeal with the accompanying frustrations, inactions, corruption and incompetence. . . .

As criticism mounted, the President and those of his associates who continued to support his policy and programs in Vietnam publicly defended the U.S. position. The President, faced with a new poll showing his popularity at its lowest ebb—23 percent[7]—and polls indicating that he trailed every major potential opponent in the 1968 Presidential race, said in a speech on October 7 that although he valued popularity, he would not abandon any of his major policies and programs at home or abroad. He said he was going to stand firm in Vietnam and on the request for a tax increase.[8]

Rusk also continued to take a strong stand, and in a news conference on October 12, as has been seen, he strongly defended administration policy, lashed out at critics, and warned of dire consequences if the U.S. did not remain committed to the war. Behind closed doors, however, Rusk, like the President, appeared to be showing considerable strain. At his staff conference on October 5, Rusk, responding in part to an article in the *New York Times* reporting on opposition to U.S. policy from within the government, which had prompted some remarks by the President at a recent Tuesday Lunch, spoke with considerable feeling about the matter of loyalty.[9] *"There is no room in this Department,"* he said, *"for those who oppose the decisions of the President.* You can keep silent, especially if you have no responsibility for the policy in question. Ideas are welcome: they should be expressed to me or the Under Secretary, or, in the case of Viet-Nam, Mr. Bundy. Ideas may be submitted freely, and without prejudice, to the proper persons within the Department. But we cannot have opposition to decisions of the President any more than dissent can be permitted among men in uniform. This is not a debating society. It is an instrument to support the policies of the President. It supports one President at a time. Either support the President or keep quiet. We're officers of the government under the President. We are not interested in personal opinions." (emphasis in original)

Rusk also spoke briefly about Vietnam. "The Administration," he said, "made a deliberate decision not to create a war psychology in the United States. There have been no war bond campaigns, etc. The decision was made because it is too dangerous for this country really to get worked up. Maybe this was a mistake; maybe it would have been better to take steps to build up a sense of a nation at

---

[7] Harris Survey, *Washington Post*, Nov. 13, 1967.

[8] *New York Times*, Oct. 8, 1967.

[9] After the staff conference, Rusk's assistant and speech writer, Ernest K. Lindley, sent a memorandum to the Policy Planning Council of the Department—it is not clear why it was sent to Policy Planning or whether other units of the Department were also informed—reporting on what Rusk had said. U.S. Department of State, Lot File 71 D 273, Memorandum for S/P—Mr. Owen from Ernest K. Lindley, "Important Statements by the Secretary," Oct. 5, 1967.

war. The course we have taken has meant expecting a great deal of our men in Vietnam, against the background of a home front going about business as usual." He added that he would be glad to have notes from any of the staff on "what you think the key questions are in regard to Vietnam."

In closing, Rusk said:

> We may come, in the next year, to the point of decision on what kind of country we're going to be. We run the risk of being lazy, of resigning with a whine and a whimper, of not being willing to pay for what needs to be done. The President's tax proposal made a lot of new doves. But we're not paying the taxes we paid in the Kennedy and Eisenhower Administrations—and we're paying far less than we paid during the Korean war. Some of us think that whines and whimpers should not be the basis for a national decision.

William Bundy also defended U.S. policy in various public speeches.[10] In an off-the-record meeting of sub-cabinet officers in October, where he was not speaking for public consumption and presumably could talk somewhat more freely, Bundy, while cautioning that it was not "a one-sided picture," said "it is my deep conviction as a cautious man—as cautious as I know how to be—that we are making very clear progress. . . ." "There are men, devoted men . . . who have served there who don't think we *are* making real progress. But I think it fair to say that they are in a marked minority and that the down-to-earth guys do really believe we are making headway." (emphasis in original)[11]

Rostow also continued to support and defend U.S. policy and to reassure the President that he was on the right course. In the middle of September, Bill Moyers, who, as noted, had left the White House at the end of 1966, allegedly in part because of differences on Vietnam, wrote to Rostow saying, among other things, that those opposed to the President's Vietnam policy were increasingly going to argue that "the game was not worth the candle," and were going to forget why the U.S. decided to become involved. "You can't win the argument over methods (the strongest power in the world pounding a rural society of 15 million into submission)," Moyers said, "but you can't lose the argument, in my judgment, over the necessity of the President having taken the stand he took."

In his reply, Rostow thanked Moyers—"it is more comfort than even you can guess to have a friend out there"—and expressed his own optimism: "I have never seen our military and civilians—here and in Saigon—more confident that we are on a winning track; nor has there been more solid evidence that the stake is the shape of all of Asia, and that Asia is gradually shaping up. This includes not

---

[10] See, for example, his address, "The Path to Vietnam," before the annual conference of the National Student Association, August 15, 1967, *Department of State Bulletin,* No. 8295 (1967).

[11] The transcript of Bundy's long speech to the sub-cabinet is in his papers in the State Department, Lot File 85 D 240 (William Bundy Papers). The speech is not dated, but on the front page there is handwritten "Sept. 12, 1967." This is not correct. The speech mentions the President's San Antonio speech, which was on September 27. In all probability, Bundy made his speech in early to mid October, possibly on October 12.

only men like Westy and the others engaged in the battle, but Bunker and Locke, Nick Katzenbach and Bill Bundy."[12]

Rostow, as noted, disagreed with McNamara's proposal for a revised course of action, and in his memorandum for the President on November 2, 1967, commenting on McNamara' memorandum of November 1, he said that although he could not predict an early end to the war, he thought that "with a little luck and reasonable performance by the South Vietnamese under the new government, the evidence of solid progress will become increasingly clear to one and all."[13]

In early December, Rostow met with John Paul Vann, who was considered to be one of the most knowledgeable Americans on the subject of Vietnam. Leonhart, White House coordinator for pacification, and Press Secretary George Christian were also there. This is the description of the meeting by Neil Sheehan, Vann's biographer:[14]

> The meeting began at 2 p.m. . . . He [Rostow] welcomed Vann and sat down next to him on the office couch. . . . Vann had decided on a dilute-the-vinegar approach. He started out by listing the positive aspects he could think of, like the organizational accomplishments of CORDS [the new U.S. organization for pacification activities, headed by Komer]. Rostow smiled. He slapped Vann on the knee. "That's great!" he said. Vann gradually shifted to the unpleasantries. Rostow left the couch, sat down behind his desk, and riffled the papers on the desktop. He interrupted Vann. Didn't Vann agree, despite these flaws he claimed to see, that the United States would be over the worst of the war in six months?
>
> Restraint deserted Vann. "Oh hell no, Mr. Rostow," he said, "I'm a born optimist. I think we can hold out longer than that."
>
> Rostow remarked that a man with Vann's attitude should not be working for the U.S. Government in Vietnam. It was close to 2:30 p.m. Rostow had another appointment.

Later in November, Rostow also took the unusual step of issuing from his office a pamphlet, printed in color, of "Statistics on the War in Vietnam," prepared by Westmoreland's headquarters. In an attached memorandum to recipients, Rostow said that the charts, which had been used by Westmoreland and Bunker in briefing the President during their trip to Washington demonstrated the "evidence of progress" in the war.[15]

The Situation in Congress at Year's End

In Congress, the ranks of those who opposed the war continued to swell, especially in the Senate. In a telephone conversation on November 6, 1967, with Marcy, chief of staff of the Foreign Rela-

---

[12] Johnson Library, Office of the President File, Moyers, Letter to Rostow from Moyers, Sept. 11, 1967, and reply from Rostow September 15.

Several weeks later, Marvin Watson sent a note to the President reporting that Moyers had told Leonard Marks that Richard Goodwin, Arthur Schlesinger, Jr., and J. Kenneth Galbraith had asked him to become chairman of a group opposing the President's Vietnam policy, but that he had refused. He said he "looks on the President as his father." Johnson Library, Office of the President File, Moyers, Note to the President from Watson, Nov. 28, 1967.

[13] Johnson Library, NSF Country File, Vietnam, Memorandum for the President from Rostow, Nov. 2, 1967.

[14] Sheehan, *A Bright Shining Lie,* pp. 700–701.

[15] "Statistics on the War in Vietnam," November 1967, from CRS files.

tions Committee, William Macomber, Assistant Secretary of State for Congressional Relations, said he wanted to check his "list of Senate 'doves' or 'dovishly inclined.'" Macomber's list was as follows (the question marks were included in Marcy's memorandum, with no indication as to whether they were Macomber's or—more likely—Marcy's):[16]

Aiken*	Kennedy, Edward
Brooke*	Kennedy, Robert
Burdick	Mansfield
Carlson* (?)	McCarthy
Case*	McGovern
Church	Metcalf (?)
Clark	Morse
Cooper*	Morton*
Fulbright	Muskie (?)
Gore	Nelson
Gruening	Pell
Hart (?)	Percy*
Hartke	Symington (??)
Hatfield*	Yarborough (?)
Javits*	Young (Ohio)

*Republicans

To the list should have been added Tydings (D/Md.), who may not have made a public announcement but had told Harry McPherson that he could no longer support the war.[17]

In the Foreign Relations Committee as of the end of 1967, of the 19 members (12 Democrats and 7 Republicans), 11 were opposed to the war: Democrats Fulbright, Mansfield, Morse, Gore, Church, Clark, Pell, McCarthy, and Republicans Aiken, Case and Cooper. Based on Macomber's list, Democrat Symington and Republican Carlson were also leaning toward opposition. Generally, the committee had tended, once the Gulf of Tonkin Resolution was passed in 1964, to operate at the perimeters of Vietnam policy, and efforts by the staff, led by Marcy, to encourage a more active role, met with little response. Fulbright felt that under the circumstances the most effective role for the committee was to seek to educate and stimulate public discussion until such time as there was a change of attitude among enough of the members of the committee

[16] National Archives, Papers of the Senate Committee on Foreign Relations, RG 46, Marcy memorandum of telephone conversation with Macomber, Nov. 6, 1967.

[17] See p. 672 above.

Toward the end of 1967, the Columbia Broadcasting System surveyed 87 Senators on their attitudes toward the war, and the results suggest that Macomber's estimate of about 30 Senators who were "doves" or "dovishly inclined" was quite accurate. Of the 87 Senators, 42 disapproved the conduct of the war; 32 approved; 11 were noncommitted. Of the 42 who disapproved, 27 [a figure close to Macomber's] wanted less military action, while 15 wanted more. On bombing policy, 18 wanted bombing stopped, 12 wanted less or a pause [again, the total of these figures—30—is what Macomber estimated], 26 approved whatever the President or the military wanted to do, and 21 wanted bombing increased. The conclusion of the survey was that the poll indicated three things: "a crumbling of the solid front support given three years ago with the Gulf of Tonkin resolution, an infectious restlessness in the Senate and among its constituents with the programs of the war, and a growing impatience with a long twilight struggle where victories do not decide, and the end cannot be seen." The results of the poll were reported in Richard H. Rovere, *Waist Deep in the Big Muddy: Personal Reflections on 1968* (Boston: Little, Brown, 1968), pp. 38–40.

and of the Senate to permit a more active role. Meanwhile, efforts to correct the "imbalance" between the Executive and the Legislature and to "restore" the constitutional war powers of Congress seemed to be in order, along with an investigation of the circumstances surrounding the passage of the Gulf of Tonkin Resolution.

There was, as will be seen, strong support within the committee and the Senate for taking the Vietnam problem to the U.N., and this consensus enabled the committee and the Senate to pass a resolution at the end of 1967 urging that this be done.

Tension between the committee and the Executive had continued to increase as more Members turned against the war, and during 1967 this led to a standoff on the subject of open testimony on the war by the Secretary of State. In the fall, the issue became full blown. In a Tuesday Lunch on October 17, Rusk told the President that he "had a problem" with the Senate Foreign Relations Committee. Fulbright, he said, had asked him to testify in public session. "I think the appearance in 1966 was a plus, but I do not want seven hours of public debate. What is your judgment?" The President replied: "The Committee is entitled to a report and a response to their questions on our national interest. I do not think you need to have it televised. . . . I would go to the hearings and hit them hard and solid." [18]

On October 19, Rusk wrote to Fulbright saying, in part, "I believe our meeting will run less risk of damaging our foreign relations if it were held in Executive Session." [19]

In an executive session of the Foreign Relations Committee on October 31 to discuss committee business, Fulbright read aloud parts of the letter from Rusk and asked the members of the committee for their advice on what to do. Hickenlooper, ranking Republican, said that the committee should hear Rusk in executive session. "I see no reason," he said, "to pillory him in public in a public session. He is going to have to get off from answering certain questions which will be asked him, and it will be embarrassing to him and it will be embarrassing to the best interests of the United States. . . ." Mansfield agreed with Hickenlooper, as did Lausche and Symington.

Aiken, supported by Cooper, also favored an executive session after which the committee would decide "whether they [administration officials] should be required to tell their story to the public or not." "I would rather get some information from him," Aiken said, than to embarrass him publicly, and I haven't had any direct information since last spring from any of the Executive Branch, and I think we should be informed even if we have to get the information in Executive Session."

Morse and Gore, however, felt strongly that Rusk should testify in public session. "These public hearings," Morse said, "are one of

---

[18] Johnson Library, Tom Johnson's Notes of Meetings, Notes of meeting Oct. 17, 1967. After the meeting, Rostow prepared a brief list of items that had been discussed at the lunch, among them that the President "passionately does not want him [Rusk] before TV." (Johnson Library, Memos to the President—Walt Rostow.) Handwritten notes by Rostow on his copy of the agenda for the meeting indicate that the President did not want the committee hearing to be televised because it would "encourage the enemy." (Same location.)

[19] The text of the letter is in the U.S. Congress, Senate, Committee on Foreign Relations, unpublished executive session transcript, Oct. 31, 1967.

the greatest checks you have on the Executive Branch of Government. . . ." Rusk had "thrown down the gauntlet to this Committee. He said to this Committee he is going to decide whether he appears before us. This is plain Executive supremacy and as long as he takes that position I don't want to hear him in private session . . . we have lost our minds if we let a Cabinet officer tell this Committee when he will appear before us and the issues on which he will not appear before us."

Gore made a similar argument: "Let us not forget that this is a government of the people. Neither this Committee nor the Executive Branch can arrogate to itself the conduct of affairs so important as to touch every home in America. True, our country is troubled, deeply divided. How do we arrive at a better state of affairs? It can only be through understanding, it can only be through discussion and debate to arrive at a unity and a consensus. I am not sure you can do that in secrecy. I am sure you ought not to attempt to do it in secrecy if we are to preserve the essentials of self-government of a great and intelligent people."

Gore suggested that the committee should communicate to the President "its concern at this threatened breakdown in interplay of two coordinate branches of government, and the bearing it will have upon the prospect of some unity in the country."

The committee agreed to hear Rusk in Executive Session for the express purpose of discussing a public session, and later that day (October 31), a letter was sent to him making that request.

On the following day, (November 1), Rusk wrote to Fulbright that he would accept,[20] and the hearing was then scheduled for November 7.

On November 6, Marcy talked by telephone with Macomber, who had called to ask whether Rusk could appear in public session without television.[21] Macomber said that what "bothered the Secretary most was the 'circus atmosphere.'" Marcy said that he doubted whether the hearing could be held without television "simply because the Committee has never sought to exclude one media." He also pointed that the "circus atmosphere" was an "unavoidable consequence of doing business with Congress."

That evening, Marcy attended a State Department reception, where Rusk asked him why the committee was insisting on a public session "in time of war." Marcy replied that Rusk's "use of the word 'war' was part of the answer—that some didn't think war restraints should be in effect." Rusk then asked "why he should provide a public forum for candidates for President like [Eugene] McCarthy. Let him get his own platform if he wants to run for President."

Rusk said, further, that in a public hearing Senators "could ask question after question, questions that he couldn't answer in public." Marcy replied that "the advantage in such a hearing was with the Secretary." And he added that Senators did not like to see the Secretary "pick his own forum, whether they be press conferences or universities and be able to avoid answering pointed questions and discussing policy questions in depth."

---

[20] U.S. Department of State, Lot File 70 D 207, letter from Rusk to Fulbright, Nov. 1, 1967.

[21] National Archives, RG 46, Papers of the Senate Foreign Relations Committee, Marcy memorandum of conversation with Assistant Secretary of State Macomber, Nov. 6, 1967.

On November 7, 1967, Rusk testified before the Foreign Relations Committee in Executive Session.[22] Fulbright said at the outset that the issue of whether Rusk should testify in public was "a matter of constitutional significance." "In this sense," he added, "the Committee has a duty to uphold a legislative prerogative. For if it is not maintained and exercised, this power will be diminished. . . ." Following a reply by Rusk,[23] there was discussion be-

---

[22] U.S. Congress, Senate, Committee on Foreign Relations, unpublished executive session transcript, Nov. 7, 1967.

On the day of the hearing, the committee staff distributed to the members of the committee a memorandum prepared by the staff on "Arguments for a Public Session with the Secretary of State." It included the following arguments in favor of open testimony:

"1. The Senate, through this Committee, traditionally has exercised in public as well as executive sessions its constitutional duty of fulfilling the Advice and Consent functions respecting treaties and nominations, and notably prior to confirmation of the appointment of the Secretary of State.

"2. According to the third clause in Section 5 of the Constitution each House exercises its own judgment concerning what part of its proceedings should not be published. By extension it may be argued that Committee proceedings should also be public unless members determine otherwise.

"3. This point number (2) is given full effect in Section 133 (f) of the Legislative Reorganization Act of 1946, which reads as follows: 'All hearings conducted by standing committees or their subcommittees shall be open to the public, except executive sessions for marking up bills or for voting or where the committee by a majority vote orders an executive session.'

"4. Now that the issue has been joined, failure to insist on a public session could establish a precedent for a Secretary of State independently to decide whether or not to appear before this Committee, and on what terms.

"5. If appointive officials are to be accountable to the electorate, the Committee public hearing offers virtually the only means for proceeding through the practice of examination by one's peers; in other words, the sole counterpart of the parliamentary question period.

"6. The Committee has always permitted the Secretary to reserve his answer for a later executive session if he judges a question too sensitive.

"7. The Secretary employed a press conference—on October 12th—to announce in effect a revised and simplified new policy basis for the Vietnam war; why should that policy be discussed openly in one forum but only in secret with the Committee?

"8. Mr. Rusk has been willing publicly to examine United States policies at press conferences and in interviews with United States and foreign newsmen, but for a year he has avoided the subject of Vietnam in open discussions with the Committee.

"9. For years, Communist and other hostile press and propaganda organs have been picking up and trumpeting statements attributed to public figures in this country—including speculation about their views in our press—and we have survived the practice. If fear of that process were carried very far, it could easily result in governmental efforts to suppress public discussion in the United States.

"10. Committee experience with 'sanitized' hearing records of executive sessions does not stimulate confidence that the public will learn much through that route; and dangerous speculation can be provoked by deletions.

"11. In sum, as a matter of public policy any Administration should wish to make its main foreign affairs spokesman available to questioning by his peers—and not solely behind closed doors."

[23] In his statement, Rusk explained why he did not want to testify in public session:

"There are some important practical considerations involved. We have substantial combat forces in the field engaged in a struggle with North Vietnamese and Viet Cong forces. They are there for reasons which are familiar to you even though some of you may not now agree with those reasons. A public discussion of the conduct of military operations, involving the Secretary of State, cannot help but be of some advantage to our adversaries. This would be particularly true with respect to intentions, future plans, estimates of the military situation and other matters bearing upon the conflict itself. Such discussions could clearly hamper the Commander-in-Chief.

"Second, it is not advantageous for the Secretary of State to be pressed publicly for details of positions which the United States *might* take in intergovernmental discussions or in negotiations to bring this situation to a peaceful conclusion. We need to be in a position to negotiate with those who can stop the shooting. It would seriously hamper such negotiations for us to be asked to disclose in advance many details which ought to be a part of negotiation itself. As the Committee knows, North Viet-Nam has been unwilling to engage in negotiations in any forum, public or private. I will be glad to go into that in as much detail as you wish in an Executive Session.

"Third, the Secretary of State faces a somewhat different problem than does a Senator in discussing the policies, the performance and the deficiencies of other countries. Senators are free to say anything that is on their minds about other countries—and do so frequently on the floor of the Senate and in public speeches. But when this is done in the presence of the Secretary of State, then I am in a most difficult position. I cannot, at one and the same time, be completely candid with my colleagues in the Senate and carry out my public responsibilities as Secretary of State in discussing either the policies or the actions of other governments. It may well

tween Rusk and members of the committee. Although Fulbright continued to stress the importance of hearing Rusk in public session, he said that it was important for there to be a continuous exchange of views between the Legislature and the Executive, and said he was "not so concerned whether that is to be in executive session or in public session." He said he did have a question in his own mind as to whether, in a time of war, a public session would be constructive. "I can picture a situation where I or some member of the Committee unintentionally may ask a question which by the mere asking of it would carry an inference which would be misunderstood . . . by the other side. . . ." In the end, Rusk said he wanted to think about the matter and would let the committee know promptly.

In comments to the press afterward, Fulbright said "If the President doesn't wish to advise with this Committee, there is no way to make him do it," adding, however, "The theory I go on is that under our system the 100 Senators and 435 Representatives have some contribution to make, that we do not rely on the infallibility of our leader as some countries do."[24]

The next day (November 8), Marcy sent the following memorandum to Fulbright:[25]

> Without much hope, but wanting to make one more try, do you think you might take the initiative to proposing a bull session in the White House on the issue of whether or not it is in the national interest for the United States to stay in Vietnam?
>
> Would it be feasible for you directly or through Senator Mansfield to propose such a session with the President, McNamara, Rusk, Russell, Mansfield, and Fulbright? Such a session would need to be without individuals who raise hackles of others. Thus, no Rostow, etc.
>
> This should not be viewed as an opportunity for the Administration people to overwhelm you with statistics—though they might try. It would be a last attempt to convey some of the "wisdom" that can conceivably develop *outside* the White House. [emphasis in original]
>
> My theory is that the White House may be hurting now—more than when you took the initiative with Bill Moyers—and this might just make them a little more inclined to listen.
>
> And finally, and in any event, you ought to keep on trying.

After the closed hearing on November 7, Mansfield had reported to the President that Senator Gore, a member of the committee, was going to ask the committee to take action to force Rusk to appear in public session.

On November 28, White House Assistant Mike Manatos reported to the President that Gore was preparing to ask the committee to take action to force Rusk to testify in public. Manatos said that Mansfield thought the administration would be in a stronger posi-

---

be that I would agree with some of the sharp criticisms which could be leveled at other governments. But for me to engage publicly in such criticism would greatly hamper the ability of the United States to work effectively and quietly to remedy the situations which are of concern both to you and to me." (emphasis in original)

[24] *Washington Post*, Nov. 8, 1967.

[25] National Archives, RG 46, Papers of the Senate Foreign Relations Committee, Marcy Chron File, Memorandum to Fulbright from Marcy, Nov. 8, 1967.

tion if it "beat Gore to the punch by taking the initiative with an announcement that the Secretary will appear."[26] Later that day, Manatos reported to the President on a meeting he had just had with Mansfield and Dirksen. Dirksen had talked to some of the Republicans on the committee, and Mansfield to some of the Democrats, and the two of them agreed that Gore did not have the support necessary to get the committee to vote to compel public testimony by Rusk.[27]

Dirksen and Mansfield, Manatos said, "believe there is nothing wrong in having Secretary Rusk appear before the committee under a time limit possibly keeping out television. They believe that the Secretary could respond to any embarrassing questions by saying that he believes that questions ought to be answered in executive session."

On November 30, 1967, the Foreign Relations Committee held an executive session in which Gore's proposal was debated at some length.[28] His motion was "that the chairman of the Committee be instructed to communicate to the President of the United States the concern of the Committee about the breakdown in public communication between the Executive and the Senate which arises from the refusal of the Secretary of State to testify before the Committee in public session on United States policy in Southeast Asia." In presenting his motion, Gore said that it had been three weeks since Rusk had testified in executive session and had told the committee that he would consider the matter and would respond promptly. "Such treatment," Gore said, "is contemptuous treatment of this Committee." "[I]f we do not press our point in this regard," Gore added, "I think it will further deny this Committee and further establish the primacy of the executive in the formulation and the execution of the foreign policy of our nation."

Fulbright said he agreed with Gore, but was unsure about the proposal. "I would think it would be kind of embarrassing," he said, if the committee sent such a letter and it was denounced and rejected.

Hickenlooper was opposed to the idea, and said he was prepared to offer a motion to table Gore's motion. He said he felt it would "tend to create an emotional, psychological situation in this country that would add to the confusion that already is bedeviling us in the world and especially within this country."

Case said he agreed with Gore, but that "in general, everybody rushes to protect the President from being hurt by usurpers in the way of Congressmen and what-not. I just don't think that it is going to do any good to squawk publicly, as a committee." "We will not get anywhere trying to force the President into doing something." Carlson agreed. Aiken suggested holding Gore's motion for further consideration.

Mundt, a conservative Republican from South Dakota, agreed with Gore's proposal. Rusk, he said, should not have "the unlimited opportunity to make statements which never are challenged and

[26] Johnson Library, WHCF Ex FG 431/F, memorandum to the President from Manatos, 12:10 p.m., Nov. 28, 1967.

[27] Same location, memorandum to the President from Manatos, 5:45 p.m., Nov. 28, 1967.

[28] U.S. Congress, Senate, Committee on Foreign Relations, unpublished executive session transcript, Nov. 30, 1967.

which are never examined in the penetrating way that we can do it. . . . On the other hand, I don't want to get involved in passing a resolution which the press is going to pick up and say that the Foreign Relations Committee has resolved to make a critical approach to the war in Vietnam. . . ."

The consensus of the committee was that Gore's proposal should not be acted upon at that time. "Let it simmer," Pell said.

After the hearing, Fulbright sent a letter to Rusk, as several members of the committee had suggested, saying that the committee had discussed the question of a public hearing, and that, "While Members were not unanimous in believing that such an appearance by you at this time would be desirable, it is fair to note that most of those present felt that a public exchange of views would be most helpful sometime before adjournment [which was expected in mid-December]. There was a strong feeling that it was proper to discuss these policies in the legislative environment, inasmuch as they are unavoidably a part of public consideration." [29]

As the White House continued to try to prevent the committee from attempting to compel Rusk to testify publicly, McPherson, the President's counsel, asked Mansfield for his support.[30] In a memorandum to the President reporting on the conversation, McPherson said: "After going over the reasons for Secretary Rusk not testifying I said, 'This is really a procedural matter. The President knows how you feel about Vietnam. But he hopes you can support him on this procedural question.' He said, 'All right, I'll try to support him. I think he's wrong, but I'll try to support him. But you ought to be aware that this could develop into a Constitutional crisis.'"

On the following day (December 8), after it had been cleared by McPherson, Rusk sent a letter to Fulbright stating that because of the "extreme sensitivity" of the military and political matters that would come up in such a hearing, "they should be fully discussed only in executive session of the Committee." He said he would testify in executive session at any time.[31]

Passage of the U.N. Resolution, November 1967

Meanwhile, the Foreign Relations Committee took up a proposal, sponsored by Morse and later by Mansfield, Church, Fulbright and Pell, among others, to seek international action on the war by taking the Vietnam problem to the U.N.[32] Ambassador Goldberg was sympathetic to this position, and in policy discussions in the State Department and with the President he generally argued for making such an effort. The President was dubious, not only because of the problem of getting the necessary votes in the Security Council, but because he apparently believed that the principal hope for a settlement lay with the U.S.R.R., and that diplomatic action to end the war, through the U.N. or otherwise, hinged on getting the U.S.S.R. to cooperate toward that end.

In addition, the President did not want the U.S. to become involved in a complex process of international debate and diplomatic

[29] Johnson Library, NSF Country File, Vietnam, letter to Rusk from Fulbright, Nov. 30, 1967.
[30] Johnson Library, WHCF, Ex FG 185, White House Name File, Mansfield, memorandum for the President from McPherson, Dec. 7, 1967.
[31] Johnson Library, NSF Country File, Vietnam, letter to Fulbright from Rusk, Dec. 8, 1967.
[32] See proposals by Church and Morse in June 1965, pp. 308–309 of pt. III of this study.

maneuvering that might interfere with prosecution of the war, especially bombing of the North.

Despite the administration's coolness toward a U.N. approach, there was continuing interest in the idea in the Foreign Relations Committee. In the fall of 1966, as will be recalled, Mansfield met with Goldberg and U.N. Secretary General U Thant to discuss a proposal Mansfield had made for using the U.N. Security Council as a medium for reconvening the Geneva Conference. U Thant was very opposed, citing opposition of the U.S.S.R. to the idea.

It will also be recalled that in the spring of 1967, the Foreign Relations Committee, at its own initiative, met in New York City with U Thant, who again expressed opposition to a Security Council approach. In April-May, Senators Mansfield and Morse met at least twice with the President in an effort to persuade him to take the Vietnam problem to the Security Council. The President continued to be dubious, but Goldberg seemed to feel that the U.S. should at least discuss the possibility with other nations, and Rusk tended to feel also that it should be explored, and that this could be done without adversely affecting U.S. Vietnam policy or operations or other interests.

In a Senate speech in August, Mansfield again raised the question of a peace initiative in the Security Council.[33] The reaction of the President's advisers, as expressed in a memorandum to the President from Rostow, was that this was not a likely possibility. Goldberg, Rostow said, had reported that there was "no possibility" of getting the Security Council to act.[34]

According to Rostow's memorandum, "The heart of the matter is not the UN, but what the USSR can and will do. You raised this as hard as you could with Kosygin at Hollybush [the summit in June 1967]. We shall see in the weeks and months ahead whether anything emerges."

As a result of increasing congressional interest, however, Goldberg was authorized in late August to explore a possible third party (Denmark) initiative in the Security Council.[35]

On August 28, Mansfield made a major speech in the Senate in which he again proposed taking the Vietnam problem to the U.N. Security Council. A number of other Senators, including Morse, Aiken, Fulbright, Cooper, Symington, Pell, Sparkman, Church, Carlson, Lausche, Allott, Hart, Mondale, Pastore and Long of Missouri, gave supporting speeches.[36] Noting that a U.S. resolution on using the Security Council to reconvene the Geneva Conference had been pending before the Security Council since February 1966 Mansfield said that although the Security Council could not be expected to "bring about a rapid settlement of the tangled issues in the Vietnam conflict . . . with its small but varied membership [it] provides a good forum for the airing of issues, for the clarification of the positions of the parties, and for mobilization of world concern."

---

[33] *CR*, vol. 113, p. 21636.

[34] Johnson Library, NSF Memos to the President—Walt Rostow, draft memorandum for Senator Mansfield, attached to memorandum for the President from Rostow, Aug. 7, 1967.

[35] U.S. Department of State, Central File, Pol 27 Viet S, Washington to Saigon (and other U.S. Embassies in the Far East) 27808, Aug. 26, 1967.

[36] *CR*, vol. 113, pp. 24287, 24437.

The President, who continued to be concerned about the effects of such a move, sent word to the State Department to make sure that Mansfield understood "that there is no undertaking to go to the Security Council unless we can get the nine necessary votes and that there is no commitment in connection with such a possible initiative that we would stop the bombing or reduce it."[37]

On September 6, Rostow telephoned Rusk's assistant, Benjamin Read, to pass along to Rusk that "the President was troubled about the attempt to get the matter into the Security Council . . . the President was afraid of being booby-trapped. Rostow wanted the Secretary to know about the President's attitude."[38]

On September 11, Morse introduced in the Senate a resolution (Senate Concurrent Resolution 44 of the 90th Congress), the operative part of which was as follows:[39]

> 1. The President should request an emergency meeting of the United Nations Security Council to consider all aspects of the conflict in Vietnam and to act to end the conflict, pledging the United States in advance to accept and carry out any decision on the matter by the Council. . . .
>
> 2. If the Security Council is unable to act, the United States should take all steps necessary to assure action on the issue by the General Assembly.
>
> 3. The United States objective in the United Nations should be to obtain—
>
> (a) support for an immediate cessation of hostilities by all parties, and
>
> (b) recommendations for appropriate measures, such as the convening of an international conference, for reaching a permanent settlement which will assure a lasting peace for Southeast Asia.

On September 12, at a Tuesday Lunch with Rusk, McNamara, Rostow, Gen. Harold Johnson (acting for Wheeler), and Christian, the President asked "if Mansfield will be back with his UN plan and does Goldberg know it won't work." Rusk said that Goldberg "knows our policy," and added, "a nose count at the UN indicated that it [Mansfield's proposal] just won't work." The President asked "why don't we take a plan to the UN, then get defeated?" Rusk replied: "some U.S. Senators such as Morse would misinterpret this as a repudiation by the world body of the United States policy in Vietnam."[40]

At an NSC meeting from 12:32 p.m. to 12:58 p.m. the next day (September 13), attended by the President, the Vice President, McNamara, Katzenbach, Deputy Secretary of Defense Nitze (who had replaced Vance), General McConnell (acting for Wheeler), Rostow, Ambassador Goldberg, CIA Director Helms, Secretary of the Treasury Fowler, USIA Director Marks, Assistant Secretary of State Sisco, Bromley Smith and George Christian, Goldberg re-

---

[37] U.S. Department of State, Central File, Pol 27 Viet S, Memorandum for Rusk from Joseph Sisco (Assistant Secretary of State for International Organization Affairs), "Possible UN Consideration of Vietnam," Aug. 29, 1967.

[38] U.S. Department of State, Central File, Pol 27 Viet 14, Read notes on telephone call from Rostow, Sept. 6, 1967.

[39] *CR*, vol. 113, p. 25957.

[40] Johnson Library, Meetings Notes File, Jim Jones' notes of meeting Sept. 12, 1967.

ported on the question of taking the Vietnam problem to the U.N.[41] He said he had talked to some members of the Security Council, and that "Our friends are timid and reluctant. They don't want to come along. They don't think the Security Council will reach a settlement." "Russia," he added, "says don't get into this."

The President asked, "Who feels we should go to the Security Council?" Goldberg said that "the general feeling is that we ought not to do it."

"The President again asked what was thought of our going to the UN and getting defeated. Goldberg said I don't think this would be considered a rebuff, although the press may say it is a rebuff."

The President asked Goldberg for his recommendation. Goldberg replied: "I would go, recognizing the great dangers. We could not come out with anything that would hurt us. I don't think anything would come out at all. There would be some who would say this was a rebuff, but this would show to the Mansfields and that group that we at least tried."

McNamara said he would favor going "if there was any possibility that it [a U.S. resolution in the Security Council] would pass. But I don't think it will and they will say it was a rebuff because of our unreasonable and inhumane action in the bombing. On balance, that would be a loss in my judgment."

Goldberg said he disagreed with McNamara. Katzenbach, however, said he agreed with McNamara.

McNamara added that he thought the results "would feed the Mansfields et al with new fuel to tell us to stop the bombing."

Vice President Humphrey said that while he wanted the U.N. to be involved, he did not think the U.S. should take the matter to the Security Council if it did not have the votes.

Goldberg said that he thought the resolution "would just flounder around into a state of disagreement and we would get credit for having tried."

"Is that a plus in relation to where we are now?" the President asked. "I feel that Mansfield might think that would be a plus."

Katzenbach responded that Mansfield "would regard those evils as we do."

On October 9, Mansfield sent a letter to all Members of the Senate in which he sought to explain and emphasize the importance of a U.N. initiative.[42] "Even if we cannot muster the votes or are estopped by a permanent member's veto," he said, "I believe we have a responsibility to pursue whatever means may be proper and open to us in the Security Council, if for no other reason than to make clear our willingness to lay our position on Vietnam formally on the line." "Of late," he said, "there have been rumors and innuendoes to the effect that 'we do not have the votes' and so, therefore, we have not moved on the matter. It seems to me, however, that if there are not nine members of the Council prepared, at this late date, to acknowledge in concert this most serious threat to the world's well-being, it is high time for this nation to clarify by a recorded vote—win or lose—who is willing and who is not willing to bring the UN into the effort to restore peace in Viet-

[41] Same location, Jim Jones' notes of meeting of the NSC, Sept. 13, 1967.
[42] For Mansfield's letter see *CR*, vol. 113, pp. 28857–28858.

nam. . . . We cannot know what the results will be until the attempt is made. In my judgment, it would have been a worthwhile effort even if consideration by the Security Council served only to clarify the various positions of those directly and indirectly involved in their conflict by bringing them together in face-to-face and open discussions."

Mansfield sent a copy of the letter to the President, who sent a note to Rostow saying, "get me a reply quickly—and I think we ought to point out the real dangers—they might handicap us."[43] A reply was drafted in the State Department, but Macomber recommended that rather than sending the letter, Rusk and Goldberg should have breakfast with Mansfield and discuss the matter.[44]

On October 25, 1967, Mansfield introduced a resolution (Senate Resolution 180 of the 90th Congress), which, by the time it was voted upon several weeks later, was cosponsored by 59 Senators, declaring the "sense of the Senate that the President of the United States consider taking the appropriate initiative through his representative at the United Nations to assure that the United States resolution of January 31, 1966, or any other resolution of equivalent purpose be brought before the Security Council for consideration."[45] Later that day, Read sent Rusk a memorandum stating that he, Katzenbach, Sisco, and Macomber suggested a letter from the President to Mansfield inviting him to a breakfast meeting at the White House to discuss the matter.[46] The next day, Rostow called Rusk to express the President's dissatisfaction with the way the matter was being handled. Rusk said he had approved the breakfast proposal, but in a talk with Mansfield the previous night he had "found him 'very rough.'" In a memorandum to the President reporting on this conversation, Rostow said he told Rusk how the President wanted the matter handled. Rusk said he had two speeches to make, and might find it difficult to make an early appointment with Mansfield. Rostow told him that the matter was urgent, and that if he could not see Mansfield with Goldberg, perhaps Katzenbach could.[47]

Fifteen minutes later, Rostow sent another memorandum to the President reporting that he had been informed by Read that Goldberg "feels quite strongly that we should accept the Mansfield resolution, reserving the timing of a UN Vietnam effort and the conditions to ourselves. He believes it preferable to the Morse resolution, and feels we will get 'run over' on this matter by the Senate."[48]

"Secretary Rusk," Read reported, "takes a position 180 degrees different [from Goldberg]."

Read told Rostow that Rusk was telephoning Goldberg "to see if he can be gotten in line for the planned confrontation with the Senate leadership in Senator Mansfield's office." (Apparently, this,

---

43 Johnson Library, NSF Country File, Vietnam.

44 U.S. Department of State, Central File, Pol 27 Viet S, Memorandum for Rusk from Sisco, Oct. 12, 1967, with handwritten note from Macomber.

45 *CR*, vol. 113, p. 30024. Among the sponsors were 12 of the 19 members of the Foreign Relations Committee and 9 of the 18 members of the Senate Armed Services Committee.

46 U.S. Department of State, Central File, Pol 27 Viet S, Memorandum for Rusk from Read, with attached draft letter from the President to Mansfield, Oct. 25, 1967.

47 Johnson Library, NSF Country File, Vietnam, Memorandum for the President from Rostow, Oct. 27, 12:45 p.m.

48 Same location, Memorandum for the President from Rostow, Oct. 27, 1967, 1:00 p.m.

rather than a breakfast meeting at the White House, was the way the President wanted the matter handled.)

On October 26, 1967, the Foreign Relations Committee began three days of open hearings on the Morse and Mansfield resolutions.[49] On November 2, Ambassador Goldberg testified for the executive branch. Before the public hearing began, the committee met with Goldberg in executive session to hear about the poll he had taken of members of the Security Council.[50] The U.S., Goldberg said, had seven and possibly eight of the nine votes needed to have an item put on the agenda of the Security Council or, as in this case, to resume consideration of an item on the agenda (the U.S. resolution had been on the agenda since 1966). Lausche asked why countries were hesitant to support the U.S. Goldberg replied that there were several reasons: "One is that in light of the explicit statement from Hanoi that it does not recognize the competence of the UN that there is no utility in proceeding. . . . Another reason is that the best way, everybody believes, to proceed, is to proceed by way of a reconvened Geneva Conference. This depends upon Soviet concurrence as a Co-Chairman. This public discussion of the matter hardens their line and makes it more difficult for them to support what they ought to support otherwise, which is a reconvening of the Conference. Other reasons are that some say they do not support American military activities there and, therefore, they won't support it [the resolution]. Others, more friendly countries, say that the discussion of the issue, faced with this intransigence, creates an inability on their part privately to use their influence. This would be more the British-Canadian position."

Goldberg, saying that he was speaking "very frankly," added that President Johnson had raised a question about seeking action by the Security Council. "[W]hen we proceed again, if we are not successful in getting the matter inscribed [voting to resume consideration of the resolution], he [the President] raised the question as to whether this would be deemed on the part of the public, on the part of the world community, as a defeat for the United States." Goldberg said he disagreed with the President. He believed that the U.N. had a responsibility, and that "if we are not successful in getting the UN to do its plain duty, I do not regard that to be a defeat for the United States. I regard that to be the performance of a plain duty under the Charter and to the international community."

Goldberg said that he agreed with the concept of the responsibility of the U.N. that underlay both the Morse and the Mansfield resolutions.[51] Referring to a comment by Morse in the hearing on October 26 that Mansfield's resolution, because it could receive broader congressional support, would be the most appropriate one to send to the President, Goldberg said that passage of the Mansfield resolution would support his efforts to get action on Vietnam by the Security Council. He promised "to persevere with all the re-

[49] U.S. Congress, Senate, Committee on Foreign Relations, *Submission of the Vietnam Conflict to the United Nations*, Hearings, October 26, 27 and November 2, 1967, on S. Con. Res. 44 and S. Res. 180, 90th Cong., 1st sess. (Washington, D.C.: U.S. Govt. Print. Off., 1967).

[50] U.S. Congress, Senate, Committee on Foreign Relations, unpublished executive session transcript, Nov. 2, 1967.

[51] Goldberg's testimony begins at p. 149 of the hearings on *Submission of the Vietnam Conflict to the United Nations.*

sources at my command" to get the Security Council to act on Vietnam. As the hearing ended, Fulbright, after a long discussion of a number of issues, urged Goldberg "to press for a vote. . . . In other words do not let the fact that you fear you may not get nine votes deter you from asking for a vote. If you don't get but one vote I would prefer that to no vote."

On November 21, the Foreign Relations Committee unanimously reported the Mansfield resolution to the Senate,[52] and on November 30 the Senate, by a vote of 82–0, adopted the resolution.[53]

Later that day, Rusk sent a memorandum to the President, drafted by Sisco, recommending a plan for raising the Vietnam question in the U.N.[54] Goldberg, he said, wanted to begin discussions promptly with members of the Security Council, based on the draft of a new resolution which, unlike the 1966 U.S. resolution, would call for discussions within the framework of the Geneva Conference as follows:[55]

> The Security Council,
>
> *Deeply concerned* about the situation in Vietnam
>
> 1. *Expresses* the view that the principles on which hostilities were brought to an end by the Geneva Accords should provide a basis for the restoration of peace;
>
> 2. *Urges* that appropriate steps be taken to reactivate the Geneva Conference machinery as the international context in which it appears that fruitful discussions looking toward a settlement are most likely to take place.

This new formulation, Rusk said, was brief, nonprejudicial, but no different substantively than the 1966 resolution.[56] With its stress on the Geneva framework, he said, it "should make the expected opposition of the Soviets and the French more embarrassing to them."

Contrary to what the State Department had told the Foreign Relations Committee, Rusk told the President that Goldberg expected to get the necessary nine votes. "There are two principal reasons: some members who hold serious reservations about involving the Security Council may be equally concerned not to embarrass the

---

[52] See Senate Report 90–798.

[53] *CR*, vol. 113, pp. 34348–34364.

[54] U.S. Department of State, Central File, Pol 27–14 Viet, Memorandum for the President from Rusk, Nov. 30, 1967.

[55] Same location, "Resolution on Vietnam," attached to memorandum for the President from Rusk, Nov. 30, 1967.

[56] This was the text of the 1966 resolution (p. 38 of the hearings on *Submission of the Vietnam Conflict to the United Nations):*

"The Security Council, "*Deeply Concerned* at the continuation of hostilities in Vietnam.

"*Mindful* of its responsibilities for the maintenance of international peace and security,

"*Noting* that the provisions of the Geneva accords of 1954 and 1962 have not been implemented,

"*Desirous* of contributing to a peaceful and honorable settlement of the conflict in Vietnam,

"*Recognizing* the right of all peoples, including those in North Vietnam to self-determination,

"1. *Calls* for immediate discussions without pre-conditions at ——— on ——— date, among the appropriate interested Governments to arrange a conference looking towards the application of the Geneva accords of 1954 and 1962 and the establishment of a durable peace in Southeast Asia; [omissions in original]

"2. *Recommends* that the first order of business in such a conference be arrangements for a cessation of hostilities under effective supervision;

"3. *Offers* to assist in achieving the purposes of this resolution by all appropriate means, including the provision of arbitrators or mediators;

"4. *Calls* on all concerned to cooperate fully in the implementation of this resolution;

"5. *Requests* the Secretary-General to assist as appropriate in the implementation of this resolution."

United States; moreover, we expect the reasonableness of the resolution may influence some doubters to support discussion. . . ."

At a Tuesday Lunch from 1:18 p.m. to 2:37 p.m. on December 5, 1967, of the President, Rusk, McNamara, Rostow, Helms, Christian and Tom Johnson, (the Vice President, who had never before attended a Tuesday Lunch, also attended), the President commented on the U.N. resolution. He said he thought it would be possible to get the nine votes, but that "this might get you where I had feared we would get. I have feared that we would be asked to stop the bombing with nothing in return. We must anticipate the worst and prepare for it." Rusk responded that "no decision had been made whether to do anything at all" (the President had not made a decision about introducing the new resolution).[57]

Subsequent consultations by Goldberg during December "failed to reveal any substantial support among Security Council members for formal UN discussion of the Vietnam conflict," and the resolution was not introduced.[58]

Tax Increase Deferred Again

After the House Ways and Means Committee voted on October 3 to postpone consideration of the 10 percent surtax until the President and Congress could agree on reducing spending. Budget Director Schultze and Council of Economic Advisers Chairman Ackley urged the President to continue his efforts *"even if in your judgment there is no chance of getting a tax increase passed."* (emphasis in original) ("Indeed," they added, "a forecast that the tax bill will not pass makes it still more imperative to take steps which would clearly fix responsibility on the Republicans. We don't need to repeat for you the consequences next year—in terms of inflation and soaring interest rates—of not having a tax increase. Responsibility for those conditions cannot help but be a major election issue.")[59]

In following weeks, the administration, together with Democratic leaders in the House and Senate, sought to find a way around impasse. On October 17, the President and several aides met from 5:35 p.m. to 6:55 p.m. with Speaker McCormack, Majority Leader Albert, and Senator Mansfield to discuss the problem. (That same day, Postmaster General O'Brien reported that there was some indication that Mills would consider reporting the tax bill if the administration would make a $4–4.5 billion cut and would also agree to appointment of a commission to study projected spending and programming in future years.)[60] The President told the leadership that Mills "wants to cut 5 to 10 billion dollars in expenditures and then in programs. This would be very difficult to do. Can you imagine our going back and cutting out programs we have passed in the last three years." "We are in an all-out, knock-down war," he added. "We must make it clear that we cannot fight a war, send

[57] Johnson Library, Tom Johnson's Notes of Meetings, Notes of meeting Dec. 5, 1967.

[58] *U.S. Participation in the UN, Report by the President to the Congress for the Year 1967,* H. Doc. 90–333, p. 61.

[59] Johnson Library, WHCF Ex LE/FI 11–4, Memorandum for the President from Schultze and Ackley, "Impasse on the Tax Increase," Oct. 13, 1967.

[60] Same location.

children to school and meet all of our other responsibilities without a tax increase."[61]

On October 19, Schultze also reported that Mills might accept a $4 billion cut.[62]

At another meeting of Democratic leaders with the President on October 31, attended by Speaker McCormack, Majority Leader Albert, and Senate leaders Mansfield, Russell Long and Robert Byrd, McCormack reported that Mills would not report the surtax bill until he was sure there were enough votes to pass it. The President said that the interest rate situation was serious. Mansfield told him to "keep pounding away for a tax bill," but that it probably would not pass until 1968.[63]

On November 18, the British announced a devaluation of the pound. The U.S. Federal Reserve Board responded by increasing short-term interest rates, and U.S. banks then raised the prime rate to 6 percent, restoring it to the record high level that had caused considerable economic distress during the latter part of 1966.

On November 20, the President met from 5:05 p.m. to 6:40 p.m. with 16 congressional Democratic and Republican leaders from the Senate and the House to talk about the tax increase. He said that, as a result of the British devaluation, action on the surtax "absolutely was imperative." He proposed a new plan which would include a reduction in fiscal 1968 expenditures of $4 billion. In questions and comments, Members of Congress indicated that they were pleased with the proposal for reducing expenditures, which Representative Gerald Ford said the administration had previously been opposing "tooth and nail."[64]

That same day (November 20), Representative Mills announced that the Ways and Means Committee would meet on November 29–30 to take testimony on this new administration proposal to reduce expenditures.[65]

At the hearing of the Ways and Means Committee on November 29, Secretary of the Treasury Fowler presented the plan to cut $4 billion (the amount that Fowler had said earlier that Mills would accept), saying, "It is my deep-seated, personal conviction, which I wish to stress with all of the earnestness at my command, that favorable action by the Congress on the proposals to be placed before you cannot be further deferred without undue and unacceptable risk to the Nation's economic and financial structure and the international monetary system."[66]

The committee took no action on the President's request, however, and Mills told reporters that he was not satisfied with the proposed plan. He said he wanted an additional reduction of $2–

---

[61] Johnson Library, Tom Johnson's Notes of Meetings, Notes of President's meeting with Congressional leadership, Oct. 17, 1967.

[62] Johnson Library, WHCF Ex LE/FI 11–4, Memorandum for the President from Schultze, Wilbur Mills and the Tax Bill," Oct. 19, 1967.

[63] Johnson Library, Meetings Notes File, Jim Jones' notes of meeting of the President with Congressional leadership, Oct. 31, 1967.

[64] Johnson Library, Tom Johnson's Notes of Meetings, Notes of meeting of President with the Bipartisan Leadership, Nov. 20, 1967.

[65] *New York Times*, Nov. 21, 1967.

[66] U.S. Congress, House, Committee on Ways and Means, *President's 1967 Surtax Proposal: Continuation of Hearings to Receive Further Administration Proposal Concerning Expenditure Cuts*, Hearings, November 29 and 30, 1967, 90th Cong., 1st sess. (Washington, D.C.: U.S. Govt. Print. Off., 1967), p. 2.

3 billion as well as evidence that there would be restraints on spending in the following fiscal year. The committee, he said, would not have time in 1967 to give further consideration to the surtax.[67]

"How are we ever going to win?"

The President, while defending his policy publicly, had, as noted, become very pessimistic about winning or even ending the war. According to John Roche, by the summer of 1967, the President "knew that something had gone desperately wrong with the war," and was convinced "that a new policy was in order." By the end of 1967, Roche contends, "Johnson, who had told me flatly shortly before Christmas that all the Joint Chiefs wanted was 'more of the same' and that he wasn't going to give it to them, began an intricate political maneuver. Its objective was to convey to the American people that everything in Vietnam was just fine, but he could be trusted to clean up the mess." "This maneuver," Roche says, "had three components: (1) a major victory over the North Vietnamese in the upcoming winter-spring offensive; (2) an offer to negotiate, combined with some kind of bombing halt; and (3) a massive effort to de-Americanize or Vietnamize the war."[68]

Roche's interpretation is borne out by various pieces of evidence, particularly the President's reaction to plans presented to him by the military during the last months of 1967, when he made it clear that he was not going to approve further increases in U.S. ground forces, that he was not going to approve more intensive bombing of the North, that he was not going to approve further expansion of the war into Laos or Cambodia or an invasion of North Vietnam, and that he expected the South Vietnamese to assume more of a responsibility for fighting the war. At the same time, as Roche also argues, the President did not expect the Communists to negotiate until they were defeated in the "winter-spring offensive,"[69] and he and most if not all of his advisers did not expect the Communists to make any serious, genuine moves toward settling the war until after the 1968 U.S. elections. Meanwhile, the U.S., while stabilizing military operations and pressing the South Vietnamese to assume a larger role, needed to maintain and to seek to improve its own military, political and diplomatic programs. Accordingly, throughout the fall of 1967, the President pressed his advisers to accelerate the deployment of all U.S. forces that had been authorized. On September 6, the JCS were asked "on an urgent basis" for a report on:

> a. What could be done to expedite deployment prior to Christmas.
>
> b. What could be done prior to March 12 [1968], the date of the New Hampshire [Presidential] primary election.

The report was completed on September 9 and was taken to a Tuesday Lunch on September 12.[70] After the lunch, the JCS were asked to recommend action on deployment. On October 4, they sub-

---

[67] *Congressional Quarterly Almanac,* 1967, p. 655.

[68] John Roche, "The Impact of Dissent on Foreign Policy: Past and Future," in Anthony Lake (ed.), *The Vietnam Legacy: The War, American Society, and the Future of American Foreign Policy* (New York: New York Univ. Press for the Council on Foreign Relations, 1976), pp. 133–134.

[69] For a discussion of the "winter-spring offensive," see pt. V of this study, forthcoming.

[70] *PP,* Gravel ed., vol. IV, pp. 528–529.

mitted their report (JCSM–505–67), which was approved by the President.[71]

The President also asked the Joint Chiefs for recommendations for U.S. actions to increase pressure on the Communists. At a Tuesday Lunch on September 12, 1967, attended by Rusk, McNamara, Rostow, Gen. Harold Johnson (acting for General Wheeler), and Christian, he asked General Johnson to have the JCS "'search for imaginative ideas to put pressure to bring this war to a conclusion.' He said he did not want them to just recommend more men or that we drop the atom bomb. The President said he could think of those ideas." He wanted "some new programs," adding that when Congress reconvened in January 1968, "they will try to bring the war to a close either by getting out or by escalating significantly."[72]

On October 17, the JCS made their report, "Increased Pressures on North Vietnam," JCSM–555–67. In a prefatory statement, the JCS explained their position:[73]

> Military operations in Southeast Asia have been conducted within a framework of policy guidelines established to achieve U.S. objectives without expanding the conflict. Principal among these policy guidelines are:
>
> a. We seek to avoid widening the war into a conflict with Communist China or the USSR.
>
> b. We have no *present* intention of invading NVN. [emphasis in original]
>
> c. We do not seek the overthrow of the Government of NVN.
>
> d. We are guided by the principles set forth in the Geneva Accords of 1954 and 1962.
>
> Although some progress is being made within this framework, the Joint Chiefs of Staff consider that the rate of progress has been and continues to be slow, largely because US military power has been restrained in a manner which has reduced significantly its impact and effectiveness. Limitations have been imposed on military operations in four ways:
>
> a. The attacks on the enemy military targets have been on such a prolonged, graduated basis that the enemy has adjusted psychologically, economically, and militarily; e.g., inured themselves to the difficulties and hardships accompanying the war, dispersed their logistic support system, and developed alternate transport routes and a significant air defense system.
>
> b. Areas of sanctuary, containing important military targets, have been afforded the enemy.

---

[71] *Ibid.*, p. 530. For the text of the JCS report of October 4, JCSM–505–67, see CMH, Westmoreland Papers, Message Files, Wheeler to Westmoreland, JCS 8356, Oct. 5, 1967.

[72] Johnson Library, Meetings Notes Files, Jim Jones' notes of meeting Sept. 12, 1967.

[73] The text of McNamara's transmittal memorandum of October 17 and of the JCS report, JCSM–555–67, October 17, together with Defense and State Department comments, are in the Department of State, Central File, Pol 27 Viet S. The text of JCSM–555–67 is also in the *Pentagon Papers*, Gravel ed., vol. IV, pp. 210–214.

On November 20, Katzenbach sent a memorandum to Warnke containing State Department recommendations on the JCS report. The earlier State Department comments, cited in the list of 10 actions recommended by the JCS (see following page), had been prepared by William Bundy. Katzenbach's recommendation differed only slightly. He said he was less favorable to item 4 (extension of naval operations) and item 10 (covert programs in North Vietnam). Katzenbach's memorandum is in U.S. Department of State, Central File, Pol 27 Viet S.

c. Covert operations in Cambodia and Laos have been restricted.

d. Major importation of supplies into NVN by sea has been permitted.

The Joint Chiefs of Staff consider that US objectives in Southeast Asia can be achieved within the policy framework set forth above, providing the level of assistance the enemy receives from his communist allies is not significantly increased and there is no diminution of US efforts. However, progress will continue to be slow so long as present limitations on military operations continue in effect. Further, at our present pace, termination of NVN's military effort is not expected to occur in the near future.

These were the ten actions recommended by the JCS (with comments by the Office of the Secretary of Defense—OSD—and the State Department and several by William Sullivan, U.S. Ambassador to Laos):

1. Remove restrictions on all militarily significant targets in NVN.

OSD—No

State—No

2. Mine NVN deep water ports.

OSD—No

State—No

3. Mine inland waterways and estuaries in NVN north of 20° N.

OSD—Yes, with prohibition against mining within 5 miles of any deep water ports and within 25 miles of Chinese border.

State—Yes

4. Extend naval surface operations (SEA DRAGON).

OSD—Yes

State—Yes, but with careful restrictions.

5. Use US Sams (TALOS) [surface to air missiles] from ships against combat aircraft.

OSD—Yes

State—No.

6. Increase air interdiction in Laos and along NVN borders.

OSD—No (since present arrangements with RLG [Government of Laos] are adequate)

State—No

Sullivan—believes more should be done, especially during the next two months, but under present arrangements with RLG. Notes that Souvanna [Phouma, Premier of Laos] would favor such an increase.

7. Eliminate operational restrictions on B–52s with regard to Laos.

OSD—Yes

State—check with Sullivan

Sullivan—Yes on night-time overflights, selected daylight bombing subject to clearance, and limited penetrations subject to clearance; No on blanket bombing authority or "indiscriminate" day-time overflights.

8. Expand operations in Laos (PRAIRIE FIRE).[74]

OSD—Yes, "examine sympathetically," have MACV and Sullivan coordinate on a selective basis.

State—Have MACV and Sullivan work out, subject to final approval here.

Sullivan—prepared to work with MACV, but wishes to retain final Washington approval; indicates clearly negative attitude on battalion- or company-size operations. No to the Gung-Ho warriors; and keep Washington involved as restraint.[75]

9. Expand operations in Cambodia (DANIEL BOONE).

OSD—No.

State—No, at least for present, [security deletion of about one line]

10. Expand and reorient NVN covert programs (FOOTBOY).[76]

OSD—Yes (as means of getting more intelligence)

State—Yes in principle, but need more information to be sure proposals do not raise political problems.

In a memorandum to the President on October 17, McNamara discussed his position on the JCS recommendations.[78] He said he agreed with six of the ten (all except numbers 1, 2, 4, and 9 on the above list), "as I believe that these actions could result in making more costly North Vietnam's aggression without serious risk of expanding the war or unnecessarily increasing US casualties." "Nevertheless," he added, "I continue to believe that actions against North Vietnam and in Laos will not in themselves destroy North Vietnam's ability and will to continue its aggression in the South, and that political, economic and military progress in South Vietnam are the critical determinants in this regard."

At a Tuesday Lunch on October 23, just after McNamara had submitted the JCS report, the President, noting that he had asked the JCS for suggestions on how to shorten the war but that all of their proposals were for action outside South Vietnam,[79] said, as was noted earlier, that the JCS report "was not what was desired,

---

[74] PRAIRIE FIRE—small cross-border U.S.-South Vietnamese reconnaissance patrols along the Ho Chi Minh Trail in Laos. See Castle, *At War in the Shadow of Vietnam*, cited above.

[75] In a response to a cable from Washington, Sullivan said, among other things (U.S. Department of State, Central File, Pol 27 Viet S, Vientiane to Washington 2358, Oct. 26, 1967): "Problem of PRAIRIE FIRE is always the knottiest because it involves a gung-ho group who, by their very nature, are always attempting to exceed the political limitations of more reasonable men everywhere. They are therefore constantly pressing against Westy and against CINCPAC for more and more reckless and irresponsible endeavors. Westy turns down a great many of their efforts and Ollie Sharp [CINCPAC] turns down even more. Occasionally they let one through in the full confidence that I will turn it down. This is largely a problem of morale for overgrown adolescents and I certainly don't wish to disappoint their inevitable image of parental rigidity. Therefore, largely for their own good, it is wise to be most severe on PRAIRIE FIRE. In general, the net effectiveness of this program is totally disproportionate to the amount of paper which it consumes; and it would not become more effective even if it were more liberally permissive."

[76] According to the JCS memorandum, this would involve "action to increase the credibility of a current national resistance movement in NVN," and action to increase intelligence collection and covert physical destruction.

[78] U.S. Department of State, Central File, Pol 27 Viet S, Memorandum for the President from McNamara, Oct. 17, 1967.

[79] Johnson Library, Tom Johnson's Notes of Meetings, Notes of meeting Oct. 23, 1967.

that it recommended actions which had previously been denied and would not now be approved."[80]

It is not clear from available documentation as to what action was taken on the JCS report of October 17 other than the dismissal of it by the President. There does not appear to have been any discussion of the report at the policymaking level, and there is no record of any reply to the JCS by McNamara or any other civilian official.

At the time the President asked General Johnson to have the JCS report prepared, Rostow asked his assistant, Ginsburgh, also to produce a plan for South Vietnam. On September 12, Ginsburgh sent Rostow a ten-point list of military measures "to accelerate progress of the war." Rostow held it until November 6, when he sent it to the President with a memorandum commenting on which of Ginsburgh's proposals seemed most important, and noting, "Once we work out such a short list, we then must hold our top-level people accountable for moving it and regularly reporting progress. That is the kind of result I should like to see from Bunker and Westmoreland's visit in Washington."[81]

MACV's Strategic Study

At about this same time, Westmoreland's headquarters produced a 68-page study of U.S. strategy for the coming year, "MACV Strategic Study, September 1967-September 1968," dated October 15, 1967.[82] According to the study, "the enemy is meeting increasing difficulty in maintaining the thrust of his effort, whereas the US/FW [free world]/RVN [Republic of Vietnam] forces are increasing in size and are becoming more proficient and experienced in developing and executing operations against the enemy." "The success of the US/FW/RVN forces is being demonstrated by the enemy's avoidance of contact, his failure to mount an offensive in the north and his increased terrorist activities. This apparent success appears to be placing US/FW/RVN forces ahead of the power curve to the extent that some change in the enemy's strategy and tactics must be anticipated." "Friendly operations," the study said, "may have degraded the enemy's capabilities to a greater extent than previous intelligence estimates indicated," and new estimates of the changed situation "raise the question as to whether the time has come for US/FW/RVN forces to make the transition to an exploitation phase of the war."

"The enemy," the study stated, "apparently has settled for a protracted war of attrition; he seems to believe that his will, patience and resources will out-last those of the Free World. This strategy implies that his will and resources will sustain him for the time required, but present evidence indicates that his time may indeed be limited. The indispensable population base appears to be slipping

[80] *PP*, Gravel ed., vol. IV, p. 536.

[81] Johnson Library, NSF Memos to the President—Walt Rostow, Memorandum for the President from Rostow, Nov. 6, 1967, with memorandum to Rostow from Ginsburgh attached.

[82] National Archives, Westmoreland-CBS Papers, "MACV Strategic Study, September 1967-September 1968, Oct. 15, 1967. There is very little available information on the conceptual origins and authorship of the study. Westmoreland's deputy, General Abrams, whose views it reflected, may have been instrumental in its drafting. For observations on Abrams' views on the war and differences between the thinking of Abrams and Westmoreland, see Lewis Sorley, *Thunderbolt: General Creighton Abrams and the Army of His Times* (New York: Simon and Schuster, 1992), pp. 201 ff.

from his grasp and he is unable to make up for the resultant loss by bringing men and supplies from the north; his strength, effectiveness and morale are deteriorating. Perhaps of greater importance, he cannot see convincing signs of our weakening will or patience."

Following a discussion of options open to the Communists, and, in each case, the possible opposing courses of action by U.S. and allied forces, the MACV study concluded with recommendations. The main effort during the period from November 1967 to mid-1968, it said, should be "multi-division offensive operations" in III Corps (the area around and to the west of Saigon), "to destroy the enemy and to neutralize his base areas." U.S. forces in IV Corps (the delta) should be limited, and the South Vietnamese Army in that area should be strengthened. In view of the "deteriorating enemy situation," consideration should be given to increased use of U.S. and other "free world" forces in pacification (Revolutionary Development) "to offset the anticipated shortage of RD cadre."

"To exploit the contingency that enemy efforts will increasingly become guerrilla in nature," the study recommended that consideration be given to:

"1. Optimum disposition and stationing of US/FW/RVN units throughout RVN, with emphasis on dispersion of battalion size units for expansion of effective territorial security for pacification.

"2. Integration of RVNAF with US/FW units.

"3. Optimum organization, equipment, and training of maneuver units to maximize their effectiveness in the guerrilla environment."

The MACV report gave the following description of "the principal roles of friendly [U.S. and allied] forces":

"Pacification—This mission is of paramount importance and operations must be expanded in all CTZs [combat tactical zones].

"Offensive—This mission will be reduced in scope to operations by highly mobile, integrated forces of brigade size in each CTZ.

"Containment—Forces must be retained in the same relative magnitude but should be integrated to prepare RVNAF for the eventual withdrawal of US/FW forces."

This MACV study is one of the most remarkable documents produced during the war—remarkable, because of its conclusions and recommendations: its conclusion that pacification was of "paramount importance" and that U.S. offensive ground action should be reduced in size and scope, and its recommendations that the U.S. should shift from large-unit search and destroy missions to smaller, more dispersed counterguerrilla forces equipped and trained for that kind of warfare; that U.S. and South Vietnamese forces should be integrated; and that South Vietnamese forces should assume more of the fighting in preparation for U.S. withdrawal. Critics of U.S. military strategy in South Vietnam had long argued against the emphasis on attriting enemy forces through large-scale search and destroy missions, most notably General Harold Johnson and the Army officers who produced the PROVN Report, as well as a number of other critics in the CIA and the State Department and nongovernmental critics such as Sir Robert Thompson. Westmoreland and his command, however, had stoutly defended the strategy of attrition as being the best choice under the circumstances, and had given the PROVN Report short shrift.

What produced such a major shift? In part, it resulted from the perception in Westmoreland's headquarters that the war was "increasingly guerrilla in nature," but it is also likely that the presence of General Abrams, who did not agree with Westmoreland's approach, may have been an important factor. In any event, the study was only a study, not an action document, and it does not appear to have had any effects on policy or operations at that time.

Soon after the MACV Strategic Study, Westmoreland received a personal letter from General DePuy,[83] who, while serving as Westmoreland's operations officer in 1965, had played a key role in developing the search-and-destroy tactics being employed by U.S. forces in South Vietnam:

> I am sure you are aware that there is a large body of what I regard as uninformed thinkers, who have become increasingly critical of search and destroy operations. These same people have convinced themselves from statistics indicating high kills per man on patrol in ICTZ [I Corps] that the most cost-effective operations are small patrols. Not having a balanced view, or any experience they then leap to the conclusion that the whole emphasis should shift to small unit patrolling—in particular, small patrols should be substituted for major unit operations in the VC base areas. They have persuaded themselves that enemy losses would then be higher, and U.S. casualties and logistic costs significantly lower: an alternative strategy of some attractiveness here.
>
> What bothers me is that as far back as 1964 you have been pressing for wide spread and large-scale reconnaissance efforts to find the enemy to be followed by larger exploitation forces as an economy of force measure and as a sensible military approach to the problem of finding and fighting an elusive enemy.
>
> Somehow, MACV is not getting credit for this kind of thinking not because you are not doing it but because perhaps you are not talking about it in a way which convinces these many analysts. . . .
>
> A concomitant misunderstanding seems to be the matter of who has the initiative. The analysts apparently have convinced themselves, largely from reports relating to who fired the first shot, that all battles are started by the Viet Cong. They do not take into account the fact that we have habitually been able to find large battles any time we entered into their base areas and remained there long enough, disrupted them sufficiently, and found their stores of supplies and ammunition.
>
> I know that you and your staff have more than enough to do, but I would recommend that in your conceptual messages or your campaign plan-type messages you explain in fairly simple terms those things which soldiers take for granted regarding the relationship between deep intelligence/reconnaissance or combat/reconnaissance by infantry elements followed by larger scale exploitation, reinforcement and pursuit. . . .

---

[83] U.S. Army Military History Institute, Carlisle Barracks, Pa., DePuy Papers, letter to Westmoreland from DePuy, Oct. 19, 1967. A copy of this letter was kindly provided by General Douglas Kinnard.

> If you could put into a message the same words that you have used so often in speaking to your commanders and troops regarding these subjects, it would forestall what may grow into a serious civilian intrusion into the business of the professional soldier. . . .

Westmoreland replied: "We are continuing operations along the lines you are familiar with and have succeeded in materially increasing our Long Range Reconnaissance capability. In addition to our efforts in developing a U.S. reconnaissance effort, we have initiated a comparable program with the ARVN. . . ." He said he thought that the idea of a message was "most timely," and that he would send it.[84]

On October 31, following a Tuesday Lunch, Wheeler cabled Westmoreland that a "major subject concerned the deteriorating public support in this country for the Vietnamese war. . . . There was a consensus of view that we have a serious problem with American public opinion; namely, how to achieve a situation wherein the ARVN [Army of the Republic of Vietnam] visibly is carrying a greater share of the combat operations.[85] Several days later, Westmoreland replied in a cable to Wheeler listing military priorities for coming months,[86] one of which was the "modernization" of the South Vietnamese Army through more and better equipment (the M–16 rifle used by U.S. troops was just being made available to the South Vietnamese, who were also short of artillery and transportation and communications equipment). Another priority was the plan for using Vietnamese units in joint and integrated search and destroy operations with U.S. forces during 1968. Wheeler replied that he was "especially pleased to see the high emphasis on modernization of RVNAF," which he added, would be one of the major subjects to be discussed with the President during Westmoreland's forthcoming trip to Washington.[87]

During his trip to Washington, as noted, Westmoreland, having taken stock of the situation in Washington and on the battlefield, decided to announce what he called his "withdrawal strategy," under which the U.S. would help the South Vietnamese to assume more of the fighting, and would plan on a phased withdrawal beginning within two years.[88] In a subsequent interview Westmoreland explained that "It was the only strategy that I could come up with that was viable if there were no change in policy, if we were not going to widen the war, and if we were not going to call up our reserves. . . . It was my strategy, and I portrayed it as such." (As noted earlier, Westmoreland cabled Abrams that he had suggested this strategy on his own initiative.) Westmoreland added that "The administration was totally noncommittal on it. They kind of nodded

---

[84] Westmoreland letter to DePuy, Oct. 30, 1967, attached to DePuy letter of October 19, cited in previous footnote. It is not known whether Westmoreland sent the message.

[85] CMH, Westmoreland Papers, Message Files, Wheeler to Westmoreland, JCS 9298, Oct. 31, 1967.

[86] Same location, Westmoreland to Wheeler, MAC 10726, Nov. 10, 1967, cited above.

[87] National Archives, Westmoreland-CBS Papers, Wheeler to Westmoreland, DTG 101539Z, Nov. 10, 1967.

[88] See p. 897 above, and Westmoreland, *A Soldier Reports*, p. 234.

their heads and did not disagree. They just listened and did nothing about it."[89]

During November-December 1967, however, Westmoreland and the JCS, despite the apparent futility of getting the President's approval, continued to recommend operations by U.S. and South Vietnamese forces against Communist forces in Laos and Cambodia as well as an amphibious hook into North Vietnam above the DMZ. As noted, when he was asked by Rostow on November 20 to comment on McNamara's memorandum proposing a stabilization of U.S. operations, Westmoreland replied, in part, that for 1968 he was thinking of using South Vietnamese forces in Laos and possibly Cambodia, as well as in a raid in force against North Vietnam above the DMZ. In a memorandum to McNamara on November 27 on "Policies for the Conduct of Operations in Southeast Asia over the Next Four Months," the JCS, as will be seen, made similar recommendations.

The JCS Recommends Strategy for 1968

At a Tuesday Lunch on October 11, from 12:55 p.m. to 1:03 p.m. with Rusk, McNamara, Rostow and Christian, which Air Force Commander General McConnell also attended, the President asked the JCS for recommendations on U.S. strategy for the coming year.[90] According to brief notes of the decisions made at the meeting, "Most important decision: President wants strategy for the next 12 months on Vietnam—military, political, negotiating. Too much vague talk."[91] This does not appear to have been followed up at the time. At a Tuesday Lunch on November 8, however, Rusk, doubtless after talking with the President, recommended that the State and Defense Departments prepare jointly a proposed plan for U.S. military and political operations in Vietnam for the following four month period.[92]

---

[89] Schandler, *The Unmaking of a President,* p. 62. Brower, "Strategic Reassessment in Vietnam: The Westmoreland 'Alternate Strategy' of 1967–1968," cited above, says (p. 35) that "By the end of 1967, the Westmoreland alternate strategy lay dormant, held down by the increasing political pressure on the eve of a presidential campaign and strong disagreement within the Defense Department over the war's strategy."

[90] In a cable that day (Oct. 11, 1967), Westmoreland gave a "personal appraisal" of the war (National Archives, Westmoreland-CBS Papers, MAC 9514, Oct. 11, 1967):

"1. With the exception of the DMZ, the enemy has evaded or attempted to evade our offensive. . . .

"2. I anticipate that the enemy will take measures over the next several months to reduce the heavy casualties we have inflicted on him thus far in 1967. Some of these measures may include: further emphasis on stationing units in the border areas where he can escape our pressure by withdrawal into North Vietnam, Laos or Cambodia; breaking up battalions and regiments in coastal areas into company size units; increased use of sapper units and attacks by fire alone.

"3. Thus, the situation at the beginning of the northeast monsoon season is conducive to initiation of wide spread offensive on all fronts—political, military, economic and psychological. RVN/US/FW forces have retained the initiative, spoiled enemy attempt to launch major offensives through the DMZ and in the western highlands, frustrated enemy efforts to disrupt pacification and election activities, expanded areas of secure population and made inroads against enemy infrastructure in several key areas.

"4. The overall strategy for the next 6 months will contain three basic points: (1) offensives to keep the enemy off-balance; (2) persistent neutralization of enemy base areas with methodical capture/destruction of his supplies and facilities; and (3) improved development in and expansion of secured population areas. . . .

"5. We are making steady progress, although undramatic. There is widespread optimism here. The air war to the north is beginning to have an impact on the enemy."

[91] Johnson Library, NSF Files of Walt W. Rostow.

[92] There are no known notes of this meeting. Information here is from *PP*, Gravel ed., vol. IV, p. 536.

It is not clear why Rusk made this request or what the report was intended to cover. There are no known notes of the meeting, and the *Pentagon Papers* says only "Secretary Rusk's proposal was expressed in broad terms. He considered the parameters should be established for political, military, and economic operations over the upcoming four months' period in order to preclude the need for weekly examinations of many small and short-range operations."[93] According to a cable from Wheeler to Westmoreland later that afternoon (November 8), which appears to be a report on the meeting, "highest authority [the President] is now thinking in terms of assigning top priority to those programs which would have a maximum impact on progress in South Vietnam during the next six months."[94] Wheeler said that some of the items being considered were:

> A. Coordinated attack on VC infrastructure. . . .
>
> B. Increased use of ARVN in integrated operations with US forces.
>
> C. Active area security and ARVN search and destroy against VC provincial battalions.
>
> D. Supplementing RD team effort with locally trained teams.
>
> E. Additional US advisors for RF and PF.
>
> F. Opening and security of LOCs.
>
> G. Various economic programs including universal elementary education, land reform, and agricultural productivity.
>
> H. Encouragement of local government responsibility and the attack on corruption.

Westmoreland replied that he agreed with the list "because these are precisely the items to which we have already been devoting urgent efforts."[95] After a description of what was being done with respect to each item on the list, he concluded: "In sum, we already well along the road toward mounting the urgent short term priority programs set forth in your message. . . ."

On November 10, Wheeler directed the Joint Staff to prepare recommendations for the JCS, and stipulated that the recommendations should cover certain matters "as a minimum," including "large ground operations in South Vietnam to include operations in the Delta region; ground operations in Laos; ground operations in Cambodia; and possible ground operations against North Vietnam."[96]

Although the lack of notes of the meeting of November 8 makes it difficult to arrive at firm conclusions about the appropriateness of this response, Wheeler's instructions, and the resulting report from the JCS, appear to have exceeded Rusk's request and to have gone far beyond the priority items that Wheeler had told Westmoreland were being considered. Moreover, he specifically requested the inclusion of ground operations in Laos, Cambodia and North Vietnam after the President had said on October 23 that he

[93] *PP*, Gravel ed., vol. IV, p. 536. This statement, which appears to have been based on notes of the meeting, is not footnoted in the Hébert (Department of Defense) edition of the *Pentagon Papers*. (The Gravel edition does not contain any footnotes.)

[94] CMH, Westmoreland Papers, Message Files, Wheeler to Westmoreland, JCS 9566, Nov. 8, 1967.

[95] Same location, Westmoreland to Wheeler, MAC 10726, Nov. 10, 1967.

[96] *PP*, Gravel ed., vol. IV, pp. 536–537.

would not approve an expansion of U.S. ground operations in Laos and Cambodia.

Why did Wheeler frame his instructions so broadly and include actions which the President had already rejected? He may have done so as a matter of course; that is, he may have wanted the document to represent the thinking of the JCS and Westmoreland as to what was needed and should be done from a military standpoint. Conceivably, he may also have done so, in part, at least, as a way of getting the President to agree to national mobilization and a call up of the Reserves. According to Perry,[97] after McNamara's testimony in the Stennis hearings, and the aborted decision of the JCS to resign, Wheeler decided, as he told General Johnson, "to let the war itself act as the catalyst" for mobilization. Having decided to try to force the President to escalate the war, Wheeler directed the Joint Staff to answer several questions on troop deployment, including how many troops over the 525,000 that had been approved would need to be called to trigger mobilization; how many troops would be needed to reconstitute the strategic reserve (troops in the U.S. and Europe that had been drawn down by deployment to Vietnam); and what political impact a call up of the Reserves would have and what mechanism had to be established in order for a call-up to take place.[98]

On November 27, 1967, Wheeler submitted the JCS report, "Policies for the Conduct of Operations in Southeast Asia over the Next Four Months," to McNamara, who sent it that day to Rusk for State Department analysis and comment.[99] In his memorandum to McNamara, Wheeler stated that, within current policy guidelines, U.S. military operations "would eventually lead to achievement of U.S. national objectives. . . ." The JCS had reviewed possible new programs and had concluded that "there are no new programs which can be undertaken under current policy guidelines which would result in a rapid or significantly more visible increase in the rate of progress in the near term." It would be possible, however, to make "additional gains . . . through the modification and expansion of certain current policies. . . ." Of these, Wheeler singled out Operation YORK II, which he said was strongly recommended by Westmoreland. (YORK II, scheduled to take place in early 1968, involved sending U.S. forces into the A Shau Valley, along the Laotian border in the western part of Quang Tin Province located in I Corps in northern South Vietnam, to reestablish control of the valley and set the stage for the invasion of Laos that Westmoreland says in his memoirs he hoped would be approved by a new administration in Washington.[100] As a part of this operation, two to three South Vietnamese battalions, with American advisers, and supported by U.S. artillery and air, were to conduct a raid across the border into "Base Area 607" in Laos for the purpose of destroying enemy supplies and munitions.)

---

[97] Perry, *Four Stars*, p. 173.

[98] *Ibid.*, pp. 173–174.

[99] U.S. Department of State, Central File, Pol 27 Viet S, Memorandum for Rusk from McNamara, Nov. 27, 1967, with attached JCS report, JCSM–663–67, Nov. 27, 1967, "Policies for the Conduct of Operations in Southeast Asia over the Next Four Months," with appendix and annexes. Also attached, for use by Rusk, were spread sheets prepared by William Bundy's office containing comments and recommendations on each of the JCS proposals.

[100] Westmoreland, *A Soldier Reports*, p. 314.

The JCS requested authority for ten modifications and expansions of current policies, principally the following:

1. To employ US and US-advised ground reconnaissance patrols throughout the DMZ.
2. The develop a guerrilla force in Laos.
3. To lift certain restrictions as DANIEL BOONE operations [reconnaissance operations in Cambodia] to include air strikes in remote border areas.
4. To expand SEA DRAGON [naval gunfire against enemy defenses and lines of communications in North Vietnam and interdiction of enemy shipping along the coast] authorities north to 21° 15′ N.
5. To modify the air strike policy in various categories to include mining of Haiphong, Hon Gai and Cam Pha.

These recommendations, as can be seen, were quite similar to the earlier JCS recommendations (JCSM–555–67, October 17, "Increased Pressure on North Vietnam") that had already been rejected by the President.

Neither the November 27 report of the JCS nor that of October 17 recommended a U.S. invasion of the southern part of North Vietnam, near the DMZ, a very politically sensitive idea that had been discussed for several years and actively considered during 1967.[101] In another memorandum in late November, however, Wheeler proposed, along with ground operations in Laos and airstrikes and limited ground operations in Cambodia, that in the spring of 1968, when weather and sea conditions permitted, the U.S. should conduct "an amphibious and airborne raid in force against NVA [North Vietnamese Army] facilities immediately north of the DMZ."[102]

The reaction of the State Department to the specific recommendations contained in the JCS plan submitted on November 27 was generally negative, except for the development of the guerrilla force for Laos, which had already been approved.[103]

More generally, State Department officials were quite concerned about the broader implications of the JCS plan. In a memorandum to Rusk on November 30, in which he commented on each specific JCS proposal, William Bundy said that "while making every effort to be reasonable and plausible," the JCS proposals "inevitably portend steady pressures for expansion."[104]

In a memorandum for Rusk on December 2, Foy Kohler, Deputy Undersecretary of State agreed with Bundy. With respect to increased bombing, Kohler said that "considerations counseling against further extension and escalation of the bombing or mining activities in the north remain valid. . . . It seems clear to me that our past escalation has in fact contributed to the harder line on the

---

[101] An initial outline of an airborne/airmobile/amphibious landing in North Vietnam—Operation BUTTSTROKE—was sent by Westmoreland to CINCPAC in the late summer of 1967. See Westmoreland's subsequent cable on the subject, CMH, Westmoreland Papers, Message Files, MAC 9619, Oct. 13, 1967.

[102] U.S. Department of State, Central File, Pol 27 Viet S, memorandum for Rusk from Read, Nov. 27, 1967.

[103] For the State Department's position, see the spread sheet cited above, and memoranda cited below.

[104] U.S. Department of State, Central file, Pol 27 Viet S, memorandum for Rusk from William Bundy, Nov. 30, 1967.

part of the Soviets and to measurable increases in Soviet military aid to the DRV [North Vietnam]. . . ."[105]

In a lengthy memorandum to Rusk on December 4, Katzenbach, both in his specific comments on each JCS proposal and in his more general comments, discussed the JCS proposals in the context of the broad strategic framework of U.S. policy.[106] JCSM–663, he said, "raises the question of what we are trying to accomplish in Vietnam and how were are going about it." If, as he believed, the Communists were pursuing a strategy of engaging U.S. forces with regular North Vietnamese forces in the border areas, thus drawing U.S. forces from the more populated areas, the U.S. would be faced with "irresistible military pressures for going after the enemy wherever they are," and "a course of ever-expanding military objectives." "There is the real possibility," Katzenbach said, "that we are embarking on a course which may well take us into a direct war against North Vietnam." "It seems to me highly likely that a year from now we may find ourselves fighting a war basically against the North Vietnamese army, with geographical limitations that now exist on the ground battle area eroding rapidly." "I think we should face the dangers now. We may be nearer the point of Chinese involvement than we think, and, in the end, the present strategy virtually foreordains it."

Katzenbach argued that each of the major recommendations of the JCS had the potential of widening and intensifying the war, and could result in larger U.S. commitments. YORK II, he said, was not an isolated request. It was a "'firebreak' issue which puts us on the road to larger commitments of U.S. forces in Laos. . . . If we are prepared to go into Laos to destroy Base 607, then I find it difficult to see what principle would prevent us from going into other parts of Laos to destroy other targets of opportunity which are almost sure to exist."

A similar problem could occur as a result of U.S. and U.S.-advised patrols in the DMZ, on the North Vietnamese side of the Provisional Military Demarcation Line (the 17th parallel). This, too, was "a 'firebreak' issue, raising perhaps more serious problems."

---

[105] Same location, Memorandum from Kohler to Read (for Rusk), Dec. 2, 1967.

Bohlen took a similar position. While in Washington for a few days, he met with the President on November 28 from 11:19 a.m. to 11:57 a.m. In his memoirs several years later Bohlen described his response to the President's question about bombing. Bohlen, *Witness to History,* p. 525:

"I told him that I was not qualified to judge the military value of bombing North Vietnam, but politically it was the worst thing that the United States had done. It forced the Soviets to extend greater assistance to North Vietnam. They attach enormous importance to maintaining their position of leadership in the Communist world, and to have turned their back on a small Communist country under assault from the great 'imperialist' power would have exposed them to criticism from the Chinese. To Peking, nonaction by the Soviets would be another proof of the revisionist and nonrevolutionary nature of the Soviet regime. Furthermore, I told Johnson, the bombing turned public opinion in Europe against us. The Europeans could see no military value in bombing small huts in rural areas. To them, the raids were an act of brutality. Walt Rostow, the President's adviser for national-security affairs, who sat in on the meeting, defended the bombing. He pointed out that Allied air raids had killed civilians in World War II but were continued because they helped the military effort. I replied that, without knowing the military effect on Vietnam, there was a difference between traditional movement of vast armies and guerrilla warfare. In traditional warfare, railroads and trucks were required to transport men and supplies. Thus bombing was effective. In guerrilla war, supplies moved on bicycles and the backs of the Vietnamese. Bombing did not stop the enemy. None of the arguments were new. Johnson had heard them from others at various times. He asked no more questions and said nothing in response to my arguments."

[106] U.S. Department of State, Central File, Pol 27 Viet S, Memorandum to Rusk from Katzenbach, Dec. 4, 1967.

"[I]f we are going to authorize this request," he said, "we should do it with the full understanding that the DMZ boundary is not likely to stick very long . . . and we will soon be faced with the much more fundamental question of operations in North Vietnam."

Expansion of U.S. ground reconnaissance patrols in Cambodia could also lead to larger problems. "I am concerned," Katzenbach said, "that this proposal is the opening step of a scenario which could well end up with the U.S. fighting up and down the eastern edge of Cambodia, with the enemy happily retreating to the west and north, luring us deeper and deeper into a political and military quagmire." "I should think that the North Vietnamese would like nothing better than to have us pursue them into Cambodia, leading to a situation in which Sihanouk either becomes more violently anti-American or is overthrown."

He concluded:

> Our present military strategy seems to me to be aimed more at victory over the DRV and is therefore somewhat inconsistent with the more limited objective of creating a viable South Viet-Nam. There are alternatives. While pressing on the political front in South Viet-Nam and the possibility of negotiated settlement in South VietNam, we could gradually decelerate the intensity of search and destroy operations in and near border areas where they lead to pressing into sanctuaries. We could make the enemy come to us . . . [W]e could give the ARVN an increasing role while using US forces to bail them out when they get into trouble, and we could relate our military actions to our political objectives in South Viet-Nam rather than to the destruction of the DRV forces with its accompanying dangers of an expanded war.

No formal action was taken by the President or by McNamara on the JCS plan of November 27, nor does it appear to have been discussed at the policymaking level. There were, however, discussions and decisions relating to several of the specific proposals, and comments on the part of plan which dealt primarily with the bombing of North Vietnam were sent by Rusk and McNamara jointly to the JCS.[107]

At a Tuesday Lunch on December 5 from 1:18 p.m. to 2:37 p.m. attended by the President, Rusk, McNamara, Rostow, Helms, Christian and Tom Johnson, McNamara reported that two cables had been received from Westmoreland concerning possible military campaigns in Laos and Cambodia.[108] With respect to the proposed operation in Cambodia—a 72-hour "pursuit by fire" in the tri-border area (where the borders of Vietnam, Laos, and Cambodia join, a short distance south of the proposed operation in the A Shau Valley) involving high volume, coordinated attacks on North Vietnamese forces just inside the Cambodian border by B–52 bombers, tactical air, and artillery—McNamara said that it raised "very serious political problems which outweigh the military gains." Rusk said he would draw a distinction between operations in Laos and in Cambodia. "If we hit the enemy in Cambodia and possibly kill Cam-

---

[107] *PP*, Gravel ed., vol. IV, p. 538.

[108] Johnson Library, Tom Johnson's Notes of Meetings, Notes of meeting Dec. 5, 1967, at 1:18 p.m.

bodian personnel, this may give them reason to commit forces against us." Both McNamara and Rusk said, however, that the Laos situation was different. McNamara said that "the border is ill defined . . . [and] the chances of getting caught are much different." Rusk said "there is not a fraction of as much a problem in Laos as there is in Cambodia." McNamara and Rusk both recommended approval of the proposed operation in Laos—YORK II, the raid against Base Area 607 described earlier—and the President agreed to approve the operation.

In his memoirs, Westmoreland confirmed what McNamara and Katzenbach had feared: the goal of Operation YORK II in the A Shau Valley was "setting the stage for the invasion of Laos that I hoped a new administration in Washington would approve. . . ."[109]

The Tuesday Lunch on December 5 continued from 6:02 p.m. to 7:15 p.m. (Wheeler, Clifford and Justice Fortas joined the group), in order to discuss further the proposal for an attack on Cambodia as part of the tri-border operation for which Westmoreland was requesting authority.[110] Rusk was strongly opposed to the proposal, saying, "we have tried all along to limit this war. 'The action which General Westmoreland is proposing would be a significant act of war against Cambodia. This would change the entire character of the war. If Cambodia is attacked, they may ask the Chinese to side with them. Then we will really have a new war on our hands.'" "'If we take this action,'" Rusk added, "'it would be absolutely essential to consult the Congress. . . . It would be a major political burden for us to bear with a minimum military gain toward ending the war.'" The President, who, it will be recalled, had previously urged reconciliation with Cambodia, in keeping with his desire to avoid widening the war, responded to Rusk: "Aware as I am of the mistakes Generals have made in the past, I place great confidence in General Westmoreland. Both he and Ambassador Bunker have recommended this action." He added: "We must tell Cambodia that we will not continue to permit them to house and protect these killers. Do we have to continue to live with this for the duration of the war?" Rusk replied: "'This problem is not really different from the one of mining Haiphong. We run the risk of enlarging the war.'" The President retorted, "I see this differently from mining Haiphong or bombing the ports."

McNamara joined Rusk in opposing the proposed attack. "'This is analogous,'" he said, "'to a land invasion [of North Vietnam] above the DMZ. This is not the most effective way to do it.'"

He continued:

> This raises a basic issue of our policy, and I have thought that this would be the issue to face us in the coming year for sometime.
>
> I believe, Mr. President that it is most unwise to expand the war beyond the South Vietnamese borders. My arguments are as follows:
>
> —This action would further divide this nation.

---

[109] Westmoreland, *A Soldier Reports*, p. 314.

[110] Johnson Library, Tom Johnson's Notes of Meetings, Notes of meeting Dec. 5, 1967, at 6:02 p.m.

—This action would further increase our problems in the United Nations.

Because of these two points, I would strongly recommend against this proposal.

"I am scared to death," McNamara added. "I am scared of a policy based on an assumption that by going somewhere else we can win the war." "The war cannot be won by killing North Vietnamese. It can only be won by protecting the South Vietnamese so they can build and develop economically for a future political contact with North Vietnam." "This is not an isolated action," he said later in the meeting, "It is a basic change of policy."

General Wheeler said he "'would not disagree with the importance Secretary Rusk and Secretary McNamara place on this issue. The real question we face is how long we can tolerate these people operating from a sanctuary. . . .'" "'The Joint Chiefs,'" he added, "'do not want to widen the war either. We only wish Cambodia would be neutral—honest to God neutral, too. Anyone else would not permit enemy troops to use their territory for sanctuaries." Rusk responded: "'I would have thought that Westy would have drug his shirttail along the Cambodian border and drawn the enemy fire. Then the rules would permit him to shoot back across the border when fired upon.'" The President asked Wheeler why Westmoreland did not take the advice that Rusk had suggested, and sweep down the border of Cambodia. McNamara replied that such an action would not draw much fire; that the North Vietnamese did not fire across the border.

Fortas and Clifford also opposed the proposed attack. Fortas said that, based on what he had heard in the meeting, there was "an overwhelming case against this action. The issue is the whole question of what you do about sanctuaries. It seems we should communicate with Sihanouk." "Domestically," he added, "we should surface the use of Cambodia as a sanctuary. . . . The sooner the American people know about this the better."

Defense Secretary-designate Clark Clifford said that Westmoreland's recommendation "does not make sense to me. . . . We need to build up a strong case to proceed to remove this sanctuary. I would be unalterably opposed to the action."

The President asked Wheeler whether the JCS agreed with the proposed attack. Wheeler replied that it was a part of the program proposed by the JCS for the conduct of the war during the following four months. (It was not.) The President replied that he wanted Westmoreland to explore "other means of getting at the enemy." "As I see it," he said, "this act could result in Cambodia declaring war against us and in their inviting China in." Rostow interjected that "he did not think Cambodia would bring the Chinese in."

In conclusion, the President, saying, "we must let Sihanouk know we will not tolerate this action any longer," suggested the possibility of renewing the attempt, which had failed in 1966, to get Sihanouk to meet with Harriman. With respect to Westmoreland's recommendation, he said he wanted to ask Westmoreland for more details, and to ask Bunker why he supported the proposal.

In a cable the following day (December 6) to Westmoreland, Wheeler said the argument had been made in the meeting that, among other things, U.S. military operations on the border, such as the proposed attack on Cambodia, "creates unnecessary pressures for escalating action against sanctuaries outside South Vietnam."[111] Westmoreland replied that he considered this "reverse reasoning."[112] "The fact," he said, "that the enemy is gainfully using these sanctuaries from which to mount his attacks is what stimulates our desire to strike them. If we elect not to protect the border provinces, the enemy would still use these sanctuaries to avoid the attacks by fire that we can apply to in-country bases. We would still be faced with the decision of attacking or granting immunity to these bases. By contacting him at the borders and thereby exposing the fact that he is making tactical use of these sanctuaries as a part of the border battlefields, we are simply putting the spotlight on a hard fact of life which cannot be ignored by the tactical commander, despite a full realization of the political implications. . . . I can see absolutely no psychological or military advantage to a strategy that would intentionally invite the war east towards the coast. It would be retrogressive, costly in casualties and refugees, and almost certainly prolong the war."

This exchange was followed by a backchannel message from Wheeler on December 23, 1967, informing Westmoreland that after several high-level meetings on the proposal for the attacks on Cambodia (the tri-border operation), any request for expansion of military operations involving Cambodia "would have little chance of approval . . . in the particularly sensitive environment which exists today."[113]

The proposals of the JCS in the memorandum of November 27 with respect to bombing North Vietnam were approved in part by the President. Ten of twenty-four new targets were approved, but the proposal to reduce the size of the prohibited zones in Hanoi and Haiphong from ten and three nautical miles to three and one and one half respectively—virtually eliminating any prohibition on bombing the two cities—was not approved.[114]

At about the same time, the JASON Division of the Pentagon's Institute for Defense Analyses issued another report on bombing which, according to the *Pentagon Papers,* "was probably the most categorical rejection of bombing as a tool of our policy in Southeast Asia to be made before or since by an official or semi-official group."[115]

---

[111] Johnson Library, NSF Country File, Vietnam, cable from Wheeler to Westmoreland, DTG 062316Z, Dec. 6, 1967.

[112] CMH, Westmoreland Papers, Message Files, Westmoreland to Wheeler, MAC 11956, Dec. 10, 1967.

[113] National Archives, Westmoreland-CBS Papers, Wheeler to Westmoreland, JCS 1109, Dec. 23, 1967. Except for the Tuesday Lunch on December 5, there are no known notes of other "high-level" meetings dealing with Westmoreland's request.

[114] *PP*, Gravel ed., vol. IV, p. 216. In a memorandum to the JCS summarizing their joint views, McNamara and Rusk said among other things, (*ibid.*, p. 538),

"a. recommend against aerial minings or bombing of North Vietnamese deep water ports. Possible military gains are far outweighed by risk of confrontation with Soviets or Chinese.

"b. recommend that strike authorization for high density population centers of government and domestic commerce continue to be controlled at the highest level of government which is most closely in touch with the political significance of air attacks in these areas.

"c. every recommendation for authorization of a new target should be considered on its own merit. The military significance of the target is, of course, a dominant factor in the evaluation of a target recommendation, but our policy is to minimize civilian casualties and this consideration must be weighed in every determination."

[115] *Ibid.*, p. 222. See pp. 222–225 for a summary of the report. The four volume JASON study, "The Bombing of North Vietnam," Dec. 16, 1967, is in the Johnson Library, NSF Country File, Vietnam. See also the excellent summary of the results of ROLLING THUNDER by Clodfelter, *The Limits of Air Power,* pp. 134 ff.

In late November a study group established within the Joint Staff of the JCS, pursuant to McNamara's suggestion to Rusk a year earlier and as a followup to the September 1967 San Antonio Formula, completed a study of what could be expected from a cessation of bombing and the onset of negotiations and what guidance should be given to military negotiators.[116]

Prospects for 1968

As 1967 drew to a close, the State Department, the CIA, and the U.S. military command in Vietnam prepared estimates of the situation at that time and the prospects for 1968. The State Department concluded that, "there is a consensus that one year from now we will be stronger than we are now, making continued progress against the VC, and slowly building up the GVN. . . ." There was also a consensus, however, "that there will not have been a decisive and undeniable breakthrough, that the enemy will still be very much with us, that it will remain difficult to produce dramatic and convincing evidence of a victory in the near future."[117]

On the military side, Westmoreland's command reported that in 1967 there had been steady progress in achieving U.S. goals and a decline in the Communists' combat effectiveness in and their control of area and population.[118] MACV plans for 1968 called for intensifying combat operations and for accomplishing 25 specific goals (which were listed), including increased effectiveness of the South Vietnamese Army. Plans were also being prepared "to phase down U.S. combat efforts concomitant with the increased effectiveness of RVAF," in keeping with Westmoreland's proposed strategy that he announced in Washington in November.

During 1968, Westmoreland's report stated,

> Our planned operations are designed to defeat the VC/NVA main forces, destroy the enemy's base areas and resources, and

[116] For a copy of the 159-page study (not counting appendices), "Study of the Political-Military Implications in Southeast Asia of the Cessation of Aerial Bombardment and the Initiation of Negotiations," Nov. 22, 1967, SEA CABIN for short, see U.S. Department of State, Lot File 85 D 240. See also the summary of the study in *PP*, Gravel ed., vol. IV, pp. 217–222.

Among other things, the study concluded that "U.S. intelligence evaluations of the impact of bombardment on NVN are sufficiently uncertain as to cast doubt on any judgment that aerial and naval bombardment is or is not establishing some upper limit on the DRV's ability to support the war in SVN. The effect on NVN itself is equally uncertain."

In a memorandum to McNamara on December 16, JCSM–698–67, the JCS took issue with the SEA CABIN study. Noting that it was a staff study and did not represent the views of the JCS, the Chiefs stressed their belief in the effectiveness of bombing and their opposition to a bombing halt as a way of spurring negotiations. (*PP*, Gravel ed., vol. IV, p. 222.) See also in the Johnson Library, Clifford Papers, CM–2902–68, Jan. 12, 1968, a memorandum from the JCS to McNamara transmitting a Joint Staff study of the military aspects of Vietnam negotiations related to the SEA CABIN study; CM–2928–68, January 20, a memorandum to McNamara from the JCS transmitting a revision of the study of January 12, and JCSM–62–68, Jan. 31, 1968, a memorandum to McNamara from the JCS transmitting a report on JCS judgments on the substantive issues raised in the SEA CABIN study.

The question of negotiating a settlement of the war was also the focus of two senior level interagency politico-military games, SIGMA I and II–67, conducted November 27-December 7, 1967 in the Pentagon by the Joint War Games Agency of the JCS. (*SIGMA-67, Final Report*, December 1967. Joint War Games Agency, Joint Chiefs of Staff, copy provided to the author by the JCS.) Participants included General Wheeler, General Taylor, General Greene, General Goodpaster, General DePuy, Colonel Ginsburgh, Paul Warnke, William Leonhart, George Carver, Philip Habib, Thomas Hughes, Leonard Meeker, and Chester Cooper.

[117] U.S. Department of State, Lot File 71 D 88, Memorandum for the Secretary from Katzenbach, "Prognosis for Vietnam, Nov. 1, 1967, with the following attachments: "1. Summary of Projections for the Next 12 Months in Vietnam," "2. Political Projection," "3. Economic Projection," "4. Anti-Infrastructure," "5. Pacification."

[118] CMH, Westmoreland Papers, Message Files, Westmoreland to Sharp, Dec. 10, 1967, "Military Operations in Vietnam."

drive him into sparsely populated areas where food is scarce. We hope to keep the enemy constantly on the move and deny him the opportunity to refit, resupply, rest or retrain in-country. The enemy losses in his main forces, destruction and neutralization of his in-country base areas and continued air and naval interdiction of his LOCs will force him to place greater reliance in sanctuaries in Cambodia and Laos. Intensified bombing of military targets in the North will further reduce his war making base and deny him the opportunity to bring his total resources to bear on the war in South Vietnam. Simultaneously, his infiltration will be further restricted by a strong point obstacle system along the DMZ, use of sensors and our Civilian Irregular Defense Group (CIDG) being redeployed to provide better surveillance and interdiction along the frontier. [CIDG consisted of small units of Montagnards operating in the border areas.] Impact on the enemy will be increased casualties, desertions, sickness and lowered morale. In-country his recruiting potential will be reduced through the increased momentum of our military offensive and pacification efforts. Prisoners of war and ralliers should increase. The attack on the VC infrastructure is expected to gain headway during the next six months. The pay off will be a greater number of the populace openly supporting the Government. In essence, every effort for 1968 will be directed towards the defeat of the enemy and the establishment of a viable government in SVN.

The CIA's estimate of the situation and comments on the outlook for 1968 concluded: [119]

—Although the long-term military and political trends have been running against the Communist effort, Hanoi has effectively adapted its tactics to cope with U.S. military pressures.

—[N]o early turning point appears likely. Given the Communists' belief that they enjoy political and psychological advantages in a protracted war, both Hanoi and the Viet Cong have some reason to view the past year with encouragement and to persevere with their policies, at least through 1968.

—Although enemy units are hurting under continued allied pressure, they remain effective enough to achieve Hanoi's immediate objective: to tie down U.S. forces on widely scattered fronts and to deny the degree of provincial security essential to the pacification program.

—In North Vietnam, Rolling Thunder operations have imposed an increasingly heavy burden. . . . Despite the achievements of the bombing program, however, no significant deterioration in North Vietnam's military capabilities or its determination to persist in the war can be detected.

—Hanoi harbors no illusions of ultimate military victory, in a Western sense. But the North Vietnamese remain confident that they can hold out, in a protracted war of attrition, longer than the U.S. They apparently remain willing and able to accept the high cost of U.S. attacks in the South and in the North, at least at present levels, in the hope that the Ameri-

[119] Johnson Library, NSF Country File, Vietnam, "A Review of the Situation in Vietnam," Central Intelligence Agency Intelligence Memorandum, SC08753/67, Dec. 8, 1967.

cans and South Vietnamese will to fight to the end eventually will weaken under the strain of military frustrations and domestic political pressures.

Rostow asked Ginsburgh to comment on the CIA memorandum. In a memorandum to Rostow on December 13, 1967, Ginsburgh took issue with a number of the CIA's conclusions. "In many places," he said, "I found it difficult to believe that the CIA document is talking about the same war we are. I believe that the Agency is overreacting to what it feels is undue optimism at top levels of government. If the document serves to caution against an expectation of a conclusion of the war before the 1968 elections, it may serve a useful purpose. In my opinion, however, it exudes an excessively pessimistic interpretation of the facts." [120]

Rostow, who said he had been asked by McNamara to bring it to the President's attention, sent the CIA memorandum to the President with a note saying that he was also attaching Ginsburgh's memorandum, and stating: "Although my own view is sympathetic to Bob Ginsburgh's, and I sometimes feel that CIA is leaning against an excessive optimism that does not exist, I would regard its conservatism as an asset to the Government, if not carried to excess."

During December, Rostow talked with an historian who was studying the making of Vietnam policy in the Johnson administration. Throughout the interview he defended U.S. policy and spoke with assurance and optimism about the progress being made. At one point he was asked about domestic opposition to the war, and he replied: "People know that 'despite its obscurities' the war is necessary in order to avoid a 'bigger and more unpleasant one later. . . . The consequences of pulling out would be something worse.' Anyhow, 'the nation is not in a bug-out mood. . . . History will salute us,' he said with certainty." [121]

As 1967 ended, the beginning of the New Year was celebrated at a party at the U.S. Embassy in Saigon. One participant says it was ". . . a massive bash . . . high hilarity, everybody letting off steam." [122] The invitation read: "Come see the light at the end of the tunnel." [123]

---

[120] Johnson Library, NSF Memos to the President—Walt Rostow, Memorandum to the President from Rostow, Dec. 13, 1967, with attached memorandum to Rostow from Ginsburgh, Dec. 13, 1967.

[121] Graff, *The Tuesday Cabinet*, p. 143.

[122] Harry Maurer, *Strange Ground*, p. 477.

[123] *Ibid.*, and Halberstam, *The Best and the Brightest*, p. 647. See also Peter Arnett, *Live From the Battlefield: From Vietnam to Baghdad: 35 Years in the World's War Zones* (New York: Simon and Schuster, 1994), p. 237. Arnett, who was there, says that the theme was chosen by some young Americans at the U.S. Mission "to poke sly fun at the official optimism."

INDEX

A

B

C

H

I

J

K

L

M

N

O

P

S

U

V

W

X

Y

Z